SUPERMAC

SUPERMAC
THE LIFE OF HAROLD MACMILLAN

D. R. THORPE

Chatto & Windus
LONDON

Published by Chatto & Windus 2010

2 4 6 8 10 9 7 5 3

First published in Great Britain in 2010 by
Chatto & Windus
Random House, 20 Vauxhall Bridge Road,
London SW1V 2SA
www.rbooks.co.uk

Addresses for companies within The Random House Group Limited
can be found at: www.randomhouse.co.uk/offices.htm

The Random House Group Limited Reg. No. 954009

A CIP catalogue record for this book
is available from the British Library

ISBN 9780701177485

The Random House Group Limited supports The Forest Stewardship
Council (FSC), the leading international forest certification organisation.
All our titles that are printed on Greenpeace approved FSC certified paper
carry the FSC logo. Our paper procurement policy can be found at
www.rbooks.co.uk/environment

Mixed Sources
Product group from well-managed
forests and other controlled sources
www.fsc.org Cert no. TT-COC-2139
© 1996 Forest Stewardship Council
FSC

Typeset by Deltatype Ltd, Birkenhead, Wirral
Printed and bound in Great Britain by
CPI Mackays, Chatham, Kent

For Robert and Kathleen Stewart

To succeed pre-eminently in English public life it is necessary to conform either to the popular image of a bookie or a clergyman.

Malcolm Muggeridge, *The Infernal Grove*

Contents

List of Illustrations

CARTOONS

Preface

The first time I met Harold Macmillan was on St George's Day, 1975, at Birch Grove, the family home near Chelwood Gate, where the daffodils shone in the spring sunshine. He had agreed to talk to me about Sir Austen Chamberlain, Lord Curzon and Rab Butler, of whom I was then writing a biographical triptych. He opened the door of Birch Grove, the only person in that vast, rambling house, and shuffled forward to greet me, for all the world like Anton Chekhov's aged manservant Firs in a Sussex production of *The Cherry Orchard*.[1] We went through to the library, where a log fire was burning in the grate. 'Now tell me exactly what it is you are writing,' he asked, 'so I can help the more.' I explained that I was writing about three prominent Conservative politicians who had reached the penultimate rung on the party ladder, but who had, nevertheless, despite expectations, remained 'the uncrowned prime ministers'. 'Oh, I see,' replied Macmillan, 'kind of failed BAs.' Already there was a wry smile on his face, and I sensed that he was going to enjoy this meeting as much as I would. 'Well, of course,' he continued, putting another log on the fire, 'if you want to make it a more amusing book, you could always add a fourth section, on George Brown ...'

Harold Macmillan transcended party. 'He was a rebel in the Tory Party in the 1930s, and, in a sense, he is a rebel still,' wrote Hugh Trevor-Roper, when Macmillan was Prime Minister.[2] Later in 1975, when Rab Butler heard that I had spoken to Macmillan, he enquired of me, 'How was Harold Macmillan when you met him? Was he the Duke's son-in-law or the crofter's great grandson?' Of course, Macmillan played both parts, and many others beside.

On the table at Birch Grove lay a copy of his firm's recent publication, a biography of Oswald Mosley by Robert Skidelsky, and initially Macmillan spoke of Mosley (a member by marriage of his wife's family) and of how Mosley's big mistake was not in crossing the floor from the Conservatives to Labour, or in attempting 'to break the mould' of British politics by forming the New Party in 1931, but in embracing extremism in the form of the British Union of Fascists, which the British public in their wisdom would never accept.

This was the prelude to an afternoon of fascinating reminiscences, including a visit to the park where President Kennedy's helicopter had landed in June 1963, and from where it had taken off, 'sailing down the valley above the heavily laden, lush foliage of oaks and beech'.[3] This was the last time Macmillan saw Kennedy, 'the loved one'. Even 12 years later, as he traced the course of the flight, tears came to his eyes.

We went into the muniment room and he showed me his dark-covered notebook diaries, volumes that I would later study in detail. He made me a cup of tea, and took me to the door, wished me luck, and waved as my car drew away up the drive.

Nine years later, Macmillan saw me again, this time in the board-room of Macmillan & Co. in Little Essex Street, to talk about Selwyn Lloyd. The visual image endures, the aged figure replicating the Bryan Organ portrait on the wall behind him, half blind, but still mentally alert and vividly reliving the past, drawing unusual and illuminating historical parallels from his long political life, comparing Selwyn Lloyd with Augustine Birrell, also a Cambridge-educated lawyer-politician with Liverpool connections, who 'always retained a deep respect for the Liberal nonconformist tradition of his Liverpool upbringing'.[4] The next year Macmillan was dead, and shortly afterwards the Birch Grove estate was sold.

The last time I went to Birch Grove, in April 1993, it was an empty shell. Indeed, this visit was a poignant experience. I was researching Alec Douglas-Home's life, and had just finished one of my regular week's work into the private papers at the Hirsel, the Home family home in Coldstream. By a combination of chance and necessity, 36 hours later I was at Birch Grove, completing research in the Macmillan papers, then at Porches Farm House on the estate, in the custody of Mrs Sylvia James. I went with Sylvia James for a last, nostalgic look at the big house.

The Hirsel was a settled world of continuity and homeliness, Labradors sleeping on the hearth, gum boots and fishing rods in the hall, and the laughter of grandchildren in the corridors. Birch Grove, by contrast, was now empty, a mixture of druggets and sheets, with long-silent dusty bell boards ('Mr Harold's Room', 'Mr Dan's Room', 'Mr Arthur's Room'). In the library, which I remembered lined with books, was a cold grate and a solitary full-sized billiard table, await-ing the final visit of the removal men. We went down corridors, into empty room after empty room, for all the world like Guy Perron and Sarah Layton in Paul Scott's *Raj Quartet*, wandering through the Raj's deserted and empty summer residence of whose vanished splendours we were 'no more than observers',[5] to the saloon where Kennedy and his entourage had discussed the future of the world in June 1963, out on to the terrace where the two world leaders had been photographed, and so on up the stairs down which Lady Dorothy Macmillan's body had been carried on a door. From the old attic bedroom, overlooking a side garden, where Macmillan had died in 1986, the distant sound of bulldozers could already be heard as the new owners began laying out an 18-hole golf course[6] over some of the best shooting land in Sussex. The Lopahins had arrived.[7]

D.R. Thorpe,
Oxford, May 2010

PRELUDE

On the night of the general election of Thursday 8 October 1959, Major Geoffrey Hoare, the High Sheriff of Essex, stepped outside the counting hall in Billericay and announced the result at one minute before 10 p.m. Billericay was the first seat to be declared, as it had been at the general election in May 1955, when the Conservatives had won by 4,206 votes. Now Major Hoare read out the 1959 figures in front of television and newsreel cameras and a large crowd, most in hats and wrapped in coats against the evening chill. Edward Gardner, the Conservative candidate, had been elected with an increased majority of 4,822 votes.[1] There were still 629 seats to be declared.

The Leader of the Opposition, Hugh Gaitskell, was in his Leeds constituency, preparing for the count in the town hall, and when his assistant, John Harris, told him the figures from Billericay, he said to his aides, 'We've lost by a hundred seats.'[2] When the final result was declared from Orkney and Shetland (the constituency of the Liberal leader, Jo Grimond) at Saturday lunchtime on 10 October, Gaitskell's prediction was fulfilled.[3] In his tenth, and what was to prove his last, election Harold Macmillan had led the Conservatives to victory with a majority of exactly one hundred.

The 1959 general election was the greatest moment of Macmillan's political career, the equivalent, for him, of Lloyd George's triumph when, on 29 June 1919, King George V, abandoning protocol, had personally greeted him at Victoria station on his return from the signing of the Paris Peace Treaty and driven with him to Buckingham Palace.[4] In 1959, Queen Elizabeth II, without compromising the monarchy's impartiality, sent Macmillan a warm letter on his re-election.

Labour responses reflected the nature of the Conservative victory. Tony Benn gloomily recorded in his diary, 'The Tory majority is 100, and the [Labour] Party will really have to reorganise itself.'[5] Patrick Gordon Walker ruefully admitted, 'The simple fact is that the Tories identified themselves with the new working class rather better than we did.'[6] It was unequivocally Macmillan's personal triumph, in strategy, timing and conduct. He had travelled the length and breadth of Britain and spoken at 74 meetings. Herbert Morrison thought the Tory revival since Suez 'was largely due to the skilful politics of Harold Macmillan, together with his intuitive understanding of a large proportion of the British people'.[7]

The visit of President Eisenhower to Britain earlier in the year, stage-managed to perfection by Macmillan, had enhanced Macmillan's position on the world stage. However, he knew that foreign policy rarely, if ever, decides the outcome of general elections. Next Friday's grocery bill is always more important. In his famous 'never had it so good' speech in Bedford on 20 July 1959, Macmillan had said: 'Taking the nation as a whole compared with six years ago, personal incomes are 40% up, and though prices have risen they have only risen by 20%.'[8] Uniquely in modern times, full employment, stable prices and a strong balance of payments coincided at the time of the 1959 general election. Such economic facts were a powerful electoral weapon, as Gaitskell himself conceded. 'The main reason for our 1955 and 1959 defeats is surely that the people were better off, and that the Tory propaganda was very effective.'[9] The Conservative election slogan – 'Life's better with the Conservatives. Don't let Labour ruin it' – seemed not so much a party political point as a self-evident truth.

In the hot summer of 1959, Macmillan was relaxing one afternoon in the garden of his Sussex residence, Birch Grove, with one of his grandsons, who regretted the seemingly ever-present drone of aircraft from nearby Gatwick Airport. Macmillan told him it was a good thing. People were going abroad on holidays they could once never have dreamed of; they would come home refreshed and happy, and in the autumn would re-elect the Conservatives. And so they did.

Indeed, the Conservative Party had improved its position over four successive elections – 1950, 1951, 1955, 1959 – a point emphasised by Anthony Eden in his letter of congratulation to Macmillan. 'It is also astonishing that the progression in the Tory majority has been so steady: 17, 60, 100,' Eden wrote. 'A form of payment by results which is something new in modern politics and very sensible.'[10] The post-mortems soon considered whether Labour could ever win again. 'Is Britain settling down into a one-party nation?' asked one of Macmillan's earliest, and best, biographers in *Anatomy of Britain*. [11] Macmillan drew two lessons from the triumph. He believed it showed that the class war was dead, and that the Conservative Party must remain on modern and progressive lines. But he also knew that political fortune was transitory. The 1959 election was the pinnacle, but from such a position there was only one route.

Macmillan's triumph was a long time coming. Stanley Baldwin and Neville Chamberlain had waited 15 and 19 years respectively from entering Parliament for the Premiership; for Macmillan the wait was

31 years. Indeed, few leading politicians have first taken any office so relatively late in their careers: he had been in the House for 16 years before he had a sniff of the humblest office. 'That was unusual,' he told James Lees-Milne. [12]

Macmillan was a man of sorrows and acquainted with grief; like Elizabeth-Jane Henchard, in the Hardy novel Macmillan admired most, he knew that 'happiness was but the occasional episode in a general drama of pain'. [13] He contemplated, and may even have attempted, suicide. In industrial Stockton-on-Tees, his pre-war constituency, his innate melancholy was acknowledged. [14]

A rebel in the 1920s and 1930s, he was never an MP of the type on whom the whips' office looked with favour. To have been correct before the war on both the key issues, unemployment and the appeasement of Nazi Germany, and to have been articulate in his criticisms, was not the quickest way to the inner governing circles of his party. Macmillan knew that there were illogical, even contradictory, responses to appeasement. Geoffrey Dawson, the imperialist editor of *The Times*, differed in his response, depending on who the dictator was. Macmillan had no time for such compromise. [15] As a result he was one of the 'troublesome young men';[16] he knew that the whips liked 'safe men' and, like Churchill, he had a career that contained elements of the steeplechase.

But what a steeplechase it was. Macmillan was at the centre of key events of the twentieth century. During the Second World War, he was the trusted adviser of Eisenhower and Alexander. After the War, he helped modernise the Conservative Party to make it relevant to new world conditions. Then in 1951 he set out on 12 years at the heart of government, beginning with his triumphant spell at the Ministry of Housing and culminating with six years as the Prime Minister who presided over Britain's transition from austerity to affluence.

Of course, his star was to fade, and he always attracted criticism from those opponents who saw him as a poseur. Aneurin Bevan, Labour's Shadow Foreign Secretary, gave free rein to his feelings. 'I have watched him carefully for years,' he declared in Manchester in March 1959. 'Behind that Edwardian countenance there is nothing.' At the Durham Miners' Gala later that year, Bevan said that Macmillan was fraudulent, 'posing like an incandescent aspidistra'. [17]

That Macmillan was a skilled actor, few would doubt, but the mask was not a pose. It was more important for what it hid, than what it revealed. What Bevan failed to acknowledge was Macmillan's chameleon-like quality, his ability to blend with, and then appeal to, a remarkably broad cross-section of mid-century British society.

*

Although Macmillan had characteristics of many successful predecessors, notably Benjamin Disraeli (for adventure) and Stanley Baldwin (for reassurance), the figure on whom he consciously modelled himself was A. J. Balfour, the only other truly intellectual prime minister of the twentieth century, with his hooded eyes, the seemingly languid appearance and apparent unflappability. Even Balfour's aphorisms could be mistaken for Macmillan's. 'When I'm at work on politics,' Balfour once told John Morley, 'I long to be in literature, and *vice versa*.'[18] Balfour's mixture of Scottish merchant antecedents and aristocratic background reflected Macmillan's persona, and confused those who mistakenly thought Balfour 'the whiff of scent on a pocket handkerchief'.[19] Macmillan knew better. 'Beneath that gentle and courteous exterior,' he wrote of Balfour, 'one sensed an iron strength of will.'[20] So it was with Macmillan, who, like Balfour, was more or less happy when being praised and not very uncomfortable when being abused, but who had 'moments of uneasiness when...being explained'.[21]

Biography, though, is a process of explanation. Macmillan's journey through life until that climactic moment on 8 October 1959 took many turns, at times contradictory, at others seemingly inexplicable – like a great lake, full of bustling activity on the surface, with white horses, gulls swooping, flotsam dipping and turning, yet underneath a permanent powerful undertow. Like Disraeli, he was passionate about improving 'the condition of the people'[22] and 'extending the co-operative effort of all those who believed in freedom'.[23] His story begins at a remote spot, the ruined Cock Farm at Lochranza, on the northern tip of the Isle of Arran in the Firth of Clyde.

PART ONE

Voices in the Air

1894–1940

Madmen in authority, who hear voices in the air, are distilling their frenzy from some academic scribbler of a few years back. I am sure that the power of vested interests is vastly exaggerated compared with the gradual encroachment of ideas. Not, indeed, immediately, but after a certain interval; for in the field of economic and political philosophy there are not many who are influenced by new theories after they are twenty-five or thirty years of age, so that the ideas which civil servants and politicians and even agitators apply to current events are not likely to be the newest. But, soon or late, it is ideas, not vested interests, which are dangerous for good or for evil.

J. M. Keynes

Balliol in Macmillan's time.

CHAPTER ONE

Working Class Ancestry

Terrible business, Roy, this insult to the Prime Minister by our old University, terrible. You know it's really a matter of class. The dons are mainly upper middle class, and they can never forgive Mrs Thatcher for being so lower middle class. But you and I, Roy, with our working class ancestry, are above that kind of thing.
Harold Macmillan to Roy Jenkins on the occasion of Oxford University's vote against granting Mrs Thatcher an honorary degree, 1985.[1]

How was Harold Macmillan when you met him? Was he the Duke's son-in-law or the crofter's great-grandson?
Rab Butler to the author, 20 November 1975

Three vistas from the rocky summit of Goat Fell, the Isle of Arran's highest point, define the history of the Macmillan clan. Argyll, Sannox and Irvine can all be seen on a clear day. These were views well known to Harold Macmillan's ancestors, who had lived in a croft at the Cock of Arran, beneath Goat Fell's northern slopes, near the village of Lochranza. Then, as now, the easy walk to the peak was a popular excursion.[2]

To the north-west of Goat Fell, on a line to the distant Paps of Jura, lies Argyll, where the known patriarch of the family, Daniel, had farmed in the eighteenth century at Dunmore, on a barren tongue of land he owned in North Knapdale. Its gaunt beauty later attracted painters of renown.[3] The Macmillans (the name was then McMillan, the Irish spelling) had earlier been vassals of the Lords of the Isles there and could trace their line back to the twelfth century Cormac, Bishop of Dunkeld, whose great-great-great grandfather had been the Scottish King Macbeth. Daniel's religious zeal was matched only by his ambitious diligence, characteristics inherited by his son Malcolm, who settled his growing family (he eventually had 10 children) in 1769 on the nearby Isle of Arran, where he hoped there would be better agricultural prospects.

At first Malcolm farmed at Sannox,[4] but he soon became the tacksman (or chief leaseholder) of farms at the Cock, the northernmost point of Arran, and it was the photograph of his croft there that Harold Macmillan later kept on his desk at 10 Downing Street.[5] A tacksman was an important figure in the isolated rural communities, as Dr Johnson discovered on his journey to the Western Islands. 'Next in dignity to the Laird is the Tacksman,' he observed, 'a large taker or leaseholder of land, of which he keeps part, as a domain, in his own hand, and lets part to under tenants.'[6]

Like his father, Malcolm was deeply religious, an elder of the Established Church, whose discouragement of the superstitious belief in witchcraft in the local community ('be these juggling fiends no more believed')[7] echoed that of the Shakespearean portrait of Macbeth, his far-distant ancestor. Thomas Hughes, author of *Tom Brown's Schooldays*, described Malcolm as 'a sort of "chief peasant"',[8] and he was remembered as a benevolent figure, generous to those poorer than himself, though conditions for him, too, were arduous. Sheep farming and peat brought in little money under a 'run-rig' system whereby tenants drew annual lots to allocate strips of arable land, with animals being tended communally. Sir Walter Scott evoked the penurious atmosphere of the region in his poem, *The Lord of the Isles*:

> On fair Lochranza stream'd the early day,
> Thin wreaths of cottage-smoke are upward curl'd
> From the lone hamlet, which her inland bay
> And circling mountains sever from the world.
> And there the fisherman his sail unfurl'd,
> The goat-herd drove his kids to steep Ben-Ghoil,
> Before the hut the dame her spindle twirl'd,
> Courting the sunbeam as she plied her toil, –
> For, wake where'er he may, Man wakes to care and toil.[9]

Care and toil was certainly the lot of Malcolm's third son, Duncan (1770–1823), born in North Sannox but brought up at the Cock. Two older sons moved to the mainland, leaving Duncan to eke out what living he could. In 1793 he married Katherine Crawford (1772–1835), daughter of William Crawford, who hailed from Ayrshire, and was another elder of the Church.[10] From his father-in-law, Duncan inherited a farm at Achog, at the north end of the village of Corrie, below Sannox Bay, and it was here that his own Daniel, grandfather of the Prime Minister and founder of the publishing company, was born on 13 September 1813, the eleventh of twelve children, four of whom had died young of tuberculosis. Daniel's younger brother, Alexander, his parents' last child, was born on 3 October 1818, though by that time the family was established on the mainland at Irvine, visible due east from Goat Fell.

The move reflected both the harsh conditions following the re-organisation of the North Arran farms in 1815 and Duncan's determination to better his family's fortunes. John Burrell, agent to the trustees of the tenth Duke of Hamilton (one of whose family seats was Brodick Castle, to the south of Corrie), had surveyed the Duke's farms in North Arran and recommended 'rationalisation', which left Duncan as one of the losers. The 'run-rig' system was ended and high grazing land given over to sheep, as a result of which Duncan was forced in 1816 to seek work elsewhere to support his family.

So ended the family's direct association with Arran, often called 'Scotland in miniature'. For Duncan Macmillan, the mining town of Irvine offered not only more promising possibilities, but essential ones, as he was facing destitution. He became a carter, transporting coal destined for Ireland to Irvine's harbour. His son Daniel, three at the time of the move, was enrolled in due course at the local common school, later Irvine Academy, an archetypal acorn moment. Duncan's two older brothers, Malcolm and William, had already anticipated the family move and were working as carpenters on building this new school, before seeking even better prospects at sea. The whole process was thus an earlier example of what Norman Tebbit told Conservative delegates his father had done in the harsh conditions of the 1930s – 'he got on his bike and looked for work'.[11]

Daniel never forgot the poverty of his early childhood. But the family, in its small way, was now established on the mainland and, as an outward sign of this new beginning, changed the spelling of its name from McMillan to Macmillan. Dr Johnson had found the atmosphere of the Western Islands oppressive. 'He felt today the weight of this barren way of passing time,' recorded James Boswell on 7 October 1773. 'He said, "I want to be on the mainland, and go on with existence. This is a waste of life."'[12] What it must have been like for those permanently cabined and cribbed on an island in the late eighteenth century can only be imagined. Advancement, as so often for Scotsmen, meant emigration, even if only in this case across the Firth of Clyde, where the Macmillans were now 'getting on with existence'.

Daniel and Alexander were nine and four respectively when in 1823 their father Duncan died, worn down by physical work and responsibility. Their seafaring uncles, Malcolm, who died in 1840, and William, who died in 1838, gave what help they could, but the greatest influence was their mother Katherine, who, befitting the

Crawford Ayrshire Covenanting stock from which she sprang, gave them a devout religious upbringing. Daniel left school at the age of 10, and on 1 January 1824 was apprenticed to Maxwell Dicks, an Irvine bookseller, at a wage of 1s. 6d a week. The drudge and poverty of toiling on the land were now a thing of the past.

Daniel's apprenticeship was successfully completed on 14 February 1831, after which he went to Stirling, where he fell ill with 'a brain fever'. Following superficial recovery, he moved to the bigger stage of Glasgow to work in Mr Thomas Atkinson's bookshop, an altogether grander enterprise.[13] He was Atkinson's shopman, but was ambitious and hoped for a partnership. Atkinson's shop was a centre of intellectual activity, and Daniel embarked on what amounted to a delayed education, reading widely and joining in discussions about the concerns of the day. The English Reform Bill was a central issue, and when the bill passed the House of Commons, there was a general illumination of the city. This was a formative time for the young Daniel.

In 1831 Glasgow was the third largest city in the United Kingdom after London and Manchester.[14] But it was also disease-ridden, and Daniel's career stalled through bad health. He returned to Irvine, where his mother nursed him. It was her death two years later that determined him to leave Scotland altogether.

His first visit to London proved an abortive experience. He failed to secure a post with Longman's, the publishers, and took various small jobs, before finding employment in Cambridge with a bookshop run by Elijah Johnson. The three years he spent here nurtured not only his commercial experience but his intellectual insights. In 1837, he secured a permanent post at Seeley's & Co, publishers and booksellers in Fleet Street. His salary was £60 a year.

Illness again drew him back to his family roots. Alexander, his younger brother, had not prospered and Daniel conceived the idea of getting him a post at Seeley's. When this materialised, also at a salary of £60 per annum, the two brothers established themselves in a boarding house in Charterhouse Square. Here it was plain living, by economic necessity, and high thinking, by choice.[15] Alexander, self-taught, put together a short collection of Shelley's poems, together with a biographical sketch, which was published by George Bell. The Macmillans now were not only selling books but writing them. Shortly they would be publishing them as well.

The key year was 1843. Anxious for independence, the Macmillan brothers set up their own bookselling business in Aldersgate Street, but this proved too distant from the traditional London book-buying public. When an opportunity came to buy the business of Richard Newby in Cambridge, they seized it at once. By then Daniel had published his first book, *The Philosophy of Training* by A. R. Craig.

George Routledge and George Cassell had started their respective houses in 1843 and 1848, and competition was fierce. The market displayed three characteristics that offered opportunities to far-sighted publishers – expanding literacy, increasing disposable income and growing leisure time. In 1845 the brothers acquired the Cambridge business of Thomas Stevenson, and set up in the important corner site of 1 Trinity Street, opposite the Senate House.[16]

Remembering his Glasgow bookselling days, Daniel knew the importance of personal links in building up a business, and 1 Trinity Street soon became a centre of literary activity. Its place in publishing history was enhanced by its associations with Wordsworth, who visited the premises to discuss *The Excursion*. It was at Trinity Street that Charles Kingsley first showed the brothers the script of *Alton Locke*; William Makepeace Thackeray was also a visitor.

The beginnings of business success also coincided with a change in the brothers' personal circumstances. Daniel was the first to be married, on 4 September 1850, to Frances Orridge,[17] a Cambridge magistrate, whose father was a chemist. In August 1851, Alexander followed suit. His bride, Caroline Brimley, was the eldest sister of the librarian of Trinity College.

Daniel and Frances had four children; their second son, Maurice Crawford, born on 5 October 1851, was to be the father of the future Prime Minister.[18] He was named Maurice after F. D. Maurice, his godfather. Another godfather was Charles Kingsley.

Daniel died on 26 June 1857 after a bout of pleurisy. He was only 43, and had been dogged by bad health throughout his short life. Alexander assumed the headship of both the family and the business, bringing his eldest son, Frederick, into a more prominent position, with the opening of a London branch at 23 Henrietta Street in 1858. The two families amalgamated their domestic arrangements, and Alexander called Frances, his sister-in-law, Mrs Daniel.[19]

Alexander, in effect, divided the firm into two branches, one bookselling in Cambridge, the other – Macmillan & Co. – in London, both bookselling and publishing. He began the practice of travelling to the London branch on Thursdays for what he called 'tobacco parliaments', informal gatherings of leading literary figures, who met to discuss issues of the day.[20] Macmillan & Co. was already establishing its 'house' style – a deep interest in matters of religion and education, and generosity of terms towards the proven authors on its list.

In 1859 Alexander moved into the lucrative shilling magazine market, publishing the first edition of *Macmillan's Magazine* on 1 November 1859, an occasion marked by a dinner at Henrietta Street for authors and potential contributors. Many such contributors became novelists published by Macmillan, including Anthony Trollope, Thomas Hardy and Henry James.[21]

Another sign of the growing financial success of the company was the education that Alexander gave his family. His ward and nephew, Maurice, and his second son, George Austin, were sent to Summer Fields, the recently founded Oxford preparatory school. From there, Maurice went on to Uppingham, whose headmaster, Dr Edward Thring, was a Macmillan author, his books on grammar and educational theory proving steady sellers. Thring was the most eminent public school headmaster of the second half of the nineteenth century, and his reforms, transforming Uppingham from a small rural grammar school into one of the foremost boarding schools in the land, with architecture to match, were the most significant of the post-Arnold era. 'In conversation,' his friends observed, 'he had but one horse to ride, and its name was "Uppingham".'[22] By winning a scholarship to Uppingham in 1867, Maurice was entering what was then arguably the finest and most progressive school in the country.

Fifty years earlier, in 1817, Maurice's own father had entered Irvine Common School. The half-century journey was far more than a geographical one. G. K. Chesterton once observed that the public schools were not for the sons of gentlemen, but for the fathers of them. 'In two generations they can do the trick.'[23] With the Macmillans they did it in one generation. Call it snobbery, or acute social awareness, there can be no doubt that Maurice's son, Harold, was to be particularly sensitive to matters of class and social placing.[24]

Maurice's time at Uppingham was the making of him. He was an immensely studious and, surprisingly, as the two rarely go together, popular pupil. In 1871 he went up to Christ's College, Cambridge, where he took a first in classics. He did not join the family firm immediately, but became classics master at St Paul's School in London from 1875 to 1883. But even here, the seeds of his future career in publishing were evident. In 1879, his book *First Latin Grammar*, reprinted several times, became the first written by a family member to be published by the family firm. At the end of 1883, he began his publishing career. Three years later he was joined in the firm by his elder brother Frederick, now with an American wife.

The two brothers and their cousin, George Austin, took Macmillan & Co. on to a new level, always alert to changes in the publishing world. W. E. Forster's Education Act of 1870, which made provision for a modicum of universal schooling, fuelled a demand for textbooks, a demand that Macmillan & Co. duly met. The firm expanded overseas, particularly in India, with their Colonial Library of 1886, the year that Maurice secured Thomas Hardy's *The Mayor of Casterbridge*.

The Macmillans were now established in the professional world of both Cambridge and London. In the next phase of Macmillan & Co., some of the foremost writers of their day became 'house' authors – Charles Kingsley, T. H. Huxley, F. D. Maurice and Lewis Carroll. Tennyson became a Macmillan author in 1884. In the next decade the firm published the first volumes of James G. Frazer's *The Golden Bough*, an event seen as marking the beginning of modern anthropology. By 1916, it had acquired the poet W. B. Yeats, the beginning of an Irish connection that was to bring the plays of Sean O'Casey to its list.

Maurice Macmillan travelled widely, and in Paris in 1883 he met a young American widow, Helen Artie Tarleton Belles, known as Nellie. They married the next year and were to have three sons – Daniel (born in 1886); Arthur, a frail child (born in 1889), ironically named after Maurice's youngest brother, Arthur Daniel, who died prematurely of tuberculosis; and Maurice Harold, always known as Harold (born in 1894).

Nellie had been born in Spencer, Indiana, in 1856, into a doctor's family, and had been raised in accordance with strict Nonconformist principles. Like Winston Churchill, Harold Macmillan thus had an American mother, a similarity he often stressed, and in September 1956 he made a pilgrimage to the family home town, where he read a lesson (on the parable of the talents) in the Methodist church his mother had attended.

Nellie was a possessive mother, driven by love and concern for her offspring. Her dominating influence was particularly acute with Harold, the Benjamin of the family. She was a woman of strong character and opinions, and her prejudices ran deep. Her religious upbringing had implanted in her the deepest distrust of Roman Catholicism, or anything she considered 'Jesuitical'. Alcohol, too, was the primrose path to ruin. Worse temptations beset the young. Her greatest fear was of her sons being exposed to what in Victorian times were euphemistically called 'unnatural practices'. At times, it seemed that Catholicism and homosexuality were inextricably linked in her mind, an unbending attitude that was to have dramatic consequences for Harold Macmillan's early life.

The family into which Harold Macmillan was born on 10 February 1894[25] at 52 Cadogan Place in London had long shed any vestiges of 'working class ancestry'. Through their industry, shrewdness and business acumen, the Macmillan cousins had established one of the great publishing houses, with a social position to match. They could have been a case study worthy of Samuel Smiles' *Self Help*. Many strands went into their make-up: muscular Christianity, a devotion to the improving aspect of education, hard work, the ability and will to take risks, self-reliance and the determination to succeed. They had made their own way. Nothing had been handed to them on a plate. They were not the leisured class of late Victorian society; they were real-life Forsytes – 'evidence of that mysterious concrete tenacity which renders a family so formidable a unit of society'[26] – and if Nellie Macmillan had her way, from Cadogan Place they would inherit the world.

CHAPTER TWO
Distant Prospects
1894–1910

Ah, happy hills! ah, pleasing shade!
Ah, fields belov'd in vain!
Where once my careless childhood stray'd,
A stranger yet to pain!
　　Thomas Gray, *Ode On a Distant Prospect of Eton College*

Oh, all the fields were summer then,
And there was time to spare.
　　　　　　　　　　　　C. Day Lewis, *First School*[1]

How should one who has only had a Scotch education be quite
at home at Eton?
　　　　　　　　　　　　　　　　James Boswell, 1789

The world into which Harold Macmillan was born in 1894 was one
of seeming stability. However, underneath the placid certainties of
late Victorian confidence, changes were afoot. On 1 March 1894
the 'Grand Old Man' of British politics, William Ewart Gladstone,
announced his resignation to the so-called 'blubbering Cabinet'.[2] His
speech was a lengthy metaphor about the solar system. He was 84.
Sixty-one years had passed since his maiden speech[3] and 50 since he
had been sworn in as a privy councillor. For 26 years his country had
known no other prime minister apart from himself, Benjamin Disraeli
and Lord Salisbury.*

Within 15 months Gladstone's successor, Rosebery, had also
resigned. 'There are two supreme pleasures in life,' he later wrote.
'One is ideal, the other real. The ideal is when a man receives the seals
of office from his sovereign. The real pleasure comes when he hands
them back.'[4]†

---

*The unfolding battle for the Liberal leadership, and Premiership, eventually won by Lord
Rosebery, was, commented Rosebery's most recent biographer, 'perhaps the strangest in
modern politics apart from the Tory succession to Harold Macmillan in 1963.'
†Of subsequent prime ministers, only for Harold Macmillan was the remark doubly untrue.
In 1957, Macmillan received his sovereign's commission with apprehension, warning the

Rosebery's brief government is best remembered for the budget that introduced death duties. 'We are all Socialists now,' declared the Chancellor, Sir William Harcourt.[5] The working man, if not yet directly represented in Parliament, soon was. The Independent Labour Party had been formed in 1893 determined 'to secure the collective ownership of all the means of production, distribution and exchange', and in the year of Macmillan's birth the fledgling organisation had two important recruits: the future Prime Minister, Ramsay MacDonald, and the future Chancellor of the Exchequer, Philip Snowden.

Economic depression in the 1890s was a backdrop to these formative political events. Fortunately for the Macmillans they were no longer dependent on the patchy income of an Arran farmstead. The second agricultural collapse in ten years had been spectacular, and the wool trade had also suffered in the face of foreign competition. The lot of the humble agricultural worker was desperate, a plight recognised in the resolutely unsentimental portrait of rural life in the novels of Thomas Hardy that Macmillan & Co. were then publishing, particularly *The Woodlanders*.

Harold Macmillan passed a lonely childhood at 52 Cadogan Place. His two brothers, Daniel and Arthur, were eight and five years older respectively, and in childhood that can be a vast chasm.

Dan preceded Harold at Summer Fields, the Oxford preparatory school ('private school', as Harold Macmillan called it, in the contemporary manner); at Eton in College as a Scholar; and at Balliol College, Oxford, where he took a First in Mods. He joined the King's Royal Rifle Corps on the outbreak of the Great War, was invalided out in 1915, and worked thereafter in the Admiralty. He attended the Paris peace conference after the war with his Eton contemporary John Maynard Keynes[6] and arranged for Keynes' influential book *The Economic Consequences of the Peace*[7] to be published by the family firm. Dan was academically brilliant, but before the war his wayward, hedonistic nature, drinking and gambling had been the despair of his parents. However, books (and the Garrick Club) proved the great loves of his mellower age, and he settled to a career in publishing, in 1936 becoming Chairman of Macmillan & Co., a post he held for nearly 30 years.[8]

Harold was a much primmer figure than Dan, though also prone to bouts of the 'black dog' of depression. He inherited Dan's cast-off

Queen that his government might not last six weeks; six years later he surrendered the seals with a regret that haunted him for the rest of his days.

clothes, saved by their frugal mother, Nellie. Worse, his education was in the shadow of Dan's meteoric successes.

Harold's other brother, Arthur, suffered from epilepsy. Nellie considered him too frail to undergo the rigours of Eton, and after Summer Fields he was educated at home, before being allowed to go up to Balliol. Arthur became a devout Anglo-Catholic, much to the concern of his mother, and but for his marriage to a divorcée would have taken holy orders. He was a clubbable figure, spending much of his time at the Athenaeum.[9] Neither Dan nor Arthur fulfilled Nellie's dynastic expectations (both had childless marriages), and her ambitions transferred to her youngest son, Harold. This was a difficult legacy for any child.

The Macmillan family home was at the heart of the Cadogan estate in Chelsea. It was an elegant and prosperous neighbourhood. Number 52 Cadogan Place was a tall house of five storeys, with basement and cellarage, overlooking private gardens, one of those precipitate residences that gave the Forsytes a crick in the neck when they looked up to take in their full magnificence.[10]

Harold's childhood abode was the small nursery at the top of the tall building. At the back it overlooked a mews. The pervasive smell of horses was one of his earliest memories, and the sound of the black-smith at work.* Dan and Arthur overlapped with Harold at Cadogan Place only in the school holidays, for by the time Arthur was being educated at home, Harold was away at Summer Fields.

Harold Macmillan's upbringing was one of the late Victorian upper-middle class, a world of day nurseries and night nurseries, walks in Hyde Park through Albert Gate to hear the military bands, and visits to London Zoo. Money was gold and silver, not paper. Harold's father, Maurice, had a little case at the end of his watch chain, which he checked and, if necessary, stocked with sovereigns before setting forth each day.[11]

Although the recently built Presbyterian Church of St Columba, consecrated in 1884, was within walking distance, along Pont Street, it was a sign of the Anglicanisation of the Macmillan family (Harold's grandfather had adopted the Church of England on moving south) that they attended Sunday worship at Holy Trinity, Sloane Street, which, with its Edward Burne-Jones stained glass, was a monument to the Arts and Crafts movement.[12] Here, past the brass doors, and among the candles and incense, the young Harold spent many a

---

*For his own children, the house was associated with the scent of chocolate.

childhood hour, as first the Reverend Henry J. Bevan, and then the Reverend Henry Reginald Gable, proclaimed the wonders of devotion and belief. Macmillan described his faith as 'the strong thing in my life', and declared in old age, 'I don't think a nation can live without religion'.

Holy Trinity may have inspired the impressionable young Harold, but his mother was suspicious of its High Church rituals and the theatricality of its services. It was one of the few areas of family life that she did not control. Pont Street would have suited Nellie's temperament. Her own home was run without extravagance, even austerely, as befitted her stern Methodist upbringing. The world of Edwardian excess and display was always kept at arm's length. A visit to Arran when Harold was eight made a deep impression on him, as his mother intended. Many were not slow to later criticise such devotion to his humble forbears as a pose, but that was a fundamental misreading of Macmillan's character. He genuinely cared about his family's past.

The surrounds of the Cadogan estate were still largely rural in the last decade of the nineteenth century, despite the District Line pushing out westwards to nearby Sloane Square. Gradually the squares and gardens were absorbed into the metropolis, and prestigious hotels and lavish department stores sprang up, competing alongside treasured local outlets such as Mr Vigo's fish shop in Sloane Street. Some of the quiet charm inevitably vanished. Harold Macmillan's early memories embraced horse-drawn hansom cabs (though Nellie thought them dangerous, so they were forbidden to her boys), lamplighters, and straw in the street to deaden the noise of traffic when confinements or death were at hand. It was a world of visiting cards and 'calling', boating on the Serpentine, the Christmas pantomime at Drury Lane, and a full complement of indoor servants.

The young Harold found the journey down to the bottom of the house tedious and lengthy, but was aware as he grew older of how much more difficult it was for the maids who brought hot water up six flights of stairs to his rooms. The installation of a bath (the Great Bath, as it was known) on the half-landing was a notable event. Mrs Cameron, the cook, was very strict in the pantry when the brothers went exploring, and Nanny Last, the centre of the children's world, and later first housekeeper for Mr Harold after his marriage, also 'spoke in capital letters'. Holidays were spent in genteel seaside resorts, first at Hunstanton in Norfolk, later at Kingsgate in Kent, the beginning for Harold of a life-long love of railways.[13]

In June 1897 Harold watched, appropriately from a bookshop, the march past of 50,000 troops, part of the celebrations of the Diamond

Jubilee of Queen Victoria, though as Mark Twain observed, the Queen was the real procession, the rest merely embroidery. Nellie had arranged an elaborate Women's Dinner to celebrate the Jubilee, and her sons were left in no doubt what a significant historical landmark had been achieved. On 19 May 1900 Harold was in Hyde Park with his French governess as news of the Relief of Mafeking spread. A very different experience came on 2 February 1901, eight days before his ninth birthday, when he watched the funeral procession of Queen Victoria from a house on the corner of Park Lane, and saw the cortège solemnly make its way to Paddington station through streets lined 60 deep with black-clad figures.

The young Harold's first schooling was at Mr Gladstone's establishment off Sloane Square, now known as Eaton House.[14] The school was chosen not only for its proximity to the family home, but for its reputation in preparing boys for Summer Fields. He had already been taught to read by his mother, and later French governesses and tutors came in to augment the learning at Mr Gladstone's. He thrived on the reading, especially in the classics, and at home loved the middle-brow adventure writers of the time, G. A. Henty, Conan Doyle and Rider Haggard. What he did not enjoy was the weekly excursion to Mr Macpherson's Gymnasium. The exercises with Indian clubs in particular proved most distressing. But *mens sana in corpora sano* (the motto of Summer Fields) was the accepted norm.

At the age of nine, Harold was taken by Nanny Last to Paddington in a four-wheeler cab and put on the train. At Oxford a waiting horse-bus took him and some other London boys to Summertown, then a village, surrounded by fields, with its post office, butcher and baker. Harold was registered as Pupil 892, son of M.C.M. (1864), for term 1903 (2). He wept himelf to sleep after a sparse meal of bread and milk. This was his introduction to boarding school.

Summer Fields[15] had been started in 1864 by Gertrude Isobel Maclaren, the second wife of Archibald Maclaren, founder of the Oxford University Gymnasium. Because his first wife, who had died in childbirth, was Gertrude's sister, the marriage was considered in some church circles to be incestuous, and indeed was proscribed under English law* until 1907.

The Maclarens kept themselves quietly to themselves in North

---

*Holman Hunt, the painter, and later a Summer Fields parent, who was to follow a similar path in 1875, went into voluntary exile abroad for some time after his marriage to his dead wife's sister.

Oxford, and by the time the school opened, no stigma was attached to them. 'Mrs', as she was universally known, was in charge of academic teaching, and her husband of physical education. The school grew and in due course more staff were employed. In 1870 a Welsh graduate of Brasenose College, the Reverend Dr Cyril Eccles Williams, had arrived, and shortly afterwards the Reverend Hugh Alington. Both married Maclaren daughters, and the brothers-in-law were to be key figures in the growing prestige of the school, which formally adopted the name Summer Fields in 1891 (it was originally designated Summerfields), to avoid postal confusion with neighbouring properties in Summertown.

Cyril Williams was in charge of the scholarship form, and was in effect headmaster, which he later became formally. He was the first person outside the immediate family circle to have a major impact on the young Harold Macmillan. His philosophy was direct. He believed in the three Cs – Chapel, Classics and Cricket. The boys felt there was a fourth, Cold Baths (not abolished until 1960). The one C in which he did not believe was Change; he was, in his own words, 'against all change, even change for the better.'[16]

For many ambitious parents, especially those who hoped their sons would win Eton scholarships, Summer Fields was *the* school of choice. Harold Macmillan gained an exacting knowledge of Latin and Greek prose, and the ability to compose as well as to translate in both languages. The reading lists included St. Mark's Gospel and the Acts of the Apostles, three books of the *Odyssey*, two of the *Aeneid*, and works by Herodotus, Horace, Ovid and Xenophon. Dickens and Scott were added to his favourite authors. Macmillan thrived on the scholarly work, though he was not keen on gymnastics and climbing ropes. The boys took an interest in the political controversies of the day, and when there was an outbreak of German measles in March 1904 the school magazine observed of the invalids, 'They were obviously not upholders of Mr Chamberlain and the protective tariff.' Nor was the young Harold. The politician he most admired was Sir Henry Campbell-Bannerman, who had become leader of the Liberal Party in the Commons in 1899.[17] Unlike the rest of his family, Macmillan supported 'CB' in his successful general election campaign of January 1906, an early sign of his rebelliousness.

For one who later became known as a renowned political actor, it is fitting that one of Macmillan's first forays on to the boards should have been as the Prime Minister. On Saturday, 16 November 1905, he was one of the stars of the school's production of *Rumpelstiltzkin*, dressed in a long cloak and crimson cape, with buckled shoes, silk stockings, knee breeches, long waistcoat and a curly judge's wig. 'Macmillan, as Prime Minister, was very obsequious and did his part excellently,' read the subsequent review in the school magazine. 'We felt very sorry when the curtain at last went down and shut out from our eyes kings, courtiers, elves and fairy land.' As he had recently been reading *David Copperfield* his performance clearly drew on the example of Uriah Heep. His other stage appearance at Summer Fields was as one of the crowd in Shakespeare's most political play, *Coriolanus*.

Eventually Harold won Eton's 'third' Scholarship. Yet even this was a disappointment: Dan had won the school's 'first' Scholarship. It took Harold many years to break free from the shadow of Dan, who was also top Scholar at Balliol, whereas Harold was 'only' an Exhibitioner. But Summer Fields had been a liberating experience for him, not least from the stultifying atmosphere of Cadogan Place. He had made friends, including an older boy, Evelyn Baring, who sympathetically told him on his first night that though his situation was critical it was not desperate. Another, who from May 1904 became a lifelong friend, was Harry Crookshank.[18]

Macmillan retained a great affection for Summer Fields which, he told a later headmaster, was like the monasteries, keeping the light of civilisation burning in the Dark Ages. He delighted that some of his grandsons and great-grandsons later attended the school. Above all Summer Fields gave him a lifelong love of the classics, deeply felt. He served the school as a governor, even after becoming Prime Minister in 1957.[19] Hugh Gaitskell, the Labour leader, gave up his equivalent post as governor of the rival Oxford preparatory school, the Dragon, on becoming Leader of the Opposition in 1955. This determined Macmillan to continue at Summer Fields, as any opportunity of being one up on both the Dragon and Gaitskell was a double bonus. In 1979 he opened the Macmillan Hall, which is used as a theatre today. In his speech he said that it was a great honour to have a building, or anything, named after oneself, but his honour was far better than that accorded Mr Gladstone by his eponymous bag, 'this obsolescent form of luggage mouldering away in some attic in your home'.[20]

The year that Harold Macmillan went to Eton, the family took possession of an estate near Horsted Keynes in Sussex with, by country house standards, a modest villa, Birch Grove. The centre of gravity of family life now moved to one of the loveliest parts of a quintessentially English county, with heather and pine and gentle rolling fields, between the Sussex Weald and Ashdown Forest. Rudyard Kipling, a near neighbour, who had bought Bateman's at Burwash in 1902, loved the area's quiet peace. Harold Macmillan was to feel the same of his adopted county. Round the house and its environs, Birch Grove possessed a seemingly endless variety of cycle routes, enjoyed by generations of children, including those of the staff.

'The King's College of Our Lady of Eton beside Windsor' was established by the charter of King Henry VI on 11 October 1440. When Harold Macmillan arrived in 1906 in College – which housed the 70 King's Scholars – over one third were from Summer Fields. For Collegers, their year of election was the key unit, as each year messed together (had tea in each other's rooms) and did not socialise much with groups a year ahead or a year behind. Such an arrangement cemented Macmillan's friendship with Harry Crookshank, and other clever Summer Field boys such as Henry Willink and Julian Lambart. College was at the heart of the school, in the oldest of the Tudor buildings. The rest of the pupils, known as Oppidans, lived in boarding houses around Eton. This was one of the reasons Macmillan had an aloof disdain for Anthony Eden, his predecessor as prime minister, as 'a town house squit'.[21] Collegers were installed in Election Hall – the Provost intoning, *Sis bonus puer* – and wore short black gowns, which further distinguished Scholars from Oppidans. They dined in College Hall, the architecture of which, dating from 1450, outclasses that of many Oxbridge college halls.

In 1906 the Collegers, dismissed as 'tugs' by the Oppidans, were 'an intellectual elite thrust into the heart of a social elite'.[22] To some extent the 70 Scholars and nearly 1,000 Oppidans in Macmillan's time[23] occupied two different schools, 'as ignorant of each other's habits, thoughts and feelings, as if they were dwellers in different zones'.[24]

The real rivalry in the shadow of Windsor Castle was not Town versus Gown, but Collegers versus Oppidans. 'Meeting Oppidans,' wrote a later Colleger, Cyril Connolly, 'was like going to smart luncheons where people seem more intimate than they are; returning to College was going on from lunch to spend all the afternoon with a bourgeois intellectual friend of long standing.'[25] This rivalry found its apogee in the annual, and nigh incomprehensible, St Andrew's Day Wall Game, 'more a trial of strength than a game'.[26] For one who had eschewed vigorous physical activity both in Mr Macpherson's Gymnasium and at Summer Fields, Macmillan nevertheless played in the Wall Game versus the Oppidans in 1909, a year that most unusually saw a goal, and gained his Wall Game Colours. A pre-match team photograph shows him, as yet unmuddied, in melancholy apprehension.

Macmillan was not popular with his contemporaries. On 5 April 1909 there was an election for places in the College Debating Society. Macmillan received 13 blackballs. At the next election, on 24 July, he received 11, a step in the right direction but not a large one.[27] The most popular boys tended to be the ones who excelled at sports. Macmillan never liked games. He enjoyed cricket, and flourished at the Field Game, an esoteric form of football, then played in the Michaelmas Half.[28] On 22 September 1908, the College Annals recorded his success. 'Macmillan opened the scoring by a good goal ... in the loose play which ensued Macmillan shot another good goal.' Two days later he was praised again. 'The ball came near Fletcher's goal guided by the skill of Macmillan who touched a rouge [a method of scoring in the Field Game equivalent to a try in rugby].'[29] He was beginning to increase in popularity as his athletic success made its modest mark. Yet the College Debating Society remained closed to him.

Collegers were under the care of the Master-in-College, one of Eton's most prestigious posts for a young, ambitious beak (teacher). The Master-in-College when Macmillan arrived was the Revd Cyril Alington. In 1908, he was appointed Head Master of Shrewsbury. He returned to Eton as Head Master in 1917, and was later Dean of Durham, and the father-in-law of Alec Douglas-Home. Alington had been appointed Master-in-College in 1904, and 'presided happily over a particularly distinguished period'.[30] Intellectual freedom was the spirit of the time. 'College shows a healthy spirit of anti-nomianism,' recorded Ronald Knox, Alington's star pupil, 'the surest proof of internal soundness.'[31] For Macmillan, Alington was a pastoral, rather than an academic, mentor.

Macmillan's main teaching came from his classical tutor, A. B. ('The Ram') Ramsay, a Cambridge chess half-blue, and a devotee of whitebait and Latin verse. He took Macmillan and his friend Julian Lambart on an Hellenic cruise and gave them their first sight of the Parthenon. An idiosyncratic figure, who at teatime asked 'Mr Kettle' if he was boiling, he was an exacting tutor, who found in the young Macmillan a willing spirit and a porous receptacle for his wisdom and knowledge. A prolific author, and editor of classical texts, Ramsay is described in the *Dictionary of National Biography* as 'probably the most significant British Latin poet of the twentieth century'.[32]

The year before Harold Macmillan's arrival at Eton, the Honourable and Reverend Canon Edward Lyttelton had been appointed Head Master. A Christian and a devout sportsman, Lyttelton had captained the Cambridge University cricket XI to victory against the Australians in 1878, had played in the FA Cup Final in 1876 for the Old Etonians versus the Wanderers, and had won an international soccer cap against Scotland. He confessed that he could never walk down the nave of a church without wondering if it would take spin. Lyttelton had previously been Head Master of Haileybury, where the future Prime Minister, Clement Attlee, had been one of his pupils. During his time at Eton, he was to be the Head Master of three more future premiers, Anthony Eden, Harold Macmillan and Alec Douglas-Home. Of no other Head Master could it be said that he had taught four prime ministers and played in an FA Cup Final.

Lyttelton inherited the school at a time of recurring scandals. In 1906 the Captain (head boy) of Williams's House was found to have been regularly abusing younger boys, a fact unknown to his housemaster. Lyttelton saw it as his duty, Heracles-like, to conduct an immediate purge. The Captain's expulsion led to the House scratching from the final of the House Football Cup, an unprecedented event.[33] The homoerotic atmosphere, however, was not unprecedented; indeed, it could be said to be endemic. 'Eton, like many public schools at the time,' the biographer of Lord Rosebery has written, 'was a hothouse of seething passion ... not least in master-pupil relationships.'[34]

In the closely knit world of London society, the 1906 scandal was soon the talk of the clubs. The news also reached the ears of Nellie Macmillan, who was beginning to wonder whether Eton was the right place for her youngest son. Two other matters at this time may have contributed to her unease.

The Cadogan Hotel, opposite the family's London home, had been opened in 1887 in the general expansion of the area. On the evening of 5 April 1895, Oscar Wilde had been arrested in Room 118.[35] This followed the collapse of his case for criminal libel against the Marquess of Queensberry, father of Lord Alfred Douglas, for leaving a card at Wilde's club, the Albemarle, accusing him of 'posing as somdomite [sic]'. The subsequent scandal, trial and imprisonment of Wilde, the most famous playwright of his day, exercised Victorian society to an unprecedented degree. John Betjeman evoked the atmosphere of affronted respectability in his famous 1937 poem on Wilde's arrest by two plain-clothes policemen:

> Mr Woilde, we 'ave come for tew take you
> Where felons and criminals dwell:
> We must ask yew tew leave with us quoietly
> For this *is* the Cadogan Hotel.[36]

Nellie, had she got wind of what was happening that April day, could easily have seen from an upper room in 52 Cadogan Place the police leaving the hotel with Wilde.[37] Whether or not she actually witnessed the aftermath of the arrest, one can easily imagine the disgust felt in the Cadogan Place community, and the accompanying gossip.

Even nearer to home was the friendship of Nellie's eldest son Dan with John Maynard Keynes.[38] Keynes was unashamedly homosexual, and Dan Macmillan was the first love of his life. At Eton, Keynes had had an affair – and one that was phsyically consummated – with Dilwyn (Dilly) Knox, an elder brother of Ronald Knox, and also an Old Summerfieldian. Bernard Swithinbank, one of Keynes' election, who unsuccessfully courted Dilly Knox, another twist in these intertwining circles, later wrote: 'In College emotion and desire were directed almost exclusively towards the male sex – I knew hardly anyone who ever thought of women. This does not mean that there was a great deal of "vice"; indeed it was looked on with disapproval, not untinged with envy, by the many who repressed their desires through shyness or virtue.'[39] Keynes was not one of those who repressed his desires, and nor was he shy or 'virtuous'.

No one can be certain how many of these Byzantine intricacies Nellie understood. She probably never suspected that Dan might have homosexual leanings, but it is unlikely that she did not pick up some confirmation of Keynes' feelings towards him. Whether Keynes ever consummated his relationship with Dan (the probability is that he did), it was not for want of trying. Both Keynes and Swithinbank, almost three years older than Dan, found him, a 16-year-old, impossibly beautiful, and at Eton he had become their 'object', an example of the friendship across the years – very rare in College – that always attracted the suspicion of both schoolmasters and parents.

Eton in the early years of the century, and for some time afterwards, was a place where some boys begged to be allowed to stay on, not to gain election to 'Pop', the exclusive school society, or to captain a house or an eleven, as their parents might have been led to believe, but because they had fallen in love with a junior. The half-mustachioed 19-year-old in School Yard was a not uncommon sight in Edwardian Eton. The atmosphere was precisely caught by John Le Carré in his novel *A Murder of Quality*, set in a thinly disguised Eton. 'They were always in mourning,' it is observed of the boys in funereal clothes, 'the small boys because they must stay and the big boys because they must leave.'[40]

In 1909, when he was 15, Harold Macmillan left Eton. Many questions remain unanswered about this early departure, the usual reason given being ill health. Was it, though, because Nellie feared that her son would be prey to 'unnatural vices'? Was he already embroiled?

Indeed, was he expelled? J.B.S. Haldane, the renowned geneticist, who was in College with him, always claimed that Harold Macmillan was sacked from Eton for homosexuality.[41] Whether or not Macmillan left 'under a cloud' has been a matter of speculation ever since.

The truth is more prosaic. Even as a boy, Macmillan was reticent about all sexual matters. He was not confident and outgoing enough to have been, in the contemporary parlance, 'a school tart', but photographs show his delicate, feminine features and he undoubtedly attracted the unwelcome attention of the rakish dandies. It is conceivable that he was being bullied. J.B.S. Haldane had endured merciless bullying, and Harold, as evinced by the number of blackballs he received in College elections, was not popular with his contemporaries. But it is more likely that Nellie had got wind that he was a potential victim of predatory older boys.[42]

Eton had initially been for Nellie an English idyll by the Thames, an attitude to the 'old culture' of Europe that would have befitted an American heroine in a Henry James novel. But now the school was inexorably associated in her mind with a different kind of Eden, full of forbidden fruit, in what Cyril Connolly described as 'the vinegar-scented cloisters'.[43] She now believed, not unjustifiably, that it was an immoral place, and shortly after her son's appearance in the Wall Game on 30 November 1909, she peremptorily took him away from the school. The fact that he had been diagnosed with a heart murmur was an additional, but not the main, factor. His father, consumed with business matters at Macmillan & Co., including the establishment of the Calcutta branch of the firm in 1907 as the Macmillan Colonial Library expanded, was not involved in the decision.

Had Macmillan been expelled, there would be evidence in the College Archives (which there is not). Such an expulsion could never have been kept confidential, and people such as Bobbety Salisbury and Oliver Lyttelton, both of whom had unswerving attitudes towards any form of homosexuality, would never have been such close friends with him.[44] In 1965, when there was a vacancy for the provostship of Eton (the resident chairman of the governing body), Macmillan let it be known that he would like to be considered. Such a candidature would have been utterly impossible had he been expelled as a boy. But the clinching fact that disproves Haldane's assertion is that Macmillan cherished his leaving book of Thomas Gray's poems, with its famous ode about Eton. No expelled boy was ever given a leaving book.

A myth has grown up that as Macmillan was unhappy at Eton, and devoted only one paragraph in his six volumes of memoirs to his time there, he did not greatly care for the school in later life. But the positives are there: close friendships, an even deeper insight into his beloved classics, and memories of the great events of the Eton school year, such as the match against Harrow at Lord's and the annual Fourth of June celebrations, commemorating the birthday of King George III, one of Eton's most generous benefactors. Macmillan's son, grandsons and, after his death, great-grandsons continued the family tradition of being educated at the school and Harold regularly alternated his neckwear between the black and narrow light blue stripe of the Old Etonian tie and that of the Brigade of Guards.

Though 'Old Etonian' increasingly became a pejorative phrase in the 1950s and 1960s, with all its associations of privilege, Macmillan delighted, tongue-in-cheek, in drawing attention to his status as the most famous living Old Etonian of them all. 'Mr Attlee had three old Etonians in his Cabinet,' he declared in 1959. 'I have six. Things are twice as good under the Conservatives.' He would dearly have loved to have become Provost. His last public appearance – on Friday, 23 May 1986 – was at the Eton College Political Society. Frail, increasingly deaf, and nearly blind, he took five minutes to walk from the Provost's dining room to his seat in Election Hall next door, where he had been installed as a King's Scholar 80 years earlier, and where a hundred boys were patiently waiting. He referred to the beauty of Eton, and how each time one visited the more enthralling it seemed. Then he added that the more one saw of the ugliness of the world, the more one was conscious of how fortunate one had been. He spoke about the 'Third Industrial Revolution' and then took questions. The last question was: 'Looking back on your long career, do you feel optimistic or pessimistic about the future of this country?' He hesitated for only a moment before rolling out a wonderful sentence: 'As I look around this room [pause] at the bright eager faces in front of me [pause] and as I listen to the intelligent questions you have asked [pause] how could I feel anything about the future of this country [pause] but optimism?' At that point he staggered a little and allowed the boy nearest him to take his arm and help him sit down. He knew he had produced the perfect words with which to finish.[45] Seven months later he was dead.

Harold Macmillan's childhood and schooling, ostensibly serene and privileged, ended in his being removed from the world-famous school where he was just beginning to find his feet. We cannot know what he suffered in terms of humiliation. But we do know that he was now at home, once more under the thumb of his ambitious mother, whose high-handed actions in the name of morality could well have made the prospects for his future years seem very distant indeed.

CHAPTER THREE

Sent Down by the Kaiser

1910–1914

Life is one Balliol man after another.

Herbert Samuel

Whatever happens, remember that the sun
will still rise over Wadham and set over Worcester.

Raymond Asquith

As it happened, Nellie had engaged a tutor for Harold during the summer holidays of 1909 before he had even left Eton. He was not falling behind with his studies – he was a Colleger and clever – so Nellie had her own agenda. If this trial run went well, then a full-time arrangement of home tutoring would be preferable to Eton, with which she was becoming increasingly disenchanted.

Harold was never very good at being a schoolboy. Undergraduate life was to be much more his métier. He was shy, withdrawn and cerebral, by no means a flannelled fool or muddied oaf, at a time when sports mattered, even in College. The peremptory end of his Eton schooling increased his already incipient sense of gloom, and even inadequacy. In addition to his friendships in College with Henry Willink, Julian Lambart and Harry Crookshank, he had regard for two other contemporaries, not in College, Oliver Lyttelton and Bobbety Cranborne, later Lord Salisbury.[1] To leave these five behind could not have been easy for the sensitive young Harold.

Any lingering doubts Nellie may have had (though she was not one given to doubts) were removed by Harold's recurring illnesses. He had almost died of pneumonia in his first year at the College (the kind of common event that made a mawkish chapter in many of the school novels of the age), and was now known to have a heart murmur.

Nellie's choice of part-time tutor, in the summer before Harold's last Half, was none other than Bernard Swithinbank, who had recently graduated from Balliol. She could not possibly have known it, but Swithinbank was, like Keynes, infatuated with her son Dan.[2] Indeed, he had been holidaying with Keynes in Burford, where the conversation had centred nostalgically on Eton and Dan.[3] Swithinbank took up his post on 2 August 1909. It cannot, one imagines, have been much fun for a 15-year-old boy in the middle of his summer holidays. But Swithinbank's tutoring of Harold, and his companionship, were deemed a success, and this success was a major factor in Nellie's decision to remove Harold from Eton at the end of the year, giving time for the necessary notice. But when Nellie needed a full-time tutor in January 1910, Swithinbank was unavailable. Her choice fell on Dilly Knox, one of the four sons of the Revd Edmund Arbuthnott Knox, Bishop of Manchester. Dilly had been at Summer Fields, first in his election to College at Eton, and a Scholar of King's College, Cambridge, where Keynes and Dan had been his contemporaries. He had taken a First in Part I of the Classics Tripos, and in 1909 had been appointed a Fellow of his college. He was very clever, and had been recommended by Dan himself. Dilly indeed was another of the Eton boys who had been part of the Keynes ménage at Cambridge. The arrangement with Dilly, however, only lasted for a few weeks. Nellie found him an unsatisfactory companion for Harold, 'austere and uncongenial'.[4] She turned instead to Dilly's younger brother, Ronald, closer in age to Harold (he was born in 1888), but, more to the point, a Balliol man and a devout Christian, unlike Dilly, who at King's had become a 'ferocious agnostic'.[5] At the time, Ronald Knox was preparing for the priesthood and was due to begin tutorial work at Trinity College, Oxford, in the Hilary (Easter) Term of 1911. So the chance of becoming private tutor to one of Dilly's friends seemed an ideal way of using a sabbatical.

Nellie was never convinced that Harold had benefited from the best available teaching at Eton. Much depended in the Eton system on the beak a boy was 'up to' for tutoring. Keynes, like Dan, had prospered under the tutelage of Samuel Gurney Lubbock, who had recognised and nurtured his special qualities.[6] The fact that Harold's classical teaching had been in the notable care of A. B. Ramsay cut little ice at the time with Nellie, a clear indication of her perfectionist demands. However, Harold felt that he had been taught so well by 'The Ram' that he now requested that his former tutor be engaged. Nellie acquiesced, and Harold always attributed any skill he had in Greek and Latin composition to Ramsay's regular visits to Cadogan Place.

Ronald Knox was initially engaged for the Michaelmas Term of 1910, because Ramsay's visits had to be fitted around Eton commitments. Nellie was a demanding, even naive, employer, and soon there were difficulties over money. In his autobiography, *A Spiritual Aeneid*, published in 1918, Knox coyly refers to Macmillan as 'C', a coyness repeated by Evelyn Waugh in his official biography of Knox, a book for which Macmillan, by then Prime Minister and busy with political preoccupations, had nevertheless afforded him much help.[7]

Knox's priority was to continue the work of 'The Ram' and Dilly in ensuring Macmillan a Balliol scholarship. But he had another mission and, finding the impressionable adolescent amenable, soon turned to spiritual matters. At Harold's request, he took him to a High Church Anglo-Catholic Mass. For the Nonconformist Nellie, who seems to have been unaware that, guided by Dan, her chosen home tutors for Harold had once been part of a 'homo-erotic set', this was a worrying development. From there it was only a short journey, geographically as well as spiritually, to the Church of the Immaculate Conception, Farm Street, the Jesuit church in Mayfair, especially as Harold found the whole ambience of ritual, incense and artistic beauty, in both music and accoutrements, profoundly impressive. When one of Knox's friends asked him if he intended making Macmillan a Catholic, Knox replied on 10 October 1910, 'I'm not making him anything yet, but biding my time. I trust I may be sent some opportunity.' A covert campaign to induce Harold to 'Pope' was bound to reach Nellie's sensitive ears, and when it did, the fierce reaction was predictable. Even at this early stage in her son's life, she had foreseen that a Roman Catholic would be disqualified from becoming Prime Minister. 'Verting', as she deemed it, was completely off limits.

She instructed Knox to confine himself to classical teaching and forbade him to discuss religious matters with her romantically inclined son, who had seen in Knox a glimpse of holiness. Knox refused, and from 27 November to 1 December had furious arguments with Nellie. What complicated things was that the tutor had now become enamoured of the handsome 16-year-old pupil, and sensed, not entirely fancifully, that the feelings were reciprocated. 'The only thing that complicates the matter,' Knox wrote frankly to his sister, 'is that I'm by now extremely (and not quite unreturnedly) fond of the boy.' The twin horrors for Nellie – 'vice' and Roman Catholicism – had returned with a vengeance. On 4 December, two days into the second general election campaign of 1910, Knox was dismissed, and sent packing on the first available train, with neither his bicycle nor his laundry. 'It's been a horrid wrench to go without saying a word to him of what I wanted to say,' he wrote to his sister. As suffering was for him an essential spiritual lesson, Knox always regarded this as one of the formative episodes of his life.[8]

So it proved for Harold Macmillan. He was devastated by the sudden removal of his first adult friend and mentor. Knox retained a special place in his affections. In June 1957, when suffering from terminal cancer, Knox stayed for some days at 10 Downing Street with Macmillan, who, after the bleak final medical diagnosis by the distinguished physican Sir Horace Evans[9], took him in his official car to Paddington station for what proved to be Knox's final return to Mells in Somerset. As they parted on the platform, Macmillan wished his former tutor well for the journey. 'It will be a very long one,' Knox replied. Much moved, Macmillan said, 'But Ronnie, you are very well prepared for it.' To Philip de Zulueta, Macmillan's (Catholic) Private Secretary, Knox, under a strict medical regime, added, 'Heaven must be better than orange juice.'[10]

From January 1911 until he took the Balliol scholarship examination that autumn, Macmillan's education was in the hands of a succession of tutors, with occasional remedial visits from 'The Ram'. It was the bleakest time of his life, largely unrecorded in his papers, unmentioned in his memoirs and unlamented by him.

On 10 February 1911, he turned seventeen. His former Eton contemporaries were just entering that unforgettable golden time of their schooldays, with position, power, accomplishment and the kind words and distant hankerings of youthful longings. There was not for Macmillan an appearance at Lord's against Harrow, to be remembered evermore, as Walter Monckton and Harold Alexander[11] and Alec Douglas-Home did; nor the prestigious Newcastle Scholarship for Classics and Divinity, a prize he could well have won in 1911 or 1912. However, this 'gap' in his Eton education might have had its positive side.

Cyril Connolly has formulated what he called 'The Theory of Permanent Adolescence', in which he postulates that 'the experiences undergone by the boys at the great public schools, their glories and disappointments, are so intense as to dominate their lives and to arrest their development'. Of his triumphant Eton contemporaries, Connolly observed that 'those who knew them then knew them at their best and fullest; now in their early thirties, they are haunted ruins'.[12] The pattern of Macmillan's life was the opposite. It was a case, in the words of Robert Browning, of 'Grow old along with me, the best is yet to be.'[13]

Macmillan's last year at Eton had been played out against the background of dramatic political events in which he took an intense interest. The politician he had admired most at the time of the 1906 general election, Sir Henry Campbell-Bannerman, had resigned from the premiership in April 1908, and, too ill to leave Downing Street, had stayed in what he called 'this rotten old barracks of a house', where he died on 22 April, the only former Prime Minister to die in No. 10.[14]* H. H. Asquith succeeded him as prime minister, and David Lloyd George became Chancellor of the Exchequer.

So swift was Campbell-Bannerman's demise that Asquith, a month after he had become Prime Minister, presented the Budget he had been preparing as Chancellor.[15] This 1908 Budget was notable for establishing the principle of differential taxation between earned and unearned income. Asquith introduced a degree of social security provision and means-tested pensions for those over the age of 70, a base on which Lloyd George, the new Chancellor, built energetically.

Lloyd George, faced with the need to raise £16m for an expansion of pensions and, in the increasingly competitive Anglo-German naval race, for more Dreadnought battleships ('We want eight and we won't wait' was the political cry of the time), cast his net ever wider. He increased death duties, and introduced Super Tax and land taxes, putting him in direct conflict with the Upper House, which he described as 'a body of five hundred men chosen at random from amongst the unemployed'.[16] In November 1909, the House of Lords rejected what Lloyd George had dubbed 'the People's Budget', an unprecedented denial of supply by the Upper House. Asquith sought a dissolution, and polling was set to begin on 15 January.

As was customary until 1918, voting took place over several weeks, and at 26 days, the January 1910 election was the longest in British history. Asquith was confirmed in office on 10 February, Macmillan's sixteenth birthday, but in a totally different political landscape from before. Though the Liberals had a total of 275 seats, they were only two seats ahead of the Conservative and Unionist Party, and did not possess an independent majority. With Labour winning 40 seats, its highest total to date, the position of the Irish Nationalist Party, with 82 seats, was to prove crucial. On 10 February, John Redmond, leader of the Irish Nationalists, 12 of whose nominal supporters were independent nationalists, declared in a threatening speech in Dublin his unwillingness to prop up the Liberals. As a result, the continuance of Asquith's government in 1910 was uncertain. The Irish had been unenthusiastic about the People's Budget, voting against the second reading. They had consented to support it only if Asquith agreed to the suspensory veto so that Home Rule could proceed, 'No veto, no

---

*King Edward VII had visited Campbell-Bannerman on his sick-bed on 4 March; the next time a sovereign would do likewise was when Queen Elizabeth II visited Macmillan in King Edward VII Hospital on 18 October 1963.

Budget' being the Irish slogan. Redmond's priority was Home Rule for Ireland, and this issue was to dominate British politics until the outbreak of the Great War in 1914, and for many years afterwards. Continued intransigence by the Lords towards the People's Budget in the months ahead led in December 1910 to a second general election, which produced a result almost identical to that in January.[17] The future of the Lords and of Ireland now became Asquith's seemingly intractable burden.

The threat of the creation of 400 Liberal peers by Asquith led to the eventual passage in November 1911 of the Parliament Bill, which limited the delaying powers of the Lords. A. J. Balfour resigned as Conservative Leader, and was replaced by Andrew Bonar Law. The future of Ireland now moved to the top of the political agenda. Macmillan later regarded the ensuing Ulster extremism as far more threatening than the unease associated with Mosley and his British Union of Fascists in the 1930s, because of the involvement of Bonar Law, the Leader of the Conservative Opposition, with his support for those who believed that 'Ulster will fight and Ulster will be right.'[18]

After the death of Campbell-Bannerman, Lloyd George became the political figure Macmillan most admired. The young Harold, with a deepening perception about contemporary events way beyond his years, respected Asquith's 'intellectual sincerity and moral nobility'.[19]* But Lloyd George, for him, was the man of action who would actually accomplish his goals. Interestingly, neither Balfour nor Bonar Law, with whom there were to be distinct parallels when he was Prime Minister himself, engaged Macmillan's sympathies to anything like the same extent at this stage as the Liberal grandees. Nellie regarded Lloyd George as a thieving opportunist. For her youngest son, reluctance simply to echo his family's traditional political sympathies doubtless played its part. Macmillan often stood out against the conventional wisdom of the time, and even at the height of his powers remained something of an outsider. Indeed, when they were together in Parliament in the 1920s, Lloyd George told Macmillan that he was 'a born rebel'.[20]

Life was lonely for Harold at this time. His brothers had left home. Daniel was in the family firm, now established in St Martin's Street, and Arthur had been called to the Bar. Their father was frequently abroad on Macmillan & Co. business, particularly in the Indian subcontinent.

---

*Later Macmillan was to enjoy Asquith's hospitality at 10 Downing Street, through his friendship with Asquith's youngest son, Cys, a Balliol contemporary.

Harold took solace in books. The latest Macmillan publications were always to hand, and in the next decade and beyond, 'house' authors such as F. S. Oliver, Rudyard Kipling and Hugh Walpole engaged his interest. Religious books by Archbishops Frederick Temple, Edward Benson and William Temple, son of Frederick, were also studied for their subtle intricacies.

Macmillan was withdrawn from Eton by his mother in December 1909, but did not go up to Balliol until October 1912. He undoubtedly returned his mother's devotion, but this lengthy gap, without the camaraderie of his peers and the boisterous give and take of school life, left its mark. His introspective melancholy, detailed attention to scholarship and eclectic reading all stemmed from this time. His ability to read very rapidly (he could devour a substantial Victorian novel in 36 hours) stood him in good stead as a minister when faced with interminable boxes.

Despite his firm grounding in the classics from Summer Fields days onwards, Macmillan felt inhibited by the experience of the Balliol examination.* All around him were the brightest and the best of his generation, some of them his urbane and confident former Eton peers. Balliol was considered the leading college of the university. 'Its Open Scholarships and Fellowships,' wrote the college's official historian, 'were the greatest distinctions in the University a young man could aspire to.'[21] Whether effortless or not, superiority was considered the natural Balliol state.

'You glance around at your competitors,' Macmillan later recalled. 'What clever faces! What intellectual brows! What application! They have all begun to write from the very first minute – apparently with easy confidence. Good heavens! Then minutes have passed – they are running well down the course. You are still at the starting gate.'[22]

His brother Dan had won the top Balliol scholarship; Harold Macmillan had to be satisfied, even though Nellie was not, with the Williams Classical Exhibition. But he made it, and Balliol, the following year, was to be a liberation.

Balliol was never just a college, more a way of life and attitude of mind. Its history can be traced back to a royal writ of 1266, but when Harold Macmillan went up on 6 October 1912, returning to the city where he had been educated as a preparatory schoolboy, and which he

---

*Chris (later Lord) Patten, a future Balliol Chancellor of Oxford, once asked Macmillan about his interview. 'In my day,' replied Macmillan, 'all they wanted to know was where you'd got your boots made.'[23]

was to love more than any other, the college still basked in the reflected fame of its celebrated Master, Dr Benjamin Jowett, who had died in 1893 after a reign of 23 years, during which time he brought Balliol to an eminence it has never surrendered. Seven of the pall-bearers at his funeral were heads of Oxford colleges, all Balliol men. The Balliol that Macmillan entered was essentially Jowett's nineteenth-century creation: meritocratic, eclectic, radical and always ready to question the prevailing orthodoxies of the day, whether in scholarship, religion or politics. One thing above all that the cherubic Jowett, clad in white tie and swallowtail coat, instilled in his undergraduates was *expectation*. From this spot they would go forth to inherit the world. One of the last invitations he sent before his death read: 'To meet members of the two Houses of Parliament, and other members of the College.'[24] Such members knew they were of the elect, and to whom they owed much of their prominence, as a Balliol verse proclaimed:

> My heart leaps up when I behold
> A rainbow over Balliol Hall,
> As though the Cosmos was controlled,
> By Dr Jowett after all.[25]

The spirit of Jowett still burned strongly in Ronald Knox's time at Balliol. Macmillan too was well aware of Jowett's posthumous hold over the college; indeed, Balliol at once engaged Macmillan's feelings more than Eton had ever done. His experience was thus the reverse of that of Knox, in whose affections Balliol never supplanted Eton, despite his admonition in *A Spiritual Aeneid* that 'One has to grow up some time.'[26] Growing up was what the young Macmillan now proceeded to do.

Balliol was the ideal engine for emancipating the confined adolescent. Its Scottish connections helped, but other factors were more important. 'There are drinkers of cocoa,' recalled Aldous Huxley of his time at Balliol, 'and drinkers of champagne.'[27] After a life so far of cocoa, Macmillan now began to enjoy finer tastes, though unlike Dan, never to excess.[28] His rooms were in the Front Quad, just off Broad Street. Little of the medieval origins of the quad remained after the nineteenth-century extensions of Alfred Waterhouse (the Front Quad's east and south ranges) and William Butterfield's chapel, and its atmosphere was one of pensive High Victorian claustrophobia. Whatever its merits as the pre-eminent college at the turn of the century, Balliol could not claim such ascendancy in its architecture, of which it has been said, '*C'est magnifique, mais ce n'est pas la gare.*'[29] Not that this worried the young Macmillan. As at Eton, he had a room of his own; the difference was that he also had a freedom he had never known before.

From the first week his loneliness vanished. His closest friend in Balliol was Humphrey Sumner, the Brackenbury Scholar of his year. Others in whose company Macmillan delighted all his life were Walter Monckton, President of the Union when Macmillan arrived as a freshman, Victor Mallet, A. P. Herbert, who was to find fame as a writer and independent MP, and Vincent Massey, later Governor-General of Canada.

Next door to Balliol, at Trinity College[30], Ronald Knox was now the Anglican Chaplain.[31] Macmillan swiftly renewed their forbidden alliance. When Nellie heard, she prevented her son attending one of Knox's reading parties in Gloucestershire, the plans for which then collapsed. But Oxford had liberated Harold, and he quietly defied his mother in his pursuit of an intense friendship with Knox.

In Ronald Knox's Trinity 'circle' was a brilliant classical scholar from Winchester, Guy Lawrence, who, despite his shyness and highly strung nature, was one of the stars of OUDS (Oxford University Dramatic Society). Dubbed 'B' by Knox in his spiritual autobiography, Lawrence and 'C' (Macmillan) were his special protégés.

Macmillan was also greatly influenced by F. F. 'Sligger' Urquhart[32], that rarity, a Catholic don, the first such tutor in Oxford since the Reformation. Urquhart, unlike his friend Ronald Knox, did not seek to convert others.[33] As a result Conservative Anglicans in the University regarded him as a benign influence. When Macmillan felt himself under increasing pressure from many quarters to convert to Catholicism, he poured out his feelings privately to Sligger Urquhart, whom he found a sympathetic and understanding listener. 'You have saved me from awful torments by letting me tell you of them,' he wrote, adding later, 'I wish Ronnie would have more sense of humour.'[34]

Sligger Urquhart was a legendary bachelor don, with a capacity for friendship. His rooms in Balliol, the bay window of which ironically overlooked the Protestant Martyrs' Memorial, became a meeting place for all manner of undergraduates. Balliol was the perfect college for Urquhart, as Jowett believed in the primacy of tutors, thus providing an atmosphere ideally suited to the Sligger style. 'He emanated a stream of gentle sympathy,' wrote Noel Annan, 'that brought others out.'[35] He is remembered for his reading parties at the Chalet des Anglais, near Saint-Gervais, in the French Alps. The first such party took place in 1891, and apart from the years of the Great War, continued under Urquhart until 1935. Invitations to these parties were a mark of special favour, extended also to selected undergraduates from other colleges. The hothouse certainly had its homo-erotic atmosphere, as Sligger 'liked handsome young men, and photographing them, but was probably celibate'.[36] Rupert Hart-Davis, who was at Balliol in the mid-twenties, described Sligger as 'a purring old doctored tom-cat, who gave lemonade parties at which he stroked the knees of rugger blues...! I've never seen a more completely homosexual man.'[37] Yet the reading parties were rigorous affairs, with mornings given over to serious study, which Macmillan enjoyed more than the mountain walks. Sligger forbade climbing, as he considered it too dangerous, though he was not always obeyed.*

Macmillan received his invitation for the party in 1913. It lasted from 2–28 July, Violet Asquith and her brother Cys visiting the company on the 14th,[39] when Rupert Brooke from King's College, Cambridge, was a guest. Travel abroad was an adventure and a revelation for the young Macmillan – the journey across the Channel, by train from Calais and two nights in Paris, before a rack-and-pinion train, the Tramway du Mont Blanc, and then a tortuous mule path to the chalet, luggage following on a cart.

His first stay in Paris was a shock. He found it 'a filthy town', and in more ways than one. His group visited the Folies Bergères, 'which we imagined like an ordinary music hall', only to find that 'the combination of Immorality and Ugliness was astonishing'. Sligger's chalet was far more to his taste. 'I believe Heaven will be rather like your Reading Parties,' he wrote to his host, after his first visit, 'and we will have excellent matches of Apostles versus a visiting side from Hell.'[40] The panoramic sight of the Vale of Chamonix, which Sligger dubbed 'the Great Wen', left an indelible impression, and evoked for the romantic young undergraduate the vision of Shelley:

> Dizzy Ravine! and when I gaze on thee
> I seem as in a trance sublime and strange.[41]

By comparison with Sligger Urquhart, other dons often seemed pro-saic, but this was not the case for Macmillan, as he was fortunate to have as his tutors two of the finest classical scholars of their day,

---

* Over the years, Urquhart's coterie in the Alps included the future MPs Robert Boothby, Dick Crossman, Quintin Hogg and Walter Monckton (important figures all in Macmillan's career), as well as Cyril Connolly, William Hayter, a future Ambassador to Russia and Warden of New College, and John Sparrow, who was Humphrey Sumner's successor but one as Warden of All Souls,[38] an appointment of which Maurice Bowra, the Warden of Wadham, observed, 'One Sparrow does not make a Sumner.' The reading parties continue to this day, and the chalet is shared with New College.

Cyril Bailey and Arthur (later Sir Arthur) Pickard-Cambridge, who took the pupils of exceptional ability, known as 'Cyril's boys' and 'Picker's boys'. Cyril Bailey also influenced Macmillan in that he was profoundly moved by the injustices of society and established the Balliol Boys' Club, bringing together the young of Town and Gown in what was then an unusual social experiment. Macmillan was in no doubt that he had joined a vibrant and unusual world. In a speech to the Balliol Society in 1957, knowing his audience, he quoted the nostalgic poem of Hilaire Belloc:

> Balliol made me, Balliol fed me,
> Whatever I had she gave me again;
> And the best of Balliol loved and led me,
> God be with you, Balliol men.[42]

The Prime Minister, H. H. Asquith, himself a Balliol man,[43] had spoken at a dinner on 22 July 1908 using words that defined the Balliol ethos. Balliol men, he said, possessed a 'tranquil consciousness of effortless superiority',[44] a phrase thereafter often used pejoratively. However, as John Jones has pointed out, 'the superiority was not effortless at all'.[45] Application, industry and talent mattered too, and Macmillan had all three in abundance.

Macmillan, later seen as the consummate actor-politician, was never attracted to OUDS. He was drawn to the Union, as the Prime Ministers Gladstone, Salisbury and Asquith had been before him, and Heath later; but not Rosebery, Attlee, Eden, Home, Wilson, Thatcher,[46] Blair or Cameron. Macmillan may not have made it into the College Debating Society at Eton, owing to the number of blackballs he received, but he made handsome amends now, and would almost certainly have been elected President of the Union in 1914–1915 if the Great War had not intervened.

For the first time, glimpses of the mature Macmillan could be discerned – the epigrammatic style, the love of anecdote with the use of apt quotation, the ability to change tone suddenly with dramatic effect. Walter Monckton, President of the Union in his first year, smoothed his path. Macmillan was elected Secretary in 1913 and Treasurer in March 1914. A great moment, and one of the highlights of his time at Oxford, was when Lloyd George visited the union in 1913. In December 1913, Macmillan spoke in favour of Asquith's government; he met Asquith that Michaelmas (Winter) term, when he came to dine in Balliol and speak to the undergraduates, a task Macmillan himself was to fulfil many times in later years, both as Prime Minister and in retirement.

Macmillan's allegiances, as befitted Balliol, were clearly on the radical side, though one contemporary, Colin Coote, thought that he was beginning to model himself on A. J. Balfour. That was a perceptive comment, for by the time he was in Downing Street, Macmillan was almost a Balfour-reborn, with the ready aphorism, the supposed (though studied) insouciance, and the underlying intellectualism.[47] Macmillan was the most purely cerebral prime minister since Balfour; the big difference was that he knew how to win general elections.[48]

At the Union, Macmillan as a freshman spoke in October 1912 in favour of the motion 'That this House approves the main principles of Socialism'. He first appeared 'on the paper' in February 1913, speaking against the public school system, arguing that it would be better for people of different backgrounds to be educated together.[49] Isis, the undergraduate newspaper, regarded this as 'a brilliant maiden speech', and they praised him frequently: he was 'decidedly amusing', 'quite brilliant', and 'his phraseology was wonderful'. He was selected to be a member of the Oxford Union team that travelled to Cambridge on 4 November 1913 for a joint debate (preceded by a lavish white-tie dinner) on the Irish situation, in which he spoke on the unjustifiable actions of the Ulster Unionists.[50] Eventually Isis became critical, thinking that his speeches smacked too much of the midnight oil, and lacked spontaneity.[51] As a learning experience, though, the Union was invaluable.

In the best tradition of political undergraduates, Macmillan joined all the clubs. He was a member of the Canning Club (Conservative), the Russell Club (Liberal) and the Fabian Club (Labour) and, as later with his London clubs, was active in all of them. Fabian Socialism was most in tune with the Balliol ethos, but this did not prevent him, after his enthusiasms for Campbell-Bannerman and Lloyd George, from delving deeply into the life of a Tory radical, Benjamin Disraeli, whose monumental multi-volumed biography by Moneypenny and Buckle was then appearing at regular intervals.[52] He read each volume fresh from the press.

Macmillan was also a member of the select Hanover Club, founded in 1911 'to promote the cause of good feeling between Germany and England', which reflected serious concerns about the international situation. More light-hearted was Balliol's Brackenbury Society, which possessed a stuffed owl called Mr Gladstone, to which members addressed comments, beginning their speeches 'Mr President, Mr Gladstone'.[53] In January 1914 a motion deprecated 'the present custom of wearing Grey bags which obtains in this University'. The minute book records that when Macmillan pleaded for the wearing of grey flannel coats, 'the house remembered an important appointment, and fled like dromedaries in a field of maize'.[54]

Despite all this varied activity, he still found time for serious work, and in Hilary term 1914 was duly awarded a First in Honour Moderations, no mean achievement.[55] The last days of peace and the glorious summer of the Trinity term were an unrepeatable idyll, approximating in Macmillan's mind to 'le plaisir de vivre' that, according to Talleyrand, departed from France for ever after the Revolution.[56]

On 28 June 1914, Gavrilo Princip assassinated the Archduke Ferdinand of Austria in Sarajevo. The governor of the Austrian provinces of Bosnia-Herzegovina had invited Franz Ferdinand to observe troop manoeuvres, and the Archduke had accepted, despite the dangers. His uncle, Emperor Franz Joseph, had been the target for an assassination by the murderous Black Hand movement in 1911. The Archduke was not so lucky. Gavrilo Princip, a Bosnian student, born like Macmillan in 1894, has been described as 'a character from a Chekhov play except that when he fired he did not miss'.[57] Indirectly, Princip, a Bosnian Serb, and reluctant subject of Austro-Hungary, thus set off a chain of events leading to the greatest military conflagration in history, and the 'sweet and carefree atmosphere'[58] of pre-war Europe was at an end.

Macmillan has given a vivid impression of the night of 28 June 1914: of a ball at one of the great London houses, accompanied by Mr Cassani's string band, a fin de siècle moment before the armageddon of war, and of hearing from the newsboys in the streets in the early hours as the ball broke up of the murder of the Archduke.[59] His account is compelling, but it may be a case of 'old men forget' and of two memories eliding. 28 June 1914 was a Sunday, unthinkable as a day in that era for a great ball, not on religious grounds, but rather because of convention. Although Gladstone routinely held Cabinet meetings on Saturday mornings, thereafter the long weekend outside London was increasingly the norm. No hostess, however grand, would have attracted guests to a Sunday evening function. Special editions of the newspapers routinely appeared for what would now be called 'breaking news'. The assassination of an obscure Austrian figure, a story that Macmillan admitted 'had no particular implication',[60] would, however, never have warranted such an early release. The issue that occupied the political classes most urgently at that time was the Irish settlement, and even dramatic developments from Dublin would not have warranted a pre-dawn edition, not least for commercial reasons, as there would have been few customers on the streets.

In fact, the news of the Sarajevo assassinations (Archduke Ferdinand's wife also perished) did not appear in the British press until 2 July, coupled with a special edition announcing the death of Joseph Chamberlain.[61] Equally, one of the last great balls of the 1914 season was on 3 August, at Dorchester House, with Mr Cassani's string band. The *jeunesse dorée* of Balliol, were among those in attendance.[62]

The weeks after the assassination were a kind of 'phoney war'. 'The Austro-Serbian crisis is wrecking Bayreuth,' the Earl of Crawford and Balcarres wrote to his wife on 27 July, after seeing only *Das Rheingold*, the first of the four Ring operas, before setting off home on what proved to be an adventurous and difficult journey out of Germany.[63] Hopes that the conflict might be avoided were dashed, and on the evening of 3 August the Foreign Secretary, Sir Edward Grey, seeing a lamplighter about his work in the courtyard below the Foreign Office, observed 'The lamps are going out all over Europe; we shall not see them lit again in our lifetime.'[64] Grey, with a composure that now seems Sir Francis Drake-like, had spent the previous day at the zoo, studying rare birds. On 4 August Britain declared war on Germany and the long garden party that had seemingly been destined to last for ever, since the end of the Boer War, was over.

Much of this image of a stable golden age had been illusory, which made the later nostalgia for its seeming certainties the more poignant. The pre-war years were ones of radical change, culturally, socially, and above all politically. Asquith's government made fiscal and constitutional decisions that were to alter the fabric of the nation for ever. Other consequential changes, almost inevitably, followed. The Labour Party established a substantial foothold in Parliament and before the next decade was out would replace the Liberals as the main party of opposition to the Conservatives. (Asquith was the last prime minister to head a purely Liberal administration.) Trade Union rights, following a series of bitter industrial disputes, were defined in law[65], and the suffragette campaign for women's votes had highlighted the limitations of parliamentary representation.[66] 'None of us,' Macmillan recalled, 'had any inkling of the nightmare world into which we were soon to be plunged.'[67]

When war broke out, Macmillan determined to volunteer, and always said thereafter that he was 'Sent down by the Kaiser'.[68] He never returned to Oxford to take Greats, the final honours school. Before embarking for France, he wrote his last letter for a long time to Ronald Knox:

I'm going to be rather odd. I'm not going to 'Pope' until after the war (if I'm alive).

1 My people. Not at all a good reason, which weighs.
2 My whole brain is in a whirl. I don't think God will mind.

But Knox minded. In the ending of his flirtation with Roman Catholicism another part of Macmillan's youth vanished, never to return.[69]

Both 'C' and 'B' disappointed Knox, Harold Macmillan because in the end he would not convert, and Guy Lawrence because he had failed to carry Macmillan with him to Farm Street when he was received there into the Catholic Church in 1915. The Knox-Macmillan-Lawrence triangle was never the same after this divergence, 'a parting of the ways', as Macmillan called it, echoing the subject of John Henry Newman's last Anglican sermon before his conversion, 'The Parting of Friends'.

Harold Macmillan had been at Oxford for only 20 months, but the experience was to nourish him for a lifetime, all the more sharply for being, as with his days at Eton, so suddenly cut short. Thereafter, it was always a case, as in the lines of Wordsworth:

> What though the radiance which was once so bright
> Be now for ever taken from my sight,
>   Though nothing can bring back the hour
> Of splendour in the grass, of glory in the flower;
>   We will grieve not, rather find
>   Strength in what remains behind.[70]

CHAPTER FOUR

To Arms

1914–1918

Was it so hard, Achilles,
So very hard to die?
Thou knowest and I know not –
So much the happier am I.

I will go back this morning
From Imbros over the sea;
Stand in the trench, Achilles,
Flame-capped, and shout for me.

Patrick Shaw-Stewart

The fighting man shall from the sun
Take warmth, and life from the glowing earth:
Speed with the light-foot winds to run,
And with the tree to newer birth;
And find, when fighting shall be done,
Great rest and fullness after dearth.

Julian Grenfell

There must be ghosts all over the country. They lie thick as
grains of sand. And we're all so horribly afraid of the light.

Henrik Ibsen

Asquith, the Prime Minister, was cheered as he went to the House
of Commons on the bright, sunny afternoon of 3 August 1914, but
he was far from cheerful himself. 'They now ring the bells, but they
will soon wring their hands',[1] he observed, and Helmuth von Moltke,
Chief of the German Staff, warned ominously of 'a war which will
annihilate the civilisation of almost the whole of Europe for decades
to come'.[2]

The Great War cast a shadow across the rest of the twentieth century. Macmillan's view, reflecting Napoleon's dictum that to understand a man fully one had to know what was happening in the world

when he was 20, was forever conditioned by his wartime experiences.

His pencilled, and sometimes bloodstained, letters to Nellie from the trenches are among the most evocative documents in his papers. They reveal unprecedented horrors, as well as touching moments. He also helped ill-educated private soldiers write their own letters home, before finding that in battle they had 'noble lustre in their eyes'.

The years between the First and Second World Wars, when Macmillan suffered acutely from survivor's guilt, were ones of censure and dread, lest such a nightmare should ever happen again. The process of obloquy began with J. M. Keynes' famous, though disputed, polemic, *The Economic Consequences of the Peace*, published under the aegis of Daniel Macmillan in 1919. How to prevent another war and the subsequent debate over 'appeasement' became one of the bitterest divides in the 1930s.[3] Those who had had direct experience of battle, including Winston Churchill, Duff Cooper, Anthony Eden and Harold Macmillan, were among the fiercest opponents of appeasement, whereas many of those who had not fought in the trenches tended to be among its advocates.

The First World War gave Macmillan a thinly disguised disdain for 'those gentlemen in England now abed', who, for whatever reason, had tasted neither the camaraderie of the trenches nor the experience of leading men in battle. 'Poor Mr Gaitskell always seems a little conscious on these occasions that he has no medals,' Macmillan recorded in his diary after a Remembrance Day service at the Cenotaph.[4] Privately, he also thought less of Knox for staying in Oxford during the hostilities.

When war broke out, Macmillan was bedridden after an appendicitis operation, then by no means a routine business. 'Sligger' Urquhart, solicitous for his protégé, made a point of visiting him when he was recuperating. Macmillan's fears though were not for his health, but of missing the war. By the time he was on his feet again, it was clear he was not going to miss anything. In convalescence, he had heard news of the retreat of the British Expeditionary Force from Mons, and the crucial defensive Battle of the Marne in September 1914, one of the most consequential among the great conflicts of military history, as its success in preventing Germany's victory through the Schlieffen Plan's swift dash to Paris ensured attritional and prolonged trench warfare.

Kitchener, the newly appointed Secretary of State for War, soon gained parliamentary approval for what he termed his 'New Armies', adding 24 divisions to the regular force. The ubiquitous recruiting posters featuring his face proclaimed the country's need for volunteers.

These volunteers were immortalised as 'The First Hundred Thousand'. Although Macmillan was not numerically one of the first hundred thousand, he was of them in spirit.[5] He was never in danger of receiving one of the white feathers distributed to those men of military age who had not volunteered.[6] In the autumn, he became a second lieutenant in the new 19th Battalion of the King's Royal Rifle Corps[7] and was posted to Southend-on-Sea, that unlikely combination of Guinness family pocket borough and popular day-trip resort of London's East Enders, reflected by its division into Southend and Westcliff-on-Sea. The London-Tilbury Railway Company, in a famous poster of 1908, advertised *Southend & Westcliff-on-Sea for Sea Breezes (Change at East Ham or Barking)*. Macmillan was billeted successively in the Queen's Hotel and the Court Hotel, Westcliff-on-Sea. The town was one of the first to be bombed. On a postcard to Sligger, Macmillan scribbled: 'Zeppelins: hurricane – peppery Colonel – Tonsilitis.'[8]

The months passed in inactivity, broken by the tedium of drill. The daily grind was not dissimilar to that described by Ian Hay in his Great War novel *The First Hundred Thousand*: 'And so the drill goes on. All over the drab, dusty, gritty parade-ground, under the warm September sun, similar squads are being pounded into shape. They have no uniforms yet: even their instructors wear bowler hats or cloth caps.'[9] Study of military textbooks, many redolent of earlier conflicts, occupied much of Macmillan's time in Southend. One such manual instructed, 'Officers of Field Rank on entering balloons are not expected to wear spurs.'[10]

The KRRC was not Nellie's idea of a prestigious regiment, and when Harold mentioned his frustration at being marooned in Southend-on-Sea, she set about engineering a transfer that would satisfy both her social requirements and her son's hopes for active service. In early 1915, Macmillan was interviewed at the regimental headquarters of the Grenadier Guards in Buckingham Gate; the questions were not demanding (and there were no enquiries about his boot-maker), and in March, one month after his twenty-first birthday, he was gazetted into the reserve battalion. As Captain Macmillan, he had now joined a company where life expectancy was six months. Victoria station was the conduit, whether to glory or to the company of Charon, largely a matter of chance. Of those who matriculated from Oxford between 1910 and 1915, 29.3 per cent were killed in the war.[11]

The Grenadier Guards is the senior regiment of the Guards division of the British Army, with the motto *Honi soit qui mal y pense*, and the Colonel-in-Chief is always the reigning sovereign. In 1915 the Guards was increased from two to four divisions, and Macmillan initially served in the 4th, marking his transit from gownsman to swordsman. He always retained elements of both.

Osbert Sitwell, a reluctant Guardsman, believed that the overriding quality of the officers was shrewd judgment of character.[12] Eventually there was to be a saying in the Guards of notable deeds in action that the man concerned had proved himself 'as brave as Macmillan'.[13]

Social standards and valour went hand in hand. No Guards officer and gentleman (the two were then taken to be synonymous) would ever carry a suitcase or a parcel. As the casualties mounted, men from the ranks became officers. Macmillan later referred to them as 'temporary gentlemen', a description he also applied at the time of the battle for the Conservative leadership in October 1963 to Lord Hailsham. Uncleared debts, cheating at cards and revealing confidences were absolute taboos, and an officer must never reverse in waltzing. Only scoundrels ever 'spoke lightly of a woman's name'.[14] Turkish cigarettes were allowed, but never Virginian.[15] One did not speak of 'mufti', rather 'plain clothes'. Self-effacement and service for the greater good were what counted above all.

Nepotism had gained Macmillan his place in the Grenadiers and he freely admitted it,[16] but the only privilege it granted him was a place further up the production line speeding the 'glum heroes up the line to death'.[17] But at Buckingham Gate, instead of glumness, Macmillan now found a surprising sense of cheerfulness, even gallows humour, among his new companions, facing, like he did, the probability of early violent death. Major George Powell,[18] later a colleague of Macmillan in the House of Commons, was in charge of instilling the Guards' traditions into the 'young' officers, a description that applied to any new recruits below the age of 45 who had not previously served.

'We belonged to a doomed generation,' wrote Osbert Sitwell of his fellow Guardsmen, 'and the enlightened Liberal statesmen then in power, men of the highest principle and attainments, and of great forensic ability, presented to it – and it included some of their own sons – the 1914 war as a coming of age gift.'[19] One such was Raymond Asquith, the intellectually brilliant Balliol-educated son of the Prime Minister, of whom H. H. Asquith was once asked at Downing Street, 'Are you the father of *the* Mr Asquith?' Raymond Asquith had transferred from a unit where there was little prospect of active service, in his case the Queen's Westminster Rifles, to the 3rd Battalion of the Grenadier Guards, in which Macmillan also served eventually. One quiet evening before the Battle of the Somme, Macmillan overheard a group of private soldiers discussing their officers. 'That Mr Macmillan tries hard,' came the reassuring verdict, 'but that Mr Asquith – he hasn't got a brain in his head.'[20]

Macmillan remembered the 1914–1918 conflict as a marching war, enlivened by songs and music; the Second World War by contrast was, for him, an experience of jeep journeys and long silences. Also, with a publisher's eye, he later noted how few Second World War writers matched the achievements of that great literary phenomenon of Georgian England, the war poets, epitomised by Rupert Brooke, Wilfred Owen and Siegfried Sassoon, though he was gratified that in 1942 during the Second War Macmillan & Co. published a different kind of masterpiece, in Richard Hillary's *The Last Enemy*.[21]

As Macmillan settled into his military career, dramatic political events were unfolding at Westminster. On 25 May 1915, Asquith formed a coalition government, thus bringing to an end what was to prove the last ever purely Liberal administration. The much-vaunted victory by Christmas had not materialised, and Asquith was being pressurised to bring a sharper focus to the conduct of the war. But by arranging a hasty and at times uneasy political alliance, he was in fact sowing the first seeds of his own eventual downfall. Labour received its first ever Cabinet post when Arthur Henderson went to the Board of Education. Although few could have realised it at the time, less than eight years later Labour was to form its first, minority, government. The old political landscape was changing for ever. Macmillan, as always, followed these events keenly.

On 15 August 1915, after a delay owing to rough weather and U-boat activity ('not the storm nor the torpedo harmed us', he wrote home the next day), Macmillan sailed with the 4th Battalion from Southampton to Le Havre. A train journey to St Omer and then a march to Blendecquesor, and he was billeted with other officers, including the company commander, Captain Aubrey Fletcher, and 'Bimbo' Tennant. His war had begun.

Arriving in France, he now began his letters home to Nellie, one of the most remarkable and detailed first-hand accounts of daily life during the Great War. On 21 August 1915 he told his mother, 'We are now part of the "3rd Gds. Bde".'[22] Although there was now another of what seemed interminable pauses until September, when the Guards division was complete, there was little doubt that they were on the verge of momentous action. Macmillan passed the time reading – *The Old Curiosity Shop* and *Master Humphrey's Clock* were two Dickens favourites, and also Walter Scott, *Heart of Midlothian* and *Rob Roy*, books that were sent out from Cadogan Place in inexpensive editions.

He read much poetry, notably Browning's *The Ring and the Book*, which Nellie sent him. After finishing the books, he always handed them on to others, and was gratified that they displaced newspapers as a priority. Eventually quite a lending library system was established. He also developed a taste for chess, and could often be found playing against some of the private soldiers or his batman. He was a bomb officer, training men in grenade-throwing – when there were grenades to throw.

In Benjamin Britten's opera *Owen Wingrave*, the pacifist hero Owen, in a lyrical outpouring, sings of how 'In peace I have found my image, I have found myself.'[23] With Macmillan it was the opposite. It was in war, both on active service in the Great War, and then in high executive command in the Second World War, that he found himself. He also developed an empathy for those who suffered with him, and for the first time an understanding of those who had not had the advantages of his upbringing and education. This was not a unique experience. Many of his contemporaries, especially Anthony Eden, his predecessor as prime minister, learnt likewise, and resolved after the war to pursue the Disraelian political ideal of 'One Nation'.

A letter to his mother on 30 August, in stubby pencil markings after an injury to his hand, which somehow adds even more to the intensity of the recollections, illustrates Macmillan's deepening awareness in telling detail:

> Dear Mother – do not worry about me. I am very happy; it is a great experience, psychologically so interesting as to fill one's thoughts. A company has just passed my house, back from a long route march, singing wonderfully the dear soldier songs, with silly words and silly tunes, but which somehow seem, sung by their great childish voices, from the depths of their very lovable hearts, the most delicate music and the most sublime poetry. Indeed, of all the war, I think the most interesting (and humbling too) experience is the knowledge one gets of the poorer classes. They have big hearts these soldiers, and it is a very pathetic task to have to read all their letters home.[24] Some of the older men, with wives & families, who write every day home, have in their style a wonderful simplicity, which is almost great literature…It is all very touching … Indeed, I think there is much to be learnt from soldiers' letters.

He also revealed his own feelings of gratitude for the sensibility his education gave him. On 10 September, he wrote to Nellie:

I have a friend who was said to have read the *Iliad* 'to make him fierce'. I confess that I prefer to do so to keep myself civilised. For the more I live in these warlike surroundings, the more thankful I am for all the traditions of the classic culture compared to which these which journalists would have us call 'the realities of life' are little but the extravagant visions of a fleeting nightmare, lacking true value or permanency.

But the quiet waiting times were coming to an end. On 11 September he penned a valedictory letter to Sligger Urquhart, to be opened in the event of his death, 'Dearest Slig – A little message of love to you in case ...'[25] And then on 24 September, the eve of the Battle of Loos, he wrote to his mother:

> Except for the guns – and these mind you, are only like thunder in the distance, we could not imagine there is war. And yet at this moment the greatest battle that the world has ever seen is just begun. On the events of the next few weeks – even the next week – the whole destinies of Europe do most certainly turn.

Macmillan's war was defined by his participation in two of the bloodiest encounters in military history, the Battle of Loos and the Battle of the Somme. During these battles he was wounded five times, and was to bear the pain and the disability of those scars for over 70 years.

On 28 September he sent home scant details of his first reverse: 'I was hit Tuesday at 5 a.m. by a *bullet* in the right hand. It entered the *back* of the hand about the middle.' He omitted to tell his mother that earlier the same day, he had received a glancing bullet wound in the head that concussed him for some time. Although the head wound was more dangerous, the wound to the hand proved the more painful, and left him with a weak handshake for life.[26]

The Battle of Loos was a crucial part of the strategy on the wide Artois-Loos offensive, and was the first large scale use of Kitchener's New Armies. Sometimes called the Second Battle of Artois, with its second phase known as the Third Battle of Artois, it began on 25 September 1915, despite the misgivings of General Haig, Commander of the First Army, and was called off on the 28th. Four days of artillery bombardment, in which some 250,000 shells were fired, led to no breakthrough.

Macmillan was in a company whose orders were to capture Hill 70, a prominent redoubt. On 3 October the Germans recaptured the Hohenzollern Redoubt, and on the 8th put in a major offensive, abandoned after heavy losses. The battle of attrition was truly joined. The British counter-attack on 13 October failed owing to a shortage of hand grenades. Heavy rain and accurate German shelling led Haig to abandon the onslaught. The use of gas also proved disastrous: the wind blew the gas back into the British trenches, resulting in 2,632 casualties. During the fighting Rudyard Kipling's son John was killed, having initially been listed as missing. Overwhelmingly those who lost their lives had no memorial, and were later commemorated on their anonymous gravestones by Kipling's epitaph 'Known Unto God'. Major-General Richard Hilton, a forward observation officer, later wrote, 'A great deal of nonsense has been written about Loos. The real tragedy of that battle was its nearness to complete success.'[27] But this was to be the pattern of many tragic operations.

During the various engagements at Loos the British suffered 50,000 casualties. Robert Graves later wrote of 'the corpse-strewn front-line'.[28] The smell of these trenches was the thing that imprinted itself most firmly on Macmillan. 'The stench from the dead bodies which lie in heaps around is awful,' he wrote home on 13 September 1916. 'We do all the burying that we possibly can, and this will of course help.' Ian Hay wrote of 'dirty work at the crossroads'.[29]*

After initial first aid, Macmillan was sent back to England. He had received his 'Blighty one' and spent the next phase of the war in a hospital in Lennox Gardens. Again his mother had arranged this, as the hospital, in the home of a family friend, Lady Mary Meynell, was known to be particularly efficient. Macmillan was in hospital until just before Christmas 1915, which he was able to spend with the family at Cadogan Place. Dan had served in the King's Royal Rifle Corps, but was invalided out in 1915 and eventually worked at the Admiralty. Arthur had been rejected for military service, because of epilepsy, but, wanting to do his bit, helped train cadets and scouts in various camps near London. The memory of this Christmas stayed with Macmillan when he returned to France. 'I have had my dinner,' he wrote home on 8 July 1916. 'I suppose you have just finished dinner too; the evening papers have come in to you, & I can see Father in his chair, & you on

---

*Another memory that did not die for Macmillan. At one of the degree ceremonies over which Macmillan presided as Chancellor of Oxford University in the 1960s, an angry crowd of protesting undergraduates threatened havoc as he led the procession of university grandees from Wadham to the Divinity School. 'It'll be all right if we get past the King's Arms,' said Macmillan reassuringly to Alan Bullock alongside him. 'You see, they'll rush us as we pass the King's Arms; it was the same in the First War, the danger spots were always the crossroads.'[30]

the sofa, & Dan & Arthur just about to go upstairs to smoke. How one remembers rooms! I always think of the library at C[adogan] P[lace] as the centre of home.'

In January 1916, Macmillan joined the reserve battalion at Chelsea Barracks. Responsibilities included mounting 'King's Guard' at St James's Palace, a ceremonial rather than a military responsibility, as the monarch had long since moved to Buckingham Palace. Nevertheless, headed writing paper – The King's Guard – was issued, and Macmillan continued writing home, albeit from Pall Mall.

When his hand wound had healed sufficiently, he headed once more for France, now as a member of the 2nd Battalion, Grenadier Guards. He sailed from Southampton on 26 March 1916, despite submarine threats. 'Tell Father not to worry about me,' he wrote to Nellie on arrival for the second time in Le Havre. 'I am sure I shall be lucky again this time.' He noticed that the towns were in a desperate state. From one – codenamed 'B' for the censor – he wrote, 'There is literally not a single house or building of any sort intact.'

On Good Friday (21 April), in charge of a platoon near Ypres, with no support, he wrote home: 'I have got my little New Testament with me, and I have read the story of the Passion in St Luke. Several of the men I found also had Testaments with them: one seeing it in my dug-out asked me to lend it him.' Daylight movement was too risky. It was rather like being back at Summer Fields. 'I am already calculating the day till my first leave!' The only highlight in the dreary routine was a personal inspection by Haig on 28 April. Macmillan contrasted this with conflicts in days past. 'The glamour of red coats – the martial tunes of fife and drum – aides-de-camps scurrying hither & thither on splendid chargers – lancers glittering and swords flashing – how different the old wars must have been.'

The year had begun with controversy over the introduction of conscription. Macmillan was in favour. 'It looks as tho' the Govt. has at last decided to take the plunge into compulsion,' he wrote home on 4 May. 'I am very glad, as it has now become obvious that it is necessary.'*

On 21 April, Sir Roger Casement, Irish rebel, was arrested on a charge of high treason. He was transported to the Tower of London, found guilty at the Old Bailey on 29 June and executed on 3 August.

---

*Ironically, it was to be Macmillan, as Prime Minister, who ended such compulsion after the Second World War. Conscription was ended in 1957, and this came fully into effect in 1960 when the last man was called up.

But the underlying scandal of the time was over the homosexual content of Casement's notorious diaries, long the subject of clubland gossip. For a while, the prurient atmosphere of the Wilde era was once more abroad in the land. With the clannishness prevalent among gentlemen of his class and era, Harold Macmillan, who closely followed national events from France, wrote only to his father about the Casement trial and its aftermath;[31] he never mentioned it in letters to his mother.

Whilst Casement was awaiting trial, news came on 6 June of the death of the War Secretary, Lord Kitchener, drowned the previous day when the SS *Hampshire* was sunk by a German mine off Scapa Flow en route to Russia. The first public hint of the tragedy was the sight of the War Office blinds being lowered as the news came through. Apart from the great psychological blow, it marked the beginning of the end for Asquith. The question of Kitchener's replacement presented grave difficulties for the balance of the coalition and Asquith's own position. 'It is all over', said Margot Asquith presciently when she heard the news of Lloyd George's promotion in July. 'It is only a matter of time before we are out of Downing Street.' And so it proved. Lloyd George replaced Asquith as prime minister on 6 December 1916 in a coup, the circumstances of which still arouse controversy.

Kitchener had had difficulties in combining a military and a political role, but Macmillan's verdict was kinder than Margot Asquith's.* 'Today we have the extraordinary news of Lord Kitchener's death,' he wrote to his father on 8 June. 'He was a great man, to whom the country owes an enormous debt. But his chief work was done...The new Armies will always be "Kitchener's Armies".'

Back with the 2nd Battalion, Macmillan was joined by his school friend Harry Crookshank in June. Their position was now by the Ypres salient. All knew that a great battle, the most dreadful in military history, was in the offing. 'These are days of anxiety,' Macmillan wrote home on 2 July, adding two days later, 'If this affair should flicker out like Loos, it will be another great blow to our prestige.' On 7 July, as they waited their turn to go over the top, Macmillan's company was visited by the Prince of Wales, who took tea in the mess.

The first day of the Somme, 1 July 1916, the costliest day in the history of British arms, saw the deaths of 20,000 men, and nearly 60,000 casualties. The attack was launched north of the Somme river

---

*Margot Asquith dismissively referred to Kitchener as not a very good man, but certainly a great poster.

between Arras and Albert, and lasted until 18 November, when it was called off. The main aim of Joffre, the French commander-in-chief, was to drain the German forces of reserves, through a battle of attrition, with territorial gain a secondary consideration. Haig accepted the plan reluctantly, as he would have preferred an offensive across the more open territory in Flanders. The planned start of the offensive, 1 August 1916, was brought forward a month to divert the Germans from their onslaught on Verdun. Haig was also at odds with Lloyd George, now politically the key figure in the prosecution of the war, particularly after his extended visit to France, when he had privately consulted the French commander, General Foch, about the competence of the British command. Haig was shocked 'that a British minister could have been so ungentlemanly as to go to a foreigner and put such questions regarding his own subordinates.'*

On 19 July, Macmillan's actions led to his being mentioned in dispatches. His mission had been to lead two men into no-man's-land on a reconnaissance, the kind of episode later dramatised by R. C. Sherriff in his play *Journey's End*. Macmillan was wounded by a German grenade, which caught him in the face. Although he could have retreated to a hospital for treatment, he opted to continue in the line.

August and September saw a period of intense training. The weather was glorious. 'We all shudder to think of a battle on such a day as this,' Macmillan wrote home on 2 August 1916. 'This is not the weather for killing people.' Their commanding officer was Colonel Crawley de Crespigny. Completely opposite in temperament to Macmillan (de Crespigny was reputed never to have read a book), he nevertheless entrusted him with important responsibilities and earned Macmillan's undying loyalty, the attraction of opposites indeed.

The company marched south to the right of the Beaumont-Hamel† sector. On the night of 14 September, with clear moonlight, Macmillan led an advance platoon to gain ground before a big push. Their return route was marked by a dead German, arm outstretched. Macmillan's orderly shook the corpse by the hand as they passed. This memory never left Macmillan.

---

*With an irony later repeated at the time of the disastrous Norwegian campaign in May 1940, the politician in charge of policy (Lloyd George as War Minister at the time of the Somme, Winston Churchill as First Lord of the Admiralty in the early days of the Second World War) became the beneficiary of the crisis that led to the replacement of the Prime Minister of the day, Asquith in December 1916, Chamberlain in May 1940.[33]
†After the conflicts, the only thing that remained of the village of Beaumont-Hamel was a small part of a stained-glass window, depicting the Virgin Mary, from the ruined church. Today this single fragment, picked up by a German soldier from the rubble, can be seen in the church, which was rebuilt in 1922.

They were back in time for the start of the attack at 6.20 a.m., and the push to Ginchy between Delville Wood and Guillemont. Caught by machine-gunners from the left flank, Macmillan was hit in the left thigh and in the pelvis, and 'rolled down into a large shell-hole, where I lay dazed, but not – at first at least – unconscious'.[34] For the next ten hours he intermittently dozed, treated himself with morphine, feigned death as Germans skirted round the shell hole, and read Aeschylus, a copy of which he happened to have in his battle dress.*

Under cover of the relative safety of night-time, a search party, led by Company Sergeant Major Norton, who had witnesssed Macmillan's fall, set out to find and rescue him. Macmillan's legs were quite unable to take his own weight, and stretcher-bearers were brought in to carry him home, the noise of their movements bringing shelling all the while from Ginchy village.

Crawley de Crespigny met the rescue party, and seeing Macmillan's plight said simply, 'Well, I think you'd better be off.' Neville Talbot, the Balliol chaplain, who was serving as an army chaplain, saw him arrive and sent on Macmillan's letter to his mother with one of his own. 'There is nothing broken and no danger,' he wrote reassuringly. 'He has had a trying time but is full of courage. I am so glad that I was able to see him go through this Dressing Station.'[35]

By the end of September, Macmillan was in hospital at Bathurst House in Belgrave Square, where he was treated on and off till December 1918, a month after the Armistice. He owed his life to the fact that one of the bullets had passed through the water bottle he was carrying in his battle dress. A series of lengthy operations extracted shrapnel and metal from his splintered bones. He became familiar with tubes,[36] and his recovery was doubted. But he survived and, unlike Harry Crookshank, who had been castrated by a shell fragment in the same action, his wounds were treatable.

As he lay immobile for months, survivor's guilt afflicted him, as did depression, the dreaded 'black dog'. But gradually, 24 at the time the war ended, he realised that the past had to be left behind and a new

---

*In May Macmillan's father had at his request sent him a batch of books, including *Prometheus Vinctus* in the original Greek. Prometheus's last words in the play could serve as a description of Macmillan's current predicament:

> Now his threats walk forth in action
> And the firm Earth quakes indeed.
> Deep and loud the ambient Thunder
> Bellows, and the flaring lightning
> Wreaths his curls around me.

beginning made. The question, as for so many, was in which direction that new start might lie.

He was lucky not to be one of the lost generation known only to God. Three quarters of a million of the adult male population of Britain did not return. Junior officers, the rank of Macmillan, suffered disproportionately more casualties than any other group. Asquith lost his son, killed by a single bullet on 15 September 1916, near Ginchy;[37] Bonar Law lost two sons. Empire losses brought the British toll to nigh on a million. Bizarre, even morbid, examples were drawn on: how long it would take the total number of the dead to march past the Cenotaph? 'If the ten million dead of the 1914–1918 War were to march in columns of fours into the gates of death,' ran another example, 'they would take eighty days and eighty nights to pass through, and for eighty days the marchers would be the British dead.'[38]

So ended Captain Macmillan's war, the most profound experience of his life. For years he could not return to Oxford; it was for him a city of ghosts and the memories were too searingly painful. Raymond Asquith, Ivo Charteris, Julian Grenfell, Patrick Shaw-Stewart, 'Bimbo' Tennant, Gilbert Talbot – the litany was endless. The death in August 1918 of Guy Lawrence caused him particular anguish. 'The act of death in battle is noble and glorious,' he had written home on 13 September, just before he was invalided back to England. 'But the physical appearance and actual symptoms of death are, in these terrible circumstances, revolting only and horrid.'[39] *Ave atque vale.*[40]

Still recuperating from his wounds and further hospital treatment, Macmillan was able to walk on crutches to Hyde Park Corner to see the crowds celebrating Armistice Day. Like Asquith, he knew that the ringing of bells would be followed by a wringing of hands. The postwar problems were only just beginning, and he determined to take his part in trying to solve them. He had written to Sligger Urquhart, 'God spares my life. Oh Slig, pray that if He spares it till the end, I may make good use of it.'[41] Such was the responsibility incumbent upon the survivors.

A new political landscape was developing. At the 1918 general election on Saturday, 14 December (the first to be held on a single day), women over the age of 30 had the vote for the first time and there was universal suffrage for men, the culmination of a long struggle going back to Chartist days and before. The result was ostensibly a triumph for Lloyd George, the man who had won the war, and who was going to build a land fit for heroes to live in (within a few years it was ironically said that he had succeeded, as one needed to be a hero to live in it). But Lloyd George was a prime minister without a party, wholly dependent for office on Bonar Law's Conservatives. Bonar Law said that Lloyd George could be prime minister for life. It would have been more accurate to say that he could be prime minister until Bonar Law decided otherwise, which became the case on 19 October 1922 at the famous Carlton Club meeting,[42] which marked the beginning of modern British politics.

Harold Macmillan entered public life as Captain Macmillan. Electioneering leaflets looked all the better for the military rank, and not only in the Conservative Party: Major Attlee was the Labour MP for Limehouse from November 1922. The same acknowledgement of military service operated after the Second World War, though interestingly the most frequent rank then was that of Brigadier (Selwyn Lloyd, Toby Low, H. R. Mackeson, Enoch Powell), because many of those entering Parliament in 1945 were older than their 1918 counterparts.[43]

One wonders why Macmillan, in the dark days of sadness and self-doubt after the First World War, did not again seek to convert to Roman Catholicism. Metaphysical problems exercised him, as always. But the ensnarements of Ronald Knox had faded, as had, more distantly, the influence of Sligger Urquhart. Macmillan was now at ease with his spiritual state, one of High Anglo-Catholicism, which he embraced, without show, for the rest of his life. The traditional liturgy, the Anglican ritual, the peace of a village church, especially St Giles, Horsted Keynes, where he now rests – all these affected him deeply. But there was another reason he did not 'Pope': he knew it would be deeply wounding, and irredeemably painful, for his mother. The Great War had liberated Harold Macmillan from much, but the old love and loyalties were as powerful as ever.

CHAPTER FIVE

ADC and Son-in-Law

1919–1923

I believe that men are beginning to see, not perhaps the golden age, but an age which at any rate is brightening from decade to decade, and will lead us some time to an elevation from which we can see the things for which the heart of mankind is longing.

American President Woodrow Wilson, speaking in
Manchester in December 1918 on the way to the Paris Peace
Conference

Tragic as it is, it is splendid to have lived in this great age – a time to which our descendants will look proudly back, as we to Elizabethan England. For there has been in it all much more of the Armada than the rude Napoleonic spirit. And more Sidneys too have been born again in England.

Harold Macmillan, letter to Sligger Urquhart

They were my close companions many a year,
A portion of my mind and life, as it were,
And now their breathless faces seem to look
Out of some old picture-book.

W. B. Yeats, *In Memory of Major Robert Gregory*

On Monday, 18 November 1918, a week after the Armistice, Lord Curzon, Leader of the House of Lords, presented an address to the Upper House congratulating the King on the conclusion of the war, and holding out his belief in 'the prospects of a victorious peace'.[1] A month later, as delegates from over 30 countries travelled to Europe for the Paris Peace Conference, scheduled to begin at Versailles in January 1919, President Woodrow Wilson of America, was even more optimistic, speaking in Manchester of an age that was about to brighten from decade to decade. These high hopes were swiftly shown to be illusory.

Wilson's arrival in Paris, to a tumultuous welcome from crowds anxious for a lasting peace, and with his Fourteen Points to hand, was a harbinger of the new diplomacy, filmed and photographed around the world. One British delegate thought Wilson was captivated by the Parisian scene 'as a debutante is entranced by the prospect of her first ball'.[2] In truth it was the reverse. The ball was entranced by the attendees, especially as the 'unwelcome nations' (no Germany, Austria, Hungary or Russia) had been refused admission. Passions ran high, with calls to 'Hang the Kaiser' and demands for Germany to pay 'until the pips squeaked'. Though initially going along with such populist cries, Lloyd George believed that an embittered Germany would be a dangerous Germany, and was also aware that Germany's former position as Britain's second largest trading partner would be imperilled if her economy was weakened artificially. He feared that if France got her demands, and the lion's share of any bounty from the settlement, she would become the dominant continental force. John Maynard Keynes, as Britain's senior Treasury representative, was appalled by what unfolded. Clemenceau, he observed 'had one illusion – France; and one disillusion – mankind'.[3]*

The Treaty of Versailles, with its 440 clauses, was signed on 28 June 1919, the fifth anniversary of the assassination of the Archduke Ferdinand of Austria in Sarajevo. The most remembered clause was about reparation terms imposed on the Germans: a sum finally fixed in London in 1921 at 132 billion marks. Lloyd George admitted, 'We shall have to do the whole thing over again in twenty-five years at three times the cost.'[4]

Keynes had already prophesied such an outcome in *The Economic Consequences of the Peace*, published at the end of 1919. Like Lenin, he believed that 'there is no subtler, no surer means of overturning the existing basis of society than to debauch the currency'.[5] Harold Macmillan had been one of the first to read this polemic, getting an advance copy of this celebrated attack on the Carthaginian Peace from his brother Dan, who had worked in Paris on the drafting of the treaty, and was the book's publisher. It made a profound impression upon Macmillan, confirming him as an incipient Keynesian, and setting him on the path to his own tract, *The Middle Way* (1938), and his expansionist economic outlook. The whole science of economics, dismal or not, now became one of his main preoccupations, and he noted approvingly how the commercial success of Keynes' book also did much to secure the financial base of Macmillan & Co. in the difficult post-war years.

---

*A pattern Harold Macmillan was to see repeated in the sixties with Charles de Gaulle.

Harold Macmillan was 25 when the Paris Conference signed off the destinies of millions. He was still recovering from his wounds, but despite this went back into the Guards' reserve battalion at Chelsea Barracks in January 1919. He had no wish to become a regular soldier; what he wanted was a change, even, though he may not have admitted it to himself, to escape from the stultifying influence of his beloved mother's overprotective nature.

He was offered such a chance by George Lloyd,[6] fated in the footnotes of history to be thought of as a prime ministerial misprint, who had been appointed Governor of Bombay in 1918 and was looking for some 'good young men' to join his staff as ADCs. Macmillan had got to know Lloyd before the war, and his military service was an outstanding recommendation to Lloyd, who also was a great enthusiast for the 'roving spirit' of the Elizabethan age.[7] Macmillan, with his romantic attachment to the world of Sir Philip Sidney, was thus ideally suited. He knew that the family firm beckoned eventually, but before settling to office routine, a chance to see the world would be ideal. India was a country he had never visited, and the consular life would indeed be a new direction.

But the best-laid plans came to naught. His wounds disqualified him from the Indian climate and the doctors were adamant that he should not go. Macmillan wrote to Sligger Urquhart of his disappointment. 'I have refused the Bombay offer,' he told him without confessing to the real reason.[8]

It was Macmillan's mother, needless to say, who eased the way to the next stage. Nellie heard that the Duke of Devonshire, Governor General of Canada since 1916, was, like George Lloyd, wanting young men to serve on his staff as ADCs. She was a close friend of Lady Edward Cavendish, the Duke's mother, and knew that many of the older, wounded servicemen, whom the Duke had taken on in wartime, were now returning home. Macmillan felt India would have been more adventurous, and tried, unsuccessfully, to get the medical opinion reversed. But Canada it was, and as he recalled, he was to find two things there – 'health and a wife'.[9]

'He arrived on Friday and he is certainly a great acquisition,' the Duke of Devonshire wrote to his wife. 'I think he will do very well and he is very keen.'[10] The new boy was soon joining in all the social activities. 'Played golf with Macmillan. He plays quite well & is much better than I am,' the Duke noted in his diary.[11]

Victor Devonshire, the 9th Duke,[12] who had served in both Balfour's government and Asquith's coalition, was to prove one of the most influential figures in Macmillan's life. In due course, Macmillan was treated as 'family' at Chatsworth, the Duke's Derbyshire seat. But first the young man caught the political bug. At Rideau Hall,[13] the Governor General's official residence in Ottawa, he developed the taste for long talks into the night on the political events of the time. When duty ADC he accompanied the Duke to his office in the Ottawa Parliament building, where he gained experience of the political process.

The Duke's role was not so much employer, rather host. He took to the young man, whose sharp intelligence and awareness of broader issues were perceptions he felt Macmillan showed beyond his years. It was said later that 'Chatsworth' found Harold Macmillan a dull dog (there was some competition to avoid the short straw of sitting next to him at formal dinners), but Victor Devonshire evidently enjoyed his company.

The three other ADCs in the service of the Duke included Lords Haddington, Molyneux and Sefton. Macmillan was seeing the aristocracy at first hand, learning their ways and imbibing their milieux. Some have claimed that, disliking sports as he did, he only took part in golf and shooting for social reasons; but this was not so, as he became surprisingly proficient at both, and very keen. Meanwhile, he was captivated by the life in Canada, its empty spaces, the friendliness of the people, and even its quasi-Scottishness. Most of his letters to Britain were not now to Nellie, but to Sligger Urquhart, to whom he communicated the excitement of a vast continent.

The Rockies charmed me very much, & we climbed some peaks & had delightful weather. But the worst of this strange vice-regal life is that one has continually to rush on to some new spot. I have only been in this country since April, but I have travelled in it over 10,000 miles! ...

I feel much stronger, physically and mentally. I am trying to 'reconstruct' (topical word) the bruised & rather shattered life which all of our generation must support.'[14]

The most important 'reconstruction' was Macmillan's growing love for Lady Dorothy Cavendish, the Duke's third daughter, another reason that the Rockies had charmed him so much, for it was on a visit to Jasper National Park with Dorothy that he realised friendship had deepened into a mutual affection. Back at Rideau Hall, they took to going in to dinner together, and Dorothy was his customary partner for bridge. The Duchess of Devonshire wrote to Macmillan saying that it had been noted that the two were spending much time together, and asked him outright what his intentions were. There may even have been a hint of forcing the issue. Macmillan was mortified at the implied solecism. 'I am afraid I am perhaps inexperienced in these matters – partly, I suppose, because I have no sisters and have never been thrown in any intimate relations with girls of my own age.' However, to the relief of Dorothy's mother, Macmillan added, 'I *am* deeply in love with her. No words which I can use can express how much I love her.'[15] On 16 December, Nellie wrote to the Duchess explaining Harold's past illnesses, his innate diffidence, but emphasising his solicitous care.[16] The reassurance was unnecessary.

Macmillan proposed and was accepted on 26 December 1919. 'Dorothy & Harold settled to call themselves engaged,' the Duke recorded in his diary that day. 'I am sure it will be alright [*sic*]. They both are radiantly happy, but do not wish anything to be said about it.'[17] Eventually the announcement of their engagement appeared in *The Times*, on 17 March 1920. On the boat home to England in the New Year, the *Empress of France*, Macmillan wrote to his future mother-in-law, thanking her for her help over the engagement. 'I have been much interested in the slight insight which I have been able to obtain into Canadian politics and conditions,' he added, 'which has been a source of much amusement & (I hope) profit to me.'[18] It was in some ways a curious letter to have written on the eve of a wedding, but one that showed that Macmillan was thinking about his career ahead.

'We are very pleased with Dorothy's engagement to Harold Macmillan,' the Duke wrote to his aunt Lucy from Government House. 'He is quite delightful and will I am sure make her very happy',[19] which rather contradicts the usual version, which is that the aristocratic Devonshires did not like their daughter marrying into 'trade'. Dorothy's elder sister, Blanche, had married a Cobbold, and the old Duke is supposed to have said with resignation, 'Well, books is better than beer.'[20]

Girls had not been important in Macmillan's life. His experience of school, university[21] and the army had left him, like Malcolm in *Macbeth*, 'yet unknown to woman'. There had been no sowing of wild oats, no 'history'. The same was true of Lady Dorothy[22] who was only nineteen at the time of her marriage. It was first love for both of them, and on the surface a strange attraction. Dorothy liked the outdoor world, golf a particular passion. Books played no part. But, as with Macmillan and Crawley de Crespigny, opposites were drawn together. Dorothy and Harold had powerful mothers and, for both young people, marriage was almost a gesture of defiance. Dorothy was not pleased when she found Nellie in residence at Birch Grove. She kept an effigy of her mother-in-law in a bedroom drawer, and was once discovered sticking pins into it.[23]

In Dorothy's lineage can be detected her fierce independence. Her mother, Evie, Mistress of the Robes to Queen Mary from 1910, was the eldest daughter of the 5th Marquess of Lansdowne, one of the last examples of the full flowering of the tradition of hereditary power. When Evie became engaged to Victor Cavendish, Lansdowne opined that he believed his future son-in-law was 'reasonably well provided for'.[24] Lansdowne was one of the foremost Whigs. Eton, Balliol, Anglo-Irish landlord, he was successively Governor General of Canada and Viceroy of India. He succeeded the 8th Duke of Devonshire as Leader of the Unionists in the House of Lords in 1900. There followed a drift to Toryism, and by 1902 he was Foreign Secretary in Balfour's Conservative administration, negotiating the Entente Cordiale with France in 1904. Macmillan was marrying into the purple line of political influence.

The marriage of Harold Macmillan and Lady Dorothy Cavendish on 21 April 1920 at St Margaret's, Westminster, was the social event of the season. 'Dorothy's wedding,' wrote the Duke in his diary. 'Really went off very well indeed.'[25] The ceremony was conducted by the future Archbishop of Canterbury, William Temple, a Cavendish cousin, and Macmillan's cousin John, a future Bishop of Guildford. Royalty attended in the persons of Queen Alexandra, the Duke of Connaught and the Duke of York, the future King George VI. King George V and Queen Mary gave Dorothy a present of a diamond brooch.

The bride's side of the congregation was socially distinguished, but the groom's side more than matched it intellectually with writers such as Lord Morley, Thomas Hardy and Rudyard Kipling, all three holders of the Order of Merit.* Kipling in addition was a holder of the Nobel Prize for literature. The couple left the church to the bridal music from *Lohengrin*. The reception was held at Lansdowne House, one of its last great functions before demolition. The next day *The Daily Graphic* divided its front page between the wedding, and Austen Chamberlain's excess profits duty in his recent Budget.[26] The young Macmillans settled at 14 Chester Square, a vast corner house, still surrounded by greenery and not yet a fashionable address. Its associations in 1920 were literary, very suitable for a young publisher.

Nellie Macmillan had already engaged a cook for Dorothy. After

---

*An honour Macmillan was to be awarded himself in 1976.

rigorous interviews, her choice had fallen on the former cook of Mrs Dudley Ward, mistress of the Prince of Wales. When asked about her qualifications, this cook had said, 'Well, the Prince of Wales was in the house almost every day to lunch & dinner, and *he* seemed quite satisfied.'[27] This was recommendation enough for Nellie, though she may not have realised the extra-culinary factors involved.

Shortly after the marriage, the Devonshires came to dinner and Macmillan made sure that everything was as it should be, white tie and all. Although the motor car was now becoming the norm, the Duke idiosyncratically still maintained his stables. On the night of the dinner Macmillan noticed that his father-in-law had arrived, from Devonshire House in Piccadilly, in a carriage and four* and this initially puzzled him, as usually in London a carriage and two horses sufficed. At the end of the successful evening, as Macmillan bade goodbye to his guests, all became clear. 'Why do you want to live halfway to Eastbourne?' asked the Duke. That was why he had four horses – he pretended it was going to be a long journey.[28]

On 27 January 1921 Dorothy gave birth to their first child, Maurice Victor[29], named after his two grandfathers. 'You would laugh to see Harold pushing the pram on Sunday morning,' Lady Dorothy wrote to her mother. 'He's awfully good at it, but does look so funny with a large cigar & terribly smart.'[30] Dorothy subsequently gave birth to three daughters, Caroline,[31] Catherine and Sarah, who were born in 1923, 1926 and 1930 respectively.

Macmillan was soon entering into the peripatetic world of the Devonshires. There was a regular routine: Ireland in April (Lismore), Bolton Abbey for the grouse shooting, Chatsworth for Christmas. At these house parties he unwound, and was always an enthusiastic participant at Lismore in 'The Game', a local variant of charades, in which, clad in striped jacket, he regularly played the part of a bookie, opposite Lord Porchester, who always played the crook. But he was most in his element at Bolton Abbey in August for the Glorious Twelfth. Once, next to Victor in the butts, he heard his father-in-law exclaim, 'These damned grouse; they won't fly straight – like a lot of Tories.'[32]

Dorothy relaxed too, or rather reverted (among family, particularly at Chatsworth) to her natural dishevelled state, no hairdresser, nails unclipped, and prone to bringing in gardening, with piles of twigs and bracken left in back corridors, before taking her place elegantly

---

* John Galsworthy's Swithun Forsyte in *The Forsyte Saga* (*The Man of Property*, Chapter III) attracted his nickname of 'Four-in-hand' because of this unusual extravagance.

at a formal dinner in the Great Dining Room, a room of which the 6th Duke observed when it was finished in 1832, 'It is like dining in a great trunk and you expect the lid to open.' Such a combination of informality and formality Macmillan, with his rather prim Presbyterian upbringing, had never witnessed before. Dorothy's openness to all, whether a gardener or a visiting head of state, was to be of inestimable benefit to him in his political career. Where he was shy and withdrawn, she was outward-going, always finding a point of contact with people she met, whether a trade union leader who lived in a village where she had taken the children for picnics when they were young, or a Cabinet minister.[33] One of her closest friends in the post-war Conservative governments was Ernest Marples,[34] at first sight an unlikely pairing, the Duke's daughter and the self-made businessman, until people realised that Marples' grandfather had been a head gardener at Chatsworth. Chatsworth, for Macmillan, was not so much overpowering as confusing.

The marriage of Harold and Dorothy Macmillan is one of the most complex episodes in two notably complex lives, happy and tragic by turns, before ending in a sunset era of the deepest devotion, 'calm of mind, all passion spent'. Some have claimed that Macmillan married to get his foot on the ladder, but although the social connections the union brought were beyond even Nellie's expectations, this is mistaken. Nor was he that classic English type, the repressed homosexual who marries for respectability (though he was certainly emotionally repressed, with the 'undeveloped heart' that E. M. Forster detected in so many from the Edwardian public school world). The truth is that he was bound by an immense tie to Dorothy, but their bond was not primarily physical in nature. It was a different kind of love, a love that proved profound and lasting, not dependent on romance. After Dorothy's sudden death at Birch Grove in May 1966, Harold was desolate, and was to find 20 years of widowerhood a period of inconsolable loneliness.

Harold Macmillan now formally joined the family publishing firm in St Martin's Street, headed at the time by his uncle Sir Frederick Macmillan. His father Maurice, his brother Dan and various cousins were partners. His father was particularly concerned with educational books and also with the overseas branches of the business, which had accounted for his many absences during Harold's childhood. Had Harold never gone into politics, his publishing career alone would have ensured his place in public life. Yet his business life, and experience of the commercial world, was to contribute to his perceptions about political life. He could read a balance sheet, whether at Macmillan & Co. or at the Treasury. He was never one of those politicians, common in later generations, who became political research assistants on leaving university and had no hinterland beyond the Westminster village.

Macmillan was to look after some of the most distinguished names on the Macmillan list – Thomas Hardy, John Maynard Keynes, Rudyard Kipling, Sean O'Casey, Hugh Walpole and W. B. Yeats. When he was a minister in the 1950s, his leaving present to his private secretaries, as he moved up the departmental ladder, was a privately printed limited edition of Yeats' poems, numbered and signed by the poet himself.[36]

The economic conditions in the early 1920s were harsh and painful. 'It is difficult to face the future with complete equanimity in any form of business. The attitude of the Trade Unions seems to be getting worse,' Macmillan wrote to Evie Devonshire on 18 August 1920. 'The thing cannot go on for ever & many people are looking round with satisfaction to the prospect of a good row & a fight, as the only means of bringing the men to their senses.'[37]

Publishers were not exempt from the general downturn, particularly after the economic collapse in April 1920, which saw the bank rate raised from 6 per cent to 7 per cent. As prices rose, so employment fell and the number of days lost to strike action soared. Industrial unrest was also endemic in the book trade, especially at the key national book distribution centre, Simpkin Marshall. A Book Trader Employers Association was established, and Macmillan became its chairman. He also chaired a specialist national body that concerned itself with the publication of educational books, juvenile books and general fiction. He worked closely with literary agencies such as A. P. Watt. For a bibliophile like Macmillan, this was fascinating work. One of his closest Eton friends, Julian Lambart, was beginning his life's work as an Eton schoolmaster at this time, and observed that he was lucky enough to be paid for doing a job that he enjoyed so much he would have done it for love. Exactly the same was true of Macmillan in publishing. Of course, doing the job you loved as a teacher or publisher was much easier if you had a private income. Macmillan was well off. But money, for him, was never there to open the door to luxury (his personal life was notably frugal); it was the key to independence. He was free to act as his conscience told him.

After the death of Thomas Hardy in 1928, Macmillan advised Hardy's widow on taxation and royalty matters, and seeing the commercial potential of *Jude the Obscure*, the author's last and most controversial novel, ensured that it continued to bring healthy returns to the estate. Macmillan adored Hardy, both the man and his books, and visited him at Max Gate, his gloomy house outside Dorchester. He said later that one needed to see a colour photograph of the man – all those blends of nut-brown, russets and lime – to appreciate the character. He wrote:

By the time I joined the firm in 1922 he was old, in his eighties. I went down to Dorset to see him, and I remember that he had a real countryman's face, rosy-cheeked and wrinkled like a fine old apple; with perhaps a touch of acidity like a Cox's pippin. Now that he was old he had become fashionable, for the English people rarely care about anything until it is old.

Although today Hardy is revered for both his poetry and his fiction, a rare accomplishment, Macmillan preferred the Aeschylean quality of the novels, and was perceptive about their particular characteristics:

Why is Hardy still so much read and studied? He is not an easy writer, his style is apt to be crabbed and his stories are often unduly complicated. But he has one vital quality: he never wrote anything he did not believe in. He has the deep sincerity of the great tragedians.[38]

W. B. Yeats visited Macmillan frequently at his office in St Martin's Street.[39] With his flowing locks and flamboyant ties, he seemed for all the world the romantic poet, but this exterior disguised his shrewd understanding of the mechanics of publishing, and a surprising formality in his professional dealings, always calling the brothers 'Mister Dan' and 'Mister Harold'.

Although publishing was fulfilling for Macmillan, his thoughts increasingly turned to a possible political career. The problem was finding a constituency that would accept an unknown beginner. In fact, Macmillan entered national politics at a time uniquely favourable for a young man wanting to gain electioneering experience: general elections were to be held in three successive years – in November 1922, December 1923 and October 1924.

On 19 October 1922, the Conservatives held their famous meeting at the Carlton Club, in which they voted two to one to leave the Lloyd George coalition, thus triggering an immediate general election. Lloyd George fell, never to hold office again. Austen Chamberlain, leader of the Conservative Party since March 1921, and main prop of the coalition, was also ousted.[40] Chamberlain was replaced by Bonar Law, who returned to the Conservative leadership he had relinquished owing to ill health 19 months earlier. Law then led the Conservatives to a crushing election victory, the first purely Conservative administration since A. J. Balfour's at the beginning of the century. Sadly, his illness (throat cancer) returned in a more virulent form, and his premiership, from October 1922 to his resignation in May 1923, was to be the shortest of the twentieth century. Law's government in November was the most aristocratic since Lord Derby's 'Who? Who?' administration of 1852.[41] The Lloyd George coalitionists were bitter in their criticism. Churchill dubbed it a government of the second eleven; Lord Birkenhead called it a government of second-class intellects.

In the election of November 1922, the 'Lloyd George National Liberals' and the 'Asquith Liberals', fighting as separate entities, won 62 and 54 seats respectively; even their combined total fell way short of Labour's total of 142. They joined together under Asquith's leadership,[42] a matter of expedience rather than conviction, but even so, they won only 159 seats in the December 1923 election, against Labour's 191. The bruised Liberals then supported the Labour Ramsey MacDonald. But in the election of October 1924, when Stanley Baldwin's Conservatives won 419 seats and Labour 151, the combined Liberals were reduced to a mere 40.

Thereafter, the Liberals were, for Macmillan, who witnessed their collapse, an increasingly irrelevant parliamentary sideshow, and the occasion for humour. 'As usual the Liberals offer a mixture of sound and original ideas,' he observed in 1961. 'Unfortunately none of the sound ideas is original and none of the original ideas is sound.'[43] Labour was, to his mind, of a different order altogether, and he toyed more than once with the idea of fighting under their banner.

At this stage, Macmillan did not want a safe seat. He wanted to learn the political ropes, gain experience, and find out more about the rough and tumble of the hustings. Such a practical approach was manna from heaven, because Conservative Central Office was inundated with applications. In Palace Chambers, Macmillan saw an understanding Conservative official. Nothing doing at the moment was the message, but we'll let you know. But by one of those chances that define life, the chairman of the Stockton-on-Tees Association, in an astrakhan-collared coat and with a flamboyant tie pin (Macmillan's first two impressions), had called. They wanted a candidate. 'The very thing for you,' said the party official. 'You can't possibly win it.'[44] So began Macmillan's connections with the ancient and historic borough of Stockton-on-Tees.[45]

Stockton-on-Tees, one of the first Incorporated Boroughs of the Municipal Corporations Act of 1835, has too often been thought of as a derelict industrial town of back-to-back, two-up two-down terraced houses, a north-east version of L. S. Lowry's Lancashire landscapes. Many would suppose its soulmate to be nearby Jarrow, the most infamous of the depressed towns of the interwar period. The truth was somewhat different, even when Macmillan first visited in 1923. More akin to the Georgian town of Yarm and spacious Northallerton, Stockton was, and is, at its centre, a handsome market town, finely situated in the Tees Valley, and beautifully laid out by the River Tees, where seals, could, and still can, be seen. The paved high street is a broad thoroughfare, the widest in England, over a quarter of a mile long, with a Town House of 1735 and Market Cross of 1768. It was at the Town House (the Town Hall) in 1810 that celebrations were held to mark the opening of the 'New Cut', a canal that straightened out an awkward bend in the Tees. At the same time, with great foresight, a resolution was moved to investigate the possibility of a railway from Stockton to Darlington.

Daniel Defoe, when he visited in the early eighteenth century, was impressed by Stockton's aura. He found great variety: both lead mining and farming were prosperous. The town was a trading port, yet its setting was rural. Norton, over the bridge to the north of Stockton's main centre, had an appealing village atmosphere with a fine green. Constituents vied to give Macmillan hospitality, and on many visits he stayed in Norton.*

The Industrial Revolution transformed Stockton's fortunes, and with shipbuilding and engineering it was to become one of the nineteenth century's boom towns. The coming of the Stockton and Darlington Railway on 27 September 1825, celebrated as a public holiday, pioneered because it was calculated to be cheaper than canal building, was the blueprint for all future railway companies in Britain, and a transforming moment in establishing Britain as the world's first major industrialised nation. The opening of the line was an event noted worldwide. The town became known as the birthplace of the railways, its economy boosted by new ease of access for working men. George Stephenson, the begetter of this new railway age, predicted at Stockton that it would be cheaper for the working man to travel by railway than to walk on foot. The rail link made it easier to bring coal from the pitheads to waterways and thence factories. In the 1920s,

---

*No question, in those days, of second homes in the constituency that could be 'flipped'.

chemical industries began to be established, including an ICI works at nearby Billingham.

But Macmillan arrived as a candidate in Stockton in 1923 just as the old manufacturing industries were experiencing what was to become a fatal decline. This brought many social problems. The growing town, with its cramped housing in the poorer districts, had suffered an outbreak of cholera in 1832, and the port declined as business moved more to nearby Middlesbrough. In the early 1920s unemployment was over 20 per cent and rising. This was a challenge for any MP of whatever party.

Macmillan had visited Stockton for several months before the election set for Thursday, 6 December 1923. In this he was helped by his wife, then expecting her second child.[46] Many people were astonished that Lady Dorothy went unabashed into what were known as 'the bad streets', canvassing in the poorer areas.

Stockton was a Liberal seat, with a fierce Radical tradition. It was a time of Depression, and the election was thought to be a two-horse race between Liberal and Labour. Macmillan was not expected to win for the Conservatives. But, in the days before Central Office funding of campaigns, he had been chosen, the local Conservative Association openly admitted, because he was in a position to bolster their failing finances. As it happened, he only just lost the seat, while pushing Labour into third place. The figures were:

Major R. Strother Stewart (Liberal)	11,734
Capt. Macmillan (Conservative)	11,661
F. F. Riley (Labour)	10,619
Liberal majority	73

He had come within a few votes of unexpected victory. More importantly, he had gained invaluable experience, while getting to know the town and its problems. Ten months later, in October 1924, there was another general election.

CHAPTER SIX

The Cleverest of the Coming Men

1923–1929

Macmillan and I caught the 8.50. Old Mrs Macmillan met us and drove me to the House of Commons. She is a nice old lady and naturally proud of her son – though she thinks that his oratorical delivery might be improved – perhaps she is right – he rather eats up his own words – but he gives out good stuff and is clearly a very able man who should go far. I look upon him easily as the cleverest of the 'coming men', though he is a trifle sententious and apt to be carried away into rather vague views which might lead him into other camps than the Conservative.

Cuthbert Headlam diary, 22 July 1926[1]

I am young enough to hope still in the Dream.
Harold Macmillan to Sligger Urquhart 7 November 1924

There is only one thing which I feel is worth giving one's whole strength to, and that is the binding together of all classes of our people in an effort to make life in this country better in every sense of the word.
Stanley Baldwin, at Stourport-on-Severn, 12 January 1925

The Conservatives had had a large majority in the 1922 election, but this was thrown away the following year. Stanley Baldwin, the ironmaster's son from Bewdley, was to be the face of interwar Conservatism and three times Prime Minister. However, his loss of controlling power after the December 1923 election temporarily cost him the premiership, after only seven short months in office. It almost lost him the Conservative leadership as well. His miscalculation was to call an early election in 1923 and to base his campaign on 'Protection'. Yet his decision was an honourable one, because Bonar Law had promised the electorate during the 1922 campaign that 'this Parliament will not make any fundamental change in the fiscal system of this country' without the electorate having the chance to vote on the matter, a specific reference to protection of imperial goods, a policy devoutly wished by the Dominion premiers. The difficulty was confining the campaign to a single issue.

'Between 1920 and 1924 the Conservative Party made three long-term decisions,' observed Maurice Cowling. 'The first was to remove Lloyd George from office. The second was to take up the role of "defender of the social order". The third was to make Labour the chief party of opposition.'[2] These were watershed decisions which were disastrous for the Liberal Party. Yet Lloyd George gave Baldwin some unlikely support, considering the part Baldwin had played in his downfall. The deposition of Lloyd George as Prime Minister in October 1922 had owed much to Baldwin's devastating speech at the Carlton Club meeting.

On that occasion Baldwin had said that Lloyd George was a dynamic force, but that 'a dynamic force is a very terrible thing; it may crush you but it is not necessarily right'.[3] Lloyd George's generosity had a poignant ring. 'To have become Prime Minister and be retiring to risk it all in favour of a great policy is fine and it is in this way that you will, whether you win or lose, get the adherence of anyone who is worth having as a follower.'[4]

Lloyd George's was not a universal view, especially among those Conservatives who felt that Baldwin, by confining himself to industrial protection, had watered down Joseph Chamberlain's vision of imperial preference. The debate between 'Protection' and 'Free Trade' was to divide Conservatives for over half a century.[5] 'I think Baldwin has gone mad,' proclaimed the disaffected Lord Birkenhead to Austen Chamberlain. 'He simply takes one jump in the dark: looks round, and then takes another. And all around him there are yawning pitfalls in which he might find his own destruction, which would matter little at any time. What is serious is that he takes our fortunes with him.'[6]

On 'Protection', Macmillan followed Baldwin's line, which was different from the 'Free Trade' line of his father-in-law. Macmillan's bold independence, a characteristic that was to delay his preferment, meant that he was the last of his parliamentary generation of future ministers to be given office.

During 1923, Macmillan visited Stockton with Dorothy for extended weekends. He experienced a new world of entertainment and relaxation, far removed from Chatsworth and Cadogan Place. Combat sports were a favourite pastime, and many was the time he was treated to an early supper and an evening of all-in wrestling. The annual dinner for the champion clog-dancer at Stockton's Hippodrome, police concerts and meetings of the Junior Imperial League ('The Junior Imps') also featured on his busy schedule. The centenary of the Stockton Railway* was a lavish occasion, celebrated by the whole community.

The visits to Stockton soon had their own established routine. He was entertained by association officers in their homes at Norton Green and Thornaby, the middle-class part of the constituency, whilst his agent, Joseph Lewis Cooke, a down-to-earth cockney who oversaw the constituency for five elections, taught him the ropes and introduced him to the working class areas. Macmillan's Stockton constituency papers are full of detailed letters from Cooke, alerting him to potential problems. Cooke oversaw arrangements for each ward, and things were run with military efficiency. Cooke's recipe for success was to win over prominent local Liberals; Macmillan believed also in door-to-door canvassing. The combination of the two approaches was to prove a winning one.

'These iron & steel trades have suffered so,' Macmillan wrote to Sligger Urquhart, '& the people have put up with all with extraordinary stoicism. I think I shall stand as Labour next time! If only we could make a coalition between the right Conservatives and the right Labourites what a good party it wd. be. And I have a vague hope that something of the kind may happen some day.'[7]

Although the Conservatives were the largest party numerically,† Baldwin knew that his hopes of forming a permanent government, in the face of a Lib-Lab alliance, were non-existent. It may not have been clear who had won, but it was clear who had lost. Nevertheless, over Christmas, he decided to face Parliament in January and force the other parties to combine against him. Asquith, who now held the ring, declared on 18 December that as the country had voted against protectionism, Labour – as the largest anti-protection party – deserved office; it would be 'a controlled experiment' under the safest of conditions.

The King's Speech was presented to Parliament on 15 January 1924. On 21 January Asquith's Liberals duly voted with Ramsay MacDonald's Labour Party and Baldwin's Conservative legislative programme was defeated by 328 votes to 256. The next day Ramsay MacDonald took office as Britain's first Labour prime minister. By his decision, Asquith had in the long term closed the door to future Liberal administrations. MacDonald's government did not 'sell out to the Bolsheviks', destroy the currency and institute free love – three

---

*Macmillan was to return to Stockton in 1975 in retirement for the 150th anniversary celebrations.
†Conservatives: 258; Labour: 191; Liberals: 159.

fears that were seriously aired by some dismayed patriots, planning to emigrate at once to Kenya. MacDonald eschewed his firebrand past; sober responsibility was to be the watchword.

John Wheatley's Housing Act was the major legislative programme of what proved to be, of necessity, a cautious government. In Scotland in particular, people still spoke decades later of 'Wheatley houses'. Macmillan greatly admired Wheatley's work, not least because of Wheatley's Keynesian belief in stimulating consumer demand as a way of increasing employment.

In Stockton, where he had narrowly lost, Macmillan at once realised that his task at the next election, which could not be far distant, would be to win over the working-class Liberal vote. It was a shrewd decision. The Liberals had held the seat since 1910, but the future threat would come from F. F. Riley, the Labour candidate, third in 1923. Riley, who contested Stockton four times, was a respected local man, General Secretary of the Postal Clerks' Association. He was MP for the constituency from 1929–1931, and died in February 1934.

Although Macmillan always dubbed 'Labour' as 'Socialist', a habit Churchill admired and indeed encouraged all Tories to do, privately he admired their finest, as Sligger Urquhart reminded him: 'I remember you saying that the best Conservatives and the best Labour men had so much in common.'[8] Macmillan did not see 'Labour' as 'Bolshevik', a term which in the twenties became shorthand for any manifestation of working-class agitation and militant trade unionism.

Far from relaxing after Baldwin's demise, Macmillan tackled the constituency with renewed vigour during 1924. On 17 June the Stockton and Thornaby Constitutional Organisation held a large invitation dinner, so that constituents could meet their Conservative candidate. Toasts were drunk to the King and the Conservative cause, coupled with the name of Captain Harold Macmillan.

The chairman of the Stockton Conservative Association was Ernest Appleton,[9] a prominent local businessman, who at once established an affinity with Macmillan because of their joint service in the Great War. Appleton was an industrious taskmaster and never spared himself when there was a project on hand, a quality Macmillan always admired. Appleton, for his part, believed that Stockton never fully realised how good Macmillan was.

The minority Labour government fell in October 1924 because of an adverse vote in the House of Commons on a matter of confidence. The next morning Ramsay MacDonald asked King George V for a dissolution of Parliament, and polling day was fixed for 29 October. Asquith's 'controlled experiment' was over.

*

Macmillan at once travelled to Stockton to kick-start his campaign. He received impressive backing from Ernest Appleton and his team, as well as senior parliamentarians, for Stockton was just the kind of constituency the Conservatives needed to win from the Liberals if they were to form a government. On the eve of the poll, Stanley Baldwin sent Macmillan a personal message of support. 'With your vigour, enthusiasm and sound political beliefs,' he wrote, 'we look to Stockton-on-Tees with confidence to put you at the head of the poll.'[10] Stockton was not to disappoint. The figures, with the defending Liberal candidate now bottom of the poll, were:

Captain Macmillan (Conservative)	15,163
F. F. Riley (Labour)	11,948
Major R. Strother Stewart (Liberal)	8,971
Conservative majority	3,215

Victor Mallet, a friend from Oxford days, who had been watching the results on a large screen in a London theatre, telegrammed Macmillan, 'We all yelled with joy at the Coliseum when your result came out.'[11]

The 1923 general election had been the first in which the wireless played a part. The British Broadcasting Company, later Corporation, first transmitted radio programmes on 14 November 1922, just in time for the results of the next day's general election to be broadcast as they came in, though too late for candidates or party leaders to campaign on air. It was a fortuitous coincidence that did much to establish the potential of the new medium.[12] Baldwin became the first national leader to master the art of 'fireside chats', speaking informally and directly from Savoy Hill, whereas MacDonald's radio broadcast was from a mass meeting in Glasgow, where different techniques applied, and which in a domestic setting sounded demagogic. By the time of the 1924 election, Baldwin had honed his technique and, far more than the Labour or Liberal leaders, fully realised the potential of the new medium. It was a lesson Macmillan learned and on which he drew with advantage when appearing on television during his own premiership.

Baldwin's Conservatives won 419 seats and Labour 151 in October 1924. Asquith's Liberals lost 116 seats and 1.4 million votes. The landslide victory of the Conservatives was helped, but not determined, by the infamous 'Red Scare', when a letter supposedly from

Gregory Zinoviev, Chairman of the Third International, to the British Communist Party, and released by the Foreign Office seemed to confirm Conservative fears of Bolshevik infiltration into the British Labour movement. The Zinoviev letter was later demonstrated to be a forgery, but by then the damage to the Labour campaign, exploited ruthlessly by Tory newspapers four days before polling, had been done. Even *The Times* ran a 'tabloid' headline: *Soviet Plot. Red Propaganda in Britain. Revolution Urged by Zinoviev. Foreign Office Bombshell.*[13] Macmillan considered the most damaging material to be the suggestion of revolutionary undermining of the armed forces.

After his landslide victory, Baldwin set about his task of reconciliation. To reunite Conservatives he needed to find posts for the former Coalitionists. He solved the Churchill 'problem' in an unexpected and controversial manner. By appointing him Chancellor of the Exchequer, a Free-Trade counterbalance to the hard-line Protectionist wing, he gave a clear sign that he had abandoned Protection. When Churchill received the offer of the chancellorship, he assumed Baldwin meant the Duchy of Lancaster, a post he had held briefly in 1915. Baldwin made it clear that he meant the Treasury, and Churchill replied, 'You have done more for me than Lloyd George ever did.' Thinking it was better to have Churchill inside the proverbial tent, rather than outside[14], Baldwin explained to the Deputy Cabinet Secretary, Tom Jones, 'It would be up to him [Churchill] to be loyal if he is capable of loyalty.'[15]

Churchill's ill-starred tenure at the Treasury from 1924–1929 was to evoke from J. M. Keynes his second famous post-war polemic, *The Economic Consequences of Mr Churchill*, which Macmillan always thought should have been called *The Economic Consequences of Montagu Norman*, then Governor of the Bank of England and the high priest of Treasury orthodoxy. After Churchill had put Britain back on the gold standard in his 1925 Budget, Keynes was scathing about the deleterious consequences this mistake would have on employment, implicitly bracketing the error with the greater perspective of Versailles by the title of his pamphlet. The pound was now fixed at the pre-war parity of $4.86, disastrous for exports. Eventually Churchill's policy, popular across all parties at first, was to be an economic failure that turned into a political failure. Macmillan recalled that only two parliamentarians, Sir Robert Horne, with his City experience, and Robert Boothby, an early Keynesian, spoke out against the decision. Despite Boothby's views, or maybe because of them, Churchill appointed him his Parliamentary Private Secretary in 1926, a post Boothby held till the government fell in 1929. Macmillan soon saw the 'consequences' in his own constituency, and in nearby manufacturing districts such as Consett.

Stanley Baldwin had advised Macmillan to specialise, and as Stockton increasingly suffered its economic downturn, Macmillan concentrated on domestic, social and industrial matters. Foreign affairs were not then in his orbit and he regretted that this meant he saw little of the Foreign Secretary Austen Chamberlain, whom, at a distance, he greatly admired, much more so than his half-brother Neville. Through his growing friendship with Boothby in the 1924 Parliament Macmillan was to see much of Churchill, and was drawn into the circle of those who discussed political issues late into the night, an immensely stimulating political baptism, and so different from a talk with Neville Chamberlain, which was, in Macmillan's view, rather like visiting the headmaster's study. His link with Churchill was not only political. Writing was another bond. Churchill remembered with gratitude that Macmillan & Co. had published his life of Lord Randolph Churchill. For Macmillan, the Churchill late-night soirées were not unlike those evenings at Balliol when undergraduates had talked on equal terms with sympathetic dons such as Sligger Urquhart. Brandy, however, replaced lemonade.

Macmillan made his maiden speech in the Commons just before 7 p.m. on 30 April 1925, in the debate on Churchill's Budget proposals. He criticised the Opposition for suggesting that the Budget was 'a rich man's budget'. In fact, said Macmillan, it concentrated on helping 'the poorer classes of Income Tax Payers'. As such it appealed greatly to 'the younger and more progressive Members of the Conservative Party', which he proclaimed himself to be. He ended by turning his attack on to the former Prime Minister, Ramsay MacDonald:

> If he thinks that he and his party have only to offer us as the true Socialism a kind of mixture, a sort of horrible political cocktail, consisting partly of the drugs of exploded economic views of Karl Marx, mixed up with a little flavour of Cobdenism, well iced by the late Chancellor of the Exchequer, and with a little ginger from the Member for Gorbals [Mr Buchanan],[16] if he thinks that this is to be the draught given to our parched throats, and that we are ready to accept it, he is very much mistaken.[17]

Sir John Marriott, following Macmillan, congratulated him 'on his very brilliant contribution to this Debate'.[18] It was a notable parliamentary debut.

*

Macmillan was immensely busy during these early parliamentary years, cramming a full day's work in St Martin's Lane at Macmillan & Co. into half a day, leaving for the House at 1.30 and staying there till late-night divisions. Dorothy gave birth to their third child, Catherine, in 1926, the year of the General Strike, so he had growing family responsibilities, and in addition, there were the regular long trips north to Stockton. In April, his father-in-law, Victor Devonshire, had suffered a grievous stroke that changed his character for ever. Macmillan was always grateful that he knew the pre-1925 Victor.

Macmillan did not neglect his constituency. One of the first rows he had to defuse after the 1924 election was about boxing tournaments and whether they should be allowed in Working Men's Clubs on Sundays, a prospect considered in some quarters as 'detrimental to Social Order and Moral Welfare'. Stockton's sabbaths remained free of pugilism. He also worked hard to get a serviceman who had lost a leg in the Great War reinstated at Ropner's, the main local shipbuilding firm, still one of the major employers. He built up a friendship with the Walford family, with whom he stayed at their house on the Green at Norton, among other hospitable venues, never imposing too long or too frequently in one place. Conservative workers vied to give him and Lady Dorothy a base, and he ensured that he got to know many influential supporters in this way by visiting them all.

The headquarters of the Stockton and Thornaby Constitutional Organisation was at a large house, Kinnoull, on Dovecot Street, now a local tax office, but Macmillan soon realised that the party needed a bigger, more public place for meetings and was instrumental in planning the Constitutional Hall, where dances, fêtes and rallies were held. He not only contributed handsomely to the project, but was the guarantor of the mortgage with Ernest Appleton. When Appleton died suddenly in 1941, Ralph Appleton, his son, then only 21, was suddenly in a position where he could be liable for losses at an uncertain time. Even though Macmillan was then fulfilling work of international importance in North Africa, he arranged at once to take on the entire risk himself to free Ralph from unnecessary worry, or possible bankruptcy. Macmillan was also instrumental in establishing two Conservative Working Men's Clubs, which he visited on a regular basis. Although he was prone to romanticising the working class, whether Durham miners, private soldiers from the Great War or the unemployed in Stockton, and although he was to prove as adept as many successful politicians in playing to the gallery, his feelings about the disadvantaged were not at heart sentimental.

The conditions Macmillan witnessed in Stockton affected him

deeply and genuinely conditioned much of his later political thinking. He was profoundly troubled by the depression and the poverty he found. He saw children without shoes and queues for soup kitchens. The Mayor's Boot Fund, which has a nineteenth-century ring, was one practical project he supported, and many were the destitute and despairing who were privately slipped a white five-pound note.[19]

A Social Services Centre was set up at the Ropner Building, site of the shipping offices, where Macmillan worked with Major Salt. Help was provided here for the young unemployed including hot midday meals, lectures, carpentry classes and training for apprenticeships. Macmillan advised 14-year-old school-leavers who planned to emigrate to Queensland and New South Wales, where there were labour shortages and attractive relocation packages. Rather in the manner that he had helped private soldiers write their letters home from the trenches, he now took it upon himself to help young people compose letters in applying for jobs. Major Salt felt that, had Macmillan's calling been in that direction, he could have been a most sympathetic schoolmaster. For his part, Macmillan told both Ernest Appleton and Major Salt that he wanted none of this work publicised, as he did not want to be seen to be trading on it. Gradually he became less shy and diffident, and the involvement in youth work was a vital learning process. When there was an eclipse of the sun on 29 June 1927, Stockton-on-Tees was one of the areas in the north of England that experienced totality, a memorable event, the educational potential of which was not neglected.

Dorothy supported her husband, giving sympathy and practical help at times of sickness, family bereavement, industrial accidents and, as happened increasingly, sudden and unexpected unemployment. Nor were more routine matters neglected, items such as the bazaar magazine and the ubiquitous lemon curd stall. At Conservative fêtes, Lady Dorothy was the undisputed champion in getting metal fish out of tanks with magnetic fishing rods.

Stanley Baldwin's second, and longest, spell as Prime Minister from 1924–1929 was a time of consolidation. Inventing himself as a latter-day Walpole, his aim above all was to seek stability. The General Strike of 1926 threatened this stability. 'Harold gets so gloomy, but I somehow can't feel that there can be any doubt as to who will win in the end,' Dorothy wrote to her mother, as there seemed no sign of an early settlement. 'Harold feels that if it is not finished by the middle of the week it will be a real long haul.'[20] The middle class experienced the crisis days in May 1926 as days of excitement – driving buses, acting as special constables – and therefore did not suffer the bitter aftermath, which left a dangerous legacy. Macmillan's view was that the strike could have been avoided, but only with a measure of state intervention in the coal industry, which was not acceptable to mainstream Conservatism. He had meetings with voluntary organisations and the local police superintendent. 'I spent some very interesting days during the troubles at Stockton,' he wrote to Ernest Appleton afterwards, 'and hope I was of some little use.'[21] In London he went each evening to Printing House Square to help in distributing special editions of *The Times*. 'I have been very struck with the growth of Parliament spirit among the Labour men,' he wrote to Sligger Urquhart. 'I have a great many friends among them & in private they all say that the strike must be called off before the Govt. negotiates.' When the strike was called off Macmillan initially had high hopes in Baldwin. 'I believe the P.M. is really the Lincoln of the day & will apply the Lincoln policy of reconciliation when this is over.'[22]

Baldwin, the Worcestershire lad, cultivated the image and *persona* of the countryman and set out to represent what later became known as Middle England. Worcestershire, the county of Elgar and the Three Choirs Festival, represented a kind of prelapsarian rural idyll and Baldwin played up to this comforting and reassuring image. He really enjoyed, it was said, leaning over a fence and scratching pigs. Such nostalgia, the political equivalent of what the composers Constant Lambert and Elisabeth Lutyens unfairly dubbed the 'Cowpat School' of inter-war English music, was very different from Macmillan's experience. The Disraelian concept of the Two Nations,[23] the rich and the poor – which Macmillan saw at first hand, from Billingham to Birch Grove, was never far from his mind.

As a result, despite his initial optimism, he felt that Baldwin had failed to make the most of a potentially favourable situation after the General Strike, which Baldwin was largely credited with ending. In September 1926 Macmillan made a speech in Parliament, in which he urged a new approach to relations between the government and the trade unions, including arbitration, and later that year he followed this up with a letter to *The Times** on industry and new democratic approaches. These initiatives gained him few friends in the ranks of the right-wing Conservatives and their supporters among the press barons.

---

* *The Times* had already spotted Macmillan as a potential minister from the 1924 intake. When a junior vacancy arose in the Admiralty in December 1926, the paper commented, 'Men like Colonel Headlam, Captain Harold Macmillan, Mr Oliver Stanley, Mr Skelton, to name no others are all of them more than equal to the standard which has been expected of under-Secretaries in the past.'[24]

Under his placid, conciliatory exterior, Baldwin was a party manager of great political skill. The Conservatives had their diehard element (represented by Colonel John Gretton[25], a fierce intriguer, whose snoring in the House after a dozen oysters often disturbed debates) and their younger progressive element (of which Macmillan was now a principal member). Indeed, Baldwin was later to say that his task in internal party politics had always been to steer a path 'between Harold Macmillan and John Gretton'.[26]

The young progressive members were dubbed the YMCA by cynical older parliamentarians. Their mentor and intellectual leader was Noel Skelton,[27] MP for Perth, and later the Scottish Universities, whose most famous contribution to forward-looking Conservative thinking was his advocacy of 'the property-owning democracy', a concept he outlined in a series of articles in the *Spectator* in April and May 1923, then published as *Constructive Conservatism*. He was a great influence on three future Conservative prime ministers – Anthony Eden, Harold Macmillan and Alec Douglas-Home. Indeed, it was Eden's speech on the property-owning democracy at the Conservative Party Conference in October 1946 that was to bring Skelton's ideas into the mainstream of Conservative thinking once again. Macmillan's later spell at the Ministry of Housing from 1951–1954 was to see the practical accomplishment of one of Skelton's main aims.

Skelton wisely was not a one-issue politician. He believed in many ideas way ahead of their time, such as co-partnership and workers' share options to improve industrial relations, referenda to resolve disputes between the two Houses of Parliament, and Conservative action on pension provision. If the Tories did not follow a progressive agenda, he felt their prospects were poor. 'Parties of the Right are psychologically incapable of taking a long view,' he wrote to Macmillan, 'or making sacrifices or taking risks to achieve it.'[28] All this was manna for Macmillan.

Skelton quickly gathered around him a like-minded group of younger MPs, among them Harold Macmillan (Stockton-on-Tees) and Robert Boothby (Aberdeenshire East). The YMCA represented a wide cross-section of constituencies throughout Britain. John Buchan (Scottish Universities), the author and future Governor-General of Canada, became a particular friend of Macmillan. Duff Cooper (Oldham) specialised in foreign policy. Yet it was over domestic issues that the YMCA became most influential. The group advocated Keynesian interventionist economic policy to combat rising unemployment, and lobbied Baldwin to ensure that reactionary elements in the Conservative Party were not given a free rein.

In one of his regular reports to King George V on parliamentary matters, Baldwin left the monarch in no doubt about his admiration for the new intake, so different from the hard-faced pre-war men. 'It is a source of satisfaction to all that this element has been largely diminished and that in its place has appeared a band of keen and ardent young Conservatives with a genuine desire to serve the public interest, rather than that of any particular class.'[29] The demographic change in Parliament was a factor in this process. At the end of the Great War, only one sixth of the parliamentary party was under 40; in the 1924 Parliament, the figure was nearly a quarter. Macmillan realised the opportunity this offered. 'We shall be able to do our small part in stirring up the old fogeys and making this government get on with the job,' he wrote to John Loder, 'the best chance we shall have and we are uncommonly lucky to have it.'[30]

The Trades Disputes and Trade Union Act of 1927, which replaced 'contracting out' of paying the political levy with 'contracting in', was described as a 'calculated and deliberate act of class hostility'.[31] Although many in the YMCA claimed the Act would be disastrous for trade union relations and give Labour activists a focus for grievance, Macmillan believed that the principle behind this contentious clause was in fact correct, a fact he emphasised in a speech at Eastbourne (Cavendish country)[32] in 1925. He was more in line with mainstream YMCA thinking when he persuaded Churchill to advocate an industrial de-rating scheme in Cabinet, which went through despite Neville Chamberlain's reservations. Introduced in Churchill's 1928 Budget, the De-Rating Bill had 115 clauses, and aimed to relieve industry from some of the pressures of taxation. Neville Chamberlain never again spoke to Macmillan during that Parliament.

Many of the older M.P.s regarded the YMCA as a prissy alliance, hence the pejorative nickname, with its suggestion of sanctimonious high-mindedness. A speech of John Buchan's in the House was interrupted by a diehard cry of 'Let us pray.' The YMCA was not part of that Roaring Twenties[33] scene of cocktails, the Charleston, nightclubs, jazz and racing cars at Brooklands; but it certainly represented a change in mood. It regarded Gretton's group as dangerous antediluvians, and saw them, together with another group, 'the Industrials', as a major block to progressive thinking and long-term electoral success. The YMCA dubbed the Industrials 'the Forty Thieves', 'hangers on of business', as Austen Chamberlain described them, full of the old and the disgruntled. 'I should like very much to know,' asked Chamberlain, 'how many young men of a decent type were numbered in its ranks.'[34]

The most important contribution Macmillan made to the political debate in these years was the booklet *Industry and the State*, published in April 1927, which he co-authored with Robert Boothby, John Loder and Oliver Stanley. A precursor to Macmillan's individual work *The Middle Way* of 1938, *Industry and the State* was imbued with the Skeltonian spirit. The authors looked at the concept of a mixed economy, with broad overall control in state hands, but detailed operation in the hands of professional managers. Collective bargaining, marketing schemes and new industrial councils were advocated, as well as workers' representation on company boards. To Macmillan's surprise, Neville Chamberlain sent him a congratulatory letter with pages of detailed comments on the 'stimulating' proposals.

Macmillan's papers are full of letters from Boothby, in that distinctive copperplate handwriting (equalled in stylishness only by that of the second Lord Hailsham). Boothby sent him cuttings and pamphlets from a myriad organisations. 'This is the sort of thing that is at least encouraging. Don't you think?' wrote Boothby of a closely argued memorandum from the Bank Officials' Association, advocating 'adequate machinery for the curtailment of the spirit of misunderstanding and suspicion which underlies most of the industrial disputes of today'. He also sent on documents on social insurance, and a Memorandum on the Mining Industry, written by two Labour politicians. 'John Strachey gave me this. It is the memorandum drawn up by himself and [Emanuel] Shinwell. He thought it might interest you.'[35] What was interesting was that two young radical Labour figures considered Macmillan the kind of Tory who would be alert to their thinking.

These notes from Boothby marked the beginning of a lengthy correspondence on the political issues of the day. Some of Boothby's later notes could be considered impertinent, coming from an MP whom promotion had left behind, suggesting policies to the Prime Minister; yet Macmillan always replied, with the utmost courtesy, commenting on individual details.

Baldwin's declining authority was marked by his retreat from a proposal to strengthen the power of the Conservative position in the Lords, and a series of by-election defeats in 1927. Macmillan had told his constituency party that any attempt to reform the House of Lords (a plan announced on 20 June 1927) was doomed to failure, as the party would never be able to agree on a scheme.[36] Even the defeat of the Revised Prayer Book[37] legislation, a proposed measure that aroused what would later be considered inexplicable controversy, was taken as a sign of Baldwin's failing touch. Cuthbert Headlam felt the issue could prove 'a hornet's nest for a good many of us at the next election'.[38] Though deeply religious, Macmillan thought the parliamentary energy and time expended during the 1927–1928 session on Prayer Book revision would have been better directed to secular problems.

Macmillan had established himself as a consequential parliamentary figure, even an inconvenient maverick, in the years of the second Baldwin government. He achieved this not by charisma (he was considered a dull dog) or by fine oratory, but by perseverance and the ability to blend chameleon-like with many diverse social groups, whether the hard drinkers in Churchill's circle, Labour figures such as James Maxton and David Kirkwood, the Clydesiders, regulars in cross-party banter in the smoking room, or his Stockton constituents. Such an approach was not unusual among the officer class, whose insular upbringing had been broadened beyond recognition through contact and shared identity with working-class soldiers during the Great War. The political aspect of this process was seen in the proselytising work of the YMCA. 'Toryism,' Macmillan was to declare in 1936, 'has always been a form of paternal Socialism.'[39]

R. A. Butler[40] always felt there were two sides to Macmillan, 'the soft heart for and the strong determination to help the underdog, and the social habit to associate happily with the overdog'.[41] This was true of many upper-class Conservatives of the time, Butler included. The Macmillans, however, moved in very elevated social circles indeed, and Harold and Dorothy were guests at the Duke of York's wedding to Elizabeth Bowes-Lyon in Westminster Abbey on 26 April 1923.

All elections can be seen as watersheds, but that of May 1929 was unique in twentieth-century parliamentary history. For the first time, women now had the vote at the same age as men, 21, and Britain had universal adult suffrage, a goal first set out (for men alone)[42] by the Chartists in their 'People's Charter' of May 1836. The electorate was increased from 21.75 million to almost 29 million, which introduced an element of uncertainty. When the Conservatives had extended the franchise with the Second Reform Act in 1867 – Disraeli's 'leap in the dark' – they had not reaped the electoral benefit. The pattern was to be repeated in May 1929, though in the longer term full female enfranchisement was to be of lasting benefit to them, something Macmillan and his wife both realised would be the case. Female voters now outnumbered male by over two million. Macmillan thereafter never neglected women's interests.

The election of May 1929 was also, at least in terms of aspiration, a genuine three-party contest. Each party put up over 500 candidates. Lloyd George, in his last bid for power, now led the Liberal Party into a general election for the first time (Asquith had resigned the Liberal leadership in 1926 and had died in 1928) and had sincere, if unrealistic, hopes of returning to Downing Street. A series of policy documents, influenced and in some cases written by J. M. Keynes, made one of the most coherent intellectual statements regarding Britain's future needs ever put before the electorate. Keynes was invited to stand as Liberal candidate for Cambridge, but declined. The most famous document was the Liberal 'Yellow Book' (so named because of the colour of its cover), *Britain's Industrial Future* of 1928. It could have been penned by the YMCA.

The overriding issue was unemployment. Lloyd George responded by issuing the manifesto *We Can Conquer Unemployment* in March 1929, advocating a programme of public works. Labour's main offering, G. D. H. Cole's *How To Conquer Unemployment: Labour's answer to Lloyd George*, was reactive, rather than original. The Conservatives were increasingly sidelined, and their slogan of 'Safety First', echoing current Ministry of Transport campaigns, together with posters showing Baldwin steering the ship of state through troubled waters, was hardly calculated to set the pulses racing. In fact, the underlying electoral battle was not between capitalism and socialism, though Baldwin and Ramsay MacDonald wished the electorate to see it as such, but between economic orthodoxy and economic unorthodoxy, a divide that transcended party boundaries.

Orthodox economic thinking was that of Montagu Norman, Governor of the Bank of England, and the Treasury. Unorthodox thinking, in the shape of Keynesian expansionism, was advocated by figures as diverse as Ernest Bevin, General Secretary of the Transport and General Workers' Union since 1922; the mercurial Oswald Mosley; Lloyd George's Liberals; and the leftish young Tories of the YMCA.

Macmillan concentrated in his campaign on industrial modernisation, and, in the wake of the Stockton centenary, the future of the railways.[43] It was clear that local goverment reorganisation – announced just before the general election – was having a negative effect on Conservative prospects. Macmillan noticed the adverse effect of rates increases, especially in home-owning areas such as Norton and Thornaby. It was also clear that his main opponent would be the Labour candidate, not the Liberal one.

Macmillan's result, which was a bitter disappointment to him was a microcosm of the national result:

F. F. Riley (Labour)	18,961
Captain Harold Macmillan (Conservative)	16.572
J. C. Hayes (Liberal)	10,407
Labour majority	2,389

By 3 a.m. on 31 May, it was clear that the results were a repeat of 1923: Baldwin had lost. For the first time, Labour were the single largest party, although without an overall majority. MacDonald's Labour Party had won 288 seats and Baldwin's Conservatives 260. Despite winning 5.3 million votes, Lloyd George's Liberals, soon to split yet again into various factions, gained only 59 seats, although they held the balance of power. Baldwin contemplated, but decided against, meeting Parliament as in January 1924. He tendered his resignation to King George V at Windsor. He had offered 'Safety First', but the voters had preferred 'Labour First'. On 8 June 1929, MacDonald and the members of his new government travelled to Windsor to receive their seals of office. Lloyd George's campaign had been in vain. For the rest of Macmillan's parliamentary career, a two-party dichotomy was the norm, with the Liberals tinkering at the edges of the system like discontented gadflies.

When Macmillan heard the result of the Stockton poll, he wept, a rare display of emotion. He was soon to weep inwardly for another reason. His wife Dorothy was beginning a passionate affair with his fellow member of the YMCA, Robert Boothby.

Out of sympathy for Macmillan's defeat in Stockton, Boothby invited the Macmillans to his father's shooting party that August. Boothby had first met Dorothy in 1928 at Beechwood, the Boothby family home in Edinburgh, and a 'society' photograph of Macmillan, Boothby and Dorothy on a golfing holiday at Gleneagles had been published in the magazines. Boothby's many letters to Macmillan nearly always concluded with the message, 'My love to Dorothy.'[44] This bravado was strangely uninhibited, though Boothby was mistaken in thinking that Macmillan was naive about the situation.

Further golfing holidays and shooting parties followed. Inevitably, given the feelings Bob Boothby aroused in Dorothy, these were only the beginning. When Macmillan realised what was happening, it was an even greater shock than his parliamentary defeat. Losing Stockton was a temporary reversal. The pain of his wife's adultery endured for the rest of his life. Canada in 1919 had given him health and a wife; ten years later, the events of 1929 were to cost him his health, and potentially his wife also.

CHAPTER SEVEN

Ebbs and Flows

1929–1935

> Apparently the Macmillan disagreement continues – I am very
> sorry about it as I always thought that Harold and Dorothy
> were a united couple. I hope they may come together again – a
> break up in the Cavendish family would be a staggering shock
> to Society!
>
> Cuthbert Headlam diary, 23 December 1932[1]

> Her hapless husband, whiskered Hal,
> Would daily greet me in the Mall
> As tho' I were his truest pal
> And no adulterer.
>
> Maurice Bowra, *The Statesman's Tragedy*

> O curse of marriage
> That we can call these delicate creatures ours
> But not their appetites.
>
> Shakespeare, *Othello*

At 5.15 p.m. on Friday, 31 May 1929, the London-bound train began
to pull out of Darlington station, as MPs and candidates returned to
the capital. The platforms were crowded with Labour voters, sporting the green and white favours of Labour's founding father, Keir
Hardie. All were eager to see Ramsay MacDonald,[2] newly elected for
Seaham Harbour and about to become Prime Minister for the second
time. A batch of newly elected Labour MPs from the Durham area
waved to their enthusiastic supporters, but standing alone at one of
the train windows was Harold Macmillan. Flourishing his electoral
colours of red and gold, the tears running down his cheeks, he bravely
called for 'Three cheers for Baldwin', but his words were drowned
out by jeers. On the train he sat with Ramsay MacDonald himself
and Hugh Dalton, newly elected MP for Bishop Auckland. Unusually
for a Labour MP, Dalton had been educated at Summer Fields, and
at Cambridge he had been taught economics by Maynard Keynes.
Macmillan felt himself with a kindred spirit.[3] Dalton, for his part,

comforted Macmillan on the journey to King's Cross by saying, 'In politics there are ebbs and flows.'[4] The returning victors were met at the station by Oswald Mosley, on the verge of government office.[5] Fortune and men's eyes no longer smiled on the Conservatives.

The result of the 1929 election was a crushing blow to the YMCA group. Duff Cooper, Cuthbert Headlam, Robert Hudson, John Loder and Terence O'Connor, like Macmillan, were all defeated. 'It is a little disappointing after all one has tried to do, but I am not at all disheartened,' Macmillan wrote to Sligger Urquhart, putting as brave a face as he could on the events. 'The people were friendly & much less bitterness than before. I quite understood their vote & sh. have been inclined to do the same. The great thing is that *everybody* has learned a lot during these years & we must go on teaching & learning.'[6]

The fate of this YMCA group – 'troublesome young men', as Macmillan described them to Churchill[7] – was not displeasing to the *Daily Mail*, which expressed the fervent hope that future candidacies should not be offered to 'semi-Socialists such as Captain Harold Macmillan'.[8] A different view came from the political correspondent of the *Yorkshire Post*, James Johnstone, who wrote prophetically:

> Captain Macmillan is full of plans for the necessary repair and reconstruction of society. His governing impulse is the desire to give to the mass of the people the fullest possible individual life. He is one of the few promising men whom this Parliament has produced. He has the affinity with the spirit of the age and the understanding of Parliamentary ways which guarantee success in the political life of the future. Some day he will be one of the guiding forces of the Conservative Party, a capable and persuasive Minister.[9]

Macmillan was now at a critical turning point. Should he abandon the political calling and concentrate on publishing, or should he find a fresh seat? Industrial Stockton was never going to be a Conservative stronghold, and nobody knew when the Conservatives might form another government. However, Macmillan decided, for the time being, to remain in the game. Meanwhile, there was plenty to keep him busy at Macmillan & Co. He became a leading light of the Publishers' Association: chair of the 'Fiction Group' and the 'Employment Group' and serving on the 'Public Relations' Committee. He travelled widely, staying at the Harvard Club of New York[10] when dealing with American business. In January 1935, as a member of the 'Indian Group' of the Publishers' Association, he was prominent with

John Buchan in ensuring that British India continued to be a signatory to the Berne Copyright Convention.[11] Buchan and Macmillan both enjoyed the world of books, and Buchan was one of the few MPs with whom Macmillan relaxed socially. Both were included by Edith, Marchioness of Londonderry, the famed interwar hostess, in her group, 'the Ark', formed of exciting figures from the world of politics and the arts. Macmillan and Buchan were doubly qualified for the Ark as they came from both worlds. Parties were held in the ballroom at Londonderry House, where nicknames were all the rage. Lady Astor[12] was Nancy the Gnat, Arthur Balfour was Arthur the Albatross, whilst Macmillan answered to the name of Harold the Hummingbird.[13] Here Macmillan mingled with Edmund Gosse and George Bernard Shaw, a publisher at home with literary men. In the midst of all his political and personal disappointments and humiliations, it must never be forgotten that publishing was his constant lodestar, his profession and living.

With a touch of defiance, several of those vying for any seats that might become vacant formed the Defeated Candidates' Association, a caucus in the waiting room of politics led by John Moore-Brabazon,[14] who had lost his seat at Chatham.[15] Among them were Macmillan, Cuthbert Headlam and Thomas Inskip.[16]

On 29 July, Harold Macmillan and Cuthbert Headlam met at 14 Chester Square. Headlam found Macmillan in a despondent mood. 'I had a talk with that dejected statesman. He does not know what to do about a seat – is, indeed, in the same quandary as myself – but his position is better than mine for he is so much younger.' Conversation soon turned to Baldwin's position, which was once more uncertain. 'He told me a lot of gossip re. the plot to get rid of Baldwin – by the newspaper peers,' wrote Headlam.[17] By the time they next had a heart-to-heart, in December 1929, the situation seemed clearer, at least for Macmillan. 'I had a long talk with Harold – who is pleased with himself having secured the Hitchin division.'[18] Headlam was not so fortunate, unsuccessfully trawling constituencies from Guildford to Huddersfield and Newcastle.

The only drawback to standing for Hitchin was Macmillan's genuine regret that he would be letting down the many friends he had made in Stockton. He discussed the situation with his Chairman, Ernest Appleton, who reassured him. 'I would be a fool not to recognise that from every point of view,' Appleton wrote on 27 January 1930, 'you are doing the right thing in standing for a Constituency nearer to London.'[19] Leonard Ropner, of the local shipbuilding family, was formally adopted as Conservative candidate for Stockton-on-Tees the same month.

Yet events did not work out. The sitting MP for Hitchen, Major Guy Kindersley,[20] who had initially supported Macmillan as his successor, showed signs of changing his mind. In the uncertain political climate, with a general election possible at any time, he now felt that it would be unfair to inflict a by-election on the Hitchin voters, especially as Lord Beaverbrook,[21] who was conducting an Empire Free Trade crusade in the pages of the *Daily Express*, might easily have supported an Empire Free Trade candidate. Beaverbrook saw Macmillan as a useful ally, but there was nevertheless a real danger of a split vote and an uncertain result in Hitchin.

Baldwin's position as Conservative leader was under increasing pressure. At a party meeting on 30 October, Major Kindersley had seconded a motion proposed by John Gretton, the prominent diehard, against Baldwin's leadership. Macmillan too was caught up in this anti-Baldwin fervour in the winter of 1929. On 5 November (an appropriately iconoclastic date), Macmillan had convened a meeting with Boothby, Edward Hulton[22] and Walter Elliot,[23] setting out their enthusiasm for Beaverbrook's Empire Free Trade crusade, in essence a plot by the press baron to oust Baldwin from the leadership.

What really angered Kindersley, though, was Macmillan's overt support for Labour MP Oswald Mosley's Keynesian ideas. Mosley had prepared a memorandum containing Keynesian solutions for solving growing unemployment. This had been rejected by the Cabinet, and Mosley had resigned as Chancellor of the Duchy of Lancaster. Kindersley wrote to Macmillan warning him that any repetition of sympathy for Mosley's Keynesian opinions would lead to Kindersley standing again in Hitchin. As Macmillan's first speech in Hitchin had been on 3 March, and Mosley's resignation on 19 May, this was a speedy falling-out. Only Macmillan's need to hang on to a candidacy – in Great War parlance he did not have 'a better 'ole to go to' – prevented him from walking away then and there; and it was not long before he wrote, with almost stubborn foolhardiness, a defensive 12-page letter to the chairman of the Hitchin Association, Lieutenant-Colonel Sir Charles Heaton-Ellis (it was a constituency of military titles), re-emphasising his position as a Conservative radical and a sceptic on Baldwin's leadership. As a result, Major Kindersley decided once and for all definitely to stand again, and Hitchin's association with Macmillan was brought to an abrupt end in February 1931.

After this reversal, Macmillan was fortunate that the situation had changed in Stockton. Leonard Ropner was unwell and had suffered a family bereavement; he felt obliged to stand down as candidate. Accordingly, Ernest Appleton had no hesitation in March 1931 in asking Macmillan to stand once again for his old seat. In May, Macmillan was rapturously received at his re-adoption meeting. The warmth of his reception reawakened all his feelings about the north. The prodigal son had returned, even though Macmillan felt guiltily that, to mix the metaphors, he had ratted, done a chicken run and re-ratted.* But, although Hitchin would have meant less travelling and been a safe Conservative seat, the chemistry was never right.

Ernest Appleton found Macmillan much changed. The old verve seemed to have gone and he exuded a melancholy air. People who had known him before felt this was owing to the bleak economic situation and possible commercial difficulties for Macmillan & Co., where he was now a senior director.[24] The real reason was very different.

On 26 August 1930, Dorothy Macmillan had given birth to her fourth child, a third daughter, Sarah. 'Had a message to say that Dorothy had got a little girl,' her father recorded in his diary.[25] It had been a difficult labour and Dorothy was laid up for many months. Macmillan too was suffering from recurrent pain from his war wounds, adding to his sense of strain and uneasiness over the situation regarding Hitchin and Stockton-on-Tees. But life at Birch Grove had its sombre side for another reason. Shortly after her confinement, Dorothy informed her husband that Robert Boothby[26] was the father of Sarah, and that she wished to have a divorce so that she could marry Bob. For any man, but particularly one of Macmillan's sensitivity, this was a double blow of pain and humiliation.[27]

Bob Boothby – he was always known as Bob – was one of those meteoric mavericks who occasionally flare across the political sky, shedding perhaps more heat than light, but always adding to the gaiety of the nation. He was an undoubted 'character', handsome and viva-cious, '*such* a jolly man', as the future Queen (later Queen Elizabeth, the Queen Mother) described him, 'a bounder, but not a cad'. In his Bentley two-seater, as in his private and professional life, Bob Boothby cut the corners, but underneath the hedonistic exterior lay a progres-sive and enlightened political mind. He was a Keynesian, and on the big issues of the age – especially unemployment and appeasement – on the side of what history would later see as the angels. Not that he was seen as such at the time. For the whips he was a disputatious rebel, one of the 'troublesome young men'.

His private life, especially by the standards of the day, could be described as unorthodox. A passionate man, he was promiscuous and

---

*Churchill had re-ratted in moving from Conservative to Liberal and back to Conservative.

bisexual, with a zest for pleasure and high living. For Lady Dorothy Macmillan, cribbed and confined for much of her time at Birch Grove, with an overbearing and unsympathetic mother-in-law living under the same roof, Boothby was the proverbial breath of fresh air. Appropriately, they first became conscious of each other in the summer of 1929 on the bracing moors of Beechwood, the Boothby family estate near Edinburgh. Boothby was a very different kind of Etonian from Macmillan. Dorothy was at first entranced by him, and soon became besotted. It was not long before they were lovers. Macmillan knew of the affair from the start but, it was soon clear, so strong were Dorothy's feelings that he was powerless to help her to bring the obsession under control. He could only nurse his wounds and stoically conceal the hurt.

Divorce in pre-war days, as shown by the Abdication Crisis of 1936, was the ultimate social solecism. While a blind eye was turned by 'society' to affairs, as long as they remained discreet, public scandal was ruinous for professional life. The lessons of Sir Charles Dilke and Charles Stuart Parnell still lurked in people's memories.[28] The Conservative Party was particularly censorious, not accepting divorcees as candidates until after the Second World War, and then only in exceptional circumstances.

The BBC, too, under the stern interwar leadership of Sir John Reith, was unbending in its attitudes. As Lord High Commissioner of the General Assembly of the Church of Scotland, Reith had influence over invitations to royal garden parties in Edinburgh. When one (excluded) dignitary pointed out to Reith that he was the innocent party in a recent divorce, Reith told him, 'That may get you into the Kingdom of Heaven, but it'll no get you into the Palace of Holyrood House.'

When Anthony Eden* remarried in August 1952, the Archbishop of Canterbury, Geoffrey Fisher, described the wedding as 'an ecclesiastical stigma of departure from a true understanding of what the Church Law requires'. Fisher's wife was once asked, at a Mothers' Union meeting, if she had ever considered divorcing her husband. 'Murder, certainly,' she replied, 'but divorce, never!'[29] Questions were raised when Eden was awarded the Order of the Garter in 1954. 'His banner is to hang with honour in a Christian church!' exclaimed one outraged correspondent. When Eden entered Downing Street in April 1955, his fitness for the premiership was questioned on the grounds that he would be unable to deal with matters of ecclesiastical preferment.[30]

Dorothy was infatuated by Boothby. Macmillan knew this; but he

---

*Still in 2010 Britain's only divorced Prime Minister.

loved her deeply and never failed in that devotion. The thought that Sarah might not have been his child was a tragedy that plagued him for years and years. Quite apart from the deep personal emotional up-heaval, there would have been profound implications for Macmillan's political career if the rumours about his wife's entanglement with Boothby ever surfaced. Macmillan was a candidate, and an uncertain one, at the time of Dorothy's claim. Divorce had serious repercussions. Walter Monckton's divorce in 1947 was reckoned to have cost him the chance of the posts of both Lord Chancellor and Lord Chief Justice.

Although Macmillan was convinced that he never wanted to grant Dorothy a divorce, when she persisted in her request he consulted the eminent solicitor Philip Frere, a partner in the firm of Frere Cholmeley.[31] Frere had been recommended by Osbert Sitwell, who had served with Macmillan in the Guards, and whose publisher he was to become in 1937 with Sitwell's volume of essays, *Penny Foolish*. Sitwell was also a friend of Daniel Macmillan and had heard that there were 'difficulties'. Frere had been Sitwell's solicitor for some time and had a reputation for unravelling delicate situations. The putative Macmillan divorce certainly qualified as such.

Macmillan's subsequent meeting with Philip Frere has a fair claim to being one that was to change the course of post-war British history. Although Macmillan was regarded by the Conservative establishment at the time as something of a gadfly, even an irritating gnat, Frere saw in him the potential for a high-flying political career. His advice was that on no account should Macmillan grant Dorothy a divorce, as this would ruin forever his chances of eventual Cabinet rank, let alone the premiership. As Macmillan was not even at the time an MP, this was to prove far-sighted advice. Most ambitious politicians harbour thoughts of a possible leadership.[32] Although the path ahead was rugged and uncertain, Macmillan was no exception, and Philip Frere was the first person, after Nellie, to entertain the idea to him.

If Macmillan wanted to 'stay in the game', then the solution was the traditional one of the estranged upper classes, what Frere termed the 'West Wing-East Wing' solution. At Birch Grove Dorothy and Harold were eventually to occupy two sitting rooms at opposite ends of the house, to which they respectively repaired after dinner. If Dorothy was willing to do so, Frere advised, she should continue in public as the loyal political wife, attending functions as before. Macmillan, for his part, should accept that there were certain needs that only Boothby could satisfy; in short, he should sanction 'an open marriage'.

Dorothy played her public part with loyalty for the next 36 years, always at Macmillan's side, as he successively climbed the ladder, at constituency meetings, party conferences, general election campaigns, international meetings and 10 Downing Street functions. As another Prime Minister's wife was later to write, 'In her public role as MP's wife Dorothy never let him down.'[33]

In his sorrow, Macmillan turned increasingly to Evie Devonshire, his mother-in-law. 'Dorothy certainly seems much happier & better,' he wrote to her two years after Sarah's birth, as the obsession with Boothby showed no signs of diminishing. 'It is very hard to know what to do best for her, but I expect it's best to leave her to recover slowly from her wounds.'

His own wounds too were deep. 'I still (for some reason or other) love her so ridiculously, that I don't dare to see too much of her. I feel it's best for her to try to forget altogether – for the present – the emotional side of life & concentrate on children, gardens, politics, etc … I care so desperately that the only way is to pretend to myself not to & to try to think about the gold standard & inflation & unemployed – about which I care hardly at all.'

Throughout the 1930s, Macmillan continued to confide in Evie, though he never mentioned the matter in letters to Victor, his father-in-law, or to his own mother, Nellie. 'The great thing for her is to be allowed to get through in her own way. How that will come about, I can't yet tell. But I do really believe that it *will* come about, in good time & given peace & calm,' he wrote to Evie in April 1934. 'The great thing is to wait – at any rate for the time being. Any attempt to influence her wd. have the opposite effect. She must make her own way through.' In March 1937, he looked back nostalgically to the immediate post-war days in Canada. 'There began here a happiness which, while it lasted, was something worth everything to me & which I wd. have again, even if I had known the sequel. I still hope that (in a different form) it will come again.'[34]

One of the few people in whom Boothby confided was Cynthia ('Cimmie') Mosley, wife of Sir Oswald. As Boothby and Macmillan were both later to burn their copies of the lovers' correspondence, the letters to Cynthia Mosley are among the few remaining documentary records of the affair. Dorothy also wrote to Cynthia, and she discussed the matter with trusted friends, something Harold never did. Dorothy once said to Quentin Crewe, 'I am by nature very faithful, I have always been faithful to Bob.'[35]

To Cimmie Mosley at the time, Dorothy declared more complex feelings:

I wish to God I knew what was the best thing to do. A bolt at the moment does seem pretty hopeless. It may well happen in the end. I've not entirely given up hope of getting Harold into a more reasonable frame of mind about divorce, but at present he's hopeless.

I'm afraid Bob must have had an awful time away. I should think he's sick of everything. He still wants to marry me, but if I don't come to him now he probably won't go on wanting to. The future looks pretty grim.[36]

Boothby likewise had confided his feelings to Cimmie:

I told Dorothy that I thought I had found a possible way through, and that in any case I couldn't go on with the life we had been leading. Indeed it has become unendurable. No basis is no meaning for me. Just an interminable series of agonising 'goodbyes' with nothing to go back to. Living always for the 'next time'. Work to hell. Nerves to hell. No-one can persuade me that a 'liaison' is anything but misery (with glorious, but oh such transitory, reprieves).

Dorothy's dependency on him was obsessional. 'Dorothy said to me tragically yesterday "Why did you ever wake me? I never want to see any of my family again. And, without you, life for me is going to be nothing but one big hurt."'[37]

Dorothy continued to pursue Boothby, and in 1935 he got married to someone else, partly to escape. His choice was her cousin, Diana Cavendish, the fourth daughter of Lord Richard Cavendish. For Macmillan, this seemed a possible closure: Bob's marriage might spell the end of his affair with Dorothy. Macmillan wrote to Evie:

I think the thing is definitely fixed now & he can't get out of it. But – like you – I shan't be happy until the ceremony is over. The great thing is that I think he has really cut a rotten figure, even in her eyes. She doesn't of course think about this now, but perhaps in later years it may help. I think in a way she has been preparing herself for this for some little time, but the actual thing is none the less a frightful blow for her. But I am so glad to know (from mutual friends) that she has no resentment agst me & realises that I have tried to do what I thought right all along. That's a great gain that has come I think in the last two years ... I care as much for her now – really more – than when we were travelling back to England fifteen years ago.

Macmillan had underestimated the power of Dorothy's obsession. Forty-eight hours before the ceremony, she was pleading with Bob to call off the wedding.

Boothby's marriage to Diana was a disaster from the start. His affections were divided between two Cavendish women, and went far deeper with the one to whom he was not actually married. He was already barred from Chatsworth because of his affair with Dorothy. His reputation reached rock bottom when, inevitably, he and Diana divorced in 1937. The Devonshire connection was an albatross round his neck. 'Once you get into the clutches of that family, by God, you haven't a hope,' he later said. 'They are the most tenacious family in Britain.'

Many years later in 1977 Boothby summed up his feelings about Dorothy to Nigel Fisher, then engaged on writing a biography of Macmillan:

What Dorothy wanted and needed was emotion, on the scale of Isolde. This Harold could not give her, and I did. She was, on the whole, the most selfish and possessive woman I have ever known. Once when I got engaged to an American heiress, she pursued me from Chatsworth to Paris, and from Paris to Lisbon. But we loved each other. And there is really nothing you can do about this, except die. Wagner was right.[38]

Boothby also discussed the matter with his own biographer, Sir Robert Rhodes James, the first to have access to the Boothby papers. Although he was rightly cautious – Boothby could always be relied upon to improve a good story – Rhodes James's conclusion is fair and authentic:

The portrayal of Boothby as 'a bounder' seducing a friend's wife is very far from the mark. In fact, it was Dorothy who seduced Boothby and who dominated him. He not only fulfilled her sexually, but gave her the fun, glamour and exciting company that her husband was unable to do. Also, Boothby was clearly a rising and successful politician, whereas Macmillan was evidently a failure, in this as in so many things. Nor is it the case that, as has been suggested, she wanted the best of both worlds – a husband and children at home, a lover in London and long holidays in Europe with him. What she wanted was to divorce Macmillan and to marry Boothby.[39]

The irony of the situation is that Boothby's affair with Dorothy marked the turning point in the political lives of both Boothby and Macmillan. Boothby's early promise was to burn out, glamorous for a while, but essentially impermanent. He ended life in the Commons as a disappointed, excluded back-bencher, better known for his broad-casting exploits on the *Brains Trust*. He was eventually rescued by the man he had cuckolded, and sent to the House of Lords in 1958, for his Indian summer as Baron Boothby of Buchan and Rattray Head. Macmillan, for his part, ended as Prime Minister.

In 1951, Boothby wrote to Quentin Crewe: 'I could never be harsh or unkind to Dorothy. I am not, by nature, an unkind person: and I love her dearly.' He admitted that 'Total monogamy – except for the fortunate few – is not a natural state for mankind.'[40] This could stand as the epitaph for a central event in three lives.

Macmillan treated Sarah as his true daughter, never letting his private sadness tinge his affections. Sarah herself never imagined that anyone else might be her father until 1947, when she was dancing in a night-club with Colin Tennant (later the 3rd Lord Glenconner). Tennant's original partner, in drunken jealousy, broke up the dance. 'What do you think you're doing with Colin? You're only illegitimate anyhow, you're Boothby's daughter.'[41] For a seventeen-year-old thinking of nothing more than enjoying parties and the admiration of young men, such as Tennant, Andrew Heath (whom she eventually married) and Quentin Crewe, it was a devastating moment.

Sadly, though, Macmillan could never dispel from his mind the thought that Sarah was Boothby's. After Dorothy's death in 1966, and Sarah's in 1970, this thought, always a disturbing presence, came to the surface again.

In February 1975, Macmillan was at a luncheon given by his son-in-law Julian Amery at 112 Eaton Square. Another guest was Bob Boothby, who lived nearby at 1 Eaton Square.[42] Macmillan asked Boothby if he might come round to see him at his flat later that after-noon. Boothby suggested 4 p.m., a time when he would be serving drinks rather than tea,[43] and the two temporarily parted. Ironically, the refreshment offered was possibly a clue to the answer Macmillan sought.

Although Boothby drank far more than would now be considered healthy, he was not unusual among politicians of that time. 'By no stretch of the words,' wrote Robert Rhodes James, 'could he be de-scribed as an alcoholic.'[44] This was not the case with Sarah, or her three siblings. Drink was the spectre that hung over Birch Grove for many years, but Sarah's alcoholism came from her Devonshire and Macmillan genes, not from Boothby's.[45]

Boothby had been for many years the chairman of the Royal Philharmonic Orchestra, a position for which he had been recommended by the orchestra's founder, Sir Thomas Beecham. The post provided Boothby with a great deal of satisfaction and, although it was unpaid, the orchestra ensured that they gave him occasional rewards. In 1975 they had just presented him with a handsome, state-of-the-art tape recorder, and Boothby hurried home from Julian Amery's that afternoon to try it. A Tchaikovsky symphony was playing on the radio and he set up a microphone and a tape to test the machine. Shortly afterwards, at about 3.30, the doorbell rang. It was Macmillan, early for his appointment. Boothby turned off the radio, but unwittingly left the tape recorder running, on the floor behind a sofa. The subsequent conversation with Macmillan was thus recorded.

Macmillan began by reiterating his hurt of 45 years. Although it was a painful subject, he wanted, for peace of mind, to know one way or another the truth about Sarah. Boothby told his old friend that, although he had known Dorothy from 1928, their actual physical affair had not begun until 'very late in 1929 or early in 1930'. As Sarah was conceived in November 1929, she could have been Boothby's, but Boothby knew that she was not. Boothby was a rakish figure, but in one thing he was very careful. Despite – or perhaps because of – having so many affairs, he ensured he never left behind what the Victorians would have called 'a vestige'.

After Boothby's revelation, everything fell into place for Macmillan. It must have been the most bittersweet of moments. Of course, contraception is not 100 per cent safe; but it is clear that Boothby certainly believed it had been in this case. Indeed, he was so open and straightforward, it must be wondered why he had not put Macmillan out of his misery decades before.

After Macmillan left Eaton Square, Boothby discovered the running tape recorder. His wife, Wanda, played back the tape with him, listening together to Macmillan's enquiries and the poignant evidence of his years of doubt and sadness. Boothby had tears running down his face.

What Boothby, famously pleasure-seeking, did not tell either Macmillan or Wanda was that, as Dorothy had aged and 'the heyday in the blood was tamed', his roving eye had taken in Sarah herself.[48] It is inconceivable that he would have attempted a 'fling' with Sarah if he had had any doubts about the efficiency of the contraception or any intimations that she might have been his daughter.

*

After Macmillan's death, Eileen O'Casey, widow of the playwright Sean O'Casey, claimed that she had had an affair with Macmillan when Dorothy was first in thrall to Boothby.[49] If true, it was out of character. Macmillan was old-fashioned, very reserved in matters of sex and morality. He allowed 45 years to elapse before he directly confronted Boothby. One of the reasons that Dorothy, a highly passionate woman, sought physical satisfaction elsewhere was because Macmillan was not interested in sex. Her claim about Sarah's paternity in all probability finished their physical relations for ever, increasing Dorothy's dependency on Boothby.

Macmillan was 36 when Sarah was born. Money was no difficulty. Nanny West looked after the three daughters at Birch Grove, and Maurice was beginning preparatory school at Durnford. Had circumstances been different, more children would perhaps have been born, for Dorothy loved the young, and a larger family would have been the natural thing for a family with no material concerns. (There had been a miscarriage in 1922 after Maurice's birth.) A second son was always considered desirable in upper-class families – a spare to the heir. Macmillan wrote to Sligger Urquhart, 'My family has just been increased by another daughter – so I now have a son & three daughters. Though I wd. like another son, I think daughters are awfully nice, & one hopes they will be kind to me in old age.'[51]

After 1930, Macmillan diverted his energies into his work. In this a parallel can be seen with Bonar Law, after the sudden and unexpected death of his wife. Politics became Law's salvation. 'It was the only thing that could occupy his mind,' wrote his biographer, Robert Blake, 'and prevent him becoming obsessed with his private tragedy.'[52] Indeed, without Macmillan's private tragedy, he might not have achieved all he did. His confidence could have been destroyed for ever, but in fact the painful experience gave him a sense of detachment and a ruthlessness that channelled his ambition.

Some have wondered, largely owing to J.B.S. Haldane's inaccurate assertion that Macmillan had been expelled from Eton for homosexuality, but also because of the emotional influence of his overbearing mother, whether Macmillan was in fact homosexual, or perhaps bisexual. There is some suggestion that he might have been emotionally damaged by his experiences at school, but no evidence at any time in his life to point to homosexual or bisexual activities. He was an asexual being, a figure perhaps more common than generally acknowledged.[53] Primness was all.

When Macmillan met the priapic President of the United States, John F. Kennedy, at Key West in Florida in March 1961, it was not just in age that they differed. During a break in their meetings on nuclear arms, Kennedy turned to Macmillan. 'I wonder how it is with you, Harold?' he enquired. 'If I don't have a woman for three days, I get a terrible headache.' It was an extraordinary observation to make to a virtual stranger, 23 years his senior, who in all likelihood had not 'had' a woman for three decades, never mind three days. Macmillan was not often lost for words, but this was one occasion when he was.[54]

Kennedy's obsession with sex was a mystery to Macmillan. In June 1963, when Kennedy stayed at Birch Grove, arrangements were made for him to attend a Catholic Mass at nearby Forest Row. Macmillan's private secretary, Philip de Zulueta, a Catholic, was deputed to accompany the President. Zulueta was astonished that on the way to the church, and back, all Kennedy was interested in was prurient detail about the unfolding Profumo affair, gossip he was intensely disappointed de Zulueta was unable to provide. When Macmillan later enquired of his secretary whether Kennedy had made any off-the-record observations about the political situation that might be of interest, he was shocked to hear what had been said, especially as it had been on the way to and from Mass.[55] Macmillan came from a generation for whom sexual matters were treated with reticence and with an intense privacy. His upbringing and religious beliefs, the personal betrayal he had suffered, and his own uninterested approach made overt display distasteful. This was one of the reasons he handled the Profumo affair so badly.

Macmillan could only watch from the sidelines as the unfolding political and economic events of 1929–1931 overwhelmed, and eventually destroyed, the second Labour government. In October 1929 came the Wall Street Crash. The subsequent fall in world commodity prices and spiralling unemployment figures (2.5 million in Britain by December 1930) cast their shadow over the global economy. The crisis of the capitalist system was at hand, and the fear of inflation, no less than the fear of hunger that was its potent offspring, was to have decisive consequences.[56]

Sir Oswald Mosley had been appointed Chancellor of the Duchy of Lancaster in MacDonald's Cabinet in May 1929, with special responsibility for unemployment questions. To later generations Mosley is known primarily as a black-shirted fascist, who was interned during the war as a security risk. His career was more polymathic. At first a progressive Conservative MP, he was the youngest member of the House of Commons, when elected in December 1918. In November 1920 he crossed the floor, and held his seat at Harrow as an Independent in the general elections of 1922 and 1923. In March 1924 he joined the Labour Party, which he served for the next seven years, welcomed by the Socialists as a figure who could bring respectability to their ranks. He was an obvious candidate for office in Ramsay MacDonald's second administration in May 1929.

On 13 December 1929, Mosley – always known as Tom to his friends – told the Prime Minister of a 'memorandum' he was preparing. When this Keynesian document was discussed in Cabinet on 19 February, the government rejected its financial unorthodoxy, and Mosley resigned to form the New Party.

Mosley's actions divided political opinion, though he secured a diverse body of support: Keynesian Liberals, Harold Nicolson (not then in the House) and many of the YMCA. Boothby thought Mosley's resignation speech in the House on 28 May 1930 was 'the greatest parliamentary *tour de force* this generation will hear'. *The Times* and the *Morning Post* were hostile, even vindictively so. The *Daily Herald* and the *Manchester Guardian* were sympathetic. So was Harold Macmillan. The New Party could be the very alliance of 'the right Conservatives and the right Labourites' that he had so long wished for. He wrote a long letter to *The Times* on 'the reactionary immobility of parties alleged to be progressive'. Mosley was trying to change the rules of the game, which presently was hardly worth playing at all. 'I hope some of my friends will have the courage to applaud and support his protest.'[57]

Rab Butler joined the controversy in an immediate riposte. 'When a player starts complaining "that it is hardly worth bothering to play" the game at all it is usually the player, and not the game, who is at fault,' he wrote to *The Times* with three other Conservative MPs. 'It is then usually advisable for the player to seek a new field for his recreation and a pastime more suited for his talents.'[58] By the standards of the time this was remarkably uninhibited in its insulting tone. Macmillan knew that Butler was the instigator of this round-robin. What aroused his animosity was that Butler had not signed the letter alone, but had surrounded himself by three others, whom he regarded as party hacks.

Whatever party loyalists might have thought, Macmillan hoped the Keynesian proposals advocated by Mosley would find fertile ground in any ensuing political debate, and he seriously considered joining the New Party. He saw in Mosley an inspiring leader: charismatic, visionary, genuinely concerned about the poor, the unemployed and the sidelined, but also, fatally, unpredictable.

Boothby was about to cause grievous pain to Macmillan personally,

but politically his influence at this transitional time was not only sagacious, but career-saving. Macmillan poured out his views on the New
Party to Boothby and confided that he was about to join its ranks
formally. Boothby, still in the House as MP for Aberdeenshire East,
and closer to parliamentary feelings on the matter, implored him to
do no such thing.

Boothby had already warned Mosley that 'our chaps won't play,
and it's no use deluding yourself that they will'. Macmillan might be
tempted, he told Mosley, 'but even on the assumption that he decided
to play (a large one), how many votes can he swing? ... What is going
to be the reaction of the great British public? I don't know. But they
might conceivably say, "By God now all the shits have climbed into
the same basket, so we know where we are." Would they be so far
out?'[59]

Whatever the temporary attractions of the New Party, Conservative
and Labour alternately would now set the political pace. To join the
New Party, Boothby warned his friend, would disqualify Macmillan
for ever from the front ranks of Conservatism. If he felt so strongly, he
would be better to make the full leap and take his chance by joining
the Labour Party. Indeed, this course might actually be preferable, as
Mosley had left 'an aristocratic vacancy' that Macmillan could fill.
Lord Carrington said later that this advice must have been the best
Boothby ever gave anybody in his notably erratic and unreliable life.[60]

So, at this low point in his fortunes, Macmillan was 'saved for the
future' by the wise guidance he had received from both Philip Frere
and Bob Boothby.

'Poor old Worthington-Evans is dead,' wrote Cuthbert Headlam in
his diary on 15 February 1931. 'This means a vacancy at St George's
Hanover Square.' Although St George's was the safest Conservative
seat in the country, the campaign for this by-election was thrown
into the melting pot when an independent 'Empire Free Trade'
Conservative candidate, Sir Ernest Petter, was run by the press lords,
Beaverbrook and Rothermere. 'If he [Petter] wins, Baldwin must go,'
wrote Beaverbrook, 'and Empire Free Trade must become the accepted
policy of the Conservative Party.'[61]

Baldwin considered resigning his seat at Bewdley and fighting the
by-election himself in a 'back me or sack me' campaign. He regarded
the issue as absolutely central to the democratic process. Was the press
or the party to decide matters of policy? In the event, Duff Cooper,
loving the gamble and the adventure, took on the official candidacy.

At the Queen's Hall on 17 March 1931, Baldwin made one of

his most famous speeches, indeed one of the most memorable of the interwar period. He concluded a devastating attack on the press barons, and their methods. 'What the proprietorship of these papers is aiming at is power,' he declared, adding a phrase suggested to him by his cousin, Rudyard Kipling, 'and power without responsibility – the prerogative of the harlot throughout the ages.' A voice from the hall cried out, 'There goes the harlots' vote.'[62]

The St George's by-election was a turning point: there was no more talk of whether Baldwin was to survive as leader or not. Duff Cooper held the seat till 1945.

There was a general election in 1931, and in the build-up Macmillan was wooed by two sides. Both Mosley and his New Party and even the Labour Party continued to make enticing noises in the hope of securing 'this troublesome young man' to their ranks.[63] Harold Nicolson met Macmillan on a train to Oxford on 30 May 1931 and recorded Macmillan's feelings of the time:

> He takes the usual young Tory view that his heart is entirely with the New Party but that he feels he can help us better by remaining in the Conservative ranks. He does not hesitate to admit that if we could obtain a certain number of seats in Parliament, most of the young Tories, all the Liberals, and a large proportion of the youngish Labour people would come over to us. He anticipates the present Government being in power for another two years. He feels that five years from now, the New Party will have its great opportunity.[64]

Such predictions were to prove inaccurate and underline the suddenness of the political crisis that was to overcome the country later that year. Nicolson's diary entry does show, however, the extent to which Macmillan was thinking ahead.

Macmillan was at a low ebb. He wondered whether it was worth 'bothering to play' the game. The Butler letter had wounded him deeply. In spite of his later unflappable image, Macmillan remained a sensitive, and at times unconfident, figure.

The combination of his political indecision and personal misery finally caught up with him, and in the summer of 1931 he had a serious breakdown. On 2 August 1931 he wrote to Sligger Urquhart to tell him he was taking 'a short holiday away from all the worries of everyday life'. The worries were such that there were rumours that he had attempted suicide.

He admitted to Urquhart, 'I have not been very well lately, having had a lot of trouble of one sort or another to contend with.'

In fact, Macmillan was admitted to the Kuranstalt Neuwittelsbach Sanatorium, near Munich, for a complete cure, physically and psychologically, a development that Nellie, his mother, ensured was shrouded in secrecy.[65] The atmosphere was not unlike that of the sanatorium in Thomas Mann's *The Magic Mountain*: 'All the days are nothing but the same day repeating itself.'[66] The only difference was that, unlike Mann's central character, Macmillan did not stay for seven years, but a few weeks. On 23 September he wrote to Urquhart with news of his progress:

> The doctor [Dr Lampe] here is, I think, very clever. He is certainly thorough & drastic – He tells me that I have only just avoided a complete & serious breakdown, which *'would have had the most calamitous consequence'*. Anyhow I do feel better after a week of his treatment. This consists of lying in bed in a semi-darkened room ... with frequent meals of which cream is the chief ingredient. Sometimes tea & cream, sometimes fruit & cream, sometimes bread & butter & cream – but always cream. This, together, with what I take to be bromide, had the result that I sleep or doze 18 hours out of the 24.

Even while convalescing, he had his eyes on political developments in Britain and told Urquhart that he would come back if there was an election.

> I do think the National Govt. was the only thing, but I am very disappointed with the Labour party. I fear they are hopelessly 'caucus-ridden' & may have missed a great chance. Even if they had plumped for inflation or repudiation, this wd. have been logical. But to admit the need for economies & then run away from making them is a very poor business.[67]

Macmillan also wrote many letters to Evie, his mother-in-law, to keep Chatsworth in touch. The first was almost identical to his first letter to Sligger Urquhart, though for 'family' he added an element of gallows humour by jesting, 'I see myself at Chiswick (is it still an asylum?) or some similar place soon!' He took every opportunity of reading. 'I have just finished the first 12 books of Homer's 'Iliad' & am glad to find I remember my Greek! Miss Austen I also find very soothing!' Political life back home in Britain also drew pungent comments. 'I gather that everyone is intriguing against everybody else &

that the Liberals, as usual, are playing their naturally rather mean game.'[68]

During Macmillan's absence in Munich, Dorothy looked after the constituency of Stockton, so that when the general election, long expected, followed in October, the association was in good order and ready for the fray. Macmillan too was refreshed and eager to get back into the House. He also wanted to be reunited with Dorothy, whose lengthy absences from Birch Grove, he suspected, might not always have been on Stockton business.

The first minority Labour government in 1924 had fallen when the Liberals had turned against them. A darkening economic situation now made MacDonald's position similarly precarious in the face of Liberal dissension. By June 1931 unemployment had reached 2,707,000, rising by another 100,000 in July. £60 million of gold reserves and foreign exchange had been lost. The government was split on the scale of economies needed. In circumstances that still arouse controversy, King George V brokered a deal on 24 August whereby MacDonald formed a National Government. Only three members of his Cabinet were willing to join him – Philip Snowden as Chancellor of the Exchequer, Lord Sankey as Lord Chancellor, and Jim Thomas as Dominions Secretary. In Labour historiography, MacDonald was now forever the Great Betrayer.

Stanley Baldwin, who became Lord President of the Council, joined the Cabinet with fellow Conservatives Samuel Hoare (Secretary of State for India), Neville Chamberlain (Minister of Health) and Philip Cunliffe-Lister (President of the Board of Trade). 'In spite of its claims', Macmillan later wrote, 'this administration was a collection of the most respectable mediocrities of all parties.'

In retrospect, the most noteworthy fact about the 1931 National Government was that there were no places for the maverick trio of Lloyd George, Churchill and Oswald Mosley, who had excluded themselves from consideration. Lloyd George had opposed the government in the 1931 election, calling for free trade, though a few weeks earlier he had been bargaining with MacDonald to enter the Labour government as Chancellor on a tariff platform. Churchill had resigned from the Conservative Shadow Cabinet in 1931 on the issue of Indian self-government. Mosley was resolutely opposed to expenditure cuts. It is a myth that Churchill and Lloyd George were 'kept out by the pygmies'. They kept themselves out – Churchill by an issue on which most progressives would oppose him; Lloyd George by chicanery. MacDonald declared that the National Government was a temporary expedient.* In fact, a National Government lasted in various guises until 23 May 1945, after Attlee brought in the Labour Party in May 1940 under Churchill's premiership.

The crisis was not over. If anything, it was only just beginning. The gold reserves continued to diminish by £2.5 million a day. On 21 September, one of the central planks of Churchill's 1925 Budget was reversed when an act was rushed through Parliament on a single day, taking Britain off the gold standard. Simultaneously, the bank rate was raised from 4.5 to 6 per cent. The pound fell from $4.86, eventually settling at $3.40.[71] Macmillan felt this gave the country a new freedom, but that the most was not made of this opportunity. Unemployment reached a peak of 2,955,000 in January 1933, and exports did not attain 1931 levels for three years.

Macmillan had followed events from the sanatorium in Munich; indeed, the drama of the unfolding crisis was one of the factors that re-ignited his interest in the endless adventure of ruling men. He wrote to his mother, Nellie, saying that though his doctors were not certain that he should risk the inevitable exertions, he intended to return to contest the Stockton seat. Too many issues cried out for his attention. A new financial order was urgently needed to cope with this crisis of capitalism, and Macmillan devoted much of the next nine years to considering how such a system might evolve. By the time MacDonald, seeking what he termed a Doctor's Mandate, had called an election for Tuesday, 27 October, Macmillan was ready to fight again.

For the only time in his five electoral contests in Stockton, Macmillan faced a straight fight with a Labour opponent, F. F. Riley, who was defending a narrow majority of 2,389. The Liberals decided to back Macmillan, largely on 'patriotic' grounds, a pattern repeated in many constituencies, to defeat Labour (non-National) candidates by tactical voting. Macmillan and the local Conservative Association had brokered an agreement with F. Kingsley Griffiths, the Liberal candidate for Middlesbrough West, by which the anti-Labour vote there could be consolidated behind one candidate, in return for a free run in Stockton. Macmillan even offered to stand down himself in Stockton and give F. F. Riley a free run if he stood as a National Labour candidate in support of MacDonald. If Riley had done so, Macmillan might have been out of Parliament for years. Though his was a principled stand, it was an anxious time for Macmillan's supporters until Riley declared that he would stand for Labour, now led by Arthur Henderson, and

---

*So was income tax for William Pitt the younger during the Napoleonic Wars.

not as the National Labour candidate. As a result, Macmillan could fight the seat, and his slogan for October 1931 was:

> Follow the lead of the distinguished Liberals
> VOTE FOR MACMILLAN
> THE NATIONAL CANDIDATE
> THUS SECURING THE NATION
> AGAINST DISASTER

He had backing from Sir Edward Grey, Sir Herbert Samuel, Walter Runciman, Sir Donald Maclean and Lady Bonham-Carter. The result was the biggest majority of his Stockton career, a result replicated across the country in the special circumstances of the time:

Captain Harold Macmillan (National)	29,199
F. F. Riley (Labour)	18,168
National majority	11,031

Nationally, the Conservatives won 473 seats, Sir Herbert Samuel's 'official' Liberals 33, John Simon's 'National' Liberals 35, Independent Liberals 4, and there were 13 National Labour. The Labour Party was reduced to a mere 52 seats. Only George Lansbury, Clement Attlee and Sir Stafford Cripps of the former ministerial team retained their seats, a result of important long-term significance for both the party and the country. Hugh Dalton, who had lost his seat in Bishop Auckland, attributed the scale of the defeat to 'the staging of straight fights almost everywhere'.[72] George Lansbury replaced Arthur Henderson as acting Labour leader, with Attlee as his deputy, despite the fact that Attlee was not even on the party's National Executive at the time.* The National Government majority in 1931 was 497. 'The importance of the election,' wrote C. L. Mowat, 'was that it gave the Conservatives, under false colours, an overwhelming strength in Parliament which they could hardly have won unaided.'[73]

Boothby's verdict was excoriating. 'It was no "National" government,' he later wrote. 'It was simply a get-together on the part of the Boys of the Old Brigade, who climbed on to the bandwagon and sat there, rain or shine, until they had brought the British Empire to the verge of destruction.'[74]

---

*Attlee became Labour leader almost by default in 1935, and then Prime Minister by acclamation in 1945.

There was no question of Macmillan, with his record of dissent, being given even the most minor of posts. His time on the back benches between 1931 and 1935 might therefore be seen as a time of limbo, waiting like so many in those 'wilderness years' for the call. In fact, he used these years as a polemicist. It was a time that could have been spent enjoying what was for many National MPs a secure and easy ride in Parliament – late-night camaraderie in the Commons bars, City lunches – with only the occasional need to attend the House for a three-line whip. That was never Macmillan's way. There were more important things to do, particularly in Stockton.

J. B. Priestley had visited Stockton-on-Tees on his famous journey through England in 1933. He found a town in sad decline, the more poignant because of its past triumphs from shipbuilding to casting the first bell for Big Ben in 1836. 'There were people about, chiefly men with caps and mufflers; but the atmosphere was not that of a prosperous town at the end of a day's work,' he observed, seeing 'grass-grown shipyards and workshops with grimy broken windows, and middle-aged men who look like old men, sucking their empty pipes and staring at nothing, and grey-faced women remembering new clothes and good meals and holidays and fun as if they had once lived in another and better world'.[75] This human dimension lay at the back of all the economic pamphlets, booklets and reports that Macmillan wrote in these years.

The massive government majority meant that party ties were loosened: Macmillan worked with political figures from many parts of the House, and indeed with those outside. Labour's deputy leader, Clement Attlee, was appreciative of his work. 'We get some support for our views,' he wrote to his brother Tom, 'from the YMCA group Macmillan, Boothby & Co who are in pretty strong enmity to the Die Hards.'[76] One figure from whom Macmillan drifted apart at this time, though, was Churchill, whose obscurantist views on Indian independence placed him firmly in a wing of the party with which Macmillan wanted to have no dealings. Only with the darkening European situation in the later 1930s did they find common cause in anti-appeasement.

For the moment, Macmillan turned to his pen. In March 1932 he published a pamphlet, *The State and Industry*, with a title confusingly similar to the booklet *Industry and the State* written by Macmillan, Boothby, Oliver Stanley and John Loder in 1927. In May 1932 he issued another policy document, *The Next Step*. Both 1932 pamphlets, with their emphasis on easier credit to aid industrial regeneration, were praised by Keynes, who regretted only that Macmillan had not been even bolder in his recommendations. With Lord Melchett, Macmillan was prominent in establishing the Industrial Reorganisation League. He spoke in favour of the Industrial Reorganisation (Enabling) Bill in the House, and combined with the defeated Arthur Henderson and the Labour intellectual G. D. H. Cole in producing a booklet entitled *Service in Life and Work*. In December 1933 he published (with the family firm) his first full book, *Reconstruction: A Plea for National Unity*, which returned to his main theme of planning. He sent a copy to Baldwin, who was frankly bored by it. The *New Statesman and Nation* heaped praise on the author. The economist Friedrich Hayek, later to be such an influence on Margaret Thatcher, thought it 'a blue print for the destruction of liberty'.

'At this stage,' Professor Donald Winch has written, 'Macmillan's views on fiscal policy were rudimentary.' His main idea was 'to favour protection of the home market as an adjunct to planning'. As a result, 'the emphasis was on restrictive measures to regulate the supply of individual commodities rather than on Keynesian measures to raise overall effective demand'.[79]

Clifford Allen was a stalwart of the old Independent Labour Party. He had been imprisoned during the First World War as a conscientious objector, and his elevation to the peerage in 1932 as Lord Allen of Hurtwood led some to think he would have been better dubbed Lord Conchie of Maidstone, where he had served a sentence of hard labour. A visit in 1920 to the Soviet Union in a joint Labour Party and trade union delegation had made a deep impression on him.

In April 1932, Allen asked 'Captain' Macmillan to write an article on the reorganisation of industry. In agreeing, Macmillan added, 'By the way, I have abandoned the use of the title "Captain".' In December 1933 Macmillan put money into a political publication Allen had started, the *Weekend Review*. Allen was to be one of the central figures in establishing the 'Next Five Years Group' in February 1933, with Harold Macmillan and the economist Sir Arthur Salter as key supporters. Macmillan became the chairman of the board of directors of *The New Outlook*, the group's newspaper. He was no sleeping chairman. He used the paper as an outlet for his ideas, many of them anathema to traditional Conservatives, including radical views on collective security, an end to the hated means test, subsidy for distressed areas, a reduction in tariffs and an acceptance and encouragement of state control over industry.

On 4 November 1932, Macmillan made a speech in the House stating, 'there is no alternative except a planned economy'.[81] He diverged from his Labour associates, however, in believing that such arrangements should not always necessarily be directed by the government; he believed even then that the Conservatives would one day have to accept the mixed economy. 'The central theme of his position at this time,' it has been commented, 'was his rejection of the association of planning with the state.'[82] In his book *Reconstruction*, Macmillan was explicit about this. 'Too often,' he wrote, 'planning is made to look like a system of bureaucratic regulation.'[83] At times, this divergence of approach went too far for Clifford Allen, and tensions arose between the two. Allen thought that Macmillan could be 'brutally pugnacious'[84], an indication of the more assertive political style Macmillan was now cultivating.

In March 1935 Macmillan published, with 14 other MPs, the pamphlet *Planning for Employment*. It concentrated on the relationship of investment and consumption in the planning equation of supply and demand. He was also drawn to the idea of 'assisted migration' to the Dominions, not realising the extent to which a significant number of orphaned and displaced young people were abused, sexually and physically, in their new homelands. In July 1935 the Next Five Years Group made a major policy statement with *The Next Five Years: An Essay in Political Agreement*. Unfortunately, political agreement was not one of the characteristics of the group, who disagreed as to the extent of Lloyd George's involvement. Macmillan was enthusiastically inclined towards Lloyd George, one of his early heroes, travelling down to Lloyd George's house at Churt on 12 August 1935 to discuss his 1935 'Council of Action'. All Macmillan's inclinations were for a merger, or at least a deal, between the Next Five Years Group and the Council of Action. Eventually the Next Five Years Group was wound up in November 1937, an indication not only of its internal disagreements, but also of the improving economic situation and the worsening foreign one.

In Parliament Macmillan attended committees on foreign policy, housing (a particular interest) and finance. In April 1935 he formed the 'Tory Planners Group'. Together with Cuthbert Headlam, he also helped to establish the 'Northern Group' of MPs, who supported the National Government but who acted as a pressure group for local interests.

Despite all this activity, Macmillan felt despondent, and often wondered if he would ever hold office. His mood at this time is vividly captured by his parliamentary neighbour at Barnard Castle, Cuthbert Headlam, who wrote in his diary on 11 March 1934:

I had a good deal of talk with Harold during the day. He is evidently still anxious for a political career, but realises that he has missed the boat. My advice to him was go on pushing his ideas and developing them but not to keep speaking and voting against the Government – and, above all else, to find a safer seat than Stockton. His only chance is to make good while the Party is in opposition, and if we are really to have a smash at the next election, it is no good anyone who wants to have a political career to stand for a seat in Co. Durham. He is a curiously self-centred man and strangely shy and prickly – and yet the more I see of him the more I like him. He tells me that he is paid £6000 a year as a salary as manager of Macmillans – seemingly the directors are his father and 2 old uncles – but when they decide to go or are taken hence he and his brother will take possession – what a wonderful business it must be even in these bad days: it made my mouth water.[88]

Although Macmillan had frequent heart-to-hearts with Headlam, many on the train to and from Darlington, his closest political friendship at this time was with Allan Young, a former Clydesider and Marxist, who had been secretary of the New Party and author of much of its manifesto for the 1931 general election. Young had broken with Mosley after his leader had turned towards fascism in the summer of 1932. Macmillan had hankered to visit Russia ever since Clifford Allen had encouraged him to do so. Now, he persuaded Young to accompany him to Moscow. These professional links were strengthened even more when Young became Macmillan's secretary in 1936.

In August and September 1932, Macmillan made a five-week visit to the Soviet Union with Allan Young. An indication of how much he was disliked by traditional Tories can be seen in the whispering campaign that now began. Bolshevism still aroused paranoiac suspicions. Even King Edward VIII was considered a dangerous subversive for his well-publicised visit to the South Wales coalfields and for declaring, 'Something must be done.' In the opinion of some Tory MPs, who saw reds under every bed, it was bad enough that Macmillan could associate with an imprisoned conscientious objector, but the fact that one of their number could undertake a visit to the Communist heartland with a Marxist Clydesider could only mean one thing – he was a fellow traveller, perhaps even some kind of agent for the KGB. In some Conservative and City quarters, these feelings never entirely vanished.*

---

* Macmillan's later friendship with Harry Dexter White,[90] the American economist who

Macmillan set sail with Allan Young for Russia from Hay's Wharf on 30 August 1932 aboard the SS *Cooperazia*. 'Eventually we found a gate, with a night watchman in charge,' Macmillan wrote to his mother. '"What do you want? Oh – the Bolshie boat! Straight in, then first right & first left, & good luck to you!"'[91]

Macmillan sent a series of 'travelogue' letters to Nellie. Delays, unpleasant food, deficient sanitary arrangements – all contributed to an uncertain start. However, anyone who had been in College at Eton was not going to be discouraged by spartan conditions. Macmillan and Young made the obligatory visit to the Hermitage Museum; but it was the 'new' Russia in which they were really interested. In each town they made a point of visiting the Working Men's Clubs. They arrived in Moscow on 9 September. They were showed the poorer areas, and Macmillan was impressed by the manner in which the equivalent of Park Lane and Mayfair had been converted into workers' flats, not an arrangement that he thought likely to be attempted for the Dorchester Hotel. A visit to the Lenin mausoleum was a required duty. As was the custom for foreigners, particularly those considered to be of important status, they were diverted past the queues. Lenin, waxed and silent, seemed a substitute religion for the Soviets. Reluctantly they agreed to their hosts' request to visit a prison, one for serious offenders. The fact that these prisoners were allowed a week's holiday a year, yet almost invariably returned, said much to Macmillan of conditions outside, and also the prisoners' likely fate if they failed to honour the arrangement. Macmillan had talks with M. Litvinoff, the Commissar for Foreign Affairs, and on the eve of their departure, the Bolshoi Theatre was the venue for a performance of Rimsky-Korsakov's *The Snow Maiden*, a work that ironically portrays a benevolent and loving Tsar, beloved by his people.

On 12 September the visitors sailed down the Volga to Nizhni-Novgorod. Here Macmillan was reminded of Canada, the vast expanses and the poor roads, with something of the same pioneer spirit. At the town hall they attended a meeting of the local Communist Party, a first for a Tory MP in the 1930s. By 23 September they were in Kharkov, where the evident boom reminded Macmillan of Chicago.

---

brokered the Bretton Woods Agreement in 1946 with Keynes, led to whisperings after White was named as a Soviet agent on 2 September 1939. Conspiracy theorists of whom there were many, ascribed Macmillan's post-war role in Europe in 1945 to his thraldom to Stalin. When Macmillan made his visit to the Soviet Union, as Prime Minister, with his Foreign Secretary, Selwyn Lloyd, in the build-up to the 1959 general election, he was warmly greeted at his designated dacha by a Soviet lady apparatchik, who seemed to know him; even this was regarded as suspicious. As C. P. Snow once observed, when you dislike somebody, imagination does the rest.

Returning to Moscow, they met various Russian commissars, including the head of Partizdat, the Communist Party's publication business. Macmillan took the opportunity to conduct some business on behalf of the family firm. Here he was in an area of his own expertise, and he discussed many questions regarding paper, bookbinding and printing, as well as distribution and sales. The Tolstoy museum was of greater interest to him than the 'anti-religious' ones. The tour ended back in Leningrad, which was celebrating Maxim Gorki week. They attended a function at which the famous author appeared, together with Stalin, who was received with tumultuous applause.

On their last morning, they were taken to the Catherine Palace, full of propaganda about the despotism of the tsars. To his amusement, Macmillan saw a drawing of his father-in-law, the Duke of Devonshire, in his robes at King George V's coronation. He asked for the caption to be translated. It read: 'Typical Boyar of the old régime in Capitalist countries, living on the exploitation of the working classes.'

Though their hosts deliberately shielded them from what would later be called the Orwellian side of the Russian system, Macmillan and Young were not deceived about the underlying reality, especially after meeting an engineer who had worked in Siberia and who told them of the conditions there. On returning to Britain – to the news that Mosley had founded the British Union of Fascists on 1 October 1932 – Macmillan felt that he had left behind a nightmare world.

The visit was of immense value to Macmillan in widening his overall view of global politics. Much of his time hitherto had been spent on domestic issues, parochial when set against the dramas that were being played out under Mussolini, Hitler and Stalin. He had a meeting with Anthony Eden, then Minister for League of Nations affairs, to give him his impressions. Russia marked an important change of emphasis in his political experience, though it confirmed his reputation among traditional Tories as a troublesome subversive.

Macmillan's business background and experience of Stockton-on-Tees gave him 'a passionate sense of commitment to radical reform which was to dominate his inter-war political career'. His problem was that all avenues to preferment seemed permanently closed. Nor could more establishment-inclined contemporaries break the mould. 'In neither party,' he was later observed, 'were the feet of the young men lifted high enough to kick out the old.'

The events of 1931 and its aftermath had confirmed Macmillan in his deep distrust of the City and the Treasury – he dubbed them 'banksters' – and this feeling endured even when he was Chancellor of the Exchequer himself. Montagu Norman still held sway in the Square Mile, and Macmillan had no time for his discredited financial orthodoxy. Macmillan remained that particular Westminster phenomenon, the distinguished, yet isolated, back-bencher, a berth similar to that which Churchill also occupied from time to time. Macmillan's odyssey – a mixture of Keynesian economics and Roosevelt's New Deal[96] – was one of the most distinctive personal crusades of the decade, but one on which his own party by and large heaped obloquy.

Macmillan remembered the early part of 1935 as a time of anxiety. The one bright spot was the Silver Jubilee of King George V and Queen Mary on 6 May.[97] 'I went with Dorothy & Harold to St Paul's,' wrote Victor Devonshire in his diary.[98] Macmillan attended the celebrations in Stockton later that week, a borough *en fête* with bunting and decorations, and was greatly impressed by the way all classes of people came together in celebration. On 9 May he was present at the parliamentary occasion, in Westminster Hall, when both Houses presented loyal addresses.

Gradually, economic worries were giving way to deeper concerns about the rise of Hitler, who had become Chancellor of Germany in 1933. The Defence White Paper on 4 March recommended an increase, albeit modest, in the armed forces. Lord Robert Cecil, President of the League of Nations Union, organised an 'unofficial' series of questions on such matters as economic sanctions and military measures in the event of attack by any nation on another. The result of this so-called Peace Ballot was published on 27 June. Eleven and a half million replies were recorded. Ten million people were in favour of sanctions; 6.7 million were in favour of military measures as a last resort, with 2.3 million opposed. The Conservatives, especially Neville Chamberlain, regarded the whole Peace Ballot as a stunt cooked up by cranks; Macmillan differed, as in so much in those days. For him, the remarkable fact to emerge was the vast number who believed, despite the recent agonies of the Great War, in using force if necessary.

For some time Ramsay MacDonald had been visibly failing, a pathetic figure arraigned on all sides by his former Labour colleagues, a target for scorn and vitriol. Macmillan, who could be cruel himself – indeed he was to see ruthlessness as one of the inevitable necessities for successful high office[99] – thought MacDonald's treatment inexcusable and hoped that one day his true stature and romantic Highland nobility would be recognised.[100]

On 5 June 1935, MacDonald presided over what was to prove

his last Cabinet as Prime Minister. Two days later he tendered his resignation to the King. Baldwin now became Prime Minister for the third time, and in the Cabinet reshuffle MacDonald took Baldwin's former job of Lord President of the Council. John Simon went to the Home Office and Samuel Hoare, disastrously as it was to prove, to the Foreign Office. Rumours abounded of an impending election, although Baldwin was not obliged to go to the country until the autumn of 1936. In the wake of the Silver Jubilee, Baldwin made his decision almost a year early. Parliament was dissolved on 25 October and polling was fixed for 14 November 1935. No one could have foreseen that it would be the last general election for nearly ten years.

Although still nominally the National Government, Baldwin was to head a predominantly Conservative one. As in 1929, but this time with better success, he promised a policy of Safety First, in difficult and uncertain times, especially in foreign policy. The Conservatives won 432 seats, Labour 154 and Samuel's Liberals 20. Ramsay MacDonald lost his seat at Seaham[101] and Herbert Samuel was defeated at Darwen. Lloyd George was returned once more for Caernarvon Boroughs, but his time was past. Any pretence that Baldwin's administration was essentially a 'national' one was fanciful at best. The size of the victory was to prove Pyrrhic. The Conservatives, who had been in power in the interwar period, either by themselves or in coalition, for all but 10 months in 1924 and the years 1929–1931, would be blamed by the post-war electorate for the failings of both unemployment and appeasement. 'One result of the victory,' wrote C. L. Mowat, 'was to increase the fine which the Conservatives had to pay later when the lease of the office fell in.'[102]

Although Macmillan faced a three-cornered fight once more in Stockton in November 1935, the campaign was low key, almost placid. He issued a statement 'To the Electors of Stockton and Thornaby', entitled *What I Stand For*. He defined this as 'a policy of Economic Reconstruction, Social Justice, International Peace'. He received pledges of support from many of the local Liberals in Stockton, despite the fact that a Liberal candidate was once more standing. He also received messages of encouragement from voters outside the constituency. J. Scott Lidgett, Warden of the Bermondsey Settlement, wrote, 'I trust you will be victorious.' He also received support from the Oxford don Gilbert Murray,[103] 'though not a member of your party'. Clifford Allen* travelled to Stockton to speak for him. Dorothy accompanied

---

*They were to fall out when Allen became a staunch pro-appeaser.

him everywhere and was received with enthusiasm. There was little doubt about the result:

Harold Macmillan (Conservative)	23,285
Susan Lawrence (Labour)	19,217
G. L. Tossell (Liberal)	5,158
Conservative majority	4,068

The only loss, apart from the Liberal deposit, was the title of 'Captain'.

Macmillan was now safely returned for Stockton once more, his fifth election in 12 years, and his third success. The previous Parliament had seen him established as a distinctive figure with an individual voice. This had brought him no ministerial post and little popularity. Would he now take office? The manner of the answer would be dramatic indeed, and totally unpredictable.

CHAPTER EIGHT

Democracy Can Do Better

1935–1940

It is not enough to deplore and condemn the political excesses
and the economic inadequacies of the totalitarian states. We
must *prove* that democracy can do better.
> Harold Macmillan, *The Middle Way* (1938)

He has cut his traces and has no political home.
> Clifford Allen on Harold Macmillan, 6 February 1936[1]

I am not a superstitious man and indeed I should not greatly
care if I were never P.M. But when I think of Father and Austen
and reflect that less than 3 months of time and no individual
stands between me and that office I wonder whether Fate has
some dark secret in store to carry out her ironies to the end.
> Neville Chamberlain to his sister Ida, 21 March 1937[2]

And so, Good-bye, grim 'Thirties. These your closing days
Have shown a new light, motionless and far
And clear as ice, to our sore riddled eyes;
And we see certain truths now, which the fear
Accused by earlier circumstances could but compromise,
Concerning all men's lives. Beyond despair
May we take wiser leave of you, knowing disasters' cause.
> David Gascoyne, *Farewell Chorus*

'All good drama has two movements,' observed W. H. Auden, 'first
the making of the mistake, then the discovery that it was a mistake.'[3]
The second half of the 1930s was to prove a great drama indeed.
Macmillan made a significant contribution in proposing solutions to
the economic downturn, and in taking a stand against appeasing the
Dictators. Both debates – over the Depression and over appeasement
– cast a long shadow.

The debate over economic policy in the 1930s was one between
Keynesianism and the financial orthodoxy of the Treasury, epitomised
by Montagu Norman, for whom Keynes's new theoretical model was

anathema. After the publication by Macmillan & Co., of Keynes's *General Theory* in 1936, one financial orthodoxy was gradually to be replaced by another. No longer was it incontrovertible that a balanced budget was the *sine qua non* of economic policy. Yet, as J. K. Galbraith has shown, it is the fate of all new conventional wisdoms to be superseded eventually. Keynes was right for his time in the 1930s; but problems changed. 'The enemy of the conventional wisdom,' Galbraith observed, 'is not ideas but the march of events.'[4]

By 1958, Galbraith, despite being a true believer, acknowledged the obsolescence of many of Keynes's ideas. In the same year, Macmillan's first Chancellor of the Exchequer, Peter Thorneycroft, together with the entire front-bench Treasury team, resigned over the level of public expenditure, one of the first shots in the long-running economic debate between Keynesianism and monetarism. Yet Macmillan was so wedded to his experiences of the 1930s that he found it difficult to accept that this sea-change had taken over economic thinking. Similarly, Eden, when confronted by Nasser over Suez in 1956,[5] could not free himself of memories of his experiences of the Dictators – Hitler, Mussolini, Stalin and Franco – in the 1930s. Thus did the past really influence the future in unexpected ways.

There were those in the 1930s who believed that re-armament was the best response to the growing threat of Hitler and Mussolini; others sincerely believed in disarmament. For the League of Nations, a policy of collective security was the best option. From the time of Mussolini's invasion of Abyssinia in 1935, however, another policy emerged, that of appeasement, a word now almost exclusively used in a pejorative sense. The failure of appeasement, transparent after German forces took Prague in March 1939 in defiance of the Munich agreement of 1938, led to a system of 'guarantees' from the British and French governments towards Romania, Greece and Poland, a pledge that was implemented only after Hitler had marched into Poland on 1 September 1939.

Macmillan was firmly in the anti-appeasement camp, alongside Churchill and Eden. 'Anti-appeasers were disproportionately the products of Eton and Oxbridge', Graham Stewart has written, facts which 'rather contradict the tendency of egalitarian commentators to claim that appeasement and the "Establishment" were irrevocably intertwined'.[6] Neville Chamberlain was an appeaser, and in this he was supported by Geoffrey Dawson, editor of *The Times*. Boothby described Dawson as 'the Secretary-General of the Establishment, and fervent advocate of Appeasement'.[7] Macmillan's view was equally scathing. When assured by the whips that appeasement must be the correct policy, because Dawson advocated it, Macmillan observed, 'The Times is always wrong, and every twenty years produces the next volume of its official history to demonstrate the fact.'[8]

Orthodoxy versus unorthodoxy, whether in economic or foreign policy, was one of the underlying conflicts of the 1930s. Another was generational. When Baldwin became Prime Minister for the third time, in June 1935, he commented that the problem with contemporary politics was that the Labour men were too old and the Conservative ones too young. As the Labour men retired or died,[9] these junior figures assumed greater prominence. But some of these Young Turks were still left out, and one such was Macmillan, who remained a back-bencher, persistently and annoyingly criticising mainstream Tory thinking. In June 1938 he published what still has a fair claim to be his most important book, The Middle Way, a summation of his thinking on the years of Depression.* The whips were not impressed.

From 1934 to 1937 the economic cycle had begun to improve, though there were still regional disparities. The Jarrow Crusade of October 1936,[10] from a town almost wholly dependent on shipbuilding, and where unemployment had been 72.9 per cent, highlighted the continuing problems of the north-east. High Wycombe, in Buckinghamshire, on the other hand, was one of the most prosperous places in Europe. Living in Sussex and representing Stockton, Macmillan saw this divergence at first hand. He understood well the aspirational goal that possession of one's own home represented. Noel Skelton had championed 'the property-owning democracy' in 1924; it was also one of Macmillan's abiding aims.

The 1930s saw a boom in housing, both private and public. Owner occupation, which had been below 10 per cent before the Great War, was 35 per cent by 1938 (and in 1961, during Macmillan's premiership, was to rise to 42 per cent). 'The place to look for the germs of the future England,' George Orwell observed in 1941, 'is in the light-industry areas and along the arterial roads.'[11] Macmillan understood this and ensured that his thinking on social matters was not entirely based on Stockton workers in terraced houses. Slough (reviled by John Betjeman in his 1937 poem), Dagenham, Barnet, Hayes, and

---

*In a speech at the Conservative Political Centre in March 1958 to mark the twentieth anniversary of its publication, he said, 'A reasonable degree of heresy is, of course, the prerogative of youth', and compared himself to Mr Feeder in Dombey and Son, 'a kind of human barrel-organ, with a little list of tunes at which he was continually working over and over again, without any variation'.

Letchworth were the suburban towns noted by Orwell. He could have mentioned Bromley and Orpington, which were successively to ease Macmillan's political journey and harbinger his downfall. The archetypal 1930s housing nirvana was the white render of the pebble-dashed semi, with its sun-trap windows, that distinctive nod to modernism in the midst of suburban conformity.

Unlike some of his patrician colleagues, Macmillan was not condescending about lower-middle-class aspiration. By 1938, people were spending £40m a year on the football pools, the same amount as on visits to the cinema.[12] Motoring too was a growing preoccupation, and across widening social groups. Car ownership and improved rail links contributed to the growth of the suburbs, where increasingly the political battles would be decided. It was the age of the Austin Seven and the Morris eight, saluting Automobile Association patrolmen, 'road houses', and the Belisha Beacon.[13] Participatory leisure was widespread – in outdoor art deco lidos, with hiking and amateur boxing also flourishing – as Britain shed much of its Victorian and Edwardian past. 'Outings' were immensely popular, whether to air shows, fairgrounds, or test matches and professional football. Billy Butlin's first holiday camp had opened in Skegness in 1937. The 'wireless' had been popular since its inception in 1922, and listening to Hitler's fanatical speech from Nuremberg on 12 September 1938, as Harold and Dorothy did at Birch Grove, convinced many, including Lord Robert Cecil,[14] their guest that night, that war was now inevitable. Television made its first tentative appearance in the London area in 1936. Sporting events such as the Boat Race were covered, and in 1938 that year's Cup Final at Wembley Stadium between Preston North End and Huddersfield Town was the first to be televised live.[15]

The growth in reading, helped by the chain of Boot's lending libraries, benefited Macmillan professionally. In the mid-1930s he was one of the first at Macmillan & Co. to spot the potential of Margaret Mitchell's American Civil War novel *Gone with the Wind*, which became one of the company's all-time best-sellers, with sales boosted by the success of the 1939 film starring Clark Gable and Vivien Leigh. Reprints of the novel by Macmillan & Co. were in multiples of 100,000.[16]

'Consumerism' flourished in the second half of the 1930s, alongside advertising, with its first steps towards market research. Brands, often American in origin, such as Kellogg's and Woolworth's, became household names. Gradually, as the worst of the Depression lifted, material standards rose, particularly in the south-east, a pre-echo of the defining image of Macmillan's own premiership. Macmillan was well attuned to these subtle social changes.

Many admired the way in which Mussolini and Hitler, through their programme of public works (such as draining the Pontine marshes, and building the autobahns), were stimulating employment in Italy and Germany. The downside was the belligerent militarism that accompanied the Dictators' policies of domestic revival. Of the Dictators – Stalin, Mussolini, Hitler and soon to include Franco – Macmillan feared Hitler the most. He felt that the British public had been too inclined to see Hitler as a kind of Charlie Chaplin figure, whereas Hitler's profound malignancy was evident to those who had read *Mein Kampf*, as Macmillan had done.[17]

'One always has to remember the difference between the old aristocrats & the new,' Macmillan wrote to 'Moucher' Devonshire on 12 October 1936. 'The Tsars ruled by divine right – duly anointed with holy oil & consecrated in their sacred office with the full strength of a mystical rite. "There's a divinity doth hedge a king." But the Stalins & the Hitlers & the Mussolinis are only crowned demagogues. They have to keep up the political ballyhoo all the time. The party congress takes the place of the cathedral.'[18]

At the end of 1935, however, Benito Mussolini – 'strutting about with his nose in the air, never addressing a word to anyone while all the Italians shouted and cheered "*Il Duce*"'[19] – was seen by many in Britain, including Anthony Eden, as a greater threat to political stability than Adolf Hitler. 'Look at that man's eyes,' Bonar Law had said in 1922 after meeting the Italian leader. 'You will hear more of him later.'[20]

Such feelings contributed to the first major foreign policy failing of Baldwin's third administration, the Hoare-Laval Pact of December 1935. Widely regarded as a cynical plan to appease Mussolini by partitioning Ethiopia, Sir Samuel Hoare's ill-starred agreement with the French Foreign Minister Pierre Laval, hastily arranged in Paris on Hoare's way to an ice-skating holiday in Switzerland, was to cost Hoare his job.[21] The Abyssinian War of 1935–1936 proved a test too far for the League of Nations' policy of collective security. The failure of the League to prevent Mussolini's aggression, and to impose effective sanctions, proved a bleak prognosis for its ability to face down any future militarism.

Macmillan was unequivocal about the infamous Hoare-Laval Pact, which he described as 'a complete sell-out to the aggressor'.[22] He correctly predicted, in a letter to *The Times*, that the pact would seriously damage the credibility of the League of Nations itself. 'It may be true that we must face the failure or collapse of the League in its present form.'[23] Popular feeling was that the government had proposed an 'exchange of half an Empire for a corridor for camels'.[24] One of the most prescient observations came from a German diplomat: 'You have found a whipping boy for Mussolini in Hoare. Now that you have relieved your feelings at Hoare's expense you will not feel any impulse to save Ethiopia by having a showdown with Mussolini.'[25]

In the succeeding furore, Hoare resigned as Foreign Secretary. After much indecision, and indeed consultation with Eden, the League of Nations Minister, as to who might replace Hoare, Baldwin ended the interview with Eden by saying, 'Well it had better be you.' With this hardly ringing endorsement, Eden travelled to Sandringham on 23 December to receive the Seals of Office from George V, in what was to prove the last month of the King's life. Eden had an audience before the formal ceremony, and found the King very friendly, even chattily indiscreet. 'HM very down on plan of Paris,' he recorded in his diary. The King added: 'I said to your predecessor: "You know what they're all saying, no more coals to Newcastle, no more Hoares to Paris." The fellow didn't even laugh.'[26]

In common with many other younger members in the House, not only Conservatives, Macmillan welcomed Eden's appointment as Foreign Secretary. * They had confidence in the man Churchill was to dub this 'one strong young figure'.[27] Moreover, his appointment was an important indication of a generational shift, particularly encouraging to former members of the YMCA.

Macmillan's relations with Eden were complex, and altered much over the years they were colleagues. At first Macmillan was envious of what he saw as Eden's easy and seemingly effortless progress. Chosen for a safe seat, Warwick and Leamington, when he was 26, Eden, who was three years and four months Macmillan's junior, had been in government since 1926, 14 years before Macmillan was to occupy even the lowliest of rungs, in spite of all the hard work Macmillan had put into his own, marginal constituency.

Eden was a glamorous, decorated war hero. He had won the Military Cross in the week of his twentieth birthday, for rescuing his wounded sergeant from no-man's-land whilst under heavy fire. Macmillan should certainly have had the Military Cross for his service in the Great War, but was unlucky in the logistics and timing. It all contributed to his nagging sense of inferiority. Eden was 'the observed of all observers', a cross between Sir Galahad and Beau Brummel.[28]

---

* At 38, Eden was the youngest Foreign Secretary since Lord Granville in December 1851.

His Homburg hat, soon dubbed the 'Eden' hat, was one of the most noted features of contemporary cartoons.[29] By comparison Macmillan, though a deeper thinker, was perceived as inelegant, drab and boring, with no outstanding features. He was still at that intermediate stage in his career when cartoonists, if they bothered with him at all, had to attach an identifying label to his tail-coat.*

The crisis following the Hoare-Laval Pact, which brought a marked increase in international tension, also raised concerns about the organisation of Britain's defence policy, leading to plans for a Ministry of the Co-ordination of Defence. Before Baldwin had decided who was to head this new department, Hitler's troops occupied the Rhineland on 7 March 1936, a defining moment in the drift towards war. Speculation was rife as to who Baldwin would choose at such a critical juncture. Neville Chamberlain, Churchill, Hoare and MacDonald were all mentioned. Hoare's over-eagerness for a swift return to high office counted against him so soon after the ill-fated pact with Laval;[30] and to general astonishment, Sir Thomas Inskip was appointed. 'After weeks of suspense as to who would be the new co-ordinating Minister of Defence,' Collin Brooks wrote in his diary, 'it is announced that the lot has fallen upon Sir Thomas Inskip, a second-rate Attorney General whose chief claim to fame is that he was a stalwart of the protestant cause in the prayer-book debates.'[34] Austen Chamberlain was convinced Baldwin's decision to overlook Churchill was 'for fear, lest Hitler take his appointment ill'.[32] Whatever the reason, Macmillan was appalled.

Macmillan's dissatisfaction with Baldwin's judgement led him to even more open dissent in Parliament. On 8 April 1936, he voted against the government on the Unemployment Insurance Bill. In a widely publicised interview in the *Star* on 25 June, he advocated a government comprising a centre party, 'a fusion of all that is best in the Left and Right and it would have to be a Left Centre rather than a Right Centre'.[33] His preferred leader for this putative government was Herbert Morrison, Labour MP for Hackney South, and Leader of the London County Council. Following the Foreign Affairs debate in the House on continued sanctions – dismissed by Neville Chamberlain as 'the very midsummer of madness' – Macmillan took the drastic step on 29 June of resigning the Conservative whip. Many felt that he had finally burnt his boats.

---

*In time, however, he was to become one of the most celebrated of all cartoonists' subjects, as Vicky's 'Supermac'.

Yet Macmillan sympathised with Eden, who had been put in an impossible position in the Foreign Affairs debate, defending a policy with which it was clear he was unhappy. Macmillan's disenchantment was with Neville Chamberlain, Baldwin's inevitable successor as Prime Minister. When in 1936 the Spanish Civil War began, a conflict Macmillan was not alone in thinking of as a trial run for a greater war, he considered Eden's policy of non-intervention in Spain to be entirely correct. As always, he had an historical parallel to hand: the Duke of Wellington's observation after the Peninsular War that 'there is no country in Europe in the affairs of which foreigners can interfere with so little advantage as Spain'.[34]

For Macmillan, 1936 was to be a defining year in other ways. On 30 March his father Maurice died, just short of his eighty-third birthday. A few weeks earlier, on 3 March, George Macmillan, son of Harold's great-uncle Alexander, had died, followed on 1 June by his uncle, Sir Frederick Macmillan. Macmillan's mother Nellie never recovered from the blow of her husband's death, and died 18 months later at the age of 81. The three partners of the second generation of Macmillan & Co. had now gone within the space of three months, and control of the publishing business passed formally to Daniel and Harold. Although in practice the two brothers had been running things for some time, they now had to decide their future course of action. After much discussion, they decided to pay the duties involved and retain the firm as a private family business.

Daniel became chairman and concentrated on the educational and Indian side of the business that his father had built up. Harold's interests reflected his parliamentary concerns. The economists J. M. Keynes, A. C. Pigou and Alfred Marshall continued to be promoted, alongside G. D. H. Cole, Lionel Robbins and Joan Robinson. After the success of *Gone with the Wind*, Macmillan added the American novelist Pearl Buck, a Nobel laureate, to their list. The novels of Thomas Hardy were one of Harold's abiding interests, and not only for commercial reasons. He knew how valuable the Mellstock edition of the novels was to their balance sheet, and he continued to advise the second Mrs Hardy until her death in 1937. In October 1936, Harold was involved in arranging the transfer and sale of various Hardy manuscripts to Toronto. He also launched a drive to promote Hardy in New Zealand, and built up a general Australian list. He was closely involved with Sir Arthur Evans[35] on his archaeological works, including a guide to the Palace of Minos at Knossos. The Irish connection continued with W. B. Yeats and Sean O'Casey.

Yet Harold was always looking for young talent to add to the Macmillan list, and one of the most fruitful partnerships he established was with Robert Byron,[36] who became a famous travel writer. Byron was something of a polymath in his early years at Macmillan & Co. under Harold's guidance. He produced two travel books, planned a history of the Great War, and wrote a satirical novel, *Innocence and Design*. Harold had high hopes that this novel, highly recommended by his senior reader, J. C. Squire,[37] might achieve sales to match one of their perennial best-sellers in this genre, A. C. Macdonell's *England, Their England*. Despite an enthusiastic review in the *Tatler* by Macdonell himself, who recognised the stable from which the book came, sales were disappointing. Harold was not disheartened, blaming the Persian setting for the commercial failure. 'I think a simpler story with an English setting would be very different,' he advised Byron. 'After all a satire is more amusing when it satirizes what one knows. This was, I think, the secret of Macdonell's success.'[38]

In April 1937, after the delivery of a manuscript Macmillan was convinced would make Byron's name, he invited him down for a weekend at Birch Grove to talk over future projects. Byron for his part was impressed by the wide range of Macmillan's publishing expertise, particularly his uncanny taste for the best possible book-jacket. Macmillan's persistence paid off. On 6 April 1937, the firm published Robert Byron's *The Road to Oxiana*, one of the classic travel books of any age. Bruce Chatwin, something of a latter-day Robert Byron himself, as a traveller-aesthete, thought *The Road to Oxiana* a 'sacred text'.[39] A less sympathetic publisher might have lost faith in Byron after *Innocence and Despair*, but not Macmillan. His loyalty was rewarded with a book of enduring quality, which was also a best-seller.

Macmillan's easy manner with Robert Byron was symptomatic of a change of mood in St Martin's. Staff noticed a new style, even in small ways. The brothers were addressed informally as Mr Daniel and Mr Harold. Letters that had previously circulated unrecorded through the office now bore a purple stamp (a system invented by Harold) marked MHM and DM to show that the brothers had read and cleared them.[40] There was a sense of renewal and it was clear that the firm was in good hands.

Another death that saddened Harold Macmillan at the beginning of 1936 was that of Rudyard Kipling, a personal friend and a stalwart of the company's list. Eight days later, King George V died and was succeeded by Edward VIII. Rumours of the new young King's infatuation with Wallis Simpson, a twice-divorced American, continued to grow during the year. When the Abdication crisis broke that December,

Macmillan observed events with mixed feelings. Although he had admired the Prince of Wales's concern with social issues, the Christian aspect of divorce was for him more important still, as he emphasised unequivocally to Baldwin in a letter on 7 December, in which he deplored declining moral standards. The subject was delicate, in the light of his own unorthodox marriage. Religious belief had been a potent factor in his own decision to refuse to give Dorothy the divorce she so passionately wanted. In the circumstances, Macmillan's main emotion was one of relief when the institution of monarchy passed to the Duke of York, who assumed the title of King George VI.

Baldwin decided to resign after the Coronation of May 1937, following the pattern of Lord Salisbury in the Coronation summer of 1902. It was an appropriate moment. In the uncertain cycle of public approbation, Baldwin stood high in 1937, full of years and honours, widely regarded as the man who had saved the monarchy. A famous cartoon by Bernard Partridge in *Punch* on 26 May 1937 to mark Baldwin's retirement, showed Farmer Bull congratulating 'The Worcestershire Lad' on his ploughing: 'Well done, Stanley: a long day and a rare straight furrow.'* Despite his reservations about Baldwin's leadership, particularly on defence matters from 1935–1937, Macmillan recognised Baldwin's era as one when Baldwin had aimed to reconcile the different classes of society. Baldwin evoked feelings of affection on the Labour benches, feelings entirely denied to his successor, Neville Chamberlain. Since his arrival in Parliament in 1923, Macmillan had known no other Conservative leader than Baldwin. For Macmillan the forthcoming Chamberlain hegemony was an untested, and faintly worrying, prospect.

Neville Chamberlain became Prime Minister on 28 May. He had been heir apparent since the Ottawa Conference of 1932, achieving at last what had been denied to his father, Joseph, and his half-brother, Austen, who had died in March 1937.

Chamberlain's Cabinet reshuffle was minimal. He needed a new Chancellor of the Exchequer, and to the satisfaction of the National Liberals, if few others, he appointed Sir John Simon, who completed

---

*In the months leading to the Coronation, Baldwin received the cheers of the crowd wherever he went, but he knew that such adulation by its very nature was impermanent. Lord Dawson of Penn[41] told him, like a slave in the Emperor's chariot in Roman times, 'You will pay for all this one day, Stanley.' It was not long before Baldwin was seen retrospectively as one of Cato's Guilty Men.[42] On his last appearance in London, in October 1947, to witness George VI unveiling a statue of King George V at Westminster, the crowd sympathetically cheered the old man once again. By this time Baldwin was increasingly deaf, and he merely asked, 'Are they booing me?'[43] Macmillan in his time was to experience similar swings of fortune. He knew it was part of the job.

the triptych of the great offices of state, having previously served as Home Secretary and Foreign Secretary.[44] Sam Hoare, the pact with Laval now conveniently ignored, if not forgotten, replaced Simon at the Home Office. Duff Cooper, the first of Macmillan's 'group' to achieve high office, took Hoare's place at the Admiralty. Lord Halifax, an increasingly important figure, became Lord President of the Council. Although Macmillan had accepted the Conservative whip again in June 1937, there was no question, after his self-imposed exile, of remaining anywhere other than firmly on the back benches, and indeed on a very distant row.

Macmillan's major project at this time was his work on *The Middle Way*, which he was to publish in June 1938. *The Middle Way*, reprinted in 1966, in essence as an appendix to the first volume of his memoirs, *Winds of Change*, was 'offered as a contribution towards the clearer formulation of the new ideas of society that have slowly been emerging since the political crisis of 1931'.[45]

On 10 May 1938, Macmillan wrote to Keynes, seeking permission to include quotations from his published works. 'I have quoted Mr Keynes at length,' he explained in the book, 'because it is better that he, being an expert on the subject, should say these things in his own way.'[46] *The Middle Way* was heavily influenced by Keynes's *General Theory*, in the publication of which Macmillan had been involved two years earlier. 'My book will be called *The Middle Way*,' he wrote to Keynes. 'It is an attempt to deal with the problem of how to accelerate economic and social progress while preserving freedom and democracy.'[47] Such a task was not to prove easy, as both freedom and democracy came under increasing threat from the continental Dictators. The central thrust of the book was Macmillan's insistence that planning was not inimical to a reasoned order of the economic system, but rather an essential component.

Despite what his parliamentary colleagues thought the dangerous leftward thrust of his political ideas, Macmillan was essentially a moderate, believing, like Keynes, that the typical Englishman was 'neither reactionary nor radical'.[48] With his faith in economic planning, he was the Conservative equivalent of Labour figures such as Douglas Jay, Evan Durbin and the economist James Meade,[49] but without the belief in centralised state control. Socialism was workable, Macmillan quipped, only in heaven, where it was not needed, and in hell, where they had it already.

For a specialist work, *The Middle Way* made a great impact. Even 60 years later it was still something of an iconic work, influencing such concepts as President Clinton's 'triangulation' and Anthony Giddens's 'The Third Way', and thus the Blair government from 1997–2007. With its details on deficiency payments under the 1932 Wheat Act, a National Nutrition Act, and technicalities such as the marginal propensity to consume, it is not the kind of book that would find a place today as a '3-for-2' offer in high-street bookshops. T. S. Eliot once said that his real audience was 200 people in Europe. Although Macmillan's audience was clearly higher than that, *The Middle Way* was not aimed at the popular market, as, say, the book of his maturity *The Past Masters* (1975) was, even more so than the six volumes of memoirs.

The Middle Way has often been described as a revolutionary work. In fact, it was a confirmation of the new orthodoxy. The conventional wisdom of Montagu Norman had been displaced. John Turner has rightly described the book as 'a rather cautious compilation of the economic revisionism of the 1930s, written up so that Conservatives need not find it too unpalatable'.[50] Macmillan's most dramatic suggestion was that the Stock Exchange should be replaced by a National Investment Board. If that frightened the horses, he also emphasised that 'it is not necessary to reduce the incomes of one class in order to increase the incomes of another',[51] a stance that would not find disfavour with the economic thinkers whose views eventually displaced Keynesianism as the conventional wisdom. His premiership was to be, above all, the practical expression of that belief.

As Europe lurched ever closer towards war, the most impressive aspect of *The Middle Way* is the manner in which Macmillan championed democracy above totalitarianism. It ends with an eloquent panegyric:

> Democracy is being revealed as much more than a political system; it is a way of life. Upon its preservation depends the future of civilisation as we have been taught to regard it. We owe it to ourselves and to posterity, as our contribution to the history of human progress, so to strengthen, enlarge, and reconstruct the very ground-work on this way of life as to enable it to endure unshaken the inner strains and external perils of the anxious days that seem to lie ahead.[52]

Neville Chamberlain had been bequeathed the bitterest of legacies. The Berlin-Rome Axis had been established in November 1936, and the German-Japanese Anti-Comintern pact of 1936 was to be merged into a triangular agreement by the inclusion of Italy on 6 November 1937. Mussolini's prediction in a speech in May 1927 that 'between 1935 and 1940 we shall have reached a point that I should call crucial in European history' was well on the way to fulfilment. On 11 December 1937 Italy was to leave the League of Nations, following the earlier example of Germany and Japan. On 11 March 1938 Germany incorporated Austria into the German Reich ('the Anschluss').

The desire for peace was an overwhelming one, and Chamberlain's attempts to appease Hitler have to be seen in that context. Vaughan Williams's cantata *Dona Nobis Pacem*, an impassioned plea for peace, had recently been premièred to great public acclaim. At its centre was a setting of John Bright's words in the House of Commons in 1855 during the Crimean War, 'The Angel of Death has been abroad throughout the land; you may almost hear the beating of his wings.'[53]

Vaughan Williams had once defined genius as 'the right man in the right place at the right time'. Unfortunately, unfolding events were soon to reveal that Chamberlain was not that man from 1937–1940. Lloyd George was one of Chamberlain's bitterest critics, saying that he saw foreign policy through the wrong end of a municipal drainpipe. It was said that Chamberlain's perceived drab provincialism made him permanently tuned to Midland Regional. 'Listening to a speech by Chamberlain is like paying a visit to Woolworth's,' declared Aneurin Bevan, 'everything in its place and nothing above sixpence.'[54]

The times required a politician with an acute sensibility and experience of international events. Unfortunately, Neville Chamberlain failed that test. As Austen Chamberlain, a former Foreign Secretary with vast experience, had told his half-brother, 'Neville, you must remember you know nothing about foreign affairs.'[55] Neville Chamberlain's experience had been exclusively on the domestic scene, with a particularly successful time as Minister of Health. In these circumstances it did not befit him to say, 'I have only to raise a finger and the whole face of Europe is changed.'[56]

The problem was exacerbated by Chamberlain having inherited Eden as his Foreign Secretary. Not only did Eden know a great deal more about foreign policy than Chamberlain; he also held opposing views on appeasement. 'I fear that fundamentally,' wrote Eden in his diary, 'the difficulty is that N. believes that he is a man with a mission to come to terms with the Dictators.' To his sister, Hilda, Neville Chamberlain wrote, 'I fear the difference between Anthony and me is more fundamental than he realises. At bottom he is really dead against making terms with the dictators.'[57] It was only a matter of time before there was a dramatic rift.

The sticking point came at the beginning of 1938 when Eden was on holiday in the South of France. For some months Eden had become increasingly exasperated by what he considered Chamberlain's ill-advised interference. Austen Chamberlain's widow, Ivy, was even having private meetings with Mussolini and his circle in Rome. 'Really that F.O.,' Chamberlain had written to his sister in October, 'I am only waiting my opportunity to stir it up with a long pole.'[58] To Eden's chagrin, Chamberlain was moving towards *de jure* recognition of Italy's Abyssinian conquest. Lloyd George and Churchill were also holidaying on the Riviera, and Eden lunched with them on 5 January to discuss the worsening situation. 'Both strongly opposed to any recognition of the Italian conquest of Abyssinia,' he wrote in his diary. 'I told them something of our efforts to ensure co-operation with the U.S. Both seemed impressed with the progress that had been made.'[59] The next day Eden wrote to Neville Chamberlain, reiterating his view that Mussolini was 'the complete gangster and his pledged word means nothing'.[60]

On 12 January, Chamberlain received a telegram from the American President, Franklin D. Roosevelt, expressing his concern. Without consulting Eden, or the Cabinet, Chamberlain applied what Sumner Welles, the American Under-Secretary of State, called 'a douche of cold water' to proposals for 'a new and comprehensive European settlement, based on the fundamental principles of international law'.[61] Eden was incandescent when he heard details of the rejection of Roosevelt's offer from his loyal Parliamentary Private Secretary, J. P. L. Thomas. He hurried home to try to repair the damage.

Relations between Chamberlain and Eden deteriorated rapidly over the next few weeks. In the end it was Spain, not Chamberlain's cold-shouldering of the Roosevelt proposals, that tilted the balance. Count Galeazzo Ciano, Mussolini's Foreign Minister and son-in-law, had insisted through Count Dino Grandi, the Italian Ambassador, that the British should go to talks in Rome on the issue of Mussolini's 4,000 volunteers fighting on the side of Franco in the Spanish Civil War. After a stormy series of Cabinet meetings on 19 February, Eden resigned as Foreign Secretary.

In retrospect, it is surprising that Eden stayed as long as he did. Halifax, who succeeded him at the Foreign Office, later wrote, 'I cannot help thinking that the difference on the actual timetable of conversations was not, & never has been the principal difference. I suspect it has been the cumulative result of a good many different things.'[62] His suspicions were correct.

The resignation of Eden from the post of Foreign Secretary on 20 February 1938 made international headlines. Rejoicing at the news, Count Ciano wrote in his diary, 'An Eden Cabinet would have as its aim the fight against the dictatorships – Mussolini's first.' He instructed Grandi 'to take any step that might add an arrow to Chamberlain's quiver'.[63] Macmillan observed unfolding events with growing incredulity, particularly as Bobbety Cranborne, his relative by marriage, and J. P. L. Thomas also resigned. Macmillan knew that many complex decisions now faced these ministerial rebels, and their back-bench supporters.

The first shots came in the debate that followed Eden's resignation. Twenty-two Conservative MPs abstained from supporting Chamberlain, including Churchill, Macmillan, Boothby and Ronald Cartland.[64] For David Margesson, Tory Chief Whip, the worrying development was that, apart from the 'usual suspects', of which Macmillan was regarded as perhaps the most suspicious, the rebels included 'respectable' Tory MPs, such as Leonard Ropner, Robin Turton, Paul Emrys-Evans and Hamilton Kerr.

The question whether the dissenting MPs, followers of Eden, should act individually or collectively was only partly answered by the informal association they built, pejoratively dubbed by the whips as 'The Glamour Boys'. These MPs faced difficult questions in their constituencies, and in the Carlton Club, where the rules stated that no member should oppose another at any election. Macmillan was one of the few who did not experience such a threat in his parliamentary base. As he funded the Stockton Constituency Conservative Association and underwrote all its debts himself, there was no question of his being made a sacrificial golden goose – not that there were political differences. The Anschluss on 11 March had concentrated many minds.

Predominantly, though not exclusively, young Conservative back-bench MPs, the Glamour Boys were united in opposition to appeasement and in their concern over the worsening European situation. Harold Nicolson, the National Labour MP, attended their gatherings, and after one 'hush-hush meeting' wrote to his wife, Vita, 'they are deeply disturbed by the fact that Chamberlain does not seem to understand the gravity of the situation'.[65] The party whips feared a back-bench campaign to reinstate Eden as Foreign Secretary, with Churchill as First Lord of the Admiralty. Macmillan actually advocated even more. On 18 March he wrote a letter to the *Northern Echo* calling for Chamberlain's removal.

The unflattering phrase 'The Glamour Boys' had been coined by Sir Joseph Ball, Director of the Conservative Research Department, as a sharper alternative to 'The Boys' Brigade', 'The Glory Boys' and 'The Insurgents' as the standard description of Eden's followers.

The phrase gained wide currency, and when Katharine, Duchess of Atholl, deselected as the Conservative candidate for the Kinross and West Perthshire by-election, stood unsuccessfully as an Independent Anti-Municheer in December 1938, she was dubbed a 'Glamour Girl' – even though she had never attended any of the group's meetings.[66]

These meetings took place on a weekly basis, usually at the Westminster houses of J. P. L. Thomas and Mark Patrick, who acted as secretaries, and Ronald Tree's house in Queen Anne's Gate, at least until it was successfully bugged by Joseph Ball. Regular attendees included Leo Amery, Duff Cooper, Paul Emrys Evans, Richard Law, son of Bonar Law, Harold Macmillan and Edward Spears. In fact Macmillan played a dual role, as he was the link with another group, Churchill's followers, known as 'The Old Guard'. Their members included Robert Boothby, Brendan Bracken and Duncan Sandys. Joseph Ball believed that the Glamour Boys were merely Churchill's courtiers, but this was very far from the truth. Eden's group was much more of a threat to party discipline, and shied away from Churchill and his followers, especially Boothby, whom they regarded as unreliable mavericks. Macmillan, therefore, was more significant than might have appeared from his relatively junior position, as he was trusted in both groups. He saw it as his function to prevent internal quarrels and to concentrate minds instead on a united anti-appeasement stance. On 17 November, together with Churchill and Bracken, he voted against the government, backing the Liberal-Labour call for a Ministry of Supply. The whips thought there was no end to his harrying tactic.

Macmillan's father-in-law, Victor Devonshire, had died on 6 May 1938. Although he had long been incapacitated after a stroke, the blow was keenly felt by Dorothy. As both Harold and Dorothy had lost beloved and influential parents within the space of a few months, something of a rapprochement was reached in their marriage. Dorothy did, after all, need more than Bob Boothby. They left the house in Chester Square and made Birch Grove their principal residence, now theirs alone, and where the growing children had space for an idyllic rural childhood. In London, Macmillan established himself in a small flat in an elegant 1883 block at No. 90 Piccadilly, no longer 'half way to Eastbourne'. The flat, between Lord Palmerston's house (by then the Naval and Military Club) and the site of the old Devonshire House, demolished in 1925, overlooked Green Park, and proved an ideal central base.[67] He found it a good place to concentrate on his writing, not only finishing *The Middle Way* in the flat, but also producing *The Price of Peace* in October 1938, and *Economic Aspects of Defence* in February 1939, in which he advocated a Ministry of Supply, a department that was created on 14 July 1939, and in which he was to gain his first government post in May 1940.

It soon became clear that the Anschluss was not the end of Hitler's territorial ambitions. In March 1938, German forces massed on the border of Czechoslovakia, as Hitler stepped up his demands for self-determination for the German-speaking areas of the Sudetenland. Ensuing events, culminating in Chamberlain's three flights to Germany in September 1938, all attempts to come to terms with Hitler and to avoid war, cast a long shadow. Careers were made and broken by re-actions to 'Munich'. Beneficiaries were the anti-appeasers – Churchill, Eden, Duff Cooper and Macmillan – who were deemed by history to have been on the 'right' side. Rab Butler was blighted. Yet judgements were not simply determined on a 'for' and 'against' basis. 'Munich' was never held against Alec Douglas-Home, even though he had actu-ally been at Munich with Chamberlain, nor against Lord Hailsham, who had initially supported Chamberlain's policy.

As Chamberlain returned from Munich, London poured out her citizens to fetch her conquering Caesar in. It was 'Peace in Our Time', and, echoing Disraeli on his return from the Congress of Berlin in 1878, Chamberlain declared 'Peace with Honour'. The King and Queen took Chamberlain and his wife, Annie, on to the balcony of Buckingham Palace to receive the acclamation of the crowds, even though the Munich Agreement was to be the subject of a division in the House of Commons the following week.[68] The overwhelming feeling was one of relief, but personal relief, not relief for Czechoslovakia, which had been abandoned to its inevitable fate. Macmillan was not immune: he shared the relief that war had been averted. 'My son would stay at school,' he later wrote, 'and go to Oxford in the autumn.'[69] Cinemas showing newsreels of the conference attracted bumper crowds. One advertised its programme: 'Chamberlain the Peacemaker: for one week only.'[70]

On 1 October, Duff Cooper, First Lord of the Admiralty, resigned. Macmillan always felt that if more members of the Cabinet had fol-lowed Duff Cooper's lead in the days after the agreement in Munich and before the Commons debate, which began on 3 October, then Chamberlain would have fallen. At the end of the first day of the debate, Macmillan sought out Hugh Dalton, who in the concluding speech had declared that Chamberlain had been outmanoeuvred by Hitler. Macmillan told Dalton that the rebel Conservatives feared that

Chamberlain could call a snap election. An alliance between Labour and these rebel Conservatives, now boosted by the arrival of Duff Cooper in their ranks, Macmillan argued, would be the best way of removing Chamberlain. Dalton and Macmillan then went on to a midnight meeting at Brendan Bracken's house in the division bell district, 8 Lord North Street. Churchill, Eden and Leo Amery were already there, with other members of both the Glamour Boys and the Old Guard. Talk centred on Labour attitudes in the event of a sudden election.

Macmillan wanted to know what support dissident Conservatives might expect from the Labour Party. Would anti-Chamberlain MPs, if deselected, be given a free run in their constituencies by Labour? Macmillan also warned that if the Opposition amendment was in the form of a censure, then it would rally potential Conservative abstainers behind Chamberlain. Everyone had to tread very carefully. Dalton, of course, was not in the business of solving Tory difficulties. The prospect of divisions in the ranks of the Conservatives was an enticing one for Labour, and Dalton would not commit himself. However, he agreed to further talks, which took place on 5 October on the eve of the vote. The agreed policy was for a block abstention, though some wavered after hearing Chamberlain's powerful speech in the House on 6 October. Nevertheless, when the division was taken, nearly 40 potential government supporters abstained, 22 of them, including Macmillan, remaining in their seats for all to see, as loyalists trooped through the division lobbies. The reputation of these dissenters was even more important than their actual numbers.

The negotiations that Macmillan had with Dalton showed him in a sharper role than before: to his opponents within his own party, he was almost Machiavellian. He was disappointed that Eden had not taken a more prominent part, and felt that the chance to depose Chamberlain had been a missed opportunity. Imperceptibly, Macmillan was moving from the grey area of cerebral pamphleteering and emerging as one of the most forceful of the discontented. The Adullamites[71] were finding a new spokesman.

By a strange quirk, eight by-elections were pending in the weeks after Munich. Their potential as a referendum on appeasement was clear.* Closest to home for Macmillan, geographically and spiritually, was the contest due in Oxford on 27 October. The by-election was caused by the sudden death of the sitting member. Oxford was a safe

---

*In the end, only three – Oxford, Bridgwater, and Kinross & West Perthshire – were fought on that single issue.

Conservative seat, as the Cowley motor works was not part of the constituency. Among those applying to be the official Conservative candidate was the future Prime Minister, Edward Heath, then still an undergraduate at Balliol. When asked what qualifications he had for the seat, he replied that as he opposed the Munich Agreement, he had the potential to be a better Foreign Secretary than Lord Halifax.[72] The Conservatives settled on Quintin Hogg, a Fellow of All Souls, son of Lord Hailsham, a former Lord Chancellor (as Hogg himself was to become) and Lord President of the Council.[73]

A three-cornered contest would have handed the victory to Hogg on a plate, so efforts were now made to consolidate the opposition. Roy Harrod wrote to the *Oxford Mail* on 18 October appealing for a Liberal-Labour agreement to unite behind a single candidate. Ivor Davies, the Liberal candidate, had already said he would stand down if Labour followed suit, so that a non-party anti-Conservative could carry the fight forward. Richard Crossman and Frank Pakenham, Oxford dons and Labour city councillors, persuaded Patrick Gordon Walker, the candidate from 1935, to stand down.[74] Reluctantly Gordon Walker agreed. Crossman and Pakenham favoured the Master of Balliol, A. D. ('Sandy') Lindsay, who had recently completed a three-year term as Vice-Chancellor of the University. After dinner in Balliol Hall on Sunday, 16 October, Lindsay announced to the President of the Junior Common Room, Edward Heath, that he was standing as an Independent Progressive candidate. As Lindsay was well known for his Labour sympathies, the Liberals initially opposed this plan, and only when a wealthy local Labour councillor defrayed the Liberals' election expenses to that date did they agree to stand aside.

Macmillan was enthused by Lindsay's candidacy. Lindsay had been one of the Balliol dons he remembered from his undergraduate days. Lindsay's political empathy for the underprivileged very much replicated his own views, though Lindsay's idealism could take a very puritanical line. He banned Lobster Newburg from Balliol menus, so as to show solidarity with the unemployed. As this dish was a speciality of the Balliol chef, the decision was not popular with the chef or the undergraduates, who did not see how it was actually going to benefit the unemployed.[75] John Betjeman evoked the atmosphere of Lindsay's mastership in *Summoned by Bells*:

> While Sandy Lindsay from his lodge looks down
> Dreaming of Adult education where
> The pottery chimneys flare
> On lost potential firsts in some less favoured town.[76]

Lindsay was to garner the support of three future prime ministers – Churchill, Macmillan and Heath. He also drew an enthusiastic undergraduate following, though the Proctors felt it unseemly to have too much involvement from 'undergraduettes'.[77] In Parliament, the Next Five Years Group was solidly behind Lindsay, though Macmillan was the only one who took an active part in the campaign. In one speech Macmillan declared that one could not always appease lions by throwing them Christians. 'A vote for Hogg is a vote for Hitler'[78] became the unofficial campaign slogan of the anti-Munich camp (much to Lindsay's distaste), but Hogg responded spiritedly with 'Vote for Hogg and save your bacon.' Hogg corresponded with Geoffrey Dawson, editor of *The Times*, who ensured that Printing House Square remained on side, giving support to the official Conservative effort.

On the eve of polling day, Lindsay addressed a packed house in Oxford Town Hall, where he was 'magnificent but inaudible'.[79] His campaign was gravely weakened when he let it be known that he would not stand again at the next general election. His opponents then made much of his 'stopgap' status and accused him of posturing. Although the Conservative majority from 1935 was halved, Hogg was elected in a 76.3 per cent turn-out, nearly 10 per cent more than three years earlier:

Quintin Hogg (Conservative)	15,797
A. D. Lindsay (Independent Progressive)	12,363
Conservative majority	3,434

Neville Chamberlain telegrammed his congratulations to Hogg. He was relieved that the Conservative candidate had been elected, but not as relieved as Stanley Baldwin had been in 1931 when Duff Cooper, now a Lindsay supporter, had fought off the press barons at St George's. Hogg's triumph was to prove temporary. The importance of the Oxford by-election was that it marked the moment that the anti-Chamberlain bandwagon began to roll. In Macmillan's career the episode was important for its illustration of how far he was to go in opposition to the 'establishment' line of his own party. It seemed he was going to be the eternal outsider.

On 5 November, the traditional Bonfire Night celebrations at Birch Grove took an unusual twist. Instead of Guy Fawkes, the effigy that year was of Neville Chamberlain, rolled umbrella and all. Macmillan even sacrificed a presentable Homburg hat to be consumed in the flames. The local village schoolchildren cheered unknowingly, but some of the

Cavendish relatives who were staying with the Macmillans were deeply offended. Also present were some 50 refugees from Czechoslovakia to whom Macmillan had given homes in various houses and cottages on the estate, following the government's decision in October to allow 350 Sudeten refugees to come to Britain. Macmillan was deeply ashamed when Nancy Astor attacked this policy in the House of Commons, saying that the Czechs were all Communists and should have been sent to Russia. He wrote to tell her that those at Birch Grove were 'quiet and cultivated people, dazed ... hard-working, courteous and grateful. With all that they have had to suffer I do not see why they should be insulted in our Parliament in addition.'[80]

A sad litany of events unfolded, almost with an air of inevitability. German troops entered Prague on 15 March 1939. On 21 March, the Lithuanian Foreign Minister was summoned to Berlin. The next day Memel was ceded to the German Reich. On 7 April, Good Friday, Mussolini's troops moved against Albania, a prelude to installing King Victor Emmanuel III of Italy on the country's throne in place of King Zog. Rumours abounded that Chamberlain was ready to overlook the conquest of Albania and enter a new Mediterranean pact with Mussolini.

'Harold Macmillan is enraged that Chamberlain should remain on,' Harold Nicolson wrote in his diary on 11 April 1939. 'He thinks that all we Edenites have been too soft and gentlemanlike. That we should have clamoured for Chamberlain's removal. That no man in history has made such persistent and bone-headed mistakes, and that we still go on pretending that all is well.'[81] Macmillan's capacity for criticism as the crisis deepened was not diminished.

After Franco's victory in the Spanish Civil War, Spain withdrew from the League of Nations on 8 May. A fortnight later, the Italo-German military alliance, the 'Pact of Steel', was announced. The Japanese government began a six-year naval expansion programme. On 23 August, the Nazi-Soviet Pact was signed and all Hitler's preparations for the invasion of Poland were in place.

Macmillan had known for some time that war was coming and that Birch Grove would be requisitioned. He prepared for this moment, and on 1 September 1939, the day Hitler invaded Poland, the first of the 70 schoolchildren who were to be evacuated to Birch Grove arrived with their teachers and nurses. Macmillan and his wife moved to Pooks, a house on the estate nearby, and stayed there for the rest of the war.[82]

Macmillan was not at Birch Grove on 1 September to welcome the evacuees. He was back in London as the final few hours of peace slipped away. On 2 September he was present in the House when Chamberlain made his statement. Macmillan feared that 'even at this late stage' (as one of his favourite Trollopian characters, Obadiah Slope, was wont to say) Chamberlain might step back from honouring the British and French guarantees to Poland. The House had expected a declaration of war. Instead, as Leo Amery wrote in his diary, 'there were some limping sentences about the French and ourselves considering what further time limit we were to put for Hitler's answer [on withdrawal from Poland]'.[83] When Arthur Greenwood, the acting Labour leader, rose to reply, he said he was speaking for his party. Leo Amery called out from the Conservative benches, 'Speak for England, Arthur.'

On the morning of Sunday, 3 September, Macmillan was with the Eden group at Ronald Tree's house at Queen Anne's Gate to hear Chamberlain's broadcast declaring war on Germany. After this lugubrious announcement, the MPs walked over to the House of Commons, where an air-raid siren was sounding. Macmillan went out on to the terrace till the sirens, which were being tested, ceased their wail. Then he went back into the chamber to hear Chamberlain's statement to the House. On Armistice Day 1918, the people had rung their bells; now, as so long predicted, they were wringing their hands. Macmillan wondered how many of his family would be there to see the next Armistice, whenever it might come. His hopes for Maurice, now 17 and about to go up to Balliol after Eton, so high after Munich, were now dispelled. Whatever role his father might be called upon to play in the forthcoming war, Maurice would be a combatant. Past agonies had returned to haunt a new generation.

Following the declaration of war, Chamberlain installed a six-man inner Cabinet to guide its prosecution. Churchill returned from the long years of exile as First Lord of the Admiralty, the post he had held at the outbreak of the Great War. 'I daresay it will work for a while,' wrote Leo Amery, 'but I think I see Winston emerging as PM out of it all by the end of the year.'[84]

The so-called Phoney War was an interlude before the main business began in Belgium and France. Scandinavia, however, was not spared early conflicts. As a direct consequence of the Nazi-Soviet Pact, Russia had attacked Finland on 30 November 1939, in the so-called Winter War.[85] Meanwhile, German U-boats were already causing havoc to British merchant shipping, there were as yet no military offensives on the Franco-German borders, and by 8 January 1940 the children who had been evacuated from London (361,192 in total) were allowed to return home. Hitler invaded Denmark and Norway on 9 April, and on 15 April the British launched an expedition to the Norwegian harbour of Narvik.[86] The Allies suffered heavy losses, and the subsequent Norwegian Debate has a fair claim to be regarded as the most important in Parliament in the twentieth century.

A dramatic intervention on the first day, 7 May, came from Sir Roger Keyes the hero of Zeebrugge in the Great War. He appeared in full Admiral of the Fleet uniform, with six rows of medals,* and made a devastating attack on British naval strategy at Narvik. After Keyes's contribution, Leo Amery delivered the *coup de grâce*, recalling the words of Cromwell to the Long Parliament. '"You have sat too long for any good you have been doing. Depart I say, and let us have done with you. In the name of God, go."'[87]

The second day's debate was opened by Herbert Morrison, who told the House that the Labour Opposition would be calling for a vote of censure. Chamberlain's reply, that he had friends in the House, led Lloyd George (now in his eighties) to declare that 'It is not a question of who are the Prime Minister's friends. It is a far bigger issue.' He continued in wounding fashion by saying that Chamberlain had called for sacrifice. 'There is nothing,' concluded Lloyd George, 'which can contribute more to victory in this war than that he should sacrifice the seals of office.'[88] Macmillan thought this unnecessarily cruel.

One voice that had remained largely silent was Churchill's. He was in a difficult position. As First Lord of the Admiralty, Narvik had been his responsibility. Macmillan knew that those who wished to remove Chamberlain from office had to tread warily lest Churchill was also brought down. Lloyd George recognized this when he declared in the debate, 'I do not think that the First Lord was entirely responsible for all the things which happened in Norway.' Churchill immediately got to his feet to take complete responsibility. Lloyd George saw his opening. 'The Right Hon. Gentleman must not allow himself to be converted into an air-raid shelter to keep the splinters from hitting his colleagues.'[89]

Churchill's winding-up speech was a vigorous defence of the government. A three-line whip was in operation for the vote, in which 33 Conservatives and eight of their National Government supporters voted with the Labour Opposition. A further 60 abstained. Although Chamberlain won the vote by 281 to 200, the government majority

---

*Macmillan who had advised Keyes to make his speech short and simple and to write it down first (advice Lloyd George had given Macmillan in 1923) was struck by the way in which Keyes's visual appearance created such an unforgettable impression, and the model was one he later used himself to considerable effect.

of 81 was way below its potential total of 213. Rebel back-benchers who voted against the government included Leo Amery, Nancy Astor, abandoning her loyalty to the 'Cliveden Set',[90] Bob Boothby, Duff Cooper, Quintin Hogg, Leslie Hore-Belisha, Sir Roger Keyes, Harold Macmillan, John Profumo, Louis Spears and Ronald Tree. The bitterness was intense. John Profumo was spat upon by Walter Elliot outside the division lobby. Hogg, who had changed his mind on appeasement since the Oxford by-election, nevertheless regretted the triumphalism that erupted in the Commons after the vote was announced. He noted that there was much 'prancing and jeering'.[91] J. C. ('Josh') Wedgwood, independent Labour MP for Newcastle-under-Lyme, struck up a refrain of 'Rule Britannia', to which Macmillan, never musical at the best of times, unconvincingly tried to contribute.

Recriminations began as Chamberlain's premiership hung by a thread. David Margesson, the Government Chief Whip, sought out John Profumo, the most junior rebel, and told him he was 'an utterly contemptible little shit' who would be ashamed of what he had done for the rest of his life.[92]

For two days the negotiations continued over Chamberlain's position.[93] Although George VI favoured Halifax as Prime Minister (Churchill's support for Edward VIII during the Abdication crisis had not been forgotten by the Palace), an opinion shared by the majority of the Conservative Party, it was not the view of Halifax himself, nor that of the Labour Party, whose price for joining what thus became a truly National Government was for Churchill to be appointed Prime Minister.

News came that Germany had invaded Holland, Belgium and Luxembourg. The way to Paris lay open. Macmillan began that fateful day, 10 May, with mundane business: he led a delegation of publishers to the Treasury to persuade John Simon to exempt books from Purchase Tax.[94] In the midst of all his preoccupations with international events, Macmillan was still heavily involved in affairs at the family publishing house. In January he had dined with J. M. Keynes at Tilton, his Sussex home, to discuss details of Keynes's forthcoming booklet *How to Pay for the War*, published by Macmillan on 27 February. The massive sales of *Gone with the Wind* had led Macmillan to plan a one-volume edition of Tolstoy's *War and Peace* jointly with the Oxford University Press.[95] Remembering his own experience of the hours, even days, of inactivity on the Western Front, he knew that books would be much in demand by the troops, the more substantial the better.

*

At 6 p.m. on 10 May, Churchill was summoned to Buckingham Palace by the King and invited to form a government. What Churchill later called 'The Great Coalition' was underway. Chamberlain retained the leadership of the Conservative Party. Churchill initially intended to make him Chancellor of the Exchequer or Leader of the House. Labour objections led to him becoming Lord President of the Council. The Labour leader, Clement Attlee, became Lord Privy Seal and Churchill's deputy. Although Churchill would have liked to have appointed Eden to the Foreign Office, Halifax's magnanimity over the premiership ensured that he remained as Foreign Secretary. The inner War Cabinet included Lord Beaverbrook as Minister of Aircraft Production. The three service ministries were filled by senior figures from each of the main parties – Anthony Eden at the War Office, Labour's A. V. Alexander at the Admiralty, and the Liberal leader Sir Archibald Sinclair at the Air Ministry. John Simon became Lord Chancellor, though the lawyers quipped, 'There'll be no moaning at the Bar, when he puts out to sea.' David Low celebrated the formation of the government with one of his most famous cartoons, 'All Behind You, Winston', showing the massed ranks, in arrowhead formation behind the new Prime Minister, rolling up their sleeves for the task ahead.[96]

The minor appointments followed in quick succession. Macmillan's invitation came on 14 May. Churchill called him to Downing Street and offered him the post of Under-Secretary to Herbert Morrison at the recently formed Ministry of Supply. Macmillan accepted at once. One of the first letters of congratulation he received was from J. M. Keynes. 'My dear Harold,' Keynes wrote, 'I saw with the greatest pleasure your official appointment – long overdue, if I may say so.'[97] Keynes was not the only one to think so. Macmillan was particularly touched to receive a letter from the London Representative of the Sudeten German refugees, many of whom were still at Birch Grove.

The 1930s had been a long haul for Macmillan. His mood on appointment to his first government post might best be summed up by a poem by D. H. Lawrence (though not one of Macmillan's favourite authors), *Look! We Have Come Through!* However, the foundations of his later success had been laid. Macmillan had learned how to cope with reversals and adversity, both personal and professional. Membership of the YMCA, the Next Five Years and the Glamour Boys had taught him much about the inner workings of the political process. He knew that fastidiousness was not always effective. Life at Westminster, 'the green-eyed jungle' as Hugh Dalton called it, was a competitive business, and he was determined to compete.

May 1940 was one of the watershed months of the twentieth century. 'The long dismal, drawling tides of drift and surrender, of wrong measures and feeble impulses,'[98] in Churchill's words, seemed at last to be over. The survival of Western civilisation was now at stake. The madmen in authority had heard voices in the air for too long. In the worldwide struggle that was to silence such voices, Macmillan was destined to be more than a minor figure, and was to come perilously close to losing his life.

PART TWO

An Insider at Last

1940–1951

The whips want the safe men, as they have always done in every party. But they don't make the future leaders of the party. I reminded Winston again that it took Hitler to make him P.M. and me an under-secretary. The Tory party wd do neither.

Harold Macmillan diary, 13 October 1954

RECHRISTENING OF BLIMP—*Cartoon by Low*

Macmillan and Butler felt that the Conservative Party should be re-named as part of the process of modernisation after the war. Cartoonist Low, with memories of the film about Colonel Blimp, remained unconvinced.

CHAPTER NINE

On the Other Side of the Fence

1940–1942

I dined tonight at the Beefsteak and sat beside Harold Macmillan. He is very much the Minister nowadays, but says that he has arrived too late to rise very high. I can see no reason (except his own personality) for his not getting on – even to the top of the tree – but he is his own worst enemy: he is too self-centred, too obviously cleverer than the rest of us.

Cuthbert Headlam diary, 24 June 1940

We hate delay, but it makes us wise.

Traditional proverb

And we are here as on a darkling plain
Swept with confused alarms of struggle and flight
Where ignorant armies clash by night.

Matthew Arnold, *Dover Beach*

Having long harassed Chamberlain, Macmillan was now on the governmental side of the fence; but he was frustrated initially not to have any specific war-related task. However, after the Russian invasion of Finland on 30 November 1939, the Cabinet had given its blessing to a working committee organising aid to Finland, then enduring the worst of its Winter War against the invading Soviet forces. As Leo Amery ran the committee, Macmillan was one of a number of members recruited, on a cross-party basis. Churchill had encouraged Macmillan to accept Amery's invitation, which gave him a quasi-official job in the war effort, especially as it could well lead to other jobs.

As the situation in Finland worsened, Macmillan was chosen, together with the Liberal peer Lord Davies, a former Parliamentary Private Secretary to Lloyd George, to go on a fact-finding mission to Finland. Macmillan's Scandinavian tour, which also incorporated Sweden, from 10 February to 1 March, was a hybrid task, halfway between back-bench and ministerial responsibility. He kept a journal, which he called 'My Finnish Diary'. As he had recently published a one-volume edition of Tolstoy's *War and Peace* with the Oxford

University Press, he took with him *Anna Karenina*, which he had not read before. He found this an even greater work, perhaps the supreme novel of all.

Exhibiting that instinct for publicity that was to characterise his later career, he obtained a white fur Finnish hat, the same he was to wear, somewhat mischievously, on his visit to Russia as Prime Minister in 1959. Scandinavia was 'like being in Toronto or Winnipeg in winter'.[1]

On 25 February, the Russian invaders broke through the Manner-heim line, a fortified system of defences on the Karelian peninsula. Macmillan knew that this was inevitable. 'Another great series of attacks is being made today,' he wrote in his journal on 12 February. 'The Finns are terribly handicapped by shortage of men.'[2] He sent cipher telegrams to both Halifax, the Foreign Secretary, and Churchill at the Admiralty, outlining the situation, but to little avail. His impression was that the British government had '"written off" the Finnish war'.[3] The Finnish government accepted Russian terms, and fighting ceased on 13 March.

Back in England, Macmillan sent a copy of his Finnish diary to Geoffrey Dawson at *The Times*, not for publication, but to let the man who had been such a stout supporter of Chamberlain's appeasement policy know some of the realities of the present war. His account did not fall on deaf ears. 'Harold Macmillan sent in a remarkable diary of his visit to Finland,' Dawson wrote in his diary, 'which I read in bed till a late hour, absorbed in it.'[4]

Macmillan regarded the British attitude to Finland's plight as shameful* and accordingly was chosen by Amery's group to speak on 19 March in the debate on Finland. From his recent first-hand experience he was able to refute Chamberlain's claims that adequate supplies had been provided. 'Harold Macmillan stated the case against the Government's delays skilfully and moderately,' Amery wrote in his diary. 'We had thought that he was the best person to present it as he could give all the figures we had got from the Finnish Legation as if they had come under his knowledge while he was in Finland.'[5]

To Macmillan's relief, Churchill, with whom the buck should have stopped, was not present in the House when he spoke. As a result, Macmillan felt he could be uninhibited. His tone was measured, but the specific details he was able to provide created a devastating picture

---

*He was not to visit Finland again until the last year of his premiership, and when he wrote an account of his 1963 visit in one of his regular, informative and informal letters to the Queen, he recalled the impression the country had made upon him 'in 1940 – during the winter war – when I felt a great admiration for this small but courageous people'.[6]

of government incompetence. The conclusion made for uncomfortable listening: 'The delay, the vacillation, changes of front, standing on one foot one day and on the other the next before a decision is given – these are patently clear to anyone. The moral of the history of these three months to be drawn for the future is, to use the phrase of Burke, "a proof of the irresistible operation of feeble counsel".'[7]

Churchill, to do him credit, was impressed. Indeed this may well have been the genesis of Churchill's later idea of employing Macmillan in the military-diplomatic role he was to be given in North Africa.[8] Macmillan's mastery of this Finnish visit was certainly to play a significant part in Churchill's choice a few weeks later of the Ministry of Supply for Macmillan's first department. Macmillan was 46 when he took up this his first government post, on 15 May 1940. On assuming office, Macmillan had to give up his directorship at Macmillan & Co., which remained in the sole control of his brother Daniel until the Conservatives were defeated in the 1945 election. He also relinquished six other directorships, including one of the Great Western Railway.

The first rung of the ministerial ladder is usually one with mundane responsibilities. The special circumstances of May 1940 meant that this was not the case with Macmillan. Within days of his appointment, Holland and Belgium had capitulated to the Nazi invaders. The evacuation of the British Expeditionary Force from Dunkirk began at the end of the month. On 14 June the Germans entered Paris, and a week later the French signed armistice terms at Réthondes, in the same railway carriage where the Germans had surrendered to Marshal Foch in 1918. If Britain was now to survive invasion, the fighting forces, especially the RAF, needed to be properly equipped. It was the job of the Ministry of Supply to ensure that they were.

Macmillan had been one of those MPs who had advocated a Ministry of Supply when he was on the back-benches, voting with Labour and the Liberals for such a department. When the ministry was established in July 1939, its function was to co-ordinate the supply of equipment to the three services. Initially it was a ramshackle organisation in which an inventive and industrious civil servant such as Oliver Franks could profitably run his own hare. Franks had a moral dimension to his puritanical work ethic that suited the times and for which Macmillan developed a profound admiration.*

---

*The same was to be true of Evelyn Sharp at the Ministry of Housing and Local Government, which Macmillan headed in 1951. Over the next 23 years, Macmillan was to work with some of the most distinguished civil servants of their generation.

Continuity at the Ministry of Supply was provided by Franks. Macmillan served as Parliamentary Secretary to three different ministers – Herbert Morrison (May-October 1940), Sir Andrew Duncan (October 1940–June 1941) and finally Lord Beaverbrook (June 1941–February 1942). 'With one Cockney, another a Lowland Scot and the third a Canadian,' he later wrote, 'I never heard a word of English spoken correctly from the Minister's chair.'[9] Only Beaverbrook, unlike his two immediate predecessors, was a member of the War Cabinet.

On taking office, Macmillan drew up a memorandum on how he felt the ministry should be organised. This became a habit, and he repeated it in the 1950s during Churchill's peacetime administration. His later style was even bolder, as often the memoranda then referred to departments with which he had no connection.

His responsibilities in 1940 were wide-ranging, and in September 1940 the junior ministerial team was strengthened by the arrival of Lord Portal as Joint Under-Secretary.[10] Macmillan had suggested such an addition to the team in his memorandum for Morrison – one Under Secretary to deal with munition production, and the other to oversee salvage and raw materials, which became Portal's task. Portal was an outstanding example of the businessman turned public servant, a type Macmillan was to bring into government in his days as Prime Minister.

Macmillan's view of Morrison was clouded by the fact that Morrison had been a conscientious objector during the First World War. Macmillan always looked down on those who had not led men in battle – Rab Butler and Hugh Gaitskell in particular – and Morrison was in a special category of contempt. Macmillan saw him as essentially timid, but he recognised that Morrison, who had led the London County Council for six years, had a big career ahead of him in the Labour Party. 'Indeed in his loyalty to me,' wrote Morrison later, 'his advice for my advancement tended to occupy his mind to such an extent that I had to remind him that we had a war job to do and that personal careers were not important.'[11] Although Macmillan was politely generous to Morrison in his memoirs, in the privacy of his diary he was outspoken, describing him as a 'dirty little cockney guttersnipe' and 'a third-rate Tammany boss'.[12] He was, he added for good measure, 'the meanest man I know'. He also lacked the basic quality of courage. 'For in addition to the physical cowardice wh[ich] used to send him down to the deep dug-out at the Ministry as soon as it was dark, not to re-emerge till morning, Morrison was the kind of man who would never take the blame for what went wrong – only the credit for what went right.'[13]

'Harold of course is desperately busy,' Lady Dorothy told her mother, '& finds his job rather uphill I think. The organisation, if any seems deplorable, & there is a constant battle with the permanent officials. However, so far everything that Morrison has suggested or done (& many of Bevin's Labour plans) have been Harold's idea, but he is naturally most careful to make the Ministers think they themselves have thought of it all!'[14] It was a technique Macmillan used to advantage with the Americans in North Africa from 1943.

Macmillan's key supporter during these fractious times was his private secretary, John Wyndham.[15] Theirs was a symbiotic relationship of the deepest significance. Macmillan appreciated Wyndham's intelligence, wit and unswerving loyalty. For his part, Wyndham achieved a prominence through his association with Macmillan he did not entirely welcome, though he accepted its inevitability as 'master' (his sobriquet for Macmillan) rose higher in the political hierarchy. Macmillan later compared their relationship to that between Disraeli and his private secretary, Montague Corry, giving him 'all the gossip of the clubs, and all the chatter of the drawing rooms'.[16] In *Endymion*, Disraeli described the ideal. 'The relations between a Minister and his secretary are, or at least should be, among the finest that can subsist between two individuals. Except the married state, there is none in which so great a confidence is involved, in which more forbearance ought to be exercised, or more sympathy ought to exist.'[17] Macmillan and Wyndham represented that ideal to unique effect.

Petworth House, Wyndham's estate in Sussex, not too far from Birch Grove, became an oasis of calm for Macmillan over the years, 'a nice little dacha', as he described it to visiting Bolshoi ballet dancers in 1956.[18] Macmillan went to few places over the next quarter of a century without Wyndham at his side. On his Commonwealth tour as Prime Minister in 1958, he was introduced to an old, dishevelled figure in a village outside New Delhi, and told, 'This is one of the largest land-owners in this district.' Bringing Wyndham forward, Macmillan introduced him to the old man. 'And this,' he said, 'is one of the largest landowners in *my* district.'[19]

Another figure Macmillan respected at the Ministry of Supply, and who was later to become a minister in his own administration, was Percy Mills.[20] Mills was another outstanding example of the industrialist-turned-public-servant. An additional recommendation for Macmillan was that his father had been a confectioner in Stockton-on-Tees. Mills was successively Deputy Director of Ordnance Factories at the Ministry of Supply, and then Controller-General of Machine Production, part of Macmillan's ministerial remit. He energised the whole business of machine-tool control, and Macmillan, then, and at Housing in the early 1950s, always regarded him as 'a first-class man'.[21]

Work at Supply was severely disrupted by the Blitz. When the Chamber of the House of Commons was destroyed, Macmillan visited the still smoking ruins and retrieved a burnt order paper as a souvenir that he kept for the rest of his life. He was bombed out of his top-floor flat at 90 Piccadilly. Palmerston's old house next door, the 'In and Out' Club, also suffered heavy damage. Macmillan moved into a flat on the first floor of 90 Piccadilly, made available to him by Hugh Walpole, a Macmillan author. From time to time he put up at 52 Cadogan Place.

With the bombs falling on London, Macmillan was concerned about his three daughters. (Maurice was now serving in the army.) The Devonshires offered sanctuary for the children at Chatsworth, but Macmillan felt that its proximity to industrial sites in Manchester made it potentially more dangerous than Birch Grove. 'At the moment H. thinks the children are better here than in Derbyshire,' Dorothy wrote to her mother. 'They [the Germans] are evidently going for works and factories & so until attempts at invasion begin we seem fairly well out of it here.'[22]

On the night of 14 October 1940, Macmillan was returning from the ministry in the Strand to his flat in Piccadilly as a raid began. There was much shrapnel, and he decided to turn into the Carlton Club, then in Pall Mall. He was having a glass of sherry with David Margesson when at 8.30 p.m. the building suffered a direct hit and the whole ceiling collapsed around them. As they made their way out, they met up with diners leaving the stricken building, including Lord Hailsham, borne from the wreckage on the shoulders of his son, Quintin Hogg. To the classically educated Macmillan, the comparison was clear:

> Aeneas, our great ancestor,
> Did from the flames of Troy upon his shoulder
> The old Anchises bear.[23]

A few days before the Carlton Club bombing, Chamberlain, mortally ill with cancer, resigned from Churchill's government.[24] As Chamberlain had retained the leadership of the Conservative Party, this raised questions of whether Churchill should remain 'above' the political struggle and allow a senior colleague such as Eden to take Chamberlain's place. However, remembering Lloyd George's fate after the Great War as a prime minister without a party, Churchill ensured that he was duly elected as Conservative leader on 9 October. In the reshuffle, Morrison became Home Secretary, where he was to establish himself as a national figure. Sir Andrew Duncan,[25] another politician from a business background, became Minister of Supply, moving from the Department of Trade. 'Duncan for Morrison at the Ministry of Supply should be an improvement,' observed Cuthbert Headlam.[26]

A Lowland Scot, with experience in both shipbuilding and banking, Duncan's character and diligence appealed to Macmillan. Not the least of his attractions was that he hailed from Irvine in Ayrshire, one of the homesteads of Macmillan's ancestors. He had also undertaken several royal commissions between the wars in Canada. Duncan was to alternate between two of the central planning departments, Trade and Supply, with their overlapping functions, throughout the war. On 29 June 1941, in a further reshuffle following Germany's invasion of Russia, he moved back for a second spell at the Board of Trade.

The German launch of BARBAROSSA, the codename for their invasion, meant that the Ministry of Supply was now responsible, in addition to its domestic military priorities, for supplying vast quantities of materials for the Russian campaign against Hitler. Churchill felt that more dynamic leadership was required. Although Duncan was a thorough and well-organised minister, he did not possess the drive the times demanded, nor the seniority, though his managerial skills were considerable. Churchill replaced him at Supply with Lord Beaverbrook,[27] Duncan's opposite in both respects.

'The general view,' wrote Cuthbert Headlam in his diary, 'is that he [Beaverbrook] may be all right at the Min. of Supply for a few weeks in order to bother people out of their inertia, but that it would be fatal to leave him there for any length of time as he has not an idea of organization.'[28]

Headlam was not the only one to have doubts. In a series of letters to her mother, Dorothy kept Chatsworth up to date with all the latest gossip:

I expect Beaverbrook will do some good but probably a good deal of harm as well. Being a crook he of course collects crooks around him. H. says the Ministry has become a mixture of a circus & a lunatic asylum. B. is absolutely unscrupulous. Most of the criticism of the Ministry of Supply in the House of Commons & Press is reputed to be engendered and paid for by Beaverbrook ... Harold keeps on saying he'll have to give up but I think he'd better try & survive a bit longer. I don't feel B. will last very long but of course he's only one of many but still he's the worst & most dangerous. Anyway he gets such bad asthma in the winter he'll probably have to give up.[29]

Beaverbrook divided opinion. Some, such as Attlee, had no time for him at all, but he appealed to those who had an unconventional approach, and who were not averse to cutting corners, from Churchill downwards. Beaverbrook was the first prima donna with whom Macmillan had worked. He found him a demanding, but generous chief, and always received great kindness from him.*

As Macmillan was also working simultaneously for Ernest Bevin,[30] the Minister of Labour, in his role as Chairman of the Industrial Capacity Committee, he soon found himself called upon to keep the peace between the two super-egos. The rows between Bevin and Beaverbrook contributed to an uneasy atmosphere in both departments. On one occasion Bevin complained to the Ministry of Supply that Beaverbrook, a fellow member of the Cabinet, had failed to attend various planning meetings. Macmillan explained, in a none too conciliatory fashion. 'He [Beaverbrook] does not attend the Production Executive because he says at two meetings on July 9th [1941] & September 2nd you shouted him down,' he wrote to Bevin on 15 November. 'He suffers from asthma and, in a shouting contest, he is bound to come off worst.'[31]

In the end it became clear that some form of central control of supply was necessary to end departmental rivalries. Macmillan produced another of his many memoranda, outlining the logistical requirements for a new department. 'A Production Ministry (to include Labour) is absolutely necessary,' he wrote to Beaverbrook on 28 October 1941. 'It is a political necessity. Dark days lie before us; the House of Commons & the nation are dissatisfied with the present production arrangements.'[32] Beaverbrook was attracted by the idea and recommended it to Churchill. Within months, a Ministry of Production was established.

As both Beaverbrook and Portal were in the Lords, Macmillan had enjoyed considerable autonomy in the Commons, where he was the sole spokesman for the Ministry of Supply. He had seen one of his vital tasks as keeping Beaverbrook and Portal in touch with back-bench feeling, much of it critical. When Beaverbrook left the Ministry

---

*This even extended to Macmillan's time as Prime Minister, when entry into the Common Market was his main strategy for Britain's post-Imperial role. Beaverbrook was in the opposite camp, fanatically so, but no personal attacks on Macmillan were allowed in his *Daily Express*.

of Supply in February 1942 to head up the newly created Ministry of Production, Macmillan had expectations that he himself might be promoted to Beaverbrook's place. However, the situation was not so straightforward. Further arguments with Bevin over the exact relationship between the Ministries of Labour and Production led to Beaverbrook's resignation from the latter department after only 12 days in office. He then left the government to campaign energetically for a Second Front. This prompted yet another reshuffle, in which Macmillan was moved to the Colonial Office, becoming Under-Secretary on 5 February 1942. Although this was a promotion of sorts, he had harboured hopes of his own department. Compensation came in the form of a Privy Councillorship, an unusual honour for a junior minister. From now on he was the Rt Hon. Harold Macmillan.

The Privy Councillorship was a sign of Churchill's regard. Churchill remembered Macmillan's time in his 'group', in the last days of peace, as being more vigorous than that of the Edenites, the Glamour Boys, whom he regarded as over-polite and gracious. Macmillan had shown a determined political drive, often with a disregard for the hierarchies, and was not always gentlemanly in execution. War was not a time for the niceties. Macmillan was willing to say things that needed saying. Churchill admired this trait and increasingly saw Macmillan as a kindred spirit.

Macmillan's spell at the Ministry of Supply from May 1940 to February 1942 had been a formative executive experience. The ministry was ideally suited for one who was committed to planning. During his time there, he had helped transform it into an organised department with immense responsibilities for the war effort and for civilian provision. The War Production Department had been hived off from the old Board of Trade, and given control over raw materials needed for both military and civilian purposes, opportunities that Macmillan seized upon. The ministry was given plenipotentiary wartime powers over factories and labour regulations. It was the classic nuts-and-bolts department, dealing with practical issues, such as ordnance factories and defence funding. Macmillan had even taken over the national survey of iron gates and railings in September 1941, requisitioning material for the war effort.[33] Beaverbrook was impressed with Macmillan's industry and vision. When it became clear that he could not take Macmillan with him to the new Ministry of Production, he recommended to Churchill that the Colonial Office might be a broader canvas for his talents.

Unlike Beaverbrook, Macmillan built up a good working relationship with Ernest Bevin, liaising with him on a wide range of issues, including the register of reserved occupations. In his visits to Tyneside and Teesside Macmillan was relieved to hear from businessmen in his own constituency that the Ministry of Supply had build up a reputation for prompter payment of accounts than either the Admiralty or the Ministry of Aircraft Production. As a businessman himself, he understood the intricacies of balance sheets and knew the importance of predicated cash flow. Macmillan could look back on his spell at the ministry with much satisfaction. One of his hopes, to be fulfilled, was that he would one day work again with Oliver Franks.

Macmillan's transfer to the Colonial Office, where his first chief was Lord Moyne,[36] came at a crucial stage of the war. Within days of his appointment news came, on 15 February 1942, of the unconditional surrender of Singapore and its garrison to the Japanese. Churchill was at a low point. He had already faced a vote of confidence in the House on the conduct of the war on 29 January. Although he had won this by 464 votes to 1, the fact that there had been a debate at all was a sign of underlying malaise. Beaverbrook's departure from the government was also a great sadness to Churchill and necessitated a government reshuffle in which Churchill's main task was to accommodate Sir Stafford Cripps, recently returned from his mission to Moscow.[35] As Cripps was regarded as the man who had brought Russia into the war, in some parliamentary circles he was even increasingly spoken of as a replacement for Churchill himself.

Cripps refused the Ministry of Supply, and was eventually appointed Lord Privy Seal and Leader of the House of Commons. The reshuffle brought a new chief to the Colonial Office, Bobbety Cranborne. For Macmillan this appointment had a piquancy. Macmillan's previous boss, Moyne, was of an older generation; but Cranborne, already twice a Cabinet Minister, was his contemporary, and now Leader of the House of Lords in addition. Personally, things could not have been more congenial. Bobbety Cranborne and Harold Macmillan were married to Cavendish daughters, and to add to the family connection, Maurice Macmillan was to marry Katie Ormsby-Gore, Cranborne's niece, in the summer.*

'It is very pleasant to be working with Bobbety; as you can imagine, a charming chief in every way,' Macmillan wrote to his mother-in-law, Evie. 'Indeed I am becoming quite respectable again!'[37] Pleasant though

---

*The close-knit family links at these high echelons of government were such that some MPs commented that the only member of Churchill's family not to be given office was the popular entertainer Vic Oliver.[36]

it was to be working with Cranborne, one of his fellow Guardsmen, there was no disguising the fact that politically Macmillan was being overtaken by his contemporaries, and even juniors. Respectability was not the same as full responsibility, and it irked him. Rab Butler was well ensconced in the Cabinet in his great work at the Board of Education. Cranborne was Macmillan's boss. Oliver Lyttelton was a member of the War Cabinet and Minister Resident in Cairo. Harry Crookshank, though mistrusted by Churchill, had received various offers of promotion from his post as Financial Secretary to the Treasury. Crookshank had even turned down the post of Minister Resident in Africa, which later was to make Macmillan's name. Yet Macmillan's time was nigh. Cranborne, Lyttelton and Crookshank were all to have their disagreements with Churchill in the next few months. In Cranborne's case there was also a damaging dispute with Beaverbrook over the High Commissioner in Canada, whom Cranborne refused to sack, as Churchill had wanted to appease Beaverbrook's wounded sensibilities following Canadian criticisms.

When Macmillan became Under-Secretary at the Colonial Office, the department oversaw 55 separate colonies, the same scale as in the days when Victor Devonshire, his father-in-law, had been Colonial Secretary in Bonar Law's government.[38] As Bobbety Cranborne had been elevated to the Lords as Baron Cecil of Essendon in January 1941, Macmillan still enjoyed considerable autonomy in the Commons.[39] John Wyndham was also again at hand to offer emotional support. Wyndham was indispensable in other ways also, securing in a deft manoeuvre the elegant Dover House, once Lord Melbourne's London residence, and recently vacated by the Scottish Office, as the Colonial Office's new headquarters. Macmillan's move from Shell Mex House, the headquarters of the Ministry of Supply, to Dover House, and the great Victorian conurbation of Foreign Office buildings at the heart of Whitehall, may have been a short one geographically, but its psychological importance was far greater.

Macmillan's first weeks in his new department were accompanied by further news of almost unrelieved gloom. After the loss of Singapore, the next major reversal was the fall of Tobruk in North Africa in June 1942. Hong Kong, Malaya, Borneo and parts of Burma also fell, with their rich supplies of tin, rubber and other resources. There were renewed fears for the futures of both Ceylon and India. The central task for the Colonial Office was to mobilise what resources there were, both in manpower and commodities, to bolster the war effort, and to help reverse these potentially fatal defeats.

However bad the news from the Far East, there remained the hope that America would come into the war. As Churchill had declared in his wireless broadcast of 27 April 1941, 'Westward, look the land is bright.'[40] Such optimism had come on the back of Lend-Lease, which Roosevelt had approved on 11 March 1941. On 22 June 1941, Hitler invaded Russia, and on 7 December, the Japanese attacked Pearl Harbour. America and Britain declared war on Japan. Germany's reaction was to declare war on America. Ultimate victory, however long it might take, was now in essence assured. Indeed, Churchill's first reaction on hearing at Chequers the news of Pearl Harbour had been, 'So we had won after all.'[41]

Macmillan was given his sideways promotion not because of his knowledge of the colonies, though of course he had valuable experience of the Dominion of Canada,[42] but because Beaverbrook had been impressed by his executive potential. He had always been a great reader. He now set about learning his new responsibilities. On arrival at the Colonial Office, he undertook a massive programme of self-education, by studying in detail the work of W. K. Hancock, 'the pre-eminent historian of the British Empire', and Margery Perham, 'the embodiment of the British Colonial conscience'.[43] He also renewed acquaintance with Sir George Gater,[44] who had been at the Ministry of Supply in Morrison's day, and who was now the Permanent Secretary at the Colonial Office. For Macmillan, Gater was in the Oliver Franks class, combining the best qualities of the Civil Service – anonymity, continuity and, notwithstanding his Labour sympathies, impartiality. He was also industrious and organised, and this suited Macmillan. In one of his first letters to Gater, Macmillan outlined his own method of working. 'Being a methodical person,' he wrote, 'I like to have records.'[45] As was now proving his custom on arriving in a new department, he submitted a far-reaching memorandum to Gater, concentrating on colonial production, in September 1942. In the same month he noted privately that he had now been working continuously since May 1940 without a holiday.[46]

Nevertheless, he was gaining a new confidence in the House – the speech in the Finland Debate had been a precursor – and made successful contributions to several debates on Colonial questions. No longer were people making for the bars and tea rooms, as they had done when he had listed economic statistics as a pre-war back-bencher. In a debate on 24 June on the future of the Colonies, he outlined what were to become post-war preoccupations. 'They [the Colonies] are four or five centuries behind. Our job is to move them, to hustle them, across this great interval of time as rapidly as we can,' he declared. 'The governing principle of the Colonial Empire should be the principle of partnership between the various elements comprising it. Out of partnership come understanding and friendship. Within the fabric of the Commonwealth lies the future of the Colonial territories.'[47]

Liaison between the Ministry of Production, that department of troubled birth, and the Ministry of Supply was now very much Macmillan's responsibility, as well as heading the Economic Department of the Colonial Office. French interests, with their colonial territories in Africa, were always a potential diplomatic difficulty. First meetings with Charles de Gaulle left Macmillan in little doubt as to how serious these difficulties could be.

Macmillan also soon became aware that progressive figures in Whitehall had a built-in suspicion about the Colonial Office, redolent as it seemed to many of past and outmoded attitudes. John Foster Dulles, the future American Secretary of State, had told the Colonial Office in July 1942 that 'deeply embedded in the mind of most Americans was a fundamental distrust of what they called "British Imperialism"'.[48] Macmillan understood this.

In 1923, his father-in-law, when Colonial Secretary, had issued the Devonshire Declaration, which had asserted that the rights of the native population should be paramount over those of the immigrant settlers in Kenya. The long-term implication of this statement, vigorously contested at the time, was some form of African autonomy. The issue had lain dormant, but in July 1942, Sir George Gater was presented with a paper by Sir Arthur Dawes, advocating a solution that would be acceptable to the white settlers. Macmillan was soon in the field with a memorandum. 'The Whites cannot afford economically to abandon their supremacy,' he prophesied. 'The Government will be torn between the rights of the settlers and their obligations to the natives.'[49] Memories of his 1932 visit to Russia led Macmillan to suggest some form of collective farming, which could release capital for the settlers and satisfy native demands. For the Colonial Office in 1942, this was a radical agenda, one to which, in a broader context, Macmillan was famously to return with his Cape Town speech on 3 February 1960 on 'this growth of national consciousness'.

One incident above all convinced Macmillan at this time that attiudes would have to change. General Orde Wingate, leader of the legendary 'Chindits', sought a meeting with Cranborne to give him first-hand information on the critical situation in Burma. 'I have had two talks with him, and found him very interesting,' Macmillan had written to the relevant civil servant. Yet bureaucratic muddle delayed the meeting. Macmillan was furious. 'If we get Colonel Wingate[50] against us as well as everybody else it will simply add to the view that we are a hidebound, obsolete, obscurant, incompetent office, grimly holding on to power with feeble, ageing, withered, trembling hands,' he minuted. 'This is a little exaggerated, but you will see the point.'[51]

As he became more accustomed to the Whitehall style, Macmillan was already showing signs of his later impishness. He did not see why Sir George Gater, and he, should battle with the Underground and buses, after 14-hour days in Whitehall. The Permanent Secretary of the Foreign Office, and the equivalent Under-Secretary, had access to the government car pool. On 4 June (for an Etonian, the better the day, the better the deed), he wrote to the relevant official. 'Whatever may be said of Colonial Policy during the last ten years, it has not been such a conspicuous failure as the conduct of our foreign affairs. Therefore why should they have a car and not us?'[52] The Treasury failed to see the logic of his argument.

The autumn of 1942 was to see the main focus of the war shift to North Africa. Lieutenant-General Harold Alexander,[53] Commander-in-Chief, Middle East, and Major-General Bernard Montgomery,[54] Commander of the Eighth Army, after Churchill had sacked General Auchinleck,[55] were to prove the key figures on the British side.[56] The battle of Alam Halfa, one of the great defensive operations, matching that of the Marne in September 1914 in long-term significance, and the second battle of El Alamein, where Rommel's hitherto invincible forces were defeated, was famously 'not the end' for Churchill. 'It is not even the beginning of the end,' he declared. 'But it is, perhaps, the end of the beginning.'[57] Not the least of its effects was to persuade the French to co-operate in the North African campaign, which now gained new impetus.

Eisenhower, all too often underestimated as a political strategist (as the British were to find to their cost at Suez in 1956), knew that North Africa was not only a military problem. The political nuances were to prove more complex. Allied Forces Headquarters in Algiers (AFHQ) was in urgent need of diplomatic reinforcement. Initially, Churchill and Eden even considered sending the Permanent Under-Secretary at the Foreign Office, Sir Alexander Cadogan, to this sensitive trouble spot. Roosevelt would only agree to such an appointment under unacceptably restrictive conditions. On 17 November, a new idea was submitted by the Foreign Office to Washington. Churchill would appoint a Minister Resident in North Africa, equivalent to the Minister Resident in Cairo. This minister would be the link between the military and the War Cabinet in London, indeed would have 'Cabinet rank'. On 19 November, Roosevelt suggested a joint American-British residency, which 'would be given authority not to administer civil functions but to hold a veto over French administrations, and to direct them in rare instances to follow certain policies'.[58] Roosevelt's candidate for the post was Robert Murphy, America's Resident Minister in North Africa since 1941. Although Roosevelt's choice was not welcome in London (Murphy was seen as being as enthusiastic for Vichy France as he was unenthusiastic about de Gaulle, and Britain), if Churchill wished to go ahead with strengthening political representation in what was becoming an increasingly vital theatre of war, he had little choice but to comply. It only remained for him to nominate his own candidate. A unified political approach was going to be vital for future developments.

Accordingly, in December 1942 Churchill made further government changes. These were necessitated not only by the situation in North Africa, but also by Stafford Cripps's resignation from the War Cabinet, and Oliver Stanley's return from military service. Stanley,[59] one of Macmillan's closest friends, was frequently spoken of as a future Conservative leader. At the beginning of the war he had declined Churchill's offer of Dominions Secretary and had returned to military service, an action reminiscent of Churchill's own decisions during the Great War. Puzzlingly for many, this had not received recognition from Churchill. On 18 November 1942, Stanley had drawn up a petition of 150 back-benchers, complaining to Churchill that their views had been ignored. Churchill's response was the time-honoured one of bringing troublemakers into the tent, where they could do less damage. On 22 November he appointed Stanley Colonial Secretary and persuaded Cripps to take on the Ministry of Aircraft Production. Eden became Leader of the House of Commons, in addition to his already considerable responsibilities as Foreign Secretary. Cranborne replaced Cripps as Lord Privy Seal Herbert Morrison entered the War Cabinet, alongside Attlee and Bevin.

The most consequential of these changes for Macmillan was the arrival of Oliver Stanley at the Colonial Office. For a junior minister Macmillan had enjoyed considerable freedom and prominence in the House of Commons under three chiefs from the Upper House: Beaverbrook, Moyne and Cranborne. Now, albeit fortuitously but not by intention, his position would be subtly reduced. The next few days were to prove crucial. Macmillan was tempted to retire from the fray, even storm out in a huff. Wiser counsels prevailed. He went to see Churchill, but only after consulting with Brendan Bracken,[60] intimate of Churchill's circle, who advised him to let things take their course. Although Bracken did not tell Macmillan so, he had advance knowledge of the way Churchill's mind was working on the forthcoming North African appointment, so the advice was both timely and career-saving. Minister residencies were now very much part of Churchill's wartime strategy for the government machine.

Much press speculation on Macmillan's next posting appeared at this time, itself a sign of his growing importance, as was the curious episode of the supposed peerage. On 2 December 1942, the *Glasgow Herald* asserted confidently that, with Oliver Stanley in the Commons, Macmillan was about to be moved to the Upper House, as the Colonial Office now needed a representative in the Lords. Macmillan, the paper stated, 'has proved a most efficient representative in the Commons'.[61] Macmillan knew that to be made a peer at this stage would limit his growing political ambitions, and he wrote, somewhat agitatedly, to the department's legal adviser, Sir Kenneth Poyser. 'Can I issue a writ?' he asked. 'It certainly holds me up to ridicule and contempt.'[62] Poyser wittily defused Macmillan's worries, saying that in Queen Victoria's time any such speculation always brought a royal veto, as the Queen refused to have peerages decided by the press.

Meanwhile, Churchill was corresponding further with Roosevelt about his choice of British minister to serve alongside Robert Murphy at AFHQ. 'I would choose an under-secretary of administrative experience whom Eisenhower might be expected to find sympathetic,' he told Roosevelt. 'For your personal information I had Harold Macmillan in mind.'[63]

On 22 December, Macmillan was summoned to Downing Street. It was one of the turning points of his life. Churchill outlined the complex situation obtaining in North Africa. Macmillan's importance, he emphasised, would lie in the relationship he could build up with Eisenhower. The two men discussed details. Churchill told Macmillan he would retain his seat in the House of Commons, so could return to the British political scene whenever his mission was over. John Wyndham could go with him. Such was the offer.

Churchill was accustomed to ministers – from Cripps to Crookshank – turning down offers he had carefully thought through. Now it was up to Macmillan. He could take time to decide if he wished. Macmillan said there was no need. He accepted the offer at once. As he said later, it was 'the big stuff'.

The years from 1940–1943 might have seemed a relative backwater in Macmillan's career, compared to the rebelliousness of the 1930s and the responsibilities that lay ahead, but they had laid the foundation for all that was to follow. Macmillan had learned much about the political and executive process from his first-hand observation of Beaverbrook, not least in Beaverbrook's clashes with Ernest Bevin. He had learned never to underestimate the importance of personal chemistry in the building of effective partnerships in government, nor the importance of what later became known as public relations. He welcomed the involvement of experts, from Sir George Gater to Percy Mills. He knew that attention to detail was the key to long-term strategical success. Persistence, patience and the long haul were also essential components.

Macmillan was clever at asking for, and taking, advice. At crossroads in his life, he had made the correct decisions, acting on wise counsel from Philip Frere about coming to an accommodation with Dorothy that excluded divorce and saved his political career; from Bob Boothby about not joining Mosley's New Party; and from Brendan Bracken about trusting Churchill eventually to make up his own mind.

In all important careers a moment arrives – 'the tide of fortune' – which, if taken, can lead on to even greater things. In March 1939 when criticised for his 'revolutionary' views, Macmillan had replied, 'You may hear that I am a bit of a "Bolshie" and sometimes make myself a nuisance in the House. Frankly, I feel it is a role that must be played by someone in the party.'[64] He was now being called upon to play a different role, and one that was to propel him firmly on to the world stage with all its attendant controversies.

As Macmillan prepared to travel to North Africa, Churchill telegraphed Roosevelt. 'He will be, I am sure, a help. He is animated by the friendliest feelings towards the United States, and his mother hails from Kentucky.'[65] Nellie had gained posthumous international mention.

CHAPTER TEN

At One Strategic Point

1942–1943

At last the armies clashed at one strategic point,
They slammed their shields together, pike scraped pike
With the grappling strength of fighters armed in bronze
And their round shields pounded, boss on welded boss,
And the sound of struggle roared and rocked the earth.

Homer, *The Iliad*, Book 4

The French want no-one to be their *superior*. The English want *inferiors*. The Frenchman constantly raises his eyes above him with anxiety. The Englishman lowers his beneath him with satisfaction. On either side it is pride, but understood in a different way.

Alexis de Tocqueville

So much bunker and not enough fairway.

Harold Macmillan, on the view from his
plane over North Africa

Macmillan's mission in North Africa was one of the strangest, yet most important, of his life. Here was a middle-ranking politician, suddenly projected on to the world stage, where Roosevelt, Churchill and General Dwight D. Eisenhower[1] were making decisions that ranked among the most significant of the twentieth century. How could he be accepted as a participant, let alone an equal, in such company? It was a sign of Macmillan's growing self-confidence that the question never really exercised him. He had been given a job by Churchill and he was going to do it.

Macmillan's first decision, before leaving Britain, was not to wear uniform. 'Among all those generals, admirals and air marshals,' he told Churchill, 'an infantry captain, even in the Grenadier Guards, would not cut a very impressive figure.' Churchill reluctantly agreed. 'I see your point,' he replied. 'You mean that between the baton and the bowler there is no middle course.'[2] The remark summed up the essential ambiguity of Macmillan's status. If he was to make a success of his assignment as Minister Resident in North Africa, it would not be through any externals, but through efficiency, strength of character and the ability to work harmoniously within a disparate team of different nationalities and cultures.

Harold Macmillan landed at Gibraltar at noon on Friday, 1 January 1943. John Wyndham was the private secretary in attendance, together with two typists.[3] Shortly afterwards, his staff was to be augmented, first by Pierson Dixon, as his Foreign Office Chief of Staff, and later by Roger Makins.[4] Macmillan's appointment had made headline news. 'Some new Government appointments were announced yesterday,' Cuthbert Headlam wrote in his diary on New Year's Day, 1943. 'Harold Macmillan comes off best – he is to go to North Africa as our ministerial representative. He should do well if he has the guts to stand up to the Americans and is clever with the French.'[5] It was a fair assessment of the delicate task awaiting Macmillan, as he moved from the shadows to the world stage. During 1943, control of the Allied war effort would pass increasingly into American hands; as a result, Macmillan's responsibilities as an international go-between multiplied, especially as he gained the confidence of the leading Americans.

Macmillan's task was fourfold. His first was to oil the wheels of the Anglo-American relationship at Allied headquarters; second, to serve as an informal head to the British civilian officials in Algiers; and third, to act as the representative of His Majesty's Government, dealing with the French. In this, his most important function was to persuade American colleagues, both civilian and military, to accept British thinking and policy regarding the French, and the eventual elevation of de Gaulle into the position of a *de facto* prime minister of France's provisional government. His final responsibility, after the fall of Tunis, was to deal with Italian questions, including the Allied Military Government of Occupied Territories (AMGOT), as the Allied forces invaded Sicily and then pushed northwards through the Italian mainland. If, in addition, he could persuade the Commander-in-Chief, General Eisenhower, of the wisdom of the policy of His Majesty's Government in the course of fulfilling those responsibilities, then his mission could be accounted a success.

After a week in Algiers, Macmillan sent Sir John Anderson,[6] Lord President of the Council, his first impressions of life at Allied Forces Headquarters (AFHQ): 'At present I think it would be rather a mistake for me to have any military officer on my staff. My whole position here is a bit anomalous, but as long as I remain a civilian – a "frock" as Sir Henry Wilson[7] used to say – I think I can get through.

The Americans do not like politicians, but they understand that they are a kind of evil necessity of nature.'[8]

His main task was to liaise at the highest level between the American and British forces in the combined Allied Command, and the first subject of friction was de Gaulle. For Macmillan, this proved a harsh baptism.

The history of France since the German occupation was complex, controversial and, to many, shameful. In June 1940, after the occupation of France, the National Assembly had reconvened in Vichy in the unoccupied zone under the premiership of Marshal Pétain. The Americans recognised the Vichy government from the outset,[9] a stance deplored in London, for whom Vichy was collaborationist. To Churchill's intense fury, Admiral François Darlan, head of the French navy, who had supported France's armistice with the Germans in 1940, did not cede French warships to the Allies. On 3 July 1940, the British, fearful lest the warships might be used against them, sank part of the French fleet at Oran in North Africa. This act made Darlan's Anglophobia even worse. Meanwhile, General de Gaulle had established the 'French National Committee' (the 'Free French') in London, declaring Vichy 'null and void'. For Pétain, de Gaulle was thus a dissident rebel. Nor did the Americans trust de Gaulle. They did not even tell him of the TORCH landings, the combined Anglo-American landings in French Morocco and Algeria, until their eve. The Americans invested their hopes in General Giraud, an anti-German Pétainist. From 1940 the British supported de Gaulle's Free French in exile, though matters were complicated by Churchill's growing personal hostility towards de Gaulle, who, he thought, showed 'many of the symptoms of a budding Führer'.[10] This, of course, was one of the reasons why the Americans were suspicious of de Gaulle. Yet Giraud also proved a disappointment to the Americans, as he was unable to rally the French in North Africa, who remained loyal to Vichy. Following El Alamein, Operation TORCH was launched on 8 November 1942, under the command of Lieutenant-General Dwight D. Eisenhower.[11] Roosevelt's administration had kept links with Vichy France and Marshal Pétain.[12] Admiral Darlan,[13] Vice-Premier in the Vichy Government, and its Foreign Minister, was in Algiers, visiting his sick son, when the TORCH operation was launched. The situation proved the catalyst for a spectacular *volte-face* by Darlan. Acting as intermediary between his own government and the American General Mark Clark, he brokered a general ceasefire on 10 November. He then decided to work for the Allies and was appointed High Commissioner for French North Africa. It was said that he had thus simultaneously betrayed Germany, Pétain and France. Roosevelt was unabashed. 'Darlan gave me Algiers, long live Darlan!' he declared. 'If Laval gives me Paris, long live Laval. I am not like [President] Wilson, I am a realist.'[14] Eisenhower had shown political realism, and the deal with Darlan had been motivated by expediency. However, it did leave open the question of who now controlled France: the Vichy regime? Darlan from North Africa? Or de Gaulle, leader of the Free French in London? Only events would tell.

On Christmas Eve 1942, Darlan was assassinated by a young French royalist. The motives remain a matter of contention, and the British may have been involved, as was asserted by the Axis at the time.[15] Eden, the British Foreign Secretary, who had been appalled by the deal with Darlan, wrote in his diary, 'I have not felt so relieved by any event for many years.'[16] On Roosevelt's instructions, Darlan was replaced by General Giraud, who, whatever else he may have been, had never been a collaborator. This brought into higher focus the battle between Giraud and de Gaulle over which of them would take power in France after the war. In this, Macmillan was a committed Gaullist.

Macmillan arrived in North Africa shortly after Darlan's murder. He was briefed by Sir Henry ('Hal') Mack,[17] formerly Head of the French Department in the Foreign Office, who had been on Eisenhower's staff throughout preparation for the TORCH landings. Afterwards, Macmillan met Eisenhower for the first time, at 4 p.m. on Saturday, 2 January at the Allied Forces Headquarters in the Hôtel St Georges in Algiers. 'Considering that neither Washington or London had informed him of my appointment (which one of his staff heard by chance on the radio),' Macmillan wrote home to Dorothy, 'the interview was quite a success.'[18] It did not seem so at the outset. Eisenhower bluntly asked Macmillan who he was, and what he was going to do. Macmillan explained that he was to liaise between AFHQ and Churchill, but at present was not *au fait* with all the political problems. Eisenhower told him that he would have plenty to learn. In any case, Eisenhower said, Hal Mack was a wholly satisfactory liaison officer. Seeking some kind of common ground, as the interview began to wind down dishearteningly, Macmillan asked Eisenhower if he knew his mother's home state. Eisenhower, thinking Macmillan meant an English county, did not see how he could possibly be expected to know it. Macmillan then explained that his mother had been born in the town of Spencer in Indiana.[19] From that moment the tone of the meeting changed. Even though Eisenhower did not treat Macmillan as an equal, even as a British minister of Cabinet rank, he thereafter regarded him as a kinsman. Eisenhower's overriding priority was to drive the Germans out of North Africa. Macmillan was at once struck by his determination.

Allied Forces Headquarters had been formed in 1942 as Eisenhower's headquarters for the North African campaigns, including TORCH. After TORCH it became the headquarters of the Supreme Allied Commander in the Mediterranean. From November 1942 it was based in Algiers, and moved to Caserta in Italy in July 1944, by which time Macmillan was involved in his second great task of the war, ensuring the transfer of power from the Allied forces pushing their way north to Rome to a government in Italy that was pro-Allied. The importance of AFHQ lay in the fact that it was the first Allied inter-service head-quarters staffed equally by British and American personnel. It was the prototype for the Supreme Headquarters Allied Expeditionary Force (SHAEF), from February 1944, which controlled the Allied invasion forces in north-west Europe.

The next day Macmillan met General Giraud for the first time. Giraud was now the French High Commissioner for North and West Africa, in the Palais d'Été, a residence to match the grandeur of his title. It was clear what high hopes the Americans had invested in Giraud; Macmillan was not to share them. He did not doubt Giraud's bravery – he heard at first hand, as many did, of his service in two wars, including his escape from a prisoner of war camp – but felt that politically he did not possess the skills to solve the many problems ahead. It was clear that any meeting between Giraud and de Gaulle would be fraught with difficulty.

Macmillan's domestic arrangements were not on the level of Giraud's *palais*. Indeed, to begin with, the harshness of the conditions he experienced with John Wyndham and the two secretaries reminded Macmillan of his time in the Great War. All of them had gone down with colds and were suffering from the after-effects of typhoid injec-tions. The first task for John Wyndham was to find more suitable accommodation. Initially, this was in the Hôtel Aletti, still suffer-ing from the deprivations of war. Such things did not easily defeat Wyndham, and within the week, Macmillan's party was installed in a villa that put him on a par with Admiral Cunningham,[20] Commander-in-Chief in the Mediterranean.

Macmillan gradually became acquainted, usually on terms of warm personal friendship, with some of the most significant figures in the war. He soon got to know the individual predilections of the vari-ous participants in the complex meetings and conferences. An early revelation was that Admiral Cunningham could not stand de Gaulle, though that hardly put him in a unique category. Initially, Macmillan found that the Americans were sceptical of his own presence, so he took particular pains to establish fruitful relationships with those close to Eisenhower. He quickly built a rapport with Lieutenant General Walter Bedell Smith,[21] Eisenhower's chief of staff, who controlled access to the great man, and with Robert Murphy,[22] a career American diplomat, who was Macmillan's direct opposite number as the US representative in North Africa. Macmillan treated Murphy with complete openness throughout their 20 months together. He showed Murphy his telegrams – they flowed from the Foreign Office in a manner quite new in Murphy's experience – and was frank in discussing difficulties.

The Casablanca Conference (codenamed SYMBOL) was held at Anfa, a suburb of Casablanca, from 14 to 23 January 1943. John Wyndham, a keen observer, thought it a utility version of the sixteenth-century meeting at the Field of the Cloth of Gold.[23] It could also have been a scene from *Antony and Cleopatra*, where the triple pillars of the world met in the Mediterranean to decide the fate of empires. Stalin ('The Red Emperor', as Macmillan dubbed him) was invited, but owing to the precarious nature of the Battle of Stalingrad felt he could not leave Russia. On the American side were President Roosevelt, who arrived at 6.20 p.m. on 14 January, after an arduous five-day journey from Washington, together with his four joint chiefs of staff; Generals Dwight D. Eisenhower and Mark Clark, with all their senior advisers; and two key civilians, Averell Harriman[24] and Harry Hopkins.[25] On the British side, Churchill brought the three chiefs of staff, Sir Alan Brooke, Sir Dudley Pound and Sir Charles Portal,[26] together with, among others, Lieutenant General Pug Ismay, Sir John Dill, Lord Louis Mountbatten, Air Marshal Sir Arthur Tedder,[27] Admiral Sir Andrew Cunningham, Major-General Sir John Kennedy[28] – and Harold Macmillan.

A photograph of the British delegation at Casablanca shows Macmillan, in pinstripe suit, in earnest conversation with Leslie Rowan,[29] one of Churchill's secretariat. This period in Macmillan's life has been characterised as 'years of being the pinky-faced moustache with glasses, on the edge of the photographs of the famous meetings of the great'.[30] Not that this perception would have worried Macmillan; he was at least in the photographs, learning all the time, and laying foundations for his later career.

For Macmillan who, 12 months earlier, had been occupying a minor post in the Colonial Office, sending out memoranda about the

Yeast Company of Jamaica, the opportunities in North Africa were an extraordinary transformation. He may not have been an Octavius Caesar, but he could lay fair claim to being a Maecenas or an Agrippa. Although 'The Red Emperor' was not present, the other two emperors were, and Macmillan dubbed Roosevelt 'The Emperor of the West', and Churchill 'The Emperor of the East'. When Eisenhower paid court to Roosevelt, Macmillan said to Bob Murphy, 'Isn't he just like a Roman centurion?'[31] The classical analogy famously went further. To Dick Crossman,[32] Director of Psychological Warfare at AFHQ, he said: 'We, my dear Crossman, are Greeks in this American empire. You will find the Americans much as the Greeks found the Romans – great big vulgar, bustling people, more vigorous than we are and also more idle, with more unspoiled virtues, but also more corrupt. We must run A.F.H.Q. as the Greeks ran the operations of the Emperor Claudius.'[33]

'Not even the Prime Minister in Britain enjoyed quite such unquestioned prestige as Harold Macmillan had earned for himself both in his own British staff and Ike's entourage,' Crossman recalled in 1964. 'I suspect it was in Algiers, where he could do all the thinking and take all the decisions while Ike took all the credit, that Harold Macmillan first realised his own capacity for supreme leadership and developed that streak of intellectual recklessness which was to be the cause both of his success and of his failure when he finally reached No. 10.'[34]

Macmillan's role at Casablanca, and that of Bob Murphy, was enhanced by the fact that neither of the two Foreign Ministers, Anthony Eden and Cordell Hull,[35] was present. Eisenhower, who had initially been dismissive about Macmillan, was surprised to find how well known he was to the President. 'Hallo, Harold, it is fine to see you – fine' was Roosevelt's initial greeting. He was also clearly one of Churchill's inner circle. What Eisenhower did not know was that such friendly intimacy stemmed from the fact that Macmillan in the past had published both Roosevelt and Churchill. Eisenhower soon came to admire Macmillan for his political efficiency. It also helped that, unlike many of Eisenhower's staff, he could converse in French. The press conference Macmillan had held in Algiers on the eve of SYMBOL greatly impressed Eisenhower, and also the manner in which Macmillan and Murphy had swiftly moved to remove the Comte de Paris, a possible focus for French monarchists, from North African territory.

SYMBOL had two main aims: first, to review progress in North Africa; and second, to chart the Allied course for the remainder of the war after the Germans had been driven out of Africa. Macmillan found the atmosphere fascinating, an invigorating blend of the formal and informal, part conference, part holiday. Notices were placed daily, outlining the timetable, a throwback to school days. When the military high command were 'let out of school' at 5 p.m., they went down to the beach and relaxed by making sandcastles. As Macmillan's responsibilities were on the political side, he regretted he could not join in. For one used to the rationing of wartime Britain, the profusion of oranges, still attached to their leaves, was the height of luxury, as were the American-style cocktails before vast dinners.

The goodwill that Macmillan discerned among the American and British participants was not reciprocated by de Gaulle and Giraud. As Macmillan's main responsibility was to establish which of the two would be most likely to be acceptable as sole French leader, this called upon all his reserves of tact and political skill. Wisely he had endeared himself to the Americans, and especially Bob Murphy, by making sure they felt they were in charge and that all the best ideas were really theirs, a technique he had already found profitable in his Ministry of Supply days. As the Americans loathed de Gaulle; and as de Gaulle was the favoured British candidate for the sole French leadership, this posed seemingly intractable problems, not least because de Gaulle was ever-conscious that Casablanca, their meeting place, was French territory.

When de Gaulle arrived on 22 January, he was installed in a villa, in conditions that he thought amounted to house arrest. For the next two days Macmillan visited him on several occasions. Working closely with Murphy, Macmillan now engineered the event for which the Casablanca Conference is best remembered – the Giraud-de Gaulle handshake on 24 January, which Macmillan described as a shotgun wedding, and one that he had doubted would ever come to the altar.[36] From this handshake came eventually, and through many tortuous moments, the formation of the Comité Français De Libération Nationale (FCNL) in Algiers in June 1943 under the joint chairmanship of Giraud and de Gaulle. Eventually, in August 1944, de Gaulle was established as the head of the GPRF (Gouvernement Provisoire de la Républic Français), because of his demonstrably greater political skills.

So ended the Casablanca Conference, a striking baptism for Macmillan in the intricacies of international diplomacy. Much of the ground for the later conduct of the war had been established. The invasion of Sicily was authorised, and the decision taken to transfer British Military forces to the Far East when Italy and Germany had been defeated. More controversially, the Allied policy of unconditional, and not negotiated, surrender was announced. The decision was also taken to launch a Combined Bomber Offensive from Britain against Germany. Only the power struggle between de Gaulle and Giraud remained unresolved by SYMBOL.

Sir William Strang,[37] Assistant Under-Secretary at the Foreign Office, wrote an account to Anthony Eden on 20 February, in which he praised Macmillan's work. On the vexed question of American enthusiasm for Giraud, he noted approvingly that 'it now appears that Mr Macmillan is bringing Mr Murphy round'.[38] Later it transpired that Roosevelt had had secret meetings with Giraud, which resulted in the so-called 'Anfa' memorandum, seeming to establish the primacy of Giraud over de Gaulle.

Roosevelt's 'understanding' with Giraud was anathema to Macmillan, and he ensured that it did not survive Churchill's scrutiny. When Churchill received the relevant documents, he was furious, and delegated to Macmillan the responsibility of sorting out the difficulty. That Macmillan's growing friendship with Murphy survived the battle of wills between the Americans and the British over the 'understanding' said much for the mutual respect they showed each other in the inevitable controversies of military diplomacy. As one historian later commented, the whole North African experience unlocked 'Macmillan's natural talent for intrigue', as well as his 'intellectual capacity'.[39]

One of Macmillan's important contributions at Casablanca had been to impress upon a reluctant Churchill that de Gaulle would be the key not only to the North African situation, but also to Anglo-French relationships after the war. To have Giraud seemingly established as leader-in-waiting did not suit the British at all, and Macmillan's swift action in alerting the Foreign Office to the 'Anfa' memorandum was the first stage in unravelling a tricky diplomatic problem. Macmillan thereafter always watched Roosevelt like a hawk.

Churchill's next delicate task for Macmillan was to resolve the problem of 'Force X', part of the French fleet that had been immobilised in Alexandria harbour since June 1940. The contingent of a battleship, four cruisers and some smaller vessels was under the command of Vice-Admiral René Godfroy, who remained loyal to Marshal Pétain and Vichy. Macmillan's commission was to negotiate a return of these vessels to the Allies.

Shortly after midnight on 21 February, as a sudden sandstorm blew up, Macmillan set off from Algiers airport, accompanied by John Wyndham and Admiral Missoffe, together with the Admiral's flag lieutenant. He was seated in the front of the plane next to the

Australian pilot. Their small Hudson plane, with neither seats nor heating, failed to clear the runway, crashed in flames, and slid into a vineyard.[40]

During the Great War, Macmillan had only survived because a bullet had been deflected from his heart by a water bottle in his tunic. His second escape from a violent death was equally fortuitous. The pilot and his navigator scrambled through the emergency exit, and with difficulty Macmillan followed suit. What Macmillan does not mention in his memoirs is that he then re-entered the plane to rescue the French flag lieutenant. John J. McCloy, Roosevelt's Assistant Secretary of War, had landed at Algiers just as Macmillan's plane crashed. Hurrying to the crash site, McCloy witnessed Macmillan's actions. 'It was the most gallant thing I've ever seen,' he later recalled, 'and I'd been in the first war and seen plenty of gallantry then.'[41]

Roger Makins, who had dashed with McCloy to the crash site, was astonished that anyone had survived. Macmillan got out of the wreckage just before the plane exploded. His eyesight was only saved because he was wearing spectacles; his moustache burned a bright blue.

When he came round from his concussion, he was on a field stretcher, just as he had been at the Somme, and his first thought was to tell his mother that he had survived. She had been dead for seven years, but such was the powerful trauma that Macmillan dimly thought he was in the trenches again. The saying in the Grenadiers had been 'as brave as Macmillan', and this was once more the case.

Macmillan was the most severely wounded of the passengers and was taken to the Maison-Carrée Military hospital nearby. His face, nastily burned, was enclosed in plaster, broken only by a special breathing mask, and it was assumed that he would be invalided home. Many distinguished visitors called at the hospital, including – to the hospital staff's astonishment – Admiral Cunningham in full uniform.

Amazingly, considering the extent of his injuries, Macmillan was discharged and allowed to do some work in his villa. Bedell Smith and Tedder visited him there and brought him up to date with the latest developments. After a week, he felt well enough to resume the journey to Cairo to sort out the problem of 'Force X' and Admiral Godfroy. He told Churchill that he would eat his hat if his mission was not successful; he felt he was on safe ground with this wager, as his hat had already been burned in the crash.

To the many MPs who sent messages of concern and sympathy, Macmillan made light of the incident. 'My accident was only due to a technical mistake on the part of the crew, the result of which might have been much worse,' he wrote to Captain Alan Graham, MP for the Wirral. 'As it is, I got off with rather a severe burning of my face, but I was able to go on with my trip a week later though still in bandages.'[42] Macmillan later had a reputation for 'unflappability'. This was not accurate; but over the North African plane crash he certainly showed a remarkable insouciance.

On 28 February, Macmillan resumed his aborted journey, this time in a Liberator with fitted seats but no heating. Beaverbrook had told him to fly again as soon as possible, and Macmillan knew that this was the right thing to do. Still in pain from his wounds and burns, he was taken first to the Scottish Hospital in Cairo, where all his bandages were skilfully removed, his face treated and shaved. Everything was done to aid his swift recuperation. 'The rigours of the North African campaign are bad in Algiers; but they exist in only a very modified form in Cairo,' Macmillan wrote on 12 March 1943 to Hal Mack, who had enquired after his progress. 'I have never seen such luxury.'[43]

From Cairo, Macmillan went by train to Alexandria, where he had his first meeting with Admiral Godfroy. Macmillan, who knew that Godfroy felt he was being bullied on Churchill's orders, trod a careful path. Macmillan also realised that any attempt at seizing the 'Force X' ships could lead to a scuttling. He understood that the Allied successes in North Africa had subtly changed the mind-set of Godfroy and was rightly confident that an agreement could be reached. The episode revealed Macmillan's talent for diplomacy that William Strang felt so vital to any success, namely one based on hard work, patience, and an innate understanding of the special problems of the time. Macmillan showed these characteristics in abundance and Churchill was immensely grateful – most of the time.

However, Macmillan did not defer to Churchill in his North African job, and the telegrams are full of brusque exchanges. Alan Brooke always said that when the day came when he (Brooke) told Churchill he was right when he believed him to be wrong, it would be time for Churchill to get rid of him. Macmillan, who believed it was better to be unpalatable than untruthful, acted in a similarly independent fashion, which for a junior newcomer showed a courageous autonomy. Throughout the difficult Godfroy negotiations, for example, Churchill was furious with Macmillan. Macmillan's tactic had been to persuade Godfroy to accept that Giraud had authority as provisional head of the French state, and that any subsequent payment to Godfroy through the Allies must come through Giraud. Although this had not been acknowledged, or agreed to by Godfroy, the payments went ahead.

'What you propose is exact opposite of what was explained, through you, to Giraud in my telegram,' Churchill telegraphed. 'No pay of any kind should reach recalcitrant squadron,' Churchill added, 'until they definitely come over to Giraud.'[44]

By this time, as Anthony Verrier has demonstrated, Macmillan was 'adroit at fielding the philippics that were regularly despatched from Downing Street'.[45] He had learned a lot from working in close alliance with a French opposite number, General Georges Catroux.[46] Macmillan and Catroux faced similar problems with their respective superiors, Churchill and de Gaulle. Catroux had adopted an insouciant stance when confronted by what he regarded as his patron's unreasonable demands, and invariably found it productive. Macmillan, caught in the middle, did likewise. 'I am afraid Admiral Godfroy will never rally in the full-blooded sense of that word. The most that he could do would be to make dainty and decorous approaches in the steps of a minuet,' he replied to Churchill. 'I cannot believe, therefore, that it would be wise at this juncture to risk throwing away all that we have achieved, largely by our own efforts, by quarrelling with Giraud on this comparatively minor point.'[47] Churchill was not happy, but Macmillan's view prevailed.

Macmillan now established a close friendship with Jean Monnet.[48] After the fall of France, Monnet had been driven by the concept of a united Europe, and in 1941, whilst working in Washington, had outlined to Paul-Henri Spaak, one-time Prime Minister of Belgium, his vision of a European Coal and Steel Union. In February 1943, he was dispatched to North Africa by Roosevelt, whose confidence he had gained, essentially to resolve the ongoing difficulties in the Giraud-de Gaulle impasse. As Monnet had the very unusual advantage of having the trust of both de Gaulle and Giraud, he was well equipped for this task. Macmillan saw at once how vital a figure Monnet would prove to be, and in long talks the two brokered the idea of the FCNL. Monnet, too, was a skilful networker and had a natural affinity with Macmillan, in method, if not in purpose.

Monnet enthused Macmillan with his grand design for the future of a united Europe.[49] Macmillan knew that Britain was 'a nation which historically only involved itself in European affairs to restore the balance of power, then willingly withdrew to its island'.[50] Monnet understood this reserve. 'The British, the Americans, the Russians have worlds of their own into which they can temporarily retreat,' he wrote on 5 August 1943. 'France cannot opt out, for her very existence hinges on a solution to the European problem.' For Monnet, that solution would be both economic and political, and ultimately involve some form of federation. 'There will be no peace in Europe, if the states are reconstituted on the basis of national sovereignty with all that implies in terms of prestige politics and economic protectionism.' What mattered to Monnet was forging what he termed 'a single economic unit', combining 'key industries needed for national defence'.[51] Monnet could fire people with the romanticism of his ideals, but even as Macmillan listened to his tale, rather in the manner of the young Walter Raleigh listening to the old seafaring greybeard in the famous painting by Millais, the roots of the eventual schism of January 1963[52] could be discerned. As Ernest Bevin, Foreign Secretary in the post-war Labour government, observed about the Council of Europe and the prospect of a European supranational government, 'If you open that Pandora's box, you never know what Trojan 'orses will jump out.'[53]

The Axis forces surrendered to Alexander on 13 May, and on 20 May Macmillan was one of those in attendance at the great victory parade and march-past in Tunis.

He flew to Tunis airport with Roger Makins, Bob Murphy and Jean Monnet. All the great military, naval and air force figures were in attendance. The civil powers were not forgotten, and Macmillan and Bob Murphy led their contingent in an open jeep decorated with their national flags. They were the most prominent civilians to be on the saluting base, as 30,000 troops marched past.

Macmillan returned to Algiers with Eisenhower in his Flying Fortress. For the first time in the war the convoy routes lay open and unthreatened. Macmillan and Eisenhower looked down on a convoy near Bizerte. 'There, General,' said Macmillan 'are the fruits of your victory.' Eisenhower, much moved, replied, 'Ours, you mean, ours.'[54] Their relationship had come a long way since the first, awkward meeting on 2 January when Eisenhower had told Macmillan he had much to learn. Neither forgot the emotion of that moment. It was one of the high spots of Macmillan's life.

The next day, in a plane provided by Eisenhower, Macmillan flew back to England for his first leave. There was much to catch up with on the domestic front. His eldest son Maurice had married Katherine Ormsby-Gore at St Mary-le-Strand on 22 August 1942 and Macmillan's first grandchild was expected. A crowded gathering of relations was at the cottage on the Birch Grove estate to welcome him. As he had left Tunis, the Bey of Tunis had presented him with the First Class Order of the 'Tunisian Medal to be Proud of'. To Macmillan the most remarkable aspect of this ribboned insignia was its resemblance to the colours of the MCC. Although bureaucrats at the Foreign Office required its return as an ineligible medal from an alien power, Dorothy found a better place for it in the children's dressing-up cupboard.

The Sussex interlude was not of long duration. De Gaulle was due in Algiers on 30 May for further negotiations over the unsettled question of the French leadership, and Macmillan returned to Africa via Gibraltar, where he had talks with Churchill and General Marshall*. The three then flew on to Algiers. At the start of the negotiations on 1 June, Giraud congratulated Macmillan on his appointment as Viceroy of India. Giraud had misinterpreted the rumours. It was Wavell who was about to be appointed to New Delhi.

Macmillan was in no doubt that the prize of French leadership must eventually be de Gaulle's. Giraud possessed none of the political ruthlessness that Macmillan believed was necessary before achieving, and then using, power. One of the outcomes of Casablanca was that de Gaulle had forestalled any attempts by the Americans to install Giraud in what he considered his own rightful place. On 25 September, the committee of the FCNL abolished the co-presidency and installed de Gaulle as President. Much of the ground had been laid by Macmillan, and not only with the French. He had also helped behind the scenes when Eisenhower had consulted him privately about de Gaulle's qualities and capabilities. The outcome of the June meetings, at which Macmillan also persuaded Bob Murphy not to give up on de Gaulle, was the formal establishment of the FCNL. So de Gaulle became President of the FCNL, which was the body for all French resistance groups opposed to the Nazis and to the Vichy régime. At this stage Macmillan sent de Gaulle a letter: 'I have always valued very highly our acquaintance – or perhaps I may be allowed to call it friendship – and I feel certain that the role which you have played during these three terrible years fits you to play a still greater one in the future. Many grave difficulties and problems lie before you. May God's blessing be with you in your work for France.'[55]

Macmillan wrote an account of de Gaulle's character after de Gaulle had become the de facto Prime Minister in August:

De Gaulle has a strong sense of his mission: to uphold the honour of France and to unite the French nation once the country is liberated. This sense of a mission does not mean there is any vanity (in the vulgar sense of the word) in his nature but there is not any humility. He has intelligence, moral courage and pride. He is intensely

---

*General George C. Marshall (1880–1959) was the author of the Marshall Plan.

suspicious, suffers from a national inferiority complex but not a personal one. Any approach to him, therefore, must be progressive and not aggressive.[56]

Not only does this memorandum give a perceptive assessment of de Gaulle's complex and essentially lonely personality (not unlike Macmillan's own), it also reveals much about Macmillan's growing sense of judgment, and awareness of the strengths and weaknesses of those with whom he served.

Macmillan's last months in Algiers contained a myriad of consequential events, including two visits from King George VI, under the name of 'General Lyon', when Macmillan's diplomacy was called upon in large and small measure, over protocol and placement. The King invited Macmillan to accompany him on his visit to Malta from 19–21 June. The entry of the cruiser *Aurora* into Valetta harbour, the King in white naval uniform on the deck, and with all vantage points lined with enthusiastic crowds against the sunrise, remained one of Macmillan's abiding memories of the war.

During this period, Macmillan kept asking for news of political events at home. His mind was imperceptibly turning to the post-war scene, and with some anxiety, as he knew that Stockton was by no means a safe parliamentary berth. On 15 July, he wrote to 'Peter' Portal:

> Affairs have been jogging along with a good many difficulties. The fact is that although the Americans on the spot are pursuing a very remarkable policy the State Department and the President are not too helpful. However, I think we shall gradually straighten things out. There is no question at all that de Gaulle must become the dominant figure because Giraud is a very unskilful politician and can always be relied upon to prove his own worst enemy – for instance, his visit to America[57] clearly makes French people think what we feel about Charles II: he was in the pocket of foreigners.
>
> What news is there at home? What is up, and what is down?[58] The Vice-Royalty was rather a surprise, I thought one of the politicians would take it. But I suppose they are all watching each other with such care that none wishes to make a false move.[59]

Alexander was made Commander-in-Chief of the Fifteenth Army Group, consisting of the American Seventh and the British Eighth Armies, in preparation for the invasion of Sicily. On 12 May 1943, Roosevelt had informed Stalin that Eisenhower had been appointed

Supreme Commander for Operation Overlord, and the Allied invasion of occupied north-west Europe.

Alexander's promotion, and Eisenhower's impending move, increased Macmillan's influence in the Mediterranean, a development not to everyone's liking. Macmillan understood this. 'It must not be forgotten that the turning over of the North Africa Command from an American to a British Commander will have important psychological consequences,' he observed shrewdly. 'We shall have to carry the Americans with us, and keep the support of Washington and American public opinion without the advantage of General Eisenhower's prestige.'[60]

Macmillan found he now had much greater freedom and he was included in all Alexander's planning meetings at Tunis over the invasion of Sicily. 'Generally speaking, I enjoy this very much more than being in England, and it is great fun being on one's own,' he wrote to James Stuart on 8 July.[61] The change in leadership brought new acquaintances. One of Macmillan's lifelong characteristics was the ability to mould around him figures whom he trusted and who could be relied upon for absolute loyalty. Now he struck up a particularly warm friendship with Lieutenant-General James (later Sir James) Gammell, who was the Chief of Staff to Jumbo Wilson,[62] successor to Bedell Smith as Chief of Staff at the Supreme Allied High command. General Gammell accompanied Macmillan on several of his journeys back to London, and Macmillan found him invaluable in his support.

When Lady Dorothy visited the field operation, she wrote to her mother about the villa. 'He [Macmillan] uses the big sitting room here as his office. There are two ways into it, one through the only other sitting room where John [Wyndham] sits on guard and writes and telephones, and the other through a little lobby. At times it becomes like a play. People are pushed in through one door while someone is pushed out of the other.'[63] Among other close companions, Macmillan also found Colonel Terence Maxwell,[64] from the Military Government Section of AFHQ, invaluable, though without the impish humour that made John Wyndham such a special friend.

Macmillan was gratified to receive congratulations from Leo Amery, who was impressed by the manner in which Macmillan had resolved the de Gaulle/Giraud difficulties. 'Evidently, all has gone increasingly smoothly in your handling of the French Committee,' he wrote on 18 October 1943. 'De Gaulle seems to have been steadily gaining strength without losing his head while Giraud seems to be settling down to the kind of position he is fit for.'[65] It was a happy time for Macmillan. Eight days earlier he had received news of the birth of his first grandchild, Alexander.[66]

Not everything ran smoothly, however, and in the privacy of his diary Alan Brooke was highly critical of Macmillan's habit of getting involved in matters that were not his concern. Macmillan's tendency to be 'viewy' had resurfaced in the debate over whether 'Jumbo' Wilson or Alexander should eventually become Supreme Commander for the Mediterranean. Macmillan favoured his old friend Alexander. Alan Brooke was furious:

> All the trouble has been caused by Macmillan who has had a long talk with the PM suggesting that Alex is the man for the job and that he, Macmillan, can take the political load off him. He [Macmillan] came round to see me for an hour this evening and evidently does not even begin to understand what the functions of a Supreme Commander should be. Why must the PM consult everybody except those who can give him real advice?[67]

In exasperation, Brooke sent for Macmillan and asked him to talk through any such matters with him before seeing Churchill. 'What I did realize very quickly whilst discussing this problem of command with Macmillan,' Brooke added, 'was that he knew he could handle Alex, and that he would be as a piece of putty in his hand; but on the other hand Jumbo Wilson was made of much rougher material which would not be so pliable and easy to handle.'[68]

Yet in March 1944 Brooke was recording how Macmillan co-operated with him in trying to save Jumbo Wilson from Churchill's wrath, after Jumbo's forthright refusal to be bullied by the Prime Minister. 'The whole problem,' Brooke recorded, 'was due to the fact that old Jumbo Wilson was not as pliable in Winston's hands as Alex would have been.'[69] This was a theme to which Brooke was to return.

Macmillan was maturing fast; he was already conscious that leadership was not a question of seeking popularity but of doing the right thing.

In November at Gibraltar, onboard HMS *Renown*, Macmillan had private talks with Churchill over the preliminary arrangements for the Tehran Conference (EUREKA). EUREKA (28 November-1 December 1943) was to co-ordinate the future strategy of the Western Allies and the USSR, and was to be notable for the presence of the Big Three, Roosevelt, Churchill and Stalin.

'I now commute – as the Americans say – between Algiers and Naples, a very exhausting life,' Macmillan wrote to 'Peter' Portal in the New Year. 'Things seem to be going on fairly well in Italy. Much the most remarkable man we have there is General Alexander – not sufficiently appreciated by our public. The change-over from American to British command here has involved a great many psychological problems which are very interesting.'[70]

An indication of how close Macmillan's thinking was to that of General Gammell can be seen in a memorandum General Gammell compiled about Anglo-American co-operation during the latter stages of the war:

> Provided the British case is a sound and true one and that it is presented with courage and courtesy and with complete frankness, the Americans will co-operate 100 per cent.
>
> If, on the other hand, they suspect there is something withheld, some *arrière pensée*, or some hidden motive which is not disclosed, immediate suspicions are aroused, the old bogey of British Imperialism and British entanglements in Europe immediately arise.[71]

This coincided exactly with Macmillan's view, and was one of the reasons why his relationship with Bob Murphy was so fruitful.

Macmillan, always anxious for the latest home news, also returned in his letter to Portal to developments at Westminster, where Aneurin Bevan was prominent among the increasingly vocal critics of Churchill's wartime strategy. The House of Commons was becoming impatient and fractious: 'Do let me know what you think of the political situation at home,' he wrote. 'It looks to me as if things were getting rather ragged. What do you think the Comrades do? Will they pull out of the Government, or will they stay in?'[72]

On a visit to England in the first week of October 1943, Macmillan met Duff Cooper, who had been invited to become the British representative with the French Committee in Algiers. Duff Cooper was doubtful; but Macmillan, liberated by his year in North Africa, persuaded him of the advantages, and of the opportunities he would have. Duff Cooper accepted, and almost a year to the day after Macmillan's arrival in Algiers touched down at the same airport. He soon realised the change in Macmillan's stature and confidence. 'We went in the evening to the reception which Harold was giving in his villa,' he recorded in his diary on the day after his arrival. 'There was a very large crowd and all the more important people in Algiers were there.'[73] In the next two months Duff Cooper learned a great deal from Macmillan about the North African situation and its underlying complexities. There was a sense of valediction about Macmillan. 'Harold said that he was gradually organizing himself out of existence,' Duff Cooper observed on 28 March 1944, 'and that he would be glad to go home.'[74]

One of the last communications Macmillan had in North Africa was from Max Beaverbrook, his erstwhile boss at the Ministry of Supply, who sent him a cutting from the *Evening Standard*:

> All those I have met who have returned from Algiers to London, whatever their differing points of view or their special remedy for the French situation agree on one point. They are unanimous in their praise of Harold Macmillan. He is not heard of often in London now, but in Algiers he is the most familiar figure amongst all the public men.
>
> He is adding to his reputation and building up a position which will give him a high place in British politics when he returns to London again. An M.P. who leaves Westminster to take up a position abroad quickly loses touch with politics at home and after a few months his name is forgotten.
>
> This rule is likely to apply to several of the M.P.s who have gone abroad during this war. Mr. Macmillan is the exception.[75]

He was indeed; he had no intention of losing touch with politics at home – or of being forgotten.

CHAPTER ELEVEN

So Many Hollow Factions

1943–1945

The speciality of rule hath been neglected;
And look how many Grecian tents do stand
Hollow upon this plain, so many hollow factions.
                                          Shakespeare, *Troilus and Cressida*

Italia! Oh Italia! thou who hast
The fatal gift of beauty, which became
A funeral dower of present woes and past,
On thy sweet brow is sorrow ploughed by shame,
And annals graved in characters of flame.
                              Byron, *Childe Harold's Pilgrimage*, IV, xlii

If there is ever another war in Europe, it will come out of some
damned silly thing in the Balkans.
                                                          Bismarck

Every form of viciousness was established in the Hellenic
world on account of the civil wars, and the simplicity that is
especially found in noble natures disappeared because it became ridiculous. The division into distrustful groups opposed
in their thinking was very extensive.
                    Thucydides, *History of the Peloponnesian War*, Book 3

On 25 May 1943, Anthony Eden, the British Foreign Secretary, addressed the War Cabinet in London on 'armistices and related problems'. He argued that Britain must approach the Soviet Union and
the United States to establish an agreed procedure regarding peace
settlements with European members of the Axis. His fear was that
without such a procedure, the Soviet Union would negotiate its own
agreements, preparing the way for Russian domination in Eastern
Europe, in which case 'we should have very shortly, after the conclusion of this war, to set about preparing for the next'.[1] Two months
after Eden's warning, the Italian king, Victor Emmanuel III, replaced
Mussolini as Italian Prime Minister with Marshal Badoglio.[2] Italy was

to be the first test of the policy of co-ordinated armistice.

As Macmillan was 'the man on the spot', the initial arrangements for this Italian armistice devolved upon Bob Murphy and himself. So far, Macmillan had been a political adviser; now, with the invasion of Sicily (Operation HUSKY) and the eventual surrender of Italy, he became an executive figure of real importance. Macmillan and Murphy brokered the armistice deal over the next few months, and, in the judgement of one recent historian, 'had since become two of the most influential people in Allied-Italian politics'.[3] Macmillan then went on to become a key player in the liberation of Greece in 1944 and in forming British policy in the Balkans.

The Italian armistice was fraught with difficulties, because the British and the Americans approached the problem from different perspectives. Additional problems were internal British ones. Also the settlement was unusual in that it was signed in two phases, the so-called 'short' armistice of 3 September, followed by the 'long' armistice of 29 September.[4]

One of the problems was the exact status of King Victor Emmanuel III of Italy,[5] and his position vis-à-vis the Prime Minister, Badoglio. From his meetings with Victor Emmanuel, Macmillan described the King to Churchill as 'physically infirm, nervous, shaky', adding, 'I do not think he would be capable of initiating any policy except under extreme pressure.'[6] Victor Emmanuel was eventually to abdicate on 11 April 1944 in the presence of Macmillan and Robert Murphy. His son, Umberto II, did not last long as regent, and in June 1944 Badoglio was replaced as Prime Minister by Ivanoe Bonomi.[7]

The root of British anxiety over Italy, which Macmillan shared, was the return of Palmiro Togliatti,[8] the Italian Communist Party leader, who had been in exile in Moscow, as Stalin's agent. After the Russians had recognised the Badoglio government on 14 March, the Italian Communists decided to work with the King, and Togliatti became a key figure. He wrong-footed the Italian anti-Communists (and the Allies) by persuading the PCI (Partito Communista Italiana) to moderate its anti-monarchy stance and join a coalition government, first under Badoglio, and later under Bonomi. The British and the Americans in Italy felt that this presaged subversion of democratic government from within. Later in the year, negotiations between the Allies and the Italian resistance leading to the Rome Protocols of 7 December 1944 were greatly influenced by developments in Greece, an example of how the problems Macmillan faced in Italy, Yugoslavia and Greece became increasingly interlinked.

One of the main objectives on the Allied side in these Rome Protocols was to prevent the CLNAI (Comitato de Liberazione Nazionale dell'Alta Italia, the Committee of National Liberations of Upper – i.e. Northern – Italy) from becoming an Italian version of the Greek ELAS movement, the National People's Liberation Army resistance group in Athens, which wielded power through its Communist-dominated political wing. 'Tagliatti is torn between loyalty to Moscow and to Italy,' Macmillan observed shrewdly. 'The former will prove the stronger; but of course it does not help the Communist Party in Italy.'[9]

Churchill was also deeply disturbed by the implications of Tagliatti's return, dubbed 'the turn round', and he sent a minute to Eden on 4 May 1944 expressing his fears. 'Evidently we are approaching a show-down with the Russians about their Communist intrigues in Italy, Yugoslavia and Greece.'[10] For his part, Macmillan feared a link-up between Marshal Tito and his Yugoslav partisans and the Communistic resistance in north-east Italy. Tito, however, seems to have been more interested in getting his hands on Trieste than in helping the Italian Communists set up a separate government in northern Italy.

Unlike the Americans, who tended 'to regard the Balkans as peripheral to the central issues in Europe',[11] the British considered the area vitally important, not just in winning the war, but because of the post-war consequences of the spread of Communism. As a result, 1944 saw an increasing rift between the two Allies, the Americans suspecting Britain of 'spheres of influence' activity against the Russians, a kind of recidivist imperialism. This mistrust culminated in the outright condemnation of Britain's policy over Italy on 5 December 1944 by Edward Stettinius,[12] who had succeeded Cordell Hull as the American Secretary of State.

Signs of this Anglo-American mistrust, which Macmillan saw as a threat to the special relationship, could be discerned as early as September 1943, at the time of the armistice settlements. 'The Badoglio-King business is going slowly forward,' wrote Eden's Private Secretary, Oliver Harvey[13] in his diary. 'The President [Roosevelt] has now weighed in and is opposed to the signature of the longer armistice terms – which we have already recommended to Eisenhower. Eisenhower and Macmillan are incredibly wooden and obstinate over it all. They hold up everything in order to argue.'[14]

Harvey's diary reflects the unease Eden felt at this time about Macmillan's growing autonomy in the Mediterranean. Macmillan provided the Foreign Office with first-hand evidence about Anglo-American relations and developments on the ground. On only one point were the British and the Americans agreed, and that was the need to keep the Communists, and, specifically, any Russian advance into the European heartland, in check. What eventually happened in Italy would be a key indicator of how the post-war settlement might unfold.

The Americans, however, differed markedly in their attitude towards the Italians, especially after the Italians changed sides in September 1943. They were more favourably disposed towards them than the British for two reasons. First, they had not fought against them for so long, and second, there was a sizeable Italian-American community in the United States.* As a result, all Italians took every opportunity to exploit these differences between the British and the Americans, and those on the right played the anti-Communist card for all it was worth. Such a situation made the task of Macmillan and Murphy exceedingly difficult, some thought nigh impossible.

Yet Badoglio had been keen to sue for terms, and these had already been discussed by Churchill and Roosevelt at the first Quebec Conference (QUADRANT), held between 17 and 24 August. Stalin was furious at the way the USA and Britain reached agreement 'with various governments falling away from Germany' and said 'that this situation cannot be tolerated any longer'.[15] Macmillan was responsible for a complex three-stage compromise proposal, one of the outstanding examples of how he had done his job 'with a skill that at the time almost amounted to a sleight of hand'.[16]

The proposals, put forward by Eisenhower on 18 October, and presented by Anthony Eden and Cordell Hull at the Moscow Conference of Foreign Ministers on 22 October, proved the basis for some measure of agreement with the Soviets, and paved the way for the establishment of the European Advisory Commission. As this led in turn to the Allied Control Commission, an important subject on the agenda at both the Yalta Conference (ARGONAUT) in February 1945 and the Potsdam Conference (TERMINAL) in July 1945, Macmillan had started an important hare, and one that proved its stamina in the difficult months ahead.

As in his Ministry of Supply days, Macmillan realised that letting others take the credit was often the key to success in unravelling a seemingly intractable problem, and he was happy for Eisenhower to receive any plaudits. He had developed an instinctive understanding of how Eisenhower operated.† 'He is still very susceptible to any minor

---

*Out of the 132 million Americans in the 1940 census, 4.6 million had either been born in Italy, or had a parent, or parents, who had. Italians were the second largest group of immigrants in the United States.

†His knowledge of Eisenhower's cautious, uncertain moods and sometimes fractious

source of irritation,' Macmillan wrote at this time, 'not so much on his own account, as on account of the delicate position in which he feels he is placed as the Commander of an Allied Army.'[17]

Such was the strain under which Macmillan had been operating now for some 18 months, it was hardly surprising that his health, never robust at the best of times, gave way in October 1943, after an unexpected visit to London.

Eden was angered to find Macmillan in England. His secretary, Oliver Harvey, wrote in his diary: 'Macmillan has suddenly appeared to A.E.'s fury. We wanted him the other end to prepare for us in Algiers. He is being packed off again. Macmillan is anxious to maintain a sort of *droit de regard* over all our French and Italian relations from his post at Eisenhower H.Q. A. E. does not wish to encourage this.' Harvey believed that Eden's awkward relationship with Macmillan, stemmed from envy, a strange emotion for Eden, who was dubbed the Beau Brummel of modern politics. Macmillan, by contrast, was still regarded as rather drab. 'He [Macmillan] is certainly a bore',[18] wrote Harvey, who was instinctively loyal to Eden. Harvey believed that Macmillan may even have had thoughts of the Foreign Office for himself, as Eden was talking at the time of the excessive burdens of combining the post with that of Leader of the Commons. In fact, Eden clipped Macmillan's wings by appointing Duff Cooper as Ambassador to the French, and Noel Charles[19] as High Commissioner (later Ambassador) in Italy. Yet Macmillan merely established good relationships with both (he was a great friend of Cooper in any case) and pressed on with his work.

Another new figure on the scene was Alexander Kirk[20] 'the American Macmillan',[21] as Harvey described him – who became the US Ambassador in Italy. The Alexander Kirk-Noel Charles-Harold Macmillan trio was to prove a formidable one in the last stages of the war in Italy, when Eisenhower departed the scene to prepare for command of the Normandy Landings (OVERLORD).

Macmillan's visit to England in the first week of October came at the same time as one of the most curious episodes in his wartime diplomacy. On 8 October 1943, the day that Macmillan, far from well, flew back to North Africa via Lisbon, Roger Makins received a letter from Lord Duncannon,[22] the British liaison officer with the FCNL in Algiers. Duncannon told Makins that Marshall Pétain, head

---

character was to be invaluable for Macmillan in rebuilding Anglo-American relations in the post-Suez days in 1957.

of the French Vichy state, was prepared to surrender to the FCNL in Algiers. His chosen intermediary was a man code-named 'Monsieur Schneider'. Although Pétain had attempted such contacts with the Allies earlier in 1943, 'Monsieur Schneider' had now made a definite offer to the FCNL, who were wanting advice from the British as to how they should proceed. 'In the eyes of many Frenchmen he [Pétain] was the legitimate leader and had influence over a large number of army officers,' Duncannon wrote. 'Pétain had told Schneider that after leaving France he would release the army from their oath to him.' The reaction of the FCNL was that this would be a welcome propaganda move before the invasion of Normandy. Makins was more sceptical. 'I suggest that Lord Duncannon should be authorised to inform the FCNL that this is a French matter on which we can express no opinion and that we cannot take any cognizance of it or do anything about it unless asked to do so by the committee of liberation,' he advised Macmillan. 'No British source should have anything to do with the affair, and no member of staff should meet M. Schneider.' Surprisingly, Macmillan agreed. In his own hand, he wrote on Makins' letter, 'The only reason for taking him out of France would be to execute him as an arch-traitor. This is very dangerous stuff indeed. I frankly fear anything in writing. Please discuss.'[23]

No records of their subsequent discussion exist, but the episode begs important questions as to why the Foreign Office and the Cabinet were not apprised by Macmillan of this offer from Pétain. As the British government's representative in North Africa, Macmillan could not, nor would he be expected to, dispatch every memorandum that came across his desk, but the implications of this one were of such high importance that it remains astonishing that he quashed it at birth. Pétain's surrender would have allowed many French forces to join the Free French troops at a crucial stage of the European war. Perhaps Macmillan feared that his relationship with de Gaulle would be subtly undermined by such a development. When de Gaulle and Macmillan met, after a longish interval, on 5 November, de Gaulle steered their wide-ranging conversation towards Pétain and his eventual fate, wryly observing that the British would not shoot Pétain after the war, but give him a villa in the south of England. (Not too near Birch Grove, one can imagine Macmillan thinking.) No mention was made by Macmillan to de Gaulle of what had transpired less than a month before, and his diaries and memoirs are likewise silent on the issue.

A new phase was now beginning in Macmillan's mission, and he moved his headquarters to Caserta, in southern Italy, where he was to spend most of the rest of the war. Churchill had asked him if he wanted to come back to some domestic post, but Macmillan wisely realised he had bigger responsibilities in Italy and preferred to see the job completed. He also had the company, socially, as well as professionally, of the British field commander he most admired, Harold Alexander. In the green-eyed jungle of Westminster, things could well have been neither as rewarding nor as congenial. Also, he was well aware that he might be in need of a new seat after a post-war election. 'I am very anxious indeed about the future of the Stockton seat for all the reasons which you can well imagine,' he wrote to Sir Ralph Assheton.[24] Inevitably, he had neglected his constituency, though Lady Dorothy had conducted a remarkable holding operation on his behalf, and Macmillan believed the best solution would be for his wife to fight the election, which he was sure she would win because of her personal popularity in Stockton, and for him to move to another constituency.

By November 1943, Macmillan had the dual title of UK High Commissioner to the Advisory Council for Italy, in addition to that of Supreme Allied Commander in the Mediterranean. RESMIN CASERTA was now his telegraphic address.

Harold Caccia[25] joined Macmillan's staff at this time, specifically to help with Italian matters. Caccia had served as Eden's Assistant Private Secretary before the war and had developed a close rapport with him. As a result he was important as a link between Eden and Macmillan, between whom relations at this time were becoming increasingly fraught. Oliver Harvey, Eden's current Private Secretary, was an Eden man through and through; Caccia was implicitly trusted by both Eden and Macmillan, the established political star and the new rising one.

Eden was sensitive about others encroaching upon his remit. It seemed to him that this was precisely what Macmillan was doing, through closely reasoned memoranda and recommendations always flowing from Algiers, and now Caserta. Also, it had not gone unnoticed by Eden that Macmillan had an easy relationship, albeit punctuated by the usual rows, with Churchill.* Both Eden and Macmillan endeavoured to catch Churchill's ear; it seemed to Eden at this time that Macmillan was better at so doing. Their relationships with Churchill were complex, but even more so with each other. Eden's approach to political life was essentially gentlemanly, reserved and modest. Any form of self-advertising was anathema to him. Macmillan, on the

---

*Twelve years later, during the Suez crisis, Eden was infuriated when he heard of Macmillan's private talks with Churchill at Chartwell about the way things were developing.

other hand, knew that politics was a down-to-earth business, and did what he felt was necessary, however many feathers he might ruffle. He was not averse to being bloody-minded. It is often forgotten that Macmillan was nearly four years older than Eden. Both were educated at Eton, where Macmillan was a Scholar and Eden a less brilliant junior. Eden, who won the Military Cross, rarely spoke about his wartime experiences in the trenches, and he cringed when Macmillan harked back to the Somme. Eden considered Macmillan a vulgarian (one could never imagine Eden inventing Premium Bonds)[26] and at heart untrustworthy. Yet politics is a vulgar business, and Macmillan had an intuitive feeling for what appealed to the electorate, and for the way in which power operated. He understood the machinery of government and knew already how to crank it into action. He was combative and knew that in politics one had to be a salesman; it was not a gentlemanly profession. Eden feared that Macmillan might pip him to the leadership of the party. The role of Crown Prince, in effect Eden's burden since 1938, was, as he himself acknowledged, 'a position not necessarily enviable in politics'.[27]

As a result, one of the most important aspects of the unfolding Italian imbroglio, with all its unfathomable complexities, was that it brought to the fore the tensions between Eden, already with six years of experience in one of the great offices of state, and Macmillan, the latecomer to executive office. The situation worried Eden more than it worried Macmillan. Macmillan had less to lose, and everything to gain; from the Mediterranean, he could go forth to inherit the political world. In that fascinating Westminster game of identifying future leaders, Macmillan was already being mentioned, even if it was a case of 'tell it not in Gath, proclaim it not in the streets of Ascot'.* Duff Cooper's wife, Lady Diana, told John Wyndham that she thought Macmillan would one day be Prime Minister, and referred to him as 'my horse', the name by which she still called him when he was actually Prime Minister, once asking John Wyndham, 'What is my horse doing today?' 'Well, at this actual moment,' Wyndham replied, to the mystification of others present, 'your horse is giving lunch to the King of Nepal.'[28]

The Italian campaign committed the southern army of Hitler's Wehrmacht (armed forces or, literally, defence power) to a defensive

---

*Another far-sighted ally was Macmillan's loyal doctor, John Richardson, who asked Macmillan at this time if he felt he would ever be Prime Minister. Macmillan knew that there were too many imponderables, but replied that if it did happen, it would be in about 12 years, not a bad prediction for something that was accomplished on 10 January 1957.[29]

operation that took it away from both the front in Normandy and that in the East, contributing eventually to the loss of both. Of course, it was also true that Allied forces were committed in Italy – but with one difference: they were not also engaged against Russia. General Marshall felt that on balance, the Allies had more forces tied up in the Mediterranean theatre than the Germans, thus weakening Eisenhower's preparations for the invasion of Europe through Normandy (OVERLORD); but of one thing he was certain – American forces were not going to be diverted eastwards. 'Say, where is this Ljubljana?' he asked Macmillan of the strategic gap that offered a viable route through to Austria from north-eastern Italy. 'If it's in the Balkans, we can't go there.'[30]

Meanwhile the Allies made their way painfully north through Italy. Their eventual victories at Monte Cassino, the Gothic line and over the River Po, geographical landmarks that favoured the defenders, came at the highest cost on both sides in human lives. The Allies were not seen universally as liberators, and many Italians were ambivalent about the bloody process unfolding on their native soil. Once in Caserta, Macmillan's acute antennae soon appreciated the troublesome potential. 'Anglo-American occupation,' he warned Eden, 'might be just as offensive to a sensitive people as the German.'[31]

Macmillan had favoured the 'short' armistice, successfully persuading Eisenhower to sign terms with the Italians on 3 September 1943. Macmillan believed that this approach would lead to a quick surrender, whilst Eden felt the negotiated terms were too lenient, preferring the more punitive 'long' armistice. He was always more sceptical than Macmillan, rightly so in the event, about the value of Italian support for the Allies militarily. However, one way Macmillan thought this difficulty could be overcome was to grant southern Italy independent national status, so that it could become a true partner in the Allied cause, and not merely a 'co-belligerent'.

Macmillan also showed a shrewdness, born of experience in the field, when he cautioned the Foreign Office over their theory that any 'armistice' would not be believed by the Italians, and their suggestion that the Pope, Pius XII, should certify it to be true in a nationwide broadcast. His urgent telegram revealed his diplomatic understanding of the situation:

I personally consider this an unwise proposal because it would
   (a) involve the Vatican to a dangerous extent
   (b) quite likely provoke and partially justify German invasion of the Vatican

(c) be almost sure to meet with a refusal

(d) compromise His Majesty's Minister at the Vatican.[32]

The government accepted Macmillan's advice and no request was put to His Holiness. Macmillan's most sagacious point was about His Majesty's Minister at the Vatican, Sir D'Arcy Osborne.[33] After 10 September 1943, when the Germans occupied Rome, Osborne would have been fatally compromised and his mission of no further use.

The capture of Rome on 4 June 1944 was one of the Allied achievements of the war. Macmillan sent heartfelt congratulations to Alexander, adding playfully as a postscript: 'It was moreover thoughtful of you as an old Harrovian to capture Rome on the 4th June.' To which Alexander mischievously replied, 'What is the Fourth of June?'[34]

Eden and Macmillan also fell out over the Dodecanese islands, and the need to amalgamate command. British Middle East Command in Cairo had failed to establish their presence in the Dodecanese, needed as bases for air attacks on Axis targets. Macmillan discussed this problem privately with Churchill on 7 October. Unification of the command arrangements was clearly desirable, and Macmillan submitted one of his forceful memoranda to Eden on 6 November 1944:

Will you consider putting into the Prime Minister's head the following plan:

(a) Send General Wilson to replace Dill at least till the end of the European war.

(b) Amalgamate A.F.H.Q. and A.A.I. and put under Alexander's command all the oddments, like Balkan Air Force, Land Forces Adriatic etc. This is essential if next year's Adriatic strategy is to succeed.

The simplification would be immense. A.F.H.Q., A.A.I., Allied Commission in Italy, Allied Military Government could all be run as a unit – probably from Rome.

And we would save man-power and nervous energy now devoted to internal stress.

I cannot see that the Americans could object.[35]

Eden had felt the failure in the Dodecanese islands was comparable to the loss of Tobruk. He was anxious to improve the command chain, but he did not see this as Macmillan's responsibility. Macmillan knew that military and political priorities were different.

A centralised AFHQ made military sense but offended the sensibilities of the Americans, who saw such a move as an attempt to consolidate British leadership in the Mediterranean. Sensitivity to such feelings had very much conditioned the manner in which Macmillan had worked with Eisenhower. General James Gammell was later to write:

> There is no shirking the fact that owing to her superior resources and manpower the United States holds the thick end of the stick, and it is no use trying to get our way by unilateral action. All we can rest upon is the honesty and sincerity of our motives, and if these are put firmly and courageously to the Americans, I am convinced from my experience here that we shall in all cases get what we want. 'Speak the truth and shame the Devil' should be our motto.[36]

Macmillan did both.

The Allied Conference in Cairo (SEXTANT) from 3 to 7 December 1943, which Macmillan attended, included discussions on future strategy, including the likelihood of Turkey entering the war on the Allied side.*

Macmillan found himself in earnest argument at one of the dinners with Andrei Vyshinsky,[37] the Soviet Deputy Foreign Minister, and in the 1930s the chief prosecutor at Stalin's notorious trials. Vyshinsky told Macmillan that he could never understand why the British had interned Oswald Mosley instead of shooting him. 'Free speech,' he declared, 'is all right, so long as it does not interfere with the policy of the Government.' Macmillan made a note to use the quotation next time he was in Stockton.[39]

Macmillan had become concerned about the top-heavy Allied administration and what he saw as the inevitable lack of clarity in preparing strategy. SEXTANT established a unified Mediterranean command, under General Sir Henry 'Jumbo' Wilson, and responsibility for the Eastern Mediterranean devolved to AFHQ on 10 December. However, this settlement left unresolved the question of Macmillan's overall responsibilities over Eastern Mediterranean matters. The Minister of State in the Middle East, Richard 'Dick' Casey,[40] had previously discharged this responsibility, but when he was made Governor of Bengal in January 1944, Casey's functions were not taken

---

*The Americans believed that Churchill's obsessive determination to draw Turkey into the war was some kind of retrospective attempt to justify the disastrous Dardanelles campaign of 1915, for which he felt responsible.[38]

over by Macmillan. Lord Moyne became the new Minister of State, an unexpected development for Macmillan, who believed that Moyne would act on his instructions regarding Balkan matters. The Foreign Office, though, as Roger Makins soon spotted, was 'not very keen on accepting the implications of the political side of the unification of command'.[41]

Pierson 'Bob' Dixon,[42] Eden's new Principal Private Secretary, saw the presence of both Moyne and Macmillan as potential for confusion. 'AE's feelings about HM are really the difficulty,' he observed.[43] As a result, Macmillan concentrated his efforts on securing Churchill's ear. 'The turning over of the North African Command from an American to a British Commander will have important psychological consequences,' he had written to Churchill at the SEXTANT Conference. 'We shall have to carry the Americans with us, and keep the support of Washington and American public opinion without the advantage of General Eisenhower's prestige. To balance this we must be able to show that the Eastern end of the Mediterranean has become, both on paper and in practice, a genuine Anglo-American undertaking.'[44] Despite this concern, the real difficulty proved to be between AFHQ and the newly 'absorbed' Middle East Command. As Marshall had made clear to Macmillan, the liberation of south-eastern Europe was not seen as an American responsibility. OVERLORD was their priority.

The establishment of a series of Balkan Affairs Committees in April 1944 was seen in the Foreign Office as an attempt by Middle East Command in Cairo to assert its own autonomy. The State Department in Washington was also angered by the lack of consultation. Bob Murphy had one of his rare disagreements with Macmillan on the issue, and in June 1944 Jumbo Wilson ordered that the work of the committees should be suspended. Roger Makins had no doubt that the difficulties arose because of Foreign Office mistrust of Macmillan, as he pointed out forcefully to Sir Orme Sargent, the Deputy Under-Secretary in London:

This Balkan Committee affair would never have happened if the directive to Macmillan had been drafted to take proper account of the unification of command of the Mediterranean and the necessity of making the political authority of the Resident Minister co-terminous with the military authority of the Supreme Commander. In fact, the directive seems to have been drawn up so as to restrict and curtail the activity of Macmillan to the greatest possible extent.[45]

When Eden saw this letter, he thought it 'revealing and disgraceful.'[46]

Yet Jumbo Wilson and Macmillan remained convinced that effective settlement of the increasingly complex Balkan situation, and the Eastern Mediterranean in general, required an agreed centralised command structure. London suspected empire-building by Macmillan, and Churchill, alerted to the situation, soon became involved. 'Surely Harold is playing too big on all this,' he agreed with Eden, 'and also most of this is premature ... pour a bucket of cold water.'[47] Eden was pleased to oblige.

In fact, the problems of Greece were far from being premature, and Churchill's displeasure with Macmillan was only a temporary blip. Unlike some, Macmillan let these sudden changes in the political weather blow over, until calmer days returned. Much of Churchill's wrath was directed towards Sir Noel Charles in Rome, especially when the Badoglio government was unexpectedly replaced in June 1944 by that of Ivanoe Bonomi, Chairman of the Rome Committee of National Liberation. 'This disaster has come about through Macmillan not being in charge of these matters,' Churchill wrote to Eden. 'If he had been in Rome at the time, this would never have happened.'[48]

In August 1944, Churchill came out to Italy to see matters at first hand. The differences between AFHQ and Cairo were not the only problem. Operation MANNA – the dispatch of British troops to Greece from an already stretched Eighth Army pushing up through Italy – was being planned. Macmillan was determined that these Balkan matters should be AFHQ's responsibility; others wondered whether the best solution might not be to wind up AFHQ entirely, now that the North African campaigns had faded into the past. Macmillan, though, was looking to a future without American involvement in the area. Bob Murphy had left the Italian theatre of war; so had Eisenhower. Fortunately, Murphy's replacement, Alexander Kirk, got on well with Macmillan, who admired, and envied, Kirk's ability to install himself in the most luxurious villas available. The British, by comparison, always seemed to Macmillan to alternate between the equivalent of 'a gentleman's residence in Portland Place' and a 'showy residence in Kensington Palace Gardens'.[49]

As the Americans were clearly reluctant to be involved militarily in Greece, except in any relief operations, Macmillan proposed to Churchill that there should be some form of agreed national devolvement that would give the British a free hand. 'We should not be hampered by the American unwillingness to take political responsibilities,' he wrote to Churchill, 'nor should we be involved in their irritating and somewhat harassing vacillations.'[50]

Macmillan's position as President of the Allied Commission, formerly the Control Commission, gave him immense authority in the Mediterranean. His predecessor was the experienced, but often politically insensitive, General Sir Noel Mason-Macfarlane.[51] Macmillan had been preferred for the post by Churchill ahead of Sir Noel Charles, the favoured candidate of the Eden camp, a decision endorsed by Roosevelt. Ambassadors such as Duff Cooper (France), Noel Charles (Italy), Reginald 'Rex' Leeper[52] (Greece), and America's Adlai Stevenson[53] (Yugoslavia) all now reported to Macmillan. Later, envoys to Romania and Bulgaria were part of his team. Only four British officers served as Allied Supreme Commanders in the Second World War – Alexander, Mountbatten, Wavell and Jumbo Wilson. Macmillan, by virtue of his position at the head of the Allied Commission, was their outstanding diplomatic equivalent. With the approval of Roosevelt and Churchill, he combined three responsibilities – British Minister Resident at AFHQ in Caserta, British Political Adviser to the Supreme Commander and Head of the Allied Control Commission.

Another area of responsibility transferred from Cairo to AFHQ under the reorganisation was that of Yugoslavia. That country's special position in the Balkan complexities was largely determined by its geographical location. When Italian forces had failed to subdue the Greeks in October 1940, Hitler of necessity had had to come to Mussolini's aid. The first consequence was that Yugoslavia had to become part of the Axis. Yugoslavia was not in itself of value to Hitler, but he needed access to Greece. Following considerable pressure, the Regent, Prince Paul of Yugoslavia, acting for the young King Peter II in exile in England, had little option but to sign the Axis Tripartite Pact (Germany-Italy-Japan) in Vienna on 25 March 1941, which in effect committed his country to acceptance of the German conquest of Greece. This prompted a coup against the government and the Regent on 27 March. The Germans and Italians then decided Yugoslavia had to be crushed. On 6 April 1941, German bombers devastated Belgrade and Yugoslavia capitulated on 17 April.

Resistance within Yugoslavia to the Regent's pact with Hitler took two forms. On one side were the Serbian Chetniks under Dragoljub Mihailović, who favoured a restoration of King Peter (shortly to come of age); on the other were the Communist forces of Josip Tito.[54] Tito's partisans were fighting both the Germans and the royalist Chetniks. Although Macmillan believed the unfolding feud was somewhat similar to that in North Africa between Giraud and de Gaulle, when the

British and the Americans backed different horses,[55] the nuances in Yugoslavia were more complex, eventually leading to a damaging rift between the British and the Americans.

The Americans supported Mihailović and his Chetniks, even though there was some suspicion that they had collaborated with both the Germans and the Italians. The view of the British government, spelled out by Churchill in the House of Commons on 2 February 1944, was to support whichever local group seemed best equipped to fight the Germans, however unpalatable its political stance. This meant Tito and his Communistic partisans. The Americans did not find this attitude convincing. Back at Westminster, Cuthbert Headlam voiced his disquiet: 'Clearly we are letting the Russians lead us by the nose as far as eastern Europe is concerned.'[56] Those Tory MPs who had suspected Macmillan of Soviet sympathies since his visit to Russia in 1932 saw his influence at work.

Macmillan was not disappointed, nor even surprised. 'It is a curious reflection in politics that nobody ever bothers about a situation which is being successfully dealt with,' he observed at this time. 'They only worry and argue about immediate difficulties. Nor is any credit gained by the solution of problems.'[57]

After the collapse of Italy in September 1943, Tito's partisans disarmed the Italians in Yugoslavia. As Tito consolidated his political and military strength, the Chetniks were correspondingly weakened. By the end of 1943, it was clear that Tito, with 250,000 men serving him, would eventually prevail, despite the young King Peter placing his hopes in Dr Ivan Subasić, the Ban (Governor) of Croatia, who was invited by the King on 1 June 1944 to negotiate with Tito and his followers about forming a government. Macmillan had the far-sighted vision of an alliance between Chetnik forces and Tito's partisans to avoid civil war. His part in the subsequent Subasić-Tito agreement of 7 December 1944 helped establish, with difficulty, a united Yugoslav government. In his meetings with Tito, he found the Marshal a dignified figure with a natural command, though Macmillan baulked at suggestions that Tito's bodyguard should stand in the dining room whenever he gave Tito lunch; it was not what gentlemen in England did. It was already clear to Macmillan that Tito would be a formidable presence in the post-war world.

Another powerful figure to emerge on to the scene was General McCreery.[58] In November 1944, General Sir Oliver Leese, Commander of the Eighth Army, took command of the Eleventh Army Group in Burma. McCreery was Leese's natural successor, and very much Alexander's man, having served under him at Dunkirk and in North

Africa. As commander of 10 Corps he played a crucial part in the Italian landings, and had proved himself reliable, innovative and calm under pressure. Anyone who was Alexander's protégé was clearly in favour with Macmillan from the start. Macmillan considered McCreery one of the ablest military commanders with whom he had worked, and his identification of the crossing of Lake Commachio, considered insuperable by Mark Clark, as the key to the vital Argenta Gap, bordered on genius.

Alongside McCreery was another key figure in Macmillan's story, Lieutenant-General Charles Keightley,[59] GOC of V Corps, and, at 42, the youngest man in the British army to lead a corps in action during the war. Keightley was to play a vital role in the final offensive of April 1945, forcing the route to Austria through the Argenta Gap. On VE Day Keightley entered Austria, where he became involved in a stand-off with Tito's partisans and the controversial repatriation of the Cossacks.

By the time the problems of Greece moved to the top of Macmillan's agenda, he had proved himself a vital figure in the settlement of the complex North African situation, the surrender of Italy and the problems arising from the dual, but disparate, resistance movements in Yugoslavia. Greece was in many ways to be an even more formidable challenge, and one that exposed him to physical danger.

The Greek government in exile, led by George Papandreou,[60] moved from Cairo to Italy at Churchill's suggestion. After the Germans had subjugated Greece in 1941, two competing resistance groups had arisen. In September 1941, EAM, the Communist National Liberation Front, was founded. By December 1941, a military wing, ELAS, the National People's Liberation Army, had broken away, taking to the mountains to conduct a guerrilla campaign against the occupation. The real struggle, however, came between EAM and EDES, the National Republican Greek League, opposed to the Greek Communist Party (KKE). An uneasy truce between the two groups was negotiated in February 1944 after winter fighting.

At a conference in Caserta in October 1944, Churchill tried to convince the Greek Prime Minister, Papandreou, that a restoration of the monarchy, under King George II,[61] was the best way forward. Macmillan was not so sure. After his experiences of Italy and Yugoslavia, he knew that monarchy was a diminishing popular asset and that the resistance groups were united on one issue, republicanism. He believed the most propitious chance of a moderate, and enduring, settlement in Greece would be best achieved by Britain distancing itself from any claims by King George II and his supporters.

The failure of Churchill's attempt in 1941 to liberate Greece from Axis control, as well as his romantic wish for the restoration of the King, hung heavily over the negotiations in 1944. The British military authorities favoured, over and above political considerations, any plan that maximised anti-Axis armed successes. The Foreign Office, and in particular Eden, looked ahead primarily to a post-war Greece that was sympathetic to Britain, monarchist if necessary, but certainly not Communist. Macmillan's task was to unravel this tangled web.

The solution was to send British troops to Greece by sea under the command of General Sir Ronald Scobie[62] to support the Papandreou government, a strategy designed to ensure that Greece became a democracy. Such a plan, so the hope went, would forestall EAM from filling any power vacuum by establishing a Communist regime, as the Germans began, in September 1944, to withdraw from the Greek islands and from the mainland. On Friday, 13 October, Macmillan embarked on HMS *Orion*, flagship of the 100-strong fleet. He was installed in the Admiral's cabin, and settled down to read *Our Mutual Friend*.*

For superstitious reasons, the ship did not weigh anchor until one minute past midnight. Minesweepers, many destined to be sunk, went ahead. Strong aerial cover was provided – and needed. Papandreou and his prospective ministers brought up the rear in a vessel with Rex Leeper in attendance. The voyage was eventful and dangerous – accompanying vessels were sunk by mines within sight of the HMS *Orion*. At one stage Junkers 88 fighter bombers approached menacingly, but were shot down by Spitfires. Macmillan watched much of this action from the deck of HMS *Orion*, and found it strangely enervating.

The fleet's entry into Piraeus was perilous, but when Papandreou eventually landed, he was greeted with acclaim. Macmillan and Leeper made a deliberate decision to stay away from all processions and public appearances so that the new government would not appear to be under British political influence. Macmillan knew what he had brokered and did not want the Caserta agreement undermined. He went ashore with General Scobie on 17 October, the day before

---

* *Our Mutual Friend* kept Macmillan occupied until his return to his Naples villa on 26 October. Without any more novels to hand, he ferreted out a volume of Shakespeare's tragedies, and embarked, appropriately, on *Troilus and Cressida*. Ulysses' words (I, iii, 78–80) had a contemporary ring:

> The speciality of rule hath been neglected;
> And look how many Grecian tents do stand
> Hollow upon this plain, so many hollow factions.

Papandreou made his processional entry. Macmillan and Scobie toured Athens, and great enthusiasm was evident whenever the crowd saw a British uniform. For the first time since Balliol days Macmillan saw the Acropolis, the Temple of Winged Victory, the Parthenon and the Theatre of Dionysus, and he marvelled afresh at the glory that had been Greece.

The country now, though, was on the verge of a destructive civil war. EAM, and its military wing ELAS, were in possession of several parts of Athens and much of the neighbouring countryside. The job of Macmillan and Scobie was to stand by Papandreou's government, newly returned from exile, until free elections could be held. The next few months were fraught with danger. Scobie and Macmillan only ventured forth rarely, and then in armoured tanks with covering forces. Although Papandreou had been greeted enthusiastically by anti-Communist crowds when he landed on 18 October, the political situation remained uncertain. Outside Athens he had little support, and it seemed likely that ELAS and its guerrilla groups would seize power.

The long-feared civil war broke out on 3 December, and British forces and those of the Greek government came close to being overrun. Fighting broke out all round the embassy, where Macmillan, Leeper and their staffs took cover. More than 50 people were there, under siege, with no heat, light or water. The situation was only partly relieved, but morale greatly so, by Macmillan's discovery of the former ambassador's supply of champagne in the embassy cellars, and unilaterally declaring it free for all. Alexander feared, not altogether fancifully, that the situation might become another Lucknow. Macmillan thought of General Gordon under siege in Khartoum.

The Communist forces, who wanted to establish Greece along Soviet lines, seemed in the ascendant. Criticism in the British Parliament was uninhibited,* and feelings in America were of outrage, as the call by Edward Stettinius for non-intervention in the internal affairs of liberated nations (5 December 1944) had shown.

As Greece descended further into civil war, Macmillan abandoned a planned visit to Washington and returned to Athens with Alexander on 11 December. Shortly afterwards, the Foreign Office sent out a press attaché, Osbert Lancaster,[63] who arrived in Athens on 13 December, in the midst of a fierce battle. Lancaster's job was to counter rumour

---

*Macmillan was temporarily in London to hear the critical and bitter speeches in the Commons, when Churchill retorted with his famous comment that 'Democracy is no harlot to be picked up in the street by a man with a tommy gun.'[64]

by communicating hard news. He and Macmillan struck up a rapport at once, Lancaster's sense of mischievous humour and unfailing cheerfulness contributing wonderfully to the air of embattled stoicism. For his part, Lancaster was captivated by Macmillan. 'I listen for hours on end to Macmillan thinking aloud,' he wrote to his publisher Jock Murray, 'a wearing but not unprofitable employment.' Both Macmillan and Lancaster were classicists, which helped. Lancaster recommended that a guard be mounted on the Acropolis, not entirely for military reasons. Macmillan whiled away many of the dangerous waiting hours by reading aloud to Lancaster Thucydides' account of the civil war in Corcyra in 427 BC, substituting the original names with those of their most untrustworthy Athenian contemporaries.[65]

Macmillan's political solution to the perilous situation, pending the arrival of military reinforcements from Italy, was to recommend a regency under Archbishop Damaskinos,[66] a respected anti-Communist figure who had not fled Greece during the German occupation. Macmillan admired his shrewdness and saw in him the hope for a transition to democracy. Not surprisingly this proposal did not find favour with Prince Paul of Greece, or, more importantly, with Papandreou. Nevertheless Macmillan pressed on, and an inclusive conference was arranged with Damaskinos in the chair. For once Macmillan's view found favour with the Foreign Office. At this point Churchill suddenly decided to come to Greece, arriving with Anthony Eden on Christmas Day.

Christmas festivities, to the chagrin of Eden, who had been peremptorily summoned from his home, took precedence over business. Negotiations did not begin until Boxing Day. Osbert Lancaster had cut some silhouettes of the Holy Family out of old index cards, and these served as decorations. A clergyman, under armed guard, took a Christmas Day service in the British Embassy, referring in his lengthy sermon to the angels as 'God's airborne division'.[67] For security, Churchill was billeted on board HMS *Ajax*, a cruiser that had taken part in the victorious Battle of the River Plate in 1939. When Damaskinos, in full archiepiscopal robes, arrived on board *Ajax* to meet Churchill, a Christmas fancy-dress party was in full swing, and initially the Archbishop was mistaken for an enthusiastic participant. Considerable diplomacy was needed by the captain to prevent Damaskinos' huffy return to the mainland.

Although Churchill had been reluctant to go against the King's feelings, and those of Crown Prince Paul,[68] he now agreed with Macmillan that Damaskinos was the best prospect for a settlement. Gradually, the deal was brokered.

Macmillan persuaded Papandreou to report to the King of the Hellenes that there was now widespread agreement for a regency proposal. In due course, Papandreou resigned as Prime Minister, to be replaced by General Plastiras,[69] an anti-Communist republican, who had enforced the abdication of King Constantine of Greece in 1922. Following Churchill's insistence, King George reluctantly appointed Damaskinos as regent. Although peace terms with EAM were still unresolved after the ceasefire of 11 January 1945, agreement was reached eventually, and the Peace of Varkiza was signed on 12 February 1945, the day after the conclusion of the Yalta Conference. It was one of Macmillan's deftest diplomatic coups in the entire war.

Rex Leeper's retrospective view was that Macmillan was 'always looking ahead, foreseeing the next difficulty and taking steps to forestall it'.[70] In Italy, too, Macmillan's irenic qualities did much to ameliorate Anglo-American tensions, particularly over preventing the Italian resistance becoming a threat to the established Bonomi government under Allied control. On 29 January 1945, Macmillan issued a document with the chief American political adviser, Alexander Kirk, re-emphasising that 'the policy of the Allied Command shall be to support the policies of the Bonomi Government'. Nothing should be done, militarily or diplomatically, that might weaken the authority of this central Government. 'Speed in getting ourselves established is the central factor: without this there is real danger of extreme Communist elements taking control.'[71] As Macmillan stressed in his memoirs, 'the lesson of Greece was that we had to get control over these movements from the start'.[72]

Macmillan had now been absent in the Mediterranean for 29 months. Back home, he was mostly known, and by no means universally revered, as the author of *The Middle Way*. His book was in the news again with the publication in 1944 of Friedrich Hayek's *The Road to Serfdom*, later a key Thatcherite text. In his 'Marginal Comment' in the *Spectator* on 7 July 1944, Harold Nicolson had taken issue with Hayek's economic philosophy and recommended him to read *The Middle Way* as a corrective. 'It might convince him that in this illogical island there exists an infinite capacity for finding middle ways.'[73] Three weeks later, Macmillan chanced upon this copy of the *Spectator*. 'You have always been a kind friend,' he wrote to Harold Nicolson. 'But I think you are also one of the very few people who read "The Middle Way" when it was published and still remember what it was about.'[74] Macmillan underestimated the impact of his book. In October 1942, William Temple,[75] recently appointed Archbishop of Canterbury, had written to Evie Devonshire, 'I have always had immense sympathy with Harold's "Middle Way", which of course his Right Wing friends regarded as rank Socialism.'[76]

In fact, Macmillan was highly regarded not only by William Temple, but also by Temple's successor as Archbishop of York, Cyril Garbett.[77] In April 1945, Garbett* made a tour of Italy, Greece and Malta. In Italy he stayed in Naples with Admiral Cunningham, Commander-in-Chief of the Mediterranean Fleet. On 3 April, Cunningham gave a dinner party at the Villa Emma (named after Nelson's Lady Hamilton) in Naples for Garbett to meet the key figures. 'Among the guests was Harold Macmillan, our very capable Minister in the Mediterranean zone,' Garbett wrote in his diary. 'He has done excellent work and is trusted by everyone. We had much interesting talk.' Both looked ahead to the post-war world. 'Macmillan says our propaganda in the past has been directed to weakening our enemies: now it should be used to strengthen our friends and to educate them about ourselves.'[79] A fortnight later, Macmillan and Garbett met again in Caserta for a longer chat. 'He is a brilliant talker and most interesting,' Garbett wrote in his diary. 'He thinks that sooner or later our relations with Russia may become acute.' This was of particular interest to Garbett, and he agreed with Macmillan that 'we must do our best to keep in with Russia if peace is to be secured'. Garbett was also impressed with what he had heard of Macmillan's second audience with Pope Pius XII. 'Macmillan likes the Pope, and has talked freely to him. On one occasion he told him that Christendom lacked the united front presented by Communism, and that he could take the first step towards it by the recognition of Anglican orders. The Pope merely smiled.'[80] As Macmillan could be 'viewy' with Roosevelt and Churchill, he obviously had no qualms about letting St Peter's successor know his opinions about almost anything.

On a visit to England in June 1944, Harold Macmillan had had a long meeting with his brother Daniel at Macmillan & Co. A rapprochement had been established with Dorothy, whose loyalty, especially in her cultivation of Stockton, was much appreciated. Harold Macmillan's first grandchild, Alexander, Maurice and Katie's son, was a blessing on his rare visits home. His daughter Caroline's engagement to a Welsh Guards officer, Julian Faber, was announced in *The Times* on 14 April 1944.[81] 'In war time marriages are always a chance, but then so they are in peace time,' Macmillan replied to a family friend, who

---

*A close friend of John Macmillan,[78] Harold's cousin, who was Bishop of Guildford.

had written with congratulations. 'It is naturally very sad for me not to be in England, but I am told she is very happy.'[82]

Macmillan was in Italy in September 1944, and met his nephew, Andrew Cavendish, serving with the 3rd Battalion Coldstream Guards. 'I saw Andrew last week in Rome,' he wrote to Andrew's mother at Chatsworth. 'He apparently got some leave and was disporting himself with his young friends in the Grand Hotel. I was much touched that he did not neglect his aged uncle, but came rushing up to me with shouts of welcome.'[83]

Letters from Italy flowed from Macmillan's pen, but he was essentially lonely, a condition he relieved by his prolific reading. Jane Austen's *Emma*, Thackeray's *Pendennis*, and what he considered the finest of all Dickens novels, *David Copperfield*, were companions at this time, as well as Boswell's *Life of Johnson* (useful, Macmillan told Dorothy in a letter, for interrupted journeys), together with three Hardy novels, *The Woodlanders*, *The Trumpet Major* and *A Pair of Blue Eyes*.

Departure is a time for retrospect and not merely farewell. Among the correspondence that came to Macmillan as his mission in the Mediterranean drew to a close, two unsought letters give some idea of the atmosphere he engendered among his circle. 'I do so want to thank you for all your kindness to me and for all the wise counsel and guidance you have given me at all times,' General Gammell wrote. 'This has been a most interesting year, and I shall always look back on it as one of the most enjoyable of my 32 years service.'[84] Roger Makins also conveyed his thanks: 'If I am able to retain and apply one tenth of what you have taught me about the management of men and affairs, and the broad human approach to politics I shall consider myself fortunate indeed – & I might add that your natural gift for diplomacy makes every kind of trained diplomat green with envy.' Makins added, 'Whenever you want an assistant I hope you know where to look.'[85]

Makins, who went on to serve in the British Embassy in Washington, now provided Macmillan with all the latest American news, including reaction to Roosevelt's re-election in November 1944 as President for a fourth term. 'The election has ended in a notable triumph for the President, a respectable popular majority, and unchanged majority in the Senate and (contrary to almost all prophecies) firm Democratic control of the House of Representatives.'[86]

Roosevelt was not to survive long. On 12 April, news came that he had died suddenly at Warm Springs in Georgia. Makins sent Macmillan background details from Washington and also let him know that the

New York Stock Exchange had surged in value on the news of the President's death. Before the month was out, Mussolini (on 28 April) and Hitler (on 30 April) were also dead. Victory in Europe Day was declared on 8 May 1945.

Thoughts of his political return to England occupied Macmillan's mind as the war entered this final phase. John Wyndham, whose wisdom Macmillan believed transcended his years, had felt he ought 'to be in the picture'[87] and, if possible, arrange some visits to Stockton, despite his international responsibilities. Macmillan knew this to be the right advice. 'I am more and more anxious to get back into English politics before it is too late,' he reflected in one letter to Wyndham Portal. 'Since I have taken up this diplomatic business I have become very fascinated by Foreign Affairs, and I think I would do better to specialise in this in future politics.'[88]

Inevitably, Macmillan had his detractors. Any figure who establishes a reputation, in whatever field, is going to leave in his wake disappointed and disenchanted rivals, as well as sceptical superiors. One of the most prominent critics was Alan Brooke, who remained wary of Macmillan's influence, particularly on Alexander. 'It is hard to tell at present who is Supreme Commander in the Mediterranean!' he had written in his diary on 18 January 1945. 'Is it Macmillan or is it Alex? Surely it is Macmillan. It is too depressing to see how Alex's deficiency of brain allows him to be dominated by others!! ... now he has selected Macmillan as his mount! His new charger may carry him over the political fences (perhaps), but will certainly crash him over the military ones!'[89]

As the war came to its conclusion in Europe, Macmillan's reputation had been completely transformed. Once regarded as having the potential of a middle-ranking minister, by 1945 he was seen as one of the makers and shakers of his age. Executive responsibility and the tug of war had given him an unimagined confidence; the old shyness, even drabness, had been cast aside: full rein was now given to his aphoristic wit, his insights and his public image. He had shown the ability to establish profitable relationships with a wide range of disparate personalities. He was that rare creature, the team player who retained his individual, often contradictory, approach. Alexander's biographer, Nigel Nicolson, who served in Tunisia and Italy, and observed Macmillan as the only civilian in Alexander's mess in Algiers and Tunis, felt Macmillan's success came through 'patrician use of great power'.[90] No longer on the edge of photographs by the end of the war Macmillan was a figure of consequence in his own right, consulted by Pope, presidents and prime ministers.

As the war came to an end, the problems of peace began. One of the most urgent was how to cope with vast numbers of discharged troops and released prisoners. On Sunday, 13 May, Macmillan flew from Eighth Army HQ to Klagenfurt in Austria. The repercussions of this short visit, dormant for many years, were eventually to blight his reputation.

CHAPTER TWELVE

Conspiracy at Klagenfurt?
May 1945

There is many a boy here today who looks on war as all glory,
but, boys, it is all hell.
> General William Sherman, 11 August 1880

Truth is a very complex thing, and politics is a very complex
business. There are wheels within wheels. One may be under
certain obligations to people that one must pay. Sooner or
later in political life one has to compromise. Everyone does.
> Oscar Wilde, *An Ideal Husband*

Which is man and which is myth? Is this fact or is it lies? What
is truth and what is fable? Where is Ruth and where is Mabel?
> Alan Bennett, *Forty Years On*

On 8 May 1945, Allied forces advanced from northern Italy into
southern Austria. In the next few weeks, hundreds of thousands of
troops surrendered to General Keightley's 5 Corps,[1] part of General
McCreery's Eighth Army. Although the majority of those who
surrendered were Germans, there were in the area troops of other
nationalities, including groups of Cossacks and anti-Communist
Yugoslavs in retreat from Yugoslavia as Tito's Communist partisan
armies advanced.

Under the general surrender terms at the end of the war it was made
explicit, after Yalta, that all forces had to surrender to the armies
against whom they had been engaged. However, the overwhelming
desire of defeated forces was to surrender to the Anglo-American
forces in the hope of more humanitarian treatment. This contributed
to the vast numbers of prisoners in that area, particularly in British
hands. The fate of prisoners, if they ended up in Soviet hands, was, to
put it mildly, uncertain.

A major crisis had blown up over Tito's threatened assimilation
into post-war Yugoslavia of the territories of Venezia Giulia (in north-
eastern Italy, including the port of Trieste) and Carinthia (in south-
eastern Austria). Alexander asked Macmillan to fly to Eighth Army HQ

at Treviso to put his generals in the picture. The message Macmillan delivered was that the line had to be held. Trieste had already been taken by Tito on 2 May, and the unresolved issue was whether that was going to be the final battle of the Second World War or the first of the Third. As military conflict between the Western Allies and Tito's Communist partisans was a real possibility, Alexander needed the whole area cleared of PoWs before any such action. The problem for the British was what to do with the forces who wanted to surrender to British or Americans rather than surrender to Soviets. 'Nothing in retrospect is more obvious about the repatriations from Austria in 1945,' Christopher Booker has rightly observed, 'than that the major factor dictating why they took place as they did was the crisis which blew up over Tito's attempt to seize Carinthia and Venezia Giulia.'[2]

On 28 April, the Chiefs of Staff had ordered Alexander to occupy Venezia Giulia, but Tito's advances had meant this was easier ordered than done, at least in the short term. When Tito refused to withdraw from the area on 10 and 13 May, AFHQ, backed by the British and American governments, prepared for a military campaign against the Yugoslav partisans. Up to that point the Venezia Giulia crisis was the cloud hanging over Macmillan's meetings. These meetings led to Macmillan being told about what was then the even more immediate threat Tito was posing in Carinthia, the area of southern Austria designated for British occupation when hostilities ceased. The issue was thus of crucial importance for the post-war settlement. Hence Macmillan's decision to fly on from Treviso to Klagenfurt, where, in his discussions with Keightley, commander of the British forces of occupation in Austria after VE Day, he was told about the complicating factor of the hundreds of thousands of surrendering Germans and other prisoners. It was in this context that he learned about the 'Cossacks' and the 'White' Russians.

The Cossacks[3] were among the many Soviet exiles of war, some of whom had served in the German armed forces. Because they came originally from communities on the borders of the Russian Empire, they were not thought of by the Nazis as Slavs. Non-Slavs had been used by the Nazis in their campaigns from 1941. Indeed Hitler regarded the Cossacks, descended from the Goths, as Aryans, and so in April 1942 specific Cossack regiments were formed, one of which was the 15th SS Cossack Cavalry Corps, under General Helmut von Pannwitz.[4] Eventually there were other Cossack forces,[5] including the 'White Russian' Schutzkorps.

In Germany, the term Cossack was often employed, not

entirely accurately, to describe Soviet citizens who had enlisted in the Wehrmacht. In Britain, the Cossacks mainly evoked memories for the pre-war generation of their displays of horsemanship at Olympia in London. In the Soviet Union, they were seen as traitors who had taken up arms against their mother country.

In the month after VE Day the Allied forces were faced with the logistical problems of billeting and feeding thousands of anti-Communist Yugoslavs and Cossacks – many with women and children and countless horses – at a time when further hostilities against Tito's partisans threatened to break out at any moment. Keightley's corps also had responsibility for 400,000 surrendered German prisoners. This unstable and volatile situation led, with tragic consequences, to enforced repatriations.

The Cossack prisoners of war, together with many of their women and children, were compulsorily returned to the Soviet authorities in Austria. Some of these Cossack soldiers committed suicide in front of their families whilst being transferred.

Many returned Cossacks were executed at once by the Russians, whilst others were dispatched to labour camps in the Soviet Union. The exact figures are impossible to determine, but members of the British 30 Military Mission in Moscow saw notices of executions in the Russian press. The personnel in Moscow also kept hearing of the deaths of former rank-and-file Cossacks, sometimes groups of them dying together. Others were reported as being given '25 years', almost invariably a death sentence,[6] although some of the 'other ranks' were released into internal exile in Russia a year after the war.

The fate of the repatriated Yugoslavs was even harsher. Thousands were slaughtered in the forests, their bodies thrown into mass graves that had been dug in advance of their arrival, in anticipation of these killings.

The question of how foreign prisoners of war should be treated after the end of the war had exercised the British Cabinet since the time of the D-Day landings the previous year. On 24 June 1944, a memorandum on repatriation was filed in the War Office after Cabinet discussion:

> This is purely a question for the Soviet authorities and does not concern His Majesty's Government. In due course all those with whom the Soviet authorities desire to deal must be handed over to them, and we are not concerned with the fact that they may be shot or otherwise more harshly dealt with than they might be under English law.[7]

On 17 July, the Cabinet considered formally what should happen to captured Russians if Soviet authorities requested their repatriation. This question arose because 1,500 Russians fighting for the Germans had been captured in France. The Cabinet conclusions record:

> After some general discussion, the Prime Minister, summing up, said that he thought we should inform the Soviet Government that we had captured these prisoners; and add that, while we did not know how they came to be fighting on the German side, they had shown every desire to be hostile to Germany. We should ask the Soviet Government what they would like us to do with these men. If they replied asking for repatriation, we should have to agree.

After further discussion, the Cabinet conclusions record that 'The War Cabinet agreed with the Prime Minister's suggestion.'[8] This matter was an early indication of how *real-politik* was going to operate. The actual distinction between 'Cossacks' and 'Soviets', which was to become a source of much later controversy, was not determined.

The matter of ultimate repatriations continued to be discussed at the highest level in London during the summer of 1944. The unpalatable implications were summed up in a letter to Anthony Eden, the Foreign Secretary, from Sir James Grigg, Secretary of State for War, on 24 August 1944:

> We are in an obvious dilemma. If we do as the Russians want and hand over all these prisoners to them whether or not the prisoners are willing to go back to Russia, we are ... sending some of them to their death; and though in war we cannot, as you point out in your minute of 2nd August, afford to be sentimental, I confess that I find the prospect somewhat revolting, and I should expect public opinion to reflect the same feeling. There is also the danger that if we hand the men back there may be reprisals on our prisoners in German hands. But I think that that risk is probably growing appreciably less, and that the Germans have probably enough to think about without keeping their eye on what happens to Russians whom they forced into the German armies.
>
> On the other hand if we don't do what the Russians wish there may be the danger that they will not be ready to co-operate in getting back speedily to us the British and other Allied prisoners who fall into their hands as they advance into Germany. Obviously our public opinion would bitterly and rightly resent any delay in getting our men home, or any infliction of any unnecessary hardship on

them, and if the choice is between hardship to our men and death to Russians the choice is plain.[9]

The War Cabinet's position was reiterated formally on 4 September 1944. Item 1 on the agenda was 'Policy regarding Prisoners of War'. Following discussion, the War Cabinet concluded:

(i) that we should agree to the Soviet Government's request to repatriate their prisoners from the United Kingdom;
(ii) that we should instruct the Middle East authorities to send back all Russians whom the Soviet authorities wished to have back, *irrespective of whether or not the men wished to return* [author's italics]; and that the practice of obtaining statements from the Soviet prisoners as to their willingness to return should be discontinued.[10]

Overshadowing all these developments was the agreement reached at the Allied conference, codenamed ARGONAUT, held at Yalta in the Crimea from 4 to 11 February 1945. Roy Jenkins has rightly commented that Yalta 'was the least successful of the wartime summits for the essential reason that the only cement which held together the Big Three, the need to defeat the massive German military machine, was rapidly losing its adhesive power'.[11] Yalta was also the most controversial of the summits because of its legacy, both in the short and long term. It soon came to be perceived as a latter-day 'Munich'; this time, the Allies were 'appeasing' Stalin.

The acquiescence shown towards the wishes of Stalin was the subject of much criticism in Parliament during the subsequent Yalta debate. Behind the scenes, views were even more forthright. On 14 February 1944 at a meeting of the Conservative 1922 back-bench committee, Victor Raikes bitterly complained that 'Poland had been utterly sold out.'[12] By the time the Yalta conference took place, the Red Army and the NKVD (KGB) held and controlled most of eastern and central Europe. This territory was already in Stalin's hands. Yalta committed the powers to free and democratic elections in Poland. Stalin broke that undertaking. It was always over-optimistic to expect he would honour it.

At Yalta, Churchill, Roosevelt and Stalin had discussed future military strategy, the shape of the post-war world, Polish frontiers, and voting rights in the embryonic United Nations. For the Americans the most immediate and vital question was the entry of the Soviet Union into the war against Japan. Of particular importance too for the British and Americans was the Declaration on Liberated Europe, in which the Big Three reiterated the aim of establishing democracy in the countries they had freed from Nazi occupation, as previously outlined in the Atlantic Charter, agreed by Churchill and Roosevelt in August 1941.[13]

However, Yalta provided the template for many other issues. Of these the question of repatriation was one of the most contentious. On 11 February a meeting was held at the Lividia Palace at 4 p.m. to agree the final *communiqué*. Item 3 read: 'The foreign secretaries [Anthony Eden, Edward Stettinius, and Vyacheslav Molotov][14] approved and signed agreements relating to liberated prisoners of war and civilians of the Three Powers in continental Europe and the United Kingdom.'[15] The operative section of this agreement was as follows:

> All Soviet citizens liberated by the forces operating under British command and all British subjects liberated by the forces operating under Soviet command will, without delay after their liberation, be separated from enemy PoWs and will be maintained separately from them in camps or points of concentration until they have been handed over to the Soviet or British authorities, as the case may be, at places agreed upon between those authorities.[16]

Who, exactly, were these 'Soviet citizens'? In the interpretation of this definition lay all the difficulties to come.

Stalin's view never entertained the niceties. The British government, on the other hand, did not consider 'White Russians' to be Soviet citizens. The term 'White Russian' was commonly used in the interwar period and afterwards to describe émigré Russians who had left or fled from the Bolshevik regime after the 1917 revolution, or during the subsequent 1918–1921 civil war. If Stalin accepted the British interpretation, then these émigrés were *not* part of the Yalta Repatriation Agreement.

Anticipating these difficulties, and long before the Cossack question had arisen, Macmillan had asked the Foreign Office on 27 July 1944 for the official definition as to what constituted a 'Soviet citizen'. Much correspondence ensued before a final definition was dispatched on 6 March 1945 (not 6 May, as stated by Count Nikolai Tolstoy in *The Minister and the Massacres*):[17]

> Under British law Soviet citizens are all persons coming from places within the boundaries of the Soviet Union as constituted before the outbreak of the present war. All persons coming from territories west of such boundaries have Polish or Baltic nationality unless

there is evidence to show in particular cases that they have acquired Soviet Citizenship by their own voluntary act. A man who has served in the Soviet Army is not a Soviet citizen if he comes from territory west of 1939 boundaries of the Soviet Union unless he has acquired Soviet Citizenship.

All persons of undoubted Soviet citizenship will be repatriated irrespective of their own wishes.[18]

This document[19] is of particular importance, 'since it makes clear that, contrary to all conjecture, there was no specific instruction to screen out *émigrés*'. This is also true of AFHQ directives of 7 and 15 March, and the conference notes on the AFHQ/Eighth Army Conference of 26/27 March, 'which make clear that ultimately 5 Corps received full authorization both for the hand-overs themselves and for the methods by which it intended to carry them out'.[20]

The papers of Macmillan's American opposite number, Alexander Kirk, give details of his day-to-day discussions with Macmillan on many matters, including the forthcoming 1945 British general election and the problems of Trieste, as well as telegrams to the State Department in Washington. 'Macmillan informed us this morning that he had received instructions from Churchill to proceed to London during the next few days in order to accept a new assignment,' Kirk reported to the State Department on 8 May. 'He hinted that he expected to receive a Cabinet post, probably the War Ministry. British Resmin [Resident Minister] stated that he believed elections would be held in England before end of June and said he felt the campaign would be a hard and bitter one.' Kirk's papers also contain copies of the 15th Army Group telegrams, requesting guidance from higher authority. One 'Top Secret' message of 16 May 1945, for instance, reads:

Probability we shall shortly find in British Occupied zone in AUSTRIA large numbers Jugoslav civilians who are Anti-TITO. They being driven out by Jugoslav forces.

If met, what is their position and should they be returned to JUGOSLAVIA if such is demanded by Jugoslavs? If not demanded what is their status?[21]

Similar telegrams requested advice over the Cossacks.

The significance in the Kirk archive of these papers, of both British and American origin, is that they counter the allegation that there was a subsequent cover-up involving destruction of key documents. These *are* the key documents, and they survive in the American archives.[22] Had the British telegrams survived fully in the British archives (and recent declassifications show that many do, replicating the relevant copies in Washington), such an allegation could never have been sustained.[23]

As the war came to a close in Europe at the end of April 1945, it was clear that the resolution of what Sir James Grigg had described as 'an obvious dilemma' over repatriation could be delayed no longer. By dint of its geographical position, Austria was to be the crucible. The Allied armies had advanced into Austria from the west, the east and the south. Eisenhower's forces were moving from Bavaria into Austria from the north. Soviet forces had taken Vienna on 13 April and the troops of Marshal Fedor Tolbukhin[24] were beginning to occupy the British zone of Austria. Field Marshal Alexander's forces were moving into Austria from north-east Italy. To complicate the situation, Tito's partisans were also about to enter southern Austria, crossing directly from Yugoslavia. As the web closed on the area of Carinthia, hundreds of thousands of German forces and those fighting with them, either voluntarily or under compulsion, were taken prisoner, together with vast numbers of refugees seeking escape from the Russian and Yugoslav Communist forces. The natural beauty of the region makes it seem particularly incongruous as a setting for such horrendous events. Brahms composed many of his most celebrated works there, and as he walked the hills and lakesides he declared that the melodies flew around so profusely he had to take care never to trample them underfoot.

In the days following VE Day, 5 Corps received the surrender of six Cossack groups, together with others who came from Soviet-controlled territory.

Also in the second week of May, anti-Tito Yugoslavs surrendered in large numbers. Among them were Croats, Slovenes and Serbs, all in fear of Tito's partisans. Ralph Stephenson, British Ambassador in Belgrade, stated that 'these anti-partisan units are without exception completely compromised by open collaboration with the Germans'.[25]

As Tito was claiming that Venezia Giulia should become part of Greater Yugoslavia, his partisans might have to be met with force, even though the Germans had surrendered and the war seemed to be over. Alexander stood firm against Tito's claim. Macmillan recorded in his diary, 'Neither British nor American troops will care for a new campaign in order to save Trieste for the "Eyeties".'[26] Consideration of the repatriation issue often neglects to give requisite attention to the fact that peace, and hard-won peaceful settlements, were genuinely threatened by Tito and his advancing partisan forces in May 1945. The military commanders wanted Carinthia cleared of prisoners of war as swiftly as possible, lest full-scale military action erupted. Such was the background.

The 'eighteen days' of Macmillan's direct involvement in the second part of the story began on 8 May. Macmillan's VE Day started at 5 a.m. as he drove from Rome to Caserta. At noon he hosted a cocktail party for all his staff, and that of Alexander Kirk, in the palace at Caserta. It was difficult to believe that the war was actually over, because the dangerous situation over Tito's claim on Venezia Giulia meant that hostilities could break out at any moment.

General Keightley's 5 Corps had found the area around Klagenfurt full of Tito's partisans, taking over public buildings and declaring Carinthia, like Venezia Giulia, to be part of Yugoslavia. On 9 May Macmillan cabled Churchill, 'In addition to trouble over Venezia Giulia Tito is engaged in a scamper into Austria; these Yugoslav troops,' Macmillan continued, 'are generally engaged in an attempt to make good their claims by de facto possessions'. As a result, 'situation is becoming very embarrassing to local British commanders ... some clear instructions must soon be issued'.[28]

On 10 May, two important meetings took place. General Keightley met Marshal Tolbulkhin, who requested the repatriation to the Soviets of all Cossacks in 5 Corps area. Meanwhile at AFHQ in Caserta, Field Marshal Alexander, who would have to implement any instructions from London on this matter, called a conference with his senior British and American advisers to discuss Tito's claims for sovereignty over Venezia Giulia. Macmillan was disheartened by the lack of progress at this conference, though not by Alexander's determination to face down Tito's demands. The next day, 11 May, Alexander received a telegram, crucial to the story, from General McCreery, who reported that the presence of Tito's partisans was making it impossible to set up the Allied Military Government (AMG). Full control of the area around Klagenfurt 'could now only be effected by full scale military operations'. Alexander decided that Macmillan must now be sent to brief the army commanders on the intricacies of the unfolding political situation. As this was being decided 'on the highest level ... Macmillan will explain it to you when he arrives'.[29]

Macmillan travelled on 12 May to Eighth Army Headquarters at Treviso, where he had a two-and-a-half-hour conference with General

McCreery. The main focus was on the Yugoslav problem, very much the priority at that stage. Macmillan showed McCreery and his staff the latest telegram he had received from Lord Halifax, the British Ambassador in Washington, about Venezia Giulia. 'I am informed in confidence by State Department that United States Government take a very serious view of the attitude of the Yugoslav Government, not only in regard to Venezia Giulia but also Klagenfurt area. They are of course conscious that Yugoslav Government would not be acting in this manner without feeling sure (rightly or wrongly) of tacit Soviet support.'[30] Macmillan also showed McCreery the covering telegram Kirk had sent to the State Department, after his previous day's meeting with Macmillan, stressing Churchill's concerns, 'particularly with regard to Yugoslav partisan activity in the Klagenfurt area'.[31]

Macmillan's original intention and instruction had been to brief McCreery. At his meeting at Eighth Army HQ he had been told that General Keightley had been requesting permission to shoot, if necessary, at Yugoslav partisans, in support of the military government. Macmillan felt it incumbent on him to bring Keightley up to date also with the latest developments. Accordingly he flew to Klagenfurt on 13 May in a Dakota. It was his first visit to Austria, and he was captivated during the 90-minute flight by the vistas of the snow-capped Alps on a perfect, cloudless day. As the plane approached Klagenfurt, mountain passes, lakes and forests came into view. He came down to earth with something of a bump on a grassy landing strip at Klagenfurt.

Macmillan began his fateful meeting with Keightley and his staff at 10 a.m. in a hut by the landing strip. The first item on the agenda was the problem for 5 Corps represented by Tito's Yugoslav partisans. General Keightley then told Macmillan of his logistical problems in dealing with the surrendered 400,000 Germans. The meeting moved on to address the question of the Soviets on Keightley's right flank, forces bolstered by Bulgar troops.

The fourth item on the agenda was the contentious one of the Cossacks and 'White' Russians. Macmillan kept a diary that he wrote up every night. His version reads:

> Among the surrendered Germans are about 40,000 Cossacks and 'White' Russians, with their wives and children. To hand them over to the Russians is condemning them to slavery, torture and probably death. To refuse, is deeply to offend the Russians, and incidentally break the Yalta agreement. We have decided to hand them over (Gen Keightley is in touch and on good terms with the Russian General [Marshal Fedor Tolbukhin] on his right), but I suggested that the

Russians should at the same time give us any British prisoners or wounded who may be in his area.[32]

The two hour meeting concluded with discussion about the evacuation of British PoWs, and problems arising from the Chetniks fleeing from the advancing Yugoslav partisans.

Macmillan then flew back to Treviso, to return the Eighth Army officers, who had accompanied him, to their HQ. At Treviso he conducted a short résumé of events with McCreery, before returning to Caserta.

The next day, 14 May, Keightley telegraphed Alexander. 'On advice [from] Macmillan [I] have today suggested to Soviet General on Tolbukhin's HQ that Cossacks should be returned to SOVIETS at once ... Cannot see any point in keeping this large number Soviet nationals who are obviously great source contention between Soviets and ourselves.'*[33]

This message, containing careless and loose wording by which 'Cossacks' mistakenly became 'Soviet nationals', which not all were, indicates the confusion over the definition, both at the time and later. Equally, Macmillan's use of the term 'White' Russians in his diary was to lead to accusations that he was a war criminal and mass murderer.

No decision was taken on any handover on 13 May and it was not until a military conference at Udine on 26/27 May, by which time Macmillan was back in England, that the matter was fully discussed. At this conference, the Eighth Army and Alexander's headquarters reached full agreement about what should be done with the Cossacks and Yugoslavs. A blanket operational order was issued on 27 May. It consisted of nine specific requirements. Two are of particular relevance. The first read: 'In accordance with an agreement made by the Allied Government all Allied Nationals are to be returned to their country. This means that the Cossacks and the Caucasians now in the Bgd area will be returned to Russia.' There was no attempt to disguise the fact that this would be a most distressing operation. The ninth directive read: 'Particularly as there are so many women and children, some of you will feel sympathetic towards these people, but you must remember that they took up arms for the Germans, thus releasing more troops to fight against us in ITALY and on the other fronts.'[35]

Macmillan's last days in Italy were disjointed and disrupted. On Saturday, 19 May he was unexpectedly called back to Chequers. He

---

*As the Cowgill report concluded, 'This was fully in line with Government and Allied policies.'[34]

found Churchill much occupied by the timetable for the post-war general election, as well as which film might be shown after dinner.[36] After bringing Churchill up to date with the situation at AFHQ, Macmillan took the opportunity on Sunday, 20 May of a brief visit to Birch Grove (the family were still in Pooks Cottage on the estate), where he saw his grandsons Alexander and Joshua (born in January 1945).

On Tuesday, 22 May, Macmillan returned to Caserta. He was not present at the discussion in G-5 branch at AFHQ, which considered the question of Yugoslav prisoners. The minutes, though, record that the advice of both Macmillan and Kirk was 'that all classes of and types of dissident and anti-Tito Jugoslavs who fall into the hands of Allied Forces either in Italy or in Austria should not be forced to return to Jugoslavia, but should be disarmed and given temporary shelter until the question of their disposition and status can be determined'.[37]

Macmillan's political meetings on 23 and 24 May were largely occupied by the Venezia Giulia problem, which throughout had been the question of overriding concern. On the evening of the 24th, he hosted a farewell party for 250 people to mark his two and a half years as Minister Resident. On 25 May, his time was occupied with an early departure to Rome for an audience with the Pope, followed by more farewell parties and a valedictory dinner with Alexander Kirk. He flew to London from Naples at 10 a.m. on 26 May.

Only after Macmillan's departure did AFHQ representatives at Eighth Army begin the discussions at Udine (26/27 May) that finally gave authorisation for the repatriation of Cossacks and Yugoslavs, and issue the instruction quoted above.

It is vital to realise that awareness of the problem posed by the presence of another group of Cossacks at the far end of Carinthia, 90 or so miles away, was only taken on board after Macmillan's visit to Klagenfurt. The key instructional telegram from 5 Corps to its divisional commanders – 'Return of Cossacks to Soviet Forces' – was issued on 24 May with details of how operations were to be conducted on the 28th. 'It is of the utmost importance that all the offers [sic] and particularly senior comds [sic] are rounded up and that none are allowed to escape,' the telegram concluded. 'The Soviet Forces consider this as being of the highest importance and will probably regard the safe delivery of the offers [sic] as a test of British good faith.'[38] It is more than probable that this order, complying with a belated Soviet demand for all senior Cossack commanders to be repatriated, stemmed from Stalin himself when he realised, doubtless through reports from Tolbukhin, that he could rely on the British to deliver a good bunch of them for his revenge, with no trouble to himself. War is indeed all hell.

*

Revulsion was experienced by many involved in the subsequent repatriations, and soldiers at all levels were profoundly shocked by what they had been ordered to do. One officer may stand as an example of these honourable and understandable feelings, Lieutenant-Colonel Robin Rose Price of the 3rd Welsh Guards, part of the 6th Armoured Division of 5 Corps. Rose Price wrote in his diary on 19 May 1945, 'Order of most sinister duplicity received i.e. to send Croats to their foes i.e. Tits to Yugoslavia under the impression they were to go to Italy.'[39] One captain under his command came to Rose Price and said that the men were on the point of mutiny, so distasteful was the task they had been ordered to do. Rose Price agreed wholeheartedly and represented to his superior officers that his battalion could not do any more. Although there was no question of disobeying orders, the strong objections were registered, and the battalion's part in the operations downgraded. The trauma of those days remained with Rose Price for the rest of his life.[40]

The last phase of the story – the accusations – belong chronologically to the 1980s.

Misgivings about the events in Carinthia in 1945 had surfaced from time to time over the years. However, it was not until the publication by Nicholas (Lord) Bethell of *The Last Secret* in 1974 that the story became more widely known. Bethell's account was the first to be based upon newly available military records, and the first to suggest that, in forcibly repatriating non-Soviet Cossacks, the British government was intentionally 'over-fulfilling' the Yalta agreement. Bethell concentrated on reconstructing in vivid detail the dreadful events of 1945, by combining first-hand recollections of, among others, General Keightley and Brigadier Tryon-Wilson,[41] Keightley's chief administrative officer at the time, with skilful use of primary sources. His findings were used as the basis for a BBC television documentary. Yet Bethell's picture was incomplete. The fate of the Yugoslavs was not covered, nor the military situation created by the advances of Tito's partisans and Tito's claims on Venezia Giulia. However, a fuse had been lit and it was not long before the slow burn of public interest was fanned by three books by Count Nikolai Tolstoy.

The first of these, in 1978, was *The Victims of Yalta*, a work of considerable scholarship, based on primary material, with a consideration of Harold Macmillan's role. Although Tolstoy had not concluded at this stage in his long investigations that Macmillan was largely responsible for what had happened, it was clear that this was the way his investigation was leading. In *Stalin's Secret War* (1981), particularly in the chapter 'Close Designs and Crooked Counsels', this focus was much sharper. In May 1983, Tolstoy followed this up with an article in *Encounter*, entitled 'The Klagenfurt Conspiracy', in which the part played by Brigadier Toby Low (later Lord Aldington),[42] Chief of Staff to General Keightley, particularly over the Yugoslavs, was first examined.[43] In 1984, Harold Macmillan, seemingly unaware of how this would add fuel to a now raging fire, published his comprehensive *War Diaries*. Armed with Macmillan's unedited diary entries for May 1945, Tolstoy now wrote an account of both the Cossack and Yugoslav repatriations, *The Minister and the Massacres* (1986). In this book he alleged that Macmillan had been part of 'the Klagenfurt conspiracy' and thus an accessory to mass murder in 1945, and that he had subsequently spent the intervening years covering his tracks and systematically destroying papers destined for the public archives.

Much was made of the fact that Macmillan had referred to 'White' Russians in his private diary entry on 13 May 1945. Yet Macmillan made no attempt to disguise this when he published his diaries. He also referred to 'White Russians' in a letter to James Grigg, the Secretary of State for War, on 18 May 1945. In this letter he listed the logistical problems faced by 5 Corps, which included 'disarming, shepherding and feeding about 400,000 Germans' and 'dealing with the White Russians and Cossacks, together with their wives and families, serving in those German forces'.[44]

At the time, both in Austria and other theatres of war, the term 'White Russian' was used to describe any anti-Communist group originating from the old Russian Empire, even if the members of that group were not in many cases ethnic Russians. The forces of General Vlasov,[45] which included Cossack formations in the 5 Corps area in Austria in 1945, were known as 'White Russians'. The term was also used by 5 Corps, as referring to those who had participated on the 'White Russian' side in the Russian civil war 25 years earlier, or who were simply refugees, exiles from these conflicts. The most common use of the phrase, though, and the one used by Keightley in his briefing of Macmillan, referred to the members of the Schutzcorps, the only surviving unit of the old Russian Imperial Army. Its members had lived in exile in Yugoslavia since the 1920s. It was in this sense that the phrase was used by Nigel Nicolson[46] in his 1st Guards Brigade SITREP on 19 May:* 'The Grenadiers today handed over the whole

---

*Ironically, Nigel Nicolson was later one of the principal witnesses against Lord Aldington in the libel case.

responsibility for the VIKIRING cage to 12 RHA and the cage itself is being rapidly cleared of its inmates. The 4,000 White Russians were sent to S VEIT, leaving the Slovenes and Serbs, for whom a different fate is intended.'[47]

The White Russians referred to in Macmillan's diary, and in his letter to Sir James Grigg, were not the Cossacks at the time in Carinthia, but the White Russian Schutzkorps, which had surrendered near Klagenfurt, together with the 15 Cossack Cavalry Corps. Nevertheless, accusations persisted that Macmillan at the meeting at Klagenfurt airport on 13 May 1945 had 'breached' the Yalta agreement and personally ordered the return of Cossacks (of whatever genre), whose numbers included those who were *not* Soviet nationals.

For some observers, Macmillan was caught up in the moral ambiguities of the hell that is war; for others, he was guilty of crimes against humanity. Unusually, for a matter of this seriousness, the extent of the charges only came to public notice decades later, and the story was a classic example of a controversy in retrospect. At the end of a long and gruelling war in the spring of 1945, the repatriations were but one factor among many others, and it is unhistorical to argue that things were otherwise. Things were done differently in the past.

The longer perspective has seen no general agreement on the extent of any culpability, while the accusations and counter-accusations have given rise to opposing and irreconcilable opinions.[48] Two examples illustrate the intensity of these feelings. 'It was wicked to hang Ribbentrop,[49] who was never a criminal,' wrote James Lees-Milne in his diary in 1985 about the judgements delivered at the Nuremberg Trials in July 1946. 'The man who deserved hanging was Harold Macmillan for sentencing all those Poles and Russians who were sent back after the war.'[50] Robert Graves, the writer, was equally outspoken. Graves was elected to an Honorary Fellowship of his Oxford College, St John's, his alma mater, in 1971, and in old age could be an embarrassment at High Table, turning to his neighbour and suddenly pronouncing on the university's chancellor (apropos of no previous conversation), 'Harold Macmillan's a murderer, you know.'[51] No former British Prime Minister had been accused of such grievous crimes, or indeed suffered the indignity of a public call for his execution.

In 1990, an independent investigation into the controversy under the chairmanship of Brigadier Anthony Cowgill,[52] published its report, *The Repatriations from Austria in 1945*. Cowgill's motive in setting up this inquiry was because he felt the honour of the British army had been impugned. He considered it a duty to get to the bottom of the matter once and for all. Fortunately, he had the time, energy and money (the inquiry was conducted entirely at his own expense) to sustain the investigations over four years.[53]

Cowgill had invited Lord Brimelow, the former Permanent Under-Secretary at the Foreign Office, a renowned expert in Russian matters, and Christopher Booker, who had researched the affair, to join him. Booker, who had initially believed that Macmillan was culpable, revised his opinion in the light of the documentary evidence the Cowgill team discovered. 'Our unequivocal conclusion,' he wrote of the extensive inquiry, 'was that Macmillan's part in the story was (a) marginal at best, and (b) that he actually knew very little about the Cossacks in Austria, apart from what he was told at the briefing at Klagenfurt airfield.'[54] Among the Cowgill inquiry report's many conclusions, based on all extant primary sources, was that 'contrary to the impression which has been widely accepted in recent years, the part played by Harold Macmillan in the repatriations as British Resident Minister was extremely small and only marginal in its consequences'. On the Yugoslav question in particular, the report was unequivocal: 'We conclude without reservation that Harold Macmillan in no sense knowingly or personally participated in any decision specifically directed to the handing back against their will of the dissident Yugoslavs.'[55]

In May 1986, before the independent Cowgill inquiry had begun, Dr Robert Knight published a detailed riposte to Macmillan's accusers, later described as 'one of those pyrotechnic academic performances'.[56] The prime military requirement in 1945, showed Dr Knight, was to prepare for the so-called 'Operation Beehive', possible military action against both Yugoslav and Soviet forces. The imperative was to clear the area of prisoners. 'Quick decisions,' he wrote, 'were made by men in a hurry, operational efficiency came first, humanity took a back seat.' In October 1990, reviewing the findings of the Cowgill inquiry, Knight returned to the matter. His opinion now was that his earlier findings of May 1986 had been vindicated, and also that Macmillan could now be completely exonerated of any blame. 'He [Brigadier Cowgill],' Knight concluded, 'correctly places the hand-overs in the context of a double crisis caused by Tito's occupation of parts of Southern Austria and Venezia Giulia, and the flood of thousands of refugees and troops of all descriptions and nationalities into the area.'[57]

It was Cowgill's team who discovered 127 unopened boxes

containing key documents. These were the papers of Alexander Kirk, held in Washington. Signals and orders provide a proper understanding of what actually happened in 1945. Kirk summed up the situation in a report to the State Department in Washington in August of that year:

> We have today been informed by Deputy Chief of Staff on behalf of Supreme Allied Commander that decision to turn over to Tito Yugoslav nationals under reference was made on grounds of military necessity in view of conditions existing at that time. It was stated that Supreme Allied Commander took note of our concurrence and pointed out that British Resident Minister [Macmillan] had concurred in proposed action but that in any case Supreme Allied Commander took his decision because of conditions existing of which he was better aware than [State] Dep[artment].[58]

Macmillan was not present at the G-5 meeting on 22 May, and was not even in Europe when the Udine meetings took place on 26 and 27 May. The key factor, which led the Cowgill inquiry to apportion no blame to Macmillan regarding repatriated Yugoslavs was that all operative decisions were taken after he had returned to England.

The accusations against him caused Macmillan anguish in his old age. Although some members of the Macmillan family disagreed as to the nature and degree of these feelings, Christopher Booker was not overstating the probability when he wrote, 'On his death bed Harold Macmillan, Earl of Stockton, was racked by the knowledge that he stood publicly accused of the most damning charges ever levelled at any British Prime Minister.'[59] Macmillan knew, at first hand, the horror of the Great War trenches, the hopelessness of the Depression, and the suffering of homeless families in the early 1950s. He was, like his friend Victor Cazalet, 'most sensible to the sufferings of others'.[60] There is no question that the Cossacks and Yugoslavs suffered hideously. These wartime memories brought forth a sense – long latent – of shame that the British army had been involved in such actions and that Macmillan, in whatever capacity, had been a part of brutal decisions justified by mere expediency.

This feeling was deepened by his awareness of his inability to defend his corner, demonstrated by what proved to be an ill-advised interview with Ludovic Kennedy on BBC television on 21 December 1984. At that stage Macmillan was infirm, nearly blind, and no longer able to cope lucidly with the complexities of recall. What he said in that interview was at times unfortunately expressed. 'I'd really nothing much to do with it [repatriation] except carry out our instructions' was not, after the Nuremberg Trials, the most appropriate form of exculpation. He also did himself no favours over some detailed points. At one stage he asserted to Kennedy that the 'Cossacks were practically savages' and that the White Russians were 'not friends of ours'.[61] In fact, most of the senior and middle-ranking Cossack officers were cosmopolitan, well informed and better educated than many of their opposite numbers in the British and American armed forces. Many of the White Russians, if not most, *were* friends and anti-Nazi.

Macmillan was nearly 91 at the time and was under the impression that he was being interviewed as part of the publicity for his most recent publication (*War Diaries*, 1984). Under close questioning from Kennedy he became visibly agitated. The overall impression, especially after it became known that sections of the recorded interview were embargoed,* was to make him appear evasive. Even in its truncated form the programme was unhelpful to Macmillan, and even convinced one of the future Cowgill inquiry team, Christopher Booker, that he was concealing the truth.

The Cowgill inquiry examined the transcript of the interview, including the sections that were not broadcast, but demonstrated that the main points Macmillan made under duress were, in fact, true. 'Despite his distress and very hazy memory as to the precise details,' the report concluded, 'the essential picture Macmillan was giving of who had agreed to the hand-over of the Cossacks was rooted in truth.'[62]

Macmillan had already become aware that silence would be interpreted as itself an admission of guilt. As a result, he had attempted long before the Kennedy interview to find out what light could be shed through primary sources on the events of 1945. On 24 June 1980, he wrote to Sir Robert (later Lord) Armstrong, Secretary of the Cabinet and Head of the Home Civil Service, to enquire about the existence of any records in the archives of the relevant government departments.[63] He was specifically interested in any responses to the telegram (quoted by Nikolai Tolstoy in *The Minister and the Massacres*) Keightley had sent to Alexander, through General McCreery, on 14 May:

On advice Macmillan today suggested to Soviet General in Tolbukhin's HQ that Cossacks should be returned to Soviets at once. Explained that I had no power to do this without your

---

* At Macmillan's own request, which did not look good either.

authority but would be glad to know Tolbukhin's views and that if they coincided with mine I would ask you officially. Cannot see any point in keeping the large number Soviet nationals clearly great source contention between Soviets and ourselves.[64]

Armstrong gave instructions for a search to be made of the relevant files in the Cabinet Office and the Ministry of Defence. The trawl, far from as rigorous as the complexities demanded, particularly as the request had come from a former Prime Minister, was largely inconclusive.[65] Keightley's telegram of 14 May 1945 was unearthed, together with one issued by Alexander on 17 May, reporting the difficulties 5 Corps faced with 'widespread commitments and responsibilities for prisoners of war', and one from the Chiefs of Staff to Alexander on 20 June, which confirmed that 'the action already taken by you with respect to the transfer of Cossacks overland to Soviet Military authorities as reported in your 0–5659 of 26th May 1945 is approved'.[66] These were the only three documents, apart from his own diary, that Macmillan had to hand when he was interviewed by Ludovic Kennedy.[67]

After Macmillan's death, significant further files, not found at the time of his original request, but which had survived,[68] were declassified, notably the Foreign Office 1020 series of the headquarters and regional files from the Allied Commission for Austria.

Macmillan was criticised for not speaking out in his own defence, and for declining to see Nikolai Tolstoy in the early part of his enquiries, though as Tolstoy himself conceded, he 'was clearly under no obligation to assist every historian approaching him'.[69] Macmillan's death in December 1986 brought no end to the debate, especially as libel was not now an issue. The need for what became the Cowgill inquiry was in fact partly prompted by the BBC interview, though mainly it was in response to the Bethell and Tolstoy publications.

In 1992, Sir Carol Mather, a military veteran who had toured the various camps in Austria containing Axis prisoners in 1945, published a firm rebuttal of the accusations against Macmillan. In his account Mather stressed the contemporary view that all those with the Germans were regarded as enemies and that the Cossacks themselves were believed to have committed grievous atrocities (this was itself disputed). He also claimed that screening of individuals was impossible and that any ultimate responsibility lay with Field Marshal Alexander, as the decisions on repatriation of Nazi collaborators had pre-dated Macmillan's involvement by many months.[70] The latter point was one that had long since been made by Christopher Booker. 'If he [Harold Macmillan] had not gone to Klagenfurt on 13 May,' Booker wrote in 1977, 'the repatriations would still have taken place (even if the Cossacks had been returned by a different route).'[71]

Macmillan was in the position in 1980 of being accused of knowing far more about the events of May 1945 than he admitted. His silence was used to build up the case that he was 'hiding something'. Yet when he tried to find documents from the period that would illuminate the situation, he was told (erroneously) on the highest authority available to him that there was little possibility, 35 years later, of unearthing more than the three telegrams Armstrong's civil servants had discovered.

When the researchers on the Cowgill inquiry conducted a transatlantic hunt, duplicates of key British documents were discovered in the papers of Alexander Kirk. Kirk's papers were for all to see in the National Archives in Washington.

The publication of the Cowgill report in 1990 led to further interest on an international level. Following an article by Robert Harris in the *Sunday Times* on 21 October 1990 claiming that the inquiry was a whitewash, Brigadier Cowgill issued a writ for libel against the newspaper, which was settled out of court, with the *Sunday Times* paying money, in respect of costs, plus a further donation to the Army Benevolent Fund in final settlement. In addition, the paper commissioned an article by Norman Stone, then Professor of Modern History at Oxford University. Professor Stone concluded:

Macmillan can be completely exonerated. The military, handing over Soviet nationals, included some foreign passport holders, without realising what they were doing until later when the process was stopped. On the Yugoslav hand-overs, there was misunderstanding, comprehensible enough in the very early days of the British occupation of that area, when our few troops were greatly overstretched.

In any event, the suggestion that there was a British plot to hand back anti-Stalinists is now ended, and so, too, is any idea that Macmillan conspired.[72]

Robert Knight, whose article 'Harold Macmillan and the Cossacks: Was there a Klagenfurt Conspiracy?' first countered the Tolstoy accusations, wrote a further account of repatriations in the light of the Cowgill report:

The unsavoury nature of this operation, and even more the fate of those sent back, especially the Yugoslavs, naturally poses moral as well as historical questions. Many of the British officers involved clearly did feel shame and regret about their involvement. In the Cold War it was politically embarrassing as well, but accusations of an establishment cover-up are nonsense. In fact the whole discussion of the repatriation conforms closely with the dynamics of contemporary history: the opening of archives after thirty years leading to sensational 'discoveries', media attention and bad history, followed after several more years by a methodical rebuttal (and fewer headlines.)[73]

In October 1990 *The Times* published an article in which Daniel Johnson commented, 'As Cowgill shows, Macmillan was telling the truth: that he had merely advised officers on the ground that Allied policy under the Yalta agreement was to hand back the Cossacks and he had, like everyone else, been unaware that large numbers of them were Russian émigrés.'[74] Many of the Cossacks, in fact, held Nansen passports, though this afforded no protection.[75]

One of the most significant responses to the Cowgill report came in the *Army Quarterly & Defence Journal* in January 1991 from a veteran of the events, Lieutenant-General Sir James Wilson,[76] a subaltern at the time in the Greenjackets. Emphasising how the report, comprehensively based on primary evidence, showed the manner in which the military chain of command operated, General Wilson demonstrated that the full documentation revealed no gap in the record, which was in fact a process of seamless continuity. He wrote:

> The documents provide a remarkable insight into how well the chain of command worked in the final stages of the war ... The professionalism of the staff work at every level comes across as outstanding; directives and signals were clear and admirably expressed, with no room left for doubt. In such circumstances, it would have been impossible to have operated a Klagenfurt conspiracy, and the idea that McCreery, for example, could have been by-passed or left in ignorance of such a design, emerges as absurd. Cowgill's team have, therefore, reached the right conclusions.[77]

Others, with recollections of the time, remain to be convinced. Major Hugh Lunghi, a member of the Military Mission in Moscow, after work as Chiefs of Staff interpreter and assistant interpreter for Churchill at Teheran, the Moscow TOLSTOY conference in October 1944, Yalta and Potsdam, was involved on the British Repatriation Committee in 1945, largely concerned with the return of Allied prisoners of war through Russia. As such he worked closely with the

Soviet counterparts, headed by the bullet-headed, and very ruthless, General Golikov.[78] Lunghi recalled:

> In Moscow, as among most people who had knowledge and experience of Russia, we were appalled to learn rather late in the day that we were forcibly returning White Russians and others who did not hold Soviet citizenship to the Soviet Union. It was all the more misguided because the Soviet side at first did not lay any claim to them. As far as I recall, Golikov did not initially refer to them at all. On the contrary the Soviet side at first said and wrote that their concern was *Soviet citizens*. We knew very well what was his, that is Stalin's, priority and why. The Cossacks and others were a late icing on the cake for Stalin.[79]

The most recent detailed study of the controversy has been by Edwyn Morris of Queen Mary College, London.[80] His conclusion is that the prime motivation of the British in dealing with the Soviet authorities was one of 'over-compliance' with the Yalta agreement, 'in order to secure a guarantee from the Soviet representatives for the direct repatriation of British prisoners in their custody'. It was neither a conspiracy nor an innocent mistake. 'Over-compliance', according to Brigadier Cowgill, after reading the Morris thesis, is not the most accurate description of what unfolded. What happened was 'full compliance' with the Yalta agreement.[81]

The decisions emanated from the top of the British government and were not independently instigated by Macmillan. As the Morris thesis demonstrated, 'The overriding objective of the British government was to secure a guarantee for the return of British prisoners.'[82] The fear at the time was that failure to repatriate 'the Cossacks' would have had deleterious consequences for British prisoners of war. The position of these PoWs was extremely vulnerable. Stalin would have had no compunction whatever about using them as a bargaining chip or holding back their release.

The Soviet side was desperately dilatory in setting up any kind of machinery to help their own PoWs. Stalin indeed cared little for the Soviet prisoners of war, whom he regarded as traitors, but he did not want to leave them in the capitalist world to spread the word about the reality of life in the USSR, which is one reason why his men bargained to get them repatriated. The Soviet system meant that virtually every decision had to be approved by Stalin personally. In addition, it seemed to those in the British Military Mission that initially the Russians were not particularly worried about their own

PoWs in British hands, until they received reports from NKVD and SMERSH[83] officers in those holding camps.

Major Hugh Lunghi confirms that when the time came, the transfers of British PoWs were eventually humanely and expeditiously conducted.[84] The overwhelming tragedy is that the corresponding transfers from the British side, because of the British wish to be 'fully compliant', and the utter ruthlessness of the Soviet authorities on Stalin's orders, could not be similarly described.

The two vast volumes of the Cowgill report and of the associated documents, whatever dissenters may make of the conclusions drawn from them, stand as one of the most remarkable and comprehensive historical investigations of recent years. Indeed, these volumes have been held up, especially in American universities, as a model of how such historical investigations should be conducted. Sadly, Macmillan was not to live to see them.

One of the pitfalls of historical interpretation is hindsight, judging yesterday's events by the different standards of the present. In May 1945, a period of total war was coming to an end, and it is difficult today to appreciate the mind-set of those times. The atomic bomb was about to be detonated over Japan. That was what the times seemed to demand. In the light of that, callous though it seems today, as one very distinguished and humane person said to the author, recalling those days, 'the Cossacks issue was very small beer'.[85]

Understandably the events aroused, and continue to arouse, a deep emotional response, containing just enough mystery to keep the controversy going. As another persecuted figure of that early summer of 1945, the fictional operatic anti-hero Peter Grimes, proclaimed, 'the case goes on in people's minds'.[86] A detailed study of the issues reveals that many of the people involved at the time had their own piece of the jigsaw in the memory bank, often with distinct visual recollections, but that the comprehensive overview could only be recreated by access to the whole documentation, a process completed by the discovery of the Alexander Kirk papers in Washington.

As a result, although there is still no consensus, and it is unlikely that there ever will be, on what happened in those dreadful days in May 1945, nor on who was ultimately responsible for the fate of the repatriated, the debate is now becoming a heavily one-sided one. A final agreed judgment cannot be made by ticking some boxes and crossing others.

Yet if the accusation that Macmillan was under obligation to Stalin, because of his alleged links to the NKVD from the time of his 1932 visit to Russia, is discounted – and the possibility, bizarre to later observers, was authoritatively assessed and dismissed in 1988[87] – then the overriding obstacle to believing that Macmillan was a war criminal, who, in the opinion of some, deserved to be hanged,[88] remains one of motive. Was he, for example, an agent of the KGB? His remarks about Palmiro Togliatti, the Soviet Communist agitator, quoted in Chapter 11, were not those of a man who had membership, sympathy or commitment to the Soviet security services. No credible motive exists for Macmillan – who was ambitious to take a prominent place in the post-war political scene in Britain – to engage in such a conspiracy with the Soviets, followed by a cover-up and 40 years of supposed deceit. 'When you have eliminated the impossible,' famously observed Sherlock Holmes, 'whatever remains, *however improbable, must be the truth.*'[89] Despite all the accusations following the events of those shameful repatriations, the case against Macmillan personally is unfounded.[90] The policy of 'full compliance', originating from the British government, was motivated by the wish for a speedy return of British prisoners of war in Soviet hands.

The essence of the whole complex matter is contained in the quotation placed as an epigram at the head of the Cowgill report:

> There was one very difficult principle that we were up against which I did not really know about to start with ... that in accordance with the general surrender everyone was supposed to surrender to the Allied Army against whom they had been fighting.
>
> Everyone in this part of the world had obviously been fighting against either the Russians or the Yugoslavs, but the devil of it was that they were prepared to do anything rather than surrender to either of these armies.[91]

It was the devil indeed. Those captured wanted to surrender either to the Americans or the British, but they fell under the terms agreed at Yalta, and were also victims of the circumstances of war as the Allies had to make preparations for the possibility of fighting Tito and his partisans in the very same area. Subsequent developments were in accordance with those surrender terms, and were decided at the highest level.

More directly involved than Macmillan in the political sphere were his superiors, Churchill and Eden; and in the military theatre of war, Alexander,* McCreery and Keightley. Macmillan's job was to tell the

---

*It is ironic that Macmillan was the one to endure shame and humiliation. His hero,

generals what those at the top had decided. He was the messenger bringing unpalatable instructions. By the time the final decisions were being taken, he was back in London as a member of Churchill's caretaker government. Stalin had got what he wanted – and he had got it at Yalta.

Edmund Burke writing of Chatham,* did not flinch from listing his faults, but concluded, 'I am sure I am not disposed to blame him.'[92] The words could stand as the final epitaph on Macmillan's part in a tragic episode.

Alexander, died in 1969 and shared none of the pain.
*William Pitt, 'Pitt the Elder', first earl of Chatham (1708–1778), British Prime Minister, 1766–1768.

CHAPTER THIRTEEN

The Possibilities of Defeat

1945

We are not interested in the possibilities of defeat; they do not exist.

Queen Victoria to A. J. Balfour, December 1899, during a period of Boer success in the early stages of the South African War

General Elections are the locks on the stream of British democracy, controlling the flow of the river and its traffic.

Sir Lewis Namier

Tyneside would like to touch the hem of your garment on Monday, Tuesday or Wednesday of next week.

Conservative parliamentary candidate for Jarrow to Winston Churchill, 30 June 1945

Clement Attlee: I've won the Election.
King George VI: I know. I heard it on the Six O'Clock news

First exchange between the King and his new Prime Minister, 26 July 1945

On 6 September 1944, Sir Henry 'Chips' Channon, MP for Southend, discussed the prospects for the post-war general election with Robin Barrington-Ward, the editor of *The Times*. 'He thinks politically there is no serious swing to the Left; and says the country is "centre of centre",' Channon recorded in his diary. 'So much for the foolish prophecy of that very nice ass Harold Macmillan who goes about saying that the Conservatives will be lucky to retain a hundred seats at the election.'[1] Ten months later the prophecy was not to prove so foolish after all.

On 22 May 1945, Churchill went to Buckingham Palace at noon to tender his resignation to King George VI as Prime Minister of the Grand Coalition. He then returned to the Number 10 annexe for lunch with his wife, a deliberate constitutional pause. At 4 p.m. the King invited Churchill to return to the palace, where he then invited him, as leader of the largest party in the Commons, to form a new administration, which became known as 'the caretaker government'. The decision Churchill had taken in November 1940 to seek election as Conservative leader had spared the King any constitutional difficulty. The position was unambiguous.

Over the next two days, Churchill appointed the members of the first predominantly Conservative administration since 1929.

He offered Bevin's former post to Macmillan. Macmillan felt that Labour and National Service was a department not suited to one who had been out of the country for so long, an attitude that showed confidence that another full Cabinet post would be offered as an alternative. Churchill then offered him the Air Ministry, which Macmillan accepted. He kissed hands and received the Seals of Office from the King on 28 May 1945, two days after returning to Britain from the Mediterranean theatre of war.

Rab Butler was now appointed Minister of Labour and National Service. Macmillan and Butler were to be the dominating figures of Conservative politics from the mid-1950s to the mid-1960s. In May 1945, most observers of the political scene would have regarded Butler as having the prior claim over Macmillan to Churchill's patronage. In October 1951, the reverse might have been the case.

Churchill then sought a Dissolution of Parliament from the King. Polling day was fixed for 5 July and, uniquely, declaration was to be deferred for three weeks until 26 July to allow for the collection and counting of the overseas forces' votes. Parliament was dissolved on 15 June. The 'caretaker' ministers were no sooner in office then they were on the election trail.

For some time Macmillan had been discreetly seeking a safer seat than Stockton-on-Tees. In September 1944, the ideal opportunity had presented itself. Duff Cooper, who had won the safe seat of St George's, Westminster, in 1931 at the height of Beaverbrook's press campaigns against Stanley Baldwin, had been unexpectedly appointed Ambassador to France. His task was to restore the diplomatic mission that had been withdrawn in June 1940. On 25 September, Duff Cooper first mooted the possibility of Macmillan being adopted as candidate in his place.[2] Macmillan replied succinctly on 5 October from Naples: 'Briefly, "Barkis is willing".'[3] On 26 October 1944, Duff Cooper wrote to Macmillan to tell him that his name as a possible successor had been extremely well received by the St George's constituency organisation. 'If I were you,' he advised, 'I would waste no time in breaking the news to Stockton.'

Matters were not quite so straightforward. Ralph Assheton had just been appointed Chairman of the Conservative and Unionist Party, and one of his first decrees was that sitting MPs must defend their present seats in the first instance. On 13 February, Macmillan wrote to Churchill pleading for the ban to be lifted. He outlined two reasons:

(1) If I stay in Parliament I hope either to be in the Government or, if we are in opposition, to be able to combine business and politics. I have therefore long felt uncertain about the physical effort of continuing at Stockton. I am fifty-one years of age and I have lived a hard life.

(2) At my age I frankly do not wish to be out of Parliament.

St George's, especially in the person of Sir John Murray, the treasurer of the constituency organisation, were pressing Macmillan to commit, but this he could not do without special dispensation. Also Lord Gage[4], a Sussex neighbour of Macmillan, was dangling the prospect of the safe seat of Lewes. Churchill seemed sympathetic to Macmillan's plight, as he wanted him to be in Parliament, but he was not going to overrule his recently appointed party chairman. Accordingly, Macmillan wrote a frank letter on 19 February 1945 to Assheton:

I saw the Prime Minister in Athens the other day. He tells me that he was perfectly prepared to allow my name to go forward for St George's in all the circumstances which you had explained to him.

I am very anxious indeed about the future of the Stockton seat for all the reasons which you can well imagine. The truth of it is that I have run it on a very personal basis for nearly twenty-two years, and as a result of the last five years it has been very largely neglected...My old retired agent, who is pensioned by me, lives in Stockton and can do a little to help, but most of the workers have faded out into different forms of war work. It would not be a great effort to revive it, but it would need somebody more or less permanently there. If this were done I think the seat could be held, but it would need a young, active, good-looking officer, full of ideals, such as I was twenty-two years ago – not a party politician growing bald and cynical.

Macmillan then made his most dramatic suggestion – that Lady Dorothy be adopted. His wife had nursed the constituency for five years, and, like Barkis, she too was willing. 'She would certainly get in,' Macmillan concluded.

Beaverbrook now got involved. He was not keen on special dispensation, as this would open the floodgates. 'If Stockton is lost you will be blamed,' he wrote to Macmillan on 22 February. 'If it is won by your successor, you will suffer ridicule as one who has taken unnecessary precautions.'

Gradually the options were closing. On 30 March 1945, Macmillan wrote to Duff Cooper. 'Events have so worked out as to make it necessary for me to go on at Stockton.' Duff Cooper blamed Churchill for the whole imbroglio. 'I am very sorry that you should have felt it necessary to turn down St George's after all,' he replied on 20 April. 'I knew that the Prime Minister was against your taking it, because he had expressed himself in that sense to me when I first mentioned it to him. I felt then, as I feel now, that he is quite wrong. Even Homer nods.'

Meanwhile Macmillan was receiving guarantees from Assheton and Beaverbrook about his future prospects, a tacit admission that he was in all likelihood going to lose the seat. On 7 April 1945, Beaverbrook wrote, 'The Prime Minister told me that if you were defeated, the party should find you a by-election. There I propose to let it rest. Churchill made the same statement to Bracken and Assheton.'[5] Two days later Assheton confirmed the promise. 'If, by bad luck, you do not get in, I have no doubt we shall be able to make some appropriate arrangement and meet the difficulty.'

Macmillan was philosophical. On 26 March, he wrote to Sir John Murray and George Gage saying that he had finally decided to stand for Stockton.*

'I fear my decision will cause a lot of trouble with St Georges's, especially after all their thoughtfulness, but I am sure it is the best thing to do,' he had written in his diary on 24 March. 'Poor Dorothy will have to undertake again those awful journeys to the North. But I feel she will always be spiritually happier in Stockton or Thornaby than in Eaton Square!'[6] Two days later, Macmillan summed up the whole experience in a letter to Lady Dorothy from Rome:

> I am sure I am right. I have a sort of instinct that it is the best course. It is curious that no matter how we try to get away from Stockton some fate drives us back there. The one thing that worries me is the work that it will mean for you. I suppose you will have to go to Stockton at least once to see how things are, and of course it

---

*The negotiations regarding St George's and Lewes were unknown to the Stockton constituency.

will always be a burden even if we win it. On the other hand, I don't really think it would really be such a nuisance as the Lewes seat which would take up a lot of time. St George's would be no trouble. But you would find it intolerably stuffy.

On 30 April, the Stockton constituency held its first association meeting since September 1939. The minutes recorded that 'Lady Dorothy was present and received a great reception.' The next day, F.W. B. Pacey, the new chairman of the association, warned Macmillan that Labour were making capital out of his lengthy absence from the constituency.

Many of the negotiations about Macmillan's political candidature had inevitably been conducted at a distance, as he had remained in Italy for the completion of his mission, with only occasional forays to London. On 26 May 1945, the great adventure on which he had embarked on New Year's Day in 1943 finally came to its conclusion. There was a send-off when he left Marcianise airfield, near Caserta, at 10 a.m. Like all partings, the occasion had its poignant air. Despite the tragedies and sufferings, the war had been a liberating experience for Macmillan. He had come of age politically and was now indisputably one of the leaders of his generation. A chapter in his life had come to an end.

Macmillan's final words before boarding the plane were with Field Marshal Alexander. 'Alex, wouldn't it be lovely to have it all to do over again?' he said to the military chief whom he admired above all. Alexander was more sanguine. 'Oh, no,' he replied. 'We might not do nearly so well.'[7]

Macmillan returned to a Britain facing the prospect of its first general election for ten years. Agents had to be found in run-down constituencies and candidates selected and confirmed. Organisational decline had left the Conservatives at a marked disadvantage. Many wives (on whom the Conservatives had traditionally depended for so much voluntary unpaid work) no longer had the domestic help that enabled them to give freely of their time. Robert Blake has identified these years as a 'twilight period between the era of cheap servants and the era of cheap washing machines',[8] in short, between the age of Baldwin and the age of Macmillan. The Labour Party, on the other hand, had always had a semi-professional paid force of party workers, many recently retired or in the reserved occupations.[9]

Churchill was soon out in the field, making a notorious radio broadcast on 4 June. 'No Socialist Government conducting the entire life and industry of the country could afford to allow free, sharp, or violently-worded expressions of public discontent,' he declared. 'They would have to fall back on some form of Gestapo, no doubt very humanely directed in the first instance.'[10] When Churchill had shown his wife Clementine the draft of this speech before the broadcast, she had pleaded with him to remove the reference to the Gestapo. Churchill had brushed his wife's objections aside.

Macmillan was horrified by Churchill's 'Gestapo' broadcast, and believed he might have been influenced by Friedrich Hayek's recently published work *The Road to Serfdom* (1944), with its assertion that central state planning inevitably meant a curtailment of freedom.[11] 'Gestapo' was offensive shorthand. In any case, Macmillan was deeply pessimistic about the eventual outcome of the election, and rightly so, because there had been a groundswell of hostility towards the Tories from 1943 to 1945 – which they had largely failed to notice. In what might be interpreted as a foolhardy and presumptuous manner, Macmillan wrote to Churchill to tell him how he felt. It was a carefully worded, even coded, letter, but the meaning was unambiguous. 'Your first broadcast has given a splendid start off to the Party, by which I mean the old *Conservative* workers throughout the country. They liked its virility and forcefulness. But it must be made clear that your warnings were against the extreme Socialist tail wagging the moderate Labour and Trade Union dog.' More important messsages needed to be delivered. Macmillan strongly advised Churchill to 'go full steam ahead with the programme of social reform prepared by the Coalition Government. This is the real appeal for the immediate future. Please forgive my interference.'[12]

Churchill was not best pleased to receive this missive, which he ignored, returning to the theme in two further radio broadcasts. He was unaccustomed to such messages, even from senior colleagues, let alone Cabinet ministers of less than a fortnight's standing. The letter confirmed Churchill in his belief that Macmillan was an opinion-ated subordinate, 'too viewy',[13] as he put it. Churchill's mistrust of Macmillan was to grow.

Hindsight, of course, shows that Macmillan was entirely correct in his analysis. Not that Churchill was ever convinced about social re-form. 'Who were those young men talking to me just now?' he asked, after he had been hearing ideas on the welfare state from a group of progressive Tory MPs. 'They're not members of our party, surely? They're nothing but a bunch of pink pansies.'[14]

Churchill did not have an easy ride during the campaign. His elec-tioneering relied far too much on past glories. The wartime cigars, a reassuring symbol a few months earlier, were now a disadvantage. Troops and civilians, who were short of cigarettes, and much else, were envious of Churchill's seemingly ready supply of luxuries. 'It's all right for him' was a widespread attitude. On 3 July, two days before polling, he was booed in Wandsworth, and stones were thrown in Ladbroke Grove. His appearances on newsreels too were coldly received in many cinemas.

Meanwhile Macmillan got down to work at the Air Ministry, acquainting himself with details of the department and its responsibilities. As he did not expect to be in office eight weeks later, he regarded this experience as a dividend for the future and a pragmatic widening of his political experience.

The Air Ministry had been created in January 1918 to oversee the transformation of the Royal Flying Corps and the Royal Navy Air Service into the Royal Air Force.

One of Macmillan's first tasks was in determining the ministry's part in distributing electoral material and ballot papers to the forces, so that votes could be returned to Britain by 22 July. He visited the Parachute Training School at Ringway, Manchester, and also studied the problem of the eventual disposal of the 180 airfields without permanent runways, places such as the Fleet Air Arm base HMS *Godwit* at Hinstock in Shropshire.[15] He co-ordinated the work of RAF Benson in Oxfordshire in conducting photographic surveys of Europe for the post-war Control Commissions, and visited the RAF in Germany. On 19 July, he wrote to Churchill in Potsdam with details of the 20 squadrons that were going to participate in a fly-past over London on 16 September, Battle of Britain Sunday.

At the back of everyone's mind, though, rather like the distant sound of thunder at a picnic, was the forthcoming election. Macmillan travelled to Stockton for his sixth campaign, and also found time to visit the nearby constituency of Seaham, where his son, Maurice, was fighting his first campaign in Emanuel Shinwell's safe Labour seat. Macmillan found the campaign curiously dull and uneventful, as though people had already made up their minds and did not wish to embarrass him after his 22 years' service. The Beveridge report of 1942, the blueprint for the post-war welfare state, was the main topic of interest, as Macmillan knew it would be. Beveridge's five targets for defeat – Want, Disease, Ignorance, Squalor and Idleness – were those that Macmillan identified also. The electorate, though, were not going to trust the Conservative Party with the implementation of Beveridge.

Election day itself, on 5 July, was unusual, as there was no town hall declaration to conclude proceedings. Three weeks later, Macmillan and Lady Dorothy returned to Stockton for the result, which came at 10.25 a.m. It was the end of his time as Stockton's MP. The result was decisive:

George Chetwynd (Labour)	27,128
The Rt Hon. Harold Macmillan (Conservative)	18,464
G. P. Evans (Liberal)	3,718
Labour majority	8,664[16]

Of all the major Conservative losses, this was the first to be announced and remained the main story for the rest of the day, another sign of Macmillan's growing prominence. In all five members of Churchill's caretaker Cabinet were defeated, and 32 junior members of his administration. For the first time nationally, Labour had a plurality of the votes cast, and an overall majority. Labour gained 239 seats and the Conservatives lost 190. Macmillan's fears had been confirmed. The post-mortem began at once.

King George VI recorded in his diary that the result was 'a great surprise to one and all'.[17] Yet with hindsight, one wonders why. Opinion polls were in their infancy, but the portents were clear. 'Why gaze into the crystal ball,' asked Aneurin Bevan, 'when you can read it in the book?' The anti-Conservative vote in July 1945 was like the bursting of a dam as the pent-up feelings, held in check for so long, were finally released.

Elections are fought on two levels – the self-interested and materialistic on the one hand, and the idealistic and altruistic on the other. When one party has the upper hand in both categories, as Labour did in 1945, a landslide follows. 'The mass of the electorate was voting in defence of full employment and against a reversion to the economic depression of the 1930s,' wrote Robert Blake of the 1945 election. 'To this sentiment was added the impetus of socialist utopianism inspired by the anti-capitalist writings of a whole intellectual generation.'[18] The voter was looking forward and Churchill's wartime status was not relevant to what Attlee called 'new world conditions'.[19] As Anthony Howard has written, 'The dole queue was more evocative than El Alamein.'[20]

After polling day on 5 July, Churchill had taken a short holiday, before travelling to the Potsdam conference to meet Stalin and Harry S. Truman. He arrived in Berlin on 15 July, his defeat already 10 days old in the as yet unlocked ballot boxes. Attlee accompanied the British delegation at Churchill's invitation, notwithstanding the 'Gestapo' gibe. The British returned to London on 25 July for the results of the General Election. The conference, ironically for Churchill, was codenamed TERMINAL.

Once the results were known, and after being charged by the King with the responsibility of forming a new government, Attlee returned to the Potsdam conference, accompanied by Ernest Bevin, the new Foreign Secretary. Stalin was mystified at the absence of Churchill and Eden, and enquired where they were. Attlee explained that there had been a general election in Britain, and that he was now Prime Minister. Stalin shook his head and said through the interpreter, 'We do things very differently in Russia.'[21]

Macmillan now also had to face up to the task of doing things differently. Publishing obviously beckoned again, now that he was no longer disqualified from directorships by office. So did family life and the gradual return from Pooks Cottage to the big house. The estate had inevitably been neglected, and much work was needed. Grandchildren were on the scene. His eldest daughter Caroline and son-in-law Julian Faber, now had their first child, Anne. In addition there were Maurice's two sons, Alexander and Joshua, whom Macmillan saw as hopeful portents for the future.

Macmillan's hunt for a new seat did not last long. On 17 July, two former Tory MPs and candidates, Sir Edward Campbell at Bromley, and Leslie Ruthven Pym at Monmouth, had died, and both were elected posthumously nine days later.[22] As the senior Cabinet casualty in the election, Macmillan was first in line for one of the immediate vacancies. Assheton and Beaverbrook honoured their pledge and ensured that the Bromley Conservatives were quickly off the mark in securing their new candidate. Randolph Churchill had also been interested in the nomination, but as soon as he heard that Macmillan was in the field, he stepped down. He wrote to Macmillan on 17 August, welcoming Macmillan's candidature at Bromley. Although the by-election was not to be held until November, Macmillan was doubly fortunate. The uncertainties of Stockton were behind him.[23] At last he had a safe seat for life, something that Anthony Eden at Warwick and Leamington and Rab Butler at Saffron Walden had enjoyed for all their political careers. In addition, the seat was within easy proximity of both Westminster and Birch Grove, indeed on the direct route between the two. On the surface, things could not have been better.

The delay until November also proved beneficial, as Macmillan had plenty of time to acquaint himself with the constituency and to meet the personnel involved. By the time he attended Bromley FC's home tie in their FA Cup fourth-round qualifying match on 3 November, he was well known to everybody. Churchill sent him a public message of support, and on 9 November, five days before polling, made a tour of the constituency with Macmillan. Although demobilisation was the predominant issue of the time, Macmillan concentrated in his campaign on the post-war agenda, extolling Beveridge and 'the Middle Way'.

On 14 November 1945, Macmillan was duly re-elected to Parliament. On a lower poll than in July, when Sir Edward Campbell's 'posthumous' majority had been 6,259, the figures were:

The Rt Hon. Harold Macmillan (Conservative)	26,367
A. Bain (Labour)	20,810
J. C. Sayer (Liberal)	5,990
Conservative majority	5,557

In the subsequent four elections Macmillan contested at Bromley, he increased his majority every time.

Macmillan was reintroduced into Parliament on 20 November by two Collegers of his election from Eton, Henry Willink and Harry Crookshank. However, Bromley never engaged him emotionally, as Stockton had done. He was grateful for the safe billet it provided, and worked conscientiously for the constituency. For Lady Dorothy, the constituency was too genteel by half. The world of trim suburban hedges and ubiquitous lace curtains was not the natural territory of a rather bohemian, dishevelled aristocrat. Peers and pitmen were one thing, but small-town bank managers and the Rotary Club were another altogether.[24]

The Conservative Party was now at its lowest parliamentary strength since the Liberal landslide victory of 1906. Balfour and his Shadow Cabinet had not then set in train the internal reforms in both organisation and philosophy necessary for renewal. That this error was not repeated in 1945 can be attributed to several important figures, notably Lord Woolton, the new chairman of the party from July 1946. In the party's ranks were politicians who were well aware how much things had to change. Macmillan was prominent among those MPs. In the next five years, in the midst of all his renewed publishing activities, he took his part in the biggest challenge the party had faced in nearly half a century, nothing less than its complete reinvention. On 26 July, a lady diner at the Savoy Hotel had been overheard declaring, 'But this is terrible – *they've* elected a Labour Government, and *the country* will never stand for that.'[25] Macmillan saw it as his task to ensure that the Conservative party would not stand for it either. He knew that change would be painful and fiercely resisted. He relished the challenge.

CHAPTER FOURTEEN

The Wooden Horse of Peace

1945–1950

The bells proclaim the immediate joy,
The horror and the killing cease:
They drag within the walls of Troy
The wooden horse of Peace.

Patric Dickinson, *A Warning to Politicians*

When parliamentary life re-established itself at Westminster in August 1945, Conservatives MPs remained in a state of shock. Initially their elected number was only 189. Ten years earlier, there had been 432 Conservatives. Tories in Birmingham, formerly a Chamberlain stronghold, lost ten out of the thirteen city seats. The percentage share of the total national vote (39.8 per cent) won by the Conservatives was even lower than that achieved in the Liberal landslide victory of 1906 (43.6 per cent). Apart from the short periods of minority Labour governments in 1924 and from 1929–1931, it was the first time since May 1915 that the Conservatives had been completely excluded from office, and never since January 1906 had their opponents in the Commons won an overall parliamentary majority.

Defeat rankled in small, daily reminders. In the first place, for many members, with memories going back to the 1920s, the Speaker was simply sitting in the wrong place. Conservatives had been accustomed, seated as MPs on the government side, to inclining their heads to the left to catch his commands. Now they faced the task of inclining their policies in that direction instead if they were ever to occupy the government benches again. The centre ground of politics had shifted.

Although Macmillan, as a Privy Councillor and former Cabinet minister, was on the Opposition front bench when he returned to the House in November 1945, he was still regarded by many as a maverick figure, 'reputed to be overprone to philander with the Socialists'.[1] Brendan Bracken regarded him as a 'Neo-Socialist' and was relieved when Macmillan's proposal to change the party's name to 'The New Democratic Party'[2] was rejected by the 1946 party conference.

Many Conservatives imagined that, once the dust had settled, Churchill would retire from the leadership to concentrate on writing his war memoirs, and indulge in travel, horse-racing and painting. They were mistaken. He did all these things, in addition to making major international speeches on 'The Iron Curtain' and 'The United States of Europe', but of retirement there was no sign. In July 1947, discontent at Churchill's frequent absences from the Commons led to the Chief Whip, James Stuart, being dispatched by five senior colleagues[3] to tell him that it was time for him to retire. Stuart got short shrift. As it turned out, Churchill's continued leadership of the Conservative Party, though deeply frustrating to ambitious senior colleagues, had its quirky advantages. Internationally, he was fêted and acclaimed, which gave the Tories a vicarious sheen. Meanwhile, below the surface, modernisers such as Macmillan had free rein to continue unhindered reform of the party's finance, organisation and philosophy, in which Churchill took little interest. The longer Churchill trod the world stage – he made his famous Fulton speech on the Iron Curtain on 5 March 1946 – the less damage he was going to do to the party's new domestic agenda.

Sir Waldron Smithers,[4] MP for Orpington, was one of the most antediluvian figures of the post-war Tory Party. He fulminated in the Westminster bars against the modernisers – 'bloody rubbish' was one of his more repeatable refrains – and when four votes were recorded at the 1947 Party Conference against adoption of *The Industrial Charter*, it was said to be Smithers and a friend putting up both hands, an observation made before Smithers badly damaged his wrist punching a wall in frustration at the party's new direction. After *The Industrial Charter*, Smithers, organist of his local village church in Kent, published a pamphlet, 'Save England', liberally spattered with Biblical quotations. 'Then considered to be on the lunatic fringe of the right,' Ian Gilmour memorably observed in 1997, Smithers 'would now probably be thought a moderate Thatcherite.'[5]

It would be a mistake to think of all such traditional Tories as peppery colonels straight from an Osbert Lancaster cartoon.[6] Sir Herbert Williams,[7] with whom Smithers was often bracketed, was, behind his bluff exterior, a figure of considerable seriousness, with an acute political brain. His reasoned opposition to the direction of much of the new policy actually contributed to the debate, enabling reformers to hone and improve the substance of their thinking. Macmillan, prominent among these reformers, welcomed such argument. His attitude was that of John Stuart Mill: 'Since the general or prevailing opinion on any subject is rarely or never the whole truth, it is only by the collison of adverse opinions that the remainder of the truth has any chance of being supplied.'[8] In such a way had the Keynesian revolution been advanced in the 1930s; a decade later, new ideas also needed debating. In a parallel that Macmillan often drew, Sir Robert Peel had fought similar battles after the defeat of 1832. Peel's Tamworth Manifesto[9] of 1834, which redefined, and established, the modern Conservative Party, had also been opposed by the 'Ultras' of his day.

Macmillan delighted in the company of the younger, progressive Conservative MPs with good war records, who had entered the House for the first time in 1945, a select band numerically. Typical of such figures was Hugh Fraser, returned for the Staffordshire constituency of Stone in July 1945. Fraser had already attracted Macmillan's attention in North Africa. 'I feel sure he will go into politics if he gets through, and he ought to do well,' he had written in his diary on 9 July 1943. 'It is curious how each generation in turn starts out with the sort of Young England idea. Disraeli left a great mark on England, and I am interested to find that the young men in the Tory party now read his novels and study his life with the same enthusiasm as we did thirty years ago.'[10]

'The young men in the Tory party' in 1945 also included Douglas Dodds-Parker, who won the North Oxfordshire seat of Banbury in July 1945. Dodds-Parker was another who had been with Macmillan in Algiers and Caserta, as liaison officer between SOE and AFHQ: 'a very fine man' in Macmillan's opinion.[11] Indeed, the 'Honourable and Gallant' Tory members were a distinct grouping in that first post-war Parliament, arousing feelings of both guilt and resentment among those whose war service had been less military. The new Tory intake in July 1945 included Brigadiers Selwyn Lloyd, MP for the Wirral, and Toby Low, MP for Blackpool North. The importance of 'a good war' was one of the few issues uniting Macmillan and Waldron Smithers.[12]

Of all those who entered Parliament in July 1945, Selwyn Lloyd[13] was to be the most intricately associated with Macmillan in the years ahead. Theirs was a strange, complex relationship, yet at its best moments one of great fruitfulness. Both had suffered harsh regimes during their school days, and had troubled marriages.[14] Lloyd had stood as a Liberal candidate before the war, and was disappointed that Oswald Mosley's New Party had failed in 1931 to establish a middle way. Both represented suburban, well-to-do constituencies, whose natural political stance was more traditionally right wing than their own. Lloyd was a determined opponent of capital punishment and, like Macmillan, established important cross-party friendships. For a time their joint careers had an almost symbiotic aspect.

The 1945 Parliament presented a unique opportunity for these new, articulate and ambitious Tory back-benchers. The party leaders were not tucked away in government (the experience for most Tory MPs in the earlier part of the century) but were accessible and anxious for newcomers to take their part in attacking the soon-to-be beleaguered Labour government. No subjects were off limits. Through numerical necessity, front-bench spokesmen were not 'Shadow Ministers', confined to their briefs, but were able to range freely over a wide remit.

Macmillan certainly cast his net widely. In a speech in the House on 5 December 1945, he returned to his 1930s themes of reconstruction, and partnership between the state and private enterprise. He became chairman of the Conservatives' Fuel and Power Committee, a post that gave him some prominence during the bitter winter of 1947, when he devised the slogan 'Shiver with Shinwell and Starve with Strachey'.[15] Labour Party intellectuals such as Harold Laski attracted Macmillan's special scorn: 'clever men who in every age were always wrong', as he put it in a speech on 1 September 1946, taking Labour 'down the slippery slope to Communism'. On 3 October 1946, the day of the opening of the Conservative Party Conference, Macmillan wrote an article advocating a fusion of the anti-Socialist forces in Parliament, music to Churchill's ears, who still hankered after a formal alliance with the Liberals.[16] Indeed, in 1947, this was partially accomplished when the small National Liberal grouping merged formally with the Tories, Vichy Liberals as Violet Bonham Carter dubbed them.

On 20 November 1946, Macmillan, already established as the party's expert on industrial matters, delivered a notable contribution to a debate on the economic situation. 'During all my political and business life, that is during almost the whole period between the two wars, the question of unemployment has in the field of home politics played the major role,' he said in the Commons. 'I believe that in this period on which we are now embarking the problem of unemployment will be replaced by the problem of production.'[17] Churchill had sat beside Macmillan on the front bench during the debate and made a point of patting him on the back when he sat down. Earlier in the year, *The Observer* had already marked Macmillan out as a potential future leader. His Keynesian past was now a positive asset, not an embarrassment.

A break with that past for Macmillan came with the sudden and unexpected death of John Maynard Keynes on 21 April 1946. Their last collaboration had been Keynes' pamphlet *How to Pay for the War*, which Macmillan had published in February 1940, but the links went back much further. Keynes' death evoked so many intense memories, of Eton and the lush Thames Valley, of Dilly and Ronald Knox, and those days when the world was young and it seemed that the golden carpet laid out before their generation, as they set out on life's journey, before the blight of war, would stretch for ever. Lydia, Keynes' widow, wrote, 'The light is gone.'[19] The same was true for Harold Macmillan. Eventually the family firm was to publish *The Collected Writings of John Maynard Keynes* in 30 volumes, an indispensable source.

The Conservative Party Conference of October 1946 at Blackpool had taken place in a spirit of optimism and renewal unimaginable 15 months earlier. Its highlight was Anthony Eden's famous speech on the property-owning democracy, renewing Noel Skelton's philosophy of 'Constructive Conservatism' from the 1920s. 'The objective of Socialism is State Ownership of all the means of production, distribution and exchange,' Eden declared. 'Our objective is a nation-wide property-owning democracy.' Following the conference, Churchill was persuaded to set up an Industrial Policy Committee. Rab Butler was named its chairman, but Macmillan was prominent among those who served on it, alongside Oliver Stanley, David Maxwell-Fyfe, Oliver Lyttelton, and a future Chancellor of the Exchequer, Derick Heathcoat Amory. Wisely, the committee also included two traditionally minded MPs, Sir Peter Bennett[20] and James Hutchison,[21] who were to be important in persuading the right wing, or at least the more open-minded of the right-wingers, to accept the principles behind *The Industrial Charter* and not reject the document out of hand.

Research in the next few months was thorough. Together with other members of the committee Macmillan travelled the length and breadth of the country, meeting industrialists and (a radical departure for those times) trade union leaders.[22] Macmillan made important speeches in Epsom, Truro and Wandsworth, outlining the committee's thinking. Critics saw this as an attempt to soften the blow when *The Industrial Charter* was eventually published, but Macmillan was unrepentant. Someone needed to play the role of John the Baptist, and he was happy to do it. As President of the National Union in 1947, Macmillan was going to be a key figure in overseeing the presentation of the Charter to the annual conference in Brighton. He believed in getting the retaliation in first. The manner in which the conference in October was steered towards endorsement was a masterpiece of political manoeuvre.

The Industrial Charter was published on 11 May, not a good day for Sir Waldron Smithers' blood pressure. Its key features were a commitment to full employment, the principles of the welfare state and acceptance of the mixed economy. Nationalisation of coal, railways and the Bank of England were accepted as a *fait accompli*. A concluding section, 'The Workers' Charter', with proposals for humanising the labour system, was potentially the most contentious for Tory hardliners, but this was balanced by a commitment to reduced taxation and an orderly end of rationing and 'controls'.

When the time came for conference to consider *The Industrial Charter* in October, Maudling was asked by Churchill to outline the proposals as background for his keynote speech concluding the conference on 4 October. '"Give me five lines, Maudling," he [Churchill] said, "explaining what the Industrial Charter says." This I did. He read it with care, and then said, "But I do not agree with a word of this." "Well, sir," I said, "this is what the Conference has adopted." "Oh well," he said, "leave it in."'[23] Maudling's paraphrase then became the basis of Churchill's endorsement, although Churchill's heart was never in it.

The Industrial Charter, despite its occasional blandness, and deliberate avoidance of over-specific proposals, was a turning point in postwar Conservative history. The Conservative Research Department was midwife to other statements, such as *The Agricultural Charter* of 1948. These charters demonstrated that the party had moved on from its pre-war laissez-faire stance, and as perception in politics is often more important than detail, they did much to pave the way for eventual victory at the polls in 1951. Devotion to Adam Smith had been replaced by respect for J. M. Keynes. Above all, *The Industrial Charter*, the most substantial, was seen, in the words of the *Sunday Express*, as 'a triumph for Mr Harold Macmillan'. The paper reminded its readers that Macmillan 'once wrote a treatise called *The Middle Way*. This is its second edition.'[24] For his part Macmillan, with the confidence of his new-found relaxed manner, had declared, 'The Socialists are afraid of it; Lord Beaverbrook dislikes it; and the Liberals say it is too liberal to be fair. What more could one want? Was ever a child born under such a lucky star?'[25]

Clementine Churchill had famously said to her husband that the Conservative defeat in the 1945 general election might well prove to be a blessing in disguise. This proved correct.[26] Senior Labour ministers, many continuously in office since 1940, were increasingly worn down by their burdens (Bevin and Cripps were both to die prematurely). Their Conservative opposite numbers, on the other hand, had time to recharge their batteries, as well as to rethink their policies. By the time of the upturn in the economy in the 1950s, the Conservatives were to catch the tide of growing prosperity, which initially was to be the defining characteristic of Macmillan's premiership. The 1945 election was a good one to lose, just as surely as defeat at Stockton had turned out to be in Macmillan's long-term interests.

Labour, however unfairly, became the party associated with austerity, queuing, rationing and controls. The atmosphere in Parliament, especially as the 1950 election neared, became increasingly acrimonious. Bevan said that the Tory Party were 'lower than vermin',[27] a remark not forgotten, and which led to the formation of 'vermin clubs' to ensure that others did not forget either. Some Tory MPs, used to the inflated majorities of the 1930s, were fastidious and remained aloof, but not Macmillan, who revelled in the increasingly combative tone of parliamentary life. He dubbed the prevailing austerity the era of 'Fish and Cripps', and his parliamentary neighbour, Herbert Morrison, 'the Lewisham Bantam', an indication of his growing acerbity. By 1949, Cuthbert Headlam recorded that Macmillan was 'making ground'.[28] This was Macmillan's intention.

As a backdrop to all this parliamentary activity, Macmillan and Lady Dorothy were busy establishing themselves in their new constituency, then embracing Bromley, Beckenham and Penge. It still retained some of its pleasant rural aspect, though the sprawl of new building was becoming more evident. A fine library had been donated by Andrew Carnegie, befitting a borough not without its literary associations. H. G. Wells was born and educated in Bromley,[29] aspects of which are recreated in his novels *Kipps* and *The History of Mr Polly*. Dr Johnson's wife is buried in the churchyard of the parish church of St Peter and St Paul, where the front left-hand pew today bears the arms of the House of Commons, together with the name of Harold Macmillan. Until his national position made attendance at the Cenotaph necessary, the Remembrance Day service in November at the parish church was one of the fixed points of Macmillan's diary. The original church, destroyed in an air raid on 16 April 1941, was rebuilt in Macmillan's time, the foundation stone being laid by Princess Elizabeth on 13 October 1949. In the calendar of the church's festal days, these patronal saints customarily appear as St Peter and St Paul *AA*, which led Macmillan to dub them 'the motoring Apostles'.[31]

Bromley was typical of the suburbs that had expanded around the major cities in the 1930s. The Bromley Manor Estate of 1936 was full of the quintessential 'sun-trap' houses of the time. After the war, Bromley, and similar boroughs, represented the aspirational dream of countless families re-establishing themselves after the disruptions of war. Demand for affordable housing was to be one of the burning issues of the post-war years. Shortages of building materials and the priorities of the export market were to constrain that demand. For those who had moved from the inner cities and been able to put down a deposit on a house, places like Bromley were a world away from their pre-war experience. Trains and buses whisked commuters to their places of work; when they returned home, for recreation there was the cricket club at Bickley Park; the Orpington & Bromley Choir; the open-air swimming pool at Southlands; golf, bowling and tennis clubs; and an abundance of parks. There was a good community spirit, with a sense of involvement and 'joining in'.

Macmillan became vice-president of the Downham Community Boys' Boxing Club, contributing money for prize funds and attending tournaments, some involving boys from the Haileybury Club in Stepney, where Clement Attlee had worked before the Great War. Good local schools, such as St Olave's & St Saviour's Grammar School, Beckenham & Penge County Grammar School and Ravensbourne School, abounded. Macmillan became a regular visitor to them all, especially on Speech Days.*

'After my work in the City, I like to be at home,' Charles Pooter† said. 'What's the good of a home, if you are never in it?'[32] Intellectuals sneered at the pretensions of the rising Pooterish lower-middle class. Macmillan's snobbery, which could have a biting edge, was never directed at such constituents; they were the future of the Conservative Party.

Bromley was then outwardly proper, even prim, though it was the birthplace, in 1957, of Siouxsie Sioux, who later appeared in bondage outfits with Sid Vicious and the Sex Pistols, to the delight of many suburban audiences. One episode indicates Bromley's reserved nature. In 1950 the Labour government had commissioned a report from Professor Kenneth Wheare[33] on film certification. As a result, local councils were given the power to ban films freely shown elsewhere. In 1955, a great brouhaha accompanied the release of the French film *The Light Across the Street*, in one scene of which the young Brigitte Bardot unbuttoned her blouse. The Bromley Highways and Buildings Committee promptly banned the film from being screened in their high street cinema. Their action merely increased the revenues of the local bus company. 'All that a Bromley resident who wanted to ogle Bardot's charms had to do,' it was noted, 'was to take a short bus ride to the next Odeon, down the road in Eltham Hill.'[34]

---

*His experience led him to quip, in 1956, when Chancellor of the Exchequer, that Budget Day was like Speech Day, a bit of a bore, but something that had to be endured.
†The 'little man' at the centre of *The Diary of a Nobody* by the Grossmiths.

Macmillan's initial concerns in Bromley were not about film censorship, but the impoverished state of the local constituency organisation, which had little in place beyond a military chairman (Major-General C. W. Norman) and an elderly agent. It was a microcosm of the woeful state of the party nationally. In contrast, the Labour Party, as Rab Butler had noted in the aftermath of the 1945 defeat, had maintained a far more professionally staffed operation, especially in marginal constituencies.

Macmillan found Bromley complacent. The constituency was a 'safe' seat; it would look after itself. Macmillan knew that this attitude was the way to ruin. Membership needed boosting, party committees re-convening (or in most instances establishing for the first time), social activities – the Young Conservatives[35] and the Junior Imperial League – encouraging. The Bromley Young Conservatives began a magazine, *New Broom*, and Macmillan gave open lectures, *The Month in Parliament*, on a regular basis, invariably to packed houses.

At first Dorothy found Bromley very difficult after Stockton. She became fond of it eventually, but never to the same degree as Stockton, which she had adored.[37] She became a stalwart of the revived tradition of summer fund-raising fêtes, as she had been in Stockton. Eventually these fetes became popular family events, transcending party allegiances, with motorcycle displays and appearances by the Dagenham Girl Pipers. Macmillan was called upon to judge competitions such as 'The Dog With the Funniest Face'.[38] He knew that people were not going to turn out of a summer's afternoon with their children to hear him expounding details of *The Middle Way*.[39]

Immediately after the war, the key issue had been demobilisation; by February 1946, the need for housing was at the top of the political agenda. An unusually large number of eviction orders had been served on Bromley constituents, and Macmillan was assiduous in following up individual cases. Constituents wrote to him at the offices of Macmillan & Co. in St Martin's Street. He bombarded Aneurin Bevan, the Minister of Health and Housing, with letters about the 'very great distress which is being caused'.[40] Chuter Ede, the Home Secretary, and the Earl of Listowel, Postmaster General, were also in receipt of Macmillan's missives on issues ranging from the Fire Service to the rates. Government red tape hindered most of his efforts. In February 1949, he wrote to one concerned constituent, 'we will do what we can but we find this Government very stubborn'.[41]

Churchill also continued to get 'viewy' missives from Macmillan. In November 1948, dismayed by what he saw as Churchill's lack of commitment to the new policies represented by the various charters, he prepared a memorandum on strategy for the next general election. He did not mince his words:

> Since many of the voters even among the higher classes are very ignorant of immediate past history, they think of you as a war chief, forgetting altogether your earlier record as a liberal reformer. If you come forward now with a policy on the lines of this memorandum, I think you can revive the principles with which you began your political life, complete the full circle to Lord Randolph Churchill, and prove that the elements that defeated your father have now been thrown out of the leadership of the Tory Party.[42]

In September 1946, Lord Woolton replaced Ralph Assheton as party chairman. Meanwhile, candidates were no longer able to be adopted on the basis of what they might be able to contribute to Party funds. This reform was as important to the future of the Conservative Party as Edward Cardwell's abolition of the purchase of commissions had been to the army in 1871. Candidates could now pay a maximum of £25 per annum (or £50 per annum if a sitting MP) into the local party funds. There had been times in Stockton when Macmillan had paid in such sums out of his private and personal funds in a single week. Pre-war that was how many constituency organisations had survived. In Bromley, Macmillan was meticulous in separating personal and political expenditure; stamps for the hundreds of Christmas cards he sent,[43] for instance, he always bought personally.

Woolton's financial reform, outlined in the two-part Maxwell Fyfe Report of 1948 and 1949, was adopted by the party conference. A consequence of this change meant that fund-raising had to involve many more people, 'a very large number of very small subscriptions, instead of relying on a very small number of very large subscriptions', as Robert Blake put it succinctly.[44] Eventually, this led to a broadening of the social background from which Tory candidates were drawn, though perhaps not as rapidly as often supposed.[45]

Although Macmillan was widely seen as a specialist in economic and domestic matters, he knew that if he was to rise to the top of the party, this perception would have to change. Indeed, he had thought deeply about the complexities of the international situation ever since the early 1930s, when he had visited Russia, a process developed further with his mission to Finland during the Winter War, and then in his North African days. Accordingly, the 1945 Parliament was the period when he began to speak more widely on foreign affairs, which he aimed to make a speciality. Few such debates went by without a lengthy contribution from Macmillan.

Two defining themes were high on the political agenda in the immediate post-war years: independence for former colonies; and a more united Europe. Initially Macmillan was antipathetic towards both concepts. Between 1945 and 1951, Attlee's Labour government gave independence to India, Pakistan and Ceylon. This was the first phase of post-war decolonisation.

Macmillan visited India twice. His second trip, with John Wyndham, took place between 24 January and 20 February 1947. Part of his time was spent in publishing business on behalf of Macmillan & Co., but he also took the opportunity of meeting Indian leaders. On 3 February he dined with Pandit Jawaharlal Nehru[46] and recorded his impressions.

> Many years of prison life – or rather preventive detention – have left a mark upon him. He is, I should judge, torn between hatred of the British & a desire to be fair & objective. He struck me as very nervous, jumpy & strained. For some months now he has had some expressions of favour. Even with the support of what remains of British authority – and it is not inconsiderable – this has taken a good deal out of him. He has found that government is not as easy as criticism.[47]

A fortnight later Macmillan met the other key political leader, Muhammed Ali Jinnah,[48] who was to be the founding father of Pakistan. Again Macmillan recorded his impressions of the meeting.

> J. is a man of striking appearance – thin, almost emaciated, with long bony fingers and a strangely shrunken, skull-like head. His voice is low & very beautiful, under wonderful control. The orator, indeed the actor, are clearly a great part of the man ... I should add that J. is obviously a man of frail & nervous type. Work & worry have taken a great deal out of him ... I felt that he, as it were, enjoyed his physical weakness. It was part of the 'act' so to speak. But I should judge that he had considerable reserves of strength, and that the strong will could still master the weak body.[49]

The description could almost be of Macmillan himself in old age.

Such meetings, well publicised back in Britain, were helping to establish Macmillan as a figure on a world stage – not that he neglected to keep in touch with news back home whilst in the sub-continent. On board ship off Bombay he recorded, 'We listen to the wireless in a detached kind of way. The only news which has given me much thrill is that Herbert Morrison has got phlebitis. How pleased Bevin will be.'[50]

From Government House in Calcutta, Macmillan sympathised with Dorothy about the bitter winter in Britain. 'We read & hear the most terrible accounts of your suffering at home,' he wrote. 'I see that my old friend Shinwell is in trouble, but I do not suppose he will be sacrificed. The Socialists seem quite impervious to criticism (like the Congress Party here) ... It seems a pity that we should have decided to give up India at this moment. It is the only place where even Shinwell cd keep warm.'[51]

Macmillan also had a long meeting with Field Marshal Archibald Wavell,[52] the Viceroy, in New Delhi. His record of the visit captures the atmosphere of the end of the Raj in a poignant manner. 'The Viceroy lives in his great house. The wonderful garden is gay with an incredible display of every English flower, all blooming at once – roses, wall flowers, violas, sylvias[sic], friesas[sic], and immense herbaceous borders. The fountains play, the vast mass of servants move silently & obsequiously about their task; the guards present arms – but it is all the shadow of a dream.'[53]

Macmillan found that Wavell was in a valedictory mood.

I feel sorry for the poor Viceroy. Charming, sincere, cultivated – but no politician, and hopelessly bamboozled by the Congress Party here & the Socialists at home ... He sits alone in his great room, with the prints of all the Viceroys, knowing that he will be the last.[54] After all these years, it is a British Field Marshal who is the 'roi fainéant' in Delhi again – like the last of the Mogul Emperors, who lingered on all through Company days. Meanwhile the Central Govt has practically ceased to function.

Macmillan saw with foreboding the impending anarchy.

Nobody really believes that anything but chaos will follow. The pretence of democracy is maintained. But India is the most snobbish & aristocratic country I have ever seen. Everyone looks down on everybody else. Everybody kicks the man immediately below him. And the imminence of our departure – the belief (now at last becoming widespread) that we have really lost our nerve & decided to go, has naturally intensified the struggle for power. When a vacuum is caused, air rushes in. The struggle is – who is to fill the place of the British Raj?[55]

One of C. Northcote Parkinson's laws was that institutions build grand new headquarters at the moment of their decline. New Delhi was the supreme example. When Georges Clemenceau saw Edwin Lutyens'[56] half-built masterwork in 1920, he observed 'This will be the finest ruin of them all.' Macmillan's observations were also rueful:

> I like the two great secretariat buildings (G.[sic] Baker)[57] in white and red sandstone. But I am not so sure about the Viceroy's House, by Lutyens. The outside is very fine – the rose & red sandstone (the local stone) & the first floor & upwards in white sandstone. This gives rather a sandwich-like effect.
>
> The state rooms are very magnificent – a sort of mixture of East & West. The rooms which one uses regularly are on the grand level & are not (in my mind) so successful ... My bedroom was enormous – about the size of the schoolroom at Chatsworth & very lofty. I also had a nice sitting room. But the furniture was just Claridge's.[58]

Macmillan returned from India with a deeply pessimistic view. The retreat from Empire, he felt, could, and should, be handled much better. As the winter of imperial withdrawal came on, Macmillan, with memories of his talks with Jean Monnet in Algiers still potent, reluctant though he was at first, began to realise that the spring of Europe could not be far behind. Although Churchill would not have accepted the inevitability of the first premise, the second was already forming in his fertile mind.

On 19 September 1946 in Zurich, Churchill called for a 'Council of Europe', a structure that would allow all to live in peace and prosperity. By 1949, this Council of Europe was meeting in parliamentary session at Strasbourg, with Harold Macmillan as one of its Conservative members. This was the era of grandiloquent plans. Lend-Lease had been ended by President Truman on 17 August 1945 after the defeat of Japan, but this was largely replaced by the Marshall Plan in 1947, offering American financial aid for a programme of European economic recovery.[59] This plan also played its part in the European movement as the Western powers organised a conference in Paris, which led to the establishment in April 1948 of the OEEC (Organisation for European Economic Co-operation). From this association developed the European Economic Community (the Common Market) and eventually EFTA (the European Free Trade Association). The next month, Robert Schuman,[60] the French Foreign Minister, launched his famous plan to combine, initially, the coal and steel industries of France and Germany. Later Schuman envisaged other European nations joining.

To a degree not often appreciated, Macmillan played a formative part in the embryonic European movement. He was a keen supporter in 1947 with Edward Beddington-Behrens[61] of the British Committee of the European League for Economic Co-operation (ELEC). Lady Rhys Williams[62] acted as the organisation's formidable secretary. With delegates such as Walter Layton,[63] the Liberal Party's spokesman on the Council of Europe, the atmosphere was one of high-minded seriousness. Macmillan was not averse to puncturing some of this intensity, whilst at the same time being fully committed to the underlying cause. Once, after a tense return from the Congress of Europe to Croydon in a light aircraft that encountered difficulties, Macmillan shouted out after the bumpy landing, 'Women and Liberals first.'[64]

In 1949, Macmillan and Beddington-Behrens helped to found the Central and Eastern European Group of ELEC, their purpose being to maintain links with Soviet-occupied countries behind the Iron Curtain. A Commonwealth conference ELEC organised in May 1951 was of great importance in formulating Macmillan's belief at that time in a strong Commonwealth/European partnership to be the counterweight to the United States. All this activity went far beyond the vision of what the Treaty of Rome eventually established.

In a speech on 17 May 1950, eight days after the Schuman Plan was launched, Macmillan was critical of Labour's cool response to proposals that he regarded as 'an act of high courage and imaginative statesmanship',[65] not least because he felt it could end centuries of Franco-German rivalry. His subsequent letter to *The Times* on 22 May, supporting Schuman's vision led to a predictable attack. Attlee's subsequent unwillingness for Britain to join in negotiations over extension of the plan was the subject of Macmillan's monthly talk about events in Parliament in Bromley that month. He remembered Monnet's vision that 'there will be no peace in Europe, if the states are reconstituted on the basis of national sovereignty with all that implies in terms of prestige politics and economic protectionism'.[66] Such defensive positions would inevitably lead to military expansion. Macmillan told Churchill that the situation now gave the Conservatives a great opportunity to seize the political initiative.

The North Atlantic Treaty Organisation (NATO) was a child of the Cold War, part product of the Berlin blockade of 1948.[67] The North Atlantic Treaty was signed in Washington on 4 April 1949, by the Foreign Ministers of 11 sovereign nations, including Britain, France and the United States. Its purpose, as with the ill-fated League of Nations in the interwar years, was to guarantee mutual assistance if any member of the alliance was attacked. It remained to be seen whether the lessons of the thirties had been learned. Macmillan was optimistic about the chances of NATO curbing Russian aggression, despite Russian advances in Eastern Europe. Again he was disappointed by back-bench Labour doubters, who criticised him heavily in a debate in the Commons on Germany on 23 March 1949. Churchill's response was to give him responsibility for the delicate matter of Germany's future European integration in the ongoing discussions at Strasbourg, by then established as a Committee of Foreign Ministers, and a Consultative Assembly of parliamentarians from the 12 member countries.

Much of this organisation owed its inception to Churchill's vision. Following his Zurich speech in 1946, Churchill had launched an all-party United Europe Movement on 14 May 1947. Macmillan was invited to serve on its committee. In May 1948, the first Congress of Europe, attended by hundreds of delegates, met at the Hague. In January 1949, talks began on the establishment of a Council of Europe. Its statute was signed on 5 May 1949, and the first session followed three months later. Macmillan was now one of the six Conservative delegates to this Consultative Assembly of the Council of Europe.[68] By the time of the assembly's second session, divisions had arisen between those who wanted co-operation, and the federalists who wanted formal integration. Macmillan was prominent as one of the British delegation who was opposed to taking the federal path. He could foresee the tensions that would arise back home, especially among sceptical Conservatives, who felt that any such European federation would compromise Britain's relationship with the Empire and the Commonwealth, and even threaten national sovereignty.*

The Strasbourg experience was important in giving Macmillan first-hand experience of the complexities of European co-operation – and this was even before de Gaulle was back in office. On the map of Europe, Strasbourg was always a place for Macmillan marked 'Here be dragons'. Things were not helped by Churchill's quasi-monarchical appearances. 'Churchill's arrival meant the usual hours,' Macmillan wrote wryly on 22 August 1949, 'no [talking] shop till 2.30 a.m. or so – and the whole pressure of that tireless and inexorable man.' He was also very critical of Herbert Morrison's performance. 'Having absolutely no knowledge or experience of foreigners, and little imagination,

---

* Such fears would return with a vengeance in the decades ahead, and split the Conservative Party from top to bottom.

Herbert clearly thought that he would reproduce Westminster at Strasbourg. He would "lead" the house; we should be a docile and fair-minded Opposition. The foreigners would stand in awe of British prestige & the power of a great Minister.'

Churchill descended on the assembly's meetings, bearing clouds of plenipotentiary power. On 15 August, a public holiday, he received the freedom of Strasbourg. 'I think he was under the impression that the public holiday was in his honour,' Macmillan observed. Churchill told Macmillan that it was 'the best fun I have had for years and years'. Fun or not, he soon flew on to Beaverbrook's villa at Monte Carlo, and Macmillan was commissioned to send him daily reports of what was unfolding in Strasbourg. 'I do not think I have ever had such tiring days,' Macmillan recorded.

Nevertheless, Macmillan found Strasbourg an absorbing experience. It propelled him on to a new stage, and as a result his name became widely known in European capitals. When Churchill suffered a stroke in late August 1949, on the eve of a vital debate on Germany's future position, Macmillan deputised for him. His speech on 5 September, in which he quoted from one of Churchill's wartime minutes on European co-operation, was the culmination of the first session of the assembly. It led eventually to Germany's invitation to become an associate member of the assembly in March 1950. A difficult political obstacle had been successfully traversed, not least because of Macmillan's skilful advocacy.

'It was a most interesting example of how a Parliament *can* work, and no doubt used to work in England, before the rigidity of parties and the growth of the power of the whips,' he wrote. 'Another important point is that there is no division bell. Only those vote who have heard the arguments. Almost no one leaves his seat for this reason during the whole sitting.'[69]

Meanwhile, the electoral clock was slowly ticking away for Labour. As the time neared, Conservative preparations intensified. Churchill hosted fortnightly gargantuan lunches in a private room at the Savoy Hotel for members of the Consultative Committee, known later as the Shadow Cabinet. So bibulous were these lunches that the amount of detailed work actually achieved was minimal. Morale-boosting and broad brush strokes were the aim. Churchill, now established in London at 28 Hyde Park Gate, dubbed the Savoy 'his advance battle headquarters'. On one occasion as the waiter brought in a huge sweet on an enormous tray, Churchill proclaimed, 'Take this pudding away, it has no theme',[70] before expounding on how politics always needed a theme. Macmillan agreed with the theme chosen – to 'set the people free' – and he was co-opted to prepare the policy statement, *The Right Road for Britain*, and then the actual 1950 manifesto, *This is the Road*.

The summer of 1950, the Golden Jubilee year of the Labour Party, and the mid-point of the century, declared a Holy Year by the Vatican, was not a golden time for many. The Cold War was at a perilous stage and the Korean War was to break out in June. Following Dalton's resignation as Chancellor of the Exchequer in November 1947,[71] and the subsequent devaluation of the pound in 1949 by his successor, Stafford Cripps, tensions in the Labour Party were running high. The mutual antipathy between Aneurin Bevan and the rising star, Hugh Gaitskell, was barely disguised. 'They have the most frightful wrangles in the Cabinet Committee on finance of Health Service,' Dalton wrote in his diary.[72]

The aftermath of devaluation influenced the choice of an election date. Gaitskell had urged Attlee to choose November 1949 or June 1950. Gaitskell's own preference was for November 1949, as the higher costs of imported goods following devaluation would not by then have increased living costs. He told Attlee that a choice of date between December 1949 and March 1950 was most unwise. His advice was not taken. 'I fear that the Tories will get a lot of Liberal votes,' Gaitskell prophesied shrewdly in his diary, 'and that this, together with redistribution, will make the contest very even.'[73]

Parliament was prorogued on 16 December 1949. On 10 January, Attlee sought an audience with the King, and polling day was set for 23 February, the first winter campaign since 1910, and one of the longest. Macmillan now prepared for his first general election campaign in Bromley. Unlike Stockton, where unusual circumstances in the 1930s had largely disguised the constituency's marginal nature, he could be confident of personal success, but the national outcome was less certain.

CHAPTER FIFTEEN

One More Heave

1950 – 1951

CHURCHILL: Am I a handicap to my party?
BUTLER: I don't think you are the asset you once were, sir.
      Churchill to the young psephologist David Butler on 20
      October 1951, five days before the general election[1]

In one corner stood an object which may be thought sym-
bolical of Mr Morrison and his planners. It was a brand-new
two penny slot machine. The shelves were bare. And on the
machine was boldy draped a label reading NOT WORKING.
      Evening Standard report on the opening of the Festival of
      Britain, May 1951

We returned to London for the General Election. I thought
the result disappointing. The conditions could not have been
more unfavourable for the Labour Party and yet more people
voted Labour than ever before. I can see little hope for the
Conservatives in the future.
      Duff Cooper diary, December 1951[2]

The Conservative Party that faced the electorate in February 1950 was
a totally different animal from that of July 1945. It was now the Whig
inheritor of the tradition of Edmund Burke, showing a 'disposition to
preserve' with 'an ability to improve', which was in essence exactly
what the Conservatives had been promising in *The Right Road for
Britain*.

Although an outright victory for the Conservatives was improbable,* the activists went at the task with a will. There was a justified
feeling that redistribution, and the introduction of postal voting in
1948, would benefit the Conservatives. Party membership stood at
2,750,000; in 1947, it had been less than a million. People had made
sacrifices during the war; now disenchantment with austerity and
regulations was palpable. Politicians' promises, like pie-crust, were
being broken.

---

*Labour then had a majority of 136 over all parties and 166 over the Conservatives.

Labour was not helped by Attlee's strategy. He had not chosen the date wisely,[3] and was to choose even less wisely when he was pressurised, not least by King George VI, to get the next election out of the way before the King's proposed Commonwealth tour in 1952.[4] Labour's historic victory in July 1945 has obscured the fact that Attlee, who led the Labour Party into five elections – 1935, 1945, 1950, 1951 and 1955 – actually had a very poor electoral record in four of them. The 1950 campaign was fought on an old register, in bad weather, and even caused the cancellation of a planned Jubilee Conference to celebrate Labour's half-century.

Labour's first election pamphlet – *Labour Believes in Britain* – could have been more accurately entitled *Labour Believes in Nationalisation*, as it contained plans to bring cement, the chemical industry, cold storage, some insurance services, meat distribution and sugar into public ownership. Despite the emphasis on public ownership, the overall thrust of Labour's message was consolidation, echoing Baldwin's 'Safety First' message of 1929, and with similar results.

The first row of the campaign was over Herbert Morrison's declaration that the anti-Labour advertising campaigns – Tate and Lyle's 'Mr Cube' appeared on sugar packets warning against nationalisation of sugar – should be reckoned as a Conservative election expense. Although legal officers did not agree with Morrison's view, Lord Woolton, the Conservative Party chairman, persuaded the firms involved to cease advertising during the actual campaign, to prevent any retrospective ambiguity. The Labour manifesto – *Let Us Win Through Together* – had none of the urgency of the equivalent document in 1945. The Conservative manifesto, eventually called *This is the Road*, was part-authored by Macmillan, and laid the foundations of the post-war consensus that operated until 1979. 'Although the document promised to stop and, if possible, reverse the process of nationalisation and to end socialist waste and bureaucracy,' wrote David Butler, 'it did completely accept the newly enacted welfare state legislation and promised to maintain full employment.'[5] This latter promise, more than any other, was calculated to exorcise the memories of the 1930s.

Macmillan's own views went even further. Since 1945 he had agreed with Labour over providing welfare on the basis of need, coupled to a progressive taxation policy. He also believed in protecting the interests of organised labour against the traditional demands of the capitalist system, and favoured a strong civil service to implement central planning. Not for the first time, very little separated Macmillan from Labour's stance.

Although Churchill made a widely publicised speech in Edinburgh on 15 February, calling for summit talks with the Russians and the Americans, his role was much reduced. Both main parties wanted to project an image of moderation, which led on the Labour side to the marginalisation of Bevan during the campaign.

The new face of the Conservative Party was the progressive trio of Eden, Butler and Macmillan, who were backed by Dr Charles Hill[6] of the British Medical Association, 'the radio doctor', in reassuring fireside chats on the wireless. Macmillan left much of the day-to-day work in the capable hands of his local agent, Sidney Aubrey, significantly one of 527 full-time Conservative agents in England and Wales.[7] After redistribution by the Boundaries Commission in 1948–1949, Bromley now stood alone as a constituency, with Beckenham and Penge becoming a new seat. As a result the electorate in Bromley was reduced to some 50,000 voters. Macmillan's result, announced on the afternoon of 24 February, was never in doubt:

The Rt Hon. Harold Macmillan (Conservative)	23,042
Mrs J. R. Elliott (Labour)	12,354
P. W. Gratton[8] (Liberal)	4,847
Conservative majority	10,688

Although the national campaign had been low-key, the turnout was 84 per cent, the highest since January 1910, and a total never again surpassed. Labour won 315 seats, the Conservatives and their supporters 298, and the Liberals 9. 'The Liberal candidate forfeited his deposit' was the phrase most repeated in the radio coverage of the results. The overall swing to the Conservatives had been 3 per cent, though in the Home Counties it was nearer to 8 per cent, an indication of the importance that seats such as Bromley would have in the coming years. It was calculated that the Conservatives won 10 of their seats through their efficient use of the postal vote.[9] Overall the Conservatives gained 87 seats.

Even more important than the number was the quality of the new intake. Aneurin Bevan described the 1950 Tory vintage – which included Edward Heath, Iain Macleod, Reginald Maudling and Enoch Powell – as the most notable in the party's history.

By contrast, many Labour stalwarts were no longer in the House. Seven ministers lost their seats. Attlee gamely declared on the steps of 10 Downing Street, with the taciturnity for which he was renowned, 'We're carrying on. That's all.'*

---

* Initially, the omens seemed quite good for Labour. There were two potentially hazardous

Labour, with a minuscule majority, had to deal with the complex fall-out from the Korean War, which broke out in June. Rearmament became a contentious issue. Meanwhile, more stalwarts departed the scene. In October 1950, Cripps, exhausted and mortally ill, resigned as Chancellor and also his seat at South-East Bristol. To the undisguised fury of Aneurin Bevan, he was succeeded at the Treasury by Hugh Gaitskell, whom Bevan later dubbed 'a desiccated calculating machine'.[10] Gaitskell's sole Budget, of April 1951, introduced prescription charges, thus negating Bevan's principle of the National Health Service (*his* National Health Service) being free at the point of use, and escalating the already bitter Bevanite–Gaitskellite split.[11] Ernest Bevin was removed from his post as Foreign Secretary on 9 March 1951 (the news arrived during the celebrations that the Foreign Office was holding for him that day, his seventieth birthday).[12] He was replaced by his old adversary, Herbert Morrison. A month later, Bevin, demoted to the non-departmental post of Lord Privy Seal, died in harness, the key to his red box in his hand.

In 1951, the government was confronted with the Abadan crisis. The Persian government, led by Dr Mossadeq, had nationalised the Anglo-Iranian oil company at Abadan, and for a while it seemed as though military intervention would follow. Macmillan took a particular interest in this potential flashpoint, as he had visited the oilfields in 1947, an example of his growing determination to acquaint himself at first hand with foreign policy issues. Arab nationalism was also growing in Egypt, and burst forth during the October 1951 election campaign, when the Anglo-Egyptian Treaty of 1936 was denounced.[13]

On 11 December 1950, Oliver Stanley died at the age of 53. He had been indisputably number 3 in the Tory hierarchy after Churchill and Eden, and as spokesman on financial affairs was probably destined to be Chancellor of the Exchequer. His death subtly altered the situation at the top of the Tory Party. No one, least of all Eden, knew when Churchill intended to retire. When he did, the post of heir-apparent, held by Eden, with some discomfort, since 1938, informally, and since 1942, formally, would be vacant.[14] The two contenders for the unofficial post of heir-presumptive were now Rab Butler and Harold Macmillan, whose rivalry was to define Conservative politics for the next 13 years.

The new Tory intake of 1950 took little time to establish themselves.

---

by-elections – West Dumbartonshire (25 April) and Brighouse and Spenborough (4 May) – and the government won both. On the most contentious issue of the day, steel nationalisation, the government survived a division by 10 votes. 'It looks as if those bastards can stay in as long as they like' was Churchill's comment, as reported in *The Times* on 10 March.

In October 1950, a group of younger MPs published *One Nation*, a clarion call for progressive policies, particularly in financing the social services. Rab Butler wrote an approving foreword to the publication by the Conservative Political Centre, and its nine contributors became known as the 'One Nation' Group, echoing the Disraelian ideal.[15] *One Nation* was to be as important to the Conservative revival as *The Industrial Charter*, endorsing as it did the Keynesian commitment to full employment. Enoch Powell had been drafted into the team because of his known expertise on housing, and it was his chapter that was to impact most on Macmillan's future career. 'In terms of its detail, its grasp and the nature of its prescriptions,' Simon Heffer has written, 'Powell's chapter was the intellectual heart of the pamphlet.'[16] It inspired not just Tory intellectuals, but rank-and-file members of the party. At the 1950 conference at Blackpool, an impassioned speech from Harmar Nicholls,[17] one of the 1950 intake, led to the adoption of the target for the next Conservative government of building 300,000 houses a year.

As a result, the Conservative's 1951 manifesto, *Britain Strong and Free*, committed the party to making housing second only to defence as a national priority. Ironically, Rab Butler, who had written such an enthusiastic foreword to *One Nation*, was disturbed by the unrealistic hysteria that seemed to have gripped the party, as the target figure was raised again and again by conference delegates in the manner of an auction.*

The Festival of Britain – the 'Tonic to the Nation', as it became known – was the special project of Herbert Morrison, ostensibly to mark the centenary of the Great Exhibition of 1851. Underneath the fun, epitomised by the Battersea Pleasure Gardens, lay an Arts Council vision of enlightenment, as in the South Bank's Dome of Discovery. For Morrison, to his delight dubbed Lord Festival, the celebration was 'a great symbol of national regeneration'.[18]

However, the festival soon became a political football, with the Beaverbrook press launching an attack on its multi-million-pound costing. Sir Waldron Smithers effectively discomfited Morrison by asking how many houses could be built with the festival's budget, and he took every opportunity of embarrassing the government. 'Has

---

*Had Butler known that from October 1951 he would be the Chancellor of the Exchequer who would have to divert scarce resources to achieving this target in what was to be Macmillan's ministry, he would have been even more worried. The more houses that were built, the higher Harold Macmillan's reputation rose, and consequently the more difficulties for Butler at the Treasury.

the Rt Hon. Gentleman,' he asked Richard Stokes,[19] the Lord Privy Seal, when the question of a festival flag arose, 'considered flying the Red Flag in order to help the fellow travellers on the other side of the House to find their way to Morrison's Folly?'[20]

Divisions went even deeper. Michael Frayn acutely observed that 'Festival Britain was the Britain of the radical middle-classes – the do-gooders; the readers of the *News Chronicle*, the *Guardian*, and the *Observer*', whom he dubbed the Herbivores, as opposed to the Carnivores, 'the readers of the *Daily Express*; the Evelyn Waughs; the cast of the Directory of Directors'. Macmillan actually thought the festival, a carnival of bread and circuses for the people, was harmless fun, much deserved after the years of hardship, and specially valuable in local communities. Political considerations, however, demanded that any stick was good enough to batter the troubled, dying Labour government, so he felt obliged to join in. The Conservatives had taken every opportunity of harassing the government, springing surprise divisions and abandoning pairings through the contentious debates on steel nationalisation. In June 1951, Parliament was asked to advance a further loan of £1m to the Festival of Britain. Macmillan declared this 'the same gross mismanagement and confusion as prevails in so many other fields'.[21] The wits had made much merrier with the South Bank Festival – 'all Heal let loose'[22] was one comment, and Rab Butler described the futuristic Skylon[23] as being like the British economy, without any visible means of support.[24]

Labour's narrow majority was causing Attlee all manner of problems, and by the summer of 1951, he had decided that he must seek a fresh mandate. He told the King at his audience on 24 June that he would ask for a dissolution in the autumn.[25] The King was facing a serious operation, due on 23 September, and one of Attlee's main considerations was to get the election out of the way before the King departed on his proposed tour to Australia and New Zealand in January 1952.[26] The King wrote to Attlee on 1 September saying that he could hardly leave the country for such a long time with the political situation in such an uncertain state.

On 5 September, Attlee wrote to the George VI requesting a dissolution of Parliament in the first week of October. Morrison and Bevan were both out of the country when the decision was confirmed at a thinly attended Cabinet on 19 September. Polling day was fixed for 25 October. Morrison heard the news from journalists in Ottawa, and was incensed by what he saw as a discourteous and hasty decision.

The new Parliament had first met on 1 March 1950 and was to be dissolved on 5 October 1951, the shortest duration since the Bonar

Law–Baldwin government of 1922–1923. In retrospect, the Conservatives could see that losing the 1950 election had been a blessing.

Churchill saw the 1951 campaign as 'one last heave'. His theme was 'Set the People Free', a slogan that chimed well with a public that had recently put the popular song 'Don't Fence Me In' high in the charts. Middle-class resentment at the increased proletarianisation of society was also an underlying current. The signs were more propitious for the Conservatives in 1951 than in 1950. Gaitskell had only just announced that the gold and dollar reserves had fallen in the year's third quarter by $600 million. The Labour Party's divisions were palpable for all to see, whereas the Conservatives more skilfully disguised their differences and projected an image of determined unity. The opinion polls were more favourable and, vitally, the number of Liberal candidates had fallen from 475 in 1950 to 109 in 1951. Macmillan faced a straight fight in Bromley.

Although television had been expanded by the opening of the Sutton Coldfield transmitter for the Midlands in 1946, and by the Holme Moss transmitter for the north of England in the month of the election, the 1951 campaign was the last one in which large political meetings predominated. The urgent foreign issue was whether Churchill was a warmonger. The *Daily Mirror*'s headline 'Whose finger on the trigger?' was to be the subject of a successful legal action by Churchill. Domestically the key issue by far was housing.

The Conservatives cancelled their proposed conference at Scarborough – a great relief to many of the 1950 intake, as it enabled them to put all their resources into the election itself.[27] Macmillan was summoned to Chartwell by Churchill on 20 September to help with the draft of his radio broadcast, and he saw his main task as ensuring that there were no more references to the Gestapo. He found Churchill optimistic, hoping for a majority of 90, but professing himself happy with 50.

As in February 1950, Macmillan toured the country. He began his campaign on 3 October in Romford and Brentwood, before moving on to Birmingham for a big rally. He took with him Walter Scott's *The Antiquary*, which he found more edifying than party pamphlets. From Birmingham, he went on to Preston to speak for his son-in-law Julian Amery, who was to be the victorious Conservative candidate, successfully defending the seat he had first won in February 1950. On 19 October, Macmillan travelled to Lincolnshire, where he spoke for his son Maurice, who was the candidate in the safe Labour seat of Lincoln.[28] He did not neglect Bromley, making several appearances in the constituency and in neighbouring areas. One meeting in the Downham area, where there was an LCC housing estate (and the local boxing club), was particularly lively, with many Labour voters present.

On election night, Macmillan opted to hear the results with Moucher Devonshire[29] in London. Dorothy went on to the party given by Lord Camrose at the Savoy, but Macmillan was too tired after all his exertions, and also, as he wrote, 'I do not like the Noel Cowards etc.'[30] The next day the Macmillans were together in Bromley for the declaration. The figures were:

Harold Macmillan (Conservative)	25,710
T.E.M. McKitterick (Labour)	13,585
Conservative majority	12,125

Because of the anomalies of the voting system, and the massive majorities Labour built up in industrial constituencies, particularly in South Wales, the Conservatives won an overall majority on a lower percentage of the total vote, (48 per cent as against Labour's 48.8 per cent.)[31] They won 321 seats, and the Labour Party 295. The Liberals were reduced to a mere six seats. Churchill's overall majority was 17. Macmillan felt that the result was 'a moral stalemate'.[32]

Stalemate or not, Churchill was back in Downing Street, elected as Prime Minister for the first time. The Cavaliers were taking over from the Roundheads. Churchill now began appointing the first purely Conservative Cabinet since his 'caretaker administration' in May 1945.

Macmillan hoped that he might become Minister of Defence, a post that would have reflected his growing interest in international matters. It was not to be. In fact, for a while, as news filtered through over the next few days of the major appointments, there was the awful thought that he might miss out altogether, or get only an insignificant post. As expected, Eden returned to the Foreign Office for the fourth time in 16 years, and also became Leader of the House. The major surprise, and disappointment for Macmillan, was that Rab Butler, eight years his junior, was appointed Chancellor of the Exchequer. Butler was surprised too. Summoned to Churchill's London home at 28 Hyde Park Gate, he found Churchill in bed and was shown a list of the Cabinet with his name pencilled in at the Treasury. Butler asked Churchill if he really wanted him to do the job. 'Yes old cock, I do.'[33]

Bobbety Salisbury became Lord Privy Seal and Leader of the Lords; Woolton became Lord President of the Council, with responsibility initially for Food and Agriculture; and Maxwell Fyfe Home Secretary and Welsh affairs. Oliver Lyttelton, whom many thought would have become Chancellor, was made Colonial Secretary. Walter Monckton became Minister of Labour and Lord Ismay Dominions Secretary. To general surprise Churchill appointed himself Minister of Defence, in addition to his responsibilities as Prime Minister. This completed the first batch of appointments on 27 October.

Macmillan was not impressed by the decisions. He thought it was a great mistake to expect Eden, at a time of international tension, to be Leader of the House as well as Foreign Secretary. As for Churchill's decision to take on Defence as well as the premiership, Macmillan was incredulous. He felt it pandered to the worst excesses of the Beaverbrook press and was esssentially a nostalgic and sentimental move, quite unsuited to the demands of the time. His feeling was not affected by disappointment at not getting the post himself. He just thought that Churchill was plainly wrong. Harry Crookshank telephoned Macmillan to share similar doubts, and had even more worrying gossip to report: these nine might be the Cabinet, a kind of peacetime 'war' Cabinet, with others, such as himself and Macmillan, in purely subordinate roles.

These doubts were removed when both Crookshank and Macmillan received summonses to Chartwell over the weekend. Crookshank was appointed Minister of Health. Macmillan was offered Housing. He was intensely disappointed, feeling that it was not his cup of tea at all. He challenged Churchill over Defence and frankly told him that it was the post he wanted. Churchill refused to give way, and offered Macmillan the Board of Trade instead, which seemed to Macmillan little better. By this time, Lady Dorothy had arrived at Chartwell and was walking with Clementine Churchill in the garden. Macmillan asked for time to consider.

He then walked round the lake with Dorothy and discussed his options. Dorothy unequivocally advised him to accept Housing. The post, though not traditionally one of the senior ones, was, in the circumstances of the time, absolutely vital. Also it would follow on from the kind of work he had done in the Ministry of Supply at the beginning of the war. Churchill had asked him to build 'houses for the people'. If he succeeded, then, like Robert Peel, he would leave 'a name sometimes remembered with expressions of good will in the abodes of those whose lot is to labour, and to earn their daily bread by the sweat of their brow'.[34] Guided by Dorothy's wise advice, Macmillan returned inside to Churchill and accepted the offer.

Only on his return to Birch Grove did Macmillan realise the enormity of the task he had taken on. At a moment that should have been one of joy and promise, he actually felt despondent, sensing his political career had stalled. On 30 October he kissed hands with King George VI, now visibly weakened, and received his seals of office.

Thus began 12 unbroken years of the highest executive command. Although Macmillan was to hold the most senior posts in government in the next few years, his time at the Ministry of Housing did indeed make his name. When Churchill said that the job would make him or mar him, perhaps neither realised the extent to which this would prove true, and how Macmillan's success in the post would pave the way for all that followed. The Conservative delegates at the 1950 Blackpool conference had, in a mood of almost unbridled optimism, raised the annual target for house building to 300,000 houses. Macmillan was about to turn their dreams into reality.

PART THREE

Believing in the Future

1951–1957

The expansionist is the optimist because he believes in the future. The deflationist is the pessimist because he fears the future.

Harold Macmillan

Macmillan drives a bull-dozer through the mountain of red tape in his successful quest to build 300,000 homes a year.

'Is that the one we swopped for Burgess?'

Guy Burgess's defection to the Soviet Union on 25 May 1951 was one of the high profile spy cases of the Cold War era.

CHAPTER SIXTEEN

Setting The People Free

1951–1954

BEVAN: Where are all the people I need for my programme?
ATTLEE: Looking for houses, Nye.
> Clement Attlee to Aneurin Bevan, Minister of Health and
> Housing, when Bevan was complaining of the shortage of
> labour for his housing programme

Farewell to office – now Local Government and Planning, but
to be renamed by Tories Housing and Local Government, in
the charge of Macmillan. He won't be able to build any more,
if as many as I. My last month (September) showed more than
17,000 completed.
> Hugh Dalton on Macmillan's appointment as Housing
> Minister, 29 October 1951[1]

England & I have need of thee – Slum Dweller
> Telegram sent to Macmillan at the Conservative Party's
> Margate conference, October 1953

When Churchill formed his peacetime administration in October
1951, it was the first purely Conservative government since Stanley
Baldwin's from 1924–1929. Expectations were high; but Britons were
anxious that autumn. The Korean War threatened a fragile global
peace, and many feared it might even be the harbinger of a third
world war. Domestically, Britain was struggling to emerge from the
inevitable austerities of the immediate post-war years. Douglas Jay's
comment that 'the gentleman in Whitehall really does know better
what is good for people than the people know themselves' was not
easily forgotten, even though the book in which it appeared may not
have been widely read.[2] On the other hand, Angela Thirkell's best-
selling novel *Peace Breaks Out* (1946) remained a favourite at the
Boots' lending libraries, reflecting as it did 'the sour bitterness with
which the Labour government was regarded by an influential section
of the community'.[3] Rationing remained in force.* Housewives queued

---

*It was not finally ended until July 1954.[4]

for offal at the butchers. Undergraduates had to hand in their ration books to college butteries. Patrons of the growing number of holiday camps were reminded, 'Please bring your ration book.'[5] The priority given to the export market meant continuing shortages. People of all political persuasions wanted to be rid of the deprivations, restrictions and controls. Churchill had promised in his election campaign to 'set the people free'. His government now had to deliver on that promise.

The Britain over which Churchill presided in 1951 was on the cusp of change. 'All periods of history are periods of transition,' Robert Blake has written, 'but some are more transitional than others.'[6] Such a defining transition was already underway, and the pace was to quicken further.

When Rab Butler, the new Chancellor of the Exchequer, first met his Treasury officials, he was told that the balance of payments deficit was £700 million, with reserves ebbing away on a scale not seen since 1931. The bank rate was raised from 2 per cent to 2.5 per cent on 7 November. In January 1952, import controls and hire purchase restrictions were imposed, together with deep capital investment cuts. Consumerism and affluence, which so characterised the later 1950s, were still distant prospects.

Socially, Britain in 1951 was not yet the ethnically diverse country it later became. The April census, the first since 1931, showed the UK population as 43,744,924. Immigration that year totalled 4.25 per cent. Grammar schools still flourished, to the aggravation of egalitarians, yet they provided a ladder of social mobility for those who passed the 11+ exam. Corporal punishment was the norm in all kinds of schools. Capital punishment* remained on the statute book. Homosexuality, even involving consenting adults in private, was illegal.

Viewed from the perspective of the twenty-first century, the early 1950s is a vanished age. Political leaders did not strum guitars, wear jeans or change nappies. Television was in its infancy. In common with the majority of his fellow citizens, Macmillan did not then own a 'television receiver', as sets were quaintly called.[7] Keeping in touch was a case of the nine o'clock news on 'the wireless'. Even then, there could be delays. For instance, Macmillan did not hear of the tragic floods in 1952 at Lynmouth in Devon for over 24 hours.

Culturally, Britain was vibrant. The Festival of Britain, which

---

*As the move towards the abolition of capital punishment gathered pace in the 1950s, Macmillan became a 'selectionist', believing that there were only some categories of murder, such as the shooting of a policeman, that should merit the ultimate sanction.

ended on 30 September 1951, had been designed to celebrate post-war recovery. Yet the festival had been 'Janus-faced', a peculiarly British piece of nostalgia, looking back to the achievements of the past, while at the same time pointing the way to 'a better future'. Of course, its planners had imagined it would be a precursor of a planned, Socialist utopia. On taking office, David Eccles,[8] the newly appointed Minister of Works, set about the demolition of the festival site on the South Bank with an eagerness some saw as bordering on the vindictive. Future visions were going to be very different.

Within four months of the Conservative victory, on 6 February 1952 King George VI died unexpectedly at Sandringham. He was only 56. Macmillan was meeting a group of advertising men when his private secretary told him the news. An emergency Cabinet was summoned and arrangements made for the Accession Council, which Macmillan attended, at St James's Palace at 5 p.m.* The young Queen, Elizabeth II, was in Kenya at the start of a Commonwealth tour en route to Australia and New Zealand. Consideration was given by the Cabinet as to whether she should return by air. Some believed flying was too dangerous, but they were overruled. On 8 February, Macmillan was present at the Privy Council meeting at St James's Palace to attend on the Queen, a moment of history that left a deep impression. Afterwards the Cabinet considered arrangements both for the King's funeral and for the Coronation. It was decided that the Coronation should not be held until 1953.

On 15 February, Macmillan, together with Lady Dorothy, attended the King's funeral at St George's Chapel, Windsor.† The death of George VI marked a break with the wartime era. Now Britain had as its head of state a young Queen, 25 years old, and noteworthy parallels were drawn with Queen Elizabeth I, who had been the same age when she came to the throne in 1558. A magazine for children, *The Young Elizabethan*, was launched in April 1953, stressing wholesome, patriotic values. The passing of the old guard was underlined when on 24 March 1953, George V's widow, old Queen Mary, died at Marlborough House. She left instructions that on no account should the Coronation – fixed for 2 June – be postponed because of any mourning.

One of the persistent myths about television in the 1950s is that

---

* By chance, Macmillan was reading at the time Charles Greville's *Journals*, with their famous description of the young Queen Victoria's Accession Council in 1837.
† 'Moucher Devonshire was very dignified as Mistress of the Robes' observed Macmillan[9].

its popularity was established by the Coronation broadcast of 2 June 1953, whereas it was actually the television coverage of King George VI's funeral, watched in countless shared 'front rooms', that sparked off the mass purchasing of sets *in time* for 2 June 1953, especially after it became known that (belated) permission had been granted for cameras in Westminster Abbey. Macmillan very quickly realised that he would have to become a master of the new medium if his career was to prosper.*

The Third Programme, first broadcast on the wireless on 29 September 1946, was revered as 'the envy of the world'. Its range led Edward Sackville-West, the novelist and music critic, to declare that the Third Programme was 'the greatest educative and civilising force England has known since the secularisation of the theatre in the sixteenth century'.[11] A typical schedule of that period included verse plays by Christopher Fry and T. S. Eliot, Alban Berg's opera *Lulu* from Vienna, celebrations of Goethe, readings of Plato's *Dialogues*, and talks by figures as diverse as Field Marshal Smuts and Max Beerbohm. On other wavelengths, *The Archers*, an 'everyday story of country folk', began on 1 January 1951, complementing the long-running and popular *Mrs Dale's Diary*. Queen Elizabeth, later the Queen Mother, listened to this teatime saga with its Pooterish concerns – 'I am worried about Jim' being one of Mrs Dale's catchphrases[12] – reputedly as it was the only way she could find out what was going on in a middle-class household. Teenagers (the term was just coming in) had their *Dick Barton – Special Agent*, while their younger siblings could *Listen with Mother*, literally, as many mothers were still then in unpaid employment running their homes and looking after these children.

Macmillan was gladdened by the continuing popularity of reading. Although, as a minister, he could not be a paid director, he continued to advise his brother Daniel in St Martin's Street, and he followed the latest trends and publishing gossip. Macmillan & Co. had one of their commercial successes in 1951 with C. P. Snow's Trollopian novel of political intrigue, *The Masters*, set in a fictional Cambridge college,[13] a book in which Macmillan himself would not have been out of place as a leading protagonist. *The Masters* was but one part of an 11–novel sequence, *Strangers and Brothers*, that uncannily covered many of the worlds that Macmillan inhabited. Also in 1951, Anthony Powell (not, to Macmillan's disappointment, one of Macmillan & Co.'s house

---

*Norman Collins, his mentor on the new techniques, told him that although the audience could be 13 million people ('And Gladstone was lucky if he got 13,000,' replied Macmillan), he should mentally imagine it as two people at home, with children popping in and out of the room.[10]

authors) published *A Question of Upbringing*, the first of the 12-novel sequence, *A Dance to the Music of Time*. Its central character, Kenneth Widmerpool, first seen emerging out of the fog on an Eton cross-country run, shared many of Macmillan's characteristics (though not all – Widmerpool had no sense of wit or humour). Widmerpool was at first a rather gauche, unconfident, emotionally stunted Etonian, tangentially involved in some nameless school scandal, and not highly regarded by his contemporaries. Yet through sheer determination and at times not entirely scrupulous ambition, he achieved a late flowering in previously unimagined positions of power.

Macmillan never had the intellectual's disdain for the culturally middle-brow, which provided such a comfort zone for many in the early 1950s. Many of the artistic successes of those days fell into that bracket. Cinema admissions in 1950 totalled 1.4 billion, with a steady programme of populist films, such as Ealing comedies and war films, appealing to a sense of patriotic nostalgia.

John Masefield[14] was a widely enjoyed Poet Laureate. His poems on national occasions may not have displayed the complexities of those of his close friend W. B. Yeats, but they were rhythmic and comprehensible, and that counted for a lot with his public. For Queen Elizabeth's Coronation, he published in *The Times* his 'Prayer for a Beginning Reign'. He saw the new reign as 'setting the enfettered spirit free',[15] a poetic exemplification of Churchill's political goal, and in keeping with the mood of optimism always associated with the news that broke that morning of the first ascent of Mount Everest by a British team led by Colonel John Hunt. The summer of 1953 was associated with other popular successes. Stanley Matthews was finally in a winning FA Cup side, Blackpool beating Bolton Wanderers in the so-called 'Matthews Final' in May. Gordon Richards won his one and only Derby (on Pinza). The next year Roger Bannister ran the first mile in under four minutes. These achievements were taken as symbols of the new age.

However, there was another side to the coin. The fifties are often seen as a time of emotional repression, inhibition, conformity and 'knowing one's place'. Formidable figures of authority, much less 'cosy' than John Masefield, symbolised a spirit of reverence. They included the Lord Chief Justice, Rayner Goddard,[16] and the Archbishop of Canterbury, Geoffrey Fisher.[17] Both had confidence in their office and an understanding of their role. They believed in church-going, capital punishment, corporal punishment (of which Fisher had been an enthusiastic provider as Head Master of Repton) and the immorality of homosexuality, although Fisher was to give a cautious welcome to the Wolfenden Report's distinction between a sin and a crime on this latter subject in 1957. Goddard presided over the 1952 Craig/ Bentley case, later seen as a miscarriage of justice that gave impetus to the abolitionist cause.*

For Macmillan, the decline in family church-going on Sunday mornings was a matter for regret.[18] He regularly read the lesson at St Giles, Horsted Keynes, when at Birch Grove; he also attended services at nearby All Saints, Danehill, and, once or twice a term, Evensong at Ardingly College. He encouraged attendance in his growing brood of grandchildren.†

The class system in the early 1950s was still pervasive, with many subtle gradations, from the entrance requirements for the Royal Enclosure at Ascot, to the annual advertisement of one leading educational employment agent in *The Public Schools Yearbook*, listing the 200-plus Headmasters' Conference Schools with which it had dealings in their supposed social pecking order.[20]

But deference was in decline. The most popular film in 1950 was *The Blue Lamp*; a decade later it was *Saturday Night and Sunday Morning*. 'The former reassuringly reaffirms the solidity of the established social order, and works by marginalising the young thug who challenges it,' observed Sue Harper and Vincent Porter, the historians of 1950s cinema. 'The latter gives a sympathetic account of a dissentient youth and his leisure time, and chronicles his uneasy settlement with marriage and consumerism.'[21] This shift in social attitudes is a central underlying theme to an understanding of Macmillan and how he moulded responses to those changes.

Macmillan gave away Sarah to Andrew Heath at her wedding at St Giles, Horsted Keynes, on 30 July 1953, a day that must have been poignant for him, as he was not absolutely sure whether Sarah was his daughter or not.‡ The Heaths were to adopt two sons. Macmillan

---

*Teenage youths involved in a burglary, Christopher Craig and Derek Bentley, were trapped on a flat roof, where a police constable was shot dead. Bentley is said to have shouted: 'Let him have it, Chris!' but it was Craig who fired the fatal shot. Craig, who at 16 was below the minimum age for a capital sentence, was imprisoned. Bentley – aged 19 but illiterate and supposedly with a mental age of 11 – was hanged in January 1953.[19]

†Maurice Macmillan's children: Alexander (born 1943), Joshua (1945), Adam (1948), Rachel (1955), David (1957); Caroline Faber's children: Anne (1944), Michael (1945), Mark (1950), David (1961), James (1964); Catherine Amery's children: Louise (1951), Theresa (1954), the twins Leo and Alexandra (1956); Sarah Heath's children, Timothy and Patrick, adopted in the early 1960s.

‡It was not until 1975 that Bob Boothby assured Harold Macmillan that Sarah was indeed Macmillan's natural daughter.

rejoiced in the youthful companionship of all his lively grandchildren. But there were other family problems.

Harold Macmillan's only son, Maurice Macmillan, was tragically afflicted with alcoholism, and now went into a nursing home for a cure. All four of Harold's children were to suffer intermittently from this blight, and drink was known as 'the Devonshire curse'. Dorothy seemed thankfully immune. Now Harold feared for Maurice's future in the family firm of Macmillan & Co. Daniel could not continue for ever (he remained chairman until his death in 1965), and Harold himself was now a minister unable to commit to publishing business.

The spell before Sarah's marriage had been fraught with difficulties. Sarah had become pregnant before the 1951 general election, and had had an abortion (then illegal, unless two psychiatrists testified to the mental damage that would otherwise be done to the mother), the outcome of which was that she was never able to have children of her own. Macmillan himself had been taken ill with gallstone trouble in July 1953, the week before Sarah's wedding. He went into St Thomas's Hospital for an operation and was luckier than Anthony Eden, whose botched gall bladder operation, the month before, was to cause him trouble for the rest of his life. Churchill had a stroke in June and was *hors de combat* for many months, though the seriousness of his illness was kept from the press.

In the six years they had been in office (1945–1951), the Labour Party had become associated with shortages and queues, allied to a burgeoning bureaucracy. This – as Mrs Churchill had percipiently commented –was a blessing in disguise for the Conservatives. By the time they were in power, the tide had turned. The Fifties were to prove a time of stable prices and full employment, an economic equilibrium never repeated. The Conservatives were well placed to catch the swell of recovery.

Macmillan was not sure that the task he had been given as Housing Minister could be accomplished. His mood was not exultant in October 1951. He feared that the problems were so overwhelming, both at home and internationally, that the electorate would react punitively at the next election with a resulting Labour landslide and a government headed by the Tories' *bête noire*, Aneurin Bevan. In Macmillan's opinion, Labour (though, like Churchill, he always referred to them as 'the Socialists') had fought the election very shrewdly by building up an atmosphere of fear – fear that unemployment would return on a scale not seen since the thirties, fear that incomes would shrink, fear that the social services would be downgraded, and, above all, fear that war would return, and in a devastating thermo-nuclear manner.

Macmillan knew that the Labour Party would hold him to account if the 'promise' to build 300,000 houses annually was not met, so he was always careful to refer to the figure as a 'target'. He was not the only one to be cautious. One of the first letters on his appointment came from Bob Boothby: 'I don't know whether to congratulate you or condole with you! On the other hand it is a fine thing to be a member of a Cabinet of sixteen; and if you can manage to build any houses at all, it will be regarded – universally – as a tremendous achievement.'[22]

Macmillan wondered how resources would be distributed between departments. There was still an empire to police, other manifold international commitments and an extensive school-building programme. At least he had Churchill's full support. His new department, the Ministry of Local Government and Planning in his predecessor Hugh Dalton's time, was now renamed the Ministry of Housing and Local Government, Churchill insisting that Housing appear in its title, as an indication of his personal commitment to the project. A further guarantee was the unequivocal statement in the party's 1951 manifesto: 'Housing is the first of the social services. It is also one of the keys to increased productivity. Work, family life, health and education are all undermined by crowded houses. Therefore, a Conservative and Unionist Government will give housing a priority second only to national defence.'[23]

Although Macmillan had enjoyed the status of Cabinet rank when 'Viceroy of the Mediterranean', he had, in essence, been a loner overseas, with considerable autonomy, ploughing his own furrow and reporting back on what he had decided. Similarly, his brief spell as Secretary of State for Air in the eight-week 'caretaker' administration was an atypical Cabinet experience, essentially holding the fort, pending the election.

So when he took his seat at 3 p.m. on 30 October at the first Cabinet of Churchill's new administration, it was the beginning of a different kind of Cabinet experience. He was now part of a team. Housing was not on the agenda that afternoon, which was dominated by defence, the economic situation, the Middle East, food and transport. Macmillan was co-opted on to one of Rab Butler's committees to formulate cuts in public spending, and on another *ad hoc* committee to prepare the King's speech. 'It looks as if I shall lose even the timber and steel I hoped to get', he wrote pessimistically in his diary. 'What a start!'[24]

Macmillan reorganised his ministry on a war footing – Action This Day. This clearly delineated, if unorthodox, command structure brought to mind the business methods of Oliver Franks. The caution, as Macmillan saw it, of his civil servants, epitomised by the kindly, but to him inadequate, presence of the Permanent Secretary, Sir Thomas Sheepshanks,[25] meant he had to do things in a radical manner, however much this alarmed and offended the traditionalists. Macmillan dubbed Sheepshanks 'the bishop', and not just because he was the twelfth child of a former Bishop of Norwich. 'Not an effective figure,' he wrote in his diary, 'wd have made a fine canon, or even archdeacon – but Permanent Secretary of the Ministry of Housing – oh no!...'[26] Hugh Dalton, who had described Sheepshanks as a man who 'will never miss a catch and never hit a six', considered him completely outclassed, as Macmillan did, by his deputy, Evelyn Sharp, 'the best man of them all' in Dalton's estimation.[27] Macmillan regarded Evelyn Sharp,*[28] as 'without exception the ablest woman I have ever known'.[29] She was the driving force behind Macmillan's success and he never forget her part in his inexorable rise. Sir John Wrigley,[30] the other Deputy Secretary, now approaching retirement, he found helpful, though not a creative dynamo like Sharp.

Macmillan saw his first task as getting a really effective figure installed as Director-General. If corners needed cutting, so be it. After some false starts, he eventually persuaded Sir Percy Mills,† to take a short-term secondment from his post as Chairman of the National Research Development Corporation. Both Whitehall, and the Labour opposition, were very wary of the new departure this appointment represented. Undaunted, Macmillan rode the storm. He was now getting used to having his own way.

Sheepshanks was deeply offended by Macmillan's use of Sir Percy Mills, a self-made businessman, as Director-General: the appointment was unconstitutional, even vulgar, and he appealed unsuccessfully to the Cabinet Secretary, Sir Edward Bridges. 'So the Bishop consults the Archbishop!' Macmillan observed wryly in his diary. 'What a lark!'[32]

Sheepshanks did not get on well with the other self-made man who was influential in Macmillan's team, his Parliamentary Secretary, Ernest Marples. Yet Marples, who had made a post-war fortune in the construction industry, had the specialised professional expertise so vital to the task in hand. The 'three Ms' – Macmillan, Mills and Marples – soon made their impact.

Mills' speedy establishment of ten Regional Housing Boards, with

---

*Evelyn Sharp was to become Permanent Secretary of the Ministry after Macmillan's time in office.

†Macmillan had known Percy Mills from wartime days, when Mills had been Machine-Tool Controller at the Ministry of Supply, involved in aircraft production. He knew Mills was a man who could deliver. A further mark in Mills' favour was that he came from Stockton-on-Tees.

the Ministry of Labour and the Ministry of Works, was a vital component in Macmillan's strategy. Red tape was cut to the minimum and
brick-making mobilised on a massive scale. Macmillan had no truck
with excuses. A Building Committee of the Cabinet was authorised,
and this gave Macmillan his first contacts with a figure who was to
become a close and important associate: Freddie Bishop.[33] Gradually
the whole government machine was being effectively mobilised behind
Macmillan's plans.

The more Macmillan at Housing prevailed, and the more Butler
at the Treasury provided funds, so the respective political fortunes of
Butler and Macmillan subtly altered. It is one of the ironies of post-war
Conservative politics that Butler not only enabled the 300,000 houses
to be built, but helped establish Macmillan in an even more advantageous position *vis-à-vis* himself in the unfolding party hierarchy. Rab
Butler's career was to reach its peak of popularity at the Conservative
Party Conference of October 1954 in Blackpool, when he called on
the youth of the party to 'Invest in Success', and prophesied, correctly,
that the standard of living in the country would double in the next
25 years. Harold Macmillan, meanwhile, was moving confidently into
his stride, his growing stature assisted by Butler's munificent support.
Another irony for Macmillan, an instinctive Keynesian, was that his
success depended not so much on central state provision as on a system of deregulation, then gathering pace, that allowed materials such
as timber and steel to be bought at low cost on the open market.

Reginald Bevins,[34] Macmillan's parliamentary private secretary at
the Ministry, and another figure in the team from a working-class
background, later recalled Macmillan's persuasiveness.

> When there was a bit of a tussle in cabinet as to whether he wasn't
> stretching our economic resources by building too many houses, he
> persuaded Churchill to leave it to him to argue it out with Rab
> Butler. Macmillan had, I think, about three nocturnal talks with
> Rab. I remember the last occasion very vividly. He had a drink with
> me in the smoking room at about midnight, which was rather late,
> and then he went off to see Rab and said would I wait for him. He
> came down at 2 o'clock into the smoking room and bought me a
> drink and said 'It's all over, Reg, I've got my own way, and I simply
> report to the Prime Minister that Rab has agreed with me.' Rab was
> tired, Macmillan had more stamina.'[35]

The housing shortage in the 1950s had two principal causes. One
was the war. Enemy action had destroyed vast swathes of property,

particularly in the capital and cities such as Coventry, Plymouth and Swansea, all of which Macmillan visited. Also many buildings had inevitably fallen into disrepair in wartime. The other was the 'post-war bulge'. The families of the baby boom generation had outlived the (sometimes reluctant) hospitality of in-laws and ageing parents, and wanted houses of their own.

The average annual total of houses built between 1945 and 1951 was 200,000. There had been a lack of skilled labour and competing claims for new schools, factories and hospitals. Macmillan benefited in his first year in office from the houses begun under Labour now nearing completion. In that first year there were 240,000 completions, between 1 November 1952 and 31 October 1953, 301,000; and in the calendar year of 1953, 318,000. Totals were displayed in the department, along the lines of a cricket scoreboard. A red-letter day was 10 December 1953, when the three hundred thousandth house that year was completed.

Macmillan believed that the Town and Country Planning Act of 1947 had limited the part played by private builders, and he determined to give this sector a freer rein. He presented a paper on the role of the private builder to Cabinet in November 1951. In December 1952 he set about steering through Parliament a new Town and Country Bill, abolishing the 1947 Development Charge, which received the Royal Assent in May 1953. Other bills he successfully established on the statute book included the Housing Repairs and Rents Act of July 1954, giving new powers to local authorities in clearance or repair of slum houses. The second phase of the Housing programme after new building, often overlooked, was the refurbishment of existing stock. Research was undertaken into existing schemes from Puerto Rico to Croydon. Ernest Marples was prominent in this work and masterminded an exhibition of three flats in Holles Street in London to show the potential of such redevelopment. Macmillan invited the Queen to open the exhibition.

Macmillan was now very much in the public eye, helped behind the scenes by the publicity machine at the Conservative Research Department. He appeared regularly in the newspapers and the cinema news-reels, a rather awkward figure, handing the key to a semi-detached house to a grateful married couple with young children. He visited Lynmouth in the wake of the disastrous floods of August 1952, after arranging for immediate help by the Ministry's engineers. Newsreels showed him picking his way tentatively through the rubble.

The great London 'smog' of December 1952 (which was to lead to the Clean Air Act of 1956) was lethal in its effects. The poisonous sulphurous fog that seeped through the capital brought to a standstill much work in the building trade. Worse was to follow in February 1953 with the East Coast flooding. Damage of between £40 million and £50 million was suffered and 25,000 houses flooded. Macmillan was instrumental (at Churchill's request) in setting up a committee of officials, and he toured the stricken areas, seeing the problems first from the air.

In March 1953, Macmillan appeared with William Deedes[36] in the first televised party political broadcast outside election time, a tightly controlled and rehearsed operation. As the programme was going out live, Macmillan spent the whole day with Deedes and Grace Wyndham Goldie[37] of the BBC at the Lime Grove studios. Mrs Goldie suggested that Macmillan and Deedes should have a rest before the broadcast, and they were allocated a couple of bunk beds in a basement for a half-hour sleep. Like Evelyn Sharp, Mrs Goldie was an effective organiser, not easily deflected from her purpose. In the enforced darkness Macmillan whispered to Deedes, 'This reminds me very much of the trenches!'

Although by later standards the programme was artificial and contrived, it was considered a successful experiment and Macmillan a new television star. Macmillan was not so sure. When Deedes asked how the housing programme in Scotland was going, Macmillan replied that Scotland had its own Secretary of State, adding (as though in one of his many clubs) 'but we work together like brothers and, indeed, we might well do so, for we are brothers-in-law.'[38]

The New Towns were a tricky area. The New Towns Act of 1946, which had outlined 14 such 'overspill' conurbations, was unpopular. Rural communities were hostile to the implicit social engineering of different classes of people being forced to mix together.* In Stevenage, for example, a 'residents' protection committee' was established, enlisting the unlikely support of the socially liberal novelist E. M. Forster, who had written nostalgically about the area in his novel *Howards End*. Only two cheers there then. Equally, Conservatives, for their part, had seen in the New Towns project a covert Labour plan to endanger safe Tory parliamentary majorities in rural areas by the introduction of vast numbers of Labour voters. Nor did many Conservatives relish the prospect of permanent 'Cockney neighbours'.

---

*The signs at one local railway station were changed to Silkingrad, after the unpopular Lewis Silkin,[39] Attlee's Minister of Town and Country Planning.

Macmillan knew that he would have to tread warily, but he also knew that the scheme was inevitable. His approach was to improve standards while minimising ill-informed opposition. He visited Crawley New Town, not far from Birch Grove, and saw that the new housing was an improvement on the cramped terraced houses of the industrial age, the kind he remembered from his days in Stockton-on-Tees. Lady Dorothy was more sensitive. When she visited Crawley, she became aware of the problems – child neglect, divorce, single parentage, poor health – beneath the outward architectural cleanliness. New Crawley, to her, was more reminiscent of the north-east than what might be thought of as leafy Sussex.

Macmillan advocated building flats 'above the shop'. He told his civil servants that in the old days merchants had not been ashamed to live on site – his Macmillan ancestors had done exactly that over the Bowes & Bowes bookshop in Cambridge – and he hoped businessmen could be encouraged likewise in the new towns. Macmillan knew that communities must feel lived in, and ensured that public houses were provided, from the start, on otherwise isolated sites. 'These sites are *not* suitable for council houses,' he instructed Sir John Wrigley, 'but very good for licensed houses.'[40] The New Towns Act of July 1953 increased advances to New Town Development Corporations from £100m to £150 million.

As Macmillan edged nearer his target, Labour MPs looked for ways to find fault. Their main charge, co-ordinated centrally, was that Macmillan had built the *quantity* of houses, but only by skimping on the *quality*. Macmillan's houses were smaller than Bevan's, an ironic criticism as Bevan in his day had been accused by his own supporters of being a Tory for having insisted on spacious dwellings. Macmillan was conscious of how this charge could stick, writing to Viscountess Davidson,[41] 'It is *not* true that the houses being built today are of a less high standard of *workmanship* than before.'

During Macmillan's time at the helm, Housing was second only to National Defence, as the 1951 manifesto had promised. In fact, Housing was the one social policy department that had its political chief in Cabinet for the full 13 years of Conservative government. Labour had forecast that the Tories would cut back on the social services after 1951; in fact, they expanded them.

Macmillan did not always understand, or affected not to bother, that Housing was technically a residual department. He frequently acted as though the many local authorities did not come into the picture at all. One figure he does not mention in his memoirs, Sydney

Wilkinson,[42] Under-Secretary and Chief Housing Aide, was vital in 'squaring' the local authorities.

Some forceful Conservatives were impatient about the pace of building. Harmar Nicholls,[43] who had been one of the most enthusiastic proponents of the 300,000 target, and Enoch Powell, who lamented the lack of a sufficiently unrestricted free-market-approach policy,[44] did not hesitate to say so. Macmillan made sure he kept such potential members of what later became known as the 'awkward squad' on side by holding monthly lunches, so that he could 'consult' them.

Housing and de-rationing were the two unequivocal successes of Churchill's peacetime administration from 1951–1955.[45] Macmillan became established as a figure of the very front rank in British politics. He had shrewdly combined a total commitment to the task in hand with keeping a weather eye open to the future and the next ministerial post. He kept his friendships in good order, notably with his wartime colleague Dwight D. Eisenhower, who was elected United States President in November 1952. Macmillan and Eisenhower exchanged warm letters at the time ('Dear Ike' – 'Dear Harold'), reminiscing on their days together in wartime in the Mediterranean.

As a Cabinet minister, Macmillan had been involved in several key issues. He was not slow in putting forward his views on all of them – from Sudanese independence to the establishment of GATT (the General Agreement on Tariffs and Trade). On 29 February, the Cabinet were asked their views on the ROBOT plan of Rab Butler to free the pound, establishing a floating rather than a fixed rate, and allowing the convertibility of some sterling holdings against the dollar. Churchill by that time had been persuaded against the idea by Lord Cherwell;[46] but Macmillan and Walter Monckton[47] alone refused to express an opinion on such a complex matter at such short notice. After considered reflection, Macmillan felt there was much to be said for Butler's proposal, the brain child of three Treasury officials, Leslie Rowan, George Bolton and Otto Clarke, from whose names the acronym ROBOT derived. The Cabinet decided otherwise.

In that ever-popular Westminster game of studying the runes to identify future prime ministers, Macmillan's name was now beginning to emerge. Some even thought he might, Claudius-like, pop in between the election and Eden's hopes. His former boss at the wartime Ministry of Supply, Lord Beaverbrook, was one such. Macmillan lunched with Beaverbrook on 23 April 1953. Although Macmillan harboured hopes of the Foreign Office at some stage, Beaverbrook thought Agriculture would be the best next step and had advised Churchill so. Beaverbrook told Macmillan to steer clear of the Foreign Office, as Churchill would always dominate foreign policy, particularly if a new Foreign Secretary lacked Eden's long experience. 'When Churchill goes there will be a contest for the leadership of the party,' he told Macmillan. 'There will be an Eden section; there will be a Butler section. You may easily slip in, as Bonar Law did between Austen Chamberlain and Walter Long.' 'Yes,' replied Macmillan, 'but who is to be my Max Aitken?'[48]

In October 1954, Churchill, still showing no signs of giving way to the ever-impatient Anthony Eden, reshuffled his Cabinet. Macmillan, who had told Churchill in June that 'it would be a very great advantage for Ministers to be installed in their new offices before and not after the summer holidays',[49] became Minister of Defence, a post for which he was well qualified, after both his wartime experience and his spell at the Air Ministry in 1945. Defence had always been a psychologically important department for the Conservatives. He approached his new task with enthusiasm, though he realised in the nature of things that he was not likely to stay there for long. However, the real talking point at Westminster, and beyond, was not the Cabinet reshuffle, but when and how the aged Churchill might be persuaded to shuffle off the stage of politics altogether.

CHAPTER SEVENTEEN

Captain of the Praetorian Guard

1954 – 1955

You know Moran, Winston ought to resign. He didn't interfere in my housing, just left it all to me. But since I have become Minister of Defence I have found that he can no longer handle these complicated matters properly. He can't do his job as Prime Minister as it ought to be done.

Harold Macmillan to Lord Moran, Churchill's doctor,
9 January 1955

H[arold] M[acmillan] is to sound the Old Man out at dinner tonight regarding his intention to resign. Feel pretty sure he will get no change.

Evelyn Shuckburgh diary, 29 December 1953

I shall certainly stand at the next election – probably as a Conservative.

Winston Churchill to Harold Macmillan, December 1953

Churchill's Cabinet reshuffle on 18 October 1954 was not well received by the press. Macmillan's move to the Ministry of Defence was the 'headline' appointment; other appointments underlined the fact that the reshuffle was, in essence, a consolidation of Churchill's position as Prime Minister for the foreseeable future.

Macmillan's spell at the Ministry of Defence proved both brief and unhappy. The service chiefs still had direct access to the Prime Minister, though possible amalgamations and reductions led to the First Sea Lord being dubbed the Last Sea Lord. Macmillan dealt with all three services, which involved close liaison with Selwyn Lloyd, now at Supply. Lloyd had initially been one of Eden's protégés, chosen by him in 1951 to be Minister of State at the Foreign Office, thwarting Butler's wish to have Lloyd at the Treasury. Macmillan also cultivated Lloyd ('a very good man', he wrote in his diary),[1] encouraging him in many ways. In January 1955 Macmillan invited his old friend Sir Percy Mills to join Lloyd and himself in one of their regular surveys of Defence and Supply matters. Afterwards he sent an account of the meeting to Rab Butler:

> We had a most interesting talk for several hours on all the organis-
> ational and industrial problems with which Selwyn is confronted.
> We discussed among others the question of whether the Ministry of
> Supply should shed its extraneous functions, e.g. care of the engineer-
> ing industry and be slimmed down accordingly. I had no idea, for
> instance, that engineering included textile and printing machinery. I
> think that Selwyn is now in a mood to approve such a plan. One of
> the great arguments for it is that it would be a new decision of his
> own and one welcome to the House and to the country.[2]

One of the most important political factors in gaining the confidence of the Chiefs of Staff was that the Defence Minister should be
a trusted confidant of the Prime Minister. Macmillan passed that test,
as well as being known and respected by Sir Rhoderick McGrigor,[3]
Sir John Harding[4] and Sir William Dickson.[5] It also helped that he
was already close friends with Sir Richard Powell,[6] who was the real
power in the ministry.

For the second department in succession, Macmillan was not greatly
impressed by his Permanent Secretary, in this case, Sir Harold Parker,[7]
who had previously been Permanent Secretary (from 1946–1948)
at the Ministry of Pensions. Macmillan did not doubt Parker's administrative skill and integrity, but felt that he lacked experience in
the defence field, and also the ability to bring fresh thinking to bear.
After experiencing the incisive minds of Oliver Franks at the wartime
Ministry of Supply and Evelyn Sharp at Housing, he had the highest
expectations of his civil servants and was a demanding political chief.
However, any professional misgivings were always masked by the
perfect, if formal, courtesy of an astute enabler.

Macmillan applied pragmatic business methods to Defence, as he
had at Housing, but the drive for targets was not always best suited to
the demands of defence policy. He soon realised that he was a much
more subsidiary figure in the overall scheme of things than he had
been at Housing. 'The task of the Minister of Defence in this country
is a very difficult one,' wrote Selwyn Lloyd. 'He is really a planner and
co-ordinator. He has no executive power. He is not even Chairman of
the Defence Committee. The Prime Minister is that.'[8]

Churchill's presence in the background was not always helpful
for Macmillan, who did not feel he had the necessary autonomy in
deciding complex strategic defence issues. The decision on the British

H-bomb had been sprung on an unprepared Cabinet in July 1954, a sign of the control Churchill exerted over defence issues. Also, for the layman there were inevitably many complex matters of great technical difficulty in the defence field. Macmillan largely resolved these with the help of the Ministry of Supply. 'Co-axial cable: where do we get it?' was a typical bread-and-butter enquiry.[9]

The running of Defence since 1951 had suffered from the unsatisfactory tenure of Churchill himself (from 28 October to 1 March 1952) and the 'non-political' appointment of Harold Alexander (from 1 March 1952 to 18 October 1954). As Alexander had been in the Lords, the Under-Secretary had been Nigel Birch;[10] now, with Macmillan in the Commons, the arrangement was reversed, and Lord Carrington[11] became Macmillan's Parliamentary Under-Secretary. His PPS was Hamilton Kerr,[12] the MP for Cambridge.*

Macmillan was not at Defence long enough to make the same impact as at Housing. Much of the direction of future policy, as well as the details of the 1955 Defence White Paper,[13] had already been settled. Britain's intention to develop an independent nuclear force, outlined in the White Paper, was confirmed by Churchill in the House of Commons on 1 March 1955, in what proved to be his last major parliamentary speech. As Minister of Defence, Macmillan ought properly to have opened this debate, but he had to defer to Churchill, who still saw Defence as his personal fiefdom. Winding up the debate on the White Paper on the second day, Macmillan defended the controversial decision on the H-bomb. The view that Britain did not need to be an independent nuclear power, he declared, was a very dangerous doctrine. 'Politically it surrenders our power to influence American policy and then strategically and tactically, it equally deprives us of any influence over the selection of targets and the use of our vital striking forces.'[14]†

In the first week of his tenure at the Ministry of Defence, Macmillan sent a friendly 'open' invitation to Field Marshal Montgomery to call on him at any time. Montgomery, now ennobled as Viscount Montgomery of Alamein, and based in Paris at SHAPE (Supreme Headquarters Allied Powers in Europe) as Deputy Supreme Commander, responded at once. At their first meeting on 8 November, Montgomery advocated

---

*When Macmillan became Prime Minister, he put in place structural changes, such as the downgrading of the three Secretaries of State to Minister of State level, and of the Defence Committee, so that his own first Defence Secretary, Duncan Sandys, enjoyed much greater autonomy within the ministry from 1957.
†By the time he was Prime Minister, Macmillan was to realise only too clearly how even that limited objective was unrealistic.

his peacetime hobby-horse, the integration of the three services and a unified defence structure. They also discussed the possible reduction of National Service from 24 to 21 months, and whether the British forces in Germany should become the Reserve Army. The two issues were related. Macmillan had already pointed out in Cabinet (on 1 October 1954) that the Labour Party would exploit any failure by the government to reduce the length of National Service, especially if this was because of increased commitments on the Continent.[15]

Some, less confident, ministers would have shied away from involvement with the tenacious field marshal, but Macmillan enjoyed their meetings. Not only did they bring back memories of wartime achievements, but Macmillan genuinely enjoyed hearing Montgomery's spiky, often iconoclastic views. Far from being discouraged by Montgomery's eagerness to 'get involved', Macmillan renewed his invitation to the field marshal in April 1955.

The everyday work in his new department began properly on 21 October, coincidentally Trafalgar Day. Macmillan flew to the NATO meeting in Paris that day with Sir Harold Parker and his private secretary, W. N. Hanna.[16] The key issue of the time was the future of the EDC (the European Defence Community). In October 1950, the French politician René Pleven had proposed the formation of a European army, his hope being that this would placate French fears about German re-armament. The six founding nations of the European Coal and Steel Community – France, West Germany, Italy, Belgium, the Netherlands and Luxembourg – had signed a treaty establishing the EDC on 27 May 1952, but the reluctance of France and Italy, in particular, to create this international army led to the French National Assembly refusing to ratify the 1952 treaty, thus strangling the embryonic EDC idea. Macmillan became Defence Minister as the Americans and the British were pressing for a Western European Union (WEU), which included Germany and Italy. The Americans saw German re-armament and integration as the best way of countering Soviet expansionism. Britain's foreign secretary, Anthony Eden, also saw the WEU as a means of ending the ruinously expensive Allied occupation of West Germany and establishing a Western European Union as a second security tier alongside the wider Atlantic alliance.

Consequently Macmillan was coming on to the scene as the work of others was reaching a critical stage. Nevertheless, solutions were needed to the central question of British defence policy – how to balance the requirements of British imperial interests worldwide with maintaining peace and security in Europe. Although the British

Empire had contracted in the late 1940s, there were still substantial commitments in Kenya and Malaya, and also the Far East after the foundation of SEATO (the South-East Asia Treaty Organisation) in September 1954. An expensive garrison was in Cyprus. Civil defence costs were soaring. British troops in 1954 totalled 800,000, and the defence budget for 1955–1956 was £1,525 million, probably more if Germany did not contribute to the costs of BAOR (the British Army on the Rhine.)

One of Macmillan's first policy statements, on 10 December 1954 – *Home Defence in a Hot War* – was on the then urgent question of civil defence. 'The Good Samaritan must be organised,' Macmillan declared, 'and not a chance wayfarer.'[17] British atomic testing had begun in Australia in October 1952, and although the Campaign for Nuclear Disarmament had not yet been founded,[18] a feeling of national unease as Britain decided to develop the H-bomb was prevalent. The Soviets had held their first 'H-bomb' test in August 1953. Macmillan felt this unease himself. In a draft on home defence policy in December 1954, he had been very pessimistic. 'We don't know what sort of bombs the Russians have, or are likely to have; how many will fall on us, or where they will fall. Nor do we really know what their effect will be.'[19]

The real importance of Macmillan's brief spell at Defence was that it gave him close insights into the Cold War world of nuclear powers, insights that were to be of great value when he became Prime Minister. There was no shortage of other problems: amphibious warfare, continued production of aircraft carriers (discussed at length in Cabinet on 5 November 1954), internal security in the Colonies, the Middle East Area Command HQ, and the future of the Simonstown naval base in South Africa. Even reducing smog appeared on Macmillan's agenda.

Thanks to Eden's diplomatic skills at the 1954 Geneva Conference, an armistice was signed between the Indo-China antagonists. International agreement was also reached on the future of Trieste in October 1954. Amid many misgivings on the Tory right, an agreement was signed on 19 October 1954 on British withdrawal from the Suez Canal Base. Occupation of West Germany was ended and the Western European Union established. The crisis over the seizure in 1951 of the Anglo-Iranian Oil Company assets was finally resolved in March 1955. On the surface, therefore, the international situation may have appeared more tranquil than for some time. Macmillan, however, was conscious that many problems could erupt without warning. President Nasser[20] took power in Egypt on 14 November 1954. Rioting broke out in Cyprus over 'Enosis', the campaign for union with Greece in

December 1955. In February 1955, Bulganin[21] became President of the USSR. Macmillan wanted to see a united Anglo-American policy, especially over Iraq and Iran. The Baghdad Pact, a mutual defence agreement between Turkey and Iraq, was signed in February 1955. Although the Americans were reluctant to sign up to this pact, Britain joined on 4 April 1955.

Personal security was necessary for Macmillan, and he was reluctantly drawn into the world of Special Branch detectives. As a result, and owing to his increasing seniority, Churchill offered him the tenancy of Dorneywood, the country house gifted to the nation in 1942 by Lord Courtauld-Thomson[22] for use by a government minister. Macmillan declined, as 'Lady Dorothy doesn't like weeding other people's gardens.'[23] Likewise, when he became Prime Minister, he did not reside at Chequers. In Birch Grove he already had his Hughenden.[24] His own house and estate provided the peace offered by Chequers and Dorneywood, which could be more profitably used by other ministers. Although Macmillan declined Dorneywood, he did express interest in the accompanying 'Dorneywood flat' in London, largely because there was not room for Dorothy to stay at 90 Piccadilly. However, he only moved into government accommodation, at 1 Carlton Gardens, when he became Foreign Secretary in April 1955, which coincided with an unaccomplished plan to rebuild the Foreign Office at Carlton House Terrace. Macmillan hoped that No. 2 Carlton Gardens, with its frontage overlooking the Mall, could then be made the Foreign Secretary's official residence, but his idea was rejected. 'The truth is that No. 1 was always a vulgar house. It was the late Lord Northcliffe's and very like him,' he wrote to Nigel Birch. 'No. 2 was a gentleman's house, but, as I say, all these are now vain dreams.'[25]

Macmillan was unfailingly thoughtful to those who served him, whether detectives, typists or cooks. His driver at this time was Bill Housden (who later chauffeured Harold Wilson). Housden was then experiencing various difficulties in finding suitable accommodation for his family near London, and Macmillan arranged for Bobbety Salisbury to make a cottage available for him to rent on the Hatfield estate, a kind act remembered gratefully.[26]

In October 1954, Maurice Macmillan contested the Wakefield by-election. His father canvassed for him on 14 October, in the midst of the Cabinet reshuffle, but their joint hopes were not high. Wakefield was a safe Labour constituency. Maurice Macmillan continued his search for a winnable seat, and the Conservative Association at Stockton-on-Tees offered him the candidacy; but Harold Macmillan advised his son against acceptance of this kindly meant and warmly sentimental suggestion. In fact, Harold was glad Maurice did not run his Labour opponent too close at Wakefield,[27] as he hoped Maurice could, with good grace, seek another, more promising, seat at the general election.

Ever since the 1945 general election, the Conservatives had tacitly been preparing themselves for life after Churchill. When Churchill regained power in 1951, it was accepted that he would serve for a while as a peacetime premier. Yet possible moments for his departure – the death of King George VI in 1952, the Coronation of Queen Elizabeth II in 1953, his stroke later that month – all passed by with no sign of any such intention on Churchill's part. In January 1955, his doctor Lord Moran wrote in his diary, 'Plainly there is a growing feeling among Winston's friends that the time has come for him to go, but only Harold Macmillan has had the guts to say so.'[28]

Unsurprisingly, Eden, the anointed successor, was frustrated by Churchill's refusal to budge. A general election was due by October 1956 and the new leader needed time to consider his options before then. Meanwhile, Churchill was increasingly vague in Cabinet, ruminating endlessly, as lunchtime passed and appointments were missed yet again. On more than one occasion Harry Crookshank asked in an obvious stage whisper, as the clock ticked towards 2 p.m., when the port was going to be handed round. It was not only Churchill's inconclusive ramblings that caused discontent. He could also prove characteristically dictatorial, presenting contentious policies as a *fait accompli*. At the Cabinet meeting on 7 July 1954, the decision to build a British H-bomb was announced and led to an embarrassing 'walkout'. The Cabinet minutes, in time-honoured fashion, gloss over this protest: 'Some Ministers asked, however, that there should be a further opportunity for reflection before a final decision was taken.'[29] Macmillan, in his diary, gave a fuller description of the disagreement: 'Harry Crookshank at once made a most vigorous protest at such a momentous decision being communicated to the Cabinet in so cavalier a way, and started to walk out of the room. We all did the same and the Cabinet broke up – if not in disorder – in somewhat ragged fashion.'[30] For Macmillan this was the moment when he became convinced that, however painful the process would be, Churchill must be made to realise he had overstayed his welcome.

Eden had a fraught meeting with Churchill on 27 August, more a sounding-out of the Prime Minister's intentions than the first stage in a coup. Churchill countered by saying it was open to Eden to lead a rebellion of five or six ministers if he so wished. 'He knew perfectly well,' Eden wrote in his diary, 'that I was the last person to want to do this after our many years of work together.'[31] It was difficult for Eden to do more, tactically or psychologically. His innate gentlemanly reserve was not suited to pressing the issue.

Macmillan had no such inhibitions. After the summer recess, he saw Churchill on 1 October, and urged him to stand down. He followed this up the next day with a letter warning Churchill that Eden was on the verge of quitting politics altogether, as he was so dispirited by the seemingly endless logjam. Macmillan hoped that the new parliamentary session could start with a new leader in place. Eden would then have a good run before an election, probably in the autumn of 1955. It was not to be. Churchill's tenacity in clinging to power surprised and shocked his colleagues, who found themselves powerless. He believed he was the one world leader capable of bringing about a summit with the Russians; in addition, he could not bear the thought of finally abandoning the stage and facing the deserts of vast eternity. Any conversations on retirement were quickly deflected.*

Parliament met for the autumn session with Churchill still firmly in place, despite a not entirely successful 'keynote' speech at the Conservative Party Conference in Blackpool on 10 October. In this speech, Churchill spoke of 1850 when he clearly meant 1950, and confused sovereignty with solvency. Writing of rank-and-file attitudes at Blackpool, Francis Boyd observed: 'They are ready for Mr Eden to take over the leadership now. They think it unfair that he should be kept waiting any longer.'[33]

Manoeuvring now took place behind the scenes. 'Don't you think it worth having another shot at getting him to go on the 80th birthday?' Macmillan wrote to Eden. 'It gives him a fine end.'[34] The celebrations duly took place and yet seemed only to serve in giving Churchill a new lease of life.

Churchill's reluctance to retire had serious implications for the Conservative Party and for the future of its three leading figures – Eden, Butler and Macmillan. For Eden, if Churchill continued in office and fought the next election, there was no telling when the long-promised torch would be passed. It was in Butler's interests, however, for Churchill to stay on, for under this scenario, the succession might conceivably skip a generation† and pass to him directly. On the other

---

*Churchill shook his head sadly over the recent death of Selwyn Lloyd's father, adding, 'Quite young too, only 90.'[32]

†Eden himself might have retired in exasperation (he had actually settled at this time on his retirement title, Lord Baltimore).[35]

hand, it was in Macmillan's interests for Eden to take over as soon as possible, as this would prevent Butler, eight years Macmillan's junior, closing Macmillan out of the premiership for ever.

Although Macmillan was older than Eden, he had not yet held one of the 'great' offices of state. He needed that experience to supersede Butler in the hierarchy, and in any Eden government he would undoubtedly achieve such rank. There was even the faint possibility, certainly entertained by Macmillan, that he might pip both Eden and Butler to the top post when Churchill eventually stepped down, depending on the timing and on Eden's health.

The autumn of 1954 was one of horrible personal tragedy for Butler, as his wife Sydney slowly succumbed to a virulent and painful cancer. Her death – on 9 December (Rab's fifty-second birthday) – left Butler, with a large and young family, understandably bereft, and, in the words of his biographer, 'oddly vulnerable'.[36] Had Sydney been by his side in the next few years (Butler remarried in 1959), political events might have turned out very differently.[37] Meanwhile, Eden had been awarded that rarest of honours, the Garter whilst still in office,[38] as a tribute to his achievement at the 1954 Geneva conference. Macmillan, too, was riding high. Churchill had no doubts as to Macmillan's increasing influence in the upper echelons of the party, calling him the Captain of the Praetorian Guard.[39] Butler, in comparison with Eden and Macmillan, was somewhat eclipsed; whether permanently or not, remained to be seen.

Four days before Christmas, Eden went to see Churchill at 10 Downing Street, hoping to discuss the timetable for a handover. 'After a long pause,' Eden wrote in his diary, 'he said "What do you want to see me about?" in his most aggressive tone.'

It was not a promising start. Churchill said there was no need for a decision before June or July 1955, but eventually agreed to meet senior Cabinet ministers the next day. 'It was all most grudging,' Eden recorded. 'There was much rather cruel "divide et impera". For instance, he asked me how I got on with Harold [Macmillan]. I said "Very well, why?" He replied "Oh, he is very ambitious."'[40]

Unsuprisingly, the meeting on 22 December resolved nothing. Eden had a gloomy conversation afterwards at the Foreign Office with Macmillan and Bobbety Salisbury. 'It was clear to us that Rab would give no help,' he wrote. 'I said that I had had my say & they agreed that no more could be expected of me. Therefore they would try to hold a meeting without W[inston] or me of the remaining colleagues before Christmas.'[41]

On 7 January 1955, Churchill invited Macmillan to lunch, ostensibly to discuss defence problems. The conversation soon turned to the handover and Churchill said that he would continue, at least until Easter, which fell that year on 10 April. On 1 February, Eden, who was about to leave for the inaugural meeting of the SEATO Council in Bangkok, received a promise from Churchill that he would retire in the last week before the Easter recess. Eden, unwisely as it turned out, considered this a firm undertaking. Whilst away in Bangkok, he heard from colleagues that Churchill was now rethinking his commitment.

On Eden's return, the matter could be dragged out no longer, and a dramatic Cabinet meeting on 14 March addressed it directly. The tension was increased because the inner circle of senior ministers (Eden, Butler, Macmillan, Salisbury and Crookshank) knew exactly what the circuitous discussion was really about – but the outer circle remained largely ignorant of the niceties. Naked anger suddenly exploded on both sides. Macmillan's account is one of the most compelling in all his diaries: 'It looked as if the meeting wd. end without the real issue being dealt with. As so often with our countrymen, it was too awkward & painful for anyone to say anything about it. Then a dramatic moment came when Eden said, slowly & without evident emotion, "Does that mean, Prime Minister, that the arrangements you have made with me are at an end?"'

Churchill was visibly rattled and began muttering about the national interest being the first priority. Macmillan's diary entry continues:

Eden then blurted out, 'I have been Foreign Secretary for 10 years, am I not to be trusted?' Churchill replied 'All this is very unusual. These matters are not, in my experience, discussed in Cabinets.' There was a long and difficult silence. Salisbury then said 'It is clear that certain plans are known to some members of the Cabinet; would it not be better if they were known to all?' Churchill said 'I cannot assent to such a discussion. I know my duty & will perform it. If any Cabinet member dissents his way is open.' After another pause, Butler made a useful intervention saying 'It's not a question of loyalty to you or your leadership, Prime Minister. It's a question of whether an election may become necessary. You have always said that you wd. not lead the party at another election. We must consider all these dates simply from the national interest. In my view another Labour government wd. be a disaster from which the country might never recover.'

Churchill had no answer to this contribution.

The meeting broke up without any firm decision one way or another. But everyone knew that it was the death knell of Churchill's career. Macmillan concluded that it was 'the most dramatic, but harrowing discussion at which I have ever been present'.[42]

The next day Churchill initiated a discussion in Cabinet on the election date, but all present knew that the eventual date would be settled by his successor. At 5.15 p.m. on 15 March, Eden held a meeting with his senior colleagues to discuss options for polling day. The meeting was split between supporters of May 1955 and October 1955. Macmillan was firmly in the camp urging an early poll. After the meeting, Eden took Macmillan aside to tell him privately that Churchill had decided that Tuesday, 5 April would be his final Cabinet.

Macmillan was present at the historic dinner party, attended by the Queen and the Duke of Edinburgh, at Downing Street on the eve of Churchill's retirement. Churchill's final Cabinet at noon the next day was another landmark occasion, never to be forgotten by those present, and even by those (as was possible in those less security-conscious days) on the pavement opposite No 10.[43] Eden was the first to arrive, avoiding as far as possible the attentions of the photographers and the cheering crowds. 'What a contrast when Macmillan arrived shortly afterwards,' wrote one bystander later, continuing:

> He ambled forwards, beaming, turned and stood in the doorway of Number 10 acknowledging applause, waving first with his right hand, then with left. One could be pardoned for wondering which one of the two was heir apparent. The way that Macmillan played to the gallery on that occasion, in complete contrast to Eden, amazed not only me. It mystified me at the time, but on thinking the matter over afterwards, I surmised that he was assuming that Eden would not last (for whatever reason) and he was making an early pitch for the succession, which, as it turned out, came rather sooner than any of the rest of us expected.'[44]

Despite all the bitter feelings of the previous few months, the valediction in the Cabinet room on 5 April was dignified and appropriate, with Eden speaking for all his colleagues in generous terms. After the Cabinet, and another pose for the cameras, Macmillan took Rab Butler (who left by a side entrance from Number 11) to lunch at Macmillan & Co. and for a private discussion on the election date. Butler was also convinced that May was the best option. In the afternoon, the senior ministers met Eden at the Foreign Office to discuss the election and to hear Eden's plans. At this meeting Macmillan was told that he would become Foreign Secretary.

Many years later, Macmillan confessed how disappointed he had been not to succeeed Churchill as Prime Minister in April 1955.[45] Eden's recent illnesses and Macmillan's own promotion to Defence had undoubtedly made him *papabile*. He was rising in the political hierarchy, just as Rab Butler, ostensibly the Conservative Party's number three after Churchill and Eden, was imperceptibly past the cusp of his career. Circumstances had pitched Macmillan into a position of direct rivalry with Eden and Butler, as he recognised in the privacy of his diary: 'I like both Butler & Eden. They both have great charm. But it has been cruelly said that in politics there are no friends at the top. I fear it is so.'[46]

CHAPTER EIGHTEEN

Nearer to the Centre

1955

A Foreign Secretary is forever poised between a cliché and an indiscretion.

Harold Macmillan, 30 April 1956

This is the devilish thing about foreign affairs: they are foreign and will not always conform to our whim.

James Reston, 16 December 1964

In England statesmen are pro-European when they belong to the opposition and anti-European when they are in power.

Paul Reynaud

This relationship (between Prime Minister and Foreign Secretary) is rarely an easy one.

Lord Gore-Booth, 1974

'So the old PM is out and the new one in,' wrote Harold Macmillan in his diary on 6 April 1955. 'It is a pretty tough assignment to follow the greatest Englishman of history, but I feel sure Eden will make a good job of it.'[1] Not everyone agreed. Lord Swinton told Churchill that Eden would be 'the worst Prime Minister since Lord North', and Hugh Dalton recorded in his diary Bob Boothby's opinion that Eden would be gone within eighteen months.[2] On the day Eden became Prime Minister, Randolph Churchill descended the steps of his London club, White's, to discover a policeman fixing a parking ticket to his car. 'The Eden terror has begun,' he declared.[3]

Yet Macmillan was genuinely optimistic about the new political era. In the House of Commons Attlee paid appropriate tribute to Churchill and then welcomed Eden generously. 'Eden's reply was excellent, in time, temper, matter & manner,' wrote Macmillan in his diary. 'A very good start. Our boys gave him no end of a cheer.'[4] After parliamentary questions a significant inner circle – Rab Butler, Macmillan, James Stuart, the Scottish Secretary, and Edward Heath, the Chief Whip – met in Eden's room at the House of Commons to finalise the composition of the Cabinet. Macmillan was to be Foreign Secretary.

Eden had been open in telling Macmillan that he would have preferred Bobbety Salisbury. Although five peers had held the post of Foreign Secretary in the twentieth century – Salisbury's own grandfather, the third Marquess; Lansdowne; Curzon; Reading and Halifax – the last occasion had been 15 years before, and Eden did not feel he could break with the seemingly accepted convention that the Foreign Secretary should be in the Commons. Though Macmillan admired Eden's frankness, it was not exactly a ringing endorsement of his own position.[5]

Macmillan's promotion left a vacancy at Defence, which was filled by Selwyn Lloyd. The other big promotion in the reshuffle was for Lord Home, who took over Lord Swinton's place at the Commonwealth Office. Though Macmillan personally regretted Swinton's departure, he agreed that it was necessary to bring on younger men. Swinton generously felt the same, disclaiming any claim to office in a letter to Eden, in which he said, 'There is a lot to be said for starting out with a team you know will stay the course.'[6] * For Macmillan, however, too many of the old guard – Woolton as Chancellor of the Duchy of Lancaster and party chairman, for example – still remained in place. Eden had not proved a good butcher. The arrangements were of an interim nature, occasioned by the decision to keep Rab Butler at the Treasury.

Butler's four arduous years as Chancellor had taken their toll. He was clearly due for a move, but the timing of Churchill's retirement did not make an immediate change easy, for Butler was due to deliver his fourth Budget on 19 April. Eden was also influenced by his feelings of compassion, following the recent death of Butler's wife. 'I can't move Rab from the Treasury,' he told his PPS, Robert Carr, 'even if in the end it proves the destruction of my Government.'[7]

Although Eden's decision was motivated by kindly understanding, it did no long-term favours to Butler, whose reputation for skilful economic management was to be severely dented in the next few months. 'Budget – tragic flop,' wrote Sir George Bolton of the Bank of England in his diary on 27 October.[8] The autumn balance of payments crisis led to Butler's emergency 'Pots and Pans' Budget of 25 October, so called because of the purchase tax imposed on kitchen and household goods. As the cumulative effect of this Budget (after the election) was to claw back many of the concessions, which had included 6d off

---

*Macmillan saw in Lord Home a future Leader of the Lords (a post he attained in 1957), though not, at that stage, a future Prime Minister.

income tax, from the pre-election Budget, it led to charges of political dishonesty. The Shadow Chancellor, Hugh Gaitskell, launched a bitter personal attack on Butler in the House of Commons: 'Having bought his votes with a bribe, the Chancellor is forced – as he knew he would be – to dishonour the cheque.'[9] Eight weeks later Butler was moved from the Treasury, to be replaced by a reluctant Macmillan.

By then accepting the non-departmental post of Lord Privy Seal, Butler had in effect ceded the eventual premiership to Macmillan. In retrospect, it would have been better all round if Macmillan had become Chancellor directly in April 1955, and Rab Butler been made Home Secretary or Foreign Secretary. The advantage for Butler would have been in avoiding the effects of the economic realities that catch up with all long-serving chancellors in the end. For his part, Macmillan would have avoided the fractious and difficult relationship that developed with Eden over the conduct of foreign policy. The political momentum in the longer term, though, was with Macmillan.

The immediate concern in April 1955, after the Cabinet posts had been allocated, was to decide on the date of the general election. Macmillan pressed for a quick poll. Butler, and most of the Cabinet, agreed, with Osbert Peake the one dissenting voice. The decision took considerable courage on Eden's part. There was no guarantee of victory. The opinion polls put the Tories variously between 48 per cent and 46 per cent, about four points ahead of Labour. Having waited so long for the top post, it would have been the ultimate irony if Eden had lasted only a few weeks, owing to an incorrect reading of the public mood.

Nevertheless, May was an option that Eden considered the most favourable. He subtly capitalised on the British sense of fair play, the belief that he 'deserved his turn', a view not limited to Conservative supporters. Also the polls were less volatile in those days and there was no strong third-party vote. Two other factors were important. Workers in the Lancashire cotton towns would be on their 'wakes weeks' at Whitsuntide (a point spotted by Butler), and as postal votes were not then available for those away on holiday, several vital north-west seats might be won by the Conservatives.[10]

Even more important was the current state of the Labour Party, in the midst of one of its perennial bouts of in-fighting. The long-running feud between the Gaitskellites and the Bevanites that was to blight the prospects of the Labour Party, even after the deaths of Bevan and Gaitskell in 1960 and 1963 respectively, was at its height. In March Bevan even suffered the withdrawal of the party whip for a short period.[11] To later eyes it seems astonishing that Attlee, by then

72, still continued as Labour leader, a post he had held for over 20 years. Despite the Labour Party's famous victory under his leadership in 1945, Attlee's electoral record was poor.* He entirely lacked Churchill's charisma; yet he had defeated Churchill despite Churchill's pugnaciousness and fame as a war leader. But the circumstances 10 years later were very different. Attlee was not a glamorous figure when set against the handsome and debonair Eden. As Bernard Donoughue was to write: 'Clement Attlee had continued as leader of the Labour Party long beyond the time when he could make any positive contribution in that role.'[12] Eden calculated, correctly, that a delayed contest, against a younger Labour leader, probably Gaitskell, would be a far greater risk.

Arrangements for the poll were soon put in hand. Ministers were sworn in at Windsor on 12 April, Butler's budget followed on 19 April, and Parliament was dissolved on 6 May. That day Macmillan attended his adoption meeting in Bromley, his tenth such since 1923. Polling day was set for 26 May, the first May election since 1929, when Baldwin had lost a large Conservative majority. More encouragingly for Eden, the two previous incoming prime ministers to seek an almost immediate mandate from the electorate – Campbell-Bannerman in January 1906 and Bonar Law in November 1922 – had been successful in their quest.

Macmillan found the next few weeks a curious limbo, not knowing whether he would still be Foreign Secretary by the end of the month, or back in St Martin's Street as a publisher. Like many privileged figures of that era, he did not depend on membership of Parliament to maintain a position in public life. He spent a family Easter at Birch Grove, where Moucher Devonshire was a guest. The Dowager Duchess, over 80, commented that Victor Devonshire would have been particularly pleased that his son-in-law was Foreign Secretary. 'So would my poor mother,' Macmillan wrote in his diary. 'What extraordinary ups and downs there are in political life! Before the war, I was a rebel agst the party; resigned the Whip, and was generally regarded as one of the many young men of whom much had been expected but had failed. Churchill rightly said "It's not a flat-race, it's a steeple chase."'[13]

The 1955 campaign was the last at which the leading political figures appeared at 'open' meetings, and travelled the length and breadth of the country with minimal security. As the national newspapers were

---

* Only Edward Heath in modern times was to have a worse record, with three defeats out of four to Attlee's three out of five.

on strike television played a more prominent part than it had done in
1951.

On 10 May, Macmillan appeared in the Conservatives' first television broadcast of the campaign. It was not a success, as he himself
admitted. The producer had arranged for Macmillan to show a small
money box representing the scant savings people had been able to
accumulate under the last Labour government. As the total under
the Conservatives was now 30 times as large, Macmillan was then
going to show a box approximating to that amount. Unfortunately,
the props man had produced a box 30 times larger in each direction;
it was thus 27,000 times bigger than the original box. As this vast
trunk, requiring two men to carry it to the studio, only arrived at
the last minute, Macmillan could not proceed with the original plan
of putting the small box on top of the second. Instead, he continued:
'Now I've got just a few more things to say to you and since I have
been pretty busy recently I have made a few notes to help me.' Putting
on his glasses, he consulted these notes, and, plainly ill at ease, read
out a prepared text: 'Things are getting better. We have got the whole
thing in our hands. There is a wonderful future before us.'[14] Things
were better for the second television broadcast on 17 May. Eden and
four Cabinet colleagues answered questions from newspaper editors.
Although unsophisticated by later standards, the format worked and
certainly proved less taxing than a solo performance.

The 1955 campaign was the dullest in living memory. More public
interest was evoked by the courageous, but unsuccessful, attempt
of the British boxer, Don Cockell, to wrest the World Heavyweight
Championship from Rocky Marciano in America on 16 May. The
election was a classic example of the outcome being determined, not
by current canvassing, but by memories of the previous campaign.[15]
In 1951, the Labour Party had campaigned on three main issues:
unemployment, which they claimed would rise to pre-war levels if the
Tories won; the welfare state, which they claimed the Tories would
dismantle; and 'Churchill's finger on the trigger', which, they asserted, amounted to war-mongering. In fact, the Tories had done well
in office. Unemployment had fallen year by year; there had been an
increase in real terms in expenditure on the social services, especially
in Macmillan's particular area, housing; and the conflicts in Korea and
Indo-China had been ended, the latter almost entirely owing to Eden's
diplomatic efforts. The swansong of Churchill's premiership had
been his call for a summit with the Russians to reduce international
tensions.

As Bromley was a safe seat, Macmillan felt free to go to NATO

The croft of the Macmillan family on the Isle of Arran.

Macmillan's American mother, Nellie, as a young woman.

Macmillan's father, Maurice, at the age of 29.

Daniel, Arthur and Harold: the three Macmillan brothers at Cadogan Place.

Macmillan (*far left*) at the Fourth of June celebrations at Eton College, 1907.

'Sligger' Urquhart at Balliol. Favoured undergraduates were invited to his reading parties on the continent.

The opening of the Battle of Loos at 6.30 a.m. on 25 September 1915 Macmillan was gravely wounded in the fierce fighting.

The marriage of
Harold Macmillan
and Lady Dorothy
Cavendish at
St. Margaret's,
Westminster, on
21 April 1920.
The guests included
Queen Alexandra,
Thomas Hardy and
Rudyard Kipling.

Captain Macmillan, M.P. for
Stockton-on-Tees, watching
the Stockton and Thornaby
sports with Lady Dorothy.

Caroline and Sarah Macmillan.

Ronald Knox, a profound
influence on the young Macmillan.

Sir Oswald Mosley with his
British Union of Fascists. Earlier,
Macmillan had to be dissuaded
from joining Mosley's New Party.

John Maynard Keynes, 'the matchless chief'.
Macmillan published Keynes's influential
works and was advised by Keynes on his
own book, *The Middle Way*.

Macmillan as 'Viceroy of the Mediterranean' in Sicily, the civilian among all the uniforms. *Back row*: Macmillan and General Bedell Smith. *Front row*: General Eisenhower, Air Marshal Tedder, General Alexander and Admiral Cunningham.

Archbishop Damaskinos and Winston Churchill in Athens, December 1944, with Osbert Lancaster *(far right)*. The Archbishop was initially mistaken as a late entrant to the Allies' Christmas fancy dress competition.

Captured Axis aircraft at Klagenfurt, scene of the chaotic surrenders which formed the background to the repatriations of the Cossacks, May 1945.

Macmillan in reforming mood at the 1949 Conservative Conference.

'All Heal let loose' – the South Bank site of the Festival of Britain with the Skylon, 1951. Rab Butler said the Skylon was like the British economy, 'it had no visible means of support'.

Anthony Eden and
Harold Macmillan at
the Geneva Conference,
1 July 1955.

Harold Macmillan
returning to 11
Downing Street after
being appointed
Prime Minister on
10 January 1957.

The Two Ernies:
Ernie Marples
and ERNIE, the
Electronic Random
Number Indicating
Equipment, as the
Premium Bonds
draw begins,
June 1957.

'A bounder but not a cad.'
Bob Boothby as Rector of
St Andrews University, 1959.

meetings in Paris. Irritatingly, though, he found time to buck up Rab Butler by sending him missives about such things as railway fares. 'We aren't going to find them going up (by mistake) on May 25th, are we?'[16] He also had a day with Churchill at Chartwell on 4 May to discuss the immediate future, including the party political broadcasts. One of the issues they talked about was the arrangement for Anthony Montague Browne[17] to be seconded from the Foreign Office to look after Churchill in retirement, an arrangement confirmed by letter on 15 June.[18]

Macmillan's main concern on the electoral front was that his son, Maurice, now standing for Halifax, should finally be elected to Parliament. He combined a tour of Yorkshire constituencies on 24 May with an evening speech in Halifax on behalf of Maurice. The meeting, open to all, was packed and enthusiastic.

Macmillan spent polling day, 26 May, in Bromley with Dorothy, touring all the committee rooms and polling stations. In the evening they attended the *Daily Telegraph* election dinner party at the Savoy Hotel. When the first result came through shortly after 10 p.m. (polls closed at 9 p.m. in those days), the swing to the Tories was clear, confirming that they would be returned. Macmillan was with Lord Woolton in Central Office at 1 a.m. when he learned that Maurice had won Halifax, a moment of profound happiness for Macmillan and his wife.

On the morning of 27 May, Dorothy and Harold left 1 Carlton Gardens (now his confirmed London residence) to attend the Bromley count. Macmillan's opponent was a future Labour minister, the young Gerald Kaufman, whom he described in his diary as 'a rather unpleasant youth' and 'very semitic'.*[19] The figures were:

Harold Macmillan (Conservative)	24,612
Gerald Kaufman (Labour)	11,473
Conservative majority	13,139

Macmillan's majority had increased by 1,014 votes since 1951, satisfactory, if not spectacular. Nationally, the results completely vindicated Eden's decision to go for an early poll. The Conservatives won 344 seats, Labour 295 and the Liberals 6. The overall majority was up from 17 seats to 60, the first time for over a century that a

---

*It was, unhappily, not unusual, particularly among the upper classes, to be dismissive of Jews in the 1930s. But to continue, even in the privacy of a diary, in such attitudes in the 1950s, in the shadow of the Second World War and in the full knowledge of what had happened to hundreds of thousands of Jewish people, reveals an unpardonable insensitivity.

non-coalition government had made such an advance. For the third successive election the Conservatives had increased their percentage of the vote; it was now 49.7 per cent, the highest percentage total attained by any party in the post-war era. For the Conservative voter, 1955 was a prelapsarian moment of stability and equilibrium. Yet a déluge of social, economic and political changes was just round the corner.

With the election won, Macmillan was able to turn his attention fully to his new responsibilities as Foreign Secretary, a task to which he looked forward with enthusiasm. For the first time in his political career, he had been given a job he really wanted and in which he hoped he could make a lasting contribution. However, events were to deny him both a long-term tenure and the success he hoped for.

One of the most important landmarks during Macmillan's period in office was the Austrian Peace Treaty of 15 May 1955,* though his own personal contribution to this diplomatic triumph was limited. The difficulty for Macmillan was that, for the second department in a row, he was overshadowed by a previous incumbent. Churchill had not been a helpful presence for him at Defence, and now Macmillan was serving Eden, who had been one of the towering twentieth-century Foreign Secretaries.[20] Eden took an almost proprietorial interest in international diplomacy. As a result any subordinate, particularly one of Macmillan's intelligence and acumen, was bound to find his position circumscribed. The feeling was mutual. In September 1955, Eden confessed to Rab Butler that he had 'found it difficult to work with so strong a character as Harold Macmillan'.[21]

Macmillan found it troublesome also. There were no major conflicts, rather niggles along the way. Symptomatic was an episode in September over the rewording of a telegram to the Russian leader, Bulganin, which was eventually resolved in Cabinet, to Macmillan's satisfaction. Yet, as Macmillan had written to Rab Butler on an earlier occasion, 'The small matters in politics are so often the occasion for great troubles.'[22]

Macmillan had excellent support from his officials, who were from a vintage diplomatic generation. His Permanent Under-Secretary was Sir Ivone Kirkpatrick, always known as 'Kirk'.[23] Kirk's intellectual brilliance, not to mention a sometimes acerbic cynicism, appealed

---

*After Stalin's death in 1953, the Allies, the occupying forces and the Austrians were able to agree terms to establish Austrian independence. This, in the shadow of the Cold War, was a considerable achievement.

to Macmillan. They saw political life from the same vantage point. Unusually for a senior diplomat, Kirk had not attended university, but the circumstances commended him to Macmillan. He had been accepted for Balliol, but had chosen instead to fight in the trenches of the Western Front, before joining the diplomatic service in 1919. His fierce antipathy to the Nazis, coupled with his pre-war stance against appeasement, also recommended him to Macmillan.

Other figures in key positions were already known to Macmillan from North African days: Roger Makins was now the British Ambassador in Washington; Piers ('Bob') Dixon was Britain's Permanent Representative at the United Nations; and Sir Anthony Rumbold was the Principal Private Secretary.[24] Sir Harold Caccia was Deputy Under-Secretary of State, and the first to brief Macmillan on the international situation for his initial NATO meetings in Paris. Also in the Private Office, and shortly to be Principal Private Secretary, was Pat Hancock, that rarity in Macmillan's life, a Wykehamist whose company he enjoyed. The Assistant Private Secretary was Andrew Stark.[25]

Macmillan always set store by his private secretaries. He knew that they were the true enablers. 'If you want to get anything done in government, it's no good going to the top,' he once recalled. 'It only antagonizes the officials. You have to know someone who knows someone who really does the job. I remember when I was in North Africa during the war, if I wanted a special aircraft it was no good my asking the Commander-in-Chief. He would have said no, and muttered something about the rules. But if I asked my Private Secretary, he would have talked on an old-boy basis to his opposite number and the whole thing would have been fixed up.'[26] He now had a team who not only 'knew someone', but also knew him.

Macmillan's first months in office show the range of his travels: Paris, Vienna, New York and San Francisco followed each other in quick succession. Moscow was his last major tour, in November. As the controversy over the 1951 defections of Guy Burgess and Donald Maclean[27] was then resurfacing, Macmillan took the opportunity on that visit to ask the Russian foreign minister, Molotov, where the British spies were in the USSR. 'That is a matter,' replied Molotov with not a flicker, 'which would require investigation.'[28]

Macmillan's first overseas visit as Foreign Secretary was to the NATO meeting in Paris from 7–10 May. The agenda was formidable – the establishment of the Western European Union, Germany's admittance into NATO, and possible summit talks with the Russians. In Paris, Macmillan renewed acquaintance with John Foster Dulles, the

American Secretary of State. He had met Dulles in May 1953, when he described him in his diary as 'the most dunder-headed man alive', moving 'from blunder to blunder'.[29] Churchill was more colourful in his exasperation, declaring that Dulles was the only bull he knew who carried around his own china shop.[30] Macmillan skilfully 'managed' Dulles by emphasising his own position as an *ingénue* from housing policy who needed guidance from Dulles in the murky waters of diplomacy. He persuaded Dulles to invite the Russians to summit talks on Germany, but, like so many of his colleagues, he was to learn the truth of Dulles' belief that 'the United States does not have friends; it has interests'.[31]

Macmillan was with Dulles at the lavish celebrations for the signing of the Austrian Peace Treaty in Vienna. The luncheons, dinners and endless toasts, a precursor of so many similar events in the years ahead, certainly confirmed Palmerston's dictum that dining was the soul of diplomacy. The Russian Commissar for Foreign Affairs, Molotov, presided at the formal ceremonies; Macmillan thought he looked like Barnard, a keeper at Hardwick Hall, one of the Devonshire properties.[32] Macmillan knew that the real work, as always on these occasions, took place in the social interaction behind the scenes. The fact that he could blend, chameleon-like, with all manner of people, whatever his private views, was to be of immense political benefit. Dulles put Macmillan's plan to Molotov and the foundations for the first Geneva summit of 1955 were laid.

This summit was dominated by Eden. The *News Chronicle* said that Macmillan 'loyally played Tenzing to Eden's Hillary'.[33] Although the Geneva gathering achieved nothing in concrete terms, it did establish a dialogue between the superpowers. Macmillan may have been a subordinate figure on the British side, but his comment on returning to England was the one to find its way into the dictionaries of quotations: 'There ain't gonna be no war.'[34]

The second Geneva Conference (of Foreign Ministers) in October was a more fraught occasion. Macmillan protested to Molotov about the Soviet encouragement of an arms race in the Levant in denial of the new 'Geneva spirit'. At the plenary session on 31 October, when Molotov proposed that both East and West German governments should be invited to further talks, Dulles said that this would not be acceptable as East Germany did not have a freely elected government. Once the remarks had been translated, Molotov took umbrage and insisted that the East German Government was just as freely elected as that in the West. Macmillan, with a carefree insouciance that he was later to display to great effect against Khrushchev at the United

Nations,[35] said that he understood the East German Government had been elected by 99 per cent of the electorate. With his experience of properly conducted democratic elections going back to 1923, he said, any such victor was not a politician, he was a walking miracle. 'This caused great glee among the Americans; polite amusement among the French,' Macmillan wrote in his diary. 'I also observed that the Russians laughed – and then suddenly stopped, looking to Molotov and Gromyko to see whether it was all right to laugh.'[36]

The press heavily criticised the White Paper on the defections of Burgess and Maclean as a whitewash.[37] Guy Burgess, Second Secretary at the Washington Embassy, and Donald Maclean, Head of the American Department of the Foreign Office, had fled to Moscow on 25 May 1951. It transpired that Maclean was already a member of the NKVD (later the KGB), and the escape of the two spies, shortly before the net closed round them, caused a major international scandal. Now, in September 1955, particular attention was paid as to why there was no examination of the events surrounding the timing of Maclean's disappearance. More damaging for MI5 was the recent revelation by a Soviet defector, Vladimir Petrov, that in fact a 'third man' had tipped off both Burgess and Maclean. On 18 September 1955, *The People* newspaper had published details of Petrov's allegations, thus giving the story general currency. Macmillan, determined to defend MI5, told Sir Dick White[38], MI5's Director-General, that there was no alternative to a statement following Petrov's allegations.

Macmillan's statement on 7 November was to a House of Commons so crowded it reminded him of Budget Day. Andrew Stark was the duty secretary, accompanying Macmillan to the Commons, and recalled it as 'a tricky and difficult moment'.[39] A Labour MP, Colonel Marcus Lipton, under the protection of parliamentary privilege, asked Macmillan directly if Kim Philby[40] was the so-called 'third man' who had warned Burgess and Maclean that their cover had been blown. This placed Macmillan in a difficult position, as he knew about MI5's ongoing inquiries into Philby. His reply skirted the delicate boundary between a cliché and an indiscretion. 'I have no reason', he replied, 'to conclude that Mr Philby has at any time betrayed the interests of this country, or to identify him with the so-called "third man", if indeed, there was one.'[41] This not entirely frank remark was to prove a hostage to fortune, which led to much criticism later as fuller details emerged of Philby's treason.

Donald Maclean had lodged in Washington with the charismatic journalist Kim Philby. History was to reveal Philby as a double agent, working for both MI5 and the Soviets, but he was not fully unmasked as a spy until some 12 years after Maclean's defection. Meanwhile, in 1955, following his 'clearance' by Macmillan in the House, Philby was enabled to revel in his status as an 'innocent' man, making a statement at his mother's flat in Kensington to demonstrate the fact. The press portrayed him as a victim. Over the next eight years, MI5 enquiries tightened the net further, and in January 1963, the year in which Macmillan was to be even more deeply embarrassed by further security matters, Philby confessed that he had indeed tipped off Burgess and Maclean. He then followed them to Russia.

Macmillan had entertained a low opinion of the non-military security services from his days in North Africa, and he now felt, rightly, that the whole spies saga was damaging Anglo-American relations. Security matters were not to be his strong point, and he was apt in post-retirement interviews to play down the importance of Burgess, Maclean and Philby, saying in one BBC interview that espionage and defection were 'not very important...it's all rather exaggerated'.[42] Certainly he was aware of the potential damage to his own position, and as Sir Dick White's biographer has written of this period, 'Macmillan had developed an instinctive wariness of any pitfalls which might hinder his ambitions.'[43]

The Home Office has traditionally been seen as the graveyard for political reputations. Among the prime ministers of the twentieth century, only the former Home Secretaries Asquith, Churchill and Callaghan have gone on to the premiership, whereas eight of the Foreign Secretaries and eight of the Chancellors of the Exchequer of the same period have done so. For Macmillan, however unfairly, the Foreign Office was now attracting some of the ill fortune normally associated with the Home Office. The fact that the Philby imbroglio was not his responsibility did not diminish the risks to his own position. The successful Austrian Peace Treaty was not his work either, but he learned to accept the plaudits and the brickbats equally.

As President of the European Coal-Steel Community (ECSC), Jean Monnet planned to relaunch the idea of a united Europe in the economic field. Accordingly, on 1 June 1955, the six foreign ministers of the Coal-Steel Community ('the Six') met at Messina – 'an improbable site for the birth-place of a great idea', wrote Hugo Young[44] – to explore the setting up of a European Common Market.

Unfortunately, the Messina conference occurred at the most unpropitious time for Britain, coinciding as it did with the transitional changes that followed in the wake of Churchill's resignation. Eden had only just moved into 10 Downing Street and Macmillan was only just established at the Foreign Office. But there is no doubt that there was an unpalatable air of *hauteur* about their prevailing attitudes.

In January 1952, Eden had made a speech in America on the question of the United Kingdom joining a federation on the continent of Europe. 'This is something,' he declared, 'which we know, in our bones, we cannot do.'[45] Eden's view was that Britain's two most important relationships, politically and economically, were with the USA and with the Commonwealth. A similar relationship with the Six would never be achievable. Rab Butler said that Eden was 'bored' by the Messina plans, 'even more bored than I was'.[46] Butler demonstrated what Alan Milward, the chronicler of post-war European reconstruction, has called 'disinvolved distaste'. At a dinner of the OEEC (Organisation for European Economic Co-operation), Butler referred to the Messina conference as 'some archaeological evacuations' in an old Sicilian town that need not concern Britain.[47]

At the time of the Messina conference, Macmillan, as Foreign Secretary, was in San Francisco, attending the tenth anniversary celebrations of the United Nations. On his return, he was more polite than Butler, if not more enthusiastic. He believed in confederation, not federation. Nevertheless, during 1955, the Six offered many overtures to Britain. The British expertise in the field of atomic energy was far in advance of that of Europe, and much needed by Euratom, the body set up to integrate and extend European co-operation over atomic policy. Had the political will been there, Britain could have joined the embryonic Common Market movement in 1955 on terms far more favourable for the Commonwealth than were available 20 years later.

These responses were typical of British mainstream opinion at the time. What need had Britain – one of the global Big Three at the Potsdam conference 10 years earlier – to concern itself with what countries like Luxembourg were thinking and doing? The attitude though was to change, as fears grew of a form of economic protectionism from which Britain was excluded. Fifty per cent of Britain's trade at the time was with the Empire and Commonwealth, and only 20 per cent with Europe, and Macmillan was well aware of the dangers of falling between the two stools, in effect antagonising both markets by a combination of perceived betrayal and condescending aloofness. Messina was a key moment, for as Alan Milward has written, 'The year 1955 was one in which German manufacturers made sudden inroads into the share of Britain's manufactures in European markets, especially in the Netherlands and Scandinavia.'[48] Sharper economic competition was on its way.

Whatever the pros and cons of 'Europe' as a political ideal, Britain suffered for its reputation as having been stand-offish, and a reluctant and late participant in the project. Gradually, the mood changed. West Germany became a sovereign state on 5 May 1955. Fears grew that France and Germany would become the dominant economic partners in Europe, with deleterious effects for Britain. 'What then are we to do?' Macmillan pondered. 'Are we to just sit back[49] and hope for the best? If we do that it may be very dangerous for us; perhaps Messina will come off after all and that will mean Western Europe dominated in fact by Germany and used as an instrument for the revival of power through economic means. It is really giving them on a plate what we fought two wars to prevent.'[50] Paul Reynaud, French Prime Minister in 1940, and now chairman of the Economic Committee of the Council of Europe, had famously observed that British statesmen were pro-Europe in opposition, and anti-Europe when in government. Macmillan was eventually to be the exception.

Cyprus had been a British crown colony since 1925. Following the Suez Canal Base agreement of 1954, the strategic importance of Cyprus, especially as an air base, precluded another withdrawal from the Mediterranean. Local interests were thus in conflict with British interests. As four-fifths of the Cypriot population was Greek, the campaign for union between Cyprus and Greece – Enosis – flared anew in 1954. An anti-British guerrilla organisation – EOKA (Ethniki Organosis Kyprion Agoniston) – led by General Grivas,[51] began a terrorist campaign on 1 April 1955. The effect of this troubled situation was to strain Anglo-Greek relations, especially after the spiritual leader of the Greek community, Archbishop Makarios,[52] was deported to the Seychelles in March 1956, because of suspicions that he was aiding and abetting EOKA. In addition, there was intense rivalry between Greek and Turkish Cypriots.

Macmillan had a low opinion of the Governor of Cyprus, Sir Robert Armitage – 'ineffective, even for a Wykehamist', he wrote in his diary after one of many frustrating meetings.[53] Much to the dismay of Armitage, who saw Cyprus as an internal question, Macmillan called a Tripartite Conference in London. The Colonial Office, which had responsibility for Cyprus, was also wary of the way Macmillan had 'taken over' the issue, not until then a Foreign Office remit. Alan Lennox-Boyd[54] though, the political head of the Colonial Office, broadly agreed with Macmillan, and it was their joint approach to the Cabinet that had led to the Tripartite Conference in August 1955. When the conference convened in London at Lancaster House,

Macmillan sought to break the deadlock by identifying the moderates from all sides, the tactic he had employed during the Greek civil war 11 years earlier. As in 1944, he drew on classical parallels, wondering if he would be a latter-day Xerxes.[55] In an unusual move for those times, he invited delegates to his own home, Birch Grove, for luncheon, walks in the garden and discussions in the library, Greeks and Turks on successive days. He felt this a more conciliatory way of dealing with intractable problems than in the formal and stultifying Whitehall atmosphere. Despite these efforts at personal diplomacy, the Tripartite Conference solved nothing, indeed broke up in disarray. Terrorist activity continued unabated in Cyprus, and some critics felt Macmillan had made the situation worse by involving the Turks, who then launched counterterrorist measures against the Greek Cypriots.

The Cyprus dilemma was neatly encapsulated by the cartoonist Illingworth,[56] who portrayed Macmillan, poised between a Greek and a Turkish suitor, with lines from John Gay's *Beggar's Opera* as a caption:

> How happy could I be with either,
> Were t'other dear charmer away!

Unsolicited, Illingworth sent the original to Macmillan, who felt it hit the proverbial nail firmly on the head. Political cartoons had become one of Macmillan's collecting specialities. Some were sent as gifts; others he asked for, and paid for, such as a drawing by Low of the rechristening of the Conservative Party in September 1946, with Macmillan (labelled: 'Mac M')* in a steamy Turkish bath, pouring water over a startled Colonel Blimp. With his walrus moustache and drooping eyelids, Macmillan was a cartoonist's dream. His enduring image as Supermac, Vicky's creation, was just around the corner.

Eden and Macmillan believed that a firmer hand was needed in Nicosia, and they appointed Field Marshal Sir John Harding as Military Governor. Macmillan received a letter from a member of the public regretting that *Gilbert* Harding,[57] a notoriously acerbic television personality, had not been appointed Governor, as he could then have been sure that somebody would have been rude to Archbishop Makarios. This was not the only subject on which Macmillan received

---

*In 1946 he had still needed a label. By 1955, such labels were superfluous – he was recognisable to all.

correspondence from the public. His in-tray contained many worried missives about the effect of H-bomb tests, politically and environmentally. As a former Minister of Defence, he had an acute understanding of the balance between 'conventional' weapons and nuclear arms. 'It has now become quite clear that there is really no protection against a nuclear attack, certainly in these islands,' he wrote to Rab Butler on 10 August. 'The only protection is the deterrent of the counter attack.'[58] Macmillan believed in the power of the deterrent, and knew that 'the bomb', once it had been invented, could not be uninvented. As a result he advocated a drastic cut-back in orthodox defence expenditure, a theme to which he was to return.

The Baghdad Pact of 1955 was designed to provide a measure of stability in the Middle East by establishing a line of Northern Tier countries along Russia's south-west frontier. Properly known by its acronym CENTO (The Central Treaty Organisation), the pact initially included Iraq and Turkey. Britain and Pakistan adhered to this on 4 April, three days before Macmillan became Foreign Secretary.

The Alpha Plan was a scheme, initially set in train by Eden and Dulles, to settle Egyptian-Israeli border disputes by providing a land link between Egypt and Jordan, with compensatory benefits for Israel. Macmillan knew that Egypt could be a crucible of unrest, especially after 1956, which was the date when British forces were due to leave the Suez Canal Base. Alpha was effectively ended as a viable plan in September 1955 by Nasser's arms deal, nominally with the Czechs, but actually with the Soviets, 'a most alarming and perilous success for the Russians', as Macmillan wrote in his diary, wary of the developments this deal could bring in its train.[59]

Macmillan was in the throes of the Alpha negotiations with Dulles when he heard the news on 16 September that Leo Amery had died at the age of 81 at 112 Eaton Square, his historic residence that had seen so much political drama. Macmillan had greatly admired Amery's dignity, never so much as over the tragedy concerning his elder son, John, who, describing himself as an anti-Communist, pleaded guilty to treason and was hanged in 1945. Leo Amery's other son, Julian, had married Harold Macmillan's daughter, Catherine. Macmillan had been instrumental in persuading Leo Amery not to accept Churchill's offer of a peerage in 1951, the effect of which would have been to limit Julian Amery's prospects of the higher offices of state. Ironically, it was to be Macmillan's own rise to the premiership that was to curtail the careers of both Julian Amery and his own son, Maurice. Macmillan was often accused of nepotism, but it did not extend to including his son or his son-in-law in his Cabinets.[60] Julian Amery asked his father-in-law if he would read the lesson at Leo Amery's memorial service. To his great regret Macmillan was unable to do so, as he would be unavoidably abroad on Foreign Office business.

Eden's Cabinet reshuffle just before Christmas 1955 is sometimes mistakenly thought of as being in response to the election on 14 December of a new, younger Labour leader, Hugh Gaitskell, the first leader of any party born in the twentieth century. In fact, Eden had been planning the changes since September. Everything hinged on Rab Butler.

An emergency autumn Budget was looking ever more likely after Butler, still Chancellor of the Exchequer, had failed to persuade the Cabinet of the need for individual deflationary measures, such as cutting the bread subsidy, to quell the run on sterling. On 22 September, after returning from an IMF meeting in Istanbul, Eden suggested to Butler that he should consider becoming Leader of the House of Commons and Lord Privy Seal. Butler knew that accepting a non-departmental job would lead to a weakening of his influence; only in retrospect did he realise how much.

The next day, Eden, after a meeting on the situation in Cyprus, asked Macmillan for his thoughts on moving from the Foreign Office to the Treasury. Macmillan was astonished and deeply disappointed. He was beginning to get the measure of the Foreign Office work and resented another rapid move after his mere eight months at Defence. The suggestion was unwelcome, and he wisely refused to be rushed. In practice, however, he had little option but to fall in with Eden's wishes, though he drove a hard, some might say almost unconstitutional, bargain.

Macmillan emphasised in a letter on 24 October that if he became Chancellor, there was no point in being an orthodox one. 'I must be, if not a revolutionary, something of a reformer.' His main concern though, in this remarkable letter, is quite clearly his future position vis-à-vis Rab Butler.[61] Macmillan asked 'for certain conditions'. The second demand was unprecedented:

A position in the Government not inferior to that held by the present Chancellor. As Foreign Secretary, I am head of the foreign front, under you as Prime Minister. As Chancellor, I must be undisputed head of the home front, under you. If Rab becomes Leader of the House and Lord Privy Seal that will be fine. But *I could not agree* [author's italics] that he should be Deputy Prime Minister.

(Incidentally this post does not exist constitutionally, and was invented by Churchill to suit quite exceptional circumstances.)

You will realise that the presence of a much respected ex-Chancellor, with all that this implies, in the Cabinet and in Whitehall must somewhat add to my difficulties, however loyal he will try to be. If he were also Deputy Prime Minister, my task would be impossible.[62]

'If you don't agree, I shall quite understand, ' Macmillan added. 'If you do, I am willing to try.'[63]

It was now a question of who would blink first. Rab Butler had been given guarantees about his position, and Eden was in a situation of immense delicacy. He tried to resolve it by giving Rab the responsibility of chairing Cabinets in his absence, though without the title of Deputy Prime Minister. A curious order of precedence was announced, headed by Lord Salisbury, the Lord President of the Council, followed by Butler and then Macmillan. Selwyn Lloyd was at Number 4 in this list. Eden had not reckoned on Macmillan, who refused to give in so easily.

'In spite of the order of precedence, the Lord Privy Seal is to preside over the Cabinet in your absence instead of the Lord President', he complained. 'This is really the introduction of the concept of Deputy Prime Minister by another means.' He was, of course, correct in this assumption. His letter continued: 'I don't press this point, as you know, from personal feeling. But, politically, a great deal is read into these niceties; and this has, as I said in my first letter, an effect on my chance of success in the job which you have asked me to undertake.'[64]

This further letter caused Eden no little difficulty. He could not easily alter the order of precedence after its publication, nor could he 'demote' Rab from the job of presiding at Cabinets in his absence.

Eventually, Eden dug his heels in and Macmillan had to accept, though with the greatest reluctance, the arrangements that had been decided. Macmillan's bold demands – and Eden's acceptance of them – had already put Macmillan in a nigh invulnerable position. But he still resented the hand that fate had dealt him.

An indication of Macmillan's mood can be seen in a letter to Dulles: 'You know with what reluctance I leave the Foreign Office. You may have seen that some of the newspapers say that I am happy to leave. Others say that the Foreign Office are happy to get rid of me. If the second statement is as untrue as the first, then I am quite satisfied.'[65]

In the privacy of his diary, he vented his frustrations more forcibly. 'I have really had rather a raw deal this last year – first with Defence, then with FO,' he observed on 22 December. 'Just as one is learning one job one goes off to another. At my age, it is not quite so easy to switch the mind on to a completely new set of problems.'[66] Macmillan's subsequent departure from the Foreign Office for the Treasury – from geography to arithmetic, as he put it to the Shadow Chancellor, Harold Wilson[67] – was a lachrymose affair.

Looking back on 1955, Hugh Gaitskell felt that Butler's position had been irretrievably damaged by his 'dishonest' October budget. 'There seems to be no doubt that Macmillan was not getting on at all well with Eden as Foreign Secretary, and that Tory opinion is rather veering round towards him as the best of the three.'[68]

The Cabinet changes were announced on 22 December. Butler and Macmillan moved to their new posts. Selwyn Lloyd became Foreign Secretary. In essence, the Foreign Office team was now the one that had operated from 1951 to 1955, when Eden had been Foreign Secretary and Selwyn Lloyd his deputy. Macmillan even referred in his diary to Lloyd as the Minister of State. Sir Walter Monckton became Minister of Defence in Lloyd's place. Iain Macleod, a rising star, became Minister of Labour. Lord Selkirk became Chancellor of the Duchy of Lancaster. To Macmillan's regret, Harry Crookshank left the government.

The ultimate irony was that Macmillan was not Eden's first choice. In October, Eden had lunched with Oliver Lyttelton, now installed in the City. 'I wish he were with us and free to go to the Treasury now,' the Prime Minister had written in his diary.[69] Neither previously as Foreign Secretary nor now as Chancellor of the Exchequer had Macmillan been Eden's preferred choice.

Fourteen months earlier, Macmillan had been a relatively junior minister at Housing. Now he was dictating terms to the Prime Minister about his reluctance to accept a second great office of state – and getting away with it. On 22 December, Macmillan and Dorothy visited 11 Downing Street, where they found 'the Prof', Lord Lindemann, installed in the upper storey of the house, where he had been allowed to lodge by Rab Butler.

That was small beer compared with what Macmillan found in the nation's balance sheets. 'The position is *much worse* than I had expected,' he wrote in his diary on 30 December. 'Butler has let things drift, and the reserves are steadily falling. If and when they are expended, we have total collapse, under Harold Macmillan!'[70]

The urgency of the situation demanded swift action. On 1 January 1956, Macmillan completed a memorandum *First Thoughts from a*

Treasury Window, a *tour d'horizon* of the economic problems facing the country, together with possible courses of action. The document soon became known to the Civil Service as *What the Butler never saw*.[71] As the dramatic year of 1956 unfolded, Macmillan kept things very close to his chest. There were many things that Butler and others were never to see.

For reasons not entirely under his control, Macmillan's eight months at the Foreign Office were a frustrating and unsatisfactory experience. As at the Ministry of Defence, he was denied the opportunity to make his own lasting mark. Many of the initiatives in both departments (especially the Defence White Paper and the Austrian State Treaty) were works set in hand by his predecessors. 'Cyprus is *my* plan. Alpha is really an *inherited* plan'[72] was a typical minute of the time. Yet Macmillan displayed, at least outwardly, a new-found confidence. Even as Minister of Housing he had not been averse to putting forward his views in Cabinet on all manner of subjects; as Foreign Secretary he was able to assume control of matters that were not strictly his responsibility. Had Alan Lennox-Boyd, at the Colonial Office, not been so amenable to Macmillan's views, and so willing to work with him, there could have been greater difficulties. Macmillan paid tribute to Lennox-Boyd's generosity in his memoirs.[73]

Alan Lennox-Boyd paved the way to Macmillan's premiership. Macmillan's dealings with those who might have prevented him becoming Prime Minister were not so cordial. His relationship with Eden, never the closest, deteriorated. Macmillan resented the manner in which he was moved around the political chessboard. Their political differences went back a long way, particularly over the Greek civil war in 1944. As troubles mounted for the Eden government, Macmillan became convinced, even before Suez, that the Crown Prince who had waited so long for his inheritance would not survive a full term in Downing Street.

Macmillan's relationship with Butler was also a distant one, and was over the years to become the frostiest among all his personal dealings, though nothing like as frosty as those with Butler's second wife, Mollie.[74] Yet Macmillan and Butler both came from the same wing of the party, 'One Nation' Tories to their fingertips. Butler recognised the importance of *The Middle Way*, just as Macmillan knew the significance of Butler's 1944 Education Act and his pioneering work in the Conservative Research Department. The gulf between the two men ran deep, even if it was not always apparent to casual acquaintances. Both could mask their real feelings. In the 1930s Butler had been a youthful party insider, though his time at the Foreign Office in the appeasement era was eventually to count against him, and not only in Macmillan's eyes. Whilst Butler prospered politically in the thirties, Macmillan was yet to start his ministerial career. He was barely surviving in the shallows, a rebel against the party establishment, irritatingly independent, and even more irritatingly to his rivals, correct in the long term on both of the key issues of the time, appeasement and the Depression. One could never imagine Butler resigning the party whip, as Macmillan had done in 1936.

At Christmas 1955, Butler was clearly seen by interested observers as the likeliest next Prime Minister. Macmillan did not share that opinion. After the demise of 'ROBOT' in 1952, he was confirmed in his view that Rab Butler was not a bare-knuckle political fighter. A series of important misjudgements in 1955 had further weakened Butler's position in the Westminster village. His first mistake was to stay at the Treasury when Eden became Prime Minister; his second was the April 1955 electioneering budget; the third was to continue as Chancellor after the election had been won in May 1955; the fourth was the 'Pots and Pans' Budget of October 1955, which stemmed from his failure to prevail in Cabinet on deflationary measures. The biggest mistake of all, however, was to accept the non-departmental post of Lord Privy Seal. Harry Crookshank told him it was 'sheer political suicide'.[75]

Macmillan never saw Butler as a serious rival for the top job after that decision. Despite the fact that he was three years older than Eden, and nearly nine years older than Butler, he began 1956 with the confident belief that in the long run he would become Britain's next Prime Minister. By January 1956, he had held successively two of the great offices of state, while Butler was at the time becalmed in a non-governmental post.

CHAPTER NINETEEN

View from a Treasury Window

1955–1956

Like inverted Micawbers, waiting for something to turn down.
Winston Churchill, on the Treasury

Being Foreign Secretary is like editing a daily paper, being Chancellor is more like a weekly paper.
Harold Macmillan, 1956

The disastrous last year of Churchill's reign, with nothing domestic getting itself settled, is now having a delayed action effect.
Sir William Haley diary, 8 January 1956

Harold Macmillan became Chancellor of the Exchequer at a difficult time for the Conservative government. The goodwill surrounding the general election victory in May 1955 had long evaporated. Even the normally supportive *Daily Telegraph* was calling for 'the smack of firm government'.[1] When Eden answered these criticisms in a speech at Bradford, rumours began that he was planning to resign. A denial from Downing Street merely fuelled speculation. 'Who would take his place?' wrote Sir William Haley, editor of *The Times*, in his diary. 'Butler is temporarily spreadeagled; his confidence has gone. Macmillan is still coming on but hasn't shone at Defence or the Foreign Office.'[2] Haley contributed to the feeling of malaise in a *Times* leader article regretting the government's lack of 'high purpose'.[3]

Major strikes had taken place throughout 1955 in the newspaper industry, in the docks and on the railways. Busmen and miners had also taken industrial action. The dock strike was especially damaging in economic terms, worsening an already difficult balance of payments problem. As Minister of Labour, Walter Monckton had been given a mandate from Churchill to appease the trade unions. Conflict was thus deferred. Oliver Lyttelton said that Monckton 'was excellent until the time came for him to say "no"'.[4] When Iain Macleod became the new Minister of Labour in the December 1955 reshuffle, a less emollient approach towards an increasingly aggressive generation of union leaders seemed likely. Outwardly, Macleod appeared a tougher prospect, but when push came to shove, conciliation remained the preferred option.

Inflation had been steadily increasing throughout 1955. In July, coal prices had actually risen by 18 per cent, by which time the trade deficit was running at £456 million, an immense sum at the time. Price inflation was running at 3.5 per cent, with wage inflation at 4.5 per cent. As Butler had made the pound convertible in the spring of 1955, the Treasury gave priority to addressing the problem of the balance of payments. Much of the detail of Macmillan's initial response to the situation was thus predetermined. In February 1956, the bank rate was raised to 5.5 per cent, the highest since 1931, followed by strict anti-inflation measures. Circumstances soon further curbed Macmillan's expansionist instincts.

The Permanent Secretary at the Treasury was Sir Edward Bridges,[5] with whom Macmillan had overlapped at Eton. Macmillan's rapid trawl through the major Whitehall departments had provided him with links to some of the finest minds in the civil service. Now he was reunited with one of the North African veterans in the person of Sir Leslie Rowan, Second Secretary in the Overseas Finance department. Also in that department was Sir Denis Rickett, a Balliol man. Other key figures among the Treasury knights included Sir Alexander Johnston and Sir Thomas Padmore. The Chief Economic Adviser was Sir Robert Hall, whom Macmillan knew from Ministry of Supply days.[6] His Private Secretaries were Louis Petch and Evan Maude.[7]

On 6 January, Macmillan had his first meeting with the Governor of the Bank of England, Lord Cobbold.[8] Their relationship was initially cautious, even at times strained. Cameron ('Kim') Cobbold warned Macmillan to be wary of making too many speeches, talking off the record to journalists and 'to stop talking about "inflation" which nobody understands'. For his part, Macmillan believed it to be essential to maintain a credit squeeze, and he pressed for the Bank to impose liquidity ratios on the clearing banks. Cobbold defended the status quo stoutly. 'Our banking system is incomparably better co-ordinated, more responsible and more willing (some critics would say too willing) to listen to official advice and requests than any other banking system in the world.'[9] This cosy arrangement was known in the trade as 'ear-stroking'.

Nevertheless, Macmillan – who privately referred to bankers as banksters[10] – preferred to have such a working association, based on frank, and not sycophantic, opinions. At bottom, both knew they were on the same side, working for what was best for the British economy.*

The atmosphere Macmillan now experienced was very different from that of the Foreign Office, the Treasury being in Anthony Sampson's words 'an intellectual, not a social, élite'.[12] Macmillan was unorthodox in that he listened to the advice of non-Treasury figures, in particular Sir Roy Harrod, who became something of an *éminence grise* in the eyes of civil servants. Harrod was an out-and-out Keynesian, an approach for which Macmillan had instinctive sympathy. The problems of 1956, though, were different from those of 1936. The feeling, not only in the civil service, was that Harrod encouraged Macmillan to be even more Keynesian than Keynes himself would have been had he still been alive. *The General Theory* cast a long shadow. Robert Skidelsky, Keynes' biographer, has observed, 'Keynes's "general theory of employment" was not quite as general as he believed.' Skidelsky believed that it was 'inconceivable' that Keynes would not have brought new ideas to bear in a new era. 'But he was no longer there, and his book was.'[13]

Macmillan's Financial Secretary at the Treasury was Henry Brooke,[14] not a persuasive speaker, but a stalwart in the machinery of government, with vast experience in local government. The fact that he was also a Balliol man was an advantage. The economic secretary was the young Edward Boyle,[15] a rising figure on the liberal wing of the Tory Party. Macmillan appreciated Boyle's understanding of the nuances of economic policy and his progressive outlook generally.

A sign of how seriously the new Labour leader Hugh Gaitskell took Macmillan's arrival at the Treasury came with his appointment of Harold Wilson[16] to his own former post of Shadow Chancellor on 14 February. Just as North Africa had been the making of Macmillan, so the shadow chancellorship propelled Harold Wilson to the forefront at Westminster. Between them, Macmillan and Wilson were to become the dominating political figures in Britain over the next 20 years. There were more similarities between them than might have at first appeared. Both were essentially outsiders in their own party, even mistrusted figures. Neither was over-fastidious about cutting corners. Macmillan protected his own back, as Wilson himself was to do on many occasions. Both were figures of considerable intellectual capacity,

---

*Later Cobbold was to record that his relations with Macmillan were the closest he had ever enjoyed with any Prime Minister, because of their partnership during his time at the Treasury, a time he regarded with affection. 'I have often been asked which Chancellor I thought the best or the worst,' he later recorded. 'I have never been willing to go beyond saying that Cripps had the most acute mind (and, contrary to general belief, a warm if shy personality) and that Macmillan was the most fun to work with.'[11]

the only prime ministers who could be said properly to understand Keynes. Their clashes over the dispatch box as their parties' Treasury spokesmen had all the razzmatazz of a circus act. Both gave as good as they got. Then, public conflict over, they would repair to the smoking room and enjoy a drink and a chat, the performance over until next time. They knew they were playing out a role in what Walter Bagehot would have called the 'dignified' part of the constitution, as opposed to the 'efficient' part.[17] They were able to adapt skilfully to the different requirements of the two functions, and both had an instinctive admiration of the other's political gifts.[18] Wilson wrote that theirs was 'a happy and stimulating relationship'.[19] The one big difference was in their attitude to the press. Wilson was paranoid about newspaper criticism, and paid meticulous attention to perceived slights, crawling over the print with a metaphorical hand lens. Macmillan's attitude was more detached, even Wildean – only one thing was worse than being talked about, and that was not being talked about.

Nineteen fifty-six was certainly a year during which Macmillan was talked about. The initial focus was the build-up to what proved to be his only budget, on 17 April. The low rate of productivity was giving cause for concern. To the amazement, and even anger, of many Conservative back-benchers, Macmillan proposed to cut spending on that most sacred of cows, conventional defence costs. 'It is defence expenditure which has broken our backs,' he warned Eden.[20] In the age of the nuclear deterrent, expenditure on conventional weaponry no longer warranted the priority it had once been granted.

Another major clash with Eden came over ending subsidies for bread and milk. Macmillan even drafted a letter of resignation on 15 February. 'I recollect one very turbulent evening in and out of No. 10 & No. 11,' Lord Cobbold recorded, 'the Chancellor eventually getting most of what he wanted.'[21] The letter remained unsent, but was kept on file in case it was needed later. The key section was unequivocal: 'A Chancellor of the Exchequer must be able, at a moment of crisis, to look for the full support of the Prime Minister and his Cabinet, and command their full support. That this is not so is no doubt my fault. But it destroys or at least greatly weakens – the value of my services. I must therefore ask you to place my resignation before the Queen for her acceptance.'[22]

In 1956, Macmillan and Peter Thorneycroft,[23] President of the Board of Trade, laid the foundations, through the so-called Plan G, of what later became the European Free Trade Area (EFTA), designed to protect Commonwealth interests, whilst at the same time encouraging economic efficiency by association with the six Messina nations. Plan G was, in essence, an attempt to build bridges between the OEEC and the embryonic EEC, the Seven,[24] and the Six. 'We have a chance which might not recur,' Macmillan and Thorneycroft wrote in the memorandum prepared for the Cabinet, 'of gaining the general support of what might be described as both the European and the Imperial wings of the Conservative Party.'[25] Thorneycroft, who had been a consistent enthusiast for European co-operation, was an important influence in steering Macmillan towards his way of thinking. Together they argued before Cabinet that Commonwealth trade would in all probability decline, and that, by being an instigator of such an organisation as EFTA, Britain had a better chance than Germany of being the dominant European influence.

Macmillan was in no doubt that there would be difficulties in selling 'this great venture' to his colleagues, but he was cheered by the quality of the younger members of the government. 'I was much impressed by the combination of knowledge and enthusiasm of these younger ministers,'[26] he wrote in his diary on 5 September after a meeting of the Cabinet's Economic Policy Committee. Plan G was formally presented to the Commonwealth Finance Ministers at a meeting at the Washington Embassy on 29 September 1956. On 12 October, Macmillan outlined the plan at the Conservative Party Conference in Llandudno.* Finally, he presented Plan G in the House of Commons on 26 November 1956, during a debate in which Maurice Macmillan made his maiden speech. Despite arguments over details at all of these stages, the ground work was established for the plan to proceed. Plan G was to prove one of the important long-term measures begun under Macmillan's chancellorship.

J. K. Galbraith, one of the most high-profile of post-Keynesian economists, always believed that politics was not the art of the possible, but the choice between the unpalatable and the disastrous. At this stage of the process of macro-economic management, Macmillan was still prepared to choose the unpalatable – defence cuts; income tax increases; and the ending of food subsidies – even if he did not always prevail. Eden flatly refused to allow income tax increases after Butler's reductions of the previous year. Difficult moments – such as

---

*Macmillan was never keen on Conservative Party conferences, with all those endless night-time discussions in out-of-season seaside hotels. Llandudno was a particular *bête noire* for Macmillan. Walking down a dingy, litter-filled corridor, he turned to a young reporter and said, 'Gladstone and Disraeli never had to put up with this.'[27]

the Farm Price Review and arguments with Germany about the cost of the British Army on the Rhine – Macmillan took in his stride. He proved very strict on wage restraint, appealing to unions to acquiesce in what was in effect a voluntary incomes policy. At the same time he urged employers to curb excess profits. It was a balancing act tried by many of his successors, with mixed success.

The one thing that stirred Macmillan's emotions above all else was the memory of conditions in pre-war Stockton. In an impassioned debate on 20 February, he declared to a hushed House of Commons: 'I cannot forget those terrible times when some 17,000 out of 25,000 able-bodied men in my constituency walked the streets unemployed.'[28] Some Treasury officials used to joke about the number of times Macmillan would mention Stockton in one day. It was no joke for Macmillan.

Further difficulties came with major redundancy programmes at the British Motor Corporation and the Standard Motor Company in Coventry. In 1954, Philip Larkin had written a famous poem, 'I remember, I remember', in which he described the throng of car workers carrying trade number plates on the railway platforms of Coventry, his birthplace. He would not have seen so many in the summer of 1956.

The electoral tide was beginning to turn against the Tories. In the autumn of 1955, support for the Government was running at 70 per cent; by the spring of 1956 it was down to 40 per cent. Worrying reversals also occurred in normally safe constituencies. In the summer of 1956, the Conservative majority of 10,196 at a by-election in one of its archetypal seats, Tonbridge, fell to 1,602. There were also adverse swings in by-elections at Torquay and Gainsborough.

Despite these reversals, Macmillan still believed that a tough Budget was appropriate. Raising the bank rate and stricter hire-purchase conditions were only a beginning. 'If the Budget does not succeed in reinforcing and fortifying what I did in February, then the outlook for the summer & autumn is very grim,' he wrote to Kim Cobbold on 23 March. 'So we must not neglect any weapons, however distasteful or contrary to our traditions.'[29] Initially, Macmillan had felt that Cobbold was not a 'big' enough man as Governor, but he came to respect Cobbold's innate authority.

Cobbold and Macmillan had detailed discussions on how far governments could, and should, control unemployment and inflation through Keynesian deficit financing. Cobbold was meticulous in keeping the Bank 'out of politics'; his main aim was to give dispassionate and reliable advice. Eventually Macmillan came to believe that a reasonably high rate of inflation was tolerable, as this would be accompanied by lower unemployment, particularly in the build-up to elections.

When Sir Edward Bridges retired, Macmillan's mind turned to the question of who should be Permanent Secretary to the Treasury. His unusual choice of Roger Makins, who had no previous experience of economic policy, was a sign of how important familiar and trusted faces were to him. Roger Makins was now at the pinnacle of the Foreign Service, Ambassador in Washington, and a strong candidate to become Head of the Diplomatic Service after Ivone Kirkpatrick. Macmillan was asking him to give up all this to become his right-hand man at the Treasury. Two days before the Budget, on 15 April, the two men met at the Treasury and Macmillan outlined his plan. Although he knew he was asking a lot, he felt that Makins was a good patriot and would see solvency as an essential prerequisite for Britain's standing, and thus for a plausible foreign policy. Discussions continued, and on 24 April, Makins accepted, on the condition that he could return to the Foreign Office after three years' 'secondment' to the Treasury.[30] In the event, Makins only got half of his promised kingdom, as he was Joint Permanent Head of the Treasury with Norman Brook.

Few Budgets are remembered over half a century later. Harold Macmillan's is one of the exceptions. Dorothy made one of her rare appearances in the Distinguished Strangers' Gallery of the House. Daniel Macmillan also attended, taking time off from the publishing business in St Martin's Street. Macmillan rose to his feet at 3.32 p.m. to address a crowded house. He spoke for nearly two hours, deftly interlinking the serious with the light-hearted. He recalled that the first Budget he had ever heard had been that of Winston Churchill. Turning towards Churchill in the chamber he added, 'It was said at the time that my great predecessor was quite surprised to find himself at the Treasury in the winter of 1924, but not half so surprised as I was, thirty-one years later.'[31] He praised Churchill for his verve, and clearly intended to match it. 'His successors have sometimes seemed more like schoolmasters than commanders,' he continued. 'To tell the truth, I have often thought of Budget Day as rather like a school speech day – a bit of a bore, but there it is. The parents and the old boys like it.' The analogy led to a felicitous reference to giving out the prizes. The difference between Speech Day and Budget Day, though, added Macmillan, was that the latter also traditionally contained some impositions.

As it turned out, Macmillan's impositions were relatively minor. His wings had been clipped, and his fiercer measures had not survived.

He held out hope that expansion would follow shortly. The difficulty was that, although industrial production was now rising, wages and salaries were rising even more, with resulting price increases. Literary references to Macaulay and Dickens sprinkled his text. One section was bound for the dictionaries of quotations. Macmillan lamented that statistics were 'too late to be as useful as they ought to be'. He then added, 'We are always, as it were, looking up a train in last year's Bradshaw.'[32]

He made it clear that his Budget was a Budget for saving. Here he sprang the great surprise for which the Budget is remembered – Premium Bonds.

This introduction of Premium Bonds was not without controversy. The head of the National Savings movement, Lord Mackintosh,[33] was initially worried about the effect they might have on regular savings, but Macmillan worked hard to persuade him to accept the idea.[34] Moral objections were raised, and two female post office workers refused to handle Premium Bond certificates on religious grounds. Civil servants in Northern Ireland had earlier rejected the opportunity to be the headquarters of the scheme for religio-political reasons, the prize eventually going to Lytham St Anne's.[35] The maximum permitted holding originally was 400 bonds (available then in units of £1) and the top prize, of which there were only four a year, was £1,000.[36] The Archbishop of Canterbury, Geoffrey Fisher,[37] denounced the whole scheme in apocalyptic terms. Harold Wilson was more succinct, describing Premium Bonds as 'a squalid lottery',[38] though when he became Prime Minister his government increased the top prize to £25,000.

Macmillan was unconcerned by the outspoken criticisms of Fisher, whom he described in his diary as 'a silly, weak, vain and muddle-headed man'.[39] Fisher was never Macmillan's idea of a successor to St Augustine. 'The Archbishop is not a good guide,' he wrote to Eden on 23 July 1956, 'no more reliable than Cranmer was.'[40] Later in the year, Macmillan and Fisher were guests at a City livery dinner. As the Church of England had recently made a profit of hundreds of thousands of pounds on investments in Trinidad oil, Macmillan expressed the hope that the Archbishop might now look a little more kindly on Premium Bonds in the wake of his own little flutter.[41]

There was an unspoken class element to Premium Bonds. In July 1956, Lord Mackintosh was preparing to advertise them, the first ever such outlay of government money – and on commercial television. Macmillan assured Eden that the decision was expedient 'on the grounds that this [ITV] is just the right medium to attract *the sort of people* [author's italics] whom we are hoping to catch with this new form of savings'.[42] Audiences for ITV were, in the patronising words of the BBC's Annual Report, 'those who turn to television for distraction'.[43] Premium Bonds appealed to such an audience, as Macmillan intended; even without a win, they were fun, 'sexy' in later parlance. By comparison, Post Office Savings books were the BBC, traditional and safe.

Macmillan was not directing Premium Bonds towards the sophisticated saver with an accountant, rather to the Mr Pooters of Bromley. He emphasised the tax-free element to the prizes and the easy availability of bonds over the post office counter. On the first available day, 1 November 1956, £5m worth of bonds were sold, the initial bond being bought in an arranged ceremony by the Lord Mayor of London, Sir Cuthbert Ackroyd. Prize-winning numbers were to be drawn by Electronic Random Number Indicator Equipment (acronym ERNIE); in 1956 the machine was the size of a small van. Fears as to ERNIE's impartiality were later allayed when it was pointed out that any imperfections in the randomness of the machine would not be detected for ten million years.[44] By the time of the first draw, at 9.15 a.m. at Lytham St Anne's on 1 June 1957, £82m had been invested. Appropriately, the draw was started by the Postmaster General, Ernest Marples, also known colloquially as Ernie. Television celebrities were later employed to publicise the results, all part of Macmillan's carefully prepared sales strategy, based on his business marketing experience.

Macmillan's reassurance in his Budget speech that 'this is not gambling, for the subscriber cannot lose' was not strictly true. The gamble was in forfeiting voluntarily any guaranteed interest on a deposit, and instead choosing the chance of a prize. The initial odds against winning any sort of prize were 2,095 to 1. For small savers, this was no disincentive. Many were accustomed to buying Christmas savings stamps in the belief that they were being frugal; actually they were giving an interest-free loan to the respective shops. Those who did not win a prize were doing the same for the government.

Macmillan's brother Daniel was seated next to Henry Brooke's wife in the Gallery, and he greeted the various measures with increasing degrees of enthusiasm. It had been Daniel who had first suggested the idea of a lottery-based form of savings to his brother. When the Premium Bonds scheme was outlined, Daniel said to Barbara Brooke,[45] 'I never thought he would be brave enough.'[46]

The scheme has outlasted all other government and private saving plans, and over 40 per cent of the population have at one stage owned Premium Bonds. Saving was the watchword of the Budget, described by Samuel Brittain as 'by far the most entertaining of the whole post-war series'.[47]

Macmillan's Budget was inevitably conditioned by the 'Pots and Pans' Budget of October 1954. Butler had delayed taking deflationary action until after the 1955 general election. He then made spending cuts for the sake of the economy as a whole, even though the Budget balance itself was favourable. Macmillan continued this economic 'fine-tuning' (a much used phrase at the time) through further demand management, both before and during his Budget. At this time the Treasury was building up a computer model of 'how the economy worked', which, it was hoped, would show the likely impact of any changes in taxation, government spending or interest rates with more precision. This belief in the possibility and effectiveness of 'fine-tuning' was the brainchild of the new generation of economists and the legacy of Keynesian thinking.

The deeper difficulty for Macmillan was how to match up policy objectives and policy instruments. He had three policy targets – price stability, low unemployment and balance of payments equilibrium. These targets could either be independent of each other or even mutually exclusive. As a result, the ideal would be to have at least as many policy instruments as independent targets. Macmillan's dilemma, and limitation, was that demand management via the budget was his only chosen instrument, yet he attempted to achieve all three targets. A compromise balance between unemployment and inflation (what was analysed in 1958 in the 'Phillips Curve')[48] had come to be acceptable, but at the time of Macmillan's Budget, the balance of payments was becoming increasingly 'out of sync' with that balance. The policy weapon, unthinkable in 1956, was a change in the exchange rate, a nettle only ultimately grasped by means of the devaluation of the pound by Harold Wilson's government in 1967.[49] In the end, Macmillan's legacy in his short spell as Chancellor was Premium Bonds and updating 'last year's Bradshaw' by a reform of official statistics. The larger issues were to be fought over at a later date.

Two days after Macmillan's Budget, which was well received by the national press, though puzzlingly to Macmillan, less so in the regional newspapers, the Russian leaders Bulganin and Khrushchev arrived on a visit to Britain. Macmillan had been involved with Eden in the invitation to B and K (or Bulge and Krush), as they became known to the popular press, at the Geneva conference in 1955. Macmillan had not been impressed by Khrushchev then, and he saw little need to revise his opinion now. 'How can this fat, vulgar man, with his pig eyes and his ceaseless flow of talk, really be the head – the aspirant Tsar – of all these millions of people and this vast country,' he wrote in his diary.[50]

Intended to relieve Cold War tension, the B and K visit if anything increased it. Sir Ivone Kirkpatrick recorded in his memoirs that the Russian leaders warned that 'they would make as much trouble for us in the Middle East as they possibly could'.[51] This was one promise they kept. Meanwhile, a drunken interpreter at a Foreign Office lunch interposed his own insulting gloss on the Russians' speeches,[52] and George Brown had an embarrassing row with the Russians at a Labour Party gathering,[53] after which Khrushchev announced that if he lived in Britain, he would vote Conservative. The Russians were jeered and spat at on a visit to Oxford. When James Stuart took them to Scotland, they were more impressed, thinking that the peasants in this outpost of the kingdom were well looked after in their dotage. The peasants were in fact members of the General Assembly of the Church of Scotland at Holyrood House.

'If we lose out in the Middle East, we lose the oil,' Macmillan wrote in his diary. 'If we lose the oil, we cannot live.'[54]

Although the Suez Canal Base was due to be vacated in June 1956, Britain still had a large deployment in the Middle East. Commitments included air squadrons in Iraq, bases in Cyprus and Malta, and a naval base in Aden. In Jordan, Britain maintained, and underwrote the costs of the Commander of the Arab Legion, Sir John Glubb, known as Glubb Pasha. The manifold difficulties of 1956, one of the most dramatic years of the century, began in January with Jordan's refusal to join the Baghdad Pact, a move Macmillan had advocated when he was Foreign Secretary. Eden and Macmillan both saw the hand of Colonel Nasser, Prime Minister of Egypt since April 1954, in Jordan's decision. Nasser's anti-British propaganda – put out through Radio Cairo – was to have an increasingly important impact in the Arab world.

Problems in Cyprus, now a vital air base after the withdrawal from Egypt, continued, and on 1 March Archbishop Makarios was exiled to the Seychelles. On the same day came news of the sacking of Glubb Pasha by King Hussein of Jordan. Macmillan's worry was of Russian infiltration if Britain cut any of the financial support for Jordan in retaliation. The next day, 2 March, Selwyn Lloyd, the Foreign Secretary, was visiting Bahrain, where his car was stoned by an angry crowd. During a subsequent debate in the House of Commons on 7 March, MPs questioned the usefulness, indeed the viability, of the Baghdad Pact. There seemed to be no end to the humiliations Britain was experiencing, all of which put pressure on Eden to respond decisively.

The catalyst proved to be the volatile situation in Egypt. Nasser's political ambitions included the formation of a League of Arab Republics, with serious repercussions for the security of Israel's borders. Nasser's domestic aim was to irrigate the Nile Valley and establish hydroelectric power by building the Aswan High Dam. To finance the project, Nasser had turned to the West for a massive loan, with the implicit threat that he would approach Russia for funds if America and Britain were not prepared to back rural electrification in Egypt. Eugene Black, President of the World Bank, imposed strict conditions on any such financing. Black met Macmillan in London on 25 January to discuss the details of British involvement.[55] 'Our concern has been to do all we can to secure that Egypt follows the western route,' Macmillan told him. 'We are anxious to do all we can to smooth the negotiations.'[56] Unfortunately these negotiations did not go well when Black met Nasser in Cairo. Macmillan looked back on this as a watershed moment in the deteriorating situation.

The last British troops from the Suez Canal Base left Port Said at 12.15 a.m. on 13 June, under the terms of the 1954 agreement. Macmillan had been concerned about the political implications of this agreement, though understanding the financial imperatives. The Suez Group of right-wing imperialist Conservative MPs, including Macmillan's son-in-law Julian Amery, had opposed the agreement from the start, denouncing it as a scuttle. Churchill was also unhappy about what he saw as the appeasement of Nasser, and cruelly observed to Eden that he did not know that Munich was situated on the Nile. Ten days later Colonel Nasser was elected President of Egypt, in traditional Soviet style by 99 per cent of the vote.

In retrospect, the outcome has an air of inevitability. Dulles informed the Egyptian Ambassador in Washington on 19 July that the American offer of a loan for the Aswan High Dam project was withdrawn. Britain, as a supporting partner in the arrangement, thus had no option but to withdraw, and the World Bank also backed out of what had previously been a joint agreement. On 26 July 1956, six weeks after the British troops had left Egypt, President Nasser announced the nationalisation of the Suez Canal Company. Let Britain and America withdraw financial aid from the Aswan High Dam project: Nasser would build the dam himself on the dues from shipping using the Suez Canal. He would also seek Soviet funding. The way was open for Russian intrusion into the Middle East, and Britain's hegemony was threatened. It was the bitterest political crisis since Munich in 1938.

CHAPTER TWENTY

The Economic Consequences of Colonel Nasser

1956–1957

> Whereas 'Suez' as a method of removing Nasser was always a non-starter, as a way of removing Eden it was brilliant.
> Remark heard by the Foreign Office minister Douglas Dodds-
> Parker

> It is not a principle of the Conservative Party to stab its leaders in the back, but I must confess that it often appears to be a practice.
> A. J. Balfour, after the Carlton Club meeting, 19 October
> 1922

The news of Colonel Nasser's nationalisation of the Suez Canal Company on 26 July 1956 reached 10 Downing Street during a formal dinner for King Feisal of Iraq and his Prime Minister, Nuri es-Said. It was the twentieth anniversary of Hitler's reoccupation of the Rhineland, as Ivone Kirkpatrick was to remind Eden. When Nuri es-Said heard what had happened, his advice was uncompromising. 'Hit Nasser,' he told Eden, 'hit him now, and hit him hard.'[1]

Britain was the controlling holder in the Suez Canal Company, with 45 per cent of the shares. A third of the ships that passed through the canal were British. Seventy million tons of oil were moved through the canal annually; 60 million of these tons were destined for western Europe. Suez was a vital conduit for Britain's energy supplies. As dinner guests left Downing Street they passed the bust of Benjamin Disraeli, who had purchased the Suez Canal shares in an audacious move in 1875. 'That's the old Jew who got you into all this trouble' was Nuri es-Said's parting shot to Eden.[2]

Macmillan was dining that evening at Fishmonger's Hall. He returned to 11 Downing Street and read himself to sleep with *Northanger Abbey*. He was not invited to the emergency meeting, which dragged on till 4 a.m. Others, less senior, were summoned from all parts of London, yet Macmillan who lived in the same building through a connecting door, slept undisturbed. The problem was the tension between himself and Eden. 'The Prime Minister had been consistently incensed by Macmillan's exceeding of his ministerial role,' as Dr Jonathan Pearson has commented. 'Therefore, Macmillan was not asked to the *ad hoc* and hastily gathered meeting.'[3] Eden did not want his Chancellor monopolising things.

Meanwhile, Lord Mountbatten, First Sea Lord, hurried from his dinner engagement at the Savoy, and Sir Gerald Templer, Chief of the Imperial General Staff, arrived shortly afterwards. Sir Dermot Boyle,[4] the recently appointed Chief of the Air Staff, who had been at the dinner for King Feisal, was fortuitously on hand to give advice on RAF involvement. Eden had a short discussion with Hugh Gaitskell, Leader of the Opposition, who had also been at the dinner. 'It is all very familiar,' Gaitskell declared. 'It is exactly the same that we encountered from Mussolini and Hitler in those years before the war.'[5] Eden invited the French Ambassador, Jean Chauvel, who was accompanied by Jacques Georges-Picot, Director-General of the Suez Canal Company,[6] and the United States chargé d'affaires, Andrew Foster. From the start he wished to emphasise the international nature of the crisis. President Eisenhower was informed at once, and arrangements were made for Robert Murphy,* the US Deputy Under-Secretary of State, to fly to London as the Secretary of State† was not available.

Four Cabinet ministers – Kilmuir, the Lord Chancellor; Home, the Commonwealth Secretary; Lloyd, the Foreign Secretary; and Salisbury, Lord President and Leader of the Lords – were already present in Downing Street, and were asked to stay. Harold Caccia, Deputy Under-Secretary at the Foreign Office, and later in the year to be Ambassador in Washington, was also present. The assembled company in the Cabinet room that night was a heterogeneous group, nationally and sartorially, some in white tie, some in black, and in one instance with no tie at all.[9] Philip de Zulueta, the duty secretary, who had brought Eden the first news of the nationalisation of the Suez Canal Company at 10.15 p.m., cautiously warned the Prime Minister in a written note that not all present were Privy Councillors.

The meeting broke up with two principles established: Nasser would have to 'disgorge' and the Chiefs of Staff should begin immediate preparations for the retaking of the canal. Had he been present,

---

* As Murphy had been Macmillan's opposite number in war-time North Africa, his presence gave Macmillan a link to the White House that was closer than Eden's, and certainly warmer. 'Bob' and 'Harold' were already good friends. The United States Ambassador, Winthrop Aldrich,[7] was recuperating from illness at the time; but during the next few months his friendship with Macmillan was to open doors. Macmillan also got on with Dulles far better than Eden ever did. During the crisis, Macmillan was to make ruthless and effective use of his links to an important trio of presidential advisers – Murphy, Aldrich and Dulles.
† 'Dulles,' Eden said in exasperation, 'as usual, is away in Peru or somewhere.'[8]

Macmillan would not have dissented from these conclusions; indeed he was initially to be the most hawkish of the Cabinet ministers and stiffened the sinews of many doubters at key moments. He regarded Nasser as 'an Asiatic Mussolini, full of insult and abuse'.[10]

'The morrow brought a very sober looking morning.'[11] Eden rang Macmillan early. Macmillan urged him to stand firm. Throughout the crisis, as Lancaster House conferences followed United Nations declarations and diplomatic missions to Egypt, Macmillan's fear was of a misjudged negotiated settlement.* His view on how to deal with Nasser was unequivocally that of Nuri es-Said.

Eden and Macmillan met just before 11 a.m. and prepared a factual statement for the House of Commons. (As 27 July was a Friday, the House was meeting in the morning.) The Cabinet convened after this Commons statement, which was well received by the Opposition, and there was unanimous agreement among ministers that a strong line was essential. At this first 'Suez' Cabinet, Eden brought ministers up to date with what had happened the previous evening. Following the review, the most important decision taken was to form an *ad hoc* Cabinet committee – to be known as the 'Egypt Committee' – chaired by Eden. Its regular members were to be Salisbury, Macmillan, Lloyd, Home and Monckton, Minister of Defence. Rab Butler, in effect the Prime Minister's deputy, was absent because of illness, but would not have been included on the Egypt Committee had he been present.[12] For Eden, with his memories of pre-war appeasement, Rab Butler was always in the company of what he disparagingly called 'the weak sisters'. Eden wanted loyal backing, not latent doubts and intellectualising about ways and means.

Macmillan's immediate task throughout the afternoon and evening was concerned with establishing what assets the Suez Canal Company, and the Egyptian government, held in London. He also prepared advice on dues claimed by the Egyptians from ships using the Suez Canal. At 10 p.m. he signed 'freezing orders' on Egyptian assets, orders that came into operation at midnight.

The initial meeting of the Egypt Committee was held at 7 p.m. on 27

---

* One of the fascinating 'What ifs?' of the Suez crisis is what might have unfolded if some sort of compromise had been agreed. The right wing of the Tory Party, already hostile to Eden over what they regarded as his 'climb-down' over the Suez base agreement of 1954, could well have forced the Prime Minister from office. Had this happened, Macmillan would undoubtedly have been the person whom they would have wanted installed in Downing Street.

July.* Four aims were established: securing the Suez Canal, ensuring the continuity of oil supplies, removing Nasser, and keeping the Russians out of the Middle East.

For Macmillan, as for Eden, the Suez crisis was primarily an economic one, albeit with important geopolitical implications. The key priority, in the days before North Sea oil, was to preserve energy supplies. 'Regime change' would be an added bonus, but not one that supplanted the overriding necessity of securing an uninterrupted flow of oil. The mistake the British government made was in believing there would be wholehearted American support for the enterprise. This over-optimistic belief failed to take account of two factors. First, November 1956 was the month of the American presidential election, what William Clark, Eden's press secretary, memorably dubbed 'the quadrennial winter of the western world'.[14] Eisenhower, unnecessarily in the event, was not confident about the outcome of this election and needed to avoid any potential embarrassments, particularly regarding the Jewish vote. Second, the United States' interests were not affected to anything like the same extent as those of Britain and France. The Americans' main worry was Russian infiltration into the Middle East. The United States would have taken a very different line if freedom of passage through the Panama Canal had been involved, but Suez was seen in Washington as essentially a European problem.

French interests were also subtly different from Britain's. Although the French had even closer historic links with the Suez Canal, in that the canal's architect, Ferdinand de Lesseps, was French, their main concern in 1956 was to prevent any Egyptian incursion into North Africa, threatening their traditional colonial territories. As a result, the newly elected Socialist government of Guy Mollet had even more need to see an end to Nasser's hegemony, a priority that would eventually lead it into a covert alliance with Israel. Also the French were still smarting from what they saw as a British rebuff over Messina, and a year later, despite their common purpose, were initially wary of being political bedfellows with the British, even after the Americans had, in effect, declared them joint pariahs.

Suez was to prove a crisis with four constituent parts. In the

---

*The first of 41 subsequent meetings, the last of which was on 9 November. Although such war committees had operated before (during the Crimean War in 1855) and were to again (during the Falklands conflict of 1982), the 1956 Egypt Committee was of special constitutional significance, as executive power was concentrated within this inner body of ministers. 'The detailed negotiations of the next few months lay with this group,' wrote the historian of the Cabinet, J. P. Mackintosh, 'though on key matters of arrangement with the French and through them with the Israelis, the Prime Minister acted with the Foreign Secretary or on his own.'[13]

cauldron of the Middle East there was already a latent conflict between the revolutionary Arabs, with Nasser as their talisman, and the Conservative Arabs, for whom Nuri es-Said was a key spokesman. There was also the unresolved question of Israel's borders and those of her Arab neighbours. Next came the question of the relationship of the Western powers with Egypt, following the recent withdrawal of Anglo-American financial backing for the Aswan High Dam project. Finally, to add to the volatile mix, there was the mutual Cold War suspicion between America and the Soviet Union. These factors were to combine with deadly effect.

Macmillan was in an unusual position as the Suez crisis erupted. Unlike Selwyn Lloyd, the Foreign Secretary, he was not directly involved in setting up the various conferences or in liaising with the United Nations, yet he had only recently been dealing at first hand with the personnel involved. He felt he still had a vested interest. As a result, Eden continued to be wary of a Chancellor who seemed to enjoy having a finger in everyone else's pies. Even as Minister of Housing in the early 1950s, Macmillan had been in the habit of issuing memoranda on foreign policy.[15] As a former Foreign Secretary, he certainly did not hold back now. He produced a financial overview in 'The Economic Consequences of Colonel Nasser', a title with Keynesian overtones. Macmillan's position during Suez gave him *carte blanche* to do as he pleased. Nominally, his responsibility was to make sure the cheques did not bounce, but he was not going to confine himself to that subordinate, albeit important, role.[16]

Eisenhower's main aim was to find out exactly what was happening, and to calm things down. Murphy arrived on 29 July. When he met Macmillan the next day, he could have been forgiven for thinking Macmillan was still Foreign Secretary. After the morning's Egypt Committee meeting, Macmillan attended Eden's working lunch at No. 10, with Robert Murphy, Andrew Foster and Christian Pineau,[17] the French Foreign Minister, together with Selwyn Lloyd and Harold Caccia. The chief item on the agenda was the composition of the proposed international conference. Murphy believed that membership should consist of those nations who were signatories of the 1888 Convention,[18] plus the United States.

Murphy had a working dinner with Lloyd and Pineau (at the Carlton Club) on 29 July. Not to be outdone, Macmillan held what was in essence a stag night for old buddies at 11 Downing Street on 30 July with Murphy and Alexander. Andrew Foster, the American chargé, made up the four. The post-dinner talk, over Macmillan's best brandy, impacted in important ways on subsequent American responses. Murphy had gained the initial impression (correctly) that the British wished to find some measure of international agreement, prior to any military action. Indeed, if the diplomatic negotiations were successful, there could well be no need for an armed intervention. The evening left Murphy in no doubt about Macmillan's political intentions. 'Although Macmillan was well pleased with No. 11 Downing Street,' he observed, 'he had aspirations to move some day to No. 10.'[19] Murphy also received an unequivocal indication from both Macmillan and Alexander that military action would be inevitable if British aims were not achieved through diplomacy. After the dinner, he headed back to the American Embassy to dispatch a warning to Eisenhower and Dulles about this worrying development, precisely the response Macmillan intended as a way of garnering full American support. Murphy's dispatch is an important Suez source:

I want to segregate one urgent note both men [Macmillan and Alexander] struck which they requested be communicated in utter secrecy to you and the President. They said British Government has decided to drive Nasser out of Egypt. The decision they declared is firm. They expressed simple conviction. Military action is necessary and inevitable. In separate conversations each said in substance they ardently hoped U.S. would be with them in this determination, but if we could not they would understand and our friendship would be unimpaired. If we were with them from beginning chances of World War III would be far less than if we delayed. They seem convinced U.S.S.R. will not intervene but they assert that a risk must be taken. Macmillan repeated over and over in language similar to that employed by Eden that government had taken the decision and that Parliament and British people are with them.

They both repeated the wish that the President clearly understood (that their) decision is firm and has been arrived at calmly and without emotion. They see no alternative. Macmillan in referring to our close wartime association in French North Africa emphasised several times his belief that as a former adviser and member of President's wartime staff he felt he could assure the President that Britain had no intention of submitting to Nasser's dictation, that British stake in M[iddle] E[ast] is vital, that a demonstration of force provided only solution. Macmillan described some of the military planning which contemplates he said the landing of three British divisions in Egypt in an operation which would take six weeks to mount. The British estimate of Egyptian resistance is low. Macmillan talked about costs. He said this operation would cost 4 to 5 hundred million pounds which they couldn't afford but they would pay. All British shipping would be allocated to it except the two Queens [the liners *Queen Mary* and *Queen Elizabeth*].

Murphy continued with a description of key figures on the British side:

Eden, Macmillan and Lloyd showed throughout unexpected calm and no hysteria. They act as though they really have taken a decision after profound reflection. They are flexible on procedure leading up to a show down; but insist, over and over again, that whatever conferences, arrangements, public postures and manoeuvres might be necessary, at the end they are determined to use force. They hope we will be with them and believe French are with them.

At dinner Macmillan and Field Marshal Alexander urged repeatedly that President as their former C. in C. (should) fully appreciate finality of British position. Macmillan several times expressed wish he could explain this orally to President. I apologise for length of this message but I am persuaded that flavour of their claim and very serious statements should be conveyed urgently as they request to the President.[20]

So far, it seemed, so good. 'We did our best to frighten Murphy all we could,' Macmillan recorded of the week's talks. 'We gave him the impression that our military expedition to Egypt was about to sail. (It will take at least 6 weeks to prepare it, in fact.)'[21]

Within minutes of receiving Murphy's letter, Eisenhower was in touch with Eden. As Murphy later wrote, 'Eisenhower was determined not to have the United States used as a cat's paw to protect British oil interests.'[22] Nevertheless, Murphy admired Macmillan's understanding of the changed realities. 'The PM [Eden] had not adjusted his thoughts to the altered world status of Great Britain, and he never did,' he later wrote. 'Macmillan (on the other hand) understood from the time I knew him in Algiers.'[23] In American eyes, this was to prove a strong recommendation in the months ahead.

Such was the alarm that this impression of immediate naval action created in Washington that Dulles was sent over post-haste to act as a restraining influence.* He saw Macmillan on 1 August, together

---

*The reverse of the situation at the Geneva conference in 1954 over Indo-China, when it was Eden doing the restraining.

with Winthrop Aldrich, now returned from illness. 'We had an hour's talk,' Macmillan wrote in his diary. 'I told Foster, as plainly as I could, that we just could not afford to lose this game. It was a question not of honour only but survival.' As Macmillan had built up a useful understanding with Dulles from his days as Foreign Secretary, he felt emboldened to spell things out in the most forceful way. From Macmillan, Dulles got a clearer indication of what Britain might be prepared to do than from any other sources. 'There was no other choice for us,' Macmillan warned him. 'I think he was quite alarmed; for he had hoped to find me less extreme, I think. We *must* keep the Americans really frightened. They must not be allowed any illusion. Then they will help us to get what we want, without the necessity for force.'[24]

Macmillan, though, like Eden, was over-optimistic in believing that the Americans would acquiesce in their militaristic plans. Much of this feeling stemmed from the fact that in Macmillan's eyes, key members of the old North African team, who had had such an intuitive understanding of each other's needs, particularly over the Greek civil war in 1944, were being reassembled. Towards the end of September, when in Washington, Macmillan still persisted in this belief, fatefully assuring Eden that Eisenhower was 'really determined, somehow or another, to bring Nasser down'.[25] What Eisenhower was really determined to do was to ensure that he was safely re-elected in November.

The first direct move following Dulles' arrival was a joint invitation from the British, French and United States governments for the original signatories of the 1888 Convention to meet. The 16 nations that used the canal most were also invited. On 12 August, the Egyptian government announced it would not be attending any such meeting. Greece followed suit. Nevertheless, 22 nations did meet on 16 August at Lancaster House, under the chairmanship of Selwyn Lloyd.

On the financial side, Macmillan calculated that preliminary military preparations in August and September would cost in the region of £12 million; if the crisis was not resolved by the end of September, then the monthly outlay thereafter would be approximately £2 million. As long as America remained 'on side', a run on the pound could be avoided.

A crucial meeting of the Egypt Committee was held on 1 August, followed by two Cabinet meetings the next day. Plans were rehearsed for what became known as Operation Musketeer. Macmillan, like Lieutenant-General Sir Hugh Stockwell,[26] Land Task Force Commander, was unhappy about the initial Musketeer plan for a landing at Alexandria. Selwyn Lloyd, who had been part of the Second Army team considering the various logistics of the Normandy invasion in 1944, was also very concerned about the difficulties of an amphibious operation with the forces available.[27] Even more worrying was the probable position after the landings: British troops would be easy targets for sniping, and without established land supplies and communications.

It was at the meetings on 2 August that the Cabinet determined, collectively, that if a diplomatic settlement failed to produce the required results, then force would be used.

A further worry for Macmillan was the information the BBC might broadcast, no wartime censorship being in place. On 3 August, together with Bobbety Salisbury, Macmillan saw Sir Ian Jacob,[28] Director-General of the BBC, to argue for restraint. Jacob was sympathetic to his concerns; but Macmillan was convinced that the BBC and the press could only be managed through a reimposition of wartime controls.

Macmillan was far more hawkish than Eden at this stage of the crisis. He believed that force would, in some form, eventually be inevitable, with or without American support; Eden, on the other hand, hoped that diplomatic manoeuvres, and American backing, would make force unnecessary. Although Eden was perturbed by Macmillan's growing sense of autonomy and keenness to put over his own views, he felt that America was being influenced in the right direction by Macmillan's 'scaremongering'.

Macmillan's independence was seen very clearly at the Egypt Committee on 3 August. Deeply disturbed about the implicit flaws in Musketeer, he had submitted a memorandum on 2 August to Eden about Israel's possible involvement, advocating that 'it would be helpful if Egypt were faced with the possibility of war on two fronts'.[29] Macmillan believed it inevitable that Israel would enter the conflict at some stage. Eden, on the other hand, was deeply shocked at the thought that Israel might become involved, and told Selwyn Lloyd to caution the Israelis against any such action. The Lancaster House conference must be allowed to take its unhindered course.

The same day, Ben Gurion, Prime Minister of Israel, noted in his diary: 'The issue confronting Eden is how to get the U.S. involved so that should action be taken, it will not be done with only the authority of France and England.'[30] Macmillan felt Selwyn Lloyd was subject to 'the PM's interference, in small as well as in large issues'.[31] Ironically, Eden felt exactly the same about the interference he was experiencing from Macmillan.

On 5 August, Macmillan saw Churchill at Chartwell, ostensibly a social visit to cheer up the lonely ex-Premier, but in reality to discuss his misgivings over Musketeer. He was convinced that Israel would have to be involved in hostilities, but at all costs an Israeli strike on Jordan must be prevented, as this would have disastrous and complicating consequences, owing to Britain's treaty obligations to come to the defence of Jordan if the country was attacked.

Macmillan's visit to Chartwell spurred Churchill into action, which was not what Macmillan had intended at all. At 11.30 p.m., Macmillan was rung by Churchill's son-in-law, Christopher Soames,[32] to say that Churchill intended to visit Chequers to tell Eden his thoughts, following his meeting with Macmillan. 'Now the fat will be in the fire!' Macmillan wrote in his diary.[33]

The next day, 6 August, a Bank Holiday Monday, Churchill was driven to Chequers. The old man stressed that wartime censorship controls should be imposed. Macmillan had told him of Ian Jacob's sympathy over the government's predicament, but also Jacob's belief that the BBC must report the facts as they unfolded. Eden could see where these opinions originated, and received news of Macmillan's visit to Chartwell with considerable irritation: his Chancellor was going behind his back and showing unwelcome autonomy beyond his departmental responsibilities.

At the Egypt Committee on 7 August, Eden was in a tetchy mood. 'I discovered later that the source of the trouble was the Churchill visit,' Macmillan wrote in his diary. 'Eden no doubt thought that I was conspiring with C[hurchill] against him. After the meeting (which was a very long one) I had it out with him and he was (as he always is) very charming and relaxed about the whole affair.'[34] Eden was not as sanguine as Macmillan thought, and Macmillan's continued diary entry smacks of self-justification. 'I had arranged many days ago, to go to dine with C, who likes company. I was horrified at the idea that C wd go to Chequers. Of course, if PM had not already discussed the whole plan with C last week, I wd not have said a word. All the same, it [Musketeer] *is* a bad plan.'[35]

On 8 August, Sir Edward Bridges, the Permanent Secretary to the Treasury, warned Macmillan of the need to protect sterling. International confidence in sterling was crucial following the fixed exchange rate system established at the Bretton Woods conference in July 1944.[36] 'Even if we don't get involved in hostilities, if the crisis continues for some time with consequent disturbance of our export trade and some loss of confidence, we may well find that economic counter-measures have to be taken in the autumn,' Bridges advised

Macmillan. 'Though it is an odious thought one cannot altogether rule out the possibilities of an autumn budget.'[37] In retrospect, it is amazing that Macmillan did not bring this warning to the Cabinet, but instead asked Bridges to consider possible contingency measures, including 6d on income tax, 6d to 1s. on petrol duty, similar rises on tobacco and even increased purchase tax and profits tax.

Meanwhile Dulles drew up a resolution for the 18 Nations in his customary legalistic manner. Whether this balanced document – recognising Egypt's sovereign rights, but also emphasising the international nature of the canal and access to it – would be accepted by Egypt was very doubtful, as the Egyptians were not attending the Lancaster House conference. Macmillan told Dulles on 23 August that 'there are only three choices: (1) Nasser voluntarily takes a proposal along the lines of the US paper; or (2) we compel Egypt to take it; (3) we accept Nasser's refusal. In the last event, Britain is finished and in so far as I am concerned I will have no part in it and will resign.'[38]

As force seemed more and more likely to be the only remaining option if a diplomatic settlement was not reached, Macmillan wrote to Eden on 24 August, employing one of his characteristic historical analogies: 'We should try to appear not as reactionary powers returning to old days of "colonisation" but as a progressive force trying to bring about a permanent and constructive settlement. We must not be like Louis 18th returning in 1815 to a dull restoration, but rather like Napoleon breaking through the Alps towards the unification of Italy.'[39]

The Treasury continued to give their financial warnings. On 7 September, Bridges told Macmillan of the 'vital necessity from the point of view of the currency and our economy of ensuring that we do not go it alone, and that we have maximum US support'.[40] Any attempt to 'shore up' the currency would be counterproductive and weaken confidence in the pound and lead to a run in the international markets. Macmillan pencilled on this memorandum. 'Yes, this is just the trouble, the US are being very difficult.'[41]

The Cabinet was already splitting into three different categories: the loyalists, who gave Eden unquestioned support throughout, were Selwyn Lloyd and Alec Home, together with Antony Head and Alan Lennox-Boyd; the covert doubters included Rab Butler, Walter Monckton and Derick Heathcoat Amory. Macmillan was in a category of his own, acting at different times as a figure to whom both the loyalists and the doubters turned for leadership and reassurance. These attitudes were mirrored by world statesmen: Sir Robert Menzies, Prime Minister of Australia, was the most loyal of the loyal throughout, together with Sid Holland, his New Zealand counterpart; doubters such as India's Prime Minister Pandit Nehru and Canada's Foreign Minister Lester Pearson became increasingly vociferous. In the Macmillan-like category all on his own was the brooding and ambiguous figure of John Foster Dulles, flitting from background to foreground, blowing alternately hot and cold.

Dulles' first concrete proposal was to create an international body to collect shipping dues and manage the canal. The Lancaster House conference (which met from 16 August to 23 August) voted to send a mission to Egypt to persuade Nasser to accept this form of administration. Macmillan was among those Cabinet ministers who would have liked Dulles to head this mission, as a sign of America's involvement and support. When it was clear that this would not happen, the choice then fell on Sir Robert Menzies. Menzies' sense of patriotic duty in agreeing to head this diplomatic initiative was much admired by Macmillan.

The main aim of the Menzies mission was to explain to Nasser in as positive a manner as possible the proposals of the 18 nations assembled in London. Menzies' approach and tone were conciliatory, but all his efforts were to no avail. The Menzies mission was effectively scuppered on the morning of 5 September, when Menzies was already running into difficulties over Nasser's intransigent attitude. On that day Eisenhower gave a press conference in which he declared: 'We [the United States] are committed to a peaceful settlement of this dispute, nothing else.'[42] Macmillan was not the only one to recognise at once that Nasser would believe force would no longer be an option if the Americans did not participate in any military action. Rejecting the Menzies mission would be seen by Nasser as an opportunity for further discussions and 'concessions'. Eisenhower's comments were extremely damaging at such a crucial stage. Unfortunately, the British political establishment failed to interpret the underlying message of this press conference. As Neville Chamberlain had put it during an earlier crisis in 1937, 'One should count on nothing from the Americans except words.'[43]

Even before Nasser had formally rejected the proposals brought by Menzies, Dulles was formulating another plan for what became known as the Suez Canal Users' Association (SCUA), the occasion for a second London conference. In Macmillan's opinion, SCUA was, 'a step towards the ultimate use of force...it should, however, serve to bring the issue to a head'.[44] Once it was clear that the Menzies mission had failed in its purpose, the Cabinet endorsed the SCUA plan on 11 September. The idea behind SCUA was that the principal user nations of the canal should band together to organise their own passage through the canal, and to collect the relevant dues, a proportion of which would be paid to the Egyptian government. The problem that Dulles did not face (a dilemma that was to return in even more dramatic form during the 1962 Cuban Missile Crisis)[45] was what would happen if these ships were blockaded and stopped. Things were not helped when Dulles told a questioner at a Washington press conference on 2 October that 'there is talk about the "teeth" being pulled out of it [SCUA]'. Then he added: 'there were never "teeth" in it, if that means the use of force'.[46]

As a self-inflicted blow, the comment was as damaging as Eisenhower's unfortunate remarks on the Menzies mission. Eden was devastated both by the content and the timing of Dulles' words. Macmillan was equally shocked, and felt that all efforts at securing some form of Anglo-American co-operation had been grievously damaged, perhaps irredeemably.

Parliament had been recalled for a special two-day debate on 12 September. Nearly two months had elapsed since Nasser had nationalised the Suez Canal Company, and the situation was still unresolved. Moreover, there seemed little chance of any satisfactory early settlement. Macmillan emphasised to Dulles that pawning the pictures in the National Gallery would be preferable to being humiliated by Nasser. At the outset of the debate, Eden outlined the thinking behind the SCUA proposals to Parliament. Macmillan felt Eden's speech was 'admirable', not least because it completely discomfited Gaitskell, whose performance in moving from his earlier 'patriotic' approach to a 'party' one Macmillan thought 'nauseating'.[47]

Coinciding with Dulles' plans for SCUA was the formulation of what became known as 'Musketeer Revise', in which Port Said replaced Alexandria as the site for amphibious landings. Macmillan had long favoured this change of plan, pressing its advantages from the beginning. A landing at Port Said would involve fewer civilian casualties than invading Alexandria.

The day after the second London conference had convened on 19 September, Macmillan departed for Washington. He was to be in the United States for 10 days, initially for a meeting of the International Monetary Fund. Related discussions with the Commonwealth Finance Ministers were also on the agenda. In Washington he stayed at the Embassy with the Ambassador, his old friend and colleague from North African days, Roger Makins.

Although Macmillan had been in America on several occasions he had never visited Spencer, his mother's home town in Indiana. To an eager American press, and photographers from *Life* magazine, he now projected himself as one of their own, a home-town boy descended from a simple pioneer family. Despite his increasing prominence in Britain, he was by no means well known in America. His visit in September 1956 altered that perception decisively. Churchill also had an American mother, and to Macmillan's satisfaction, the parallel was not missed by the local media.

Macmillan, accompanied by Makins, his Principal Private Secretary Evan Maude, and David Butler, personal assistant to the Ambassador, flew to Indianapolis in a four-seater Heron aircraft. Macmillan was engrossed throughout the flight in Thackeray's *Vanity Fair*. Despite the fact that important financial meetings on Plan G lay ahead, Macmillan was never seen to study any economic papers during the next few days.[48] The party was received at Indianapolis by Eugene C. Pulliam, a forceful newspaper magnate of considerable local importance. Reporters from his publication, the *Indianapolis Star*, were on hand to report the event. Pulliam had laid on a luncheon for 100 local grandees, whom Macmillan addressed. The tacit agreement was that this speech would be 'off the record'. In this Middle West state, traditionally isolationist, Macmillan combated any suggestion of 'colonialism' in Britain's response to Nasser. He spelt out warnings, very much in the manner he had employed with Bob Murphy at the end of July, about British intentions. He was hawkish and uninhibited. The ambassadorial party was concerned about how all this would be taken by their hosts. However, Macmillan got a great welcome from 'these very sincere folks',[49] as he described them, and he moved on to recall his American roots. The audience gave him a raucous 'Hoosier' welcome, 'Hoosier' being the traditional nickname for a native of Indiana.

After the luncheon, Makins and Macmillan, and the two secretaries, flew on to Bloomington, where Macmillan, with the kind of grand ceremony that he was later to revel in on Encaenia days as Oxford's Chancellor, received an honorary degree, and much praise from President Wells, head of Indiana University, about his 'Hoosier' connections. The whole campus was *en fête*. Brahms' *Academic Festival Overture* was played by the university orchestra as a prelude to the ceremonies. Macmillan reversed the order of subjects in this second speech of the day. He began, again in a sentimental manner, about his roots, which the audience absolutely adored. Changing the tone, he then moved on to stress the importance of Anglo-American resolve against Communism and standing together at this time of crisis. He knew well how to appeal to different audiences, and the speech made a great impact.

The next day, as Macmillan was breakfasting with President Wells, David Butler perused the newspapers, especially the *Indianapolis Star*, which had full details, in a rather sensationalised form, about Macmillan's Suez 'warnings' of the previous day. Butler sought out Macmillan, apprehensive about what the Chancellor's reaction would be to these details being published of a speech ostensibly delivered under Chatham House rules. Far from being discomfited, Macmillan, wily operator, was hardly surprised at all. He had a message for the American people about the importance of sticking together, and the more people who heard it the better.

After breakfast and a tour of the university, President Wells took his visitors to Spencer, home town of Macmillan's mother. Here Macmillan met elderly people who remembered both his grandfather, Dr Joshua Belles, and his mother, Nellie Belles. He read the lesson about the parable of the talents at the local Methodist church. It was an event of great emotion for Macmillan, feeling as though his mother was looking down upon him as he spoke. After the service, the party visited his grandfather's old house, before going on to the cemetery, where Macmillan laid a wreath on his grandfather's grave and saw other family plots.

The flight back to Washington was exceedingly uncomfortable, even perilous, as the small Heron was buffeted to and fro. Macmillan remained implacable throughout, quietly turning the pages of *Vanity Fair*, which he finished before the plane finally touched down in Washington.

The next day he was invited by Eisenhower for a private meeting at the White House. He was accompanied by Roger Makins, who took notes of the conversation, and who was astonished at the lack of focus in their ruminatory talks. Macmillan was the only senior British politician accorded such an interview during the Suez crisis, yet for Makins he did not make the most of the opportunity that was provided.

Eisenhower was not entirely candid during this meeting. His main political aim at this time was still to gain re-election. Anything that obscured that goal was treated with extreme caution. However, for Macmillan it was like old times in AFHQ, about which the two men reminisced nostalgically. Makins thought Macmillan wholly unwarranted in his subsequent optimism about the degree of forthcoming American support. Certainly, America had a general wish to see the canal made secure for free international passage. However, it was clear to Makins that any military aid to ensure such an outcome was not going to be forthcoming before the presidential election. And by the time winter set in, it would be too late. Macmillan did not seem to Makins to register this underlying reality.[50]

Yet on his return to Britain, Macmillan gave Eden assurances that were simply not justified. 'As usual with Ike,' he wrote, 'it was rather rambling and nothing very definite.' Nevertheless, he saw the meeting as helpful. 'Ike is really determined, somehow or other, to bring Nasser down,' he continued. 'I explained to him our economic difficulties in playing the hand long, and he seemed to understand. I also made it clear to him that we <u>must</u> win, or the whole structure of our economy would collapse. He accepted this.'[51] It was to prove a costly miscalculation.

Following his 35-minute meeting at the White House (longer than had been planned), Macmillan had a two-and-a-half-hour meeting with the IMF, in which he stressed that the British aim was to maintain the strength of sterling. There was no hint that international support for sterling would not be forthcoming. Again Macmillan was more reassuring to Eden than realities justified.

After lunch, accompanied by Makins, he saw Dulles at the State Department. The initial talks did not go well. Dulles was angered by the Anglo-French referral of the whole Suez question to the Security Council of the United Nations. He had not been consulted about this and felt affronted. Macmillan let the storm blow itself out. More dispiriting, though, was Dulles' belief that the British and the French should 'play it long'. Macmillan pointed out unequivocally that Britain could not afford to wait six months. Talks then moved on to financial matters, and Dulles was seemingly more conciliatory, telling Macmillan that he had already seen George Humphrey, the US Treasury Secretary, about easing conditions regarding the post-war loan.[52]

Macmillan met Humphrey the next day (26 September). Humphrey treated him to a long monologue on the economic woes of America itself. The Middle East crisis was not mentioned at all. Macmillan mistakenly assumed that Humphrey was not thus concerned about its ramifications. Humphrey exhibited considerable charm towards Macmillan in this meeting and suggested further meetings after the presidential election to discuss such matters as the financial arrangements for NATO. He emphasised that America must support Britain during the current troubles because of the ramifications for the American economy if things unravelled in Europe.

For the third time Macmillan left a crucial meeting with a senior

American figure believing that Britain was being promised more than actually would be forthcoming. Communicated in such terms to Eden on his return, these misapprehensions were to have a deleterious effect on future developments. Macmillan's political antennae, usually acute, seem to have deserted him during these two days. With hindsight, this was his conclusion too. In his memoirs he admits that in his assumptions he was proved 'tragically wrong'.[53]

Macmillan returned to Britain on 1 October. After the Washington economic talks – and jet lag – it took him a couple of days to readjust. He found Butler very worried at the Cabinet on 3 October, and on 4 October pessimistically recorded in his diary, 'The Suez situation is beginning to slip out of our hands.'[54] With winter approaching, the window for an amphibious landing would soon be closed. Macmillan's diaries also closed for the next few months. The manuscript comes to an abrupt halt on 4 October and is resumed on 3 February 1957, when he gave a résumé of the events of the previous four months.[55]

The focus now shifted to the United Nations, where Selwyn Lloyd was engaged in patient talks with Dr Mahmoud Fawzi,[56] his opposite number. These talks were making progress – 'a good natured preamble to a missing treaty', as Lloyd described them[57] – when the Foreign Secretary was summarily ordered back to Britain following an unexpected French initiative.

Lord Home, the Commonwealth Secretary, always believed that if Lloyd and Fawzi, who were on the verge of an agreement over the so-called Six Principles (they were adopted by the Security Council on 13 October), had been allowed to continue their negotiations, the situation could have been saved.[58] Ironically, these Six Principles eventually became the template for the final settlement in 1957.

The French plan, put to Eden at Chequers by Major General Maurice Challe, Chief of the French Air Staff, and Albert Gazier, French Minister for Social Affairs, was for the Israelis to invade Egypt. The French and the British would then intervene to 'separate the combatants' – the *casus belli* necessary – and thus secure the canal. Selwyn Lloyd later called this 'The Plan for which I did not care';[59] nor did he care for being dragooned into clandestine meetings at a villa at Sèvres, outside Paris, with French and Israeli representatives.[60]

Macmillan, however, welcomed the French plan. As early as 3 August he had been advocating Israeli involvement. 'I feel that he [Eden] must make use of Israel against Egypt',[61] he had written in his diary after sending Eden a detailed memorandum.

Contrary to popular belief, the Cabinet *was* informed of the Sèvres meetings (as was the Queen by her Prime Minister).[62] Nevertheless, 'collusion' has remained the most controversial aspect of the whole Suez affair, with obloquy being heaped upon Eden. 'Liberal' opinion, in particular, but not exclusively, was uniformly hostile to Eden as more details of the subterfuge emerged some years after the event.

The historian Andrew Roberts has characteristically put an alternative view. 'The worst part of the liberal internationalist mantra over Suez, however, was their outraged moral sensibilities over collusion with Israel. Without secret diplomacy and alliances, let alone plans of attack, Britain could not have won the Napoleonic wars, or managed to stave off involvement in every European conflict between 1856 and 1914.' Moreover, the consequence of the secret negotiations protected the lives of the Allied forces. 'Without collusion,' Roberts continues, 'the Israelis would not have destroyed one-third of the (Soviet-built) Egyptian air force, which would otherwise have been directed against British servicemen.'[63] Some episodes have to remain secret (Attlee confined news of Britain's commitment to the nuclear option in 1947 to a small inner circle). As Robert Blake has written of Suez: 'There must have been a great deal of *suppressio veri* – principally of course in connection with the charge of "collusion". No one of sense will regard such falsehoods in a particularly serious light. The motive was the honourable one of averting further trouble in the Middle East, and this was a serious consideration for many years after the event.'[64] Macmillan certainly lost no sleep over 'collusion'.

The latter part of the Suez crisis, after the long preliminaries, was nasty, brutish and short. The invasion of Port Said was duly launched on 5 November, with British parachute landings to the west of the city, and French ones to the south. The immediate military objectives were soon achieved, though with many civilian casualties. By dawn on 6 November, 3,000 soldiers had landed from assault crafts. The pathway to the canal itself, only 48 hours away, was opened. The military objectives may have been accomplished, but the political ramifications were soon to bring the action to its humiliating end.

In short, the Americans pulled the plug, by triggering massive selling of sterling and simultaneously refusing British access to IMF funds unless there was a ceasefire. The markets plunged.

Macmillan was at the centre of the ensuing storm. Before offering any financial help, the Americans demanded withdrawal from Egypt in addition to the ceasefire. Macmillan's melancholy task was to pass this information on to the Cabinet. The strong line he had previously advocated was now seen to be unviable, as the Treasury reserves were insufficient to stave off the financial consequences of military action. Eden had no option but to announce the ceasefire, which was agreed in Cabinet on 6 November.

Eisenhower meanwhile had won the presidential election handsomely. At the start of his second term, he faced two crises simultaneously – Suez and the contemporaneous Soviet invasion of Hungary, now being debated in the United States. Rarely had the Cold War seemed so dangerous. Obloquy poured down on Eden in the Commons, where he was at bay from the Opposition in the rowdiest scenes. At one stage, the Speaker had to suspend the session. Eden's health finally gave way under the strain, and Macmillan moved to centre stage in the final phase of the crisis.

The key figures in this end game were Macmillan, Butler, and Salisbury. Butler was *ipso facto* the Deputy Prime Minister, and the favourite to succeed Eden, whenever the moment came. Only Randolph Churchill, tipped off by the ever-astute observer Lord Beaverbrook, publicly declared that Macmillan would be chosen.[65] Butler lifted no finger to aid his cause, and was not seen by the Americans as a Prime Minister in waiting. Macmillan, meanwhile, continued to tell Winthrop Aldrich that *he* was 'Eden's deputy', despite the fact that Butler was acting Prime Minister. Shrewdly, Macmillan realised that the strongest candidate would be the one most acceptable to Washington.

Macmillan played his wartime links with Eisenhower for all they were worth. His main aim was to persuade the Americans of the need for an Anglo-American meeting, with himself representing Britain. As Chancellor of the Exchequer, Macmillan was now a pivotal figure, more so than at any other time of the crisis, because of the need for American support of sterling. George Humphrey had bluntly told him, 'You'll not get a dime from the US Government until you've gotten out of Suez.'[66] Macmillan responded, 'That's a frosty message you have for me, George.' 'Well, it's a frosty place I'm ringing from' was Humphrey's response, before he rang off.[67] He was calling from a domesticated meat safe, to which he had retreated in order to speak on the telephone to Macmillan in privacy.

Eisenhower foresaw that Eden was in the last phase of his premiership. Macmillan was the President's favoured successor. Ever since their days together in North Africa, Eisenhower had admired Macmillan's style and intelligence. He also believed that Macmillan had a decisive political touch. Macmillan was a 'buddy', whereas Butler was virtually unknown to Eisenhower. In any case, Butler was not a figure one could imagine drinking bourbons with Eisenhower into the small hours after a leisurely game of golf.[68]

On the afternoon of 16 November, Macmillan had been at Ambassador Winthrop Aldrich's residence in Regent's Park, trying to arrange an urgent meeting with Eisenhower in Washington. Aldrich recorded details of their talk. 'Macmillan said to me that perhaps he, Macmillan, could go to Washington as "Eden's deputy" as Eden himself "might not be well enough to come".' Aldrich was clear about the implications. 'I cannot help wondering whether this might not be a hint that some sort of movement is on foot in the Cabinet to replace Eden.'

Aldrich's appointment had not been primarily a political one; he was a social figure, chosen as a reward for his fund-raising contributions to the Republican Party. 'The Aldriches are really very charming people – the nice, simple, rich, and rather old-fashioned Americans one likes so much,' Macmillan had written in his diary on 19 August 1953. 'He is a great friend of Eisenhower.'[69] Both Bobbety Salisbury and Macmillan were close to Aldrich, regularly meeting him socially, often with their wives, and both found Dulles very 'sticky'.[70] As the crisis approached its conclusion, Macmillan seized upon Aldrich, resident in London, as his link to Eisenhower and the White House.

Macmillan was now visiting Aldrich on a daily basis. On the afternoon of 18 November, he began to negotiate with Aldrich about what support the United States might give over sterling and oil supplies if the worst came to the worst. He promised Aldrich that he could persuade 'a sufficient number of Conservative backbenchers to insure a majority in favour of withdrawal from Egypt'.[71] Aldrich telephoned Herbert Hoover, who was acting as Secretary of State during Dulles' illness,* to say that if such assurances were forthcoming, 'the Cabinet is to be completely reshuffled'.[72]

Eden's health now gave an unexpected turn to events.[73] On the evening of 18 November, his doctor, Sir Horace Evans,[74] called on Macmillan at 11 Downing Street to say that he had advised the Prime Minister that it was essential for him to have a complete break from his duties. The news confirmed what Macmillan had already been telling Aldrich, as recently as that afternoon, when Aldrich recorded that Macmillan seemed 'only too willing to outline Eden's planned vacation to recoup his health'.[75] It had been decided that Eden should recuperate in Jamaica at Goldeneye, the house of Ian and Ann Fleming.

---

*Dulles was in the Walter Reed Hospital, where he was undergoing treatment for cancer.

Macmillan thought that this was a grave mistake, and he told Evans so with some vehemence. Even Ann Fleming, through whose good offices Goldeneye had been made available, had her doubts. 'Torquay and a sun-ray lamp would have been more peaceful and patriotic,' she concluded.[76]

Salisbury had been with Macmillan in 11 Downing Street when Evans called. After they had been told the news, the two men discussed the situation. Although Butler was designated as the acting head of government, it was clear that policy would be decided by a triumvirate of Butler, Macmillan and Salisbury. Of this triumvirate, Macmillan was to prove the most pro-active.

On 19 November, a public announcement was made about the Prime Minister's health, and the lobby was told that Butler would now be in charge of the government whilst Eden was away. The same day Macmillan gave a different impression to Aldrich, after which Aldrich sent the following telegram to the State Department: 'Macmillan is desperately anxious to see the President at earliest possible opportunity & apparently consideration being given to appointment of Macmillan as Deputy Prime Minister during Eden's absence in order that such meeting might take place after withdrawal British troops!'[77]

The fact that Aldrich appended an exclamation mark to this telegram spoke volumes. Nevertheless, Eisenhower was also told by Aldrich that Macmillan had given assurances that if he became Prime Minister, America would find him more amenable than the present incumbent of Number 10. 'Macmillan,' Aldrich added in a later dispatch, 'faced with London's precarious economic situation, asked "if you can give us a fig leaf to cover our nakedness", he would arrange the withdrawal of British troops from Egypt and the replacement of Eden.'[78] Rather belying his reputation as merely a social Ambassador, Aldrich told Eisenhower that he was now convinced that Eden would not survive politically, quite apart from any issue of health. Eisenhower, sensing the way the wind was blowing, encouraged Aldrich to have further frequent meetings with Macmillan, so as to ascertain any developments. 'To some observers,' one American academic has concluded, 'it appeared that Eisenhower, and certainly Macmillan, were attempting to ease Eden from power.'[79]

Aldrich's next meeting took place at noon on 21 November. So as to be even-handed, both Butler and Macmillan were there. Afterwards, Aldrich telegrammed the State Department, 'Macmillan indicated British Cabinet changes which he has previously forecast will take place within the next few days.' So seriously was Eisenhower taking the prospect of a sudden change in the British political leadership that he held a meeting on 24 December with three of his senior advisers (George Humphrey, Herbert Hoover and Brigadier General Andrew J. Goodpaster, the President's Defense Liaison Officer) to consider who might eventually replace Eden as Prime Minister. The Treasury Secretary, George Humphrey, was in favour of Butler, but Eisenhower stressed the advantages of Macmillan. He described Macmillan to his colleagues as 'a sraight, fine man, and, so far as he is concerned, the outstanding one of the British he served with during the war'.[80] How far Washington influenced the replacement of Eden is still a matter of controversy. 'There is sufficient evidence,' concluded Steven Z. Freiberger, who has studied the matter closely, 'to suggest that Washington was heavily involved behind the scenes.'[81]

Butler was concerned about the effect of Eden's illness on both public opinion and the troops still in Egypt. Communications with Goldeneye were poor and major decisions, such as the timing of the final withdrawal, would have to be checked with Eden, which delayed their implementation. The Edens left for Jamaica on 23 November. In retrospect, this might well have been the time for Eden to have retired from his burdens. His full medical recovery was not assured, and the speculation about his future continued unabated in his absence.

Once Eden was 'safely' in Jamaica, Macmillan pursued the American link even more assiduously, as well as having further meetings with Churchill, his old wartime chief, at Chartwell. The British press did not know about this. 'Macmillan is telling journalists that he intends to retire from politics and go to the morgue [the House of Lords],' Brendan Bracken wrote to Lord Beaverbrook on 7 December. 'He declares that he will never serve under Butler. His real intentions are to push his boss out of No. 10 and he has a fair following in the Tory Party.'[82] The extent of that following was about to be confirmed in dramatic fashion.

On 22 November, Butler made a statement in the House of Commons about the withdrawal of British troops from the Canal Zone, commending the 'effective intervention' of the United Nations.[83] He was in an unenviable position as the public face of the government, defending its stance and putting the best spin he could on policies to which he had never been committed. Now he would wrongly be seen as the man who had urged withdrawal of British forces, and as a result he faced criticism from constituency chairmen and party supporters throughout the country. For many of these Tories, Butler simply lacked dependability in a crisis. The spectre of pre-war appeasement was raised again.

Party feelings were running very high at Westminster when Butler and Macmillan appeared before the 1922 Committee of Conservative back-benchers that evening in an attempt to calm the situation. Butler's appeal for party unity fell on deaf ears. He spoke for ten minutes, outlining matters factually and dispassionately, but during questions it became clear that he did not know full details of the Tripartite Declaration of May 1950 of the Americans, the British and the French, a central tenet of their joint Middle Eastern policy. Butler then made a mistake: he suggested that Macmillan might like to add a few words about oil. 'This was invitation enough.'[84]

The assembled company of Tory back-benchers knew that the two candidates to succeed Eden were on trial. The meeting was not so much about Suez; rather a microcosm of an American primary election. Macmillan was not going to waste his opportunity by giving bald facts on oil supplies. In any case, petrol rationing, which had just been imposed, was not an issue on which to dwell. Instead, he launched on a virtuoso performance lasting some 35 minutes, speaking of 'the long adventure of politics, full of hard knocks but still a game more worth playing than any other'. Although some of the younger MPs may not have picked up the reference, this was a sly riposte to the letter that Butler had written to *The Times* on 28 May 1931.*

In a wide-ranging *tour d'horizon*, Macmillan rehearsed his famous analogy from North African days (and many subsequent occasions) of the British being the Greeks and the Americans the Romans, the British with the ideas and the Americans with the power. Butler's speech had been flat and uninspiring; Macmillan's was a St Crispin's Day rallying call, expansive not only in language, but also in its gestures, which at one point 'nearly caused poor Rab to fall backwards from the adjacent seat'.[85] By the time Macmillan sat down to rapturous applause, it was clear that Butler's last lingering hopes (already very faint) of becoming Prime Minister were over. In his speech, Macmillan had not been concentrating on Suez; what he intended, and achieved with ease, was to reach for the crown.

For Enoch Powell, it was 'one of the most horrible things that I remember in politics'.[86] Thereafter he always regarded Macmillan with distrust. Yet Powell, not for the last time, was overstating the position. Macmillan's performance at the famous 1922 Committee meeting was *real-politik*, and the simple truth was that he knew the rules of the game better than the increasingly hapless Rab. Ian Orr-Ewing,[87]

---

* About Macmillan's support for the Mosley memorandum and whether the game of politics was worth playing (see Chapter 7).

secretary to the 1922 Committee in 1956, was in no doubt as to the significance of the speech. 'A great number, I should think 90 per cent of the people as they went out of that room, would have supported Harold Macmillan.'[88] This was the day that ensured Macmillan would be the next Prime Minister. As F. E. Smith had observed, 'The world continues to offer glittering prizes to those who have stout hearts and sharp swords.'[89] Macmillan may have been the gownsman for much of his career, but when the times required it, he was well equipped to be the swordsman too.

On 24 November, the day after the Edens had flown to Jamaica, the General Assembly of the United Nations passed a motion (by 63 votes to 5) condemning the actions of Britain and France and demanding withdrawal of the Allied troops from the Canal Zone. Britain and France found themselves increasingly isolated. On 27 November, Macmillan gave his sternest warning yet to the Cabinet that the only way that American goodwill could be sustained, and possible threats to sterling withdrawn, was by 'an immediate and unconditional undertaking to withdraw the Anglo-French force from Port Said'. Over the next few days, it became clear that Macmillan's prognosis was correct and on 30 November the Cabinet bowed to the inevitable.[90] Selwyn Lloyd was left to make a statement to the House of Commons on 3 December. He was savaged by the opposition and the painfulness of the occasion was never forgotten by those who witnessed it. Even Lloyd's humiliation was held against Butler. Back-benchers wanted to know why Butler, as acting head of the government, had not made the statement.[91]

Tory back-benchers were not Macmillan's only supporters. On 26 November, Lord Moran discussed the situation with Churchill. Moran wondered if Eden would be able to continue as Prime Minister on his return from Jamaica. 'I am very doubtful,' Churchill replied. 'I'd like to see Harold Macmillan as Prime Minister, but they may ask Lord Salisbury. I cannot understand why our troops were halted. To go so far and not go on was madness.'[92]

When the financial crunch came, Macmillan was the Cabinet minister who in effect ended the invasion. Such decisiveness, even at a moment of national humiliation, was to give him enormous influence and prestige among worried Tory back-benchers, as a man of resolution and authority. The unfortunate Rab Butler, who had actually been consistent throughout, and had been landed with the nigh impossible job of acting as the government's spokesman during Eden's absence in Jamaica, was seen as a spineless ditherer because of the doubts he had expressed to back-benchers. Nor did Macmillan's ambitions stop at playing at Foreign Secretary. Eden, after Churchill's warning, saw him as a potential threat and someone covetous of his job, as Prime Minister, which, in the opinion of Eden's secretary, 'he probably was.'[93]

In addition, Macmillan had closer contacts with the American political elite than any other British politician of the day. Butler, the official deputy to Eden, was trying to hold the party together, defending a policy about which he had always had doubts. Macmillan was talking on a personal basis with 'Ike', 'Foster', 'Bob' and 'Winthrop'. The Americans regarded him as the Prime Minister in waiting, which was exactly the impression he wished to create.

It has been suggested – the Machiavellian theory – that Macmillan had urged Eden to take military action against Egypt, knowing that it would fail and that he would thus become Prime Minister.[94] He was certainly no shrinking violet when it came to pushing forward his own claims (one of the reasons he was successful in achieving them), but such a scenario does not bear scrutiny. Macmillan was a sincere patriot who wanted Britain to be extricated from the dilemma in which she found herself. He knew the military risks involved, and calculated the odds on success at only '51 to 49'.[95]

The Edens returned from Jamaica on 14 December. 'Everyone looking at us with thoughtful eyes,' Clarissa Eden recorded in her diary.[96] Rab Butler with one of his quizzically ambiguous comments noted that Eden looked well, physically. Macmillan continued to be preoccupied by the financial implications and emphasised to Eden how dependent the British were on the Americans. On 20 December, the Governor of the Bank of England, Lord Cobbold, wrote to Macmillan in unequivocal terms:

> I believe that H.M. Government have no option but to undertake an immediate review of public expenditure which, on the figures involved, must inevitably cover policy as well as administration.
> It is my firm belief that unless radical measures are taken early, we shall drift (and drift rather quickly) to a position where the currency cannot be held and our way of life will have to be changed.[97]

Even though Macmillan had warned his colleagues about the 'Economic Consequences of Colonel Nasser', this was a bleak message of confirmation.

Nasser's timing and tactics were impeccable throughout the crisis.

From the moment he nationalised the Suez Canal Company on 26 July 1956, the Allies were on the back foot and never regained the initiative. The Arab peoples rallied round Nasser from the start, sensing that this was their moment to be taken seriously on the world stage. Eden, by contrast, was bedevilled by short-sighted allies in Washington, too many faint-hearted colleagues and liberal internationalism, of which the United Nations were the high priests. When the final balance sheet was reckoned, Nasser had prevailed on every count. The British, as has been seen, had four main aims over the Suez crisis: to secure the Suez Canal, to ensure continuity of oil supplies, to shatter Nasser, and to keep the Russians out of the Middle East. The results of the crisis were that the Suez Canal was blocked, oil supplies were interrupted, Nasser became the acknowledged leader of Arab nationalism and the way was left open for Russian infiltration into the Middle East.

Equally costly, in the long term, was the damage done to Anglo-French relations. After 1956, the French increasingly turned towards Germany as their main European partner. Indeed, Chancellor Adenauer of Germany said to Guy Mollet after Suez, 'Europe will be your revenge.'[98] So it eventually proved with de Gaulle's return to power in France in 1958.*

Suez proved once and for all that Britain was no longer able to 'go it alone'. The reality was well articulated by General Sir Charles Keightley, the supreme military commander, in his final Suez dispatch: 'The one overriding lesson of the Suez operation is that world opinion is now an absolute principle of war and must be treated as such. However successful the pure military operations may be they will fail in their object unless national, Commonwealth & Western world opinion is sufficiently on our side.'[99] Such a lesson was one of which Margaret Thatcher was well aware at the time of the Falklands War in 1982; unfortunately, the lesson was not heeded at the time of the Iraq invasion in 2003.

Eden appeared in the Commons on 17 December, but only one Tory MP rose to wave his order paper. His appearance at the 1922 Committee on 18 December, with memories of Macmillan's performance still fresh for many back-benchers, was uneasy.[100] Questions were beginning to be asked about 'collusion'. Whilst not addressing the matter directly, Eden stated, correctly, that there are some operations that demand complete secrecy.

---

*Macmillan's government was fatally wounded in the end not by growing economic difficulties, or lurid espionage and sex scandals, but by the uncompromising attitude of de Gaulle in vetoing Britain's application to join the Common Market in January 1963 (see Chapter 28).

On 20 December, however, in the Commons, Eden was closely questioned by Gaitskell about 'collusion'. He denied that there was foreknowledge that Israel would attack Egypt. This was what Churchill might have called 'a terminological inexactitude'.

Over Christmas at Chequers, Eden asked Kilmuir, the Lord Chancellor, outright whether he should continue. Although Kilmuir urged him to carry on, he was under the impression that Eden would not do so. Salisbury and Butler told Eden privately that if his health was not fully restored by Easter, then changes would be necessary at the head of government.

On 3 January 1957, after presiding at his penultimate Cabinet, Eden had a private meeting with Macmillan about the dwindling reserve fuel stocks, authorising, if necessary, access to Admiralty supplies at Trincomalee.[101] On 4 January, Macmillan wrote to Eden: 'The Suez operation has been a tactical defeat. It is our task to ensure that, like the retreats from Mons and Dunkirk, it should prove the prelude to a strategic victory.'[102] He received an oblique rebuff on 7 January, when Eden told the whole Cabinet, 'I do not think that the events of Suez can be reckoned as a tactical defeat. It is much too early to pronounce on an operation of this kind.'[103] Macmillan was unaware that the Prime Minister was on the verge of resignation.

The first political colleague to hear of Eden's decision to resign was Salisbury.[104] The two old friends met at 9.45 a.m. on 5 January, and Eden told Salisbury that medical opinion gave him no alternative. 'He was obviously sad but quite calm,' Salisbury recorded. 'Better to make the change now. That was the advice he had already been given by Norman Brook.' It was almost 19 years since Bobbety Salisbury and Anthony Eden resigned together from Neville Chamberlain's government.

On 8 January, the Edens travelled to Sandringham, staying overnight. Eden discussed the situation with the Queen in two phases. First, he spoke informally at Sandringham of the inevitability of his resignation. His intention was to smooth the way for the Queen in the first such situation Her Majesty had faced in her reign. Privately, Eden told Sir Michael Adeane, the Queen's Private Secretary, that evening that the Cabinet should now be canvassed as to their view and that Lord Salisbury was the right person to undertake this task. Before leaving Sandringham on the morning of 9 January, Eden wrote to Churchill (on Sandringham writing paper), forewarning him of the news. 'I did not want you to know by any hand but mine.'[105]

The next day, at his formal resignation audience at Buckingham

Palace, Eden moved into his second phase and spoke in a more structured fashion about the procedures. He recorded some, but by no means all, of the details of the audience in a memorandum. 'The Queen made no formal request for my advice,' he recorded, 'but enabled me to signify that my own debt to Mr Butler while I have been Prime Minister was very real and that I thought he had discharged his difficult task during the three weeks while I was away in Jamaica very well.'[106]

The question of Eden's 'advice' about the succession has been a matter of some disagreement over the years. 'It is untrue, though often alleged, that the Queen did not consult him about his successor,' Robert Blake wrote in his notice of Eden's life in the *Dictionary of National Biography* (1986). 'He never revealed his choice, nor was it necessarily decisive, but there is good evidence that he did not recommend Butler.'[107] The accurate story is not quite so clear cut.

Eden had been determined to follow all the proprieties in his departure from Downing Street, and was irritated, to put it no more strongly, by the myths that persisted many years after the event. On 27 November 1970, Lord Avon, as he had then become, wrote to Sir Michael Adeane, so that a proper record could be placed in the Royal Archives about the 1957 resignation audience:

> I notice that Mr Macmillan's memoirs recently serialised (*Riding the Storm*) repeat the statement first made in Lord Kilmuir's memoirs,[108] that the Queen did not ask my advice about my successor. Mr Macmillan adds that neither did I volunteer such advice. These statements are incorrect. Her Majesty followed the constitutional procedure and asked me my advice as to her choice of successor. As I consider that all communications between the Sovereign and her Prime Minister are confidential, I do not propose to state here what that advice was, except to say that the course subsequently followed was consistent with that advice.[109]

As Professor Vernon Bogdanor has written of this memorandum, 'the word "advice" is perhaps inappropriate here'. In fact, Eden did not opt formally for either Butler or Macmillan. As the present author has written in his notice of Eden's life in the *Oxford Dictionary of National Biography* (2004), 'In a farewell audience, he [Eden] gave no formal advice to the Queen as his successor, whom he assumed would inevitably be Macmillan.'[111] The correct parallel to draw is with the case of Bonar Law in May 1923, the previous occasion on which the then monarch (King George V) had had to choose between two candidates for the premiership (Stanley Baldwin and Lord Curzon). Bonar Law declined to give formal 'advice' to King George V that month, though this did not prevent others from representing to the King's private secretary, Lord Stamfordham, what that advice might have been. This reluctance on Law's part was not owing to his advanced throat cancer, but because he believed – and feared – that Lord Curzon was the inevitable choice and that whatever he, as outgoing Prime Minister, 'advised' would have no effect on the outcome. He wanted no part in helping Curzon to assume the mantle of Prime Minister. In fact, his reticence was academic, as the King, after seeking extensive advice, chose Stanley Baldwin.[112]

Eden was in a similar position in January 1957. Although the extent of his illness was not as severe as Bonar Law's, his political antennae were finely tuned and he knew that Macmillan was the inevitable choice. Anything he said was not going to alter the way back-benchers were thinking. However, as he believed that Macmillan had been disingenuous over financial matters and self-serving and disloyal during the latter stages of the Suez crisis, he was not going to add his recommendation to the overwhelming view of the Cabinet and the party. So he confined himself to generous words about Butler.

On the night that Macmillan became Prime Minister, Eden's wife, Clarissa, wrote to Butler:

> Dear Rab,
>   Just a line to say what a beastly profession I think politics are – and how greatly I admire your dignity and good humour.
>   Yours ever,
>   Clarissa[113]

In the words of Rab Butler's official biographer, Anthony Howard, this was 'a very touching letter from Clarissa Eden, which, without being explicit, managed to convey the impression that the choice made by the Palace owed nothing to any recommendation offered by the outgoing Prime Minister'.[114] This accurately sums up the position of Eden's involvement.

Back in London, Lord Salisbury was already preparing, with the assistance of the Lord Chancellor, Lord Kilmuir, to take the views of the Cabinet. The Palace, in the person of Sir Michael Adeane, had already seen Salisbury to confirm that in due course the Queen would wish to seek his advice. Adeane also wanted to know if the Queen should seek advice from Churchill. 'I replied that I thought she most certainly should,' Salisbury recorded. 'The British people would expect that he should be consulted.'[115]

After Eden had announced his resignation to the Cabinet at 4 p.m. on 9 January, 'very bravely and without emotion', as Salisbury recorded, the Cabinet (apart from Macmillan and Butler) were invited one by one to Salisbury's room in the Privy Council office. Almost all of those summoned to meet Salisbury and Kilmuir broke the tension of the moment by saying that it was like a visit to the headmaster's study.[116]

'Well, which is it?' each one was asked, directly, by Salisbury. 'Wab or Hawold?' The vote for Macmillan was overwhelming. 'All of them voted for Harold,' recorded Salisbury, 'with the exception of P[atrick] B[uchan]-H[epburn], who was for Rab* & S[elwyn] L[loyd], who, to our astonishment, refused to come down one way or the other. The L[ord] C[hancellor] was greatly shocked by this, which was indeed very surprising in a senior member of the Cabinet.'

Salisbury had never been a supporter of Butler's candidacy for the Premiership. The two had been on opposing sides in the great appeasement debates of the late 1930s, and when Salisbury had resigned, with Eden, in February 1938, it was Butler who had replaced him as Under-Secretary at the Foreign Office. Staunch Conservatives of that generation had never forgiven Butler for his supposedly defeatist attitude in a talk he had in St James's Park on 17 June 1940, the very day that France fell to the Germans, with the Swedish envoy to London, Björn Prytz.[117]

To make assurance doubly sure, Salisbury did not call in the Cabinet to see him in order of seniority, but according to their known commitment to Macmillan. On the table in front of him he had a sheet of paper with two columns marked *Macmillan* and *Butler*. The mounting number of votes for Macmillan was thus clearly visible to those entering the room, in case any waverers thought Butler still had a chance.[118]

The Cabinet was not the only section of the party to be consulted. The Chief Whip, Edward Heath, the chairman of the party, Oliver Poole, and the chairman of the 1922 Committee of Conservative back-benchers, John Morrison, had all been asked to ascertain views. The consultations were extensive, and on the morning of 10 January the results were telephoned to Lord Salisbury and Lord Kilmuir, or confirmed in person. Heath told Salisbury that 'the Suez Group would refuse to follow Rab, who they regarded as having been weak-kneed throughout, while the left wing of the Party, though they would have

---

*Patrick Buchan-Hepburn was not retained in Macmillan's new Cabinet.

preferred Rab would accept Harold'. In a second interview Poole told Salisbury that Tories saw Rab as the scapegoat. 'He would therefore, at the moment, be a very unpopular choice with the rank and file of the party in the country.' John Morrison had already rung from his home on the Isle of Islay to deliver the pro-Macmillan verdict of the back-benchers.

There was a groundswell of backing for Macmillan, not only among back-benchers, but also among party workers and local constituency chairmen. Second, and more significantly, there was a small minority who were opposed to Butler at any price. As so often in Conservative leadership contests – May 1923 in particular, and later in October 1963 – the principle of negative choice was crucial. Who was against you was more important than who was for you.

The soundings were not selective. Many Conservative MPs were away that week at the Council of Europe meeting in Strasbourg. In fact, the first that many of those in Strasbourg knew of the dramatic events in London was when a foreign delegation at the Council told them, 'Your PM's resigned.' Shortly afterwards, the whips were on the telephone to find out the views. Robert Boothby later recalled the events of that week:

> It is, however, quite untrue to say there was a small cabal of senior ministers who manoeuvred Macmillan into the leadership of the party. The party was consulted extensively, and at every stage. I was abroad at the time, and they even took the trouble to ring me up to find out who I wanted. There was no doubt the overwhelming majority of the party preferred Macmillan to Butler. If there'd been a vote it would have been exactly the same.[119]

Many who would have been thought of as natural Butler supporters had conceded that Butler was not the man to lead the Conservative Party in the wake of Suez. These views were in due course communicated to the Palace. On the morning of 10 January, Sir Michael Adeane,[120] the Queeen's Secretary, saw Churchill, Lord Salisbury, Lord Waverley and Lord Chandos. Independently all four recommended Macmillan over Butler. Adeane told Salisbury privately that Churchill's recommendation was for Macmillan.[121] Later that morning, a group of Butlerite MPs rang Julian Amery at breakfast at Strasbourg. Their message was a simple one. They had switched their support to Macmillan and they asked Julian Amery to let his father-in-law know of their decision. Amery rang Macmillan at 11 Downing

Street and passed on the news.[122] Thus Macmillan had three hours' advance notice of the inevitable decision in his favour.

During the morning of 10 January, Macmillan waited in 11 Downing Street for the summons, passing the time in reading *Pride and Prejudice*; 'very soothing', as he described it.[123] At 11.55 a.m., Adeane rang and asked him to be at the Palace for 2 p.m. Macmillan ordered lunch with Dorothy sharp at one, as the Palace wanted to see him. 'What do *they* want?' asked Lady Dorothy, concerned at the time with a grandchild's illness. When Macmillan appeared for lunch in a morning coat, all became clear. During his half-hour audience with the Queen Macmillan famously, and inaccurately, prophesied that he did not think his government could last six weeks. Many MPs, even those who had supported him, wondered if he could last three. In such a low-key manner did Macmillan achieve his mother's overriding ambition.

The first message he received on his return was from his sister-in-law, Mary ('Moucher'), Duchess of Devonshire, who mentioned Nellie in her letter, saying how pleased she would have been. At St Martin's Street, Daniel Macmillan was told excitedly by one of his publishing staff, who had heard the news on the wireless, 'Mr Macmillan's been appointed Prime Minister.' 'No,' replied the chairman of the family firm, 'Mr Harold has been appointed Prime Minister.'[124]

Few of the participants in the Suez crisis emerged with their reputations enhanced. Macmillan was no exception. Like Shakespeare's Henry IV, there were many 'bypaths and indirect crook'd ways'[125] by which he had met his crown. Four charges are customarily brought against him. First is the 'Machiavellian' suggestion that he pushed Eden onwards into a disastrous venture that he knew would fail, thus securing his position as Eden's successor when the situation inevitably imploded. Even by the standards of far-fetched conspiracy theories, this is unsustainable. The overwhelming feeling in Cabinet from the outset was for decisive action, including force if necessary. Had Macmillan cherished such bizarre tactics, he would have been pushing at an open door, with no guarantee of success. Indeed, had suspicions emerged of such a plan, it could have been the one factor to have delivered the premiership to Butler. Macmillan did not believe that any military action was pre-doomed to failure, though he was well aware of the risks.[126]

Second, there is the charge that he was devious over the financial situation, giving a falsely pessimistic account of the figures to the Cabinet to hasten withdrawal. This accusation is not so easily dismissed. On 13 November Macmillan told the Cabinet that gold and currency reserves had fallen by £100 million, when the real figure was £31.7 million. Treasury records show total sterling assets on 30 September to have been £3,607 million. By 31 December they were £3,622 million, a total fall during *the whole period* of the crisis of £84 million.[127] Diana M. Kunz, historian of the financial side of the Suez crisis, concluded, 'it seems obvious that Macmillan knew that he was misleading the Cabinet', as there was little chance of his misinformation being discovered.[128] The whole saga is very puzzling, as from 30 July to 18 December Macmillan sent Eden regular, precise and accurate weekly Treasury figures.[129] The exaggerated figure on 13 November alarmed an already anxious Cabinet, who were not aware of the background pressure George Humphrey had been putting on Macmillan. Humphrey had refused to back Macmillan's request on 5 November for IMF support for the pound. When in addition Macmillan heard that oil sanctions were being discussed in New York, it was for him the nadir of the whole crisis. 'Oil sanctions!' he exclaimed. 'That finishes it.'[130] Macmillan was only too aware that the cupboard would be bare in 1957 if things continued at the present rate, even if the specific details he gave to the Cabinet (but not to Eden in writing) were inaccurate. As Jonathan Pearson has observed, 'It is therefore possible that Macmillan exaggerated the figures to ensure the panic, or had miscalculated the figures and frightened himself.'[131] Such misinformation, though – if it was deliberate – was not for self-promotion. Financial insolvency would be the ultimate condemnation of his chancellorship. The figures emphasised the utter seriousness of the situation and concentrated minds. Macmillan may have cried wolf – at moments of crisis he was prone to exaggeration. When he had become Chancellor he instructed his private secretary to prepare a '<u>very pessimistic</u>' paper on the economic situation to present to Cabinet. 'We must treat them as the Fat Boy did Miss Rachael Wardle. *It takes a lot to make Ministers' flesh creep – they are all hardened.*'[132] Bob Murphy had experienced this 'flesh-creeping' approach at the outset of the crisis, when Macmillan had advocated frightening the Americans into supplying Britain. By November, Macmillan was one of the first to understand that Britain would in the end have to acquiesce and go along with what the Americans wanted – complete withdrawal. The figures he presented to Cabinet ensured that this was accepted by the Cabinet as inevitable.

Third, as Harold Wilson put it, Macmillan was 'first in, first out'. In the circumstances of November 1956, 'first in, first out' was not so much inconsistency as pragmatism. As Chancellor, Macmillan knew what the Americans could and would do if Britain did not go along with their wishes. At such moments one has to cut one's losses, however painful the process might be. In a strange way this U-turn actually worked to Macmillan's advantage, and not only among the more robust back-benchers. He had been decisive at the outset of the crisis, and he was now being seen as equally decisive at the moment of its ultimate resolution. By contrast Butler appeared an equivocal figure, always a doubter over Suez, but never, it seemed, with the courage to come out and say so, unlike Sir Anthony Nutting[133] and Sir Edward Boyle, who both resigned from the government. Butler had, in fact, been consistent throughout; but consistency was not what was needed at this dire moment of financial blackmail by the Americans. The presidential election had cast a long shadow over the crisis.

Finally, Butler's supporters always maintain that Macmillan, instead of concentrating on the political matters in hand, poured all his energies into a ruthless (and successful) campaign to deny their man what they felt was his rightful inheritance of the premiership. The manner in which Butler was outmanoeuvred has not commended itself to the fastidious. The British character has never taken kindly to 'vaulting ambition', preferring chance to crown a king without his stir. Overt self-promotion is often counterproductive. Yet fastidiousness discounts the realities of the political process, especially at times of crisis. From 16 November, Macmillan knew, earlier than most, that Eden would not remain as Prime Minister in the long term. For a man who had been, however improbably, disappointed in April 1955 not to have been chosen as Prime Minister, this was Macmillan's moment of destiny. To have held back now that his first real chance (and perhaps the only one) had arisen was inconceivable. Timing is everything in politics and Rab Butler was just on the wrong square of the chessboard at the wrong time.

Rarely do prime ministers accede to the post in a 'tidy' manner, as the example of two of the greatest, Lloyd George and Churchill, could testify. Macmillan genuinely believed, just as the two wartime predecessors had in 1916 and 1940, that he was the man best equipped for the premiership and for retrieving the situation. Such self-confidence was not dishonourable. Fortunately for Macmillan, his view was shared by the vast majority of his parliamentary colleagues. Rab Butler found – and was to find again in October 1963 – that few are presented with the key to Number 10 on a velvet cushion.

Macmillan's age made the window available to him to succeed to the premiership a very narrow one, but he did not miss it.[134] Had Eden continued in office much longer, Macmillan, as the senior man, over three years older than Eden and nearly nine years older than Butler, would have been disqualified by age. It was the Attlee/Morrison situation in reverse. Attlee had continued as Labour leader until December 1955, and it stopped Morrison; Eden did not go on, and it stopped Butler. In January 1957 Butler was at his most vulnerable, disadvantaged by his almost supine loyalty to the Prime Minister he privately thought had made a grave error of judgement. Politics can indeed be a 'beastly profession'. Macmillan learned a lot about reversals on his political journey. By contrast, Rab Butler had had an assured and golden time at Westminster, rising effortlessly up the political ladder; Rab's rebuffs – when they came – were all the more painful.

Bitter rivalries are one of the distinctive features of political life – Fox and Pitt, Gladstone and Disraeli, Lloyd George and Baldwin, Churchill and Attlee, Gaitskell and Bevan, Heath and Thatcher, and, most recently, Blair and Brown. That between Macmillan and Butler was one of the fiercest, as internal party rivalries tend to be, and long outlived their time in office, continuing posthumously through the claims of their adherents. The tension between the two was not a creative one. In that, their rivalry most closely resembled that between their contemporaries Gaitskell and Bevan, which so bedevilled the Labour Party in opposition. Butler never forgave Macmillan for beating him to the top of Disraeli's greasy pole, whilst Butler's second wife, Mollie, never forgave Macmillan for the outcome of the leadership contest of October 1963. In small but significant ways Macmillan had not been helpful to Butler. When Butler was editing a history of the Conservative Party in the mid-1970s, Macmillan declined to give interviews to contributors 'because it was Rab's book'. Butler soldiered on, and in public had to make the best of a bad job. 'After all,' he consoled himself, 'it's not every man who *nearly* becomes Prime Minister of England.'[136]

Eden never forgave Eisenhower and Dulles for the collapse of American support at the key stage of the crisis. Though both Eisenhower and Dulles were later to admit that their Suez policy had been a mistake, this was of little retrospective consolation. Eden had believed that there would have at least been benevolent neutrality; but even that was not forthcoming when the crunch came. Dulles was dead in 1959; Eisenhower left office in January 1961. They passed into history as far as Eden was concerned. Macmillan though seemed ever-present, a Prime Minister who survived on the back of Eden's troubles. His presence in Downing Street was always a bitter reminder to Eden of how the last days of Suez had unfolded. Rab Butler was renowned for his so-called 'Rabbisms', oblique and ambiguous comments, of which one of the most famous was that Eden was the best Prime Minister we had got.[137] Eden, though, was capable of his own form of seemingly opaque, but discernible, indignation. 'There are always weak sisters in any crisis,' he wrote in his memoirs, 'and sometimes they will be found among those who were toughest at the outset of the journey.'[138]

PART FOUR

Top of the Greasy Pole

1957–1986

The great man of the age is the one who can put into words the will of his age, tell his age what its will is, and accomplish it. What he does is the heart and essence of his age; he actualises his age.

G.W.F. Hegel, *Philosophy of Right*

"I TOLD YOU THIS SORT OF STUFF WILL FETCH 'EM BACK INTO THE OLD CINEMA . . ."

With Heathcoat Amory as Chancellor and bell-ringing Party Chairman Lord Hailsham, the Tory faithful look forward to defeating Gaitskell at the 1959 election.

CHAPTER TWENTY ONE

Rebuilding

1957

The first thing is to get power. The next is to do something
with it.

C. P. Snow, *Corridors of Power*

Such a position was never occupied by any Greek or Roman,
and, if it only lasts two months, it is well worth while to have
been Prime Minister of England.

Thomas Young, Lord Melbourne's secretary, 1834

On 10 January 1957, the *Brighton Evening Argus* led with two stories
of pressing interest for local people. Progress on the new £7.8m South
Terminal for Gatwick airport was one; the second was an analysis
of the prospects of promotion from the Third Division South of the
Football League for Brighton & Hove Albion after their 2–0 defeat
of Swindon Town at the weekend.[1] The dramatic political events that
day at Westminster were relegated to an inside paragraph, headlined
'Local Man becomes Prime Minister'. In this laconic manner Harold
Macmillan's arrival in Downing Street was announced in his adopted
county of Sussex. Like his hero Disraeli in 1868, he had finally
climbed to the top of the greasy pole. The *Brighton Evening Argus*,
reflecting the mood of many, nevertheless felt his appointment was a
story without legs.

The first person Macmillan met after his return from the Palace was
the Chief Whip, Edward Heath. The party owed Heath a great debt for
the way he had managed the divisions (both personal and parliamentary) during the fraught atmosphere of the Suez months. Macmillan
personally owed much to Heath, who had suggested to Butler that
Macmillan should be allowed to speak at the famous meeting of the
1922 Committee on 22 December, recognising that if Butler alone
spoke it could lead to ill-feeling.[2] The opportunity was not missed by
Macmillan.

Heath was to be a vital figure throughout the Macmillan premiership. They met every day during the week, and Heath was often a

weekend guest at Birch Grove or Chequers. As a bachelor with no family commitments, he was on hand whenever needed. Macmillan found him reliable, professional and well-organised. The fact that Heath had demonstrably had a 'good war' was also a component of their relationship. Heath's memories of Macmillan went back to university days and Macmillan's support for A. D. Lindsay in the 1938 'Munich' by-election in Oxford. The fact that both were Balliol men was a bonus. It might have been thought that Macmillan, with his Chatsworth and Eton connections, would not have been in tune with Heath, this thrusting technocrat, who had risen from relatively humble origins. Such a view misses the point about Macmillan's political approach. He was in tune with most people and Heath's meritocratic rise was the logical conclusion of 'One Nation' Conservatism. The future of the country lay in the channelling of such talent. The partnership of Macmillan and Heath was a creative and complementary one. 'Macmillan liked to take a broad strategic view of politics, drawing sweeping parallels from Herodotus or Trollope,' Heath's biographer John Campbell has aptly written, 'Heath was a good foil, the man of detail who could bring him back to practical reality.'[3] For his part, Heath always admired Macmillan's courage.[4] The opportunities Macmillan gave Heath were the key to Heath's eventual leadership of the Conservative Party.

Macmillan's characteristic invitation when forming his government was 'Would you like to join my shooting party?'[5] The king-makers, Salisbury and Kilmuir, were reappointed to their former posts – Lord President of the Council and Leader of the House of Lords in Salisbury's case, and the Woolsack in Kilmuir's. Far more delicate in terms of Cabinet-making was the problem of Rab Butler. Macmillan's two meetings with Butler on 10 January were, inevitably, difficult. The bitterness Butler felt at his rejection by the party to which he had devoted such public service never left him. Now, on top of his great disappointment at being denied the premiership, he lost out on the subsidiary prize of the Foreign Secretaryship, which he coveted. Macmillan knew that Butler wanted to move to the Foreign Office, but he was determined not to accede to this request. By keeping Selwyn Lloyd in post he would declare that he was not going to apologise for Suez. Eden had gone; and Macmillan, in a graphic phrase, later wrote that 'one head on a charger is enough'.[6]

Harold Macmillan's account in his memoirs of his discussions with Rab Butler glossed over the facts. 'It was therefore,' Macmillan wrote, 'a great relief to me when Butler chose the post of Home Secretary.'[7]

This was not true; and Butler pointed it out with some acerbity in his own memoirs.

Macmillan, nevertheless, depended heavily on Butler over the next six years, and his Number Two was the essential glue that bound the team together. Both Harold and Rab were liberal and progressive, ranged against the antediluvian 'floggers and hangers' always so evident at Tory Party conferences. Yet, as John Campbell has written, 'judged on the conventional political spectrum it is impossible to say which was more to the left or right'.[8] What was incontestable was that the 'right' always preferred Macmillan to Butler, even if it was a closer call on the left of the party.

Butler called these frustrating, even disillusioning times, his 'years of Pooh-Bah'.[9] At times Macmillan appeared to take him for granted as a kind of No. 10 'butler', a pun that provided the cartoonists with a convenient shorthand image. In addition to his new responsibilities as Home Secretary, Butler continued as Lord Privy Seal and Leader of the House of Commons,* a post he held until 9 October 1961, an uneasy threefold responsibility.

Selwyn Lloyd's secretaries at the Foreign Office had watched the comings and goings in Downing Street and were mistakenly convinced that Lloyd's days were numbered. Macmillan saw Lloyd at No. 10 at 11 a.m. on 11 January. Simply, and without preamble, he asked him if he would stay at the Foreign Office. Selwyn Lloyd agreed at once. 'You don't look very happy about it,' said Macmillan. 'Oh yes,' replied Lloyd, 'I'm just composing a face of disappointment for the newspaper reporters outside.'[10] In this manner Selwyn Lloyd continued as Foreign Secretary, returning to King Charles Street, as the political wags put it, through a long arch of raised eyebrows.[11] 'I had little doubt that he would ask me to stay on when he became Prime Minister,' Lloyd wrote in his diary, 'otherwise it would seem like a repudiation of the [Suez] policy.'[12]

There was also a less positive reason for Macmillan's decision. He worried that if Lloyd was liberated from office, there was no telling what uncomfortable beans he might spill. This was a fundamental misreading of Lloyd's character. Indeed Macmillan was to find Lloyd, like Heath, the most loyal of colleagues.

Their relationship was positive and interdependent, despite the fact Macmillan took Lloyd for granted, referring privately to his Foreign Secretary as 'a little country notary' and 'a middle class lawyer from

---

*Although Stanley Baldwin had been Leader of the House during his three premierships, in the changed circumstances of the 1950s it was an unnecessary additional burden for Butler.

Liverpool', the latter the title Lloyd chose for his uncompleted memoirs.[13] Macmillan indulged in a sensibility completely different from
that of Lloyd. Macmillan relaxed with a Jane Austen; with Lloyd it
would be a Georgette Heyer. Macmillan liked to ruminate over late-
night glasses of whisky upon grand designs and lofty concepts; Lloyd
was a devotee of ITV's *Robin Hood*.[14] Yet underneath Macmillan's
insouciance (a French interpreter once translated 'unflappability' as
'Macmillanisme'), especially when about to embark upon an important speech, he could be a bag of nerves. Lloyd's steadiness, acting
as Sancho Panza to Macmillan's mercurial Don Quixote, calmed the
Prime Minister's edginess very effectively, particularly at the international summits in Bermuda, Moscow and Paris.

What Macmillan wanted in foreign affairs was continuity (and
also the ability to retain a controlling interest) under safe pairs of
hands. David Ormsby-Gore[15] and Commander Allan Noble[16] were
the Ministers of State at the Foreign Office, with Ian Harvey as
Under-Secretary. Ironically, the first of a series of scandals that were to
bedevil Macmillan's government soon came from this Foreign Office
team. In November 1958, Ian Harvey[17] resigned after disclosure of an
assignation with a guardsman in St James's Park.[18] Initially, Macmillan
refused Harvey's resignation, but Harvey's position became untenable
after his conviction on 10 December 'for gross indecency'.

Macmillan's premiership can be divided into four phases, approximat-
ing to the spells in office of his four Chancellors of the Exchequer
– Peter Thorneycroft, Derick Heathcoat Amory, Selwyn Lloyd and
Reginald Maudling.

To succeed himself at the Treasury, Macmillan first chose Peter
Thorneycroft, then President of the Board of Trade. Sir Robert Hall,
Chief Economic Adviser to the Treasury, wrote in his diary that
Thorneycroft was 'the best of the possibles; very pleasant, but also
clear and firm'.[19] Macmillan's problem was that Thorneycroft refused
to behave like an acquiescent Keynesian. Heavily influenced by his
Treasury team – Nigel Birch as Economic Secretary and Enoch Powell
as Financial Secretary – Thorneycroft believed in 'sound' money,
and imposed tough measures, including a deflationary package in
September 1957.

Thorneycroft's relationship with Roger Makins, whom Macmillan
kept on as Permanent Secretary, was never easy. In retrospect, it can be
seen that Thorneycroft was not going to be long for No. 11.* Indeed,

---

*Many years later, after Thorneycroft had served as chairman of the party during Margaret when Sir Robert Hall considered resignation over Thorneycroft's deflationary approach, Makins dissuaded him by saying that there would be a new Chancellor before too long.[20]

The other dispositions were more straightforward. Iain Macleod,[22] a rising star, whose relationship with Macmillan was eventually to sour spectacularly, remained as Minister of Labour. Alec Home continued at the Commonwealth Office. As Macleod's standing with Macmillan dipped, so Home's was to rise. David Eccles succeeded Thorneycroft at the Board of Trade. Lord Hailsham became Minister of Education, the beginning of a Cabinet career that was to span 30 years. Henry Brooke (Housing and Local Government), Harold Watkinson (Transport and Civil Aviation), Jack Maclay (Scottish Office) and Dr Charles Hill (Chancellor of the Duchy of Lancaster) also became Cabinet ministers for the first time. A much underestimated figure, Derick Heathcoat Amory,[23] continued at Agriculture, Fisheries and Food. Though four senior ministers – Gwilym Lloyd George, Walter Monckton, Patrick Buchan-Hepburn (a known supporter of Rab Butler) and James Stuart – went to the Lords, the general impression was of musical chairs rather than wholesale butchery. The Cabinet numbered 18, a more manageable and effective unit than became the later custom.

On 22 January, Macmillan was formally elected Conservative Party leader in Church Hall, Westminster. He was proposed by Salisbury and seconded by Rab Butler, a painful moment for Butler, despite the outward courtesies. The motion was passed unanimously. In his acceptance speech, Macmillan began by quoting Disraeli: 'To use Disraeli's phrase, we must be conservative to conserve all that is good and radical to uproot all that is bad. So it is that we have never been, and I trust that while I am your Leader we never will be, a Party of any class or sectional interest.' He went on to remind the party that social reform did not begin with the Socialists in 1945: 'Our structure of social services has been built up by centuries of conservative and liberal thought and action. What distinguishes both these points of view from the Socialist is this. We believe that unless we give opportunity to the strong and able we shall never have the means to provide real protection for the weak and old.'[24]

Within days of taking office, Macmillan was in receipt of unsolicited advice from the Archbishop of Canterbury, Geoffrey Fisher. Eden had been similarly treated during the Suez crisis. Macmillan, for

---

Thatcher's premiership, Macmillan referred to him as 'that fellow who looks like a butler, with a pretty Italian wife – can't remember his name'.[21]

whom Fisher was to become a *bête noire*, was determined to close the door on him. 'The Archbishop of Canterbury will write and talk to me about politics,' he confided to his brother Arthur on 11 February. 'Can you with your expert knowledge, think of a way I might retort? Is there no heresy which he leaves unrebuked, no Canon Law openly defied, no liberalism lapsing into infidelity of which I could remind him? I should dearly like to counter-attack by invading *his* territory.'[25]

Macmillan identified several areas in which rebuilding would be necessary. Confidence in the government had to be restored and a new spirit established. The Suez Canal had to be cleared, together with all the financial difficulties and complications of compensation for those whose assets had been seized by Nasser. The Suez affair also had to be buried. Macmillan, throughout his premiership, resisted all attempts at an inquiry or an official history,[26] a stance also adopted by his successors in Downing Street. 'I believe that our best interests will be served if we concentrate on the future and do not revive controversy,' he wrote to Lord Lansdowne on 5 February. 'I hope that in time the value of what we did will no longer be questioned.'[27]

The most difficult task of all was restoring relations with the United States. 'The Anglo-American alliance was from the outset central to Macmillan's conduct of foreign policy,' Nigel John Ashton has written, 'and he set out his stall as Prime Minister uniquely placed to handle relations with Washington.'[28] Such rebuilding had inevitable implications for Britain's dealings with Europe and the Commonwealth, and was to prove one of the most difficult of juggling acts.

The economic situation was of critical importance. The relationship between Macmillan and Thorneycroft was to undergo severe strain over the deflationary measures of September 1957, which, as A. E. Holmans has written, 'implied a very substantial shift of policy priorities away from "high and stable" employment or "full employment" towards stability of the internal price level'.[29]

One area in which Macmillan worked towards a change of mood was in Downing Street itself, which he sought to make a still centre of outward harmony. With characteristic aplomb, he placed upon the Cabinet door the message 'Quiet calm deliberation disentangles every knot.' He made sure that this coded distancing of himself from the frenetic atmosphere of the Suez crisis became widely known. He maintained a strong central control over government strategy. His skill lay in disguising autocracy, making subordinates feel they were individual contributors to the general debate. Cabinets did not have the self-indulgent meanderings of Churchill's latter phase, nor the overt tensions of Eden's time. Disagreements on policy simmered, which meant that the explosions when they came made more of an impact.

Cabinet ministers had to decipher the literary and historical allusions with which Macmillan spiced his contributions. They had to know exactly who, say, Pecksniff or Obadiah Slope[30] were, to appreciate the full richness of Macmillan's scorn for his opponents, and sometimes his own colleagues. Remembering the conspiratorial atmosphere in Eden's Cabinets, Macmillan removed the racks of writing paper from the Cabinet table, so that ministers could not slip each other surreptitious notes.[31]

Macmillan's business background meant that he kept office hours, at least with his secretaries and ministers. Though he heard 'the chimes at midnight' himself, he avoided late-night meetings. He ensured that most of the paperwork was dealt with on the same day, an echo of Churchill's wartime approach of 'Action This Day'. Macmillan was very efficient in dealing with paperwork, and boxes were always ready for the secretaries each morning. Two other boxes were put out. The 'Dip' box contained all the material from the previous day, a means whereby the secretaries could catch up with overall business. The other was the 'Discard' box, full of unused material from Macmillan's speeches that might be put to good use at a later date.*

On 11 January, when he had been Prime Minister for over a day, Macmillan dined with Oliver Franks, and enthusiastically compared his job to the excitement of owning a new car. One turned the key and the engine started smoothly; one tried the brakes and the steering, and found they were reliable; the seats were comfortable; and one could control the whole machine. All that needed to be decided was the direction in which to travel.[33]

Like Churchill, Macmillan was not an early riser, but he did not work in bed till lunchtime with a cat as a hot-water bottle. He was solicitous in having morning meetings to keep up with 'events'.[34] In these, Edward Heath as Chief Whip, his successive parliamentary private secretaries, and Norman Brook, the Cabinet Secretary, were regular attenders. Others were called in as necessary. The Private Office at No. 10 was one of the vintage teams. Freddie Bishop was the Principal Private Secretary; Philip de Zulueta was the Foreign Affairs Secretary; with Neil Cairncross looking after the domestic side. On the advice of Charles Hill, Macmillan appointed Harold Evans[35] as his press officer, to replace William Clark, who had resigned from the post in November following Suez disagreements with Eden.

---

* Macmillan mystified Harold Wilson by asking him if he had a 'Discard' box.[32]

Almost inevitably, Macmillan eventually turned to his close friend John Wyndham, who served, from 21 May, in an unpaid capacity, as one of Macmillan's closest confidants.[36] At times, Petworth, Wyndham's house in Sussex, was an alternative Chequers. Philip de Zulueta and John Wyndham were to be with Macmillan throughout his premiership.

During his six-year premiership, Macmillan had three parliamentary private secretaries: Bobbie Allan, whom he had inherited from Eden; Anthony Barber, a future Chancellor of the Exchequer, and Knox Cunningham,[37] a redoubtable Ulsterman, who had been a heavyweight boxing blue at Cambridge in 1931.

On 17 February, Macmillan brought Eden, now convalescing in New Zealand, up to date. 'I have taken on your nice Bobbie Allan, who is most helpful,' he wrote. Elsewhere, as he frankly admitted, things were not so easy.

> The party at home is of course in a very confused state. In the house they are standing up pretty well, but we have a lot of trouble ahead of us; partly the Canal, the Middle East and all the rest, and partly the economic situation and partly things like the Rent Bill. What I am hoping to do is to get all the troublesome things over in the first six months, so that we may hope for a bit of light at the end of the tunnel. But I must frankly say that it is a pretty difficult job. However, one can only do one's best ... Sooner or later the Americans will come round. If they don't, Europe is finished, for I am certain that the Russians are determined to get hold of the Middle East, and that is why they are so angry even about the Eisenhower Declaration,[38] weak as it is in many ways.[39]

Congratulations flowed in to 10 Downing Street, Evelyn Waugh combining good wishes with the suggestion that Ronald Knox, whose life he was then writing, should be awarded the Order of Merit.[40] In his letter, Lord Beaverbrook, Macmillan's former boss at the wartime Ministry of Supply, reminded Macmillan that he had always predicted this moment. Potentially, two of the most significant letters came from President Eisenhower and John Foster Dulles. In fact, Eisenhower sent Macmillan two letters, one an official message for publication, and the other a private letter of welcome on Eisenhower's distinctive DDE inscribed writing paper. Wisely, Macmillan felt that 'it better to be the pursued than the pursuing'.[41]

Much was made of the fact that Macmillan entertained Edward Heath to a meal of oysters, game pie and champagne at the Turf

Club on the night he became Prime Minister. High living* was thus mistakenly thought to be the characteristic of the new regime. In fact, plain living was the characteristic of Macmillan's domestic life. His taste was for simple nursery food, or cold meats, especially roast beef, and raspberries from the garden. Before leaving Downing Street on Fridays, he partook of a good Scottish 'high tea', which meant that Mrs Bell, the cook at Birch Grove, was not obliged to provide a meal at a late and uncertain hour. Macmillan then had the benefit of a leisurely free evening ahead of him on arrival for his country weekend. If 'Bloomsbury' had got wind of Macmillan's fondness for 'high tea', they would have shuddered and considered it very 'bedint'.[43]

Life at 10 Downing Street was overshadowed by the knowledge that before long the whole architectural complex was going to need a major overhaul. As a result, the Macmillans did not make any extensive domestic alterations, or arrange for redecoration. They accepted the house as it was. In 1957, Macmillan set up the Crawford Committee to consider what remedial work was necessary. No. 10 and No. 11 were scheduled for major renovation, including underpinning, as the staircase was sinking, and No. 12 (the whips' office) was to be completely rebuilt. The Macmillans moved to Admiralty House further up Whitehall on 1 August 1960, only returning to No. 10 on 2 October 1963. Macmillan much preferred Admiralty House, a residence steeped in history, and, to his mind, more elegant and convenient in every way.

In Downing Street, the Macmillans made the flat on the second floor (where Sir Henry Campbell-Bannerman, his early political hero, had died in May 1908) their main living quarters. Lady Dorothy used the first-floor room on the north-west corner as her private abode (the 'boudoir', as Macmillan called it), whilst Macmillan made his study in the room overlooking the park. The growing brood of grandchildren were frequent visitors and the main hallway was soon full of tricycles, scooters and toys. For an 'official' house, No. 10 Downing Street, in Macmillan's time, was a very 'lived-in' building, and consequently welcoming in an informal way to all kinds of visitors.

Birch Grove was always Macmillan's favoured bolt-hole. He was happy that Selwyn Lloyd, divorced, and with a young daughter, Joanna, was able to use Chequers.[44] Macmillan never relaxed at Chequers, but the house made a splendid, and secure, venue for a variety of official

---

*If Butler had been chosen, Macmillan wrote afterwards, 'there would have been plain living and high thinking'.[42]

gatherings during his premiership. Many Cabinet ministers found it a suitable backdrop for their own political meetings.[45]

The Britain over which Harold Macmillan now presided was on the cusp of change. This was particularly true of the skilled, aspirational lower-middle class, whose material gains symbolised the transformations of the Macmillan era. Two influential books examined aspects of this process.

In 1957, Richard Hoggart published *The Uses of Literacy*, in which he analysed the way in which the mass media influenced attitudes among the working class in the north of England. Hoggart saw an 'emerging classless class', as the working and middle classes began to merge, at a time 'when they [the working class] no longer have such strong economic pressure as makes them feel the great importance of loyal membership of their known groups'.[46]

In his seminal book *Culture and Society*, published in 1958, Raymond Williams pinpointed a further essential truth about that transformation. 'A dominant class can to a large extent control the transmission and distribution of the whole common inheritance,' he observed. In essence, such a goal was what Macmillan had striven for since his Stockton days. By 1958 it was thought by many, Williams wrote, 'that the working class is becoming more "bourgeois", because it is dressing like the middle-class, living in semi-detached houses, acquiring cars and washing machines'. He added a cautionary and perceptive note. 'It is not "bourgeois" to possess objects of utility, nor to enjoy a high material standard of living ... the worker's envy of the middle-class man is not a desire to be that man, but to have the same kind of possessions.'[47] Macmillan intuitively understood this distinction; the key factor was to bring material advantages across the whole social spectrum.

At times Macmillan resembled a benevolent uncle at a family birthday party, reassuring and comfortable, rather like the crumpled cardigans he favoured; at other times, he could be censorious, though in the manner of the local vicar at Sunday Matins (his own favoured service in Horsted Keynes), quite crisp when one looked beneath the surface, but never too sharply disconcerting to frighten away the congregation he needed to keep on side.

Memories of the pre-war depression had not yet faded when Macmillan became Prime Minister. Yet the improving social conditions, as the country moved from austerity to affluence, a process that now accelerated under Macmillan, meant there was less discontent. The main concern was whether the improvements could be sustained.

Memories of the Second World War now had a nostalgic glow, nurtured by the patriotic films of the time, such as *The Dam Busters*.[48] If a new war came, the fear was that it would be a nuclear conflict. The first CND protest march from London to the Aldermaston atomic research establishment (a later reversal of the direction of the route ensured more participants) took place on 4 April; 1957 also saw the appearance of Nevil Shute's novel *On the Beach*, which gave a graphic portrait of Armageddon. Despite these Cold War fears, the great mass of what later became dubbed 'Middle England', epitomised by Macmillan's own Bromley constituents, was domestically a much more settled, even grateful population. There was an inbuilt deference, with respect for authority and for the wartime generation of politicians. National Service was generally accepted. Crime rates were low.

The prerequisite for such contentment was security. Freedom from financial anxiety, efficient health and education provision, and a nice place to live, with good transport links: these were the things that counted more than what Archbishop Makarios was getting up to in Cyprus. Although foreign affairs was Macmillan's passion, and economics his hobby, he knew that general elections are rarely, if ever, decided by foreign policy. What matters most is next Friday's grocery bill. From his first day in Downing Street, Macmillan had his eyes on the next general election, and the need for success in that contest conditioned his whole approach.

The domestic scene was an opportunity, not a handicap. The manufacturing base had not yet receded, unemployment was hardly an issue and trains still ran to village stations. Increasingly, the people of Middle England owned their own homes, yet were not overburdened with crippling mortgages. Indeed, many 'ordinary' people did not have mortgages at all, but paid for their homes outright.[49] The Rent Act of 1957, which decontrolled some private sector rents, caused inevitable controversy among tenants, owing to consequent price increases. The Act demonstrated the Tory belief that the free market was the best solution to Britain's housing shortage, and was the third part of their housing strategy. First, council housing had been relegated from general need to specific; second, private owner occupation had been encouraged; now rented accommodation was to be a free market. The argument in favour of the legislation was that controls had inhibited landlords from improving existing properties and also from increasing existing supply. It was believed that mobility of labour would now be encouraged and that overcrowding and underoccupation would both be reduced. In the north of England, Wales and Scotland, some of these factors worked. However, the provisions did not take into account demographic changes. In London, where demand was highest, the availability of stock was actually reduced. Larger houses were subdivided and sold off, and pressure was put on tenants to vacate such properties. As M. J. Barnett has observed, 'freedom not from control, but to make a fair return, was what landlords required'.[50]

The Conservatives were anxious not to appear to be favouring these landlords. The exploitations of what became known as 'Rachmanism', after an unscrupulous Polish-born London landlord, Peter Rachman,[51] were particularly damaging. For owner-occupiers, such hazards of the rental market did not arise. They were far removed from the crowded immigrant population in areas such as Notting Hill, later the epicentre of 'gentrification'. A pleasant semi-detached house in a leafy suburb could be bought for £1,500 to £2,000, a figure affordable with prudent saving or legacies from parents or grandparents. Suburbia was the Utopia of the Macmillan age.[52]

In 1958, the Cabinet, belatedly in the opinion of many, considered immigration from the New Commonwealth (Africa, the Caribbean, India, Cyprus, Malta and Gibraltar). Lord Hailsham reported in June 1958 that the coloured population of Britain was 180,000, an increase of 40,000 over 1957.[53] Race riots in Notting Hill in the summer of 1958 raised concerns about social cohesion, and not all responses were liberal-minded. In 1962, Macmillan's government brought in the Commonwealth Immigration Act, which set up a voucher scheme for skilled workers, not applicable to the predominantly white Old Commonwealth (Australia, New Zealand, Canada and South Africa) or Eire. The Labour Opposition criticised the Act as racist and discriminatory, which led Macmillan to describe Gaitskell as 'the kind of cad that only a gentleman can be'.[54] Many in Middle England were not condemnatory of this Act.

The children of this Middle England, if not of the immigrant population, went to schools that were run with structured discipline; the brighter – and luckier – ones to grammar schools. One problem was the uneven provision of grammar school places in different regions; another that the secondary modern schools did not have the 'parity of esteem' for which Rab Butler had hoped when he formulated the 1944 Education Act. The drive for comprehensive schools in the state system was already under way when Macmillan became Prime Minister. The first such landmark establishment was Kidbrooke School in 1955.

Michael Young,[55] who had drafted the 1945 Labour Party election manifesto, perceptively argued in The Rise of the Meritocracy (1958) that such a reform would actually lead to a different kind of inequality from the old class-based one. Those 'left behind', when merit was the criterion, would, bluntly, have no excuse on which to fall back. Also, with increased affluence, Young foresaw 'the decline of the labour movement', as 'parents harboured ambitions for their children rather than for their class'.[56] Macmillan rode that wave with consummate skill.

As more pupils could benefit from an academic education than the places available, the 11+ examination became one of the dreaded mountain ranges that children had to scale – or fail to scale. A teacher – or 'schoolmaster' in the grammar or public schools – although not of the same standing as the local GP, as portrayed in the long-running television drama *Doctor Finlay's Casebook* (first broadcast in August 1962), was not far behind. The police, even without the officer class of the armed forces, were similarly respected, and a programme such as *Dixon of Dock Green* (first broadcast in July 1955), was a wistful memory of a community spirit already under threat. Its popular successor as a police television series, *Z Cars* (from January 1962), reflected a shifting perception of social conditions.

University grants meant that students ('undergraduates', at Oxford and Cambridge) could receive the benefits of higher education without incurring huge debts. Graduates entered an employment market full of opportunity, and when conscription for National Service was ended in the early 1960s, such careers were not interrupted for two years. Those born in the 1940s, who came to political consciousness in the Macmillan era, enjoyed a legacy denied to both preceding and later generations.

Television loomed large as a leisure activity, especially after the start of independent television in September 1955. There were no remote controls in those days to change channels (limited in any case by later standards), and all broadcasts, until July 1967, were in black and white. TV programmes were a staple of conversation, at home, work, and on the buses and trains. For example *Panorama*, the BBC's 'weekly window on the world', was in its golden era, thoughtfully explaining complex issues of current affairs in a non-patronising way, with the reassuring Richard Dimbleby,[57] a kind of Macmillan of the BBC, as a paternal figurehead. In 1957, *Panorama* broadcast its famous April Fool's Day hoax on the spaghetti harvest, a bumper crop owing, said Dimbleby in his most sonorous tones, to the effect of the mild winter on the spaghetti weevil. It was as though the Archbishop of Canterbury had been discovered dancing the 'twist', a popular gyration of the time. The 'spaghetti hoax' was mischievous fun, but Richard Dimbleby with a twinkle in his eye was not what people expected from 'Auntie'.[58]

People could take things seriously. Holidays were planned months ahead, not involving flights to some Spanish resort, but the family Morris Minor (usually painted grey), carefully packed with the necessary items for a fortnight's adventure. Routes were planned weeks ahead. The Automobile Association could provide individual itineraries on request, their fold-over pages a staple item for the passenger in the front seat, before the day's journey to resorts such as Bridlington or Scarborough. The pecking order of these seaside resorts was of byzantine complexity: Skegness could not match Filey, and Torquay trumped Great Yarmouth. In 1936, Skegness was the site of the first Butlin's holiday camp,[59] the success of which was built on an inclusive camaraderie. After the war, Filey became Butlin's showpiece holiday camp, aimed at a more discerning clientele. Many holidaymakers went to the same resort and guest house year after year, their choice of venue itself a form of social definition. An Eastbourne family was clearly 'doing better' than a Hastings one, and Lytham St Anne's was markedly 'superior' to Blackpool. Clothes were still formal, even on holiday: a jacket on the beach, grandad in his suit and hat, children clad against the sun.

Sport was an obsession, football clubs the focus of local support. A star centre-forward might well live in the next street. The FA Cup Final was a national event, broadcast simultaneously on BBC and ITV. In 1958, Macmillan was invited to take tea with the winning team, Bolton Wanderers. The Cup Final hymn, 'Abide with Me', was reverently sung by the crowd, led by a master of ceremonies in a white suit.

Cricket was a participatory pastime, village greens all over the land resounding at weekends (but on Sundays only in the afternoon, after Church)[60] to the sound of willow on leather. Substantial cricket teas, provided by stalwart armies of wives and girlfriends, were almost as important as the match itself, trestle tables loaded with urns and paper plates with substantial sandwiches, pork pies, cheeses, celery, 'Empire' biscuits, cakes with 'hundreds and thousands' on brightly coloured icing, and fizzy 'pop' for the children, which enticed them in from their own little interval games on the boundary. Macmillan batted in local Bromley matches to support his constituency fêtes. County cricket still maintained its division between the amateurs and the professionals, and the Gentlemen versus Players fixture at Lords was still an annual event, as were several public school fixtures, not only Eton versus Harrow, a fixture that Macmillan made a point of attending, in a morning suit.

Home truly was where the heart was. The growing popularity of

'Do it Yourself' (DIY) occupied many weekends, and the garden, for those lucky enough to have one, became an extension of the living space. Michael Flanders and Donald Swann first performed their long-running review *At the Drop of a Hat* on New Year's Eve 1956, a few days before Macmillan became Prime Minister. One of its numbers astutely observed that 'the garden's full of furniture and the house is full of plants'.[61]

After the 1959 general election, Macmillan declared that the class war was over. So did John Major more than 30 years later. Yet class is always part of the fabric of British society. Nancy Mitford's ironic book, *Noblesse Oblige* came out in 1956. Did one say toilet or lavatory, serviette or napkin, notepaper or writing paper, mantelpiece or chimney piece? Did one have dinner as the midday meal, or lunch? When was the evening meal – was it high tea at six (Macmillan's secret favourite) on return from the workplace, which in many cases was not far distant from the home, or a later 'supper'? A full-scale 'dinner' was often a special weekend occasion for guests, with courses kept warm on a 'hostess' trolley.

Britain in 1957 was almost a prelapsarian age. Re-adjustment was disconcerting, particularly for older generations used to traditional and deferential ways. Macmillan's colleague from wartime Athens days, Osbert Lancaster, illustrated the humorous side of this transition in his popular 'pocket cartoons' in the *Daily Express*, featuring a bemused upper-class figure, Maudie Littlehampton, vainly attempting to come to terms with the advancing tide of modernity.[62] As the title of Lionel Bart's musical in 1959 put it, *Fings Ain't Wot They Used to Be*.

'I am always hearing about the Middle Classes,' Macmillan wrote to Michael Fraser, joint director of the Conservative Research Department on 17 February 1957. 'What is it they really want? Can you put it down on a sheet of notepaper, and then I will see whether we can give it to them?'[63]

Macmillan's critics have always maintained that his Achilles heel was 'short-termism', particularly over economic matters. The shadow of 1930s Stockton still lay heavy over his calculations. After all, it was Keynes himself who had said that in the long term we are all dead, and Macmillan frequently stressed the importance of the here and now. 'All through my life I have heard people talk about the long-term problems,' he wrote to Peter Thorneycroft on 22 January, as Budget plans were being formalised. 'This is an excuse to avoid short-term ones.'[64] From the start of his chancellorship, however, Thorneycroft stressed the importance of financial prudence. He would not give the middle classes what they wanted if it was detrimental to the overall health of the economy.

Thorneycroft faced a demanding timetable if his first (and, in the event, only) Budget was to be ready for 9 April 1957. On 7 February, he reduced the bank rate by 0.5 per cent to 5 per cent, but it would not be long before retrenchment became the order of the day. On the weekend of 24/25 February, at a Chequers meeting attended by Salisbury, Butler, Thorneycroft, Lloyd, Sandys and Home, the new Defence White Paper of Duncan Sandys came under close scrutiny. The outcome was that the defence budget was to be reduced to £1,450 million for 1957/1958, from the planned £1,598.7 million of 1956/1957. The main point of the White Paper was the ending of conscription. On 12 March 1957, Thorneycroft reported to Macmillan that initial cuts had brought the total for 1957/1958 down to £1,475 million. Macmillan warned that defence spending was impacting adversely on scientific and technological research. As a result, a complete review of defence priorities was necessary.[65] Even though it had implications for employment, Macmillan became increasingly sceptical about a vast commitment to conventional defence spending in a nuclear age.

Nevertheless, he urged tax cuts, which Thorneycroft duly delivered in the Budget. A limited relief in surtax – what was dubbed 'Room at the Top' after the best-selling novel of the time by John Braine[66] – was the 'headline' measure, welcomed or reviled depending from which part of the political spectrum it was viewed. Entertainment tax was also cut, that on live theatre and sport completely. Thorneycroft helped young home-owners by cutting the purchase tax on kitchen goods and furniture from 30 per cent to 15 per cent. The supplementary duty on petrol, which had been imposed (at 1s. a gallon)[67] during the Suez crisis, was also removed. Overall the tax burden was reduced by £100m. Thorneycroft also announced the Radcliffe Commission on the Monetary System, which gave the Governor of the Bank of England, Lord Cobbold, some hope that the government might be willing to bring in control of the money supply.

Although the Budget was well received by the press, there were tensions between Macmillan and Thorneycroft. As the outgoing Chancellor of the Exchequer, Macmillan still had a proprietorial interest in economic affairs, and did not give Thorneycroft a free rein. The ghost of Keynes (and his disciple Roy Harrod, who had Macmillan's ear) still loomed large in economic planning. Thorneycroft's wish was to take Sir Frank Lee, his trusted Permanent Secretary at the Board of Trade, with him to the Treasury, but Macmillan did not allow this move.[68] Macmillan was in an awkward position, as Roger Makins had only recently transferred, at Macmillan's own repeated request, to the Treasury. Makins had left Washington dutifully, but with regret. He had told John Foster Dulles 'how truly sorry' he was to be giving up his post as Ambasssador.[69] Had Makins now been displaced at the Treasury by Lee, after having been pressurised into giving up his diplomatic career, it could have put severe strains on his relationship with Macmillan. So Thorneycroft had to give way.

Another relationship that needed careful handling was that with Eisenhower. Harold Caccia, the British Ambassador in Washington, heard on 22 January that Eisenhower wanted to meet Macmillan as soon as possible. Although Caccia initially thought 'a later date than March'[70] would be preferable, to allow for detailed preparation, when it became clear that such an offer was 'most unlikely to recur' in the near future, Caccia advised that any *communiqué* 'should be as concrete and specific as possible'.[71] Norman Brook warned Macmillan that Eisenhower was 'ageing and tends increasingly to deal in generalities'.[72] A summit meeting was arranged in Bermuda from 21–24 March, a couple of weeks before the Budget. 'I feel that Eisenhower's inviting himself as our guest to Bermuda,' Macmillan confided to Eden, 'was in itself meant to be a friendly gesture.'[73] Macmillan had taken the precaution of consulting the French first, not that this courtesy was to do him much long-term good.

The British contingent consisted of Macmillan, accompanied by Norman Brook, the Cabinet Secretary, and Freddie Bishop; Selwyn Lloyd, the Foreign Secretary, with Patrick Dean and John Graham; plus an unusually large retinue of back-up staff. Dulles had already flown in by air and was installed at the Mid-Ocean Golf Club, the American headquarters. Eisenhower, not in the best of health, arrived later, having taken a leisurely and restorative sea voyage. Macmillan was particularly pleased that Bob Murphy was part of the American team, as it added to the sense of an old boys' reunion.

The whole island was *en fête*. The Union Jack and the Stars and Stripes flew from all public buildings. When Eisenhower landed at Hamilton, the band played the 'Star-Spangled Banner' twice and an 84-gun salute was fired, which Eisenhower said was 'a lot of explosions in the cause of peace'.[74] The only discontent was expressed by the golf professional at the Mid-Ocean Club, because his shop had to close for the duration.

Despite the recent Suez debacle, Eisenhower and Macmillan greeted each other like long-lost friends. Selwyn Lloyd, acting as a 'pair' for

Dulles, felt isolated as Macmillan and Eisenhower sat long into the night reliving their days in North Africa. Despite the unseasonal weather, Lloyd took early-morning swims with Dulles (who sported uncharacteristically gaudy shorts), while security men hovered with snorkels.

Eisenhower let Macmillan know, through Dulles, how personally affronted he felt by continued criticism of him in the British press. Differences about Egypt and Nasser also contributed to the tension. In addition, Eisenhower was not happy about the effect British defence cuts might have on NATO. Gradually, though, the atmosphere improved. Macmillan was always effective in a gregarious setting, and his reflections on the sweep of history from Queen Victoria's days and the fall of the Austro-Hungarian Empire helped set current problems in their context. During the conference he was getting reports about difficulties at home, but he did not betray any sense of these anxieties. The final protocol showed agreement in three areas: the Americans would work with the Military Committee of the Baghdad Pact; intermediate range ballistic missiles would be provided for Britain; and nuclear tests would, for the time, continue. Disagreements still remained over the Middle East, but Caccia was able to work, post-Bermuda, with officials at the State Department to minimise these. The conference ended amiably. The sun shone at last. Ike got some golf at the Mid-Ocean Club, finding the famous fifth hole over Mangrove Lake a difficult proposition. Macmillan now relaxed. 'Not at all like an experience in the modern world,' he said. 'More like meeting George III at Brighton.'[75]

Macmillan returned to London to find problems over Cyprus. On 28 March, the government announced that Archbishop Makarios would be released from detention in the Seychelles, where he had been exiled since March 1956, a decision Macmillan had made before leaving for Bermuda, but confirmed there in consultation with Lloyd, after Eisenhower requested Makarios' release.

During Macmillan's time in Bermuda, EOKA (the National Organisation of Cypriot Fighters) had issued leaflets saying that a ceasefire would follow if Makarios' detention was ended. Macmillan was prepared to take the risk, even giving up Cyprus if necessary. 'There was little point in him going to Bermuda and claiming a new start,' S. J. Ball has written, 'if Britain was made to look like an imperialist dinosaur by a Cypriot priest.'[76] Salisbury refused to accept the decision as either inevitable or right and resigned from government. Macmillan swiftly reshuffled his team. Lord Home added the leadership of the

Lords to his responsibilities as Commonwealth Secretary in the Lords, and became Lord President of the Council.

Bobbety Salisbury later poured out his feelings to Anthony Eden: 'I cannot with the best will in the world get on with your successor. It isn't that I don't think him a very able man. I do; and if I had to advise the Queen again, I should give the same advice as before. But his mind and mine don't click; and he knows that as well as I do. So it is really better that he should go his own way; and run things his own way.'[77]

Salisbury's resignation was a moment of immense symbolic importance for Macmillan. As Anthony Sampson has observed, 'Macmillan did not feel entirely on top of the aristocracy until he had not only bcome Prime Minister, but had sacked his cousin Lord Salisbury.'[78] The departure was also important for the aristocratic tradition in British public life. Chatsworth and Hatfield could no longer sneer at the shy, bespectacled, goofy-toothed bore, 'Mr Harold', as they had done in pre-war days. 'Bad teeth in politics are not good,' Howard Brenton's Macmillan says in the opening speech of the play *Never So Good*. 'It's cruel, but people will always make moral judgments from appearances.'[79] Macmillan had had his teeth fixed, a sign of his seriousness; he had seen off Salisbury, a sign of his resolve. 'Mr Harold' was now without question a leader of consequence.

Many had mistakenly thought that a Conservative government needed a Cecil to bolster its standing. After all, 'the Cecils are deaf to the howling of the mob'.[80] Yet when Bobbety Salisbury – a scion of the Cecil family – resigned, not a dog barked. The Cecils, were not, after all, indispensable to a Conservative government. It was the most ineffective resignation since Lord Randolph Churchill had 'forgot Goschen' in December 1886.[81] Life carried on, and Macmillan now dominated his Cabinet, by age, by experience and by subtlety. He had shown that he knew how to operate the levers of power.

Salisbury had, in effect, been driven into resigning by Macmillan. Outwardly the formal proprieties were maintained. 'One thing comforts me,' Macmillan wrote in reply to Salisbury's letter of resignation, 'you refer to my old friendship: that we can surely keep.'[82] In private, Macmillan, who always thought the Cecils had resigning minds, recorded in his diary what he really thought. 'All through history, the Cecils, when any friend or colleague has been in real trouble, have stabbed him in the back – attributing the crime to qualms of conscience.'[83]

Salisbury's departure cleared the way for Macmillan to run his government in the way he wanted, not always having to look over his shoulder to see what the imperialist right wing of the party was thinking. The second wave of decolonisation could now proceed more smoothly, and in 1957 Ghana, Malaya and Singapore all became self-governing. Macmillan now exhibited a new confidence. If he could see off Bobbety Salisbury, then Hugh Gaitskell, 'the sanctimonious Wykehamist with gestures like an Armenian shopkeeper', would remain merely an irritant.

Several issues were on the agenda in Parliament on 1 April. The government had announced in March that H-bombs would be tested on Christmas Island. Macmillan knew how divisive this issue was for the Labour Party. Even Gaitskell's sympathetic biographer, Philip Williams, admitted how successfully Macmillan took the initiative in the House that day. 'The Prime Minister skilfully diverted attention from Salisbury's resignation two days earlier (which he did not even mention) and from Suez (so contentious within his own party) to the nuclear issue.' He asked Gaitskell directly 'to say whether in office Labour would stop the tests, abandon the bomb, and so accept both permanent conscription and military inferiority against Russia'.[84] Forced on to the back foot, Gaitskell could only equivocate and say that such a decision would be taken in government. The Tory press savaged him for his reply.

The Suez debate was also a hurdle successfully cleared, at least as far as the voting went. The Opposition censure motion was defeated by 308 votes to 259. Macmillan had taken nothing for granted. He spent the whole of Sunday, 12 May, drafting his statement, which he made at 3.30 p.m. on 13 May. He then worked late on 14 May in Downing Street for his opening speech in the debate. Nevertheless, he was thrown by the continual barracking and catcalls from the Opposition benches and admitted that his speech was not a success. He was still deeply upset by the news of the sudden and mysterious death of his brother Daniel's wife.

An unexpected reprieve for Macmillan came on the last day of the debate (17 May), when the speech of the Shadow Foreign Affairs spokesman, Aneurin Bevan, failed to make an impact. 'It was rather like my speech yesterday, though (I think) worse',[85] Macmillan wrote in his diary. Macmillan's own speech, winding up the debate, was, by contrast, extremely effective, pointing to the divisisons between Gaitskell and Bevan on the Eisenhower Doctrine. 'The whole Tory party stood up and cheered me,' he wrote of the scene when the vote was announced. 'At the Speaker's Chair, I turned and bowed. It was an extraordinary and spontaneous act of loyalty and touched me very much. How odd the English are! They rather like a gallant failure. Suez has become a kind of Mons retreat. Anyway, we're through this particular trouble – at least for the moment.'[86]

Macmillan's initial prophecy of a mere six weeks' government was now quite superseded. His hold over the party, though not complete, was improving all the time. He was beginning to inspire not merely loyalty, but also affection. The Tories really had found a 'card', and they rejoiced in Gaitskell's discomfiture.

The return of John Wyndham to the team had helped. 'We seem to have got over quite a number of jumps in this Grand National Course,' Macmillan wrote to him, 'and having just managed to pull the old mare through the brook with the same jockey up, and the Cecil colours fallen, I am plucking up my courage.'[87]

In fact, the summer of 1957 proved a time of stability, even popular success. The H-bomb tests on Christmas Island had gone well. Macmillan received the Freedom of Bromley in a colourful ceremony. A visit to Edinburgh for the General Assembly of the Church of Scotland was followed by a day's golf at Muirfield. He wrote thanking the Honourable Company of Edinburgh Golfers for allowing him to play on 'your magnificent course'.[88] On the way south he revisited old haunts and spoke to an enthusiastic crowd at Stockton Race Course. He also presided with aplomb over the conference of Commonwealth Prime Ministers from 26 June to 5 July. Its success was the genesis of Macmillan's Commonwealth Tour of 1958, the first such ever undertaken by a serving Prime Minister. Churchill had attended one of the formal dinners and Macmillan proved an attentive host, smoothing over political differences. Even *The Times*, not the most sympathetic of observers of Macmillan's government declared that 'the Conference has been a personal success for Mr Macmillan'.[89]

Although it was not the most important speech of his career, Macmillan's declaration, on 20 July 1957 at Bedford football ground, that 'most of our people have never had it so good' was certainly the most famous. The phrase 'never had it so good' became the iconic description of his age, and provided many authors with titles,[90] as well as images for many cartoonists.

As with many other utterances remembered most of all for a single, captivating phrase – Margaret Thatcher's 'There is no such thing as Society',[91] for instance – the 'never so good' speech has been misinterpreted in popular mythology. Critics have taken it as an example of Macmillan's smug materialism, complacent and self-satisfied. Nothing could be further from the truth. The speech was not complacent; it was a warning *against* complacency. The famous phrase by which the speech is remembered was first used that afternoon at Bedford as a rebuke and rejoinder to a persistent heckler. '"*You've* never had it so good",' Macmillan later told David Butler, then researching his book on the 1959 general election, 'was actually delivered at a young boiler-suited heckler and was meant to contrast his position with that of pensioners on a fixed income; i.e. aimed at a particular person, not the electorate at large.'[92]

The speech had been planned to celebrate the Silver Jubilee of Alan Lennox-Boyd's time as MP for Bedford. Macmillan used the occasion to give a grand *tour d'horizon* of Britain's economic position. Thorneycroft had warned him that Britain was living beyond its means, and that inflation was now a real danger. The recent run on the pound had seen gold reserves falling, and even devaluation, usually associated with Labour governments,[93] could not be ruled out. It was against this background that Macmillan spoke. The weather may have been fine, and the children happily munching on candy floss[94] ('the candy floss society' was what critics later dubbed the era), but Macmillan put a damper on the proceedings. He warned people against thinking that the good times would endure indefinitely. 'What is beginning to worry some of us is "Is it too good to be true?", or perhaps I should say "Is it too good to last?"'[95]

Bedford was one of the last great examples of a major political speech freely open to the public. Gladstone had regularly addressed thouands in his day on the slopes of Mount Snowdon, and Churchill had been brought up in the same tradition of mass gatherings. Macmillan's 'never so good' speech was not a ticketed event. Later, 'spin doctors' would have counselled against the risks. There was no need in July 1957. Despite the economic warnings Macmillan delivered, the people cheered, which either showed they had not fully understood the message, or that they approved of the messenger. Macmillan's speech was one of the last manifestations of a dying tradition, before television largely took over. The fact that he could hold a big crowd in thrall was a clear indication of how far he had come from the shy back-bencher of his early days. The transition was the product of hard work and careful preparation. Macmillan had even taken advice from members of the popular comic act the Crazy Gang[96] on how to project himself to an audience.

By the time of the parliamentary recess, Macmillan could be pleased, on balance, by the way things had gone.

'Macmillan is cool, calm and radiates self-confidence,' noted the

Indianapolis Star. 'He has been Prime Minister for only six months, but he has already managed to change completely the British political scene. There is above all a marked improvement in United States–British relations.'[97] Selwyn Lloyd, who had observed Macmillan at this time as closely as any, recorded his own interim verdict on the Prime Minister's style:

He believed in the Presidential form of Government. He modelled himself upon an American President, with subordinates, not colleagues. He could be close to some, and treat them as intimate and trusted friends, just as Eisenhower was close to Foster Dulles and George Humphrey. But most of his ministers he would talk about as though they were junior officers in a unit he commanded. He welcomed Lord Salisbury's resignation in 1957 because it removed the only member of the Cabinet who was a contemporary and his equal in experience and authority. He regarded the Cabinet as an instrument for him to play upon, a body to be moulded to his will and it was entertaining to watch him handle with infinite pains the obstinate or the uncertain. Very rarely did he fail to get his own way, but by determined and subtle persuasion.[98]

August saw Macmillan taking his customary holiday at Bolton Abbey with the Devonshires, followed by a spell in the Highlands, where he played classic golf courses, including Dornoch[99] and Brora. From there he went to Balmoral as the weekend guest, with Lady Dorothy, of the Queen and Prince Philip. Although the Queen and Macmillan came to understand each other's ways, this first visit was not easy. Macmillan was unsure whether the visit was social, with 'shop' relegated to the margins, or a Highlands version of his weekly audiences with the Queen at Buckingham Palace.[100] The robust opinions of Prince Philip came as a shock. 'I don't altogether like the tone of his talk,' Macmillan confided to his diary. 'It is too like that of a clever undergraduate, who has just discovered Socialism.'[101] Macmillan used his Cabinet as a sounding board, often floating kites to see the reaction. He did not find it so welcome when he was the sounding board.

The illusory summer calm was now disrupted by fresh trouble in the Middle East, where there was rebellion against the rule of the Sultan of Muscat and Oman. The Eisenhower Doctrine did not apply to what the Americans considered internal difficulties. When Britain alone went to the aid of the Sultan, deploying the RAF, Macmillan thought 'the Americans are behaving outrageously to us about Oman', and he dispatched stiff telegrams to Eisenhower. 'He answers agreeably enough,' Macmillan recorded, 'but does nothing.'[102] The potential for a another Suez-type Anglo-American rift was considerable, but further trouble brought a change of attitude from the Americans.

The second Middle East crisis was potentially serious. The Russians were threatening a Communist takeover of Syria. As oil from Saudi Arabia and Iraq passed through Syria, Britain and America could not stand aside. On 9 October, Macmillan wrote to Eisenhower proposing a meeting in Washington. His underlying purpose was to build on the foundations laid at Bermuda, but with specific reference to the Russian threat. His request fell on fruitful ground. Shortly before Macmillan's departure for Washington, the Russians had launched their first Sputnik[103] satellite, which, bleeping as it went, put a girdle around the earth in 95 minutes, not quite as swiftly as Puck, but still a worrying portent of what might be expected by way of the Soviet capacity to launch missiles.[104] 'The Russian success in launching the satellite has been something equivalent to Pearl Harbour,' Macmillan wrote in his diary. 'The American cocksureness is shaken.'[105] Sputnik was a wake-up call. Only if America and Britain worked together against such threats could their mutual interests be protected.

Joint action with the Americans had the desired effect. The Russian leader Nikita Khrushchev said the whole episode had been misunderstood and that there was no threat of Russian incursion into Syria. Macmillan wrote warmly to Eisenhower, saying that he was 'tremendously impressed by the work our people have been doing together on the Syrian problem'. It was like the Anglo-American partnership in the war. 'I would like to see this sort of co-operation continued with a view to our working out together the role of the free countries in the struggle against Communist Russia.'[106] Although Bermuda had made more headlines, the co-operation over Syria was of deeper significance.

The visit to Washington from 23–25 October proved far more substantive than Bermuda. One of Macmillan's concerns was the McMahon Act of 1946 and future sharing of nuclear information between Britain and America. The American Atomic Energy Act of 1946, sponsored by Brian McMahon, the Democrat Senator from which it took its name, had decreed that no information on atomic technology should be shared with other nations, even friendly allies. This seemed to Macmillan a lasting reproach to the British scientists who had helped on the Manhattan Project that had created the atomic bomb in 1945. On arrival he found that Eisenhower felt the same. Eisenhower described the McMahon Act as 'one of the most deplorable incidents in American history'.[107] Working groups were established on nuclear co-operation. The same month, the Queen made a visit to America to mark the three hundred and fiftieth anniversary of the foundation of Jamestown, Virginia. The combination of the two visits helped to exorcise the spirit of both Suez and George III. A Declaration of Common Purpose was signed between Britain and America.[108]

When Macmillan addressed the House of Commons at the opening of the new session on 5 November, he was able to proclaim with justification that 'this new situation in the United States will be of far-reaching importance to us all'.[109] The situation, for the first time since Suez, had been transformed.

What had not been transformed was the economic situation, following Thorneycroft's earlier dire warnings. On 24 August, Macmillan had discussed the weakness of sterling with his Chancellor. The battle lines were rapidly drawn. Thorneycroft believed that it was essential to reduce the money supply, and he found Leslie Rowan his best ally in the forthcoming struggles. Protecting sterling was paramount. Macmillan was reliant, over-reliant for many, on advice from Roy Harrod. On 7 September Macmillan received a forceful missive from Harrod.

> The idea that you can reduce prices by limiting the quantity of money is pre-Keynesian. Hardly any economist under the age of 50 subscribes to it. If it were supposed the Conservatives were associated with any such idea, that might drive many middle of the way economists into the ranks of Labour and what is more Gaitskell could probably succeed in galvanizing them all into lambasting and ridiculing this policy. I do sincerely hope that no goverment speaker subscribes to such an antiquated doctrine.[110]

Harrod's advice was a considerable annoyance to Sir Robert Hall and his successor as the government's Chief Economic Adviser, Sir Alec Cairncross, who had to devote additional time, in their already crowded schedules, to preparing replies for him.[111]

On 19 September, Thorneycroft raised the bank rate from 5 per cent to 7 per cent. Although Macmillan did not like the move, he could hardly complain, as he had raised the rate himself the previous year. Evelyn Baring, who had told the young Macmillan on his first night at Summer Fields that his situation was critical but not desperate, could have repeated his comment. On 1 October, Baring, now an important figure in the City, wrote to Thorneycroft, 'We have great hopes that this rise in bank rate may have a restraining influence on the amount of money borrowed from the banks, with the resultant strengthening of our reserves.'[112]

More damaging was the question of whether there had been a leak of the intended change in the bank rate, as many dealers sustained major losses. There were calls for an inquiry, which Macmillan authorised, on advice from the Conservative Party's chairman, Oliver Poole, a senior figure at Lazard's. The Bank Rate Tribunal, under Lord Justice Parker, began its deliberations on 26 October. When it reported on 21 January 1958, it concluded that there was no justification to allegations that there had been improper disclosures. Thorneycroft had already commented sardonically that 'the main complaint in the City appeared to be not that there had been a leakage of information but there had not'.[113]

One of the more curious, and better-hidden, events of Macmillan's first year in Downing Street was the Windscale fire on 10 October. The incident is not mentioned in Macmillan's memoirs, yet the potential for ecological damage, as well as political, was immense. On 10 October, a graphite core in the nuclear reactor in the village of Seascale in Cumberland, had caught fire, releasing radioactive iodine into the atmosphere, one of the worst such nuclear accidents until the Chernobyl disaster in 1986. There was a threat to milk supplies in 150 farms in the 200 square miles around the site. Cinema newsreels showed urns of milk being emptied into drains. Evacuation of the area was not ruled out.

Macmillan ordered an immediate inquiry under Sir William Penney.[114] He was committed to nuclear research, recognising the importance of a co-ordinated defence and energy policy. Calder Hall, the first of Britain's civil nuclear power stations, supplying electricity to the National Grid, had been opened by the Queen in 1956. Ironically, since the Americans at this time were proving more open over nuclear matters, Macmillan felt that he was not justified in reciprocating over many of the technicalities of Calder Hall, as the details were too sensitive commercially. Meanwhile, CND was making much of the running in influencing public opinion against anything 'nuclear'. Macmillan received Penney's report on 'Windscale' on 28 October. This identified faults in procedure and organisation, and recommended reforms. 'How are we to deal with Sir W. Penney's report?' Macmillan pondered in his diary on 30 October. 'It has, of course, been prepared with scrupulous honesty and even ruthlessness.'[115] If the full extent of the failings at Windscale were to be revealed publicly, Macmillan feared the US–UK nuclear collaboration might be seriously jeopardised, with the accident being used as ammunition by those in America who did not want to help Britain.

Macmillan decided on partial release of Penney's report, on grounds of national security and international relations. This (unjustly) led to the suspicion that Penney had conducted a whitewash.

'Windscale' was eased by the simultaneous controversy over the Bank Rate Tribunal, the Opposition never quite deciding on which to concentrate. Had Macmillan maintained a blanket of total secrecy over 'Windscale', he could have been accused of another 'Sèvres' (collusion and cover-up), but he handled the fall-out, political as well as scientific, with a ruthlessness quite the equal of Penney's report. Limited release fulfilled its purpose, while trans-Atlantic co-operation on nuclear policy was not jeopardised. Lord Plowden, Chairman of the Atomic Energy Authority, believed that Macmillan was fully justified, in the circumstances of the time, in restricting the publication of Penney's conclusions.[116] As the accident came at a relatively early stage of Britain's nuclear programme, 'Windscale' made everyone very safety conscious, and eventually led to the Nuclear Installations Inspectorate.

In the autumn of 1957, however, the enduring worry for Macmillan was not Sputnik, Syria, or Windscale, but the continuing debate over the future direction of economic policy. The Bedford speech had been delivered in the wake of Thorneycroft's warnings. 'We must be bold; caution is no good,' Macmillan wrote in his diary. 'All our political future depends on whether we can combine prosperity with stability.'[117] His aim, first and foremost, was to bring the country sustained prosperity. He agreed with his literary hero Trollope: 'After all, what is it that the Prime Minister of such a country as this should chiefly regard? Is it not the prosperity of the country?'[118]

On 1 September, Macmillan had set out his guidelines, and what he saw as the main dilemma, in a memorandum distributed to Cabinet:

To challenge a demand for more wages by a series of strikes is like King Canute trying to keep back the tide if (as seems to be the case) the demand for more wages is carried forward all the time on the rising tide of an ever increasing demand for labour. But all Trade Union leaders are in fact the same as any other merchant in a capitalist society. The commodity which they control is labour. The demand for labour is greater than the supply. Therefore, like those who control any commodity in such a situation, they cannot do anything except put up the price.[119]

What he could not have anticipated was the resignation of the entire Treasury team.

CHAPTER TWENTY TWO

Local Difficulties and Wider Visions

1958

I thought the best thing to do was to settle up these little local difficulties and then to turn to the wider vision of the Commonwealth.

Harold Macmillan, 7 January 1958

The Chancellor of the Exchequer and his two other ministers had resigned and Harold Macmillan gets into an aeroplane to go and fulfil an engagement in Australia the next morning. The press and television people come up and ask, 'What about these resignations?' He says, 'It's just a little local difficulty', and goes off to Australia. A frightfully good way of running a government.

John Wyndham

When in trouble, delegate.

James H. Boren

The financial crisis that erupted in January 1958 was one of the most dramatic of Macmillan's premiership. Its origins lay in the run on sterling and the subsequent emergency 'September measures' of 1957. Voluntary pay restraint had not worked. Both Eden and Macmillan had tried in May 1956 to persuade industry to keep to a price 'plateau', a forlorn attempt met with 'shattering silence'.[1] Thorneycroft now tacitly put aside the consensual post-war commitment to full employment in favour of establishing stability in internal price levels. Yet wage settlements continued to creep up alarmingly. In the summer of 1957, railway workers got a pay rise of 5 per cent, having rejected a pay tribunal award of 3 per cent. Then shipbuilding workers and engineers were awarded 6.5 per cent. On 20 July, the *Financial Times* declared that the government had 'given up the fight on inflation'.[2] The journalists had mistaken the Chancellor. Peter Thorneycroft never gave up. In July 1957, Macmillan, in close consultation with Thorneycroft, set up a three-man Council (soon dubbed 'the three wise men') on Prices, Productivity and Incomes, under the chairmanship of Lord

Cohen.[3] The Council's terms of reference were: 'Having regard to the desirability of full employment and increased standards of life based on expanding production and reasonable stability of prices, to keep under review changes in prices, productivity and the level of incomes (including wages, salaries and profits) and to report thereon from time to time.'[4] It was thus in essence the forerunner of the quest for a national incomes policy. It was not part of the government machine, more a body to inform the country of the development of, and the rationale behind, economic policy.

The contribution of Sir Dennis Robertson[5] to the Council's deliberations soon demonstrated that both wage and price rises were symptoms of excess demand, hence the need to restrain spending. Thorneycroft found this body far more supportive of his aims than Macmillan's placeman at the head of the Treasury, Roger Makins. 'He only comes in one day in three,' Thorneycroft complained to Powell, 'and when he does he's against me.'[6]

Meanwhile, there was growing discontent among core white-collar Conservative voters. Suburban voters, epitomised by the electorate in Macmillan's own constituency of Bromley, felt that their interests were being neglected. 'The mood today is to criticise everything,' Macmillan had written to Anthony Eden: one of many letters to his predecessor at this time in which he unburdened his feelings. 'It may pass, but I have never known the press and public so sensitive or so hyper-critical. I think it is really because they are all so terribly well off. English people never seem to show their best except when they are in great trouble.'[7]

Thorneycroft warned Macmillan that prices 'unless substantially checked will prove economically damaging and electorally disastrous'.[8] Roy Harrod was warning about the threat of rising unemployment. Macmillan bizarrely suspected that Thorneycroft and his two Treasury ministers – Powell and Birch – were plotting a challenge to his leadership, a view shared by his Chief Whip, Edward Heath,[9] and an indication of Macmillan's paranoia at the time.

The Treasury team and Thorneycroft's advisers were divided on how best to stem the rise in inflation. Should it be by a wages policy, or by controlling the money supply? Soon, Thorneycroft came to believe that 'a measure of deflation in the economy' would be necessary, and gave instructions to that effect to his officials on 7 August. The influence of Nigel Birch and Enoch Powell, both firm believers in sound money, was very evident in the subsequent deflationary response of 19 September, which was a new drive to halt inflation and maintain the value of sterling abroad. Not only was the bank rate hiked up to 7 per cent, the highest since the early 1920s, but public-sector investment was to be held for two years. The measures were described as 'early day monetarism' by John fforde, the historian of the Bank of England.[10]

'What Thorneycroft and those who thought like him were concerned with,' G.C. Peden has written, 'was the level of bank advances and the level of bank liquidity, arising from the financing of government expenditure through the sale to the banks of Treasury bills; no attempt was made to measure the money supply as a whole.'* [11]

Robert Hall, a Keynesian through and through, was horrified by the policy of economic restraint advocated by Thorneycroft. 'They would not listen to any suggestion,' he wrote in his diary, 'that what they were saying did not make much sense as economics.'[13] Hall was only dissuaded from resignation by Roger Makins, who advised him to back off, as it would not be too long before there was a new Chancellor.[14]

Macmillan too was receiving conflicting advice. The Robertson school, instinctively opposed to Keynesianism, believed that the problem was 'demand' inflation: 'too much money chasing too few goods', the Quantity Theory. On the other hand, the Roy Harrod school, which Macmillan followed, believed the problem was 'cost-push' inflation, brought about by trade union power. Concerned at the size of pay settlements, Macmillan circulated a minute to ministers on 10 August 1957 telling them to limit their departments' current expenditure in 1958/1959 to 1957/1958 levels.[15] Thorneycroft had good reason at this stage to think that he had Macmillan's support. When details of spending programmes were worked out, the difference between what Thorneycroft thought necessary by way of cuts, and what the Cabinet was prepared to back, was £50 million out of a total of £4,000 million. Had the timetable allowed it, an acceptable figure could probably have been negotiated.[16] After all, £50 million amounted (depending on the precise statistics followed) to half a penny per head of the tax-paying population, and only 1 per cent

---

*Nevertheless, the Thorneycroft resignation was later seen by Thatcherites as the first shoots of what they regarded as realism. Margaret Thatcher's appointment of Thorneycroft as Conservative Party chairman in 1975 was a tacit acknowledgment of her approval of his stance. Similarly, Macmillan's choice of Stockton, a place of pre-war unemployment, as the name of his hereditary earldom on his ninetieth birthday in 1984 was a coded rebuke to the whole drift of Thatcherite monetarist policy. Some arguments are never resolved.

Interestingly, when Mrs Thatcher became Prime Minister in 1979, she asked Macmillan for his advice on economic policy. In his first response Macmillan harked back to 1958: 'The so-called "money supply" policy may be useful as a guide to what is happening, just as a speedometer is in a car,' he wrote, 'but like the speedometer it cannot make the machine go faster or slower.'[12]

of government expenditure. However, Macmillan's departure on 7 January for his Commonwealth tour made this impossible in the time available. By the time of the Christmas recess, Macmillan had clearly backed down from the firmness of his 7 August instruction on public spending. Even the September measures, backed by the Cabinet at the time, were no longer sacrosanct in his mind. This change of heart was puzzling to Thorneycroft and has never been satisfactorily explained. The key surely is that the shadow of pre-war depression was never forgotten by Macmillan. It was increasingly clear that he did not want to preside now over any repetition.

Macmillan and Thorneycroft met on 22 December, the Prime Minister coming up to London specially from Birch Grove for the meeting. Thorneycroft spelt out his concerns about the civil estimates, concentrating particularly on the cost of pensions, education and agricultural subsidies. 'The Chancellor wants some swingeing cuts in the Welfare State expenditure,' Macmillan recorded in his diary, 'more, I fear, than is feasible politically.'[17] Macmillan placed political considerations at this time above economic ones.

Thorneycroft wanted overall cuts of £153 million, and spending ministers were asked to consider options over Christmas. By the time the Cabinet met again in the New Year, a figure of £100 million had been painfully negotiated. Thorneycroft, though, was not satisfied. On 1 January, the Treasury informed ministers of proposals to end the family allowance for the second child, together with an increase in the NHS element of the National Insurance stamp. At a meeting next day of a small group of senior ministers (Macmillan, Thorneycroft, Butler, Hailsham and Sandys), Thorneycroft made it clear that he would resign if the 1958/1959 estimates were not at the same level as those for 1957/1958. The lines were drawn.

On one side were the money supply theorists, on the other the Keynesians. In political terms it was a straight clash between Thorneycroft and Macmillan.

At eleven o'clock on Friday, 3 January, the Cabinet met in a tense atmosphere. Its numbers were boosted by the attendance of John Boyd-Carpenter, the Minister of Pensions and National Insurance, Derek Walker-Smith, the Minister of Health, and Reggie Maudling, the Paymaster General. Although Duncan Sandys, the Minister of Defence, offered a further £5m cut in his department's expenditure, the overall gap in reductions, give or take, was still in the region of £50 million, and this was Thorneycroft's sticking point. Duncan Sandys warned that cuts beyond the extra £5 million he had proposed were the absolute limit. Military cuts could lead to the resignation of the Secretary of State for War (John Hare) and the Chief of the Imperial General Staff (Field Marshal Sir Gerald Templer), and, by implication, himself. Failure to curb civil costs threatened the resignation of the Chancellor.

The meeting then moved on to consider civil expenditure. Both Boyd-Carpenter and Walker-Smith spoke out against the proposed changes to family allowances, and possibly to the NHS. Maudling took a tougher line, which his biographer postulates 'may have been influenced by his hopes of promotion in the event of the Chancellor resigning'.[18] If so, he was to be disappointed. As further negotiations were clearly going to be necessary, the Cabinet adjourned until 4.30 p.m.

At the resumption, Macmillan outlined in detail the suggested economies. Talk then centred on the National Insurance fund, to which Thorneycroft responded 'somewhat ungraciously', according to John Boyd-Carpenter.[19] Eventually the Cabinet adjourned at 6 p.m. for 30 minutes to allow Thorneycroft, at his own request, to consider his position.

When the Cabinet reassembled half an hour later, Thorneycroft and Kilmuir, the Lord Chancellor, were not present. Gallows humour prevailed as Rab Butler, the Home Secretary, was then asked whether he ought not to have the lake in St James's Park dragged.[20] At 6.42 Kilmuir reappeared, to be asked by his fellow lawyer, Lord Hailsham, whether the jury was going to be out for much longer. Responding in kind, Kilmuir said that he was the foreman come to ask a question. He then outlined Thorneycroft's conditions if he was not to resign. Arguments followed on details, but Macmillan drew the inconclusive meeting to an end. Further discussions would take place over the weekend, 'and if on Monday agreement couldn't be reached, following discussions at weekend, he would have to consider question of placing resignation of [the] Government in the hands of the Queen'.[21] Macmillan, of course, had no such intention. His tactical ploy was to bring the issue to a head, if necessary by forcing Thorneycroft out, almost goading him to depart. Macmillan had survived Salisbury's departure; Thorneycroft's, though inconvenient, would not be fatal.

On Sunday, 5 January, Macmillan saw Thorneycroft at 10.30 a.m. and appealed to him to accept the Cabinet's collective view. Thorneycroft was not in a conciliatory mood, and Macmillan rightly suspected the influence of Nigel Birch and Enoch Powell in his Chancellor's obduracy. Macmillan regarded the first as a 'cynic', the second as 'a fanatic'.[22] Birch and Powell had already agreed between themselves that if the Chancellor went, they would go also.[23] Macmillan and Powell, in particular, had a great and lasting distaste for each other, stemming from the time when Macmillan had outmanoeuvred Butler at the 1922 Committee meeting on Suez in December 1956. When Powell later returned to Cabinet as Minister of Health, Macmillan always made sure he was seated in a place where he would not be forced to see Powell's piercing eyes.

There was no turning back. At 10.30 a.m. on 6 January, Thorneycroft saw Macmillan and gave him his letter of resignation. He also handed over similar letters from Nigel Birch and Enoch Powell. At the Cabinet meeting at 11 a.m., Macmillan read out the three letters to his colleagues. The rest of the day was occupied with the consequent reshuffle, a visit to the Queen at Buckingham Palace with a list of the proposed changes, a reception for the Commonwealth High Commissioners, and final preparations for his departure the next morning on the Commonwealth tour.

The exchange of letters between Macmillan and Thorneycroft was unexpectedly crisp on both sides. 'I am not prepared to approve estimates for the Government's current expenditure next year at a total higher than the sum that will be spent this year,' Thorneycroft wrote. 'Your proposed departure from this country on the 7th January has made it essential that a decision of principle upon this matter be taken now.' Macmillan's reply, mistakenly dated 1957, was equally forthright. 'Your resignation at the present time cannot help to sustain and may damage the interests which we have all been trying to preserve.'[24]

Lord Cobbold, the Governor of the Bank of England, sent Macmillan a barely disguised rebuke. 'I should always feel chary about resignations over comparatively small figures but feeling as he does on the question of principle, I myself think he is right.' For Cobbold, Thorneycroft's departure marked a missed opportunity to get the economy under control. 'I am very sorry, because I felt that with P.T.'s courage and with you behind him at No. 10, we were on an improving wicket from the currency's point of view.'[25]

How was Macmillan now to adhere to the broad outlines of Thorneycroft's policy, without openly admitting it? This required a conjuring trick that he would delegate to the new Chancellor.

Macmillan could afford Thorneycroft's resignation, embarrassing though its timing was; what he had to avoid were mass resignations from the Cabinet. Individual spending ministers were fighting their corner for their own departments. Thorneycroft's departure would keep such ministers on board, not to mention allowing the possibility of economic expansion before the next election. The crisis, however, beginning with the run on sterling and the fall in the reserves, and ending with the Treasury team's resignation, was not, as Macmillan claimed, 'a little local difficulty', but a turning point in post-war economic policy. David Kynaston has described it as 'one of the classic episodes of post-war British history – political and social, as well as financial.'[26] Ahead lay all the landmarks of a stop/go economy – George Brown's National Plan of 1964, the Wilson freeze of July 1966, devaluation in 1967, the Heath/Barber era leading to rampant inflation, and the coal crisis of 1972.*

Thorneycroft's September measures were not actually about 'the supply of money', as it was, and is, understood by economic theory. The September 1957 rise in bank rate was primarily prompted by the need to protect the foreign exchange reserves. The control of public expenditure in the 1958 Budget was to keep aggregate demand under control, thus preventing an escalation of inflation. With no increase in Government spending to be financed it would also keep bank advances steady. In that sense, Thorneycroft did not represent, as often supposed, the first shoots of Thatcherite monetarism. Even Enoch Powell, the driving force behind the resignations, said it was but 'a gleam in the eye' of monetarism.[27]

Macmillan could not complain about Thorneycroft's resignation; he had threatened resignation himself a year earlier over milk and bread subsidies. The difference was that then his will prevailed. The importance of Thorneycroft's resignation was that it demonstrated in sharp focus the fault line between the post-war consensus-driven Keynesians, committed to the 1944 goal of full employment, and those, both economists and politicians, who believed that only by slaying the dragon of inflation could unemployment be permanently reduced and kept low. The contrasting choices were financial and political. Macmillan favoured the political, but it was not expediency. He held a different view, which – whether right or wrong – was as much based on principle as Thorneycroft's was. Arguably, Macmillan was right.

How incomes should be redistributed was the insoluble problem, and not only for Macmillan's government. 'The trade unions saw redistribution away from profits, property incomes, and higher salaries

---

*The Thorneycroft resignation was a Conservative version of that of Aneurin Bevan from the Labour Cabinet in April 1951, albeit in reverse form. The difference then was that the three resigning ministers (Bevan, Harold Wilson and John Freeman) were against the imposition of deflationary measures. Also, owing to Macmillan's swift handling of the fall-out, and Thorneycroft's unwillingness to rock the boat further, a major party split on economic direction was avoided, at least until Mrs Thatcher took up the monetarist cudgels two decades later.

in favour of wages as being part of their purpose', A. E. Holmans has written. 'The "discontented middle class" plus some at least in the City and in business management wanted the exact opposite. Anything that conciliated the one would offend the other.'[28] Successive governments oscillated between the two objectives for 20 years. Peter Thorneycroft's departure marked only a temporary end to the doctrine of economic liberalism underpinned by sound money.

Thorneycroft's resignation was not entirely unexpected to Macmillan, even if the exact timing was. He had already considered who might be the new Chancellor, so the suddenness of Thorneycroft's departure, on the eve of Macmillan's Commonwealth tour, caused less difficulty than it might have done. Macmillan's choice fell on Derick Heathcoat Amory, whose pre-war business career in the textile industry in Tiverton had instilled in him a loathing of unemployment. The appointment was essentially a holding operation. Although Macmillan thought Amory rigid and not over-clever, he was still for Macmillan the outstanding 'Stockton' candidate for the post. He was also a saintly figure with a profound sense of duty, who would take on any task he was asked to do, however unpalatable. The 'daring' appointment would have been to promote Reginald Maudling, the Paymaster General, to the post.[29] If Macmillan had not been about to depart the country, this might have been negotiated. Other possible candidates, also with economic experience, were either too junior (John Boyd-Carpenter, Derek Walker-Smith and Aubrey Jones) or too embroiled in important tasks (Selwyn Lloyd).

Macmillan rightly calculated that Amory's appointment would restore business confidence in the government. Moreover, Amory was not only a 'safe pair of hands', but, Macmillan believed, more malleable than Thorneycroft. Amory delivered, at the same time maintaining there was no departure from previous policy. Many believed him, and those who did not favoured the change in any case. Amory's work on the Agriculture Act of 1957 had led him to liaise with the Treasury on price support for farmers, so he was not coming to his task without first-hand knowledge of the prevailing economic conditions.

Macmillan's choice of Amory strengthened his hold even further over the post-Salisbury Cabinet. He now had a Foreign Secretary and a Chancellor, 'neither of whom', wrote Edmund Dell, 'had regarded themselves as serious contenders for the high positions they now held and both of whom were prepared to defer to their maker'.[30] One of the precepts of the American Democratic politician James H. Boren was 'when in trouble, delegate'. Macmillan went one better. He delegated the immediate problems to his new Chancellor, whilst at the same time maintaining overall control, as Amory was soon to find.

The consequential mini-reshuffle was quickly organised. The post of Economic Secretary to the Treasury was left vacant for the time being, though Reginald Maudling was drafted in to help. Roger Makins directed that, among other things, 'Mr Maudling would take the parliamentary work, including the Parliamentary Questions, which would normally fall within the Economic Secretary's sphere.'[31]

The next day the Cabinet showed solidarity by loyally seeing Macmillan off on his Commonwealth tour from Heathrow airport. In a strange way, the episode strengthened Macmillan's position. Interviewed before boarding his plane, he referred to the events surrounding Thorneycroft's resignation as 'these little local difficulties', then 'goes off to Australia – a frightfully good way to run a Government', as John Wyndham recorded.[32] The public thought so too, and the moment became the most celebrated example of Macmillan's 'unflappability'. However, as so often, the outward pose disguised Macmillan's very real (albeit unfounded) fears about the survival of his government. From Pakistan in a letter to the Chief Whip he admitted that the whole business had been 'a very serious shock'.[33]

Shrewdly, Macmillan realised that Thorneycroft's principled stance had struck a chord with an important segment of Conservative support, and in 1960 he brought him back into government as Minister of Aviation, and subsequently, from 1962, as Minister of Defence.

A few weeks before his tour, Macmillan had received a letter from a schoolgirl in Newcastle, inviting him to her twelfth birthday party on 11 January 1958. So assured was the letter that the secretarial team took the precaution of asking if the family were known to the Prime Minister. Macmillan had never heard of them, but he took time to write back to the little girl, explaining why he could not be there. 'I shall be leaving England early in the New Year on my Commonwealth Tour when I shall be visiting India, Pakistan, Ceylon, Singapore, New Zealand and Australia. If you will look at your school atlas, you will see what a very long journey it will be.' On his return, he got another letter from the girl saying that she had followed his journeys in her atlas, and that when she grew up she would also like to be Prime Minister.[34]

Macmillan's party included Lady Dorothy, Norman Brook, John Wyndham, Neil Cairncross, Harold Evans, and Jane Parsons from the team of Number 10 secretaries, known as Garden Room Girls.[35] The first stop was Delhi. Memories of the Raj were still discernible, not least in the lavish receptions. The Macmillans were guests at a garden party and a dinner at the former Viceregal Lodge, which Macmillan had last visited in Lord Wavell's final phase as Viceroy. At one stage during the banquet, Prime Minister Nehru asked Macmillan, 'I wonder if the Romans ever went back to visit Britain?'[36]

Political talks followed, mainly on the disputes over Kashmir. Nehru told Macmillan that progress was not possible on the issue as the Pakistan government seemed to change every few months. Nehru was more optimistic about his Five Year Plan and its part in stemming Communist pressures. Macmillan felt this was right. 'The Congress Party is in a sense in the position of the Irish Party after Home Rule,' he wrote, 'it cannot just live on the claim that it made the revolution.'[37] Macmillan laid a wreath at Raj Ghat, the spot where Gandhi had been cremated on the banks of the Jumna River. Vast crowds greeted him. 'You've only got to raise your hands and say "my friends!" and you get an immediate response.'[38]

From India he went on to Pakistan, a much less stable country politically. There were none of the welcoming crowds of New Delhi, nor the high intellectualism that characterised Indian politics. Macmillan found it like travelling from Hampstead or North Oxford to the shires.[39]

Ceylon was altogether cheerier. Macmillan addressed the Parliament on 17 January and was taken to the Temple of the Tooth in Kandy. A brief stop in Singapore saw the most overtly political event of the whole tour, the Annual Conference of the Commissioner for South-East Asia, a gathering determining defence policy for the region, and so important that the permanent Under-Secretary of the Foreign Office, Derick Hoyer Millar, had flown out to attend. From Singapore, Macmillan had a long flight to New Zealand.

Macmillan always saw New Zealand, not just geographically, as a southern hemisphere version of Scotland. The welcome he received was heart-warming. Even after passing his first anniversary as Prime Minister, he was still finding his way, though he was skilful at disguising his diffidence and lack of confidence. Australia did wonders for his self-esteem. In other countries he had been received with respect, and, in New Zealand, enthusiasm. In Australia it was genuine affection. Undoubtedly it helped that the Australian Prime Minister was Macmillan's old friend, 'Bob' Menzies. Macmillan's speeches emphasised Australia's links with the 'Old Country', and the benefits on both sides of migration. On 31 January he addressed the Australian Cabinet. He also brought up the potentially difficult subject of Britain's possible future trading links with Europe. He spent his sixty-fourth birthday in Tasmania.

Macmillan made an astute decision when he opted to arrive at Melbourne airport at 5 p.m. As he explained later to Lord Carrington, Britain's High Commissioner in Australia, this would be when the offices were closing. Also, owing to strict licensing laws, the pubs closed at 6 p.m., so the people would be in a good mood, spilling out in large numbers by the time he arrived on the processional route from the airport.[40] He calculated correctly. The Melbourne crowds gave him a rousing welcome, even though many may not have known exactly who he was.

Throughout the 'bedding-in' period of his premiership, Macmillan had kept up contacts with his two predecessors. He lunched with Churchill at Chartwell on 5 January at the height of the Thorneycroft resignation crisis. The day before, news had broken of the death of one of their wartime colleagues, Sir John Anderson (Lord Waverley), an occasion for reminiscence and gratitude. Churchill liked to be in the know, and he reciprocated by informing Macmillan on 22 March of the early plans for Churchill College, Cambridge, which would be the war leader's national memorial. Macmillan found both Churchill and Eden invaluable as sounding boards, and on 15 March he lunched with the Edens at their home in Wiltshire, and shared his thoughts about his tour.

He had weekly audiences with the Queen, with whom he now discussed his impressions of his Commonwealth tour. As Head of the Commonwealth, the Queen had undertaken a similar, but even more ambitious, six-month tour in 1954. Now Monarch and Prime Minister compared notes; Macmillan found the Queen's views immensely valuable.

The benefits of the Commonwealth tour, though, seemed short-lived. Two by-elections were lost, and on 27 March, Mark Bonham-Carter, the Liberal candidate, won Torrington, Devon, with a majority of 219, overturning a Conservative majority of 9,000.[41] Although Torrington was a narrow Liberal victory numerically, Macmillan felt the psychological impact would be severe. 'I'm afraid the triumph of the Asquiths (Violet Bonham Carter and her son) will encourage the Liberals elsewhere.'[42] Since November 1956, the Liberals had been led by Jo Grimond,[43] son-in-law of Lady Violet Bonham Carter, an attractive, popular figure who was reviving Liberal fortunes.

The Liberals were for Macmillan a thorn in the side of the

Conservatives, helping Labour by siphoning off votes that he hoped would come to a progressive Conservative Party. He took every opportunity of belittling them.

The pressure on Derry Amory when he arrived at the Treasury was to bring a halt to the rise in the cost of living. This required a careful balance if he was not to spark off another hike in wage settlements. Foreign investors must not be frightened off either. In fact Amory established a fine record in that his two and a half years as Chancellor saw prices rise by less than 1 per cent, an enviable achievement, particularly as the pressures from Macmillan (backed by Roy Harrod) were always for expansion.

The bank rate was cut to 6 per cent on 20 March. In the Budget on 15 April Amory introduced tax cuts of £50 million, which made some wonder what all the fuss had been over Thorneycroft. 'I would like to re-emphasise,' Amory said in his Budget speech, 'that, as a Government, we are convinced that the long-term welfare of this country demands a steady expansion of our national economy. That is the objective of all our policies. We shall not, therefore, keep the brakes on one day longer than we must. We dislike restrictions intensely, and we are eager to resume expansion.'[44] The words could have been Macmillan's himself, but delivered as they were by Amory, with his reputation as a rather cautious figure, they did nothing to alarm the markets.

The financial press saw the Budget as a personal triumph for Amory. Macmillan owed much to Amory's nimble footwork. Yet he described the Budget as a 'good, but humble little package'.[45]

During 1958, Amory introduced other measures to stimulate the economy. The ceiling on credit was ended in July. Hire purchase restrictions were eased in September, and ended completely in October. The fall in import prices, which brought price stability nearer, enabled him to plan for a more expansionist package in his election-year Budget in 1959. The down side, which curbed any sense of complacency, was on the industrial front. The lorry drivers at Smithfield meat market went on strike on 21 April, and this dispute soon spread to the docks. A bus strike began on 5 May; simultaneously a rail strike was threatened, which would have been a catastrophic combination. On Sunday, 6 May, Macmillan held talks with the relevant ministers. Eventually a rail strike was averted, though not one on the London Underground. By October unemployment had risen from 1.9 per cent to 2.2 per cent. On 20 November, the bank rate was reduced to 4 per cent and in December, as de Gaulle's government in France devalued the franc,

Macmillan's government made sterling held by non-residents convertible into dollars. The rate was $2.80 dollars to the pound, a rate held until the Labour devaluation in 1969, when the rate fell to $2.40. Despite all the changes and industrial difficulties, the balance of payments at the end of the year was in surplus by £455 million.

Macmillan knew that Cyprus was 'not a Colonial problem but an international problem',[46] and in May 1958 he launched yet another initiative, which aimed at an agreed co-operation between London, Ankara and Athens, the so-called 'Tridominion'.[47] In August, he visited Athens, Ankara and Nicosia in an attempt to gain acceptance for his new plan. Despite the efforts of both Sir Hugh Foot (whom Macmillan had appointed as the new Governor in January 1958) and Alan Lennox-Boyd (the Colonial Secretary), there was an increase in the activities of EOKA. Macmillan reported to the Cabinet on 8 September that 'it had now become clear that the Greek Government would not accept any plan for the future administration of Cyprus which involved their sharing the government of the Island with Turkey, or acquiescing in the physical presence in Cyprus of any symbol of Turkish authority'.[48] An important breakthrough came in December 1958, with Selwyn Lloyd gaining acceptance for the concept of 'sovereign bases' from both parties to the dispute.[49] Lloyd discussed this plan at a NATO Ministerial Council meeting with Evangelos Averoff, the Greek Foreign Minister, and Fatin Zorlu, his Turkish counterpart.

On 19 February 1958, during a routine two-day foreign affairs debate, Aneurin Bevan, the Shadow Foreign Affairs spokesman, made a convoluted speech trying to explain his position on one of the big issues of the day, unilateral disarmament. In replying, Lloyd gave his prepared speech with no reference to Bevan's difficulties. As Macmillan wrote later, 'A more agile parliamentarian would have torn Bevan to pieces.'[50] Although Lloyd, much distressed by a missed opportunity, and feeling that he did not have the confidence of his colleagues, offered his resignation, Macmillan refused it. Macmillan knew that criticism of Lloyd was vicarious criticism of himself and his government. After the Treasury resignations he could not afford another, particularly from one of the 'great' offices of state. Paradoxically, the incident strengthened Lloyd's position in the government; Macmillan knew that the two of them would stand or fall together.[51]

Selwyn Lloyd, who had been Foreign Secretary for nearly two and a half years, now found Macmillan most attentive, even assiduous, in consulting him. 'There was hardly a day when I was not in touch with him,' Lloyd recalled. 'If I was overseas, by telegram; if the House was in recess, by telephone; more usually by seeing him at No. 10.'

One of Macmillan's characteristics was very striking for Lloyd: 'He had the desire to communicate personally as frequently as possible with other Heads of Government.'[51] On the stage of the superpowers, there were two key figures with whom Macmillan needed to establish good working relationships – Eisenhower in America, and Khrushchev in Russia. He had cultivated the American link assiduously. Khrushchev was a new challenge. The leadership of Russia had changed dramatically on 27 March when Bulganin was ousted as the Prime Minister. Khrushchev was now his country's dominating figure. Macmillan was to have no illusions about Khrushchev, and had not been taken in by his smiling outward bonhomie. In the 1930s, Anthony Eden had deduced that Mussolini's gross table manners were an indication of his inner character;[53] Macmillan now deduced the same about this 'obscene figure; very fat with a great paunch; [who] eats and drinks greedily'.[54] His first impressions of Khrushchev did not betray him. 'Much more impulsive than Stalin,' he wrote to Churchill about Khrushchev on 7 August 1958, 'and, if possible, even more crooked.'[55] As Macmillan got to know Khrushchev better, he added, in the privacy of his diary, that he was 'a kind of mixture between Peter the Great and Lord Beaverbrook'.[56] He was always wary of the Russian bear, yet determined to use the animal to his advantage.

In Europe, the two dominating figures were Charles de Gaulle, President of France, and Konrad Adenauer, Chancellor of West Germany. De Gaulle came to power after the revolt of right-wing military extremists in Algeria, at the time an integral part of metropolitan France,* had led to the fall of the Fourth Republic, following which de Gaulle formed a 'government of national safety' on 29 May 1958. Four months later, the constitution for the Fifth Republic was approved in a referendum, and de Gaulle became President on 21 December, with powers that he had sought since the end of the war. Adenauer's path to power was less complex. He had first been elected Chancellor of West Germany in 1949, and remained in the post until his retirement in 1963, combining that office with that of Foreign Minister between 1951 and 1955. Macmillan and Adenauer had overlapped on the diplomatic scene in 1955.

Macmillan realised that Adenauer's real aim was to cultivate a Franco-German alliance that would be the driving force in Europe. Exactly where Britain would fit into this scenario was an unresolved

---

*Algeria became independent in 1962.

problem. Adenauer had ambitions for Germany to become a nuclear power and was forthright in his defence of German interests. He even rebuked Macmillan in December 1957 about the BBC's Reith Lectures[57] on the radio that month, which he felt had been unhelpful and 'inspired by the British Government'.[58] But he came to realise that Macmillan could be invaluable as a counter to de Gaulle's overweening ambitions for France. Macmillan, for his part, hoped that Adenauer would be supportive of his hopes for a European Free Trade Area, which he had discussed when Adenauer paid a state visit to Britain in April 1958.* The General had not by then returned to take over the destiny of France, so Macmillan rightly saw Adenauer's support as crucial to this scheme of economic expansion. It was not a one-way process. Later in the year, Adenauer was to find Macmillan a real prop in time of trouble.

On 17 September 1958, de Gaulle proposed, in a letter to Eisenhower and Macmillan, that the 'Triple Directorate' of the non-Communist world should be the United States, France and Britain. There were no prizes for guessing who de Gaulle thought should take the part of Lepidus in the triple pillar of the world.[59] Adenauer, who was aghast at de Gaulle's initiative, was not even to be an attendant lord. When Macmillan visited Bonn in October, Adenauer's fury had still not abated. 'In the afternoon, with various officials present, he tried to control himself – after dinner he showed his disgust and resentment,' Macmillan wrote in his diary. 'I tried to calm him down as much as I could.'[60]

Nevertheless, Macmillan was forthright with Adenauer where British interests were concerned. The next day, 9 October, he outlined his thinking on future economic integration and defence commitments. 'It would be very bad if the United Kingdom found herself economically isolated,' he wrote. 'No British Government could continue to take part in the military defence of a continent which had declared economic war upon her. The United Kingdom would become isolationist. We could not have a Europe which was militarily united and economically divided.'[61]

Macmillan reported back to Selwyn Lloyd with some satisfaction that his message had alerted Adenauer to the strength of British feelings and even alarmed the European leaders. 'I hardly think we could

---

*The original Free Trade Area proposal, based on the so-called Plan G, was a British scheme to contain (in more senses than one) the newly founded EEC in a broader West European entity. When it was vetoed by the French at the end of 1958, Britain set up the European Free Trade Association (EFTA) of non-EEC West European countries, which it hoped would lead to some sort of deal with the EEC.

justify remaining in NATO and keeping four divisions of our troops at considerable expense to defend militarily a group of countries who were carrying on an economic war against us,' he wrote of this warning. 'I have already said something pretty stiff to de Gaulle but then he will have forgotten it by now. I said the same to Adenauer the other day. He was shocked but impressed. We may be accused of the usual perfidy[62] if we do not make it clear while there is still time how serious we would consider a breakdown and how it would cause us to review all our commitments. Fortress Britain might be our right reply.'[63]

The uneasy affinity – partnership would be too strong a word – between Macmillan and de Gaulle went back to wartime North African days. In many ways they knew each other too well. They had similar hopes and fears, particularly about the Soviet threat and Germany's place in the new Europe. Both remembered the once Great Power status of their respective countries; both knew inwardly that it could never truly be the same again. But unlike de Gaulle, Macmillan never saw himself as a latter-day Louis XIV, believing that 'L'État, c'est moi.'[64] Although Macmillan happily received the de Gaulles at Birch Grove, de Gaulle did not reciprocate with an invitation to Macmillan to visit his private home at Colombey-les-Deux-Églises. He preferred the grandeur of Rambouillet, where 'our guests were made to feel the nobility behind the geniality, the permanence behind the vicissitudes, of the nation which was their host'.[65]

May brought a full-blown crisis in the Lebanon. Nasser was wanting to force Lebanon, and Jordan, into his United Arab Republic. President Camille Chamoun, who was pro-Western, appealed to Britain and America in the face of this threat from Egypt, Syria and the Yemen. King Hussein of Jordan also sought British support. Macmillan dispatched Selwyn Lloyd to Washington for talks with Dulles. 'Fortunately the Americans have learned a lot since Suez,' he recorded in his diary. In Cabinet it was 'agreed that we would join with the U.S. in saying to President Chamoun that if he decided to ask for military help to preserve the independence of Lebanon we would give it'.[66] In June, Macmillan flew to Washington to see Eisenhower. The Middle East, over which there was still Anglo-American divergence, was not the main item on the agenda, though it soon pushed its way to the forefront of the talks. Macmillan was taking the lead on the possibility of a summit on disarmament. He had spoken to both de Gaulle and Adenauer on this matter before departing for America. On 23 May, Adenauer had written to Macmillan, welcoming his initiative. The indications from Paris were more opaque.

The June visit to Washington was a combination of hard political haggling, ceremonial degree days, and receptions. In Indianapolis on 8 June, Macmillan attended a publishers' dinner, but his hosts mistakenly sifted him into a party for the American Automobile Convention at the same hotel. The Prime Minister was extricated only after he had done his best to keep up a conversation on gaskets and petrol pricing.[67] To the delight of Lady Dorothy, who accompanied her husband on the tour, the final visit en route to England was to Ottawa and Government House. The Macmillans had last been there together in 1920 as a newly engaged couple.

On his return to London, Macmillan reported to the Cabinet. On the positive side, he was hopeful that the Americans would be supportive of friendly Arab powers, whilst at the same time distancing themselves from Nasser's grandiose schemes. Macmillan wrote to Adenauer, and paid a visit to de Gaulle in Paris. 'I'm off to see de Gaulle,' he wrote to Pamela Berry, 'which will be rather amusing.'[68] He knew it would not be, and it proved anything but. The French still remembered that the British had done nothing at the Bermuda Conference to advance their hopes for an independent nuclear capability. On his side, Macmillan was frustrated by de Gaulle's coolness about a Free Trade Area and his ambiguous messages about a possible summit of the superpowers.

On his return from America, Macmillan had received a letter from Khrushchev, assertive and barbed, questioning whether the West really wanted talks on renouncing the use of nuclear weapons. (The most recent, successful British H-bomb test had been on 29 April.) Macmillan replied in conciliatory terms about the importance of settling any differences that existed. But nuclear matters still cast their shadow, metaphorically and in reality. The French wanted to continue with their nuclear research,* which was for de Gaulle 'a *sine qua non* of an independent foreign policy, as well as vital status symbol'.[69] An eight-power conference began in Geneva on 1 July on the scientific detection of nuclear explosions. Macmillan hoped that some agreement could be reached, a compromise admittedly, whereby America, Russia and Great Britain suspended nuclear tests for two years, whilst the French continued their experiments. The next day he heard from Eisenhower that the McMahon Act of 1946, banning the sharing of nuclear information, had finally been repealed. Such collaboration had been an important goal for Macmillan, something he had described as the 'great prize'.[70]

However, within 12 days a new crisis had erupted. On 14 July,

---

*Their first atomic bomb test was on 2 March 1960.

Selwyn Lloyd telephoned Macmillan with the news of a coup in Baghdad. King Feisal of Iraq had been assassinated, along with the Crown Prince and the Prime Minister, Nuri es-Said, one of Britain's most loyal supporters in the region.[71] President Chamoun now called for the military support Macmillan had promised in May. The subsequent landing of American troops at Beirut by the US Sixth Fleet, and two British paratroop battalions in Jordan, displayed an Anglo-American co-operation that Macmillan still regretted had not been displayed at Suez. There were, however, still differences. Macmillan believed that a permanent military presence in the area was necessary to maintain stability; the Americans were reluctant to be drawn further into the Middle East morass. Nevertheless, a sign of the new easiness of Macmillan's restored relationship with Eisenhower was that he could even joke about this in the build-up to the military action. At 10.45 p.m. on 14 July, he spoke to Eisenhower (on an unprotected line in those pre-'hotline' days). 'I said "You are doing a Suez on me", at which the President laughed,' Macmillan wrote in his diary. 'All the same I think I made it clear that we really must expect the Americans to stand by us and to see the thing through.'[72]

Despite complications, such as the inadvertent failure to seek permission to overfly Israeli airspace, Macmillan carried the day, by a majority of 62, in the House of Commons debate on military intervention. 'There is none of the rancour of Suez,' he observed.[73] His overriding aim at this time remained to convene a summit of the major powers, and an unexpected opportunity arose when Khrushchev suggested, on 19 July, a Five Power Conference on the volatile situation in the Middle East.

Further afield, another crisis broke with unexpected suddenness on 23 August 1958, when Mao Tse-tung's Communist government of mainland China began the bombardment of the offshore islands of Quemoy and Matsu. These islands were held by the Nationalist forces of Chiang Kai-shek, which, following their defeat by Mao Tse-tung, now occupied Formosa. Eisenhower's position had always been to support Chiang Kai-shek's government, and in 1954 he had even pledged American support in the event of any attack on Quemoy or Matsu. Macmillan knew what an acute dilemma this posed for Britain. 'Our own view is that the Chinese (Communists) have an unanswerable case to the possession of these islands,' he wrote in his diary.[74] 'But if we abandon the Americans – morally I mean, they need no active support – it will be a great blow to the friendship and alliance which I have done so much to rebuild and strengthen. If we support them, the repercussions in Far East, India and through the Afro-Asian group in the Middle East may be very dangerous. At home, Parliament and public will be very critical of any change from our public position three years ago. So there we are!'[75]

One danger would be that Khrushchev would become involved, especially after Dulles' brinkmanship on 4 September in threatening a nuclear response if the Chinese occupied Quemoy. Khrushchev and Eisenhower were soon trading insults, which delighted Mao and may (according to some interpretations) have been the main Chinese motive for provoking the crisis in the first place. On 6 September, as the Americans built up a naval presence in the Formosa Straits, Macmillan wrote to both Eisenhower and Dulles urging caution. Eventually Dulles began to compromise, and the crisis petered out, in as puzzling a way as it had suddenly erupted. For a while nuclear war might have been one of the outcomes. Macmillan wondered what the moral of it all had been. His initiatives with Eisenhower had been largely inconsequential, as had the intervention of Nehru and Robert Menzies. The true lesson was that, at this stage of the Cold War, in an atmosphere of mistrust and brinkmanship, the players of consequence were America, Russia and China – and that Britain had been relegated to a subordinate role.

On 21 April 1958, Macmillan cleared his schedules to talk with Evelyn Waugh, then researching his life of Ronald Knox. Macmillan was generous in allowing Waugh access to private letters. His own holiday reading included Churchill's four volumes of his *History of the English Speaking Peoples*.[76] Apart from some of the vivid descriptions of military episodes, Macmillan found them dull. On 25 June, at one of the last Encaenias presided over by Lord Halifax, Chancellor of Oxford University, Macmillan received an honorary degree. In the afternoon he planted a tree at Summer Fields. His summer break was the usual Devonshire gathering at Bolton Abbey, and there was also golf with Dorothy at Blairgowrie, Gleneagles, Muirfield and Nairn, classic courses all. Music was never one of Macmillan's interests. His tastes were middle brow. He went to the new musical *My Fair Lady* in London in July. The next month he took Ava Waverley, not long bereaved, to Lehár's *The Merry Widow*. Hospitality from the Earl of Drogheda, chairman of the Royal Opera House, Covent Garden, in the form of Mussorgsky's *Boris Godunov*, was one of Macmillan's few experiences of grand opera since Rimsky-Korsakov's *The Snow Maiden* during his Russian visit in 1932. The death scene in *Boris Godunov*, sung by Boris Christoff, was memorable, though, as Lord

Drogheda admitted in his memoirs, 'it took over three hours to get there'.[77]

In April 1958, Hugh Gaitskell had told the Prime Minister, as a courtesy, that he intended to take a holiday in the Soviet Union. Macmillan strongly advised against Gaitskell's acceptance. 'I must be frank and say that if I were in your position I should not accept this invitation. The fact of your going to spend your holiday in the Soviet Union might be misunderstood abroad. There is the further point that in view of the high cost of living in the Soviet Union, you would presumably be the guest of the Soviet Government with an inevitable sense of obligation.'[78] Gaitskell was furious. He had not asked for Macmillan's advice; he had informed him of his intention. However, the position changed in June 1958, when news came that the Russians had executed Imre Nagy and Pal Meleter, the Prime Minister and the Military Commander of Hungary, who had both been seized in Budapest in November 1956 during the Russian invasion. Gaitskell knew that he could not travel to Russia in the wake of this atrocity.

Eventually an invitation came for March 1959, by which time Macmillan had pre-empted the Leader of the Opposition and got himself invited instead.[79] 'That's the trouble when you have a super-tactician like MacWonder,'[80] said a disappointed Gaitskell.

Always wanting to be abreast of the latest technological developments, Macmillan became the first Prime Minister to be interviewed live in a television studio. His questioner, Robin Day, was comfortably ensconced in a swivel chair, whereas the Prime Minister was placed in a hard-backed wooden seat, reminiscent of Summer Fields days. Seeing the Prime Minister's discomfort, Robin Day offered to swap seats. 'Not at all,' replied the Prime Minister. 'I know my place.'[81] In the autumn, the State Opening of Parliament was televised for the first time, and on 6 November the cartoonist Vicky published his famous cartoon depicting Macmillan as 'Supermac', an image that was eventually to confound its creator's original intention.

On the morning of 5 December 1958, Harold Macmillan opened Britain's first stretch of motorway (albeit only eight and a quarter miles), the Preston by-pass, later part of the M6. 'A fine thing in itself,' he told the enthusiastic crowds, watching the ceremony from a bridge, 'but a finer thing as a symbol, as a token of what is to follow.'[82] As Macmillan cut the ribbon, he quoted, in a deliberately exaggerated Scottish accent, the words of Robert Burns. 'I'm now arrived, thanks to the gods, thro' pathways rough and muddy.'[83] It was an appropriate metaphor for his political year.

Although it was not recognised as such at the time, the Life Peerage

Act of 1958 was to prove one of the most important legacies of the Macmillan government. Lords reform, included in the Conservatives' 1951 election manifesto, was an unresolved issue Macmillan had inherited. Lord Salisbury had feared that without reform the Lords 'will die on its feet'. In 1956 he believed that 'it is very feeble now'.[84] In the nineteenth century, Bagehot had prophesied of the Lords that 'its danger is not in assassination, but atrophy; not abolition, but decline'.[85] Inaction thus suited Labour very well. By 1957 nothing had been achieved, not least because of the Labour Party's refusal to co-operate. As Bernard Crick pointed out, Labour seemed 'quite happy that the composition of that House should remain indefensible'.[86]

Life peerages encouraged a spirit of professionalism in the Upper House, a necessary move after the introduction of reimbursements for peers in 1957. Now MPs could retire as life peers to the red benches of the Upper House, without lumbering their politically active sons with an unwanted hereditary peerage, always a consideration for Macmillan, who did not want to inhibit the career of his own son, Maurice.[87] Of course, 'non-political' figures were also beneficiaries. As Vernon Bogdanor has pointed out, 'One important consequence of the Life Peerages Act was the admission into the Lords not only of party politicians but also of experts from all walks of life who were able to make important contributions to the work of the upper house.'[88] The Bill was included in the Queen's Speech on 5 November 1957, and aroused public interest.*

Lord Home had outlined the government's intentions in October 1957. Backwoodsmen in the Lords had been taken aback, not least by Home's confirmation that the proposed measure would allow the introduction of lady peeresses. 'Taking women into a parliamentary embrace,' he said in the Lords, with a ribaldry considered very daring in 1957, 'seemed to be only a modest extension of the normal functions of a peer.'[90] Home introduced the Bill in the Lords on 21 November, and the measure received the Royal Assent on 30 April 1958. Macmillan announced the names of the first 14 life peers, 10 men and four women, on 24 July 1958.

The headline appointment was that of Bob Boothby, MP for East Aberdeenshire, who metamorphosed into Baron Boothby of Buchan and Rattray Head. Even for those outside the gossipy Westminster

---

* As in 1911 (the Parliament Act), church congregations enjoyed the hymn containing the lines:

> There is room for fresh creations
> In that upper house of bliss.[89]

village, who did not know the personal history, this elevation brought delight and dole in equal measure. The background was simple. Boothby had written to Macmillan asking directly for a peerage. 'Of course he must have it,' Macmillan said to John Wyndham, who had first read the letter with some discomfort. Macmillan then told Boothby, 'You can be the last of the old [hereditary peer], or the first of the new [life peer].'[91] Boothby chose the latter. Macmillan's underlying motive for elevating Boothby to the Lords was the pleasure he knew it would give to Dorothy.[92] It also had the added benefit of removing Boothby, an increasingly maverick MP, from the Commons.[93]

'I only hope that you will, as I believe you will, enjoy the platform that the other House will give you,' Macmillan wrote to Boothby. 'It will enable you to put forward your contributions in a much better atmosphere than the House of Commons now has.'[94]

Lady Violet Bonham Carter, who was herself to be granted a life peerage in 1964 (as Baroness Asquith of Yarnbury), appeared on 19 August with Boothby on a television discussion about 'The Establishment'. Boothby railed against this sinister, high-minded and wrong-headed body, and its deleterious effect on his own career. Lady Violet, not unreasonably, said that Boothby had not done badly out of the Establishment. 'Why there he is plastered with decorations – titles, Knighthoods & Life Peerages rain down on him. He emerges drenched & dripping from the Fount of Honour & then shakes himself like a dog getting out of dirty water.'[95]

Kay Elliot, who had failed to be elected to the constituency of her late husband, Walter Elliot, at the Glasgow Kelvingrove by-election in March, was also included in the list.[96] An incidental pleasure for Macmillan was that asking Gaitskell for the names of Labour nominees caused the Opposition leader some difficulty, as his party was divided about the future of the Lords. A reformed and better-functioning Upper Chamber would pose difficulties for Labour firebrands wanting changes that were a great deal more radical.

One of Macmillan's motives was to redress the imbalance in the hereditary Upper House. Jo Grimond was grateful for the platform that life peerages were to afford Liberals in public service at a time when few were able to win seats in the Commons. Gaitskell too came to see the advantages, and, though the decision was not universally popular among his parliamentary colleagues, nominated half a dozen for the Upper House. 'I shall go very cautiously in this matter of life Peerages,' Macmillan wrote to a colleague, 'since one of the main purposes of the legislation is to improve the working of the Upper House, particularly on the Labour side.'[97] So it proved. The reform was not a Trojan Horse of destruction, but the salvation of the Upper House, though one with many unintended consequences.[98] The Act also closed the issue for the Conservatives for the immediate future, and no further mention was made of Lords reform in the 1959 election manifesto.

On 10 November 1958, Khrushchev announced that if there was no negotiated end to Berlin's four-power status, then control of Allied access to Berlin would pass to the East German government. Such a breach of the Potsdam Agreement had the most dangerous implications, and it markedly increased Cold War tensions, especially as Khrushchev had already compared Adenauer and de Gaulle to Hitler and Mussolini. Khrushchev followed up this threat at a Kremlin press conference on 27 November. Declaring that West Berlin had become 'a sort of malignant tumour', he added that the Soviet Union had 'decided to do some surgery'. He announced that he had given Western ambassadors a 28–page document that morning with a clear ultimatum. Unless Western powers withdrew their troops from West Berlin,[99] Russia would sign a peace treaty with Walter Ulbricht, the East German leader, ending any Allied rights in Berlin. The deadline was 27 May 1959.

Thus began 'the Berlin Crisis', the greatest post-war threat to world peace until the Cuban Missile Crisis of October 1962. Macmillan was in no doubt as to what the stakes were. 'Are we really prepared to face war over Berlin?' he asked himself in a delayed diary entry. The situation was almost a rerun of the crisis surrounding the Berlin Airlift in 1948. 'What matters,' Macmillan judged correctly, 'is whether civil and military supplies actually reach Berlin.'[100] After Khrushchev's first pronouncement, Adenauer appealed to Macmillan to act as peace-broker. Macmillan agreed, sending a personal appeal to Khrushchev on 22 November. Khrushchev's various evasive and contradictory replies Macmillan dismissed as 'blandishment, if not blarney'.[101]

Macmillan knew that the Allies were now in for the long haul, and as there was going to be no easy resolution, patience was of the essence. He was soon co-ordinating the Western response. Adenauer came over to London on 7 December, full of concern over Berlin. Macmillan thought that Adenauer was showing signs of ageing. 'He wrings his hands and says that Russia and the West are like two express trains rushing to a head-on collision.'[102] To prevent such a scenario, Macmillan warned Dulles, now in the last months of terminal cancer, that 'we must not slip into the 1914 position – mobilisation sliding into war'.[103] There were disagreements with de Gaulle, who was belligerent, believing the West should call the Russian bluff. Adenauer and Macmillan knew that the French lacked the firepower to back up such a stance, and saw de Gaulle's attitude as one likely to increase nuclear conflict. Macmillan's strategy was more subtle. 'The whole art of dealing with an opponent who is indulging in "brinkmanship" consists of not allowing him to get into a position in which he has to choose between war and humiliating retreat.'[104] He saw the crisis as the ultimate justification for a new East–West summit, of the kind envisaged by Churchill in May 1953. His own visit to Moscow, scheduled for February 1959, would now be even more important.

On 31 December, Macmillan had a meeting with Alec Home, mainly about Commonwealth matters, but the talk soon turned to whether there should be a spring or autumn election. He was now facing up to the loneliest of all prime ministerial decisions. He had not forgotten the mistake of Attlee in calling an ill-advised, and unnecessary, election in February 1950, nor the brave initiative of Eden in May 1955 in facing the electorate at once. So much hinged on what Macmillan decided. After nearly two years' work, he had no wish to go down as the Tory leader who threw it all away by a foolish choice. The economy would have to be the deciding factor.

Robert Hall looked back on 1958 in his diary. 'The New Year opens with the economic position very much better than it was a year ago except that production is low and the outlook for private investment a bit off,' he wrote. 'On the other hand we have got all the Thorneycroft policies reversed quite smoothly, the reserves and the pound have had good years, and the latest (November) production and (December) unemployment confirm my feeling that we are on the turn.'[105] Hall's comments came on the first anniversary of the Thorneycroft resignation. On 6 January 1958, although he had disguised it, Macmillan was in despair about the prospects for his Government's political survival. He was now, in the words of the title he gave to the fourth volume of his memoirs, 'Riding the Storm'.

CHAPTER TWENTY THREE

Porpoises in the North Sea

1959

Even porpoises had been spotted in the North Sea.
Harold Macmillan on the glorious summer of 1959[1]

There are complaints here and there and on many specific issues, but – in the main – scarcely anyone here in Great Britain seems any longer to feel there is anything fundamentally wrong. On the contrary, Great Britain on the whole, and especially in comparison with other countries, seems to the British intellectual of the mid-1950s to be all right and even much better than that.
American sociologist Edward Shils, on British society in the
mid-1950s[2]

The simple fact is that the Tories identified themselves with the new working class rather better than we did.
Patrick Gordon Walker

Macmillan knew that the majority of voters make up their minds which way to vote long before any campaign formally begins. So he realised it was vital for him to establish in the minds of the electorate the key factors most conducive to electoral success.

His platform was Amory's Budget on 7 April 1959. Growth was now well under way, and Amory delivered the package Macmillan wanted. The Budget certainly contributed in a major way to eventual victory in the autumn, but it also laid the foundations for the economic difficulties of 1961–1963, a repeat of the pattern of 1955 after Butler's first Budget that year. To Amory's credit, he spotted the difficulties lurking ahead and pressed Macmillan, unsuccessfully, to back the remedial action he wanted in 1960. 'Orthodox economists and officials,' Samuel Brittain has observed, 'have ever since regarded the 1959 Budget as an object lesson in the dangers of trying to go too fast.'[3] Amory kick-started a boom that was already under way. Industrial production in the next year rose by almost 11 per cent. The burden on the taxpayer was reduced considerably. Purchase tax was cut by one sixth, and the duty on beer came down by twopence. The effect of these measures alone was to reduce the retail price index by nearly a point. The standard rate of income tax was cut by ninepence. The repayment of post-war credits was speeded up. Investment allowances on plant and machinery were restored to the generous levels of 1954.

The Budget was well received by the press, and more importantly for Macmillan, by the voters. The only criticism was that little had been done for old age pensioners. (Macmillan himself was to become a pensioner on 10 February, his sixty-fifth birthday celebrated with a dinner at No. 10.) In June, John Boyd-Carpenter, the Minister of Pensions and National Insurance, announced an increase in National Assistance of £32m. 'The Opposition were much taken aback,' Macmillan noted approvingly in his diary.[4]

Macmillan had begun 1959 with a four-day visit to the north-east, accompanied by Lady Dorothy. On 14 January, he called in at the Conservative Association offices in Stockton, a nostalgic visit that gave pleasure on both sides. The programme was an intensive one, up to 12 hours a day, touring factories, attending mayoral receptions and making speeches. Macmillan's main concern was to assess electoral prospects, and he was not encouraged by the condition of manufacturing industry. 'Order books are thin,' he wrote in his diary, 'and I feel sure we must do more "reflation" if we are to avoid a serious increase in unemployment.'[5] Jack Simon, the Solicitor General, and MP for Middlesbrough West, thanked Macmillan for visiting his constituency, but was also concerned about employment prospects. 'The general feeling was that there was unlikely to be a marked upturn before the summer,' he wrote to Macmillan, 'and the confidential advice I was given by well-wishers in the Employment Exchanges was that from their point of view an autumn General Election would be better for the government than a spring one.'[6] Macmillan's north-east tour confirmed him in that view.

The next month Macmillan travelled with Selwyn Lloyd to Russia to meet Khrushchev, taking up the invitation Khrushchev, and the now deposed Bulganin, had given to Eden on their visit to Britain in 1956. Macmillan was away from 21 February to 3 March, even though John Richardson, his doctor, did not feel he was fit to travel at the time. The delegation included Norman Brook, the Cabinet Secretary, Tom Brimelow and Pat Dean from the Foreign Office, and the experienced Ted Orchard as chief interpreter. One of the key figures in making the visit a success was Sir Patrick Reilly,[7] whom Macmillan had appointed as Ambassador to Moscow at the age of only 48. The Cold War was at a critical stage. 'Macmillan,' Sir John Ure has written, 'wanted an envoy of high intellect and absolute integrity whom he could trust to report the scene in all its complexity and who would be neither brow beaten nor provocative.'[8] Reilly did not disappoint. 'I do not think Khrushchev's incipient megalomania is as yet nearly as dangerous as Hitler's,' he had told Macmillan, 'and I think the odds are against it becoming so.' Khrushchev was 'a normal human being, with a normal family life'. He had lost a son in the war. 'There is no Khrushchev *mystique* here.'[9]

Although the electoral advantages of this tour were clear, not to mention the pleasure Macmillan gained from trumping Gaitskell's plans for a similar visit, the motives were more complex. Since Khrushchev's Berlin ultimatum in November 1958, international tension had been escalating dangerously. Lloyd had spoken to Macmillan in December 1958 about the possible benefits of such a visit. The West was in hopeless disarray over Berlin. 'If nothing was done before May (when the ultimatum expired),' he recalled, 'I really wondered whether with Foster Dulles' illness we could have preserved any sort of common front.'[10] Macmillan agreed, and preparations were put in hand.

A sign of how important Macmillan considered the visit came with his choice of present – a King George I walnut bureau bookcase, eight feet high – which was shipped to Moscow in advance.[11] When Macmillan presented this gift to Khrushchev he pointed out six secret drawers at the back. 'Very useful for political purposes,' he added. Khrushchev did not get the joke.[12]

Not that Khrushchev was reticent in telling his own jokes. Selwyn Lloyd reminded him of his 1956 visit to London and of his comment at the ill-fated Labour party dinner that if he lived in Britain he would vote Conservative. 'Was this still the case?' asked Lloyd. 'Certainly,' replied Khrushchev. 'Bulganin was the one who was going to vote Labour and look where that had got him.'[13] Macmillan too, though far from well, tried to be in lively form: on being told that *dobry den* meant 'Good day', he greeted everyone with the words 'double gin'.[14]

Macmillan had hoped to be taken to the circus. However, there were several interminable cultural evenings instead. Prokofiev's last ballet *The Stone Flower* was particularly heavy going. His hosts asked Macmillan how he had enjoyed the performance. Macmillan tactfully picked out one dramatic scene, the arrival of the Demon King in a futuristic aerial contraption. 'I liked the sputnik,' he replied, to general approval.[15] Further cultural delights awaited the visitors. An exhibition was organised at the Hermitage of modern French pictures,

many of which had never been shown before, as they were at odds with Socialist realism. At the government dacha at Semenovskoye, reminiscent of the days of Turgenev and Pushkin, with troikas in the snow and caviar, not marmalade, at breakfast, clay pigeon shooting was arranged and holes were cut in the ice so that the visitors could fish. However, there was a darker side, and security was a nightmare. Sir Patrick Reilly had set up a tent in his study at the Embassy, within which confidential discussions took place against a tape of cocktail party noise and the sound of rushing water. Surprisingly, Khrushchev himself had suggested a walk in the garden, as his office was probably bugged.*

On 22 February, when discussions began in earnest, Khrushchev repeated his determination that West Berlin should be a 'free' city. Macmillan countered by outlining alternative agendas: German reunion could see Berlin as the capital city; if German division continued, West Berlin should be West Germany's and East Berlin East Germany's; alternatively, the whole of Berlin could be a free city. Khrushchev was unyielding. Talks on disarmament and the possibility of a superpower summit followed over the next two days. With some emotion, Macmillan recalled the tragedy of the Great War that the combatants had stumbled into, and the evil forces that had occasioned the second. Khrushchev agreed that it was incumbent upon them to avoid a third.

The low point of the visit came on 24 February, when Khrushchev unexpectedly made a virulent speech about the capitalist system while Macmillan and Selwyn Lloyd were away visiting a nuclear research station. When details of the speech came through the next morning,

---

*On 12 May 1974, Macmillan dined in Rome with Muriel Spark, one of the writers in the Macmillan stable. She was researching the security angle for her new novel *Abbess*, and asked Macmillan if he had ever used bugging devices. 'Well, at least I was never such a damn fool as to bug myself,' he replied. He recalled the Khrushchev incident of 1959 and how he had remained cautious, even outside in the garden, as he suspected that the trees had microphones, 'an idea soon planted in the opening pages of *Abbess*'.[16]

['Vicky'—*New Statesman*]

Macmillan and Lloyd walked and talked with their advisers in the snow-strewn grounds of their dacha, keeping clear of trees in the park, away from possible microphones. Despite his reputation for unflappability, this was one of those occasions when Macmillan was very worried; indeed, on the verge of abandoning the tour. Lloyd and Reilly stiffened his courage.

On 26 February, Khrushchev called off his visit to Kiev with the British party, because he said he had to have a new filling, an episode which went down as the 'toothache insult'. Macmillan courteously said that he would be sorry to miss Khrushchev's company. Selwyn Lloyd went one better by saying that the previous dentist must have used a British drill. At this, Khrushchev broke into broad smiles, almost like a naughty schoolboy who has been caught out but who is determined to pretend otherwise.

There were fewer alarums during the rest of the tour. Indeed, Macmillan's hopes for a summit had produced a Soviet proposal that the way might be paved for such a meeting by holding a conference of Foreign Ministers first.[17] Macmillan felt that this was the most important result of his Moscow visit, and he reported the details to Eisenhower, de Gaulle and Adenauer. Macmillan's dispatches to other Allied leaders covered the full spectrum of the talks, particularly on disarmament. Meanwhile, Khrushchev offered to extend his 27 May deadline on Berlin.

Reilly later saw the 'toothache' episode as a turning point of the visit. 'Mr K. frankly behaved abominably,' he recorded. 'But to his credit he seems to have realised it and at the end he made up for it. The PM and the Foreign Secretary handled the whole thing brilliantly. I knew the PM would of course. It was all the more remarkable, however, since he was so tired and unwell much of the time, and the programme was gruelling. What I did not expect was that Lloyd would be so good. He was quite first class and they make an admirable team and obviously get on splendidly.'[18]

Macmillan learned more in his 10 days in Russia about Khrushchev than he could possibly have done in months of correspondence. He knew that he was dealing with a leader who was ruthless, even barbaric, yet at the same time curiously vulnerable. He noticed that Khrushchev had an impressive control over details, never spoke from notes, but could get confused by the subtleties of complicated arguments. He soon became aware of Khrushchev's almost child-like delight in being flattered, his desire to be the centre of attention, and his impetuousness, all of which first-hand experience was to be invaluable in the future, particularly during the Cuban Missile Crisis of October 1962.[19] For his part, Khrushchev realised that Macmillan was an equally determined politician, not easily deflected from his goals. The Russian leader's extrovert and crude behaviour was a tactic that had not cowed his guest, who thereafter remained something of an enigma for Khrushchev.

Macmillan went with Selwyn Lloyd to Paris to report to de Gaulle on the Moscow visit. De Gaulle was not impressed, seeing Macmillan's Russian excursion as motivated principally by electoral considerations. He told Macmillan how worried Adenauer was about Khrushchev's threats. 'The position over Berlin had destroyed the illusion in which they had been living that Germany had recovered its position of greatness,' de Gaulle said. 'Now they had realised they were dependent on others.'[20] Macmillan knew this, which was why Bonn was on his agenda.

Adenauer also gave Macmillan cold comfort. He was suspicious of Britain's plans for withdrawing troops from Central Europe. He also feared, wrongly, that Britain and Russia had arranged some secret pact about East Germany of which he was being kept in ignorance.[21] The atmosphere of the talks was far from friendly. Macmillan insisted that East Germany should be represented at the forthcoming meeting of foreign ministers in May. For his part, Adenauer made it clear that he wanted any summit with the Soviets to include talks on Germany as a whole, East and West, not just the Berlin ultimatum, and these bargaining points were accepted. Adenauer believed, not unjustly, that France and Germany were the new ruling powers in Europe and he had little regard for British attempts to force the pace over a summit, massaging Khrushchev's ego at the same time. The increasingly incompatible views of Macmillan and Adenauer on foreign policy stemmed from the dissimilar perspectives from which they viewed the diplomatic failures of 1913–1914 and the appeasement crisis before the Second World War. The lesson Macmillan drew was that negotiations were preferable to confrontation, the Churchillian precept that 'to jaw-jaw is always better than to war-war.'[22]

In his dealings with Adenauer, Macmillan was not being 'anti-German', however much German politicians might have thought otherwise. He saw the Berlin crisis as analogous to the complex diplomatic breakdown before the Great War, rather than the rigid confrontations before the Second World War. The Soviet Union for Macmillan was not like Nazi Germany under Hitler. Unlike Adenauer, he did not believe that negotiations over Berlin, whatever their result, would decisively influence the East–West balance of power. For one thing, the growth of missile technology had rendered parameters such as German frontiers less relevant than they had been in 1938. Adenauer, inevitably, had a different national focus.

After Macmillan's visit to Moscow, Adenauer's attitude hardened, which was of enormous significance in connection with Britain's subsequent attempt to join the EEC.

From Germany, Macmillan flew with Selwyn Lloyd to Ottawa. A visit to Rideau Hall was a nostalgic experience, especially as Macmillan's bedroom was that used by Lady Dorothy as a drawing room over 40 years earlier. John Diefenbaker, the Canadian Prime Minister, was a sympathetic audience.

The final stop on this diplomatic excursion was in Washington. By now, Dulles was in the last stages of the cancer that was to claim his life in May, so Macmillan and Lloyd went with Eisenhower to see him in the Walter Reed Hospital. It was a sad meeting, especially as Dulles was, in Macmillan's words, '*against* almost everything'.[23] Dulles was not in favour of a summit, was not keen on the Foreign Ministers' conference scheduled for Geneva, and felt that the West should 'tough it out' over Berlin. Macmillan was torn between sympathy for Dulles' state and the need to answer the points. Afterwards, he much regretted arguing with a dying man. The subsequent talks with Eisenhower at Camp David, mainly on contingency plans in the event of a blockade of Berlin, were realistic and fruitful. Their agenda also contained talks on the economy and a ban on atomic testing. Before leaving America, Macmillan paid a last, private call on Dulles.

Eisenhower was in the last stages of his two-term presidency, aware that he was not as young as he was. (Adenauer was 82 and de Gaulle four years older than Macmillan, who was himself 65.) Dulles' funeral took place in Washington on 27 May, the date of Khrushchev's original Berlin deadline, and was the occasion for a big Foreign Ministers' conference.

'We must have a summit,' Macmillan told Selwyn Lloyd in June. 'I feel all this so strongly that if a Summit does not take place I should have to express my feelings in public even at the cost of separating myself from the other Three.'[24] Macmillan and Lloyd had an almost symbiotic relationship at this time, which was strengthened by a bizarre article that appeared in *The Times* on 1 June. The article – headlined *Prime Minister's Plans for Mr Selwyn Lloyd* – claimed that Macmillan had taken Lloyd aside and told him that in these troubled times 'enough is enough' and that he would soon be moved from the Foreign Office. As the Russians saw *The Times* as the British equivalent of *Pravda*, the story had a considerable impact and the diplomatic wires were soon buzzing. Macmillan was furious with Sir William Haley, the editor of *The Times*. Randolph Churchill claimed the article had been orchestrated by Rab Butler as a means of removing Lloyd as a potential rival for the eventual party leadership.[25] Unlike Eisenhower, Macmillan was about to seek re-election. He did not want *The Times*, which he had mistrusted since pre-war appeasement days, upsetting the apple cart.

The economic signs after Amory's Budget were promising. During 1958, owner-occupiers in Britain had first outnumbered those who rented their homes. This continued housing boom fuelled sales of 'big ticket' consumer items such as televisions, washing machines, refrigerators and ovens. The Americanisation of British consumer habits was well under way. In 1959 there were 286 supermarkets in Britain. Two years earlier there had been 80; by 1961 there were 572.[26] The marketing boom was not limited to major purchases or the large-scale outlets. A similar upwards trend could be seen in smaller shops, particularly the more sophisticated and expensive. The appearance (from 1950 onwards) of the many cookery books of Elizabeth David revolutionised the culinary habits of the aspirational.[27] The Continent suddenly seemed more accessible. The first cross-Channel hovercraft left for France on 25 July. Freshness, innovation and adventure were in the air. Britain no longer seemed stuck in the past.

The continuing road-building programme had many commercial offshoots, such as the publication of new maps and gazetteers, an increase in motorists taking up AA and RAC membership, and petrol stations expanding to become local shops, particularly in rural areas. The number of cars in Britain had doubled since 1952. The Mini, designed partly in response to the fuel shortages caused by the Suez crisis, first rolled off the production lines on 8 May 1959. The plants at Cowley and Longbridge were to be kept at full capacity, as the model rapidly became one of the icons of the 'swinging sixties'.[28] In 1959, the total of new motorbike licences topped 200,000, a phenomenon that the poet Thom Gunn described in his poem 'On the Move'.[29]

On 2 November, the first stretch of the M1, from Watford to Rugby, was opened by Ernest Marples, the Transport Minister, who hailed the project as a symbol of 'the bold, exciting and scientific age in which we live', then, before cutting the ribbon, warned motorists, in the days before a 70 mph speed limit, 'to take it easy'. His words were unheeded and Marples looked on with some trepidation as the first cars raced down the slip road from the Luton Spur roundabout. 'My God,' he asked, 'what have I started?'[30]

Road deaths in 1959 totalled 6,520,[31] and as a result double white lines made their first appearance. Sales of cars and bikes had increased because people could afford them. Unemployment, inflation and the bank rate had all come down. At the same time the average weekly wage had almost doubled since 1951. Opinion polls showed a general optimism that this pattern would continue. Consumerism was the new goal and the platform for electoral success. The final piece of the jigsaw Macmillan needed before committing to an election date was success in foreign policy. His hopes hinged on the question of Cypriot independence.

Prospects of a speedy Cyprus settlement had stalled after the release of Makarios in 1957. Much of the problem centred on whether Cyprus should be granted full Commonwealth status after independence. Using a characteristic clubland analogy, Macmillan wondered whether Cyprus should be 'the RAC or Boodles?'[32] Makarios had no intention of Cyprus being accorded RAC membership.

On 17 February, the plane bringing Adnam Menderes, the Turkish Prime Minister, to the Cyprus conference in London crashed at Gatwick with many fatalities. Miraculously, Menderes was not among them, as he was in the middle part of the aircraft, which had withstood the impact.[33] News of the crash was held back from Evangelos Averell, Foreign Secretary of Greece, and Fatin Zorlu, the Foreign Minister of Turkey, already in London, until it was clear Menderes had survived. Macmillan had an instinctive feeling for Menderes. 'I have myself been involved in an aircraft crash and I know what an unpleasant experience this is and what a shock to one's whole system,'[34] he wrote at once to the Turkish Prime Minister. In fact, the tragic event concentrated minds and there was sympathy for Menderes among the already assembled delegates, many of whom visited him in hospital. The timetable of the day was disrupted, and after a late Downing Street dinner, Macmillan went with the Greek Prime Minister, Constantine Karamanlis, at 10.30 p.m. to the London Clinic. At that hour they could not see Menderes, but the symbolism of their joint visit was not lost on the Turkish delegation.

At the end of Sir John Harding's governorship of Cyprus in December 1957, Macmillan had appointed the liberal-minded Sir Hugh Foot[35] as his successor. Although Foot had his disagreements with Alan Lennox-Boyd, the Colonial Secretary, the two respected each other and proved a creative, if disparate, partnership. Macmillan knew Foot was vital in his quest for conciliation. When deadlock loomed in tortuous negotiations, Macmillan's response was to turn to Foot. 'Now wheel on the idealist' was his usual cue.[36] Foot's views matched Macmillan's, and not only over Cyprus. 'Once a decision to hand-over to an independent government is made,' he wrote, 'it is best to go ahead at top speed, so that no-one can have second thoughts or suggest that Great Britain is giving something grudgingly.'[37] Macmillan's real skill was not just in seeing possible stumbling blocks in advance, but also in disguising from the Tory right wing how swiftly he intended Britain to pursue a broad policy of colonial disengagement, particularly in Africa.

A Cyprus agreement was finalised on 19 February. Macmillan's aim had always been to partition the island into a Turkish and Greek settlement, with Britain retaining bases in case of Communist infiltration. Achieving this solved two problems: the desire of the Chiefs of Staff to maintain a military presence, because of the strategic importance of the island in the Mediterranean; and the fear that after independence, Cyprus would carry through Enosis, union with Greece, with the danger of Communism in Athens. The sovereign bases would permit a speedy response to any such threat. Overall, the agreement was an example of Macmillan's pragmatism in the face of changing realities. The imperialist wing of the Tory Party, a thorn in Macmillan's side, was deeply suspicious of the withdrawal. Yet the need to cut costs, and a change in global priorities, meant that the way was clear for a peaceful disengagement.

In the House of Commons on the evening of 19 February, Macmillan rightly declared the Cyprus agreement to be 'a victory for reason and co-operation'.[38] Some Conservative back-benchers were far from happy, but Macmillan was let off the hook, not for the first time, by a political miscalculation by the Opposition. 'Gaitskell made the mistake of sneering (instead of a generous reply) and I *went for* him,' he wrote in his diary. 'This was very pleasant for our party, and they cheered rapturously.'[39]

Subsequent negotiations over the sovereign bases, first by Selwyn

Lloyd, and then by Julian Amery, Under-Secretary at the Colonial Office, continued after the February 1959 settlement. Ironically, Amery, one of the most ardent of the Tory imperialists, lived in Cyprus for four months, and personally paved the way for Cyprus to become an independent Commonwealth country (on 16 August 1960), with Archbishop Makarios as the first President.* Amery's view, supported by Macmillan, was that the importance of Cyprus had been as a staging post for Suez, limited in any case, and with Suez gone, the costs in both human and financial terms of keeping the island were unjustifiable. Macmillan was to be even more expedient over Empire in the next phase of decolonisation.

Nevertheless, this process, even when there was the political will for such transition in the governing power, was to prove extremely complex, especially in its timing. Macmillan knew that a prerequisite for any post-independence stability was the need for an indigenous non-British elite that was able to make sovereignty work. Singapore gained its independence on 3 June 1959, and the initial prognosis was optimistic, not least because Britain was able to maintain military facilities in the area. Africa was to prove more awkward. Macmillan knew the reason only too well. 'The Africans are not the problem in Africa, it is the Europeans who are the problem.'[40]

The history of what eventually became the Central African Federation in 1953 (Southern and Northern Rhodesia and Nyasaland) can be traced back to the days when Macmillan's father-in-law, the Duke of Devonshire, was Colonial Secretary in the early 1920s. In the famous 'Devonshire Declaration' of 1923, Victor Devonshire had asserted that 'the interests of the African natives must be paramount, and that if, and when, those interests and the interests of the immigrant races should conflict, the former should prevail'.[41] Macmillan's views on the future of Africa showed that he had not forgotten that principle, a stance that earned him the obloquy of many in the Tory ranks.

The settlers of Northern and Southern Rhodesia favoured amalgamation, and the Central African Federation was established in October 1953. Thereafter the Colonial Secretary had responsibility for the territories of Northern Rhodesia and Nyasaland; whilst the Commonwealth Secretary was the conduit between the British and the federal government, and oversaw the government of Southern Rhodesia, which had the largest proportion of white settlers. Federation

---

*Independence for Cyprus and membership of the Commonwealth did not, unhappily, end the long-simmering mistrust between the Turkish and Greek communities.

made economic sense, combining the copper belt in the north with the predominantly agricultural countries of Southern Rhodesia and Nyasaland. Politically, though, the situation was fraught, because the African population in all three territories strongly, and at times violently, opposed federation, as they feared the permanent domination of the white settlers. When Roy Welensky[42] became Prime Minister of the federation in 1956, these fears increased.

Cyprus helped Macmillan's electoral prospects, but Africa provided an unwelcome counterbalance. Indeed Macmillan even felt that events there could 'well blow this government out of office'.[43] He became ever more determined to advance African self-government.[44]

On 3 March, as Macmillan was returning to London from Moscow, news broke that 11 inmates had been beaten to death during a riot at Hola Camp in Kenya, where hard-core Mau Mau supporters were detained. The Mau Mau were a secret society among the largest and most powerful of the indigenous tribes in Kenya, the Kikuyu. In October 1952, they had instigated a campaign to drive white farmers out of Kikuyu lands. Violence was also directed at those Africans thought to be collaborators with the ruling colonial power. There was bloodshed on all sides and a state of emergency was declared. The Mau Mau leader, Jomo Kenyatta,[45] was arrested and sentenced to seven years' hard labour in April 1953. In prison, Kenyatta became the focus for nationalist aspirations.*

In 1954, the Cabinet had authorised a policy of compulsory labour as part of the process of 'rehabilitating' 70,000 Mau Mau supporters who were held in detention camps. This policy had been successful, and by 1959 the number in detention was less than 1,000. 'The Hola Massacre', as it became known, put into sharp focus the conditions in these camps[47] and the issue moved at once to the head of the political agenda. The government's embarrassment was skilfully exploited by the Opposition. Macmillan admitted that 'we are in a real jam'[48] and told the Cabinet on the day of the parliamentary censure motion that 'the Government would have to admit frankly in the debate that the way in which the policy [of 'rehabilitation'] had been applied on this occasion at Hola had undoubtedly been wrong'.[49]

Macmillan now had to use all his political dexterity to hold his team together. He knew that the massacre was a watershed for British

---

*Like Archbishop Makarios, previously imprisoned in the Seychelles, Kenyatta was eventually released, once again to the fury of Bobbety Salisbury and many Tory back-benchers. The same process of imprisonment and release was repeated with Dr Hastings Banda[46] in Nyasaland. Makarios, Kenyatta and Banda were all to become presidents of their respective republics.

colonial policy and he was confirmed in his belief that the old ways of governing in Africa were no longer sustainable, a view shared above all among his Cabinet colleagues by Iain Macleod.[50]

The problems of Kenya had long pre-dated Macmillan's government. Hopes that the new constitution of November 1957, which increased African representation in the legislative council (legco), would provide stability had been overoptimistic and were now completely dashed by the events at Hola Camp. In addition, confusing signals were emerging from London as to the future of Kenya. Lennox-Boyd, the Colonial Secretary, had said at the 1958 Conservative Party Conference that the British government would continue to be responsible for Kenya, and at the Conference of Colonial Governors in London in January 1959 he had predicated a timetable of independence for Tanganyika by 1970, Kenya by 1975 and Uganda by 1972/1973.[51] The white settlers in Kenya, who had been encouraged by both Labour and Conservative governments to establish farmsteads there, and who had lived through the worst of the Mau Mau terrorism, were anxious about a renewal of violence. So there was mistrust on both sides.

The first reports of the outrages at Hola reached Lennox-Boyd as he was about to announce his retirement from politics at the next election to rejoin the board of Guinness.[52] Macmillan now refused to allow him to make this statement, lest it be thought he was resigning over Hola.[53] Macmillan was anxious throughout the crisis to keep Lennox-Boyd on board so that he could 'present voters at the 1959 General Election with the image of a party fully united behind the Colonial Secretary'.[54] In this he succeeded, though many corners were cut on the way.

Macmillan's path was smoothed by the existence of the Conservative Party's Commonwealth Affairs Committee, which acted as a useful safety valve. Here disgruntled Tory MPs could, and did, vent their frustrations without inhibition. Having had their say, these backbenchers were then restrained in their public criticisms, so as to avoid giving succour to the Opposition's attacks.

It became clear that Evelyn Baring, the Governor of Kenya, had too readily accepted the version of events from his officials, and had told Lennox-Boyd that the 11 deaths were caused by drinking poisoned water. Lennox-Boyd had then reported as such to the Commons. When the pathologist's report showed that the true cause was that the Africans had been beaten to death, there was no holding back the tide of bitter criticism.

The first debate on the massacre took place on 16 June in the wake of the publication of the first of three White Papers on Hola.[55] There were fierce personal attacks on both Lennox-Boyd and Baring, particularly from the former Labour Solicitor General, Sir Frank Soskice[56] who said that events at Hola had 'shocked and dismayed civilised opinion all over the world'.[57] Matters were not helped by the recent announcement that one of the officials at Hola was to be awarded the MBE.* Lennox-Boyd offered Macmillan his resignation, but this was refused.

The issue arose again a month later, following the debate on 17 July on the second White Paper on Hola. The earlier pattern was repeated, with calls for heads to roll, and a refused resignation. Macmillan told his Colonial Secretary that if he went then, it would be inevitable that the Governor would also have to go, together with the Minister of State at the Colonial Office, Lord Perth, and the Under-Secretary, Julian Amery. With an election looming, such a mass resignation would have had incalculable effects. Even though a third White Paper exonerated the government in general, and attached no personal blame to the Colonial Secretary or Governor, Lennox-Boyd again unsuccessfully pressed the case for his resignation.

As if the Kenyan situation was not crisis enough for Macmillan's government, on the very same day as the deaths in Hola camp – 3 March – the Governor of Nyasaland, Sir Robert Armitage,[60] declared a state of emergency. The escalating violence had left him with little option. Riots were widespread throughout the country, as nationalist groups rebelled against proposed constitutional reforms. Hastings Banda and hundreds of his supporters were held. Eventually a patched-up peace of sorts was established. The two crises in Kenya and Nyasaland thus ran contemporaneously, each providing fodder for the Opposition. Lennox-Boyd, having made his speech on Hola in the early hours of 28 July in the House of Commons, had to make a second one later that same day on Nyasaland.

The whips scheduled the Debate on Nyasaland for what turned out to be the small hours of 28 July (no newspaper headlines therefore that day) and on the eve of the summer recess. Yet the debate was to be remembered for a speech of remorseless logic and powerful emotion by Enoch Powell, whom Macmillan described in his diary as 'a sort of Fakir'.[61] Powell's criticism of the government was far more effective than the Opposition's. First describing events at Hola as 'a great administrative disaster', Powell warmed to his theme: 'It is argued that this is Africa, that things are different there. Of course

---

* Subsequent enquiries showed that the officials who had been sent down to Hola to investigate had made a far from comprehensive inspection of the site (or the bodies) and had spoken to few of those actually running the camp.

they are. The question is whether the difference between things there and here is such that the taking of responsibility there and here should be on different principles...we cannot, we dare not, in Africa of all places, fall below our own highest standards* in the acceptance of responsibility.'[62]

Macmillan's immediate concern was that the violence should not escalate any further. He amended Lennox-Boyd's minute of instructions to Armitage, by adding that if weapons were used to disperse crowds, they should be used 'in such a way as not to cause casualties, as, for example, in the old days troops "fired over the heads of the mob"'.[63]

A Commmission of Inquiry was promptly set up to look into the Nyasaland emergency. It was a time for commissions. On 17 March, the Cabinet also took the decision to set up a Royal Commission on the future of the Central African Federation. Macmillan was determined that this commission should be bi-partisan, which is why he chose to head it the conciliatory figure of Walter Monckton, whose job as Minister of Labour in the Churchill government had been to appease the trade unions.[64]

The chairman of the Nyasaland Commission was chosen, not by Macmillan, but by Lord Kilmuir, the Lord Chancellor. Macmillan thought Kilmuir's choice of Patrick Devlin[65] politically ill advised. 'I was away in Russia when the Devlin Commission was chosen,' Macmillan wrote in an uncharitable diary entry, which shows Macmillan himself in an unattractive light:

Why Devlin? The poor Lord Chancellor – the sweetest and most naive of men – chose him: He was able, a Conservative; runner-up or nearly so for Lord Chief Justice. I have since discovered that he is (a) *Irish* – no doubt with that Fenian blood that makes Irishmen anti-Government on principle, (b) a *lapsed* Roman Catholic. His brother is a Jesuit priest; his sister a nun. He married a Jewess, who was converted, and was *received* a Catholic, c) a hunchback, d) bitterly *disappointed* at not being made Lord Chief Justice.'[66]

Of the Devlin Report itself, Macmillan added, 'I am not at all surprised that this report is dynamite.'[67]

The Report was dynamite indeed. On the first page it stated: 'Nyasaland is – no doubt only temporarily – a police state where it is

---

*Macmillan knew all too well that the highest standards had not been maintained, and Powell's remarks hit home. Yet he appreciated intellectual brilliance when he saw it and in July 1960, Powell was to return to government as Minister of Health.

not safe for anyone to express approval of the policies of the Congress Party, to which before 3 March, 1959 the vast majority of politically-minded Africans belonged, and where it is unwise to express any but the most restrained criticism of government policy.'[68] Macmillan was livid. Such was not the language of government White Papers, certainly not that of a gentleman, even if what it said was in practice true. In fact, one of the three commissioners, Sir Percy Wyn-Harris,[69] had to be dissuaded from writing a minority report, dissenting from Devlin's robust criticism of Armitage's abuse of power. Rumours persisted that pressure was put on Devlin to rewrite parts of the report.[70]

The Cabinet took the unusual, but not unprecedented, step of rejecting the report.[71] Sir Robert Armitage had two days to draft a response to Devlin's work of four months. Over a frantic weekend at Chequers, Lord Kilmuir, the Lord Chancellor, Sir Reginald Manningham-Buller,[72] the Attorney General, and Julian Amery, Under-Secretary at Colonies, helped him put together a joint response. Armitage did not equivocate. 'I must place on record,' he wrote, 'my regret that the commission should have felt it necessary to refer to Nyasaland as being at present "a police state"'. He continued, 'these words will I believe be quoted out of context and misused throughout the world, and in particular in Nyasaland'. Armitage was correct in his prognosis. Though Nyasaland is a long-forgotten controversy, mention of the Devlin Report immediately evokes the words 'police state'.

The two documents – the Devlin Report and Armitage's dispatch – were then considered at a Cabinet meeting on 20 July. It was the most difficult occasion since the Thorneycroft resignation Cabinets in January 1958. Macmillan drew on all his political guile to hold the team together. Before the Cabinet at 11.30 a.m., he saw first Butler, then Lennox-Boyd, whilst the Cabinet, who had been able to read the Devlin Report over the weekend, were given copies of Armitage's dispatch, which they read whilst Macmillan, Butler and Lennox-Boyd sat outside in the Downing Street garden. Lennox-Boyd again said that he must resign. Rab Butler told him that this would be wrong, if not impolitic. Macmillan added that if Lennox-Boyd agreed, he would ask each member of the Cabinet to give his view before he gave his own. It was a shrewd tactic.

When the Cabinet assembled, Macmillan said that he had an offer of the Colonial Secretary's resignation and wanted to hear the views of each member. He began by asking for the views of the two lawyers who had drafted part of the addendum to Armitage's dispatch, Kilmuir and Manningham-Buller. Both declared that Lennox-Boyd and Armitage should stay in office. Faced with this opening to the innings, few of the lower-order batsmen were likely to differ. It was an individual ballot, but not a secret one. The votes were marshalled more subtly than at an Eatanswill election,* but just as effectively. When all had declared in favour of the Colonial Secretary and the Governor, Macmillan said that such was his view also, and that if the Cabinet had decided otherwise, he would have resigned as Prime Minister.

The debate on the Devlin Report – specifically on the government's decision, curate's egg-like, to accept only parts of it – took place on 28 July, hours after the conclusion of the debate on Kenya. The government had a majority of 63. The successful mood surrounding the Cyprus settlement seemed a distant memory.

Macmillan saved Lennox-Boyd, but he knew that after the election, he would, if the Conservatives were returned to power, have to appoint a Colonial Secretary responsive to progressive opinion in Britain and sympathetic to nationalist opinion in Africa. 'Empire' divided the Conservatives at that time in the way that 'Europe' was to do later. Hardline back-benchers, with their racist prejudices and 'little Englander' attitudes, were the despair of Macmillan, who knew deep down that the outrage expressed by Devlin and Powell was right.

The summer of 1959 was glorious. As *The Economist* observed: 'The sun is shining down on Britain's packed beaches in the first hot summer since 1955 and in an atmosphere of easy holiday contentment the literally floating voter feels no burning desire for change.'[73] To add to the 'feel-good' atmosphere, the England cricket team won all five of its Test matches (against India), three of them by an innings.

Macmillan knew that the ideal launch pad for his election campaign would be to have Eisenhower as a personal guest at Downing Street. As a Republican, Eisenhower had no desire to see a Labour government in office; on the other hand, he resented the way in which Macmillan was attempting to control his movements if he visited Europe in the autumn. Eisenhower had also been warned by his advisers of a possible hostile reception, as the British had not forgiven him for Suez.[74] In any case, with the Foreign Ministers' Conference in Geneva far from being resolved, it was by no means certain that he would be travelling to Europe at all. Macmillan, though, could be very persuasive and he drew on all the reserves of goodwill latent from their wartime association. When it became clear that Eisenhower would after all be visiting Europe for talks, before Khrushchev's visit

---

* *The Pickwick Papers* by Dickens, about corrupt pre-Reform Bill elections.

to the United States in September, Macmillan made sure that London was on the itinerary. The Foreign Office made it known to Christian Herter, Dulles' successor as Secretary of State, that 'if he [Eisenhower] does not come to the U.K., this will be an insult to the Queen'.[75] This may have been melodramatic, but it worked. On 7 August, it was announced from Buckingham Palace that the Queen was expecting her third child.[76] As a result, the royal hospitality for Eisenhower would be in Balmoral, not London. It was an invitation Eisenhower could not refuse.

'The Eisenhower visit is now more or less fixed for August 28,' Macmillan wrote to Rab Butler, after the long and at times difficult negotiations with the White House. 'I think all this has worked out much better than I had dared to hope some weeks ago. We seem to have acquired quite a lot of credit. The moral is one never knows in politics: sometimes things work out well and sometimes badly. The only thing is to cash in when they turn out well.'[77]

And cash in Macmillan did. The most powerful man in the world was revealed as an intimate 'buddy' of the Prime Minister. On 27 August, people turned out to line the route from Heathrow, and it took the motorcade two hours to reach Grosvenor Square, Eisenhower's old wartime headquarters. Suez was quite forgotten. As the crowds grew ever denser round Grosvenor Square, Harold repeated to Ike, 'I would never have believed it, I would never have believed it.'[78]

There was a holiday atmosphere about the visit. Not only did Eisenhower enjoy his stay in the Scottish Highlands with the Queen at the start, he ended his tour with a private call at Culzean Castle in Ayrshire, where he had been given an apartment in perpetuity by the people of Scotland in gratitude for his wartime service.

Macmillan entertained Eisenhower at Chequers, taking him incognito on 30 August to Oxford to look round Magdalen and Christ Church. The next day they drove – to the concern of security men – in an open-top car to St Paul's Cathedral to see the American Chapel. Again there were enthusiastic crowds lining the streets. That evening Macmillan gave a dinner at 10 Downing Street for Eisenhower, attended by Churchill, Attlee and Eden, all of whom spoke. What was most remembered about this evening, though, was the 'informal' pre-dinner talk between the two old wartime comrades, relaxed in dinner jackets, a conversation the country was able to share live on television. Such an occasion was unprecedented and gave a vicarious and glamorous glimpse of power, combined with gracious living, that resonated deeply.

Eisenhower gave a return dinner at the American Embassy on 1

September for his old compatriots from the war. Macmillan stylishly asked to be placed at table not as the Prime Minister, but lower down as 'Political Adviser AFHQ', so that Alexander and Alanbrooke could sit next to the President. Churchill attended also, as did Montgomery, and several field marshals, admirals and marshals of the Royal Air Force. In his speech Macmillan said, to general amusement, that even when he was a publisher he had never seen so many authors in one room.[79]

On 7 September, Macmillan, in the afterglow of the Eisenhower visit, travelled to Balmoral, to ask – not advise – the Queen formally for a dissolution of Parliament. He was determined to preserve this prerogative of the Crown, which 'might be of vital importance at a time of national crisis'.[80] After dinner, the company was shown *I'm All Right Jack*, a popular film that contributed in no small measure to the negative view of trade unions and even in its way to the eventual Conservative victory.[81] The next day the Cabinet was informed of Macmillan's decision and a public announcement was made that dissolution would be on 18 September, with polling day on 8 October. An added bonus for Macmillan was that the news disrupted the TUC Conference at Blackpool.

In fact, Macmillan caused maximum inconvenience to Labour and their paymasters three times that election year. In February there had been his well-publicised visit to Russia, which meant that Gaitskell's similar plans had to be delayed. When Gaitskell, and Bevan, eventually travelled to Russia in August, all the media concentration was on Eisenhower's visit to Britain, which completely overshadowed coverage of Gaitskell's tour. Then on 8 September, at the end of the Russian visit, as Gaitskell and Bevan were about to fly on to Poland, they had to return post-haste to Britain when Macmillan announced the dissolution of Parliament.[82]

The general election campaign of 1959 was predominantly a national rather than a local affair. The focus throughout was very much on the leaders, a process intensified by the widespread television coverage. In 1955, 40 per cent of the population had a television; by 1959, the figure was over 70 per cent. The daily press conferences – the Battle of Smith Square, as it was dubbed by the journalists[83] – were covered on television news bulletins.

At the outset of the campaign, two thirds of the electorate thought Macmillan was doing a good job as Prime Minister. Unemployment was falling, and production was up. Income tax was at 38.75 per cent, as opposed to 47.5 per cent in 1951. In spite of all these indicators, the

Labour leader, Hugh Gaitskell (7 per cent ahead in the polls in June 1957), was confident of victory, and in the first days of the campaign the Opposition seemed to be making headway, the reversal of the normal electoral pattern. Overall the election fell into three phases: a quiet initial period, followed by 10 days of vigorous Labour attacks, leading to a Conservative counter-attack in the last week and a half.

Macmillan had observed the courtesies. He invited Anthony and Clarissa Eden to Birch Grove for the weekend,[84] and travelled to Chartwell to 'consult' Churchill. The kind of campaign now unfolding, though, was not one with which Churchill was familiar. The Conservatives were to spend £113,000 on an advertising campaign run by Colman, Prentis and Varley, the public relations firm who devised the slogan 'Life's better under the Conservatives. Don't let Labour ruin it.'[85] Posters with this message had appeared on the hoardings every month since January. The slogan fulfilled one of Macmillan's beliefs, that propaganda must be understandable. He also believed that the important aspect of political advertising was not the colour on the poster, but the legibility of the message. This successful slogan was both understandable and legible. Advertising, especially after the advent of commercial television in September 1955, was now a growing influence on both consumer spending and public attitudes. Although the Conservatives embraced the new techniques enthusiastically Macmillan was always wary lest 'public relations' became a substitute for policy.

The public perception according to the polls was that Macmillan was 'fun', whereas Gaitskell was 'dry'. Although this worked to Macmillan's advantage, the reverse was actually more truthful. Macmillan had now reverted to his earlier pre-war earnestness in pursuit of votes, whereas Gaitskell's private life was adventurous.[86] Their lifestyles were also very different. One could not imagine Macmillan putting aside his favourite Victorian novels, rolling back the carpets at Birch Grove and leading the dancing, something Gaitskell often did when partying at his home in Frognall Gardens in Hampstead.[87]

The combination of well-directed central and local spending (264 per cent higher than Labour's), combined with the efficiently organised campaign, directed by Lord Hailsham, the party chairman, and Lord Poole, former, now deputy, chairman, gave the Conservatives a distinct edge. The importance of the postal vote (a six-to-one lead in marginals) also bore evidence of a campaign that left no stone unturned. Such thoroughness was necessary. The Labour campaign was considered the best, technically, that they had waged up to that point. However, Macmillan took nothing for granted. He wrote rather touchingly in his diary midway through the campaign, 'It is rather a strange feeling to lie in bed in this room at No. 10 (which I have occupied for nearly three years) & wonder whether I shall be here in 10 days' time.'[88]

Gaitskell made some fundamental errors. 'Compared with pre-war, most people are a good deal better off,' he admitted in the *Daily Mail* on 30 July. This was indeed so, but the voters, particularly those who read the *Daily Mail*, did not associate such progress with Labour. Gaitskell was on sounder ground when he added, 'There are signs of the breaking up of traditional loyalties.'[89] There were indeed, but the break-up was not to Labour's advantage. The Labour veteran Hugh Dalton recorded a dispiriting post-election talk with Jim Callaghan. 'He says children of Socialists in Housing Estates often voted Tory. One old boy in Cardiff told him that his son had said, "All right, Dad. Labour may suit you, but I'm voting Conservative this time."'[90] Although Labour won votes from voters who were disillusioned by Suez and appalled by Kenya and Nyasaland, this was more than counterbalanced for the Conservatives by the increase in their working-class support. Suez had passed into history and was hardly mentioned at all by the candidates.

Although a March 1959 Gallup poll said that 60 per cent of the public did not know what the Liberal Party stood for, the Liberals, who fielded 216 candidates, substantially increased their overall vote (by nearly one million) for the first time since 1929. Jo Grimond, the Liberal leader, was well liked across the political spectrum.

The Tory manifesto, *The Next Five Years*, was published on 11 September. With Labour's enthusiasm for the new comprehensive schools, education was an important issue. Many financially stretched middle-class voters, now unable to afford for their children the private education they had experienced themselves, were desperately worried about the threat to the grammar schools.[91] 'We shall defend the grammar schools against doctrinaire Socialist attack,' the Tory manifesto declared, 'and see that they are further developed.'[92]

Fifty-seven members of the Conservative Bow Group stood as candidates. To Macmillan's delight, 10 of them were returned to Parliament, six for the first time. The Bow Group had been founded in 1951 as a progressive Tory equivalent of 'intellectual Socialism' and the Fabian Society. Macmillan encouraged the Bow Group – a political 'think tank' before the phrase became generally used – in many ways, launching their quarterly magazine *Crossbow* in 1957.[93]

Macmillan stumped the country, travelling 2,500 miles and making 74 speeches, the first big one in Manchester on 23 September. All his speeches were carefully checked for errors or clashes by the Conservative Research Department and their relevant departments throughout the campaign before delivery. For an overworked man of 65, prone to hypochondria, and always carrying the burden of his war wounds, such an intensive programme showed considerable stamina. Dr Richardson was in attendance, and kept him on the road.

On 28 September, Eisenhower and Khrushchev announced that the way was open for a Summit. Beaverbrook's *Daily Express* blazoned the news as *MACMILLAN'S TRIUMPH*.[94] On the same day, unemployment figures showed a fall of 22,000 in the previous month. On 30 September, news came that output in August 1959 was up 8 per cent on the equivalent month in 1958, and on 2 October, gold and dollar reserves were revealed to have increased by £13m in September.

The twenty-eighth of September was to be a crucial day in other respects, for on that day Gaitskell made the blunder that psephologists have always identified as the turning point of the campaign.[95] In a speech in Newcastle he pledged no increase, in normal peacetime circumstances, in income tax. Macmillan was not alone in realising that Gaitskell, in turning the election into an auction, had made a fundamental mistake. The next day at Labour's Transport House daily press conference, Morgan Phillips, the party's national secretary, was asked further about the report that Labour would reduce purchase tax on essential items. Phillips said that it was a Labour commitment. Gaitskell was furious, for he knew that the double pledge was now turning into an electoral liability. 'How rapidly moods in an Election change!' Richard Crossman wrote in his diary.[96] Labour never regained the initiative.[97] Macmillan, stoking up old Labour divisions, took the opportunity of reminding voters that in his only Budget in April 1951, Gaitskell had put 6d on income tax 'and for good measure he put a charge on spectacles and teeth under the health service'.[98]

On 5 October, Field Marshal Montgomery weighed in, declaring that anyone who now voted Labour 'must be completely barmy, absolutely off his rocker and should be locked up in a lunatic asylum as a danger to the country'. In perspective this Blimpish[99] intervention seems comic, but 'Monty' was a figure of massive popularity, especially amongst the working-class veterans of the campaigns of the Western Desert and Normandy, and the outburst was not counterproductive. Montgomery deeply admired Macmillan, believing him 'to be a great man in international affairs who deserved to be allowed to put Europe to rights'.[100] Macmillan would have preferred this endorsement, on the day that Montgomery declared he was to become a Conservative, in more measured tones. It was left to Lord Hailsham, the party chairman, welcoming his new recruit, to say, 'I think these fighting men have a colourful means of expressing themselves.'[101]

On 6 October, two days before polling, Macmillan delivered the last television party political broadcast of the campaign.* It was master-minded by Norman Collins, a key figure in the early days of inde-pendent television. Macmillan was rather fearful of any mistakes in the live broadcast that evening. Unbeknown to him, Collins recorded the rehearsal at the tiny ATV Foley Street studio in Nottingham. Macmillan was so relaxed the rehearsal was the version used, some-thing Collins had planned all along. When Macmillan realised that the broadcast was in the can, literally, he said gratefully to Collins that it was 'like going to the dentist to have a tooth out and to be told that it has already been drawn'. The BBC, who had been expecting to broadcast the Prime Minister live, were furious that they had instead to transmit a production of their rivals. To soothe ruffled feathers, Macmillan said he would accompany the can of the film to the BBC studios, and honour was satisfied.

Collins advised Macmillan to deliver his speech standing, and to walk between his desk, where letters were conveniently placed, and an enormous globe, which he deftly turned, giving the intended impres-sion that here was a man who had the world in his hands. 'This final broadcast,' the record of the 1959 Election concluded, 'regarded as the most important in the election, was widely acclaimed – even the *Daily Mirror* applauded it. The picture was conveyed of the Prime Minister as a relaxed and confident statesman, fully in touch with domestic and international problems.'[102]

On polling day, Macmillan and Lady Dorothy, by his side throughout the campaign, toured Bromley and then settled down in the evening to see the first results. By 1 a.m., Gaitskell had conceded the elec-tion, an American innovation that his dejected colleagues thought unnecessary. The Macmillans went to Smith Square an hour later to congratulate the party workers. To their delight, Maurice Macmillan and Julian Amery had both increased their majorities, in Halifax and Preston respectively. Later that day, 9 October, Macmillan went down to Bromley for the declaration of his own result. The figures were:

Harold Macmillan (Conservative)	27,055
A. J. Murray (Labour)	11,603
Conservative majority	15,452

---

*It became one of the most famous in post-war election history, not least because it later provided the basis in 1961 for Peter Cook's impersonation of Macmillan in the sketch TVPM in *Beyond the Fringe*. For one who had never found television easy, to be dubbed the TV PM was a belated compliment.

Macmillan's majority from 1955 had increased by 2,313. When the final result of the election, Jo Grimond's seat in Orkney and Shetland, was declared on 10 October, the scale of the landslide was clear. The Conservatives had won 365 seats, Labour 258 and the Liberals 6, a majority of 100 seats over all other parties.

'It has gone off rather well,' Macmillan wrote, with considerable understatement, in his diary.[103] It had indeed. The Tories had confronted a tougher task than in 1951 or 1955, as they faced an invigorated Opposition, and a resurgent Liberal Party. Yet they still increased their number of votes, from 13,296,569 in 1955 to 13,749,830 in 1959.

The accepted explanation was that prosperity won the day for the Conservatives. Yet the reasons were more complex and went deeper. As Richard Crossman wrote in his diary, 'Tory voters are far more afraid of another Labour Government than Labour voters are afraid of another Tory Government.'[104] The 1959 general election took place at a particularly transitional moment in British society. The old shibboleths were under threat. Allegiances were changing as the old working class became more distinctly capitalist in outlook. When Noel Skelton had proclaimed the benefits of the property-owning democracy in the 1920s, he was thinking primarily of the benefits for those enabled by such economic advance. The real benefit politically, though, proved to be for the Conservative Party.

Voting Tory was a sign of 'going up in the world', no less than home ownership, a car, or a first foreign holiday. Macmillan understood this, and had pitched much of his appeal at this aspiring section of the lower-middle class. 'To build is the laborious task of years,' he had said in his final television broadcast on 6 October, two days before the general election. 'To destroy can be the foolish act of a single day.' The implication was clear – 'Don't let Labour ruin it' had proved a telling slogan.

Macmillan told David Butler that the election had been won because of progressive policies and the glorious summer. 'Even porpoises had been spotted in the North Sea,' he recalled. The results showed how many agreed with this diagnosis. The trade unionist Ray Gunter told David Butler that Macmillan was the cleverest man in politics.[105]

Even the *Observer*, bane of the Tory Party during Suez, took a mellow view. 'The true interest of the Tory Party clearly lies in the continuation of that secret and unacknowledged alliance between the leadership and the younger progressives, such as the Bow Group, which Mr Macmillan himself has encouraged and which has been fruitful in bringing forward new ideas. If this happens, the country need not regret its choice.'[106]

The 1959 election showed that Macmillan appealed to a remarkably broad cross-section of British society: the deferential working class, who believed that the governing class knew their business, and that it was best to let them be about it; the military veterans, who admired his Great War record, in an age when MPs who had seen active service were referred to in the House of Commons as Honourable and Gallant; the aspiring lower-middle class, who wanted their children to have educational opportunities denied to themselves in pre-war days; the Rotary Club members in his Bromley constituency, who thought him a Prime Minister who actually looked like a Prime Minister; the left-of-centre Keynesian economists, who saw the author of *The Middle Way* as a kindred spirit; the intellectual and university world (the constituency that was Gaitskell's strong point), which admired his innate seriousness on the big issues; the business world, which knew that he was a man of vast commercial experience who could actually read a balance sheet; Disraelian 'One Nation' Conservatives, who wanted 'Tory men and Whig measures'; the world of letters, who were in reverence at his links with writers such as Hardy and Yeats; the religious community (though not Archbishop Fisher), for his loyal churchmanship; the patriots, who applauded his unambiguous pursuit of British interests; what might be called the 'Chatham House' constituency, who admired his approach to the second phase of decolonisation; and the aristocrats, who saw him as one of their own, though he was really a Forsyte businessman who had married into the aristocracy, rather than being an aristocrat himself. Gaitskell, in contrast, 'always came over as rather wooden and patronising'.[107]

Macmillan was in no doubt as to the way ahead. 'The great thing is to keep the Tory Party on *modern* and *progressive* lines.'[108]

After his great election victory, Macmillan began the task of forming his new Cabinet. Rab Butler was no longer pressing to become Foreign Secretary. Work at the Home Office was absorbing his full attention and he was sufficiently politically astute to realise the disadvantages of flitting from post to post. Macmillan, though, was always willing to flatter Butler, whether through guilt or sympathy, and he now asked him to take on, in addition to the two jobs Butler already had as Home Secretary and Leader of the House, the post of Conservative Party Chairman. It was yet another prestigious hat for him to wear. The reality, though, was that the hat did not actually mean much politically.

Butler's acceptance of the party chairmanship was a mistake on his part. The post of party chairman is immensely important in the run-up to an election; since the Tories had just been returned for a full term, it was inevitably now low-key. Second, as Anthony Howard, Butler's biographer, has noted, 'there were bound to be difficulties in combining the essentially cheer-leading job of Chairman of the Party with the traditionally non-partisan role of Leader of the House'.[109] Butler's thoughts at that time were not entirely concentrated on politics. On 21 October he married Mollie Courtauld,* widow of August Courtauld, the famous Arctic explorer. Butler's first wife, Sydney (a cousin of August Courtauld), when she was dying of cancer, had always hoped that Butler would one day marry Mollie.[110]

Butler's appointment meant a curious double demotion for Lord Hailsham, who later wrote that he was 'fed up with being cold-shouldered and snubbed after I had given my very best and achieved success in a seemingly impossible task'.[111] He would have been even more fed up if he had been able to read Macmillan's diary. 'Lord Hailsham,' he wrote, 'is really not safe.' He added, 'Hailsham is in a very overexcited condition and keeps giving ridiculous "press conferences" – but no doubt he will quieten down soon.'[112] In his own words, Hailsham was 'received frostily'[113] at Number 10 and offered the choice of a return to his former post at the Ministry of Education, or the new post of Science and Technology, coupled with the sinecure post of Lord Privy Seal. Hailsham thought it impossible to return to Education after the chairmanship of the party, so with some reluctance he accepted Science and Technology. The press reaction was not good. What could this distinguished classicist know about science? Alec Home took over from Hailsham as Lord President of the Council. Selwyn Lloyd, now a hardy perennial in the upper reaches of government, remained at the Foreign Office, continuing his Sancho Panza role.

Derick Heathcoat Amory now asked Macmillan to honour their agreement. He would, if pressed, accept a minor post, but the Treasury was too much of a burden, and he wanted to go back to his business interests in Devon. Macmillan persuaded him to stay on until after the 1960 Budget.

Alan Lennox-Boyd's retirement enabled Macmillan to put Iain Macleod in charge of the Colonies, a key promotion giving Macleod the clear opportunity of establishing himself as a successor-in-waiting. Duncan Sandys was not best pleased to be offered the Ministry of Supply, with the remit to break it up and form a new ministry of aviation. The 'self-made' men, always important for Macmillan in

---

* Mollie Butler was to become the most determined of Macmillan's critics.

Cabinet-building, Harold Watkinson and Ernest Marples, went to Defence and Transport respectively. Edward Heath became Minister of Labour, with his old job as Chief Whip going to Martin Redmayne. Heath had arguably been the most successful of all post-war Chief Whips, and Redmayne was not in the same league. Reggie Maudling received a significant promotion to become President of the Board of Trade, with Freddie Errol moving from the post of Economic Secretary to become his Minister of State. They became a powerful duo.[114] David Eccles returned, with some reluctance, to Education, the post he had held from 1954–1957. Lord Carrington, returning from his three-year spell as High Commissioner in Australia, became First Lord of the Admiralty.

The allocation of some of the minor posts outside the Cabinet did not go entirely smoothly. Jocelyn (Jack) Simon, who had first cautioned Macmillan against an early election back in January, became Solicitor General after Sir Harry Hylton-Foster had been translated, following some Labour discontent, to the speakership. Aubrey Jones, whom Macmillan had once asked if there had been a Sligger Urquhart at his alma mater, the London School of Economics, was bitterly disappointed that his old Ministry of Supply was to be broken up. He returned to the back benches after being offered only a minor post. 'The son of a coal miner,' Macmillan noted of Jones after their awkward interview, 'but he looks like, and is like, a rather overlaid and stylish effete younger son of a Duke.'[115]

Surprisingly, for a reshuffle that seemed simple on the surface, there were many bruised egos.* The winners were the young Turks who had first entered Parliament in that vintage generation of 1950 – Heath, Macleod and Maudling. One seemingly minor change was to be of unexpected later significance. Anthony Barber, who had been Macmillan's eyes and ears as Parliamentary Private Secretary since 1958, was promoted to the post of Economic Secretary to the Treasury. To replace Barber, Macmillan chose Sir Knox Cunningham, the blunt-speaking Ulster Unionist MP for South Antrim. Cunningham was what in parliamentary circles was known as 'colourful'. Such a choice comes with risks. Although Cunningham was the most loyal and industrious of Macmillan's circle (he called his memoirs *One Man Dog*), his political antennae were not on the same level of sophistication as the sharpest of Westminster operators.[117]

---

*In 1916, when Lloyd George offered Balfour the Foreign Secretaryship, Balfour exclaimed, 'You put a pistol to my head, I must accept.'[116] Unfortunately, there are never enough pistols to go round, and this was the case in 1959. Macmillan, though, was in a position of such personal strength that he could do exactly as he wished.

Macmillan's own prestige was at its height, and Labour was breaking out into factional discord. On 23 December, Macmillan wrote to Rab Butler, conscious of how much Butler had done for the party organisation: 'I think we have got through the first lap of the parliamentary year very successfully and I am most grateful to you. A lot of troublesome matters have been dealt with and the new Members have begun to find their feet. Nevertheless it will not be an easy house to manage – unless of course things get very bad: English people are always easier to handle in adversity than in prosperity!'[118]

Yet such is the unexpected and volatile nature of politics, that this situation did not last. From the peaks of success, there is only one way to go.

CHAPTER TWENTY FOUR

Return to Africa

1960

The wind of change is blowing through this continent, and,
whether we like it or not, this growth of national consciousness is a political fact.

> Harold Macmillan, speaking to both Houses of the South
> African Parliament, 3 February 1960

Like a sleeping hippo in a pool, suddenly it gets a prod from
the white man and wakes up; and it won't go to sleep again.

> Harold Macmillan, on Africa, 1960

Westward the course of empire takes its way;
The first four acts already past.
A fifth shall close the drama with the day:
Time's noblest offspring is the last.

> Bishop Berkeley, 1752[1]

At the beginning of 1960, Macmillan had undisputed power and the
time to use it as he chose. He had not been complacent about the
outcome of the general election. Indeed, he had admitted in reply to
Anthony Eden's letter of congratulation that 'there were moments
during the Election in which I was rather concerned'.[2] He was determined, though, that whichever party formed the next administration it
should have access to properly reseached policy options.

Macmillan had adopted this approach from the beginning of his
premiership. In 1957 he had commissioned an analysis of the costs
of Empire, and weighed them against the benefits. In 1957–1958 he
established a committee of permanent secretaries, under the chairmanship of Sir Norman Brook, Cabinet Secretary, to examine, no less,
Britain's position in the modern world. In the autumn of 1959, in
conditions of secrecy akin to the Joint Intelligence Committee, a third
initiative followed, the Future Policy Study Group, chaired by Sir
Patrick Dean, then head of the Foreign Office defence department.
This study group considered the 'Next Ten Years', twice as many as
Stalin used to examine, Macmillan joked.[3]

The Future Policy Study Group was staffed by Whitehall's brightest and best, under-secretaries from the Foreign, Colonial and Commonwealth Offices, plus Treasury mandarins, and equivalent ranks of civil servants from the Ministries of Defence, and Fuel and Power. The group considered three questions. 'What will the world be like in ten years' time? What will Britain's position in it be? What should be done about it?' This was 'globe-turning' on a grand scale.

Such long-term assessments inevitably produced contradictory responses. Macmillan, however, did not seek glib or 'easy' solutions. The important thing was to identify likely pan-global trends and consider the various options rationally. One of the results of cost-benefit analysis of Empire from 1957 meant that 1960 was the year in which National Service, that two-year hiatus and rite of passage for dissociated and often disgruntled youth,[4] finally ended, another Macmillan initiative of which many Tory back-benchers disapproved.

Cabinet committees were not a new invention. 'The English way is a committee,' Walter Bagehot had written in 1867, 'we are born with a belief in a green cloth, clean pens and twelve men with grey hair.'[5] In February 1936, Tom Jones, Deputy Cabinet Secretary, had recorded that the Cabinet Office bred committee like rabbits.[6] The breeding did not diminish.*

Cabinet committees allowed groups of Cabinet ministers and their advisers to work on policy away from Downing Street, whilst at the same time keeping the larger body informed and involved. † Many were fruitful. The committee in 1959 on University Population led, as planned, to what became the Robbins Report on Higher Education in September 1963, one of the most significant developments of the Macmillan years.

After EFTA was established in 1959, the ministerial Free Trade Area Committee quietly had its name, but not its membership, changed to the Economic Association Committee.[9] Macmillan was by now convinced that closer European economic association for Britain was not only inevitable, but desirable. If only, said the Europhiles with hindsight, he had felt the same when he was Foreign Secretary at the time of the Messina conference in 1955. Macmillan kept his cards

---

*With the advent of the welfare state, the nationalisation programme of Attlee's government and the attachment to Keynesian economics, the burden on Cabinet became overladen. Delegation was overwhelmingly to committees, though in 1961 Macmillan was to put a second Treasury minister in the Cabinet Room, the Chief Secretary, to relieve the workload of centralised direction.[7]

†Macmillan used this committee system extensively, so much so that one of the first things his successor, Sir Alec Douglas-Home, did was to take a swathe to the many such bodies that had reached the end of their natural life.[8]

very close to his chest. All the inevitable problems about loyalty to the Commonwealth, butter mountains, the price of prunes and what Gaitskell called 'the end of a thousand years of history'[10] could wait. Potential opponents – in both Africa and Europe – did not fully realise what was afoot until Macmillan's policies were well advanced. As Jacqueline Tratt has pointed out, 'the Anti-Common Market League did not come into existence until August 1961',[11] a month after Macmillan had announced to Parliament his plans to apply for membership of the European Economic Community.

If the application to join the Common Market was one prong of the fork of 'Future Policy', the other was to seal a Test Ban Treaty. These twin aims were at the heart of the remaining years of the Macmillan premiership. Macmillan's thoughts were already looking ahead to the May summit in Paris.

Looking ahead was also true in another delicate area. Churchill had celebrated his eighty-fifth birthday in November. The Queen had made it known to Macmillan at their meeting at Sandringham before he departed for Africa that when the sad event of Churchill's death occurred, the monarch would issue 'Her Royal Command for a State Funeral'. Macmillan was asked to inform the Earl Marshal. Accordingly, he wrote to the Duke of Norfolk on 4 January. 'The only comparable man in our history seemed to me to be the Duke of Marlborough and Wellington,' he wrote, adding that the Queen felt 'it is quite right that you should do as much of the detailed planning as is possible beforehand'.[12] Discussions had also been held about the sensitive question, much desired by the Duke of Edinburgh and Lord Mountbatten, that future royal descendants should be named 'Mountbatten-Windsor'.[13]

The day after setting these funeral plans into motion, Macmillan went to Africa. Ever since his days in North Africa in 1942, the continent had been a talisman for him, as it had been for the great Victorian explorers. When H. M. Stanley (of 'Dr Livingstone, I presume?' fame) died in 1904, he was buried in the churchyard of St Michael and All Angels at Pirbright in Surrey. Above Stanley's grave was placed a huge granite monolith from Dartmoor, on which was carved the single word *AFRICA*.[14] It would not have been out of place as a memorial to Macmillan, for Africa was witness to two of his greatest contributions – at AFHQ during the Second World War, and as the harbinger in 1960 of the eventual ending – after a long struggle – of apartheid in South Africa.[15]

Macmillan and Lady Dorothy set out from Heathrow on 5 January.[16]

They were away until 15 February, during which time Macmillan celebrated his sixty-sixth birthday. With them was the Cabinet Secretary, Sir Norman Brook, 'looking', as Anthony Sampson wrote, 'like a casual tourist who just happened to be following'. Sampson added, 'The local officials took little notice of him, and few of them realised that he was the central cog in the British Government machine.'[17] Tim Bligh, the Principal Private Secretary, and the ubiquitous John Wyndham were close at hand. Sir David Hunt[18] and James Hugh Robertson of the Colonial Office made up the main party.

The first stop was Ghana, what a bowler might have called 'a loosener' before a long and difficult spell, as the country had attained its independence in 1957. Dr Kwame Nkrumah,[19] the Prime Minister, was, however, steering Ghana towards a one-party state, and did not make it easy for Macmillan to meet opposition leaders. From his own wartime service in the Colonial Office, Macmillan knew that the economic potential for Ghana, particularly through sales of cocoa, was very high, and he showed himself well informed of the issues. In a less fastidious age, he also took the opportunity of meeting Macmillan & Co. representatives in Ghana to help in boosting sales in any way he could.[20]

From Accra, he flew to Lagos. He was met here by the Governor General of Nigeria, Sir James Robertson,[21] a Balliol man, and father of James Hugh Robertson of Macmillan's party. Thanks to Robertson, Nigeria was moving relatively smoothly towards eventual independence. Indeed, the Nigerian government, which received Dominion status on 1 October 1960, and remained a republic within the Commonwealth three years later, asked Robertson to stay on after independence, so grateful were they for his stewardship during transition.

On 12 January, Macmillan addressed the Nigerian Council, the equivalent of the Cabinet. During the lengthy discussion that followed, Sir Norman Brook outlined the procedural work of the British Cabinet and the workings of government. On this part of the tour at least there was no underestimating by the local officials of the primacy of Brook's position in the British system. The only down side was a casual remark by Macmillan implying that the Central African Federation was not necessarily a permanent structure. Roy Welensky, who was Prime Minister of the Federation of Rhodesia and Nyasaland, was enraged when he heard the rumours, coinciding as they did with a member of the Monckton Commission, Sir Hartley Shawcross, not ruling out secession from the federation, and Iain Macleod suggesting that the release of Dr Banda was essential if any headway was to be made in Nyasaland.

On 18 January, Macmillan landed in Salisbury, the capital of the Central African Federation. Welensky was still fuming and Macmillan tried, not altogether successfully, to calm him down by saying that he supported the federation. Welensky, who was now the dominating figure in Central African politics, was uncompromising. 'The sight of big powers scuttling out of colonial responsibilities makes me sick,' he said.[22] Outwardly, the grace of the Governor General's residence, where the party was entertained by Lord Dalhousie in lavish splendour, may have reflected the old colonial ways on a vice-regal scale, but Macmillan knew what undercurrents were building. The white settlers reflected unbending attitudes, and were uninhibited in expressing their extremist views – and not only when well lubricated in the clubhouses of their suburban golf clubs. The key feeling Macmillan took away from his time in Rhodesia was its uncertainty.

Salisbury was the base from which Macmillan visited Lusaka in Northern Rhodesia, the copper belt and the Victoria Falls. On 25 January, his party arrived in Nyasaland. Dr Hastings Banda was still in jail, and discussions here were tense.

On his return to Salisbury, Macmillan raised the question of Dr Banda's release; he now knew that this was inevitable, indeed a prerequisite for any hopes for stability. But talks with Roy Welensky revealed a nigh-unbridgeable gulf. It seemed that much would depend on the eventual report of the Monckton Commission, due in October. At the Colonial Office, meanwhile, Macleod was already pushing for Dr Banda's release. Alec Home always maintained that 'Macmillan was a wind of change man and Macleod was a gale of change man.'[23]

Macmillan faced up to the prospect of hostility in South Africa with some apprehension. There would inevitably be demonstrations – one group of blacks unfurled banners saying 'We've never had it so bad' – and although he could cope with this, having developed over the years the necessary carapace, he knew that his reception from the white political leaders would be far from placid. Hugh Trevor-Roper noted that there was at least an even-handedness about Macmillan's treatment. 'The PM,' he wrote, 'was in darkest Africa, moving from place to place with hectic rapidity, being pelted with brick bats by black men in Nairobi and by white men in Cape Town.'[24]

When Macmillan landed at Bechuanaland, he was met by Sir John Maud,[25] the British High Commissioner in South Africa, as well as in the territories of Swaziland, Basutoland and Bechuanaland. Like Macmillan, Maud was an old Summerfieldian and King's Scholar at Eton. At mischievous moments, Macmillan regretted that Maud had blotted the educational triptych by becoming an alumnus of

Gaitskell's New College, rather than his own Balliol. Maud's links with South Africa were long-standing. He had received a postgraduate Rhodes Travelling Fellowship, which first took him to South Africa in 1932, where he was invited to write the history of local government in Johannesburg. Macmillan had chosen him for the key post of South African High Commissioner at the beginning of 1959. Macmillan needed someone of integrity, undoubted intellectual excellence and proven industry.[26] He knew that in Maud he had a trusted adviser* for the sensitive tasks ahead. One of the first of these tasks was seeking some form of rapprochement with the South African Prime Minister, Dr Henrik Verwoerd.[27]

As the Minister of Native Affairs in 1948, Verwoerd had been responsible for enforcing the policy of apartheid, separate development for whites and non-whites. Macmillan saw Verwoerd as a kind of latter-day John Knox, who was convinced that only he was right. In their discussions, Verwoerd told Macmillan that in South Africa there was strong opposition to the Queen being the head of the Commonwealth. A referendum was shortly due on whether South Africa should become a republic.

The old colonial past was still evident. Harold and Dorothy stayed at Groote Schuur, Cecil Rhodes' house in the Dutch colonial style on the slopes of Table Mountain. The contrast between the beauty of the landscapes and the poverty and deprivation of the black townships made a profound impression upon Macmillan.

Macmillan went down a gold mine in Baragwanath, changing into overalls, heavy boots and a helmet with a lamp. After visiting the rock face, he briefly participated in processing the gold into oblong shapes the size of a cake tin. These gold bars were then stacked by the workers into a number of blocks worth millions of pounds, like a scene from Wagner's *Das Rheingold*. Many native ceremonies, in truth too many, were staged for the benefit of the visitors. Lady Dorothy found these particularly tiring, as she had badly torn her leg on entering an aeroplane in Northern Rhodesia, and the wound had to be cleaned and stitched twice during the visit. At the new Bantu University, near Pietersburg, vast crowds gathered. 'Charming, just like Derby Day,' observed the Prime Minister. He was the centre of attention, but only until an ice cream van appeared, when hundreds, whooping with excitement, turned tail for refreshment. A wild hunting dance was staged in front of young girls, wearing beads, which, Macmillan was assured, signified their virginity. Unfortunately for the realism of the chase, the

---

*Patrick Reilly had been equally valuable in Russia, and for similar reasons.

man playing the part of the monkey, draped in an animal skin, was also wearing two sock suspenders.[28]

At 10.30 a.m. on 3 February, Macmillan addressed both houses of the South African Parliament in the Parliamentary Dining Room, the former Chamber of the Cape Colony Parliament. The atmosphere was at first friendly, almost carefree, as the South Africans welcomed an undoubted world figure on to their stage.[29] Macmillan began with soothing noises, stressing his delight at being present in 'your beautiful country'. His speech lasted for 50 minutes, and an apprehensive atmosphere soon developed as he expressed 'a deep preoccupation with what is happening in the rest of the African continent'. Macmillan spoke of the awakening of national consciousness throughout the world, most recently in Asia. The implications were clear. South Africa could no longer ignore external opinion or pressures.

> Today the same thing is happening in Africa, and the most striking of all the impressions I have formed since I left London a month ago is of the strength of this African national consciousness. In different places it takes different forms, but it is happening everywhere. The wind of change is blowing through this continent,* and, whether we like it or not, this growth of national consciousness is a political fact. We must accept it as a fact, and our national policies must take account of it.'[31]

This crucial passage was received in total silence. When Macmillan sat down, there was a smattering of polite applause. Dr Verwoerd rose to reply, saying that the white man had rights also in South Africa. This response was rapturously applauded. The next evening – 4 February – in a farewell radio message to the peoples of South Africa, Macmillan reiterated his message.

The importance of the 'wind of change' speech was profound. More than that, it was one of the finest and bravest speeches delivered during the twentieth century. 'South Africa can never be the same again,' Lady Maud, wife of the High Commissioner, wrote in her

---

*The authorship of Macmillan's celebrated 'wind of change speech' has been variously attributed. Sir John Maud, Sir Norman Brook, Lord Home, Julian Amery and Sir David Hunt all took a part in its preparation. The first drafting, however, was made by Sir John Johnston, the Deputy High Commissioner in South Africa.[30] There was much tinkering with this earliest version. At a time when de Gaulle was trying to persuade the French to prepare to leave Algeria, Macmillan knew that he had to spell out similar truths, however unpalatable.

diary, noting the 'furious resentment' and 'wilful blindness' of the Nationalists 'in not seeing things they don't want to admit'.[32] Anthony Sampson was not alone in thinking the speech the best of Macmillan's career, not least because of its restraint and clarity. A cartoon at the time depicted Macmillan delivering the speech above the caption 'O pardon me, thou bleeding piece of earth That I am meek and gentle with these butchers.'[33]

Had Macmillan been assassinated in its aftermath, as Verwoerd nearly was on 9 April 1960, his place in history would have been secure. Both in timing and content the effects of the speech resonated for years. The clear declaration proved to be a key moment in the struggle for black nationalism in South Africa, as well as for further independence movements throughout Africa. It was also a watershed in the changing attitudes towards the apartheid regime of Dr Verwoerd and a major contribution to the ongoing pattern of decolonisation.

A fortnight later, a new power-sharing deal was established in Kenya. In 1960, British Somaliland, Nigeria and Sierra Leone all gained their independence. Tanganyika was to follow on 1 May 1961, a month that also saw Dr Verwoerd taking South Africa out of the Commonwealth on 31 May. By his words Macmillan was declaring that black people were correct in claiming the right to rule themselves and was tacitly accepting that it was the British government's responsibility to promote the creation of societies that upheld the rights of all individuals. Not only South Africa, but the whole Commonwealth, should move towards racial equality.

Over the years, a steady stream of visitors to Britain from the former colonial territories, particularly Africans, made the pilgrimage to pay their respects at Harold Macmillan's grave at St Giles, Horsted Keynes.[34] A similar sense of respect was experienced by David Faber, Macmillan's grandson, then MP for Westbury, while on a Lords and Commons cricket tour in South Africa in 1995. After a match in Cape Town, a dinner was held in the very same room in which Macmillan had made his 'wind of change' speech in 1960. Appropriately, David Faber was invited to make the post-match vote of thanks, after which many members of the ANC came up to say, with much emotion, how much Macmillan's speech meant to them.

Reaction at the time from the white population in South Africa was predictably hostile. Trouble loomed in unexpected ways, both comic and tragic. The English Folk Dance and Song Society now declared its reluctance to undertake a tour of South Africa, arranged earlier, if its members' safety could not be guaranteed.[35] Dr Verwoerd led the opposition to Macmillan's speech from the start. Violence was not long delayed. The Sharpeville massacre of 21 March 1960, in which South African police fired on an anti-apartheid demonstration about the pass laws, left 67 Africans dead and more than 200 wounded.

Opinion in Britain was sharply polarised. Right-wing Conservatives formed the Monday Club in November 1961 'to oppose Government policy in Africa and to promote true Conservatism in other fields'.[36] Churchill was appalled by the speech and was highly critical in private of Macmillan. Lord Lambton, the unconventional, free-spirited MP for Berwick-upon-Tweed, who loathed Macmillan, publicly declared that 'for the sake of a phrase he has confounded a Continent'.[37]

The final days of Macmillan's visit included a state dinner in Cape Town, at which Dr Verwoerd was morose and distant. There was relief on both sides when Macmillan finally set sail on the *Capetown Castle*, bound for Las Palmas, where he transferred to the *Britannia* for the last part of the long voyage home. After a six-week tour of 20,000 miles,[38] during which he had kept the Queen informed of his progress by special dispatches, Macmillan was looking forward to some relaxation before he arrived back in Britain. On the evening of his sixty-sixth birthday, he watched a cowboy film, *The Big Country*, after a celebration dinner. The ship's company presented him with a large birthday cake, which gave Macmillan an almost child-like delight. Reports of the international impact of the 'wind of change' speech were still resonating. Macmillan chuckled at the thought of the world seeing his African tour as 'a move of profound and statesman-like wisdom', Harold Evans recorded in his diary, 'whereas (he says) it was just to get away from London in the middle of winter'.[39]

In the midst of dispatches to and from Rab Butler, Macmillan received an unexpected radio telephone call from his son Maurice, who had recently been lunching with Hugh Trevor-Roper. Maurice had heard from Trevor-Roper that there was a move afoot to nominate the Prime Minister for the vacant chancellorship of Oxford University. Maurice had been asked to assess his father's feelings. Macmillan was intrigued by the idea, but needed to consult colleagues before deciding.

The death of Lord Halifax on 23 December 1959 had left many an honorific office vacant.[40] Among the most prestigious was the chancellorship of Oxford University, largely a ceremonial sinecure.

An easy passage to the Oxford chancellorship was anticipated for Sir Oliver Franks. He was nominated by Sir Maurice Bowra, the Warden of Wadham and the acting Vice-Chancellor of the University. There had not been an election for the post since the Lords Cave and

Asquith had contested the succession to Curzon in 1925, and initially there seemed no reason to suppose that there would be one now.

Supporters of Franks, however, had overlooked the delight that Hugh Trevor-Roper[41] took in academic intrigue, which some claimed had contributed to his own advance. Macmillan, whose firm had published Trevor-Roper since the time of his first book on Archbishop Laud in 1940, had recommended him to the Queen for the Crown appointment of Regius Professor of Modern History* at Oxford in 1957.

Trevor-Roper was grateful to Macmillan, but the main reason he instigated, and then undertook the management of, the campaign to elect the Prime Minister was because he found Franks so stultifyingly boring, 'intellectually ordinary, and of dull, puritan, not to say sanctimonious virtue'.[45] Trevor-Roper wanted to save Oxford from the 'solemn, pompous, dreary, respectable *Times*-reading world which hates elections (indeed, hates life)' and install a representative of the 'irreverent, genial, unpompous world, which holds exactly opposite views'. For this purpose he had initially considered Lord Salisbury, but soon decided that Macmillan was his man, if only he could get him to the starting post. Trevor-Roper had powerful allies, who also delighted in the prospect of upsetting Bowra's apple cart. Sir Roy Harrod, for example, Macmillan's close friend, regarded Franks as the 'bum-faced purveyor of last year's platitudes'.[46]

There was another reason why Trevor-Roper's camp did not want Franks as Chancellor: Franks lived in North Oxford and might actually get involved in university matters. That was not, in their opinion, what a Chancellor should be doing at all. Lord Halifax had very wisely kept his distance. A Prime Minister, who would bring undoubted dignity to the office, could hardly be popping down to the Sheldonian every week.

Trevor-Roper correctly surmised that his scheme would appeal to the mischievous side of Macmillan's personality. It was a shrewd judgement. Trevor-Roper knew that Macmillan was at heart a rebel. 'In this sense he is very like Winston Churchill, whom he greatly admires,' he wrote. 'Throughout his career, as throughout Winston's,

---

* 'Heaven knows whom Macmillan will give us as Regius Professor,' Isaiah Berlin had pondered. 'I have a feeling that Alan Taylor, despite all his real ability, has somehow gone too far astray.'[42] Berlin was correct in his prognosis: A.J.P. Taylor's rejection made him thereafter an embittered opponent and critic of Macmillan. (As a supporter of Labour, he had not been a fan anyway.) 'Honours and appointments go to Mr Macmillan's relatives,' Taylor wrote in the *New Statesman* shortly afterwards, 'or to those who entertain him by talking amusingly at lunch.'[43] Macmillan's motives in preferring Trevor-Roper for the Regius professorship were not dissimilar to those of Bernard Shaw in writing *Saint Joan*. When asked why he had chosen that subject, Shaw replied that someone had to save her from John Drinkwater.[44]

the official Tory party has been against him, or at least (even when, ultimately, accepting him as its leader) has distrusted him. He is in the great tradition of Disraeli and Winston as opposed to that other of Bonar Law and Baldwin – men, who by their mediocrity, really represented instead of commanding the dull, impersonal, conventional respectable forces of the Establishment.'[47]

When Macmillan discussed the prospect with some of his colleagues, he found them wary. Lord Kilmuir warned him that he had nothing to gain and everything to lose. 'You risk your neck for something you don't really need,' he said, to which Macmillan replied, 'You might say the same about fox-hunting.'[48] More seriously, as he warmed to the task, Macmillan told Trevor-Roper that everything hinged on the attitude of Balliol. By good fortune, the Master of Balliol, Sir David Lindsay Keir, had been abroad when Bowra had been nominating Franks, so he had not been swept up into the Bowra camp. Trevor-Roper set to work at once mobilising the Balliol vote.

Macmillan's second requirement before accepting was that he should have more than the 149 nominations that Bowra had secured for Franks. In the end, Trevor-Roper secured 200 nominations, including 33 professors. The game was afoot.

Macmillan and Franks, of course, took no part in the campaign. On a personal level, Macmillan's deep admiration for Franks' abilities as one of the outstanding civil servants of his generation remained undiminished. He had not forgotten the wartime Ministry of Supply days.

As Oxford graduates had to be MAs to vote, the university reaped a windfall of £1,500 in composition fees as a marquis, three barons and 50 knights, including Sir David Eccles from the Cabinet, upgraded their Bachelor of Arts degrees.* Voting had to be in person, and in academic dress, so on the two polling days, the great and the good descended on Oxford, laden with aged, or borrowed, gowns. The university was *en fête*. The election was a cross between Eatanswill and a Gaudy. Balliol laid on lunch for 150 people. Trevor-Roper recorded that Christ Church 'seemed to groan under hams and bottles from dawn to dusk', adding, 'Queen's [Franks' college as an undergraduate and as Provost, 1946–1948] no doubt administered suitably frugal refreshment to the Franksites.'[49]

Voting crossed 'party' lines. Hugh Gaitskell voted for Franks, but Richard Crossman delighted in voting for Macmillan and letting it

---

*The fee for taking an MA degree was £5.

be known that he had done so. (Actually he had merely told Isaiah Berlin, but that amounted to the same thing.) When the votes were announced, in Latin in the Gothic Divinity School, there was a nice symmetry about the figures – Haroldus Macmillanus 1,976, Oliverus Frankus 1,697. 'The PM himself is delighted,' rejoiced Trevor-Roper. 'So am I. Oh frabjous day!'[50]

Macmillan's election to the chancellorship of Oxford University had coincided with ongoing controversies over alleged fraud in the recent ballot held by the Electrical Trades Union for its general secretary.[51] Anthony Wedgwood Benn, referring to 'the recent medieval frolics in the City of Oxford', congratulated Macmillan in the House of Commons on 'having proved by his own tremendous victory in a ballot held in Latin, open for all to see, that the Establishment has nothing to learn from the Electrical Trades Union'. Macmillan's face puckered in delight. 'Except this,' he replied, 'that I think that on this occasion, the Establishment was beaten.'[52]

Although in the greater scheme of things, Macmillan's election to the chancellorship of Oxford was unimportant, the manner in which he embraced the fun of the chase was a paradigm of his career. The whole episode – a *Zuleika Dobson* occasion', as Richard Crossman described it, 'with crocuses in the park'[53] – could have provided the plot for a novel by C. P. Snow. The election had all the necessary ingredients: the mischievous in-fighting of the academic world, which so appealed to the iconoclast in Macmillan; the clash of powerful egos; and dramatic reversals of fortune.[54] For once Maurice Bowra was hoist by his own petard.[55] Macmillan thoroughly enjoyed the contest, even though forced to watch from the sidelines. One suspects he would have enjoyed it even if he had lost, but more to the point, he revelled for the next quarter of a century in his place at the heart of the city he loved above all others. His chancellorship enabled him to exorcise the ghosts of his long-lost companions, the dead of the Great War. On that spring day in Oxford, the bookie, Macmillan, had triumphed over the clergyman, Franks. Whether there would be similar success in the Paris summit in May remained to be seen. Khrushchev was a formidable bookie.

CHAPTER TWENTY FIVE

Turning Points

1960–1961

Let us hope that Pitt will have the last word: 'We will save
England by our exertions and Europe by our example.'
Sir Frank Lee memorandum, 22 April 1960[1]

The budget when produced had been very popular. Budgets,
like babies, are always little loves when first born. But as their
infancy passes away, they also become subject to many stripes.
The details are less pleasing than was the whole in the hands
of the nurse.
Anthony Trollope, *The Prime Minister*, 1876

There is a glare in some men's eyes which seems to say,
'Beware I am dangerous'...A mischievous excitability is the
most obvious expression of it.
Walter Bagehot, *Biographical Studies*, 1867

For Macmillan, the Paris summit in May 1960 marked the moment
when his luck began to run out. Up to that point, his premiership
had enjoyed great fortune, not all of it owing to himself. He had
been lucky to have come to office at a time of cyclical upturn in the
economy and when the Labour Party was bedevilled by internal strife.
Although Labour was more unified by the time of the 1959 election,
through necessity rather than inner conviction, their campaign was
fatally undermined by Gaitskell's mistaken pledge on income tax.
However, even if Gaitskell had not made this mistake, the odds are
that Macmillan would have won the election anyway. His government
was not going to lose whilst the tide of prosperity flowed so strongly.

Macmillan had been lucky on the international stage as well. His
1959 visit to Khrushchev had played well with the public. Eisenhower
willingly co-operated in rebuilding the old Anglo-American relationship, not least with his pre-election visit to Downing Street in August
1959. 'Suez' and all its attendant controversies had slipped quietly
from the collective memory. Napoleon would have approved of such a
lucky general. However, Paris was the beginning of a downward trend.

The early part of 1960 also involved Macmillan in a variety of responsibilities, including an exhausting and exhaustive state visit from President and Madame de Gaulle. On 16 February, he had an audience with the Queen, three days before the birth of Prince Andrew, to give a first-hand account of his long African tour. As always, he found the monarch well briefed on all the issues, and, thanks to his dispatches, clear on all the details concerning Cyprus, Nyasaland and Ghana. The next day Macmillan held a meeting with Derick Heathcoat Amory and Lord Cobbold. The Chancellor and the Governor of the Bank of England were greatly worried about the rate of consumption.

Before the summit, always there in the background, like 'the raven o'er the infected house, boding to all',[2] Macmillan travelled to Rambouillet (12–13 March) and Washington (27–31 March) for preliminary talks with de Gaulle and Eisenhower respectively.

Britain in 1960 had the capacity to make nuclear warheads, but did not have the effective means of delivering them.[3] The fixed Blue Streak rocket system for nuclear warheads was considered outdated by the Chiefs of Staff, owing to new Russian air defence systems. It was also prohibitively expensive and had been cancelled on 20 February by the Cabinet Defence Committee. Macmillan's purpose in visiting Eisenhower therefore was not only to prepare the ground for the May summit, but also to seek a replacement for Blue Streak on the best possible terms. Eisenhower offered Britain Skybolt, a new long-range air-to-ground missile system. In the long term, though, Macmillan wanted Polaris, a submarine missile system, and he regarded Skybolt as an interim measure.

Macmillan's talks with de Gaulle were conducted entirely in French, which was a mistake that added to the strain and responsibility. A month earlier, France had exploded its first nuclear device, and when de Gaulle spoke of the Big Three it was clear to Macmillan that he meant America, Russia and France. The French, however, wanted to explore nuclear co-operation with Britain, but Macmillan was looking westward to America. 'We have got to have this thing over here whatever it costs,' Ernest Bevin, the Foreign Secretary, had said of the atomic bomb in October 1947, adding, 'We've got to have the bloody Union Jack flying on top of it.'[4] Macmillan was open with de Gaulle about British concerns. For de Gaulle, any difficulties the British experienced over Skybolt would not be unwelcome, for then perhaps the British and the French could combine in the end after all.

Macmillan was deeply concerned by the 'acceleration' plan of the

German President of the European Commission Walter Hallstein[5] for the reduction of internal tariffs by the Six. The proposed cuts, up to 20 per cent, would be extremely damaging to the Seven. Macmillan expressed his concerns to de Gaulle. 'I pressed him strongly *not* to accelerate the tariff reductions between the Six next July (as is now being proposed) because this would increase the discrimination and might have very serious results,' he wrote in his diary. 'Although I came back to this several times, I could get no firm promise from him.'[6]

Macmillan returned to this question of tariffs in Washington in his first sustained talks with Christian Herter, the new Secretary of State, following Dulles' death in 1959. On 28 March, he met Herter and Douglas Dillon, the Under-Secretary of State, and emphasised how anxious he was about Hallstein's plan. He even compared it to Napoleon's economic blockade of Britain in 1807 and how alliance with Russia then had been necessary to curb French ambitions. On 30 March, the *Washington Post* published an exaggerated account of these discussions, which fluttered the dovecotes in Paris and Bonn. Macmillan had to issue a statement denying the more dramatic details. 'However, it may in the end do more good than harm,' he wrote in his diary. 'It may make the 6 begin to realise how seriously we take this proposed Hallstein "acceleration" plan.'[7]

In a more encouraging mode, Macmillan was much impressed by the progress Herter had made with the Russians on banning nuclear tests. Paradoxically, much of Macmillan's time with Eisenhower at Camp David, the presidential retreat, was spent on talks aimed at sustaining Britain's independent nuclear capacity following the difficulties in developing its own missile system. Eisenhower was in good form, despite his anger at the recent publications of Montgomery's memoirs and Alanbrooke's diaries.[8] The talks on joint defence systems went better than Macmillan had anticipated.

Macmillan told the Queen of these developments on his return. His main concern about Blue Streak, apart from the defence considerations, had been that rocket installations in a small country such as Britain caused anxiety, especially when installed anywhere near large population centres. The Queen's Speech in November 1960 outlined a new agreement: the British got Polaris, and the Americans got a sheltered anchorage for their submarines in Holy Loch on the Clyde. Macmillan told the Commons that the arrangement was 'in the tradition of Anglo-American co-operation in joint defence established in peace time more than twelve years ago and carried on by successive British Governments.'[9] Inevitably, the American submarine base became the focus of much controversy, with CND vociferous in their opposition, as well as much of the population in the west of Scotland.[10]

The Skybolt/Polaris agreements in 1960 showed how closely bound Britain was under the American nuclear umbrella. How far Britain's nuclear capacity was now 'independent', (as Macmillan – and in his time Ernest Bevin – wished) was not precisely defined. Harold Watkinson, the Minister of Defence, admitted, 'we should be dependent on American goodwill: no promise by an American administration could be a guarantee of the future. We should be seen by the world to be independent.'[11] Derick Heathcoat Amory also believed that the decision had been taken in an uncharacteristically impromptu manner by Macmillan. He wrote to Watkinson of the 'great disadvantage in making such a commitment on the spur of the moment, with no examination of the merits of the alternative courses'. Amory felt that Macmillan was 'plunging wildly from one weapon to another'.[12] For his part, Watkinson thought that the Americans 'might be wrong in pinning so much of the future of the deterrent on submarine based weapons like Polaris'.[13] It was more than likely that the Russians would develop an effective response, even to Polaris.

In April, de Gaulle came to London on a state visit. Macmillan paid close attention to all the details, with their attendant festivities,[14] particularly as it had been clear at Rambouillet in March that de Gaulle was not regarding the event with much enthusiasm. So no expense was spared in making his visit a success. Buckingham Palace was illuminated with firework displays of the Cross of Lorraine. Not even Eisenhower, when he had visited Britain in 1959, had received such attention. Macmillan knew that he had much wooing to do. From his first days in Algiers, he had recognised that de Gaulle was a tough nut. 'It is very difficult to know how to handle him,' he had written in his diary on 14 June 1943. 'I'm afraid he will always be impossible to work with.'[15] The intervening 17 years had not changed things.

Morning dress was the order of the day for the de Gaulle visit. The Duke of Edinburgh acted as joint host. Field Marshal Alexander was assigned to de Gaulle's staff for the duration, and the old wartime links were stressed at every opportunity. Macmillan was with the Queen at Victoria station on 5 April to welcome de Gaulle's party from Gatwick, a signal honour that the monarch went forth to receive the august visitor. In fact, de Gaulle was not best pleased that the Queen had not been at the airport, where he was first welcomed on to British soil by the Duchess of Kent.[16]

The next three days were crammed with engagements. There was a formal dinner at Buckingham Palace, and lunch at the Mansion House. De Gaulle gave a return dinner for his hosts at the French Embassy. The programme included visits to Churchill and the Queen Mother. A gala command performance was given at Covent Garden on 7 April by the Royal Ballet (no 'sputniks' descending from above this time). 'Very long,' Macmillan wrote of the evening. 'I got home exhausted.'[17]

President de Gaulle addressed both Houses of Parliament in Westminster Hall. When Macmillan had recently done the same in Cape Town, he had been racked with nerves, and physically sick beforehand.* He was deeply impressed, and not a little envious, of the aplomb with which de Gaulle carried off the occasion. A copy of his address, in English, was on every seat; de Gaulle then proceeded to give the entire speech, in French, word perfectly, without a note, having committed it to memory.

For Macmillan, one of the most impressive sights of the visit was the tall figure of de Gaulle inspecting scarlet-coated pensioners, and stooping to talk to them, at Chelsea Hospital. The venue, which reminded de Gaulle of Les Invalides, obviously touched him greatly, though the lunch at the hospital afterwards, hosted by Macmillan and Lady Dorothy, was tense, because the Great Hall was filled with captured French eagles and standards.[19]

Unfortunately, it was a sad time for Macmillan personally, as the Dowager Duchess of Devonshire – 'Moucher' – had recently died, so he was unable to go to the Guildhall luncheon. In addition, Daniel, his brother, had undergone an operation for cancer. Macmillan made time, nevertheless, for further talks prior to the vital Paris summit in May. He visited de Gaulle in his suite at Buckingham Palace and found him in private more relaxed than of late. He could not persuade de Gaulle to go to Chequers, though, and the President also declined an honorary degree at Oxford, something Macmillan could have easily arranged and would have delighted in bestowing.

In the midst of all this diplomatic activity, Macmillan had also been heavily involved in the preparation of Derick Heathcoat Amory's Budget, which was delivered the day before de Gaulle's arrival in Britain. Of Amory's three Budgets, the April 1960 package was the one that has attracted most criticism. The internal tensions, between

---

*Such vomiting was not unusual when Macmillan had a big speech to deliver, and as a precaution he always lunched alone before Prime Minister's Question Time, then held on Tuesdays and Thursdays.[18]

Macmillan's political aims and Amory's economic ones, were never satisfactorily resolved. Macmillan wanted expansion, Amory and the Treasury wanted to rein back. Currency reserves had fallen and Amory had warned Macmillan when he was in Africa what he felt needed to be done. Although Macmillan had agreed to an increase in the bank rate, many of Amory's other fiscal proposals were heavily fought over in Cabinet and watered down.

An important change had taken place at the Treasury on 1 January 1960 when Sir Frank Lee[20] became Joint Permanent Secretary, alongside Sir Norman Brook, in charge of financial economic policy, in place of Sir Roger Makins, who had become Head of the UK Atomic Energy Authority. Makins had never been entirely happy in his role at the Treasury. In retrospect, Macmillan realised that by asking Makins to transfer from Washington he had curtailed what was already one of the outstanding post-war diplomatic careers. By contrast, Lee was a Treasury man through and through, having first worked there as a principal in 1940. Subsequently, he had been on Keynes' Treasury delegation to Washington at the end of the war, and then in 1948, after Keynes' death, he was again posted to Washington to work on the distribution of Marshall aid.

Lee was to become one of the key figures during the second half of Macmillan's premiership, not just in the Treasury, but also as an impassioned advocate of European integration. He had worked closely with Peter Thorneycroft, that spectre at the Stocktonian feast, so closely that Thorneycroft had wanted to take Lee with him to the Treasury in 1957.[21] Both Lee and Thorneycroft were enthusiasts for closer formal trading association ties with Europe. The logical conclusion of their advocacy was to seek membership of the EEC. Lee's appointment to the Treasury marked one of the turning points in this process.

Sir Frank Lee's memorandum, *The Six and the Seven*, delivered to Heathcoat Amory on 22 April 1960, 'stands out as the definitive document that was to set Britain on a new course, not only in terms of trade but also in terms of Britain's political role and outlook'.[22] There were many staging points on Macmillan's Damascene journey towards conversion to the European idea, but the Lee memorandum was one of the most vital.

The background to Amory's Budget was one of rising demand, especially in public investment and consumption. There was no slack in the economy. National output was up 14 per cent. Unemployment had recently fallen by 1.8 per cent, and after three years of stagnation, the economy was expanding. Amory was concerned about the threat to the balance of payments, and wished to restrain credit, in particular by imposing stricter controls on hire purchase and calling for special deposits in the clearing banks. These new measures were applied from 28 April. Macmillan had already agreed, somewhat reluctantly, to the second rise in bank rate that year, which took effect on 23 June.[23] The overall shape of the Budget was agreed at Cabinet on 24 March, though Macmillan subsequently did much tinkering with Amory's text.

The effect of Amory's Budget was broadly neutral. The new Profits Tax rate of 2.5 per cent and 2d on tobacco brought in £40m. To balance this, £9m was allocated on post-war credit repayments, and concessions of £30m, including an increase in housekeepers' allowances and an end to the tax on cinema tickets. Obviously, as some wags put it at the time, the more people who saw *I'm All Right Jack* the better. Amory had wanted a more severe Budget, but Macmillan, mindful of the criticism Rab Butler's post-election 'Pots and Pans' Budget of October 1955 had attracted, did not want his chancellor to suffer the same obloquy. Give with one hand and take away with the other may have been Amory's wish; fundamentally, Macmillan would have liked to give with the other hand as well. There were similar tensions between Macmillan and successive chancellors until Reginald Maudling went to the Treasury in July 1962.

With the 'Consolidation Budget', as Macmillan dubbed it, launched to a largely favourable press, he began to look anew over the Easter recess at the changes that would be necessary in the wake of Amory's retirement. Selwyn Lloyd was the most suitable successor. By the summer of 1960, Lloyd had been at the Foreign Office for four and a half years, and was due for a move. As Macmillan had now decided that entry into Europe was the most painless way of making the British economy more competitive, he required a Chancellor with an international overview. Neither of the other possible candidates – Henry Brooke and Reginald Maudling – had such experience.

Amory also favoured Lloyd as his successor. Indeed, he had told Lloyd on 4 November 1959 that he was going to resign within a matter of months and that he wanted a serious talk about Treasury matters. Rumour spreads quickly at Westminster, and on 22 November, 'Crossbencher' in the *Sunday Express* was forecasting 'Derry Amory's retirement – and the "durable" Mr Lloyd as his successor, because by then Harold M. will be diverting his attention to home politics again and will want someone to fetch and carry'.[24] When Lloyd dined with Rab Butler on 18 January, talk soon turned to the Cabinet reshuffle. Rab Butler also saw Lloyd as the natural successor to the Treasury, in which case 'Harold might make Duncan Sandys Foreign Secretary, because he is always fascinated by cads.' A week later Lloyd dined with Amory.[25]

Harold and Dorothy celebrated their ruby wedding on 21 April. After all the storms it was a case now of 'calm of mind all passion spent'.[26] Photographs reveal the inner peace and acceptance that they shared. Pictures of the ceremony of the granting of the Freedom of the City of London in December 1961 show the two in an open carriage, for all the world like any contented Darby and Joan enjoying a day out.

Before Macmillan finalised his summer reshuffle, the Paris summit came – and went. It proved a terrible diplomatic embarrassment for the Western alliance. The seeds of the disaster were sown on 1 May when one of the high-surveillance American U2 spy planes, then conducting covert photographic reconnaissance missions on a regular basis in Soviet airspace, was shot down near Sverdlovsk in the Ural mountains. From that moment the summit was doomed. The American pilot, Gary Powers, was captured, interrogated and put on trial. 'God knows what he will say when tortured!' Macmillan wondered in his diary. The British had also been conducting similar flights – 'some very successful ones', according to Macmillan[27] – using surplus planes from the Americans. Russian intelligence knew that such missions had been operating since 1956, but Russian technology – in the shape of SA2 guided missiles – had only recently been developed to deal with such high-flying aircraft. The wreck of the U2 plane was the first prize they could display to the world, and the Soviet propaganda machine did not miss the opportunity.

'The Americans have committed a great folly,' Macmillan wrote in his diary of the loss of the U2 spy plane. To guard against such an eventuality, which he had considered inevitable sooner or later, he had cancelled British flights well in advance of the summit.[28] He was furious with Eisenhower for not doing likewise, and then with Christian Herter for ill-advised remarks. Macmillan advised Eisenhower to make no further comments before the summit.

In many ways the U2 episode was also an embarrassment to Khrushchev on the eve of the summit, as it now forced him to play an unwanted role, to satisfy the requirements of his own domestic audience and internal political critics. He would have much preferred to have had a summit.[29] A meaningful dialogue on Berlin, possibly gaining some concessions from the West, would have been far more productive for him. From the moment Gary Powers was in Russian hands, such a conclusion was no longer politically possible.

Although all sides in this dangerous stage of the Cold War knew that espionage happened as a matter of routine, to have it publicly revealed in such a stark manner ceded the initiative to a belligerent Khrushchev. The Russian leader now heaped obloquy upon the Americans, in particular Christian Herter, the Secretary of State, whose comments were interpreted as confirmation that such flights would continue.

Khrushchev certainly did not hold back. 'You must understand that we Russians always go whole hog,' he declared. 'When we play, we play and when we fight, we fight.'[30]

Macmillan travelled to Paris on 15 May with the row about the U2 plane still rumbling on. He was now determined to be the conciliatory go-between. At a first meeting with Eisenhower and de Gaulle on 15 May, harsh words were exchanged on Berlin. Macmillan told de Gaulle the worst scenario would be to proclaim military support over Berlin and then find it impossible to deliver.

Khrushchev came to the British Embassy at 4.30 p.m. on 15 May. He was full of demands if the summit was to continue. It was clear to Macmillan that Khrushchev's aim was to humiliate Eisenhower as much as possible so as to extract a full apology. Macmillan pleaded with Khrushchev for reasonableness and emphasised the importance the whole world attached to a successful period of *détente*. Although Khrushchev was well disposed towards Macmillan – the memories of the Moscow visit were still fresh – it was clear that the odds were against the summit continuing.

'Harold went to breakfast with Ike,' Selwyn Lloyd wrote in his diary.

> They have drawn up a statement for the President to make, stating that the overflights had been discontinued and would not be resumed. We went on to the Elysée for the 11 a.m. meeting with the Russians. It was tense. K. asked to speak first, then rose to his feet & made a tough speech ... Ike made his reply with dignity. Harold and de Gaulle appealed for reason, de Gaulle saying that he could not understand all this fuss about overflying – the Soviet satellite passed through French air space 18 times a day.'[31]

Khrushchev was not best pleased with this essentially conciliatory remark by de Gaulle. Everything hinged on Khrushchev's attitude on the morrow.

The next day was even worse. Macmillan described it as 'one of the most agonising as well as exhausting which I have ever been through except, perhaps, in battle'.[32] At the first morning session, 'Khrushchev tried to pulverize Ike (as Micawber did Heep) by a mixture of abuse, vitriolic and offensive, and legal argument,' Macmillan recorded in his diary (unusually he wrote this retrospectively, as there was no time on the day). 'It was a most unpleasant performance,' he concluded.[33] Khrushchev was adamant that there should be a public apology from Eisenhower, punishment of offenders and a promise of no further overflying. Eisenhower left the meeting publicly humiliated.

During the course of the day, Macmillan then saw de Gaulle, Eisenhower and Khrushchev individually, in an attempt to save the summit. De Gaulle believed, rightly as it proved, there was no hope, as the Soviets had predetermined to sabotage the conference. Eisenhower's advisers had obviously wanted him to respond in kind to Khrushchev, but that was not his style. Macmillan, employing the tactics he was to use with President Kennedy during the Cuban Missile Crisis in October 1962,[34] said the important thing was to give Khrushchev an 'escape route' that he could take without losing face, even if this meant a full diplomatic apology. Khrushchev would not back down otherwise.

Much to the annoyance of Selwyn Lloyd and Sir Gladwyn Jebb,[35] the British Ambassador in Paris, Macmillan then visited Khrushchev at the Russsian Embassy, with Freddie Bishop and Philip de Zulueta in attendance. 'This is government by private secretary,' Lloyd protested to Bishop. 'Well, the only alternative is government by politician,' replied Bishop.[36] Jebb, who had provided rare wines from the embassy cellars to celebrate the summit, had been sidelined during Suez meetings in Paris in October 1956, and did not appreciate a repeat performance. It was a new experience for Lloyd, who wrote in his diary: 'I tried to stop him [Macmillan] seeing K that night, but Harold was rather incited by the Private Secretaries to do it. In fact he was too tired and in any case we wanted time.'[37] Although Khrushchev was again polite to Macmillan, a total contrast to his rudeness to both Eisenhower and de Gaulle, he was unbending.

The summit petered out in a series of perfunctory and mournful meetings. De Gaulle summoned a meeting of the main delegates at the Elysée on 17 May. Khrushchev did not attend, which was the final nail. However, the next day the Russians did respond to a British invitation to come round and say their farewells at the embassy, a courtesy not extended to the French or the Americans.*

---

*Selwyn Lloyd compared the atmosphere to that in a dentist's waiting room, and at a

The Paris summit was an international disaster on a spectacular scale, casting a shadow over Eisenhower's last months in the White House. Back home in Washington, he entered a period of deep depression and was testy with Christian Herter, when the Secretary of State said that the United States needed to regain its leadership. Eisenhower denied that the leadership had ever been lost. President de Gaulle remained calm outwardly, but he knew the damage done to the Western alliance was deep. More surprisingly, Khrushchev was also weakened. The Soviet military had been against his attempts at *détente*, and if he did not get concessions on Berlin he would be weakened still further in their eyes. One theory is that when Khrushchev realised that the Western alliance would press ahead with plans for installing a NATO military presence in West Berlin come what may, then no summit was better than one in which the Soviets failed to get what they wanted. The U2 episode was therefore a convenient excuse on which to base his tantrums, and the Paris summit proved a significant step on the path to his eventual downfall in 1964.[39]

For Macmillan, no less than Eisenhower, the Paris catastrophe marked the end of his hopes for diplomatic advances through superpower 'summitry'. Macmillan actually emerged from the summit with some personal, if no political, credit. Although physically exhausted (one diplomat mistakenly thought he was the worse for drink),[40] his strenuous conciliatory efforts to save the situation were impressive. Nevertheless, the net result was failure, and Macmillan saw it as the most tragic moment of his life.[41]

Macmillan had a long talk with Selwyn Lloyd on 24 May about the future shape of his administration. The Chancellorship of the Exchequer was discussed directly for the first time. Macmillan said he was 'v. disappointed in Maudling' and claimed that 'Brooke would just be a Treasury spokesman'. To tempt Lloyd to fall in with his wishes, Macmillan dangled the prospect of the eventual leadership of the party if he agreed to go to the Treasury. 'He said he was sure that Butler could not lead the party – he would not hand over to him,' Lloyd wrote in his diary of their talk. 'I was at the perfect age – I ought to go to the Exchequer in my own interest – the race for the leadership was very open.'[42]

The conversation marked a watershed. For the first time, Macmillan was contemplating the shape of the government after his departure,

---

moment of pause in the desultory small talk said, in all too audible a stage whisper, 'This is the moment when Gladwyn will tell us the vintage of the claret.'[38]

and it was not a government he felt Butler would ever head. 'It was very important from my point of view', Lloyd recorded of Macmillan's view, 'because if ever I was to lead the party, I must have experience away from Foreign Affairs.'[43]

Lloyd was not, in fact, concerned about the leadership.[44] He understood that dangling it was part of Macmillan's tactics, and he knew it was unlikely ever to fall to him. What he was worried about was doing a good job for the country if he became Chancellor. He warned Macmillan against disappointment. 'I told him he was wrong if he expected any originality. I had v. orthodox ideas about taxation and public expenditure.'[45] Macmillan nevertheless persisted in trying to persuade Lloyd to move. His alternative, if Lloyd refused, was Henry Brooke, whom he dismissed as 'just a Treasury spokesman'.[46]

Of course, if Lloyd did move to the Treasury, then Macmillan would have to find a new Foreign Secretary. He asked Lloyd if he thought Home could do the job. Lloyd thought Home would be well equipped after his long spell at Commonwealth Relations. Significantly, the only drawback, for both Macmillan and Lloyd, was not Home's membership of the Lords,* but his health.

Before approaching Home, Macmillan consulted Derick Hoyer Millar,[47] the Permanent Under-Secretary at the Foreign Office, about the physical demands of the job. The advice he got was that as Home was free of constituency duties, a lot of the burden was already removed, a point that Lloyd with his large, geographically scattered constituency in the Wirral had already made to Macmillan. Thus reassured, Macmillan decided to broach the matter directly with Home.

'Lord Home to luncheon,' he wrote in his diary on 3 June. 'I asked him whether, *if* I decided to ask Selwyn Lloyd to take the Exchequer (when D. Heathcoat Amory goes) he would take Foreign Office. He seemed rather flabbergasted† but recovered slowly.'[48] Home did not rush into accepting, but asked for time to consider the implications and consult his wife, Elizabeth. He was not a falsely modest man and knew that the post was a natural progression from the Commonwealth Office. He was confident he could acquit himself well. If people did not like a peer in the Foreign Office, so be it.

On 11 June, Macmillan closed the first part of his reshuffle bargain when Lloyd agreed to become Chancellor. 'Selwyn Lloyd is ready and (after the shock) anxious for the change,' Macmillan wrote in

---

*No Foreign Secretary had been in the Lords since Halifax in 1938. In 1955, Eden had drawn back from appointing Lord Salisbury, the man he favoured, as Foreign Secretary.
†The general expectation was that Home was pencilled in for the Scottish Office in any reshuffle.

his diary. 'He has had five years as Foreign Secretary, which is an immense strain. He must realise that to go to the home side makes him a possible rival to Butler in considering the succession. Although he is not ambitious in any wrong sense, he is conscious of Rab's weakness and oddness (which seems to grow not lessen)'.[49]

Lloyd and Macmillan met at Petworth and settled the details. In a manner reminiscent of Macmillan's own translation to the Treasury in December 1955, Lloyd made some demands. He asked to stay on in 1 Carlton Gardens,* the Foreign Secretary's London residence. He wanted to keep Antony Acland as his private secretary, and Inspector Wren as his principal detective. The most audacious of his requests was that he should be granted a three- to four-year minimum spell at the Treasury to get public expenditure under control and to bring to fruition any plans that he and his advisers thought desirable. Macmillan gave Lloyd his word at Petworth on 10 June that he would not be prematurely removed from the Treasury and could expect to stay there until the next general election in 1963–1964. In retrospect, it is astonishing that Macmillan agreed to this fourth request,† but he wanted Lloyd in the job, his hands were tied.

In a manner that would be impossible in a later era, these appointments were kept under wraps and not announced until 27 July. Meanwhile, Harold Macmillan presided on 22 June at his first Encaenia[50] as Chancellor of Oxford. It was a ceremony at which he was to preside for close on a quarter of a century. His first list of honorary graduands included Selwyn Lloyd, Alec Home and one of his oldest friends from Summer Fields, Eton and Great War days, Harry Crookshank. The Archbishop of York, Michael Ramsey, soon to be Macmillan's choice for Lambeth Palace, was also on the list. It was a golden summer's day, the only cloud being that between a festal lunch at All Souls and a Gaudy at Christ Church, Macmillan was constantly called to the telephone to speak to Derry Amory about the next day's rise in the bank rate.

One of the key requirements of Home's appointment was that a Cabinet minister in the Commons should be appointed as the Foreign Office No. 2. Macmillan and Home, after considering, but not for long, the claims of Freddie Erroll, decided that the post should be offered to Edward Heath, the Minister of Labour. He was appointed Lord Privy Seal with responsibility for Europe.[52] As John Campbell

---

*Downing Street was about to undergo a major reconstruction, with Macmillan moving to Admiralty House for three years.

†Two of the other three requests did not work out in the long term, and Acland never moved with him to the Treasury at all.

has written, 'with this appointment Heath found his life's cause'.[53] Lord Home's appointment caused a storm. It was denounced as the worst appointment since Caligula made his horse a consul in ancient Rome. 'There is a furious controversy going on,' Lloyd wrote in his diary. 'Comment on my own translation was rather lost in the row about Home.'[54]

The consequential changes soon followed. Hailsham succeeeded Home as both Leader of the Lords and Lord President of the Council. Duncan Sandys took over as Commonwealth Relations Secretary. John Hare succeeeded Heath at the Ministry of Labour. To replace Hare at the Ministry of Agriculture, Fisheries and Food, Macmillan chose Christopher Soames, Churchill's son-in-law. He also moved to repair the damage caused by the Treasury resignations of 1958. Peter Thorneycroft accepted the post of Aviation, with a seat in the Cabinet. Enoch Powell became Minister of Health, not a Cabinet post, but one with a Cabinet minister's salary and a Privy Councillorship. Two of the firmest believers in the principle of sound money had now, ironically, been appointed by Macmillan to two of the most high-spending departments. Yet there was no place for Nigel Birch, fiercely anti-Keynesian in his continued criticisms of Macmillan's spendthrift policies.

On 8 August, Macmillan moved into Admiralty House. Although his secretariat was not enthusiastic, he preferred the expansiveness of this historic residence to the higgledy-piggledy nature of Downing Street.

On 10 August, Macmillan, accompanied by the new Foreign Secretary, Lord Home, left for talks with Adenauer in Germany. 'I am not at all looking forward to our visit to Bonn,' he wrote. 'Dr Adenauer has deceived me before, over the great economic issue. He promised to support the [plan for an industrial] free trade area. But, under French pressure, he went back on his promises.'[55] In the event, the British party was welcomed warmly and some progress was made, though Macmillan was not deceived into believing that Adenauer's primary allegiance was other than to de Gaulle. Macmillan had already told the Queen, 'in the present state of Europe, if we are to reach agreements helpful to this country, so long as de Gaulle remains in power, the French are the key'.[56]

When Macmillan returned to Britain, the threatened power strike had been called off, but an unofficial shipping dispute was escalating, with consequential damage to the export trade. Elsewhere, 'Cyprus goes "on" and "off" – like a dish at a cheap restaurant,' Macmillan wrote in his diary.[57] The island became independent on 16 August.

Violence, as vehement as it was unexpected, erupted in July 1960 in the Congo. 'It is more like the Crazy Gang than anything I can remember,' Macmillan admitted in his diary.[58]

On 30 June, the government in Brussels had granted independence to the former Belgian Congo, which it had administered since 1908. Within days, African troops in the Congolese Force Oublique had mutinied against their European officers. Chaos ensued. Initially, it seemed that the Congo, far larger than the Central African Federation, which it bordered, would be a Belgian matter. However, Britain, America and the United Nations were soon drawn into the ensuing morass as a series of crises unfolded.

In 1890, the novelist Joseph Conrad returned from a visit to the Congo Free State, then under the control of King Leopold II of the Belgians, deeply depressed by the commercial exploitation he had found there. 'The conquest of the earth,' he wrote later in *Heart of Darkness*, 'which mostly means the taking it away from those who have a different complexion or slighter flatter noses than ourselves, is not a pretty thing when you look into it too much.'[59] Commerce, in the shape of the mineral wealth of the province of Katanga, was still to be at the heart of this later darkness.

The new Congo Republic was initially designed to be a unitary state governed from Leopoldville by President Kasavubu and his Prime Minister, Patrice Lumumba. Differences between Kasavubu and Lumumba led to the latter's overthrow in a military coup in September, when the Congolese army commander Colonel Mobutu, backed by the United States and Belgium, established a new government. In May, Moise Tshombe, leader of the Konakat party, had won control in the provincial elections of the legislature of Katanga, the south-eastern province of the Congo, rich in mineral resources. He became Prime Minister of the provincial government. On 11 July, he announced the secession of this province from the Congolese state, declaring Katanga independent under his leadership.

Civil war tensions rose when Lumumba fell into Katangese hands and was murdered in unexplained circumstances in January 1961. Tshombe's military backing came from a white mercenary army. Many vested interests played their part, and Tshombe was also backed by American and European businessmen, not to mention right-wing back-benchers in the Conservative Party, who saw him as a stout opponent of Communism. In an increasingly complex situation, the Belgians sent in troops that were soon in action against Congolese forces. Russia solidly supported Lumumba and used the Congo as the basis for vitriolic anti-Western propaganda, whilst sending technical equipment and supplies to Lumumba. The United Nations were also drawn in, sending troops, which eventually overthrew Tshombe in January 1963.[60]

The Congo from the start was a potential tinderbox, which even threatened at one stage to become a latter-day Sarajevo, certainly in Macmillan's eyes. On the anniversary of the outbreak of the Great War on 4 August, he wrote in his diary, 'Ever since the breakdown of the Summit in Paris I have felt uneasy about the summer of 1960. It has a terrible similarity to 1914. Now Congo may play the part of Serbia.'[61] The fear was that as the United Nations would not back Lumumba in his struggles against Tshombe, Lumumba would turn to Russia, as indeed he did. The situation was very reminiscent of Egypt after the collapse of American support for the Aswan High Dam project in July 1956. Communist infiltration was the overriding spectre for the politicians, just as surely as access to Katanga's mineral resources was for international businessmen.

Macmillan was troubled by the unfolding complexities. He accepted that an independent Katanga, whether linked to Belgium or not, would be in Britain's interests, especially if it maintained good relations with the Central African Federation. He believed that stability in the Katangan part of the copper belt would be beneficial for neighbouring Northern Rhodesia. Also an independent Katanga was more likely to safeguard British investment in the leading mining company in the area, an important consideration for right-wing Conservative back-benchers. Yet conflict between Katanga and the Congo Central Government now seemed inevitable. Macmillan was advised by Philip de Zulueta, his foreign affairs secretary, that 'it would probably be safest not to take sides until the situation became clearer'.[62] The fact that initially Macmillan accepted this advice indicated an untypical lack of confidence.

In the Federation of Rhodesia and Nyasaland, Sir Roy Welensky was deeply aggrieved by Macmillan's ambiguous part in the tangled situation. The release of Hastings Banda from prison had been the sticking point for Welensky. At the same time, he was suspicious, in the event rightly so, that the imminent Monckton Report would pave the way for the secession of Northern Rhodesia and Nyasaland from the Central African Federation. Welensky was a fervent supporter of Tshombe, whereas in Ghana, President Nkrumah led support from the newly independent African states for Lumumba.

Macmillan made an unsuccessful attempt to placate Welensky, whom he was to describe in his diary as 'an emotional Lithuanian Jew'.[63] On 14 July 1960, the Cabinet had decided to support the use of United Nations troops in the Congo, but only to restore order, not in any way to threaten Katanga. United Nations troops, for any purpose, were anathema to Welensky, and Macmillan knew the whole situation required delicate handling and continual surveillance. He sent Welensky a lengthy memorandum after this Cabinet, with his analysis of the Congolese situation. 'There will be very many fishing with glee in these troubled waters who will try and divide our two countries and discredit us. We must not allow them to score.'[64] It was to prove a vain hope. Macmillan wrote that the first task must be restore order. 'With all its risks, the United Nations seems to offer the best hope of achieving this and keeping the Communists out.' Welensky did not agree. He saw United Nations involvement as the thin end of a very dangerous wedge. Macmillan's memorandum showed a pessimism bordering on melancholy. 'Our troubles alas are now world wide,' he concluded. 'We are having many difficulties with the Russians over the aeroplane flights and the whole world situation is becoming darker.'[65]

Welensky had been intensely suspicious of Macmillan for some time, and he now began a long-running correspondence with Lord Salisbury. Increasingly Salisbury became the focus for disenchanted Monday Club Tories, who disliked Macmillan's colonial policy, and his obvious empathy with the liberally minded Bow Groupers. Uninhibited MPs such as Lord Lambton, who loathed Macmillan, weighed in. 'Tony never ceased to drive his own long knife into Macmillan, in speech and in writing, whenever he could,' Jock Colville recalled. 'They even had an unseemly dispute on the steps of Westminster Cathedral after the memorial service for President Kennedy.'[66]

Salisbury was vocal in his informed criticisms of Macmillan, starting a 'Watching Committee'[67] in December 1960 as a conduit for opposition to the Prime Minister. It was the end of long years of intimate friendship between the two men. When Salisbury made his infamous broadside attack on Iain Macleod, the Colonial Secretary, in the House of Lords on 7 March 1961, denouncing him as being 'too clever by half', few were in doubt that this was a vicarious attack upon Macmillan himself. In fact, Salisbury had used exactly the same phrase about Macmillan in a letter he had sent to Anthony Eden in 1957. 'I don't think I am meant for politics, especially Harold's kind,' he had written to the former premier. 'He is *too clever by half* for me.'[68] Eventually, Macmillan secretly put Lord Salisbury under close MI5 observation.[69] It was not MI5's only involvement in surveillance for Macmillan. In July 1963, in the wake of the Profumo scandal, Macmillan had the Cabinet Room, its Waiting Room and the Prime Minister's Study electronically bugged. Apart from a short interval after Macmillan's resignation in October 1963, this system continued until James Callaghan ordered the devices to be removed in 1977.

Russian propaganda attacks on the West for its 'imperialist' agenda in the Congo, and for the unforgotten U2 spy plane incident, were becoming increasingly shrill during the summer of 1960. Khrushchev declared that he would be addressing the United Nations General Assembly in New York in September. Macmillan, who discussed the matter with the Queen at Balmoral on his September visit, decided that he must also attend in person. Events were to prove this a fortuitous decision.

On 29 September 1960, Macmillan was addressing the General Assembly of the United Nations on control of nuclear weapons. When he reached a passage referring to the fact that no country would welcome a large number of officials from abroad on its sovereign territory, Khrushchev began banging the table repeatedly with his shoe and shouting out disruptively.[70] Macmillan paused, looked up and said quietly, 'Well, I'd like it translated, if you would.'[71] This impromptu retort to Khrushchev's incivility was devastatingly effective. Macmillan emerged as the sharp-witted, unflustered senior statesman of the Western alliance. At a time when America was entering its quadrennial winter of the presidential election, such an image was doubly reassuring. As so often in politics, it was the small things, rather than the weighty speech or lengthy diplomatic dispatch, that made the biggest public impact. The episode was long remembered.

Macmillan had intended before travelling to America that the West should present a calm, united front in the face of any Russian bluster. Khrushchev's explosion, whether premeditated or not, made Macmillan's task in achieving this aim even easier.[72] By contrast, even a formal meeting Macmillan had with President Nasser of Egypt, who was also attending the United Nations, was civilised and purposeful.

When Macmillan returned to London, he received an advance copy of the Monckton Report, which was to be published on 11 October 1960. One of its conclusions, that Northern Rhodesia and Nyasaland should, if they wished, secede from the Central African Federation, was neither unexpected nor unwelcome to Macmillan. The problem was the response of Roy Welensky, who felt that he had been betrayed. Welensky had understood that British promises, dating back to 1953, had guaranteed no secession from the Central African Federation. Lord Salisbury felt that Welensky had been let down, and wrote in no uncertain terms to tell him so.

'There will no doubt be allegations that Sir Roy Welensky has been badly treated in this matter,' Macmillan admitted to his secretary, Tim Bligh. 'It could be argued that my statements in the House of Commons, the terms of reference, and the private assurances which I gave from time to time in my messages to Sir Roy, made it clear that the recommendation for secession or the contemplation of the break-up of the Federation was not within the terms of reference.'[73] Welensky's anger knew no bounds. He believed that Macmillan had acted dishonourably, though such a bitter view says more about the incandescence of Welensky's rage than about the morality or otherwise of Macmillan's stance.

Salisbury urged Welensky to publish Macmillan's private correspondence,[74] and deft footwork was needed if the commission was not to be stillborn. Lord Home told his Minister of State, Lord Perth, privately that they would have to 'fudge'.[75]

The publication of the Monckton Commission's report on 11 October 1960 inevitably heightened the tensions. 'It is quite clear to me,' Welensky wrote to Macmillan, 'that the commission has approached its task principally from the standpoint of appeasement of African nationalism.'[76] He believed the report was a breach of faith and wanted Macmillan to join him in dissociating himself from its conclusions, which presaged majority rule as well as secession. Macmillan refused. In utter frustration, Welensky considered plans for a unilateral declaration of independence, and even planned at one stage to kidnap the Governor of Northern Rhodesia.[77] Africans had always seen the Federation as the covert means of maintaining white domination. Now the boot was firmly on the other foot and the settlers did not like it. The African leaders were not best pleased either.

In December 1960, the Lancaster House Review Conference on the future of the Federation was marred by several walk-outs, Dr Hastings Banda and Joshua Nkomo among them. Macmillan managed to persuade Dr Banda to read one of the lessons in the church of St Peter and St Paul at Ellesborough, near Chequers, that weekend. But it was an uneasy time, and further constitutional meetings were postponed until early in 1961.

As Colonial Secretary, Iain Macleod's attitude towards the pace of decolonisation was far to the left of the traditional imperialist Tory back-benchers – even, some suspected, of Macmillan himself. What made matters worse for these back-benchers was the unconcealed delight with which Macleod rejoiced in the discomfiture of the white colonial settlers. Macleod was becoming a turbulent minister, a genie that Macmillan himself had let out of the bottle.

On 17 February 1961, during the Northern Rhodesian Conference in London, Macleod tendered his resignation to Macmillan in Admiralty House. With difficulty, Macmillan persuaded him to hold off. 'We may have a Boston Tea Party (Welensky declaring the Federation independent and seizing the colony of Northern Rhodesia), or an African blood bath (riots all over British Africa), accentuated if Colonial Secretary were to resign,' he wrote. Yet his hands were tied, as Macleod knew. 'If Colonial Secretary had resigned, I think Government would have fallen,' Macmillan admitted. 'All the younger men in the party would have gone against us.'[78]

For a proportion of the Tory party, Macleod was now a *persona non grata*, whilst at the same time being a liberal hero to others. So the prime requisites for bitter divisions were firmly in place. By August 1961, Macmillan was actually avoiding one-to-one meetings with Macleod. When more objections arose from Macleod about constitutional proposals, Macmillan minuted Tim Bligh, 'I am not very anxious to discuss it alone with him.'[79]

Lambton's animus towards Macleod as Colonial Secretary was, if anything, even stronger than Salisbury's. Macleod warned Macmillan that there was 'no doubt about the venom towards you and towards myself'.[80] Martin Redmayne, the Chief Whip, advised Macmillan that Lambton was pressing for an interview. 'I wonder whether it might not pay to let him get all this off his chest if you could find the patience to listen to it,' he wrote to the Prime Minister. 'If you were to see him, you could say very little but I feel that there is a possibility that it might put a stop to some of his worst mischief.'[81]

Macmillan accordingly agreed to see Lambton on 2 August. Lambton was uncompromisingly frank, as was his way. He told Macmillan directly that all the people he had met on his recent visit to Africa 'had made adverse remarks about the Colonial Secretary'. He pointed out that Welensky had not been on speaking terms with Macleod for over ten months. Macmillan admitted to Lambton 'that he was aware that this feeling existed in some quarters in Africa; it was very sad'.[82]

Right-wing criticism continued nevertheless. As Macmillan knew from his own rebellious times during the Chamberlain era, a leader can ignore such criticisms, but eventually the cumulative effect can be very destructive.

The only solution was to move Macleod. On 9 October 1961, he became Chairman of the Conservative Party and Leader of the House of Commons, with the non-departmental title of Chancellor of the Duchy of Lancaster. As Butler had found in 1957, the simultaneous demands of party chairman and Leader of the House were contradictory responsibilities. Tub-thumping and emollience did not go hand in hand. Macleod's farewell speech, surveying his time as Colonial Secretary, at the Conservative Party Conference in Brighton that October, was seen by his opponents as a provocative swan song, and by his supporters as the greatest of his career. He ended his speech by quoting Robert Burns' lines about men the world over being brothers 'for a' that'. When Macleod's successor at the Colonial Office, Reginald Maudling, first met his officials shortly afterwards, he said, 'I suppose I'm looking at a lot of people who believe in the "brotherhood of man".'[83]

There had been little evidence of brotherhood in the Congo. Patrice Lumumba, Prime Minister of what had formerly been the Belgian Congo, was assassinated on 17 January 1961 (though his death was not confirmed until 13 February) and the greatly respected Dag Hammarskjöld,[84] Secretary General of the United Nations, was killed (on 18 September 1961) in a plane crash. Hammarskjöld had been flying to Northern Rhodesia for ceasefire talks with Moise Tshombe, President of the secessionist Congolee province of Katanga, when his plane came down.

The death of Lumumba has given rise to many conspiracy theories. Britain was not entirely blameless in the process of subterfuge. A frank document in the Foreign Office archives drafted by H.T.F. Smith,[85] then a member of the African Department, explored the dangers of Lumumba 'coming out on top' in the internecine power struggles in the Congo:

> I see only two possible solutions to the problem. The first is the simple one of ensuring Lumumba's removal from the scene by killing him. This should in fact solve the problem since, so far as we can tell, Lumumba is not a leader of a movement within which there are potential successors of his quality and influence. His supporters are much less dangerous material. The other possible approach is for a constitution to be worked out which places far more power in the hands of the President and in such a way that even if the President (for example Kasavubu) is a less formidable person than the Prime Minister (i.e. Lumumba) the President's powers are safeguarded and those of the Prime Minister limited.[86]

Such an outcome, if not the method, would have suited Macmillan, who regarded Lumumba, often high on drugs, as 'a Communist and probably a Russian agent'.[87] The matter of Lumumba's 'removal' had even been discussed in New York at the time of the General Assembly. On 27 September, Macmillan, accompanied by Lord Home, the Foreign Secretary, had met Eisenhower and Christian Herter to discuss the Congo. Andrew Goodpaster, Eisenhower's staff secretary, recorded Britain's continued concerns about Lumumba, fearful that, if unchecked, he could open the Congo to Communist infiltration. 'Lord Home raised the question why we are not getting rid of Lumumba at the present time,' Goodpaster recorded. 'He [Home] stressed that now is the time to get rid of Lumumba.'[88] 'Getting rid of Lumumba' was a euphemism. When Shakespeare's Iago urged the unfortunate Roderigo to remove Cassio, Roderigo asked, 'How do you mean, removing of him?' Iago had to spell it out. 'Knocking out his brains.'[89] Diplomatic niceties prevented such directness. The actual circumstances of Lumumba's death remain murky and the turn of events seems to have taken Macmillan by surprise, even though he had been present at discussions about the possibility.

'Lumumba has been caught by Col. Mobutu's troops and brought back to Leopoldville,' Macmillan wrote in his diary in December 1960. 'This is good news; but I fear they will kill him (and perhaps eat him) which will bring discredit on the Congo Government.'[90] Mobutu's forces did indeed kill Lumumba, who was shot by firing squad, with some of his supporters. The latest research on the matter attributes the responsibility directly to the Belgian government, with United Nations connivance. Eisenhower had ordered the CIA to take action, but they were pre-empted. There is no record of any direct British involvement.[91]

On 28 October, in the midst of the continuing Congolese problems and Welensky's resentment over the Monckton Report, Macmillan completed the second phase of his earlier ministerial reshuffle. It was not well received. Julian Amery, Macmillan's son-in-law, became the Minister for Air. The Duke of Devonshire, Macmillan's nephew by marriage, was appointed Under-Secretary at the Commonwealth Relations Office, a great surprise, even to the appointee. Hugh Fraser, a regular with Macmillan and Andrew Devonshire at Bolton Abbey shooting parties, was named as the Under-Secretary at the Colonial Office. Joe Godber became Under-Secretary at the Foreign Office, the platform from which he was to rise to be a significant figure in the Test Ban Treaty negotiations in 1963.

Many mistakenly thought the appointment of the Duke of Devonshire too obvious an attempt to appease Bobbety Salisbury, also related by marriage to the Devonshires, then incandescent about Macmillan's unfolding African policy. Accusations of nepotism were openly brandished about. Lord Lansdowne, Lady Dorothy's cousin, was already an Under-Secretary at the Foreign Office. Macmillan's son's brother-in-law, David Ormsby-Gore (later Lord Harlech), was shortly to become Ambassador to America. Macmillan fended off these accusations.[92] But his manner and choice of words were insensitive. He told Nigel Fisher, the liberal-minded Tory MP for Surbiton, that 'Andrew [Devonshire] is awfully good with the natives. The Devonshires have always been good with the natives.'[93]

Duncan Sandys was ungracious towards Andrew Devonshire on his arrival at the Commonwealth Relations Office, telling him bluntly that his appointment would cause resentment. And so it did. Andrew Devonshire was unabashed about Macmillan's patronage. 'I have always wondered whether his urge to dispense favours stemmed from a feeling that neither the Cavendish or Cecil families quite regarded him as one of them; and showing he could bestow patronage on their children was his response,' he wrote of the figure he and his wife always called 'Uncle Harold'. 'Even so, I like to think he was too shrewd an operator to risk employing people, particularly relations, who weren't up to the job.'[94]

Macmillan's son Maurice was chosen to move the address at the start of the new parliamentary session. He showed a light touch. 'Speaking as the only back-bench member of my family,' he began.[95] Even Gaitskell was disarmed.

In November, with the Congo still in turmoil, Macmillan went to Rome with Selwyn Lloyd for economic talks on Europe, what he called the Sixes and Sevens. On 23 November, he had an audience with the Pope, John XXIII. His last such papal audience (with Pius XII) had been in May 1945, on the eve of his return to England at the end of the Second World War. Vatican officials were solicitous in their welcome, and proudly showed Macmillan some of their great artistic treasures, including a marble bust of the Emperor Augustus. When asked his opinion, Macmillan said – to the mystification of his hosts – 'I think it looks awfully like Douglas Jay.'[96]

The responsibility for the Queen's safety if a royal tour to Ghana proceeded had exercised Macmillan greatly. If the Queen was advised by the government to cancel plans because of the deteriorating political situation in Africa, then Macmillan feared that Ghana would leave the Commonwealth, thus leaving another vacuum for the Russians to fill.

In the event, the Queen made a successful tour in November 1961. Of all the services the Queen uncomplainingly fulfilled for the country, this risky venture was one that Macmillan admired more than any other during his term as Prime Minister.

From early in 1960, Macmillan had wondered who would be the Democratic Party's nominee to face Vice-President Nixon in November's American Presidential Election. In April, Nixon had told Selwyn Lloyd that the most formidable opponent for him would be Senator John F. Kennedy. 'Nixon seemed to think that if there was no recession he should beat everyone except Kennedy,' Lloyd recorded. 'About him he seemed doubtful.'[97] It was an accurate prognosis, though, at that stage, Nixon felt his opponent would in all likelihood be Senator Hubert Humphrey. Nixon had underestimated the power, determination and money of the Kennedy clan. After a fiercely fought campaign in which Kennedy's Catholicism was used against him, Kennedy received the nomination of his party at the Democratic Party's convention at Los Angeles on 16 July 1960. Eleven days later, Nixon swept to the Republican nomination by 1,321 votes to 10 on the first ballot.

Macmillan felt that Nixon's first mistake, as incumbent Vice President, was to agree to a series of four television debates with Kennedy. Such a confrontation inevitably favoured the 'challenger'. Macmillan would never have entertained the idea of debating with Gaitskell. Moreover, Nixon had been Vice President for eight years. By contrast, Kennedy was a fresh face for a new age.

Macmillan saw the first of the Nixon–Kennedy television debates on 26 September when he was in America for the meeting of the United Nations General Assembly. Eisenhower saw Macmillan shortly after the broadcast and asked him how he thought the debate had gone. Macmillan's answer confirmed Eisenhower's fears. Nixon, Macmillan said, would find it very difficult to counter Kennedy's youthful vigour and charisma.

Macmillan prepared himself accordingly. 'I do not feel that Kennedy will be bad for us,' he wrote in his diary three days before the poll. 'He will perhaps have ideas and be attracted by ideas.'[98] In the event, the result was closer than anyone imagined. Nixon, looking to future presidential elections, was a good loser.

Macmillan was now 66; Kennedy was 43. On both sides of the Atlantic, the rising generation was knocking at the door, demanding to be let in.[99] Harold Wilson, the 44-year-old Shadow Chancellor, had challenged Gaitskell for the Labour leadership at the party's Scarborough conference in October 1960, winning 81 votes against

Gaitskell's 166. Macmillan was not surprised by the opposition to Gaitskell that the ballot revealed. 'There are moments when his false, perjured face irritates me beyond measure,' he had written in his diary. 'I gather from my Labour friends that he has the same effect on them.'[100]

Political life was not the only area where a younger generation was making an impact. The first version of the long-running satirical review *Beyond the Fringe* had opened on 22 August 1960 at that summer's Edinburgh Festival. Its target was not so much 'the establishment', as complacency in any area of British life.[101] The same was to be true of the magazine *Private Eye*, the brainchild of four ferociously talented alumni of Shrewsbury, who had worked on its pioneering model while still at the Shropshire public school.[102] *Private Eye* became required reading, not only among the political class, its investigations surreptitiously enjoyed even by some of its intended victims.

Another phenomenon of the time also transcended social barriers. In August 1960, a group of five young Liverpool musicians set off to fulfil a booking in Hamburg. Their old Austin van bore a temporary sign – THE BEATLES. The 'fab four', as they eventually became known worldwide to their adoring audiences, epitomised the new classlessness in both demeanour and dress. There was none of the iconoclasm associated with their contemporaries, The Rolling Stones. Three of the Beatles were actually from the solidly respectable, even staid, suburban middle class, and were grammar school educated. Only Ringo Starr, the drummer, had an unimpeachably working-class background.[103]

The new fashion was to be unfashionable. As one of the icons of the age, Twiggy, said, 'The sixties were a time when ordinary people could do extraordinary things.'[104] The decade was characterised by the disappearance of the deference many senior figures in public life, though never Macmillan, had unthinkingly accepted as their due. Macmillan, with his drooping moustache, off-duty plus fours and speeches full of learned literary allusions, was never the glass of fashion or the mould of form, yet he had not been widely characterised as an out-of-touch old fogey.

The gap between the traditional world and the new, informal age had been seen in sharp focus at the time of Princess Margaret's wedding in May 1960. Macmillan had first heard of the forthcoming engagement when visiting the Queen at Sandringham in January, before his African tour. His telling of the story improved over the years. The final version had him being greeted by an agitated Duke of Gloucester: 'Thank heavens you've come, Prime Minister. The Queen's in a terrible state; there's a fellow called Jones in the billiard room who wants to marry her sister, and Prince Philip's in the library wanting to change the family name to Mountbatten.'[105]

The groom was Anthony Armstrong-Jones, a 'commoner' in the parlance of the time.[106] The Duke of Gloucester, and some of the old courtiers, may have been apprehensive, but generally the marriage was seen as a welcome, even democratic, sign of a breaking down of the old protocols.[107] The fact that Armstrong-Jones was an Etonian and his remarried mother a countess was conveniently ignored.[108] Such differences between appearance and reality were often blurred in the sixties. President Kennedy's appearance on the world stage was rapturously greeted on both sides of the Atlantic by those who saw it as a sign of modernity and 'unstuffiness'. The fact that the Kennedy machine, built on the fortunes of his bootlegging father, the pre-war appeasing American Ambasssador in London, Joe Kennedy, had largely bought the presidency was not mentioned.

The sixties was to be full of such paradoxes. *Beyond the Fringe*, a show so popular that the Queen asked Alec Home to arrange a private visit for her,[109] spawned many offspring, increasingly less affectionate and cosy. One of the most influential of these was the television programme *That Was The Week That Was* (known as TW3), which was first broadcast on 24 November 1962. The career of the then Director General of the BBC, Sir Hugh Carleton Greene,[110] was itself one of the key turning points of the sixties. Greene's stated aim was to turn down the central heating at the BBC and throw open the windows. TW3 was one of the symbols of that approach. In the 1930s, Greene had worked in Berlin and remembered the political impact of the cabaret revues, where the audience was an integral part of the show. He envisaged TW3 as an extension of that tradition – entertaining, disrespectful, witty and iconoclastic.[111]

Unlike *Beyond the Fringe* and *Private Eye*, TW3 immediately reached a nationwide audience. Bernard Levin, whose rudeness towards his targets made him the Gilbert Harding of the 1960s, and Millicent Martin, who rounded off each show with a song on the week's events, became national figures. Before the days of video-recording equipment TW3's Saturday nights became a no-go area for social engagements.[112] The impact of the show was well summed up by a *Punch* cartoon of March 1963, which showed a professional couple watching the show. 'Stop laughing, you fool,' the lady berated her husband. 'They're taking the mickey out of people like us.'[113] The central figure, the anchor of TW3 and general all-round scourge of the

Establishment, was the young David Frost, fresh from Cambridge. Yet in time, he too, like Macmillan, would become a duke's son-in-law and an Eton parent.[114]

'It is not easy nowadays to convey the sensational audacity, the explosively liberating effect of hearing the Prime Minister of the day impersonated or judges, bishops, police chiefs and army officers,' wrote Michael Palin. 'It was shocking and thrilling.'[115]

Macmillan was not shocked. He knew it was better to be mocked than ignored. After the first edition of TW3, Reginald Bevins, the Postmaster General, the minister with responsibility for licensing the BBC, was asked if he intended to do anything about the show. 'Yes, I will,' replied Bevins. He received a crisp note from Macmillan the next day, 'Oh, no, you won't.'[116]

The prosecution of Penguin Books for publishing D. H. Lawrence's 1928 novel *Lady Chatterley's Lover* was the visible moment when the old Britain confronted the new age – and lost. Even the American presidential election was sidelined, as enticing details emerged from the High Court before the world's press. The prosecuting counsel, Mervyn Griffith-Jones, Old Etonian and holder of the Military Cross, asked the jury, 'Is it a book that you would even wish your wife or your servants to read?' The laughter in court showed how much the prosecution had misjudged the mood. 1960 was not 1860.

CHAPTER TWENTY SIX

Seeing Beyond the Trees

1961

> That was the great thing about Jack. He could always see
> beyond the trees.
>   Harold Macmillan on President Kennedy, 23 April 1975[1]

'I fear that 1961 will be for all of us a year full of great difficulties all over the world,' Macmillan wrote to President de Gaulle on 22 December 1960.[2] In the privacy of his diary he was equally pessimistic:

> We are only now beginning to realise, as the weeks go by, the full extent of the Summit disaster in Paris. For me, it is the collapse of the work of two or three years. For Eisenhower, it means an ignominious end to his Presidency. For Khrushchev, a set back to his more conciliatory and sensible ideas. For the world, a step nearer ultimate disaster.[3]

So concerned was Macmillan with the troubled international scene that he produced a long memorandum over Christmas to focus his thoughts and guide his colleagues. The memorandum served as the basis for his first meeting with President Kennedy, which was due to be held in Washington in April 1961. The document was soon known by the Private Office as 'The Grand Design', dealing as it did with the West's economic, political and defence problems. Macmillan knew it was only a matter of time before Khrushchev built up the pressure again on Berlin, and he wanted the West to prepare a co-ordinated response.

'The Grand Design', prompted by the impending change of American leadership, comprehensively rehearsed two of Macmillan's key concerns – 'the uncertainty about our relations with the new economic, and perhaps political, state which is being created by the Six countries of continental Western Europe; and the uncertainty of American policies towards us.'[4] Macmillan knew that de Gaulle would be a pivotal figure in the post-summit phase. 'De Gaulle's Europe is not strong enough to be a third force without Britain,' he observed.

'He wants us in, but only after we have "chosen Europe" instead of the United States. We must somehow persuade him that this idea of choice is false and out of date. Unity is the only way.'[5]

At the end of January, Macmillan had talks with de Gaulle at Rambouillet, his second such meeting within a year. Macmillan was cautious. He did not want President Kennedy to feel that Britain and France had arranged things between themselves without reference to American interests. For his part, de Gaulle wondered why Britain always seemed 'to follow exactly in the wake of the Americans'.[6] Yet a middle way, with Britain as the honest broker between America and Europe was not on de Gaulle's agenda either, as he made clear to Adenauer.

Macmillan sent Adenauer an account of his Rambouillet talks, prior to their own meeting in London at the end of February. Macmillan was clear in his mind that if any 'fixing' was being done, then it was between the French and the Germans, with Britain on the margins. He felt that Britain was curiously vulnerable and isolated in this transitional political phase. First reports from Harold Caccia, British Ambassador in Washington, indicated that Kennedy was not overimpressed with either de Gaulle's political vision or Macmillan's tripartite ideas as outlined in 'The Grand Design'.

In preparation for their first meeting, Macmillan read Kennedy's book of speeches, *The Strategy of Peace*. He also took advice from Harold Caccia about how to approach the scheduled April meeting. For Macmillan there was an unexpected bonus in Kennedy's presidency. Not only did Macmillan have relatives by marriage in his own administration, he now had a relative by marriage in the White House. The President's sister Kathleen ('Kick') Kennedy had married Andrew Devonshire's elder brother, Billy Hartington, in May 1944. Billy was killed in action by a sniper's bullet on 10 September 1944. Then in 1948 Kick Kennedy died in an air crash. She was buried in the village churchyard at St Peter's Church, Edensor, across the park from Chatsworth.[7]

Andrew Devonshire and his wife Deborah (Debo, born Deborah Mitford) were guests on Inauguration Day in Washington on 20 January 1961. Kennedy spotted them and sent a message to them to come and sit by him. The connection between the Kennedys and the Devonshires went back to pre-war days in London, when Joe Kennedy was the American Ambassador. Joe Kennedy lived in Princes Gate, near the Devonshires' house in Rutland Gate. The families had 'grown up together', the young, in particular, forging a bond that time and separation had not eroded. Later that evening, at the Inaugural Ball, Andrew and Deborah Devonshire were seated in the President's box. Kennedy told Deborah that he was looking forward to seeing Macmillan, 'Uncle Harold', before too long.[8]

Macmillan and Kennedy first met, not, as scheduled, in Washington, but, unexpectedly, at the American Naval Base at Key West in Florida. Macmillan had arrived in Trinidad on the first stage of his West Indies tour on 24 March 1961 when he received an urgent message from Kennedy (so urgent that it arrived at 4 a.m.) The crisis in Laos, a kingdom in northern Indo-China torn by civil war since 1954, and in a constant state of political flux, was so serious that Kennedy wanted to see Macmillan at once. The suggestion from the White House was that the two leaders should meet the very next day. This sudden request was not entirely to Macmillan's liking. It was not that he objected to a round trip of 3,600 miles for luncheon, as he put it laconically, rather that he would have preferred to have met in an orderly manner after he had been fully briefed.

Nevertheless, Macmillan decided at once that he must travel to Florida. He observed the proprieties by consulting Rab Butler and Edward Heath in London, together with Alec Home, who was in Karachi.* 'I did not wish to <u>accept</u> meeting with President without general approval,' he wrote in his diary, 'for I fear it may cause a scare in the world and trouble in Parliament.'[9]

To the surprise of many, including Macmillan, the two leaders found they had much in common. There was a chemistry between them. Both still bore the scars and accompanying pain of serious war wounds. They understood the military mind. Macmillan was impressed by the trouble Kennedy had taken in providing a ceremonial welcome, bands, a guard of honour and a 19-gun salute. 'Although we have never met and belonged to such different generations,' he wrote in his memoirs, 'he was just forty and I was nearly seventy, we seemed immediately to talk as old friends.'[10] The meeting was purposeful and brisk, no lengthy lunch, just a plateful of meat sandwiches.

Harold Caccia had travelled from Washington on the President's plane, which had landed just before Macmillan's, and he briefed Macmillan before the formal talks began. The Eisenhower administration had spent five years (and over 300 million dollars) in trying to establish Laos as a pro-Western anti-Communist outpost on the

---

*On his way to Bangkok for a SEATO meeting.

borders of China and North Vietnam. At the time of Kennedy's inauguration, the Soviets had massively increased their military support in the region to the insurgent Communist forces of the Pathet Lao, and Kennedy was under pressure from the Pentagon to back a military operation by SEATO. Opinion is divided on whether Kennedy himself favoured such a plan. David Nunnerly believed that he did and was consequently disappointed by 'Macmillan's failure to react more strongly to his premonitions about the Laotian crisis'.[11] This was not Macmillan's impression. He felt Kennedy was unwilling to be pressurised by the Pentagon against his instincts.

Macmillan cautioned restraint, because he believed that American problems in south-east Asia were self-inflicted, albeit largely by the previous administration. His fear was that American involvement in the area would be damaging to the Atlantic alliance, both politically and in terms of resources. Also Macmillan sensed that Kennedy was at the time preoccupied with preparations for a possible invasion of Cuba at the Bay of Pigs and thus wary of further military commitments, an early example of how he was considering several moves ahead on the diplomatic chessboard. Not for the first time, as Macmillan later put it, Kennedy was seeing beyond the trees.

Macmillan knew that the Chiefs of Staff in London would not consider military intervention desirable. In the wake of Suez, Macmillan himself had no wish for British forces to be imbroiled in south-east Asia. He played the role of the cautious, experienced family uncle, reining back the impulses of an impatient and restless nephew. Not that Kennedy needed much dissuasion.

Kennedy had all manner of military top brass in attendance in his entourage; Macmillan had Tim Bligh and Harold Caccia, plus secretarial help. 'It is always more important at these international conferences,' Macmillan wrote in his diary, 'to have good shorthand girls than to have generals and admirals.'[12] In the longer term, the importance of the Key West meeting[13] was not the discussion on Laos, but the fact that it marked the beginning of what was to become an important partnership for both Kennedy and Macmillan. Kennedy was shortly to meet Khrushchev for the first time, so he took the opportunity to glean information about the Soviet leader's character and methods, something Macmillan was able to provide from his own experience. Increasingly, Macmillan 'offered the words of comfort the president in his lonely solitude seemed to crave, and which Joe Kennedy was no longer in a position to provide'.[14] In short, in both personal and professional dealings with the President, Macmillan truly was established in the President's mind as father figure.

*

Before Kennedy departed from Key West, he raised the question of the next British Ambassador in Washington. Kennedy was 'emphatic for David Gore', telling Macmillan that Gore was 'the most intimate friend' of his brother Robert, the Attorney General.[15] Ormsby-Gore had stayed *en famille* with the Kennedys at their holiday compound at Hyannis Port on several occasions since 1954, and was one of those talented figures with whom Kennedy liked to surround himself. Kennedy did not need to spell out his long-held opinion that 'Gore was the most intelligent man he had ever met'.[16] In asking for Ormsby-Gore as Britain's envoy, the President was knocking at an open door. Macmillan knew that Robert Kennedy was the *éminence grise* of the new administration, and he had already decided on Ormsby-Gore for the post. Harold Caccia, through no fault of his own, had been somewhat marginalised in Washington after Suez.[17] The new era required a man in whom the President had absolute trust. Of all Macmillan's hunches, the appointment of Ormsby-Gore (known as 'Macmillan's special representative to the court of King John')[18] was the one that was most triumphantly vindicated.

Other European ambassadors, such as Hervé Alphand, the French envoy, were distinctly jealous of Ormsby-Gore's privileged position in Washington, which contributed to de Gaulle's mistrust of the British and the Americans when they got together. Macmillan confirmed Ormsby-Gore's appointment to Washington in May 1961, and Gore took up his post in the autumn of that year. 'The appointment will, of course, be criticised by Lord Beaverbrook,' Macmillan wrote to Ormsby-Gore, 'but all sensible people will feel, as I do, that we are all under a great obligation to you and your wife for agreeing to accept the post.'[19]

Macmillan returned to Trinidad the same day. It had been a long journey for his beef sandwiches, but a worthwhile one in every way. On 28 March, his small team moved on to Barbados, where he was able to lunch with the Edens, who had a holiday home, Villa Nova, on the island. Messages meanwhile were coming from Lord Home in Bangkok: Kennedy's 'restraint' over Laos did not seem to have got through to the American delegation. Macmillan was not unduly worried. Kennedy had told him that he would keep their conclusions under wraps, as 'everything leaks from the State Department'.[20]

On 4 April, Macmillan flew from the West Indies to Washington for his second, and lengthier, meetings with Kennedy and his team. Lord Home was now in Washington, hotfoot from Bangkok. Home's work had impressed Macmillan, who was glad that the 'dual' appointment, with Edward Heath as Lord Privy Seal, acting for the Foreign Office in the Commons, was proving its worth. 'The Foreign Secretary and Lord Privy Seal have handled this crisis very well,' he wrote.[21] Although few could have predicted it in April 1961, Home and Heath were to be his two successors as Conservative prime ministers.

The three days in Washington were much more formal than Key West, but Macmillan found his private meetings with Kennedy to be of the greatest value. Kennedy admitted to having worries, particularly that he did not have a majority in Congress, and also the situation he faced in Cuba. Macmillan was more concerned about the latter. 'That young man is going to do something foolish about Cuba,' he said privately.[22]

In his opening address to an audience that included Dean Rusk, the Secretary of State, and the former Secretary of State, Dean Acheson, Macmillan outlined his concerns about the recent Soviet advances and the consequent need to have a unified Allied response. He told his audience of the growing strength of the 'Six' in Europe. Kennedy stressed how important it was for Britain to become part of the 'Six'. The advantages for America – and the European countries – in having to deal with one trade bloc, not two (the 'Seven'), were clear. Also, if Britain was within the 'Six', it would have a better opportunity of exerting political influence independently of both de Gaulle and Adenauer.

'It is fun knowing you,' Macmillan wrote to Kennedy on his return to Britain, 'and I look forward to going on working with you.'[23] Macmillan felt there was something almost eighteenth century about the grace and bearing of both 'Jack' and 'Jackie', as the couple soon became known to him. 'They certainly have acquired something we have lost,' he wrote, 'a casual sort of grandeur about their evenings, always at the end of the day's business, the promise of parties, and pretty women, and music and beautiful clothes, and champagne, and all that.'[24]

On 12 April, Macmillan sent the Queen a lengthy account of his contacts with the new administration in Washington. In his letter, he observed that Kennedy had made many shrewd moves. First, he had kept older, experienced figures such as Averell Harriman, Adlai Stevenson and Dean Acheson in his circle, and had also appointed several black men to his administration. Second, he was a good listener, and his obvious charm and charisma made a marked contrast to the 'elderly' Eisenhower administration. Kennedy's Catholicism had been an issue during the presidential election, but it was of no importance to Macmillan. Robert Menzies, the Australian Prime Minister, had also dismissed dislike of Kennedy's religion as irrational prejudice. 'I am not afraid of the Pope,' he had written to Macmillan. 'I am afraid of Papa!'[25] Now that he was getting to know Kennedy, Macmillan could dismiss this latter concern also. Indeed, he was also impresssed and encouraged by the way that Kennedy, despite the obvious filial ties, was subtly distancing himself from the pre-war ambassadorial legacy of Joe Kennedy in London as a supporter of appeasement.

Macmillan's admiration for the new President was not rose-tinted. He sensed an insecurity and lack of confidence. Kennedy should have been unassailable, but the manner of his victory over Nixon had dented his confidence. 'How did I manage to beat a guy like this by only a hundred thousand votes?' he had asked in frustration.[26] As a result, he felt he needed to prove himself. Macmillan soon realised that Kennedy liked to be the centre of attention, could be easily pleased by such attention, and, equally, could just as soon be offended.

Macmillan established a close understanding with many of the key figures in Kennedy's entourage. He much admired the new Secretary of State, Dean Rusk,* whom he privately nicknamed 'the biscuit man',†[28] not a sign of disparagement, rather of Macmillan's feeling of ease, even affection. Referring to de Gaulle privately at this time as 'the little pinhead' was, however, not affectionate.

Two of Kennedy's advisers – Schlesinger and Galbraith – were impresssed by Macmillan. Outwardly Macmillan had a 'languid Edwardian appearance', but underneath, Arthur Schlesinger knew that there was 'a sharp, disillusioned mind' and 'a vivid sense of history'.[30] John Kenneth Galbraith, the celebrated economist, liked the 'elegance, information and style' that was always revealed in Macmillan's letters.[31] David Bruce, the American Ambassador, told Dean Rusk that although Macmillan gave the 'impression of being shot through with Victorian languor', he was actually 'a political animal, shrewd, subtle

---

*The thing that Macmillan admired about Rusk was that he did not seek to shift responsibility for failings on to the shoulders of others, rather he appropriated the blame himself. When Macmillan was saying farewell to Kennedy and Rusk after their visit to Britain in June 1962, uncharacteristically he put his arm round Rusk. 'I've got to know you better,' he said. 'Jack has been telling me that you were opposed to the Bay of Pigs but that after it happened you acted as if you had done it yourself.'[27]

†This fondness for nicknames was a characteristic of the English upper classes, the Mitfords in particular. When Macmillan became Foreign Secretary, a guide to 'who was who' had been circulated to embassies.[29]

in maneuver'. After Kennedy's death, Bruce contributed a memoir on the Kennedy–Macmillan relationship. 'The frequency and frankness of their interchanges,' he wrote, 'had few parallels.'[32]

The fact that Macmillan had a reputation for shrewdness in 'maneuver' appealed to Kennedy. At this early stage of his presidency he was interested in asking the questions and storing away the responses in his memory bank, an approach Macmillan felt wholly admirable. Macmillan also admired Kennedy's dislike of discursiveness.

Macmillan's fondness for trans-Atlantic talks with the new President (they had seven such meetings in three short years) made rich fodder for the satirists. Peter Cook did not miss his opportunity in his impersonation of the British Prime Minister: 'I then went to America, and there I had talks with the young, vigorous President of that great country, and danced with his very lovely lady wife. We talked of many things, including Great Britain's role in the world as an honest broker. I agreed with him, when he said that no nation could be more honest, and he agreed with me, when I chaffed him, and said that no nation could be broker.'[33]

Macmillan returned to Britain, after his lengthy tour, via Ottawa, where he stayed at Government House, with its nostalgic associations with Lady Dorothy. Shortly after his return, he heard of the failure of the Bay of Pigs.* The honeymoon mood in Washington soon vanished, and Kennedy was now subject to vicious personal attacks, and not only from Republicans. Macmillan knew how visceral the hatred of the American right could be for figures such as Roosevelt on the liberal left, and he admired immensely the manner in which Kennedy withstood the obloquy now poured upon him. Macmillan's main fear was that the fiasco in Cuba would turn Kennedy towards military involvement in Laos, a crisis showing no sign of early resolution.

Macmillan was shortly to have his third series of meetings with Kennedy, when the US President came to Europe for his first encounter with the French President. The White House asked Macmillan for written briefings before this important meeting. Kennedy was to press de Gaulle, not with overt success, on the reunification of Europe. From Paris, he went on to his infamous first meeting with Khrushchev: the Soviet leader mistakenly believed that the young President was an inexperienced political figure who would be an easy 'pushover'.

The Kennedys arrived in London on 4 June (always a day of

---

*The Bay of Pigs incident (17 April 1961) was an unsuccessful attempt to topple Cuba's leader, Fidel Castro, through an invasion of Cuba by a CIA-trained force of Cuban exiles, backed by the American government. The failure was a severe embarrassment to President Kennedy, who said he wanted 'to splinter the CIA into a thousand pieces and scatter it into the wind'.

celebration for Macmillan, from schooldays at Eton to the fall of Rome in 1944). This was the glamorous moment when 'Camelot', as the Kennedy White House was now sentimentally being dubbed, came to town. In the midst of a busy programme, including the christening of his sister-in-law's baby and a dinner at Buckingham Palace, Kennedy gave Macmillan a lengthy account of his impressions of de Gaulle and Khrushchev. He communicated his disappointment with both meetings, and Macmillan felt that a less buoyant character would have been more despondent. The visit ended with a gathering of the clans at a private lunch Macmillan hosted at his new home, Admiralty House. The Kennedys and the Macmillans were there in force, as were those who 'overlapped' – figures such as Andrew and Debo Devonshire, David and Sissy Ormsby-Gore, and David Bruce[34] and his wife Evangeline.

The relationship between Kennedy and Macmillan was one of ideas, and one in which Kennedy was willing to listen, not wanting to offer instant solutions to complex issues. Macmillan was neither unrealistic nor over optimistic about his new friendship. Kennedy appealed to the young and to the liberally minded; in time, Macmillan was to be an unsympathetic figure, indeed target, for both groupings. Macmillan obviously gained by being so closely associated with the Kennedy stardust, but he was too shrewd politically to think that this would last for ever. In strict bilateral terms, Macmillan understood that the much-vaunted 'special relationship' was actually a myth, but he knew that it was a useful myth. The events of the next two years were to show the nature and extent of that usefulness.

CHAPTER TWENTY SEVEN
Searching For A Role
1961–1962

Great Britain has lost an empire and has not yet found a role.
> Dean Acheson, 5 December 1962

In the life of any government, however safe its majority, there comes a moment when the social movements of which it had once been the expression turn inexorably against it.
> Christopher Booker, *The Neophiliacs*, 1969[1]

Politics is not the art of the possible. It consists in choosing between the unpalatable and the disastrous.
> J. K. Galbraith to President Kennedy, 2 March 1962

On returning to Britain in 1960, Michael Young, the entrepreneurial author of *The Rise of the Meritocracy*, noticed how drab and dispiriting things seemed compared to his recent experience on the Continent. The contrast was for him epitomised by one telling detail: the chipped white cups in the tea room at the port of Dover. Young made this the title of a celebrated pamphlet. Although *The Chipped White Cups of Dover*[2] was primarily a call for consumer reform, Young's image symbolised for many the indifferent service they encountered in their everyday lives. Young had been instrumental in founding the Consumers' Association in 1957, with its magazine *Which?*, intended to educate consumers into making more informed choices.[3]

Something of Young's feeling rubbed off on Macmillan after his recent experience of the grace and glamour of America's first family. Although there were no chipped white cups in the VIP lounge at Heathrow airport, Macmillan had been conscious of areas of public provision where improvements were still needed. Penguin Books published a series of books in 1961 examining the theme of *What's Wrong with Britain*, looking critically at institutions as diverse as the churches and the trade unions. The most influential of these questioning publications proved to be Michael Shanks' *The Stagnant Society*.[4] 'The Modernisation of Britain' was thus one of the main themes of Macmillan's premiership, and he presented a memorandum with this title to the Cabinet for consideration in 1962. The difficulty for Macmillan was that by that time the Conservative Party was not seen as 'modern'. President Kennedy appealed to the young and to liberals. Increasingly the Conservatives seemed to appeal to neither. One could hardly imagine, say, Sir Reginald Manningham-Buller shopping in Carnaby Street. Macmillan knew he had difficult choices to make, but he felt that those who grumbled could help also. 'If only all the people who write, lecture, broadcast and even preach about economic growth did some useful work,' he wrote in his diary, 'the increase in manpower would perhaps enable us to achieve it.'[5]

A distinct change of mood came over Britain in 1960. Until then, people felt things were getting better, as compared with the interwar and war years. At the start of the new decade, many people began to observe not how well Britain was doing, but how other countries seemed to be doing much better. Many solutions were considered: entry into Europe, planning, an incomes policy. The aim was to raise the rate of growth to 4 per cent, but that had not been achieved since mid-Victorian times. What actually lay ahead was a lower rate of growth, combined with conflict with the unions, and in that lay the demise of the Macmillan government.

Of all the issues, 'Europe' was to prove the most problematical, especially after de Gaulle had been strengthened by a Gaullist absolute majority in the Assembly, the first absolute majority in modern French history, and by his victory in the referendum on direct election of the President. Without these, he would not have been in a strong enough position to veto Britain. Reginald Maudling, President of the Board of Trade, had been present at the abortive free-trade negotiations in Paris in June 1961, and he presciently predicted that Britain would not secure entry into Europe, because of the French. On 24 June, he sent Macmillan his views prior to a weekend meeting of ministers at Chequers. Of the French obduracy he wrote, 'it seems to me to be pointless to be talking about any negotiations with them ... I should like to suggest that one of the things we might discuss this weekend is whether in the light of this wholly negative French attitude a complete change in our tactics may not be necessary'.[6] The failure to do so casts doubts on Macmillan's negotiating tactics. In hindsight, he should not have quibbled so much, but simply accepted the treaty and then tried to secure concessions later.

In December 1962, Dean Acheson, the veteran American politician, pronounced that 'Great Britain has lost an Empire and has failed to find a role.' Ironically, the speech (entitled 'Our Atlantic Alliance:

The Political and Economic Strands') was delivered at the Key West military base where Macmillan had first met President Kennedy and had seemingly been absorbed into the world of the new frontiersmen. Acheson did not mince his words. 'Great Britain, attempting to work alone and to be a broker between the United States and Russia, has seemed to conduct policy as weak as its military power.'[7] The search for a role had preoccupied Macmillan since his 1959 general election victory. It was particularly galling to have it trumpeted to the world that his country was still searching.

Acheson's speech caused tremendous offence in Britain. Realising this, President Kennedy telephoned Macmillan personally to soothe injured feelings.[8] Reginald Maudling, by then Chancellor of the Exchequer, and rapidly emerging as the likeliest successor to Macmillan, observed perceptively that 'British opinion was angry with him [Acheson] precisely because what he said was fundamentally true.'[9] Indeed, as Dr Peter Catterall has observed, Acheson 'summed up the self-doubts and criticism the British themselves were experiencing at the time'.[10]

Macmillan was not complacent. Many areas of British life were now being subjected to fierce scrutiny in the cause of improved efficiency. Several of the reports and commissions that abounded at this time were the result of Macmillan's own initiatives. One of the first had been the Crowther Report, *Fifteen to Eighteen*, on the future of secondary education, published in 1959.[11] Geoffrey Crowther[12] had been in the wartime Ministry of Supply from 1940 to 1941, where Macmillan had first noted his talents. Crowther's report was an influential document, not all the contents of which were to Conservative tastes. He recommended the expansion of comprehensive schools (an enduring controversy for the Conservatives, as sharp as that over Europe), the raising of the school leaving age to 16 (not achieved until 1972, during the premiership of Edward Heath), and an exam of less demanding academic rigour to supplement GCE O levels (what eventually became the GCSEs, from September 1986). Crowther also addressed the wasteful 'drop out' of pupils from education, at the very time when they needed more training for their adult careers.

The Crowther Report was followed by the Robbins Report on *Higher Education*[13], published in 1963, and one of the most far-reaching legacies of Macmillan's premiership.[14] Robbins recommended a doubling of university places and the immediate elevation to university status of the Colleges of Advanced Technology. He was particularly keen that the proportion of science students and women in tertiary education should be increased. John Boyd-Carpenter, then

Paymaster General, warned the Cabinet that the cost of the 10-year programme, if Robbins' recommendations were accepted, would be in the order of £3,500 million, a doubling of current expenditure.[15] Nevertheless, the main conclusions were accepted by the government.

The Robbins Report established the principle that university places should be provided for all who could benefit from them. Robbins reflected the prevailing mood of the time, rather than setting it in train. New 'plate-glass' universities were already under way; indeed, two of them – Sussex and East Anglia – were already open before Robbins reported. This expansion of higher education did not meet with universal approval. Kingsley Amis, Director of Studies in English at Peterhouse, Cambridge, in 1961, had already proclaimed that 'more means worse', saying that he was not so much concerned with the untapped pool of talent, but rather the tapped pool of untalent, a debate that still continues.[16]

The Newsom report of 1963, *Half Our Future*,[17] looked at educational provision for those in secondary-modern schools. Macmillan also appointed inquiries to look into other areas of British life, such as consumer protection (one of Michael Young's hobby-horses), the ports, town planning, and a royal commission on the Press, headed by Lord Shawcross, which recommended a more powerful Press Council.[18] The Buchanan Report, *Traffic in Towns*,[19] published in November 1963, was commissioned by Ernest Marples and looked at the consequences of increased car ownership. Roads, with Marples at Transport, were still seen very much as the future.

Macmillan appointed the Pilkington Committee on Broadcasting on 13 July 1960 with the remit of considering the future of broadcasting. Its chairman was the industrialist Sir Harry Pilkington,[20] a former president of the Federation of the Bank of England, and one of a seemingly endless supply of the 'great and the good' to head such inquiries at the time. The committee contained a diverse group, ranging from Joyce Grenfell to Richard Hoggart. Peter Hall, director of the Shakespeare Memorial Theatre in Stratford (shortly to become the Royal Shakespeare Company), was also a member, until pressure of outside commitments forced him to withdraw (on 27 January 1961). As Billy Wright, the former England football captain, served on the committee, the popular press tended to refer to the members as 'the team'.[21]

Richard Hoggart, the most influential committee member, had not expected that such 'a largish disparate group' should 'so steadily and firmly reach a common mind'.[22] Much of this was owing to Hoggart's persuasiveness and the evidence submitted. The Pilkington Committee reflected the views of the high-minded professional classes, many of whom did not watch television regularly, or even possess a set.* The attitudes expressed in the Pilkington report were reminiscent of the 'improving' atmosphere surrounding the planners of the Festival of Britain. T. S. Eliot, for instance, was approached for his opinions. Ironically, Macmillan the begetter of the Pilkington Committee, was very middle-brow in his artistic tastes (though not, of course, in his literary tastes). He went to the first night of John Osborne's play *Luther*, starring Albert Finney, on 5 September 1961 at the Phoenix Theatre, but he found Lionel Bart's *Oliver!*, a popular musical of the time, a far more entertaining evening.

The Pilkington Report was published in June 1962[23] and was at once seen as a vindication of the BBC under the director generalship of Sir Hugh Carleton Greene. As *The Times* observed, it was three cheers for the BBC and none for ITV.[24] The committee's conclusion about commercial broadcasting provision was unambiguous. 'The service falls well short of what a good public service of broadcasting should be.'[25] ITV was criticised, in particular, for its populist recycling of American crime programmes and Westerns. Hoggart's really telling point, though, was not that ITV provided too much light entertainment, but that they did not provide enough *high-quality* light entertainment. The scene at the ITA headquarters on the day of publication was described as not so much *Coronation Street* as 'Consternation Street'.[26]

The Pilkington Report had unintended consequences, few beneficial to the Macmillan government. As the conclusions were so critical of independent broadcasting, there was now accelerated lobbying for commercial radio, and indeed 'pirate' radio stations were set up offshore. Such outlets were what would later be dubbed 'alternative', and, as they were implicitly critical of the establishment, proved very popular. The overall effect of the Pilkington Report, which was heavily criticised as elitist and patronising, was thus to make the Macmillan government seem out of touch; in short, too much T.S. Eliot and not enough Cakes and Ale.

Yet Pilkington's judgements and assumptions were not confined to educated members of the intelligentsia. The issues were ones of taste, not class. The TUC had passed a resolution (No. 42) at their conference in 1960 for an inquiry into the state of the arts, aimed at making them more 'accessible'. Arnold Wesker, the playwright, became the key proselytising figure in bringing 'sweetness and light' to otherwise barren areas. Wesker founded Centre 42, housed in a derelict railway

---

* Macmillan had a set at Birch Grove, but it was in the servants' hall.

building, the Roundhouse, in north London, which became a centre of artistic excellence. Matthew Arnold would have approved.

Macmillan wanted to examine the whole transport infrastructure, rationalise where necessary and establish realistic priorities. Attlee's Labour government had combined railways, road haulage, the docks, inland waterways and London Transport into a British Transport Commission, far too unwieldy for its purpose. Ernest Marples, Transport Minister since the 1959 election, was just the kind of pro-active figure Macmillan wanted to shake things up. Marples had been invaluable for Macmillan when he was at the Ministry of Housing in the early 1950s. In December 1960, Macmillan had decided to separate the British Transport Commission into its constituent parts, and to establish a new British Railways Board. Marples was now given his head. He appointed Dr Richard Beeching,[27] technical director of ICI, to head British Rail, at a salary of £24,000 per annum, by far the largest salary of any nationalised industry head. This vast sum contributed to Beeching's unpopularity, even before he started wielding his infamous axe. British Rail's debts were written off, but the proviso was that trains now had to compete in the market.

This goal suited Beeching, ironically a daily rail commuter himself from East Grinstead. He had never thought of railways as a public service; for him, the system had to be run as a business, and if lines were unprofitable, or underused, then they would have to be closed. He believed, illogically, that once such lines had been axed, the rest would become profitable. 'Beeching's fundamental mistake,' the railway historian Christian Wolmar has written, 'was to underestimate the contribution of branches to the economics of the railways and he was wrong to assume that people who travelled by rail would happily shift to buses.'[28]

Marples believed that the future of transport in Britain lay in roads. Yet road and rail were inextricably linked. The growth in road usage was to have deleterious effects on railway finances, quite apart from polluting the environment. Bottlenecks, particularly around the major conurbations, and on holiday routes at Bank Holidays, were the scourge of the long-suffering motorist. In an era known for its slogans and banners, 'Marples' Jams are best' was one of the wittiest.

When Beeching reported on 27 March 1963, his proposal was that one third of Britain's 18,000 miles of railways should close. The East Grinstead line was not one of those threatened.[29] Many rural areas were to be cut off completely. Public outrage greeted the report, now dubbed 'Beeching's Axe'. Yet the Macmillan government largely accepted his recommendations. The physical legacy was a countryside of abandoned stone bridges, derelict platforms and overgrown viaducts, awaiting some future railway archaeologist. The human legacy was less picturesque. The irony was that Macmillan, who was to be so unsympathetic to the later Thatcherite monetarist revolution,[30] presided over what was one of the most purely market-driven exercises in post-war British politics. Beeching's report contributed to the growing unpopularity of the government, particularly among Home Counties commuters, fearful that their essential rail links to the capital might be under threat. As the later spoof music-hall song put it:

> Oh, Dr Beeching what have you done?
> There were lots of trains to catch,
> but soon there will be none,
> I'll have to buy a bike, 'cos I can't afford a car,
> Oh, Dr Beeching what a naughty man you are![31]

The support of the people who needed the bicycles would be vital for the Conservatives if they were to win a fourth successive election victory. 'Beeching' eroded that support.

The economic legacy of the Beeching cuts was even more damaging than the physical and human ones, not least in that its corrosive effects could be predicted. The extensive closures did not bring profitability to the rail system. Initial savings were £30 million annually, but losses were over £100 million.[32] At the heart of the exercise was an anomaly. Beeching was applying market forces to the economics of railway provision. Yet this approach was compromised by overriding political considerations where deemed necessary. The Central Wales line, for instance, passed through so many marginal constituencies that neither Conservative nor Labour governments dared close it. Ironically, the most expensive operations in terms of subsidy – the 'East Grinstead' commuter services – were recognised, even by Beeching, as inviolable, because of the political and social upheavals that would be caused by their closure.

Macmillan's ready acceptance of the Beeching Report is one of the puzzles of his career. Railways were never going to be profitable in an increasingly post-industrial age; it was wishful thinking to imagine otherwise. Unlike Margaret Thatcher, who hardly ever travelled on a train if she could help it, Macmillan was a railways man through and through. His career was inextricably linked with the historic birthplace of the railways – from Stockton-on-Tees to Darlington. A former director of the Great Western Railway before nationalisation, he still retained, and frequently used, his lifetime gold pass, granting him free rail travel. His late-night journeys back to Haywards Heath station from London were part of his routine.

The legacy of the 'Beeching Axe' was injurious on several grounds, social, ecological, financial and political. The closure of underused branch lines isolated many rural communities and damaged much economic activity, from tourism to farming. Stratford-upon-Avon, for instance, was eventually to lose its direct link to London. The closure failed to return the rail network to profitability and the consequent increase in road traffic (road haulage in particular) had deleterious ecological effects, a factor not foreseen at the time. The most damaging message of Beeching, though, was that the railways were now a secondary transport priority, and accordingly should be run to a business model, not as a social provision, a change that would never have been contemplated over health and education. The subsequent controversies gravely harmed Macmillan's government, obloquy that was deserved, but which could easily have been avoided.

Macmillan's fundamental miscalculation was compounded by his insensitivity over the future of Philip Hardwick's historic Doric Euston Arch of 1837. 'Hardwick's Doric Arch at Euston is the supreme justification of the Greek revival in England,' the poet John Betjeman had declared resoundingly in 1933. 'If vandals ever pulled down this lovely piece of architecture, it would seem as though the British Constitution had collapsed.'[33] In January 1960, the British Transport Commission proposed to demolish Euston station, with its famous Grade II listed Great Hall.[34] The Euston Arch was also scheduled for demolition. The heritage lobby was up in arms, with John Betjeman prominent among those who sought to preserve the arch. Yet Macmillan seemed to treat their concerns with indifference.

J. M. Richards,[35] editor of the *Architectural Review*, led a concerned team of architects and conservationists, including Betjeman, to see Macmillan on 24 October 1961. 'Macmillan listened – or I suppose he listened,' Richards recalled. 'He sat without moving with his eyes apparently closed. He asked no questions; in fact he said nothing except that he would consider the matter.'[36] Demolition of the arch began in December 1961. An article in the *Architectural Review* savaged the decision, saying the destruction of the arch was 'wanton and unnecessary', and had been connived at by the government, 'the face of official apathy and philistinism'.[37]

Macmillan never regretted the decision to implement the Beeching Report. Indeed, in defensive mode, he paid Beeching an extravagant and fulsome compliment in his memoirs, saying that 'the nation owes him a deep debt of gratitude'.[38] The decision on the Doric Arch, though, he later felt to be a mistake, and not just on sentimental grounds. In relative terms the financial costs were small. The anonymous Euston station today, compared to its handsome and historic predecessor, is an even more powerful symbol of reduction than the chipped white cups of Dover. The conjunction of 'Beeching' and the Euston Arch was a sign that Macmillan's instinctive political feel was no longer quite as sure as it had been. The danger, as always, is that such a trickle soon accelerates into an unstoppable surge.

'I rather enjoy patronage,' Macmillan admitted. 'I take a lot of trouble over it. At least it makes all those years of reading Trollope seem worthwhile.'[39] However, unlike the Archdeacon Grantlys of Trollope's world (not to mention some of his predecessors as Prime Minister), Macmillan's main concern when deliberating over these appointments was primarily theological, rather than political. To the surprise of many in the Conservative Party, he had nominated the Socialist Dr Mervyn Stockwood for the bishopric of Southwark in 1958. Edward Heath even went so far as to express his concern directly to Macmillan. 'You looked annoyed,' said Macmillan to Heath at a routine meeting in November 1958. 'I *am* annoyed,' replied Heath. 'You've made a Commie a bishop.'[40]

It fell to Macmillan to appoint a new Archbishop of Canterbury on the retirement of Dr Geoffrey Fisher in 1961. Fisher had never been one of his favourite prelates. Macmillan resented, as had Eden, Fisher's pronouncements during the Suez crisis in 1956, not to mention his fierce attack on the 'squalid' Premium Bonds the same year. Macmillan's position remained that of Stanley Baldwin in the 1920s, who once said that he did not advise the archbishops on the Athanasian Creed, and in return he did not expect to be lectured on the General Strike.

Macmillan also wanted a figure in contrast to the outgoing Archbishop, following the custom that had prevailed in archiepiscopal appointments, certainly in the twentieth century.[41] Macmillan's favoured candidate for the post of Primate of All England, Dr Michael Ramsey, was not only a complete contrast to Fisher, but was also Archbishop of York. The natural consideration when there was a vacancy at Lambeth was to look first at the acknowledged number two.[42] 'I thought we had had enough of Martha,' Macmillan said later, 'and it was time for some Mary.' Ramsey's churchmanship was sympathetic to the Oxford Movement, which Macmillan himself favoured.

Fisher was not best pleased. He had been influential in recommending Stockwood to Macmillan for the bishopric of Southwark, and had assumed, wrongly, that he would have the same influence when it came to the appointment of his own successor. His favoured candidates were Dr Donald Coggan, the evangelical Bishop of Bradford, and Dr Robert Stopford, the Bishop of Peterborough, whom he admired for his work with Christian educational bodies and as episcopal secretary for the 1958 Lambeth Conference. When it became clear that the decision was to be for Ramsey, Fisher sought an urgent meeting with Macmillan. It did not go well. 'Dr Ramsey is a theologian, a scholar and a man of prayer. Therefore he is entirely unsuitable as Archbishop of Canterbury,' Fisher informed the Prime Minister. 'I have known him all my life. I was his Head Master at Repton.' Macmillan replied, 'You may have been Dr Ramsey's Head Master, but you are not mine.'

Fisher had further reason to be displeased. As their talk came to an end, Macmillan added, 'Of course, this will mean a lot of changes when you go, there will be York to be filled.' He realised his mistake at once, adding quickly, 'That is to say if Ramsey is appointed.'[43] Macmillan, unusually, wanted to announce the appointment of Canterbury and York together, and went ahead without consulting Fisher about the candidates for York. As Fisher had wanted Dr Coggan to be appointed to Canterbury, he could not therefore, from an ecclesiastical point of view, object to Coggan's eventual translation to the northern province. However, Fisher had wanted Coggan, if he did not go to Canterbury, to go to London, which he regarded, from his own experience as bishop there during the war, as a more difficult and challenging responsibility than York. He also felt the whole issue was being rushed. There was no need to name successors so quickly. Macmillan's withers were quite unwrung – the Queen was shortly to be out of the country – and indeed Fisher's case collapsed when Coggan made it clear to Macmillan that he would much rather move to York than to London.[44]

Macmillan confirmed Ramsey's appointment to Canterbury on 20 January 1961. He had already written to Fisher. 'I have thought over most carefully what you said to me last Thursday about the choice of your successor. It is, of course, a difficult decision.' He was aware of Fisher's regard for Dr Coggan, and hoped that Coggan's translation to York would be welcome. 'With the Queen's agreement I propose to offer this to the present Bishop of Bradford, Dr Coggan. I hope you will feel, in spite of what you thought it right to say to me, that this conjunction of choice will serve to meet some of the dangers which you foresaw.'[45] Fisher was furious that he had not been consulted before the York appointment was a *fait accompli*, and was not appeased even when Dr Stopford was translated from Peterborough to London.

Macmillan outlined his ecclesiastical thinking to a more responsive figure in the person of Mervyn Stockwood. 'I think we have in Dr Ramsey a great theologian and a great apologist.'[46] Stockwood agreed.

After these alarums, Macmillan was relieved to be able to turn to less contentious matters, when he acted upon the recommendation of his son-in-law, Julian Amery, that one of his constituents, Tom Finney, the celebrated Preston North End footballer, should be included in that year's Birthday Honours List. Thanks to Macmillan, Finney was awarded an OBE that June.[47]

The question of South Africa's continued membership of the Commonwealth if, as the Prime Minister Dr Verwoerd wished, the country became a republic, hung heavily over the Commonwealth Conference, which began at Lancaster House on 8 March 1961, against the background of the break-up of the Rhodesian government. Macmillan's fear, correctly as events turned out, was that if South Africa on becoming a republic failed to be re-elected to the Commonwealth by fellow member nations, the apartheid system would continue unchecked for a much longer period.

The Prime Minister of Canada, John Diefenbaker, made it clear that South Africa would not have his country's support. Despite Macmillan's attempts, no compromise was possible, and he advised Verwoerd to give up any thought of readmission to the Commonwealth. Verwoerd agreed, and on 14 March, with a heavy heart and his voice breaking, Macmillan told a silent House of Commons that South Africa would be leaving the Commonwealth. Roy Welensky was scathing about Macmillan's emotional Commons speech, accusing him of crocodile tears,[48] but the black dog of depression was something Macmillan never fully shook off at times of crisis, and South Africa's departure from the Commonwealth brought on waves of sadness and pessimism.

March 1961 was one of the low spots of Macmillan's premiership. He wrote in his diary of the nervous strains he felt. 'I have had little sleep – sometimes not more than two or three hours a night.'[49] The domestic financial crisis continued, with a real possibility of the collapse of sterling. War in Laos threatened stability in south-east Asia. British troops were poised for Kuwait, if the situation there deteriorated. (They were dispatched on 1 July.) In addition, the potential for trouble in Rhodesia seemed limitless. One interlude at this time provided much needed relief.

On 12 April, the Russian cosmonaut Yuri Gagarin was launched into space aboard Vostok 1 and became the first human to orbit the earth. Macmillan sensed that, in the Cold War atmosphere of the time, this pioneering flight by Vostok 1 would be exploited more by the Soviets for its publicity value than its scientific one. When the dog Laika had been launched into space aboard Sputnik 2 on 3 November 1957, the Russian propaganda machine had made much of how far ahead they were of the Americans in the space race. Gagarin's flight was hailed in similar fashion. Everything had gone smoothly, so much so that some pundits felt the most hazardous part of the trip was the massive bear-hug Gagarin received from Khrushchev on his return to Moscow airport.

Macmillan calculated that it would not be long before Gagarin toured the West. The invitation came from an unexpected quarter, the Manchester Foundry Workers, and Gagarin arrived in Britain on 11 July for a four-day visit. The Cabinet discussed at length how he should be received officially. The arrival at the airport was low-key, occasioning much press criticism. Hurriedly, Gagarin was invited to a lunch that the Queen was hosting on 14 July. The guests included Lord Mountbatten, Sir John Hunt and Bud Flanagan of the Crazy Gang, so Gagarin and his interpreters added to the cosmopolitan air.

Afterwards, Gagarin processed slowly down the Mall in an open-topped Rolls-Royce, specially numbered YG 1 by the Foreign Office, to be received by Macmillan at Admiralty House. So vast were the throngs that Gagarin was delayed. Macmillan was with John Wyndham in Admiralty House awaiting their guest, and they could hear the resounding cheers of the crowds from outside. As the minutes passed, Macmillan and Wyndham went up into Admiralty Arch to see what was happening. The scene that greeted them was almost like a Coronation or Jubilee day, with enthusiastic multitudes milling around waving Union Jacks and Soviet flags. A beaming Gagarin was clearly revelling in all the adulation, standing up in the back of the Rolls-Royce and acknowledging the cheers. Macmillan turned to John Wyndham. 'Of course,' he said, 'it would have been far worse if they had sent the dog.'[50]

Selwyn Lloyd's first Budget was delivered on 17 April 1961. Much was riding on its success, for the economy, for Selwyn Lloyd person-ally, and also for Macmillan. The time lag between the announcement of fiscal changes and their impact on consumers meant that the 1961 Budget would have a vital effect on the election in 1963 or 1964. As a result, Macmillan was very pro-active in the run-up to Budget Day, so much so that on 16 March Lloyd wrote to complain.

The idea that you are now preparing the Budget does not in my view enhance your prestige. Whether you are in fact doing it is quite a different matter. But the build up of your colleagues is a fact more important for you, provided of course you trust them. On the general issue your prestige is so high and the smooth working relations with your ministers so good that it is not helpful to portray the image of 'Mac Winston' trying to do everything himself.'[51]

Lloyd followed this point up in a meeting on 17 March. As a result he found that the Prime Minister was notably emollient towards him in the remaining weeks before Budget Day. Macmillan had encouraged Lloyd on his appointment to break away from his Treasury advisers and to go his own way, telling him that the Treasury would never have come up with a plan as audaciously inventive as Premium Bonds. For the moment he let Lloyd go his own way, but the free rein was not to last.

Lloyd continued to see the main economic problem of 1961 as inflation, particularly for its effect on the export market. After separate meetings with the TUC and the Federation of British Industries in January, he conceived the idea of what was later to become the National Economic Development Council ('Neddy'), the major institutional legacy of his time as Chancellor. Macmillan approved of this initiative and worked closely with Lloyd to establish the consultative body in the autumn. He could hardly do otherwise. The plan echoed much of his own corporatist approach in *The Middle Way*.

Lloyd was determined to restrain the rise in personal consumption. The main features of his Budget, which he designed to be counter-inflationary, were the two regulators allowing the government to vary taxes, either way, by 10 per cent, without recourse to a Budget. (This was a 10 per cent variation on the percentage of the current rate, not a 10 per cent change in the tax itself.) The first regulator applied to Customs and Excise revenue duties and to Purchase Tax. The second regulator, if needed, would apply to the employers' share of the National Insurance stamp. The two regulators showed Lloyd's willingness to try new ideas, the 'Premium Bond' factor.

The introduction of the regulators was the high point at that time of 'fine-tuning' the economy, giving flexibility in tax rates and in the timing of changes. It was the culmination of the view of Keynesian economists (though as later events were to show, not necessarily those of Keynes himself) that the economy could be steered with some precision to achieve targets of price stability, high employment and balance of payments equilibrium. Ironically, it was the view that Macmillan had himself earlier questioned with his comment about 'last year's Bradshaw'. Overall, Lloyd's approach was to shift from monetary to fiscal measures, a reflection of the Treasury/neo-Keynesian view that the economy can be more predictably controlled by taxation than by interest rates, the influence of which on spending is uncertain.

The headlines, though, were on Lloyd's raising of the starting point for surtax exemption level to £4,000. His advisers had thought £3,000 the most he could 'get away with' politically, but Lloyd insisted on doubling the existing exemption level, unchanged at £2,000 since the days of Lloyd George's 'People's Budget' of 1909. In practice, the result was even bolder, for by applying the income tax allowance of two-ninths on earned income up to £4,000, the effective starting point became £5,000. Profits tax rose by 2.5 per cent; motor vehicle tax went up to £15, and 2d a gallon went on fuel. A big surprise was the introduction of a 10 per cent tax on television advertising revenue. The City was relieved to hear that there was to be no Capital Gains Tax. Overall Lloyd budgeted for a deficit of £69m, with a surplus above the line of £506m (in practice the deficit was £211m over the year.)[52] There was a shift from monetary to fiscal measures, and of the burden of taxation from individuals to companies.

The Budget was well received, though Labour criticised the raising of the surtax exemption level. The *Financial Times* declared that 'the elements of a really first-class economic policy now exist'. The *Manchester Guardian* saw the budget as 'a radical departure in British economic policy ... a bold programme of tax reforms far surpassing anything attempted by any other Conservative Chancellor since the war'.[53] The element of flexibility that Lloyd had introduced into taxation by the regulators was particularly welcome. Macmillan was well pleased, and, to Lloyd's delight so were the party's back-benchers. Nevertheless, so swiftly do circumstances change, it was to be the end of Lloyd's honeymoon period at the Treasury.

Despite the favourable reception of the Budget, pressure on sterling continued through the summer of 1961. The German mark had been revalued upwards on 5 March during the Budget preparations. As Peter Thorneycroft had found as Chancellor in 1957, speculative funds had flowed in anticipation of the revaluation. The exodus of short-term funds to the German markets was just as unwelcome to Lloyd. An unofficial dock strike in May contributed to the June trade deficit of £80m. Feelings grew that the pound might have to be devalued. On 25 July, Lloyd announced in the House of Commons what became known as the 'July measures', in effect an unofficial Budget. The regulator came into operation for the first time. Lloyd employed the full 10 per cent increase on consumer tax rates, and also raised the bank rate to 7 per cent. Yet the Treasury and the Bank of England (in the person of Lord Cromer,[54] the new Governor) had wanted even more severe curbing of consumer spending.

The breaching of the 'pay pause' was not long delayed. The electricity pay settlement in November was clearly excessive, occasioning a personal rebuke by Macmillan to the Electricity Council at his room in the House of Commons. The question of whether an incomes policy could ever be made to work, especially as, in this instance, the Chancellor and the Minister of Power, Richard Wood, had not co-ordinated the government policy, was an awkward dose of political reality.

In any assessment of the overall shape of Macmillan's years in Downing Street, the 'July measures' of 1961 inevitably loom large. In retrospect, it was the moment when public opinion began to move decisively against the government. The 'pay pause' announced by Lloyd affected in particular groups of public workers such as nurses and teachers, who had a large measure of public support but, unlike the electricity workers, little industrial muscle. Although the pay pause ended in March 1962, it was replaced by a policy known as the 'guiding light', an attempt to limit wage rises to 2.5 per cent. Backbenchers were now in an edgy mid-term mood. Minds were already concentrating, especially among those MPs with marginal seats, on electoral survival.

Privately, Macmillan was thinking of introducing, against Treasury advice, or Lloyd's wishes, an expansionist economic policy. The inevitable conclusion of such thinking would be the removal of Lloyd as Chancellor, despite Macmillan's assurances to him at Petworth in June 1960 that he would have a full term to reform economic policy. Lloyd's position was not under any immediate threat, but he was not as secure as he had been led to believe. Macmillan had shown great kindness to Lloyd over his personal difficulties, and Lloyd's political antennae did not detect the edge that was entering their relationship. The same thing was happening with Iain Macleod.

Another dramatic moment in what was proving to be a tumultuous summer came on the weekend of 12–13 August. Berliners awakened on the Sunday morning to find that overnight the Soviets had closed the border to East Berlin. The most visual sign of the Cold War – the Berlin Wall – was in the early stages of construction. Macmillan was at Bolton Abbey, shooting with the Devonshires, when the news broke. (Some even felt that the Soviets had decided on 'the Glorious Twelfth' for the operation in the belief that the British ruling class would be otherwise engaged.) Macmillan felt the key thing was for the West to avoid doing anything foolish in response. Displaying a deliberate calmness (though keeping in touch with Alec Home), the Macmillans went on, as arranged, to Gleneagles for golf. As Macmillan was coming down the long eighteenth hole back to the clubhouse on his first day in Perthshire, journalists came on to the fairway to question him. Angered by this intrusion, he incautiously declared that the situation had all been got up by the press, a stance he regretted and later withdrew. These first anxious days over the new Berlin crisis was the time when Lord Home impressed Macmillan anew by his steady diplomatic skill.

Two days after the July measures, the Cabinet formally decided to apply to join the EEC. One watershed in a week might seem to be enough – for the July measures were certainly a watershed – but the commitment to the Common Market began a new chapter in the long island history and was an even greater one.

Macmillan was attempting the difficult, if not impossible task, of satisfying three different constituencies – the Americans, the Commonwealth, and the other members of the Seven. He formally informed President Kennedy, the Commonwealth heads of state and the prime ministers of Eire and South Africa of his forthcoming announcement to Parliament.

From North African days, when he had worked so closely with Eisenhower, Macmillan had always had deep Atlanticist instincts. Kennedy's emergence, far from diminishing such feelings, had actually increased them. Like Churchill in wartime, Macmillan believed that 'westward, look, the land is bright'.[55]

However, he believed that Britain must now be the link between Europe and America. This idea had been germinating since Council of Strasbourg days in the late 1940s, which makes the missed opportunities of the Messina conference of 1955 even more regrettable. Enhanced Western unity – quite apart from the trading issues – would be vital in the next phase of the Cold War. Macmillan outlined these ideas for his ministers in a paper of December 1960, 'The Grand Design', which became the basis for Cabinet discussions. Its aim, set out in the preamble, was 'to call attention to the need to organise the great forces of the Free World – U.S.A., Britain and Europe – economically, politically and militarily in a coherent effort to withstand the Communist tide all over the world'.[56]

Macmillan always saw European unity in terms beyond the economic ones enshrined in the Treaty of Rome, but Freddie Bishop had warned him that such a formal alliance would be 'a reappraisal which might well be very agonising indeed'.[57] Beaverbrook's *Daily Express* was vehemently opposed to the idea from the start. For Beaverbrook, the Common Market meant one thing – 'political subjection'.[58]

Although there were Euro-sceptics in Macmillan's Cabinet, notably Hailsham and Maudling, as well as 'little Englanders' in the constituencies, in the early 1960s 'Europe' was a more divisive issue for Labour than the Conservatives. Gaitskell was to declare that European federation would mean 'the end of a thousand years of history'.[59] Macmillan was scathing about Labour's view of 'a federal Europe without Britain – unconscious of the fact that it hands Europe on a plate to Germany, and destroys in a day the fruits of our hard-won victory in two wars'.[60]

The key to membership of the EEC was clearly de Gaulle. Preliminary discussions on Britain's application began, significantly, in Paris, not Brussels, on 10 October. They took place against the worrying background of extensive Russian nuclear tests and the deployment of British and American tanks in Berlin. President de Gaulle suggested that it might be fruitful for Macmillan and himself to have private talks, not at Chequers, but more informally at Birch Grove.

The visit of the de Gaulles to Birch Grove began on 24 November 1961. Supplies of the President's special blood group were needed, and the Foreign Office explained that it had to be kept in a refrigerator. Not surprisingly, Mrs Bell, the Macmillans' devoted cook, took objection, so a special freezer was installed in the coach house. After de Gaulle's visit, the space was needed there too, and the equipment was dispatched to some remote area on the estate, where, with what survives of the General's blood, it evidently still remains, rusting away.[61]

The massive security led to detectives and armed policemen tramping through the surrounding fields and woods. Journalists also attempted entry to the estate, and a *Daily Mail* man was bitten by an Alsatian. To de Gaulle's barely disguised annoyance, the head keeper, Mr Blake, came into the house to point out that next Monday's shoot would be completely ruined if the interruptions continued.

The talks were no easier. Berlin, as so often at this time, was the sticking point. No agreement could be brokered as to a unified Anglo-French response. At one point, Macmillan, in frustration, said, 'Oh, well let's have a war then.'[62] Other difficulties arose over the EEC. Macmillan emphasised that with Adenauer, de Gaulle and himself in power in their respective countries, the right time for British entry to the EEC had arrived. President de Gaulle, as always, was sceptical of what he regarded as Commonwealth hangers-on, such as Australia and Canada. There were too many imponderables for the man Macmillan privately dubbed 'the Emperor of the French'.[63]

Emperors do not like being upstaged. Macmillan's fourth meeting that year with President Kennedy in Bermuda from 20 to 23 December made de Gaulle both suspicious and envious. He did not like to think that Britain and America were arranging things behind his back. There had been earlier difficulties over America's attitude towards the embryonic French nuclear programme. Despite Macmillan's punctiliousness in sending both de Gaulle and Adenauer a full report on his return, the presence on the international stage of Kennedy worried de Gaulle.

By December 1961, Kennedy and Macmillan had come to an understanding of each other's methods and foibles, and the talks were brisk and businesslike. Berlin, nuclear tests, the disarmament meetings in Geneva, the Congo, Cuba, Goa, China and the Common Market were all on the agenda. Macmillan felt that Kennedy was better informed and more effective on specific detailed issues, such as the Congo, whereas on the broader canvas he felt the new President was still finding his way.

1961 had proved to be a difficult year; 1962 brought no respite. The decline in Macmillan's standing with the electorate, only partly discernible to the psephologist in 1961, became palpably clear in the course of 1962, which was littered with confusions, miscalculations and reverses. The public mood was fractious and volatile. As the seeming promised land of uninterrupted affluence and economic growth was now proving more of a chimera than anticipated, scapegoats were sought. Protests – from CND rallies in Trafalgar Square to unprecedented mockery of the ruling classes in the media – became a regular part of British life. In March 1962, this was to exemplify itself in an unprecedented manner.

The parliamentary vacancy at Orpington, a constituency bordering Macmillan's at Bromley, was caused by the appointment in the autumn of 1961 of the sitting Conservative MP, Donald Sumner, as a county court judge. It was an archetypal Home Counties 'safe' seat, with a majority at the 1959 election of 14,760. But these were not normal times. Orpington was not, in estate agent's parlance, quite as 'desirable' as Bromley, or its other neighbouring constituency, Beckenham. The social mix was diverse, from overspill pre-war council estates at its northern boundary to leafy habitat nearer the Green Belt. Here lived the younger, aspirational professionals – Macmillan's children – without tribal loyalties to the established main parties.

Philip (later Sir Philip) Goodhart, MP for Beckenham, later commented that 'now the extent and growth of this social mobility can be seen for the first time'.[64] Beckenham retained Penge, near Crystal Palace, as part of the constituency. Penge's many local Labour councillors, whose supporters remained loyal to the party at national elections, served to 'inoculate' Beckenham against the 'virus' there (as Tories saw it) of growing Liberalism. No such protection existed in Orpington. So when Labour voters switched tactically to the Liberals, the Conservative cause was doomed.[65] Dissatisfaction was setting in over the pay pause and the feeling that middle-class living standards were being eroded, relative to blue-collar workers. Eric Lubbock, the Liberal candidate, proved to be the ideal lightning conductor for such feelings.

Conservative Central Office tacticians realised, though they did not admit it, that a careful approach might be needed to avoid the embarrassment of a reduced majority. The writ for the by-election was not moved immediately, as the party strategists preferred to wait for the new electoral register in February. The postal vote, always efficiently garnered by the Conservatives, would thus, so the thinking went, disadvantage the Labour Party, who had come second in 1959. What the Conservatives did not anticipate was how this decision would galvanise the Liberals, already well organised at local government level, into righteous indignation about the delay. Jeremy Thorpe, victor at Devon North in the 1959 election, and Eric Lubbock displayed a flair for publicity by delivering a petition to the House of Commons, protesting at the disenfranchisement of the electorate in Orpington.

Eric Lubbock was just the kind of candidate to appeal to disaffected Conservatives, '"a gent" to his finger tips', as Lady Violet Bonham Carter noted approvingly.[66] He was not a bearded, sandal-wearing eccentric, so often glimpsed at the time at fringe meetings at Liberal Party conferences, brandishing CND pamphlets, but an Old Harrovian and a Balliol man, who had served in the Welsh Guards. Ironically, he supported unilateral disarmament, but he did not look as though he did. He was also the heir to the Avebury peerage. Some voters mistook him for the Conservative.

The deferential vote was thus safe for the Liberals. Lubbock campaigned energetically. On all sides, he was seen as a sincere and personable candidate. Moreover, he was a well-known and respected local councillor, and his young children attended Orpington schools. The Lubbocks had lived in the borough for generations. His father had been the Squire of Orpington, as had his ancestors, and, Caesar-like, had bequeathed his woods to the local authority.[67]

Although Eric Lubbock campaigned in the accepted political uniform of the day, a dark three-piece suit, he was far from being a crusty stereotype. By profession he was a trained engineer, just the kind of 'new man' who was productively useful for the country. One of the things Harold Wilson was to call for in his famous 'White Heat' speech about the modernisation of Britain at the Labour Conference in September 1963 was more engineers.

By contrast, the Conservative Party candidate, Peter Goldman, was not attractive to the floating voter, 'a curiously repellent personality, dark, smug' in Lady Violet Bonham Carter's opinion.[68] He was seen as a cerebral outsider, imposed on the constituency organisation, which had a tradition of local candidates and a shortlist of 99 hopefuls. In short, he was an old-fashioned 'carpet-bagger', even to local Tories. These perceptions underestimated his abilities. Macmillan saw him as having Cabinet potential.[69] Goldman had been one of the most significant and progressive intellectual figures in the Conservative Research Department, admired by both Rab Butler and Iain Macleod.[70] The 'safe seat' of Orpington was his reward. Yet he was just the wrong candidate for the constituency at that time.

An underlying element of anti-Semitism also bedevilled Goldman's candidature. His campaign was seen as aloof and old-fashioned, depending too much on local volunteers. All the ingredients for an upset were thus in place, though few could have predicted its extent. As early as 14 December the *Daily Mail* posed the question 'Will the word Orpington be engraved on the coffin of the Macmillan government?' A month later, the *Daily Mail* was confidently predicting a shock Liberal victory.[71]

Polling day was set for 14 March. The previous day the Liberals scored a spectacular advance, widely reported in the morning newspapers, at the by-election at Blackpool North, caused by Sir Toby Low's elevation to the peerage as Lord Aldington. A Conservative majority of almost 16,000 had been slashed to just 973, which gave the Liberals in Orpington the impetus for one final push. Tactical voting also benefited them, as polls showed that Labour was trailing. An anti-Conservative coalition thus combined to produce one of the most sensational by-election victories in post-war history. The Conservative majority of 14,760 was turned into a Liberal one of 7,855.

A series of disappointing by-elections followed at Middlesbrough West, Macmillan's former seat of Stockton-on-Tees, Derby North, Montgomeryshire and West Derbyshire. On 12 July, the Tories came third at Leicester North-East. The next day Macmillan sacked one-third of his Cabinet.

*

The build-up to the Night of the Long Knives, as Macmillan's cull-ing of his Cabinet colleagues was soon dubbed, though Butler always called it 'the Massacre of Glencoe', provoked Jeremy Thorpe, who had done so much to secure Liberal victory at Orpington, to declare, 'Greater love hath no man than this, that he lay down his friends for his life.'[72] The months between Orpington and Friday 13 July showed Macmillan at his most ruthless, and, ultimately, his most ineffectual.

The post-mortems over Lubbock's victory began at once. Yet Orpington, like so many 'triumphs', was to prove a false dawn for the Liberals. By-elections, fertile grounds for the 'protest' vote, are not the same as general elections. The Conservatives regained the seat in 1970. The immediate effect of Orpington was to delay other impend-ing peerages Macmillan had planned, to avoid further by-election embarrassment, and to instil the firm belief in local constituency organisations, of all parties, that adopting a non-local candidate was something to be done in only exceptional circumstances.

Selwyn Lloyd continued his painstaking preparations for his second, and last, Budget, unaware that the vultures were already gathering. He dined with Macmillan on 4 March to discuss the Budget propos-als, which Lloyd recorded were 'accepted without demur'. They soon moved on to future plans. Macmillan told Lloyd that he would have to decide six months before the next election whether he would con-tinue as Prime Minister or not, one of the first indications that he was already thinking he might not fight another campaign. He went on to discuss the reconstruction that would be necessary, as win or lose, the team must consist of people who would continue after the election. For Macmillan this meant a group centring on Lloyd, Henry Brooke, Frederick Erroll, John Hare, Edward Heath, Reggie Maudling, Duncan Sandys and Christopher Soames.

To Lloyd's surprise, there was no mention of Iain Macleod in this list. What did not surprise him, though, was Macmillan's blunt con-clusion about Rab Butler. 'Butler would not stay on,' he said, 'unless PM or prospect of it.' As in January 1957, Macmillan added, advice must be given to the Queen, if he stood down, by senior figures in the Lords, in this case Home and Kilmuir.[73]

Four days after this remarkable example of what Henry James called 'the terrible fluidity of self revelation',[74] the bank rate fell to 5.5 per cent. On 22 March, it fell to 5 per cent. Ambitiously, Lloyd now felt it was realistic to aim for a growth target of 4 per cent. The financial disenchantment of the middle classes was very much in his mind as he put the final touches to his Budget. Very damagingly for him, these last-minute details were strongly criticised, to the point of alteration, by the Cabinet. The main point at issue was the abolition of Schedule A, against which the Liberals had campaigned. The view in Cabinet was that Lloyd should now take the plunge on Schedule A. The Conservative Party Conference at Scarborough in October 1960 had passed a motion calling for the ending of this income tax on privately owned houses, so resented by owner-occupiers. In his original proposals, which now had to be reprinted at the last minute, Lloyd had not allowed for immediate abolition of Schedule A, but accepted that its days were now numbered. As a result, the Budget Red Book, available in the vote office after the Chancellor has sat down, proved to be only a partial summary of Lloyd's proposals, owing to late tinkerings.

Lloyd rose to deliver his second Budget at 3.22 p.m. on 9 April. He praised the work of the NEDC, then continued by stating his intention to abolish Schedule A in the future,[75] at a cost of £60m to the Exchequer in a full year. His most important innovation was a short-term Capital Gains Tax, minuscule by later standards. Differential Purchase Tax rates were consolidated at 10 per cent. Overall Lloyd budgeted for an above the line surplus of £443m in a revenue of £6,807m. This compared with an actual surplus above the line in 1962–1963 of £410m, as against the £506m for which he had budgeted the previous April. It was a long, complex and rather dull Budget, with little to grab the headlines. That was until he came to what he had thought an innocuous tax, 15 per cent on confectionery, ice cream and soft drinks, yielding £30m in 1962 and £50m in a full year, not insignificant sums when the deficit for 1961–1962 had been £211m and the expected deficit in the next financial year was £74m. As so often, it is the unexpected detail that makes the headlines. Newspaper comment concentrated on the sweets tax. So did Lloyd's own family. His sister wrote to him from Hoylake the next day, 'Well, well! Taxing the poor children's pocket money!'[76] William Rees-Mogg headed his account the next Sunday, 'Mr Lloyd's last Budget.'[77] One of the few people who congratulated Lloyd was Macmillan himself. 'That was the best speech I have ever heard from you both in manner & matter,' he wrote.[78] Notwithstanding that generous compliment, Rees-Mogg's prophecy would soon be fulfilled.

On 11 April, Macmillan wrote to Lloyd about the 1963 Budget, telling him that he should proceed 'on the assumption that the economic situation allows an expansionist Budget and substantial reductions of taxation. Do not leave it too late.'[79] Bank Rate fell to 4.5 per cent on 26 April. Things seemed set fair. But the political going was about to get increasingly tough, with further by-election reverses to come, and as with Peter Thorneycroft before him, Selwyn Lloyd was to find that in such a situation he no longer retained Macmillan's unequivocal support.

Selwyn Lloyd's chancellorship was to founder not on the rocks of Orpington, or even on the unpopular sweets tax or his failure to establish a formal income policy, but on the series of cumulative political difficulties that arose for the government at the time. The final straw was to be the disastrous Leicester North-East by-election on 12 July. The Conservative candidate came a poor third and the share of the vote fell from 48.1 per cent at the 1959 general election to 24.2 per cent.

Macmillan planned to make the Cabinet changes in an ordered manner after the summer recess. These plans were thrown into disarray by Rab Butler's indiscretion at a lunch with Lord Rothermere, proprietor of the *Daily Mail*, on Wednesday, 11 July. Butler, who was privy to Macmillan's intentions (indeed, he had pressed for Lloyd's removal from the Treasury), told his host of Macmillan's long-term intentions, dramatically different from the plans discussed with Lloyd in April. The next day, the details were blazoned across the front page of the *Daily Mail* in an article by Walter Terry, the paper's political correspondent, headlined MAC'S MASTER PLAN.

Macmillan was horrified. He now felt he had to act before the summer recess. Lloyd was summoned to Admiralty House at 6 p.m. It was an emotional meeting for both men. Macmillan bluntly told his Chancellor that he would have to go. Lloyd could not believe that all the compliments and encouragement he had received from Macmillan since the Budget counted for nothing. He was even more shocked when Macmillan said he believed there was a conspiracy against him within the party, and that Lloyd, by implication, was part of it. Nothing could have been further from the truth as far as Lloyd was concerned. Macmillan, though, was to be the more discomfited by the meeting. He suggested first that Lloyd might like to go into the City and make money. The chairmanship of Martin's Bank was becoming vacant and he would be the ideal candidate. Lloyd said that he had no intention of going into the City. Macmillan then suggested he might take a peerage. Lloyd turned down this offer also. He said he would not abandon his constituents in the Wirral. After further desultory conversation, the two men parted at the head of the stairs, Macmillan in obvious distress. 'I was sad for him as well as for myself,' Lloyd later wrote, 'because I thought he was damaging his own position, perhaps beyond repair.'[80]

The events of the next few days were to be one of the most damaging errors of Macmillan's entire premiership, and he was never to recover the initiative. His main aim in replacing his Chancellor was to make the government more attractive to the electorate. By appointing Reginald Maudling, he hoped to generate an expansionist economic policy in good time for the next election. Selwyn Lloyd became an unfortunate victim of the changes. Macmillan would have liked to have moved Lloyd to the Home Office. The necessary government restructuring would then have been achieved, with no political casualties. Under this scenario, Butler would have vacated the Home Office to occupy a newly created post, as in fact happened; Lloyd would fill Butler's shoes, and Maudling would then replace Lloyd at the Treasury, a neat and tidy solution.

In 1957, Macmillan's long-term plan was to let Lloyd see out the Suez aftermath as Foreign Secretary and then transfer him to the Home Office at the next convenient juncture. However, it was then made clear to Macmillan by Lloyd himself that such an appointment was impossible. As Lloyd had risen up the ranks of the Cabinet, filling major post after major post, some felt that he might soon become only the second politician (after Sir John Simon) to hold the three great offices of state under the premiership – Foreign Secretary, Chancellor and Home Secretary. There was, however, an insuperable obstacle.

Unusually for a Conservative politician of those days, Lloyd was a vehement opponent of capital punishment. He had worked in the 1940s with the Labour MP Sidney Silverman for its abolition, and always voted against the continuance of the death sentence when the issue was debated in Parliament. To save confusion, he had asked Macmillan in January 1957 not to consider him for the Home Office in any future reshuffle, as he would never be able to advise the Queen in the proper dispassionate manner on the prerogative of mercy in capital cases. His instinctive feeling would always be for a reprieve, whatever the legal circumstances.[81] So that route was closed in July 1962.

Philip de Zulueta believed that a better way would have been to make Lloyd, with his legal background, Lord Chancellor in place of Kilmuir, who was due to be replaced shortly in any case.[82] Macmillan's solution, well-intentioned, was different. Rather than casting off Lloyd alone into the lifeboat, he decided to call in the chips of various ministers who had intimated they would not be serving after the next election, a matter he had already discussed with Lloyd after the Budget. Unfortunately, when faced with this sudden reality, minister after minister was reluctant to be forced out. When Lord Kilmuir was told he was to be replaced, he protested that one's cook would have been given more notice. Macmillan replied that it was easier to find Lord Chancellors than cooks. One sacking led to another. Macmillan told Harold Watkinson, Minister of Defence, that he needed a younger team, and then replaced him with Peter Thorneycroft, an older man.[83] Dr Charles Hill, Lord Mills, Jack Maclay and David Eccles, who had entertained hopes of becoming the new Chancellor, and who disdainfully declined the Board of Trade, were also dismissed, making a total of one third of the Cabinet of 21. The political carnage was unparalleled, and, as Selwyn Lloyd predicted, was to damage Macmillan more than anyone else.

The key figure at the centre of the whole disastrous episode was not, in fact, Selwyn Lloyd, but Rab Butler, whose ill-advised indiscretions had triggered off the reshuffle in the first place. The continuing unstable situation in Rhodesia had convinced Macmillan that a new approach was needed to resolve the problems of the Central African Federation. One of the often overlooked changes of the Night of the Long Knives was Macmillan's decision to amalgamate the old Colonial Office with the Commonwealth Relations Office, under Duncan Sandys. As so often when he needed help, Macmillan turned to the increasingly put-upon, Rab Butler, proposing that he should become Deputy Prime Minister (what else had Butler been for the last five years?), a post unknown to the constitution, as King George VI had reminded Churchill on more than one occasion. Butler would also become First Secretary of State (an office peremptorily wound up on 18 October 1963) and the minister in charge of the Central Africa Office. By, reluctantly, accepting the grandiose but essentially empty titles bestowed upon him, Butler had moved into a cul-de-sac of government, in effect confined to work on the Central African Federation. The fact that he accomplished this difficult task most expeditiously, winding up the Federation at the Victoria Falls conference in the summer of 1963, was little compensation. Moving from the post of Home Secretary cut him off from the great offices of state, and expansive civil service support.[84] It was not an ideal waiting room for 10 Downing Street.

Although he was devastated by the abruptness of his sacking, Lloyd wisely decided that 'a bitter resentment against Macmillan would destroy my peace of mind'.[85] He believed that forgiveness was the best form of revenge and from that moment on was punctiliously loyal, writing a letter of good wishes to Macmillan on the eve of the no-confidence debate which followed the sackings on 26 July. Macmillan later told Rab Butler that it was perhaps the nicest letter he had ever received.[86] For his part, Macmillan was consumed by a sense of guilt at his mismanagement of the man who had been privy to all his counsels. When Lloyd first appeared in the Commons after his sacking, he was cheered to the echo on all sides. Macmillan, by contrast, entered to silence from the government side and jeers from the Opposition. Lloyd experienced a new popularity, though he knew that the more the House boosted him, the more they were getting at Macmillan. 'The PM looked pale and ill,' he noted. 'As he left after his questions he turned and looked for a moment at where I was sitting on the third bench below the gangway.'[87]

On the way into the Commons for the no-confidence Debate, Macmillan took Lloyd aside and said he would like a word with him. The meeting was arranged for the evening of 1 August at Admiralty House. Tim Bligh met Lloyd and told him, 'He is spending all his time thinking of how to bring you back.'[88] The conversation was one of the most curious Lloyd ever experienced. Macmillan began by saying how sorry he was about it all. Lloyd replied that his main regret was the damage that it had done to Macmillan. 'He said that he had made a mistake,' Lloyd recorded. 'He had been rushed. One day he would tell me the conspiracy again him which had forced his hand ... Butler had been plotting to divide the party on the Common Market, and bring him down. He realised that he had made a mess of it ... His only anxiety was Europe. He would fight an election on that, perhaps lose, and then the Party and not the Queen would choose the next leader.' Lloyd told Macmillan that the fatal defect in the government was having the Leader of the House and the chairman of the party as one and the same person. Macmillan said he would attend to that. What Lloyd did not spell out was what he thought was the fundamental mistake at the heart of Macmillan's whole career, 'thinking unemployment a worse enemy than uncontrolled inflation'.[89]

After a confessional hour on both sides, the two men parted. Macmillan pledged to keep in touch. Lloyd's impression was of a beleaguered leader, ensconced in the last redoubt. 'I am afraid that my conclusion after the interview was one of his utter ruthlessness, and his determination to retain power by the sacrifice of even his closest friends. He was now concerned to conciliate me, because I had become a possible danger.'[90]

Macmillan was wrong about Lloyd, who was, in fact, the most loyal of the loyal. As for conspiring against the Prime Minister, Lloyd would not have recognised a plot even if it had been placed in front of him. He was not that kind of politician. Any danger, therefore, was not going to stem from that source. Macmillan, though, was not in the clear. Lloyd's supporters were soon to speak out. Anthony Eden (now Earl of Avon) declared at a Young Conservatives rally at Leamington Spa on 21 July that Lloyd had been harshly treated. Nigel Birch, a persistent critic of Macmillan since the 1957 Treasury resignations, had already taken to the correspondence columns of *The Times*: 'For the second time the Prime Minister has got rid of a Chancellor of the Exchequer who tried to get expenditure under control. Once is more than enough'.[91] For a former minister to censure the Prime Minister from whose patronage he had once benefited was highly unusual; but for a former Prime Minister to criticise publicly a successor from his own party was then virtually unprecedented.[92]

One episode made a poignant footnote to the month's events. When Selwyn Lloyd hurriedly had to find a flat in London after his sacking, he left behind his black Labrador, Sambo,* in the care of Mrs Kathleen Hill, the curator at Chequers. A fortnight after the Night of the Long Knives, Macmillan held a Conservative forum at Chequers. As he sat on the terrace that balmy July evening, chatting expansively about the middle way ahead, other members of the entourage gradually became aware of the inquisitive presence of Sambo, walking along the line of the assembled company, vainly looking for his master. The dog eventually settled in front of Macmillan, gazing mournfully up at him. Those who were present never forgot the frisson that went through the gathering, nor the studied disregard with which Macmillan ignored the animal, knowing better than most what memories its presence evoked.[93]

Other problems that were now looming on the horizon Macmillan was not able to disregard so easily.

---

*In a different age, the British Foreign Secretary could call his dog Sambo without attracting criticism.

CHAPTER TWENTY EIGHT

Opening Pandora's Box

1962–1963

When sorrows come they come not single spies
But in battalions.

Shakespeare, Hamlet, 4,v,78–79

Keep a lid on things.
  Harold Macmillan's instruction to Sir Roger Hollis, Director
General of MI5, 1962.[1]

As he rose like a rocket, he fell like the stick.
Thomas Paine on Edmund Burke, 1792.

The greatest test of courage I can conceive is to speak the truth
in the House of Commons.

William Hazlitt, 1820

In the spring of 1962, the Cabinet Secretary, Sir Norman Brook, warned Macmillan that MI5 had discovered that an Admiralty clerk was selling state secrets in clubs round Victoria. 'Nonsense', replied Macmillan. 'There are no clubs round Victoria.'[2]

Macmillan had been embarrassed by security matters ever since he had, on advice, mistakenly cleared Kim Philby in 1955; equally, there were those who believed something suspicious had hung about Macmillan's own dealings with the Soviets ever since his visit to Russia in 1932.[3] As Christopher Andrew has observed, 'Macmillan hated spy scandals and, partly for that reason, disliked direct contact with the Security Service on counter-espionage matters.'[4]

As Foreign Secretary in Eden's government, Macmillan had enjoyed good relations with Sir Dick White,[5] then head of MI5. His dealings with Sir Roger Hollis,[6] who succeeeded White in 1956, were less cordial.* Indeed, Macmillan found Hollis an unsatisfactory director of the security services, not least because of the confluence of scandals that erupted in 1962 and 1963. He saw the names of these spies as a

---

* After retirement, Hollis himself was investigated for links with the KGB, and cleared.

litany of shame – George Blake, Ethel Gee, Harry Houghton, Peter and Helen Kroger,[7] Gordon Lonsdale, John Vassall and Anthony Wraight. Some of the later investigations, exposures and trials proved more damaging than others, but in the febrile atmosphere of espionage and counter-espionage of the Cold War at the time, always looking for 'reds under the bed',[8] the cumulative effect was of a government that had lost control of its own security operations ever since the defection of Burgess and Maclean.

The exposure of a spy ring at the Underwater Detection Establishment at the Portland naval base in 1961, involving a clerical officer, Harry Houghton, a record-keeper, Ethel Gee and 'Gordon Lonsdale' (actually a Soviet agent, Konon Trofmovich Molody) was a sensational development.[9] Investigations led to the discovery of documents, devices and a secret radio transmitter at the Krogers' suburban home in Ruislip. In March 1961, the Lord Chief Justice, Lord Parker, sentenced the five 'Portland spies' to lengthy periods of imprisonment.

The Portland spy case was followed almost at once by the unmasking of George Blake, a 39-year-old officer within SIS itself. Blake confessed under interrogation on 5 April 1961. Macmillan's dismay was compounded by the fact that the Blake case was one of the first intelligence matters he had to disclose to President Kennedy.

The Admiralty clerk to whom Norman Brook had referred was John Vassall.[10] An active homosexual, at a time when such practice was illegal in both Britain and Russia, Vassall had been photographed in compromising circumstances at a party in Moscow in 1954. Under threat of blackmail, and then in receipt of financial inducements, he supplied his KGB controllers with secrets, first from the Moscow embassy and then from the Admiralty.

Suspicions were aroused by Vassall's lavish lifestyle in his Dolphin Square flat, his Savile Row suits and extensive foreign holidays, far beyond the means of his modest salary. Leads had already been given to the CIA and MI5, following the defection of Anatoli Golitsyn to the United States on 15 December 1961. Vassall was arrested in September 1962. His trial was so sensitive that much of it took place in camera. On 22 October 1962 he was found guilty and sentenced to 18 years' imprisonment.

On the same day, in Moscow, the KGB arrested Colonel Oleg Penkovsky, the deputy head of the foreign section of the GRU (Soviet Military Intelligence), who had long been the most important source within the Kremlin for both the CIA and MI6. Whilst visiting Britain, in charge of a Soviet delegation, in April and July 1961, Penkovsky had secretly met Sir Dick White. For some time thereafter he had been providing highly classified information on Soviet missile capability, including technical information, which had alerted the Americans to the nature of the hardware being installed secretly in Cuba in 1962. Macmillan was told of these meetings by White in 1961 and was aware, before he was told by Kennedy, of Soviet intentions in Cuba.

Also on the same day, 22 October, at 7 p.m., Eastern Standard Time, President Kennedy broadcast the news of the presence of Soviet missile sites in Cuba. 'Within the past week unmistakable evidence has established the fact that a series of offensive missile sites is now in preparation on that imprisoned island,' he said. 'The purposes of these bases can be none other than to provide a nuclear strike capability against the Western Hemisphere.'[11] The Cuban Missile crisis, what Harold Macmillan called 'this terrifying episode',[12] had begun. For the next few days, a period never to be forgotten by those who lived through it, the world was on the brink of annihilation.

Macmillan's influence in the crisis has been a matter of disagreement. McGeorge Bundy, Kennedy's National Security Adviser, later recorded that Macmillan's advice 'was not very important', though he did concede that, on both Berlin and Cuba, Macmillan had been 'a pretty tough guy'.[13] Percy Cradock, in his history of the Joint Intelligence Committee, wrote that 'Britain's role was peripheral'.[14]

On the other hand, Nigel Fisher made the pertinent point that 'Kennedy put a high premium on Macmillan's advice', adding 'indeed, had he not, the daily telephone conversations would not have been worth the time and trouble, since they went far beyond the requirements of co-operation between allies and were not in fact shared with other Western leaders'.[15] The question is whether Macmillan was more than 'the Grecian' advising the 'Roman'. What is clear is that Macmillan learned how to identify the hidden messsages in the tone of Kennedy's speeches, and, knowing how serious things were from what was not said, enabled him to sort out his thoughts before the next telephone discussion.

Lord Home, who, as Foreign Secretary, was present alongside Macmillan during many of the transatlantic telephone calls between the Prime Minister and the President, believed that there was, in fact, a whole raft of British advisers whose influence was significant. Apart from Macmillan, he listed David Ormsby-Gore, the British Ambassador in Washington; Sir Frank Roberts, the British Ambassador in Moscow,[16] and Herbert Marchant, 'our man in Havana'.[17] Macmillan was the keystone of the arch. Kennedy later told Home on several occasions 'how much he valued being able to talk with Mr Macmillan and with the British because he could do so without reserve – something he could not do with any other people'.[18]

Despite, or rather because of, his own undisputed place at the epicentre of the Western world, Kennedy was actually a very lonely man. He needed reassurance. Outwardly, compartmentalising his routine, he seemed untroubled. He entertained Andrew and Deborah Devonshire to private functions *en famille* at the very height of the crisis, as though he did not have a care in the world.[19] However, as his brother, Robert Kennedy, the Attorney General, revealed in his book on the crisis,[20] John F. Kennedy behind the scenes consulted on a unique scale. He was particularly keen to seek out advice from older men with memories of Munich and first-hand experience of the Second World War. Those such as Macmillan whose experience went back even further, to the Great War, were in a special category. Kennedy had, in American parlance, to 'cover all bases'. If he did not, there might well be no more bases, metaphorical or actual, in East or West. People were acutely aware of this doomsday scenario.[21]

For example, Colonel Leigh Maxwell, a military attaché in Moscow, was asked by Marshal Rotmistrov, in charge of dealing with Western figures, how long he would last if war broke out. 'About two hours,' Maxwell replied. 'Goodness,' said the Marshal, 'I didn't think London's defences were that bad.' 'Marshal,' explained Maxwell, 'you asked how long *I* would last; *I* am here in Moscow.'[22]

The heart of Macmillan's advice lay not in military or political details, but in his emphasis on a psychological approach. Macmillan stressed to Kennedy that the primary requirement was to afford Khrushchev an exit strategy, whereby he could step back from the brink without losing face.[23] In the end, such a door was opened to Khrushchev by Kennedy with his concessions on the five American launch sites in Turkey – the 'other missiles of October', as they were to be called.[24]

Macmillan, remembering his 'Laos dash' to Key West in March 1961, offered to come to Washington, but the crisis was developing at such a breakneck speed, after Kennedy's broadcast to the American people, that the President preferred to keep in contact with him through regular telephone calls, at all times of day and night. He liked to report to Macmillan at midnight, Washington time, so Macmillan got little uninterrupted sleep during the crisis.

Kennedy's first call to Macmillan came during the night of 22 October, at 12.30 a.m. London time.[25] Macmillan asked Kennedy outright, 'How do you see a way out of this?' Kennedy had announced a quarantine zone, 800 miles from Cuba. Macmillan wanted to know

'What are you going to do with the blockade? Are you going to oc-cupy Cuba and have done with it or is it just going to drag on?' Would the blockade eventually include 'things like oil and all the rest of it in order to bring down the Castro government'? At this stage, Kennedy told him that the blockade was confined to 'offensive weapons of war in order not to give [him] a complete justification for Berlin'.

Macmillan saw Cuba through the prism of both Suez and the failed 1960 Paris summit, reminding Kennedy that 'we've always found that our weakness has been when we've not acted with sufficient strength to start with'. Kennedy was thinking in terms of a meeting with Khrushchev. Macmillan, remembering the 1961 Vienna meeting between the two men, was not convinced:

> If we are forced to a conference all the cards are in this man's hand. But, however, you explained to me what are the possible develop-ments you may have to take. And if we do have to talk to him, and meet him, in the last resort the more cards in our hands the better, in my view. You may say that's rather tough, and perhaps rather cynical, but I think the more cards in our hands the better, and I would be very happy to see them in your hands.[26]

Kennedy knew Macmillan well enough by now to realise that he could be both tough and cynical.

Many of the background details had already reached Macmillan from Ormsby-Gore in Washington. Ormsby-Gore was the most important of all the British during the crisis, as he was co-opted personally into many of the key meetings. Indeed, it was he who suggested, with Macmillan's agreement, that the United States should change the quarantine zone of the naval blockade off Cuba to 500 miles, from the original plan of 800 miles, as this would give Khrushchev more time to consider his options, as the Russian ships sailed towards the exclusion zone.

Ormsby-Gore reported rapidly changing moods in Washington. Macmillan knew how close Ormsby-Gore was to Kennedy, and he used Ormsby-Gore as a conduit for his views. He confided in his Ambassador, knowing that his nuanced views would be communi-cated directly to Kennedy, in the appropriate diplomatic manner. For instance, after receiving Kennedy's first call, Macmillan wrote bluntly to Ormsby-Gore:

> Is he [Kennedy] (a) leading up to a position in which he can seize

the Island as might have come off some months ago or (b) is he preparing for a conference with Khrushchev which, if it once starts, must develop into a conference of world powers.

You will realize, for your personal information only, that I could not allow a situation in Europe or in the world to develop which looks like escalating into war without trying some action by calling a conference on my own, or something of the kind to stop it.[27]

Macmillan gave a worried Cabinet a full update at their meeting on 23 October. At 5 p.m he saw the Labour leader, Gaitskell, together with George Brown[28] and Harold Wilson, and gave them details on Privy Councillor terms. He followed this meeting with a visit to Buckingham Palace for an audience with the Queen, during which he outlined the details of the growing threats. At the end of the crisis, Sir Michael Adeane, the Queen's Private Secretary, wrote to thank Macmillan for keeping the Queen so comprehensively in touch.

The crisis unfolded in two phases. Initially, there was disbelief: the feeling that the gung-ho Americans were replicating the Bay of Pigs. Berlin had always been seen as the likeliest flash-point for a nuclear stand-off. Then came irrefutable photographic evidence that missiles were being installed in Cuba, and that America was in range. When David Bruce, the American Ambassador in London, brought this material to Macmillan on 22 October, Macmillan's initial reaction was that the Americans would now realise under what shadow the British people had been living for many years. Although the undeniable truth, this observation was not the most tactful. Macmillan, with memories of Suez, felt Kennedy would be justified in invading Cuba straight away, a stance he came to regret, as delving deeper, he felt Khrushchev's underlying purpose was probably to trade Cuba for Berlin.

Kennedy's second telephone call to Macmillan came at 11.30 p.m. (British time) on 24 October. Alerted in advance, Macmillan had Home, the Foreign Secretary, and Sir Harold Caccia, the former British Ambassador to Washington and now Permanent Secretary at the Foreign Office, on hand. The first Soviet ships had turned round, but others were still coming towards the exclusion zone.

On 25 October, Kennedy and Macmillan spoke alone from 11 p.m. till after midnight. On 26 October, there were phone calls covering two and a half hours from 11.30 till 2 a.m. Macmillan supplemented these calls by sending teleprint messages, filling in the details on outstanding points.

The most significant conversation took place on 24 October.

Kennedy asked Macmillan directly whether he should 'take out' Cuba, or 'whether we should hold off and use Cuba as sort of hostage in the matter of Berlin'.[29] Wisely Macmillan avoided a peremptory answer and said he would think over the options. However, he was able to tell Kennedy that British intelligence had revealed that 'Russian ships not so far on in the queue are returning via Baltic or Russian ports.' His teleprinted response a few hours later was that Kennedy should avoid a military confrontation. Macmillan addressed the '$64,000 question' Kennedy had posed. 'After much reflection, I think that events have gone too far. While circumstances may arise in which such action would be right and necessary, I think we are now all in a phase where you must try to obtain your objectives by other means.' He advised Kennedy to propose a system of United Nations inspection in Cuba 'to stop work on the major military installations so long as the negotiations last'. He wanted the President to call off the blockade in return for a standstill. 'At the same time you will no doubt continue with your military build up for any emergency. This may be as important a factor for persuading the Cubans to accept as in other directions.'[30]

Kennedy responded to Macmillan's message just after 11.00 p.m. (London time) on 25 October. On the United Nations proposal Macmillan had felt the point at issue was 'immobilizing the weapons in Cuba, which is your major point, isn't it?' Kennedy agreed, but said that confrontation at the edge of the exclusion zone was the first hurdle.[31]

When they next spoke, for two and a half hours on 26 October, Macmillan again advised against any United States military action. 'At this stage any movement by you may produce a result in Berlin which would be very bad for us all, that's the danger now.'[32]

Macmillan knew that all now hinged on the actions taken by the Soviet ships (one called *Gagarin*) still on the high seas, as they approached the exclusion zone. By Saturday, 27 October, the crisis had reached a new peak. The American U2 pilot who had provided photographic evidence of the building of the missile sites was shot down and killed. The same day Kennedy received two contradictory letters from Khrushchev. The first was, in essence, a capitulation in return for a guarantee that there would be no invasion of Cuba; the second, much tougher, demanded negotiations about the American missiles in Turkey.[33] Kennedy's masterstroke was to ignore the second letter and reply to the first. To Macmillan's delight, this manoeuvre (suggested by McGeorge Bundy) became known as the 'Trollope Ploy'. McGeorge Bundy had remembered a scene from Trollope's

The American Senator, in which one of the characters interpreted an ambiguous message as an offer of marriage and accepted it.

On 27 October, Macmillan authorised British V bombers in Lincolnshire to be placed on alert condition 3, one of 15 minutes' readiness.[34] The night of 27/28 October, longer because of the move from daylight standard time in America, was the most anxious time, as Khrushchev's response to Kennedy's letter of 24 October, stating that the missile sites had to be dismantled, was awaited. Macmillan called a Cabinet for the Sunday, 28 October. The 'Precautionary Stage', as the recent 'Nuclear Retaliation Procedures' detailed it, was on the agenda.[35] Macmillan was planning to make arrangements, if necessary, for the key government personnel to evacuate to the secret underground bunker, near Corsham, between Bath and Chippenham, codenamed TURNSTILE.[36] However, as members of the Cabinet were having lunch before their meeting, news came of Khrushchev's agreement to dismantle the bases in Cuba.[37] The crisis was over.

Macmillan's reaction revealed his exhaustion. 'It's like a wedding when there is nothing left to do but drink the champagne and go to sleep.'[38] In the light of what was to happen a little over a year later, Kennedy's reaction was gallows humour indeed. 'This is the night to go to the theatre,' he said to Arthur Schlesinger, 'like Abraham Lincoln.'[39]

The sense of relief was profound, on all sides. 'If way to the Better there be,' one of Macmillan's favourite in-house authors, Thomas Hardy, had written, 'it exacts a full look at the Worst.'[40] For 13 days that look had come unnervingly close. Yet Macmillan always felt that the Cuban Missile Crisis had its positives. The leaders of the superpowers now realised what could ensue from a miscalculation, so such a crisis would never arise again. Castro survived and Cuba was not invaded.

Many in the West felt grateful to Khrushchev for sparing them the horrors of nuclear war, much as people had been grateful to Hitler for seemingly making 'peace in our time' in September 1938. Macmillan felt grateful that the American President at the time was Kennedy, who had avoided an impulsive response. In old age, Macmillan said he had two recurring nightmares: the first was of the trenches of the Great War; the second was what would have happened if Cuba had gone wrong.[41]

During the missile crisis, President de Gaulle had remained aloof, retiring to Colombey-les-Deux-Églises,[42] and declining to receive the American Ambassador. Macmillan knew how touchy de Gaulle was about 'the special relationship', from which he felt excluded.

The President could interpret any meeting between the British and the Americans as a plot against himself. Accordingly, Macmillan was determined to see de Gaulle personally, before he flew to Nassau to negotiate with Kennedy over a replacement for the cancelled Skybolt system.

The meetings at Rambouillet from 15 to 16 December, though they began with high hopes, soon revealed de Gaulle's inner feelings.[43] He had been strengthened recently by the return of the Gaullist party in the legislative election, and though never lacking in confidence, this shift in the French political temper gave him an uninhibited determination.

The Saturday morning was a time for shooting. The President did not participate,[44] but came out in a battered old Citroën car for the last drive, installed himself behind Macmillan, and commented 'Pas de chance' whenever Macmillan, disconcerted, missed a shot. After lunch, de Gaulle and Macmillan went for a walk in the woods, an idea suggested by de Gaulle. They were accompanied only by de Gaulle's interpreter and Philip de Zulueta, Macmillan's Private Secretary. Macmillan insisted on conversing with de Gaulle in French. He returned from the walk believing things had gone well. Philip de Zulueta was not so sure. The session in the evening seemed successful, but the plenary meeting the next morning scotched all British hopes. Macmillan, now regretting the lack of an interpreter of his own, summoned one from the British Embassy, as well as the Ambassador, Sir Pierson ('Bob') Dixon. In a long and tortuous speech, de Gaulle declared that though he was in favour of eventual British membership of the EEC, he was not convinced that the time was yet right. Macmillan declared himself shocked and dismayed.

De Gaulle was further angered by Macmillan's imminent visit to see Kennedy in Nassau about missiles, though the nuclear issue was really a fig leaf. The key issue for de Gaulle was the Common Agricultural Policy, without which, he believed, there would be riots in Paris, as there had been in Algiers. With Britain in the Common Market, there would be no immediate inclusive Common Agricultural Policy.

At the French Council of Ministers on 19 December, de Gaulle made some deliberately disparaging remarks about Macmillan, soon leaked to the press. 'We prefer the Britain of Macmillan to that of Labour and would like to help him to stay in power,' de Gaulle declared.[45] 'But what could I do, except sing to him Edith Piaf's song, Ne pleurez pas, Milord.' It was a strange way to show his preference.

Macmillan had only one day in London to nurse his bruised feelings before he flew to Nassau in the Bahamas for his first meeting with Kennedy since the Cuban Missile Crisis. He was accompanied by Alec Home and Peter Thorneycroft. The failure of Skybolt tests in 1962 had forced a rethink on both sides of the Atlantic alliance. Nassau was to prove a watershed in British defence policy. If these talks failed, then Home believed it could have necessitated a general election on their return.[46] Macmillan anticipated talks as difficult as those with de Gaulle. Yet the results were far better than he could have expected. He often pondered on Kennedy's motives. The historian of Skybolt, Richard Neustadt, offers a convincing explanation:

> By December 1962, three months after the Cuban crisis – if not, indeed, before – President Kennedy was privately more Macmillanite than McNamerian...This was part of the bond between these two chiefs of government, JFK and the PM, part of the way they viewed the human condition, wryly, with an underlay of tragedy, part of the reason that the former treated the latter's pleas with more consideration than Macmillan himself may have expected.[47]

Robert McNamara, Kennedy's Defence Secretary, had anticipated 'a very, very, very difficult meeting'.[48] Britain's independent nuclear deterrent depended on a satisfactory replacement for Skybolt. Without such a deterrent Macmillan believed Britain would be impotent in international counsels – 'naked in the Conference chamber', as Aneurin Bevan had once put it.[49] Macmillan saw Nassau as the last chance to sustain even the pretence of superpower status.

As so often, Ormsby-Gore's influence over Kennedy was to be of immense help to Macmillan. On the flight to Nassau with Kennedy, Ormsby-Gore explained the implications. As a result, Kennedy felt under an obligation to accommodate Britain's defence needs.

Kennedy's advisers were not pleased when Kennedy agreed to give Britain Polaris on favourable terms, thus preserving Britain's independent nuclear capability. Nor was de Gaulle, because this agreement meant that there was no longer any need for Britain to join a multilateral force, a supranational NATO alliance that would have included France.

Whilst the Nassau talks continued, Khrushchev sent a letter to Kennedy offering the possibility of a nuclear Test Ban Treaty incorporating international verification within the borders of the Soviet Union. Until then, access to the Soviet Union itself had been the sticking point of any agreement.

Macmillan had kept Butler fully informed of the Nassau negotiations.

Butler presided at a Cabinet at Admiralty House on 21 December. The main consideration for the Cabinet, as they examined Macmillan's four detailed telegrams, was how far the proposed agreement 'could be publicly defended as maintaining an independent United Kingdom contribution to the nuclear deterrent'.[50] At a full Cabinet on 3 January 1963, Macmillan was at his most masterful and reassuring, putting the best possible gloss on Nassau, 'a realistic compromise, in present circumstances, between independence and interdependence'.[51] The Cabinet accepted this. In truth they had little option. Polaris missiles were being made available at a competitive price, though the British would have to produce their own warheads, and, in addition, the Americans were prepared to pay 50 per cent of the future development costs.

Kennedy's decision was more political than military. Most insiders at the Pentagon thought an independent British nuclear deterrent was, at best, irrelevant; at worst, proliferation. Macmillan saw the deterrent as Britain's ticket to the top table. Kennedy knew the dangers Macmillan would face domestically if the Nassau talks failed, and because of Ormsby-Gore's clear and sympathetic advocacy, he was prepared to help. The irony was that the day after the conference, Skybolt, the discarded missile, was tested again – and this time it was successful.

Over New Year, and for several weeks to come, Britain was in the grip of the most bitter winter since 1947. 'I wish we were still in the Bahamas,' Alec Home wrote to President Kennedy, 'as we are snowed in.'[52] It was an apt metaphor for the year that lay ahead. Overshadowing everything was de Gaulle's attitude to Britain joining the EEC. 'We do not expect much from de Gaulle except obstinacy and non-cooperation,' Macmillan wrote in his diary on New Year's Eve, 'but we must try.'[53]

On 14 January 1963, the day the Brussels negotiations about British entry actually restarted after the Christmas and New Year break, de Gaulle held a press conference at the Elysée Palace – no town hall or television studio for the 'new Louis Quatorze' – and declared that the time was not right for British entry. Britain, he said, was 'insular, she is maritime, she is linked through her exchanges, her markets, her supply lines to the most diverse and often the distant countries; she pursues essentially industrial and commercial activities, and only slightly agricultural ones'. Moreover, Britain had failed to put 'Europe' first, 'without restriction, without reserve, and in preference to anything else'.[54] In de Gaulle's eyes, the Commonwealth and America still mattered more to Britain than Europe did. The only thing missing from de Gaulle's denunciation was a reference to Agincourt and perfidious Albion.

De Gaulle feared that the UK would be an American 'Trojan horse' inside the EEC, and was anxious lest British entry upset the delicate economic balance of the bargain between French agriculture and German industry upon which the EEC was based.

Macmillan always felt that the comment of the French Agriculture Minister to his British opposite number, Christopher Soames, had the ring of truth. With the Six, the Minister asserted, there were five hens and one cock; if Britain joined, there would be two cocks.[55]

Although Macmillan put a brave face on de Gaulle's veto, in private he despaired. 'All our policies at home and abroad are in ruins.'[56] Sir Michael Fraser, Director of the Conservative Research Department, put flesh on the bones of the disaster: 'Europe was to be our *deus ex machina*: it was to create a new contemporary political argument with insular Socialism; dish the Liberals by stealing their clothes; give us something *new* after 12–13 years; act as a catalyst of modernisation; give us a new place in the international sun. It was Macmillan's ace, and De Gaulle trumped it.'[57]

Four days after de Gaulle's veto, Hugh Gaitskell, the Labour leader, died at the age of only 56, following a mysterious and sudden illness. The antipathy between Macmillan and Gaitskell had been mutual and well known, so Macmillan had to avoid even the faintest hint of insincere sanctimony in the tributes he delivered, both nationally and in Parliament. He decided that he should broadcast to the nation, and he spoke in generous terms, even movingly, as Churchill had done in November 1940 on the death of Neville Chamberlain, despite their differences. Some people were hard to please. 'Macmillan's tribute was the most revolting since he and Gaitskell hated each other,' wrote Tony Benn in his diary. 'Indeed one of the curious factors operating to check bi-partisanship in politics has been this personal hatred.'[58] The next day, 19 January, Macmillan moved the adjournment of the House, the first time this had ever happened for a Leader of the Opposition who had not previously been Prime Minister.

Inevitably, Labour would now be electing an even younger leader, fresh and ready for the challenge, against a Prime Minister who had just passed his sixth anniversary in office. Gaitskell had been 13 years Macmillan's junior; Harold Wilson, elected Labour leader on 14 February, was 22 years younger. Macmillan knew that Wilson would prove a formidable opponent. Gaitskell had been one of Westminster's clergymen; Macmillan and Wilson were both political bookies. They were sharp on their feet, quick thinkers in debate, ready with the apt riposte, which made their clashes at the dispatch box extremely lively. Of course, they were old hands at the game, as Wilson had been Shadow Chancellor in 1956, facing Macmillan at the time of Suez. In the past, both had been rebels against the party establishment, and both were skilful actors in the game of politics. They enjoyed the chase, and honed their skills accordingly. Macmillan felt none of the personal animosity towards Wilson that he had for Gaitskell. After heated exchanges on the floor of the House, they would meet for a quiet drink. Wilson knew he was up against one of the most effective parliamentarians of the age, while Macmillan found Wilson amusing. In short, a mutual respect soon developed.

Macmillan, wounded by de Gaulle, was a politician who had passed the cusp of his career; Wilson, by contrast, was on the rise, the British Kennedy, destined for Downing Street, it seemed. As a result, Wilson often outplayed Macmillan on the floor of the House, not something the Prime Minister was used to. Their battles made politics interesting.

The question not only of the future leadership of the Conservative Party, but the method of determining that leadership was already being discussed. Humphrey Berkeley, the MP for Lancaster, had made a speech to the Chelsea Young Conservatives arguing that the whole process of choosing the next leader needed examining. He proposed that some form of electoral system should be introduced. The reaction of the party hierarchy was not dissimilar to Ernest Bevin's on the Council of Europe in 1949 – 'If you open that Pandora's box, you never know what Trojan horses will jump out.'[59] Lord Aldington, the deputy party chairman, was horrified. 'Humphrey,' he asked in disbelief, 'surely you are not advocating one man one vote, are you?' Berkeley was made to feel as though he 'had suggested that the leader of the party should be elected by the entire adult population of the African continent'.[60]

On 5 January, Macmillan appointed Lord Hailsham minister with responsibility for the north-east. The area had always had a special resonance for Macmillan. To focus on its problems, as well as those in Scotland, where the decline in shipbuilding and heavy industry was having its deleterious effect on employment, was an essential priority. Unfortunately, Hailsham, always a politician for the photo-opportunity, whether ringing bells or sporting capacious swimming trunks at seaside party conferences, now appeared in the north-east in a flat cap, a source of ridicule for the satirists. A serious initiative was quickly dubbed a gimmick.

The fallout from the Vassall affair continued to concern Macmillan. The Cuban Missile Crisis had confirmed how important espionage was proving to be in the Cold War. Much of the information on Khrushchev's intentions over Berlin, and the technical information on the proposed missiles for Cuba, had come from Colonel Oleg Penkovsky. One of the key pieces of information from Penkovsky was that the Russians were then still behind the Americans in their technology. For this, he was to pay the heaviest price after his arrest.[61]

The Radcliffe Report[62] into security in Britain, which Macmillan had commissioned following the Portland case, had reported in early 1962 that infiltration of the civil service unions by Communists had reached 25 per cent. Radcliffe had recommended increased security vetting and a continuation of the D-Notice system.[63] Macmillan always felt that Sir Roger Hollis had mishandled the Vassall case. Hollis had been exultant. 'I've got this fellow, I've got him,' he told Macmillan. To say that Macmillan was not best pleased is an understatement. 'When my gamekeeper shoots a fox,' he told Hollis, 'he doesn't go and hang it up outside the Master of Foxhounds' drawing room; he buries it out of sight.' Hollis was told he should have followed the same course with Vassall. 'Better to discover him, and then control him, but never catch him.'[64] As a result of the Vassall trial, opposition politicians and investigative journalists trawled through the subplots to see what further information damaging to the government could be unearthed. As rumour followed rumour, Macmillan called Lord Radcliffe into service again to conduct a tribunal into the accusations.

Macmillan's fears were justified. Of all the scandals that beset his twilight days at No. 10, none (not even the Profumo affair) was to be so profoundly damaging.[65]

Thomas Galbraith,[66] by then Under-Secretary at the Scottish Office, had formerly been Civil Lord at the Admiralty, where Vassall had been his Private Secretary. Prurient insinuations now circulated that there had been a homosexual relationship between Galbraith and Vassall, and that there were incriminating letters. Macmillan always shrank from indelicate matters, and now demons were coming to haunt him. Public attitudes towards homosexuals in Britain were then both unforgiving and vindictive (as figures as diverse as Alan Turing,[67] Benjamin Britten[68] and the MP Ian Harvey had found). In the 1950s, the Lord Chancellor, Lord Kilmuir, had authorised an active police drive against homosexuals, which led to unsavoury entrapments, blackmail and harassments. The Radcliffe Tribunal eventually exonerated Galbraith, but by that time he had resigned (Macmillan did not try to dissuade him) and the damage was done.*

The Vassall Debate in the Commons in early November 1962 was a public relations disaster for the government. Patrick Gordon Walker, the Shadow Defence Minister, launched a powerful attack on the Admiralty's handling of the whole affair. There was particular anger on the opposition side that the Radcliffe Tribunal would be conducted by three civil servants and would not be a full public inquiry. Peter Thorneycroft, the Minister for Defence, adopted an ill-advisedly light-hearted approach. So hostile was the press reaction that it seemed that Lord Carrington, the First Lord of the Admiralty, would have to resign, which he offered to do.[69] Although the Radcliffe Tribunal eventually cleared both Carrington and Galbraith, absolving them of any blame, the story did not end there.

Two journalists, Brendan Mulholland of the *Daily Mail* and Reginald Foster of the *Daily Sketch*, were imprisoned on 7 March for refusing to disclose their sources about Vassall.[70] A debate on their imprisonment followed in Parliament on 21 March, the occasion on which, under parliamentary privilege, the Labour MPs Reginald Paget, George Wigg, Barbara Castle and Richard Crossman raised the matter of the rumours surrounding John Profumo and a 19-year-old call girl named Christine Keeler. The press splashed the story across all the front pages the next morning. 'The real interest of the affair,' Crossman wrote in his diary, 'is the hostility between the press and the Government, which makes the press willing to leap at anything.'[71]

Of the many constituent parts of the Vassall saga, it was the imprisonment of Mulholland and Foster that marked the turning point in the attitude of the press towards the government. From that moment, the majority of the press criticised Macmillan at every opportunity. As Tony Benn was to observe later, 'Once you alienate journalists, they won't find anything good in what you do.'[72]

John Profumo, MP for Stratford-upon-Avon, and, since 1960, Secretary of State for War in the Macmillan government, had been involved with Christine Keeler in the summer of 1961. He had met Keeler at Cliveden, Lord (Bill) Astor's home, during a weekend visit. On the evening of 8 July, after dinner, Astor and Profumo wandered over to the estate's swimming pool, shielded by hedges, not far from the big house. They were drawn by sounds of merriment. Stephen

---

*Macmillan brought Galbraith back into the government as a Parliamentary Secretary at Transport under Ernest Marples on 3 May 1963, acknowledgment that he had been mistreated.

Ward, an osteopath with many 'society' clients, including Bill Astor, had the tenancy of Spring Cottage down by the Thames on the Astor estate. He was allowed to use the pool[73] and he was there that evening with several girls. Christine Keeler, clutching a towel around herself to cover her nakedness, was introduced to Profumo by Astor. Profumo's subsequent affair with Keeler was very brief and in normal circumstances might have been as quickly forgotten. But the circumstances were not normal.

Christine Keeler was simultaneously sharing her favours with Captain Evgeni Ivanov, assistant Soviet naval attaché at the Russian Embassy in London and a GRU agent. The security service had been watching Ivanov for some time. Stephen Ward was also well known to them because of his suggestion to MI5 in June 1961 that Ivanov could perhaps be persuaded to become an agent. In 1962 Ward had been involved in some of the murkier edges of the security aspects of the Cuban missile crisis.

When MI5 discovered that Profumo had strayed, albeit unwittingly, into the Ward/Ivanov web, Sir Roger Hollis decided that Sir Norman Brook, the Cabinet Secretary, should be informed.[74] Brook saw Profumo on 9 August 1961 and told him about Ivanov, warning him to be wary. Profumo misinterpreted this as a covert indication that MI5 knew about his affair with Keeler. In fact, MI5 did not have actual confirmation of the affair until 28 January 1963.[75] Information was now filtered through to Macmillan. MI5 were concerned with the security aspects. But Macmillan was aware also of the rumours about Profumo's private life. Was this adulterous affair, if true, just too painful a reminder of the great sorrow of his own life for Macmillan to handle? Where matters of infidelity were concerned, Macmillan preferred, ostrich-like, either to hope they did not exist, or that, if they did, they would soon go away. 'Profumo', on the contrary, ran and ran.

'A Minister is said to be acquainted with an extremely pretty girl,' declared Reginald Paget, Labour MP for Northampton, in the House of Commons on 21 March 1962, adding, 'as far as I am concerned, I should have thought that that was a matter for congratulation rather than inquiry.'[76] At the opposite extreme came the censorious verdict of Lord Hailsham during an explosive television interview with Robert Mackenzie: 'A great party is not to be brought down because of a squalid affair between a woman of easy virtue and a proved liar.'[77] Reginald Paget described this as 'a virtuoso performance in the art of kicking a fallen friend in the guts'.[78]

*

Law officers began to investigate the rumours. The Attorney General, Sir John Hobson (no relation of Profumo's wife, Valerie Hobson, the actress), deeply committed at the time to his work on the Radcliffe Tribunal regarding the Vassall case, interviewed Profumo at 11 p.m. on 28 January, the day MI5 received confirmation that Profumo was seeing Keeler. Hobson told Profumo to be absolutely frank. Profumo related the events of July 1961 at Cliveden, and said that subsequently he had many times visited Stephen Ward at his flat when Keeler was present. On two occasions Keeler was there alone when he arrived. Profumo insisted that there had been no impropriety in his relationship with Keeler, a story which, tragically, he was to stick to, even on the floor of the House of Commons. Hobson warned that if there was any truth in the rumours that were circulating, then Profumo would have to resign. Profumo repeated his denial of impropriety. The fact that Hobson had been at the same school as Profumo (Harrow), the same college (Brasenose, Oxford) and had even served in the same regiment during the war (the First Northamptonshire Yeomanry) made him reluctant to disbelieve Profumo. Nevertheless, he remained suspicious and contacted both the Solicitor General, Sir Peter Rawlinson, and the Chief Whip, Martin Redmayne.

A few days later, Profumo appeared before both Hobson and Rawlinson. They told him it was absolutely vital that he should be truthful. Profumo admitted that he had given Keeler a cigarette lighter that she had admired, but again flatly denied any impropriety. He blamed the vindictiveness of the press. He had no intention of resigning. On 3 February he instructed counsel to sue when the opportunity arose and to seek injunctions.

After this meeting, the two law officers told Macmillan that they were not convinced Profumo was telling the truth, even though, by engaging solicitors, it seemed he was prepared to repeat his story on oath. Martin Redmayne and Tim Bligh were now brought in. At this point, Macmillan should clearly have seen Profumo himself, face to face. But he did not feel that it would be productive. A gentleman had given his word; it would reflect badly if that word was not believed. The truth is that such a meeting would have been difficult for Macmillan, painful and embarrassing, and he ducked it.

Instead of seeing Profumo himself, Macmillan consulted David Bruce, the American Ambassador in London. Bruce saw Thomas Corbally, a New York business consultant, whom he knew had become a friend of Stephen Ward following treatment for a knee injury. Corbally knew both Christine Keeler and Mandy Rice-Davies, another of the girls who had been swimming at Cliveden, as well as Ivanov.

On 29 January, Corbally provided a written account. He had already given details of the scandal to Hugh Fraser, Macmillan's Secretary of State for Air.[79] Bruce gave Corbally's account to Macmillan, who now had, independently, more information than his law officers, especially about Ward's activities.*

Without the persistence of George Wigg, Labour MP for Dudley,[80] the Profumo affair might yet have died the death. But Wigg harboured a grievance towards Profumo after being slighted by him in the House in 1962, and the Keeler affair gave him every opportunity of indulging in what became known as 'wiggery-pokery'. Prurience was not Wigg's motivation; more revenge against Profumo and what he saw as an effete and inefficient establishment, defending its own over issues of morality.†

Thursday, 21 March was the day the rumours were raised in the House of Commons with statements, under parliamentary privilege, by Reginald Paget, Barbara Castle, George Wigg and Richard Crossman. After this, Henry Brooke, the Home Secretary, summoned Hollis to ask about MI5's involvement, as 'he felt he ought to know the facts'.[81] Hollis denied that MI5 had been sending anonymous warning letters to Profumo's wife; their only concern had been to make Profumo aware of Ivanov's GRU contacts.

The statements about the rumours broke in the evening, and on a Thursday. The law officers and the Chief Whip, in consultation with Macmillan, determined that Profumo had to make a statement in the House the next day, which was almost upon them, so late had the story broken. Parliament sat at 11 a.m. on Fridays in those days and time was of the essence. Had the episode occurred, say, during the Friday-morning session of Parliament, a weekend would have been available for a considered response; maybe, in the cold light of day, even a resignation by Profumo.

Profumo was summoned to a meeting in the Chief Whip's room for 2.30 a.m. As he had taken a sleeping draught, he was still groggy, when he arrived with his solicitor at 3 a.m. He was met by the two law officers, Sir John Hobson and Sir Peter Rawlinson; the Chief Whip, Martin Redmayne; Iain Macleod, the Leader of the House; and

---

*All this while, the FBI in America were investigating the affair (some even wondered if their womanising President was involved in some way). In 1986 they released the information under the codename of 'Bowtie'. In these files, Corbally asserted that if Stephen Ward had not spoken so openly to everyone, then Profumo would never have been disgraced. Corbally could have added that the same would have been true if he himself had been more circumspect.

†An ironic footnote to 'Profumo' came in 1976, when Wigg was charged with accosting women, whilst 'kerb-crawling' near Marble Arch.

William Deedes, Minister without Portfolio, in charge of government information. Again, Macmillan failed to be there.

A statement was drawn up, again denying any impropriety, which was typed out by William Deedes on an old typewriter he kept in his room at the House. Later that morning at 11 a.m., with Macmillan sitting beside him, and with Butler and Macleod there in support, Profumo made his statement from the front bench. He denied any impropriety. As he sat down, Macmillan patted him on the shoulder.

Rumours persisted. It was said that Profumo had lied to the House, a far worse offence than any perceived moral failing. Summoned back to London from a holiday in Italy on 3 June, he confessed all. The next day he resigned his office, his parliamentary seat at Stratford-upon-Avon, and, most painfully of all, his membership of the Privy Council.

Life after Parliament for Profumo was one long process of atonement. He devoted his time to charitable work at Toynbee Hall in the East End, work for which he received the CBE in 1975, on the recommendation of the then Prime Minister, Harold Wilson, who had played a part in his downfall. Profumo sought no publicity for his commitment to Toynbee Hall, but remained self-effacing. When it was suggested in 1989 by the Principal of Brasenose, Lord Windlesham, that he become an Honorary Fellow, he declined lest the press raked up the story again and brought unwelcome publicity to his former college.[82]

Recriminations were painful. There were calls for the ministers who had seen Profumo in the small hours that Friday morning to resign as well. Macmillan said that if they went, he would go also. Martin Redmayne and Sir Peter Rawlinson both tendered their resignations, which were refused. On 17 June, a debate took place on the scandal. The Opposition concentrated on the security aspects. Wilson was at his sharpest, though some felt with a touch of sanctimony. Macmillan emphasised that he had not colluded in Profumo's lie. He was in a dilemma, though. The more he demonstrated (truthfully) that he had acted honestly, the more he laid the government and himself open to the charge of incompetence. The nominal Conservative majority was 98; it fell to 57.[83]

Inevitably, an inquiry was needed and Macmillan appointed Lord Denning to prepare a report.[84] During his investigations, Denning found some of the evidence so disgusting that he sent the lady shorthand typists from the room. Denning delivered his report to the

Cabinet on 16 September. When it was published ten days later at 12.30 a.m., 4,000 copies were sold in the first hour at the HMSO in Kingsway. Sales in Britain alone topped 100,000. Harold Wilson was given an advance copy. When Macmillan heard that Wilson's reaction was that 'there was not much in it', he said that what Wilson really meant was 'well, not much in it for me.'[85]

After Bill Astor's death in 1966, Cliveden was turned into an hotel. 'My dear boy, it always has been,' said Macmillan when he was told.[86]

Intensely worried that there might have been some Soviet plot to destabilise his government, Macmillan sent for Sir Dick White, the former MI5 director general, in whom he had implicit trust. There was no such empathy with Sir Roger Hollis, the current MI5 director general. Macmillan and White met on 17 June 1963, 12 days after Profumo's resignation. MI5 and the SIS were instructed by Macmillan 'to look into the possibility that the Russian Intelligence Service had a hand in staging the Profumo Affair in order to discredit Her Majesty's Government'.[87] Sir Alec Douglas-Home, Macmillan's successor as Prime Minister, was eventually to receive the report, which showed there was no such plot.

Macmillan handled the Profumo affair as badly as anything during his premiership. There were things he just did not want to believe or to confront. Some of the blame can be laid at the door of his Parliamentary Private Secretary, Sir Knox Cunningham, who did not have the acute political antennae needed at the time. Macmillan's repugnance was genuine and deeply felt. 'I do not remember ever having been under such a sense of personal strain,' he confessed in his diary. 'Even Suez was "clean" – about war and politics. This is all "dirt".'[88]

'Profumo' was never a spy scandal with security breaches. The cases of George Blake and John Vassall were far more serious and politically damaging. Nor was it security that interested the press and public. The media fed, frenzy-like, on the whole surrealistic saga: the trial of Johnny Edgecombe, Keeler's West Indian boyfriend, a marijuana dealer who fired shots at Ward's mews flat in Marylebone, where Keeler and Mandy Rice-Davies lived for a while; the charges against 'Lucky' Gordon, another of her West Indian lovers, for wounding her. Stephen Ward was put on trial for living off immoral earnings, and killed himself with an overdose before sentencing. Titillating details were leaked about Ward's orgies, attended by politicians wearing nothing but their socks. When Denning's Report appeared,[89] the episode was political manna for the Opposition.

David Bruce sent full reports to the State Department in

Washington. On 18 June, the day after the Profumo Debate, he wrote that Macmillan would survive until after the President's proposed visit to Europe, but that thereafter 'his replacement cannot be too long delayed'. Macmillan had become, Bruce wrote, 'an electoral liability'.[90] The next day, in a telegram marked PRIORITY, he advised that 'on past record Conservative Party capable of moving with brutal speed when fountainhead of leader's authority had dried up'.[91] The telegram coloured Kennedy's view of Macmillan as a tired leader when they met at Birch Grove a fortnight later.

Tired leader or not, Macmillan stayed on, and one of the unregarded consequences of 'Profumo' was that it denied Reginald Maudling his best, and, in the event, his only chance of becoming Prime Minister.

The last Budget of Macmillan's premiership had been delivered by Reginald Maudling on 3 April. The mood surrounding it was even more apprehensive than that of a year earlier when Selwyn Lloyd had failed to rally the troops. 'Waiting for Maudling' was how Harold Evans, Macmillan's press secretary, described it. 'All now depends on the budget. If it fails to revive the party, it seems inevitable that the senior backbenchers will get together to decide on a successor and to convey a demand to the P.M. that he should go.'[92]

Macmillan knew how vital the Budget was, not only for the party's electoral prospects, but also for his own survival. To ensure that Maudling delivered, he bombarded him with memos and letters, urging an expansionist course. On 20 February, he urged his Chancellor to go for 'the big stuff – the national plan, the new approach, the expand or die'.[93] He suggested tax reductions of £400m. 'The economy is not really moving forward yet at all,' he added, by way of a reminder, on 6 March.[94] Twelve days later, Lord Cromer, the new Governor of the Bank of England, also emphasised to Maudling 'the need for a Budget to stimulate the level of the economy'.[95] Cromer argued for concessions in the range of £200–300 million. At a meeting on 22 March, Macmillan urged Maudling 'to go for a more extensive range of tax concessions'.[96] In the end, Maudling listened more closely to his Treasury advisers: his Budget had £269m of concessions.

Macmillan hoped this package would satisfy the voters. He was confident that Maudling would make a good impression in the House of Commons on Budget Day. Not only was Maudling intellectually the most able of all Macmillan's Chancellors, he was also better presentationally than either Amory or Lloyd. Unlike his two immediate predecessors, he was unconventional, even slightly rakish, in both tastes and appearance. On one occasion he arrived at an early evening meeting in Downing Street sporting a midnight-blue velvet dinner jacket. 'Ah Reggie,' said Macmillan, 'off to the 100 Club again?' He then turned to the other ministers. 'Plays the drums, y'know.'[97]

Whatever else, his speech promised not to be dull. He appalled his officials by suggesting that he might deliver some of it 'off the cuff'.[98] Another sign of his unconventional approach was that he believed in announcing the major tax changes early on, rather than keeping his audience in suspense. Although he did not introduce any tax relief concessions on mortgage interest payments, he did abolish the hated Schedule A tax, as promised by Selwyn Lloyd a year earlier, thus encouraging further home ownership. When it came to direct taxation, Maudling had two options. He could either cut the standard rate of income tax by 6d, or go for an increase in the thresholds of the tax-free personal allowances. The advantage of this latter course would be that it would help the poorer section of society and have a more immediate effect on consumer spending. After heated debates in pre-Budget Cabinets, with John Boyd-Carpenter, the Chief Secretary to the Treasury, arguing for the direct income tax cut, Maudling opted for the second course, taking 3,750,000 people out of income tax completely.[99] He hoped (in vain) that this would encourage the trade unions to moderate their wage demands. Boyd-Carpenter felt it was 'an opportunity missed'.[100]

The 'guiding light' on wage settlements was raised to 3.5 per cent, not that powerful trade unions paid much notice, either to the new level or the old one. As with the sweets tax in Lloyd's Budget the previous year, it was a minor change that grabbed the headlines. Maudling exempted domestic home brewers of beer from the need to obtain an excise certificate. In his memoirs he boasted that the growth of home brewing was entirely owing to his initiative.[101]

Press reception of the Budget was favourable. So, for Maudling, were the subsequent opinion polls. His standing with the public now eclipsed that of all his senior colleagues. His approval rating was 33 per cent. Macmillan's was 25 per cent, Butler's 23 per cent and Hailsham's 13 per cent. Within the parliamentary party, Maudling's levels of approval were even higher. On 12 July, the *Daily Telegraph* reported that his standing at Westminster was 70 per cent. It seemed inevitable that he would be Macmillan's successor, the sooner the better for most Tory MPs.

Harold Wilson, the new Labour leader, feared such an outcome. 'You know what our directive is,' Wilson told Richard Crossman, 'to keep Macmillan as our most valuable asset... The one thing I am really frightened of is Maudling.' Crossman saw this as very perceptive, and wrote in his diary: 'Maudling is Harold [Wilson]'s own age, a figure comparable to him. As long as he has Macmillan opposite him, old, effete, worn out, a cynical dilettante, the contrast between Harold's character and Macmillan's is an overwhelming advantage to Harold and the Labour party. There would be no such sharp contrast between Harold Wilson and young Maudling.'[102]

It is often asserted that the Profumo affair accelerated Macmillan's departure from the premiership. In fact its consequences were the exact opposite, prolonging his time in office by some four months. Macmillan was not brought down by Profumo; he was brought down by his prostate.[103]

In the summer of 1963, Macmillan did indeed give serious consideration to retirement. President de Gaulle's veto in January was a blow from which he never recovered. Adenauer was on the verge of retirement in Germany. Pope John XIII died on 3 June and Robert Schuman, architect of the Schuman Plan in 1950 and advocate for European integration, on 4 September. Guy Burgess, the defector, died in Moscow on 30 August, and, eventually, news came of the execution of Oleg Penkovsky, the secret agent, on 16 May. All these deaths gave Macmillan a whiff of mortality.

Another factor influenced him. In recent reshuffles, looking for the stars of the next generation, he had given the 'Young Turks' their heads in the hope that one would emerge ahead of the others as the acknowledged leader-in-waiting around whom the party could unite. The problem of the succession in 1963 was not that there was no candidate, but that there were several. Macmillan knew that Butler could never now become leader. So, in his heart of hearts, did Butler. John Morrison, Chairman of the 1922 Committee, had told Butler in June (just as he was leaving for the Victoria Falls conference) that 'the chaps won't have you', an unpalatable fact confirmed to Butler by members of the 1922 Executive he consulted.[104]

The first of these 'Young Turks', Edward Heath, as Lord Privy Seal, had been in charge of the EEC negotiations. If they had been successful, Heath would probably have become leader of the party in 1963 rather than 1965. But the negotiations had not been a success, and at the time Heath's reputation was rather in eclipse. Iain Macleod had been made Leader of the House of Commons and party chairman. He was a very good orator (his career had been launched when Churchill heard him declare in 1952 that 'a debate on the National Health Service without the Right Honourable Gentleman [Aneurin Bevan] would be like putting on *Hamlet* with no one in the part of the first gravedigger'),[105] but in truth was better in the House than outside it. Macmillan was also aware of how unpopular Macleod was in certain influential sections of the Tory party. In addition, he had come to realise that Macleod, who was racked with pain owing to his war injuries, far more debilitating than Macmillan's own, would not have been up to the job of leader physically. Enoch Powell was another whose star brightened the scene for a while, but his was an idiosyncratic talent, and he and Macmillan had a mutual suspicion of each other.

Maudling was now at the apogee of his career, and had Macmillan stepped down in the summer of 1963, he would have been the obvious, indeed almost inevitable, successor. Maudling pursued 'the dash for growth' because he believed in it, not because Macmillan ran him as his puppet. On 20 June, the *Daily Telegraph* published an article showing the extent of Maudling's support. According to a sample poll, 147 Tory MPs had him as their first choice as Macmillan's successor,[106] whereas the 1922 Committee believed that his support actually ran at 'between 60 and 70 per cent of Conservative MPs'. In the summer of 1963, Maudling met Rab Butler by chance in the street outside his Hans Place flat. They engaged in some desultory chat, before Butler, with some emotion, placed his hand on Maudling's shoulder and said, 'Of course Reggie, when you become leader I will be very happy to serve under you.'[107]

Macmillan was aware that Maudling was not everybody's cup of tea. He was considered lazy and too 'laid back'. Actually, as Treasury officials knew, he was so accomplished intellectually that he could dispatch his work in a fraction of the time his predecessors had taken.[108] On 6 July 1963, Maudling made a speech at Sawston in Cambridgeshire, in which with vigour and determination he addressed the issues surrounding 'Profumo'. His biographer concludes that 'Reggie's position was never so strong again as it was in the first two weeks of July 1963.'[109]

However, because of 'Profumo', there was no vacancy. Macmillan knew that he had to carry on, as any other course would have given the impression that he had been driven from office by scandal, spies and sleaze.

By the autumn, Maudling's star had mysteriously faded. Three factors had by then transformed the situation. First, Macmillan was seen as the architect behind the signing of the Test Ban Treaty in Moscow on 25 July.[110] This triumph coincided with his end-of-session speech to the 1922 Committee, which calmed the troops and largely dispelled any move towards a change in the leadership. Second, with the Budget out of the way, and the long summer recess, Maudling was not in the public, or parliamentary, eye, and found himself rather on the margins. The third, and most important, development, though, was the Royal Assent on 16 July to the Bill that allowed hereditary peers to disclaim their titles, following the spirited campaign by Tony Benn to avoid elevation to the Upper House. The implications of this Bill were not fully realised at the time, though Anthony Howard, in a celebrated article in the *New Statesman* on 14 December 1962, had predicted, with uncanny precision, what actually unfolded 10 months later. Howard's article was entitled: 'Mr Home and Mr Hogg'. At a stroke, two fresh candidates were eligible to join the field. Maudling was no longer the 'new' candidate.

CHAPTER TWENTY NINE

Guided Democracy

October 1963

> I nearly rang you up about six times during the turmoil, but thought it was not fair to worry you with my concerns. I think it has all come out pretty well, but would love sometime to tell you the whole story – a very strange one – and what is behind Macleod and Powell at this moment, I wonder.
>
> Selwyn Lloyd to Sir Anthony Eden, 28 October 1963[1]

In April 1963, Macmillan appointed Lord Poole[2] as joint party chairman with Iain Macleod. Selwyn Lloyd felt this fudged the issue; he would have preferred one chairman, not two. Poole, with his Eton, Christ Church and City links, was just the kind of Tory who got under Macleod's skin, and the two did not like each other. 'Under these circumstances,' Nigel Fisher observed in his biography of Macleod, 'it was surprising that the new arrangement worked as well as it did.'[3]

Poole was an experienced electioneer. He had contributed to *The Right Road for Britain*, the 1950 manifesto. As party chairman from 1955–1957, and then as deputy chairman from 1957 under Lord Hailsham's flamboyant leadership, he had proved an effective financial manager. He also understood the importance of constituency links with Central Office, and of political advertising, of which he was an important pioneer. The 1959 campaign – 'Life's better with the Conservatives; don't let Labour ruin it' – owed much to his input. He had also demonstrated a sure touch over election timings, having persuaded Macmillan not to go to the country in the spring of 1959, but to wait until the autumn. Macmillan was confident that Poole would energize the party's electoral machine, however much the implicit demotion might irritate Macleod. In an attempt, not entirely successful, to soothe troubled feelings, he spelled out the range of Macleod's responsibilities. 'You will control the political field, the presentation and planning of policy and of the Election Manifesto,' he wrote to Macleod on 16 April.[4] On the surface this did not seem to leave much for Poole to do, but both Macmillan and Macleod knew that this was not the case.

Poole's importance over the next seven months lay in his ability to tell Macmillan what he needed to know, not what he might want to hear. Unless the party pulled itself together, Poole wrote bluntly, 'there is a real possibility of an election defeat in 1964 on the scale of 1945'.[5] He believed that the best course would be for Macmillan to retire in orderly fashion before the end of 1963, and was not reticent in pressing this view. Macmillan had opened his own Pandora's box.

Churchill had been persuaded by his family to say, somewhat reluctantly, that he would not be standing again at the next election. This prompted suggestions that Macmillan should also bow out. Poole read the letters, many very forthright, that came into Central Office. The Liverpool Conservative Association had passed a resolution that 'there should be a change in the leadership, and as soon as possible'. The Denbigh association felt 'that the Government image was one of an elderly administration, out of touch with the people, too "old school tie", and badly in need of new blood'.[6] Donald Johnson, the MP for Carlisle, defied the three-line whip for the Profumo debate, preferring to play golf instead. He later said, 'I have encountered nobody but Rip Van Winkle still living in the days of Harold Macmillan.'[7] Maurice Macmillan and Julian Amery, son and son-in-law, were now seen with Macmillan at Westminster, talking to him in the Smoking Room and flanking him in the corridors.

At Nassau in December 1962, Khrushchev had indicated that some form of agreement over a Nuclear Test Ban, even involving inspection within the Soviet Union, might be possible. On 8 June, he wrote to President Kennedy, agreeing to the opening of negotiations. Kennedy welcomed this potential for a breakthrough, and appointed the experienced Averell Harriman as his representative at the Moscow talks. Macmillan needed to send a similarly heavyweight negotiator.

His choice fell on Lord Hailsham, a clear indication of how his thoughts were developing on the eventual leadership. Success in Moscow, Macmillan reckoned, would surely cement Hailsham's position as the leader-in-waiting.

Such tactics were only possible because of the lengthy campaign, now nearing its conclusion, that Tony Benn had waged for nearly three years to allow peers to disclaim their inherited titles. On 17 November 1960, Benn's father, the 1st Viscount Stansgate, died and Benn was automatically disqualified, as the 2nd Viscount, from continuing to sit as MP for Bristol South East.[8] Two days later, Benn had a meeting with Rab Butler, Leader of the House, to discuss the question of disclaiming his peerage. Butler was friendliness itself and said, rather patronisingly, that Macmillan would certainly wish 'these little points examined'. Benn wrote in his diary: 'I got the idea that he was vaguely on my side, which was clearly quite wrong. He went on: "By the way, one thing: would your scheme permit Quintin [Hailsham] to come back?" So I said, "Well, no, it wouldn't really." So he said, "Ah, well that's all right."[9]

By the summer of 1963, however, it was no longer 'all right' for Rab Butler. The Peerage Bill, now approaching the end of its tortuous passage through Parliament, was on the verge of receiving the Royal Assent. On 18 January 1963, the Cabinet had considered the timetable. Their collective decision was that existing hereditary peers and new hereditary peers would have a window of six months in which to disclaim their titles. On 15 May, a statement was made in both Houses declaring that the Peerage Bill would be operative *after* the next general election. The Labour opposition, however, wanted the measure to be introduced at once. Not unnaturally, Tony Benn agreed.

Initially, the Cabinet adhered firmly to their original decision. Macleod, whose position as a possible contender for the leadership might be affected if Hailsham returned to the Commons, was not in favour of early introduction of the Bill. However, on 27 June, the Cabinet discussed the matter again. It was agreed, surprisingly after only five minutes' discussion, Butler not dissenting, that if an amendment to this effect was moved and carried in the Lords, it should be accepted.[10]

Lord Hailsham was the Cabinet Minister most immediately affected. Before Hailsham left for the Soviet Union, Lord Poole told him to prepare himself for the leadership of the party.[11] Poole was getting ahead of events, as Tim Bligh pointed out to the Prime Minister on 4 July. 'As at present drafted,' he wrote, 'Quintin has to wait until Parliament has dissolved before he can exercise a disclaimer.'[12] That would be of no use to Hailsham, as things stood, or to Macmillan, if he retired in the autumn. Whether Macmillan fought the election or not, Hailsham would not have the opportunity of disclaiming as the Bill stood at that time.

Lord Salisbury led a 'revolt' in the House of Lords pressing for the Peerage Act to come into force immediately on receiving the Royal Assent. Support came from Labour peers such as Lord Shackleton and Lord Silkin. Salisbury may have thought this would discomfit Macmillan, his sworn enemy for six years. Actually, Salisbury's initiative suited Macmillan's purposes ideally. Hailsham would be *papabile*, if necessary, *before* the election. An Opposition amendment was duly tabled, seeking to make the Bill commence at the time of the Royal Assent.

Two weeks later, the Lord Chancellor, Lord Dilhorne, reported to the Cabinet that the Conservative peer Lord Swinton, backed by Lord Silkin, had tabled a further amendment to propose allowing peers who succeeded before the Act came into force a window of 12 months, instead of six, to disclaim their peerages.

Although Philip Swinton had left the Cabinet in April 1955, he remained an influential and active figure in the Lords, often consulted by senior Conservatives, including Macmillan, who valued his impartial judgement. In August, Macmillan stayed with Swinton in Yorkshire for three days' shooting; it was during this holiday that Swinton persuaded him not to retire. Tim Bligh's letter to Macmillan on 4 July had pointed out the disadvantages for Hailsham of not making the changes with immediate effect, as the Opposition had wanted. Now a Conservative peer was the one who paved the way for the Opposition amendment. Swinton was the enabler and 'front man' for Salisbury, but it was Dilhorne, prompted by Lord Poole and Tim Bligh on behalf of Macmillan, who had alerted him to what was needed.

On 16 July 1963, the House of Lords voted by 105 votes to 25 in favour of Swinton's amendment, which now had the air of a cross-bench measure. With memories of the conflicts of the past and a desire to see the issue settled, the Cabinet, although Macleod still had reservations, accepted the Lords' amendment and the Bill became law on 31 July. The two peers possibly in line for the premiership now had until 31 July 1964 to decide whether to disclaim their titles and become 'Mr Hogg' and 'Mr Home'. Mollie Butler, Rab Butler's wife, was in no doubt about the implications. She felt that Rab, like Mercutio in *Romeo and Juliet*, had received a wound 'not so deep as a well, nor so wide as a church door, but 'tis enough, 'twill serve.'[13]

After the embarrassments and dramas surrounding Vassall and Profumo, Macmillan greatly looked forward to President Kennedy's stay at Birch Grove.[14] The visit took place on 29–30 June and proved to be the last time the two leaders saw one another. In later years, Macmillan looked back on these few days with much emotion and could not recall them without his eyes misting over. It was like a country house weekend. The whole area was in celebratory mood. Schoolchildren were invited to line the drive down from the main gate to the house. CND protestors were in evidence on the road outside with banners demanding an end to nuclear tests. In the light of the Moscow talks on that very issue, Macmillan felt their presence seemed unnecessary.

Kennedy arrived in Sussex following his successful visit to Berlin, where he had declared to enthusiastic crowds, 'Ich bin ein Berliner.'[15]

From Germany he had gone on to Ireland, before diverting by helicopter to Chatsworth, where he visited his sister's grave at Edensor. As a result, his arrival at Birch Grove was delayed, but it was the only hitch of the 24-hour visit. Generous presents were given and received. Kennedy gave Lady Dorothy a gold dressing table, embossed with her initials. So vast were the numbers of police, advisers and press that hotels were booked for miles around. J. M. Keynes, a good Sussex man in his later days, would have approved of the multiplier effect on the county's local economy. Maurice Macmillan housed David Ormsby-Gore and some of the American support team at Pooks, his house on the Birch Grove estate. The main house accommodated Kennedy and his security team, Dean Rusk, McGeorge Bundy and Alec Home.

Although Macmillan in his memoirs stressed the garden party atmosphere, there were also important, and sometimes difficult, talks. Kennedy put forward further American views on the Multilateral Force (MLF) that had been discussed at Nassau. Macmillan had never enthused about the MLF, at that stage a rather nebulous idea of a European naval task force, manned by Europeans but controlled by America. 'Do you really expect our chaps to share their grog with the Turks?' he had said to George Ball, the Under-Secretary of State. He knew the MLF downgraded Britain's global position, putting her on a level with France and Germany, even, heaven forbid, the Benelux countries. The Test Ban talks were Macmillan's priority.

Hailsham was briefed by the Americans on the forthcoming talks in Moscow, but the tone of the discussions made it clear that Averell Harriman was regarded by the Americans as the key player, with Hailsham filling a supporting role. Other British figures, Peter Thorneycroft, Duncan Sandys and Ted Heath, also attended some of the meetings, but the core of the visit was the face-to-face talks between Macmillan and Kennedy. As a result, many 'attendant lords' were left twiddling their thumbs.

A press conference was held, largely to involve the huge numbers of officials who had been sidelined until then. As the main issues on the Multilateral Force and the Test Ban talks had already been covered in private meetings, Macmillan and Kennedy decided to discuss the future of NATO. Kennedy, largely to fill the time, mooted the possibility of the future commander of NATO being a British, Canadian, French or Italian officer. 'Or perhaps a Russian?' suggested Macmillan impishly. Joining in the spirit of the moment, Kennedy solemnly added, 'Mr Prime Minister, I think that is a proposition that needs much serious discussion.'

On the Sunday morning, Sir Philip de Zulueta, a Catholic, took

Kennedy to Mass at Forest Row. Kennedy left by helicopter after lunch, never to see Macmillan again. The meeting, their seventh, was a sad one in other respects. Their parting was one of great emotion. Macmillan had been shocked to see Kennedy's physical appearance. He was in pain from his war wounds, and a rocking chair (costing £3) had to be hurriedly acquired. Kennedy, already briefed by David Bruce, saw a Prime Minister suffering from wounds from an even earlier war, tired, older; and he doubted whether Macmillan would last the year.

Of all their meetings, the Birch Grove visit of June 1963 was the most relaxed socially, but the most unproductive politically.

However, as Macmillan had hoped, Kennedy's visit improved his poll ratings. On 2 August the *Daily Mail* reported that the Tories were 6 per cent behind Labour; two weeks earlier, the figure had been 20 per cent. The Test Ban Treaty talks gave out hopes of even further improvement. On 12 July, Macmillan saw Averell Harriman in London on his way to Moscow. He was greatly impressed by Harriman's grasp of the details and the soundness of his views on France and Germany. The Moscow talks began on 15 July. Hailsham sent reports on the almost daily changes in Khrushchev's position on such things as internal inspections within Soviet territory. On 25 July, after many alarums, the ship finally reached port: an agreement had been achieved. Macmillan made a statement to a packed House of Commons at 11 p.m. It was the last substantive achievement of his premiership and a fitting one on which to end. The signing of the treaty was fixed for 5 August.

After a lengthy period when nothing had seemed to go right for Macmillan and his administration, the Test Ban Treaty was a welcome and important change in fortune. It paved the way for later developments such as the Non-Proliferation Treaty of 1968 and the Strategic Arms Limitation treaties of the 1980s.

Cheered by the success of the talks, Macmillan began to reconsider retirement. The opinion polls improved in the wake of the news from Moscow, while the lack of an agreed successor encouraged him to stay on.

On 2 August, David Ormsby-Gore brought President Kennedy up to date with the change in plan: 'The Prime Minister is in such a state of euphoria after the Test Ban agreement that Alec [Home] doubts whether he now has any intention of retiring. This may lead to trouble as an overwhelming majority of the Conservatives in Parliament are convinced he should make way for a younger man in the shape of Reggie Maudling this autumn.'[16]

Ormsby-Gore was right about Macmillan's change of plan, but his belief that Maudling would be the likely successor was no longer so certain. The Peerage Bill had become law two days earlier. Parliament had adjourned for the summer on 2 August and was not due to assemble again until 24 October for Prorogation, prior to the Queen's Speech. Maudling was not in the news to the same extent as at the time of his Budget.

On 8 August, a new sensational story took over the front pages: the Great Train Robbery in Buckinghamshire. During the night, a Royal Mail train from Glasgow was targeted by a team of 15 thieves in a highly organised logistical operation. As it was just after a Bank Holiday weekend, the carriages were unusually full of valuables. Overall 120 bags were stolen, yielding in bank notes alone £2.6m.[17] Despite the fact that the driver, Jack Mills, received grievous injuries from an axe handle, preventing him from ever working again, the robbery evoked admiration for the skill with which it had been planned.

Two days before the Great Train Robbery, Macmillan, accompanied by Lady Dorothy, had set off for a 'working' holiday to Finland and Sweden. He had not been in Finland since the days of the 'Winter War' in 1940. Although exhausted by the travelling, he enjoyed seeing the country again, its vast lakes and beauty. In Stockholm, Alec Home, hotfoot from Moscow, joined him on the Swedish part of the tour. He told the Swedish Cabinet about the Moscow agreement and the optimistic atmosphere surrounding the signing ceremonies. Macmillan returned from Scandinavia on 13 August. Two days later, he lunched with Alec Home at Dorneywood, the Foreign Secretary's country residence, and spent most of the afternoon discussing strategy for the autumn. He then went on to Bolton Abbey for his annual shooting party with the Devonshires, before visiting Philip Swinton in Yorkshire for a further three days. For the first time for a long while, he was able to relax and put aside the pressing political problems of the day.

On his return south, Macmillan spent much of September at Chequers, reading and relaxing before the arduous autumn programme. Oliver Poole kept him in touch. 'There has never been a time when political and lobby correspondents have found it so easy to find both members of the Government and back benchers ready to talk to them,' Poole wrote on 28 August. 'The Profumo affair was the incident which released these emotions.' Whatever unfolded in the autumn, Poole emphasised that it was 'important that the opinion of back benchers should not seem to have been ignored'.[18]

Macmillan received the Denning Report on the Profumo affair on 17 September. Although public interest focused on sections with lurid titles such as 'The Man in a Mask' and 'The Man without a Head', MPs were more concerned with Part Three: 'Where Lies the Responsibility?' The security services were exonerated. 'I do not think they should be found at fault,' Denning concluded.[19] The police were criticised for not taking a full statement from Christine Keeler on 1 February, hardly a hanging offence. Ministers did not escape completely scot-free. In the final paragraph, Denning pointed out that Profumo's conduct had created 'a *reasonable belief* that he had committed adultery'. This was not a matter for the security forces or the police, he said. 'It was the responsibility of the Prime Minister and his colleagues, and of them only, to deal with this situation: and they did not succeeed in doing so.'[20]

Some of the newspapers tried to claim that Denning had blamed Macmillan. But the scandal, in truth, was no longer headline news. Macmillan, as intended, had stayed in office to see through the publication of the report. Now he was free to work out the details of his exit strategy, if indeed he did decide to retire after all. During the next four weeks he was constantly changing his mind.

On 11 September, Macmillan had a long talk with Rab Butler. He knew that Butler was dreading yet another rejection after Macmillan stood down. Macmillan then saw Home who was distressed at the prospect of Macmillan's retirement, as he feared that 'there will be complete disunity in the party and that great troubles will follow'.[21] Meanwhile, Macmillan kept the Queen fully informed of his intentions at all stages, aware that a lot of the responsibility, and possible blame, would devolve on the monarch if there was a contested and difficult succession. He wrote to the Queen on 5 September saying he had not yet decided on whether to stay or go. However, at his audience on 20 September, he said he would be announcing at the party conference his intention to step down in January. On Monday, 30 September, Philip Swinton lunched with Macmillan at Chequers and spent four hours alone with him. Macmillan told Swinton that he had decided, after all, to retire, and that he thought Hailsham would be the best successor, a view he was also to communicate to Hailsham.[22]

Macmillan moved back into Downing Street on 2 October, the hurdle of the Denning Report now successfully behind him. Although Admiralty House had been more spacious, he was glad to be back among familiar historic surroundings.

As the party conference in Blackpool neared, he began to get messages telling him that he must stay on, to avoid the blood-letting that might follow. The last Cabinet meeting before Blackpool was scheduled for 8 October. Macmillan knew he had to make a decision by then. On 6 October, he discussed the situation with his son Maurice, whose links with back-bench feeling were closer than Macmillan's own. Macmillan told Maurice that he was moving towards the idea of staying for another two to three years. Maurice felt that, although a fourth successive victory would be difficult to achieve, the peace and prosperity that the government had brought Britain gave it a fair chance. Dining with Alec Home that evening, Macmillan confessed to having second thoughts: he was anxious lest the interval between an announcement on 12 October and eventual retirement in January left him as a lame-duck premier.[23]

On 7 October, the eve of the crucial Cabinet, Tim Bligh told Macmillan that Cabinet opinion was now in favour of his staying. At 5.30 p.m., Oliver Poole called. Macmillan outlined his fear that he would be seen to be deserting the ship, which could have a damaging effect on crucial marginals, also that he would appear to be quitting following pressure by the discontents. Inevitably, the subsequent succession battle would be highly divisive. After dinner, he was joined by Dilhorne, Butler, Home and Sandys. Their discussion chewed over the same points. Macmillan went to bed, having firmly decided to carry on.

The best-laid plans, though, do not survive what Macmillan called the stroke of fate. During the night of 7–8 October, Macmillan was laid low by prostate trouble.

Much has been made of the fact that Sir John Richardson, Macmillan's doctor, was on holiday when the medical emergency arose. Things were in fact smoothly handled. Lady Dorothy summoned Dr Lionel King-Lewis,[24] who was at Downing Street by 5 a.m. King-Lewis consulted Richardson by telephone. Richardson recommended that Alec Badenoch, the foremost consultant urologist in the country, should be summoned.

By the time Richardson reached Downing Street at 4.45 p.m. on 8 October, Macmillan had been examined, and given initial treatment and relief, and as a result, had felt sufficiently recovered to hold a Cabinet meeting (his last ever) at 10 a.m.

The Cabinet meeting went on for three hours, but Macmillan, in great pain, twice had to withdraw. In one of the intervals, Lord Dilhorne said that if the situation required it, he would offer himself, as he was not a candidate, to sound Cabinet opinion on the leadership.

Home followed suit, disclaiming interest in the succession and offering his services.*

When Macmillan, who had only the night before telephoned the Queen's Assistant Private Secretary, Sir Edward Ford,[25] to say that he intended to continue in office, returned for the second time to Cabinet, looking much the worse for wear, Lord Hailsham said 'Prime Minister, wherever you go, you know that our hearts go with you.' Enoch Powell, in his account of the events, observed 'I had never heard a more effective *coup de grâce*.'[26]

After the fraught Cabinet, there followed a medical consultation between Sir John Richardson, Alec Badenoch and Dr King-Lewis. 'My tasks, as they appeared to me,' Richardson recorded, 'were to get him into the frame of mind where he would agree not to go to Blackpool, and would plan for the future on the supposition that he was going to have an operation more or less immediately. After some discussion he accepted these ideas...The Prime Minister was beginning to feel that the hand of Providence was working and that "man proposes and God disposes".'[27] Alec Badenoch's son, David Badenoch, also a consultant urologist, has written a memorandum for the historical record, based on conversations with his late father.[28] It was decided that Macmillan should be admitted to King Edward VII Hospital for Officers 'in order to undergo surgery to the prostate to relieve the obstruction causing his urinary retention'.

Astonishingly, Macmillan summoned up the strength at 8 p.m. to attend a cocktail party for the staff of 10 Downing Street to celebrate their return to the building after its refurbishment. At this party he told Butler and Home privately that he would have to stand down. They were the only Cabinet ministers to be told at this stage. Butler wanted to know whether in that case he should take responsibility for delivering the closing speech at the conference on Saturday, 12 October. Macmillan said it was a problem he would have to think over. At 9 p.m. he was driven to the hospital. The BBC announced at 9.41 that Macmillan would undergo an operation for prostatic obstruction. 'It is expected that this will involve his absence from official duties for some weeks and he has asked the First Secretary, Mr R. A.

---

*Home's intervention was, not unnaturally, to be the cause of controversy. Enoch Powell considered it a firm pledge, which Home abandoned when pressure was put on him to stand for leader. As a result, Home 'ran' initially, in Powell's opinion, as an 'undeclared' candidate, not subject to the scrutiny to which his rivals were being ruthlessly exposed. It was one of the reasons Powell refused to serve in Home's Cabinet, a decision which contributed to the Conservatives' narrow defeat at the October 1964 general election.

Four Tory Chancellors

Peter Thorneycroft (*above*); Derick Heathcoat
Amory (*above right*); Selwyn Lloyd (*below*);
Reginald Maudling (*right*).

The visit of the American President in August 1959: Eisenhower arriving at St Paul's Cathedral with Macmillan. Pre-election publicity was rarely so successful.

Lord Home as Foreign Secretary, 1960. 'Steel painted as wood' was how Harold Macmillan described Home to the Queen, 'the old governing class at its best'.

Major Geoffrey Hoare, High Sheriff of Essex, announces the figures at Billericay, the first constituency to declare, just before 10 p.m. on 8 October 1959. When Hugh Gaitskell, the Labour leader, heard the result, he said to his aides: 'We've lost by a hundred seats.'

Harold Macmillan after hearing his own result in his Bromley constituency, 9 October 1959.

Macmillan reviewing the First King's African Rifles in Lusaka at the start of his African tour, 22 January 1960.

Khrushchev, the Cold War Warrior. 'How can this man really be the head – the aspirant Tsar – of all these millions of people?' wondered Macmillan.

'Of course, it would have been far worse if they'd sent the dog.' Macmillan welcomes the first man in space, Yuri Gagarin, to Admiralty House, July 1961.

'United we stand.' Charles de Gaulle and Konrad Adenauer at a demonstration in favour of European union. Bonn, 9 May 1962.

One of Macmillan's 'discoveries', novelist Muriel Spark, outside the offices of Macmillan & Co. in St Martin's Street in 1961.

Affairs of state in 1963: Mandy Rice-Davies and Christine Keeler.

Seeing beyond the trees: President Kennedy with Harold Macmillan at Birch Grove, 30 June 1963. It was the last time the two leaders met.

The Queen and the Duke of Edinburgh with Jacqueline Kennedy and her children and Lord Harlech (David Ormsby-Gore) at the dedication of the British memorial to President Kennedy at Runnymede, 14 May 1965. Jacqueline Kennedy was so deeply moved by Macmillan's tribute that she was unable to deliver her own speech.

Old men remember:
Macmillan and Tito years after the
controversies of Venezia Giulia.

Macmillan with his son Maurice
in the summer house at Birch Grove.

Macmillan at an Encaenia as Chancellor
of Oxford University. Successive grandsons
from Balliol acted as his train-bearer,
in this case David Faber.

Butler, to take charge of the government while he is away.' There was no indication of any imminent resignation.

The following day, 9 October, an early edition of London's *Evening Standard* carried the headline: TORIES ON THE BOIL: CRISIS OVER THE LEADERSHIP HEADS FOR SHOWDOWN.[29] It did indeed. When the news broke that Macmillan was in hospital, many senior Conservatives began ringing the Buckingham Palace switchboard.*

First in the field was Sir Charles Mott-Radclyffe, MP for Windsor and vice-chairman of the 1922 Committee, who rang from his home in Norfolk to say that Rab Butler could not conceivably be chosen. Other MPs rang with equally strong views they wished to communicate, setting out why Hailsham, Maudling and – even as early as 9 October – Home should not be candidates. Interestingly, those who rang were all expressing negative choices. No recommendations were offered as to who should be preferred.[30]

The same day, 9 October, Butler travelled to Blackpool and promptly moved into the Prime Minister's suite (Room 127) at the Imperial Hotel, where he went into immediate consultation with Iain Macleod and Lord Poole. It was obviously in Butler's interests to be seen as the leader-in-waiting. The decision that he should give the final rallying speech, was, however, to rebound on him.

In Blackpool, Macleod was now under the mistaken impression that the message he had received from Philip Woodfield, one of Macmillan's secretaries in Downing Street, during the evening of 8 October, had been a sign that he was in the special confidence of the Prime Minister, whereas in fact he had been told the developing news in his capacity as joint party chairman. When further 'special' messages failed to arrive, this added to Macleod's sense of discontent, although it was not the methodology of selecting a successor he eventually objected to, but the result.

Until 1963, Blackpool had always been a 'lucky' venue for the Conservative Party Conference. The annual conference had been held there in 1950, 1954 and 1958; in each instance the year following had seen a Conservative election victory. The 1963 conference changed this perception for ever, and Rab Butler, for one, could never visit the Lancashire resort again.[31] From the start of the week, when a young holidaymaker was tragically drowned in the sea opposite the Imperial Hotel, the whole affair seemed jinxed.

---

*The numbers of Sir Michael Adeane, the Queen's Private Secretary, and the two assistant private secretaries, Sir Martin Charteris and Sir Edward Ford, were not ex-directory.

*

Home remained in London at the hub of events, unlike Butler, now at one remove in Blackpool. During the morning of 9 October, Home was with Macmillan considering the timing of the announcement that Macmillan would not be leading the party into the next election. If the resignation was announced during the conference, it could be seen to favour Hailsham, a darling of the constituency associations since his high-profile chairmanship of the party in the late 1950s, and his recent prominence at the Test Ban talks in Moscow. Nor would it be disadvantageous to Home, highly regarded by party activists. On the other hand, if the announcement was delayed until Parliament reassembled, it would favour Butler and Maudling, the leading candidates in the Commons. Home urged Macmillan to put an end to the already feverish speculation.

Butler, meanwhile, was clearly apprehensive about the way things were moving, for he rang Tim Bligh to tell him to remind the Prime Minister that the proceedings at Blackpool were a rally and one did not take a serious decision at a rally. He therefore hoped that all references to the future leadership would now be put on hold until Parliament reassembled, a shrewd assessment of the dangers to his prospects if the conference became the equivalent of an American nominating convention.

Macmillan decided that news of his intention overrode these considerations. Tim Bligh and Sir Knox Cunningham now began preparing a letter for Home to read out at the conference.* While it was being drafted and typed, Macmillan turned to Home's own position. Why should Home not make himself available? He was a senior and respected figure, attracted (as yet) no animosity, and the Peerage Act, combined with an impending by-election at Kinross and West Perthshire, afforded him his opportunity and a speedy return to the Commons. Such a suggestion was not new, nor had Home himself discounted the possibility.†

Once the letter announcing Macmillan's impending retirement had been drafted and checked, Home flew to Blackpool. On that day *The*

---

*As that year's President of the National Union of Conservative Associations, a fortuitous coincidence that contributed to the eventual outcome, Home was ideally placed to be the bearer of a message from the Prime Minister. Butler's supporters later felt this placed Home too much in the conference spotlight and that the letter should have been read out by Butler as Deputy Prime Minister.

†What was interesting was Macmillan's timing, *preceding* Hailsham's melodramatic announcement of his intention to disclaim (the action generally accepted as ending his candidature at the very moment it began) suggesting that Macmillan already felt that Hailsham might not stay the course.

Times first mentioned Home's name as a possible fourth candidate (in addition to Butler, Hailsham and Maudling). When Home arrived at the Tower Ballroom, where the main sessions were held, John Boyd-Carpenter was in the midst of a reply on Local Government Finance, and, to the obvious impatience of delegates, Home's speech was delayed. After half an hour, he finally came to the microphone. The audience was hushed.

Home explained that he had come from the Prime Minister's hospital bedside that morning (here was a man at the heart of events was the immediate impression) and that he had been asked to read out the Prime Minister's letter 'as soon as I could after arriving at Blackpool'. The operative part of Macmillan's message was unequivocal: 'It is now clear that, whatever might have been my previous feelings, it will not be possible for me to carry the physical burden of leading the Party at the next General Election...In these circumstances I hope that it will soon be possible for the customary processes of consultation to be carried on within the party about its future leadership.'[32] The problem was that there were no customary processes.

After a period of jockeying, the starting gun had now been fired for the race ahead. First out of the blocks was Lord Hailsham. Randolph Churchill, his counterproductive cheer-leader, had already arrived at Blackpool hotfoot from America, like some latter-day Chaucerian Pardoner, dispensing 'Q' for Quintin buttons, which he pinned on every available jacket lapel, including at one stage Rab Butler's. Hailsham, meanwhile, was alienating delegates in a different way. He appeared in public in the lobby of the Imperial Hotel with his infant daughter Kate (goddaughter of Harold Macmillan), whom he fed from her bottle.* Another misjudgement followed. At the end of a fringe meeting that evening, Hailsham said 'I wish to say tonight that it is my intention after deep thought to disclaim my peerage.' In scenes that some hostile critics later distastefully compared to a Nuremberg rally, his remaining words were lost in the general enthusiasm – enthusiasm not shared by the platform party. 'Martin Redmayne, Chief Whip, stony and prefectorial, clearly not best pleased,' Dennis Walters, MP for Westbury, and one of Hailsham's main aides, wrote in his diary, 'Michael Fraser rather embarrassed.'[34]

Macmillan was soon apprised of developments at Blackpool. He

---

*Edward Heath was appalled. 'Never discount the baby food,' he said, 'as a factor in disqualifying Hailsham.'[33] For many Conservatives of that generation, the proper person to be dispensing such nourishment was the nanny – and in private.

grasped that the combination of events had been fatal to Hailsham's chances of success. It would have been far better if Hailsham had followed Talleyrand's precept – not too much zeal. The Americans, especially Averell Harriman, had been very irritated by Hailsham's legalistic nit-picking over the final drafts of the Test Ban Agreement. Gromyko had been similarly umimpressed by Hailsham's emphasis at one crucial stage on the importance of 'the indefinite article in English'.[35] Washington, briefed by David Bruce from London of Macmillan's impending demise, was aghast at the prospect of a Hailsham premiership.

The pivotal figure in steering grass-roots opinion towards Home at Blackpool was Selwyn Lloyd. Following his sacking in the Night of the Long Knives in July 1962, Lloyd had not withdrawn Achilles-like into his tent, but had skilfully rehabilitated himself with the rank and file by travelling the country in the worst winter since 1947 to produce his report on the party organisation. As a result, many of these party workers, agents, volunteers and constituency chairmen were prepared to listen to what he had to say about the leadership. Lloyd also had influence with Martin Redmayne, the Chief Whip.

It was a powerful combination. Lloyd quietly spread the claims of the Foreign Secretary. By 11 October, the Lord Chancellor, Lord Dilhorne, the Chief Whip, and the party's senior back-benchers were all firmly in Home's camp. That day, Dilhorne, Lloyd and Redmayne went for a walk along the sea front to discuss the next stage.* Here they were accosted by a Labour-voting old-age pensioner, who told them that his Socialist household recognised in Home the qualities needed to lead the nation. Lloyd later recalled that this pensioner represented 'the gnarled voice of truth'.[36]

The same day, 11 October, Home's speech to the conference, on Foreign Affairs, was rapturously received. Nigel Birch pronounced to all and sundry after the speech, 'I'm an Alec Home man. There aren't any other possibilities. He's *going* to get it.'[37] If Home's stock was rising, just as Hailsham's was fading, the position of Butler and Maudling was more indeterminate. Neither was a great orator, certainly not in the bear-pit of the party conference. Both still faced the hurdle of the beauty contest of making conference speeches; both, for different reasons, failed to impress.

Maudling's speech was more suited to a Treasury planning meeting

---

* The private walk in the open air reminded Lloyd of similar outdoor talks he had had with Macmillan when they were in Russia in 1959, away from prying bugging devices.

than an excitable conference. 'Our plans for education, housing and overseas aid will lay a heavy burden on the Exchequer' was not a statement to raise the temperature among delegates wanting to take the battle to Labour. On *That Was the Week That Was*, Bernard Levin declared: 'if not the dullest speech in history, it would do until the dullest was made'.[38]

Butler's speech was sadder still. The executive of the National Union, not Macmillan, had decided that Butler should, after all, deliver the closing speech at the final rally on 12 October. It proved to be a poisoned chalice. Before the afternoon speech Alec and Elizabeth Home had lunched with Rab and Mollie Butler at the Imperial Hotel. During the lunch, Home dropped a bombshell. He casually mentioned that he was seeing his doctor in London the next week. Surprisingly, Butler did not immediately grasp the significance of the remark and asked him why. 'Because I have been approached about the possibility of my becoming the leader of the Conservative party,' replied Home.[39] Stunned and devastated, Butler unsurprisingly failed to rouse the Tories.

Macmillan's operation took place at 11.30 a.m. on Thursday 10 October. The David Badenoch memorandum reads:

> So as to avoid any likelihood of complications arising during the surgery, as had occurred during the operation on Anthony Eden, AWB [Alec Badenoch] had two experienced and skilled urological surgeons assisting, David (later Sir David) Innes Williams and Joseph Smith. Harold Macmillan underwent surgery to his large benign prostate by open retropubic enucleation of the prostate.

The key detail here is that Macmillan's condition was *benign*. He knew this before his decision to resign. It is incorrect to state, as so often, that Macmillan, in the initial absence of Sir John Richardson, believed that the condition was malignant, and that he resigned prematurely only to regret this decision ever after. The Badenoch memorandum continues:

> By the time of the resignation, the histology of the prostate was known to be benign – a fact that was discussed with Macmillan well before his resignation. At no time was Macmillan led to believe that he had a cancer of the prostate by AWB, and even if he had a cancer, it would not have been a cause on its own to resign from office with immediate effect.

For Macmillan, the sudden affliction resolved all the conflicting emotions and doubts he had experienced about his future. Although he had decided on 7 October to stay on, it was a decision conditioned mainly by his wish to delay a damaging succession battle. In his heart, he knew that his time was complete. His illness provided him with the perfect opportunity to retire with good grace, not pushed out by 'Profumo' or the dissidents within his own party.

It was clear to AWB and his team [the Badenoch memorandum continues] that Macmillan used his acute illness as a vehicle for resignation in order to extricate himself from an increasingly difficult political position after the Profumo scandal following which there had been persistent speculation in parliament and the press as to a change of leadership. He (Macmillan) stated to AWB that the illness 'came as manna from heaven – an act of God'.[40]

David Badenoch wrote to *The Times* on 12 January 1994 about Macmillan's resignation, pointing out that 'the histology of the prostate showed benign hyperplasia and Macmillan was aware of this fact'. Far from believing he had cancer, Macmillan 'expressed great relief that he had reason to leave the political crises which he had faced'.[41]

Although the operation was a success, Macmillan stayed in hospital afterwards for an unusually long time, even for the 1960s, not owing to any post-operative medical complications, but so that he could be secluded from the bustle of Downing Street, and receive Cabinet ministers and other figures in privacy, as the succession battle was joined. Lady Dorothy was meant to be the only visitor allowed over the weekend, but in fact Macmillan needed to speak to Dilhorne, Home and Swinton.

He began formally receiving visitors at the King Edward VII Hospital on Monday, 14 October. Lord Home and Tim Bligh arrived at 10.45 a.m. Home gave Macmillan first-hand accounts of the events in Blackpool, with Tim Bligh taking notes. Aware that controversy would be inevitable, however things worked out, Macmillan now ensured that everything was recorded, so that copies could be kept in the Royal Archives and his own papers. The initial part of the leadership battle had been played out in public in Blackpool, full of sound and fury; the second and decisive part, which now followed in London, was conducted in private meetings, at the hospital and in ministers' houses, notably Enoch Powell's in South Eaton Place.

Also on 14 October, Macmillan prepared a memorandum for

Butler, his deputy, outlining a formal way of assessing opinion. His recommendation was that Lord Dilhorne should poll the Cabinet; the Chief Whip should sound out the opinion of members of the House of Commons, including ministers not in the Cabinet; Lord St Aldwyn, Chief Whip in the House of Lords, should canvass peers taking the whip, including junior ministers; and the joint party chairman Lord Poole,[42] Mrs Shepherd, Chairman of the National Union of Conservative Associations in 1963, and Lord Chelmer, Chairman of the Executive Committee of the National Union, should sound out the constituency parties. Much of the latter work had already been conducted in Blackpool the previous week, but Macmillan wanted to set down the complete process for the record.

The Cabinet was to accept this proposal unanimously at its meeting on Tuesday, 15 October. In practice, this procedure was a more formalised version of the process that had taken place in January 1957 when Macmillan was chosen to succeeed Eden. As then, all sections of the party had their opportunity to make their views known. Yet, as Francis Bacon once observed, 'It is hard in all causes when voices shall be numbered but not weighed.'[43]

Another indication that the leadership contest was approaching its resolution had came on Monday, 14 October, when the Queen returned from Balmoral to London. On the same day, Sir Michael Adeane, the Queen's Private Secretary, saw Elizabeth Home, without her husband's knowledge, to discuss the situation. Adeane wanted to know, in confidence, if Alec Home would accept the premiership were he invited to form, or try to form, a government. Elizabeth Home told him that if the situation demanded it, Home would serve.[44] Adeane went on to visit Lord Swinton at his London flat after dinner that evening. Swinton told him that his two preferences were Rab Butler as Prime Minister with Alec Home staying as Foreign Secretary; or the reverse, with Home as Prime Minister and Butler taking his place at the Foreign Office. Philip Swinton had already discussed this scenario with Macmillan in two telephone calls on the Sunday and Monday evenings.[45] Macmillan had also consulted Anthony Eden, now Earl of Avon, whose preferences, in order, were Hailsham, Butler and then Home.

Tuesday 15 October was to prove a pivotal day. The key members of the Cabinet visited Macmillan individually at the King Edward VII Hospital. Rab Butler went in first, at 10 a.m., before the crucial Cabinet. He agreed with the four-way process for assessing party opinion. In the afternoon, after the Cabinet, Macmillan was visited successively by Home, Maudling, Macleod, Hailsham and Heath. Home told him that the Cabinet had unanimously agreed to the four-way method of canvassing party opinion. From 10.30 p.m. to 11.20 p.m., Tim Bligh took notes from Macmillan on each interview. The first draft of a detailed account for the Queen was also prepared. This 'Tuesday Memorandum', as it became known, to distinguish it from the final document, the 'Thursday memorandum', was aptly described by Professor Peter Hennessy as 'one of those richly revealing, thinking aloud, deeply personal historical fragments which will be referred to any time a scholar wishes to visit the demise of the Macmillan premiership'.[46]

The tone of the 'Tuesday Memorandum' is one of perceptive elegance, the Macmillan style *par excellence*. 'Had he been of another generation, he would have been of the Grenadiers and the 1914 heroes,' Macmillan wrote of Home. One of Home's key qualities, according to Macmillan, was the ability to think about the question under discussion and not about himself. 'It is thinking about themselves that is really the curse of the younger generation – they appear to have no other subject that interests them at all and all their books, poems, dramas and all the rest of it are almost entirely confined to this curious introspective attitude towards life, the result no doubt of two wars and a dying faith.'[47]

The most important information Macmillan noted down in his records on 15 October came from Home himself. 'David Ormsby-Gore had rung up in a great state,' he told Macmillan, 'to say that if Lord Hailsham was made Prime Minister this would be a tremendous blow to Anglo-American relations and would in fact end the special relationship.'[48] It was clear to Macmillan that the choice would be between Home and Maudling.

It is often thought that, following Lord Hailsham's scenes at Blackpool, Macmillan 'switched peers' and devoted all his energies to securing the succession for Lord Home. Things were not as straightforward. Macmillan certainly had no doubts that Hailsham had 'put himself out of court by his stupid behaviour in the foyer of the Imperial Hotel at Blackpool'.[49] He also believed that Butler's campaign would never get off the ground. The fact that Macmillan discounted Butler as his successor, for which he has been forever criticised, was a perfectly legitimate opinion for him to hold, and one shared by many people at all levels of the party. It was equally legitimate for figures such as Enoch Powell and Iain Macleod to take exactly the opposite view. Difficult choices are part of the bloodstream of politics.

The question, as so often in Conservative leadership struggles, was not how many people were for you, but how many were against you. Rab Butler was cursed with too many figures resolutely opposed to his candidacy; after Blackpool, Hailsham joined him in the same boat. A few days earlier, Macmillan had suggested to Lord Dilhorne that he might consider becoming a candidate, a scenario that John Morrison had also advocated, telling Dilhorne not to discount his own candidature as a dark-horse peer.[50] Dilhorne had discussed the issue with Macmillan, before deciding that his proper part in events should be as a sounder of Cabinet opinions, a task he now fulfilled, in Butler's words, 'like a large Clumber spaniel sniffing the bottoms of the hedgerows'.[51]

Although he was not the senior Private Secretary at Buckingham Palace, the courtier who was to become the pivotal figure was Sir Edward Ford. In October 1963, he became the conduit between Buckingham Palace and the King Edward VII Hospital. There was later criticism, particularly from Enoch Powell, that it was constitutionally wrong for Macmillan to discuss the identity of his possible successor with the Queen when he was no longer formally Prime Minister. Macmillan was, in fact, responding throughout to a direct request from the Palace. Sir Edward Ford had made it very clear to him that the Queen would be seeking his advice. The Palace was well aware from the start that the process of transition would be a complex, contentious matter. There were too many possible candidates for it to be otherwise. Losers would become unpredictable loose cannons.

Unlike the situation in 1923 and 1957, the Palace knew that the monarch would be placed in a nigh-impossible position, having to decide between seven, even in some scenarios, eight, candidates. In both 1957 and 1963, the Queen acted not on the basis of her personal views, but on the views of the Tory Party. In 1963, it was no longer a direct choice between 'Wab or Hawold?', as Lord Salisbury had described the options to the Cabinet in January 1957. It was now Wab or Hailsham or Heath or Home or Macleod (certainly in Macleod's mind) or Maudling or Powell or Dilhorne. The situation was unprecedented, and, after later internal party organisational changes, unrepeatable. Macmillan has often been blamed for ending the Royal Prerogative. It was the Palace that conceded this prerogative, by establishing the 'you choose, we send for' formula. If Macmillan had washed his hands of the whole business, as Bonar Law had done in May 1923, it would have been a recipe for chaos. Pleading inanition on his part was not an option. The monarch wanted not guidance, but one name only. He had to deliver.

Contingency plans were already in place for the processes to be followed constitutionally if, and when, Macmillan resigned. On 16 June, just before the Profumo debate in the Commons, Alec Home had written to Macmillan, first to wish him well, but, more importantly, to let him know that he had recently discussed with Sir Michael Adeane, at Adeane's request, what should happen if the government was defeated. Home's advice to Adeane was that it was vital to keep the monarch out of any ensuing controversy over the succession. Thus was formulated the process of 'you choose, we send for'. It was agreed that the monarch would in due course take no part in discussing the merits of the various candidates, would express no preference, but would stay above the internal party controversies by summoning the person whose name was presented to the Palace by the Conservative Party. This was conceding an important principle, but the alternative would drag the monarch into internal party politics.

In 1957, as in 1923, the monarch had been faced with a choice between two candidates (Macmillan and Butler, and Baldwin and Curzon respectively). Advice was taken extensively, but, in both instances, the monarch decided the outcome. After October 1963, that prerogative in effect no longer operated, especially after the Conservatives adopted a formal electoral process in July 1965, as the Labour Party had already done.

Professor Ben Pimlott has asserted that the Queen was culpable in 1963. 'Her decision to opt for passivity,' he wrote, 'and in effect to collude with Macmillan's scheme for blocking the deputy premier, must be counted the biggest political misjudgement of her reign.'[52] Leaving aside the question of whether Macmillan did indeed have such a scheme (he had no need to 'block the deputy premier', as Butler was highly unlikely to be chosen), if the Queen had subsequently become more deeply involved in the process, she would have been inexorably drawn into internal party politics, which would have been the real misjudgment.'[53]

The monarch's permanence and legitimacy stem from being above politics, staying aloof from the often murky and grubby activities of transient parliamentarians. Had the Queen started involving herself in October 1963 in discussing the relative merits of the contradictory views of, say, Sir Charles Mott-Radclyffe and Iain Macleod, she would at once have stepped irretrievably over the dividing line between the dignified and the efficient. With Macmillan in hospital, Sir Edward Ford now dusted down, so to speak, the 'you choose, we send for' arrangement.

*

The October 1963 battle for the Conservative leadership succession had two unique features. First, it occurred during a party conference, which was soon transformed into the equivalent of an American nominating convention. Second, the extra-parliamentary rank and file were actively involved throughout, had access to ministers and were canvassed for their views by the system put into place.

In 1911, when Balfour resigned the leadership, the party grandees moved to ensure that constituency representatives at the party conference, about to take place on 16 November in Leeds, should not have a role in the decision. Lord Balcarres, the Conservative Chief Whip, thought a prompt ballot among Unionist MPs would solve the problem. Walter Long, one of the candidates, protested that there was 'nothing so undignified as a ballot for the leadership', thus pre-empting Lord Aldington by 52 years. The problem in 1911 was that, in addition to Long, there were two further candidates, Austen Chamberlain and Bonar Law. Some form of alternative vote thus seemed unavoidable. Balcarres then decided to take 'soundings' (what Macmillan may have recalled when he talked of the 'customary processes'). It soon became clear that neither Long or Chamberlain would command a majority, and so both were persuaded to stand down in favour of Bonar Law.

The 1963 leadership contest mirrored that of 1911 in several, but by no means all, respects. Rab Butler was the Austen Chamberlain, always playing the game and always losing it. Lord Hailsham was the Walter Long, of whom Austen Chamberlain said, 'if he could always have three drives off the tee, he might do very well, for his third shot was generally a good one, but the first two went here and there all over the place'.[54] Both had enemies who were opposed to their selection at any price, as was true of Chamberlain and Long in 1911. So the previously unregarded candidates, Bonar Law (1911) and Alec Home (1963), emerged as the compromise winners.

'Great leaders of parties are not elected, they are evolved,' declared Captain Ernest Pretyman, MP for Chelmsford, in 1921, remembering the events surrounding Bonar Law's emergence 10 years earlier. 'It will be a bad day for this or any party – to have solemnly to elect a leader. The leader is there and we all know it when he is there.'[55] The system Macmillan set in train in October 1963 was because the Conservative Party in October 1963 did *not* know where their leader was.

In the course of the subsequent consultation process, MPs were initially asked three questions. The first was for their preferred outright choice to succeed Macmillan; then their second choice; finally, the name of anyone they would oppose.[56] As in many Conservative leadership battles, the principle of negative choice was to prove vital.[57]

Who was *against* a candidate was to be more significant in determining the final result than who was *in favour*. As Hailsham fell from the race as a serious contender after Blackpool, a fourth question was then added, asking for views on Home. This process Professor Vernon Bogdanor has aptly described as 'guided democracy'.[58]

On Wednesday, 16 October, Macmillan's day began with a visit from Philip de Zulueta at 10.30 a.m. From then until 5 p.m. he saw Cabinet ministers. Those ministers who were not in London were rung up for their views. Significantly, Macmillan sent for Selwyn Lloyd, who went in at 12.30 p.m. They discussed the events of the last few months and the performances of Butler and Hailsham; it was clear to both men that neither of these two would be the next Prime Minister. Lloyd's preference was for Home. In the corridor outside Macmillan's hospital room, Lloyd was more forthright with Tim Bligh, knowing his views would get back to Macmillan. He told Bligh frankly that, from his experience over the previous year going round the constituencies for his party report, he knew there was strong opposition to Butler among many party workers and, for some reason, particularly among women. Both Butler and Hailsham would have a substantial number of opponents. Home would be the unity, compromise candidate, a latter-day Bonar Law. Lloyd concluded by telling Bligh that he also thought the Opposition in the House of Commons would find Home far more formidable when he got there than they now expected.[59]

Not all senior figures felt likewise. Reginald Bevins had thought it a joke when Redmayne had asked him for his views on Home, and when assured it was not, declared that if Home became leader, the Tories would never win a seat in Liverpool, where he was MP for the Toxteth division.[60] Supporters of Butler and Hailsham always felt that the whips pressed too hard the supplementary question about Home, inviting the response they wanted.[61]

Another Cabinet minister at the hospital, Duncan Sandys, was also firmly in favour of Home, not as a compromise between two undoubtedly deadlocked figures, Butler and Hailsham, but on his own merits. Macmillan's final visitor of the day was Edward Heath, who told him that the party had won in 1955 and 1959 with the moderate vote, and that Hailsham would not be attractive to that vote. Butler, in Heath's opinion, ought by now to have justified his claim to the leadership, but the fact was that he had not and he would be an uninspiring leader. The only way to prevent a split was by drafting Alec Home.

Of Macmillan's other visitors that day, none ruled out Home completely, which was not the case with Butler and Hailsham. Peter

Thorneycroft was for Butler or Hailsham, but if party unity was overriding, then the choice should be Home. Edward Boyle was for Butler, or perhaps Home, who would attract the moderate, wavering votes more than Hailsham. Afterwards Boyle felt he had been too enthusiastic about Home (Butler was his definite preferred option) and he told Tim Bligh this. Bligh wrote an account of this conversation and gave it to Macmillan. Christopher Soames felt that Hailsham would not attract the wavering vote, even though the public did not see Hailsham as a peer in the same way as they did Home. Interestingly, Macmillan felt the same regarding Hailsham, whom he described as a 'temporary gentleman', rather like officers in the Great War promoted from the ranks.[62] The main priority for Soames, though, was to pick someone who could unite the party. Home could do this, but not Hailsham. Rab Butler was not even mentioned. John Hare was for Home. Henry Brooke nominated Rab as his first choice, then Home. Keith Joseph was for Butler, with Home in his team as Foreign Secretary; if Butler was not acceptable, Joseph was against Hailsham and preferred a shift to the next generation. Macleod and Hailsham did not express a preference, as both considered themselves candidates. Macmillan felt that Hailsham was not conscious of how he had lost ground by his behaviour at Blackpool.

By the end of the day, Macmillan was clear that Home was the candidate most generally acceptable, largely because he was the only one not (at that stage) *un*acceptable. He noted that Maudling had hardly featured at all in the preferences.

On Thursday, 17 October, the decision was finally taken for Home. Sir Knox Cunningham recorded details of all the conversations Macmillan had that day, on 17 closely filled sheets of Basildon Bond writing paper.[63] Rab Butler was Macmillan's first visitor, but the discussion was on government business, not the leadership. Butler was followed, in separate groups, by the four canvassers of party opinion: Lord Poole, joint party chairman, and the party officials Lord Chelmer and Mrs Shepherd at 10.48 a.m.; Lord Dilhorne, the Lord Chancellor, at 11.00; John Morrison, chairman of the 1922 Committee, at 11.33; Martin Redmayne, the Chief Whip, at 11.42; and Lord St Aldwyn, Chief Whip in the Lords, at 12.07. Finally, before lunch, Macmillan saw another former Cabinet Minister, James Stuart, who was unequivocally in favour of Home, his Minister of State at the Scottish Office in the early 1950s.

Poole and the two party officials reported that the more one got away from Westminster, the greater was Hailsham's support, adding the caveat that many in the constituencies had not realised at Blackpool that Home was a possible candidate. Lord St Aldwyn said that peers were two to one in favour of Home, with Butler in second place. Martin Redmayne reported that Home and Butler were front-runners, with Hailsham third and Maudling a 'bad fourth'. His figures were: Home 87 first choices, Butler 86, Hailsham 65, Maudling 48, Macleod 12 and Heath 10. However, he reported that 'when one came on to the second choices, Home had much the best of it'. Home also had the lowest number of 'definite aversions'. Ultimately, this preponderance of second choices was decisive, as it had been for Bonar Law in 1911.

The most controversial evidence was Lord Dilhorne's list of the Cabinet's first preferences, a source criticised and disputed ever since. According to Dilhorne's record, ten Cabinet ministers had Home as their first choice (and this did not include Macmillan or Home, who did not vote), four were for Maudling, three for Butler and two for Hailsham. The exact figure for Maudling on the original sheet of paper was changed by Dilhorne, initially from three to five, and then (in Philip de Zulueta's handwriting) from five to four. Those choosing Home as their first alternative preference, according to Dilhorne, included Iain Macleod; the others were Boyle, Deedes, Dilhorne, Hare, Heath, Marples, Noble, Sandys and Soames.

The main controversy has been over Macleod's inclusion in the list of Home supporters, whereas the question mark should have been over Boyle, whose first preference had been for Butler, with Home as a (distant) second choice. Macmillan had Tim Bligh's note about Boyle's 'back-tracking' from his position of 'over-enthusiasm' for Home. Clearly, Dilhorne did not.

Boyle was a supporter of Butler. His vote was incorrectly allocated. But had his vote been given to Butler, as it should have been, it would not have made any material difference. The importance of the error was not mathematical, but in the doubt it cast over the legitimacy of the whole exercise. If Dilhorne had got Boyle wrong, where else could he not be trusted? Supporters of Butler were in no doubt that Macleod's listed preference for Home was incorrect. Sir Ian Gilmour even publicly asserted that Dilhorne had deliberately falsified the Cabinet's views.[64]

Macleod is clearly recorded as voting for Home, but Dilhorne did not get this wrong, nor, apart from Boyle, any others. Macleod was playing a double game of tactical voting, well in character. His hope was for a complete deadlock, which would favour him as a second, and preferred, compromise candidate when the first compromise candidate aroused opposition. Nigel Lawson, like Macleod a future editor of the *Spectator* and Chancellor of the Exchequer, and at the time a political adviser to Harold Macmillan, has written a penetrating account of Macleod's part in the succession crisis. 'I have little doubt,' he declared, 'that Dilhorne got it right, and that Macleod did indeed vote for Home.' This was confirmed to Lawson by Philip Woodfield, one of Macmillan's secretarial team, who spoke to Lawson of 'Macleod's vote for Home as recorded in the Dilhorne document' and 'was in no doubt as to its accuracy'. Butler also was not surprised when he was told of the Dilhorne figures. 'Macleod was very shifty, much more than you think,' he commented.[65] Tory grandees had always felt this instinctively, most famously Lord Salisbury, when he declared that Macleod was 'too clever by half'.[66]

On this occasion Macleod played his hand badly. 'His game plan was essentially to support Home in order to stop not only Hailsham but Butler as well, and then, when Home decided that he was not prepared to take on the job after all, to allow his own name to go forward to break the deadlock,' Lawson wrote. 'Hence his crucial vote for Home in the Dilhorne soundings, and hence his fury, and public support for Butler – as belated as it was public – when he realised that he had been too clever by three-quarters.'

Nor was this the end of the damage Macleod did to the Conservative party that autumn. Lawson's verdict is blisteringly accurate. 'His petulant refusal to serve under Home and the extended explanation he gave for it both deprived the government of its most effective political street fighter and undermined the new prime minister's legitimacy.'[67] Macleod's 'extended explanation' came in a review he wrote in the *Spectator* of Randolph Churchill's book *The Fight for the Tory Leadership*, which he described as 'Mr Macmillan's trailer for the screenplay of his memoirs'.[68] Both Macmillan and Hailsham had helped Randolph Churchill over his book, which was a partial account of the leadership struggle. Macleod's review, full of inaccuracies, countered one partial view by presenting a different partial one. The ensuing row led to colleagues cutting Macleod in the House and finished forever his chance of becoming Tory leader.

The most perceptive account of the Macleod article came from Robert McKenzie:

The tenor of Macleod's article curiously suggests that he assumed that the *first* choices of the Cabinet Ministers would (and should) be of decisive importance. Martin Redmayne emphasised, however, that those conducting the operation were seeking what might be called 'the highest common factor' of agreement. On this basis, even if Home did not have the largest number of first choices among ministers [which in fact he did], he might, if he had overwhelming 'second-choice' strength (and faced little outright hostility), be considered to have the 'strongest' Cabinet backing. Macleod also seems to have been greatly surprised and exasperated that during the decisive period of the enquiries the Cabinet did not meet (presumably to arrive at a collective judgment as to who should succeed to the leadership). With no less than six of its members possible contenders for the succession – including its presiding officer, R. A. Butler – this would have been not only an unprecedented, but very probably an unworkable, procedure. After more than a decade in the Cabinet Macleod appears to have forgotten that on the occasion of the choice of a new leader it is the machinery of *party* and not of *government* which takes precedence.[69]

Home always believed that the Macleod article was the single most important factor in denying the Conservatives victory in October 1964 in the closest election contest for over half a century. He knew that much of what Macleod asserted was plainly wrong, but one point worried him above all. Macleod said that by choosing Home from the Lords, the party had admitted it was unable to find a candidate in the Commons. Home asked Macmillan for his advice on how to deal with this issue if it arose during the election. Macmillan's reply was pungent. Home should point out that the world of journalism had been unable to find a new editor of the *Spectator* from among its own ranks, but had resorted to choosing Iain Macleod.[70]

After lunch on 17 October, Lord St Aldwyn, Lord Dilhorne, Lord Poole and Martin Redmayne met Macmillan in his room to finalise the recommendation for the Queen. Knox Cunningham kept detailed notes of all that was discussed. Macmillan stressed that he was a collector of views, adding that a good argument for a man was not just that he had no enemies; it might also mean that he had no character. He also wanted to know if Maudling would appeal to those voters he called 'the Orpingtonians'. Poole felt Maudling would represent 'that class of person' better than Home. Macmillan went on to ask about Hailsham. How did he stand in the north-east? In a curiously lateral response, Redmayne said that Home had more widespread support in the country, including the north-east, than might be thought. Macmillan remained cautious. It would all be a tremendous gamble, he said. The key thing was for the new Prime Minister to dominate the House of Commons. Dilhorne reckoned that Home's reputation as

Foreign Secretary made him a bigger figure than Hailsham. Macmillan agreed that Home had dominated party committees more than anyone he had known. At that moment Knox Cunningham knew the decision would be for Home. Macmillan, anticipating trouble, added that it was vital for the Cabinet to unite behind whoever was chosen. There must be no bickering. His thoughts were very much for the Queen.[71] The Palace wanted a clear recommendation and an end to the matter.

Drawing the meeting to a close, Macmillan said that he would now prepare a second and final memorandum, relating what he had been told. On 15 October, he had written to the Queen, stating, 'I am anxious that everything done so far should be amply recorded in writing and not give rise to the kind of confusion by which previous crises have afterwards been poisoned with very ill effects to all concerned.'[72] His aim throughout was to protect the Queen from controversy. He would prepare his resignation, and as he was unable to go to the Palace to resign, he anticipated that the monarch would visit him, as Edward VII had called on Campbell-Bannerman during his final illness in Downing Street in March 1908 to bid farewell to his Prime Minister. A new, updated memorandum would be ready for the Queen by 10.30 a.m. on the Friday morning, 18 October.

Macmillan then asked that the news be discreetly disseminated. 'It will be terrible for Rab,' he said. Poole said that Rab Butler knew he had no real chance, but the rejection would be painful nevertheless. Macmillan asked to be put through to Home on the telephone. The three vital matters to be settled were Hailsham, the chancellorship and the Foreign Secretaryship, an implicit assumption that Hailsham would not be offered either of these great offices of state. Macmillan said he was not keen for Rab to be given the Foreign Secretaryship. It would please Rab, but there were too many ongoing initiatives which Rab would not grasp. Macmillan, however, accepted it might be the price of Butler agreeing to serve. The obvious figure, to his mind, to be Foreign Secretary was Ted Heath. Dilhorne felt a lot of difficulty could be avoided if Hailsham could be persuaded to stay on in the Lords and abandon his impetuous decision to disclaim his peerage. When Home was put through on the telephone, Macmillan told him he would formally be recommending his name to the Queen as his successor. The meeting had lasted for 56 minutes, and had brought to an end a chapter in British political history.[73]

The news spread with a rapidity that only the Westminster village can manage. As Macmillan had feared, there was immediate dissent. The famous 'midnight meeting' at Enoch Powell's South Eaton Place home was convened, attended by Powell, Macleod, Maudling, Erroll and Lord Aldington.[74] Selwyn Lloyd and Martin Redmayne were also later summoned by Powell. Redmayne was asked to tell Macmillan later that morning (Friday had already dawned) of the objections to the recommendation of Home. Surrounded by the balloons and streamers of his daughter's birthday party in the upstairs drawing room at South Eaton Place, Powell presided over a group whose fervent hope was that Rab would now hold out and deny the premiership to Home. 'For becoming a Prime Minister a man must be ready to shoot it out,' Powell later remarked.[75] Powell presented Butler with the loaded revolver, but Butler would not pull the trigger. Too much weight has been given to Powell's point. If Butler did not have sufficient support, as was manifest, was there any trigger to pull? And had he failed to serve, he would have seemed merely a bad loser, a spoiler.

Meanwhile, Macmillan was writing his final, revised 'Thursday Memorandum' for the Queen, a document he always regretted not printing in full as an appendix to his final volume of memoirs, *At the End of the Day*.[76] The 'Thursday Memorandum' begins with a factual account of the procedures adopted since 14 October for canvassing opinion throughout the party, both at Westminster and in the country. It then outlines all the information Macmillan had received and sets out a clear recommendation for Lord Home, adding that if the Queen made this choice, she would incur no blame and would be held to have chosen a man generally backed by all the various sections to whom a Prime Minister must look for the support of his administration, particularly as regards foreign affairs. Macmillan then covered what might be called the 'small print'. Lord Home would have to seek election to the House of Commons. As he was a Knight of the Thistle, he would in future be known as Sir Alec Douglas-Home, Alec being a well-known diminutive in Scotland.

Macmillan knew that the Palace wanted *one* name. Faced with the evidence that was provided by all wings of the party, the only possible single-option recommendation, enabling the Palace to avoid involvement, was Lord Home. 'The outcome, the selection of Lord Home cannot be said to have seriously misrepresented Conservative opinion at the time,' Vernon Bogdanor has written. 'Macmillan was widely criticized for foisting Lord Home on an unwilling party. Yet it is doubtful if criticism of Macmillan is justified. He lacked both the means and the will to secure the premiership for Home against the wishes of the party as a whole. He was unable to impose his first choice, Lord Hailsham, and he could not have secured the succession of Home had the latter not genuinely enjoyed the confidence of the party.'[77] In the end, Rab Butler, blocked by the 1922 Committee in the summer, confirmed Home as Prime Minister, by agreeing to serve as Foreign Secretary.

The next morning, Redmayne gave Macmillan details of the 'midnight meeting' at South Eaton Place, but, as Knox Cunningham recorded, 'the Prime Minister was firm and Tim [Bligh] set out for the Palace carrying the letter of resignation'. Macmillan and Knox Cunningham then prepared an addendum for the Queen, covering the overnight happenings, so that the monarch would be up to date with the current situation.[78] In this postscript Macmillan recalled the offer of the premiership to Lord Aberdeen by Queen Victoria at Osborne House on 18 December 1852. Aberdeen had only kissed hands the following day, on securing the agreement of Lord John Russell, whom he regarded as an essential buttress of his administration, to serve as Foreign Secretary. Macmillan advised that Lord Home should similarly be invited to sound out first the *possibilities* of forming a government. If he failed in this attempt, a frequent occurrence in Victorian times, then the Queen could entrust the commission to other hands and no censure would attach itself to the Palace.

The Queen arrived at the King Edward VII Hospital at 11 a.m.[79] on Friday, 18 October for the last act of Macmillan's premiership. Macmillan had put on a silk shirt and saw the Queen in a downstairs room, his legs covered by a rug.[80] The Queen stayed for 40 minutes while Macmillan read out the memorandum. This third and final draft shows him toning down his earlier criticisms of Hailsham, particularly his being 'impulsive, even arrogant', and is notably even-handed, putting the pros and cons of all the candidates. Like Hercule Poirot disentangling a mystery, Macmillan went through the names of all the suspects, before picking out the one least expected.

The Queen agreed that Lord Home was the candidate most likely to command general support, but asked about the implications of the midnight meeting. (Telephone calls had also been made to the Palace, as on the first night of the crisis, notably by Dennis Walters of the Hailsham camp, complaining about the methods employed and the outcome.) Macmillan said that the significance of the midnight meeting would be tested if and when Lord Home attempted to form a government. The Queen agreed to summon Lord Home to the Palace. As she left the hospital, the memorandum was placed in a huge white envelope and given to Sir Michael Adeane, a scene that reminded Knox Cunningham of Tenniel's drawing of the Frog Footman in *Alice in Wonderland*.[81]

Lord Home arrived at the Palace at 12.30 pm, after which a statement was issued: 'The Queen has received the Earl of Home in audience and invited him to form an administration.' Home said he would attempt to do so and would return to tell the Queen the outcome of talks with his colleagues. The initiative, though, was his, as the *locum tenens*. 'He has got the loaves and the fishes,' said Lord Beaverbrook, the master-mind behind Bonar Law becoming leader of the Conservative Party in November 1911. 'There is no stopping him now.'[82] Nor, despite the refusal of both Macleod and Powell to serve, was there any stopping Home. At 2.45 p.m., he saw Butler, who initially reserved his position. If Butler had intended to pull the trigger of the loaded revolver, this was the moment, but it was not in his nature. He called to mind all the splits in the party at the time of Peel and the Corn Laws, and had no wish to see the process repeated. 'I don't know what's happening,' he had said to Sir Freddie Bishop, as he had sat alone at the Cabinet table on 16 October after the meeting that day, adding, 'but I do really.' When Bishop asked him what he would do if the outcome was as he feared, Butler replied, 'I shall behave with dignity.'[83]

A crucial meeting followed at 3.15 p.m., when Home saw Reginald Maudling, who was also initially non-committal. Home said that if Maudling was holding out in the hope that Rab Butler would become Prime Minister, he was mistaken. If Home failed to form an adminis-tration, the task would fall to Maudling himself. (Home later came to believe that he could have formed an administration without Butler, but not without Maudling.)[84] Meetings continued for the rest of the day.

Late in the evening there was a quadrilateral meeting between Home, Hailsham, Butler and Maudling, at which Hailsham agreed to serve. This proved the breach in the dyke. The next morning Maudling said he would continue as Chancellor and Butler agreed to become Foreign Secretary, the post he had so wanted in January 1957. So Butler became only the second politician to have held the three great offices of state, Chancellor of the Exchequer, Home Secretary, and Foreign Secretary. Chequers, though, was never his. Poignantly, its postal address is Butlers Cross.[85]

Just as Eisenhower and Dulles had later felt that they had been wrong over their attitude to Britain over Suez, so Macmillan and Home both came in time to think that it might have been better if Rab Butler had become Prime Minister in 1963. Home acknowledged that the public had seen Butler as the heir apparent, and anyone else was seen in some sense as an 'unnatural' successor. The controversies had done the Tories immense damage, yet it was largely self-inflicted, for the mass of the party would not have had Butler at any price. Macmillan's sudden illness had come at exactly the wrong moment, on the eve of the conference. 'With benefit of hindsight, I think that it was a mistake to try to obtain views during the hurly burly of that Blackpool conference,' Dilhorne later admitted. 'It should have been done when things were calmer and people had more time for reflection.'[86]

Macmillan soon had it made clear that he was no longer Prime Minister. With almost indecent haste, Post Office engineers were disconnecting the scrambler telephone in his hospital room. He had been Prime Minister for six years and 281 days. Of these days, the last ten had been the most painful of all. His papers show that he felt the controversy intensely and resented the way he was, and continually has been, misrepresented. 'The press has tried to represent that Alec Home was my personal choice,' he wrote to John Morrison on the day Home became Prime Minister. 'You know well the immense trouble I took to get the views of the Cabinet, the House of Commons, the House of Lords and the Conservative Party generally. I think if you can help to get this about among members it will do a lot of good. I was not really anything more than a convenient recipient of this information, and the means by which this advice could be given to the Queen.'[87] Knox Cunningham, who was at Macmillan's side throughout, always took pains to stress how unfairly Macmillan had been treated by history. 'You are well aware,' he wrote to the author in 1975, 'that it is thought that Harold Macmillan made a personal recommendation of his successor in 1963 with a view to preventing Rab from becoming Prime Minister. This is not true. Recently a reference to this occurred in the Press (one can never kill a story such as this) and Harold Macmillan asked me to give him a note of events. This I did and the enclosed memo. refers to two passages in his sixth volume *At the End of the Day* and my unpublished book *One Man Dog*. I told him about your book [*The Uncrowned Prime Ministers*] and he suggested that I should send you the enclosed document for information.'[88]

In 1964, Knox Cunningham attended the Quatercentenary production of the *Wars of the Roses*, the cycle of Shakespeare's history plays, in Stratford-upon-Avon, John Profumo's former constituency, as he noted.[89] 'All in all it was a good school in the art and practice of treachery', he wrote to Macmillan of the production, adding 'and not very different from Westminster in 1963!'[90] The treachery was not Macmillan's.

CHAPTER THIRTY

Leaving the Green Room
1963–1986

I've known every Prime Minister to a greater or lesser extent
since Balfour, and most of them have died unhappy.

Lord Hailsham, 1997[1]

'Let me not live', quoth he,
'After my flame lacks oil, to be the snuff
Of younger spirits.'

Shakespeare, *All's Well That Ends Well*, I, ii, 58–60

Father Time is not always a hard parent, and, though he tarries
for none of his children, often lays his hand lightly upon those
who have used him well; making them old men and women
inexorably enough, but leaving their hearts and spirits young
and in full vigour.

Charles Dickens, *Barnaby Rudge*

Harold Macmillan's premiership was one of the most significant and
eventful of the twentieth century. His tenure was similar in length to
that of Clement Attlee (who served for six years and three months),
longer than that of Lloyd George, but shorter than Asquith, Baldwin,
Churchill, Wilson or Thatcher. As with Attlee, his period in office was
in one continuous spell, punctuated by a general election.

'I am convinced that it is essential to have a cumulative period of
office of at least five years,' Roy Jenkins has written, 'in order to rank
as a Prime Minister of major impact.'[2] Although this stern judgement
may be questioned over Balfour and Heath, and, conversely, may be
untrue about some who have served more than five years, Macmillan
clearly qualifies as being in the front rank. For six years he defined his
age. Opponents reacted to his agenda. Only towards the end of his
time in Downing Street did the new Labour leader, Harold Wilson,
make the political weather.

Domestically, Macmillan was the Prime Minister who presided over
the transition from austerity, the age of fish and Cripps as he called it,

to a widespread affluence, which he feared people took too much for granted. He knew how quickly such prosperity could wither on the vine. Much of the new prosperity, he knew, was owing to the economic cycle, but it still needed careful shepherding. On the world stage, even more importantly, the Macmillan era was one of reappraisal of Britain's global role. The retreat from Empire, its pace disguised from the more antediluvian Tories, was managed as humanely as any such retreat in history.

For much of his time Macmillan resembled a successful Napoleonic general who rode his luck. This made the reversal when it came the more dramatic and painful. More important for him in the long run than economic success was keeping the Conservative Party on progressive lines. Despite his aristocratic connections, he was never an old-style Tory. He had contempt for many of his back-benchers, some of whom felt he was never a Tory at all. His experience as an MP was not with the county, rural voter; in his two constituencies he represented the industrial working class and the suburban lower-middle and middle class: in short, the mass of Britain. Echoing Disraeli's objective, Macmillan wrote in 1971 of his relationship with the Conservative Party, 'I succeeded in making it a national party, covering a very wide range of classes, interests and individuals.'[3]

'He was throughout his long political career,' Derek Walker-Smith, one of Macmillan's long-serving ministers, has written, 'at his most impressive and convincing when speaking to smaller and somewhat rarified gatherings, where his great intellectual quality and the challenge of his evocative reasoning had their greatest impact.'[4] Some of this flavour came over in his many television interviews, notably the ruminative ones with Robert McKenzie over the publication of successive volumes of his memoirs.

Macmillan's life after Downing Street was multi-layered. Part of this was owing to the unexpectedly lengthy time afforded him, of 23 years and 72 days, almost exactly one quarter of his life. Among prime ministers, only James Callaghan has lived to a greater age. What distinguished Macmillan's 'retirement' was the variety of his activities. He remained a lonely figure inwardly, though not a loner, and he needed to busy himself to keep the black dog at bay.

'It has always seemed to me more artistic when the curtain falls on the last perfomance to accept the inevitable *E finita la commedia*,' he wrote. 'It is tempting, perhaps, but unrewarding to hang about the green room after final retirement from the stage.'[5] He was being teasingly disingenuous. The lure of the greasepaint proved too much.

He did leave the green room from time to time, but only for the main stage itself. The controversies that had accompanied his active political career did not diminish. In some respects they even increased, for he had firm views on the way Britain was going and, particularly during Margaret Thatcher's premiership, was not reluctant to express them. The fact that these views were usually in coded form did not diminish their force or cogency.

Gladstone, referring to Peel after 1846, said that 'Former Prime Ministers are like untethered rafts drifting around harbours – a menace to shipping.'[6] Rosebery, who survived his own Downing Street days by 34 years, believed that ex-prime ministers, if invited to serve again in Cabinet, always proved to be 'a fleeting and dangerous luxury'.[7]

The first priority in the weeks after Macmillan's resignation was a successful recuperation. As Alec Badenoch made clear to his patient, all would be well within a few weeks. So it proved, physically. Some of the mental scars of the aftermath of October 1963 took longer to heal. Yet by 31 October, Macmillan was back at work at Macmillan & Co. in St. Martin's Street, once more a publisher. In addition, he was soon active in advising and encouraging his successor in Downing Street, Alec Home.

One of the key questions for Home was the timing of the general election. Macmillan was clear that Home should play it long. They met on 26 March 1964 to discuss the options. Macmillan then sent Home a lengthy memorandum, setting out the reasons for choosing October. Much of his advice was influenced by his memories of 1959:

Date of Election. I am coming more and more a partisan for October and for the following reasons:

a) The party has been thoroughly upset by R. P. M. [Retail Price Maintenance].[8]

b) Since the Bill cannot be carried till the middle of May, this confusion will injuriously affect a June election.

c) It is always an advantage to an Opposition to have Parliament in session. It is therefore an advantage to the government to have an interval between the end of parliament and the election. This was proved in 1959.

d) The decision will ultimately be on almost Presidential lines. Therefore, the longer Wilson has to become i) a bore ii) mistrusted as a crook, the better.

e) After a summer holiday, the mood of the people is better. It was in 1959.

Against this is the argument 'You are hanging on to the bitter end etc.' But I think you could meet this (at least to some extent) by a clear and simple statement of intentions in April.[9]

This advice was important, as Lord Blakenham,[10] the new party chairman, who had replaced Lord Poole and Iain Macleod, was a firm advocate of a spring election in 1964, which led to him being dubbed 'the March Hare' at Conservative Central Office.[11] Home duly decided on an autumn election and announced the fact, again on Macmillan's advice, before the results of the Greater London Council elections on 9 April, correctly anticipated to be bad for the government. Macmillan told Home that he would not be standing for Parliament again. He had no desire to emulate the embarrassingly long sunset of Churchill in the House.

To the surprise of many, though not those who knew him best, in April 1964 Macmillan turned down the offer of both an earldom and the Garter.[12] The only honour he coveted was the Order of Merit, which, like the Garter, was in the personal gift of the sovereign and limited to 24 recipients at any one time. Having turned down the Garter for a second time, he was awarded the Order of Merit (the 134th person to be so honoured) on 2 April 1976. 'Thank you ma'am,' he wrote to the Queen, 'for making an old man happy.'[13] He preferred to be in the company of Henry James and Thomas Hardy than to be an aristocrat, however elevated, in the peerage.

Installed in his office at Macmillan & Co., Macmillan had two priorities: modernisation of the family publishing house, and writing his memoirs. He took over the chairmanship of the business in 1963 from his brother Daniel, who died in December 1965. He held this position till 1974, when he assumed the role of president, which he held until his own death. Those in St Martin's Street were soon aware that 'Mr Harold' was a sharp observer of all aspects of the business, and that change could be expected.[14]

Macmillan was entering a world very different from that he had last known in 1951. An under-used ground-floor room, overlooking the National Gallery, was converted into a table-tennis room, very popular during the lunchtime break. Once, as Macmillan was going out to lunch, he looked quizzically through the window at the scene of merriment. At a routine board meeting later that afternoon, he said ruminatively, 'You know, they sell very good curtains at Harvey Nichols.'[15]

The memoirs, originally planned, and advertised, to be in three volumes, as Anthony Eden's had been, eventually ran to six, as Churchill's war memoirs had done. Three reasons contributed to this decision. First, once Macmillan had surmounted the difficulties of the structure of the first volume, a comprehensive survey of European history from 1914 to 1939, he found that writing was absorbing, even therapeutic, work. 'I am beginning to be a little frightened by the magnitude of the task,'[16] he had written in his diary at the outset. He had dedicated help, particularly from David Dilks, who had worked with Eden on his memoirs. 'If I can get Mr. Dilks to help me, I shall be very lucky.'[17]

Second, Macmillan had a multiplicity of primary material to hand, stretching back to Great War days, in the form of letters, journals and diaries. The muniment room at Birch Grove was crammed with boxes containing this archive.[18] Third, there was no editor at Macmillan brave enough to curb the chairman's prolixity and take the blue pencil to the project.

Jack Kennedy was assassinated in Dallas on 22 November 1963. The events of that terrible day were forever etched in Macmillan's memory. He was profoundly affected by the tragedy, as though it had been the closest of family bereavements. The fact that the two leaders had so recently met made the sudden news the more painful and poignant. There was no question of Macmillan being able to appear on television, as George Brown, deputy Labour leader, was to do, clearly the worse for wear, that Friday evening. On the Monday, though, he had recovered his composure and saw it as his duty to pay tribute to Kennedy in the House of Commons. A stillness settled over the Chamber as Macmillan spoke of the fallen President and 'the sudden and cruel extinction of a shining light'.[19]

Macmillan's correspondence with Jackie Kennedy was to be one of the most touching of his latter years, and he made a point each year of writing to the President's widow, so that his message of comfort would reach her for the anniversary. At midnight on 31 January 1964, on the eve of moving out of the White House, Jackie Kennedy wrote a heartfelt letter to Macmillan. 'The two greatest men of our time – you and Jack', she wrote. 'How marvellous you were with him ... he always kept in his office a picture of you.' Macmillan, who had suffered so much in his own long life, saw himself as a lightning conductor for Jackie Kennedy's grief, and he encouraged her to write whenever she felt she wanted to unburden herself. In reply to her last White House letter, he wrote simply, 'May God bless you, my dear child. You have shown the most wonderful courage to the outer world. The hard thing is really to find it *inside*.'[20] In one of the last letters that Jackie Kennedy (by then Jackie Onassis) wrote to Macmillan, she recalled how his letter of condolence in November 1963 had been like a life-raft for her.[21]

Macmillan helped to sustain and support Jackie Kennedy at Runnymede on 14 May 1965 when the Queen inaugurated the national memorial for President Kennedy on historic British soil, bequeathed in perpetuity to the American people. Jack's brothers, Robert and Edward, were also present, as well as David Ormsby-Gore, now Lord Harlech. Macmillan's speech, the first of the afternoon, in which he spoke of 'that grim day nearly two years ago when we heard the news', moved Jackie Kennedy so much she was unable to deliver her own speech, in which she had intended to refer to John Buchan's tribute to Raymond Asquith – 'he loved his youth, and his youth has become eternal'.[22]

Three years later Macmillan had to comfort the Kennedy family again, when Robert Kennedy was assassinated in June 1968 in Los Angeles, whilst campaigning for the presidency. He also broadcast to the nation about Robert Kennedy, and this touched such a chord with the British people that he received one of the biggest correspondences ever from the public.[23]

The various contracts for his memoirs were signed in time for Macmillan to pen the first lines of what was to total in the end nearly three million words on 4 August 1964. It was the fiftieth anniversary of the outbreak of the Great War, which had so defined his life and those of his contemporaries. 'I should very much dislike anybody writing a book about me while I am alive,' Macmillan had written to Quentin Crewe in 1957. 'When I am dead nobody will want to.'[24] Yet he was under no illusions. When Sir Roy Harrod, Keynes' official biographer of 1951, complained in 1969 in the most vigorous terms about Macmillan's plans to commission a new life of Keynes, Macmillan pointed out the incontrovertible truth about such prominent public figures: 'People will continue to write new books about him and nothing will prevent this.'[25]

Macmillan accepted his 'fate' in a speech at Gray's Inn in December 1968. 'I read books, I have published books; I have even written books,' he told the assembled benchers. 'I suppose some day somebody might even write a book about me.'[26] Before that happened, Macmillan, like Churchill, wanted to set down his own version of events.

The six volumes of the Macmillan memoirs, appearing at regular intervals between 1966 and 1973, received a muted welcome. The general opinion was that they were 'heavy going'. Yet the first and last volumes were best-sellers, and much publicity attended the television interviews with Robert McKenzie. The middle four volumes were steady, rather than sensational, sellers and this militated against a paperback release.[27] One response from Rab Butler was characteristically biting. In the preface to his own well-received memoirs, *The Art of the Possible*, Butler wrote, 'I have eschewed the current autobiographical fondness for multi-volume histories, and have preferred a single book which is not too heavy for anyone to hold up and doze over in bed.'[28] Memories of 1963 were still sharp. What Macmillan could have said by way of response was that he did at least write his books himself. Much of Butler's elegant single volume was actually written by Peter Goldman.[29]

Winds of Change (1966), the title taken from Macmillan's famous 1960 Cape Town speech, was the most accomplished of the six volumes, a classic account of an important transitional period. It was also the book that appealed most to a non-specialist audience. The events were near enough in time for many of the readers to have lived through them. Nostalgia for a vanished age was evoked, yet with a perceptive understanding of how things had to change, the underlying paradox of Macmillan's whole career.

'*La douceur de la vie*' that Talleyrand had praised in pre-revolutionary France was brilliantly evoked by Macmillan, particularly in his account of pre-war Oxford. The story he had to tell was a dramatic one too, focusing on two central twentieth-century issues – the Depression and appeasement. He did not indulge in false modesty. The book clearly revealed his opinion that he was 'right' on both issues.

The potential audience for Macmillan's second volume, *The Blast of War* (1967), was a narrower one. This was a work of military history and without the partisan controversies that readers had become accustomed to in the many accounts of the Second World War, notably Montgomery's memoirs of 1958. Later, when the accusations over the Cossacks were beginning, Macmillan published his *War Diaries* (1984) to put primary material into the public arena. These diaries were an important unexpurgated addition to the public debate, though some of the material was used against him. *The Blast of War* never achieved the drama and immediacy of *Winds of Change*.

Now well into his stride, and marshalling his material skilfully, Macmillan wrote one of the best accounts of the post-war Attlee and Churchill governments in *Tides of Fortune* (1969). As with the first volume, the book was essentially a history of an important transitional period in British society. The first-hand observations on Attlee's ministerial team had a piquant immediacy that was greatly revealing, and when he came to the Churchill years, Macmillan was able to give one of the most perceptive accounts of how a government actually operates, particularly in his account of 1951–1955, when he himself played an important executive part. *Tides of Fortune* is the most under-rated volume of the series.

Riding the Storm (1971), which covered Suez, suffers from a reticence that other, more candid accounts, notably Anthony Nutting's *No End of a Lesson* (1966) and Hugh Thomas' *The Suez Affair* (1966), had already superseded. Readers have to look with a hand lens between the lines in Macmillan's account to ascertain 'what really happened'. Nevertheless, he pushes the narrative on with great vigour, the drama being inherent in the events. Surprisingly, considering his disappointment at the American response, Macmillan shows himself well aware of the dilemmas that Dulles faced.

Pointing the Way (1972), which looks at the events of 1959–1961, is a work of considerable poignancy, as Macmillan was now having to address disappointment and failure, notably the 1960 Paris summit, which is vividly described. The portrait of de Gaulle, in the light of what was to unfold in January 1963, has an air of inevitable piquancy. The book remains one of the most perceptive inside stories of the pressures on an incumbent Prime Minister, as fortunes turn against him, and is far franker than the Suez volume.

At the End of the Day (1973) attracted special attention for its detailed accounts of the Cuban Missile Crisis and the October 1963 leadership situation. Since in both instances Macmillan gave a version that his critics did not want to believe, the volume was underestimated. The book matched the commercial success of *Winds of Change*. A reception was held at the Dorchester to mark the publication of the sixth volume and the completion of the series. Hugh Trevor-Roper, who had played his own part in the story, gave the first speech, concentrating on the importance of literature in Macmillan's life. Edward Heath, the Prime Minister, then paid generous tribute to the man who had done so much to set him on the path to 10 Downing Street. He was followed by Harold Wilson, shortly to be Prime Minister again himself, who in a masterly speech revealed the respect, even affection, he had for Macmillan. In the days when they faced each other over the dispatch box, Wilson said, debate was proper debate and not just a repetitious catalogue of *'prises de positions'*. His speech reminded many of the parliamentarians present of Macmillan's own techniques, on which Wilson had so assiduously modelled himself. Macmillan, chairman of his own publishing house, then concluded the proceedings. In such surroundings, and with such an audience, he was in his element, and the old actor-manager gave a vintage performance, evincing from one of his political opponents the grudging, yet admiring, remark, 'There's no ham like old ham!'[30]

Many famous actors of the day thought Macmillan had missed his vocation by not going on the stage. One such was Sir Donald Wolfit, who thought of Macmillan as a latter-day Scarlet Pimpernel, with 'the same lazy eyes, so well described by Orczy, the lazy voice – the mask which that mythical figure adopted to hide his magnificent activity and active brain'.[31]

The six books represent a remarkable achievement for a man who was nearly 80 when the final volume appeared. Often criticised as self-serving, the memoirs do in fact contain admissions of where things went wrong and mistakes were made. Apart from *Winds of Change*, they may not be books to nod over in bed, as Rab Butler delighted in pointing out, yet the series is a candid contribution to an understanding of Britain's place in the world in the twentieth century, and a vital source of primary information for students of the period.

Two years after the last volume, Macmillan published *The Past Masters* (1975), an unashamedly popular book, lavishly illustrated, aimed at the 'coffee table market'. When told by the sales department that the book had not sold particularly well in Japan, he replied, 'Well, they don't have coffee tables in Japan!'[32] Harold Wilson was to target the same market with his *A Prime Minister on Prime Ministers* (1977), in which he assessed Macmillan from his first-hand perspective as Leader of the Opposition in 1963. 'The long Macmillan tenure of 10 Downing Street had been a fascinating premiership,' he concluded. 'His opponents enjoyed his consummate style as much as did his friends. But behind the public nonchalance was the real professional.'[33]

The model for *The Past Masters* was Churchill's *Great Contemporaries*. Macmillan gave vivid sketches of the people he had known in a crowded life, particularly the key prime ministers of his time – Lloyd George, Ramsay MacDonald, Baldwin, Chamberlain and Churchill. He devoted a whole chapter to the Chamberlain family, extolling the virtues of what Joseph Chamberlain had done in Birmingham 'to improve the condition of the people'.

Improving the condition of the family publishing house also occupied Macmillan while he was working on the memoirs. Publishing, in common with other industries in the mid-1960s, was undergoing a rapid process of reappraisal. Macmillan knew that modernisation was vital for future prosperity. In 1965, he oversaw the move from St Martin's Street, selling the building and site to developers, to Little

Essex Street, rented on very advantageous terms commercially. Little Essex Street did not have the 'character' or history of the old buildings, but it made for more efficient production. Another key project in the general restructuring was a purpose-built office and warehouse in Basingstoke, where Palgrave Macmillan, an academic label, was to be based. 'Went to Basingstoke to the Macmillan building there. It is a splendid place & well designed,' Macmillan wrote in his diary, adding with prudence, 'I wish it had not cost quite so much.'[34]

Macmillan & Co.'s reputation, despite its global potential, was of a rather sleepy, albeit venerable firm, over-dependent on its valuable backlist, out of date and vulnerable. Macmillan, who had the instinctive respect of his managers in the task, set about altering such perceptions. He saw the potential of marketing paperbacks. Pan Books, initially jointly owned by Macmillan (which held 51 per cent of the equity) and Collins, regularly proved to be what Thomas Hardy had called a milk cow. Between 1973 and 1987 sales grew from £4.9 million to £26.5 million. One of the key figures among the directors was Alan Maclean,[35] whom Macmillan trusted implicitly, and of whom he had heard justifiably good reports from Maurice, whose close friend Maclean was.

One of the most discerning signings was of the novelist Muriel Spark for her first novel, *The Comforters*, in 1957. As her fame grew, Spark became dissatisfied with the marketing of her books and there were rows with Maclean, her editor. When Macmillan returned to the firm in 1963, he did much to soothe troubled feelings, as other publishers hovered for her signature. Invitations to Birch Grove followed. 'He admired her writing,' Spark's biographer has commented, 'and although she doubted whether he understood it, she found him easy, witty company.' Whether he understood the novels or not, he certainly admired them, and when *The Mandelbaum Gate* was published in 1965, he wrote to tell Spark that it 'was not only her best novel but also a great one by any standards'.[36]

Macmillan was much amused when Maclean received an urgent telex from India: PLEASE SEND AT ONCE FIFTY BOUND UNJACKETED GIRLS OF SLENDER MEANS.[37] His own telex messages, brisk and to the point, as he embraced modern technology, were reminiscent of Churchill's wartime 'Action This Day' instructions. An indication of the improved state of the company can be seen by comparing its annual sales figures. In 1963 these amounted to £12.5 million; in 1983 sales were £40 million, and rising.

Two major new projects, overseen by Macmillan as chairman, re-established and cemented the firm's reputation as a leading house.

These were the *New Grove Dictionary of Music*, 12 years in the making, published in 1980 in 20 volumes, under the editorship of Stanley Sadie, and *The Dictionary of Art*, published in 1996 after Macmillan's death in 34 volumes, under the editorship of Jane Turner. The first edition of Grove had appeared in 1886, and was frequently updated. The 1980 edition was a completely new work, and was itself regularly expanded. The second edition of the *New Grove* in 2001 ran to 29 volumes. Macmillan saw the *New Grove*, and its companion piece *The Dictionary of Art,* despite the capital risks, as noble and worthy projects, proving to any doubters that the publishing house was in the business long-term and would, as a result, be recruiting the best talent in publishing.

Macmillan travelled to New York in 1980 to help launch the *New Grove*. A spectacular party was held at the Waldorf Astoria, attended by such American musical luminaries as Leonard Bernstein and Virgil Thomson. Macmillan spoke not only at the Waldorf Astoria, but also on American breakfast television 'chat shows', a new experience for a man of 86.

Macmillan knew the importance of the long-term approach in publishing. When the copyrights of Thomas Hardy were about to expire in 1978, he arranged for the complete works to be reissued in paperback and handsome hardbacks as further protection against competition. He oversaw expansion in Africa and Asia. He was an indefatigable traveller on behalf of the firm, undertaking major tours of China, Australia, India, Nigeria, Egypt and Japan. He enjoyed China as much as anywhere. 'I know now that the Chinese are truly civilised,' he reminisced. 'They eat banquets at a sensible hour, don't hang around for long speeches and let you go home to your own whisky and soda by 9 o'clock.' On his return from China, he wrote to Nicholas Byam Shaw, who had accompanied him: 'I doubt, at my age, that I shall ever try anything of the kind again and, indeed, I was rather hesitant about attempting this journey.'[38] He was then in his mid eighties. 'He had the capacity to broaden any argument,' wrote Byam Shaw, 'to explore untapped possibilities in an otherwise ordinary proposal.'[39]

Macmillan was always rather envious of what he saw as Oxford University Press's favoured tax position. As Chancellor of Oxford University, he was once sitting next to the publisher Graham C. Greene at a publishing conference in Oxford. 'Who owns the OUP?' he asked. 'You do, sir,' replied Greene. 'Well, we should sell it,' he said, not entirely in jest.[40]

*

Although the literary establishment could be condescending towards C. P. Snow, Macmillan rated him highly, not least because of the novelist's combination of the Trollopian characteristics of narrative drive and intrigue. (Snow wrote a biography of Trollope for Macmillan & Co. in 1975.) The *Strangers and Brothers* series began in 1940 and the sequence occupied Snow for 30 years, until the final volume, *Last Things*, was completed in 1970. The first three volumes had been published by Faber, up to *Time of Hope* in 1949. One of the last executive publishing decisions Macmillan had made before returning to ministerial office in 1951 had been to encourage Horatio ('Rache') Lovat Dickson,[41] chief editor and director, to poach Snow from Faber. The results amply vindicated this decision. In 1951, Macmillan published *The Masters*, a political allegory surrounding the events of the election of a new master at a Cambridge college, a thinly disguised portrait of Christ's, Snow's own college. Macmillan always regarded it as the finest of the whole series, and one of the most underrated of post-war novels. Macmillan and Snow became close friends, and the character Lord Hillmorton in Snow's 1974 novel *In Their Wisdom* (not part of the *Strangers and Brothers* sequence) was loosely based on Macmillan.[42]

As Macmillan returned to the firm in 1963, Snow was completing the ninth novel of the series, *Corridors of Power*, topically examining a (fictional) political scandal at Westminster. Snow always took great care over the detail of his typescripts, paying particular attention to the title. He was unsure whether he should call the novel *Corridors of Power*. 'The fact that I invented the phrase and that it is my cliché doesn't alter the case;'[43] he said. He had first used the phrase in his novel *Homecomings*, describing public life as 'the official world, the corridors of power, the dilemmas of conscience and egotism'.[44] Despite Snow's reservations, Macmillan was in no doubt that the title was the correct one.[45] The phrase had already entered the language, as shorthand for the world of power and influence. When Macmillan, as Chancellor of Oxford University, attended the one hundred and fiftieth anniversary celebrations of the Cambridge Union in 1975, he met Rab Butler, then Master of Trinity, for the first time in ten years. In a rather awkward atmosphere, as they processed to dinner at Magdalene College, supporting each other arm in arm, Macmillan said, 'We're in the corridors of power now, Rab,' which left Butler speechless.[46]

Macmillan was not convinced, such was his own attention to detail, about the Sidney Nolan painting for the front of the dustjacket of *Corridors of Power*. The title and the name of the author appeared only on the spine, which he thought bizarre. He encouraged Maclean to send a photographer to the Foreign Office to take an appropriate photograph, but as Nolan had been commissioned to design all the Snow covers, the photo was not used.

Snow sent Macmillan the typescript of *Corridors of Power* in May 1964. Macmillan, always a quick reader, devoured the book over a weekend. He found it a splendid read, although not as assured artistically as *The Masters*. However, he picked up inaccuracies about parliamentary procedure and sent a telegram to Snow, who was in New York, warning him of these. Snow asked Macmillan if he would be able to advise on the solecisms. Macmillan not only pointed out these details ('Civil servants do not go into an official box during prayers in the House of Commons'), but began to redraft certain episodes, to their benefit. Snow was immensely grateful and incorporated these new scenes, which to his mind made Macmillan almost part author. 'This is the first novel a former Prime Minister has taken a hand in since *Lothair*,' he wrote to Macmillan.[47] The novel, expected to sell 20,000 copies, did four times as well.

Macmillan closely followed the progress of the remaining books in the series and on 8 December hosted a party for Snow at the Ritz to celebrate the completion of *Strangers and Brothers*.

When Keynes' official life by Roy Harrod was published by Macmillan & Co. in 1951, it was rightly acclaimed as an essential contribution to understanding the Keynesian model and its impact on twentieth-century economic policy. However, Harrod was reticent about revealing aspects of Keynes' character and personality, particularly his homosexuality. In the climate of the time, this was understandable. Although the details of Keynes' private life were well known in circles such as the Bloomsbury Group, no mention of it, in a more discreet age, ever reached the press.[48] When James Lees-Milne interviewed Harold Macmillan in 1979, whilst researching his official life of the bisexual writer, and sometime MP, Harold Nicolson, linked to Bloomsbury through his wife Vita Sackville-West, he asked Macmillan coyly if Members of Parliament had known about Nicolson's 'curious married life and his propensities'. Macmillan, shy and fastidious as always when confronted with delicate matters, was 'aghast'. 'No, in no sense whatever,' he replied. 'In fact I don't think I knew then. I don't think anyone did. Besides, it was not a subject which we would discuss.'[49]

The same reticence was true about Keynes, even six years after his death. Harrod was certainly not going to be the one to lift the veil.

Not only was the atmosphere of the early 1950s unsuited to such revelations, but Harrod deliberately avoided muddying the economic legacy by including frank details of Keynes' private life. 'Part of the purpose of Harrod's book was to clinch the success of the Keynesian Revolution in Britain and America,' wrote Robert Skidelsky. 'He was quite clear that this involved suppresssion of anything in Keynes's life which might set Americans against him.'[50]

By the late 1960s, as more became known of Keynes' circle, following the publication of Michael Holroyd's outstanding, and uninhibited, two-volume biography of Lytton Strachey (1967 and 1968), Harold Macmillan – fearing muck-raking that he could not control – realised that a new, responsible biography of Keynes was overdue. Accordingly, he approached Robert Skidelsky, then of Nuffield College, Oxford, to write what would be, in essence, the second official biography. Macmillan had been impressed by Skidelsky's first book, *Politicians and the Slump*; he was to be even more impressed by his life of Oswald Mosley, which his firm published in 1975.[51] Macmillan followed his hunches; he was proved right in having confidence in Skidelsky (as indeed he had been right to back Robert Byron).

Macmillan knew that commissioning a new biography would create a delicate situation with Sir Roy Harrod (who had been knighted, on Macmillan's recommendation, in 1959). Harrod regarded his biography of Keynes as the final, proprietorial, received word[52], and himself, with some justification, as one of the surviving members of that group of economists who had touched the hem of the garment of the master. Before undertaking to teach economics at Christ Church, he had moved to King's College, Cambridge, to be tutored by Keynes. At King's, he was drawn into that magic circle of Cambrige economists, Richard Kahn, Dennis Robertson and Joan Robinson in particular, who had read the *General Theory* of 1936 in all its draft versions. The subsequent propagation of Keynesianism was evangelical in its fervour and long survived Keynes' death in 1946. An American economist, Harry Johnson, put it best when he said, 'In post-war Cambridge they still talked about "Maynard" as if he might walk into the room at any moment.'[53] Harrod's 1951 biography was part of this hagiology, not that Harrod was ignorant of Keynes' 'propensities'. Indeed, he perceptively felt that Keynes' fundamental weakness was that he was unable to conceive of a friendship or attraction or sympathy which was not also erotic. But in 1951 this remained a page unturned.

Accordingly, Macmillan trod carefully. He wrote to Harrod on 4 July 1969 in advance of any public announcement, outlining the firm's intention to commission a new life of Keynes. Although he had anticipated difficulties, he had not foreseen the extent of Harrod's uncompromising anger.

'I was deeply distressed to get your letter,' Harrod replied three days later. 'If you continue with your project, that will be, I think, the most unpleasant thing that has happened to me in my life.' This was followed by a blanket refusal to allow any quotations or reproductions from his 1951 biography. Macmillan replied on 15 July, saying that he too was distressed, to receive Harrod's letter. 'Keynes was so great a man, like Churchill, people will continue to write new books about him and nothing will prevent this.' Macmillan explained that as a modern biography was inevitable, it was better that such a book should be published 'under our control'.

Harrod remained unconvinced. In an attempt to dissuade Macmillan from proceeding, he explained: 'If we are to have a biography that is more outspoken about homosexual matters than mine, your *own* brother would have to figure in it in a prominent way. He was Maynard's first love and perhaps, in some ways, his deepest. When it became apparent that they would have to be separated, Daniel going to Oxford [Balliol] and he to Cambridge [King's], Maynard was quite heartbroken.'[54] Although this letter gave Macmillan 'great pain', it was with the combination of courtesy and steel that characterised many of the awkward moments of his life*, that he made it clear that the Skidelsky commission would proceed.[55]

The three-volume Skidelsky biography, joined the Snow project, the *New Grove* and the *Dictionary of Art* as Macmillan's legacy, confirming his belief in, and commitment to, long-term planning.

On 15 January 1965, as it became clear that Churchill was dying, Macmillan went to London to record two tributes, the first for a British audience, and the second for America and Canada. In the latter he said, 'Born of an American mother – as I, too, am proud to be – he has handed on to his successors his passionate belief that the freedom – perhaps even the survival – of the civilised world, depends upon the closest association between the two branches of the English Speaking Peoples.' As he emphasised to the British audience, what Churchill had taught above all else was how to be courageous.[56]

The news of Churchill's death came early on a Sunday morning. As usual when at Birch Grove, Macmillan, who was very upset, was due to read the lesson at St Giles, Horsted Keynes. In consultation with the vicar, he changed the plannned lesson and chose instead

---

*The interview, for instance, with Selwyn Lloyd on 12 July 1962, when dismissing him.

the passage 'Let us now praise famous men' from Chapter 44 of Ecclesiasticus. Of the many tributes broadcast that day, Macmillan felt that 'no-one quite brought out what tremendous fun Churchill was'.[57] Churchill's state funeral, the first for a commoner since that of the Duke of Wellington in 1852, took place at St Paul's Cathedral on 30 January. Macmillan was one of the 12 pall-bearers, together with his great contemporaries from the wartime generation, Alexander, Attlee, Avon, Bridges, Ismay, Menzies, Mountbatten, Normanbrook, Portal, Slim and Templer. It was a bitterly cold day, and the elderly mourners, freezing on the steps of St Paul's, were eventually provided with chairs, 'but what we needed was a brazier', wrote Macmillan, who feared for the health of both Attlee and Ismay.

Macmillan found time as he continued with his memoirs to assist historians, of whose company he felt himself now a fellow practitioner. Randolph Churchill, who had embarked on his father's official biography, died in 1967, aged only 57. At his funeral in Suffolk, Macmillan met the young Martin Gilbert, to whom the task of writing the official biography of Winston was now entrusted. Macmillan offered whatever help he could, and was as good as his word, inviting Gilbert down to Birch Grove, visiting him at Gilbert's own home, and sending letters and reminiscences whenever the need arose.[58] He was just as punctilious over less grand projects. In 1974, a pupil at Alleyn's School in South London wrote to ask him about Munich, which he was studying for his A levels. Macmillan replied with insights that the student would not readily have found elsewhere.

Following the Conservatives' narrow defeat (by just four seats) at the October 1964 general election, Alec Douglas-Home decided to step down as party leader, having introduced a new electoral system to replace the 'customary processes'. Three candidates stood on 28 July 1965 under the new rules – Edward Heath, Reginald Maudling and Enoch Powell. Macmillan, though he had no vote in the new procedure (he would have done under the old one),[59] backed Heath for the leadership. 'I feel sure that Ted is the best choice. He is a stronger character than Maudling.'[60] The first ballot, after which Powell was eliminated, and Maudling conceded, was Heath 150, Maudling 133 and Powell 15. Macmillan now had the satisfaction of seeing one of his protégés, and a Balliol man, as party leader. Heath remained close to Macmillan, taking his advice at troubled moments.

On 22 May 1966, Lady Dorothy was at Birch Grove, preparing to attend a point-to-point meeting, the kind of local outing she so much enjoyed. As she was putting on her boots, she collapsed in the hall and died at once of a massive coronary. She was two months short of her sixty-sixth birthday. The light went out of Harold Macmillan's life. As they aged, Dorothy and Harold had grown increasingly close. He had never wavered in the deep love he had felt for her, ever since those far-distant days at Rideau Hall in the aftermath of the Great War. Now he was bereft, with a profound, lonely sorrow that never left him. It is not given to everyone to be able to express their inner feelings, as Macmillan admitted when he wrote to Dorothy for her sixtieth birthday: '60 years is a long time. Many happy memories, many sad ones. I hope you feel that those who love you have tried to make it happy. Your children and grandchildren love you very much – so, in his own rather inarticulate way, does your husband, who is grateful for years of partnership.'[61]

Macmillan's last entry in his diary was written the day before her death; he never resumed it.

Dorothy had died intestate, and Macmillan now instigated over-due dispositions, making Birch Grove over to Maurice. The grief of Dorothy's death had been, and was to be, replicated in other ways too. His grandson Joshua, Maurice's second son, had died in tragic cir-cumstances, whilst an undergraduate at Balliol in 1965. His divorced daughter Sarah also died tragically, after a fall on 26 March 1970, at the age of only 39, leaving two young adopted sons to her father's care. When John Wyndham, as close to him as a son, died in 1972, at the age of only 52, Macmillan wrote an affecting personal tribute in *The Times*, and later wrote the notice of his life for the *Dictionary of National Biography*.

In his loneliness, Macmillan often journeyed back to Chatsworth, initially for a weekend, and then for months at a time. He was solici-tously cared for on these extended visits by the Devonshires' butler, Henry. It was feared that he might set fire to things with his cigar ash in the wicker baskets, but Henry made sure this never happened.[62]

Chatsworth, with all its memories, was now a great comfort to Macmillan. He had always been gregarious, and the varying company drew him out. On 19 June 1965, he was one of the guests at the twenty-first birthday celebrations of the Devonshires' eldest son, Peregrine. With his intuitive sense, he realised that there was some-thing puzzling about the atmosphere, a tangible froideur. Eventually, all became clear. Sir Oswald Mosley, husband of Diana, Deborah Devonshire's sister, was in attendance. In 1965, Mosley was very much *persona non grata* in Britain. The British Union of Fascists and Mosley's wartime imprisonment had not been forgotten. As the guests assembled in the Painted Hall, ready to go into dinner, there was no sign of 'Uncle Harold'. Then he appeared, at the top of the great staircase, supported by Mosley. Slowly he came down the stairs and walked the whole length of the Painted Hall, arm in arm with Mosley in front of all the guests.[63] He was making a gesture. Macmillan and Mosley were colleagues of old, and, despite disgrace and disagreement, Mosley was family.

On 30 August 1967, a year after Dorothy's death, Lord Boothby married Wanda Senna. She was 33 years younger than Boothby; yet the two were to be blessed with 20 years of happy, devoted marriage. To Macmillan's surprise, Boothby asked him if he would like to meet Wanda; to Boothby's even greater surprise, Macmillan said he would very much like to. The three met at Boothby's flat at 1 Eaton Square. When Harold and Wanda were briefly alone for a few moments that afternoon, Macmillan said to the new Lady Boothby that he was glad that Bob had married again. 'Bob is lucky in that he is now a happy man,' he said, adding, 'whereas I am not.'[64]

Shortly before his remarriage, Boothby had written a lengthy article for the *Daily Mail* about his affair with Lady Dorothy. Macmillan was with the historian Kenneth Rose at Julian Amery's house in Eaton Square the day the article appeared. He was clearly very distressed about it, and asked Rose how much Boothby would have been paid. When Rose told him that he thought the going rate was two to three thousand pounds, a vast sum at the time, Macmillan said, 'I would have willingly paid him that not to write such an article.'[65]

On 18 June 1970, Heath, against the predictions of the opinion polls, won the general election. Macmillan felt it a just reward for stubborn persistence against all the odds. He knew how older Tories had patronised Heath, who had once appeared at a function in a white dinner jacket. When Maudling had worn a blue velvet smoking jacket, it was a cause for give-and-take banter. Heath was not so lucky, occasioning snide and snobbish remarks about waiters. He felt this social exclusion deeply,[66] and Macmillan knew it contributed to the carapace he constructed around himself, making it difficult for him to relate naturally to both his contemporaries and his juniors.

On 6 March 1971, Heath hosted a dinner for Macmillan at Chequers, attended by many of the Cabinet and Macmillan's former colleagues. Macmillan spoke of the looming problems: 'The English people do not like power. They distrust power and fight it when it appears. It has always been so. They broke the power of the barons in the Middle Ages, they broke the power of the Crown under Charles I, then the landlords in the Reform Bill, then the press, then the middle class. Now it is the trade unions. It has happened all before, dear boy.'[67]

Another celebratory dinner that lived long in the memory was the one Heath gave at Downing Street for Alec Home's seventieth birthday in July 1973. The evening was marked with musical entertainments and over-ran so much that Macmillan went downstairs to ring Birch Grove to say that he would not be coming back that evening. 'All these madrigals,' he said, 'now I'm going to have to doss down here.' Later he went along to have a last look at the Cabinet room in the half-light. 'All those many years I have spent in this room,' he reminisced to Robert Armstrong who was with him. 'Is that the 'phone on which I used to talk with Jack Kennedy during the Cuban missile crisis?' Armstrong forbore to tell him that the 1962 telephone calls had actually taken place in Admiralty House.[68]

Towards the end of 1973, it seemed the Heath government might founder in its long-running and bitter struggles with the trade union movement. Reggie Dilhorne advised Macmillan on 15 January 1974 to take the peerage due to him as a former Prime Minister, telling him he would be needed as a calming influence in the Upper House.[69] Macmillan had no wish (at that stage) to go to the Upper House, an institution he compared to a mausoleum, and felt he did not need a platform in Parliament to make an impact.

The industrial unrest of late 1973, together with the three-day week, power cuts and walk-outs, led Heath to call a 'Who Governs Britain?' election, a strategy Macmillan felt very risky, as it is always difficult to confine any campaign to a single issue of one party's choosing. On 28 February, despite polling more votes than Labour, the Conservatives won four fewer seats (297 to 301). As the Liberals refused to join with Heath, he resigned as Prime Minister, and Harold Wilson formed a minority Labour government

1974 was the first year since 1910 to have two elections. With his memoirs finished, Macmillan was eager for his advice to be heard on important matters. He spoke informally to the Queen, and also went down to Wiltshire to see the Avons, trying to persuade his predecessor to back him as a figure who could provide the focus for national unity. (As Macmillan was in neither House, how exactly he was going to play this part was not clear.) Eden had no wish to be drawn into these manoeuvres and Macmillan got short shrift, though generous hospitality. The rift between the two, as Martin Gilbert found when he worked with both men on his Churchill biography, was long-lasting, Eden always feeling he had been let down by Macmillan over Suez.

Macmillan deliberately withheld himself from the February 1974 election, as he wanted to remain 'untainted' so as to be able to participate in the aftermath, which he foresaw would be messy and partisan. He explained his strategy to Michael Fraser in a talk at the Carlton Club on 12 February. He had been considering making a personal intervention in the campaign, but had decided against it so that he could, 'if things went wholly wrong', be one of 'a small group of fairly detached elder statesmen to advise the Queen in the event of some National Government having to be found outside the normal Party system'. Fraser noted in his record that Macmillan 'felt, quite naturally, that if he intervened in the campaign this would make him ineligible for the other activity'.[70]

Wilson's government was narrowly returned in the general election of October 1974. As Wilson settled in to what was his fourth premiership, Macmillan knew that Heath's time as Tory leader was limited. He also knew that Heath, despite the abrupt ending to his short premiership, had altered Britain in a way not often managed by those who had ruled for much longer. Under Heath's watch, for good or ill, Britain had finally joined Europe, something de Gaulle had denied Macmillan. In February 1975, the inevitable challenge came, not as expected from one of the senior Cabinet members, but from Margaret Thatcher, the Education Secretary. For a time, Macmillan's son-in-law, Julian Amery, considered standing in the second ballot, before deciding against it.[71]

The first ballot, on 4 February saw Thatcher taking what proved to be an unstoppable lead. She polled 130 votes, with Heath on 119 and Hugh Fraser on 16. Heath immediately withdrew from the contest. Others then joined the race, but it was too late. Thatcher had seized the initiative. On 11 February, she became Conservative leader after polling 146 votes, an absolute majority over her four opponents. William Whitelaw received 79 votes, Sir Geoffrey Howe 19, James Prior 19 and John Peyton 11. The Thatcher years had begun. On 3 May 1979, Thatcher won a decisive election victory, the first of three. Macmillan was not happy with the sense of triumphalism, especially at the 1979 Blackpool conference, so different from that of 1963. He had now become something of a national treasure, and British Rail named a train after him, which took many delegates to Blackpool that October.

*

In the summer of 1979, Macmillan chose Alistair Horne to be his official biographer. Alan Maclean had initially looked through the list of distinguished Macmillan authors (there were several possibilities), before the decision was made. Horne's reputation had been established with his trilogy on the Franco-German conflict, of which the central panel of the triptych, *The Price of Glory: Verdun 1916* (1962), won the Hawthornden Prize. *A Savage War of Peace: Algeria 1954–1962* (1977) won both the Wolfson Literary Award and the *Yorkshire Post* Book of the Year Prize.

Horne's initial reluctance to accept the commission led to a meeting at Birch Grove, during which he admitted that he was not sure he was a very good Tory. 'Nor was I, dear boy!' replied Macmillan,[72] after which there was no turning back. In the interim, for the Horne biography was contracted not to appear in Macmillan's own life-time, Macmillan co-operated with Nigel Fisher on a biography that appeared in 1982, with no access to papers, and on condition that Boothby's affair with Lady Dorothy was not mentioned. The two Horne volumes, which stand as the keystone of the arch of Macmillan studies, appeared in 1988 and 1989.

Macmillan's attitude to Thatcher changed over the years. He admired her determination and knew that winning the leadership in 1975 was a massive achievement. Macmillan had been an outsider himself, but Thatcher was an outsider twice over, coming from the lower-middle class and as a woman. When Mrs Thatcher became leader of the Tory Party in February 1975, she asked if she might meet Macmillan for advice. Courteous to the last, Macmillan invited her to Birch Grove for lunch. Mrs Thatcher was talking on arrival. She continued to talk over drinks, during lunch, over coffee and as she was leaving. As her car drove away, Macmillan turned to one of his grandsons who had been at the lunch and said, 'Do you ever get the feeling that you have just failed geography?' When four years later she became Britain's first female Prime Minister, Macmillan knew it was an historic moment. He felt she possessed in abundance that Churchillian quality he most admired: courage. Nevertheless, he always retained a certain impish-ness in her presence. Unveiling the Oscar Nemon bronze head of Mrs Thatcher at the Carlton Club in January 1979, he said, in an all too audible stage whisper, 'Now I must remember that I am unveiling a bust of Margaret Thatcher, not Margaret Thatcher's bust.'[73]

The Falklands War in 1982 exhibited the Churchillian courage most clearly, and at its outset, Macmillan called on the Prime Minister. His support was not clandestine. He arrived at the front door of Downing

Street, which Mrs Thatcher much appreciated at a 'wobbly' time. His advice over the next two hours was invaluable, telling the Prime Minister how military campaigns had been managed before, from the Second World War to Suez. At Macmillan's suggestion, Thatcher set up a key executive command chain, establishing a small inner war Cabinet, with its echoes of Lloyd George in 1916. The success of the Falklands campaign owed much to Macmillan's initial advice.

When the Franks Report (Thatcher's Denning Report), on the causes and conduct of the Falklands War, was published in January 1983, Macmillan wrote to Thatcher on the happy outcome. His letter had a touch of mischief.* 'I am glad to observe that the time honoured judgment in the famous case of Albert and the Lion has been respected by these distinguished Privy Councillors. "The magistrate gave the opinion that no one was really to blame."'[74]

The attitudes of Macmillan and Thatcher to the problems the country faced were utterly different and the rift between them gradually widened. 'Monetarism' was the complete antithesis of Stockton Keynesianism, a rebuke to Macmillan's whole political philosophy. Thatcher was never burdened by sentimentality towards brow-beaten groups, such as, in her opinion, Macmillan had exhibited towards the miners. For his part, Macmillan thought she was too governessy, and told her so.

As an old-fashioned 'gentleman', it was not in Macmillan's nature to be brusque towards a lady. He knew that many of the 'gentlemen' in Thatcher's first Cabinets were similarly inhibited. The fact that Heath did not hold back in his criticisms was proof to older Conservatives who often actually agreed with those criticisms that he was never really one of them. Macmillan's criticisms were always more subtle.

The most famous 'rebuke' from Macmillan to Thatcherism came at a meeting of the Tory Reform Group at the Carlton Club on 8 November 1984. His target was the programme of privatisation. 'First the Georgian silver goes,' he said. 'And then all that nice furniture that used to be in the saloon. Then the Canalettos go ...'[76] The analogy caused great damage, as Thatcher's biographer John Campbell has observed. 'The image of ministers, like a lot of dodgy house-strippers,

---

*Later that year, his underlying sense of mischief was on display again. On election night, 9 June, he was watching the results at the Carlton Club. When Norman St John Stevas was safely returned for Chelmsford, Macmillan commented 'Good. Now he can be Speaker, and then it will be like Gilbert and Sullivan.'

knocking down the nation's heirlooms at a cost well below their true worth subtly undermined Mrs Thatcher's carefully created reputation for thrifty house keeping.'[77]

This was playing to the gallery. The ranks of Tuscany could scarce forbear to cheer. Yet the analogy was not exact. Macmillan had style, and the 'family silver speech' was stylish above all else. It was also knowing and very mischievous. Macmillan understood perfectly well that his comparison was not an exact representation, but the phrase stuck, as he intended. The true analogy was that the family silver (a declining, not an appreciating, asset at the time) was not being sold and lost to the family, but was being transferred to another branch of the family and saved. The state had so many necessary responsibilities that it was better at the time to shed those it did not have to control, especially when they could be run more efficiently under different control. It was not asset-stripping, it was transfer.

The 'family silver' was far from being the last rebuke. On his ninetieth birthday on 10 February 1984, Macmillan belatedly and unexpectedly accepted an earldom. When Disraeli had done likewise in 1876, he had taken the title of Earl of Beaconsfield, a purely geographical choice, as the place near his country home, Hughenden Manor. Macmillan had two constituencies to choose from; but for him there was only one. The Earl of Bromley did not trip from the tongue. The Earl of Stockton, on the other hand, had no element of bathos. The rebuke came in the association of Stockton with an earlier age of unemployment. The choice was a deliberate statement about Thatcherism.

The Lords became Macmillan's public platform in his last years. On 23 January 1985, when the House was first televised, he was one of the initial speakers. When it was known he was on his feet, the bars and tea rooms always emptied as peers flocked to hear this last contact with Edwardian Britain. He did not disappoint.

On 8 December 1985, Macmillan went to Downing Street for the last time for a dinner to celebrate the 250th anniversary of Sir Robert Walpole's move to Number 10, which established the house as the official residence of the First Lord of the Treasury. The dinner was attended by the Queen and the Duke of Edinburgh and all living former prime ministers. A subsequent photograph of the assembled company, which inevitably made its way on to the front cover of *Private Eye*, had Macmillan at the centre, stooping slightly on his walking stick, as he turned to Denis Thatcher. 'I don't remember you being Prime Minister,' was the *Private Eye* caption.[78]

In these last years, Macmillan continued to visit Oxford as Chancellor, usually staying with Anthony Kenny at Balliol. Some younger dons started a campaign for a more 'vigorous' Chancellor; Macmillan said he was quite happy to stand down, but only for somebody older. His mischievous speeches, especially at his ninetieth birthday celebrations at Balliol, continued to captivate his audiences. As he was nearly blind, he learned them by heart, disguising his artfulness. He spliced his observations with irreverences, and, like Dickens, presented 'the tragic and the comic scenes, in as regular alternation, as the layers of red and white in a side of streaky bacon'. Rule one in politics, he often declared, was NEVER INVADE AFGHANISTAN, and the ideal combination of a club was 75 per cent gentlemen and 25 per cent crooks, 'which is what makes White's so fascinating'.[79]

Clubs had always been an important part of Macmillan's life, even more so after Dorothy's death. The Carlton was very special for him, and in 1977 he took over its presidency at the age of 83. He had been a member since 1929. Within a few months of becoming president, he was instrumental in merging the Carlton and the Junior Carlton Clubs, thus securing the financial future of both at an uncertain time for clubland. 'Much opposition to the merger was expected but Macmillan's skill and charisma seemed to mesmerise antagonists,' the minutes of the vital meeting in October 1977 record. 'The scheme was approved, and the meeting over in eight minutes.'[80]

When Macmillan came to London, the Carlton was his base if he had to stay overnight, although this was something he preferred not to do. He never stayed in town if he could help it. Buck's in Clifford Street was another favourite haunt; he loved its low-key intimacy. Pratt's, owed by the Duke of Devonshire, was a club where he met younger political figures and caught up on all the gossip at lunchtime. If he had to attend a dinner, his usual pattern was to make for 3 Chester Square, the home of Julian Faber,[81] his son-in-law, where he could change and relax.

Macmillan's retirement was a varied one, and he much valued the interaction with the business community he had through Julian Faber. It brought him into contact with the City in many guises, attending boardroom lunches and livery dinners. The fact that he was always received with affection by bankers and businessmen was also gratifying. When Julian Faber was chairman of Willis Faber, he got his father-in-law to perform many ceremonial tasks for the company, such as laying the foundation stone for, and later opening, the Willis Faber headquarters in Ipswich, a state-of-the-art building designed by Norman Foster. For his part, Julian Faber was able to help Macmillan over many administrative matters that became difficult for him as he declined into old age and blindness.

Macmillan also enjoyed staying with Julian and Lady Caroline Faber at their country base, 1 Coastguard Cottage, at Sandwich, near Royal St George's Golf Club. Here he loved to be taken on drives to Broadstairs and Margate and to get out of the car and walk the front. More often than not, he was accosted by members of the public, something that would not have been possible in a later security-conscious age. Figures such as Robert Runcie, Archbishop of Canterbury, and E.W. Swanton, the great cricketing scribe, were invited to informal dinners at Coastguard Cottage, events that kept Macmillan busy and involved in matters beyond politics. As a result, Julian Faber, largely because he was not a political animal, opened up a different world of contacts.

Macmillan got much of the inside political news from another son-in-law, Julian Amery, who lived, when in Sussex, at Forest Farm House, Chelwood Gate, near Birch Grove. The proximity of the houses was a boon to Macmillan, as he could see his Amery grandchildren. He was very good with young children; their bustle and high-spirited activity intrigued him, even when he was quietly puffing on his pipe and listening to his favourite authors on 'speaking books'.

Macmillan also loved visiting schools. He presented the prizes at Eastbourne College, with its Devonshire connections. Summer Fields, his preparatory school in north Oxford, was like an extension of the family. He had made a visit in 1958, as Prime Minister, with Lady Dorothy, to plant a tulip tree on the masters' lawn. In December 1979, he opened the Macmillan Hall in the grounds, and followed closely the progress of his many grandsons who were pupils there. Ardingly College was near Birch Grove, and he received an open invitation from the Head Master, Christopher Bulteel, to come to Evensong whenever he wished. It became a familiar sight for the pupils on Sundays to see the stooped, elderly figure walking slowly into the chapel, though as he came anonymously many did not realise that a former Prime Minister was in their midst.[82] Eton, with all its memories, was also a place he loved visiting, and he spoke on occasion to their Political Society and corresponded regularly with successive provosts and head masters until the end of his life.

One of Macmillan's biggest disappointments was that he had not become Provost of Eton in 1965, when Harold Caccia was appointed. He would have loved to have been appointed, not for the kudos or as a sinecure, but as a means of 'getting something done'. He would have been an active Provost, more so than circumstances allowed him to be as Chancellor of Oxford University, though Roy Jenkins, his successor as Chancellor, was to take that post to a new level.[83]

As staff retired at Birch Grove, Macmillan became increasingly dependent on part-time help. He persuaded Maurice and Katie Macmillan to come to Birch Grove to live with him and be companions for him in his old age. It was a wrench for his son and daughter-in-law to leave Highgrove, near Tetbury, which they sold to the Prince of Wales,[84] Katie, in particular, being reluctant about the move.

Macmillan's two closest female friendships in his old age were with Ava Waverley and Eileen O'Casey, widows of two great men, Sir John Anderson and Sean O'Casey. Ava Waverley harboured thoughts (futile ones) of a possible marriage with Macmillan now that they were both widowed. But Eileen O'Casey, who had a perceptive intelligence, and whose friendship was deeper that that of Ava's, knew this was never going to be the case. As a result, she was always more relaxed in his presence and more of a comfort to him than Ava Waverley ever was. He liked taking 'contrary' views and teasing the person he was speaking to, particularly if that person was in any way 'grand', and Ava Waverley never quite knew how seriously to take some of the things he said.

Macmillan continued to take a keen interest in contemporary events. He was fascinated by Michael Heseltine's walk-out from the Thatcher Cabinet on 7 January 1986. By chance he saw, or rather heard, as he was by then virtually blind, this dramatic event live on television, when staying with Pamela Egremont. He said that he would like to meet Heseltine to hear all about it. As Pamela Egremont knew Heseltine, a meeting was arranged, and Heseltine took the aged former Prime Minister through the whole saga. The two men got on, not least because Macmillan saw in Heseltine something of his younger self, a rebel against the prevailing orthodoxies of the time.[85]

On 10 March 1984, Maurice Macmillan died, the second of Harold's children to predecease him. It was exactly a month since Harold's ninetieth birthday and the granting of the earldom that had made Maurice briefly Viscount Macmillan of Ovenden. Over the years Maurice had 'got better', but he had 'not really got better', and there was an element of release after his last illness, emphysema, exacerbated by his heavy smoking. He was buried in the family plot at St Giles, Horsted Keynes. Further legal dispositions were now made over the Birch Grove estate. Things were arranged so that when Macmillan himself died, his estate came to £51,114.[86]

Harold Macmillan never recovered from Maurice's death.

The end when it came was mercifully swift. Macmillan died after a short illness on 29 December 1986 in the small upstairs side bedroom at Birch Grove, where he had increasingly retreated in his last months. It had become his favourite room in the whole vast empty house. The funeral took place at St Giles Church, Horsted Keynes, on 5 January 1987. The mourners included 64 members of his family, the prime minister Margaret Thatcher, and two former prime ministers, Alec Home and Edward Heath. The hymns included 'Fight the Good Fight', 'The King of Love my Shepherd is' and 'I Vow to Thee My Country.' Macmillan preferred to rest in a quiet corner of an English country churchyard,* rather than what Edmund Burke called 'the tomb of the Capulets'.[87] He was buried beside Dorothy and next to the graves of his parents, his son Maurice and his daughter Sarah.[88] The granite block marking Dorothy's grave had already borne for some years his own incomplete inscription, HAROLD MACMILLAN 1894–.

Memorial services were held in many places associated with Macmillan. The first was at St Mary, the University Church, Oxford on 7 February 1987, celebrating his long chancellorship of the university. On 10 February, on what would have been his ninety-third birthday, a memorial service, attended by Prince Charles, was held at Westminster Abbey, 'that temple of silence and reconciliation where the emnities of twenty generations lie buried'.[89] Alec Home gave the address.[90] On the same day, a service was held in South Africa, and others followed in all the 'territories' where the Macmillan publishing house was represented.

Later, the family placed a memorial tablet on the north wall of St Giles' Church.

---

*As did Asquith, Churchill and Eden.

ENVOI

In 1967, Macmillan exhorts Harold Wilson and George Brown to seek
their fortunes in the Common Market, despite the formidable obstacles
still posed by de Gaulle.

A great Premier must add the vivacity of an idle man
to the assiduity of a very laborious one.
                    Walter Bagehot, *The Economist*, 2 January 1875

'All political lives,' Enoch Powell famously observed, 'end in failure, because that is the nature of politics and human affairs.'[1] Harold Macmillan's career is no exception. From the moment that President de Gaulle delivered his devastating rejection of Britain's application to join the Common Market on 14 January 1963, Macmillan's strategy lay in ruins. Rudderless, all that he now needed was the opportunity to make a graceful exit and hand on the torch to the next generation. Even this was denied him by events beyond his control. First there was the unfolding imbroglio of the Profumo affair in the summer of 1963, and second the suddenness of his illness in the autumn, after he had decided that he would fight the next election. A messy departure followed. One of the most eventful and significant premierships of post-war Britain ended in turmoil and recrimination.

Some had seen the incipient signs of failure earlier. The Vassall affair, and the subsequent tribunal, turned the press against Macmillan and all his doings. The Night of the Long Knives was a grievous miscalculation; once the first minister had toppled, sacking followed sacking, like a row of dominoes. Macmillan's one-time political boss, Lord Beaverbrook, was wont to say at times of political crisis, 'Who's in charge of the clattering train?' In the summer of 1962, many felt like asking the same, and as Nigel Birch cruelly observed to Macmillan's face in the Commons – revenge being a dish best served cold – it was 'never glad confident morning again'.[2]

Macmillan was by then a man out of touch with the modern generation. 'I do not live among young people much myself,' he had admitted on 17 June 1963, leaving a hostage to fortune. The thrusting worlds of 'the New Men' (as C.P. Snow called his 1954 novel), Harold Wilson and 'the white heat of the technological revolution' were the future. Macmillan's demise marked the moment when it was no longer advisable or profitable for Etonians to wear their old school tie.

Of course, there were those who could never stand Macmillan. Not that this worried him. A thick skin is a prime requisite for the leadership in any walk of life. There were people he disliked, such as Morrison, Gaitskell and Butler, who had not fought in the war. Yet paradoxically he got on perfectly well with Wilson and Home, neither of whom had fought. It is difficult to avoid the conclusion that failure to have served one's country in wartime was just his rationalisation for people to whom he did not warm, anyway.

By the early sixties, Macmillan, struggling to retain the grandeurs of the past, with its social system and petty snobberies, was seen by many people, and not just political opponents, as the epitome of all that was wrong with anachronistic Britain. This was an unfair charge. He did not live in the past. He pursued his aims on matters such as Europe and Africa by indirection – something Harold Wilson always admired. Indeed, in retirement, Macmillan became something of the nation's Ancient Mariner. He loved to relate tales of his past experience, to colleagues and opponents alike, drawing lessons for the direction of future policy (as Harold Wilson found in conversations about Europe).

Macmillan understood that he had to cater for the national mood of self-deception, for instance the inherent belief that Britain, despite Suez, remained a major world force. His first television speech as Prime Minister in January 1957 emphasised that Britain had been a Great Power, was a Great Power and would continue to be so, provided that everyone pulled together and got on with the job, Tory sentiments indeed.

Yet critics eventually saw him as the poseur, the fraudulent actor-manager, like John Osborne's Archie Rice rehearsing his outdated act in a once opulently decorated theatre where the stucco was now peeling.[3] What was often forgotten was how much Macmillan was an outsider, even in his own party. He was an old-style paternalist Whig, not a dyed-in-the-wool Tory. Nor was he, despite the general belief, an aristocrat. He was a businessman who had married into the aristocracy. When he won the chancellorship of Oxford in 1960, it was as a rebel candidate. As he paraded through the streets of Oxford in yearly Encaenia ceremonies, successive Balliol-educated grandsons acting as train-bearers, people saw it as the Establishment in full flow. Yet as Macmillan pointed out at the time, the Establishment did not actually win the chancellorship election. Such apparent contradictions contributed to his complex image. He could never be pigeonholed. The essence of his persona was as elusive as mercury.

In his seminal book *Britain Since 1918*, David Marquand admitted, with some surprise, his discovery that 'Harold Macmillan, that master of irony and specialist in ambiguity, emerges from my story as the nearest thing to a great Prime Minister in the post-war years.'[4] Macmillan *was* a great Prime Minister for much of his time in Downing Street, though not quite in the supreme category occupied by Lloyd George,

Churchill, Attlee and Margaret Thatcher. Yet even that quartet had their dying fall. Titans too smell of mortality.

The Labour government from 1945–1951 was associated in the public mind with austerity, scarcity, rationing and queues; Macmillan's government was associated with prosperity, affluence and the good life. His abiding achievement, by a combination of the luck of the economic cycle and careful planning, was to be the Prime Minister who led Britain from that immediate post-war world of deprivation to the years of plenty. His reward was the triumphant result of the 1959 election. Moreover, once scarcity had been replaced by comfort, there was no going back.

In the 1940s, a holidaymaker at a Butlin's camp had gratefully enthused: 'eggs and bacon for breakfast and fresh peaches for lunch, it was an absolute dream'.[5] In Macmillan's Britain this was not seen as a dream, but expected as a right. The aspiring lower-middle-class family, unforgettably recorded in the Giles cartoons of the period, was no longer content with the limited horizons of the past. As material standards rose, those who lived through both the grey late 1940s and the affluent 1950s never forgot the contrast.

Moreover, the welfare state was not curbed under Tory rule, as Labour activists had prophesied. If anything, the collectivist drive that Macmillan directed from the Ministry of Housing brought a new level of social provision, which not only improved living standards, but eroded the support that working-class people had traditionally given to Labour. The political opportunity afforded by this important transition was not one that Macmillan let slip.

Macmillan was throughout a leader and a presence. There were always two levels to him. On the one hand were the human factors, the problems of the day; but there was always a deeper, more serious, spiritual dimension, which put the perils and dangers of this fleeting world in context. Perceptively, it has been observed that 'Harold Macmillan displayed a ruthless Machiavellian instinct licensed by his sense that the things of this world were finally insubstantial.'[6] The everyday never mattered to him as much as the eternal questions, which gave him an ability to carry on through adversity. In retirement in Cockermouth, when visiting the Wyndhams (by then Lord and Lady Egremont),[7] he was driven out one day as a great storm was building over the lakes, like a scene from Wordsworth, 'in grandeur and in tumult'.[8] He got out of the car, cloak flapping in the gathering winds, to look for a while at the dark clouds scudding in over the hills. 'Well, nobody can alter that,' he proclaimed, as he got back in.[9]

*

Macmillan was the first post-war Conservative Prime Minister to break free from the shadow of Churchill, and to redefine the Conservative Party by winning a general election on the back of economic prosperity. He put to rest the ghost of the 1930s. Churchill, as a peacetime Prime Minister, was always being compared with what he had been; Macmillan was simply the thing he was. He had style in abundance, was a star on the world stage, and for much of the time successfully disguised Britain's international decline. He knew that the special relationship with America was the useful myth, brilliantly sustained by his friendships with Eisenhower and Kennedy.

He did not 'change' Britain in the way that Margaret Thatcher did – there was never any 'Macmillanism' – but then in 1957 the country did not need a wholesale overhaul. It needed economic growth.

Thatcher's legacy has been so powerful that one of the difficulties in assessing Macmillan's has been obscured. A broader perspective is needed if he is to emerge fully. The problem is compounded because his principal detractors have been Thatcherites. Their main criticisms of him are threefold: that he underestimated the danger of inflation because of his memories of the 1930s; that his 'Keynesian' planning policies – 'Nicky' and 'Neddy'* in particular – led to a statism that inhibited economic growth; and that entry into Europe was a mistake and, in any case, as Reginald Maudling predicted, unrealistic.

There is an element of truth in all three charges, but not the whole story. Selwyn Lloyd, Macmillan's Chancellor from 1960–1962, wrote at the time of his sacking in July 1962 that Macmillan's biggest mistake was in believing unemployment to be more important than inflation. Yet the position is not as black and white, as there is an inevitable trade-off between unemployment and inflation. The problem can be approached by governments from different directions. In both pre-war and post-war Germany, for example, for decades inflation was so traumatic an experience that it conditioned that country's response to economic policy. Selwyn Lloyd with his middle-class upbringing of rectitude, and a concern about 'the value of money', was similarly disposed. He was convinced that attempting to tackle unemployment first, rather than inflation, was putting the cart before the horse, as the first aim was inevitably jeopardised if inflation was not brought firmly under control.

Macmillan saw things differently and with a greater underlying understanding of the interlinking economic realities. His searing

---

*Nicky = National Incomes Commission; Neddy = National Economic Development Committee.

experience was the Depression in pre-war Stockton, and this, together with his affinity with Keynesian ideas, hung heavily over the way he thought about financial policy. There was always an element of 'sufficient unto the day' about Macmillan – let the morrow look after itself – an approach that echoed Keynes' belief that 'in the long run we are all dead'.[10]

Yet Macmillan knew that control of the money supply could not guarantee price stability, because the rate at which money balances are spent (the velocity of circulation) can vary in the short run. It is that spending that determines the level of economic activity and is influenced by fiscal policy, trade cycles, and the random shocks and 'animal spirits' that Keynes saw driving the economy in the short run.

Macmillan has been accused of ignoring the dangers of inflation, yet in his time in office it averaged only 2 per cent. As this figure rose in the decades ahead, Macmillan was increasingly identified as the fountainhead. The free-marketeers rejected his whole economic approach and philosophy.

Many Conservatives, including Churchill, were antagonised by the manner in which Macmillan hastened the end of Empire, even though he was pushed into it by his Colonial Secretaries Maudling and Macleod.

The explorer Stanley had a granite plinth erected above his grave bearing the single word AFRICA. This would have been a suitable monument for Macmillan also, as two of his greatest achievements occurred in that troubled continent. In North Africa during the war, Macmillan's executive capacity was demonstrated in its most potent and influential manner, through personal dealings and administrative expertise, linked to a perceptive understanding of the underlying strategy needed for the war effort in a vital theatre. He came of age in those years, and had he never held office after the war, his service as Viceroy of the Mediterranean would have been enough to secure his reputation as a figure of consequence and international importance. Then, in 1960, in South Africa, his speech in Cape Town on the Wind of Change, still remembered affectionately by the black population, was a vital staging post on the long journey to freedom that ended apartheid.

The greatest criticism of Macmillan, the more painful as it came in the latter stages of his life when he was unable to defend himself, was, of course, the controversy over the repatriation of the Cossacks in May 1945. Posthumously, much detailed research, notably, but not exclusively, by the Cowgill Inquiry, was able to establish the truth about this tragic event. As a result, the accusation that Macmillan was 'a war criminal' is now seen merely as a blot that has been removed from his reputation.

Macmillan's 'conversion' to the idea of European integration was a complex and lengthy process. In February 1959, Reginald Maudling, then Paymaster General, said in the House of Commons 'that for us to sign the Treaty of Rome would be to accept the ultimate goal, political federation in Europe, including ourselves'.[11] Macmillan was aware of this, which is why he approached the question of an application cautiously and in stages. After the 1959 election victory, he wrote to Maudling: 'What do you think of GATT [the General Agreement on Tariffs and Trade]? I know the Americans always cheat where their interests are concerened. Some people feel that on the whole we do better without all the various GATT agreements. Do you share this view?'[12]

Maudling did not. 'The GATT is the best set of international trading rules that we have, and we should be unwise to get rid of it until we can see something better to put in its place.'[13]

Macmillan respected this forthrightness, despite the difficulties that might be engendered with the Americans and the Commonwealth. The European Free Trade Association (EFTA), which was established in November 1959, was from the start dominated by the British. Herein lay the difficulty of Europe for Britain.

The Messina conference of 1955 had occurred at the moment of the handover of power from Churchill to Eden. Macmillan became Foreign Secretary in Eden's Cabinet, but failed to attend Messina, where Britain gained a reputation for being arrogant and standoffish. When Britain eventually became involved in negotiations, it was inevitably cast in the role of latecomer to the European project.

In short, Britain had made the worst of both worlds – missing the opportunities afforded by Messina, and experiencing numerous difficulties in gaining eventual acceptance. The country joined the EEC (at the second attempt) but memories of earlier attitudes were never forgotten by the powerful European alliance of France and Germany. Macmillan must take his portion of the blame for the lack of clarity and commitment in the British approach to European membership.

Time erodes even the brightest prime ministerial legacies. Harold Wilson always said that he would be remembered for one achievement – the Open University. Macmillan has his unexpected memorial also. Two of his initiatives still endure: Premium Bonds (1956) and life peerages (1958).

Few Chancellors who deliver only one Budget leave a lasting legacy.

Macmillan's sole Budget of 1956 is an exception. Premium Bonds are sometimes inaccurately compared to the later National Lottery, yet Macmillan's scheme did not involve the loss of the original 'stake'. What was voluntarily sacrificed by the purchaser of a Premium Bond (though this may not always have been understood by the customer) was a guaranteed return of interest for the hope of a larger prize, possibly a very large windfall. As interest rates recently fell to a negligible level, Premium Bonds became an attractive 'gamble' for all levels of investors, and today the scheme flourishes as never before.

The introduction of life peerages also had unexpected consequences. When Macmillan brought in the constitutional change in 1958, some saw the measure as a Trojan horse, weakening the structure, and possibly the very existence, of the Upper House. Such predictions were proved wrong. Life peerages eventually became the 'acceptable' part of a bicameral system, and the means by which the Lords was given a form of validation. Any future for the House of Lords lies now not in its hereditary, but in its 'life' principle.

Macmillan had style, vision, breadth of view and compassion Of course, there were failings, and he knew it himself. 'On the whole,' he wrote to Jack Kennedy, 'it is not the things one did in one's life that one regrets, but rather the opportunities missed.'[14]

Even as the public turned against him, Macmillan retained his individuality. C. P. Snow wrote to him:

> Prime Ministers in the long run survive in history according to whether their intelligent contemporaries find them psychologically interesting. You are the only Prime Minister for a long time, Churchill excepted, who has evoked any such interest. That, of course, is why you attract some hostile attention from the revue writers and the like: but if you didn't there would be something very wrong.[15]

Macmillan always remained a psychologically interesting Prime Minister, and his survival in history is assured. He was both vivacious and assiduously laborious, those seemingly contradictory twin prerequisites Walter Bagehot felt so necessary to sustain a great premiership. His final *envoi* to the nation, written in May 1973, was one of guarded optimism:

> Nothing in my long experience or in my observations of the youth of today makes me fear that the people of Britain, in every walk of life, will shrink from the new challenge or fail to rise to the level of

events. But to do so they must restore and strengthen the moral and spiritual, as well as the material, base on which they have rested for so many generations through so many troubles and tribulations.[16]

Time has not eroded the relevance or the essential truth of Macmillan's message.

The Memorandum for the Queen
18 October 1963

LEADERSHIP OF THE CONSERVATIVE PARTY
MR MACMILLAN'S RESIGNATION

October 18, 1963
Madam,

Mr Macmillan with his humble duty to The Queen.

As Your Majesty knows, I reached the conclusion, when I was taken ill last week, that I could not hope to continue to conduct Your Majesty's business for any extended period. Although I am encouraged by the good reports I have received from my doctors, I remain in that mind and I now tender my resignation with the assurance that I shall ever be

Your Majesty's
faithful and obedient servant,
Harold Macmillan

TOP SECRET   MEMORANDUM BY THE PRIME MINISTER

(Handed to The Queen at the Hospital on 18.10.63)

On October 14, it seemed to me necessary to sound opinion in Conservative circles regarding the situation that would follow my early resignation as Prime Minister. I therefore issued a directive to the First Secretary of State asking him to arrange that the Lord Chancellor should take steps to ascertain the opinions of the Cabinet; the Chief Whip in the House of Commons those of Junior Ministers and Members of the House of Commons; the Chief Whip in the House of Lords those of Members of the House of Lords who are either Junior Ministers or regular supporters of the Government; and Lord Poole those of the leaders of various organisations in the Conservative Party. This directive was read to the Cabinet and no objection was made. While waiting for their detailed reports I saw a number of my senior colleagues and got a general idea from them of the way opinion was moving. These included: the Chief Whip, the Lord Chancellor, the Foreign Secretary, the First Secretary of State, the Chancellor of the Exchequer, the Lord President, the Leader of the House of Commons, and the Lord Privy Seal; the Minister of Defence, the Minister of Education, the Minister of Agriculture, the Minister of Labour, the Home Secretary and the Minister of Housing and Local Government, and the Commonwealth Secretary.

I received the reports on the morning of Thursday, October 17, from the Lord Chancellor who came alone; the Chief Whip who was supported by Major Morrison, Chairman of the Conservative 1922 Committee and with whom I had a separate conversation; Lord St Aldwyn; and Lord Poole, who was accompanied by Lord Chelmer and Mrs Shepherd, the latter two doing most of the speaking.

At 3.00 p.m. I held a meeting of the four groups together at which were present: the Lord Chancellor, Lord St Aldwyn, Lord Poole and the Chief Whip.

As a result I feel able (and quite apart from any personal opinion I might have of my own as to who would make the most suitable Prime Minister in the conditions which confront the Nation today) to make the following appreciation of opinion in those forces which are the most dominant in the Conservative Party. Naturally these opinions give full weight to a variety of considerations since it is known that whoever is asked by The Queen to form an Administration must become Leader of the Conservative Party and in this capacity fight a General Election within a year.

I find on analysis that this is the broad view.

(i) *Cabinet*:

The Lord Chancellor gave the views of his Cabinet colleagues. This showed that Lord Home had a substantial lead. The Lord Chancellor expressed his personal view that Lord Home was now a well known figure abroad and best fitted to continue and exploit our Foreign Policy aims. In the Lord Chancellor's view everyone in the Cabinet will be prepared to serve under Lord Home if he is chosen. This was not so true of some of the other names mentioned.

(ii) *Junior Ministers and Conservative Members of the House of Commons*:

Major John Morrison, MP, the Chairman of the 1922 Committee of Conservative and Unionist Back Benchers, gave his view that the person who would command the most support in the House of Commons is Lord Home. There were strong blocks of Members who were antagonistic to all the other likely candidates. If Lord Home would accept, the Party in the Commons would rally round him. If he would not, the Members would probably prefer Mr Maudling and Mr Butler in that order, but there was not much in it. There was strong support for Lord Hailsham but a bigger block who were anti.

The Chief Whip presented the views which he had collected from Junior Ministers and Conservative Members of the House of Commons. He stated that through his whips he had collected the views of some 300 Members. Lord Home came first; and then either Mr Maudling–Mr Butler or Mr Butler–Mr Maudling as second or third choices. In his view Lord Hailsham was out of the running.

(iii) *Junior Ministers and regular supporters in the House of Lords*:

Lord St Aldwyn gave the views of Junior Ministers and regular supporters in the House of Lords. He produced figures showing that support for Lord Home was in the ratio of two to one.

(iv) *Conservative Organisations, viz. Area Chairmen, Young Conservatives, Women's Advisory Committee, Trade Unionists and Candidates*:

Lord Poole, Lord Chelmer and Mrs Shepherd gave the views of certain Party organisations. They had held meetings with Area Chairmen, Officers of Women's Advisory Committee, Young Conservatives and Conservative Trade Unionists. The view expressed was that there was a clear determination in the Party to rally behind whoever is selected.

Lord Hailsham still commanded the majority support of the constituencies, although rather less than he had at Blackpool. Mr Butler was second choice. There was support for Lord Home, but they had not been asked to consider him specifically as many people thought that he had, at Blackpool, refused to be considered. If Lord Hailsham and Mr Butler were eliminated there was great support for Lord Home. A great many had said that if Lord Home could be persuaded to accept this was the answer. A straight vote had not been taken between Lord Hailsham and Lord Home.

I deduce that before Lord Home's name began to be seriously considered as a potential Prime Minister, in the general view the choice lay between Mr Butler and Lord Hailsham. Mr Maudling, who had been thought of earlier in the summer before the Peerage Act 1963 had come to the fore and at a time when there was a possibility of my Administration being brought to a sudden end by some critical division, had been in the running with Mr Butler. But it is now clear that in spite of a slight revival in the last day or two the whole contest has been publicised as one between Mr Butler and Lord Hailsham. On the one side, long experience, devoted service to the Party, absolute integrity of character, great political skill, and the moral and intellectual inspiration of the Conservative Party after the 1945 collapse. On the other, Lord Hailsham, a man of the highest moral standing, keen churchmanship, strong opinions, a great orator, a fine public performer, able to enthuse in a way that recalls some of the older leaders of opinion in the past, and perhaps the most favoured election winner.

Nevertheless, it soon emerged that there were very strong opponents of each. There were those for instance who thought that Mr Butler with all his qualities was a dreary figure who would lead the Party to inevitable defeat or to a worse defeat than was necessary. These sections included not only members of the House of Commons but strong sections in the party Organisation. On the other side there were those who thought that Lord Hailsham, in spite of his great qualities, was somewhat unpredictable. This included the more old fashioned people who are shocked at the gimmicks and inescapable advertising which play an important role in political life. (Incidentally there is nothing new in this because I have heard, all through my life, the same criticism of Sir Winston Churchill from the days of Sidney Street with his coats, hats, cigars, romper suits and all the rest of it.) But apart from this question of taste I think there is a real sense of alarm lest under the tremendous stress of world politics Lord Hailsham would not be able to remain sufficiently calm to handle the kind of situation which only too frequently arises.

When we come to the position of Lord Home it is noticeable that apart from being the first choice of very large groups as set out earlier he seems to be the second choice of everybody. Nobody is against him and indeed everyone seems to think he has all the qualities except the great disadvantage of being a 'right-down regular' peer. Strange as it may seem, Lord Hailsham is hardly thought of as a peer any more. But the fourteenth Earl – will he not be the source of attack, ridicule, etc. that will be insupportable or too damaging? This seems to be the only fear expressed by anyone. Cabinet colleagues would work loyally under Lord Home as their chief. Members of Parliament would feel that they were efficiently and strongly led; organised bodies of the Party who already have a deep respect for Lord Home as representing qualities, which although often derided are still admired, would rally round him.

If Your Majesty would make this choice you would incur no blame and would be held to have chosen a man generally supported by all the various sections to whom a Minister must look for the support of his administration. I am bound to say that if we are able to persuade Lord Home to undertake this task, as I think Your Majesty will be able to do, I can think of nobody to whom I would more willingly commit the further stages, particularly in the realm of foreign affairs, of the policies which I have tried to pursue during my tenure of office. It will be an advantage that he is already so well known and liked by the main figures, including Mr Gromyko and Mr Khrushchev, as well as Mr Rusk and President Kennedy. On the home front I feel that a situation will develop not unlike that when I recommended Your Majesty to appoint Lord Home Foreign Secretary. This was regarded at first with great derision. It was violently attacked in the House of Commons and it was not too well received in the Conservative Party. The fact that he is now regarded as one of the most successful of my colleagues is due entirely to Lord Home's having been able, by his character, to overcome the disadvantages which he had to face. Even the most bitter opponents or the most critical debaters find beneath an apparently meek demeanour something very firm and tough. He is well able to give a good account of himself. At any rate, it will be interesting to watch these encounters when they take place.

It must, I think, be a condition that if Lord Home accepts Your Majesty's nomination he should take advantage of the Peerage Act and seek immediate election to the House of Commons. I think it has been generally agreed in recent years that it would be difficult to have a peer as Prime Minister. Your Majesty's grandfather established that in the case of Lord Curzon. The passing of the Act allowing a peer to sit in the House of Commons has now made it almost impossible.

Since your Majesty has conferred the honour of Knight of the Thistle on Lord Home he is of course, even when he gives up his Peerage, a Knight. I hope it will be possible for him to be called Sir Alec Home. Alec is, after all, a well known diminutive of Alexander and all over Scotland, where Alexander is a very common name, Alec is in ordinary use. Therefore I hope no difficulty will be found if this is what he would wish. The pedants of heraldry may make some objection; but since they have allowed Sir Austin Richard William Low

APPENDIX

to be known in heraldry as Sir Toby Low I trust they will allow Sir Alexander to be known as Sir Alec.

Your Majesty has asked for my advice. I thought it right to prepare myself against this possibility and hence set out my thoughts on paper in this memorandum. Your Majesty may care to have a copy for the Royal Records and I will keep a copy. I think in the present circumstances this is a wise course to take in order to safeguard Your Majesty's position.

October 17, 1963

Since obtaining the reports from the four sources to which I have referred and compiling this memorandum on the night of October 17, I have this morning received accounts of movements among certain Ministers to oppose the choice of Lord Home. It remains the fact that out of the Cabinet Ministers, not less than ten when asked who they would like to succeed me in the event of my resignation answered the question, Lord Home. One or two of these may of course now be changing their position; but this is the information which the Lord Chancellor gave me yesterday. I would judge that what is happening is that the rival forces of the defeated parties (if I may use such an expression) that is of Mr Butler and Lord Hailsham are now trying to join together in a last-minute agreement amongst themselves to support Mr Butler. I still do not think that this alters the immediate situation, although it may of course affect Lord Home's success in forming an Administration should Your Majesty entrust him with the task. After all there is nothing unusual in a Minister having to take soundings and enter into negotiations before an Administration can be successfully formed, and there is nothing that is reported in today's newspapers as a result of last night's efforts by certain ministers to alter the advice which I have given to Your Majesty. If Lord Home fails to form an Administration likely to command the support of the House of Commons, he will no doubt report this to Your Majesty and Your Majesty can then entrust the commission to other hands.

October 18, 1963

Select Bibliography

Private Papers

1 Macmillan Papers
The Macmillan Papers are in the Bodleian Library, Oxford. The Macmillan Publishing Archive and other related material is at the British Library.

2 Other Private Papers
Winthrop Aldrich Papers (Harvard University, Boston)
Earl Alexander of Tunis Papers (National Archives, Kew)
Lord Allen of Hurtwood Papers (Thomas Cooper Library, University of South Carolina, Columbia)
Nancy Astor Papers (Reading University)
Earl Attlee Papers (Bodleian Library, Oxford, and Churchill College, Cambridge)
Earl of Avon Papers (Birmingham University, courtesy of the Avon Trustees)
Countess of Avon Papers (courtesy of the Countess of Avon)
Earl Baldwin Papers (Cambridge University Library)
Lord Beaverbrook Papers (House of Lords Record Office)
Ernest Bevin Papers (Churchill College, Cambridge)
Sir Isaiah Berlin Papers (Bodleian Library, Oxford)
Sir George Bolton Papers (Bank of England)
Lady Violet Bonham Carter Papers (Bodleian Library, Oxford)
Lord Boothby Papers (courtesy of Lady Boothby)
Viscount Boyd of Merton Papers (Bodleian Library, Oxford)
Sir Maurice Bowra Papers (Wadham College, Oxford)
Lord Broxbourne Papers (courtesy of Sir Jonah Walker-Smith)
Lord Butler of Saffron Walden Papers (Trinity College, Cambridge)
Dr David Butler Papers (Nuffield College, Oxford)
Nicholas Byam Shaw Papers (courtesy of Nicholas Byam Shaw)
Lord Caccia Papers (Eton College Library)
Sir Alexander Cadogan Papers (Churchill College, Cambridge)
Sir Austen Chamberlain Papers (Birmingham University Library)
Neville Chamberlain Papers (Birmingham University Library)
Viscount Chandos Papers (Churchill College, Cambridge)
Chartwell Papers (Churchill College, Cambridge)
Viscount Cherwell Papers (Nuffield College, Oxford)
Sir Winston Churchill Papers (Churchill College, Cambridge)
William Clark Papers (Bodleian Library, Oxford)
Lord Cobbold Papers (Bank of England)

Lady Diana Cooper Papers (Eton College Library)

Brigadier Anthony Cowgill Papers (courtesy of the late Brigadier Anthony Cowgill)

Sir Stafford Cripps Papers (Nuffield College, Oxford)

Viscount Crookshank Papers (Bodleian Library, Oxford)

Sir Knox Cunningham Papers (in private possession)

Lord Dacre Papers (Christ Church, Oxford)

Lord Dalton Papers (Nuffield College, Oxford)

Geoffrey Dawson Papers (Bodleian Library, Oxford)

Sir Patrick Dean Papers (Bodleian Library, Oxford)

The Devonshire Collection (Chatsworth, courtesy of the Duke of Devonshire)

Sir Pierson Dixon Papers (courtesy of Mr Piers Dixon)

Sir Douglas Dodds-Parker Papers (Magdalen College, Oxford, courtesy of the late Sir Douglas Dodds-Parker)

Lord Duncan-Sandys Papers (Churchill College, Cambridge)

Dwight D. Eisenhower Papers (Eisenhower Presidential Library, Abilene, Kansas)

Paul Emrys-Evans Papers (British Library)

Lord Fisher of Lambeth Papers (Lambeth Palace Library)

Sir Nigel Fisher Papers (in private possession)

Lord Fraser of Kilmorack Papers (Bodleian Library, Oxford)

Lieutenant-General Sir James Gammell Papers (Imperial War Museum)

Lord Gladwyn Papers (Churchill College, Cambridge)

Lord Gordon-Walker Papers (Churchill College, Cambridge)

Lord Hailes Papers (Churchill College, Cambridge)

Lord Hailsham Papers (Churchill College, Cambridge)

J.B.S. Haldane Papers (National Library of Scotland)

Sir William Haley Papers (Churchill College, Cambridge)

Lord Halifax Papers (Borthwick Institute, York)

Lord Hankey Papers (Churchill College, Cambridge)

Thomas Hardy Papers (Eton College Library)

Sir Roy Harrod Papers (British Library)

Lord Home of the Hirsel Papers (courtesy of the 15th Earl of Home)

Lord Hore-Belisha Papers (Churchill College, Cambridge)

Viscount Inskip Papers (Churchill College, Cambridge)

John F. Kennedy Papers (Kennedy Presidential Library, Boston, Massachusetts)

Lord Keynes Papers (King's College, Cambridge)

Earl of Kilmuir Papers (Churchill College, Cambridge)

Alexander C. Kirk Papers (National Archives, Washington DC)

Hugh Lunghi Papers (courtesy of Mr Hugh Lunghi)

Viscount Margesson Papers (Churchill College, Cambridge)

Viscount Monckton of Brenchley Papers (Bodleian Library, Oxford)

Lord Morrison of Lambeth Papers (Nuffield College, Oxford)

Sir Charles Mott-Radclyffe Papers (Middle East Centre, St Antony's College, Oxford)

Earl Mountbatten of Burma Papers (University of Southampton)
Lord Normanbrook Papers (Bodleian Library, Oxford)
Viscount Norwich Papers (Churchill College, Cambridge)
Sir Patrick Reilly Papers (Bodleian Library, Oxford)
Lord Reith Diaries (unpublished material, BBC Written Archives, Caversham)
Kenneth Rose Papers (courtesy of Kenneth Rose)
Sir Horace Rumbold Papers (Bodleian Library, Oxford)
5th Marquess of Salisbury Papers (Hatfield House, Hatfield)
Lord Selwyn-Lloyd Papers (Churchill College, Cambridge)
Lord Sherfield Papers (Bodleian Library, Oxford)
Viscount Simon Papers (Bodleian Library, Oxford)
Earl of Swinton Papers (Churchill College, Cambridge)
Lord Thorneycroft Papers (Southampton University)
Viscount Thurso Papers (Churchill College, Cambridge)
Dame Irene Ward Papers (Bodleian Library, Oxford)
Baron Wakehurst Papers (Parliamentary Archives)
Sir Roy Welensky Papers (Rhodes House, Oxford)
Lord Wilson of Rievaulx Papers (Bodleian Library, Oxford)
Sir Horace Wilson Papers (National Archives, Kew)
Earl of Woolton Papers (Bodleian Library, Oxford)

3 *Oral History Transcripts* (Kennedy Presidential Library)
McGeorge Bundy
Chester Cooper
Sir Alec Douglas-Home (later Lord Home of the Hirsel)
Lord Gore-Booth
Averell Harriman
Sir Patrick Reilly
Dean Rusk
Sir Humphrey (later Lord) Trevelyan
Sir Michael Wright

Public and Institutional Records

1 *State Papers* (National Archives, Kew)
State Papers (Public Records Office of Northern Ireland – PRONI – Belfast)
Annual Report and Accounts of the British Broadcasting Corporation, 1956–57, Cmnd 267, Stationery Office, 1957
British Documents on the End of Empire, Series A Volume 4: The Conservative Government and the End of the Empire 1957–1964, Part I High Policy, Political and Constitutional Change, Part II Economics, International Relations, and the Commonwealth, ed. by Ronald Hyam and Wm Roger Louis, Stationery Office, 2000
British Documents on the End of Empire, Series B, Volume 9: Central Africa,

Part I Closer Association 1945–1958, Part II Crisis and Dissolution 1959–1965, ed. Philip Murphy, Stationery Office, 2005*

Committee on Higher Education (The Robbins Report), Cmnd 2154, 1963, HMSO

Documents on British Foreign Policy, 1919–1939, Series 1, Series 2, Series 3, ed. E. L. Woodward, W. N. Medlicott and Douglas Dakin; M.E. Lambert and Rohan Butler; J. P. T. Bury, Gillian Bennett and Keith A. Hamilton, HMSO, 1946–1997

Documents on British Policy Overseas, Series 1, Volume 1, ed. Rohan Butler and M. E. Pelly, HMSO, 1984

Documents on British Policy Overseas, Series 1, volumes 1 and 2, ed. Roger Bullen and M. E. Pelly, HMSO, 1986 and 1985

Enumeration of the Inhabitants of Glasgow, John Cleland, 1831, Glasgow City Archives

15 to 18: Report of the Central Advisory Council for Education, England (Chairman Sir Geoffrey Crowther), Vol. 1, Report, July 24, 1959, HMSO

Half Our Future (The Newsom Report), 1963. A Report of the Central Advisory Council for Education, HMSO, 1963

Hola Camp: Documents relating to the deaths of eleven Mau Mau detainees at Hola Camp in Kenya, Cmnd 778, HMSO, June 1959

Hola Camp: Further Documents relating to the deaths of eleven Mau Mau detainees at the Hola Camp in Kenya, Cmnd 816, HMSO, July 1959

Indians in Kenya: memorandum, Cmnd 1922, HMSO, 1923

Lord Denning's Report: The Circumstances Leading to the Resignation of the Former Secretary of State for War, Mr J. D. Profumo, Cmnd 2152, HMSO, September 1963

Memorandum on relations between the United Kingdom, the United States and France in the months following Egyptian nationalisation of the Suez Canal Company in 1956, National Archives, Kew, FO 800/728

Record of Proceedings and Evidence in the Inquiry into the deaths of eleven Mau Mau detainees at Hola Camp in Kenya, Cmnd 795, HMSO, June 1959

Report Concerning the Disappearance of Two Former Foreign Office Officials, Cmnd 9577, HMSO, September 1955

Report of the Committee on Broadcasting (The Pilkington Report), 1960, Cmnd 1753, 5 June 1962, HMSO

Report of the Nyasaland Commission of Inquiry (The Devlin Report), Cmnd 814, HMSO, 16 July 1959

Report on the Royal Commission on the Press, 1961–1962, Cmnd 1811, September 1962, HMSO

---

*Volumes kindly donated to the author by Mrs Susan Kyle from the library of the late Mr Keith Kyle.

The Reshaping of British Railways (The Beeching Report), British Railways
Board, HMSO, 1963
Security Procedures in the Public Service (The Radcliffe Report), Cmnd 1681,
April 1962, HMSO
Statement on Defence, Cmnd 9391, HMSO, February 1955
Traffic in Towns (The Buchanan Report), 1963, Penguin Books, Harmonds-
worth, in association with HMSO, 1963

2 *Other Records*
Annual Conference Reports of the National Union of Conservative and
Unionist Associations
Annual Register
BBC Written Archives (Caversham Park, Reading)
Balliol College, Oxford
Bank of England Archives
Burke's Peerage, 3 volumes, Boydell, 2003
Eton College
Foreign Relations of the United States, Volume XVI: The Suez Crisis, 26 July–
31 December 1956, ed. Nina J. Noring, Department of State, Washington
DC, 1990
Keesing's Contemporary Archives, 1945–1977
Labour Party Annual Conference Reports
Mass Observation files (Sussex University)
News International plc, Archives (*The Times* Archives and Record Office,
London)
Oxford University Calendar (Clarendon Press, Oxford)
The Repatriations from Austria in 1945: The Cowgill Inquiry and *The Report
of An Inquiry*, 2 volumes, Sinclair-Stevenson, 1990
State Department Files, National Archives, Washington
Stockton Conservative Association Papers, Bodleian Library
Stockton Conservative Association Papers, Records and Diaries (Stockton-
on-Tees Conservative Association)
Summer Fields, Oxford
Who's Who 1924–1987 (A. & C. Black)
Who Was Who 1897–1980 (A. & C. Black)

3 *Published Official and Party Documents*
Annual Register
Conservative Party Archives (Bodleian Library, Oxford)
Report on Social Insurance & Allied Services (December 1942), Cmnd 6404

The Press and Periodical Literature
1 *National and Foreign*
*Daily Express, Daily Graphic, Daily Herald, Daily Mail, Daily Mirror,
Daily Record, Daily Telegraph, Daily Worker, Evening Dispatch, Evening
News, Evening Standard, Financial Times, Glasgow Herald, Guardian,*

Independent, Indianapolis Star, Manchester Guardian, Morning Post, Morning Star, New York Herald Tribune, New York Times, News Chronicle, News of the World, Observer, The People, Scandia, The Scotsman, Sun, Sunday Chronicle, Sunday Express, Sunday Telegraph, Sunday Times, The Times

2 *Local and Regional*
Belfast Telegraph, Birmingham Daily Mail, Birmingham Post, Brighton Evening Argus, Bromley Times, Darlington and Stockton Times, Glasgow Herald, Isis, Kent Messenger, Labour Chronicle, Midland Daily Telegraph, Newcastle Journal, North Eastern Daily Gazette, Northern Echo, Oxford Mail, Ripon and Richmond Chronicle, Western Daily Press, Yorkshire Post

3 *Journals and Periodicals*
Apollo, Architectural Review, Army Quarterly & Defence Journal, Atlantic Monthly, Church Times, Contemporary British History, Contemporary Record, Crossbow, Diplomatic History, Economic History Review, The Economist, Encounter, English Historical Review, Eton College Chronicle, Foreign Affairs: An American Quarterly Review, Historical Journal, History Today, Illustrated London News, Intelligence and National Security, International Affairs, The International History Review, Journal of Politics, Life, Listener, London Review of Books, London School of Economics Quarterly, Macmillan News, Middle Eastern Affairs, New Statesman & Nation, New York Review of Books, Newsweek, Paris Match, Parliamentary Affairs, Picture Post, Private Eye, Publishing News, Punch, Spectator, Star, The Summer Fields Magazine, Tatler, Times Literary Supplement, Twentieth Century British History

Published Works By Harold Macmillan
1 *Books and Pamphlets* (all published by Macmillan)
Industry and the State (with Robert Boothby, John Loder and Oliver Stanley), 1927
Reconstruction: A Plea for a National Policy, 1933
Planning for Employment, 1935
The Next Five Years, 1935
The Middle Way, 1938 (revised edition, 1966)
The Price of Peace, 1938
Economic Aspects of Defence (with Paul Eizig and Thomas Balogh), 1939
Winds of Change 1914–1939, 1966
The Blast of War 1939–1945, 1967
Tides of Fortune 1945–1955, 1969
Riding the Storm 1956–1959, 1971
Pointing the Way 1959–1961, 1972
At the End of the Day 1961–1963, 1973

· *The Past Masters: politics and politicians*, 1975
War Diaries: Politics and War in the Mediterranean January 1943–May 1945, 1984
The Macmillan Diaries: The Cabinet Years 1950–1957 (ed. Peter Catterall), 2003
The Macmillan Diaries: The Premiership 1959–1966 (ed. Peter Catterall), 2011

2 *Other Published Works* (pamphlets and treatises published by Macmillan)
The State and Industry, 1932
The Price of Peace, October 1938
Why Britain Fights, 1940

Secondary Sources
1 *Published Works*
(All books are published in London, unless otherwise indicated)
Dean Acheson, *Present at the Creation: My Years in the State Department*, Hamish Hamilton, 1970
Paul Addison, *The Road to 1945*, Jonathan Cape, 1975
Richard Aldous and Sabine Lee (ed.), *Harold Macmillan and Britain's World Role*, Macmillan, 1996
Nicholas Aldridge, *Time to Spare?: A History of Summer Fields*, David Talboys Publications, Oxford, 1989
Joseph and Stewart Alsop, *The Reporter's Trade*, Bodley Head, 1960
Stephen E. Ambrose, *Eisenhower The President Volume 2, 1952–1969*, Allen & Unwin, 1984
_____ *Eisenhower: Soldier and President*, Pocket Books paperback edition, 2003
Julian Amery, *Joseph Chamberlain and the Tariff Reform Campaign: The Life of Joseph Chamberlain Volume Six 1903–1968*, Macmillan, 1969
_____ *Approach March: A Venture in Autobiography*, Hutchinson, 1973
Leo Amery, *My Political Life: Volume Two War and Peace 1914–1929*, Hutchinson, 1953
_____ *My Political Life: Volume Three The Unforgiving Years 1929–1940*, Hutchinson, 1955
Mark Amory (ed.), *The Letters of Ann Fleming*, Collins Harvill, 1985
Christopher Andrew, *The Defence of the Realm: The Authorized History of MI5*, Allen Lane, 2009
Rick Atkinson, *An Army at Dawn: The War in North Africa 1942–1943*, Little Brown, 2003
Phyllis Auty and Richard Clogg (ed.), *British Policy towards Wartime Resistance in Yugoslavia and Greece*, Macmillan, 1975.
Walter Bagehot, *The English Constitution*, Fontana Paperback edition, 1963
Simon Ball, *The Guardsmen: Harold Macmillan, Three Friends, and the World They Made*, Harper Collins Publishers, 2004

Stuart Ball (ed.), *Parliament and Politics in the Age of Baldwin and MacDonald: The Headlam Diaries 1923–1935*, The Historians' Press, 1992

_____ *Parliament and Politics in the Age of Churchill and Attlee: The Headlam Diaries 1935–1951*, Royal Historical Society, Cambridge University Press, Cambridge 1999

Paul Barker, *The Freedoms of Suburbia*, Frances Lincoln, 2009

John Barnes and David Nicholson (ed.), *The Leo Amery Diaries: Volume One 1896 – 1929*, Hutchinson, 1980

_____ *The Empire at Bay: the Leo Amery Diaries 1929 – 1945*, Hutchinson, 1988

M. J. Barnett, *Politics of Legislation: the Rent Act of 1957*, Weidenfeld & Nicolson, 1969

C. J. Bartlett, *A Political History of Anglo-American Relations since 1945*, Longmans, 1992

Lewis Baston, *Reggie: The Life of Reginald Maudling*, Sutton Publishing, 2004

Francis Beckett, *Macmillan*, Haus Publishing, 2006

Sally Bedel Smith, *Grace and Power: The Private World of the Kennedy White House*, Aurum Press, 2004

Tony Benn, *Years of Hope: Diaries, Papers and Letters 1940–1962*, Hutchinson, 1994

_____ *Out of the Wilderness: Diaries 1963 – 1967*, Hutchinson, 1987

_____ *More Time for Politics: Diaries 2001–2007*, Hutchinson, 2007

Humphrey Berkeley, *Crossing the Floor*, Allen & Unwin, 1972

Isaiah Berlin, *Enlightening: Letters 1946–1960*, ed. Henry Hardy and Jennifer Holmes, Chatto & Windus, 2009

Nicholas Bethell, *The Last Secret*, Deutsch, 1977

John Betjeman, *Summoned By Bells*, John Murray, 1960

Reginald Bevins, *The Greasy Pole*, Hodder & Stoughton, 1965

Earl of Birkenhead, *Walter Monckton: The Life of Viscount Monckton of Brenchley*, Weidenfeld & Nicolson, 1969

Robert Black (ed.), *To the Hebrides: Samuel Johnson's Journey to the Western Islands of Scotland and James Boswell's Journal of a Tour to the Hebrides*, Birlinn Limited, Edinburgh, 2007

Robert Blake, *Disraeli*, Methuen paperback edition, 1969

_____ *The Conservative Party from Peel to Thatcher*, Methuen, 1985

Robert Blake and C.S. Nicholls (ed.), *The Dictionary of National Biography 1971–1980*, Oxford University Press, Oxford, 1986

_____ *The Dictionary of National Biography 1981 – 1985*, Oxford University Press, Oxford, 1990

Martin Blumenson, *Mark Clark*, Jonathan Cape, 1985

Vernon Bogdanor, *The Monarchy and the Constitution*, Clarendon Press, Oxford, 1995

_____ *The New British Constitution*, Hart Publishing, Oxford, 2009

Vernon Bogdanor and Robert Skidelsky (ed.), *The Age of Affluence*, Macmillan, 1970

Christopher Booker, *A Looking-Glass Tragedy: The Controversy over the Repatriations from Austria in* 1945, Duckworth, 1997

_____ *The Neophiliacs: a study of the revolution in English life in the Fifties and Sixties*, Collins, 1969

Christopher Booker and Richard North, *The Great Deception: Can the European Union Survive?*, Continuum, 2005

Cherie Booth and Cate Haste, *The Goldfish Bowl: Married to the Prime Minister* 1955–1997, Chatto & Windus, 2004

Lord Boothby, *I Fight to Live*, Gollancz, 1947

_____ *My Yesterday, Your Tomorrow*, Hutchinson, 1962

_____ *Recollections of a Rebel*, Hutchinson, 1978

Tom Bower, *The Perfect English Spy: Sir Dick White and the Secret War* 1935–1990, Heinemann, 1995

Maurice Bowra, *New Bats in Old Belfries*, Robert Dugdale, Oxford, 2005

John Boyd-Carpenter, *Way of Life: The Memoirs of John Boyd-Carpenter*, Sidgwick & Jackson, 1980

Henry Brandon, *Special Relationships: a foreign correspondent's memoirs from Roosevelt to Reagan*, Macmillan, 1989

Howard Brenton, *Never So Good*, Nick Hern Books, 2008

Asa Briggs, *The BBC: The First Fifty Years*, Oxford University Press, Oxford, 1985

_____ *The History of Broadcasting in the United Kingdom Volume* 5: *Competition* 1955–1974, Oxford University Press, Oxford, 1995

Douglas Brinkley, *Dean Acheson: The Cold War Years* 1953–1971, Yale University Press, New Haven, 1992

Sam Brittan, *Steering the Economy*, Penguin Books, Harmondsworth, revised edition, 1971

Merry and Serge Bromberger, *Secrets of Suez*, Pan Books and Sidgwick and Jackson, 1957

David Butler, *The British General Election of* 1951, Macmillan, 1952

_____ *The British General Election of* 1955, Macmillan, 1955

David Butler and Anne Sloman, *British Political Facts* 1900–1975, Macmillan, 1975

Lord Butler, *The Art of the Possible*, revised paperback edition, Penguin Books, Harmondsworth, 1973

Mollie Butler, *August and Rab: A Memoir*, Weidenfeld & Nicolson, 1987

Alec Cairncross (ed.), *The Robert Hall Diaries, Vol. II* 1954–1961, Unwin Hyman, 1991

John Campbell, *Edward Heath: A Biography*, Jonathan Cape, 1993

_____ *Margaret Thatcher Volume Two: The Iron Lady*, Jonathan Cape, 2003

Tim Card, *Eton Renewed: A History from* 1860 *to the Present Day*, John Murray, 1994

Edward Carpenter, *Archbishop Fisher: His Life and Times*, The Canterbury Press, Norwich, 1991

Lord Carrington, *Reflect on Things Past: The Memoirs of Lord Carrington*,

Collins, 1988

Owen Chadwick, *Michael Ramsey: A Life*, Clarendon Press, Oxford, 1990
_____ *Britain and the Vatican during the Second World War*, Cambridge University Press, 1986.

Sir Austen Chamberlain, *Politics from Inside: An Epistolary Chronicle 1906–1914*, Cassell, 1936

Lord Chandos, *The Memoirs of Lord Chandos*, The Bodley Head, 1962
_____ *From Peace to War: A Study in Contrasts 1857–1918*, Bodley Head, 1968

John Charmley, *Duff Cooper: The Authorized Biography*, Weidenfeld & Nicolson, 1986

Randolph S. Churchill, *The Fight for the Tory Leadership: A Contemporary Chronicle*, Heinemann, 1964

Winston S. Churchill (Jr), *His Father's Son: The life of Randolph Churchill*, Weidenfeld & Nicolson, 1996

Alan Clark, *The Tories: Conservatives and the Nation State 1922–1997*, Weidenfeld & Nicolson, 1998

Ronald Clark, *The Life and Work of J. B. S. Haldane*, Hodder & Stoughton, 1968

Sir Edward Clarke, *The Story of My Life*, John Murray, 1918

Peter Clarke, *A Question of Leadership: Gladstone to Thatcher*, Hamish Hamilton, 1991
_____ *The Cripps Version: The Life of Sir Stafford Cripps 1889–1952*, Allen Lane, The Penguin Press, 2002

Michael Cockerell, *Live from Number 10: The Inside Story of Prime Ministers and Television*, Faber and Faber, 1988

H. L. Coles and A. K. Weinberg, *Civil Affairs: Soldiers become Governors*, Washington, USPGO, 1964

John Colville, *The Fringes of Power: Downing Street Diaries 1939–1955*, Hodder, 1985
_____ *Those Lambtons!*, Hodder & Stoughton, 1988

Henry Colyton, *Occasion, Chance and Change: A Memoir 1902–1946*, Michael Russell, Norwich, 1993

Chris Cook, *Sources in British Political History 1900–1951*, 5 volumes, Macmillan, 1975

Chris Cook and John Ramsden (ed.), *By-Elections in British Politics*, Macmillan, 1973

Giles Cooper, *Everything in the Garden*, included in *New English Dramatists 7*, Penguin Books, Harmondsworth, 1963

Colin Coote, *Editorial: Memoirs*, Eyre & Spottiswoode, 1965.
_____ *A Companion of Honour: The Story of Walter Elliot*, Collins, 1965

Brigadier Anthony Cowgill, Lord Brimelow and Christopher Booker, *The Repatriations from Austria in 1945: The Report of An Inquiry*, Sinclair-Stevenson, 1990
_____ *The Repatriations from Austria in 1945 – Cowgill Inquiry: The*

Documentary Evidence reproduced in full from British, American, German and Yugoslav Sources, Sinclair-Stevenson, 1990

Maurice Cowling, *The Impact of Hitler: British politics and British policy 1933–1940*, Cambridge University Press, Cambridge, 1975

Percy Cradock, *Know Your Enemy: How the Joint Intelligence Committee Saw the World*, John Murray, 2002

Quentin Crewe, *The Autobiography of an Optimist*, Hutchinson, 1991

Stanley Crooks, *Peter Thorneycroft*, George Mann Publications, Winchester, 2007

J. A. Cross, *Lord Swinton*, Oxford University Press, Oxford, 1982

N. J. Crowson (ed.), *Fleet Street, Press Barons and Politics: The Journals of Collin Brooks 1932–1940*, Royal Historical Society, Cambridge University Press, Cambridge, 1998

Sir Knox Cunningham, *One Man Dog: My Times with Harold Macmillan 1959–1963*, privately printed, 2006

Robert Dallek, *John F. Kennedy: An Unfinished Life 1917–1963*, Allen Lane, 2003

Tam Dalyell, *Dick Crossman: A Portrait*, Weidenfeld & Nicolson, 1989

Alex Danchev and Daniel Todman (ed.), *Field Marshal Lord Alanbrooke: War Diaries 1939–1945*, Weidenfeld & Nicolson, 2001

Richard Davenport-Hines, *The Macmillans*, Heinemann, 1992

_____ (ed.), *Letters from Oxford: Hugh Trevor-Roper to Bernard Berenson*, Weidenfeld & Nicolson, 2006.

Charles de Gaulle, *Memoirs of Hope*, Weidenfeld & Nicolson, 1971

Andrew Devonshire, *Accidents of Fortune*, Michael Russell, Norwich, 2004

Deborah Devonshire, *Memories of Andrew Devonshire*, Landmark Publishing, Ashbourne, 2007

_____ *Home to Roost and Other Peckings*, John Murray, 2009

David Dilks (ed.), *The Diary of Sir Alexander Cadogan 1938–1943*, Cassell, 1971

Benjamin Disraeli, *Coningsby*, Colburn, 1844

_____ *Endymion*, Longmans, Green & Co., 1881

_____ *Sybil or The Two Nations*, Penguin Books, Harmondsworth, 1980

Sir Douglas Dodds-Parker, *Political Eunuch*, Springwood Books, 1986

Bernard Donoughue and G.W. Jones, *Herbert Morrison: Portrait of a Politician*, Weidenfeld & Nicolson, 1973

J. C. R. Dow, *The Management of the British Economy 1945–60*, Cambridge University Press, Cambridge, 1964

Lord Drogheda, *Double Harness*, Weidenfeld & Nicolson, 1978

David Dutton, *Anthony Eden: A Life and Reputation*, Arnold, 1997

_____ *Neville Chamberlain*, Arnold, 2001

James Eayrs, *The Commonwealth and Suez*, Oxford University Press, 1964

Anthony Eden, *The Eden Memoirs: Full Circle*, Cassell, 1960

_____ *The Eden Memoirs: Facing the Dictators*, Cassell, 1962

_____ *The Eden Memoirs: The Reckoning*, Cassell, 1965

_____ *Another World: 1897–1917*, Allen Lane, 1976

Clarissa Eden, *A Memoir: From Churchill to Eden*, Weidenfeld & Nicolson, 2007

Ruth Dudley Edwards, *Harold Macmillan: A Life in Pictures*, Macmillan, 1983

Lord Egremont, *Wyndham and Children First*, Macmillan, 1968

Dwight D. Eisenhower, *The White House Years: Mandate for Change 1953–1956*, Heinemann, 1956

Leon D. Epstein, *British Politics in the Suez Crisis*, Pall Mall Press, 1964

Harold Evans, *Downing Street Diary: The Macmillan Years, 1957–1963*, Hodder & Stoughton, 1981

David Faber, *Speaking for England: Leo, Julian and John Amery – The Tragedy of a Political Family*, Simon & Schuster, 2005

_____ *Munich: The 1938 Appeasement Crisis*, Simon & Schuster, 2008

J. S. fforde, *The Bank of England and Public Policy, 1941–1958*, Cambridge University Press, 1992

Herman Finer, *Dulles over Suez*, Heinemann, 1964

Nigel Fisher, *Iain Macleod*, Deutsch, 1973

_____ *The Tory Leaders: Their Struggle for Power*, Weidenfeld & Nicolson, 1977

_____ *Harold Macmillan*, Weidenfeld & Nicolson, 1982

Penelope Fitzgerald, *The Knox Brothers*, Flamingo, 2002

Pascal Fontaine (ed.), *Jean Monnet: A Grand Design for Europe*, OOP, Luxembourg, 1988

Hugh Foot, *A Start in Freedom*, Hodder & Stoughton, 1964

Steven Z. Freiberger, *Dawn Over Suez: The Rise of American Power in the Middle East, 1953–1957*, Ivan R. Dee, Chicago, 1992

Aleksandr Fursenko and Timothy Naftali, *Khrushchev's Cold War: The Inside Story of an American Adversary*, W. W. Norton, New York, 2006

J. K. Galbraith, *The Affluent Society*, Penguin edition, Harmondsworth, 1965

_____ *Ambassador's Journal: A Personal Account of the Kennedy Years*, Houghton Mifflin, Boston, 1969

John P. S. Gearson, *Harold Macmillan and the Berlin Wall Crisis, 1958–1962: The Limits of Interest and Force*, Macmillan, 1998

E. Brice Geelhoed and Anthony O. Edmonds, *Eisenhower, Macmillan and Allied Unity, 1957–1961*, Palgrave Macmillan, Basingstoke, 2003

E. Bruce Geelhoed and Anthony O. Edmonds (ed.), *The Macmillan-Eisenhower Correspondence, 1957–1969*, Palgrave Macmillan, Basingstoke, 2004

Martin Gilbert, *Winston S. Churchill: Volume V 1922–1939*, Heinemann, 1976

_____ *Finest Hour: Winston S. Churchill 1939–1941*, Heinemann, 1983

_____ *Road to Victory: Winston S. Churchill 1941–1945*, Heinemann, 1986

_____ *Never Despair: Winston S. Churchill 1945–1965*, Heinemann, 1988

_____ *In Search of Churchill: A Historian's Journey*, Harper Collins, 1994

_____ (ed.), *Plough My Own Furrow: The Story of Lord Allen of Hurtwood as told through his writings and correspondence*, Longmans, 1965

Ian Gilmour, *Whatever Happened to the Tories: The Conservative Party since 1945*, Fourth Estate, 1997

Lord Gladwyn, *The Memoirs of Lord Gladwyn*, Weidenfeld & Nicolson, 1972

Grace Wyndham Goldie, *Facing the Nation: Television and Politics 1936 – 1976*, Bodley Head, 1977

Laurence Goldman (ed.), *Oxford Dictionary of National Biography, 2001– 2004*, Oxford University Press, Oxford, 2009

Philip Goodhart, *The 1922: The Story of the Conservative Backbenchers' Parliamentary Committee*, Macmillan, 1973

_____ *A Stab in the Front: The Suez Conflict 1956*, Wilton 65, Windsor, 2006

John Grigg, *1943: The Victory That Never Was*, Penguin Books, Harmondsworth, revised edition, 1999

Jo Grimond, *Memoirs*, Heinemann, 1979

G. Grossmith and W. Grossmith, *The Diary of A Nobody*, Penguin Books, Harmondsworth, 1965 paperback edition.

Lord Hailsham, *The Door Wherein I Went*, Collins, 1975

_____ *A Sparrow's Flight: Memoirs*, Collins, 1990

Sue Harper and Vincent Porter, *British Cinema of the 1950s: The Decline of Deference*, Oxford University Press, 2003

Kenneth Harris, *Attlee*, Weidenfeld & Nicolson, 1982

Brian Harrison, *Seeking a Role: The United Kingdom, 1951–1970*, Clarendon Press, Oxford, 2009

R. F. Harrod, *The Life of John Maynard Keynes*, Macmillan, 1951

Max Hastings, *Nemesis: The Battle for Japan, 1944–45*, Harper Press, 2007

Ian Hay, *The First Hundred Thousand*, Seeley Service & Co. edition, 1975

Sir William Hayter, *A Double Life*, Hamish Hamilton, 1974

Sir Edward Heath, *The Course of My Life: The Autobiography of Sir Edward Heath*, Hodder & Stoughton, 1998

Simon Heffer, *Like the Roman: The Life of Enoch Powell*, Weidenfeld & Nicolson, 1998

_____ *Great British Speeches: A Stirring Anthology of Speeches from Every Period of British History*, Quercus, 2007

Nicholas Henderson, *The Private Office Revisited*, Profile Books, 2001

Peter Hennessy, *Whitehall*, Secker and Warburg, 1989

_____ *Never Again: Britain 1945–1951*, Jonathan Cape, 1992

_____ *Muddling Through: Power, Politics and the Quality of Government in Postwar Britain*, Victor Gollancz, 1996

_____ *The Prime Minister: The Office and Its Holders Since 1945*, Allen Lane, 2000

_____ *The Secret State: Whitehall and the Cold War*, Allen Lane, The Penguin Press, 2002

_____ *Having It So Good: Britain in the Fifties*, Allen Lane, 2006

_____ (ed.), *Cabinets and the Bomb*, Oxford University Press for the British Academy, 2007

J. D. Hoffman, *The Conservative Party in Opposition, 1945–1951*, MacGibbon & Kee, 1964

A. E. Holmans, *Demand Management in Britain*, Institute of Contemporary British History, 1999

James Holland, *Italy's Sorrow: A Year of War, 1944–45*, Harper Press, 2008

Lord Home, *The Way the Wind Blows: An Autobiography*, Collins, 1976

Michael F. Hopkins, Saul Kelly and John W. Young, *Washington Embassy: British Ambassadors to the United States, 1939–77*, Palgrave Macmillan, Basingstoke, 2009

Alistair Horne, *Macmillan 1894–1956: Volume 1 of the Official Biography*, Macmillan, 1988

_____ *Macmillan 1957–1986: Volume 2 of the Official Biography*, Macmillan, 1989

Anthony Howard, *RAB: The Life of R.A. Butler*, Jonathan Cape, 1985

_____ *Crossman: The Pursuit of Power*, Jonathan Cape, 1990

_____ (ed.), *The Crossman Diaries*, Magnum paperback condensed version, 1979

Michael Howard, *Grand Strategy, Volume 4*, HMSO, 1968

Geoffrey Howe, *Conflict of Loyalty*, Macmillan, 1994

Emrys Hughes, *Macmillan: portrait of a politician*, Allen & Unwin, 1962

George Hutchinson, *The Last Edwardian at No. 10*, Grafton Books, 1980

Ronald Hyam, *Empire and Sexuality*, Manchester University Press, Manchester, 1991

Julian Jackson, *France: The Dark Years 1940–1944*, Oxford University Press, 2001

Alan James, *Britain and the Congo Crisis, 1960–63*, Macmillan Press, Basingstoke, 1996.

Antony Jay (ed.), *The Oxford Dictionary of Political Quotations*, revised second edition, Oxford University Press, Oxford, 2005

Douglas Jay, *Change and Fortune: A Political Record*, Hutchinson, 1980

Roy Jenkins, *A Life at the Centre*, Macmillan, 1991

_____ *Portraits and Miniatures*, Macmillan, 1993

_____ *Churchill*, Macmillan, 2001

John Jones, *Balliol College A History: Second Edition Revised*, Oxford University Press, 2005

Thomas Jones, *Whitehall Diary Volume II 1926–1930*, Oxford University Press, 1971

_____ *A Diary with Letters 1931–1950*, Oxford University Press, 1954

Robert Kennedy, *Thirteen Days: The Cuban Missile Crisis*, Macmillan & Co., 1969

Anthony Kenny, *A Life in Oxford*, John Murray, 1997

J. M. Keynes, *The Economic Consequences of the Peace*, Macmillan paperback edition, 1984

_____ *A Tract on Monetary Reform*, Macmillan & Co., 1923

_____ *The General Theory of Employment Interest and Money*, Macmillan, 1936

Earl of Kilmuir, *Political Adventure, The Memoirs of the Earl of Kilmuir*, Weidenfeld & Nicolson, 1964

Cole C. Kingseed, *Eisenhower and the Suez Crisis of 1956*, Louisiana State University Press, Baton Rouge, Louisiana, 1995

R. J. L. Kingsford, *The Publishers' Association: 1896–1946*, Cambridge University Press,

Sir Ivone Kirkpatrick, *The Inner Circle: Memoirs of Ivone Kirkpatrick*, Macmillan, 1959

James Knox, *Robert Byron*, John Murray, 2003

_____ *Coronets & Cartoons: The Genius of Osbert Lancaster*, Frances Lincoln, 2008

Ronald Knox, *A Spiritual Aeneid*, Burns & Oates, 1950

Diana B. Kunz, *The Economic Diplomacy of the Suez Crisis*, University of North Carolina Press, 1991, Chapel Hill and London

Keith Kyle, *Suez*, Weidenfeld & Nicolson, 1991

_____ *Suez: Britain, France and the Endgame in Egypt*, I.B. Tauris, 2002

David Kynaston, *The City of London Volume IV: A Club No More 1945–2000*, Chatto & Windus, 2001

_____ *Austerity Britain: 1945–1951*, Bloomsbury, 2007

_____ *Family Britain: 1951–1957*, Bloomsbury, 2009.

Richard Lamb, *The Failure of the Eden Government*, Sidgwick & Jackson, 1987

_____ *The Macmillan Years 1957–1963: The Emerging Truth*, John Murray, 1995

Ann Lane, *Britain, the Cold War and Yugoslav Unity, 1941–1949*, Sussex Academic Press, Brighton, 1996

Barbara Leaming, *Jack Kennedy: The Making of a President*, Weidenfeld & Nicolson, 2006

James Lees-Milne, *Through Wood and Dale: Diaries 1975–1978*, Michael Russell, 2007

_____ *Beneath A Waning Moon: Diaries, 1985–1987* (ed. Michael Bloch), John Murray, 2003

Bernard Levin, *The Pendulum Years: Britain in the Sixties*, Icon Books paperback edition, 2003, Cambridge

Selwyn Lloyd, *Suez 1956: A Personal Account*, Jonathan Cape, 1978

Wm Roger Louis, *Ends of British Imperialism: The Scramble for Empire, Suez and Decolonisation*, I. B. Tauris, 2006

_____ *Penultimate Adventures with Britannia: Personalities, Politics and Culture in Britain*, I.B. Tauris, 2007

Wm Roger Louis and H. Bull, *The Special Relationship: Anglo-American Relations since 1945*, Clarendon Press, Oxford, 1986

Wm. Roger Louis and Roger Owen (ed.), *Suez 1956: The Crisis and its Consequences*, Clarendon Press, Oxford, 1991 paperback edition

Andrew Lownie, *John Buchan: The Presbyterian Cavalier*, Constable, 1995

W. Scott Lucas, *Divided We Stand: Britain, the US and the Suez Crisis*, Hodder & Stoughton, 1996 paperback edition

Oliver Lyttelton, Viscount Chandos, *The Memoirs of Lord Chandos*, Bodley Head, 1962

Peter Mangold, *The Almost Impossible Ally: Harold Macmillan and Charles de Gaulle*, I. B. Tauris, 2006

R.B. McCallum and Alison Readman, *The British General Election of* 1945, Oxford University Press, Oxford, 1947

Iverach McDonald, *The History of 'The Times': Volume V Struggles in War and Peace, 1939–1966*, Times Books, 1986

Malcolm MacDonald, *Titans and Others*, Collins, 1972

Donald MacDougall, *Don and Mandarin: Memoirs of an Economist*, John Murray, 1987

Robert McKenzie, *British Political Parties: The Distribution of Power within the Conservative and Labour Parties*, Heinemann, 1967

Leo McKinstry, *Rosebery: Statesman in Turmoil*, John Murray, 2005

John P. Mackintosh, *The British Cabinet*, 3rd edition, Stevens & Sons, 1977

_____ (ed.), *British Prime Ministers of the Twentieth Century, Volume 2: Churchill to Callaghan*, Weidenfeld & Nicolson, 1978

Alan Maclean, *No, I Tell a Lie, It was the Tuesday ...*, Kyle Cathie Limited, 1997

David S. McLellan, *Dean Acheson: The State Department Years*, Dodd, Mead & Company, New York, 1976

Robert McLellan, *The Isle of Arran*, David & Charles, Newton Abbot, 1985 edition

James Margach, *The Abuse of Power*, W. H. Allen, 1978

David Marquand, *Ramsay MacDonald*, Jonathan Cape, 1977

Stanley Martin, *The Order of Merit: One Hundred Years of Matchless Honour*, I. B. Tauris, 2007

Carol Mather, *Aftermath of War: Everyone must Go Home*, Macmillan, 1992

H. C. G. Matthew, Brian Harrison and Laurence Goldman (ed.), *Oxford Dictionary of National Biography*, 60 volumes, and online updates, Oxford University Press, 2004 – 2009.

Reginald Maudling, *Memoirs*, Sidgwick & Jackson, 1978

Ernest R. May and Philip D. Zelikow (ed.), *The Kennedy Tapes: Inside the White House during the Cuban Missile Crisis*, W. W. Norton, New York, 2001

Robert Menzies, *Afternoon Light: Some Memories of Men and Events*, Cassell, 1967

Keith Middlemass, *Power, Competition and the State, Volume One: Britain in Search of Balance, 1940–1961*, Macmillan, 1986

Keith Middlemass and John Barnes, *Baldwin: A Biography*, Weidenfeld & Nicolson, 1969

Alan Milward, *The Rise and Fall of a National Strategy, 1945–1963: The*

United Kingdom and the European Community, Vol. 1, Frank Cass, 2002

Anthony Moncrieff (ed.), *Suez: Ten Years Later*, BBC Publications, 1967

Anthony Montague Browne, *Long Sunset: Memoirs of Winston Churchill's Last Private Secretary*, Cassell, 1995

Joe Moran, *On Roads: A Hidden History*, Profile Books, 2009

Lord Moran, *Winston Churchill: The Struggle for Survival 1940–1965*, Sphere paperback edition, 1968

Charles Morgan, *The House of Macmillan 1843–1943*, Macmillan, 1943

Janet Morgan (ed.), *The Backbench Diaries of Richard Crossman*, Hamish Hamilton and Jonathan Cape, 1981

_____ *Diaries of a Cabinet Minister: Volume One, Minister of Housing, 1964–1966*, Hamish Hamilton/Jonathan Cape, 1975

John Morley, *Recollections: Volume 2*, Macmillan & Co., 1917

Herbert Morrison, *An Autobiography*, Odhams, 1960

Charlotte Mosley (ed.), *The Letters of Nancy Mitford and Evelyn Waugh*, Hodder & Stoughton, 1996

_____ *The Mitfords: Letters between Six Sisters*, Fourth Estate, 2007

Oswald Mosley, *My Life*, Nelson, 1968

Charles Mott-Radclyffe, *Foreign Body in the Eye: A Memoir of the Foreign Service Old and New*, Leo Cooper, 1955

C.L. Mowat, *Britain between the Wars 1918–1940*, Methuen paperback edition, 1968

David Murphy, Sergei A. Kondrashev and George Bailey, *Battleground Berlin: CIA vs KGB in the Cold War*, Yale University Press, 1997

Philip Murphy, *Party Politics and Decolonization: The Conservative Party and British Colonial Policy in Tropical Africa, 1951–1964*, Clarendon Press, Oxford, 1995

_____ *Alan Lennox-Boyd: a biography*, I. B. Tauris, 1999

Robert Murphy, *Diplomat among Warriors*, Collins, 1964

Christopher Murray, *Sean O'Casey: Writer at Work*, Gill & Macmillan, Dublin, 2004

Richard E. Neustadt, *Report to J. F. K: The Skybolt Crisis in Perspective*, Cornell University Press, Ithaca, New York, 1999

H. G. Nicholas, *The British General Election of 1950*, Macmillan, 1951

Harold Nicolson, *Diaries and Letters: 1930–1962*, ed. Nigel Nicolson, 3 volumes, Collins, 1966, 1967, 1968

_____ *Diaries and Letters: 1930–1964*, ed. Stanley Olson, Penguin Books, Harmondsworth, paperback edition, 1984

_____ *The Harold Nicolson Diaries 1907–1963*, ed. Nigel Nicolson, Weidenfeld & Nicolson, 2004

Nigel Nicolson, *Alex: The Life of Field Marshal Earl Alexander of Tunis*, Weidenfeld & Nicolson, 1973

_____ *Long Life: Memoirs*, Weidenfeld & Nicolson, 1997

_____ (ed.), *Vita and Harold: The letters of Vita Sackville-West and Harold Nicolson, 1910–1962*, Weidenfeld & Nicolson, 1992

John Julius Norwich (ed.), *The Duff Cooper Diaries: 1915–1951*, Weidenfeld & Nicolson, 2005

David Nunnerly, *President Kennedy and Britain*, Bodley Head, 1972

Anthony Nutting, *No End of a Lesson: The Story of Suez*, Constable, 1967

Lynne Olson, *Troublesome Young Men: The Rebels who brought Churchill to Power in 1940 and helped to save Britain*, Bloomsbury, 2007

George Orwell, *The Lion and the Unicorn: Socialism and the English Genius*, Secker & Warburg, 1962

Stephen Parkinson, *Arena of Ambition: A History of the Cambridge Union*, Icon Books, 2009

Peter Paterson, *Tired and Emotional: The Life of Lord George-Brown*, Chatto & Windus, 1993

G. C. Peden, *The Treasury and British Public Policy, 1906–1959*, Oxford University Press, 2000

Henry Pelling, *Churchill's Peacetime Ministry, 1951–1955*, Macmillan Press, Basingstoke, 1997

Alicia C. Percival, *Very Superior Men: Some Early Public School Headmasters and their Achievements*, Charles Knight & Co., 1973

Sir Charles Petrie and Alistair Cooke, *The Carlton Club 1832–2007*, The Carlton Club, 2007

Ben Pimlott, *Hugh Dalton*, Jonathan Cape, 1986

_____ *Harold Wilson*, Harper Collins, 1992

_____ *The Queen: A Biography of Elizabeth II*, Harper Collins, 1996

_____ (ed.), *The Second World War Diary of Hugh Dalton 1940–45*, Jonathan Cape, 1986.

_____ *The Political Diary of Hugh Dalton 1918–40, 1945–60*, Jonathan Cape, 1986

Chapman Pincher, *Their Trade is Treachery*, Sidgwick & Jackson, 1981

Edwin Plowden, *An Industrialist in the Treasury: The Post-War Years*, André Deutsch, 1989

Douglas Porch, *Hitler's Mediterranean Gamble: The North African and the Mediterranean Campaigns in World War II*, Weidenfeld & Nicolson, 2004

Mark Pottle (ed.), *Champion Redoubtable: The Diaries and Letters of Violet Bonham Carter 1914–1945*, Weidenfeld & Nicolson, 1998

_____ (ed.) *Daring to Hope: The Diaries and Letters of Violet Bonham Carter 1946–1969*, Weidenfeld & Nicolson, 2000

J. B. Priestley, *English Journey*, Penguin Books, Harmondsworth, paperback edition, 1977

David Profumo, *Bringing the House Down: A Family Memoir*, John Murray, 2006

Martin Pugh, *We Danced All Night: A Social History of Britain Between the Wars*, Bodley Head, 2008

John Ramsden, *The Age of Churchill & Eden, 1940–1957*, Longman, 1995

_____ *The Winds of Change: Macmillan to Heath, 1957–1975*, Longman, 1996

_____ *An Appetite for Power: A History of the Conservative Party since 1830*, Harper Collins, 1998

_____ *Don't Mention the War: The British and the Germans since 1890*, Little, Brown, 2006

Jean Redcliffe-Maud, *High Commission to Embassy: South Africa 1959–1963*, Englang Publishing, Cirencester, 1990

David Reynolds, *Britannia Overruled: British Policy and World Power in the 20th Century*, Longman, 1991

_____ *In Command of History: Churchill Fighting and Writing the Second World War*, Allen Lane, 2004

Robert Rhodes James, *Rosebery*, Weidenfeld & Nicolson, 1963

_____ *Anthony Eden*, Weidenfeld & Nicolson, 1986

_____ *Bob Boothby: A Portrait*, John Curtis, Hodder & Stoughton, 1991

_____ (ed.), *Chips: The Diaries of Sir Henry Channon*, Weidenfeld & Nicolson, 1967

_____ (ed.), *Memoirs of a Conservative: J.C.C. Davidson's Memoirs and Papers, 1910 – 1937*, Weidenfeld & Nicolson, 1969

Daniel Ritschel, *The Politics of Planning: The Debate on Economic Planning in Britain in the 1930s*, Clarendon Press, Oxford, 1997

Andrew Roberts, *Eminent Churchillians*, Weidenfeld & Nicolson, 1994

_____ *A History of the English-Speaking Peoples since 1900*, Weidenfeld & Nicolson, 2006

Frank Roberts, *Dealing with Dictators: The Destruction and Revival of Europe 1930–1970*, Weidenfeld & Nicolson, 1991

Trevor Robertson, *Crisis: The Inside Story of the Suez Conspiracy*, Hutchinson, 1965

Stephen Robinson, *The Remarkable Lives of Bill Deedes: The Authorised Biography*, Abacus revised paperback edition, 2008

Kenneth Rose, *Superior Person: A Portrait of Curzon and His Circle in late Victorian Britain*, Weidenfeld & Nicolson, 1969

_____ *The Later Cecils*, Weidenfeld & Nicolson, 1975

Anthony Sampson, *The Anatomy of Britain*, Hodder & Stoughton, 1962

_____ *Macmillan: A Study in Ambiguity*, Allen Lane, 1967

_____ *The Anatomist: The Autobiography of Anthony Sampson*, Politico's, 2008

Dominic Sandbrook, *Never Had It So Good: A History of Britain from Suez to the Beatles*, Little, Brown, 2005

_____ *White Heat: A History of Britain in the Swinging Sixties*, Little, Brown, 2006

Martin P.C. Schaad, *Bullying Bonn: Anglo-German Diplomacy on European Integration, 1955–61*, Macmillan Press, Basingstoke, 2000

Arthur M. Schlesinger, Jr, *A Thousand Days: John F. Kennedy in the White House*, Houghton Mifflin, Boston, 1965

Thomas J. Schoenbaum, *Waging Peace and War: Dean Rusk in the Truman, Kennedy & Johnson Years*, Simon & Schuster, New York, 1988

Victoria Schofield, *Wavell: Soldier & Statesman*, John Murray, 2006

Anthony Seldon, *Churchill's Indian Summer: The Conservative Government 1951–1955*, Hodder & Stoughton, 1981

Anthony Seldon and Stuart Ball (ed.), *Conservative Century: The Conservative Party since 1900*, Oxford University Press, Oxford, 1994

Michael Shanks, *The Stagnant Society: A Warning*, Penguin Books, Harmondsworth, 1961

Tony Shaw, *Eden, Suez and the Mass Media: Propaganda and Persuasion during the Suez Crisis*, I.B. Tauris, 1996

Robert Shepherd, *A Class Divided: Appeasement and the Road to Munich 1938*, Macmillan, 1988

_____ *The Power Brokers: The Tory Party and Its Leaders*, Hutchinson, 1991

_____ *Iain Macleod*, Hutchinson, 1994

Avi Shlaim, *The Iron Wall: Israel and the Arab World*, Penguin books edition, 2001

Avi Shlaim, Peter Jones and Keith Sainsbury, *British Foreign Secretaries since 1945*, David & Charles, Newton Abbot, 1977

Evelyn Shuckburgh, *Descent to Suez: Diaries 1951–1956*, ed. John Charmley, Weidenfeld & Nicolson, 1986

Michael Sissons and Philip French (ed.), *Age of Austerity: 1945–1951*, Penguin Books, Harmondsworth, 1964

Osbert Sitwell, *Great Morning*, Macmillan & Co. paperback edition, 1957

Noel Skelton, *Constructive Conservatism*, Blackwood, Edinburgh, 1924

Robert Skidelsky, *Politicians and the Slump: The Labour Government of 1929–1931*, Penguin Books, Harmondsworth, 1970

_____ *Oswald Mosley*, Macmillan, 1975

_____ *John Maynard Keynes: Hopes Betrayed 1883–1920*, Macmillan, 1983

_____ *John Maynard Keynes: The Economist as Saviour 1920–1937*, Macmillan, 1992

_____ *John Maynard Keynes: Fighting for Britain 1937–1946*, Macmillan, 2000

Gaddis Smith, *Dean Acheson*, Cooper Square Publishers, New York, 1972

Philip Snow, *Stranger and Brother: A Portrait of C. P. Snow*, Macmillan, 1982

_____ *A Time of Renewal: Cluster of Character, C. P. Snow and Coups*, Radcliffe Press, 1998

Mary Soames, *Clementine Churchill*, Cassell, 1979

_____ (ed.), *Speaking for Themselves: The personal letters of Winston and Clementine Churchill*, Doubleday, 1998

Martin Stannard, *Muriel Spark: The Biography*, Weidenfeld & Nicolson, 2009

Graham Stewart, *Burying Caesar: Churchill, Chamberlain and the Battle for the Tory Party*, Phoenix, 2000

Hew Strachan, *The First World War: Volume 1*, Oxford University Press, 2001

James Stuart, *Within the Fringe*, Bodley Head, 1967

Earl of Swinton, *Sixty Years of Power*, Hutchinson, 1966

Terry Tastard, *Ronald Knox and English Catholicism*, Gracewing Publishing, Leominster, 2009

William Taubman, *Khrushchev: The Man, His Era*, Free Press paperback edition, 2003

A. J. P. Taylor, *The Origins of the Second World War*, Penguin Books, Harmondsworth, 1964

_____ *Politics in Wartime*, Hamish Hamilton, 1964

_____ *English History 1914–1945*, Oxford University Press, 1965

_____ *Beaverbrook*, Penguin Books, Harmondsworth, 1974

Frederick Taylor, *The Berlin Wall: 13 August 1961 – 9 November 1989*, Bloomsbury, 2006

Mary Van Rensselaer Thayer, *Jacqueline Kennedy: The White House Years*, Little Brown, Boston, 1971

Kevin Theakston, *Leadership in Whitehall*, Macmillan, 1999

Alan Thompson, *The Day Before Yesterday*, Sidgwick & Jackson, 1971

Neville Thompson, *The Anti-Appeasers: Conservative Opposition to Appeasement in the 1930s*, Clarendon Press, Oxford, 1971

Andrew Thorpe, *The British General Election of 1931*, Clarendon Press, Oxford, 1991

D. R. Thorpe, *The Uncrowned Prime Ministers: a study of Sir Austen Chamberlain, Lord Curzon and Lord Butler*, Darkhorse Publishing, 1980

_____ *Selwyn Lloyd*, Jonathan Cape, 1989

_____ *Alec Douglas-Home*, Sinclair-Stevenson, 1996

_____ *Eden: The Life and Times of Anthony Eden First Earl of Avon 1897–1977*, Chatto & Windus, 2003

Nikolai Tolstoy, *Victims of Yalta*, Hodder & Stoughton, 1977

_____ *Stalin's Secret War*, Jonathan Cape, 1981

_____ *The Minister and the Massacres*, Hutchinson, 1986

David Torrance, *The Scottish Secretaries*, Birlinn, 2006

Michael Tracey, *A Variety of Lives: A Biography of Sir Hugh Greene*, Bodley Head, 1983

Selwyn Ilan Troën and Moshe Shemesh, *The Suez-Sinai Crisis 1956: Retrospective and Reappraisal*, Frank Cass, 1989

Jacqueline Trott, *The Macmillan Government and Europe: A Study in the Process of Policy Development*, Macmillan, 1996

John Turner, *Macmillan*, Longman, 1994

Ann Tusa, *The Last Division: Berlin and the Wall*, Hodder & Stoughton, 1996

Anthony Verrier, *Assassination in Algiers: Churchill, Roosevelt, and the Murder of Admiral Darlan*, Macmillan, 1990

John Vincent (ed.), *The Crawford Papers: The journals of David Lindsay twenty-seventh Earl of Crawford and tenth Earl of Balcarres 1871 – 1940, during the years 1892 to 1940*, Manchester University Press, 1984

SELECT BIBLIOGRAPHY

Dennis Walters, *Not Always with the Pack*, Constable, 1989

Geoffrey Warner, *Pierre Laval and the Eclipse of France*, Eyre & Spottiswoode, 1968

Philip Warner, *The Battle of Loos*, Wordsworth editions, Hertfordshire, 1976

Harold Watkinson, *Turning Points: A Record of our Times*, Michael Russell, Salisbury, 1986

Evelyn Waugh, *The Life of the Right Reverend Ronald Knox*, Chapman & Hall, 1959

Sir Roy Welensky, *Welensky's 4000 Days: The Life and Death of the Federation of Rhodesia and Nyasaland*, Collins, 1964

Nigel West, *Molehunt: The full story of the Soviet Spy in MI5*, Weidenfeld & Nicolson, 1987

John Wheeler-Bennett, *Special Relationships: American Peace and War*, Macmillan, 1975

Hugh Whitemore, *A Letter of Resignation*, Amber Lane Press Ltd, Charlbury, 1997

L.G. Wickham Legg and E.T. Williams (ed.), *The Dictionary of National Biography* 1941–1950, Oxford University Press, 1959

Charles Williams, *The Last Great Frenchman: A Life of General de Gaulle*, Little, Brown & Company, 1993

_____ *Adenauer: The Father of the New Germany*, Little, Brown and Company, 2000

_____ *Harold Macmillan*, Weidenfeld & Nicolson, 2009

E.T. Williams and Helen H. Palmer (ed.), *The Dictionary of National Biography* 1951–1960, Clarendon Press, Oxford, 1971

E.T. Williams and C.S. Nicholls (ed.), *The Dictionary of National Biography* 1961–1970, 1981

Francis Williams, *A Pattern of Rulers*, Longmans, 1965

Philip Williams, *Hugh Gaitskell: A Political Biography*, Jonathan Cape, 1979

_____ (ed.), *The Diary of Hugh Gaitskell* 1945–1956, Jonathan Cape, 1983

Roger Wilmut (ed.), *The Complete Beyond the Fringe*, Methuen, 1987

Harold Wilson, *Memoirs: The Making of a Prime Minister* 1916–1964, Weidenfeld & Nicolson/Michael Joseph, 1986

_____ *A Prime Minister on Prime Ministers*, Weidenfeld & Nicolson/Michael Joseph, 1977

Donald Winch, *Economics and Policy: A Historical Study*, Hodder & Stoughton, 1969

Jay M. Winter, *The Great War and the British People*, Palgrave Macmillan, Basingstoke, second edition, 2003

Christian Wolmar, *Fire & Steam: A New History of the Railways in Britain*, Atlantic Books, 2007

J.R.T. Wood (ed.), *The Welensky Papers: A History of the Federation of Rhodesia and Nyasaland*, Graham Publishing, Durban, 1983

C. M. Woodhouse, *British Foreign Policy since the Second World War*, Hutchinson, 1961

S. J. Woolf (ed.), *The Rebirth of Italy 1943–1950*, Longman, 1972

Lord Woolton, *The Memoirs of the Rt Hon. the Earl of Woolton*, Cassell, 1959

G. D. Worswick and P. H. Ady (ed.), *The British Economy in the Nineteen-Fifties*, Clarendon Press, Oxford, 1962

Peter Wright, *Spycatcher: The Candid Autobiography of a Senior Intelligence Officer*, Viking, New York, 1987

Hugo Young, *This Blessed Plot: Britain and Europe from Churchill to Blair*, Macmillan, 1998

Kenneth Young, *Rhodesia and Independence: A Study in British Colonial Policy*, J. M. Dent, 1967

_____(ed.), *The Diaries of Sir Robert Bruce Lockhart: Volume One 1915–1938; Volume Two 1939–1965*, Macmillan, 1973 and 1980

Michael Young, *The Rise of the Meritocracy*, Penguin Books, Harmondsworth, 1961

_____ *The Chipped White Cups of Dover*, Unit 2, 1960

Philip Ziegler, *Mountbatten: the Official Biography*, Collins, 1985

_____ *Wilson: the Authorised Life*, Weidenfeld & Nicolson, 1993

_____ *Osbert Sitwell*, Chatto & Windus, 1998

2 Articles, Essays, Lectures and Pamphlets

R. K. Alderman and Martin J. Smith, 'Can British Prime Ministers be given the push by their Parties?', *Parliamentary Affairs*, July 1990

R. J. Aldrich, 'Intelligence, Anglo-American Relations and the Suez Crisis, 1956', *Intelligence and National Security*, Vol. 9, No. 3, July 1994

Winthrop Aldrich, 'The Suez Crisis: A Footnote to History', *Foreign Affairs*, January 1967

Nigel John Ashton, 'Harold Macmillan and the "Golden Days" of Anglo-American relations revisited, 1957–63', *Diplomatic History* 29 (4), Blackwell Publishing, 2005

W. H. Auden, 'Some Reflections on Opera as a Medium', 1952, in Edward Mendelson (ed.), *W. H. Auden: Prose, Volume III, 1949–55*, Princeton University Press, Princeton, USA, 2008

David Badenoch, 'Memorandum on the events surrounding Harold Macmillan's operation, October 1963', privately printed

S. J. Ball, 'Banquo's Ghost: Lord Salisbury, Harold Macmillan, and the High Politics of Decolonization, 1957–1963', *Twentieth Century British History*, Vol. 16, No. 1, 2005

Peter J. Beck, '"The Less Said about Suez": British Governments and the Politics of Suez's History, 1955–1967', *The English Historical Review*, Vol. CXXIV, No. 508, June 2009

Christopher Booker, 'The Victims of Tolstoy', *Sunday Telegraph*, 21 October 1990

Alan Bullock, 'Most Honoured Chancellor: A Personal Reminiscence', *Oxford Magazine*, No. 17, Noughth Week, Hilary Term, 1987.

SELECT BIBLIOGRAPHY

Peter Catterall, 'Macmillan and Europe, 1950–1956: The Cold War, the American Context and the British Approach to European Integration', *Cercles*, 2002

_____'The Prime Minister and his Trollope: Reading Harold Macmillan's Readings', *Cercles*, 2004

_____ 'Identity and Integration: Macmillan, Britishness and the Turn Towards Europe', pp. 161–78 in Gilbert Millat (ed.), *Angleterre ou Albion, entre fascination et répulsion*, Lille University, Lille 3, Charles de Gaulle, 2006

Bernard Crick, 'The Life Peerages Act', *Parliamentary Affairs*, Vol. XI, No. 4, 1957

Sir Patrick Dean, 'Memorandum by Sir Patrick Dean – 1986', Patrick Dean Papers

Professor David Dilks, 'The Office of Prime Minister in Twentieth-Century Britain', 18 November 1992, Hull University Press, 1993

_____ 'De Gaulle and the British', 22 June 1994, Paris, printed privately

Sir Michael Fraser, 'The Conservative Research Department & Conservative Recovery after 1945', circulated privately, August 1961

Peter Hennessy and Caroline Anstey, 'Moneybags and Brains: The Anglo-American "Special relationship since 1945"', Strathclyde *Analysis* Paper No. 1, Department of Government, University of Strathclyde, 1990

Peter Hennessy and Mark Laity, 'Suez – What the Papers say', *Contemporary Record*, Vol. 1, No. 1, Spring 1987

Robert Henriques, 'The Ultimatum: A Dissenting View', *Spectator*, 6 November 1959

Matthew Jones, 'Macmillan, Eden, the War in the Mediterranean and Anglo-American Relations', *Twentieth Century British History*, Vol. 8, No. 1, 1997

Daniel Jonson, 'Macmillan: a vindication that came too late', *The Times*, 19 October 1990

Saul Kelly, 'A very considerable and largely unsung success: Sir Roger Makins' Washington Embassy, 1953–1956', *Anglo-American Relations in the Twentieth Century* (ed. Jonathan Hollowell), Macmillan, 2000

Saul Kelly and Anthony Gorst (ed.), 'Whitehall and the Suez Crisis', *Contemporary British History* (Special Issue), Vol. 13, No. 2, Frank Cass Publishers, Ilford, 1999

Robert Knight, 'Harold Macmillan and the Cossacks: Was there a Klagenfurt Conspiracy?', *Intelligence and National Security* (1), 1986

_____ 'The decisions of men in a hurry', *Times Literary Supplement*, 19–25 October, 1990

Keith Kyle, 'Suez Revisited', Lecture to the Thackeray Society, Reform Club, 30 March 2000

Diana Kunz, 'Did Macmillan Lie over Suez?', *The Spectator*, 3 November 1990

Nigel Lawson, 'The sick PM, his waiting successor and the unexpected assassin', *Daily Telegraph*, 3 October 2004

_____ 'Robot and the Fork in the Road: How Churchill might have made Thatcher Unnecessary', *Times Literary Supplement*, 21 January 2005

Sir Donald Logan, 'Suez: Meetings at Sèvres 22–25 October 1956. Narrative', Donald Logan Papers

_____ 'Comments' (Memorandum on the Suez Section of Richard Lamb's *The Failure of the Eden Government*, Sidgwick & Jackson, 1987), Donald Logan Papers

William Roger Louis, 'Harold Macmillan and the Middle East Crisis of 1958', *Proceedings of the British Academy*, 94, 207–28, London, 1996

_____ 'All Souls and the Suez Crisis of 1956', Chichele Lecture, Oxford University, 2006

W. Scott Lucas, 'Suez, the Americans and the Overthrow of Anthony Eden', *London School of Economics Quarterly*, pp. 277–84, September 1987

Hugh Lunghi, 'Yalta – Forty Years On', privately printed, 1985

Geoffrey Marston, 'Armed intervention in the 1956 Suez Canal crisis: the legal advice tendered to the British Government', *The International and Comparative Law Quarterly*, Vol. 37, 1988

Victor Mauer, 'Harold Macmillan and the Deadline Crisis over Berlin 1958–9', *Twentieth Century British History*, Vol. 9, No. 1, 1998

Tim Rayment, 'The Massacre and the Ministers', *Sunday Times*, 7 April 1996

Andrew Roberts, 'Betrayal of the brave at Suez', *Sunday Times*, 20 October 1996

Avi Shlaim, 'The Protocol of Sevres, 1956: anatomy of a war plot', *International Affairs*, Vol. 73, 3, 1997

Noel Skelton, 'The Conservative Task: A Property Owning Democracy', *Yorkshire Post*, 23 January 1930

Norman Stone, 'Judgment best left to history', *Sunday Times*, 30 December 1990

D. R. Thorpe, *The Glamour Boys*, reference group essay, *Oxford Dictionary of National Biography*, Oxford University Press, online edition, May 2006

_____ 'A Psychologically Interesting Prime Minister', essay in the programme booklet for Howard Brenton's play *Never So Good*, National Theatre publications, 2008

Nikolai Tolstoy, 'The Klagenfurt Conspiracy', *Encounter*, May 1983

Geoffrey Warner, '"Collusion" and the Suez Crisis of 1956', *International Affairs*, Vol. 55, 1979

_____ 'The United States and the Western Alliance, 1958–63', *International Affairs*, Vol. 71, 1995

Lieutenant-General Sir James Wilson, 'The Repatriations from Austria in 1945: The Cowgill Inquiry – Report and Documentary Evidence', *Army Quarterly & Defence Journal*, January 1991

3 Theses, etc.

Dr Chris Ballinger, *An Analysis of the Reform of the House of Lords, 1911–2000*, Oxford D Phil thesis, 2006

Edwyn Morris, 'The Repatriation of the Cossacks from Austria in 1945', Queen Mary and Westfield College, 2009

M.T. Thornhill, 'Britain and the Egyptian Question, 1950–54', PhD Thesis, Oxford, 1995, Bodleian Library, Oxford

Broadcast Programmes

1 *Radio*
(Transcripts in BBC Written Archives, Caversham)

'A Canal Too Far', presented by Peter Hennessy, BBC Radio 4, 31 January 1986

'Assignment: Suez – The Propaganda War', BBC World Service, 31 October 1996

'Nasser's Eden', by Howard Brenton, BBC Radio 4, 30 October 1998

'Neither War nor Peace at 10 Downing Street', BBC Radio 4, 1997

'Suez: Ten Years After', BBC Radio, July 1966

2 *Television*

'At the End of the Day', Harold Macmillan/Robert McKenzie interview, BBC TV, 1973

'The Day Before Yesterday', Thames Television, 1971

'End of Empire', Granada Television, 1985

'Reputations: R. A. Butler', by Anthony Howard, BBC Television, 13 July 1983

'The Suez Crisis', BBC1, 22 October 1996

'Suez: A personal view by historian Andrew Roberts', BBC2, 23 October 1996

'Television and Number 10', BBC Television, 1988

'Never Had It So Good?', BBC4 Television, 10 December 2007

3 *Video material*
British Pathé News, 'A Year to Remember: 1945–1957', British Pathé News Ltd

4 *Gramophone recordings*
'British Prime Ministers: 1924–1964', BBC Records, REB 39M, 1969

5 *Map*
Isle of Arran, Ordnance Survey, Landranger Map 69, Southampton, 2007

NOTES

PREFACE

1 Surprisingly for one who could have been a character from a Chekhov play (a name he spelt Tchekov), Macmillan was not an admirer of the plays, much preferring the short stories. But he made an exception for *The Cherry Orchard*. Harold Macmillan, *War Diaries: The Mediterranean 1943–1945*, Macmillan, 1984, entry for 13 April 1945, p. 734.

2 Hugh Trevor-Roper to Bernard Berenson, 23 March 1960. *Letters from Oxford: Hugh Trevor-Roper to Bernard Berenson*, edited by Richard Davenport-Hines, Weidenfeld & Nicolson, 2006, p. 297.

3 Harold Macmillan, *At the End of the Day*, 1961–1963, Macmillan, 1973, p. 475.

4 Pat Jalland, notice of Augustine Birrell's life in *Oxford Dictionary of National Biography; Volume 5*, Oxford University Press, 2004, p. 849.

5 Paul Scott, *A Division of the Spoils*, Heinemann, 1977, p. 335.

6 In 2005, David Faber took me over part of this golf course, pristine and largely unused, and in the distance was the shuttered big house, once in the summer of 1963 the centre of the political world.

7 Lopahin was the merchant who developed the Ranevsky estate in *The Cherry Orchard*, chopping down the cherry trees before the family departed.

PRELUDE

1 1955 Billericay result: Richard Body (Conservative) 24, 327; B. R. Clapham (Labour) 20, 121; Conservative majority, 4,206. 1959 Billericay result: E. L. Gardner (Conservative), 29, 224; Mrs R. A. Smythe (Labour - Co-op), 24, 402; P. Sheldon-Williams (Liberal) 9, 347; Conservative majority, 4,822.

2 Billericay was a demographic microcosm of the whole country, hence Gaitskell's accurate forecast. With great dignity Gaitskell conceded the election on television at 1 a.m. Aneurin Bevan was furious that he made this American-style 'concession'. In fact, he could have made it three hours earlier.

3 But not that of *The Times*, which had predicted a majority of 22. *The Times*, 8 October 1959.

4 King George VI had wanted to greet Neville Chamberlain

personally on 30 September 1938 at Heston Airport on his return from the Munich Conference, but was dissuaded. Her Majesty Queen Elizabeth the Queen Mother to the author, 22 March 1991.

5 Tony Benn, *Years of Hope: Diaries, Letters and Papers 1940–1962*, Hutchinson, 1994, p. 317.

6 D. E. Butler and Richard Rose, *The British General Election of 1959*, Macmillan, 1960, p. 197.

7 Herbert Morrison, *Herbert Morrison: An Autobiography*, Odhams, 1960, p. 320.

8 Speech at Bedford, 20 July 1957.

9 Cited in Anthony Sampson, *Anatomy of Britain*, Hodder and Stoughton, 1962, p. 109.

10 Anthony Eden to Harold Macmillan, 29 October 1959. MS Macmillan dep. c. 310, fol. 62. Macmillan Papers, Bodleian Library, Oxford.

11 Sampson, op. cit., p. 106. I am very grateful to the late Anthony Sampson for sharing with me his insights into Macmillan's character and career. His book *Macmillan: A Study in Ambiguity* (Allen Lane, 1967) remains an indispensable assessment.

12 James Lees-Milne, *Through Wood and Dale: Diaries 1975–1978*, Michael Russell, 2007, p. 205.

13 Thomas Hardy, *The Mayor of Casterbridge*, Chapter XLVI. In the 1920s, Macmillan looked after Hardy's publishing interests at Macmillan & Co.

14 Although the affair of his wife,

Lady Dorothy Macmillan, with the Tory MP Robert Boothby was the cause of this depression, his constituents believed it was because of business worries. Ralph Appleton to the author, 18 July 2007. As a key worker in the Conservative Constituency Association in Stockton-on-Tees, and later chairman, Ralph Appleton knew Macmillan as well as any in the area, but he did not know about the Boothby-Lady Dorothy affair until the 1980s, and then only from publications.

15 Private information.

16 Harold Macmillan to Winston Churchill, 1 January 1928. Churchill Papers, Churchill College, Cambridge, 18/85.

17 Speech at Manchester, 22 March 1959. Speech at Durham, 18 July 1959.

18 Kenneth Young, *Arthur James Balfour*, G. Bell, 1963, p. xiv.

19 Lloyd George's opinion, as recorded in Thomas Jones' diary, 10 June 1922. Keith Middlemass (ed.), *Thomas Jones Whitehall Diary, Volume 1, 1916–1925*, Oxford University Press, 1969, p. 201.

20 Harold Macmillan, *The Past Masters*, Macmillan, 1975, p. 24.

21 Young, op. cit., p. xi.

22 The theme of Disraeli's speech at the Crystal Palace, 24 June 1872.

23 John Fforde, *The Bank of England and Public Policy, 1941–1958*, Cambridge University Press, 1992, p. 657.

CHAPTER ONE

Working Class Ancestry

1 Quoted in Anthony Kenny, *A Life in Oxford*, John Murray, 1997, p. 190. I am grateful to Sir Anthony Kenny for describing the scene to me on the steps of Balliol Hall, where the conversation took place. Another interpretation of these events is held by some in Oxford. Macmillan had suggested the honorary degree to Geoffrey Warnock, Vice Chancellor of Oxford University from 1981–1985, knowing that a nonagenarian chancellor of the university would not be denied, but also, with impish mischievousness, that the proposal would be controversial. He thus lit the blue touchpaper and then retired to watch the subsequent fireworks.

2 As the author can remember from childhood holidays in Arran in the 1950s. The name Goat Fell derives from the Gaelic, *goadh bhein*, 'mountain of the winds'. At 2,867 feet, Goat Fell just fails to qualify as one of Scotland's 284 Munros, named after Sir Hugh Munro, who compiled the list of mountains over 3,000 feet in 1891.

3 John Piper's *Kilmory Chapel, Argyll* (1975) is one of the finest of such paintings of the area.

4 Two third cousins of Harold Macmillan, Catherine McKillop and Catherine Mackay, still lived at Sannox at the time of Macmillan's death in 1986.

5 Harold Macmillan habitually referred to himself as a crofter's grandson. In fact, he was a crofter's great-great-grandson, so the 'working class ancestry' goes back even further.

6 Robert Black (ed.), *To the Hebrides: Samuel Johnson's Journey to the Western Islands of Scotland and James Boswell's Journal of a Tour to the Hebrides*, Birlinn Limited, Edinburgh, 2007, p. 185.

7 *Macbeth*, V, viii, 19.

8 Charles Morgan, *The House of Macmillan, 1843–1943*, Macmillan, 1943, p. 7.

9 Sir Walter Scott, *The Lord of the Isles* (1815), Canto 5, Stanza 1.

10 The family tree printed in the endpapers of Ruth Dudley Edwards, *Harold Macmillan: A Life in Pictures*, Macmillan, 1983, mistakenly names Malcolm, the father-in-law, as the husband of Katherine Crawford.

11 Norman Tebbit, speech to the Conservative Party Conference at Blackpool, 15 October 1981, a venue that in October 1963 had heard the news of the resignation of Harold Macmillan as prime minister.

12 Black (ed.), op. cit., p. 325.

13 The notice of Thomas Atkinson's life in the *Oxford Dictionary of National Biography* states, 'The assertion that Daniel Macmillan, the publisher, in his youth worked as a shopman for Atkinson is apocryphal.' Rosemary T. Van Arsdell, 'Thomas Atkinson', *Oxford Dictionary of National*

Biography, Volume 2, Oxford University Press, 2004, p. 847. If so, the story is nevertheless well documented in early histories of the Macmillan family and should be rehearsed, with the proviso that, if Atkinson was not Daniel's employer, work in the book trade in Glasgow was part of his experience and the general points made about the influence this had on his future career as a founding publisher still stand.

14 John Cleland, *Enumeration of the Inhabitants of Glasgow 1831,* Glasgow City Archives.

15 When Harold Macmillan became prime minister in January 1957, some newspapers, noting that he had dined at the Turf Club with his Chief Whip, Edward Heath, opined that if Butler had been chosen there would have been 'plain living and high thinking'. Harold Macmillan, *Riding the Storm,* Macmillan, 1971, p. 196. Such observations belied the puritan streak that ran deep in the Macmillan family line, and, in particular, in Harold Macmillan's character.

16 Later Cambridge generations, who knew the building at 1 Trinity Street as the Bowes & Bowes bookshop, may not have realised that Macmillan & Co. began trading there in the nineteenth century. In fact, Robert Bowes (1835–1919) was Ayrshire born, a grandson of Duncan Macmillan and thus an uncle of Daniel and Alexander Macmillan. He worked for Macmillan & Co. in Henrietta Street, where he

managed the bookshop, and from 1863, when the Macmillan brothers moved permanently to London, returned to Cambridge, branching out himself into both bookselling and publishing. He formed Bowes & Bowes with his own son, George Brimley Bowes. The shop at 1 Trinity Street is now the retail outlet of Cambridge University Press.

17 Frances Orridge (1821–1867), the maternal grandmother of the future Prime Minister, became a partner in the business in her widowhood.

18 The other children were Frederick Orridge Macmillan, born 5 October 1851; Katherine Macmillan, born 5 April 1855, and Arthur Macmillan, born on 13 May 1857. Alexander and his wife had five children, the second son George Austin, born in 1855, being particularly close to his cousin, Maurice.

19 A characteristic family quirk that survived to the bell board in the servants' quarters at Birch Grove House in Sussex, labelled 'Mr Harold's room' and the like.

20 Regulars included Maurice and Kingsley, his nephew's godfathers, and luminaries such as Tennyson, Thomas Palgrave (of future, *Golden Treasury* fame for the firm in 1861), Coventry Patmore and Thomas Hughes, whose *Tom Brown's Schooldays* (1857) was to be one of the company's enduring successes, and which fixed a particular image of Dr Arnold, the reforming headmaster of Rugby School, firmly in the

public consciousness. This image was ruthlessly deconstructed by Lytton Strachey in *Eminent Victorians* in 1918.

21 *The Portrait of a Lady*, described by F. R. Leavis as 'James' finest achievement and one of the great novels of the English language' (*The Great Tradition*, Peregrine Books, Harmondsworth, 1962, p. 179), is arguably the most enduring literary work ever published by Macmillan & Co., not discounting the poems of W. B. Yeats and the novels of Thomas Hardy's maturity.

22 Alicia C. Percival, *Very Superior Men: Some early Public School Headmasters and their achievements*, Charles Knight & Co., 1973, p. 183.

23 G. K. Chesterton, *What's Wrong with the World*, Cassell, 1910, p. 231.

24 Of both his Cabinet Secretary, Norman Brook (Wolverhampton Grammar School) and his last Chancellor of the Exchequer, Reginald Maudling (Merchant Taylor's), Harold Macmillan was to comment: 'no background'. Norman Brook in conversation with Lord Moran. Lord Moran diary, 3 August 1959. *Winston S. Churchill: The Struggle for Survival* 1940–1965, Sphere paperback, 1968, p. 796. SELO 180 (3). Selwyn Lloyd Papers, Churchill College, Cambridge.

25 Two contemporaries who were to impinge greatly on Harold Macmillan's political career were also born in 1894, Nikita Khrushchev, future leader of Russia, on 17 April, and Robert Menzies, future Prime Minister of Australia, on 20 December, as was Gavrilo Princip, the assassin of Archduke Ferdinand of Austria at Sarajevo in June 1914, the event that sparked the First World War.

26 John Galsworthy, *The Man of Property*, Chapter 1.

CHAPTER TWO

Distant Prospects 1894–1910

1 A poem referring specifically to Summer Fields and inspired by Day Lewis' time as a master there in the 1930s.

2 Crocodile tears contributed to the lachrymose atmosphere. Tributes were read from documents yellowing with age. The Conservatives (and Queen Victoria) did not even display token respect towards the GOM, which for the Cecils had always stood for 'God's Only Mistake'.

3 On 3 June 1833 on the emancipation of slaves in the West Indies.

4 Leo McKinstry, *Rosebery: Statesman in Turmoil*, John Murray, 2005, p. 300.

5 Quoted in Robert Rhodes James, *Rosebery*, Weidenfeld & Nicolson, 1963, p. 384.

6 John Morley, *Recollections: Volume 2*, Macmillan & Co., 1917, p. 97.

7 Whether the influence was beneficial or not is still debated by historians, politicians and economists.

8 Daniel's wife Margaret died

in 1957 in what *The Times* in its obituary notice of Daniel (7 December 1965) described, without elaboration, as 'tragic circumstances'. In fact, his wife died in her bath after a heart attack, and the poignant circumstances were increased by the fact that Daniel did not at first realise that his wife was dead. Private information. Arthur's wife, Peggy, died in 1974.

9 Harold Macmillan was to outdo both his brothers by belonging to seven clubs.

10 No blue plaque marks the house today as the birthplace of the Prime Minister, although eight doors along, a plaque records that William Wilberforce, slavery abolitionist, lived at number 44 (now 43B) and died there in 1833. Surprisingly, no Macmillan residence in London has a blue plaque.

11 Maurice was a calm man, who rarely got excited, but one morning after breakfast he announced that the most extraordinary thing had happened that would change the world. A man called Blériot had flown a box-kite apparatus 400 yards. In 1979, at the age of 85, Macmillan was to fly to Singapore on Concorde in six hours.

12 John Betjeman felt that the church only needed a bishop's throne to be the Cathedral of West London.

13 Harold Macmillan was on the board of the Great Western Railway for 11 years from 1929, and then from 1945–1947 until nationalisation. Along with his fellow directors, his compensation included a gold pass, allowing unlimited free rail travel, of which he availed himself to the end of his life. British Railways later named a locomotive after him. In old age, Macmillan would always try to get the last train back to Haywards Heath, rather than stay in London, because the guards and the station master looked after him so well.

14 Eaton House is still a feeder for Summer Fields, and has been attended by several of Macmillan's great-grandchildren. His son-in-law Julian Amery was there too.

15 Details of Harold Macmillan's time at Summer Fields are from the archives at the school. I am grateful to the archivist, Nicholas Aldridge, for his help and advice.

16 A remark overheard by Julian Amery, Harold Macmillan's future son-in-law, when a pupil at the school. Nicholas Aldridge, *Time to Spare? A History of Summer Fields*, David Talboys Publications, Oxford, 1999, p. v.

17 There was no leader of the Liberal Party as a whole when the party was out of office, so there was no guarantee that CB, as he was universally known, would become prime minister. But in January 1906 he won one of the great election landslide victories of the century, and was prime minister till May 1908.

18 A friendship analysed in Simon

Ball, *The Guardsmen: Harold Macmillan, Three Friends, and the World They Made*, Harper Collins, 2004.

19 It was the inaugural Board of Governors on which he served, the moment the school changed from being privately owned to being a charitable trust. Both his son-in-law, Julian Faber, and his grandson, David Faber, subsequently became governors too. David Faber became Head Master of the school in 2010.

20 Harold Macmillan speech at Summer Fields, December 1979.

21 Private information.

22 Bernard Crick, *George Orwell: A Life*, Penguin edition, Harmondsworth, 1982, p. 101.

23 In 1908 the number of boys at the college was 1,045.

24 As Disraeli described the rich and the poor in *Sybil*, 1844, Book ii, Chapter 5, though it would be incorrect to see Collegers as poor and Oppidans as exclusively wealthy, both in Macmillan's time and now. But the divergent experience remains. Private information.

25 Cyril Connolly, *Enemies of Promise*, Penguin edition, Harmondsworth, 1961, p. 245.

26 Tim Card, *Eton Renewed*, John Murray, 1994, pp. 109–10.

27 College Debating Society minutes, 5 April and 24 July 1909. College Archives. I am grateful to the two King's Scholars who entertained me to luncheon in College Hall in June 2004 and then gave me a tour of College, having bookmarked in advance all references to Macmillan in the College Annals.

28 Eton parlance for the winter term. The Field Game is now played in the Lent Half.

29 'In the Field', 22 and 24 September 1908.

30 Card, op. cit., p. 145.

31 'College Annals', 1902. Eton College Archives.

32 D. K. Money, notice of A. B. Ramsay, *Oxford Dictionary of National Biography*, Volume 45, Oxford University Press, 2004, p. 912. Of his elevation to Cambridge, the same article observes, 'Ramsay had no pretensions to be a serious academic; he was therefore considered a suitable College Master.' Ibid., p. 911.

33 Card, op. cit., p. 125.

34 William Johnson, later William Johnson Cory (1823–1892), author of 'Heraclitus'. He famously wrote of Rosebery that 'he is one of those who likes the palm without the dust', never a criticism that could be made of Macmillan.

35 Now the Wilde Suite.

36 John Betjeman, 'The Arrest of Oscar Wilde at the Cadogan Hotel', *Collected Poems*, John Murray, 1958, p. 18. Homosexual relations were illegal in Great Britain until 1967, when the law was relaxed regarding consulting adults in private over the age of 21.

37 There is an uninterrupted view between the two buildings.

38 James Lees-Milne, *Through Wood and Dale: Diaries 1975–1978*, Michael Russell,

Norwich, 2007, p. 205.

39 Bernard Swithinbank, 'Note on Eton in JMK's time', 9 March 1948. Keynes Papers, King's College Cambridge. Quoted in Robert Skidelsky, *John Maynard Keynes: Volume One Hopes Betrayed 1883–1920*, Macmillan, 1983, p. 104.

40 John le Carré, *A Murder of Quality*, Victor Gollancz, 1962, Chapter 1. Although le Carré asserts that Carne, his fictional school in the novel, is just that, its physical characteristics are a blend of Sherborne, his own school, and Eton, where he taught in the 1950s. Two of the characters, Terence Fielding and Susan Hecht, are based on Eton figures of that era, Oliver van Oss and Grizel Hartley.

41 'Haldane was, in all likelihood, motivated by malice.' Ball, op. cit., p. 19.

42 Such abuse of younger boys was common. Selwyn Lloyd, Macmillan's Foreign Secretary and Chancellor, was to suffer from similar unwelcome attentions from a group of senior boys at Fettes in 1918, three of whom were expelled as a result. Lloyd's contemporary, Michael Tippett, the composer, was removed from Fettes by his parents after his mother heard of the homosexual activity. D. R. Thorpe, *Selwyn Lloyd*, Jonathan Cape, 1989, pp. 17–18.

43 Connolly, op. cit., p. 234.

44 Oliver Lyttelton once declared that 'all buggers should be shot'. Private information.

45 Eton College Archives. I am grateful to the former Provost of Eton, Sir Eric Anderson, who was Head Master at the time of Macmillan's final visit, for his account of the evening.

CHAPTER THREE

Sent Down by the Kaiser 1910–1914

1 Willink, Crookshank, Lyttelton and Salisbury were all future ministerial colleagues. See Simon Ball, *The Guardsmen: Harold Macmillan, Three Friends and the World They Made*, Harper Collins, 2004.

2 R. F. Harrod, *The Life of John Maynard Keynes*, Macmillan, 1951, p. 32.

3 Robert Skidelsky, *John Maynard Keynes, Volume One: Hopes Betrayed 1883–1920*, Macmillan, 1983, p. 237.

4 Penelope Fitzgerald, *The Knox Brothers*, Flamingo paperback edition, 2002, p. 109.

5 Ibid., p. 56.

6 Lord Skidelsky to the author, 27 February 2008.

7 Waugh's biography of Knox was in fact published on 8 October 1959, the day of Macmillan's general election victory.

8 Evelyn Waugh, *The Life of the Right Reverend Ronald Knox*, Chapman & Hall, 1959, pp. 106–7.

9 Sir Horace, later Baron, Evans (1903–1963) was physician to Queen Elizabeth II from 1952 until his death, and *inter alia* to Sir Anthony Eden.

10 Harold Macmillan, *Winds of*

Change: 1914–1939, Macmillan, 1966, p. 43. The Hon. Lady de Zulueta to the author, 27 February 2008.

11 Both Alexander and Monckton played in the most famous of the Lord's encounters, 'Fowler's Match' in 1910. R. St L. Fowler almost single-handedly retrieved an impossible situation for Eton, who won by nine runs, to national acclaim 'in a way that now seems incomprehensible'. Letters addressed to 'Fowler's Mother, London' proved sufficient. Tim Card, *Eton Renewed*, John Murray, 1994, pp. 133–4. See footnote 14 for similar efficiency in the case of Campbell-Bannerman.

12 Cyril Connolly, *Enemies of Promise*, Penguin Books, Harmondsworth, 1961 edition, p. 271.

13 Robert Browning, *Rabbi Ben Ezra*.

14 Sir Henry Campbell-Bannerman (1836–1908), MP for Stirling Boroughs, 1868–1908; Prime Minister, 1905–1908. Campbell-Bannerman's last recorded words were reputedly 'This is not the last of me.' Universally known as CB, so great was his fame, and so efficient were the postal services of the day, that letters sent to him in Scotland, then known as North Britain, addressed 'CB NB', reached him in Perthshire the day they were posted in London.

15 Roy Jenkins, *The Chancellors*, Macmillan, 1998, p. 159.

16 Speech at Newcastle, 9 October 1909.

17 1974 was the only other year in the twentieth century that saw two general elections - in February and October. The indecisive outcome of the February election led Macmillan to harbour unrealistic thoughts of returning as a caretaker prime minister of a National Government. (See Chapter 30)

18 As in his speech at Blenheim Palace, 29 July 1912.

19 Macmillan op. cit., p. 96.

20 Ibid., p. 166.

21 John Jones, *Balliol College: A History*, second edition, Oxford University Press, 2005, p. 186.

22 *The Times*, 18 October 1975, in an interview on the twelfth anniversary of his resignation as Prime Minister.

23 *Spectator*, 14 January 2006.

24 Kenneth Rose, *Superior Person: A Portrait of Curzon and his Circle in late Victorian England*, Weidenfeld & Nicolson, p. 45.

25 Fitzgerald, op. cit., p. 76.

26 Ibid., p. 142.

27 Aldous Huxley, *Limbo*, Chatto & Windus, 1946, p. 28.

28 Drink was to be a curse not only of the Macmillan family, but also of the Cavendishes, into which family Dan had married in 1920. Harold Macmillan knew what the temptations had done for his family and adopted prudence as a deliberate policy.

29 Marshal Caurobert observed of the Charge of the Light Brigade at Balaclava, '*C'est magnifique, mais ce n'est pas la guerre.*' The adapted variation, a famous Oxford saying, has been applied to both the University Museum opposite Keble and to Balliol.

30 The rivalry between 'Bloody Balliol' and Trinity was of long standing, Trinity men largely being dismissive of Balliol's 'progressive' leanings and its place as the first Oxford college to admit African and Indian undergraduates. In 1935 when the film *Sanders of the River* was shown in an Oxford cinema, the scene of 'natives' in a canoe was greeted by ribald Trinity shouts of 'Well rowed, Balliol!'

31 Knox was received into the Roman Catholic Church by the Abbot of Farnborough Abbey.

32 Macmillan once discussed university life with his Minister of Supply from 1957–1959, Aubrey Jones, who took a first-class degree at the London School of Economics. Macmillan affected puzzlement at the lack of collegiate life and the fact that Jones had to return, commuter-like, to a London suburb each evening. As a last, unsuccessful attempt at finding some common ground, he enquired of an incomprehending Jones, 'Did you have a Sligger Urquhart?' Aubrey Jones to the author, 25 November 1986. Urquhart's nickname metamorphosed from 'sleek one' through 'slicker' before eventually finalising as 'sligger'. Urquhart's pupil Anthony Powell partly based his character Professor Sillery in *A Dance to the Music of Time* on Urquhart and his Balliol salon.

33 Urquhart was instrumental in getting Knox appointed to the Oxford Catholic chaplaincy in 1926.

34 Harold Macmillan to F. F. Urquhart, 10 December 1912 and 4 August 1913. MS Macmillan dep. c. 452. Macmillan Papers, Bodleian Library, Oxford.

35 Noel Annan, *The Dons: Mentors, Eccentrics and Geniuses*, Harper Collins, 1990, p. 78.

36 John Jones, notice of F. F. Urquhart, *Oxford Dictionary of National Biography*, Volume 55, Oxford University Press, 2005, p. 949.

37 Rupert Hart-Davis to George Lyttelton, 7 February 1959. Rupert Hart-David (ed.), *The Lyttelton Hart-Davis Letters: Volumes Three and Four 1958–1959*, John Murray paperback edition, 1986, p. 198.

38 Sir Hubert Henderson (1890–1952), father of the diplomat Sir Nicholas Henderson, was briefly Warden of All Souls from 1951 until ill health forced him to resign in January 1952, a month before his death.

39 Balliol College Archives.

40 Harold Macmillan to F. F. Urquhart, 4 August 1913. MS Macmillan dep. c. 452, loc. cit.

41 Shelley, *Lines written in the Vale of Chamonix*.

42 Hilaire Belloc, *To the Balliol Men Still in Africa*.

43 Macmillan was to be the next Balliol prime minister. His Chief Whip, Edward Heath, would be the third Balliol prime minister of the century.

44 *The Times*, 23 July 1908.

45 Jones, op. cit., p. 227.

46 In Margaret Thatcher's time

at Somerville, women were excluded from the Union, but it is doubtful she would have participated, even if eligible.

47 Colin Coote, *Editorial: Memoirs*, Eyre & Spottiswoode, 1965, p. 35.

48 A. J. Balfour lost three general elections in January 1906, January 1910 and December 1910, a melancholy record equalled by Edward Heath (March 1966, February 1974 and October 1974).

49 A theme to which Macmillan returned in his book *The Middle Way* in 1938, not that this had prevented him from sending his own son Maurice to Eton.

50 MS Macmillan dep. c. 453, loc. cit.

51 *Isis* record of Union debates, 1912–1914. Macmillan was later much influenced by Churchill's technique of rehearsing speeches meticulously in advance. Effectiveness was for him more important than spontaneity.

52 Volume 1 was published in 1910; the sixth and final volume appeared in 1920.

53 Even though Gladstone was a Christ Church man.

54 Jones, op. cit., p. 245.

55 The leaders of the three parties at the 1959 general election, Harold Macmillan (Conservative), Hugh Gaitskell (Labour) and Jo Grimond (Liberal) all possessed Firsts from Oxford, Gaitskell from New College, Grimond from Balliol.

56 A remark recorded by François Guizot.

57 A J. P. Taylor, *Politics in Wartime*, Hamish Hamilton, 1964, p. 68.

58 Osbert Sitwell, p. 241. It may be that Macmillan was thinking subconsciously of the ball before the Battle of Waterloo in 1815.

59 Macmillan op. cit., pp. 45–6.

60 Ibid., p. 46.

61 Sir Edward Clarke, *The Story of My Life*, John Murray, 1918, p. 113.

62 An evening memorably recreated by Alan Bennett in *Forty Years On*.

63 The Earl of Crawford to the Countess of Crawford, 27 July 1914. John Vincent (ed.), *The Crawford papers: The journals of David Lindsay twenty-seventh Earl of Crawford and tenth Earl of Balcarres, 1871–1941, during the years 1892 to 1940.* Manchester University Press, 1984.

64 G. M. Trevelyan, *Grey of Fallodon*, Longmans, Green & Co., 1937, p. 266. Ironically, it was the sight of the gas lamps being turned up that led to Grey's famous metaphor about them being extinguished.

65 The Trade Union Act of 1913 reversed the Osborne Judgment of 1909 that had prevented trade union funds from being used for political purposes.

66 Most, but not all, women over 30 were to gain the vote in 1918, and all women over 21 in 1928.

67 Macmillan, op. cit., p. 6.

68 A remark rehearsed on several occasions, including to the author, 23 April 1975.

69 Waugh, op. cit., p. 142.
70 Wordsworth, *Immortality Ode*.

CHAPTER FOUR

To Arms 1914–1918

1 Quoting Sir Robert Walpole on the declaration of war with Spain in 1739.
2 Helmuth von Moltke, 29 July 1914.
3 One of the best recent accounts is David Faber, *Munich: The 1938 Appeasement Crisis*, Simon & Schuster, 2008.
4 Harold Macmillan diary, 13 November 1960, MS Macmillan dep. d. 40. Macmillan Papers, Bodleian Library, Oxford.
5 In the first week of August 1914, 8,193 men enlisted; in the next week 43,354, and in the third week 49,982. Over 60,000 enlisted in the last week of the month. By 12 September a total of 478,893 men had enlisted since 4 August, one of them Harold Macmillan.
6 The portly G. K. Chesterton was accosted in Regent Street during the Great War and, though disqualified by both age and health from military service, was asked by a feather-wielding lady, 'Why aren't you out at the front?', to which he replied, 'If you go round to the side, you will see that I am.'
7 The KRRC, the Green Jackets, was Anthony Eden's regiment during his service in the Great War, and one he rejoined in August 1939, before being recalled to government office.

It was a regiment for which Eden had a lifelong respect and affection.
8 Harold Macmillan to F. F. Urquhart, January 1915. MS Macmillan dep. c. 452, loc. cit.
9 Ian Hay, *The First Hundred Thousand*, Seeley Service & Co. edition, 1975, p. 10. A. J. P. Taylor regarded Hay's novel as the best expression of the spirit of 1915. A. J. P. Taylor, *English History 1914–1945*, Oxford University Press, 1965, p. 52.
10 Harold Macmillan, *Winds of Change*, Macmillan, 1966, p. 63.
11 Jay M. Winter, *The Great War and the British People*, Palgrave Macmillan, Basingstoke, second edition, 2003. Table of University Casualties by matriculation year.
12 Osbert Sitwell, *Great Morning*, Macmillan & Co., 1957 edition, pp. 10–11.
13 C. R. Coote, *Editorial: The Memoirs of Colin R. Coote*, Eyre & Spottiswoode, 1965, p. 35.
14 From a narrative painting by John Arthur Lomax (1857–1923), popular at the time.
15 Nigel Nicolson, *Alex: The Life of Field Marshal Earl Alexander of Tunis*, Weidenfeld & Nicolson, 1973.
16 Macmillan, op. cit., p. 64.
17 Siegfried Sassoon, *Base Details*.
18 Evelyn George Harcourt Powell (1883–1961). Conservative MP for Southwark SE, 1931–1935.
19 Sitwell, op. cit., p. 274.
20 One of the few stories Macmillan could later be prevailed upon to tell of his service. The memories were

otherwise too painful for easy recall. MS Macmillan dep. d 1/1, loc. cit.

21 Keith Douglas, Alun Lewis and Sidney Keyes, who was killed at the age of 20, in April 1943, are the nearest equivalents to Wilfred Owen and his many contemporaries from the Great War.

22 All of Macmillan's original 1915 letters to both his mother and father can be found in MS Macmillan dep. d 1/1. A typed and bound volume containing a full typed transcript is in MS Macmillan dep. 1/2. The original 1916 letters are in MS Macmillan dep. 2/1, with the bound transcript volume in MS Macmillan dep. 2/2. Loc. cit.

23 Myfanwy Piper, libretto of *Owen Wingrave*, Faber Music, 1970.

24 This duty was necessary for reasons of censorship, lest any military details were inadvertently leaked.

25 Harold Macmillan to F. F. Urquhart, 11 September 1915. MS Macmillan dep. c. 452, loc. cit.

26 Macmillan's weak handshake, a potential disadvantage in politics, never in fact discomfited him in public life, unlike Rab Butler's, which his opponents did not forget, although it was the result of a childhood accident in India.

27 Philip Warner, *The Battle of Loos*, Wordsworth editions, Hertfordshire, 1976, p. 1.

28 Robert Graves, *Goodbye to All That*, Penguin edition, Harmondsworth, 1960, p. 132.

29 Hay, op. cit., p. 146.

30 Alan Bullock, 'Most Honoured Chancellor: A Personal Reminiscence', *Oxford Magazine*. No. 17, Nought Week, Hilary Term, 1987.

31 Letter to his father on 13 May 1916.

32 Quoted in Lyn Macdonald, *Somme*, Michael Joseph, 1983, p. 306.

33 The same could be claimed of Macmillan's ascent to the premiership from the Treasury after the downfall of Eden after the Suez Crisis in January 1957.

34 Macmillan, op. cit., p. 88.

35 The Revd N. S. Talbot to Mrs Nellie Macmillan, 16 September 1916. MS Macmillan dep. d 2/1, loc. cit.

36 The next time Macmillan had protruding tubes was in King Edward VII Hospital in October 1963, when he was visited by the Queen at the height of the Conservative leadership struggle prior to his resignation as prime minister. He told the author that his greatest anxiety prior to the Queen's visit was not the political crisis, but the fear that he might not look decent when his monarch arrived. Harold Macmillan to the author, 23 April 1975.

37 Raymond Asquith's grave can be found in the British War Cemetery on Guillemont Road. The epitaph on his headstone is from *Henry V*:
Small time, but in that small most greatly lived
This star of England.

38 Alan Bennett, *Forty Years On*, Faber and Faber, 1969, p. 54. The schoolmaster in Bennett's play supplying this information to his class then added, 'In the light of that information, I want you to calculate (1) the width of the gates of death to the nearest centimetre and (2) the speed in miles per hour at which the column was marching.' Light-heartedness was easy after the event, as in the sketch 'Aftermyth of War' in *Beyond the Fringe* (1961) on Battle of Britain pilots.

39 Harold Macmillan to Mrs Nellie Macmillan, 13 September 1916. MS Macmillan dep. d. 2/1, loc. cit.

40 'Hail, and farewell evermore.' Catullus, *Carmina*, ci.

41 Harold Macmillan to F. F. Urquhart, 3 August 1916. MS Macmillan dep. c. 452, loc. cit.

42 See Chapter 5 for an account of this meeting.

43 'We'll reduce all the Tory Brigadiers to the ranks, when the Red Revolution comes,' recorded Hugh Dalton in his diary on 15 March 1951. Ben Pimlott (ed.), *The Political Diary of Hugh Dalton* 1918–40, 1945–60, Jonathan Cape, 1986.

CHAPTER FIVE

ADC and Son-in-Law
1919–1923

1 *Hansard*, 18 November 1918.

2 Quoted in Margaret MacMillan, *Peacemakers: The Paris Conference of 1919 and Its Attempt to End War*, John Murray, 2001, p. 11.

3 John Maynard Keynes, *The Economic Consequences of the Peace*, Macmillan, 1984 paperback edition, p. 20.

4 Quoted in David Reynolds, *Summits: Six Meetings that Shaped the Twentieth Century*, Allen Lane, 2007, p. 30.

5 Robert Skidelsky, *John Maynard Keynes: Hopes Betrayed* 1883–1920, Macmillan 1983, p. 386.

6 George Ambrose, first Baron Lloyd of Dolobran (1879–1941), MP for West Staffordshire 1910–1918; Governor of the Bombay Presidency 1918–1924; MP for Eastbourne 1924; High Commissioner for Egypt and the Sudan, 1925–1929; Colonial Secretary 1940–1941; Leader of the House of Lords, 1941.

7 John Charmley, *Lord Lloyd and the Decline of the British Empire*, Weidenfeld & Nicolson, 1987, p. 31.

8 Harold Macmillan to F. F. Urquhart, 25 October 1918. MS Macmillan dep. c. 452. Macmillan Papers, Bodleian Library, Oxford.

9 Harold Macmillan, *Winds of Change*, Macmillan, 1966, p. 110.

10 The Duke of Devonshire to the Duchess of Devonshire, 14 April 1919. Box N 16/6373. Devonshire MSS, Chatsworth.

11 The Duke of Devonshire diary, 14 April 1919. Devonshire MSS, Chatsworth.

12 Victor Christian William Cavendish, 9th Duke of

Devonshire (1868–1938).
Liberal Unionist MP for
West Derbyshire 1891–1908;
Financial Secretary to the
Treasury, 1903–1905; Civil Lord
of the Admiralty, 1915–1916;
Governor General and
Commander-in-Chief of Canada,
1916–1921; Secretary of State
for the Colonies, 1922–1924.

13 The main bedrooms at Rideau
Hall are all named after a
former Governor General.
In the 1990s the Devonshire
family gave a Regency mirror
from Chatsworth to hang in the
Victor Devonshire bedroom. The
9th Duke of Devonshire thought
Rideau Hall 'very comfortable
and homelike'. The Duke of
Devonshire diary, 13 November
1916. Devonshire MSS,
Chatsworth.

14 Harold Macmillan to F. F.
Urquhart, 29 September 1919.
MS Macmillan dep. c. 452, loc.
cit.

15 Harold Macmillan to the
Duchess of Devonshire, undated
letter of December 1919. Box
G4/3207, Devonshire MSS,
Chatsworth.

16 Nellie Macmillan to the Duchess
of Devonshire, loc. cit.

17 The Duke of Devonshire diary,
26 December 1919. Devonshire
MSS, Chatsworth.

18 Harold Macmillan to the
Duchess of Devonshire, 28
January 1920. Box A 28/1032,
Devonshire MSS, Chatsworth.

19 The Duke of Devonshire to
Lady Frederick Cavendish, 15
January 1920. Box K5/4688,
Devonshire MSS, Chatsworth.

Lord Frederick Cavendish was
murdered on 6 May 1882 in
Phoenix Park, Dublin on his
arrival to take up the post of
Chief Secretary to Ireland.

20 Anthony Sampson, *Anatomy of
Britain*, Hodder & Stoughton,
1962, p. 326.

21 Summer Fields and Eton are
still all-male establishments.
Balliol admitted women as
undergraduates in 1979.

22 Lady Dorothy Evelyn Cavendish
was born on 28 July 1900 and
died on 21 May 1966.

23 Lady Caroline Faber to the
author, 16 February 2008.

24 Quoted in Richard Davenport-
Hines, *The Macmillans*,
Heinemann, 1992, p. 169.

25 The Duke of Devonshire diary,
21 April 1920. Devonshire MSS,
Chatsworth.

26 *Daily Graphic*, 22 April 1920.

27 Box A 28/1043, Devonshire
MSS, Chatsworth.

28 Lady Caroline Faber to the
author, 16 February 2008.
On one occasion that summer
Macmillan bicycled from Chester
Square to Eastbourne.

29 Dorothy had a difficult labour
- the baby was 8lb 10z. The
following year, in July 1922,
she was to suffer a miscarriage.
Maurice Victor, Viscount
Macmillan of Ovenden, PC
(1921–1984), MP for Halifax
(1955–1964) and Farnham
(1966–1984), where the present
author got to know him as a
constituent; Economic Secretary
to the Treasury, 1963–1964,
Chief Secretary to the Treasury,
1970–1972; Secretary of State

for Employment, 1972–1973, Paymaster General, 1973–1974; Chairman, Macmillan & Co., 1967–1970.

30 Lady Dorothy Macmillan to the Duchess of Devonshire, 23 July 1922. Box N18/4665, Devonshire MSS, Chatsworth.

31 Lady Caroline was later to set up her family home with her husband Julian Faber at 3 Chester Square in 1961.

32 Harold Macmillan, *The Past Masters: Politics and Politicians 1906–1939*, Macmillan, 1975, p. 195.

33 Deborah, Dowager Duchess of Devonshire, to the author, 15 October 2007.

34 Alfred Ernest, Baron Marples (1907–1978), businessman, Parliamentary Secretary to Harold Macmillan at the Ministry of Housing and Local Government, Paymaster General and Minister of Transport. The acronym for the electronic random number indicating equipment to choose Premium Bond prize winners was his colloquial Christian name, ERNIE.

35 The Hon. Lady de Zulueta to the author, 23 May 2008.

36 Sir John Graham who showed the author his handsome volume.

37 Harold Macmillan to the Duchess of Devonshire, 18 August 1920. Box A28/1034, Devonshire MSS, Chatsworth.

38 Harold Macmillan, 'The Mind of the Writer', Thomas Hardy Papers, Eton College Library.

39 The site of the office has long been subsumed into the extensions to the National Gallery.

40 Austen Chamberlain was the only Conservative leader during the 20th century until William Hague who did not also go on to become Prime Minister. In the early 21st century there were suddenly two more, Iain Duncan Smith and Michael Howard.

41 So called because the ailing Duke of Wellington, on being told by Lord Derby of the names of the (to him) unknown peers, grunted 'Who? Who?' after each of the names was revealed.

42 H. H. Asquith was Leader of the Liberal Party from 1908 to 1926, even when out of Parliament from 1918 to 1920 after losing his seat in the 1918 Election. Lloyd George only became Leader of the Liberal Party after 1926, by which time it was no longer one of the two major parties.

43 Speech on 7 March 1961. Nevertheless the Liberals could claim the last laugh, as their spectacular victory in a by-election in the previously safe Conservative seat of Orpington in March 1962 began a process that ended with Macmillan's departure from Downing Street in October 1963.

44 Macmillan, op. cit., p. 139.

45 Macmillan's grandson, David Faber, MP for Westbury from 1992 to 2001, first stood as a Conservative candidate in his grandfather's old constituency Stockton (then Stockton North) in 1987.

46 Lady Caroline Faber was later

to tramp the same streets in support of her son, David, Conservative candidate in the 1987 election.

CHAPTER SIX

The Cleverest of the Coming Men 1923–1929

1 Stuart Ball (ed.), *Parliament and Politics in the Age of Baldwin and MacDonald: The Headlam Diaries* 1923–1935, The Historians' Press, 1992, p. 96.
2 Maurice Cowling, *The Impact of Labour* 1920–1924, Cambridge University Press, 1971, p. 1.
3 Stanley Baldwin, speech at the Carlton Club, 19 October 1922.
4 Quoted in Keith Middlemass and John Barnes, *Baldwin: A Biography*, Weidenfeld & Nicolson, 1969, p. 245.
5 For a comprehensive overview of the controversy, and Macmillan's culminating part in it, see the Epilogue in Julian Amery, *Joseph Chamberlain and the Tariff Reform Campaign: The Life of Joseph Chamberlain Volume Six* 1903–1968, Macmillan, 1969, pp. 993–1055.
6 F. E. Smith to Austen Chamberlain, 15 August 1923. Austen Chamberlain Papers, Birmingham University Library. AC/35/2/24.
7 Harold Macmillan to F. F. Urquhart, 16 January 1924, MS Macmillan dep. c. 452. Macmillan Papers, Bodleian Library, Oxford. The feelings expressed in this letter account for Macmillan's enthusiasm

initially for the idea of Oswald Mosley's New Party in 1930. See Chapter 7.
8 F. F. Urquhart to Harold Macmillan, 30 October 1924. MS Macmillan dep. c. 46/1, loc. cit.
9 Ernest Appleton, who died in 1941, was the father of Ralph Appleton, a key worker for Macmillan in the 1945 election, and David Faber's chairman in 1987. Stockton details were given by Ralph Appleton to the author at his home in Norton, often a base for Macmillan, on 17 July 2007, and in extended correspondence subsequently. Ralph Appleton could remember canvassing for Macmillan as a schoolboy in the 1929 election campaign.
10 Stanley Baldwin to Harold Macmillan, 21 October 1924. MS Macmillan dep. c. 46/1, loc. cit.
11 Ibid.
12 The impact of broadcasting, even in its early days, on the social life of Britain between the wars was far-reaching. 1923, which saw the first 'radio' election, was also the year in which a commentary on the FA Cup Final, between West Ham United and Bolton Wanderers on 28 April, was broadcast live for the first time. In 1922, news of the result of the equivalent match between Huddersfield Town and Preston North End only filtered back gradually to the north of England by word of mouth. As Sunday papers were not widespread

in Nonconformist areas, many people in Huddersfield did not know the result, a 1–0 defeat for their team, until the national papers arrived on Monday, an interval of nearly 48 hours. (Information to the author from a family member who had been at the 1922 Cup Final.)

13 *The Times*, 25 October 1924.

14 The American President Lyndon B. Johnson was to make frequent use of this analogy in a more earthy manner.

15 Thomas Jones diary, 8 November 1924. Quoted in Middlemass and Barnes, op. cit., p. 282.

16 George Buchanan (1890–1955), Labour, later Independent Labour Party, MP for Glasgow Gorbals, 1922–1948.

17 *Hansard*, 30 April 1925.

18 Ibid. Sir John Marriott (1859–1945), Conservative MP for Oxford, 1917–1922, and for York, 1923–1929.

19 Ralph Appleton to the author, 17 July 2007.

20 Lady Dorothy Macmillan to the Duchess of Devonshire, 7 May 1926. Box G20A/3646. Devonshire MSS, Chatsworth.

21 Harold Macmillan to Ernest Appleton, 19 May 1926. MS Macmillan dep. c. 51, loc. cit.

22 A reference to the American President Abraham Lincoln (1809–1865) and his desire for unity after controversy 'with malice towards none'. Harold Macmillan to F. F. Urquhart, 9 May 1926. MS Macmillan dep. c. 452, loc. cit.

23 Outlined by Disraeli in his novel *Sybil or The Two Nations*, 1845, Book ii, Ch. 5.

24 *The Times*, 7 December 1926. Cuthbert Headlam was chosen to replace J. C. C. Davidson in this junior post on 16 December 1926 following Davidson's appointment as party chairman.

25 Colonel John Gretton (1867–1947), Conservative MP for Derbyshire South, 1895–1906; Rutland, 1907–1918; Burton, 1918–1943; created Baron Gretton, 1944. Chairman of the brewers Bass, Ratcliffe & Gretton. Gretton was the leading diehard figure in the interwar period, and convenor of the 'Conservative Group', also known as the 'Gretton Group'.

26 R. A. Butler Memorandum, 19–21 July 1935. G6/57. Lord Butler of Saffron Walden Papers, Trinity College Cambridge.

27 Noel Skelton (1880–1935) was widely seen as a potential future Tory leader. His premature death was a grievous blow to those in the party who saw him as the great champion of progressive thinking. His biographer, David Torrance, establishes Skelton as a key figure in Conservative thinking in the interwar years, and an underlying influence through to the time of David Cameron's leadership of the party in the twenty-first century. David Torrance, *Noel Skelton and the Property-Owning Democracy* (forthcoming).

28 Noel Skelton to Harold Macmillan, 5 November 1929. MS Macmillan dep. c. 862, loc. cit.

29 Stanley Baldwin to King George V, 18 Febrary 1927. Box 62. Baldwin Papers, Cambridge University Library.

30 Harold Macmillan to John Loder, 5 November 1924. John de Vere Loder, 2nd Baron Wakehurst Papers, Parliamentary Archives.

31 *Hansard*, 2 May 1927. The new arrangements reduced the Labour Party's income from such affiliation fees by a quarter. The Act was repealed by MacDonald's 1929 Labour government.

32 The Duke of Devonshire had extensive interests in Eastbourne.

33 One could hardly imagine members of the YMCA at one 1922 London music hall attraction, 'Naughty Fifi, the Comic French Chanteuse and Mimi her Eccentric Accompanist'.

34 Sir Austen Chamberlain to Ida Chamberlain, 2 November 1930. AC 5/1/519. Austen Chamberlain Papers, Birmingham University Library.

35 Robert Boothby to Harold Macmillan, 2 November 1926, and undated letter. MS Macmillan dep. c. 359, loc. cit. John Strachey (1901–1963), Labour MP, Birmingham Aston 1929–1931, Dundee, 1945–1950; Dundee West, 1950–1963. Emanuel Shinwell (1884–1986), Labour MP, Linlithgow 1922–1924, 1928–1931, Seaham, 1935–1950, Easington 1950–1970. Both were ministers in Attlee's post-war Labour government. Strachey succeeded Shinwell as Secretary of State for War in 1950.

36 Torrance, op. cit., p. 108.

37 Since the war, the Church of England had been working on a Prayer Book revision that would have given greater latitude to Anglo-Catholic practice. Evangelical and Presbyterian opposition was predictably fierce.

38 Cuthbert Headlam diary, 16 December 1927. Ball (ed.), op. cit., p. 137.

39 Anthony Sampson, *Macmillan: A Study in Ambiguity*, Penguin Books, Harmondsworth, 1968, p. 39.

40 R. A. Butler (1902–1982), later Baron Butler of Saffron Walden, Conservative MP for Saffron Walden, 1929–1965, was to be one of the central figures in Macmillan's political story, and Macmillan in his. Holder of the three great offices of state, Chancellor of the Exchequer, Home Secretary and Foreign Secretary, like Sir John Simon before him, and James Callaghan afterwards, Butler could have become Prime Minister on three occasions, June 1953, January 1957, when Macmillan was preferred, and October 1963, when Alec Douglas-Home emerged as the dark-horse candidate. With hindsight Butler always believed that June 1953, when Churchill and Eden were both laid low with illness, was his best opportunity. Lord Butler to the author, 20 November 1975.

41 Quoted in Sampson, op. cit., p. 28.

42 William Lovett (1800–1877), one of the original Chartists, had wanted full enfranchisement of women also, but his colleagues felt this would have been ridiculed and weakened their case for full male voting rights.

43 Ironically, in 1962 Macmillan's government was responsible for the biggest contraction of the railway network with the infamous Beeching Axe. See Chapter 27.

44 As in Robert Boothby to Harold Macmillan, 25 December 1929. MS Macmillan dep. c. 455, loc. cit.

CHAPTER SEVEN

Ebbs and Flows 1929–1935

1 Stuart Ball (ed.), *Parliament and Politics in the Age of Baldwin and MacDonald: The Headlam Diaries 1923–1935*, The Historians' Press, 1992, p. 256.

2 Ramsay MacDonald (1866–1937) of necessity moved to many constituencies during his parliamentary career. He was Labour MP for Leicester, 1906–1918; Aberavon, 1922–1929; Seaham Harbour, 1929–1931; and National Labour MP for Seaham Harbour, 1931–1935, when he was defeated by Emanuel Shinwell in the November general election by 38,380 votes to 17,882. MP for Scottish Universities, 1936–1937. He returned to the House of Commons in unusual, though not unique, circumstances. Noel Skelton died suddenly during the 1935 general election campaign and was elected posthumously. MacDonald won the subsequent by-election for the Scottish Universities in 1936. Macmillan was to return to the House of Commons in 1945 after his defeat in Stockton-on-Tees at a by-election following the posthumous election of Sir Edward Campbell, the candidate and former MP for Bromley from 1930. Leslie Ruthven Pym, Unionist MP for Monmouth, was also elected posthumously after his death on 17 July 1945. Polling day in 1945 was on 5 July, and to allow for collection of worldwide postal votes from troops overseas, the declaration was on 26 July.

3 In 2004, the former Labour MP Tony Benn commented in his diary about establishment figures such as senior civil servants and judges greeting him warmly at a function at the Oxford Union. 'I was saying how nice everyone was to me and Lissie [Benn's daughter] commented, "Well, it is all about class, you realise." They are nice to me because I am part of their class. She is shrewd about that.' Tony Benn, *Diaries 2001–2007: More Time for Politics*, Hutchinson, 2007, p. 175. Exactly the same was true of the relationships between public school Labour Members of Parliament and Harold Macmillan, with the conspicuous exception of Hugh Gaitskell, where mutual antipathy ran deep.

4 Hugh Dalton, *Call Back*

Yesterday: Memoirs 1887–1931, Muller, 1953, p. 212.

5 Sir Oswald Mosley (1896–1980) was spoken of at different times as both a future Conservative and Labour leader. His political journey was one of the most complex in interwar politics. MP for Harrow, 1918–1924 (Conservative to 1920, Independent to 1924, Labour from 1924); Smethwick, 1926–1931 (Labour to 1931, then the New Party); Chancellor of the Duchy of Lancaster, 1929–1930; Leader of New Party, 1931 to 1932, and of the British Union of Fascists, 1932–1940. Imprisoned, 1940–1944. His first wife Cynthia Blanche Mosley (1898–1933), MP for Stoke, 1929–1931 (Labour to February 1931, then New Party), was the daughter of Lord Curzon. Mosley married Diana Guinness (née Mitford) in 1936. As Deborah Mitford, Diana's sister, was in 1941 to marry Andrew, the future 11th Duke of Devonshire (1920–2004), Mosley became part of the extended Macmillan family, a fact Macmillan never forgot, even after their political estrangement from 1932.

6 Harold Macmillan to F. F. Urquhart, 3 June 1929. MS Macmillan dep. c. 452. Macmillan Papers, Bodleian Library, Oxford.

7 Harold Macmillan to Winston Churchill, 1 January 1928. Churchill Papers, Churchill College, Cambridge. 18/85.

8 *Daily Mail*, 22 June 1929.

9 Quoted in Nigel Fisher, *Harold Macmillan: A Biography*, Weidenfeld & Nicolson, 1982, p. 32.

10 A club that still evokes the 1920s spirit of Scott Fitzgerald and the Great Gatsby.

11 R. J. L. Kingsland, *The Publishers' Association: 1896–1946*, Cambridge University Press, 1970, pp. 91, 151, 165 and 123.

12 Nancy Witcher Astor (1879–1964), Conservative MP for Plymouth Sutton, 1919–1945, was the first woman member of Parliament.

13 Andrew Lownie, *John Buchan: The Presbyterian Cavalier*, Constable, 1995, p. 224.

14 John Moore-Brabazon (1884–1964), Conservative MP, Chatham, 1918–1929; Wallasey, 1931–1942. Created Lord Brabazon of Tara, 1942.

15 Chatham was always one of those closely fought marginal seats that help to decide the national result. 'Why do I emphasise the importance of the Royal Navy?' asked the then Leader of the Opposition, Harold Wilson, when campaigning there during the 1964 general election, 'Because you're in Chatham,' came a heckler's reply.

16 Thomas Inskip, Conservative MP, Bristol Central 1918–1929; Fareham, 1931–1939. Created Viscount Caldecote, 1939. To the dismay and astonishment of many of Macmillan's group, he was made Co-ordinator of Defence, 1936–1939.

17 Ball (ed.), op. cit., 29 July 1929, p. 178.

18 Ball (ed.), op. cit., 5 December 1929, p. 181.

19 Ernest Appleton to Harold Macmillan, 27 January 1930. MS Macmillan dep. c. 455, loc. cit.

20 Guy Kindersley, Conservative MP for Hitchin, 1923–1931.

21 William Maxwell Aitken, 1st Baron Beaverbrook (1917), was Conservative MP for Ashton, 1910–1916, and a minister in Lloyd George's Coalition Government and Winston Churchill's Wartime Government, notably as Minister of Aircraft Production, 1940–1941. He was instrumental in making Bonar Law Prime Minister in 1922, and in making and unmaking many other careers later.

22 Sir Edward Hulton (1906–1988) had been the unsuccessful Conservative candidate in the Leek Division of Staffordshire in 1929, and failed to enter Parliament for the second time in 1931 when he contested Harwich. His true fame was to come later in publishing.

23 Walter Elliot (1888–1958), Conservative MP for Lanark, 1918–1923; Glasgow Kelvingrove, 1924–1945, 1950–1958, and Scottish Universities, 1946–1950. His first wife was killed in 1919 in a climbing accident on their honeymoon in Skye. In April 1934 he married Katherine ('K') Tennant, whose sister Peggy was married to John Loder. Noel Skelton had long hoped that 'K' Tennant would accept his hand in marriage. 'K' Elliot was included in Macmillan's first list of life peerages in 1958 and remained a lifelong friend.

24 Ralph Appleton to the author, 17 July 2007.

25 The Duke of Devonshire diary, 26 August 1930. Devonshire MSS, Chatsworth.

26 Robert John Graham, Baron Boothby of Buchan and Rattray Head (1900–1986), Conservative MP for East Aberdeenshire, 1924–1958, PPS to Winston Churchill as Chancellor of the Exchequer, 1926–1929; Under Secretary at the Ministry of Food, May-October 1940; among the list of the first life peers in 1958.

27 The following account of the Boothby affair is based on interviews with the late Lord Boothby, Lady Wanda Boothby, his second wife, and the Boothby papers in private possession of Lady Boothby.

28 Dilke was not to recover from his involvement in the infamous Crawford divorce case in 1886, and Parnell's career was ruined when he was cited as co-respondent in the O'Shea divorce case of November 1890.

29 Private information.

30 In fact, one of Eden's first tasks on entering Downing Street was to recommend a new bishop for the diocese of Peterborough. For pre-war attitudes to divorce, see D. R. Thorpe, *Eden: The Life and Times of Anthony Eden First Earl of Avon 1897–1977*,

Chatto & Windus, 2003, pp. 104 and 423. Such attitudes did not die out easily. The author's father was killed in the Second World War. When his remarried mother met with his putative housemaster in 1956, the first question of the housemaster, seeing that the mother's surname was different from that of the new pupil, was 'Who was the guilty party?'

31 Information from Philip Frere's nephew by marriage, Brian Rees.

32 In September 1975, Reginald Maudling, Conservative leadership candidate in 1965, unequivocally told the author, 'Everyone wants to become leader.'

33 Cherie Booth and Cate Haste, *The Goldfish Bowl: Married to the Prime Minister* 1955–1997, Chatto & Windus, 2004, p. 44.

34 Harold Macmillan to the Duchess of Devonshire, 20 September 1931 and 1 October 1931, 10 April 1934, 13 March 1937. Box Z12, Box E13/2318, Box E13/2319. The Devonshire Collection, Chatsworth.

35 Quentin Crewe, *The Autobiography of an Optimist*, Hutchinson, 1991, p. 72. When Sir Alistair Horne was commissioned to write the official life of Harold Macmillan in 1979, he was given unrestricted access to the Macmillan papers, then at Birch Grove. The only condition imposed upon him was that he should not publish any letters between Dorothy and Boothby. As he found no such letters

the issue did not arise. (Private information.)

36 Lady Dorothy Macmillan to Lady Cynthia Mosley, January 1933. Boothby Papers, File M, Letter 69.

37 Robert Boothby to Lady Cynthia Mosley, 14 September 1932. Boothby Papers, File M, Letter 689.

38 Lord Boothby to Sir Nigel Fisher, 21 October 1977. Boothby Papers, File M, letter 389. Macmillan co-operated with Fisher on the biography - Nigel Fisher, *Harold Macmillan: A Biography*, Weidenfeld & Nicolson, 1982 - only on condition that Lady Dorothy's affair with Boothby was not mentioned. Nevertheless, Fisher always hoped to give the first public account of the affair, and wrote to Boothby, 'It might be best to hold up publication of the book till after Harold dies, in order not to upset him.' Sir Nigel Fisher to Lord Boothby, 21 November 1977. Boothby Papers, File M, Letter 391. Macmillan's continued longevity put paid to this plan.

39 Robert Rhodes James, *Bob Boothby: A Portrait*, John Curtis, Hodder & Stoughton, 1991, p. 114.

40 Robert Boothby to Quentin Crewe, 15 August 1951. Boothby Papers, File M, Letter 171.

41 Ibid. p. 71.

42 The placing of blue plaques on the homes of the famous is an arbitrary matter. A plaque at 1 Eaton Square records that it

was the home of Lord Boothby from 1946 until his death. No such plaque adorns the portals of Macmillan's birthplace, 52 Cadogan Place, or his first London home, 14 Chester Square.

43 When the author interviewed Lord Boothby on 14 December 1974, he was served a tumbler of neat whisky at 2 p.m.

44 Rhodes James, op. cit., p. 384.

45 The Devonshire family suffered from alcoholism in many generations.

46 Rhodes James, op. cit., p. 114.

47 'The historian should bear in mind that between about 1880, when limitation started, and 1940 or so, when the use of the sheath at any rate became more general in all classes, he has on his hands a frustrated people.' A. J. P. Taylor, *English History 1914–1945*, Oxford University Press, p. 166. An account of how the different social classes dealt with contraception in the interwar years is contained in Martin Pugh, *We Danced All Night: A Social History of Britain between the Wars*, Bodley Head, 2008, Chapter 8.

48 Although Sir Robert Rhodes James knew of this when he wrote his biography of Boothby in 1991, he limited any reference to the opaque sentence 'There was also an episode, too sensitive to relate, when Sarah was an adult', but reading between the lines the reader could guess his meaning. Sir Robert Rhodes James to the author, 2 March 1999. Rhodes James, op. cit., p. 120.

49 *Sunday Times*, 1 April 1973.

50 Francis Beckett, *Macmillan*, Haus Publishing, 2006, p. 28.

51 Harold Macmillan to F. F. Urquhart, 10 September 1930. MS Macmillan dep. c. 452, loc. cit.

52 Robert Blake, *The Unknown Prime Minister: The Life and Times of Andrew Bonar Law, 1858–1923*, Eyre & Spottiswoode, 1955, p. 62.

53 In *Empire and Sexuality*, Manchester University Press, Manchester, 1991, Ronald Hyam places Macmillan firmly in this category, in which he also includes Winston Churchill, General Gordon and Sligger Urquhart.

54 Alistair Horne, *Macmillan 1957–1986: Volume II of the Official Biography*, Macmillan, 1989, p. 290.

55 The late Sir Philip de Zulueta to the author, 11 November 1986.

56 Details of the economic difficulties of this period can be found in Robert Skidelsky, *Politicians and the Slump: The Labour Government of 1929–1931*, Penguin Books, Harmondsworth, 1970.

57 *The Times*, 27 May 1930.

58 Ibid. 28 May 1930. Butler's fellow signatories were Viscount Lymington, MP for Basingstole; Harold Balfour, MP for the Isle of Thanet; and Michael Beaumont, MP for Aylesbury.

59 Robert Boothby to Sir Oswald Mosley. Boothby Papers. File M, undated and un-numbered letter,

though clearly written sometime in October 1931.

60 Lord Carrington to the author, 21 January 2008.

61 A. J. P. Taylor, *Beaverbrook*, Penguin Books, Harmondsworth, 1974, p. 400.

62 Keith Middlemass and John Barnes, *Baldwin: A Biography*, Weidenfeld & Nicolson, 1969, fn p. 600. Various versions of the exact words have circulated, another being 'Now Stanley's lost us the tarts' vote as well.'

63 See Chapter 7.

64 Harold Nicolson diary, 30 May 1931. Harold Nicolson, *Diaries and Letters 1930–1964*, ed. Stanley Olson, Penguin Books, Harmondsworth, 1984, p. 26.

65 The sanatorium had been built initially as a spa in 1885, but later specialised in mental illness. It was destroyed by Second World War bombing.

66 Thomas Mann, *The Magic Mountain*, Chapter 5.

67 Harold Macmillan to F. F. Urquhart, 2 August 1931 and 23 September 1931. MS Macmillan dep. c. 452, loc. cit.

68 Harold Macmillan to the Duchess of Devonshire, 20 September 1931 and 1 October 1931. Box Z12. Devonshire MSS, Chatsworth.

69 See David Marquand, *Ramsay MacDonald*, Jonathan Cape, 1977, Chapters 25 and 26.

70 From the foreword by the Earl of Stockton to John Barnes and David Nicholson (ed.), *The Empire at Bay: The Leo Amery Diaries 1929–1945*, Hutchinson, 1988, p. xi.

71 In the mid-twentieth century the pound was to be devalued at 18–year intervals, each time under a Labour Prime Minister - 1931 (Ramsay MacDonald), 1949 (Clement Attlee) and 1967 (Harold Wilson).

72 Hugh, op. cit., p. 297.

73 C. L. Mowat, *Britain Between the Wars 1918–1940*, Methuen & Co., University paperback edition, 1968, p. 420.

74 Robert Boothby, *I Fight to Live*, Gollancz, 1947, p. 93.

75 J. B. Priestley, *English Journey*, Penguin Books, Harmondsworth, 1977 paperback edition, pp. 320–1.

76 Clement Attlee to Tom Attlee, 29 February 1932. Attlee papers, fo. 46. Bodleian Library, Oxford.

77 Daniel Ritschel, *The Politics of Planning: The Debate on Economic Planning in Britain in the 1930s*, Clarendon Press, Oxford, 1997, pp. 182 and 192.

78 Beckett, op. cit., p. 34.

79 Donald Winch, *Economics and Policy: A Historical Study*, Hodder & Stoughton, 1969, p. 217.

80 Reported in Hugh Dalton's diary, 1 January 1932. Ben Pimlott (ed.), *The Political Diary of Hugh Dalton: 1918–40, 1945–60*, Jonathan Cape, 1986, p. 164.

81 *Hansard*, 4 November 1932.

82 Ritschel, op. cit., p. 193.

83 Harold Macmillan, *Reconstruction: A Plea for a National Policy*, Macmillan, 1933, p. 10.

84 Martin Gilbert (ed.), *Plough My Own Furrow: the story of*

Lord Allen of Hurtwood as told through his writings and correspondence, Longmans, 1965, p. 321.

85 Ritschel, op. cit., p. 257.

86 Pugh, op. cit., p. 195.

87 Gilbert (ed.), op. cit., p. 321.

88 Ball (ed.), op. cit., 11 March 1934, p. 296.

89 Private information.

90 Harry Dexter White (1892–1948), American economist, Director of Monetary Research at the US Treasury, 1938–1945. He was first named as a Soviet agent to Adolphe Berle, US Assistant Secretary of State, on 2 September 1939. President Roosevelt dismissed the idea of a Soviet agent within his administration as absurd. But he was wrong.

91 Harold Macmillan to Nellie Macmillan, 30 August 1932. MS Macmillan dep. e.1, loc. cit.

92 Ibid.

93 Ritschel, op. cit., p. 191.

94 Colin Coote, *Editorial: Memoirs*, Eyre & Spottiswoode, 1965, p. 151.

95 Lord Lawson to the author, 18 June 2008.

96 The term used to describe President Franklin D. Roosevelt's economic and social policies, particularly during his first two administrations. The first New Deal was from 1933–1935, and the second from 1935–1939. Roosevelt was the last US President to serve more than two terms.

97 King George the fifth and Queen Mary the four-fifths, as the wags put it.

98 Duke of Devonshire diary, 6 May 1935. The Devonshire Collection, Chatsworth. Macmillan writes in his memoirs that he was in Stockton on Jubilee Day itself. His visit was on 7 May 1935, when the celebrations were still in full swing.

99 Macmillan's son Maurice once pondered with his father why his own political career had fallen so far short of his father's. 'Because you weren't ruthless enough' was his father's explanation. (Private information.)

100 It was, in David Marquand's *Ramsay MacDonald*, Jonathan Cape, 1977.

101 MacDonald was to be returned as Member for the Scottish Universities in a by-election caused by the fact that Noel Skelton, who died on 22 November, four days before the new Parliament assembled, was elected posthumously. Macmillan, as has been noted in note 2, was to be returned for Bromley in 1945 in similar circumstances.

102 Mowat, op. cit., p. 556.

103 Gilbert Murray Murray (1866–1957), internationalist; Regius Professor of Greek, Oxford University, 1908–1936; Liberal candidate, Oxford University, 1919–1928; Chairman, Executive Council, League of Nations Union, 1923–38. Virginia Woolf considered him so immaculate in taste that she wondered how he ever had the boldness to beget children.

CHAPTER EIGHT

Democracy Can Do Better
1935–1940

1 Martin Gilbert (ed.), *Plough My Own Furrow: The Story of Lord Allen of Hurtwood as told through his writings and correspondence*, Longmans, 1965, p. 323.

2 NC 18/1/999. Neville Chamberlain papers, Birmingham University Library. Joseph Chamberlain, Neville Chamberlain's father, and Austen, Neville Chamberlain's half-brother, failed to become Prime Minister, though both were predicted to do so.

3 W. H. Auden, 'Some Reflections on Music and Opera' (1952).

4 J. K. Galbraith, *The Affluent Society*, Penguin Books, Harmondsworth, paperback edition, 1965, pp. 25 and 22.

5 On 3 November 1956, when Eden's broadcast to the nation about the forthcoming invasion of Egypt at the height of the Suez crisis, All Souls College in Oxford was holding its annual Gaudy. Guests included Lord Halifax, a proponent of appeasement, and Eden's successor as Foreign Secretary in 1938. Dinner was delayed so that the High Table guests could see Eden's television broadcast on the butler's television in a back room in the Warden's Lodgings. After Eden had finished there was a long silence, eventually broken by Halifax saying, 'That's the trouble with Anthony, he always did have this thing about dictators.' Professor Wm Roger Louis to the author, 2 November 2006, after the All Souls Chichele lecture, 'All Souls and the Suez Crisis of 1956'.

6 Graham Stewart, *Burying Caesar: Churchill, Chamberlain and the Battle for the Tory Party*, Phoenix paperback edition, 2000, p. 333.

7 Robert Rhodes James, *Bob Boothby: A Portrait*, Hodder & Stoughton, 1991, p. 175.

8 Kenneth Rose papers. The 4th volume of the official history of *The Times*, covering the Dawson years, published in 1952, not only demonstrated, but admitted Dawson's errors. On 6 August 1969, the paper admitted its mistake over appeasement in a leading article.

9 Arthur Henderson was the first of the big figures from the first two Labour govermments to die, on 20 October 1935. Philip Snowden, in rural retirement in Tilford, died on 15 May 1937. Ramsay MacDonald died at sea on 9 November 1937, and George Lansbury on 7 May 1940, the day the Norwegian Debate began in the House of Commons, the event that was to bring down the curtain on a distinct era in British politics.

10 200 of Jarrow's unemployed, supported by the local MP, Ellen Wilkinson ('Red Ellen'), set out to the capital on 5 October 1936, arriving in London on 31 October. Even more than Stockton-on-Tees, Jarrow depended on shipbuilding as its major source of employment.

The Jarrow Crusade was far from unique among the interwar hunger marches, but it was the one that became symbolic of the age. An ironic painting by Thomas Dugdale (1880–1952), *The Arrival of the Jarrow Marchers in London, 1936,* showed an elegant lady, cigarette holder in hand, looking out of her apartment on the crowds outside, her pinstriped-trousered husband sitting uninterested beside her.

11 George Orwell, *The Lion and the Unicorn: Socialism and the English Genius,* Secker & Warburg, 1962 edition, p. 42.

12 C. L. Mowat, *Britain between the Wars,* Methuen, 1968, fn p. 501, and p. 501.

13 Road houses, large and inexpensive eating places, neither restaurant nor public house, grew up along the arterial roads in this period. They were usually placed so that car journeys could be conveniently broken on a day's outing. That on the Hog's Back, south of Guildford, halfway from London to the South Coast, was an archetypal example. Belisha beacons, illuminated amber globes on black and white posts at pedestrian 'zebra' crossings, were introduced by Leslie Hore-Belisha (1893–1957), a Simonite Liberal, when Minister of Transport in 1934 in the National Government, and were named after him. Launching the scheme at a crossing in Camden Town, Hore-Belisha narrowly escaped being run down by a speeding sports car. Though he was Neville Chamberlain's Secretary of State for War from 1937–1940, the Belisha beacons are his one claim on posterity, and Belisha beacon pencils were popular at the time. Macmillan thought him a prime example of a politician who did not last the course.

14 Viscount Cecil of Chelwood (1864–1958). Robert Cecil, 'Bob' to family and friends, had been, among other things, MP for Hitchin, Macmillan's one-time putative constituency, from 1911–1923, Lord Privy Seal, 1923–1924, Chancellor of the Duchy of Lancaster, 1924–1927. In the 1930s he was renowned as one of the architects of the League of Nations and President of the League of Nations Union, 1923–1945. He was awarded the Nobel Peace Prize in 1937. Lady Dorothy had been taught German by her governesses and was able to translate much of Hitler's speech that night, though the gist of it was clear, even to non-German speakers.

15 On 1 September 1939, the television transmitter from Alexandra Palace - which could be used as an aircraft direction finder - was closed down during the broadcast of a Mickey Mouse cartoon. When the television service was resumed on 7 June 1946, apologies were made for the break in transmission, and the interrupted Mickey Mouse cartoon was completed.

16 Charles Morgan, *The House*

of Macmillan 1843–1943, Macmillan, 1943, p. 230. Facsimile 50th anniversary editions of the novel also enjoyed great success in 1986.

17 The Labour Prime Minister Harold Wilson boasted that he had never read Karl Marx's *Das Kapital*. Macmillan had.

18 Harold Macmillan to Lady Alice-Mary 'Moucher' Cavendish, later Duchess of Devonshire, 12 October 1936. Box Q 28. Devonshire MSS, Chatsworth.

19 A description of Mussolini at the Stresa Conference of 1935. Cuthbert Headlam diary, 17 April 1935. Stuart Ball (ed.), *Parliament and Politics in the Age of Baldwin and MacDonald: The Headlam Diaries 1923–1935*, The Historians' Press, 1992, p. 331.

20 A prophetic remark made to his secretary, Edith Watson, quoted in Robert Blake, *The Unknown Prime Minister: The Life and Times of Andrew Bonar Law 1858–1923*, Eyre & Spottiswoode, 1955, p. 486. Edith Watson, still in No. 10 Downing Street during Neville Chamberlain's premiership, was to make a prophetic remark of her own in 1938, telling Jock Colville that Lord Dunglass (later Sir Alec Douglas-Home) would be Prime Minister one day. 'I shall be dead before it happens, but on the day Lord Dunglass becomes Prime Minister I hope you will remember what Miss Watson said.' Jock Colville did.

21 A full account of the Pact and the circumstances leading up to it can be found in J. A. Cross, *Samuel Hoare: A Political Biography*, Jonathan Cape, 1977, Chapter 6.

22 Harold Macmillan, *Winds of Change: 1914–1939*, Macmillan, 1966, p. 443.

23 *The Times*, 18 December 1935.

24 Hugh Dalton reporting on the mailbag he had received, 19 December 1935. Ben Pimlott (ed.), *The Political Diary of Hugh Dalton, 1918–40, 1945–60*, Jonathan Cape, 1986, p. 197.

25 Hans Dieckhoff to Arnold Toynbee, quoted in Cross, op. cit., p. 264.

26 Anthony Eden diary, 23 December 1935, AP 20/1/15. Avon Papers, Birmingham University Library. Anthony Eden, *Facing the Dictators*, Cassell, 1962, p. 317.

27 Quoted in Martin Gilbert, *Winston S. Churchill: Volume V 1922–1939*, Heinemann, 1976, p. 903.

28 Eden was even to live in Beau Brummel's former house in Chesterfield Street. George 'Beau' Brummel (1778–1840) was a renowned dandy and socialite, whose fashionable dress made him the 'observed of all observers'.

29 Together with the Duke of Wellington, Eden was to be one of only two prime ministers to have had an article of clothing named after him.

30 Cross, op. cit., p. 269.

31 Collin Brooks journal, 14 March

1936. N. J. Crowson (ed.), *Fleet Street, Press Barons and Politics: The Journals of Collin Brooks, 1932–1940*, Royal Historical Society, 1998, p. 160. Collin Brooks (1893–1959), an influential interwar journalist, was in the press baron Lord Rothermere's inner circle. He supported Rothermere in his campaigns against Baldwin's leadership, and later became a stout defender of Neville Chamberlain's appeasement policy.

32 Sir Austen Chamberlain to Hilda Chamberlain, 15 March 1936. AC 5/1729. Austen Chamberlain Papers, Birmingham University Library.

33 *Star*, 25 June 1936.

34 Macmillan, op. cit., p. 473.

35 Sir Arthur Evans (1851–1941), archaeologist, and Keeper of the Ashmolean Museum, Oxford.

36 Robert Byron (1904–1941), traveller and writer, as befitted a distant relative of Lord Byron, was a passionate admirer of Greece. His most famous book, *The Road to Oxiana*, was a bravura and serious account of the culture of Persia and Afghanistan. He was part of the Harold Acton set at Oxford in the 1920s, a vigorous opponent of appeasement, and greeted the outbreak of the Second World War by declaring, 'Well, there's one thing to be thankful for: the post-war decadence ought to be even better than the last.' Tragically, he was not to survive the war, going down with his torpedoed ship in February 1941, two days before his 36th birthday.

37 J. C. Squire (1884–1958), Georgian poet and literary editor, was one of the figures gently parodied in A. C. Macdonell's *England, Their England*. Macmillan found Squire's views as a reader consistently dependable. The only occasion they diverged was over C. P. Snow's *The Masters* (1951), which Macmillan thought Snow's finest novel.

38 Quoted in James Knox, *Robert Byron*, John Murray, 2003, p. 355.

39 Ibid., p. xiii.

40 Macmillan Publishing File. MSS Add. 54789. British Library.

41 Lord Dawson of Penn (1864–1965), physician to Edward VII and George V, was shown in 1986 to have hastened George V's passage in his last illness by injecting him with a mixture of morphine and cocaine. This revelation post-dated the contemporary jingle, 'Lord Dawson of Penn/Has killed lots of men/So that's why we sing/God Save the King.'

42 *Guilty Men* by 'Cato', published in 1940 (the authors were Michael Foot, Peter Howard and Frank Owen), by selective quotation, particularly from Baldwin's speeches, successfully established a partial interpretation of the complexities of 1930s defence policy in the public mind.

43 Keith Middlemass and John Barnes, *Baldwin: A Biography*, Weidenfeld & Nicolson, 1969, p. 1070.

44 A record matched later only by Rab Butler and James Callaghan.

45 Harold Macmillan, *The Middle Way*, Macmillan, 1966 paperback edition, p. 5.

46 Ibid., p. 254.

47 Harold Macmillan to J. M. Keynes, 10 May 1938. Macmillan Publishing File. Add. MSS 55204. British Library.

48 J. M. Keynes, 'The English National Character', March 1901, an essay he wrote as a 17-year-old schoolboy, and a view from which he never later dissented. Quoted in Robert Skidelsky, *John Maynard Keynes: Volume One Hopes Betrayed 1883–1920*, Macmillan, 1983, p. 91.

49 Douglas Jay (1907–1996), MP for Battersea North, 1946–1983, Economic Secretary to the Treasury, 1947–50, Financial Secretary, 1950–51, President of the Board of Trade, 1964–67, life peer, 1987. When Macmillan visited Pope John XXIII in February 1960, before the papal audience he was shown the bust of the Emperor Augustus by proud Vatican officials. When asked his opinion, he replied, 'I think it looks awfully like Douglas Jay.' Evan Durbin (1906–1948), economist and politician, author of *The Politics of Democratic Socialism*, 1940. MP for Edmonton, 1945–48. Drowned in Cornwall, saving his daughter and another child from heavy surf. James Meade, 1907–1995, economist, one of Keynes' disciples; he wrote the first Keynesian textbook, *An Introduction to Economic Analysis and Policy*, in 1936.

50 John Turner, *Macmillan*, Longman, 1994, p. 36.

51 Harold Macmillan, *Middle Way*, op. cit., p. 374.

52 Ibid., p. 376.

53 Vaughan Williams's *Dona Nobis Pacem* had first been performed in Huddersfield on 2 October 1936. It made the kind of impact that Benjamin Britten's *War Requiem* was to make in 1962 at the height of the Cold War. Vaughan Williams later said that he was the first composer to have set words spoken in Parliament to music.

54 Quoted in John Campbell, *Nye Bevan and the Mirage of British Socialism*, Weidenfeld & Nicolson, 1987, fn p. 74.

55 Quoted in David Dutton, *Neville Chamberlain*, Arnold, 2001, p. 195.

56 Neville Chamberlain to Ida Chamberlain, 8 August 1937. NC 18/1/1015. Neville Chamberlain Papers, Birmingham University Library.

57 Anthony Eden diary, 17 January 1938. AP 20/1/18. Avon Papers, Birmingham University Library. Neville Chamberlain to Hilda Chamberlain, 15 October 1938. NC 18/1/1073, loc. cit.

58 Neville Chamberlain to Hilda Chamberlain, 24 October 1937. NC 18/1/1025, loc. cit.

59 Anthony Eden diary, 5 January 1938. AP 20/1/18, loc. cit.

60 Anthony Eden to Neville Chamberlain, 6 January 1938. FO 954/6A. National Archives, Kew.

61 Sumner Welles, *Seven Decisions That Shaped History*, Harper and Brothers, New York, 1951, p. 27. Account of Anthony Eden's Resignation. Viscount Cilcennin papers, Carmarthen Record Office. MS Cilc. Coll. 61.

62 Lord Halifax 'A Record of Events connected with Anthony Eden's resignation February 19th-20th 1938', Halifax Papers, the Borthwick Institute of Historical Research, York. File A4 410 411.

63 Count Ciano diary, 20 February 1938. *Ciano's Diary 1937-1938*, Methuen, 1952, p. 61.

64 Ronald Cartland (1907-1940), progressive Conservative MP for King's Norton, 1935-1940, was one of the four MPs, together with Macmillan, Boothby and Leo Amery, later dubbed 'troublesome young men' because of their opposition to Chamberlain. As he was 65 in 1938, Amery might not have been young, but he was certainly troublesome, delivering the *coup de grâce* to Chamberlain in the Norwegian Debate in May 1940. Cartland was killed on active service at Dunkirk.

65 Harold Nicolson to Vita Sackville-West, 9 November 1938. Nigel Nicolson (ed.), *The Harold Nicolson Diaries, 1907-1963*, Weidenfeld & Nicolson, 2004, p. 180.

66 The official Conservative candidate, W. McNair Sneddon, had a majority over the Duchess of Atholl of 1,313 votes. He regretted it had not been one more, as then it would have been the same as the date of Bannockburn.

67 Among its later manifestations, 90 Piccadilly was the Lebanon Tourist and Information Office.

68 Queen Elizabeth the Queen Mother told the author that this was a constitutional mistake. Queen Elizabeth the Queen Mother to the author, 19 March 1990.

69 Macmillan, *Winds of Change*, op. cit., p. 562.

70 David Dutton, *Neville Chamberlain*, Arnold, 2001, p. 55.

71 'The Adullamites' was the name given by John Bright to the Liberal MPs who seceded from the Reform Party in 1866 and opposed the Franchise Bill, 'everyone that was in distress and everyone that was discontented'. The reference was to 1 Samuel, xxii, 1-2. Like Disraeli in 1866, Macmillan played a prominent part behind the scenes in 1938.

72 Edward Heath, *The Course of My Life*, Hodder & Stoughton, 1998, p. 59.

73 Details of Hailsham's campaign can be found in HSML 2/43/1-9. Hailsham Papers, Churchill College, Cambridge.

74 Richard Crossman (1907-1974), MP for East Coventry, 1945-74, and Cabinet Minister in the Wilson governments. He was to work closely with Macmillan in North Africa as Deputy Director of Psychological Headquarters, Algiers, 1943. Frank Pakenham, later 7th Earl of Longford

(1905–2001), Student (Fellow) in Politics at Christ Church, Cabinet Minister in the Attlee government, and Leader of the Lords in the first two Wilson governments. Patrick Gordon Walker, Baron Gordon-Walker (1907–1980), Secretary of the University Labour Party, MP for Smethwick, 1945–1964. He was briefly Foreign Secretary from October 1964, whilst out of Parliament, following his defeat at the 1964 general election in a racist campaign; subsequently he lost the seat at Leyton that had been vacated for him, in January 1965.

75 Lord Hailsham, *A Sparrow's Flight: Memoirs*, 1990, p. 122.

76 John Betjeman, *Summoned by Bells*, Chapter 9, John Murray, 1960.

77 *Picture Post*, 5 November 1938.

78 A slogan coined by Julian Amery, Macmillan's future son-in-law. Julian Amery, *Approach March: A Venture in Autobiography*, Hutchinson, 1973, p. 113.

79 Chris Cook and John Ramsden, *By-Elections in British Politics*, Macmillan, 1973, p. 155.

80 Harold Macmillan to Nancy Astor, 13 November 1938. MS 1416/1/2/188. Lady Astor Papers, Reading University.

81 Harold Nicolson diary, 11 April 1939, Nigel Nicolson (ed.), op. cit., p. 186.

82 When Birch Grove temporarily housed a school, they stayed in another house, Gosses, on the estate.

83 Leo Amery diary, 2 September 1939. John Barnes and David Nicholson, *The Empire At Bay: The Leo Amery Diaries 1929–1945*, Hutchinson, 1988, p. 570.

84 Leo Amery diary, 3 September 1939, ibid., p. 571.

85 Macmillan's fact-finding mission to Finland is examined in Chapter 9.

86 A flotilla of five British destroyers had entered the ice-free Narvik harbour, a vital port for the German war effort, where they were able to sink two German destroyers and destroy six merchant ships, but not before the Germans had landed 2,000 occupying troops. The British flotilla was prevented from leaving the harbour by five German destroyers from neighbouring fjords and, caught in crossfire, suffered heavy losses. The commander of the British flotilla was killed. Although two destroyers managed to make their escape to open sea, Narvik was not the kind of decisive action that the British, buoyed up by the success of the Battle of the River Plate in December 1939, had expected.

87 *Hansard*, 7 May 1940.

88 Ibid., 8 May 1940.

89 Ibid.

90 The name given to the group of appeasers who met at Nancy Astor's house, Cliveden.

91 Lord Hailsham, op. cit., p. 138.

92 David Profumo, *Bringing Down the House: A Family Memoir*, John Murray, 2006, p. 77. In fact, in May 2003, a motion was carried in the

House of Commons saluting the last surviving 'gallant and honourable gentleman' who had helped to bring Churchill to power 63 years earlier.

93 See Robert Blake, 'How Churchill became Prime Minister', Robert Blake and Wm Roger Louis (eds.), *Churchill: A Major New Assessment of his Life in Peace and War*, Oxford University Press, 1993, Chapter 15, pp. 257–273.

94 R. J. L. Kingsland, *The Publishers' Association 1896–1946*, Cambridge University Press, p. 168.

95 As a publisher, Macmillan had uneasy relations with the Oxford University Press. He considered their privileged position regarding bibles and prayer books, not to mention some associated subsidies, unfair to other commercial publishers. The *War and Peace* project was thus a rare collaboration.

96 Sir David Low (1891–1963), one of the most celebrated cartoonists of the age. 'All Behind You, Winston' appeared on 14 May 1940. His cartoons ridiculing the Dictators in the 1930s did much to alert public opinion to the coming dangers. In his last years he published many cartoons critical of the Macmillan government, which he dubbed 'Micawber Ministry'.

97 J. M. Keynes to Harold Macmillan, 25 May 1940. Add. MSS 55204. Macmillan Publishing File, British Library.

98 Quoted in Gilbert, op. cit., p. 903.

CHAPTER NINE

On the Other Side of the Fence 1940–1942

1 Harold Macmillan, 'My Finnish Diary', 13 February 1940. MS Macmillan dep. c. 1/2. Macmillan papers, Bodleian Library, Oxford.

2 Ibid., 12 February 1940.

3 Ibid., 15 February 1940.

4 Geoffrey Dawson diary, 7 March 1940. John Evelyn Wrench, *Geoffrey Dawson and Our Times*, Hutchinson, 1955, p. 407.

5 Leo Amery diary, 19 March 1940. John Barnes and David Nicholson (ed.), *The Leo Amery Diaries 1929–1945*, Hutchinson, 1988, p. 585.

6 Harold Macmillan to Queen Elizabeth II, 5 September 1963. MS Macmillan dep. c. 578, loc. cit.

7 *Hansard*, 19 March 1940.

8 See Chapter 10.

9 Harold Macmillan, *Blast of War: 1939–1945*, Macmillan, 1967, p. 82.

10 Wyndham Raymond, 1st and last Viscount Portal of Laverstocke (1885–1949), not to be confused with his kinsman, Charles Frederick, Viscount Portal of Hungerford, (1893–1971), Chief of the Air Staff. Wyndham Portal, Under-Secretary Ministry of Supply, 1940–1942, Minister of Works & Buildings, 1942–1944, became known for the wartime pre-fabricated 'Portal houses', an influence on Macmillan's housing policy from 1951. After

the war Portal became chairman of the Great Western Railway, a company in which Macmillan resumed his directorship whilst in Opposition. Portal presided over the Olympic Games in London in 1948.

11 Herbert Morrison, *An Autobiography*, Odhams, 1960, p. 300.

12 Harold Macmillan diary, 21 June 1951. Peter Catterall (ed.), *The Macmillan Diaries: The Cabinet Years 1950–1957*, Macmillan, 2003, p. 82.

13 Harold Macmillan diary, 24 October 1951, ibid., p. 109. Anthony Eden had a totally different view of Morrison and felt it a 'national misfortune' that Morrison did not succeed Attlee as Labour leader in 1955. AP 7/26/1. Avon Papers, Birmingham University Library.

14 Lady Dorothy Macmillan to the Duchess of Devonshire, undated letter of 1940. Box E 21. Devonshire MSS, Chatsworth.

15 John Edward Reginald, first Baron Egremont (1920–1972) was Macmillan's private secretary at the Ministry of Supply 1940–1942; the Colonial Office, 1942; in North-West Africa, 1943–1945; and at the Air Ministry, 1945. In 1955, when Macmillan became Foreign Secretary, Wyndham once more became his private secretary. He could not accompany Macmillan to the Treasury in December 1955, because of the conflict of interest that would have arisen over Wyndham's negotiations with the Treasury regarding death duties on the family estates. However, when Macmillan became Prime Minister in 1957, and the negotiations over the art collection at Petworth House had been completed, Wyndham rejoined his 'master'. He was created first Baron Egremont in Macmillan's resignation honours list. Macmillan wrote the notice of John Wyndham's life for *The Dictionary of National Biography* and dedicated his *War Diaries* to him.

16 Robert Blake, *Disraeli*, Methuen & Co. paperback edition, 1969, p. 449.

17 Benjamin Disraeli, *Endymion*, Longmans, Green & Co., 1881, Chapter 49.

18 The Dowager Lady Egremont to the author, 24 June 2008.

19 Anthony Sampson, *Anatomy of Britain*, Hodder & Stoughton, 1962, p. 356.

20 Percy Herbert, first Viscount Mills (1890–1968), was a key figure in Macmillan's drive to build 300,000 houses in Churchill's 1951 government; he became Minister of Power under Macmillan, 1957–1959; Paymaster-General, 1959–1961; and Minister without Portfolio, 1961–1962, when he was one of the seven ministers dismissed on 13 July 1962 in Macmillan's 'Night of the Long Knives'.

21 Harold Macmillan diary, 2 November 1951, Catterall (ed.), op. cit., p. 116.

22 Lady Dorothy Macmillan to the Duchess of Devonshire, 26 June 1940. Box E 21. Devonshire

MSS, Chatsworth.

23 Shakespeare's account in *Julius Caesar*, I, ii, 111–113, derived from Virgil, *Aeneid*, II, 721ff. A similar comparison is made in Churchill's war memoirs and Harold Nicolson's diary. A full account of the drama is in Charles Petrie and Alistair Cooke, *The Carlton Club 1832–2007*, The Carlton Club, 2007, pp. 160–173.

24 Chamberlain died on 9 November 1940.

25 Andrew Rae Duncan (1884–1952), MP City of London, 1940–1950; President, Board of Trade, January-October 1940, and June 1941–February 1942; Ministry of Supply, October 1940–June 1941, and 1942–1945.

26 Cuthbert Headlam diary, 3 October 1940. Stuart Ball (ed.), *Parliament and Politics in the Age of Attlee: The Headlam Diaries 1935–1951*, Cambridge University Press, 1999, p. 221.

27 William Maxwell Aitken, first Baron Beaverbrook (1879–1964), newspaper proprietor and politician, was a renowned political fixer. It was largely owing to him that Bonar Law replaced Lloyd George as Prime Minister in 1922. His later campaign to remove Baldwin was not successful. Although Beaverbrook divided opinion, his work as Minister of Aircraft Production in particular was vital for Britain's survival in 1940. Macmillan was fascinated by Beaverbrook, though wary of his potential for mischief.

28 Cuthbert Headlam diary, 10 July 1941. Ball (ed.), op. cit., p. 262.

29 Lady Dorothy Macmillan to the Duchess of Devonshire, July 1941. Box E 21. Devonshire MSS, Chatsworth.

30 Ernest Bevin (1881–1951), General Secretary, Transport & General Workers' Union, 1922–1940; Labour MP Wandsworth Central, 1940–1950; Woolwich East, 1950–1951; Minister of Labour & National Service, 1940–1945; Foreign Secretary, 1945–1951. His part in the removal of Labour's leader, George Lansbury, in 1935 was as ruthless as anything done by Beaverbrook. His biographer describes him as belonging 'to that small group of men who can be said to have had a decisive impact on the history of their own times'. Alan Bullock, *Ernest Bevin: Foreign Secretary 1945–1951*, Oxford University Press paperback edition, 1985, p. 857.

31 Harold Macmillan to Ernest Bevin, 15 November 1941. MS Macmillan dep. c. 267, loc. cit.

32 Harold Macmillan to Lord Beaverbrook, 28 October 1941. A. J. P. Taylor, *Beaverbrook*, Penguin Books, Harmondsworth, 1974, p. 640.

33 A curious incident concerned Stanley Baldwin's gates at his home, Astley Hall, near Bewdley. The Ministry of Supply had instructed local authorities to requisition gates and railings for the war effort, unless they were 'of special artistic merit or historic interest'. Baldwin's

gates had been given to him by the Worcestershire Conservative Association to mark his retirement in 1937. Baldwin pleaded for the gates to be spared, on the grounds of artistic worth. His appeal, in December 1941, was successful. Questions were subsequently asked in the House of Commons, a Conservative back-bencher, Alan Graham, stating uncharitably 'that it is very necessary to leave Lord Baldwin his gates in order to protect him from the just indignation of the mob'. *Hansard*, 4 March 1942.

34 Walter Edward Guinness, first Baron Moyne (1880–1944), Financial Secretary to the Treasury, 1923 and 1924–1925; Minister of Agriculture, 1925–1929; Secretary of State for the Colonies and Leader of the Lords, 1941–1942; Deputy Minister of State in Cairo, 1942; Minister Resident in the Middle East, 1944. He was assassinated in Cairo on 6 November 1944 by members of the Stern Gang.

35 Sir Stafford Cripps (1889–1952), Labour MP for East Bristol, 1931–1950; South-East Bristol, 1950. British Ambassador to the Soviet Union, 1940–1942; Lord Privy Seal and Leader of the House of Commons, 1942; Minister of Aircraft Production, 1942–1945; President of the Board of Trade, 1945–1947; Minister of Economic Affairs, 1947; Chancellor of the Exchequer, 1947–50. The main purpose of his mission to Moscow had been to establish relations with Russia following the divorce between Hitler and Stalin. Unusually he remained an MP whilst ambassador, thus easing his path back into mainstream politics. A subsequent mission to India did not prove as successful. His spartan lifestyle became symptomatic of the 'Age of Austerity' after the war. Churchill observed of Cripps, 'There, but for the grace of God, goes God.'

36 Vic Oliver, the music hall comedian, had married Churchill's daughter, Sarah, in New York in December 1936. They were divorced in 1944. When Randolph Churchill, the Prime Minister's son, tried to pull rank in Cairo during the war, he was unusually lost for words by the reaction. 'Don't you know who I am?' he had demanded angrily of some hapless subordinate. 'Yes,' came the reply. 'You're Vic Oliver's brother-in-law.'

37 Harold Macmillan to the Duchess of Devonshire, 7 July 1942. Box Q 11. Devonshire MSS, Chatsworth.

38 India had its own Secretary of State, Leo Amery, whose younger son Julian was to marry Macmillan's daughter, Catherine, in 1950.

39 Cranborne did not succeed his father as Marquess of Salisbury until 1947. His early elevation to the Lords in January 1941, taking one of his father's baronies, Cecil of Essendon, though he retained

use of his courtesy title, was because Anthony Eden, once again Foreign Secretary from December 1940, wanted Cranborne to speak in the Lords on Foreign Affairs.

40 From the final line of Arthur Hugh Clough's poem *Say Not the Struggle Naught Availeth*.

41 Quoted by Roy Jenkins, *Churchill*, Macmillan, 2001, p. 800.

42 The Colonies and Dominion Affairs were two separate departments at the time. They were amalgamated as a Department for Commonwealth Relations in August 1966.

43 Wm Roger Louis, *Ends of British Imperialism: The Scramble for Empire, Suez and Decolonisation*, I. B. Tauris, 2006, pp. 1044 and 978. Details of Macmillan's vast preliminary reading on colonial questions can be found in MS Macmillan dep. c. 277, loc. cit. Sir Keith Hancock (1898–1988) was an Australian Rhodes Scholar at Balliol, Fellow of All Souls, 1923–1930, and held Chairs successively at the Universities of Birmingham, Oxford and London. Dame Margery Perham (1895–1982) gave the Reith Lectures in 1961 under the title of 'The Colonial Reckoning'. Their liberal ideas on the legacy of Empire were a profound influence on Macmillan.

44 Sir George Gater (1886–1963), educated at Winchester and New College, first made his name in educational administration, particularly in the expansion of state secondary schools. In the 1930s Gater worked with Herbert Morrison at the LCC on housing matters and the establishment of the Green Belt. During the war he was a civil servant of distinction in the Home Office, the Ministry of Supply and the Colonial Office. Macmillan did not normally care overmuch for Wykehamists. He once described Hugh Gaitskell to the author as 'a sanctimonious Wykehamist with gestures like an Armenian shopkeeper', and David Eccles as 'possibly the only Old Wykehamist who could be mistaken for an Old Harrovian'. George Gater was an exception.

45 As shown by his insistence on providing a full written record for the Royal Archives of the events surrounding his resignation in 1963, not that this diligence has prevented most commentators from interpreting these events as they wish, rather than as they really happened.

46 MS Macmillan dep. c. 275, loc. cit.

47 *Hansard*, 24 June 1942.

48 Quoted in Macmillan, op. cit., p. 179.

49 CO 965/57. National Archives, Kew.

50 Major-General Orde Wingate (1903–1944) led two Chindit operations in Burma. He was killed in an air crash on 24 March 1944 returning from the successful beginning of the second. Field Marshal Wavell described the manner of his death as befitting his life, 'swift,

meteoric, headlong'. On the memorial tablet placed in the porch of the chapel of his old school, Charterhouse, is Churchill's epitaph, 'A man of genius who might well have become also a man of destiny.'

51 Harold Macmillan to Mr Thornley, 22 May 1942. MS Macmillan, loc. cit.

52 The Fourth of June, King George III's birthday, is the principal festival of celebration at Eton. Harold Macmillan to Mr Howard, 4 June 1942. MS Macmillan, loc. cit.

53 Harold Alexander, first Earl Alexander of Tunis (1891–1969), was the patrician soldier *par excellence*, unruffled in crisis, compassionate in victory. He was one of Macmillan's closest friends. After the war he was Governor General of Canada from 1946–1952. Churchill made him Minister of Defence in his peacetime government. Self-effacing to a degree, Alexander was lunching quietly one day in a corner of the dining room at White's in full field marshal's uniform, with baton at his side, prior to attending a military memorial service. 'Who is that distinguished figure?' asked an occasional member of the club of the steward. 'That, sir,' replied the steward, 'is the Earl of Caledon's younger brother.'

54 Bernard Law ('Monty'), first Viscount Montgomery of Alamein (1887–1976), was Britain's greatest field commander since Wellington. His capacity for annoying

his colleagues, especially the Americans, was legendary. From 1951 he was, among many other things, Chairman of the Governors of St John's School, Leatherhead. On one of his visits to the school he was taken initially to see a junior history lesson. 'What are you studying?' he barked. 'History, sir,' replied a nervous boy. 'History - then you must be studying me!' (Private information.)

55 Sir Claude Auchinleck (1884–1981), field marshal, resisted Churchill's frequent demands for offensives he regarded as premature, owing to lack of resources. Churchill's patience was finally exhausted after the fall of Tobruk, and Auchinleck became one of the most high-profile military dismissals of the Second World War. His name is commemorated on a memorial to the ten field marshals of the war in the crypt of St Paul's Cathedral.

56 Montgomery was not Churchill's first choice to head the Eighth Army. This was Lieutenant-General William 'Strafer' Gott, who was killed in an airbus en route to Cairo (for a bath) on 7 August 1942.

57 Speech at the Lord Mayor's Luncheon at the Mansion House, 10 November 1942.

58 President Franklin D. Roosevelt to Winston S. Churchill, 19 November 1942. William Kimball (ed.), *Churchill and Roosevelt - the Complete Correspondence, Vol ii Alliance Forged, November*

1942–*February* 1944, Princeton University Press, New Jersey, 1984, p. 22.

59 Oliver Stanley (1896–1950), Conservative MP for Liverpool Edge Hill, 1923; Westmorland, 1924–1945; Bristol West, 1945–1950. Member of the YMCA. The culmination of his career was as Colonial Secretary, 1942–1945. In opposition in the post-war era, he was on the committee that drew up the 1947 Industrial Charter and was very much third in the Conservative hierarchy after Churchill and Eden, and seen as a possible future leader of the party. His premature death in December 1950 opened up significant new possibilities for both Macmillan and R. A. Butler.

60 Brendan, Viscount Bracken (1901–1958), Conservative MP for North Paddington, 1929; Bournemouth East and Christ Church, 1945–1952. Parliamentary Private Secretary to Churchill at the Admiralty, 1939; Minister of Information, 1941; First Lord of the Admiralty, 1945. Bracken was a key figure in Churchill's appointment as Prime Minister, and one of his closest intimates. He was distrusted by many. Clementine Churchill did not take kindly to the (untrue) rumour that he was Churchill's illegitimate son.

61 *Glasgow Herald*, 2 December 1942.

62 Harold Macmillan to Sir Kenneth Poyser, 2 December 1942. MS Macmillan, loc. cit.

63 Winston S. Churchill to President Franklin D. Roosevelt, 11 December 1942. Kimball (ed.), op. cit., p. 71.

64 Quoted in Anthony Sampson, *Macmillan: A Study in Ambiguity*, Penguin Books, Harmondsworth, 1968, p. 57.

65 Winston S. Churchill to President Franklin D. Roosevelt, 27 December 1942, Kimball (ed.) op. cit., p. 90.

CHAPTER TEN

At One Strategic Point
1942–1943

1 Dwight D. Eisenhower (1890–1969), general and 34th President of the United States 1953–1961. Command of the Allied invasion of French North Africa was his breakthrough, no less than Macmillan's political task as Minister Resident in North Africa was for him. 'Ike', as he was colloquially known in America, won more popular votes than any previous candidate in the presidential election of November 1952. Eisenhower left presidential office in January 1961. Macmillan built skilfully on his wartime links with Eisenhower throughout the four years, 1957–1961, that they coincided as heads of government of their respective countries.

2 Harold Macmillan, *The Blast of War* 1939–1945, Macmillan, 1967, p. 217.

3 One of whom, Miss Campbell,

had been Macmillan's secretary at the Colonial Office.

4 Sir Pierson ('Bob') Dixon (1904–1965) joined the Foreign Service in 1929, and was Principal Private Secretary to two Foreign Secretaries, Anthony Eden and Ernest Bevin. He was Britain's Permanent Representative at the United Nations during the Suez crisis of 1956. As ambassador in Paris from 1960, he was leader of the British delegation negotiating entry into the Common Market. Roger Makins, first Baron Sherfield (1904–1996), entered the Foreign Service in 1928, first in the list, and was assistant to Macmillan at AFHQ from January 1943 to September 1944. A tall, imposing figure, he was ambassador in Washington, 1952–1956, when guests at his crowded parties arranged to 'meet you at the British Ambassador'. Makins was recalled to London by Macmillan to become, in an unorthodox dichotomy, Joint Head of the Treasury, 1956–1959, with Sir Norman Brook. Both Dixon and Makins wrote diaries invaluable for the historian.

5 Cuthbert Headlam diary, 1 January 1943. Stuart Ball (ed.) *Parliament and Politics in the Age of Churchill and Attlee: The Headlam Diaries 1935–1951*, Cambridge University Press, 1999, pp. 340–350.

6 John Anderson, first Viscount Waverley (1882–1958), Home Secretary and Minister of Home Security, 1939–1940, during which time the eponymous Anderson air-raid shelters became a feature of life on the home front; Lord President of the Council, 1940–1943; Chancellor of the Exchequer, 1943–1945. Anderson's widow, Ava, became one of Macmillan's closest friends, and their correspondence over the years gives a unique insight into Macmillan's life.

7 Sir Henry Wilson Bt (1864–1922), Chief of the Imperial General Staff, 1918–1922. One of the most influential commanders of the Great War, a 'brass-hat' (soldier) to his fingertips, not 'a frock' (politician). He was assassinated by two Irish Republicans on the doorstep of his London home in Eaton Place in June 1922. Not to be confused with Sir Henry ('Jumbo') Wilson (see f-n 62).

8 Harold Macmillan to Sir John Anderson, 7 January 1943. MS Macmillan dep. c. 283. Stockton Papers, Bodleian Library, Oxford.

9 As did 40 other countries, including Canada, China and Japan.

10 Note for the Cabinet, 13 July 1943. FO 371/36301. National Archives, Kew.

11 Eisenhower was a figure of considerable importance in Macmillan's life. Macmillan's close links with Eisenhower from North African days was a contributory factor in his rise to the premiership.

12 Vichy was the name given to

the French collaborationist government, headed by Marshal Pétain (1856–1951), based in the city of Vichy.

13 Admiral François Darlan (1881–1942) served as Vice Premier and Foreign Minister in the Vichy government. He was assassinated on Christmas Eve, 1942.

14 Julian Jackson, *France: The Dark Years* 1940–1944, Oxford University Press, 2001, p. 447.

15 See Anthony Verrier, *Assassination in Algiers: Churchill, Roosevelt, de Gaulle and the Murder of Admiral Darlan*, Macmillan, 1990.

16 Anthony Eden diary, 24 December 1942. AP 20/1/22. Avon Papers, Birmingham University Library.

17 Sir Henry Mack (1894–1974), British Civilian Liaison Officer to the Supreme Allied Commander in North Africa. Ambassador to Iraq, 1948–1951, Argentina, 1951–1954. 'I delight in Hal.' Macmillan wrote in his diary (27 April 1945), 'always fresh and interesting.' Harold Macmillan, *War Diaries: Politics and War in the Mediterranean, January 1943–May 1945*, Macmillan, 1984, p. 745.

18 Letter reprinted in ibid., p. 4.

19 Macmillan made a pilgrimage to Spencer in September 1956, at the height of the Suez crisis, with Sir Roger Makins, British Ambassador to America, and Dr David Butler, then working in the British Embassy as personal assistant to the Ambassador.

20 Admiral Andrew Browne Cunningham, Viscount Cunningham of Hyndhope, KT (1883–1963), known as ABC, was arguably the greatest British admiral since Nelson. Later in 1943 he became the navy's representative on the Chiefs of Staff Committee. He once said, 'It takes the navy three years to build a ship but three hundred years to build a tradition.'

21 Lieutenant-General Walter Bedell Smith (1895–1961), Eisenhower's Chief of Staff from September 1942 till the conclusion of hostilities in 1945. He later served as American Under-Secretary of State during Eisenhower's first presidency.

22 Robert Murphy (1894–1978) was the personal representative of President Roosevelt in French North Africa and Chief Civil Affairs Officer on General Eisenhower's staff. As such he was Macmillan's opposite number at AFHQ. Macmillan later said that he had never had such a fruitful professional relationship with anyone as he did with Murphy in those North African days.

23 The extravagant and gilded meeting at Balinghem, near Calais, between Henry VIII and Francis I of France in 1520 to increase the bond of friendship between the two kings. Lord Egremont, *Wyndham and Children First*, Macmillan, 1968, p. 80.

24 William Averell Harriman (1891–1986), Roosevelt's Special Representative to the United Kingdom and the USSR,

US Ambassador in Moscow, 1943–1946, and in Britain, 1946. Thereafter, he became an extraordinarily influential ambassador-at-large for the United States in several key roles. His third wife Pamela, who died in harness as American Ambassador to France in 1997, was first married to Randolph Churchill. As chief American negotiator at the Limited Test Ban Treaty talks in Moscow in August 1963, Harriman experienced what he considered the eccentric behaviour of Lord Hailsham, Macmillan's representative, and was the crucial figure in imposing what was, in essence, an American veto on Hailsham's candidature later that year for the premiership. See Chapter 29. Harriman was a prime example of H. A. L. Fisher's dictum that the wheels of history are seldom turned by the poor.

25 Harry L. Hopkins (1890–1946), special wartime envoy to President Roosevelt, and later President Truman. He was greatly respected by both Stalin and Churchill, who said that if Hopkins had ever been eligible for a peerage, his title should have been 'Lord Root of the Matter'.

26 Alan Francis Brooke, Field Marshal, the 1st Viscount Alanbrooke (1883–1963), known as 'Brookie', CIGS from 1941–1945, and a key figure in the conduct of the war. See Andrew Roberts, *Masters and Commanders:*
How Roosevelt, Churchill, Marshall and Alanbrooke Won the War in the West, Allen Lane, 2008. Alanbrooke was always suspicious of Macmillan's politicking, and the two had a prickly relationship. Sir Dudley Pound (1877–1943), First Sea Lord, 1939–1943. Illness forced his early retirement and he died on Trafalgar Day, 21 October, 1943. Charles Frederick Algernon, Viscount Portal of Hungerford (1893–1971), Chief of the Air Staff, 1940–1945, known to all as Peter. His most painful task in the war was to tell Anthony Eden of the loss of his son, Simon, on active service in Burma.

27 Hastings Lionel, Baron Ismay (1887–1965), known as Pug, Chief Staff Officer to the Prime Minister from 1940. Macmillan admired, and somewhat envied, his ebullient cheerfulness. Sir John Dill (1881–1944), personal representative of Winston Churchill, in Churchill's capacity as Minister of Defence. Based in Washington after Pearl Harbor in December 1941, Dill brokered a unique relationship with Marshall, and was honoured by burial in Arlington National Cemetery, the US chief of staff as his pallbearers. Louis Francis Albert Victor Nicholas, first Earl Mountbatten of Burma (1900–1979), known as 'Dickie', Chief of Combined Operations, 1943, Supreme Commander South-East Asia, 1943–1946, last Viceroy of India, 1947, First Sea Lord, 1954–1959, Chief of the Defence

Staff, 1959–1965. His meteoric career overlapped at several key moments with Macmillan's, though not without tensions on both sides. Arthur William, first Baron Tedder (1890–1967), Head of Mediterranean Air Command from February 1943, and a trusted confidant of Eisenhower, whom he served as deputy for Operation Overlord in 1944. He was Chancellor of Cambridge University, 1950–1967, overlapping with Macmillan's chancellorship of Oxford University for seven years. Macmillan felt that he had that indefinable quality of greatness that was apparent at once when he entered a room.

28 Major-General Sir John Kennedy (1893–1970), Director of Military Operations, including intelligence, in 1944, and later Governor of Southern Rhodesia. His military career never recovered from his advice that in the worst scenario Egypt might have to be abandoned, which led to Churchill saying in his wrath that he should be made an example of, like Admiral Byng. It is not unknown for him to be confused with his famous namesake, the 35th President of the United States.

29 Sir Leslie Rowan (1908–1972), civil servant. Assistant Private Secretary to Neville Chamberlain, 1933–1937; Private Office of Winston Churchill, 1941–1945; Private Secretary to Clement Attlee, 1945–1947; Permanent Secretary, Ministry of Economic Affairs, 1947; with Sir Stafford Cripps at the Treasury, 1947–1949; Economic Minister in Washington, 1949–1951, Head of Overseas Finance Department at the Treasury, 1951–1958. Macmillan considered him one of the very best of the Treasury knights.

30 Howard Brenton, *Never So Good*, Nick Hern Books, 2008, p. 47.

31 John Grigg, 1943: *The Victory That Never Was*, Penguin Books, Harmondsworth, 1996, p. 60.

32 Richard Howard Stafford Crossman (1907–1974), Deputy Director, Political Warfare, 1943; Assistant Chief of the Pyschological Welfare Division, SHAEF, 1944–1945; Labour Cabinet Minister, 1964–1970; notable diarist of the post-war political scene. When Macmillan stood for the chancellorship of Oxford University in 1960 against Oliver Franks, the Establishment candidate, Crossman voted for Macmillan with what he called a delicious sense of irresponsibility.

33 *Sunday Telegraph*, 9 February 1964.

34 Ibid.

35 Cordell Hull (1871–1955), Secretary of State in Roosevelt's four administrations.

36 Macmillan, op. cit., p. 245.

37 William, first Baron Strang of Holmesfield (1893–1978), Permanent Under-Secretary at the Foreign Office, 1949–1953. Because of his lack of an Oxbridge education, some dubbed him 'the suburban

diplomat', but never Macmillan, who greatly admired his ability, tact and kindness.

38 Sir William Strang to Anthony Eden, 20 February 1943. FO 371/36119. National Archives, Kew.

39 Verrier, op. cit., p. 255.

40 The history of the Second World War is full of the tragic litany of plane crashes in which the famous, no less than the unknown, perished: General Gott (1942), the Duke of Kent (1942), Leslie Howard (1943), General Sikorski and Victor Cazalet (1944), Glenn Miller (1944) and Air Marshall Sir Trafford Leigh-Mallory (1944). Eden's son, Simon, perished in a crash in Burma (1945).

41 Quoted in Alistair Horne, *Macmillan 1894–1956: Volume One of the Official Biography*, Macmillan, 1988, p. 174.

42 Harold Macmillan to Captain Alan Graham (1896–1964), 12 March 1943. MS Macmillan dep. c. 283, loc. cit. Alan Graham was MP for the Wirral from 1935–1945 and influential in securing the candidacy for his successor as MP, Selwyn Lloyd.

43 Harold Macmillan to Sir Henry Mack, 12 March 1943. MS Macmillan dep. c. 282, loc. cit.

44 Winston Churchill to Harold Macmillan, 12 April 1943. FO 660/91. National Archives, Kew.

45 Verrier, op. cit., p. 256.

46 General Georges Catroux (1877–1969), de Gaulle's Delegate General and Plenipotentiary for the Levant; Governor General of Algeria, 1943; Minister for French North Africa, September 1943; and one of the original members of the FCNL.

47 Harold Macmillan to Winston Churchill, 4 May 1943. FO 660/91. National Archives, Kew. The long delay before Macmillan's reply is an indication of his growing confidence in his own position.

48 Jean Monnet (1888–1979), 'father of Europe', political adviser to General Giraud in North Africa, founder member of the FCNL.

49 See Chapter 18.

50 Ann Tusa, *The Last Division: Berlin and the Wall*, Hodder & Stoughton, 1996, pp. 105–106.

51 Jean Monnet, Memorandum of 5 August for the FCNL, quoted in Pascal Fontaine (ed.), *Jean Monnet: A Grand Design for Europe*, OOP, Luxembourg, 1988.

52 When de Gaulle vetoed the British application to join the Common Market.

53 Sir Roderick Barclay, *Ernest Bevin and the Foreign Office*, Latimer, 1975, p. 67.

54 Dwight D. Eisenhower diary, 21 May 1943. Dwight D. Eisenhower Library, Abilene, Kansas, USA. File 1652.

55 Harold Macmillan to General de Gaulle, 4 June 1943. FO 660/49. National Archives, Kew. A year later to the day, Macmillan was congratulating Alexander on the capture of Rome. See Chapter 11.

56 Harold Macmillan, 'Notes on General de Gaulle', 20 October 1943. MS Macmillan dep. c. 285, loc. cit.

57 A visit interpreted by Gaullist supporters as a last attempt by Giraud to bolster his support with Roosevelt.

58 An echo of King Lear's comment on court views: 'Who loses and who wins; who's in, who's out.' *King Lear*, V, iii, 15.

59 Harold Macmillan to Air Chief Marshal Sir Charles Portal, 15 July 1943. MS Macmillan dep. c. 282, loc. cit.

60 Harold Macmillan memorandum on 'Organization of Resident Minister's Work, Mediterranean Theatre', December 1943–March 1944. MS Macmillan dep. c. 284, loc. cit.

61 Harold Macmillan to James Stuart, 8 July 1943. MS Macmillan dep. c. 282, loc. cit.

62 Field Marshal Henry 'Jumbo' Maitland, Baron Wilson (1881–1964), the least recognised of all the great Allied commanders of the Second World War, Commander-in-Chief Middle East, 1943, and then Supreme Allied Commander in the Mediterranean, 1944. Macmillan felt he had an unusual combination of shrewdness and kindness.

63 Lady Dorothy Macmillan to Evie, Dowager Duchess of Devonshire, 17 May 1944. Box F 15. Devonshire MSS, Chatsworth.

64 Colonel Terence Maxwell (1905–1991) was an important figure in the Military Government Section of AFHQ. Son-in-law of Sir Austen Chamberlain, he had been invited, but declined, to take over Chamberlain's

constituency, Birmingham West, after his death in 1937. Both before and after the war, he was an important figure in banking and industrial circles, though Macmillan had advised him on the possibility of a post-war political career. The late Colonel Terence Maxwell to the author, 20 August 1974.

65 Leo Amery to Harold Macmillan, 18 October 1943. MS Macmillan dep. c. 282, loc. cit.

66 Alexander Macmillan was born on 10 October 1943. His father, Maurice, died a month after Harold Macmillan's 90th birthday celebrations in 1984. Alexander Macmillan thus became the 2nd Earl of Stockton on his grandfather's death in 1986.

67 General Sir Alan Brooke diary, 8 December 1943. Alex Danchev and Daniel Todman, *War Diaries 1939–1945: Field Marshal Lord Alanbrooke*, Weidenfeld & Nicolson, 2001, p. 493.

68 Ibid.

69 General Sir Alan Brooke diary, 7 March 1944, ibid., p. 529.

70 Harold Macmillan to Air Chief Marshal Sir Charles Portal, 24 January 1944. MS Macmillan dep. c. 282, loc. cit.

71 Memorandum on Anglo-American relations, 15 December 1944. Lieutenant-General Sir James Gammell Papers, File 73/14/1. Imperial War Museum.

72 Harold Macmillan to Air Chief Marshal Sir Charles Portal, 24 January 1944, MS Macmillan dep. c. 282, loc. cit.

73 Duff Cooper diary, 4 January 1944. John Julius Norwich (ed.), *The Duff Cooper Diaries 1915–1951*, Weidenfeld & Nicolson, 2005, p. 284.

74 Duff Cooper diary, 28 March 1944, Norwich, op. cit., p. 300.

75 MS Macmillan dep. c. 283, loc. cit.

CHAPTER ELEVEN

So Many Hollow Factions
1943–1945

1 CAB 65/34. National Archives, Kew.

2 Marshal Pietro Badoglio (1871–1956), Prime Minister of Italy, July 1943–June 1944. Macmillan thought he was an Italian version of Giraud, but with more humility, and peasant shrewdness.

3 James Holland, *Italy's Sorrow: A Year of War, 1944–45*, Harper Press, 2008, p. 247.

4 The 'short' armistice, signed in secret by General Giuseppe Castellano, covered only the military surrender, repatriation of prisoners of war and Italy's status as an Allied base. The 'long' armistice, signed between Eisenhower and Badoglio, ceded complete control to the Allies over all aspects of the Italian state. The Allied Military Government that was formed to administer Sicily had its remit extended to Italy.

5 King Victor Emmanuel III (1869–1947), King of Italy, 1900–1946, acquiesced in Mussolini's takeover of the Italian state in 1922, but appointed Badoglio to succeed Mussolini as Prime Minister in July 1943. He fled Rome when the Germans were on the point of occupying it in September 1943.

6 Harold Macmillan, 'Report on Mission to Italy, 14–17 September', PREM 3 242/11A, National Archives, Kew.

7 Ivanoe Bonomi (1873–1951) had served as Italian Prime Minister, 1921–1922. At this time he led the anti-Fascist CLN.

8 Palmiro Togliatti (1893–1964), leader of the Italian Communist Party for 40 years. Minister without Portfolio in the Badoglio government, 1944, and later Vice-Premier in the post-war De Gasperi government.

9 Harold Macmillan diary, 30 April 1945 (the day of Hitler's suicide). Harold Macmillan, *War Diaries: Politics and War in the Mediterranean, January 1943–May 1945*, Macmillan, 1984, p. 747.

10 Winston Churchill to Anthony Eden, 4 May 1944. FO371/43636. National Archives, Kew.

11 Ann Lane, *Britain, the Cold War and Yugoslav Unity, 1941–1949*, Sussex Academic Press, Brighton, 1996, p. 42.

12 Edward R. Stettinius Jr (1900–1949), famed for his administration of the Lend-Lease Agreement, American Under-Secretary of State, September 1943–November 1944, Secretary of State, November 1944–June 1945, when he became the first American Ambassador to the United Nations.

13 Oliver Charles, first Baron Harvey of Tasburgh (1893–1968), private secretary to Anthony Eden, 1936–1938 and 1941–1943. Harvey succeeded Duff Cooper as Ambassador in Paris in 1948, a post he held until 1954.

14 Oliver Harvey diary, 21 September 1943. John Harvey (ed.), *The War Diaries of Oliver Harvey,* 1941–1945, Collins, 1978, p. 297.

15 Marshal Stalin to President Franklin D. Roosevelt and Winston S. Churchill, 22 August 1943, USSR Foreign Ministry Archives, quoted in Geoffrey Warner, 'Italy and the Powers, 1943–49', in S. J. Woolf (ed.), *The Rebirth of Italy,* 1943–50, Longman, 1972, pp. 32–3.

16 Elisabeth Barker, *Churchill and Eden at War*, Macmillan, 1978, p. 90.

17 Harold Macmillan memorandum, 17 August 1943. MS Macmillan dep. c. 288. Macmillan Papers, Bodleian Library, Oxford.

18 Oliver Harvey diary, 8 October 1943, Harvey (ed.), op. cit., p. 305.

19 Sir Noel Charles (1891–1975), the High Commissioner in Italy from 1944–1947, representative of HM Government, with the personal rank of ambassador. Macmillan admired his charm, but not his speed of thinking.

20 Alexander C. Kirk (1888–1979), wealthy American diplomat, had served as the US Minister in Egypt, Saudi Arabia and Greece before becoming the US representative of the Advisory Council for Italy, US Adviser to the Supreme Allied Commander Mediterranean (SACMED) and Ambassador to Italy, 1944. Macmillan felt that his mind was not a naturally creative one. The 127 boxes of Kirk's wartime papers in the National Archives, Washington DC, are one of the fullest surviving accounts of the contentious events at Klagenfurt, regarding the repatriations from Austria in 1945. See Chapter 12.

21 Oliver Harvey diary, 14 October 1943, Harvey (ed.), op. cit., p. 308.

22 Frederick Edward Neuflize Ponsonby, Viscount Duncannon (1914–1993), GSO2, West and North Africa; 1st Secretary British Embassy, Paris, 1944–1948. Duncannon succeeded his father as 10th Earl of Bessborough in 1956. He was devoted to Stansted, his home in Sussex, and especially its chapel, the stained-glass windows of which are described in Keats' poems *The Eve of St Agnes* and *The Eve of St Mark*. The Earl of Bessborough to the author, 8 May 1966.

23 Lord Duncannon to Roger Makins, 8 October 1943. Roger Makins to Harold Macmillan, 11 October 1943. Harold Macmillan to Roger Makins, 11 October 1943. FO 660/149. National Archives, Kew.

24 Harold Macmillan to Sir Ralph Assheton, 19 February 1945. MS Macmillan dep. c. 283, loc. cit. Ralph Assheton, first Baron Clitheroe, (1901–1984), MP for

Rushcliffe, 1934–1945, City of London, 1945–1950, Blackburn West, 1951–1955, Chairman of the Conservative Party, October 1944–July 1946. As chairman of the party during the 1945 general election campaign, Assheton adopted a strict policy of sitting MPs defending their existing seats, which was to prevent Macmillan moving to Duff Cooper's constituency at St George's, Westminster. See Chapter 13.

25 Harold Anthony, Baron Caccia (1905–1990), Assistant Private Secretary to Anthony Eden, 1935–1938, and to Lord Halifax, 1938–1939; Vice President of the Allied Control Commission in Italy, 1944; political adviser in Greece, 1945, and Minister in the Athens Embassy. After the war, Caccia was Ambassador in Austria, 1951–1954, and Ambassador in America (during Suez) from 1956–1962. He was Permanent Under-Secretary at the Foreign Office in 1962, and Head of the Diplomatic Service, 1964–1965. Harold Macmillan was deeply disappointed when the Fellows of Eton College chose Caccia to be Provost of Eton in 1965, a post he had craved. Caccia's papers, now at Eton College (though the author saw them when they were still at the Caccia home in Builth Wells), are one of the unsung source materials for his age.

26 A popular savings scheme introduced by Macmillan in his 1956 Budget, whereby investors did not receive a guaranteed return, but instead participated in a lottery that paid out prizes, funded by the accumulated interest, to the lucky numbers. Eventually the top prize was to be £1 million.

27 Anthony Eden, *Full Circle*, Cassell, 1960, p. 266.

28 John Wyndham, *Wyndham and Children First*, Macmillan, 1968, p. 109.

29 Alistair Horne, *Macmillan 1894–1956: Volume One of the Official Biography*, Macmillan, 1988, p. 214. John Samuel Richardson, Bt, Baron Richardson of Lee (1910–2004), was Macmillan's personal physician over many years. Macmillan referred to him affectionately as 'my caddy'.

30 Quoted in Holland, op. cit., p. 254.

31 Harold Macmillan to Anthony Eden, 4 October 1943. MS Macmillan dep. c. 285, loc. cit.

32 Harold Macmillan to Anthony Eden, 7 September 1943. FO 371/37333. National Archives, Kew.

33 Sir D'Arcy Osborne (1884–1964) was the British Minister to the Holy See, 1936–1947. The episode is an example of Macmillan's deep interest in religious matters, particularly those with an underlying political connection. In December 1943, Cardinal Griffin was unexpectedly nominated as Archbishop of Westminster. Macmillan believed Ronald Knox should have been chosen.

34 Harold Macmillan to General

Harold Alexander, 4 June 1944.
General Harold Alexander to
Harold Macmillan, 5 June. MS
Macmillan dep. c. 285, loc. cit.

35 Harold Macmillan to Anthony
Eden, 6 November 1944. MS
Macmillan dep. c. 282, loc. cit.

36 Lieutenant-General Sir
James Gammell, 'Notes on
Anglo-American relations
with particular reference to
the present situation in Greece
and Italy', 15 December 1944.
Gammell papers, Imperial War
Museum.

37 Andrei Yanuarievich Vyshinsky
(1883–1954), Public Prosecutor,
Foreign Minister and Chief
Soviet Delegate to the United
Nations, where his speeches
seldom lasted less than two
hours. Vyshinsky was infuriated
when Selwyn Lloyd, the British
Minister of State, responded to
one four-hour speech by saying
there was a Russian proverb that
the cow that makes the most
noise gives the least milk. It was
a Polish proverb, Vyshinsky
insisted.

38 In January 1915 Churchill
had advocated sending a naval
force through the Dardanelles
to Constantinople in the hope
of rallying Turkey's Balkan
opponents to the Allied cause.
The failure of the campaign
haunted Churchill for the rest of
his days.

39 Harold Macmillan diary, 3
December 1943. Macmillan, op.
cit., p. 317.

40 Richard Gavin Gardiner, Baron
Casey (1890–1976), Australian
politician, Governor General

of Australia, 1965–1969.
Macmillan admired his integrity,
but felt him over-parted in
Mediterranean politics.

41 Roger Makins to Sir William
Strang, 6 January 1944. FO
800/432. National Archives,
Kew.

42 Sir Pierson John Dixon, always
known as Bob (1904–1965),
diplomat, Britain's Permanent
Representative at the United
Nations during the Suez
crisis, Ambassador to France,
1960–1965, when de Gaulle
vetoed Britain's application to
join the EEC. His diary is one
of the great sources for these
tempestuous events.

43 Pierson Dixon diary, 2 January
1944. Dixon papers (in private
possession).

44 Harold Macmillan to Winston
Churchill, 8 December 1943.
PREM3/272/1. National
Archives, Kew.

45 Roger Makins to Sir Orme
Sargent, 14 June 1944. FO
800/277. National Archives,
Kew. Sir Orme Sargent
(1884–1962), known as Moley,
was Deputy Under-Secretary at
the Foreign Office, 1939–1946,
and Permanent Under-Secretary,
1946–1949. 'He knew all the
answers,' observed his colleague
Sir Robert Vansittart, 'When
politicians did not want them he
went out to lunch.'

46 Anthony Eden diary, 23 June
1944. AP 20/1/24. Avon Papers,
Birmingham University Library.

47 Winston Churchill to Anthony
Eden, 22 May 1944. PREM
3/66/6. National Archives, Kew.

48 Winston Churchill to Anthony Eden, 14 June 1944. AP 20/12/335. Avon Papers, Birmingham University Library.

49 Harold Macmillan to Wyndham Portal, 23 August 1944. MS Macmillan dep. c. 288, loc. cit.

50 Harold Macmillan, 'Organisation of the Mediterranean Command', 16 August 1944. PREM 3/272/4. National Archives, Kew.

51 Lieutenant General Sir (Frank) Noel Mason-Macfarlane (1889–1953), always known as Mason-Mac. When British military attaché in Berlin before the war, he offered to shoot Hitler to further the prospect of world peace. He stood as a Labour candidate in the 1945 general election, defeating Brendan Bracken in Paddington North. Macmillan thought him a military man lost in the political entanglements and a regular *prima donna*.

52 Sir Reginald Wildig Allen Leeper (1888–1968), Ambassador to the Greek Government, 1943–1946, Ambassador to Argentina, 1946–1948.

53 Adlai Stevenson (1900–1965), US presidential candidate, 1952 and 1956, American Ambassador to the United Nations, 1961–1965.

54 Marshal Josip Broz, known as 'Tito' from 1922 (1892–1980). General Secretary of the Yugoslav Communist Party, 1937–1980; leader of the partisan resistance movement, 1941–1945; named Marshal of Yugoslavia, November 1943;

head of the provisional and federal government, 1943–1945; Prime Minister, 1945–1953; President, 1953–1974; President for Life, 1974–1980.

55 Harold Macmillan, *The Blast of War,* 1939–1945, Macmillan, 1967, p. 526.

56 Cuthbert Headlam diary, 23 February 1944. Stuart Ball (ed.), *Parliament and Politics in the Age of Churchill and Attlee: The Headlam Diaries* 1935–1951, Cambridge University Press, 1999, p. 399.

57 Harold Macmillan to Sir Wyndham Portal, 9 May 1944. MS Macmillan dep. c. 282, loc. cit.

58 General Sir Richard McCreery (1898–1967), General Alexander's Chief of Staff during the campaigns in the Western Desert, 1943; Commander of the Eighth Army's 10th Corps at Salerno and Monte Cassino; Commander of the Eighth Army, 1944–1945.

59 Lieutenant General Sir Charles Frederick Keightley (1901–1974), Commander of the 6th Armoured Division in North Africa; Commander 5th Corps, 1944–1945; Commander of the British Army of the Rhine (1948–1951), Far East land forces, 1951–1953, and Middle East land forces, 1953–1957, when he was the army commander in the Suez operation of 1956.

60 George Papandreou (1880–1968), Prime Minister of Greece, 1944, veteran Liberal politician, and fiercely anti-Communist.

61 King George II (1890–1947), King of the Hellenes, in exile in London after the German occupation of Greece, internationally recognised as head of state. The prospect of his return to Greece in 1944 exacerbated a volatile situation. The King spent his last years in a rented house in Chester Square (where the Macmillans had begun their married life) with his English mistress.

62 Lieutenant General Sir Ronald Scobie (1893–1969), GOC Malta, 1942; Chief of Staff to General Jumbo Wilson, 1943; GOC III Corps, 1943, and Commander of the British forces in Greece, 1944–1946; Lieutenant of the Tower of London, 1951–1954. Despite his deserved reputation as the man who had saved Greece from Communism, Macmillan was very judgemental about Scobie, regarding him as an overpromoted and fundamentally stupid man.

63 Sir Osbert Lancaster (1908–1986), classicist and cartoonist. Press attaché in Greece, 1944–1946. His 'Maudie Littlehampton' cartoons were one of the most telling social commentaries on the era of Macmillan's premiership.

64 Hansard, 8 December 1944.

65 James Knox, Cartoons and Coronets: The Genius of Osbert Lancaster, Frances Lincoln, 2008, p. 55. The parallels with the politics of the ancient civil war were uncanny. See Chapters 69–90 of Book 3 of Thucydides.

66 Archbishop Damaskinos of Athens (1891–1949). On Armistice Day, 11 November 1944, Macmillan thought Damaskinos' presence, alongside British chaplains, immensely impressive and dignified.

67 Knox, op. cit., p. 55.

68 Crown Prince Paul of the Hellenes (1901–1964), King of Greece, 1947–1964; brother of King George II, and also in exile in London after the German occupation of Greece. The brothers were first cousins of the Duke of Edinburgh.

69 General Nikolaos Plastiras (1883–1953), Prime Minister of Greece, January-April 1945. Macmillan found him an endearing figure, describing him as 'really quite a dear'. Harold Macmillan diary, 13 March 1945. Macmillan, War Diaries, op. cit. Churchill was told, 'Sir, the Greeks have a new Prime Minister, General Plastiras, pronounced plaster-arse', to which he replied, 'Let's hope he doesn't have feet of clay.'

70 Quoted in Nigel Fisher, Harold Macmillan: A Biography, Weidenfeld & Nicolson, 1982, p. 115.

71 Harold Macmillan and Alexander Kirk Policy Document, 29 January 1945, quoted in H. L. Coles and A. K. Weinberg, Civil Affairs: Soldiers becoming Governors, Washington, USPGO, 1964, p. 544.

72 Macmillan, War Diaries, op. cit., p. 670.

73 Spectator, 7 July 1944.

74 Harold Macmillan to Harold Nicolson, 26 July 1944. MS Macmillan dep. c. 282, loc. cit.

75 William Temple (1881–1944), Archbishop of York, 1929–1942, Archbishop of Canterbury, 1942–1944. Some were surprised that Temple, a Labour Party supporter, was not passed over, on political grounds, as Churchill's recommendation to the King for Canterbury on Cosmo Gordon Lang's retirement. 'The only half-crown article in a penny bazaar' was Churchill's view. Macmillan was always greatly impressed by Temple's ministry.

76 The Archbishop of Canterbury to Evie, Dowager Countess of Devonshire, 8 October 1942. Box 15. Devonshire MSS, Chatsworth.

77 Cyril Forster Garbett (1875–1955), Bishop of Winchester, 1932–1942; Archbishop of York, 1942–1955. Macmillan always found Garbett's views illuminating and interesting, especially on international affairs. Garbett became a kind of roving ambassador for the Anglican Church, and a fierce opponent of Communism, which belied his reputation in the Northern Province as a rather shy and retiring figure.

78 The Rt Revd John Victor Macmillan (1877–1956), Bishop of Guildford, 1934–1949.

79 Dr Cyril Garbett diary, 3 April 1945. Charles Smythe, *Cyril Forster Garbett: Archbishop of York*, Hodder & Stoughton, 1959, pp. 319–20.

80 Dr Cyril Garbett diary, 28 April 1945, ibid., p. 328. Pope Pius XII (1876–1958) was elected Pope in March 1939. His wartime stance remains one of controversy. (See Owen Chadwick, *Britain and the Vatican during the Second World War*, Cambridge, 1986.) Macmillan had wartime audiences with Pius XII on 18 November 1944 and 25 May 1945.

81 Macmillan's religious sensibilities were such that he had not wanted his daughter to marry during Lent. Easter Day in 1944 was on 9 April.

82 Harold Macmillan to Lady Isabel Browne, 28 April 1944. MS Macmillan dep. c. 284, loc. cit.

83 Harold Macmillan to the Duchess of Devonshire, 9 September 1944. Box P 28. Devonshire MSS, Chatsworth.

84 Lieutenant General Sir James Gammell to Harold Macmillan, 15 December 1944. MS Macmillan dep. c. 285, loc. cit.

85 Roger Makins to Harold Macmillan, 1 October 1944. MS Macmillan dep. c. 282, loc. cit.

86 Roger Makins to Harold Macmillan, 10 November 1944. MS Macmillan dep. c. 284, loc. cit. American presidents are now limited to two terms after the 22nd Amendment to the United States Constitution of 21 March 1947.

87 John Wyndham to Harold Macmillan, May 1944. MS Macmillan dep. c. 282, loc. cit.

88 Harold Macmillan to Wyndham

Portal, 9 May 1944. Ibid.

89 Alex Danchev and Daniel Todman (ed.), *War Diaries 1939–1945: Field Marshal Lord Alanbrooke*, Weidenfeld & Nicolson, 2001, p. 646.

90 Nigel Nicolson, *Alex: The Life of Field Marshal Earl Alexander of Tunis*, Weidenfeld & Nicolson, p. 193.

CHAPTER TWELVE

Conspiracy at Klagenfurt? May 1945

1 The British 5 Corps comprised 6 Armoured Division (under Major General Horatius Murray), 46 Infantry Division (under Major General Steven Weir) and 78 Infantry Division (under Major General Robert Arbuthnott). 5 Corps was part of the Eighth Army, together with 13 Corps (under Lieutenant General John Harding). Eighth Army was one of the constituent parts of 15 Army Group under the American general Mark Clark. The supreme commander of these forces was Field Marshal Harold Alexander, then based in Caserta, north of Naples. His two political advisers were Harold Macmillan and the American Alexander C. Kirk.

2 Christopher Booker, *A Looking Glass Tragedy: The Controversy over the Repatriations from Austria in 1945*, Duckworth, 1997, p. 275.

3 There were four main groups of Cossacks - the Don, Kuban, Terek and Zaporozhian Cossacks - but also other groupings from different areas.

4 General Helmut von Pannwitz (1898–1947) established Cossack volunteer forces from 1942 and led them in action against Yugoslav partisans. Although not subject to repatriation to Russia as a German national, he insisted that he should share the fate of his men and surrendered voluntarily. He was executed in Moscow in January 1947.

5 These units were the Domanov Cossacks, the Cossack 'Training Unit', the Caucasians, the 1st Ukrainian Division, and, of great importance in understanding the terms employed, the White Russian Schutzkorps under Colonel Anatoly Rogozhin.

6 Major Hugh Lunghi, a member of 30 Military Mission, to the author, 29 March 2009.

7 Patrick Dean memorandum, 28 June 1944. WO 32/1137. National Archives, Kew. This document shows that the advice on repatriation emanated from the Foreign Office, not the military.

8 CAB 65/43. National Archives, Kew.

9 Sir James Grigg to Anthony Eden, 24 August 1944. FO 371/40444. National Archives. Kew.

10 CAB 65/43. National Archives, Kew. Those present at this Cabinet meeting were Winston Churchill, in the chair, as Prime Minister; Anthony Eden, Foreign Secretary; Ernest Bevin, Minister of Labour and National Service;

Herbert Morrison, Home Secretary; Sir John Anderson, Chancellor of the Exchequer; Oliver Lyttelton, Minister of Production; and Lord Woolton, Minister of Reconstruction.

11 Roy Jenkins, *Churchill*, Macmillan, 2001, p. 778.

12 Sir Philip Goodhart, *The 1922: The Story of the 1922 Committee*, Macmillan, 1973, p. 134. Victor Raikes (1901–1986), then a flight lieutenant, was Conservative MP for Essex SE, 1931–1945; Liverpool Wavertree, 1945–1950; and Liverpool Garston, 1950–1957.

13 The first breach of this commitment came as early as March 1945 when Stalin established a minority Communist government in Romania.

14 Vyecheslav Molotov (1890–1986). As People's Commissar of Foreign Affairs from 1939, Molotov had signed the Nazi-Soviet Pact with Ribbentrop that August. He was second only to Stalin in the Soviet hierarchy. He fell from grace during the Khrushchev era in Russia, but his name lived on through the eponymous 'Molotov cocktail', a hand-made petrol bomb, widely used from the Spanish Civil War onwards.

15 PREM 3/51/6. National Archives, Kew.

16 FO 916/1189. National Archives, Kew.

17 Nikolai Tolstoy, *The Minister and the Massacres*, Century Hutchinson, 1986, p. 215.

18 Foreign Office directive of 6 March 1945. Alexander Kirk Papers, 711.4 TS. National Archives, Washington. The document in the Kirk papers is the only known copy to have survived and was discovered, together with other key papers from Macmillan's AFHQ Office, by Brigadier Anthony Cowgill in 1989, subsequent to the publication of Tolstoy's *The Minister and the Massacres* in 1986.

19 In the 127 boxes of Alexander Kirk papers in the National Archives in Washington.

20 Anthony Cowgill, Lord Brimelow and Christopher Booker, *The Repatriations from Austria in 1945: The Report of an Enquiry*, Sinclair-Stevenson, 1990, p. 195.

21 Alexander Kirk to the State Department, 8 May 1945. Alexander Kirk Papers, USNA (TS) (o). National Archives, Washington. Military Government Staff, Austria to AFHQ, 15 May 1945. Alexander Kirk Papers, USNA (TS) (r). National Archives, Washington.

22 Their appearance in the public domain is entirely owing to Brigadier Cowgill. 'By a remarkable feat of detective work over four years, Cowgill managed to track down all the missing signals and orders necessary to a proper understanding of what had happened. In particular, thanks to inspired guesswork, he discovered in a Washington archive 127 unopened boxes containing many key documents

previously thought lost.'
Obituary of Brigadier Anthony
Cowgill, *Daily Telegraph*, 9
November 2009.

23 Some British operational
telegrams were lost in a lorry
fire in Caserta at the time.
Others, as is the custom with
all national records, were
'weeded'. It would have saved a
lot of trouble had they not been
weeded so extensively, but their
full significance was not realised
before the controversy arose.

24 Marshal Fyodor Ivanovich
Tolbukhin (1894–1949) had
conquered Belgrade with the
help of Tito's partisans in
October 1944, and Vienna on
13 April 1945, and was now
occupying the Austrian city of
Graz.

25 Ralph Stephenson to Anthony
Eden and to Harold Macmillan,
28 April 1945. FO 371/48812.
National Archives, Kew.
Sir Ralph Stephenson was
Ambassador in Cairo during
the Suez crisis. A misprint in
the index of the first edition
of Eden's memoir *Full Circle*
(1960) referred to him as 'Sir
Ralph Richardson'. A keen-eyed
reader wrote to Eden, 'I presume
he must have been "acting"
for Sir Ralph Stephenson.'
AP7/18/118A. Avon Papers,
Birmingham University Library.

26 Harold Macmillan diary, 9
May 1945. Harold Macmillan,
*War Diaries: Politics and War
in the Mediterranean, January
1943–May 1945*, Macmillan,
1984, p. 753.

27 Count Nikolai Tolstoy to the
author, 2 April 2008.

28 Harold Macmillan to Winston
Churchill, 9 May 1945. FO
371/48813. National Archives,
Kew.

29 General McCreery to Field
Marshal Alexander, 11 May
1945. Field Marshal Alexander
to General McCreery, 11 May
1945. FO 1020/42. National
Archives, Kew.

30 Lord Halifax to Anthony Eden,
10 May 1945, repeated to
Resmed (Caserta) and the British
Military Mission in Moscow. FO
371/48814. National Archives,
Kew.

31 Alexander C. Kirk to Edward
Stettinius, 12 May 1945. USNA
Diplomatic State Dept 119/
Control Italy. Alexander Kirk
Papers, National Archives,
Washington.

32 Harold Macmillan diary, 13
May 1945, Macmillan, op. cit.,
p. 757.

33 General Keightley to Field
Marshal Alexander, 14 May
1945. WO 170/4241. National
Archives, Kew.

34 Cowgill et al., op. cit., Volume
I, p. 226.

35 'CAUCASIAN and COSSACK
Personnel', Comd 36 Infantry
Brigade Personal Message, 27
May 1945. WO 170/4461.
National Archives, Kew.

36 This was a common problem for
those attending meetings with
Churchill, whose fondness for
late-night films was well known,
as was Hitler's.

37 G-5 AFHQ Brief 'Dispositions
of Displaced Persons, etc., in N.
Italy and Austria', 22 May 1945.

AFHQ G5 Reel 16–1. Alexander Kirk Papers, National Archives, Washington.

38 5 Corps to Divisions, 24 May 1945. WO 170/4241. National Archives, Kew.

39 Lieutenant Colonel Robin Rose Price diary, 19 May 1945. WO 170/4982. National Archives, Kew.

40 Kenneth Rose, then serving in the 3rd Welsh Guards, to the author, 14 December 2008.

41 Brigadier Edward Tryon-Wilson (1909–1991) won the DSO at the Battle of Monte Cassino and was later awarded a military CBE. He added the name Wilson after a post-war family inheritance.

42 Toby Low, first Baron Aldington (1914–2000), Brigadier BGS 5 Corps Italy, August 1944–June 1945; Conservative MP, Blackpool North, 1945–1962; Deputy Chairman, Conservative Party, 1959–1963; Chairman, Sun Alliance and London Insurance Co., 1971–1985; Warden, Winchester College 1979–1987.

43 The legal case - Aldington v. Watts, Tolstoy and Century Hutchinson Ltd - arose after the circulation of a pamphlet, 'War Crimes and the Wardenship of Winchester College', by Nigel Watts, who had an insurance dispute with Lord Aldington, then Chairman of the Sun Alliance and London Insurance Co., and Warden of Winchester College, and marked the ending of a later stage of the Klagenfurt Conspiracy charges.

The case was heard in the High Court from 3 October to 30 November 1989. The jury found in favour of Aldington and awarded him libel damages of £1.5 million, plus costs. Aldington's vindication was also a posthumous vindication for Macmillan. In its reports of the trial, *Private Eye* referred to Aldington as Lord Allalongtimeago and Tolstoy as Count Tallstory.

44 Harold Macmillan to Sir James Grigg, 18 May 1945. Cited as Key Document 176 (Birch Grove Archives) in the Cowgill report. Cowgill et al., op. cit., Volume 2, p. 174.

45 Lieutenant General Andrey Vlasov(1900–1946), Commander of the Second Shock Army, and prominently involved in the defence of Moscow, was captured by the Germans in July 1942. The loss of his army, given the order by Vlasov to disband, led to his hanging in August 1946.

46 Nigel Nicolson (1917–2004), son of Harold Nicolson and Vita Sackville-West, and, like Macmillan, a product of Summer Fields, Eton and Balliol, and a publisher (co-founder of Weidenfeld & Nicolson); Captain Grenadier Guards in Tunisian and Italian campaigns; biographer of Field Marshal Alexander (1973); Conservative MP for Bournemouth East and Christchurch, 1952–1959, where he succeeded Brendan Bracken on Bracken's elevation to the peerage. Nicolson's rivals for the

vacant parliamentary candidacy included Roy Harrod and John Wyndham. He was elected at a by-election on 6 February 1952, the day of the death of King George VI. He was deselected by his constituency organisation after his stance against Sir Anthony Eden's Suez policy.

47 1st Guards Brigade SITREP No. 3, 19 May 1945. WO 170/4404. National Archives, Kew.

48 The following account is based on talks with the late Lord Aldington, Lord Armstrong of Ilminster, Christopher Booker, the late Lord Brimelow, the late Brigadier Anthony Cowgill, Major Hugh Lunghi, Edwyn Morris, the late Nigel Nicolson and Count Nikolai Tolstoy among others. The essential documentation is contained in Cowgill et al., *The Repatriations from Austria in 1945: The Report of an Inquiry*, Sinclair-Stevenson, 1990, and *The Repatriations from Austria in 1945: Cowgill Inquiry - The Documentary Evidence reproduced in full from British, American, German and Yugoslav Sources*, Sinclair-Stevenson, 1990. Also important are Booker, *A Looking-Glass Tragedy*, op. cit.; and Robert Knight, 'Harold Macmillan and the Cossacks. Was There a Klagenfurt Conspiracy?', *Intelligence and National Security*, Volume 1, May 1986, No. 2, Frank Cass. Brigadier Tryon-Wilson, senior administrative officer (DA & QMG) in 5 Corps in 1945, also worked on the early stages of the Cowgill report, though he voluntarily withdrew when judgements were being formulated on decision-making processes in which he had been involved. A recent, and most valuable, addition to the essential bibliography is a thesis by Edwyn Morris, *The Repatriation of Cossacks from Austria in 1945*, Queen Mary and Westfield College, London, 2008.

49 Joachim von Ribbentrop (1893–1946), dealer in wines and spirits: German Ambassdor to London, 1936–1938; German Foreign Minister, 1938–1945, in which office he signed the Nazi-Soviet non-aggression pact with his opposite number Molotov on 23 August 1939. His hanging at Nuremberg on 16 October 1946 was botched and he strangled to death after the drop had failed to kill him instantly.

50 James Lees-Milne diary, 24 March 1985. James Lees-Milne, *Beneath a Waning Moon: Diaries, 1985–1987* (ed. Michael Bloch), John Murray, 2003, p. 15. As has been noted earlier, Harold Macmillan had shown great kindness to James Lees-Milne over his biography of Harold Nicolson.

51 Private information from one so addressed. Robert Graves (1895–1985), almost Macmillan's exact contemporary, was the author of 135 books, the most famous of which was the classic account of the Great War, *Goodbye to All That*.

52 Brigadier Anthony Cowgill, MBE (1915–2009), soldier and engineer, developed the waterproofing of tanks prior to the D-Day landings. He served on Field Marshal Montgomery's 2nd Army staff from Normandy to Luneberg Heath, where he was present at the surrender of German forces in May 1945; member of the Partition Commission in India, 1947; served in the Korean War; Chief Industrial Engineer to Rolls Royce, 1969; British Management Data Foundation, 1979–2009.

53 Some critics of the Cowgill report erroneously claimed that the inquiry had been covertly financed by the Foreign Office from the start. This assertion is examined by Edwyn Morris in his thesis on the controversy. Brigadier Cowgill confirmed to the author on 13 July 2009 that the inquiry was completely independent. Even if the assertion had been accurate, it does not follow that the inquiry was partial. Morris op. cit., p. 40.

54 Christopher Booker to the author, 5 August 2008.

55 Cowgill et al., op. cit., pp. 226 and 159.

56 Knight op. cit. Norman Stone, 'Judgement best left to history', Sunday Times, 30 December 1990.

57 Robert Knight, 'The decisions of men in a hurry', Times Literary Supplement, 19–25 October 1990.

58 Alexander Kirk to James F. Byrnes, 14 August 1945. Kirk Papers (7114.5 Yugo) (o). National Archives, Washington.

59 Booker, op. cit., p. 1. On the disagreements in the Macmillan family, Christopher Booker to the author, 21 December 2008.

60 Hugh Dalton tribute to Victor Cazalet, cited Robert Rhodes James, Victor Cazalet: A Portrait, Hamish Hamilton, 1976, p. 288.

61 Transcript of BBC television programme, 'Macmillan at War: In Retrospect', broadcast, in part, on 21 December 1984. BBC Records, Caversham.

62 Cowgill et al., op. cit., Volume 1, p. 216.

63 This action was prompted by the family, as Macmillan could not have done this by himself at that stage. David Faber to the author, 15 May 2009.

64 General Keightley to General McCreery, 14 May 1945. WO 170/4241. National Archives, Kew.

65 The subsequent discovery of material that would have countered some of the wilder allegations against Macmillan was a considerable embarrassment to the Ministry of Defence. The late Brigadier Anthony Cowgill to the author, 13 July 2009.

66 General Alexander to Combined Chiefs of Staff, 17 May 1945. FO 1020/42. National Archives, Kew. Combined Chiefs of Staff to Field Marshal Alexander, 20 June 1945. FO 371/48825. National Archives, Kew.

67 Lord Armstrong of Ilminster to

the author, 29 January 2009.

68 Christopher Booker has drawn attention to the 'over-zealous weeding of almost all British official papers which had taken place over the decades since the war' in Booker, op. cit., p. 120.

69 Tolstoy, op. cit., p. xvi. Given the language Tolstoy used publicly about him, it is not surprising that Macmillan did not agree to meet him.

70 See Carol Mather, *Aftermath of War: Everyone Must Go Home*, Brassey's (UK), 1992, particularly Chapter XVI, 'The Klagenfurt Conspiracy: The dog that didn't bark in the night, 13–14 May', pp. 104–108. Sir Carol Mather (1919–2006), Conservative MP for Esher, 1970–1987, was recommended for an immediate MC after his actions at Nijmegen during the Battle of Arnhem.

71 Booker, op. cit., p. 435.

72 Stone, op. cit.

73 Knight, op. cit., 19–25 October 1990.

74 Daniel Johnson, 'Macmillan: a vindication that came too late', *TheTimes*, 19 October 1990.

75 Nansen passports were for stateless persons and had been pioneered by the Norwegian explorer and diplomat Fridtjof Wedel-Jarlsberg Nansen (1861–1930). Issued by the League of Nations from 1922, they were internationally recognised.

76 Lieutenant General Sir James Wilson MC (1921–2004) ended his distinguished military career as GOC SE District, 1974–1977. He was also on the Sports Council, 1973–1982, the Council of the CBI, 1977–1985, and was Association Football Correspondent for the *Sunday Times* for many years.

77 Lieutenant General Sir James Wilson, *Army Quarterly & Defence Journal*, January 1991.

78 General Filip Golikov (1900–1980), a veteran of the winter war in Finland, Chief of Military Intelligence, 1940–1941, Deputy Commander Stalingrad Army Group, 1942–1943, and Chief of Soviet Repatriation Commission, 1944–1946.

79 Major Hugh Lunghi to the author, 18 March 2009. Documentation on this operation is included in 'Report on activities of personnel from 30 Military Mission, Moscow, who went to Odessa to deal with repatriation of British PoWs, 28 March 1945'. WO 208/1860. National Archives, Kew.

80 Morris, op. cit.

81 The late Brigadier Anthony Cowgill to the author, 13 July 2009.

82 Morris, op. cit., p. 25.

83 Narodnyi Kommissariat Vnutrennikh Del, the People's Commissariat for Internal Affairs. SMERSH was the main counter-intelligence directorate, its name an acronym for *Smert Shpionam* (Death to Spies).

84 Hugh Lunghi to the author, 18 March 2009. One distinguished figure who read an early draft of this chapter recalled a friend who had been the navigator in a glider-towing aircraft that was shot down during the Arnhem

operation. He ended up in
a camp on the Baltic in East
Germany, but was freed and
repatriated by the Russians. The
fate of countless similar Allied
prisoners of war could easily
have been very different.

85 Unattributable interview.

86 Montagu Slater, libretto for
Benjamin Britten, *Peter Grimes*,
Boosey and Hawkes, 1945.

87 Johnson, op. cit..

88 Following the executions of
William Joyce (Lord Haw-Haw)
and John Amery in December
1945, some felt that P. G.
Wodehouse, who had broadcast
from Nazi Germany during the
war, should have suffered the
same fate.

89 Sir Arthur Conan Doyle, *The
Sign of Four*, Lippincott's
Magazine, February 1890.

90 Later allegations that General
Keightley had been 'precipitate
in beginning the prisoner
exchange and negligent in
failing to identify those who
had valid claims to remain as
refugees in the 5th corps area'
were found after investigation
to be unfounded. Anthony
Farrar-Hockley, notice of
the life of General Keightley,
*Oxford Dictionary of National
Biography*, Volume 31, Oxford
University Press, 2004, p. 36.

91 Brigadier T. P. D. Scott, 38 Irish
Brigade, May 1945. Cowgill et
al., op. cit., p. 1.

92 Edmund Burke, 'Of Lord
Chatham'.

CHAPTER THIRTEEN

The Possibilities of Defeat 1945

1 Sir Henry Channon diary,
8 September 1944. Robert
Rhodes James (ed.), *Chips: The
Diaries of Sir Henry Channon*,
Weidenfeld & Nicolson, 1967,
p. 393. This was not Channon's
only *faux pas* at this time. At a
fashionable post-war wedding,
Channon surveyed the glittering
scene at the reception, and said
to Lady Emerald Cunard, 'This
is what we've been fighting for',
to which Lady Cunard replied,
'What, are they all Poles?' Ibid.,
p. 414.

2 All details and letters
regarding the putative St
George's candidature are in
MS. Macmillan dep. c. 143.
Macmillan Papers, Bodleian
Library, Oxford.

3 The message Mr Barkis, a
Yarmouth carrier, asked young
David Copperfield to convey to
Clara Peggotty, David's devoted
nurse, indicating Barkis's desire
to marry her. Charles Dickens,
David Copperfield, Chapter 5.
The reply was characteristic of
Macmillan's delight in literary
allusions, particularly Dickensian
ones. Stafford Cripps he
compared to Mrs Pardiggle in
Bleak House and Aneurin Bevan
to Madame Defarge in *A Tale of
Two Cities*. To be Pecksniffian
was one of the worst solecisms.
In 1952, Macmillan thought
Basildon New Town was 'pure
Martin Chuzzlewit'.

4 The Gage family were Keynes'
landlords at Tilton House.

5 Bracken was found Bournemouth East after his defeat in July 1945, but Assheton was not so lucky, and never sat in the Commons again.

6 Harold Macmillan diary, 24 March 1945. Harold Macmillan, *War Diaries: The Mediterranean 1943–1945*, Macmillan, 1984, p. 723.

7 Quoted in Max Hastings, *Nemesis: The Battle for Japan, 1944–45*, Harper Press, 2007, p. xxv.

8 Robert Blake, *The Conservative Party from Peel to Churchill*, Eyre & Spottiswoode, 1970, p. 264.

9 Rab Butler believed this was one of the great unregarded disadvantages for the Conservatives at the 1945 election. By the time the problem was addressed it was too late. The late Lord Butler to the author, 20 November 1975.

10 Radio broadcast, 4 June 1945.

11 Keynes, whose White Paper on Full Employment had also been published in 1944, corresponded with Hayek about *The Road to Serfdom*. 'Morally and philosophically I find myself in agreement with virtually the whole of it,' he had written to Hayek on 28 June 1944. But virtually was not the same as totally. Where one drew the line between the demands of planning and the demands of freedom lay at the core of the argument. 'You agree that the line has to be drawn somewhere, and that the logical extreme is not possible. But as soon as you admit that the extreme is not possible,' he continued, 'you are, on your own argument done for, since you are trying to persuade us that so soon as one moves an inch in the planned direction you are necessarily launched on the slippery path which will lead you in due course over the precipice.' J. M. Keynes to Friedrich Hayek, 28 June 1944. Quoted in Robert Skidelsky, *John Maynard Keynes: Volume Three Fighting for Britain 1937–1946*, Macmillan, 2000, pp. 284–5. Hayek's book was later to be a central plank in Thatcherism.

12 Harold Macmillan to Winston S. Churchill, 8 June 1945. MS Macmillan dep. c. 284, loc. cit.

13 Information to the author from the Countess of Avon, Churchill's niece.

14 Nigel Nicolson, *Long Life: Memoirs*, Weidenfeld & Nicolson, 1998, p. 141.

15 The author spent VE Day, as a child, at RAF Hinstock, a rural outpost of the Fleet Air Arm operation.

16 Sir George Roland Chetwynd (1916–1982), a graduate of King's College, London, was MP for Stockton 1945–1962. When Macmillan set up the National Economic Development Council in 1962, Chetwynd was invited to be a member. He served on it from 1962–1967.

17 Quoted in Anthony Howard, 'We are the Masters Now: The General Election of 5 July 1945', in Michael Sissons and Philip French (ed.), *Age of Austerity: 1945–1951*, Penguin Books,

Harmondsworth, 1964, p. 15.

18 Blake, op. cit., p. 266.

19 Speech outside Transport House, 26 July 1945.

20 Howard, op. cit., p. 17.

21 This exchange was not the only example of confusion during the second half of the Potsdam conference. At a concluding vodka and caviare reception hosted by the Russians, Bevin is reputed to have said to Stalin, ''Ere, Joe, this jam tastes fishy.'

22 I am grateful to the late Lord Pym for writing with details of the date of his father's death on the same day as Sir Edward Campbell, a day therefore of some consequential importance in post-war Conservative history. 17 July was also to be the date, 60 years later, of Sir Edward Heath's death in 2005.

23 The seat was later divided, and Stockton South was held by the Conservatives in the 1987 election.

24 A point emphasised to the author by Lady Caroline Faber.

25 Quoted in Howard, op. cit., p. 16.

CHAPTER FOURTEEN

The Wooden Horse of Peace 1945–1950

1 Earl of Crawford diary, 14 November 1934. John Vincent (ed.), *The Crawford Papers: the Journals of David Lindsay twenty-seventh Earl of Crawford and tenth Earl of Balcarres 1871–1940, during the years 1892 to 1940*, Manchester

University Press, 1984, p. 555.

2 *The Times*, 2 September 1946.

3 Rab Butler, Harry Crookshank, Bobbety Salisbury (as Cranborne had become in April 1947), Oliver Stanley and Lord Woolton.

4 Sir Waldron Smithers (1880–1954), MP for Chislehurst, 1924–1945; Orpington, 1945–1954.

5 Ian Gilmour, *Whatever Happened to the Tories: The Conservatives since 1945*, Fourth Estate, 1997, p. 33.

6 'But Colonel, they have no whites to their eyes!' declared Maudie Littlehampton in a 1960s cartoon, armed and behind barbed-wire barricades, as mods and rockers laid waste to the Brighton sea front.

7 Sir Herbert Williams (1884–1954), MP for Reading, 1924–1929; Croydon East, 1950–1954.

8 John Stuart Mill, *On Liberty* (1859), Chapter II.

9 Peel's 'Tamworth Manifesto', eponymous with his constituency, was the first such document in British history, directly addressing electors. Peel's belief, in a political era of great transition, in 'conserving the things that needed conserving, and reforming the things that needed reforming', was to give the party its name, and also save it from electoral extinction. As the character Lord Monmouth said in Disraeli's novel *Coningsby*, 'Peel is the man; suited to the times and all that; at least we must say so and

try to believe so; we can't go back.' Disraeli, *Coningsby*, Book VIII, Chapter 3.

10 Harold Macmillan diary, 9 July 1943. Harold Macmillan, *War Diaries: Politics and War in the Mediterranean January 1943–May 1945*, Macmillan, 1984, p. 144. 'Young England', a romantic paternalistic Tory philosophy of the 1840s, sought to instil better understanding between different classes of society, and was espoused, eventually, by Macmillan's hero Disraeli. Robert Blake described 'Young England' as 'the reaction of a defeated class to a sense of its own defeat' and 'the Oxford Movement translated by Cambridge from religion into politics'. Robert Blake, *Disraeli*, Eyre & Spottiswoode, 1966, p. 171.

11 Harold Macmillan diary, 9 July 1943. Macmillan, op. cit. When Douglas Dodds-Parker was declared the winner, narrowly, at Banbury on 26 July within the town hall, he said he would go out and speak to the crowds. The returning officer had to tell him that there were no crowds to address. The late Sir Douglas Dodds-Parker to the author, 23 September 1986.

12 Another was the low opinion both shared of Herbert Morrison. 'We all listened in last night (the family and I) to your broadcast,' Waldron Smithers wrote to Anthony Eden on 7 January 1953, 'and when you had finished, I played the National Anthem on the piano! It was a dignified & statesmanlike speech & such a relief to have a gentleman as Foreign Secretary after that dreadful Herbert Morrison.' AP 20/21/93. Avon Papers, Birmingham University Library.

13 John Selwyn Brooke Lloyd, Baron Selwyn-Lloyd of the Wirral (1904–1978), MP for the Wirral, 1945–1976; Minister of State at the Foreign Office, 1951–1954; Minister of Supply, 1954–1955; Secretary of State for Defence, 1955; Foreign Secretary, 1955–1960; Chancellor of the Exchequer, 1960–1962; Lord Privy Seal and Leader of the House of Commons, 1963–1964; and Speaker of the House of Commons, 1971–1976. Macmillan could be condescending towards Lloyd. He described him privately as 'a middle class lawyer from Liverpool', which Lloyd planned to use as the title for his (unfinished) memoirs. In March 1984, Harold Macmillan discussed Lloyd's career with the author. He described Lloyd as a latter-day Augustine Birrell, another liberal lawyer-politician from Liverpool and Chief Secretary for Ireland in Asquith's government. More playfully, he asked the author where Lloyd 'came from'. When reminded that it was the Wirral (a fact that could not even have temporarily slipped his mind), he gestured with his hand, 'That's up there, isn't it, juts out?' and then after an interminable pause, *sotto*

voce, 'Funny place to come from.' The late Lord Stockton to the author, 20 March 1984. No geography was taught at Eton in Macmillan's day.

14 Selwyn Lloyd was divorced in 1957, after six years of marriage. He never remarried.

15 Emanuel Shinwell was Minister of Fuel and Power and John Strachey Minister of Food.

16 *Daily Telegraph*, 3 October 1946.

17 *Hansard*, 20 November 1946.

18 *The Observer*, 20 January 1946.

19 Robert Skidelsky, *John Maynard Keynes: Volume Three Fighting for Britain 1937–1946*, Macmillan, 2000, p. 478.

20 Lord Bennett of Edgbaston (1880–1957), MP for Edgbaston, 1940–1953, one of the few surviving Birmingham Conservative members at the time. Bennett had worked in the Ministry of Supply, 1939–1940, before entering Parliament.

21 James Hutchison (1893–1979), Unionist MP for Glasgow Central, 1945–1950; Scotstoun, October 1950–1959. Hutchison had served in North Africa during the war.

22 On taking office as Prime Minister in 1997, Margaret Thatcher declared that there would be 'no more beer and sandwiches at No. 10' for trade union leaders.

23 Reginald Maudling, *Memoirs*, Sidgwick & Jackson, 1978, pp. 45–6.

24 *Sunday Express*, 15 May 1947.

25 Speech to the Constitutional Club, May 1947.

26 Although Churchill's response had been, 'It seems to be pretty well disguised at the moment.'

27 Speech at Manchester, 4 July 1948.

28 Cuthbert Headlam diary, 28 January 1949. Stuart Ball (ed.), *Parliament and Politics in the Age of Churchill and Attlee: The Headlam Diaries 1935–1951*, Cambridge University Press, 1999, p. 570.

29 A blue plaque marks the site of his birthplace at 47 High Street.

30 When the author visited the church, he met by chance an elderly lady who was changing some flowers. 'We loved him so much,' she said of Macmillan, 'he was a wonderful MP.'

31 Private information. *AA* is used as shorthand to indicate the plural of apostle.

32 G. Grossmith and W. Grossmith, *The Diary of a Nobody*, Penguin Books, Harmondsworth, 1965, p. 19.

33 Sir Kenneth Wheare (1907–1979), constitutional expert, Rector of Exeter College, Oxford, 1956–1972, and Vice-Chancellor of Oxford University, 1964–1966.

34 Sue Harper and Vincent Porter, *British Cinema of the 1950s: The Decline of Deference*, Oxford University Press, 2003, pp. 237–8.

35 'Do you know a man called Ronald Kray? And his brother Reginald Kray?' asked Macmillan of Robert Boothby in Howard Brenton's 2008 play *Never So Good*. 'I don't think I …' replied Boothby. 'What

are they, Young Conservatives?'
Howard Brenton, *Never So
Good*, Nick Hern Books, 2008,
p. 84. The Young Conservatives
were not exclusively political in
purpose; the organisation was
traditionally seen as a middle-
class marriage mart.

36 The immediate post-war era was
still one in which the political
meeting drew vast crowds,
before they were superseded
by television. *The Month in
Parliament* talks by Macmillan
were not overtly political, more
an insider's view of what had
been happening at Westminster,
enlivened by gossip and studied
indiscretions.

37 Lady Caroline Faber to the
author, 16 February 2008.

38 Usually the one that most
resembled Ernest Bevin won.

39 Those wishing such details today
should turn to 'Searching for
the Middle Way: The Political
Economy of Harold Macmillan',
in E. H. Green, *Ideologies of
Conservatism*, Oxford University
Press, 2002.

40 Harold Macmillan to Aneurin
Bevan, 5 February 1946.
MS Macmillan dep. c. 192.
Macmillan Papers, Bodleian
Library, Oxford.

41 Harold Macmillan to S. E. D.
Draper, 16 February 1949. Ibid.

42 November 1948, 'Most Secret'
Memorandum. MS Macmillan
dep. c. 251, loc. cit.

43 The list of Bromley recipients
alone in 1950 covered five
typed foolscap pages, in double
columns with single spacing.

44 Robert Blake, *The Conservative
Party from Peel to Churchill*,
Eyre & Spottiswoode, 1970, p.
261.

45 Edward Heath, Iain Macleod,
Reginald Maudling and Enoch
Powell, four of the star entrants
to Parliament among the 1950
vintage, are often cited as
examples of this process of
democratisation. They were
nevertheless products of schools
such as Fettes (Macleod) and
Merchant Taylor's (Maudling),
and colleges such as Balliol
(Heath) and Trinity, Cambridge
(Powell). 'The Peasants' Revolt'
that brought Mrs Thatcher to
prominence was still some way
off.

46 Pandit Jawaharlal Nehru
(1889–1964), Prime Minister of
India after independence from
1947–1964.

47 'India: A Diary', MS Macmillan
dep. d. 4, loc. cit.

48 Muhammed Ali Jinnah
(1876–1948), Governor General
of Pakistan, 1947–1948.

49 'India: A Diary', MS Macmillan
dep. d. 4, loc. cit.

50 Ibid.

51 Ibid.

52 Field Marshal the Earl Wavell
(1883–1950), the most cultured,
and taciturn, of the great field
commanders of the Second
World War, which led Churchill
and Attlee, who both played
fast and loose with his career,
to underestimate his essential
greatness of spirit. His anthology
of poetry that he knew by heart,
Other Men's Flowers (1944),
remained in print for decades.

53 'India: A Diary', MS Macmillan

dep. d. 4, loc. cit.

54 Wavell and Macmillan were both wrong in this assumption. After lunch on the very day of Macmillan's visit, Wavell received a letter from Attlee, written on 31 January, informing him that his term of office as Viceroy was being terminated with a month's notice. 'Not very courteously done,' Wavell observed in his journal. Macmillan's diary account of the day shows that he was unaware of this development. A week later Wavell was told he was to be succeeded by Lord Mountbatten, who had first been interviewed about the post by Attlee on 18 December 1946, whilst Wavell was in London. The next day, Wavell had discussions in Downing Street with Attlee about the next phase of negotiations about the British withdrawal from India, completely unaware that he was, in later parlance, a 'dead man walking'. The episode, which the Prime Minister referred to as 'a change of bowling', is not one on which apologists for Attlee care to dwell. The last two viceroys of India lie a few miles apart in Hampshire: Wavell in the cloister garth on the north side of the chantry at Winchester College; Mountbatten, assassinated in 1979, in Romsey Abbey.

55 'India: A Diary', MS Macmillan dep. d. 4, loc. cit.

56 Sir Edwin Landseer Lutyens (1869–1944), the greatest British architect since Christopher Wren, and some claimed even greater. Fittingly, his ashes were placed in the crypt of St Paul's Cathedral.

57 These buildings were in fact by Sir Herbert Baker (1862–1946), whose dispute with Lutyens over the Raisina Hill gradient, which obscured the view of Viceregal Lodge, led to Lutyens' observation that he had met his Bakerloo. Lord Halifax, who had been Viceroy of India (as Lord Irwin) from 1926–1931, compared them architecturally to the building in Munich where the Munich Agreement was signed.

58 'India: A Diary', MS Macmillan dep. d. 4, loc. cit. Interestingly, Robert Byron also shared some of Macmillan's misgivings about New Delhi.

59 The Marshall Plan had been announced by General George Marshall (1880–1959) in a speech at Harvard on 5 June 1947.

60 Robert Schuman (1886–1963), a passionate advocate of European integration.

61 Sir Edward Beddington-Behrens, MC (1897–1968), a key British figure in the embryonic European movement. Vice President, European League for Economic Co-operation, 1949; Chairman, Central and European Conference, 1952; Chairman, European Industrial Conference, 1958; Chairman, Political and Economic Conference of the Seven, 1960; and Chairman, Conference on Central and Eastern Europe,

Brussels, 1963; author of *Why
Britain Must Join Europe*, 1966.

62 Lady (Juliet Evangeline)
Rhys Williams (1898–1964),
unsuccessful Liberal candidate
for Pontypridd in a by-election
in 1938, and for Ilford North
in 1945. Honorary Secretary
of the Economic Section of
the Congress of Europe at the
Hague, 1948; member of the
United Europe Movement,
1947–1958.

63 Walter Thomas, first Baron
Layton (1884–1966), economist,
and Deputy Liberal Leader in
the Lords, 1952–1955, stood
unsuccessfully for Parliament
three times in the 1920s. With
Keynes and Beveridge, he was an
important influence on Liberal
opinion, notably when chairman
of the *News Chronicle* from
1930. His biographer, the late
David Hubback, told the author
in 1986 that Layton was one
of the greatly underestimated
figures in public life.

64 A cry in which Peter
Thorneycroft also joined. Harold
Macmillan, *Tides of Fortune:
1945–1955*, Macmillan, 1969,
p. 162.

65 Ibid., p. 189.

66 Jean Monnet memorandum, 5
August 1943, for the Comitié
Français de Libération Nationale
(CFLN).

67 The Russians had blockaded
Berlin from March 1948,
preventing rail access from
the west. Three months later a
road blockade followed. The
Americans and the British,
who had been granted zones

of occupation at the Yalta
conference, organised an airlift.
Even though the Russians lifted
the blockade in May 1949,
the airlift continued lest they
reimposed it without warning.
Berlin was thereafter a focal
point in the Cold War stand-off
between the superpowers.

68 The six were Churchill, Robert
Boothby, David Eccles, David
Maxwell Fyfe, Macmillan and
Ronald Ross of the Ulster
Unionists. There were 11 Labour
members, including Dalton and
Morrison, and one Liberal.

69 These European papers are in
MS Macmillan dep. c. 11/1–3,
loc. cit.

70 Interview with R. A. Butler
in Alan Thompson, *The Day
Before Yesterday*, Sidgwick &
Jackson, 1971, p. 86.

71 Dalton resigned after a leak of
Budget details to John Carvel,
the lobby correspondent of the
London evening paper, *Star*. The
reaction of the Tory MP Nigel
Birch was, 'My God! They've
shot our fox.'

72 Hugh Dalton diary, 11
September 1950. Ben Pimlott
(ed.), p. 485. *The Political
Diary of Hugh Dalton 1918–40,
1945–60*, Jonathan Cape, 1986,
p. 1055.

73 Hugh Gaitskell diary, 27 January
1950. Philip Williams (ed.),
*The Diary of Hugh Gaitskell
1945–1956*, Jonathan Cape,
1983, p. 161.

CHAPTER FIFTEEN

One More Heave 1950–1951

1 Dr David Butler to the author, 16 November 2001.
2 Duff Cooper diary, retrospect on 1951. John Julius Norwich (ed.), *The Duff Cooper Diaries 1915–1951*, Weidenfeld & Nicolson, 2005, p. 486.
3 Labour prime ministers have by and large not been lucky in their choice (or non-choice) of election dates. Apart from Attlee in 1950 and 1951, Harold Wilson suffered a surprise defeat in June 1970, and the shunning of an election by James Callaghan in 1978, and by Gordon Brown in 2007, proved catastrophic for Labour.
4 In fact the King's illness (he died on 6 February 1952) meant that his place on the tour was taken by Princess Elizabeth and Prince Philip. Had speedy long-distance air travel been the norm in 1951, as it was in February 1974, when the Queen returned from Australia for the aftermath of a sudden election, Attlee could well have carried on as Prime Minister until the mid-1950s.
5 David Butler, *British General Elections since 1945*, Blackwell, 1989, pp. 10–11.
6 Charles Hill, Baron Hill of Luton (1904–1989), the voice of the BMA in its opposition to Aneurin Bevan's plans for state-salaried general practitioners, entered Parliament for Luton in 1950 as a 'Conservative and Liberal'. Postmaster-General, 1955–1957; Chancellor of the Duchy of Lancaster, 1957–1961; Minister of Housing and Local Government, 1961–1962, Hill was one of the seven Cabinet victims of Macmillan's Night of the Long Knives in July 1962. Subsequently he became Chairman of the Independent Television Authority, 1963–1967, and then Chairman of the BBC, 1967–1972.
7 Labour, which had such a residual advantage with agents in 1945, only had 279 in 1950.
8 P. W. Gratton advertised himself in his election address as having been educated at 'Stowe and Bryanston', which Macmillan felt was taking progressiveness too far.
9 H. G. Nicholas, *The British General Election of 1950*, Macmillan, 1951, pp. 8–9.
10 In an interview on 28 April 1959. Bevan denied he was specifically referring to Gaitskell, but few believed him.
11 It is often mistakenly said that Bevan resigned as Health Secretary following Gaitskell's Budget. Bevan had in fact been Minister of Labour and National Service since January 1951. The Health Secretary at the time was Hilary Marquand, who was consulted by Gaitskell before the budget as to whether the cuts should come in hospital building or through prescription charges. Marquand opted for prescription charges.
12 Uniquely all members of the Foreign Service, from the humblest to the Permanent Under-Secretary, had contributed

sixpence to this celebration as a token of their affection and respect.

13 The Anglo-Egyptian Treaty had been negotiated by Anthony Eden in his first spell at the Foreign Office and provided for British troops to defend the Suez Canal Zone for 20 years. Rights of passage through the Suez Canal were established as 'a universal means of communication'.

14 In June 1942, Churchill had formally advised, in the event of his death, that the King should send for Eden as Prime Minister.

15 The original nine members were Cub Alport, Robert Carr, Richard Fort, Edward Heath, Gilbert Longden, Iain Macleod, Angus Maude, Enoch Powell, and John Rodgers. Disraeli had warned in his novel *Sybil* (1845) of the dangers of the division of the country into two nations - the rich and the poor.

16 Simon Heffer, *Like The Roman: The Life of Enoch Powell*, Weidenfeld & Nicolson, 1998, p. 157.

17 Harmar, Baron Harmar-Nicolls (1912–1980), MP for Peterborough, 1950–1974.

18 Bernard Donoughue and G. W. Jones, *Herbert Morrison: Portrait of a Politician*, Weidenfeld & Nicolson, 1973, p. 492. Morrison's grandson, Peter Mandelson, saw the Millennium Dome as a similar project, and a tacit tribute to his grandfather.

19 R. R. Stokes (1897–1957), MP for Ipswich, 1938–1957; Minister of Works, 1950–51; Lord Privy Seal and Minister of Materials, 1951.

20 *Hansard*, 19 June 1951.

21 Ibid., 25 June 1951.

22 Heal's in the Tottenham Court Road is a well-known supplier of contemporary furniture.

23 The Skylon was a vertical architectural sculpture, seemingly hanging in mid-air, and illuminated from within at night. It anticipated later development of tensioned structures, such as the Millennium Dome, and became the visual symbol of the festival.

24 Michael Frayn, 'Festival', in Michael Sissons and Philip French (ed.), *Age of Austerity 1945–1951*, Penguin Books, Harmondsworth, 1964, pp. 331, 345 and 348.

25 Kenneth Harris, *Attlee*, Weidenfeld & Nicolson, 1982, p. 486.

26 The King's health was to prevent such a tour.

27 For wealthy MPs, such as Macmillan and Butler, party conferences were just one of the regular events in the political calendar. For those less fortunate, they were a nightmare of expense and entertaining, which left several seriously out of pocket.

28 Maurice Macmillan was to enter Parliament first as MP for Halifax in 1955.

29 Mary, Dowager Duchess of Devonshire (1895–1988).

30 Harold Macmillan diary, 25 October 1951. MS Macmillan dep. d. 9. Macmillan Papers, Bodleian Library, Oxford.

31 In the 26 general elections of the 20th century, only three - 1929, 1951 and February 1974 - resulted in the party winning the most votes winning fewer seats than its main opponent. 1951 was the only one of these close elections in which the Conservatives prevailed. Throughout the 1950s, no winning party gained less than 46.1% of the vote (Labour in 1950). The winning Conservative proportion of the vote in 1955 and 1959 was 49.7% and 49.4% respectively.

32 Harold Macmillan diary, 28 October 1951. MS Macmillan dep. d. 9, loc. cit.

33 The late Lord Butler to the author, 20 November 1975.

34 Resignation speech of Sir Robert Peel to Parliament, 28 June 1846.

CHAPTER SIXTEEN

Setting the People Free
1951–1954

1 Hugh Dalton diary, 29 October. Ben Pimlott (ed.), *The Political Diary of Hugh Dalton, 1918–1940, 1945–1960*, Jonathan Cape, 1986, p. 565.

2 Douglas Jay, *The Socialist Case*, 2nd edition, Faber & Faber, 1947, p. 258. Although some reviewers discerned an anti-*dirigiste* approach to pricing policy in the relevant chapter, that was not what Tory propagandists seized upon. Douglas Patrick Thomas, Baron Jay (1907–1996), Labour MP, Battersea North, 1946–1983; Economic Secretary to the Treasury, 1947–1950; Financial Secretary to the Treasury, 1950–1951; President of the Board of Trade, 1964–1967. He was sceptical about both nationalisation and European entanglements.

3 Robert Blake, *The Conservative Party from Peel to Thatcher*, Methuen paperback edition, 1985, p. 264.

4 Ham and tea were de-rationed in October 1952; sweets and chocolate in February 1953; sugar in September 1953; butter, margarine, cooking fat and cheese in May 1954; and bacon and meat in July 1954. In the 1940s it had been said that only in an innings by Denis Compton was there no rationing.

5 Brochure for Brean Sands Holiday Resort, Somerset.

6 Robert Blake, *Disraeli*, Methuen paperback edition, 1969, p. 270.

7 In 1950, the total of television licences was 656,649; by 1960, the total was 10,469,753.

8 David McAdam, first Viscount Eccles (1904–1999), MP for Chippenham 1943–1962; Minister of Works, 1951–1954; Minister of Education 1954–1957 and 1959–1962; President of the Board of Trade, 1955–1957; a victim of Macmillan's Night of the Long Knives in July 1962. See Chapter 26. Macmillan said that Eccles was possibly the only Old Wykehamist who could be mistaken for an Old Harrovian, a put-down remark of byzantine

complexity, fully comprehensible only to a particular coterie. Others, less subtle, dubbed him 'smarty boots'.

9 Harold Macmillan diary, 1–7 June 1953. MS Macmillan dep. d. 13, Macmillan Papers, Bodleian Library, Oxford.

10 Lord (Alexander) Stockton on 'Based on a True Story', BBC Radio 4, 1 January 2009. Norman Collins (1907–1982), a publisher at Victor Gollancz, joined the BBC, becoming head of the corporation's television service in November 1947. After being passed over as director of television in October 1950, he became one of the key figures in pushing for an end to the BBC's broadcasting monopoly, and in establishing independent television. Director and chairman of Independent Television News.

11 Quoted in Asa Briggs, *The BBC: The First Fifty Years*, Oxford University Press, 1985, p. 250.

12 At the same time, Macmillan was writing to a Deputy Secretary in the Ministry of Works, 'I am worried about bricks.' Harold Macmillan to Eric Seal, 30 October 1952. MS Macmillan dep. c. 290, loc. cit.

13 Based on Christ's College, where Snow had been a Fellow.

14 John Edward Masefield (1878–1967), Poet Laureate 1930–1967. His ashes were buried in Westminster Abbey next to Robert Browning's.

15 *The Times*, 2 June 1953.

16 Rayner, Baron Goddard (1877–1971), Lord Chief Justice,

1946–1958. The most fervent of anti-abolitionists of capital punishment. On a visit to the High Court as a schoolboy in the early 1950s, the author saw Lord Goddard sitting in judgement in full panoply, a tremulous experience.

17 Geoffrey Francis, Bacon Fisher of Lambeth (1887–1972), Bishop of Chester, 1932–1939; Bishop of London, 1939–1942; Archbishop of Canterbury, 1942–1960. Fisher was a fierce critic of Anthony Eden over the Suez crisis, and described Harold Macmillan's Premium Bonds scheme in his 1956 budget as 'squalid'.

18 Harold Macmillan to the author, 23 April 1975.

19 Bentley's conviction was declared unsafe by the Court of Appeal in July 1998. At the time controversy centred on whether Bentley had meant 'let the policeman have the gun' or 'shoot'.

20 The top five - Eton, Harrow, Winchester, Rugby and Charterhouse - were fixed in stone, but minor shiftings in the lower placings were the subject of much interest, and anxiety.

21 Sur Harper and Vincent Porter, *British Cinema of the 1950s: The Decline of Deference*, Oxford University Press, 2003, p. 1.

22 Robert Boothby to Harold Macmillan, 1 November 1951. MS Macmillan dep. c. 252, loc. cit.

23 *Britain Strong and Free*, 1951 Conservative Party policy statement.

24 Harold Macmillan diary, 30 October 1952. Peter Catterall, p. 116. Peter Catterall (ed.) *The Macmillan Diaries: The Cabinet Years*, 1950–1957, Macmillan, 2003

25 Sir Thomas Sheepshanks (1895–1964), a key figure in the wartime civil service in Home Security and Reconstruction. Permanent Secretary at the Ministry of Town and Country Planning, 1946–1951, and at its successor, the Ministry of Local Government and Planning, later Housing and Local Government, 1951–1955. Macmillan saw his austere aspect as a peculiarly Wykehamist characteristic.

26 Harold Macmillan diary, 11 May 1952. MS Macmillan dep. d. 11, loc. cit.

27 Hugh Dalton diary, 25 March 1951. Pimlott, op. cit., pp. 515–16.

28 Dame Evelyn Adelaide, later Baroness, Sharp (1903–1985), Permanent Secretary, Ministry of Housing and Local Government, 1955–1956, the first woman ever to achieve such rank. 'I should prefer to have been a man,' she said in an interview in 1966, 'then I could have had a career and marriage too.' Evelyn Sharp became known to a wider public with the publication of the diaries of a future Minister of Housing, Richard Crossman, in the 1970s. Crossman's prickly relationship with Sharp was owing to the collision of two dominating personalities, of a quite different order to Macmillan's unproductive

interaction with Sheepshanks.

29 Harold Macmillan, *Tides of Fortune: 1945–1955*, Macmillan, 1969, p. 460.

30 Sir John Crompton Wrigley (1888–1977), Local Government Board, 1912; posts in the Ministry of Health 1919–1951; Joint Deputy Secretary Ministry of Housing and Local Government, 1951–1952. Wrigley found Percy Mills (see below) an abrasive presence and took retirement a little earlier than planned owing to their personality clashes.

31 Percy Herbert, 1st Viscount Mills (1890–1968), son of a wholesale confectioner in Stockton-on-Tees, wartime civil servant, businessman; Minister of Power, 1957–1959, Paymaster General, 1959–1961; Minister without Portfolio, 1961–1962. He left office in Macmillan's Night of the Long Knives on 13 July 1962.

32 Harold Macmillan diary, 31 March 1952. MS Macmillan dep. d. 11, loc. cit.

33 Sir Frederick Bishop (1915–2005), always known as Freddie, a ubiquitous and indispensable civil servant from the days of the Attlee government to the Wilson one, Private Secretary to both Sir Anthony Eden and Harold Macmillan during their premierships. Macmillan gave Bishop the original copy of the famous notice he placed on the Cabinet door in January 1957, 'Quiet calm deliberation disentangles every knot.'

34 Reginald Bevins (1908–1996),

MP Toxteth division of Liverpool, 1950–1964; PPS at Housing and Local Government, 1951–1953, Ministry of Works, 1952–1957, Housing and Local Government, 1957–1959; Postmaster General, 1959–1964.

35 Quoted in Alan Thomson, *The Day Before Yesterday*, Sidgwick & Jackson, 1971, p. 96.

36 William Francis, Baron Deedes of Aldington (1913–2007), MP Ashford, 1950–1974; Minister without Portfolio, 1962–1964; editor of the *Daily Telegraph*, 1974–1986. Immortalised as the recipient of Denis Thatcher's (fictional) letters in the long-running 'Dear Bill' feature in *Private Eye*.

37 Grace Murrell Wyndham Goldie (1900–1986), one of the most influential of television producers. Goldie pioneered the election results broadcasts from the 1951 general election onwards, enlisting experts such as David Butler and Robert McKenzie as presenters.

38 Michael Cockerell, *Live from Number 10: The Inside Story of Prime Ministers and Television*, Faber & Faber, 1988, pp. 17–18. James Gray, first Viscount Stuart of Findhorn (1897–1971), Secretary of State for Scotland, 1951–1955, was married to Lady Rachel Cavendish, Lady Dorothy's sister.

39 Lewis, first Baron Silkin (1889–1972), Minister for Town and Country Planning, 1945–1950. Labour MP for the Peckham division of Camberwell. Ironically, population changes led to the abolition of his parliamentary seat for the 1950 election.

40 Harold Macmillan to Sir John Wrigley, 3 December 1951. MS Macmillan dep. C. 290, loc. cit.

41 Frances Joan, Viscountess Davidson and Baroness Northchurch (1894–1985), elected as Conservative MP for Hemel Hempstead, the constituency of her husband J. C. C. Davidson, when he was elevated to the peerage in 1937. She was the only woman Conservative candidate returned at the 1945 election, and held the seat until she stepped down in 1959.

42 Sydney Frank Wilkinson (1894–1988), entered the civil service in 1913. After a commission in the Great War, he served as secretary to Kingsley Wood, Walter Elliot and Malcolm MacDonald, before posts at the Ministry of Health, and Housing and Local Government.

43 Baron Harmar-Nicholls of Peterborough (1912–2000), MP for Peterborough 1950–1974, was a fiercely outspoken backbencher on issues that concerned him.

44 Simon Heffer, *Like the Roman: The Life of Enoch Powell*, Weidenfeld & Nicolson, 1998, p. 189.

45 Anthony Seldon, *Churchill's Indian Summer: The Conservative Government 1951–1955*, Hodder & Stoughton, 1981, p. 250.

46 Frederick Alexander Lindemann, Viscount Cherwell (1886–1957),

Professor of Experimental Philosophy (Physics) at Oxford University; influential adviser and friend to Churchill; Paymaster-General, 1942–1945 and 1951–1953.

47 Walter Turner, first Viscount Monckton of Brenchley (1891–1965), lawyer and politician, confidant of Edward VIII during the abdication crisis; MP for Bristol West, 1951; Minister of Labour, 1951–1955; Minister of Defence, 1955–1956; Paymaster-General, 1956–1957. David Margesson, Chief Whip, called him 'the old oil can'.

48 Following the resignation of Balfour as Tory leader in November 1911, the two main candidates, Austen Chamberlain and Walter Long, were deadlocked. Following manoeuvrings by Max Aitken, the future Lord Beaverbrook, Bonar Law emerged as a compromise, and victorious, candidate. See D. R. Thorpe, *The Uncrowned Prime Ministers*, Darkhorse Publishing, 1980. The pattern was to be repeated in the Tory leadership contest of October 1963, with Macmillan, in many people's eyes, the Max Aitken figure, and Lord Home the unexpected victor. See Chapter 29.

49 Harold Macmillan to Winston Churchill, 18 June 1954. MS Macmillan dep. c. 291, loc. cit.

CHAPTER SEVENTEEN

Captain of the Praetorian Guard 1954–1955

1 Harold Macmillan diary, 17 January 1953. MS Macmillan dep. d. 20. Macmillan Papers, Bodleian Library, Oxford.

2 Harold Macmillan to R. A. Butler, 19 January 1955. MS Macmillan dep. c. 295, loc. cit.

3 Admiral of the Fleet Sir Rhoderick Robert McGrigor (1893–1959), a veteran of the Battle of Jutland in 1916 and the sinking of the *Bismarck* in 1941, McGrigor became First Sea Lord and Chief of the Naval Staff in December 1951.

4 Field Marshal John Allen Francis, first Baron Harding of Petherton (1896–1989), Chief of Staff to Field Marshal Alexander in Italy; Chief of the Imperial General Staff, 1952–1955. Macmillan had worked with Harding before, particularly over the aftermath of Harding's campaign against Tito's Yugoslav partisans at Trieste in May 1945, often called the first victory of the Cold War.

5 Marshal of the Royal Air Force Sir William Forster Dickson (1897–1987), Chief of the Air Staff, 1 January 1953–1 January 1959, when Macmillan made him the first Chief of the Defence Staff.

6 Sir Richard Powell (1909–2006), Deputy Secretary, Ministry of Defence, 1950–1956, Permanent Secretary, 1956–1959; Permanent Secretary, Board of Trade, 1960–1968. Sir Richard

Powell discussed the post-war Ministry of Defence with the author in 1986.

7 Sir Harold Parker, MC (1895–1980), joined the Treasury in 1919, and became Permanent Secretary at Pensions, 1941–1946; Permanent Secretary, Ministry of Defence, 1948–1956.

8 SELO 249 (4). Selwyn Lloyd papers, Churchill College, Cambridge.

9 MS Macmillan dep. c. 295, loc. cit.

10 See Chapter 16.

11 Peter Alexander Rupert, 6th Baron Carrington, born 1919, Parliamentary Secretary, Ministry of Agriculture and Fisheries, 1951–1954, and at the Ministry of Defence, October 1954–November 1956; High Commissioner in Australia, 1956–1959; 1st Lord of the Admiralty, 1959–1963; Minister without Portfolio and Leader of the House of Lords, 1963–1964; Secretary of State for Defence, 1970–1974, for Energy, 1974; Foreign Secretary, 1979–1982; Chairman Conservative Party Organisation, 1972–1974.

12 Sir Hamilton Kerr (1903–1974), educated Eton and Balliol, MP for Cambridge, 1950–1966; PPS to Duff Cooper at the Admiralty; PPS to Macmillan, 1954–1956, at Defence, the Foreign Office and the Treasury.

13 'Statement on Defence', Cmd 9391. February 1955. HMSO.

14 *Hansard*, 1 March 1955.

15 Cabinet Minutes, 1 October 1954. CAB 128/27, National

Archives, Kew.

16 W. N. Hanna, private secretary to Harold Macmillan and Selwyn Lloyd at the Ministry of Defence, guided the author through the intricacies of 1950s defence policy in a wide-ranging interview in 1986.

17 MS Macmillan dep. c. 295, loc. cit.

18 CND was launched by Bertrand Russell and Canon John Collins on 17 February 1958. Its peak was in the years 1960–1961 when it had more members than any pressure group in Britain since the Anti-Corn Law League in the 1840s.

19 MS Macmillan dep. c. 295, loc. cit.

20 Gamal Abdel Nasser (1918–1970), President of Egypt, 1954–1970, and the focus for Arab nationalism in the Middle East.

21 Nikolai Bulganin (1895–1975), Soviet Prime Minister 1955–1958. He was ousted from the premiership by Nikita Khrushchev in March 1958. 'B and K', as they were known, made a famous visit to Britain in April 1956.

22 Courtauld Greenwood, 1st Baron Courtauld-Thomson (1865–1954) was following in the enlightened footsteps of Arthur, Viscount Lee of Fareham (1868–1947), who had presented his country house, Chequers, to the nation in 1917 for the use of the Prime Minister in perpetuity, together with a handsome endowment for its upkeep. Many of those who have experienced

both residences have preferred Dorneywood.

23 Harold Macmillan to the author, 23 April 1975. Lord Home, whose private residence was in Scotland, occupied Dorneywood as Commonwealth Secretary and Foreign Secretary, 1955–1963, and for a time as Prime Minister, 1963–1964; Selwyn Lloyd was granted the tenure of Chequers whilst Chancellor of the Exchequer, 1960–1962.

24 Thanks to Lord George Bentinck and his two brothers, Disraeli had been able to secure Hughenden Manor, near High Wycombe, in 1848. This proved the launch pad for his parliamentary career. Birch Grove was in what might be called the 'Hughenden line' of 20th-century prime ministerial country houses from Hatfield (Salisbury), through Astley (Baldwin) to Chartwell (Churchill) and the Hirsel (Home). Nowadays such residences tend to be acquired after leaving office.

25 Harold Macmillan to Nigel Birch, 8 September 1955. MS Macmillan dep. c. 30, loc. cit. 2 Carlton Gardens was once the London home of Lord Kitchener. It is now used by the Privy Council Office.

26 The late Bill Housden to the author, November 1981.

27 Although Maurice Macmillan raised the Conservative percentage of the vote, Labour won 21,882 votes to his 15,714.

28 Lord Moran diary, 24 January 1955. Lord Moran, *Winston*

Churchill: The Struggle for Survival 1940–1965, Sphere Books paperback edition, 1968, p. 660.

29 Cabinet Minutes, 8 July 1954. CAB 128/27. National Archives, Kew.

30 Harold Macmillan diary, 8 July 1954. MS Macmillan dep. d. 20, loc. cit.

31 Anthony Eden diary, 27 August 1954. AP 20/1/30. Avon Papers, Birmingham University Library.

32 Information from the Lloyd family.

33 *Spectator*, 15 October 1954.

34 Harold Macmillan to Sir Anthony Eden, 9 September 1954. AP 20/17/192. Avon Papers, Birmingham University Library.

35 D. R. Thorpe, *Eden: The Life and Times of Anthony Eden First Earl of Avon 1897–1977*, Chatto & Windus, 2003, p. 423.

36 Anthony Howard, *Rab: The Life of R. A. Butler*, Jonathan Cape, 1987, p. 213.

37 This was very much the view of Robert Armstrong, one of Butler's secretaries at the Treasury, 1954–1955. Lord Armstrong of Ilminster to the author, 29 January 2009.

38 In the 20th century, only two previous Foreign Secretaries, Sir Edward Grey in 1912 and Sir Austen Chamberlain in 1925, had received this signal honour.

39 Lord Moran diary, 20 January 1955. Moran, op. cit., p. 660. The Praetorian Guard were crucial in sustaining the political power of the Emperor in the Roman Republic. Ironically,

as Churchill admitted to Lord Moran, Macmillan had now transferred his allegiance to the opposing camp.

40 Anthony Eden diary, 21 December 1954. AP 20/1/30, loc. cit.

41 Ibid., 22 December 1954.

42 Harold Macmillan diary, 14 March 1955. MS Macmillan dep. d. 20, loc. cit.

43 This was still the case when Harold Wilson held a similar dinner on 23 March 1976 to mark his retirement. The author witnessed the departure of the Queen and the Duke of Edinburgh from Downing Street after the dinner.

44 Letter to the author, 18 February 2005, from W. D. G. Chalmers, who was outside 10 Downing Street on 5 April 1955.

45 Martin Gilbert, *In Search of Churchill*, Harper Collins, 1994, p. 246.

46 Harold Macmillan diary, 17 July 1952. MS Macmillan dep. d. 11, loc. cit.

CHAPTER EIGHTEEN

Nearer to the Centre 1955

1 Harold Macmillan diary, 6 April 1955. MS Macmillan dep. d. 20. Macmillan Papers, Bodleian Library, Oxford.

2 J. A. Cross, *Lord Swinton*, Oxford University Press, 1982, p. 284. Hugh Dalton diary, 1 April 1955. Ben Pimlott (ed.), *The Political Diary of Hugh Dalton* 1918–1940, 1945–1960, Jonathan Cape, 1986, p. 284.

Boothby was only three months out in his forecast.

3 Winston S. Churchill, *His Father's Son: The Life of Randolph Churchill*, Weidenfeld & Nicolson, 1996, p. 336.

4 Harold Macmillan diary, 6 April 1955, loc. cit.

5 In 1960 Macmillan did not feel similarly restricted when he appointed Lord Home to the Foreign Office, nor did Mrs Thatcher in 1979 with the appointment of Lord Carrington.

6 The Earl of Swinton to Sir Anthony Eden, 7 April 1955. SWIN 174/6/3. Swinton Papers, Churchill College, Cambridge.

7 Lord Carr of Hadley to the author, 20 May 1997. Robert Carr (born 1916), MP for Mitcham 1950–1974, was Eden's PPS, 1951–1955. An original member of the 'One Nation' Group of the 1950 parliamentary intake, he held various Cabinet posts in the Heath government, including that of Home Secretary, 1972–1974.

8 Sir George Lewis French Bolton (1900–1982), a key official in the Bank of England, 1931–1957, and one of the main proponents in 1952 of the ROBOT scheme for a floating rate of exchange for sterling. Sir George Bolton diary, 27 October 1955. File C160/27. Bank of England Archive.

9 *Hansard*, 27 October 1955. Gaitskell's attack was ironic in that Butler and himself had been seen, mistakenly, by many commentators as twin halves

of what became known as 'Butskellism', a shared belief in economic demand management. 'Poor Mr Butskell,' observed Gaitskell's biographer, 'a short life, wrecked by schizophrenia.' Philip M. Williams, *Hugh Gaitskell: A Political Biography*, Jonathan Cape, 1979, p. 318.

10 The key to Edward Heath's unexpected general election victory in June 1970 was the success in the north-west.

11 At a meeting of the Labour Party's NEC on 30 March 1955, the party whip was restored to Bevan by 14 votes to 13, a clear indication of the current internal divisions.

12 Bernard Donoughue and G. W. Jones, *Herbert Morrison: Portrait of a Politician*, Weidenfeld & Nicolson, 1973, p. 534. Bernard Donoughue wrote the section on Morrison's life from 1940.

13 Harold Macmillan diary, 7 April 1955, loc. cit.

14 Michael Cockerell, *Live from Number 10: The Inside Story of Prime Ministers and Television*, Faber & Faber, p. 30.

15 A point emphasised to the author by Dr David Butler, 25 January 1995.

16 Harold Macmillan to R. A. Butler, 15 April 1955. MS Macmillan dep. c. 302, loc. cit.

17 Sir Anthony Montague Browne born 1923, entered the Foreign Service in 1946; seconded as Private Secretary to the Prime Minister, 1952–1955, an arrangement continued until Churchill's death in 1965

through Macmillan's initiative. 'It would be impossible to overrate the service which Anthony rendered Winston in the last ten years of his life,' Churchill's daughter has written. Mary Soames, *Clementine Churchill*, Cassell, 1979, p. 459.

18 MS Macmillan dep. c. 302, loc. cit.

19 Harold Macmillan diary, 30 May 1955. MS Macmillan dep. d. 21, loc. cit.

20 Roy Jenkins considered the key figures among 20th-century Foreign Secretaries to be Lord Lansdowne, Sir Edward Grey, Lord Curzon, Ernest Bevin and Sir Anthony Eden. Roy Jenkins, *Nine Men of Power*, Hamish Hamilton, 1974, p. 64. Despite the undoubted claims of Ernest Bevin, a case can be made for Eden, owing to his three periods in office from 1935–1938, 1940–1945 and 1951–1955, as the most important of them all.

21 Lord Butler, *The Art of the Possible*, Penguin Books, Harmondsworth, 1973, p. 182.

22 Harold Macmillan to R. A. Butler, 7 February 1954. MS Macmillan dep. c. 291, loc. cit.

23 Sir Ivone Augustine Kirkpatrick (1897–1964), Permanent Under-Secretary, 1953–1957. His diplomatic service in Rome and Berlin in the 1930s had given him a profound distaste for totalitarian dictatorships, which influenced his response to the Suez crisis in 1956, when he was a firm supporter of Eden's policy.

24 Sir Anthony Rumbold (1911–1983) was a second

secretary in North Africa in 1944. Macmillan much admired his intelligence, industry and charm. Principal Private Secretary to the Foreign Secretary, 1954; Assistant Under-Secretary at the Foreign Office, 1957; Ambassador to Thailand, 1965–1967; Ambassador to Austria, 1967–1970.

25 Sir Patrick Hancock, (1914–1980), Principal Private Secretary to the Foreign Secretary, 1955; Ambassador to Israel, 1959–1962; Norway 1963–1965; Italy, 1969–1974. Sir Andrew Stark (1916–2000), Assistant Private Secretary to the Foreign Secretary, 1953–1955; Ambassador to Denmark, 1971–1976.

26 Nicholas Henderson, *The Private Office Revisited*, Profile Books, 2001, p. 158.

27 Guy Francis de Moncy Burgess (1911–1963), sometime member of MI6 and Second Secretary at the Washington Embassy, 1950–1951, and Donald Duart Maclean (1913–1983), member of the diplomatic service from 1935, by which time he was already a member of the NKVD (later the KGB); Head of the American Department of the Foreign Office, 1950–1951. Their defection to Moscow on 25 May 1951, in the midst of the Korean War, was a major scandal, leading to American suspicions that atomic secrets had been leaked and a cooling in Anglo-American relations owing to Washington's low opinion of British security. The defection

had important consequences for Macmillan & Co. Alan Maclean, Donald's brother, though free of all suspicion of espionage, could not continue work at the Foreign Office. In a change of career he moved into publishing and became one of the most important figures in the post-war history of the company.

28 Harold Macmillan diary, 2 November 1955. MS Macmillan dep. d. 24, loc. cit.

29 Harold Macmillan diary, 2 May 1953. MS Macmillan dep. d. 13, loc. cit.

30 A *bon mot* first used privately at the 1953 Bermuda conference, and oft repeated during the Suez crisis.

31 Speech on 1 December 1958, a prime example of what Henry James called 'the terrible fluidity of self-revelation'.

32 Harold Macmillan diary, 15 May 1955. MS Macmillan dep. d. 20, loc. cit.

33 A reference to Sir Edmund Hillary and Sherpa Tenzing, who had made the first ascent of Mount Everest on 29 May 1953, the final stages of which were led by Hillary. Quoted in Anthony Sampson, *Macmillan: A Study in Ambiguity*, Pelican Books, Harmondsworth, 1968, p. 106.

34 Statement at a London press conference, 24 July 1955.

35 See Chapter 25.

36 Harold Macmillan diary, 31 October 1955. MS Macmillan dep. d. 24, loc. cit. Andrei Gromyko (1909–1989) was the Soviet Deputy Foreign Minister, 1954–1957, and the Foreign

Minister, 1957–1985. He was known to his opposite number in Britain, Lord Home, Foreign Secretary, 1960–1963, and 1970–1974, as the Abominable No-Man.

37 *Report Concerning the Disappearance of Two Former Foreign Office Officials* (1955), Cmd 9577.

38 Sir Dick Goldsmith White (1906–1993), Director General of MI5, 1953–1956; Head of MI6, 1956–1968.

39 Quoted in Tom Bower, *The Perfect English Spy: Sir Dick White and the Secret War 1935–1990*, Heinemann, 1995, p. 157.

40 Harold Adrian Russell (Kim) Philby (1912–1988), spy; representative of the Secret Intelligence Service (MI5) in Washington from 1949, where Maclean lodged with him. MI5 had their suspicions about Philby but at the time of Macmillan's statement did not have the concrete evidence for a prosecution. After fleeing to Russia in 1963, Philby became a Soviet citizen; he was awarded the Order of Lenin in 1965, and given a prestigious funeral by the KGB.

41 *Hansard*, 7 November 1955.

42 BBC 1 interview, 9 September 1969. BBC records, Caversham.

43 Bower, op. cit., p. 156.

44 Hugo Young, *This Blessed Plot: Britain and Europe from Churchill to Blair*, Papermac paperback edition, 1999, p. 78.

45 Speech at Columbia University, on accepting an honorary degree, 11 January 1952.

46 Quoted in Richard Lamb, *The Failure of the Eden Government*, Sidgwick & Jackson, 1987, p. 69.

47 Alan Milward, *The Rise and Fall of a National Strategy, 1945–1963: The United Kingdom and the European Community*, Vol. 1, Frank Cass, 2002, p. 229. Speech by R. A. Butler, 21 June 1955.

48 Ibid., p. 230.

49 A rare split infinitive in Macmillan's papers.

50 Harold Macmillan to Sir Edward Bridges, 1 February 1956. T 234/100. National Archives, Kew. This letter was written to his Permanent Secretary at the Treasury within weeks of becoming Chancellor of the Exchequer. Economic considerations concentrated Macmillan's mind on the implications of Messina.

51 George Theodoros Grivas (1898–1974), Greek army officer, and creator of EOKA.

52 Archbishop Makarios III (1913–1977), President of the Cypriot Republic, the Etnarch, the national and spiritual leader of Cyprus. Grivas regarded Makarios' acceptance of Commonwealth membership for Cyprus in August 1960 as treason.

53 Harold Macmillan diary, 2 September 1955. MS Macmillan dep. d. 22, loc. cit.

54 Alan Tindall Lennox-Boyd, 1st Viscount Boyd of Merton (1904–1983), MP for Mid Bedfordshire, 1931–1960; Minister of

Transport, 1952–1954, and from 1953, Civil Aviation; Colonial Secretary, 1954–1959.

55 Xerxes spent three years on intensive diplomatic and military preparations before launching an unsuccessful invasion of Greece in 480–479 BC. Macmillan's analogy was fear that a small island such as Cyprus might defeat and defy the forces of a great empire, just as Xerxes had been defeated by the resistance of a few Greek cities.

56 Leslie Gilbert Illingworth (1902– 1979), cartoonist, particularly in the *Daily Mail* and *Punch*. Malcolm Muggeridge thought his political insights even greater than Low's.

57 Gilbert Harding (1907–1960) had taught in Cyprus before the war and was disenchanted by British rule in the island. Ironically, he was a close friend from Cambridge days of both Field Marshal Harding's successor as Governor, Sir Hugh Foot, and of Selwyn Lloyd, who was to succeed Macmillan as Foreign Secretary.

58 Harold Macmillan to R. A. Butler, 10 August 1955. MS Macmillan dep. c. 302, loc. cit.

59 Harold Macmillan diary, 22 September 1955. MS Macmillan dep. d. 23, loc. cit.

60 Julian Amery never reached the Cabinet; Maurice Macmillan only did so after his father's retirement, as Chief Secretary to the Treasury, 1970–1972; Secretary of State for Employment, 1972–1973; and Paymaster General, 1973–1974.

61 Professor Peter Hennessy has described the exchanges as 'perhaps the most bizarre correspondence I have ever read in the National Archives between a senior Cabinet minister and a premier'. Peter Hennessy, *Having It So Good: Britain in the Fifties*, Allen Lane, 2006, p. 377.

62 Harold Macmillan to Sir Anthony Eden, 24 October 1955. PREM 5/228. National Archives, Kew.

63 Ibid.

64 Harold Macmillan to Sir Anthony Eden, 9 December 1955, loc. cit.

65 Harold Macmillan to John Foster Dulles, 21 December. MS Macmillan dep. c. 305, loc. cit.

66 Harold Macmillan diary, 22 December 1955. MS Macmillan dep. d. 24, loc. cit.

67 Harold Wilson, *A Prime Minister on Prime Ministers*, Weidenfeld & Nicolson, and Michael Joseph, 1977, p. 308.

68 Hugh Gaitskell diary, 16–21 January 1956. Philip M. Williams (ed.), *The Diaries of Hugh Gaitskell 1945–1956*, Jonathan Cape, 1983, p. 422.

69 Sir Anthony Eden diary, 16 October 1955, AP20/1/13. Avon Papers, Birmingham University Library.

70 Harold Macmillan diary, 30 December 1955. MS Macmillan dep. 24, loc. cit.

71 The late Sir Thomas Padmore to the author, 1986.

72 Minute, 9 June 1955. FO 371/115869. National Archives, Kew.

73 Harold Macmillan, *Tides of*

Fortune 1945–1955, Macmillan, 1969, p. 664.

74 Lady Butler of Saffron Walden (1907–2009) married Rab Butler in 1959. Mollie Butler was the great keeper of Rab Butler's flame and her antipathy towards Macmillan was legendary. See the obituaries in *The Times* and the *Daily Telegraph* (19 February 2009). On one occasion she said to the author, 'Mr Thorpe, when you realise that Mr Macmillan was an evil man, you will be well on your way to an understanding of post-war politics.' For her, Rab could do no wrong. When Lady Butler read the account of Macmillan's sacking of seven Cabinet ministers in an advance publisher's proof copy of the author's *Selwyn Lloyd*, she rang the author to see if a word could be changed in the sentence 'Butler leaked details of Macmillan's long-term intentions.' D. R. Thorpe, *Selwyn Lloyd*, Jonathan Cape, 1989, pp. 339–40. Although accepting that this was quite true (Butler had told Walter Terry of the *Daily Mail* of the forthcoming Cabinet changes), Lady Butler felt that 'leaked' had a pejorative ring. When asked what would be preferable to her as a substitute at this late stage, in the six-letter space, Lady Butler suggested 'was charmingly indiscreet'.

75 Lord Woolton diary, 24 October 1955. MS Woolton 3, Department of Western MSS, Bodleian Library, Oxford.

CHAPTER NINETEEN

View from a Treasury Window 1955–1956

1 In a famous article by Donald McLachlan, published on 3 January 1956.

2 Sir William Haley diary, 8 January 1956. HALY 13/9. Haley papers. Churchill College, Cambridge.

3 *The Times*, 2 January 1956.

4 Quoted in Andrew Roberts, *Eminent Churchillians*, Weidenfeld & Nicolson, 1994, p. 276.

5 Edward Ettingdene, first Baron Bridges (1892–1969), son of the Poet Laureate Robert Bridges, won the Military Cross in the Great War. Bridges first worked for the Treasury in 1917. He was appointed Cabinet Secretary in 1938; in 1945 he became Permanent Secretary to the Treasury and head of the civil service, a post he held till 1956. Macmillan regarded Bridges as 'one of the greatest' (diary, 24 April 1956). MS Macmillan dep. d. 21. Macmillan Papers, Bodleian Library, Oxford.

6 Sir Denis Hubert Fletcher Rickett (1907–1997) joined the Treasury in 1947. Principal Private Secretary to Clement Attlee, 1950–1951; Economic Minister at the Washington Embassy, 1951–1955; Third, later Second, Secretary in the Overseas Finance division, 1955–1968; Vice President of the World Bank, 1968–1974. Like Sir Edward Heath, Rickett lived in the close of Salisbury Cathedral

in retirement. Sir Alexander Johnston (1905–1994), Home Office, 1928–1935; Ministry of Reconstruction, 1943–1945; Deputy Cabinet Secretary, 1948–1951; Third Secretary at the Treasury, 1951–1958; Chairman of the Board of Inland Revenue, 1958–1968. Sir Thomas Padmore (1909–1996), Inland Revenue, 1931–1934; Treasury, 1934–1962; Permanent Secretary at the Ministry of Transport, 1962–1965. Robert Lowe, Baron Roberthall (1901–1988), Director of the Economic Section of the Cabinet Office from 1947–1961 (retitled Chief Economic Adviser in 1953); Principal of Hertford College, Oxford, 1964–1967. These four Treasury mandarins helped the author in 1986 over the work of the post-war Treasury and, in particular, Selwyn Lloyd's chancellorship.

7 Sir Louis Petch (1913–1981), Principal Private Secretary to the Chancellor of the Exchequer, 1953–1956. Evan Maude (1919–1980), Principal Private Secretary to the Chancellor of the Exchequer, 1956–1958.

8 Cameron Fromanteel, first Baron Cobbold (1904–1987), joined the Bank of England during Montagu Norman's governorship in 1933. He was Governor of the Bank of England, 1949–1961.

9 6 January 1956. File G3/115. Lord Cobbold to Harold Macmillan, 26 March 1956. File G1/74. Bank of England Archive.

10 Private information.

11 File G15/19. Bank of England Archive.

12 Anthony Sampson, *Anatomy of Britain*, Hodder & Stoughton, 1962, p. 272.

13 Robert Skidelsky, *John Maynard Keynes: Fighting for Britain 1937–1946*, Macmillan, 2000, p. 499.

14 Henry Baron Brooke of Cumnor (1903–1984), MP for Lewisham West, 1938–1945, and Hampstead, 1950–1964; Financial Secretary to the Treasury, 1954–1957; Minister of Housing and Local Government and Minister for Welsh Affairs, 1957–1962; Home Secretary, 1962–1964. As the satirists sharpened their pens in the early 1960s, he was to receive even more obloquy than Macmillan.

15 Edward Charles Gurney, Baron Boyle of Handsworth (1923–1981), baronet; MP for Handsworth, 1950–1970; held a variety of economic and education posts before entering the Cabinet as Minister of Education, 1962–1964; Vice Chancellor of Leeds University, 1970–1981.

16 James Harold Wilson, Baron Wilson of Rievaulx (1916–1995), President of the Board of Trade, 1947–1951, the youngest Cabinet minister since Pitt the Younger; Prime Minister 1964–1970, 1974–1976.

17 In Chapter 1 of his book *The English Constitution* of 1868, Walter Bagehot (1826–1877) described the dignified parts of

the constitution as 'those which excite and preserve the reverence of the population'; the corollary was the efficient parts, 'those by which it, in fact, works and rules'.

18 A fact volunteered by both Macmillan and Wilson to the author on more than one occasion.

19 Harold Wilson, *A Prime Minister on Prime Ministers*, Weidenfeld & Nicolson/Michael Joseph, 1977, p. 308.

20 Harold Macmillan to Sir Anthony Eden, PREM 11/1326. National Archives, Kew.

21 File G15/19. Bank of England Archive.

22 Harold Macmillan to Sir Anthony Eden, 15 February 1956. MS Macmillan dep. c. 304, loc. cit.

23 George Edward Peter, Baron Thorneycroft (1909–1994), MP for Stafford 1938–1945, and Monmouth, 1945–1966; President of the Board of Trade, 1951–1957; Chancellor of the Exchequer, 1957–1958; Minister of Aviation, 1960–1962; Minister of Defence, 1962–1964; Secretary of State for Defence (combining the three service ministries), 1964; chairman of the Conservative Party, 1975–1981. See Chapter 22 for the Thorneycroft resignation. As will be argued, this proved to be one of the key watersheds of post-war politics.

24 The original members were Austria, Denmark, Great Britain, Norway, Portugal, Sweden and Switzerland.

25 'United Kingdom Commercial Policy. Memorandum by the Chancellor of the Exchequer and the President of the Board of Trade', 28 July 1956. CAB 129/82, National Archives, Kew.

26 Harold Macmillan diary, 5 September 1956. MS Macmillan dep. d. 27, loc. cit. Apart from Thorneycroft, Derick Heathcoat Amory (Minister of Agriculture), David Eccles (Minister of Education), Iain Macleod (Minister of Labour) and Duncan Sandys (Minister of Housing and Local Government) were particular enthusiasts. Salisbury and Butler were not so easily convinced.

27 Dr David Butler to the author, 23 April 2009.

28 *Hansard*, 20 February 1956.

29 Harold Macmillan to Lord Cobbold, 26 March 1956. MS Macmillan dep. c. 303, loc. cit.

30 Events conspired to prevent this. From 1960–1964 Makins ended his official career as Chairman of the UK Atomic Energy Authority.

31 All Budget references are from *Hansard*, 17 April 1956.

32 A reference to the then ubiquitous Bradshaw railway timetable, often referred to in Victorian literature. George Bradshaw (1801–1853) had first published his guide to railway timetables in 1839. The scope of the publication grew with its popularity and long survived Bradshaw's death. The last Bradshaw appeared in 1961, just as Macmillan and Dr Richard Beeching were taking an axe

to Britain's railway system. See Chapter 27. At a time of economic fine-tuning, Macmillan was admitting that we do not know where we are now, never mind where we will be in a year's time.

33 Harold Vincent, 1st Viscount Mackintosh of Halifax (1891–1964), head of National Savings movement from 1946; a staunch Methodist, Mackintosh was chosen as the public face of Premium Bonds to reassure those, such as Nonconformists, who were unhappy about any form of public lottery.

34 File C40/426, January-February 1956. Bank of England Archive.

35 Ibid.

36 Half a century later these figures were 30,000 and £1m.

37 Geoffrey Francis, Baron Fisher of Lambeth (1887–1972), Head Master of Repton, 1914–1932; Bishop of Chester, 1932–1939; Bishop of London, 1939–1945; Archbishop of Canterbury, 1945–1960. Fisher was a persistent thorn in the side of both Eden and Macmillan.

38 Hansard, 17 April 1956.

39 Harold Macmillan diary, 21 July 1956. MS Macmillan dep. d. 26, loc. cit.

40 Harold Macmillan to Sir Anthony Eden, 23 July 1956. MS Macmillan dep. c. 320, loc. cit.

41 Harold Macmillan, Riding the Storm, 1956–1959, Macmillan, 1971, p. 50.

42 Harold Macmillan to Sir Anthony Eden, 31 July 1956. MS Macmillan dep. c. 306, loc. cit.

43 Annual Report and Accounts of the British Broadcasting Corporation, 1956–57, p. 8, Cmnd 267, Stationery Office, 1957.

44 1 May 1959. File C40/426. Bank of England Archive.

45 Barbara Muriel, Baroness Brooke of Ystradfellte (1908–2000), DBE, 1960; President of the National Union of Conservative Associations, 1969.

46 Lord Brooke of Sutton Mandeville to the author, 18 April 2009.

47 Samuel Brittain, Steering the Economy: The Role of the Treasury, Penguin Books, Harmondsworth, 1971, p. 205.

48 Alban Williams Housego Phillips (1914–1975), New Zealand economist, Reader in Economics, London School of Economics, 1954–1958; Tooke Professor of Economic Science and Statistics, University of London, 1958–1967; author of The Relationship between Unemployment and the Rate of Change of Money Wages in the United Kingdom 1861–1957 (1958). 'The Phillips Curve' was the model describing the inverse relationship between inflation and unemployment, implying that governments could control unemployment and inflation with a Keynesian policy. The trade-off would be that a tolerable rate of inflation would be associated with lower unemployment. Political considerations would determine what rate was tolerable. It

is interesting to note that Germany's choice was generally a lower rate of inflation, their national consciousness seared by the experience of hyperinflation during the Weimar Republic, whereas Britain, in Macmillan's time, opted for a lower rate of unemployment, a direct consequence of his memories of pre-war Stockton-on-Tees.

49 On 18 November 1967, the pound was devalued from $2.80 to $2.40. Even then some economists maintain that the devaluation was delayed too long.

50 Harold Macmillan diary, 22 July 1955. MS Macmillan dep. d. 22, loc. cit.

51 Sir Ivone Kirkpatrick, *The Inner Circle: Memoirs of Ivone Kirkpatrick*, Macmillan, 1959, p. 262.

52 See D. R. Thorpe *Selwyn Lloyd*, Jonathan Cape, 1989, pp. 203–4. Even a quarter of a century later, some members of the Foreign Service were not happy that these details had been revealed.

53 George Alfred, Baron George-Brown (1914–1945), MP for Belper, 1945–1970; Minister of Works, 1951; Secretary of State for Economic Affairs, 1964–1966; Foreign Secretary, 1966–1968. In 1975, Macmillan suggested to the author that he include George Brown in *The Uncrowned Prime Ministers*, a study of Sir Austen Chamberlain, Lord Curzon and Rab Butler, as it would make 'for a more amusing book'.

54 Harold Macmillan diary, 12 January 1956. MS Macmillan dep. d. 25, loc. cit.

55 The initial figures mooted were $200 million from the World Bank, $130 million from the USA and $80 million from Britain.

56 FO 371/119048. National Archives, Kew.

CHAPTER TWENTY

The Economic Consequences of Colonel Nasser 1956–1957

1 A remark noted in various accounts of the Suez crisis, including one of the first, Hugh Thomas, *The Suez Affair*, Weidenfeld & Nicolson, revised edition, 1986, p. 38.

2 W. Scott Lucas, *Divided We Stand: Britain, the US and The Suez Crisis*, Hodder & Stoughton paperback edition, 1996, p. 142.

3 Jonathan Pearson, *Sir Anthony Eden and the Suez Crisis: Reluctant Gamble*, Palgrave Macmillan, 2003, p. 33.

4 Sir Dermot Alexander Boyle (1904–1993), Chief of the Air Staff, 1956–1959.

5 Speech in the House of Commons, *Hansard*, 2 August 1956.

6 Though, surprisingly, he was not allowed to join in the political discussions and was left waiting in an adjoining room, much to his annoyance.

7 Winthrop Williams Aldrich (1885–1974), United States Ambassador to the Court of St

James, 1953–1957. Aldrich was a leading Republican fund-raiser and had been influential in persuading Eisenhower to run for the presidency. As a member of White's, he was the recipient of much accurate gossip about internal Conservative Party politics.

8 Iverach McDonald, *The History of 'The Times': Volume V, Struggles in War and Peace 1939–1966*, Times Books, 1986, p. 26.

9 Although tielessness was later to become fashionable, in 1956 it was almost an H. M. Bateman moment.

10 Harold Macmillan diary, 27 July 1956. MS Macmillan dep. d. 27. Macmillan Papers, Bodleian Library, Oxford.

11 Jane Austen, *Northanger Abbey*, 1818, Chapter XI.

12 FO 371/121748. National Archives, Kew. Though he was never formally a member of the Egypt Committee, Butler did later take to turning up invited, and even on occasion chaired the Committee in Eden's absence.

13 J. P. Mackintosh, *The British Cabinet*, 3rd edition, Stevens & Sons, 1977, p. 24.

14 William Clark papers, MS Eng. 4814, Bodleian Library, Oxford.

15 D. R. Thorpe, *Eden: The Life and Times of Anthony Eden First Earl of Avon, 1897–1977*, Chatto & Windus, 2003, p. 190.

16 In this Macmillan's position was analagous to that of a pre-war accountant of the Yorkshire County Cricket Club, who offered opinions on policy, only to be told by aggrieved committee members to desist, as he was 'now't but scorer'. Private information.

17 Christian Pineau (1904–1995), French wartime resistance fighter and politician. After a variety of ministerial posts, Pineau was for two days (17–19 February 1955) Prime Minister of France, but the National Assembly refused to invest his Cabinet. French Foreign Minister (February 1956–May 1958) when he signed the Sèvres Protocol for France in October 1956 and the Treaty of Rome in 1957, Pineau told the author in 1986 that as the Suez crisis reached its conclusion, the French and the British put aside earlier differences, but that afterwards they soon resurfaced.

18 The Suez Canal Convention of 1888 had been signed in Constantinople between Turkey and the European Powers and had established that 'The Suez Maritime Canal shall always be free and open, in time of war as in time of peace, to every vessel of commerce or war, without distinction of flag.'

19 Robert Murphy, *Diplomat among Warriors*, Collins, 1964, p. 462.

20 Robert Murphy to John Foster Dulles, 31 July 1956. *Foreign Relations of the United States (FRUS)*, Volume XVI, document 33.

21 Harold Macmillan diary, 30 July 1956. MS Macmillan dep. d. 27, loc. cit.

22 Murphy, op. cit., p. 467.

23 Ibid., p. 381.

24 Harold Macmillan diary, 1 August 1956. MS Macmillan dep. d. 27, loc. cit.

25 Harold Macmillan to Sir Anthony Eden, 26 September 1956. PREM 11/1102. National Archives, Kew.

26 Sir Hugh Charles Stockwell (1903–1986), always known as Hughie, Commandant of the Royal Military Academy, Sandhurst, 1948–1950; Commander of the Land Forces in Malaya, 1952; Commander of 1st British Corps, 1954–1956; Land Forces Commander in Port Said and Suez, 1956; Deputy Supreme Allied Commander, Europe, 1960–1964. The French military command did not find Stockwell an easy colleague.

27 The vast majority of Cabinet ministers in 1956 had first-hand military experience from the Second World War; some, such as Macmillan, also had experience of the Great War.

28 Sir Edward Ian Claud Jacob (1899–1993), assistant military secretary to the War Cabinet, and Cabinet, 1939–1946, Deputy Military Secretary, 1951–1952; Director-General of the BBC, 1952–1960. Jacob was a stout defender of the editorial independence of the BBC during the Suez crisis.

29 CAB 134/1216. National Archives, Kew.

30 David Ben-Gurion diary, 3 August 1956. Quoted in Selwyn Ilan Troën & Moshe Shemesh (ed.), *The Suez-Sinai Crisis 1956: Retrospective and Reappraisal*, Frank Cass, 1990, p. 292. Ben-Gurion could not have imagined at this stage his own future part in the joint venture, when the disappointment with America's response led France and Britain into murkier waters. Machiavelli once said that there was always a tension between politics and morality. If Munich was the failure of an idealistic view of foreign policy, then Suez was the opposite, where national interests had a greater priority than fulfilling a wider moral purpose.

31 Harold Macmillan diary, 3 August 1956. MS Macmillan dep. d. 27, loc. cit.

32 Arthur Christopher John, Baron Soames (1920–1987), MP for Bedford, 1950–1966; Secretary of State for War, 1958–1960; Minister of Agriculture, Fisheries and Foods, 1960–1964; British Ambassador in Paris, 1968–1972; Lord President of the Council and Leader of the House of Lords, 1979–1981; Governor of Southern Rhodesia, 1980. During Churchill's indisposition during the summer of 1953, government business was largely continued by Jock Colville and Christopher Soames.

33 Harold Macmillan diary, 5 August 1956. MS Macmillan dep. d. 27, loc. cit.

34 This may have been the impression Macmillan gleaned, but Eden remained deeply suspicious of Macmillan's conduct and motives. Private information.

35 Harold Macmillan diary, 7

August 1956. MS Macmillan dep. d. 27, loc. cit.

36 Bretton Woods was an international financial conference held in New Hampshire, USA in July 1944. The 28 nations who participated laid the foundations for the International Monetary Fund (IMF) and for a World Bank. The IMF was designed to maintain fixed exchange rates by helping member countries meet balance of payments deficits (for example, the United Kingdom in 1976) and the World Bank was intended to make loans available for major projects vital for a country's development (as, initially, for the Aswan High Dam project in Egypt in 1956).

37 Sir Robert Bridges to Harold Macmillan, 8 August 1956. T236/4188. National Archives, Kew.

38 Harold Macmillan to John Foster Dulles, 23 August 1956. *FRUS*, op. cit., Volume XVI, document 97.

39 Harold Macmillan to Sir Anthony Eden, 24 August 1956. MS Macmillan dep. c. 304, loc. cit. As a postscript, Macmillan added, in imitation of Dulles' legal jargon: 'If there is an Arabic word which means the same as "co-prosperity sphere" it would be very useful!'

40 Sir Robert Bridges to Harold Macmillan, 7 September 1956, loc. cit.

41 Harold Macmillan to Sir Robert Bridges, 10 September 1956, loc. cit.

42 FO 371/119126. National Archives, Kew.

43 Neville Chamberlain to Hilda Chamberlain, 17 December 1937. NC/18/1/1032. Neville Chamberlain papers, Birmingham University Library.

44 Cabinet Minutes, 11 September 1956. CAB 128/30, National Archives, Kew.

45 See Chapter 27.

46 Roger Makins dispatched details of Dulles' remarks on 2 October 1956. PREM 11/1174. National Archives, Kew.

47 Harold Macmillan diary, 12 September 1956. MS Macmillan dep. d. 27, loc. cit.

48 Dr David Butler to the author, 23 April 2009.

49 Harold Macmillan diary, 22 September 1956. MS Macmillan dep. d. 27, loc. cit.

50 The late Lord Sherfield to the author, July 1995.

51 Harold Macmillan to Sir Anthony Eden, 26 September 1956. PREM 11/1102. National Archives, Kew.

52 Negotiated by J. M. Keynes in 1945.

53 Harold Macmillan, *Riding the Storm: 1956–1959*, Macmillan, 1971, p. 138.

54 Harold Macmillan diary, 4 October 1956. MS Macmillan dep. d. 27, loc. cit.

55 It has been claimed that Macmillan destroyed his diaries for these months on Eden's orders. See Peter Catterall (ed.), *The Macmillan Diaries: The Cabinet Years* 1950–1957, Macmillan, 2003, p. 607. Eden gave no such orders. Macmillan mislaid Volume 24 of the blue-backed volumes shortly

after he had completed Volume 23 (up to 4 October 1956) and then genuinely was unable to resume writing nightly entries owing to the pressure of events. Harold Macmillan diary, 3 February 1957. MS Macmillan dep. d. 28, loc. cit. Although 'conspiracy' theories can be superficially attractive, in this instance there was no cover-up. It would not have been in Eden's interests to have suppressed a primary source of the day-to-day events from such an important participant, nor was it in his character to require a colleague to do such a thing.

56 Dr Mahmoud Fawzi (1900–1981), Egyptian Foreign Minister, 1952–1958; Prime Minister, 1970–1972; Vice President of Egypt, 1972–1974. Macmillan regarded Fawzi as a very slippery customer, but Selwyn Lloyd established a cordial working relationship.

57 Terence Robertson, *Crisis: The Inside Story of the Suez Conspiracy*, Hutchinson, 1965, p. 144.

58 The late Lord Home of the Hirsel to the author, June 1990.

59 SELO 129 (1). Selwyn Lloyd papers, Churchill College, Cambridge.

60 See D. R. Thorpe, *Selwyn Lloyd*, Jonathan Cape, 1989, pp. 229–40, for a full account based on Selwyn Lloyd's papers.

61 Harold Macmillan diary, 3 August 1956. MS Macmillan dep. d. 27, loc. cit.

62 See D. R. Thorpe, *Eden: The Life and Times of Anthony Eden*

First Earl of Avon 1897–1977, Chatto & Windus, 2003, pp. 513–19 and 585–9.

63 Andrew Roberts, *A History of the English-Speaking Peoples since 1900*, Weidenfeld & Nicolson, 2006, p. 432.

64 Robert Blake, Eden chapter, in J. P. Mackintosh (ed.), *British Prime Ministers in the Twentieth Century, Volume 2: Churchill to Callaghan*, Weidenfeld & Nicolson, 1978, pp. 112–13.

65 In an article in the *Evening Standard* on 10 January 1957.

66 Russell Braddon, *Suez: Splitting of a Nation*, Collins, 1973, p. 11.

67 Private information.

68 Following a severe accident to his hand as a child in India, Rab had been largely disqualified from team games. His lack of athleticism was well known. In the early 1960s one of Butler's secretaries was the future Cabinet Secretary, Robin (later Lord) Butler, an Oxford rugby blue. Letters addressed to R. Butler had a habit in Whitehall of landing on the wrong Butler's desk. Rab decreed that all communications ambiguously addressed to R. Butler should come to him first. One such note read 'You have been selected to play in the Harlequins first XV on Saturday. Please be at Twickenham by 1.30 p.m.' Rab Butler sent this on to Robin Butler with a covering note, 'I am afraid I am not available on Saturday. Please could you deputize for me?' Private information.

69 Harold Macmillan diary, 19 August 1953. MS Macmillan dep. d. 13, loc. cit.

70 Harold Macmillan diary, 19 August 1956. MS Macmillan dep. d. 27, loc. cit.

71 *FRUS*, op. cit., pp. 1150–2.

72 Ibid., p. 1163.

73 The definitive account of Eden's health is given by David Owen in his book *In Sickness and in Power: Illness in Heads of Government during the last* 100 *years*, Methuen, 2008, pp. 109–40. Eden's full medical records were previously made available only to Sir Robert Rhodes James and the present author for their respective biographies of Eden, but Lord Owen was the first medic to have access.

74 Horace, Baron Evans of Merthyr Tydfil (1903–1963), physician to Queen Mary, 1946–1953; to King George VI, 1949–1952; and to Queen Elizabeth II from 1952 until his death in 1963.

75 *FRUS*, op. cit., p. 1152.

76 Mark Amory (ed.), *The Letters of Ann Fleming*, Collins Harvill, 1985, p. 188.

77 Record of Aldrich-Hoover telephone conversations. *FRUS*, op. cit., p. 1163.

78 Winthrop Aldrich, Telegram 2814 to the Department of State, 19 November 1956. *FRUS*, op. cit., p. 1163.

79 Cole C. Kingseed, *Eisenhower and the Suez Crisis of* 1956, Louisiana State University Press, Baton Rouge, 1995, p. 140.

80 Ann Whitman diaries, Box 19, November 1956. Eisenhower Papers, Eisenhower Library, Abilene, Texas.

81 Steven Z. Freiberger, *Dawn Over Suez: The Rise of American Power in the Middle East,* 1953–1957, Ivan R. Dee, Chicago, 1992, fn, p. 266.

82 Brendan Bracken to Lord Beaverbrook, 7 December 1956. Beaverbrook Papers, House of Lords Record Office, File BK C/17. Beaverbrook was a lurking presence throughout the Suez crisis, keen to know all the 'drama'. Even the fierce guard dog at Goldeneye, Eden's retreat, was called Max after the press lord.

83 *Hansard*, 22 November 1956.

84 As Jane Austen observed of Mrs Bennet in Chapter One of *Pride and Prejudice* when Mrs Bennet's husband gave her *carte blanche* to tell him her views. Macmillan was to be reading *Pride and Prejudice* on 10 January 1957 when he received the summons to Buckingham Palace.

85 Philip Goodhart, *The* 1922: *The Story of the Conservative Backbenchers' Parliamentary Committee*, Macmillan, 1973, p. 175.

86 Simon Heffer, *Like the Roman: The Life of Enoch Powell*, Weidenfeld & Nicolson, 1998, p. 210.

87 Charles Ian, Baron Orr-Ewing (1912–1999), MP for North Hendon, 1950–1970.

88 Quoted in Alan Thompson, *The Day Before Yesterday*, Sidgwick & Jackson, 1971, p. 161.

89 Frederick Edwin, First Earl of Birkenhead (1872–1930), MP for Walton, 1906–1918, West Derby, 1918–1919; Lord

Chancellor, 1919–1922. Smith made his remark about the glittering prizes during his rectorial address at Glasgow University, 7 November 1923. Macmillan had recently supported Butler in his successful bid to become Rector of Glasgow University. When Butler was installed as rector he was infamously pelted with tomatoes and flour bombs, and drenched with fire extinguishers. In 1959 Macmillan was mooted as Butler's successor; unsurprisingly Butler advised him to steer well clear of standing.

90 CAB 128/30. National Archives, Kew.

91 Ibid.

92 Lord Moran diary, 26 November 1956. Lord Moran, *Winston Churchill: The Struggle for Survival* 1940–1965, Sphere paperback edition, 1968, p. 743.

93 Sir Guy Millard interview with Dr Jonathan Pearson, 25 February 1998. Pearson, op. cit., p. 33. Sir Guy Millard expressed the same views to the author on more than one occasion.

94 This theory is considered in a balanced manner by Anthony Sampson. Anthony Sampson, *Macmillan: A Study in Ambiguity*, Penguin Books, Harmondsworth, 1967, p. 123.

95 Thomas, op. cit., p. 138.

96 Lady Eden diary, 14 December 1956, Countess of Avon Papers.

97 Lord Cobbold to Harold Macmillan, 20 December 1956. G15/19. Bank of England Archive.

98 Quoted in Percy Cradock, *Know*

Your Enemy: How the Joint Intelligence Committee Saw the World, John Murray, 2002, p. 132.

99 Sir Charles Keightley memorandum of 12 November 1956. AIR 8/1940. National Archives, Kew.

100 Brendan Bracken to Lord Beaverbrook, 23 January 1957. Beaverbrook Papers, loc. cit., File BK C/17.

101 T 172/2152. National Archives, Kew.

102 Harold Macmillan to Sir Anthony Eden, 4 January 1957. CAB 129/84. National Archives, Kew.

103 CAB 129/84, loc. cit.

104 Salisbury's record of the events regarding the change of Prime Minister are recorded in '1957': Manuscript Memorandum by the 5th Marquess of Salisbury. Salisbury Papers, Hatfield House. File B: 1956–1960.

105 Sir Anthony Eden to Sir Winston Churchill, 9 January 1957. Chartwell Papers, Churchill College, Cambridge, 2/216.

106 Sir Anthony Eden, Note on Resignation Audience. AP 20/33/12A. Avon Papers, loc. cit.

107 Robert Blake, notice of Anthony Eden's life, *Dictionary of National Biography*, 1971–1980, Oxford University Press, 1986, p. 271.

108 The Earl of Kilmuir, *Political Adventure: The Memoirs of the Earl of Kilmuir*, Weidenfeld & Nicolson, 1964. Opponents of Kilmuir declared the memoirs

were so inaccurate that the author even left the letter 'r' off the second word of the book's title.

109 The Earl of Avon to Sir Michael Adeane, 27 November 1970. AP 23/2/20A. Avon Papers, loc. cit.

110 Vernon Bogdanor, *The Monarchy and the Constitution*, Clarendon Press, Oxford, 1995, fn p. 94.

111 D. R. Thorpe, notice of Anthony Eden's life, *Oxford Dictionary of National Biography Volume* 17, Oxford University Press, 2004, p. 677.

112 See D. R. Thorpe, *The Uncrowned Prime Ministers*, Darkhorse Publishing, 1980, pp. 142–51.

113 Lady Eden to R. A. Butler, 10 January 1957. Quoted in Lord Butler, *The Art of the Possible: The Memoirs of Lord Butler*, revised paperback edition, Penguin Books, Harmondsworth, 1973, p. 197.

114 Anthony Howard, *RAB: The Life of R. A. Butler*, Jonathan Cape, 1987, fn p. 248.

115 Salisbury memorandum '1957', loc. cit. Other Salisbury quotations are also from this memorandum.

116 Kilmuir also gives details of these meetings in his memoirs, op. cit., pp. 285–6.

117 Björn Prytz (1887–1976), Swedish diplomat and businessman, Swedish Minister in London, 1938–1947. Anti-appeasement Tories never forgave Rab Butler for what they saw as his 'lukewarm'

attitude amounting to defeatism in his talk with Prytz. Thomas Munch-Petersen has written an account of the episode. See his article '"Common Sense Not Bravado": The Butler-Prytz Interview of 17 June 1940', *Scandia*, 52:1 (1986). The present author also considered the issue in a letter to *The Times*, 9 May 1997, written at the request of the late Lady Butler of Saffron Walden.

118 The late Lord Amery of Lustleigh to the author, 6 February 1975.

119 Alan Thompson, *The Day Before Yesterday*, Granada Publishing, 1971, p. 161.

120 Michael Edward, Baron Adeane (1910–1984), Principal Private Secretary to the Queen, 1954–1972. Adeane was the son-in-law of Lord Stamfordham, Private Secretary to King George V, when Stanley Baldwin was preferred to Lord Curzon as Prime Minister by the monarch. Uniquely, Adeane was the monarch's Private Secretary when two such choices had to be made, in January 1957 and in October 1963.

121 Martin Gilbert, *'Never Despair' Winston S. Churchill*, 1945–1965, Heinemann, 1988, p. 1227.

122 The late Lord Amery of Lustleigh to the author, 6 February 1975.

123 Harold Macmillan, *Riding the Storm 1956–1959*, Macmillan, 1971, p. 184.

124 Private information.

125 *Henry IV Part 2*, 4, 3, 314

126 Points he was to make to Mrs Thatcher at the outbreak of the Falklands conflict in 1982. Private information. Anthony Sampson, as has been seen, considered the overall 'Machiavellian' charge to be unfounded in his biography of Macmillan in 1967. Alistair Horne, in the first volume of his official life of Macmillan in 1988, gives a comprehensive overview of the charge from the point of view of both critics and supporters of Macmillan. His view is rightly that such a charge is unsustainable. Alistair Horne, *Macmillan 1894–1956: Volume 1 of the Official Biography*, Macmillan, 1988, p. 453.

127 William Roger Louis, 'Harold Macmillan and the Middle East Crisis of 1956', *Proceedings of the British Academy*, 94, 207–28 (1996).

128 Diana M. Kunz, *The Economic Diplomacy of the Suez Crisis*, University of North Carolina Press, Chapel Hill and London, 1991, pp. 132 and 205.

129 Copies in MS Macmillan dep. c. 305, loc. cit. The figures did not always show a reversal. In the week of 11 September 1956, for instance, the reserves actually increased by $133 million.

130 Reported to Keith Kyle by Marshal of Royal Air Force Sir William Dickson. Keith Kyle, *Suez*, Weidenfeld & Nicolson, 1991, p. 440. The remark is also quoted in Selwyn Lloyd, *Suez 1956: A Personal Account*, Jonathan Cape, 1988, p. 206.

131 Pearson, op. cit., p. 163.

132 The Dickensian reference is to Joe, the fat boy in Chapter 8 of *The Pickwick Papers*, who wanted to make old Mrs Wardle's flesh creep by telling her that her spinster daughter, Rachael, had been seen kissing Mr Tupman. Memorandum, 2 January 1956. MS Macmillan dep. c. 306. loc. cit.

133 Sir Harold Anthony Nutting, third baronet (1920–1999), MP for the Melton division of Leicestershire, 1945–1956. Nutting was one of the great white hopes of the post-war Conservative Party, even dubbed 'Eden's Eden'. Ironically he was to follow the path of resignation Eden had taken in February 1938; the difference was that Nutting resigned his seat over Suez and never returned to the Commons. Harold Macmillan told him his reticence in not making the customary resignation speech in the Commons, which could have involved mentioning 'collusion', would one day bring him the leadership of the party. See obituary of Sir Anthony Nutting by D. R. Thorpe, *Independent*, 3 March 1999.

134 Nor did Lord Home, in an even narrower window, six years later. See Chapter 29.

135 Private information. The book was *The Conservatives: A History from their Origins to*

1965, George Allen & Unwin, 1977, edited by Butler, who also contributed a foreword and an epilogue.

136 The late Lord Butler of Saffron Walden to the author, 20 November 1975.

137 In response to an interviewer's question at London Airport on 8 January 1956. When Sir Michael (later Lord) Fraser retired as chairman of the Conservative Research Department in 1974, Butler said there was no one's leaving dinner he would rather attend.

138 Anthony Eden, *Full Circle*, Cassell, 1960, p. 557.

CHAPTER TWENTY ONE

Rebuilding 1957

1 Brighton & Hove Albion narrowly missed promotion in the 1956–1957 season, but were promoted as champions the next season, the year the Queen opened the new extensions to Gatwick Airport.

2 Edward Heath, *The Course of My Life: My Autobiography*, Hodder & Stoughton, 1998, p. 176.

3 John Campbell, *Edward Heath: A Biography*, Jonathan Cape, 1993, p. 99.

4 The late Sir Edward Heath to the author, 4 March 1999.

5 *The Times*, 6 June 2005. To anyone inheriting the post of a formidable predecessor, he would often add, 'A bit like going in to bat after Bradman.'

6 Harold Macmillan diary, 3

February 1957. MS Macmillan dep. d. 28, Macmillan Papers, Bodleian Library, Oxford.

7 Harold Macmillan, *Riding the Storm: 1956–1959*, Macmillan, 1971, p. 186.

8 John Campbell, *Pistols at Dawn: Two Hundred Years of Political Rivalry from Pitt & Fox to Blair & Brown*, Jonathan Cape, 2009, p. 245.

9 A reference to the character in W. S. Gilbert's *The Mikado*, who holds several different offices at once.

10 D. R. Thorpe, *Selwyn Lloyd*, Jonathan Cape, 1989, p. 271.

11 Ibid., p. 268.

12 Selwyn Lloyd diary, 11 January 1957. SELO 88 (3). Selwyn Lloyd Papers, Churchill College, Cambridge.

13 Thorpe, op. cit., p. 1.

14 One weekend when Selwyn Lloyd and his daughter Joanna were staying with Rab and Mollie Butler, Lloyd was anxious to locate the whereabouts of a television so that Joanna could watch *Robin Hood*. As the clock moved to the appointed hour, Butler said, 'You don't have to go Joanna, we know who really wants to see it.' Thorpe, op. cit., p. 440.

15 William David Ormsby-Gore, fifth Baron Harlech (1918–1985), Conservative MP for Oswestry, 1950–1961; Minister of State at the Foreign Office, 1957–1961; British Ambassador to the United States, 1961–1965. Ormsby-Gore was considered the 11th member of Kennedy's Cabinet, and was uniquely

qualified to be the hyphen that joined and the buckle that fastened the worlds of Camelot and Birch Grove. His part in re-establishing 'the special relationship' between Britain and America was of supreme importance.

16 Commander Sir Allan Herbert Percy Noble (1908–1982), Conservative MP for Chelsea, 1945–1959; Minister of State at the Foreign Office, 1956–1959. Like so many of his political generation, particularly Conservatives who entered the House of Commons for the first time in 1945, Noble had had 'a good war'.

17 Ian Harvey (1914–1987), Conservative MP Harrow East, 1950–1958; Joint Parliamentary Under-Secretary at the Foreign Office, 1957–1958. Harrow East has proved something of an unlucky constituency for a few MPs. Harvey's book *To Fall Like Lucifer* (1971) gave a frank account of the scandal that brought him down. At a time when homosexuality was illegal in Britain, and the Lord Chancellor, Lord Kilmuir, was encouraging high-profile prosecutions of publicly known homosexuals, the implications of Harvey's downfall had serious implications for homosexual members of Macmillan's Cabinet. Macmillan himself could have been implicated by association, as Harvey was an Anglo-Catholic intimate of Ronald Knox, who had introduced him to Macmillan.

See Simon Ball, *The Guardsmen: Harold Macmillan, Three Friends, and the World They Made*, Harper Collins, 2004, p. 340.

18 When Churchill heard of the scandal he remarked, 'And on the coldest night of the year too; makes one proud to be British.'

19 Alec Cairncross (ed.), *The Robert Hall Diaries 1954–1961*, Unwin Hyman, 1991, p. 94.

20 G. C. Peden, *The Treasury and British Public Policy, 1906–1959*, Oxford University Press, 2000, p. 487.

21 Alan Clark, *The Tories: Conservatives and the Nation State 1922–1997*, Weidenfeld & Nicolson, 1998, p. 387.

22 Iain Norman Macleod (1913–1970), Conservative MP for Enfield West, 1950–1970. After war service - he landed in Normandy on D-Day - Macleod cut his political teeth in the Conservative Research Department in opposition. An original member of the 'One Nation' group of Conservatives, he was soon spotted as a rising talent by Churchill, who made him Health Minister, 1952–1955. Subsequently, Macleod served as Minister of Labour, 1955–1959; Colonial Secretary, 1959–1961; Chancellor of the Duchy of Lancaster, 1961–1963; and Conservative Party chairman, 1961–1963. He died in harness as Chancellor of the Exchequer in June 1970 after only four weeks in office.

23 Derick Heathcoat, first Viscount Amory (1899–1981).

Conservative MP for Tiverton, 1945–1960); Minister of Pensions, 1951–1953; Minister of State, Board of Trade, 1953–1954; Minister for Agriculture, Fisheries and Food, 1954–1958; Chancellor of the Exchequer, 1958–1960. Just as his successor at the Treasury, Selwyn Lloyd, thought that he had been confused with another MP (Geoffrey Lloyd) on being appointed to the government by Churchill in 1951, so Amory thought Churchill had intended to promote Julian Amery. The inn sign of a Northallerton pub - 'The Jolly Minister' - depicts him on horseback as Minister of Agriculture.

24 Macmillan, op. cit., p. 203.

25 Harold Macmillan to Arthur Macmillan, 11 February 1957. MS Macmillan dep. c. 321, loc. cit. Arthur Macmillan had published *What is Christian Marriage?* (Macmillan & Co., 1944) and had a special interest in matters of Church doctrine.

26 See Peter J. Beck, '"The Less Said about Suez": British Governments and the Politics of Suez's History, 1956–1967', *The English Historical Review*, Vol. CXXIV, No. 508, June 2009.

27 Harold Macmillan to Lord Lansdowne, 5 February 1957. MS Macmillan dep. c. 337, loc. cit.

28 Nigel John Ashton, 'Harold Macmillan and the "Golden Days" of Anglo-American relations revisited, 1957–1963', *Diplomatic History* 29 (4), Blackwell, 2005, p. 7.

29 A. E. Holmans, *Demand Management in Britain 1953–1958*, Institute of Contemporary British History, 1999, p. 172.

30 Seth Pecksniff was an unctuous and hypocritical character in Dickens' *Martin Chuzzlewit*; Obadiah Slope was an oleaginous and ambitious vicar in Trollope's *The Warden* and *Barchester Towers*.

31 Lord Home of the Hirsel to the author, 9 August 1990.

32 Nigel Fisher, *Harold Macmillan: A Biography*, Weidenfeld & Nicolson, 1982, p. 182.

33 The late Lord Franks to the author, 1986.

34 'Events, dear boy, events' became one of his most famous sayings.

35 Sir Harold Evans Bt (1911–1983), public relations adviser to the Prime Minister, 1957–1964. Not to be confused with his namesake, also Sir Harold, editor of *The Times* and *Sunday Times*. Harold Evans was to publish a diary of his time with Macmillan, *Downing Street Diary: The Macmillan Years, 1957–1963*, Hodder & Stoughton, 1981, an invaluable guide to the atmosphere of those years.

36 Wyndham had been with Macmillan when he was Chancellor, but left whilst issues regarding death duties on Petworth House were resolved, so that there could be no conflict of interest.

37 Robert Alexander, Baron Allan of Kilmahew (1914–1919), MP for South Paddington, 1951–1966; PPS to the

Prime Minister 1955–1958. Anthony Perrinott Lysberg, Baron Barber of Wentbridge (1920–2005), MP for Doncaster, 1951–1964, Altrincham and Sale, 1965–1974; Minister of Health, 1963–1964; Chancellor of the Exchequer, 1970–1974. Sir Samuel Knox Cunningham, Bt (1909–1976), MP (Ulster Unionist), 1955–1970; PPS to the Prime Minister, 1959–1963. Knox Cunningham, like Robert Allan, was a graduate of Clare College, where both won blues, Cunningham, as the university's heavyweight boxing champion. He was a loyal benefactor to his alma mater, Fettes College, and in 1967 became the 'Visitor' to a new boarding house, one of whose members was Tony Blair, the future Prime Minister. The house, a modern concrete structure, was soon dubbed Fort Knox.

38 The Eisenhower Doctrine was a new departure in American foreign policy, named after the President's message to Congress on 5 January 1957, which recommended that American forces should protect Middle East countries against threats from any nation 'controlled by international Communism'. The doctrine did not survive the death in May 1959 of Dulles, who had formulated its details, underestimating the reaction of Arab nationalism to outside intervention.

39 Harold Macmillan to Sir Anthony Eden, 17 February 1957. MS Macmillan dep. c.

320, loc. cit.

40 Macmillan told Waugh that the Order of Merit was in the gift of the monarch and not subject to a submission from the Prime Minister. Nevertheless, Macmillan did try, unsuccessfully, to secure the OM for A. L. Rowse in 1960. MS Macmillan dep. c. 319, loc. cit. Waugh's biography of Knox was published on the day of the 1959 general election, a time therefore of double celebration for Macmillan.

41 Macmillan, op. cit., p. 195.

42 Ibid., p. 196.

43 The epithet Harold Nicolson and Vita Sackville-West used to describe anything they thought 'common'.

44 The terms of the original Chequers Trust laid down a list of alternative tenants in the event that Chequers was not needed by the Prime Minister. This designated hierarchy was headed by the Chancellor of the Exchequer and the Foreign Secretary.

45 The author is grateful to Lady Thatcher for arranging private tours of both 10 Downing Street and Chequers in 1986.

46 Richard Hoggart, *The Uses of Literacy*, Pelican paperback edition, Harmondsworth, 1958, p. 285.

47 Raymond Williams, *Culture and Society: 1780–1950*, Pelican paperback edition, Harmondsworth, 1961, pp. 310–11.

48 It was once said of one of these films that it must have been a

very early one, as the ubiquitous actor Nigel Patrick was only a second lieutenant.

49 This may not have been the most efficient way of organising finances, but the spirit of Micawber's warning about debt was still abroad in the land.

50 M. J. Barnett, *Politics of Legislation: The Rent Act of* 1957, Weidenfeld & Nicolson, 1969, pp. 252–3. Barnett's critical account shows clearly how the unintended consequences of the Rent Act actually reduced availability of housing, especially in London.

51 'Rachmanism' entered the Oxford English Dictionary as a definition of the unscrupulous exploitation of poor and vulnerable tenants, often immigrants. The name derived from the notorious practices of Peter Rachman (1919–1962) in the late 1950s.

52 Paul Barker's *The Freedoms of Suburbia*, Frances Lincoln, 2009, is a paean to the place where 84% of Britains now live, giving 'most people what they want most of the time, at a price they can afford', ibid, pp. 15–17

53 'Commonwealth Immigrants', Lord Hailsham memorandum, 20 June 1958. CAB 129/93. National Archives, Kew.

54 Harold Macmillan diary, 22 November 1961. MS Macmillan dep. d. 44, loc. cit. Macmillan's diaries are littered with disobliging references to the Labour leader, Hugh Gaitskell, whom he loathed. His published memoirs 'sanitise' this feeling.

55 Michael Dunlop, Baron Young of Dartington (1915–2002), sociologist, first chairman of the National Consumers' Association. *The Rise of the Meritocracy* considered the implications for society, analysed by Plato in *The Republic*, of what happens when children are moved upwards - towards the ranks of the Guardians - according to their merit and capability. It was then incumbent upon the identified and successful to work for the interests of the whole community.

56 Michael Young, *The Rise of the Meritocracy*, Pelican paperback edition, Harmondsworth, 1958, p. 140. The three seminal publications by Raymond Williams, Richard Hoggart and Michael Young in 1957–1958 certainly justified Pelican's advertising slogan 'Pelicans, as you'd expect/Suit the adult intellect.'

57 Richard Dimbleby (1913–1965), the most famous broadcaster of his day, inextricably linked with national occasions such as the Coronation, the State Opening of Parliament and royal weddings and funerals. During the 1962 Cuban Missile Crisis, a mother rang the BBC to seek Dimbleby's reassurance that it would be safe for her children to go to school the next day. Only then would she allow them to do so.

58 The nickname by which the BBC was known, first affectionately, later pejoratively.

59 The Butlin's holiday camps were satirised in the BBC television comedy series *Hi-de-Hi!*, first broadcast on 1 January 1980. The opening film credits for the programme featured Macmillan at his count at Bromley in the 1959 general election.

60 The Lord's Day Observance Society made its presence strongly felt in the 1950s. Complaints were registered when Peter Thorneycroft, the Chancellor of the Exchequer, gave the Queen his private briefing on the 1957 Budget on a Sunday, as the Queen was departing for a state visit to France on the Monday. Thorneycroft, a committed Christian, had attended morning service at his local church, as, of course, had the Queen. The Lord's Day Observance Society nevertheless asserted that he should have visited Windsor on the Saturday.

61 *At the Drop of a Hat* (1962). The affectionate and gentle review of Michael Flanders (1922–1975) and Donald Swann (1923–1994) was on the verge of being superseded by much sharper satire. When Flanders and Swann staged *At the Drop of Another Hat* in 1967, they observed that since their first show the hypocrisies of society had been stripped bare of their comforting veneer, and that it was obviously time for them to put the veneer back again. Flanders and Swann would never have portrayed a Chancellor of the Exchequer (Reginald Maudling) ending a meeting with the unemployed by saying, 'Well, I've got work to go to, even if you haven't', as *That Was the Week That Was* did in 1963.

62 One such cartoon at the time of the Mods and Rockers confrontations showed Maudie Littlehampton, armed with a machine gun, behind a barbed-wire barricade on Brighton sea front. 'But Colonel,' she said to the commanding officer, 'they have no whites to their eyes.' There was an underlying class element to these riots. The 'Mods', on scooters, were by and large middle class grammar-school-educated; the 'Rockers', on motorcycles, were working class. It was not just Capulets v. Montagues.

63 Harold Macmillan to Michael Fraser, 17 February 1957. PREM 11/1816. National Archives, Kew.

64 Harold Macmillan to Peter Thorneycroft, 22 January 1957. T172/2152. National Archives, Kew.

65 PREM 11/1768. National Archives, Kew.

66 John Braine (1922–1986), one of the disparate group of 'Angry Young Men' of the late fifties. His novel *Room at the Top* portrayed the upward progress of the ambitious working-class hero, Joe Lampton.

67 5p in decimal coinage.

68 Such transfers were not unknown. Sir Ian (later Lord) Bancroft followed Rab Butler round many Whitehall departments, at Butler's request.

The late Lord Bancroft to the author, July 1975.

69 Sir Roger Makins to John Foster Dulles, 19 July 1956. State Department Decimal Files, Box 2305.

70 Sir Harold Caccia to Sir Ivone Kirkpatrick, 22 January 1957. PREM 11/1835. National Archives, Kew.

71 Sir Harold Caccia to Harold Macmillan, 1 February 1957. PREM 11/1835, loc. cit.

72 Sir Norman Brook to Harold Macmillan, 6 February 1957. PREM 11/1835, loc. cit.

73 Harold Macmillan to Sir Anthony Eden, 17 February 1957, loc. cit.

74 Quoted in John Dickie, *'Special' No More, Anglo-American Relations: Rhetoric and Reality*, Weidenfeld & Nicolson, 1994, p. 98.

75 Joseph and Stewart Alsop, *The Reporter's Trade*, Bodley Head, 1960, p. 332.

76 S. J. Ball, 'Banquo's Ghost: Lord Salisbury, Harold Macmillan, and the High Politics of Decolonization, 1957–1963', *Twentieth Century British History*, Vol. 16, No. 1, 2005, p. 79.

77 Lord Salisbury to Sir Anthony Eden, 23 July 1957. AP23/60. Avon Papers, Birmingham University Library.

78 Salisbury was Macmillan's cousin by marriage. Anthony Sampson, *The Anatomy of Britain*, Hodder & Stoughton, 1962, p. 325.

79 Howard Brenton, *Never So Good*, Nick Hern Books, 2008,
p. 5.

80 Lady Robert Cecil, 6 April 1923. Quoted in Kenneth Rose, *The Later Cecils*, Weidenfeld & Nicolson, 1975, p. 33.

81 Lord Randolph Churchill had resigned from the government of Bobbety Salisbury's grandfather, the 'great' Lord Salisbury, 3rd Marquess, believing he was indispensable and irreplaceable. Salisbury promptly appointed George Goschen as Chancellor of the Exchequer, which led Churchill to say that he had 'forgot Goschen', just as surely as Napoleon had 'forgot Blücher'.

82 Harold Macmillan to Lord Salisbury, 29 March 1957. MS Macmillan dep. c. 320, loc. cit.

83 Harold Macmillan diary, 31 March 1957 MS Macmillan dep. d. 28, loc. cit.

84 Philip M. Williams, *Hugh Gaitskell: A Political Biography*, Jonathan Cape, 1979, p. 453.

85 Harold Macmillan diary, 15 May 1957. MS Macmillan d. 28, loc. cit.

86 Harold Macmillan diary, 17 May 1957. Ibid.

87 Lord Egremont, *Wyndham and Children First*, Macmillan, 1968, p. 161.

88 Harold Macmillan to Colonel Evans-Loube, 29 May 1957. MS Macmillan dep. c. 320, loc. cit.

89 *The Times*, 6 July 1957.

90 In addition to Howard Brenton's play, *Never So Good*, op. cit., Peter Hennessy wrote *Having it So Good: Britain in the Fifties*, Allen Lane, 2006, and Dominic Sandbrook, *Never Had it So*

Good: A History of Britain from Suez to the Beatles, Little Brown, 2005.

91 In an interview with *Woman's Own* magazine, 31 October 1957. The speech was routinely condemned as 'uncaring'. Its message was in fact the complete opposite.

92 Interview with Dr David Butler, 9 July 1964. David Butler Archive, Nuffield College Oxford.

93 As in 1931, 1949 and, a further 18 years on, in 1967.

94 'Candy floss' was a mass of spun sugar, often in bright colours, wrapped round a stick, a confection popular in the 1950s, to the despair of dentists.

95 The speech has not been published in full. The material in Simon Heffer, *Great British Speeches*, Quercus, 2007, pp. 200–2, is only a short extract. To read the complete speech, from the actual cards Macmillan used to deliver it (MS Macmillan dep. c. 740, loc. cit.) was an unforgettable 'archive' moment.

96 'The Crazy Gang', comprising Bud Flanagan, Chesney Allen, Jimmy Nervo, Teddy Knox, Charlie Naughton, Jimmy Gold and 'Monsewer' Eddie Gray, flourished as popular review artists from 1931 to 1962. Their combination of vulgarity and sentimentality was immensely popular. In July 1961, Bud Flanagan was to be a guest at one of the Queen's Buckingham Palace lunches. A fellow guest was the first man in space, the Russian Yuri Gagarin. (See

Chapter 27.)

97 *Indianapolis Star*, 21 July 1957.

98 SELO 314 (2). Selwyn Lloyd Papers, Churchill College, Cambridge.

99 A course that could have hosted the Open Championship had it not been for its geographical remoteness.

100 The same was true with the decade of visits of the Blairs to Balmoral. Eventually the Queen took to inviting mutual friends to make up a house party to ease things along. Private information.

101 Harold Macmillan diary, 1 September 1957. MS Macmillan dep. d. 29, loc. cit.

102 Harold Macmillan diary, 16 August 1957 and 20 August 1957. Ibid.

103 'Sputnik' meant travelling companion.

104 In Shakespeare's *A Midsummer Night's Dream*, Puck boasted that he could put a girdle round the earth in 40 minutes.

105 Harold Macmillan diary, 23 October 1957, MS Macmillan dep. d. 30, loc. cit.

106 Harold Macmillan to President Dwight D. Eisenhower, 10 October 1957. PREM 11/2461. National Archives, Kew.

107 Quoted in Dickie, op. cit., p. 100.

108 Published as Appendix Three in Macmillan, op. cit., pp. 756–9.

109 *Hansard*, 5 November 1957.

110 Sir Roy Harrod to Harold Macmillan, 7 September 1957. PREM 11/2973. National Archives, Kew.

111 The late Sir Alec Cairncross

to the author, 1986. Sir Alexander Kirkland Cairncross (1911–1998), economist and government adviser. After important wartime service in the Cabinet Office, the Board of Trade and the Ministry of Aircraft Production, Cairncross became Professor of Applied Economics at Glasgow University, 1951–1961; Chief Economic Adviser and Head of the Treasury's Economic Section, 1961–1964; head of the Government Economic Service, 1964–1967; and Master of St Peter's College, Oxford, 1969–1978.

112 Quoted in David Kynaston, *The City of London, Volume IV: A Club No More*, 1945–2000, Chatto & Windus, 2001, p. 87.

113 G 3/10, 18 October 1957. Bank of England Archives.

114 William George, Baron Penney (1909–1991), mathematical physicist, first came to prominence with his scientific advice on the D-Day landings. As the Attlee government explored the possibility of developing the atom bomb, Penney, who had seen the devastation at Nagasaki, became Chief Superintendent of Armament Research on 1 January 1946. The nuclear reactor at Windscale had been commissioned the previous month. Penney was instrumental in the development of both the British A-bomb and the H-bomb. He was Macmillan's chief adviser on nuclear policy and attended Macmillan's summits with both Eisenhower and Kennedy.

115 Harold Macmillan diary, 30 October 1957. MS Macmillan dep. d. 28, loc. cit. The report was published as a White Paper, *Accident at Windscale No. 1 Pile on 10 October 1957*, Cmnd 302 (HMSO, November 1957).

116 Peter Jay, notice of the life of Edwin, Baron Plowden, *Oxford Dictionary of National Biography 2001–2004*, Oxford University Press, Oxford, 2009, p. 845.

117 Harold Macmillan diary, 24 August 1957, MS Macmillan dep. d. 29, loc. cit.

118 Anthony Trollope, *The Prime Minister*, 1876, Chapter LXXX.

119 'The Economic Situation', Prime Minister's Memorandum, 1 September 1957. CAB 129/88. National Archives, Kew.

CHAPTER TWENTY TWO

Local Difficulties and Wider Visions 1958

1 *The Economist*, 19 May 1956.

2 *Financial Times*, 30 July 1957.

3 Lionel Leonard, Baron Cohen of Birkenhead (1888–1973), judge, one of the great and the good of his generation, whose services were indispensable to successive governments for tribunals and Royal Commissions. He headed the

Council on Prices, Productivity and Incomes from 1957–1959. The other two members were Sir Harold Howitt and Sir Dennis Robertson. Sir Harold Howitt, MC (1886–1969), accountant, believed that the existence of the CBI and the TUC meant some form of regulation of the industrial economy was the price that had to be paid for full employment.

4 G. D. N. Worswick and P. H. Ady (ed.), *The British Economy in the Nineteen-Fifties*, Clarendon Press, Oxford, 1962, p. 55.

5 Sir Dennis Home Robertson (1890–1963), economist, Sir Ernest Cassell Professor of Economy in the University of London, 1939–1944; adviser to HM Treasury, 1939–1944; and Professor of Political Economy at the University of Cambridge, 1944–1957. As a thoroughgoing Keynesian sceptic, Robertson was a key influence on Thorneycroft's deflationary policies. Initially a supervisee and friend of Keynes, they diverged in the 1930s after Robertson wrote a dismissive review of *The General Theory*. Keynes encouraged his followers, particularly Joan Robinson and Richard Kahn, though there were others, to attack Robertson. He thus became an isolated and academically sidelined figure in post-war Cambridge after Keynes' death, even when holding the chair of economics at the university. However, Robertson was highly regarded in the City and was a great supporter of the Bank of England's policy of 'sound finance'.

6 Simon Heffer, *Like the Roman: The Life of Enoch Powell*, Weidenfeld & Nicolson, 1998, p. 232.

7 Harold Macmillan to Sir Anthony Eden, 29 September 1957. MS Macmillan dep. c. 310, Macmillan Papers, Bodleian Library, Oxford.

8 Peter Thorneycroft to Harold Macmillan, 30 July 1957. HF 396/01. National Archives, Kew.

9 Harold Macmillan diary, 31 January 1958. MS Macmillan dep. d. 30, loc. cit. Edward Heath, *The Course of My Life*, Hodder & Stoughton, 1998, p. 186.

10 John ffforde, *The Bank of England and Public Policy, 1941–1958*, Cambridge University Press, Cambridge, 1992, p. 586.

11 G. C. Peden, *The Treasury and British Public Policy, 1906–1959*, Oxford University Press, Oxford, 2000, pp. 486–7. For Powell's influential role in the Thorneycroft resignation, see Heffer, op. cit., pp. 217–34.

12 Harold Macmillan to Margaret Thatcher, 20 August 1980. MS Macmillan dep. c. 571, loc. cit.

13 Robert Hall diary, 22 October 1957. Alec Cairncross (ed.), *The Robert Hall Diaries, 1954–61*, Unwin Hyman, 1991, p. 126.

14 Peden, op. cit., p. 487.

15 Harold Macmillan minute, 10 August 1957. M 405/57. National Archives, Kew.

16 The late Lord Thorneycroft to the author, 1986.

17 Harold Macmillan diary, 22 December 1957. MS Macmillan, dep. 30, loc. cit.

18 Lewis Baston, *Reggie: The Life of Reginald Maudling*, Sutton Publishing, 2004, p. 127.

19 John Boyd-Carpenter, *Way of Life: The Memoirs of John Boyd-Carpenter*, Sidgwick and Jackson, 1980, p. 136.

20 The late Lord Boyd-Carpenter to the author, 1986.

21 Boyd-Carpenter, op. cit.

22 Harold Macmillan diary, 6 January 1958. MS Macmillan dep. d. 30, loc. cit.

23 Heffer, op. cit., p. 229.

24 Peter Thorneycroft to Harold Macmillan, 6 January 1958. Harold Macmillan to Peter Thorneycroft, 6 January 1958. MS 278 A 962/1/9. Thorneycroft Papers, Southampton University.

25 Lord Cobbold to Harold Macmillan, 6 January 1958. G3/78. Bank of England Archives.

26 David Kynaston, *The City of London, Volume IV: A Club No More 1945–2000*, Chatto & Windus, 2000, p. 83.

27 Peden, op. cit., p. 487.

28 A. E. Holmans, *Demand Management in Britain 1955–58*, Institute of Contemporary British History, 1999, p. 262.

29 The late Reginald Maudling to the author, September 1975.

30 Edmund Dell, *The Chancellors: A History of the Chancellors of the Exchequer, 1945–1990*, Harper Collins, 1996, p. 243.

31 'Division of ministerial responsibilities', 9 January 1958. T 199/631. National Archives, Kew.

32 Quoted in Alan Thompson, *The Day Before Yesterday*, Sidgwick and Jackson, 1971, p. 167. Macmillan's first stop was in fact in Delhi.

33 Harold Macmillan to Edward Heath, 12 January 1958. T 18/58. National Archives, Kew.

34 Correspondence in MS Macmillan c. 336, loc. cit. Harold Macmillan's letter to Miss Gillian Paul was dated 30 October 1957.

35 The late Jane Parsons gave the author many insights into life at No. 10 Downing Street over the years from the perspective of the Garden Room.

36 Anthony Sampson, *Macmillan: A Study in Ambiguity*, Pelican Books, Harmondsworth, 1968, p. 138.

37 Harold Macmillan diary, 8 January 1958. MS Macmillan dep. d. 30, loc. cit.

38 Sampson, op. cit., p. 138.

39 Harold Macmillan, *Riding the Storm: 1956–1959*, Macmillan, 1971, p. 390.

40 Lord Carrington to the author, 21 January 2008.

41 Kelvingrove and Torrington were to be regained at the general election in October 1959. 'To my great joy we got back Torrington,' Macmillan wrote in his diary, 'Lady Violet Bonham Carter has been routed.' Harold Macmillan diary, 9 October 1959. MS Macmillan dep. c. 20, loc. cit.

42 Harold Macmillan diary, 28

March 1958. MS Macmillan dep. d. 31, loc. cit.

43 Joseph, Baron Grimond of Firth (1913–1993), Liberal MP for Orkney and Shetland, 1950–1983. Educated, like Macmillan, at Eton and Balliol. Grimond was Liberal leader from 1956–1967. His patrician bearing and integrity were increasingly attractive to Conservatives as Macmillan's political appeal waned in the latter years of his premiership. There were few kinder figures at Westminster. The author vividly remembers interviewing Lord Grimond (on 26 November 1985) a few moments after he had heard of the death of his sister, Nancy. Grimond would not hear of postponing the talk (about Selwyn Lloyd) and gave the author over an hour of his time, when his thoughts must have been elsewhere.

44 *Hansard*, 15 April 1958.

45 Harold Macmillan diary, 14 April 1958. MS Macmillan d. 31, loc. cit.

46 Harold Macmillan memorandum for the Cabinet, 9 July 1957. CAB 129/88. National Archives, Kew.

47 Cabinet Conclusions, 13 May 1958. CAB 128/32. National Archives, Kew.

48 Cabinet Conclusions, 8 September 1958. CAB 128/32/2. National Archives, Kew.

49 The Sovereign Base areas of Akrotiri and Dhekelia became the two British-administered areas on Cyprus after the island became an independent sovereign state in 1960. It was important for the United Kingdom to retain military bases on the island because of the strategic location of Cyprus in the Mediterranean. Lloyd's solution had enduring merit. The Hon. Sir Humphrey Maud, High Commissioner in Cyprus, 1988–1990, to the author, 16 September 2009.

50 Macmillan, op. cit., p. 472.

51 Later, Lloyd's dismissal as Chancellor of the Exchequer in the Night of the Long Knives in July 1962 was a vital moment in Macmillan's own decline. See Chapter 27.

52 SELO 180(4). Selwyn Lloyd Papers, Churchill College, Cambridge.

53 D. R. Thorpe, *Eden: The Life and Times of Anthony Eden First Earl of Avon*, 1897–1977, Chatto & Windus, 2003, p. 159.

54 Harold Macmillan diary, 22 July 1958 and 19 July 1955, MS Macmillan dep. d. 22, loc. cit.

55 Harold Macmillan to Sir Winston Churchill, 7 August 1958. MS Macmillan dep. c. 324, loc. cit.

56 Harold Macmillan diary, 4 March 1959, MS Macmillan dep. c. 20, loc. cit.

57 The BBC had instituted the Reith Lectures in 1948 in honour of their first Director-General, Lord Reith. The first series was delivered by Bertrand Russell.

58 Charles Williams, *Adenauer: The Father of the New Germany*, Little Brown, 2000, p. 452.

59 In Shakespeare's *Julius Caesar*, Mark Antony described Lepidus

to Octavius Caesar as 'a slight unmeritable man, meet to be sent on errands'. *Julius Caesar*, IV, i, 12–13.

60 Harold Macmillan diary, 8 October 1958. MS Macmillan d. 33, loc. cit.

61 Harold Macmillan to Dr Konrad Adenauer, 9 October 1958. PREM 11/2328. National Archives, Kew.

62 'Perfidious Albion' had long been a French gibe against England.

63 Harold Macmillan to Selwyn Lloyd, 15 October 1958. PREM 11/2532. National Archives, Kew.

64 A remark, maybe apocryphal, to the Parliament de Paris, 13 April 1655, but one that perfectly described de Gaulle's view of his national role.

65 Charles de Gaulle, *Memoirs of Hope*, Weidenfeld & Nicolson, 1971, p. 211.

66 Harold Macmillan diary, 13 May 1958. MS Macmillan d. 31, loc. cit.

67 MS Macmillan dep. c. 25, loc. cit.

68 Harold Macmillan to Lady Pamela Berry, 28 June 1958. MS Macmillan dep. c. 323, loc. cit.

69 Peter Mangold, *The Almost Impossible Ally: Harold Macmillan and Charles de Gaulle*, I. B. Tauris, 2006, p. 101.

70 Harold Macmillan diary, 24 October 1957. MS Macmillan dep. d. 30, loc. cit.

71 Nuri es-Said had attempted to escape Baghdad disguised in woman's clothes, but he was recognised and butchered by a lynch mob.

72 Harold Macmillan diary, 14 July 1958. MS Macmillan dep. d. 32, loc. cit.

73 Ibid., 17 July 1958.

74 Both Churchill and Eden had enunciated this position in 1955.

75 Harold Macmillan diary, 28 August 1958. MS Macmillan dep. d. 33, loc. cit.

76 Two volumes appeared in 1956, the third in 1957 and the last in 1958.

77 The Earl of Drogheda, *Double Harness*, Weidenfeld & Nicolson, 1978, p. 364. Drogheda had been elected chairman of the Royal Opera House, following Lord Waverley's death in January 1958.

78 Harold Macmillan to Hugh Gaitskell, 18 April 1958. MS Macmillan dep. c. 323, loc. cit.

79 See Chapter 23.

80 Hugh Gaitskell letter of 21 February 1959. Quoted in Philip M. Williams, *Hugh Gaitskell: A Political Biography*, Jonathan Cape, 1979, p. 519. When Gaitskell eventually visited Moscow in August 1959, all the press attention was on Eisenhower's visit to see Macmillan at the same time, so Gaitskell lost out twice, Macmillan's intention.

81 Michael Cockerell, *Live from Number 10: The Inside Story of Prime Ministers and Television*, Faber and Faber, 1988, p. 61.

82 'Prime Minister opens first motorway', MT 121/22. National Archives, Kew.

83 Robert Burns, 'Epigram on the Roads'.

84 Lord Salisbury memorandum, March 1956. FO 1109/350. National Archives, Kew.

85 Walter Bagehot, *The English Constitution*, 1867, Chapter IV.

86 Bernard Crick, 'The Life Peerages Act', *Parliamentary Affairs*, Volume XI, Number 4, 1957, p. 458.

87 Leo Amery, who died in 1955, refused a peerage so as not to hinder Julian Amery's political career.

88 Vernon Bogdanor, *The New British Constitution*, Hart Publishing, Oxford, 2009, p. 155.

89 From 'There is a wideness in God's mercy' by F. W. Faber.

90 *Hansard*, 30 October 1957.

91 Robert Rhodes James, *Bob Boothby: A Portrait*, Hodder & Stoughton, 1991, pp. 388–9.

92 Private information.

93 Dr Chris Ballinger, *An Analysis of the Reform of the House of Lords, 1911–2000*, Oxford DPhil Thesis, 2006, f-n 86, p. 189.

94 Harold Macmillan to Sir Robert Boothby, 12 July 1958. MS Macmillan dep. c. 323, loc. cit.

95 Quoted in Mark Pottle (ed.), *Daring to Hope: The Diaries and Letters of Violet Bonham Carter, 1946–1969*, Weidenfeld & Nicolson, 2000, p. 207.

96 The full list of the first life peers was: Sir Robert Boothby (Baron Boothby of Buchan and Rattray Head); Victor John Collins (Baron Stonham); Mary Irene Curzon (Baroness Ravensdale of Kedleston); Dame Katharine Elliot (Baroness Elliot of Harwood); Sir William Jocelyn Ian Fraser (Baron Fraser of Lonsdale); Sir Charles John Geddes (Baron Geddes of Epsom); Daniel Granville West (Baron Granville-West); Dame Stella Isaacs, Marchioness of Reading (Baroness Swanborough); Victor Ferrier Noel-Paton (Baron Ferrier of Culter); Sir Edward Arthur Alexander Shackleton (Baron Shackleton); Sir John Sebastian Bach Stopford (Baron Stopford of Fallowfield); Stephen James Lake Taylor (Baron Taylor); Sir Edward Frances Twining (Baron Twining); and Barbara Frances Wootton Wright (Baroness Wootton of Abinger). A 15th life peer, Sir Hubert Lister Parker (Baron Parker of Waddington of Lincoln's Inn), was added to the list in September 1958.

97 Harold Macmillan to Sir Edward Beddington-Behrens, 7 July 1958. MS Macmillan dep. c. 323, loc. cit.

98 The extent to which later prime ministers were to use life peerages as a convenient device for bringing unelected figures into government could not have been anticipated.

99 Whether Khrushchev was aware of how his language mirrored that of Neville Chamberlain's ultimatum of 3 September 1939 to Hitler is unclear.

100 Harold Macmillan diary, 5 January 1959. MS Macmillan dep. d. 34, loc. cit.

101 Macmillan, op. cit., p. 576.

102 Harold Macmillan diary, 16 January 1959. MS Macmillan dep. d. 34, loc. cit.

103 Ibid., 4 February 1959. Dulles died on 24 May 1959.

104 Harold Macmillan diary, 7 December 1958. MS Macmillan dep. d. 33, loc. cit. This was the crux of Macmillan's advice to President Kennedy during the Cuban Missile Crisis in October 1962. See Chapter 27.

105 Sir Robert Hall diary, 6 January 1959. Alec Cairncross (ed.), *The Robert Hall Diaries 1954–1961*, Unwin Hyman, 1991, p. 185.

CHAPTER TWENTY THREE

Porpoises in the North Sea 1959

1 Harold Macmillan interview on 9 July 1964 with Dr David Butler on the 1959 general election. David Butler archive, Nuffield College, Oxford.

2 *Encounter*, April 1955.

3 Samuel Brittain, *Steering the Economy: The Role of the Treasury*, Pelican Books, Harmondsworth, 1971, p. 225.

4 Harold Macmillan diary, 15 June 1959. MS Macmillan dep. d. 36. Macmillan Papers, Bodleian Library, Oxford.

5 Harold Macmillan diary, 16 January 1959. MS Macmillan dep. d. 34, loc. cit.

6 Sir John Simon to Harold Macmillan, 16 January 1959. MS Macmillan dep. c. 312, loc. cit.

7 Sir D'Arcy Patrick Reilly (1909–1999), Fellow of All Souls, passed first into the diplomatic service in 1933, and filled a series of increasingly important appointments with distinction. That rarity in Macmillan's life, a Wykehamist he profoundly admired, Reilly became Ambassador to Moscow, 1957–1960; Deputy Under-Secretary Foreign Office, 1960–1964; and Ambassador in Paris, 1965–1968, where he and his wife were treated with disgraceful rudeness by the Foreign Secretary, George Brown. On leaving the foreign service, another important ambassadorial figure of the time, Sir Evelyn Shuckburgh, publicly rebuked Brown for his behaviour. Reilly was a vital witness for historians.

8 Sir John Ure, notice of the life of Sir D'Arcy Patrick Reilly, *Oxford Dictionary of National Biography, Volume* 46, Oxford University Press, Oxford, 2004, pp. 426–8. I am grateful to the late Sir Patrick Reilly for many of the first-hand details of Macmillan's visit to Russia.

9 Sir Patrick Reilly to Harold Macmillan, 25 August 1958. PREM 11/5115. National Archives, Kew.

10 SELO 88 (3), Selwyn Lloyd Papers, Churchill College, Cambridge. News was received of the terminal nature of Dulles' cancer during preliminary meetings at Chequers for the visit.

11 *Daily Telegraph*, 24 February 1959. President Obama's gift to Prime Minister Gordon Brown

when they first met at the White House in 2009 was a boxed set of DVDs, which reputedly were unplayable on British systems.

12 The late Sir Patrick Reilly to the author, 1997. Silver candlesticks were also given to Khrushchev, and a silver tea service and a china dinner service were presented to Mrs Khrushchev. Equally lavish gifts were bestowed upon the British visitors, including the journalists accompanying the party.

13 The late Sir Patrick Reilly to the author, 1986.

14 The late Lord Barber to the author, 1986.

15 Harold Evans, *Downing Street Diary: The Macmillan Years,* 1957–1963, Hodder & Stoughton, 1981, p. 79.

16 Martin Stannard, *Muriel Spark: The Biography*, Weidenfeld & Nicolson, 2009, p. 402. There was even an echo of Chaucer's *The Knight's Tale*:
But sooth is seyd, go sithen many yeres,
That feeld hath eyen and the wode hath eres.

17 This conference of foreign ministers began in Geneva on 11 May 1959.

18 Sir Patrick Reilly memorandum, 8 March 1959, sent by him to the author in 1986.

19 See Chapter 27.

20 Record of the President de Gaulle-Macmillan talks, 10 March 1959. FO 371/145616. National Archives, Kew.

21 Record of Chancellor Adenauer-Macmillan talks, 13 March 1959. PREM 11/2717, loc. cit.

22 Winston Churchill speech at the White House, 26 June 1954.

23 Harold Macmillan diary, 20 March 1959. MS Macmillan dep. d. 35, loc. cit.

24 Harold Macmillan to Selwyn Lloyd, 10 June 1959. PREM 11/2685. National Archives, Kew.

25 D. R. Thorpe, *Selwyn Lloyd,* Jonathan Cape, 1989, p. 292.

26 Brian Harrison, *Seeking a Role: The United Kingdom 1951–1970,* Clarendon Press, Oxford, 2009, p. 335.

27 Elizabeth David (1913–1992), influential cookery writer. Her most famous book was *French Provincial Cooking* (1960). Elizabeth David recipes were not attempted at Birch Grove. Macmillan's taste was for simple nursery food provided by Mrs Bell.

28 In many respects the sixties began not with the Beatles' first LP, or the Lady Chatterley trial, but with the appearance of the Mini on 8 May 1959.

29 Thom Gunn, *On the Move* (1957).

30 Joe Moran, *On Roads: A Hidden History*, Profile Books, 2009, pp. 27–8.

31 *Hansard,* 12 April 1961.

32 Quoted in Harrison, op. cit., p. 111. The hierarchy of London clubs is as complex and intricate as those of public schools or seaside resorts. Suffice it to say that Boodles is one of the most socially prestigious.

33 Selwyn Lloyd, much impressed by this fact, always made a point thereafter when flying to book

what he called 'the Menderes seat' in the middle part of the aircraft.

34 Harold Macmillan to Adnam Menderes, 20 February 1959. MS Macmillan dep. c. 323, loc. cit.

35 Hugh Mackintosh Foot, Baron Caradon (1907–1990). His important diplomatic and colonial responsibilities included the governorship of Jamaica 1951–1957; the governorship of Cyprus, 1957–1960; and the British ambassadorship to the United Nations, 1964–1970. It was calculated that during his career he had overseen the enfranchisement of six million people.

36 Hugh Foot, *A Start in Freedom*, Hodder & Stoughton, 1964, p. 151.

37 Sir Hugh Foot to J. D. Higham of the Colonial Office, 6 February 1959. CO 926/721. National Archives, Kew.

38 *Hansard*, 19 February 1959.

39 Harold Macmillan diary, 19 February 1959. MS Macmillan dep. d. 34, loc. cit.

40 Harold Macmillan minute (No. 527), 28 December 1959. PREM 11/3075. National Archives, Kew.

41 *Indians in Kenya: memorandum*, Cmd 1922, HMSO, 1923, p. 9.

42 Sir Roland (Roy) Welensky (1907–1991), Prime Minister of the Federation of Rhodesia and Nyasaland, 1956–1963. Welensky was a larger-than-life political bruiser (he had been the heavyweight boxing champion of the Rhodesias from 1926–1928). When asked once if he understood Africans, he said, 'Considering that when I was a lad I swam bare-arsed in the Makabusi with the piccaninns, I think I can say I know something about Africans.' After his premiership, his wax model was removed from display in Madame Tussauds in London. Its vast bulk was then utilised in the reconstruction, among others, of the figure of Selwyn Lloyd, then returning to high office as Speaker. D. R. Thorpe, *Selwyn Lloyd*, Jonathan Cape, 1989, p. 363.

43 Harold Macmillan diary, 13 July 1959. MS Macmillan dep. d. 36, loc. cit.

44 Macmillan's four Colonial Secretaries, whose approach to decolonisation was very different, were Alan Lennox Boyd, from July 1954 to October 1959; Iain Macleod, October 1959 to October 1961; Reginald Maudling, October 1961 to July 1962, and Duncan Sandys, July 1962 to October 1964. Lennox Boyd's strength was the relationship he built up with the colonial governors. By contrast, Macleod ruffled many feathers, not least on the Conservative back benches. Maudling was more emollient, though less forceful. Duncan Sandys proved the toughest and most obdurate of the four. Nehru said that Sandys reminded him of the kind of Englishman who used to put him in jail.

45 Jomo Kenyatta (*c*. 1895–1978), President of the Kenya African

Union, June 1947; first Prime Minister of a self-governing Kenya, June 1963; and President of the Republic of Kenya in December 1964.

46 Dr Hastings Banda (c. 1898–1997), leader of the Nyasaland National Congress, 1958; imprisoned March 1959– June 1960; Prime Minister of Nyasaland (Malawi from 1964), 1963; President of Malawi, 1966; Life President, 1971.

47 Conditions that evoked unwelcome memories of the treatment of Chinese labourers in South Africa during Balfour's premiership. Guantánamo Bay was a more recent example.

48 Harold Macmillan diary, 9 June 1959. MS Macmillan dep. d. 35, loc. cit.

49 Cabinet conclusions, 11 June 1959. CAB 128/33. National Archives, Kew.

50 Robert Shepherd, *Iain Macleod: A Biography*, Hutchinson, 1994, p. 159.

51 In the event, Tanganyika gained its independence in 1961, Uganda in 1962 and Kenya in 1963.

52 Lennox-Boyd's wife, Lady Patricia, whom he had married in December 1938, was a Guinness, and Lennox-Boyd had served as a director of Arthur Guinness & Co. in the 1940s.

53 Harold Macmillan to Alan Lennox-Boyd, 15 March 1959. PREM 11/3051. National Archives, Kew.

54 Philip Murphy, *Party Politics and Decolonization: The Conservative Party and British Colonial Policy in Tropical Africa, 1951–1964*, Clarendon Press, Oxford, 1995, p. 147.

55 *Hola Camp: Documents relating to the deaths of eleven Mau Mau detainees at Hola Camp in Kenya*, Cmnd 778, HMSO, June 1959.

56 Sir Frank Soskice, Baron Stow Hill (1902–1979), Solicitor-General, 1945–1951; Home Secretary, 1964–1965; Lord Privy Seal, 1965–1966.

57 *Hansard*, 16 June 1959.

58 *Hola Camp: Further Documents relating to the deaths of eleven Mau Mau Detainees at Hola Camp in Kenya*, Cmnd 816, HMSO, July 1959.

59 *Records of Proceedings and Evidence in the Inquiry into the deaths of eleven Mau Mau detainees at the Hola Camp in Kenya*, Cmnd 795, HMSO, July 1959.

60 Sir Robert Perceval Armitage (1906–1990), colonial governor. Governor of Cyprus, 1954–1956, and Governor of Nyasaland, 1956–1961. Armitage was fated to preside over two of the most contentious and controversial missions of the 1950s. More than most he could feel let down by Macmillan when, after his retirement, the government went back on its promise that the Central African Federation would never be abandoned.

61 Harold Macmillan diary, 24 July 1959. MS Macmillan dep. d. 36, loc. cit.

62 *Hansard*, 27 July 1959. Powell's speech, one of the finest he ever

made, actually began at 1.15 a.m. on 28 July. Lennox-Boyd's was even later.

63 Harold Macmillan to Alan Lennox-Boyd, 7 March 1959. PREM 11/2787, National Archives, Kew.

64 The Monckton Commission finally reported, in ambivalent terms, in October 1960. See Chapter 24.

65 Patrick Arthur, Baron Devlin (1905–1992), judge in the King's Bench Division, 1948; Court of Appeal, 1960–1964.

66 Lord Parker of Waddington was chosen to succeed Lord Goddard as Lord Chief Justice in 1958. The three 'runners-up' were Lord Kilmuir, the Lord Chancellor; Lord Devlin; and Reginald Manningham-Buller, the Attorney General. The choice was difficult for Macmillan. Kilmuir preferred to stay by Macmillan's side in the government, not that this was to save him in the Night of the Long Knives in July 1962. Manningham-Buller was too similar in outlook to Goddard. Both Manningham-Buller and Devlin had been involved in a legal *cause célèbre* the year before - the trial of Dr John Bodkin Adams - Devlin as judge, Manningham-Buller as the unsuccessful counsel for the prosecution. Devlin, who thought Manningham-Buller's conduct of the prosecution of Dr Bodkin Adams was clumsy, stupid and perverse, was aggrieved at being passed over.

67 Harold Macmillan diary, 13 July 1959. MS Macmillan dep. c. 20, loc. cit.

68 *Report of the Nyasaland Commission of Inquiry (The Devlin Report)*, Cmnd 814, HMSO, 16 July 1959, p. 1, paragraph 2.

69 Sir Percy Wyn-Harris (1903–1979), colonial governor and mountaineer. Wyn-Harris had been settlement officer for Kikuyu land claims before the war. His governorship of Gambia, 1949–1958, was the longest governorship of the twentieth century. Wyn-Harris made the first ascent of the Nelion peak of Mount Kenya with Eric Shipton in 1929. In the 1930s, he was considered one of the stout spirits among the climbers of the British Everest expeditions.

70 Lord Devlin told the author in 1986 that this was not the case, though he vividly remembered the hostility towards him after the publication of the report.

71 Details are in the Cabinet Minutes, CAB 128/32, National Archives, Kew.

72 Reginald Edward Manningham-Buller, first Viscount Dilhorne (1905–1980), Conservative MP for Daventry, 1943–1950, South Northamptonshire, 1950–1962; Solicitor General, 1951–1954; Attorney General, 1954–1962; and Lord Chancellor, 1962–1964. As a law officer, Manningham-Buller was involved in several key events during the Macmillan premiership: the aftermath of the Devlin Report, the Vassall

tribunal, the Profumo affair, and the leadership controversy of October 1963. A heavily built figure, with a commanding and at times ruthless presence, he was known, perhaps inevitably, as 'Bullying Manner'.

73 *The Economist*, 25 July 1959.

74 Stephen E. Ambrose, *Eisenhower: Soldier and President*, Pocket Books paperback edition, 2003, p. 512.

75 Harold Macmillan diary, 27 July 1959. MS Macmillan dep. d. 36, loc. cit.

76 Prince Andrew was born on 19 February 1960.

77 Harold Macmillan to R. A Butler, 10 August 1959. MS Macmillan dep. c. 310, loc. cit.

78 Ambrose, op. cit., p. 512.

79 Harold Macmillan diary, 1 September 1959. MS Macmillan dep. d. 37, loc. cit.

80 Ibid., 7 September 1959. Constitutional experts have often wondered whether the Queen advised Harold Wilson not to ask for a further dissolution after the two largely indecisive elections of February 1974 and October 1974. In conversation with Harold Wilson in 1981, the author asked Wilson if this was the case. The change in atmosphere was immediate. Wilson, who had been open and transparent until that point, clammed up and became evasive.

81 *I'm All Right Jack* was one of the most overtly political of the comic films of the 1950s. The picture it paints of the challenge by the bloody-minded trade union steward Fred Kite (played by Peter Sellers) is 'vicious rather than just boisterous'. Sue Harper and Vincent Porter, *British Cinema of the 1950s: The Decline of Deference*, Oxford University Press, Oxford, 2003, p. 112. 'If that doesn't win you the election,' said one who had seen the film with Macmillan, 'nothing will.'

82 The key source for figures and other details quoted in this account is David Butler and Richard Rose, *The British General Election of 1959*, Macmillan, 1960. I am deeply grateful to Dr David Butler for discussing the niceties of this and other elections with me over the years and for giving me access to his research archive on elections at Nuffield College, Oxford.

83 Both the main party headquarters were in Smith Square, Westminster.

84 Eden never gave a personal endorsement of Macmillan during the campaign. The memories of November 1956 still resonated.

85 In the 27 months leading up to the election, the Conservatives spent £460,000 on political advertising, a vast sum for the time.

86 As with Boothby's affair with Lady Dorothy Macmillan, Gaitskell's long-standing affair with Ann Fleming, wife of Ian Fleming, author of the James Bond novels, was well known in political circles.

87 Philip Williams, *Hugh Gaitskell: A Biography*, Jonathan Cape, 1979, p. 522.

88 Harold Macmillan diary, 27 September 1959. MS Macmillan dep. c. 20, loc. cit.

89 *Daily Mail*, 30 July 1959.

90 Hugh Dalton diary, 11 October 1959. Ben Pimlott (ed.), *The Political Diary of Hugh Dalton 1918–40, 1945–60*, Jonathan Cape, 1986, p. 696.

91 Conservative ministers and MPs routinely sent their children to private schools, as did many prominent Labour MPs. Attlee, Gaitskell, Wilson and Callaghan all educated their children privately. The threat to the grammar schools did not therefore affect such MPs directly. Tony Blair was the first Prime Minister to send his children to a state school.

92 Butler and Rose, op. cit., p. 54.

93 File PPB 1. Conservative Party Archive, Bodleian Library, Oxford.

94 *Daily Express*, 29 September 1959.

95 Butler and Rose, op. cit., p. 63.

96 Richard Crossman diary, 30 September 1959. Janet Morgan (ed.), *The Backbench Diaries of Richard Crossman*, Hamish Hamilton and Jonathan Cape, 1981, p. 782.

97 *Annual Register*, 1959, p. 35.

98 Speech to the Chartered Accountant Students' Society, 5 October 1959.

99 Colonel Blimp, the epitome of the reactionary diehard, was a character invented by the cartoonist Low in 1934. Churchill tried to get the film version, *The Life and Death of Colonel Blimp*, banned in 1943.

100 Alun Chalfont, *Montgomery of Alamein*, Weidenfeld & Nicolson, 1976, pp. 323–4.

101 Lord Egremont, *Women and Children First*, Macmillan, 1968, p. 186.

102 Butler and Rose, op. cit., p. 88.

103 Harold Macmillan diary, 9 October 1959. MS Macmillan dep. c. 20, loc. cit.

104 Richard Crossman diary, 9 October 1959, Morgan (ed.), op. cit., p. 786.

105 David Butler archive, loc. cit.

106 *Observer*, 1 October 1959.

107 Dominic Sandbrook, *Never Had It So Good: A History of Britain from Suez to the Beatles*, Little, Brown, 2005, p. 93.

108 Harold Macmillan diary, 9 October 1959. MS Macmillan dep. c. 20, loc. cit.

109 Anthony Howard, *Rab: The Life of R. A. Butler*, Jonathan Cape, 1987, p. 269.

110 Ibid., p. 268.

111 Lord Hailsham, *A Sparrow's Flight: Memoirs*, Collins, 1990, p. 326.

112 Harold Macmillan diary, 11 October 1957. MS Macmillan dep. d. 20, loc. cit. As political leopards, no less than real ones, do not change their spots, it seems incredible that Macmillan should initially favour Hailsham as his putative successor in October 1963, when exactly the same pattern of behaviour emerged. See Chapter 29.

113 Hailsham, op. cit., p. 327.

114 And not only in politics. Tipping the scales jointly

at over 35 stones, they had lengthy duels at the tennis courts in Cadogan Gardens (opposite Macmillan's birthplace), at which point 'small children and animals using the gardens were known to take fright and flee'. D. R. Thorpe, obituary of Lord Erroll of Hale, *The Independent*, 26 September 2000.

115 Harold Macmillan diary, 18 October 1959, loc. cit.

116 A story Lord Beaverbrook was told by Bonar Law, and which he often recounted at times of reshuffles.

117 In 1967, Captain Terence O'Neill, Prime Minister of Northern Ireland, complained to Macmillan about Cunningham's part in Ulster politics. 'Since shedding the anonymity and discretion of his P.P.S. role, he has proved in many ways a great embarrassment to us all,' O'Neill wrote. Cunningham had, among other things, contributed to the Revd Ian Paisley's paper, the *Protestant Telegraph*, and O'Neill hoped that a quiet word from Macmillan might calm Cunningham down. 'Of course I am out of everything now but if I can do anything I will,' Macmillan replied. 'But you Ulstermen are an obstinate and stiff-necked race. However, if you were not we would not have survived the Celtic onslaught in the past.' Captain Terence O'Neill to Harold Macmillan, 2 June 1967, and

undated reply from Macmillan. CAB/9J/6/11, Public Records Office of Northern Ireland, Belfast (PRONI). I am grateful to Professor Geoffrey Warner for drawing my attention to this correspondence.

118 Harold Macmillan to R. A Butler, 23 December 1959. MS Macmillan dep. c. 310, loc. cit.

CHAPTER TWENTY FOUR

Return to Africa 1960

1 Bishop Berkeley, 'On the Prospect of Planting Arts and Learning in America'.

2 Harold Macmillan to Sir Anthony Eden, 10 October 1959. MS Macmillan dep. c. 326. Macmillan Papers, Bodleian Library, Oxford.

3 'The Balance Sheet of Empire', 1957. CAB 134/1555. 'The Position of the United Kingdom in World Affairs', 1958. PREM 11/2321. 'Study of Future Policy, 1960–1970', 1960. CAB 134/1935. National Archives, Kew.

4 The experience of National Service was one way in which the different classes of society were thrown together in a manner that would not have happened normally. Nevertheless, the memory of many public schoolboys, particularly ones with sporting flair, was of a golden time, with endless summers of cricket. Personal information.

5 Quoted in Anthony Sampson, *Anatomy of Britain*, Hodder &

Stoughton, 1962, p. 247.

6 Thomas Jones, *A Diary with Letters: 1931–1950*, Oxford University Press, p. 176.

7 Henry Brooke was the first to occupy this post. On 1 November 1968, John Diamond became the first Chief Secretary to become a full member of the Cabinet, in the second Wilson administration.

8 D. R. Thorpe, *Alec Douglas-Home*, Sinclair-Stevenson, 1996, p. 326.

9 A similar switch of emphasis can be seen from the early 1930s when the National Government's Disarmament Committee changed its name to the Rearmament Committee in 1934.

10 Gaitskell's description of what European federation would mean, Labour Party Conference, Scarborough, 3 October 1962.

11 Jacqueline Tratt, *The Macmillan Government and Europe: A Study in the Process of Policy Development*, Macmillan Press, Basingstoke, 1996, p. 86.

12 Harold Macmillan to the Duke of Norfolk, 4 January 1960. MS Macmillan dep. c. 328, loc. cit. Far from being reluctant to consider such intimations of mortality, Churchill embraced the planning stage enthusiastically. The route by boat from St Paul's Cathedral along the Thames would mean that the rail journey to Bladon, Churchill's final resting place near Blenheim Palace, would begin at Waterloo. The Duke of Norfolk pointed out that

Waterloo was not the most convenient station for starting a journey into Oxfordshire. Churchill reputedly overruled the Duke's concern, saying that de Gaulle would be coming to the funeral and that 'de Gaulle must go to Waterloo'.

13 On 8 February 1960 a statement in Council declared that royal descendants, with some exceptions, would be named 'Mountbatten-Windsor'.

14 Details of Stanley's dates were later appended on a metal plaque.

15 Memories of the great days at AFHQ had not endured in the public consciousness. In 2008, A. N. Wilson wrote of 'that vast continent upon which, until he became Prime Minister, Macmillan had never set foot: Africa'. A. N. Wilson, *Our Times: The Age of Elizabeth II*, Hutchinson, 2008, p. 87.

16 I am grateful to the late Anthony Sampson, who accompanied the tour throughout, for recounting to me his impressions of the key moments, especially the reception in Cape Town of the 'wind of change' speech, which he witnessed personally.

17 Anthony Sampson, *Anatomy of Britain*, Hodder & Stoughton, 1962, p. 244.

18 Sir David Wathen Stather Hunt (1913–1998) Foreign Affairs Secretary to Clement Attlee, 1950–1951, and to Sir Winston Churchill, 1951–1952; Deputy High Commissioner, 1954–1954; Head of Central African Department, CRO, 1956–1959;

Under-Secretary of State, CRO, with responsibility for Africa; Deputy High Commissioner, Nigeria, 1960–1962; High Commissioner, Kampala, 1962–1965; High Commissioner, Cyprus, 1965–1967; High Commissioner, Nigeria, 1967–1969; Ambassador to Brazil, 1969–1973. Sir David Hunt came to wider public notice as the winner of the BBC's *Mastermind* in 1977, and then as the first 'Mastermind of Masterminds', 1982.

19 Dr Kwame Nkrumah (1909–1972), Prime Minister of Ghana, 1957–1960; President of the Republic of Ghana, 1960–1966, when he was overthrown in a military coup. At the height of his powers, when Macmillan visited, Nkrumah was the undisputed leader of the pan-African movement, through his hosting of the All African People's Convention in April 1958.

20 Combining publishing with politics on his travels was a regular practice for Macmillan, particularly in Africa over educational books. Graham C. Greene to the author, 15 September 2009.

21 Sir James Wilson Robertson (1899–1983), Governor General of the Federation of Nigeria, 1955–1960, was firmly in the tradition of that distinguished Scottish thread in Balliol life. Macmillan regarded Robertson as 'a man of outstanding courage' (letter to the Queen, 18 January 1960) and Sir Hugh

Foot described him as one who 'took all Nigeria into his big, bear-like hug'. Sir Hugh Foot, *A Start in Freedom*, Hodder & Stoughton, 1964, p. 103.

22 Quoted in Kenneth Young, *Rhodesia and Independence: A Study in British Colonial Policy*, J. M. Dent, 1967, p. 49.

23 The late Lord Home of the Hirsel to the author, 10 April 1991.

24 Hugh Trevor Roper, 23 March 1960. Richard Davenport-Hines (ed.), *Letters from Oxford: Hugh Trevor-Roper to Bernard Berenson*, Weidenfeld & Nicolson, 2006, p. 298.

25 John Primatt Redcliffe, Baron Redcliffe-Maud (1906–1982), Permanent Secretary, Ministry of Education, 1945–1952, and of Ministry of Fuel and Power, 1952–1959; High Commissioner in South Africa, 1959–1963; Master of University College, Oxford, 1963–1976.

26 Maud was not a dry-as-dust diplomat of the old school. Privately, he did a wickedly accurate impersonation of Dr Verwoerd, which rather shocked some visitors, who did not think it appropriate that a High Commissioner should be imitating the Prime Minister of the country to which he was accredited. Private information.

27 Dr Hendrik Frensch Verwoerd (1901–1966), Prime Minister of South Africa, 1958–1966. After the Sharpeville shootings, an unsuccessful attempt was made to assassinate Verwoerd on 9 April 1960. Verwoerd led South

Africa out of the Commonwealth in 1961. He was assassinated on 6 September 1966. *Private Eye* had a cover photograph of four Zulu warriors jumping for joy, above a headline, 'Verwoerd: A Nation Mourns'. *Private Eye*, 17 September 1966.

28 Jean Redcliffe-Maud, *High Commission to Embassy: South Africa 1959–1963*, Englang Publishing, Circencester, 1990, p. 122–3.

29 I am grateful to the late Anthony Sampson, who witnessed the speech from the gallery, for telling me of the changing moods among Macmillan's audience. The speech is reprinted in full as Appendix One in Harold Macmillan, *Pointing the Way: 1959–1961*, Macmillan, 1972, pp. 472–82.

30 The late Sir David Hunt to the author, 1986. See also Roger Westbrook, notice of the life of Sir David Hunt, *Oxford Dictionary of National Biography: Volume 28*, Oxford University Press, 2004, p. 837. Sir John Johnston (1918–2005), an alumnus of Banbury Grammar School, one of the many such distinguished grammar schools that flourished in Britain. Johnston was successively Deputy High Commissioner, South Africa, 1959–1961; British High Commissioner, Sierra Leone, 1961–1963, and in the Federation of Rhodesia and Nyasaland, 1963, Rhodesia, 1964–1965, Malaysia, 1971, and Canada, 1974–1978.

31 Address by Mr Macmillan to both Houses of the Parliament of the Union of South Africa, Cape Town, 3 February 1960. DO 35/10570. National Archives, Kew.

32 Lady Maud diary, February 1960 retrospect. Redcliffe-Maud, op. cit., p. 135.

33 Anthony Sampson, *The Anatomist: The Autobiography of Anthony Sampson*, Politico's, 2008, p. 94, and to the author on more than one occasion. The cartoon caption is from *Julius Caesar*, III, i, 254–5.

34 Father John Twisleton to the author, 28 February 2010.

35 Bernard Levin, *The Pendulum Years: Britain in the Sixties*, Jonathan Cape, 1970, pp. 204–5.

36 Ian Gilmour, *Whatever Happened to the Tories: The Conservative Party since 1945*, Fourth Estate, 1997, p. 157.

37 Sir Anthony Montague Browne to the author, 1998. Anthony Montague Browne, *Long Sunset: Memoirs of Winston Churchill's Last Private Secretary*, Cassell, 1995, p. 307. Lambton was able to sit in the Commons, as his title, since 1941, of Viscount Lambton was a courtesy one. When he succeeded in 1970 to the titles of 6th Earl of Durham, Viscount Lambton and Lord Durham, he disclaimed them under the terms of the 1963 Peerage Act, so as to be able to remain in the Commons.

38 Not 13,000, as Macmillan stated in his memoirs.

39 Harold Evans diary, 15 February

1960. Harold Evans, *Downing Street Diary: The Macmillan Years* 1957–1963, Hodder & Stoughton, 1981, p. 107.

40 Halifax had succeeded Lord Grey of Fallodon as Chancellor of Oxford in 1933. Among his many other honours, he had been the Chancellor of the Order of the Garter, Grand Master of the Order of St Michael and St George, High Steward of Westminster, President of the Pilgrims, Colonel in Chief of the Yorkshire Dragoons, and also had the gift of a dozen livings and presided over many institutions, including Pusey House.

41 Hugh Redwald Trevor-Roper, Baron Dacre of Glanton (1914–2003), historian and college head. Regius Professor of Modern History at Oxford, 1957–1980; Master of Peterhouse, Cambridge, 1980–1987. Trevor-Roper's most famous work was arguably *The Last Days of Hitler* (1947). The most damaging blow to his reputation was his mistaken authentication in 1983 of 60 handwritten volumes, supposedly Hitler's diaries, but actually the work of a confidence trickster in Stuttgart.

42 Sir Isaiah Berlin to Charles Webster, 28 January 1957. Isaiah Berlin, *Enlightening: Letters* 1946–1960, edited by Henry Hardy and Jennifer Holmes, Chatto & Windus, 2009, p. 567.

43 *New Statesman*, 6 July 1957. Such a public expression of his bitterness went a long way in many people's minds to explain why Macmillan had been right not to appoint Taylor.

44 John Drinkwater (1882–1937) had written a series of stolid plays on historical figures such as Abraham Lincoln, Mary Stuart and Oliver Cromwell, the latter being first performed in the year of the premiere of Shaw's *Saint Joan* in 1923.

45 The late Lord Franks told the author in 1986 that as soon as Macmillan was nominated, he knew he would lose.

46 Davenport-Hines (ed.), op. cit., pp. 295, 307 and 290.

47 Ibid., p. 297.

48 Ibid., p. 300.

49 Ibid., p. 304.

50 Ibid., p. 307.

51 In 1959, John Byrne stood against the general secretary of the ETU, Frank Haxell, and was supposedly defeated. Writs were issued, and in 1961 the High Court confirmed that 'fraudulent and unlawful devices' had been employed, and declared Byrne to be secretary.

52 *Hansard*, 8 March 1960.

53 Zuleika Dobson was the heroine of the eponymous novel of 1911 by Max Beerbohm, which fantasised about the fatal effect of a visit to Oxford of a beautiful maiden. Richard Crossman diary, 4 March 1960. Janet Morgan (ed.), *The Backbench Diaries of Richard Crossman*, Hamish Hamilton and Jonathan Cape, 1981, p. 819.

54 All of which are present in Macmillan's favourite C. P. Snow

novel, *The Masters*.

55 Bowra, surveying the great and the good on crowded lawns at a Wadham function when he was Vice Chancellor of the University, was asked what collective noun he would use to describe heads of houses. He replied, 'A lack of principals.'

CHAPTER TWENTY FIVE

Turning Points 1960–1961

1 PREM 11/3133. National Archives, Kew. The exact words of William Pitt the Younger in a speech at Guildhall in 1805 were 'England has saved herself by her exertions, and will, as I trust, save Europe by her example.'

2 *Othello*, IV, i, 21–22.

3 In 1961, *Beyond the Fringe* satirised these difficulties in the sketch 'Civil War': 'The British Sea-Slug is a ludicrously cumbersome vehicle, depending as it does on a group of highly trained runners carrying it into enemy territory.' Roger Wilmut (ed.), *The Complete Beyond the Fringe*, Methuen, 1987, p. 80.

4 Alan Bullock, *Ernest Bevin: Foreign Secretary*, Oxford University Press paperback edition, Oxford, 1985, p. 352.

5 Professor Walter Hallstein (1901–1982), West German statesman, first President of the European Commission, 1958–1967. Hallstein once berated Reginald Maudling, then President of the Board of Trade, for referring to him as Doctor rather than Professor Hallstein.

Lewis Baston, *Reggie: The Life of Reginald Maudling*, Sutton Publishing, 2004, p. 130.

6 Harold Macmillan diary, 13 March 1960. MS Macmillan dep. d. 38, Macmillan Papers, Bodleian Library, Oxford.

7 Ibid., 30 March 1960.

8 Field Marshal Montgomery, *Memoirs*, Collins, 1958, and Arthur Bryant, *Triumph in the West*, Collins, 1958, a heavily censored selection of the Alanbrooke diaries. Eisenhower was angered by Monty's trenchant criticisms of his limited understanding of military strategy and later in the year even considered the book to have damaged Republican chances in the November 1960 presidential election. Alanbrooke's diaries also displayed a low opinion of Eisenhower's abilities as a general.

9 *Hansard*, 1 November 1960.

10 Living in Renfrewshire at the time, the author can remember the general sense of anxiety about the submarine base, which nevertheless became a popular destination for many Sunday motorists.

11 Harold Watkinson memorandum, February 1960. AIR 19/998. National Archives, Kew.

12 Derick Heathcoat Amory to Harold Watkinson, 22 April 1960. PREM 11/3261. National Archives, Kew.

13 Harold Watkinson, *Turning Points: A Record of our Times*, Michael Russell, Salisbury, 1986,

p. 141. Watkinson was very critical of Macmillan's defence strategy at this time. The late Lord Watkinson to the author, 1985.

14 One of the often unregarded demands of official functions, especially royal ones, was the reception, usually at 10 p.m., for those not invited to the dinner. This could involve scores of people, all of whom needed to be welcomed. The arrangement was not a new one. 'They count as Tories,' said Lady Bracknell in Oscar Wilde's *The Importance of Being Earnest* of the Liberal Unionists. 'They dine with us, or come in the evening at any rate.' At this time, Macmillan took to asking the Queen to be excused from some of these receptions when his programme was very heavy.

15 Harold Macmillan diary, 14 June 1943. Harold Macmillan, *War Diaries: Politics and War in the Mediterranean, January 1943–May 1945*, Macmillan, 1984, p. 122.

16 Peter Mangold, *The Almost Impossible Ally: Harold Macmillan and Charles de Gaulle*, I. B. Tauris, 2006, p. 93.

17 Harold Macmillan diary, 7 April 1960. MS Macmillan dep. d. 38, loc. cit.

18 Harold Macmillan, *Winds of Change: 1914–1939*, Macmillan, 1966, p. 41.

19 FO 371/15396. National Archives, Kew.

20 Sir Frank Godbould Lee (1903–1971). After many important postings in the Treasury, including working with J. M. Keynes on the end of Lend-Lease in 1944 and the British loan agreement. Lee said that working for Keynes was akin to being one of Lucifer's followers in *Paradise Lost*, 'rejoicing in their matchless chief'. After working in Washington in 1948 on the distribution of Marshall aid, Lee became Permanent Secretary to the Ministry of Food, 1949–1951; Permanent Secretary to the Board of Trade, 1951–1960; and Joint Permanent Secretary to the Treasury, 1960–1962, from which he retired prematurely owing to a heart attack. Lee was Master of Corpus Christi College, Cambridge, from 1962 until his death.

21 Stanley Crooks, *Peter Thorneycroft*, George Mann Publications, Winchester, 2007, p. 79. 'One of the greatest permanent secretaries a man could ever wish to have' was Thorneycroft's view of Lee. 'I wanted to take him with me to the Treasury. I believe that history would have been a little different if I had managed that.' Speech of 7 June 1993. Ibid., pp. 260–1.

22 Jacqueline Tratt, *The Macmillan Government and Europe: A Study in the Process of Policy Development*, Macmillan Press, Basingstoke, 1996, p. 95.

23 The bank rate was to be reduced to 5.5% on 27 October and to 5% on 8 December.

24 *Sunday Express*, 22 November 1959.

25 SELO 308 (1). Selwyn Lloyd

Papers, Churchill College, Cambridge.

26 Milton, *Samson Agonistes*, 1, 1758.

27 Harold Macmillan diary, 7 May 1960. MS Macmillan dep. d. 38, loc. cit.

28 Ibid.

29 David Reynolds, *Summits: Six Meetings that Shaped the Twentieth Century*, Allen Lane, 2007, p. 161.

30 *New York Times*, 12 May 1960.

31 Selwyn Lloyd diary, 16 May 1960, SELO 308 (1), loc. cit.

32 Harold Macmillan, *Pointing the Way: 1959–1961*, Macmillan, 1972, p. 204.

33 Harold Macmillan diary, 16 May 1960. MS Macmillan dep. d. 39, loc. cit. The Dickensian allusion was very characteristic of Macmillan.

34 See Chapter 27.

35 Hubert Miles Gladwyn, first Baron Jebb (1900–1996). Private Secretary to Sir Robert Vansittart and Sir Alexander Cadogan before the war, and acting Secretary General of the United Nations at its inception afterwards, Jebb was one of the towering figures of the diplomatic service. His two missions were as British representative at the United Nations, 1950–1954, and Ambassador to France, 1954–1960. Jebb, by then Lord Gladwyn, told the author in 1986 that he was never convinced by Macmillan's attempts at 'summitry'. Jebb was a figure of some grandeur, if not hauteur, and was not best pleased to hear of Selwyn Lloyd's epigram, 'You're a deb, Sir Gladwyn Jebb.'

36 D. R. Thorpe, *Selwyn Lloyd*, Jonathan Cape, 1989, p. 304.

37 Selwyn Lloyd diary, 16 May 1960. SELO 308 (1), loc. cit.

38 Thorpe, op. cit., p. 304.

39 Aleksandr Fursenko and Timothy Naftali, *Khrushchev's Cold War: The Inside Story of an American Adversary*, W. W. Norton, New York, 2006, p. 288.

40 Peter Mangold, *The Almost Impossible Ally: Harold Macmillan and Charles de Gaulle*, I. B. Tauris, 2006, p. 137.

41 BBC interview, 6 June 1972.

42 Selwyn Lloyd diary, 23 May 1960. SELO 308 (1), loc. cit.

43 Selwyn Lloyd diary, 24 May 1960. SELO 180 (4), loc. cit.

44 Though the headline in the *Daily Worker* on 10 January 1957 had been 'EDEN QUITS - NEW PREMIER TODAY: Selwyn Lloyd the hottest tip'.

45 SELO 180 (4), loc. cit.

46 SELO 308 (1), loc. cit.

47 Frederick Robert Hoyer Millar, first Baron Inchyra (1900–1989), always known as Derick. A key figure in the formation of NATO and Permanent Secretary on the NATO Council, 1952. High Commissioner in Germany, 1953–1955, and first Ambassador in Berlin since Sir Nevile Henderson, 1955–1957; Permanent Under-Secretary at the Foreign Office, 1957–1961.

48 Harold Macmillan diary, 3 June 1960. MS Macmillan dep. d. 39, loc. cit.

49 Ibid., 11 June 1960.

50 The annual ceremony of commemoration of the founders and benefactors at Oxford University, at which the Chancellor bestows honorary degrees.

51 On 23 June 1960 the bank rate was raised to 6%.

52 The same arrangement was to operate in 1979, when Lord Carrington was Foreign Secretary in the Lords with Sir Ian Gilmour as his number two in the Commons as Lord Privy Seal.

53 John Campbell, *Edward Heath: A Biography*, Jonathan Cape, 1993, p. 112.

54 Selwyn Lloyd diary, 28 July 1960. SELO 308 (1), loc. cit.

55 Harold Macmillan diary, 6 August 1960. MS Macmillan dep. d. 39, loc. cit.

56 Harold Macmillan to the Queen, 23 December 1959. PREM 11/3480. National Archives, Kew.

57 Harold Macmillan diary, 15 February 1960. MS Macmillan dep. d. 38, loc. cit.

58 Harold Macmillan diary, 16 September 1960. MS Macmillan dep. d. 40, loc. cit.

59 Joseph Conrad, *Heart of Darkness*, I, 1902.

60 Moise Tshombe (1919–1969) nevertheless became Prime Minister of the Congo Republic in July 1964, but fled to exile in Spain in 1965 in the wake of corrupt elections. The then President of the Congo, Mobutu had Tshombe tried for treason in his absence and he was condemned to death. Captured in July 1967, Tshombe was imprisoned in Algeria where he died of a heart attack on 29 June 1969.

61 Harold Macmillan diary, 4 August 1960. MS Macmillan dep. d. 39, loc. cit.

62 Memorandum by Philip de Zulueta to Harold Macmillan, 13 July 1960. PREM 11/2883. National Archives, Kew.

63 Harold Macmillan diary, 25 February 1962. MS Macmillan dep. d. 54, loc. cit.

64 Harold Macmillan to Sir Roy Welensky, 14 July 1960. PREM 11/2883. National Archives, Kew.

65 The correspondence is in the Welensky Papers, Rhodes House, Oxford.

66 John Colville, *Those Lambtons!*, Hodder & Stoughton, 1988, p. 167. The late Sir John Colville told the author in 1986 he had never witnessed such antipathy as that shown by Lord Lambton to Macmillan.

67 This Watching Committee was based on the one Salisbury's father, the 4th Marquess, had formed in 1940 with the aim of destabilising Neville Chamberlain. Macmillan had been a prominent member of that Watching Committee. It was not a question of poacher turned gamekeeper, more poacher transformed into the hare.

68 The Marquess of Salisbury to Sir Anthony Eden, 21 May 1957. AP 23/60. Avon Papers, Birmingham University Library.

69 After a meeting with the

Commonwealth Relations Secretary, Duncan Sandys, and the Colonial Secretary, Iain Macleod, on 16 June 1961. PREM 11/3492. National Archives, Kew.

70 When the author visited the United Nations on 12 March 2008, guides were pointing out where Khrushchev had been sitting at the time of his outburst.

71 Interpreters told Macmillan later that the actual words Khrushchev had used were, 'You sent your planes over our territory, you are guilty of aggression.' Macmillan's speech, and Khrushchev's intervention, can be heard on a BBC long-playing record, 'British Prime Ministers, 1924–1964', BBC REB 39M, 1969. The wording of the retort to Khrushchev was slightly different from that recalled by Macmillan in his memoirs.

72 Macmillan always attributed the interruption to the fact that his speech had not been pre-released like many at the time. As a result his comments on nuclear inspection were new to Khrushchev. The short delay, because of the time for translation, between Macmillan's mention of this and Khrushchev's outburst shows clearly that it was this issue that riled the Soviets.

73 Harold Macmillan to Timothy Bligh, 22 September 1960. PREM 11/3078. National Archives, Kew.

74 Lord Salisbury to Sir Roy Welensky, 27 September 1960. WP 665/2. Welensky Papers, Rhodes House, Oxford.

75 Lord Perth minute, 16 June 1959. CO 1015/1704. National Archives, Kew. The late Lord Perth told the author in 1991 that there was a lot of such politicking to get the commission launched.

76 Sir Roy Welensky to Harold Macmillan, 22 September 1960. DO 35/7502. National Archives, Kew.

77 Donal Lowry, notice of Sir Roy Welensky, *Oxford Dictionary of National Biography, Volume 57*, Oxford University Press, Oxford, 2004, p. 995.

78 Harold Macmillan diary, 22 February 1961. MS Macmillan dep. d. 41, loc. cit.

79 Harold Macmillan to Timothy Bligh, 28 August 1961. The underlining is in Macmillan's own hand on the letter. PREM 11/3497. National Archives, Kew.

80 Iain Macleod to Harold Macmillan, 25 July 1961. CO 1015/2442. National Archives, Kew.

81 Martin Redmayne to Harold Macmillan, 25 July 1961. PREM 11/3496. National Archives, Kew.

82 Record of meeting between Harold Macmillan and Lord Lambton, 2 August 1960. PREM 11/3496. National Archives, Kew.

83 Robert Shepherd, *Iain Macleod*, Hutchinson, 1994, p. 255.

84 Dag Hammarskjöld (1905–1961), second Secretary

General of the United Nations. Hammarskjöld, enhanced the reputation of the UN throughout his distinguished term of office. Although Macmillan praised Hammarskjöld in his memoirs, particularly for his patience and impartiality, in the privacy of his diary he was less complimentary.

85 Sir Howard Frank Trayton Smith (1919–1996), Ambassador to Moscow, 1976–1978. As was the custom in those days, Sir Howard's *Who's Who* entry did not state that from 1979–1981 he was Director General of MI5.

86 Minute to Lord Home by H. F. T. Smith, 28 September 1960. FO 371/146650. National Archives, Kew.

87 Harold Macmillan diary, 10 July 1960. MS Macmillan dep. d. 39, loc. cit.

88 Memorandum of Conference with the President, 27 September 1960. AWF-IS, Box 25B, Folder 5. Eisenhower Papers, Dwight D. Eisenhower Library, Abilene, Kansas, USA.

89 *Othello*, IV, ii, 229–31.

90 Harold Macmillan diary, 3 December 1960. MS Macmillan dep. d. 40, loc. cit.

91 Ludo de Witte, *The Assassination of Lumumba*, Verso, 2001. In a review of the book in the *New York Review of Books*, 'The Tragedy of Lumumba', 4 October 2001, Sir Brian Urquhart, former Under-Secretary General, 1974–1986, stoutly defends the United Nations against charges of involvement.

92 Anthony Sampson was to include in his 1962 edition of *Anatomy of Britain* a fold-out insert of the many intertwining family relationships of the Macmillan government.

93 Conversation recalled in Nigel Fisher, *Harold Macmillan: A Biography*, Weidenfeld & Nicolson, 1982, p. 265. 'Being good with the natives' was always a cause for patrician admiration in the Tory Party of those days. The late Lord Colyton told the author in 1992 that this was one of the secrets of Anthony Eden's popularity in liberal-minded political circles.

94 Andrew Devonshire, *Accidents of Fortune*, Michael Russell, Norwich, 2004, p. 65.

95 *Hansard*, 1 November 1960.

96 Private information. Douglas Jay, the Labour Cabinet Minister, had particularly aquiline features.

97 SELO 308 (1), loc. cit.

98 Harold Macmillan diary, 2 November 1960. MS Macmillan dep. d. 40, loc. cit.

99 Henrik Ibsen, *The Master Builder* (1892), Act One.

100 Harold Macmillan diary, 17 December 1959. MS Macmillan dep. d. 37, loc. cit.

101 *Beyond the Fringe*, in various manifestations, ran on both sides of the Atlantic until 1966. It confirmed the burgeoning reputations of its four original stars - Alan Bennett, Peter Cook, Jonathan Miller and Dudley Moore - who became 'national treasures'. All four were Oxbridge graduates, and Cook and Miller had been

educated at Radley and St Paul's respectively. These Young Turks were not in charge of the tumbrils. The author's memory of seeing the revue in 1962 was of a solidly middle-class audience, with some dinner jackets in the stalls, and two coaches from Tunbridge Wells outside the Fortune Theatre.

102 Christopher Booker, Paul Foot, Richard Ingrams and William Rushton. Rushton was to be *Private Eye*'s link with the satirical television show *That Was The Week That Was* from 1962–1963.

103 *Sunday Times*, 21 October 1962. At that stage the group consisted of John Lennon, Paul McCartney, George Harrison, Stuart Sutcliffe and Pete Best. Stuart Sutcliffe left of his own accord, but Pete Best, the drummer, was dropped in favour of Richard Starkey, who had the stage name Ringo Starr. 'The Beatles,' wrote Dominic Sandbrook, 'had sacked Best with little more compunction than Harold Macmillan showed when dismissing Chancellors.' Dominic Sandbrook, *Never Had It So Good: A History of Britain from Suez to the Beatles*, Little, Brown, 2005, p. 469.

104 Twiggy (Leslie Hornby) on the 'Fashion' menu of her website, www.twiggylawson.co.uk.

105 Harold Macmillan in conversation with Alistair Horne.

106 So was Lady Elizabeth Bowes-Lyon when she had married the Duke of York, later King George VI, in 1923.

107 When Armstrong-Jones was ennobled as Lord Snowdon in 1961, Macmillan unfairly observed that it was 'making a mountain out of a molehill'.

108 Anne, the Countess of Rosse, was known in certain circles as Tugboat Annie, 'because she drifted from peer to peer'.

109 D. R. Thorpe, *Alec Douglas-Home*, Sinclair-Stevenson, 1996, p. 262.

110 Sir Hugh Carleton Greene (1910–1987), Director General of the BBC, 1960–1969, was one of the seminal figures of the sixties, as anti-Establishment as his great predecessor Lord Reith, whom he somewhat resembled physically, had been a personification of the Establishment. He worked as a journalist in Germany, 1933–1939, and after the war was Controller of Broadcasting in the British Zone in Germany, 1946–1948. He was chairman of the Bodley Head, the publishing house of his brother, Graham Greene. Such a powerful figure divided opinion. For many he was 'the other great DG' after Reith; for Mary Whitehouse he represented all that was wrong with British society.

111 Graham C. Greene to the author, 15 September 2009.

112 Television had a powerful hold. The same phenomenon was seen in 1967 with the Sunday night episodes of *The Forsyte Saga*, which meant that many

churches changed the time of evensong.

113 Cartoon by Anton, *Punch*, 20 March 1963.

114 And not what Macmillan would have called 'any old duke'. Frost's father-in-law was the Duke of Norfolk, Earl Marshal of England and the premier peer of the land.

115 Michael Palin, *Observer*, 15 January 1995.

116 Michael Cockerell, *Live from Number 10: The Inside Story of Prime Ministers and Television*, Faber and Faber, 1988, p. 85.

CHAPTER TWENTY SIX

Seeing Beyond the Trees 1961

1 In conversation with the author at the spot where President Kennedy's helicopter had taken off from Birch Grove on 30 June 1963.

2 Harold Macmillan to President Charles de Gaulle, 22 December 1960. MS Macmillan dep. c. 330. Macmillan Papers, Bodleian Library, Oxford.

3 Harold Macmillan diary, 30 June 1960. MS Macmillan dep. d. 39, loc. cit.

4 'The Grand Design'. Memorandum by the Prime Minister, 29 December 1960. PREM 11/3325. National Archives, Kew.

5 'Short Version of the Grand Design', prepared by Philip de Zulueta. PREM 11/3311, loc. cit.

6 Macmillan-de Gaulle talks, 28–29 January 1961, FO 371/161097, National Archives, Kew.

7 President Kennedy visited his sister's grave in June 1963 on his way to stay with Macmillan at Birch Grove. Subsequently his two brothers, Robert and Edward, also visited Edensor. The President was greatly touched by the epitaph on his sister's headstone, 'Joy she gave. Joy she has found.'

8 An account of the presidential inauguration is given in Deborah Devonshire, *Home to Roost and Other Peckings*, John Murray, 2009, pp. 83–92.

9 Harold Macmillan diary, 25 March 1961. MS Macmillan dep. d. 41, loc. cit.

10 Harold Macmillan, *Pointing the Way: 1959–1961*, Macmillan, 1972, p. 336.

11 David Nunnerly, *President Kennedy and Britain*, Bodley Head, 1972, p. 28.

12 Harold Macmillan diary, 26 March 1961. MS Macmillan dep. d. 41, loc. cit.

13 A full account is contained in 'Key West Meeting: Record of discussion held at the United States Naval base, Key West, Florida, 26 March 1961'. PREM 11/3313, National Archives, Kew.

14 Barbara Leaming, *Jack Kennedy: The Making of a President*, Weidenfeld & Nicolson, 2006, p. 359.

15 Ibid.

16 Nunnerly, op. cit., p. 41.

17 A fact the late Lord Caccia admitted to the author in 1985.

18 Nunnerly, op. cit., p. 40.
19 Harold Macmillan to Sir David
   Ormsby-Gore, 24 May 1961.
   MS Macmillan dep. c. 331, loc.
   cit.
20 Macmillan, op. cit., p. 345.
21 Harold Macmillan diary, 4 May
   1961. MS Macmillan dep. d. 42,
   loc. cit.
22 McGeorge Bundy, Interview,
   1 March 1964. Oral History
   Project, John F. Kennedy
   Presidential Library, Boston.
23 Harold Macmillan to John
   F. Kennedy, 10 April 1961.
   T216/61. National Archives,
   Kew.
24 Quoted in Mary Van Rensselaer
   Thayer, *Jacqueline Kennedy:
   The White House Years*, Little
   Brown, Boston, 1971, p. 247.
25 Sir Robert Menzies to Harold
   Macmillan, 28 March 1960.
   PREM 11/3609. National
   Archives, Kew.
26 Robert Dallek, *John F. Kennedy:
   An Unfinished Life, 1917–1963*,
   Allen Lane, 2003, p. 299.
27 Thomas J. Schoenbaum, *Waging
   Peace and War: Dean Rusk
   in the Truman, Kennedy and
   Johnson Years*, Simon and
   Schuster, New York, 1988,
   p. 276. The Bay of Pigs was
   the disastrous CIA-sponsored
   invasion of Cuba in April 1961.
28 The late Lord Home to the
   author, 9 August 1990.
29 The many Mitford spin-off
   books almost invariably contain
   such a glossary. How else was
   the general reader to know that
   'Cake' was the Queen Mother?
30 Arthur Schlesinger was Special
   Adviser to John F. Kennedy,
   1961–1963. Arthur M.
   Schlesinger Jr, *A Thousand
   Days: John F. Kennedy in the
   White House*, Houghton Mifflin,
   Boston, 1965, p. 376.
31 John K. Galbraith was the
   United States Ambassador to
   India, 1961–1963. John Kenneth
   Galbraith, *Ambassador's
   Journal: A Personal Account of
   the Kennedy Years*, Houghton
   Mifflin, Boston, 1969, p. 8.
32 Ambassador David Bruce to
   Dean Rusk, 13 December
   1961. State Department
   Correspondence files, John
   F. Kennedy Presidential
   Library, Boston. David Bruce,
   memorandum on Kennedy and
   Macmillan, Oral History Project
   written statement, 1964, John
   F. Kennedy Presidential Library,
   Boston.
33 Roger Wilmut (ed.), *The
   Complete Beyond the Fringe*,
   Methuen, 1987, p. 54. Talks
   in Bonn were treated in similar
   fashion. 'I spoke with the
   German Foreign Minister, Herr
   ... Herr and there, and we
   exchanged many frank words in
   our respective languages.' Ibid.
34 David Kirkpatrick Este Bruce
   (1898–1977), American
   Ambassador in London, 1961–
   1969. Bruce was a figure of great
   influence in Anglo-American
   relations in the sixties. He had
   been one of the candidates for
   Secretary of State before Rusk
   was appointed. His dispatches
   to the State Department in
   Washington in 1963 give one
   of the most detailed accounts
   of Macmillan's political decline.

His informed description of how Lord Home eventually emerged as Prime Minister in October 1963 scotches many inaccurate myths.

CHAPTER TWENTY SEVEN

Searching for a Role 1961–1962

1 Christopher Booker, *The Neophiliacs: a study of the revolution in English life in the Fifties and Sixties*, Collins, 1969, p. 167.

2 Michael Young, *The Chipped White Cups of Dover*, Unit 2, London, 1960.

3 To Young's disappointment, *Which?* became the bible of middle-class consumers.

4 Michael Shanks, *The Stagnant Society: A Warning*, Penguin Books, Harmondsworth, 1961.

5 Harold Macmillan diary, 16 February 1962. MS Macmillan dep. d. 45. Macmillan Papers, Bodleian Library, Oxford. The same frustration was later expressed by Lady Thatcher to the late Hugo Young, a persistent and articulate critic of free-market views. 'Why don't you do something useful, Hugo?' she implored. 'Like starting a small business.' (Private information.)

7 Speech at Key West, 5 December 1962.

8 David Nunnerly, *President Kennedy and Britain*, Bodley Head, 1972, p. 1.

9 Reginald Maudling, *Memoirs*, Sidgwick & Jackson, 1978, p. 233. See Chapter 28 for a discussion of how Maudling lost his position as the heir apparent to the premiership.

10 Dr Peter Catterall, 'Roles and Relationships: Dean Acheson, "British Decline" and Post-War Anglo-American Relations', in Antoine Capet and Aissatou Sy-Wongu (ed.), *La 'relation spéciale' entre le Royaume-Uni at Les États Unis*, Rouen University Press, Rouen, 2003, p. 117.

11 *Fifteen to Eighteen*, Report of the Central Advisory Council for Education (Chairman: Sir Geoffrey Crowther), 24 July 1959, HMSO.

12 Geoffrey, Baron Crowther (1907–1972), businessman, editor of *The Economist*, 1938–1956; Chairman of the Advisory Council for Education, 1956–1960; and first Chancellor of the Open University, 1969.

13 *Higher Education* (The Robbins Report), Cmnd 2154, HMSO, 1963.

14 The government of Sir Alec Douglas-Home accepted the conclusions of the Robbins Report on 24 October 1963, a few days after Macmillan's resignation as Prime Minister.

15 Cabinet Conclusion C (63) 173, 1 October 1963. National Archives, Kew.

16 *Encounter*, July 1960. The author can recall Kingsley Amis, in appropriate costume and wig, taking part in a re-creation of an 18th-century cricket match, with curved bats and two stump wickets, on Parker's Piece at Cambridge in the summer of

1963. Such activities were not part of Harold Wilson's vision of 'the white heat of the technological revolution'.

17 *Half Our Future* (The Newsom Report), 1963, A report of the Central Advisory Council for Education, HMSO, 1963.

18 *Royal Commission on the Press, 1961–1962*, September 1962, Cmnd 1811, HMSO.

19 *Traffic in Towns* (Report by Sir Colin Buchanan), November 1963, Penguin Books, Harmondsworth, in association with HMSO, 1963.

20 Harry William, Baron Pilkington (1905–1983), Director of Pilkington Brothers, Ltd, 1934–1980.

21 Asa Briggs, *The History of Broadcasting in the United Kingdom: Volume V Competition*, Oxford University Press, Oxford, 1995, p. 269.

22 *The Listener*, 13 November 1980.

23 *Report of the Committee on Broadcasting 1960*, Cmnd 1753, 5 June 1962, HMSO.

24 *The Times*, 28 June 1962.

25 *Report of the Committee on Broadcasting 1960*, op. cit., para. 207, p. 64.

26 *Daily Mail*, 28 June 1962. The Independent Television Authority (ITA) became the Independent Broadcasting Authority (IBA) in 1972.

27 Richard, Baron Beeching (1913–1985), had worked on armament design in the wartime Ministry of Supply, before joining the technical department of ICI. He came to public notice

as, first, chairman of the British Transport Commission from 1960, and then chairman of the British Railways Board, 1960–1965.

28 Christian Wolmar, *Fire and Steam: A New History of the Railways in Britain*, Atlantic Books, 2007, p. 286.

29 The north Oxfordshire village of Charlbury still retains a small railway station, a direct, pre-Beeching rail link to London. Villagers attribute this to the fact that Sir Peter Parker (1924–2002), chairman of British Rail from 1976 to 1983, lived there, and a garden is gratefully maintained at the station in his memory.

30 See Chapter 30 for an analysis of Macmillan's relations with the Thatcher government.

31 A song inspired by Will Hay's 1937 film *Oh, Mr Porter*, from the BBC TV comedy series *Oh, Doctor Beeching!* (1995–1997).

32 Wolmar, op. cit., p. 286.

33 *Architectural Review*, Volume 74, September 1933.

34 One of the author's vivid memories of the early 1950s is of the Great Hall at Euston Station and of the Doric Arch, through which he passed for five years, in contrasting mood depending on whether he was returning to boarding school or going home.

35 Sir James Maude Richards (1907–1992), architectural correspondent of *The Times*, 1946–1971. Richards was appalled when Sir William Haley, editor of *The Times*,

published a leading article at the height of the controversy over the Euston Arch, declaring that it was not worth saving.

36 Gavin Stamp, 'Steam ahead: the proposed rebuilding of London's Euston station is an opportunity to atone for a great architectural crime', *Apollo: the international magazine of art and antiques*, October 2007.

37 'The Euston Murder', *Architectural Review*, April 1962.

38 Harold Macmillan, *Pointing the Way: 1959–1961*, Macmillan, 1972, p. 370.

39 Speech in Oxford, June 1959.

40 Bevis Hillier, *Betjeman: The Bonus of Laughter*, John Murray, 2004, p. 306.

41 Randall Davidson had succeeded the very different figure of Frederick Temple in 1903. Cosmo Gordon Lang, likewise a contrast to his predecessor, succeeded Davidson in 1928. In 1942, William Temple, from the Christian Socialist tradition, became Archbishop of Canterbury - 'the best half crown article in a penny bazaar' as Churchill commented after appointing him. After Temple's premature death in 1944, Churchill appointed Fisher to succeed him.

42 Not that this guaranteed the succession for the Archbishop of York. Mrs Thatcher appointed the Bishop of Bath and Wells to Canterbury in 1990, rather than the Archbishop of York. In previous centuries, York was more regarded as a top job in itself, and between 1396 and 1862, only six Archbishops of York moved to Canterbury.

43 Edward Carpenter, *Archbishop Fisher: His Life and Times*, The Canterbury Press, Norwich, 1991, p. 749.

44 Owen Chadwick, *Michael Ramsey: A Life*, Clarendon Press, Oxford, 1990, pp. 103–7.

45 Harold Macmillan to the Archbishop of Canterbury, 17 January 1961. MS Macmillan dep. c. 330, loc. cit.

46 Harold Macmillan to Dr Mervyn Stockwood, 25 January 1961. Ibid.

47 This was upgraded to a CBE in 1992. Six years later, Tom Finney received a knighthood.

48 Roy Welensky, *Welensky's 4000 Days*, Collins, 1964, pp. 304–5.

49 Harold Macmillan diary, 24 March 1961. MS Macmillan dep. d. 41, loc. cit.

50 Information from a Bank of England official who heard the story from John Wyndham.

51 Selwyn Lloyd to Harold Macmillan, 16 March 1961. SELO 240 (4). Selwyn Lloyd Papers, Churchill College, Cambridge.

52 'Above the line' surpluses and 'below the line' deficits were terms that became obsolete in 1963. 'Below the line' deficits were financial transactions (interest received from, loans made to, and repaid by, for example, nationalised industries), and if the deficit there was greater than the surplus 'above the line', the government would be a net borrower during the

year, and would hope to be selling, among other things, more of Macmillan's Premium Bonds to plug the gap. The 'above the line' figure is what really matters - the balance of government income and actual expenditure. The important thing is whether the surplus was increasing (reducing aggregate demand) or falling (increasing demand). Lloyd's second budget, in 1962, aimed for a smaller surplus than 1961, and to that extent would be seen as reflationary, although compared with the outcome for 1961 it was fairly neutral.

53 *Financial Times*, 18 April 1961. *Manchester Guardian*, 18 April 1961.

54 George Rowland Stanley Baring, 3rd Earl of Cromer (1918–1991), banker and diplomat, Governor of the Bank of England, 1961–1966; Ambassador in Washington, 1971–1974.

55 Arthur Hugh Clough, *Say Not the Struggle Naught Availeth*. Churchill had quoted this poem in his famous rallying wartime broadcast of 27 April 1941, extolling the support of Roosevelt for the British war effort.

56 Macmillan, op. cit., p. 323.

57 Frederick Bishop to Harold Macmillan, 22 April 1960. PREM 11/3133. National Archives, Kew.

58 A. J. P. Taylor, *Beaverbrook*, Penguin Books, Harmondsworth, 1974, p. 826.

59 Speech at the Labour Party Conference, 3 October 1962.

60 Harold Macmillan diary, 16 November 1950, MS Macmillan dep. d. 6, loc. cit.

61 Harold Macmillan to the author, 23 April 1975.

62 Harold Evans, *Downing Street Diary: The Macmillan Years 1957–1963*, Hodder & Stoughton, 1981, p. 174.

63 Harold Macmillan diary, 29 November 1961. MS Macmillan dep. d. 44, loc. cit.

64 Letter to the *Daily Telegraph*, 23 March 1962.

65 Sir Philip Goodhart to the author, 2 June 2008.

66 Lady Violet Bonham Carter diary, 14 March 1962. Mark Pottle (ed.), *Daring to Hope: The Diaries and Letters of Violet Bonham Carter 1946–1969*, Weidenfeld & Nicolson, 2000, p. 250.

67 'He hath left them you/And to your heirs for ever: common pleasures/To walk abroad and recreate yourself.' *Julius Caesar*, III, ii, 240–2. As a result of this bequest, Orpington's council, uniquely in local government, employed a gamekeeper. Jo Grimond, *Memoirs*, Heinemann, 1979, p. 203.

68 Lady Violet Bonham Carter diary, 14 March 1962, Pottle (ed.), op. cit., p. 250.

69 The late Peter Goldman to the author, 1976. Though Macmillan's words to the defeated Goldman might be seen as tactful sympathy, this opinion was shared by many other Tory grandees.

70 Goldman had written much of

Iain Macleod's biography of Neville Chamberlain (1961) and was to perform a similar service over Butler's memoirs, *The Art of the Possible* (1971).

71 *Daily Mail*, 26 January 1962.

72 D. E. Butler and Anthony King, *The British General Election of 1964*, Macmillan, 1965, p. 16.

73 Selwyn Lloyd's record of meeting of 4 March 1961. SELO 88 (3). Selwyn Lloyd Papers, loc. cit.

74 Preface to the 1903 New York edition of *The Ambassadors*.

75 His successor, Reginald Maudling, honoured that pledge in his 1963 Budget.

76 Mrs Rachel Clayton to Selwyn Lloyd, 10 April 1962. SELO 88 (3), loc. cit.

77 *Sunday Times*, 15 April 1962.

78 Harold Macmillan to Selwyn Lloyd, 9 April 1962. SELO 88 (3), loc. cit.

79 Harold Macmillan to Selwyn Lloyd, 11 April 1962. SELO 88 (3), loc. cit.

80 SELO 180 (4), loc. cit.

81 Information from the late Michael Marshall, Selwyn Lloyd's solicitor, in 1985.

82 The late Sir Philip de Zulueta to the author, 1986.

83 The late Lord Watkinson to the author, 1985.

84 See Anthony Howard, *RAB: The Life of R. A. Butler*, Jonathan Cape, 1987, pp. 291–4, for an account of Butler's feelings.

85 SELO 180 (4), loc. cit.

86 D. R. Thorpe, *Selwyn Lloyd*, Jonathan Cape, 1989, p. 352.

87 SELO 53 (1), loc. cit.

88 SELO 180 (4), loc. cit.

89 SELO 184 (3), loc. cit.

90 Ibid.

91 *The Times*, 14 July 1962.

92 In a later era it was to become almost commonplace.

93 Evidence from several Cabinet ministers and officials who were present.

CHAPTER TWENTY EIGHT

Opening Pandora's Box 1962–1963

1 Tom Bower, *The Perfect English Spy: Sir Dick White and the Secret War* 1935–90, Heinemann, 1995, p. 295.

2 Private information.

3 The unfounded rumour that Macmillan had himself been a KGB agent still surfaced from time to time. When Churchill became Prime Minister in October, he would have received a security briefing from the then Director General of MI5, Sir Percy Sillitoe. Macmillan would never have been appointed to the Cabinet in 1951, and certainly not to the post of Minister of Defence in 1954, if there had been any hint, at whatever distance in time, of these rumours in MI5 files.

4 Christopher Andrew, *The Defence of the Realm: The Authorized History of MI5*, Allen Lane, 2009, p. 484.

5 Sir Dick Goldsmith White (1906–1993), intelligence officer, Director General of MI5, 1953–1956; head of SIS (the Secret Intelligence Service), 1956–1968; co-ordinator of

intelligence, Cabinet Office, 1968–1972.

6 Sir Roger Henry Hollis (1905–1973), intelligence officer, Director General of MI5, 1956–1963. After retirement he was himself investigated for links to the KGB. On 25 March 1981 the Prime Minister, Margaret Thatcher, in response to growing public rumours about the investigation, announced in the House of Commons that his name and reputation had been fully cleared.

7 The alias of Morris and Lona Cohen, who were convicted of spying in 1961.

8 When Evgeni Ivanov was found to be involved with Christine Keeler at the time of the Profumo Affair, it was said that it was not 'reds under the bed' but 'reds on top of the bed'.

9 The atmosphere at the time contributed much to the popularity of the James Bond novels of Ian Fleming.

10 William John Christopher Vassall (1924–1996), Admiralty official and spy.

11 Ernest R. May and Philip D. Zelikov (ed.), *The Kennedy Tapes: Inside the White House during the Cuban Missile Crisis*, W. W. Norton, New York, paperback edition, 2002, p. 183.

12 Harold Macmillan, *At the End of the Day: 1961–1963*, Macmillan, 1973, p. 220.

13 McGeorge Bundy, Oral History Interview, 1970. John F. Kennedy Presidential Library, Boston.

14 Percy Cradock, *Know Your Enemy: How the Joint Intelligence Committee Saw the World*, John Murray, 2002, p. 190.

15 Nigel Fisher, *Harold Macmillan*, Weidenfeld & Nicolson, 1982, p. 299. Professor Peter Hennessy, after researching the primary records of the Cuban Missile crisis for his forthcoming book on the 1960s, also believes that Macmillan's involvement should not be disregarded. Professor Peter Hennessy to the author, 3 November 2009.

16 Sir Frank Kenyon Roberts (1907–1998), diplomat; Ambassador to Yugoslavia, 1954–1957; Ambassador to Russia, 1960–1962; Ambassador to the Federal Republic of Germany, 1963–1968. Sir Frank Roberts told the author that he was convinced war would not break out over Cuba, as there was no panic buying of supplies by citizens in Moscow. The late Sir Frank Roberts to the author, 1991.

17 Sir Herbert Stanley Marchant (1906–1990), diplomat, began his career as a schoolmaster at Harrow, 1928–1939; Ambassador to Cuba, 1960–1963; Ambassador to Tunisia, 1963–1966. Lord Home of the Hirsel's views on Macmillan, Ormsby-Gore, Roberts and Marchant, discussions with the author, 1990–1995, from which many subsequent details also derive. With characteristic modesty, Lord Home downplayed his own, not insignificant, part, especially in the advice he gave to Macmillan

before crucial telephone calls to Washington.

18 Sir Alec Douglas-Home, 17 March 1965 interview, John F. Kennedy Oral History statement, John F. Kennedy Presidential Library, Boston.

19 Deborah, Dowager Duchess of Devonshire, to the author, 15 October 2007.

20 Robert F. Kennedy, *Thirteen Days: The Cuban Missile Crisis*, Macmillan, 1969, *passim* a book for which Macmillan provided an affectionate foreword.

21 Lord Hailsham baptised his own newly born daughter as a precaution.

22 *The Times*, 6 January 2007.

23 A point Lord Home had made to Macmillan. The late Lord Home to the author, 9 August 1990.

24 The Americans had deployed 15 Jupiter IRBMs in Turkey in early 1962. This was Khrushchev's 'excuse' for the Cuban deployment.

25 The complete transcripts of Kennedy's telephone conversations with Macmillan during the Cuban Missile crisis are in Cuba-General-Macmillan Telephone Conversations, 10/62–11/62 folder, National Security Files, Box 37. John F. Kennedy Presidential Library, Boston. These transcripts were later placed in the National Archives at Kew (PREM 11/3690), but the author read the transcripts in Boston.

26 Kennedy-Macmillan telephone conversation, 22–23 October 1962, PREM 11/3690, loc. cit.

27 Harold Macmillan to Sir David Ormsby-Gore, 22 October 1962. PREM 11/3689. Telegram 7396. National Archives, Kew.

28 George Alfred, Baron George-Brown (1914–1985), Labour MP for Belper, 1945–1970; First Secretary of State and Secretary for Economic Affairs, 1964–1966; Foreign Secretary, 1966–1968. Macmillan thought him one of the rudest men he had ever encountered, and ruder when sober than when drunk. Brown's weakness for alcohol brought the euphemism 'tired and emotional' into the political vocabulary.

29 Kennedy-Macmillan telephone conversation, 24 October 1962, PREM 11/3690, loc. cit.

30 Harold Macmillan to John F. Kennedy, 25 October 1963, PREM 11/3690, telegram 24020, loc. cit.

31 Kennedy-Macmillan telephone conversation, 25 October 1962, PREM 11/3690, loc. cit.

32 Kennedy-Macmillan telephone conversation, 26 October 1962, ibid.

33 In fact the missiles were Turkish property; it was the warheads that were owned by the Americans.

34 Peter Hennessy, *The Secret State: Whitehall and the Cold War*, Allen Lane 2002, p. 40.

35 'Nuclear Retaliation Procedures', 23 January 1962. DEFE 25/49. National Archives, Kew.

36 Andrew, op. cit., p. 329.

37 Hennessy, op. cit., p. 172.

38 Harold Evans diary, 28 October 1962. Harold Evans, *Downing Street Diary: The Macmillan*

Years 1957–1963, Hodder &
Stoughton, 1981, p. 224.

39 Arthur M. Schlesinger, Jr,
*A Thousand Days: John F.
Kennedy in the White House*,
Houghton Mifflin, Boston, 1965,
p. 758.

40 Thomas Hardy, *In Tenebris*.

41 Peter Hennessy, *The Prime
Minister: The Office and its
Holders since 1945*, Allen Lane,
2000, pp. 102–3.

42 Peter Mangold, *The Almost
Impossible Ally: Harold
Macmillan and Charles de
Gaulle*, I. B. Tauris, 2006, pp.
180–1.

43 I am grateful to the late Sir
Philip de Zulueta in 1986, and
Sir Michael Jenkins, then in the
Paris Embassy, on 1 April 2008,
for details of the Rambouillet
visit.

44 An echo of the time they had
met at Tipasa in North Africa on
13 June 1943, when Macmillan
had bathed naked in the
Mediterranean, whilst de Gaulle,
in military uniform, had sat
watching on a rock. Mangold,
op. cit., p. 1.

45 Report from the Paris
Embassy to the Foreign Office,
21 December 1962. FO
371/171443. National Archives,
Kew.

46 The late Lord Home to the
author, 9 August 1990.

47 Richard E. Neustadt, *Report
to JFK: The Skybolt Crisis in
Perspective*, Cornell University
Press, Ithaca, New York, 1990,
p. 137.

48 Peter Hennessy and Caroline
Anstey, 'Moneybags and Brains:
The Anglo-American "Special
Relationship" since 1945',
Strathclyde *Analysis* Paper No.
1, Department of Government,
University of Strathclyde, 1990,
p. 11.

49 Aneurin Bevan speech at the
Labour Party Conference,
Brighton, 3 October 1957.

50 Cabinet minutes, 21 December
1962. CAB 128/36. National
Archives, Kew.

51 Cabinet minutes, 3 January
1963. CAB 128/37. National
Archives, Kew.

52 Lord Home to President
Kennedy, 7 January 1963.
Kennedy Papers. President's
Office Files (POF), Box 127,
Folder 5. John F. Kennedy
Presidential Library, Boston.

53 Harold Macmillan diary, 31
December 1962. MS Macmillan
dep. d. 48. Macmillan Papers,
Bodleian Library, Oxford.

54 President de Gaulle press
conference, 14 January 1963.

55 Harold Macmillan, *At the
End of the Day: 1961–1963*,
Macmillan, 1973, p. 365.

56 Harold Macmillan diary, 28
January 1963. MS Macmillan
dep. d. 48, loc. cit.

57 Dr David Butler file of interviews
for his book on the 1964 general
election. Nuffield College,
Oxford.

58 Tony Benn diary, 18 January
1963. Tony Benn, *Out of the
Wilderness: Diaries 1963–1967*,
Hutchinson, 1987, p. 1.

59 A remark first reported by
Bevin's secretary, Sir Roderick
Barclay, often quoted by Euro-
sceptics.

60 Humphrey Berkeley, *Crossing the Floor*, Allen & Unwin, 1972, p. 28.

61 Some reports state that Penkovsky was killed by a single bullet shot to the back of the head; others, more chillingly, claim that a film exists of him being bound by piano wire to a board and then cremated alive, feet first.

62 *Security Procedures in the Public Service* (The Radcliffe Report), Cmnd 1681, April 1962, HMSO.

63 A D-Notice is a request by the Joint Services, Press and Broadcasting Committee of the House of Commons to journalists to refrain from publishing matters concerning national security.

64 Alistair Horne, *Macmillan 1957–1986: Volume II of the Official Biography*, Macmillan, 1989, p. 461.

65 See below.

66 Sir Thomas Galbraith (1917–1982) was Unionist MP for the Hillhead Division of Glasgow from 1948 until his death on 2 January 1982. Roy Jenkins, leader of the Social Democratic Party, captured the seat at the by-election in March 1982. On 2 January, a member of Jenkins' team had left a garbled message on the answerphone - 'Galbraith is dead.' Instead of realising that this meant a by-election at a winnable seat, Jenkins thought that the economist John Kenneth Galbraith had died, and began preparing condolences for Galbraith's 'widow'. Private information.

67 Alan Mathieson Turing (1912–1954), computer scientist, and the brains behind the Enigma code-breaking success at wartime Bletchley Park, committed suicide, after police investigated his private life.

68 The composer Benjamin Britten (1913–1976) was interviewed by police during Kilmuir's 'clamp-down'.

69 Macmillan would not hear of Carrington resigning, though Carrington had felt it a matter of honour, as at the time when he did resign from the government on the morning of 5 April 1982, when Argentina invaded the Falklands Islands. It was the day of Rab Butler's memorial service in Westminster Abbey and there was no time to reprint the order of service, which still listed Carrington, who read the first lesson, as Foreign Secretary.

70 An opinion widely held in Fleet Street was that Mulholland and Foster were in an impossible position, as they had no sources to reveal. Anthony Howard to the author, 3 March 2008.

71 Richard Crossman diary, 27 March 1963. Janet Morgan (ed.), *The Backbench Diaries of Richard Crossman*, Hamish Hamilton and Jonathan Cape, 1981, p. 989.

72 Tony Benn, *More Time for Politics: Diaries 2001–2007*, Hutchinson, 2007, p. 166.

73 As the author found, on a visit to Cliveden in the summer of 2009, the pool still exists for hotel guests, much as it was in Ward's day.

74 Details of the security aspects of the Profumo affair are in Andrew, op. cit., pp. 494–501.

75 Ibid., p. 497.

76 *Hansard*, 21 March 1963.

77 BBC Television interview, 13 June 1963.

78 Quoted in David Profumo, *Bringing the House Down*, John Murray, 2006, p. 194.

79 David Corbally obituary, *Daily Telegraph*, 28 April 2004.

80 George Edward Cecil, Baron Wigg (1900–1983). Labour MP for Dudley, 1945–1967; Paymaster General, 1964–1967. Like Macmillan, Wigg was greatly influenced by the social vision of A. D. Lindsay, the interwar Master of Balliol.

81 Andrew, op. cit., p. 498.

82 Professor Vernon Bogdanor to the author, 8 November 2009.

83 Not 69, as some people liked to joke.

84 *Lord Denning's Report: The Circumstances Leading to the Resignation of the Former Secretary of State for War, Mr J. D. Profumo*, Cmnd 2152, HMSO, September 1963.

85 Profumo, op. cit., p. 199.

86 Ibid., p. 155.

87 Andrew, op. cit., p. 500.

88 Harold Macmillan diary, 7 July 1963. MS Macmillan dep. d. 49, loc. cit.

89 Cmnd 2150, HMSO, September 1963.

90 David Bruce to the Secretary of State, 18 June 1963, Box 171, Folder 4. John F. Kennedy Presidential Library, Boston.

91 David Bruce to Dean Rusk, 19 June 1963, Telegram 5130, Department of State Papers. John F. Kennedy Presidential Library, Boston.

92 Harold Evans diary, 31 March 1963. Evans, op. cit., p. 260.

93 Harold Macmillan note to Reginald Maudling, 20 February 1963. PREM 11/4202. National Archives, Kew.

94 Written addition by Harold Macmillan on a Treasury memorandum, 6 March 1963. Ibid.

95 Lord Cromer to Reginald Maudling, 18 March 1963. Ibid.

96 Record of meeting between Harold Macmillan and Reginald Maudling, 22 March 1963. Ibid.

97 Lewis Baston, *Reggie: The Life of Reginald Maudling*, Sutton Publishing, 2004, p. 178.

98 Ibid., pp. 192–3.

99 John Boyd-Carpenter, *Way of Life*, Sidgwick & Jackson, 1980, p. 169.

100 Ibid., p. 170.

101 Reginald Maudling, *Memoirs*, Sidwick & Jackson, 1978, p. 112.

102 Richard Crossman diary, 22 June 1963. Morgan (ed.), op. cit., p. 1005.

103 A point emphasised by Sir Alistair Horne at the seminar on biographical writing held at St Antony's College, Oxford, on 28 September 2009 to celebrate the 40th anniversary of the Horne Fellowship at St Antony's.

104 Philip Goodhart, *The 1922: The Story of the Conservative Backbenchers' Parliamentary Committee*, Macmillan, 1973, p. 191.

105 *Hansard*, 27 March 1952.
106 Article by Harry Boyne, *Daily Telegraph*, 20 June 1963.
107 The late Reginald Maudling to the author, 4 September 1975.
108 A point emphasised to the author by several ministers and civil servants.
109 Baston, op. cit., p. 200.
110 See Chapter 29.
111 Lady Home of the Hirsel told the author that this article, more than any other factor, alerted Lord Home to the possibility that he could become Prime Minister. The late Lady Home of the Hirsel to the author, 9 August 1990.

CHAPTER TWENTY NINE

Guided Democracy 1963

1 Selwyn Lloyd to Sir Anthony Eden, 28 October 1963. AP 23/44/56. Avon Papers, Birmingham University Library.
2 Oliver Brian Sanderson, first Baron Poole of Aldgate (1911–1993), Conservative MP for Oswestry, 1945–1950, when he left Parliament for the City. Head of the Conservative Political Centre, 1950; Joint Party Treasurer, 1952; Conservative Party Chairman, 1955–1957; Deputy Party Chairman, 1957–1959; Joint Party Chairman, 1963–1964.
3 Nigel Fisher, *Iain Macleod*, Andre Deutsch, 1973, p. 231.
4 Harold Macmillan to Iain Macleod, 16 April 1963. MS Macmillan dep. c. 335. Macmillan Papers, Bodleian Library, Oxford.
5 Lord Poole to Harold Macmillan, 28 August 1963. MS Macmillan dep. c. 355, loc. cit.
6 John Ramsden, *The Winds of Change: Macmillan to Heath, 1957–1975: A History of the Conservative Party*, Longman, 1996, p. 190.
7 Ibid., p. 192.
8 When the 13th Earl of Home, father of Alec Douglas-Home, then Lord Dunglass, had died on 11 July 1951, Dunglass, until that moment MP for Lanark, had attempted to re-enter the Commons to retrieve his spectacles. Doorkeepers barred his entry, as he was already a member of 'another' place. D. R. Thorpe, *Alec Douglas-Home*, Sinclair-Stevenson, 1996, p. 139.
9 Tony Benn, *Years of Hope: Diaries, Papers and Letters, 1940–1962*, Hutchinson, 1994, p. 360.
10 Cabinet Minutes, 27 June 1963. CAB 128/37. National Archives, Kew.
11 Lord Hailsham, *A Sparrow's Flight: The Memoirs of Lord Hailsham of St Marylebone*, Collins, 1990, pp. 348–9.
12 Tim Bligh to Harold Macmillan, 4 July 1963. Quoted in Thorpe, op. cit., p. 261.
13 *Romeo and Juliet*, III, i, 92–4. The late Lady Butler of Saffron Walden to the author, 20 July 1995.
14 Macmillan gives a detailed, though over-romanticised, account of the Kennedy visit in his memoirs. Harold Macmillan, *At the End of the Day:*

1961–1963, Macmillan, 1972, pp. 471–5. The author is grateful to the late Sir Philip de Zulueta for describing other details of the visit in 1986.

15 Unfortunately, in idiomatic German, *ein Berliner* is a jelly doughnut. Kennedy should not have included the word *ein*.

16 Sir David Ormsby-Gore to President John F. Kennedy, 2 August 1963. Kennedy Papers (President's Office Files POF6/26/22). John F. Kennedy Presidential Library, Boston.

17 Approximately £30m by later reckonings.

18 Lord Poole to Harold Macmillan, 28 August 1963. MS Macmillan dep. c. 355, loc. cit.

19 Denning Report, Paragraph 283.

20 Ibid., Paragraph 286.

21 Harold Macmillan diary, 18 September 1963. MS Macmillan dep. d. 50, loc. cit.

22 Lord Swinton memorandum, 'Prime Minister's Resignation, October 1963'. SWIN 174/7/9. Swinton Papers, Churchill College, Cambridge.

23 As Tony Blair was to find in his last spell in Downing Street.

24 I am grateful to the late Dr Lionel King-Lewis for discussing the events surrounding Macmillan's retirement with me in 1986.

25 Sir Edward Ford (1910–2006), tutor to King Farouk of Egypt, 1936–1937; Assistant Private Secretary to King George VI, 1946–1952; and to Queen Elizabeth II, 1952–1967. I am grateful to the late Sir Edward Ford for discussing with me

in 1991 details of the events surrounding the Macmillan resignation.

26 Enoch Powell, 'Narrative of the Events of 8–19 October 1963 so far as known to me directly', dictated on 20–23 October 1963. POLL 1/6/28. Enoch Powell Papers, Churchill College, Cambridge.

27 Sir John Richardson, 'Memorandum on Harold Macmillan's illness, written at the time' and given to Macmillan on 8 August 1972 as background material for the last volume of his memoirs. MS Macmillan dep. c. 962, loc. cit.

28 I am grateful to David Badenoch for providing me with a copy of this memorandum and for discussing related issues, particularly the oft-repeated myth that Macmillan resigned believing his condition was malignant.

29 *Evening Standard*, 10 October 1963.

30 The late Sir Edward Ford to the author, 1991.

31 The late Lord Butler of Saffron Walden to the author, 20 November 1975.

32 The original copy of this letter, from which Home read, is in the Home Papers at the Hirsel, Coldstream.

33 The late Sir Edward Heath to the author, 4 March 1999.

34 Dennis Walters, *Not Always with the Pack*, Constable, 1989, p. 125.

35 Record of the talks in Moscow. FO 371/171229. National Archives, Kew.

36 D. R. Thorpe, *Selwyn Lloyd*, Jonathan Cape, 1989, p. 375.

37 *Sunday Times*, 13 October 1963.

38 Lewis Baston, *Reggie: The Life of Reginald Maudling*, Sutton Publishing, 2004, p. 206.

39 D. R. Thorpe, *Alec Douglas-Home*, Sinclair-Stevenson, 1996, p. 296.

40 Quotations from David Badenoch memorandum, 'AWB and Harold Macmillan', 2008.

41 David Badenoch letter to *The Times*, 12 January 1994.

42 Obviously the other joint party chairman, Iain Macleod, could not be involved in this capacity, as he was a potential candidate for the leadership.

43 Francis Bacon, 'Of Church Controversies', *Essays*, 1625.

44 The late Lady Home of the Hirsel to the author, 9 August 1990.

45 SWIN 174/7/8. Swinton Papers, loc. cit.

46 *Independent on Sunday*, 1 January 1995.

47 Harold Macmillan, first draft Memorandum for the Queen, 15 October 1963, 'The Tuesday Memorandum'. PREM 11/5008. National Archives, Kew. The comment on the younger generation was included among the Macmillan entries in the *Oxford Dictionary of Political Quotations* after extracts from the memorandum were first published in Thorpe, *Douglas-Home*, op. cit., pp. 301–2.

48 Thorpe, *Douglas-Home*, op. cit., pp. 298–9.

49 Macmillan, op. cit. PREM 11/5008, loc. cit.

50 The late Lord Margadale (John Morrison) to the author, 1991.

51 D. J. Dutton, notice of the life of Reginald Edward Manningham-Buller, first Viscount Dilhorne. *Oxford Dictionary of National Biography Volume 8*, Oxford University Press, Oxford, 2004, p. 626. The Dilhorne family much resented the fact that the Lord Chancellor was always portrayed as a figure out of P. G. Wodehouse for his part in the events of October 1963. Kenneth Rose to the author, 10 January 2007.

52 Ben Pimlott, *The Queen: A Biography of Elizabeth II*, Harper Collins, 1996, p. 335.

53 D. R. Thorpe, obituary notice of Professor Ben Pimlott, *The Independent*, 14 April 2004.

54 Austen Chamberlain, *Politics from Inside: An Epistolary Chronicle 1906–1914*, Cassell, p. 372.

55 Captain Ernest Pretyman speech at the meeting to confirm Austen Chamberlain as party leader on 21 March 1921. Conservative Party Archives, Bodleian Library, Oxford.

56 The late Sir Knox Cunningham to the author, March 1975, cited in D. R. Thorpe, *The Uncrowned Prime Ministers*, Darkhorse Publishing, 1980, p. 233.

57 In 1911, Bonar Law was chosen because he was not Chamberlain or Long; similarly in 1923, Baldwin was chosen because he was not Curzon. Even as recently as 1990, John Major was chosen because he was not Michael Heseltine.

58 Vernon Bogdanor, 'The Selection of the Party Leader', in Anthony Seldon and Stuart Ball (ed.), *The Conservative Century: The Conservative Party since 1900*, Oxford University Press, Oxford, 1994, p. 76.

59 Selwyn Lloyd, record of talk with the Prime Minister, 16 October 1963. SELO 61 (6). Churchill College, Cambridge. The record Tim Bligh drew up is identical in all respects to Lloyd's, an indication that the Macmillan record is a reliable account of the interviews at the King Edward VII Hospital.

60 Reginald Bevins, *The Greasy Pole*, Hodder and Stoughton, 1965, p. 143. Bevins did lose his seat at the 1964 election.

61 See Ramsden, op. cit., pp. 204–5, for examples of this pressurising.

62 The late Harold Macmillan to the author, 23 April 1975.

63 These sheets are now in Macmillan's papers at the Bodleian Library, but Sir Knox Cunningham made them available to the author on 8 April 1975.

64 *London Review of Books*, 27 July 1989.

65 Nigel Lawson, 'The sick PM, his waiting successor and the unexpected assassin', *Daily Telegraph*, 3 October 2004. I am grateful to Lord Lawson for discussing these issues with me on 18 June 2008.

66 Speech in the House of Lords, 7 March 1961.

67 Lawson, op. cit.

68 *Spectator*, 17 January 1964.

69 McKenzie, op. cit., f-n p. 594.

70 The late Lord Home of the Hirsel to the author, 9 August 1990.

71 A point made to the author by both Lord Home and Harold Macmillan.

72 Harold Macmillan to Her Majesty the Queen, 15 October 1963. MS Macmillan dep. c. 578, loc. cit.

73 Details from the notes taken by Sir Knox Cunningham, loc. cit.

74 When discussing this meeting, in the room in which it had taken place, with the late Enoch Powell in 1986, the author was told that he was occupying the very chair in which Iain Macleod had sat.

75 Alan Thompson and John Barnes, *The Day Before Yesterday: an illustrated history of Britain from Attlee to Macmillan*, Granada Publishing, 1971, p. 219.

76 The late Harold Macmillan to the author, 23 April 1975. The 'Thursday Memorandum' is published for the first time as an appendix to the present volume, belatedly fulfilling Macmillan's wishes.

77 Vernon Bogdanor, *The Monarchy and the Constitution*, Clarendon Press, Oxford, 1995, pp. 96–7.

78 The Friday addendum to the 'Thursday Memorandum', Knox Cunningham papers.

79 Not eleven o'clock at night, as the Channel 4 television documentary *Ten Days that Made the Queen* (April 2006) asserted.

80 As Macmillan explained to the author, 'I had a tube in my penis, so I needed to be made decent.' The late Harold Macmillan to the author, 23 April 1975.

81 The late Sir Knox Cunningham to the author, 8 April 1975.

82 A. J. P. Taylor, *Beaverbrook*, Penguin Books, Harmondsworth, 1974, p. 846.

83 The late Sir Frederick Bishop to the author, 1991.

84 The late Reginald Maudling to the author, 4 September 1975. The late Lord Home to the author, 9 August 1990. Had Lord Home failed in his attempt, the Queen would not have got involved in further talks with her former Prime Minister, or any other senior Conservative figures, but issued a second invitation (Maudling), and, if necessary, a third (Butler). The late Sir Knox Cunningham to the author, 8 April 1975.

85 Thorpe, *Douglas-Home*, op. cit., p. 319.

86 Lord Dilhorne to Alistair Horne, 18 June 1980. Quoted in Alistair Horne, *Macmillan 1957–1986, Volume II of the Official Biography*, Macmillan, 1989, p. 687.

87 Harold Macmillan to John Morrison, 19 October 1963, MS Macmillan dep. c. 355, loc. cit.

88 The late Sir Knox Cunningham to the author, 6 March 1975. The manuscript of *One Man Dog: The Memoirs of Harold Macmillan's Private Secretary* is in the possession of the Drapers' Company in London. On 8 April 1975, going through the details of his memoirs with the author, Sir Knox Cunningham, with some feeling, even 12 years after the events, said that the reason the inaccuracies of October 1963 remain 'the myth that will not die' was because it was the one consolation remaining to disappointed supporters of Butler.

89 The Stratford-upon-Avon constituency was by then held by Angus Maude.

90 Sir Knox Cunningham to Harold Macmillan, 6 September 1964. MS Macmillan dep. c. 442, loc. cit.

CHAPTER THIRTY

Leaving the Green Room 1963–1986

1 *Oxford Dictionary of Political Quotations*, Oxford University Press, Oxford, 2005 edition, p. 157.

2 Roy Jenkins, *Portraits and Miniatures*, Macmillan, 1993, p. 124.

3 Harold Macmillan to Desmond Donnelly, 1 April 1971. MS Macmillan dep. c. 538. Macmillan Papers, Bodleian Library, Oxford.

4 Derek Walker-Smith, *Politics - Game or Art?*, unpublished memoirs, typescript p. 6, courtesy of the Hon. Jonah Walker-Smith. Derek Colclough Walker-Smith, Baron Broxbourne (1910–1992), Conservative MP for Hertford 1945–1983; Chairman of the 1922 Committee, 1951–1955;

holder of various ministerial posts, including Minister of Health, 1957–1960. Macmillan wrote a preface to Walker-Smith's scholarly 1933 book *The Protectionist Case in the 1840s*, much approving of his conclusion that Disraeli was 'not dead, but only sleeping'.

5 Harold Macmillan, *At the End of the Day: 1961–1963*, Macmillan, 1973, p. 520, '*La commedia e finita*' (the comedy is ended) are the closing words of Leoncavallo's opera *Pagliacci*.

6 Quoted in Roy Jenkins, *The Chancellors*, Macmillan, 1998, p. 187.

7 A reference to Arthur Balfour, who became Foreign Secretary in 1916.

8 The abolition of RPM was a contentious issue in 1964, impacting adversely on small shopkeepers, considered a bedrock Conservative constituency.

9 Harold Macmillan to Sir Alec Douglas-Home, 27 March 1964. Home Papers, the Hirsel, Coldstream.

10 John Hugh Hare, first Viscount Blakenham (1911–1982), Conservative MP for Woodbridge, 1945–1950; Sudbury and Woodbridge, 1950–1963; Secretary of State for War, 1956–1958; Minister for Agriculture, Fisheries and Food, 1958–1960; Minister of Labour 1960–1963; Conservative Party Chairman, 1963–1965. In the notice of Blakenham's life in the print edition of the *Oxford Dictionary of National Biography: Volume 25*, Oxford University Press, Oxford, 2004, pp. 255–6, it is stated that Blakenham's preference was for an autumn election. This was corrected in a later online edition.

11 The late Lord Fraser of Kilmorack to the author, 6 April 1995.

12 *The Times*, 11 April 1964.

13 Stanley Martin, *The Order of Merit: One Hundred Years of Matchless Honour*, I. B. Tauris, 2007, p. 399.

14 I am grateful to Nicholas Byam Shaw, sales manager in the early 1960s at Macmillan and Co., subsequently Macmillan Publishers Ltd, and managing director, 1969–1990, for his help over Macmillan's post-Downing Street publishing career.

15 Nicholas Byam Shaw to the author, 24 June 2009.

16 Harold Macmillan diary, 25 April 1964. MS Macmillan dep. d. 52, loc. cit.

17 Ibid., 18 June 1964. Professor David Dilks (born 1938), Professor of International History, University of Leeds, 1970–1991; Vice-Chancellor, University of Hull, 1991–1999. Professor Dilks edited the diaries of Sir Alexander Cadogan, and wrote a two-volume account of Lord Curzon's viceregalship of India and a biography of Neville Chamberlain.

18 Harold Macmillan took the author into the muniment room at Birch Grove on 23 April 1975 and proudly showed him the contents of some of the boxes.

19 *Hansard*, 25 November 1963.

20 Mrs Jacqueline Kennedy to Harold Macmillan, 31 January 1964. MS Macmillan dep. c. 553, loc. cit. Harold Macmillan to Mrs Jacqueline Kennedy, 18 February 1964, ibid.

21 Mrs Jacqueline Onassis to the Earl of Stockton, 13 May 1984. MS Macmillan dep. c. 653, loc. cit.

22 Barbara Leeming, *Jack Kennedy: The Making of A President*, Weidenfeld & Nicolson, 2006, pp. 390–2 and 139.

23 The correspondence is in MS Macmillan dep. c. 552, loc. cit.

24 Harold Macmillan to Quentin Crewe, 6 August 1957. MS Macmillan dep. c. 321, loc. cit.

25 Harold Macmillan to Sir Roy Harrod, 15 July 1969. MS Add 72732. Harrod Papers, British Library.

26 Speech at Gray's Inn, 15 December 1958. MS Macmillan dep. c. 764, loc. cit.

27 Nicholas Byam Shaw to the author, 24 June 2009.

28 Lord Butler, *The Art of the Possible: The Memoirs of Lord Butler*, Penguin Books, Harmondsworth, 1973, p. ix.

29 Goldman also wrote much of Iain Macleod's controversial biography of Neville Chamberlain (1961).

30 Details from *Macmillan News*, Winter 1973/4, Volume 2, No. 2, the internal newsletter of the publishing house.

31 Sir Donald Wolfit to Lord Hailsham, 5 August 1959. Sir Donald Wolfit (1902–1968) was one of the great 'larger than life' actors of his generation. As with C. P. Snow in his world, Wolfit's peers were condescending towards him, Hermione Gingold remarking 'Olivier is a *tour-de-force*, and Wolfit is forced to tour.' Baroness Orczy (1865–1947) published *The Scarlet Pimpernel* in 1905 to great acclaim. Lord Hailsham gave Macmillan Wolfit's letter. It is now in MS Macmillan MS dep. c. 311, loc. cit.

32 Nicholas Byam Shaw to the author, 24 June 2009.

33 Harold Wilson, *A Prime Minister on Prime Ministers*, Weidenfeld & Nicolson and Michael Joseph, 1997, p. 326.

34 Harold Macmillan diary, 21 July 1964. MS Macmillan dep. d. 52, loc. cit.

35 Alan Maclean (1924–2006), editorial director of Macmillan for many years. He had been in the diplomatic service, latterly as private secretary to Sir Gladwyn Jebb in New York, 1950–1951, but when his brother Donald Maclean defected to the Soviet Union in 1951, Alan left the Foreign Office for publishing, although he was completely cleared by MI5 of any involvement in his brother's treachery.

36 Martin Stannard, *Muriel Spark: The Biography*, Weidenfeld & Nicolson, 2009, pp. 230–1, 260 and 317.

37 *Independent*, 6 October 2006.

38 Harold Macmillan to Nicholas Byam Shaw, 8 November 1979. Nicholas Byam Shaw Papers.

39 Details from Nicholas Byam

Shaw's tribute to Macmillan in *Publishing News*, 1987.

40 Graham C. Greene to the author, 13 September 2009.

41 Horatio Lovat Dickson (1902–1985), always known as Rache, chief editor and a director of Macmillan for many years.

42 Philip Snow, *Stranger and Brother: A Portrait of C. P. Snow*, Macmillan, 1982, p. 187.

43 Ibid., p. 132.

44 C. P. Snow, *Homecomings*, Macmillan, 1956, Chapter 22. In Chapter 14 of the same novel, he described them as 'those powerful anonymous *couloirs*'.

45 When advising Lord Home about his memoirs, Macmillan stressed the importance of choosing an apt title. D. R. Thorpe, *Alec Douglas-Home*, Sinclair-Stevenson, 1996, p. 452.

46 Stephen Parkinson, *Arena of Ambition: A History of the Cambridge Union*, Icon Books, 2009, p. 290. As Macmillan waited in his car after dinner to be driven down the hill over Magdalene Bridge to the Union, he asked where Rab had gone. He was told that he was walking to the Union. 'Walk?' said Macmillan. 'He can't walk, he's too fat.' Ibid.

47 C. P. Snow to Harold Macmillan, 22 May 1964. Macmillan Publishing Archive, Add. MSS 72742. British Library. *Lothair* (1870) was an immensely popular novel by Disraeli, which went into eight editions in the year of its publication.

48 A parallel can be found in the way that King Edward VIII's affair with Mrs Simpson remained hidden from the general public until a few days before the Abdication.

49 James Lees-Milne, *Through Wood and Dale: Diaries 1975–1978*, Michael Russell, Norwich, 2007, p. 205. What Macmillan would have made of Michael Bloch's frank biography of James Lees-Milne himself, *James Lees-Milne: A Life*, John Murray, 2009, does not bear close contemplation.

50 Robert Skidelsky, *John Maynard Keynes: Volume Three, Fighting for Britain 1937–1946*, Macmillan, 2000, p. 492. Lord Skidelsky discusses the whole question of the Harrod biography, on pp. 491–8.

51 When the author met Macmillan at Birch Grove in April 1975, Skidelsky's newly published life of Mosley was on Macmillan's desk, and was the first topic of conversation.

52 As the second official biographer of Sir Anthony Eden, I was aware of the delicacy of the situation regarding the first such biographer, Sir Robert Rhodes James.

53 I am grateful to a later Cambridge economist, Graham Jones, for these details.

54 Robert Skidelsky felt that Harrod overplayed the position of Daniel Macmillan among Keynes' loves (Arthur Lee Hobhouse at Cambridge, for one, was a far deeper involvement) in the hope of scotching a new biography.

Lord Skidelsky to the author, 27 February 2008.

55 Harold Macmillan to Sir Roy Harrod, 4 July 1969, 15 July 1969 and 19 August 1969. Sir Roy Harrod to Harold Macmillan, 7 July 1969, 18 July 1969, 5 August 1969 and 19 August 1969. Macmillan Publishing Archive, Add. MSS 72742. British Library. Discussing Keynes and Daniel Macmillan in his biography, Roy Harrod confined himself to the comment 'Maynard was especially fond of Daniel Macmillan.' It was left to the reader to decipher how fond. R. F. Harrod, *The Life of John Maynard Keynes*, Macmillan, 1951, p. 34. The three-volume life of Keynes by Robert Skidelsky (1983, 1992 and 2000) was acclaimed as one of the towering biographies of the post-war age. Skidelsky became so immersed in Keynes' life that he even lived in Tilton House, Keynes' home in Sussex.

56 MS Macmillan dep. c. 535, op. cit.

57 Harold Macmillan diary, 24 January 1965. MS Macmillan dep. d. 52, op. cit..

58 Martin Gilbert, *In Search of Churchill: A Historian's Journey*, Harper Collins, 1994, pp. 239–47.

59 The vote was confined to Conservative MPs in the Commons.

60 Harold Macmillan diary, 27 July 1965. MS Macmillan dep. d. 53, loc. cit.

61 Harold Macmillan to Lady Dorothy Macmillan, 3 August 1960. MS Macmillan dep. c. 596, op. cit..

62 Deborah, the Dowager Duchess of Devonshire to the author, 15 October 2007.

63 Ibid.

64 Lady Boothby to the author, 8 August 2006.

65 Kenneth Rose to the author, 20 September 2009.

66 A point made to the author by the late Lord Fraser of Kilmorack on more than one occasion.

67 Quoted in Edward Heath, *The Course of My Life: My Autobiography*, Hodder & Stoughton, 1998, p. 462.

68 Lord Armstrong of Ilminster to the author, 29 January 2009.

69 Note in MS Macmillan dep. c. 538, loc. cit.

70 Record of talk of 12 February 1974, Microfilm 97. Lord Fraser of Kilmorack Papers, Bodleian Library, Oxford.

71 By chance, the author was with Julian Amery at 112 Eaton Square on 6 February 1975, the night all the London evening papers had blanket headlines on his possible intentions. Our discussion was on Sir Austen Chamberlain, Lord Curzon and Lord Butler for my book *The Uncrowned Prime Ministers*. It seemed the telephone would never cease, as colleagues rang, telling him to stand, or to desist. Julian Amery found all this very ironic, as, he said, it was in the very same upstairs double drawing room in 112 Eaton Square that his father

had orchestrated many of the manoeuvres over the events in the earlier part of the century when Chamberlain and Curzon had failed to be chosen as Tory leader. As we parted he told me that unlike Austen Chamberlain, he would not play the game and lose it, but would not enter the contest at all, as the telephone calls had made it clear he did not have broad enough support to be a serious runner. The late Julian Amery (later Lord Amery of Lustleigh) to the author, 6 February 1975.

72 Alistair Horne, *Macmillan 1894–1956: Volume 1 of the Official Biography*, Macmillan, 1988, p. xi.

73 Professor Keith Middlemas to the author, 22 April 2010, and Sir Charles Petrie and Alistair Cooke, *The Carlton Club 1832–2007*, The Carlton Club, 2007, p. 209.

74 Harold Macmillan to Margaret Thatcher, 19 January 1983. MS Macmillan dep. c. 482, loc. cit. Stanley Holloway's droll recitation of the tale of Albert Ramsbottom, a boy swallowed by a lion at Blackpool Zoo, was one of the most popular music-hall turns of the 1930s.

75 Professor J. Mordaunt Crook to the author, 13 June 2008.

76 Speech to the Tory Reform Group, 8 November 1985.

77 John Campbell, *Margaret Thatcher: Volume Two, The Iron Lady*, Jonathan Cape, 2003, p. 240.

78 *Private Eye*, Christmas issue, 13 December 1985.

79 Charles Dickens, *Oliver Twist*, 1837, Chapter 17. Balliol College Records of Macmillan's Chancellorship of Oxford University.

80 Petrie and Cooke, op. cit., pp. 197–8.

81 David Faber to the author, 19 March 2010.

82 David Gibbs, Old Ardinian, and former Head Master of Chigwell School, to the author, 1988.

83 Lady Caroline Faber to the author, 31 January 2007.

84 It is some indication of the world in which the higher Tories lived at this time that the Macmillan family should sell Highgrove to the Prince of Wales, and that Rab Butler should sell Gatcombe to the Queen, as a residence for Princess Anne, later the Princess Royal.

85 Pamela, the Dowager Lady Egremont, to the author, 24 June 2008, and Lord Heseltine to the author, 25 September 2009.

86 Probate, 1 June 1987.

87 Letter from Edmund Burke to Matthew Smith, 1750.

88 His daughter Catherine, wife of Julian Amery, is buried at the Church of St John the Baptist, Lustleigh, Devon, with other members of the Amery family.

89 Lord Macaulay essay on Warren Hastings.

90 The full text of this address is printed as Appendix II in D. R. Thorpe, *Alec Douglas-Home*, Sinclair-Stevenson, 1996, pp. 467–9.

ENVOI

1 Enoch Powell, *Joseph Chamberlain*, Thames and Hudson, 1977, p. 151.
2 Robert Browning, *The Lost Leader*.
3 Eras can be defined by their artistic landmarks. Key works that illuminated characteristic moments of the Macmillan era - in its changing social assumptions and over the Cold War - were John Osborne's play *The Entertainer* (1957), and Benjamin Britten's *War Requiem* (1962).
4 David Marquand, *Britain Since 1918: The Strange Career of British Democracy*, Weidenfeld & Nicolson, 2008, p. xii.
5 Paul Addison, *Now the War is Over: A Social History of Britain 1945-51*, BBC Books and Jonathan Cape, 1985, p. 116.
6 Peter Clarke, *The Cripps Version: The Life of Sir Stafford Cripps 1889-1952*, Allen Lane, 2002, p. 531.
7 John Wyndham had been ennobled as the first Baron Egremont in Macmillan's resignation honours list.
8 William Wordsworth, *The Prelude*, Book 2.
9 The Dowager Lady Egremont, to the author, 24 June 2008.
10 J. M. Keynes, *A Tract on Monetary Reform*, Macmillan & Co., 1923, *Collected Writings of J. M. Keynes, Volume IV*, p. 65.
11 *Hansard*, 12 February 1959.
12 Harold Macmillan to Reginald Maudling, 25 October 1959. BT 11/5711. National Archives, Kew.
13 Reginald Maudling to Harold Macmillan, 27 October 1959. *Ibid.*
14 Harold Macmillan to President John F. Kennedy, 5 January 1962. MS Macmillan dep. c. 357. Macmillan Papers, Bodleian Library, Oxford.
15 Sir Charles Snow to Harold Macmillan, 1962. Macmillan Publishing Archive, British Library.
16 Harold Macmillan, *At the End of the Day 1961-1963*, Macmillan, 1973, p. 523.

Acknowledgements

Surprisingly for such a complex personality, Harold Macmillan has not attracted the number of studies devoted to substantial political figures such as Baldwin, Neville Chamberlain and Eden. Even prime ministers such as Rosebery, Balfour and Bonar Law, who served much shorter spells in Downing Street, have recently been accorded major 'second-generation' studies. Although 50 years after he became Prime Minister there are welcome signs of a renewal of interest in Macmillan's career, the reason for this comparative neglect is that the official two-volume biography by Sir Alistair Horne, published in 1988–1989, was so dominant that revisiting the subject was effectively closed. Macmillan had been 'done'.

However, things move on, more archival material becomes available, and the historical perspective alters. My first thanks therefore must be to Sir Alistair Horne, for his generous encouragement to me on embarking on this project, for his help and advice, and for the leads he has given me. As a former Alistair Horne Fellow at St Antony's College, Oxford, I was already heavily in his debt. He had also helped me over my earlier books.

I was the first historian, after the publication of Sir Alistair Horne's biography, to be given free and unlimited access to the Macmillan archive, still then in its unexpurgated, uncatalogued state at Porches Farm House on the Birch Grove estate, before its transfer to the collection of Western manuscripts at the Bodleian Library, Oxford.

Harold Macmillan had loomed large in my previous four books. Indeed, in the lives of Anthony Eden, Selwyn Lloyd, Rab Butler and Alec Douglas-Home, he was the central supporting figure, and I had told his story obliquely by relating theirs. Now the 'point of view', which one of the Macmillan authors, Henry James, felt to be so crucial, alters. Macmillan himself is the prism through which these events are seen.

Over the past 35 years, I have interviewed the vast majority of people closely involved with Macmillan's career, including all the prime ministers from Macmillan to Thatcher, ten Foreign Secretaries, ten Chancellors of the Exchequer and eight Home Secretaries, plus the principal civil servants and ambassadors, in addition to many of their counterparts from abroad. Their names are recorded in the prefaces of my previous books and to repeat hundreds of them here is unnecessary. Suffice it to say that the following, in addition to Harold Macmillan himself, sadly all departed, remain central witnesses:

Lord Aldington, Lord Amery of Lustleigh, Lord Barber, Sir Frederick Bishop, Lord Boothby, Lord Boyd-Carpenter, Lord Brimelow, Lord Broxbourne, Lord and Lady Butler of Saffron Walden, Lord Caccia, Sir Alec Cairncross, Lord Callaghan of Cardiff, Sir Knox Cunningham, Lord Devlin, Sir Nigel Fisher, Lord Franks, Lord Fraser of Kilmorack, Lord Hailsham of St Marylebone, Sir Edward Heath, Lord Home of the Hirsel, David Hubback, Sir David Hunt, Lord Inchyra, Lord Jenkins of Hillhead, Aubrey Jones, Lord Lambton, Viscount Macmillan of Ovenden, Lord Margadale of Islay, Reginald Maudling, Col. Terence Maxwell, Nigel Nicolson, Lord Perth, Enoch Powell, John Profumo, Lord Rawlinson, Sir Patrick Reilly, Lord Roberthall, Lord Sherfield, Lord Soames, Lord Thorneycroft, Lord Watkinson, Lord Wilson of Rievaulx, Sir Philip Woodfield, and Sir Philip de Zulueta.

I am also most grateful to the following people, who have given generously of their time to talk to me, in many cases on more than one occasion, about aspects of Harold Macmillan's life and career:

Sir Eric and Lady Anderson, Ralph Appleton, Lord Armstrong of Ilminster, the Countess of Avon, David Badenoch, Francis Beckett, the late Sir Harold Beeley, Lady Bligh, Professor Vernon Bogdanor, Christopher Booker, Lady Boothby, Lord Brooke of Sutton Mandeville, the late Sir Julian Bullard, Dr David Butler, Nicholas Byam Shaw, Neil Cairncross, Lord Carrington and the late Lady Carrington, Dr Peter Catterall, the late Lord Charteris of Amisfield, the late David Clarke, Michael Cockerell, the late Sir John Coulson, the late Sir John Colville, the late Lord Colyton, Lady Colyton, the late Maurice Couve de Murville, the late Brigadier Anthony Cowgill, Patrick Croker, Tam Dalyell, the late Sir Robin Day, the late Sir Patrick Dean, Professor David Dilks, Mr Piers Dixon, the late Sir Douglas Dodds-Parker, the Dowager Duchess of Devonshire, the late Chris Dunn, the Dowager Lady Egremont, Lady Caroline Faber, David Faber, James Faber, Dr Robert Gasser, the late Lord Gilmour of Craigmillar, the late Lord and Lady Gladwyn, Sir Philip Goodhart, the late Lord Goodman, Sir John Graham, Graham C. Greene, the late Lord Greenhill of Harrow, Dr Cameron Hazlehurst, the late W. N. Hanna, Charles Hastings, Simon

Heffer, the late Sir Nicholas Henderson, Professor Peter Hennessy, the late Mrs Kathleen Hill, Sir Alistair Horne, Anthony Howard, Sylvia James, Sir Michael Jenkins, Dr Harry Judge, Sir Anthony Kenny, the Revd Anne Kiggell, the late Keith Kyle, the late Richard Lamb, Lord Lawson of Blaby, Frederick Leishman, the late Sir Donald Logan, Andrew Lownie, Hugh Lunghi, the Hon. David Macmillan, Dr Peter Mangold, Sir Humphrey Maud, the late Iverach McDonald, Professor Keith Middlemas, Sir Guy and Lady Millard, Anthony Moncrieff, Sir Anthony Montague Browne, Sir John Morgan, Edwyn Morris, Niall Murphy, the late Sir Anthony Nutting Bt, the late Sir Thomas Padmore, the late Professor Ben Pimlott, the late Christian Pineau, the late Sir David Pitblado, the late Sir Richard Powell, Brian Rees, Lord and Lady Rees-Mogg, the late Sir Robert Rhodes James, Peter Riddell, the late Sir Frank Roberts, Kenneth Rose, the late Sir Archibald Ross, the late Sir Algernon Rumbold, the late Anthony Sampson, Anthony Shone, Christopher Sinclair-Stevenson, Lord Skidelsky, Christopher Spence, Adam Sisman, Sir Peter Tapsell, Professor Kevin Theakston, Count Nikolai Tolstoy, David Torrance, the late Lady Anne Tree, Father John Twisleton, Professor Geoffrey Warner, Michael Wheeler-Booth, Lady Williams of Elvel, Lord Windlesham, Professor Blair Worden, the late Sir Denis Wright, Philip Ziegler and the Hon. Lady de Zulueta.

I am particularly grateful to Professor Peter Hennessy for much help and encouragement over the years. I also acknowledge the help of Dr Saul Kelly in allowing me to see his study of Sir Roger Makins (Lord Sherfield) at the typescript stage, and for many stimulating conversations on the Anglo-American relationship in the 1950s.

I am indebted to many other individuals and institutions for their help with the research:

Brigid Avison for help over the Macmillans and Arran; Nicolas Barker; Alan Bell; Dr Tim Benson of the Political Cartoon Society for advice over cartoons; Mr and Mrs Michael Binns; the Very Revd Keith Jones, Dean of York, for help over Macmillan's ecclesiastical appointments; Dr Martin Maw, Jill Davidson and Jeremy McIlwaine, successive Conservative Party archivists at the Bodleian Library, Oxford; Ruth Northley of *Whitaker's Almanac*; Christine Penney, former Librarian of the Special Collections at the University of Birmington Library for help over the Avon Papers, the Austen Chamberlain Papers and the Neville Chamberlain Papers, housed in the Heslop Room at the University of Birmingham; Andrew Peppitt, archivist of the

ACKNOWLEDGEMENTS

Devonshire Collection at Chatsworth; Michael Simmonds, Director of the Conservative Political Centre, and Alistair Cooke, Michael Mates MP and the Executive of the Conservative Party 1922 Committee; Helen Langley, Curator of Modern Political Papers at the Bodleian Library, and Michael Hughes for help over the Sherfield Papers at the Bodleian; the staff of the Vere Harmsworth Library at the Rothermere American Institute, Oxford University; Lady Boothby for giving me unrestricted access to the papers of her late husband, Lord Boothby; Dr David Butler for giving me access to his archive at Nuffield College on the post-war general elections; Dr John Jones and Mr Alan Tadiello of Balliol College, Oxford; Dr Simon Robbins, Archivist, Imperial War Museum; Ben White, Assistant Archivist at the Bank of England; Mrs Grace Smaill of the Brodick Museum, Arran; the staff at the Churchill Archives Centre, Churchill College, for their unfailing help and advice, in what is the foremost British equivalent of the American Presidential Libraries; Dwight E. Strandberg, Archivist, Dwight D. Eisenhower Library, Abilene, Kansas, USA; Ms K. V. Bligh, Archivist (Modern Collections) at the House of Lords Record Office; Dr Simon Rutter of the Imperial War Museum; Dr Richard Palmer, Librarian and Archivist, and Miss Melanie Barber, Deputy Librarian and Deputy Archivist, at Lambeth Palace Library; Mrs Penelope Hatfield, Archivist at Eton College Library, and Dr Michael Meredith; Dr David Holloway for help over Russian matters; Jonathan Smith, Manuscript Cataloguer at Trinity College Library, Cambridge; at St Antony's College, Oxford, the Librarian, Ms Rosamund Campbell, Mrs Clare Brown, Archivist of the Middle East Centre, and the Librarian of the Middle East Centre, Mrs Diane Ring; at Magdalen College, Oxford, the Archivist, Dr Robin Darwall-Smith, for help over the Douglas-Dodds Parker Papers; at Nuffield College, Oxford, the Archivist, Mrs Eleanor Vallis; Nathan Williams, Reading University Special Collections; Sir Jonah Walker-Smith for help over the Broxbourne Papers; at the Hartley Library, Southampton University, Dr C. M. Woolgar, for help over the Mountbatten Papers; Dr Cliff Davies, Archivist of Wadham College, Oxford, for help over the Sir Maurice Bowra Papers; at News International plc, Eamon Dyas, Group Records Manager, and Sarah Hepworth, Assistant Archivist at *The Times* Archives and Record Office; and at Wolfson College, Oxford, Dr Mark Pottle of the Lady Asquith of Yarnbury Research Project, and Dr Anne Deighton.

Others who have helped in various valuable ways, and to whom I am extremely grateful, include Sir Eric Anderson, former Provost of Eton

College, for access to the Eton College Archives and Eton's holdings of the Lord Caccia and Thomas Hardy Papers; Lady Anderson; Dr John Avison over medical matters; David Badenoch for his memorandum on the events surrounding the operation conducted by his father, Alec Badenoch, on Macmillan in October 1963; the late Peter Baldwin; James Bayliss; Alan Bell; Philippa Blake-Roberts of the Harold Macmillan Book Trust; Susan Bradley; Tom Bristowe; Frances Cairncross and Hamish McRae for help over the Robert Hall Diaries; Professor Richard Cooper; Alistair Cooke, expert on all aspects of Conservative history; Richard Crawford; John Davies; Hugh Gammell for help over the career of his grandfather, the late Lieutenant-General Sir James Gammell; Cary Gilbart-Smith for help over Harold Macmillan's references to classical literature; Lord Heseltine; Robert and Rosie Ingram; Graham and Vanessa Jones; Dr Norman Jones; Robert and Kay Kellock; Nigel Jaques; Andrew Lownie; John Mollo; the late Mary Myles; John and Elizabeth Peters; Anne Shiel; David Torrance for letting me see the manuscript of his biography of Noel Skelton, and for his many insights into Scottish politics; David Twiston Davies; George Walker; Frank Wiseman; the Revd John Witheridge; Philip Ziegler and Dr Ernst Zillekens.

The typescript has been read, either in part or whole, by various people, and I am particularly grateful to the Countess of Avon, Professor Vernon Bogdanor, Christopher Booker, the late Brigadier Anthony Cowgill, David Faber, Hugh Gammell, Graham C. Greene, Graham Jones, Hugh Lunghi, Dr Edwyn Morris, Stephen Shuttleworth, Adam Sisman, Lord Skidelsky, Christopher Spence, Professor Geoffrey Warner and the Revd John Witheridge for their insights. Responsibility for the final version and the interpretation of events, however, is mine alone.

Since 1997, I have been indebted also to Lord Windlesham, the former Principal, Professor Roger Cashmore, FRS, current Principal, and the Fellows of Brasenose College, for electing and re-electing me to senior membership of Brasenose College. Nobody could have enjoyed a more hospitable or helpful environment in which to pursue research.

For insights into Harold Macmillan, both his family life and the public career, I am especially grateful to David Faber, devoted grandson, former MP, historian, author and valued friend. His input and encouragement over the years have been of the utmost importance and, as his grandfather would have applauded, fun.

I owe much to Penelope Hoare, the nonpareil of editors, and to Parisa Ebrahimi and Jane Selley, all of whom have worked tirelessly to prepare this volume for publication. Also at Chatto & Windus, Becky Hardie, Sue Amaradivakara, Neil Bradford, Katherine Murphy and Nicky Nevin are acknowledged with thanks.

The author and publishers are grateful to the following for permission to publish copyright material:

Extracts from Harold Macmillan's private diary, private letters composed by Harold Macmillan, extracts from Harold Macmillan's published works and private letters composed by Lady Dorothy Macmillan in the Harold Macmillan Archive at the Bodleian Library, Oxford, are published by kind permission of the Trustees of the Harold Macmillan Book Trust.

Crown copyright material at the National Archives, Kew, is reproduced by permission of The National Archives of the United Kingdom. Grateful acknowledgements to the Countess of Avon for extracts from the Avon Papers in the custody of the University of Birmingham and from her diary; the Syndics of Cambridge University library for a letter by Stanley Baldwin in the Earl Baldwin of Bewdley Papers at Cambridge University library; Earl Baldwin of Bewdley for unpublished letters by Stanley Baldwin in the Macmillan Papers at the Bodleian Library, Oxford; David Badenoch for extracts from his memorandum on the medical aspects of the events of October 1963; the Bank of England Archive for extracts from the correspondence of Governors of the Bank of England and other material in its copyright. 'To the Balliol Men Still in Africa' by Hilaire Belloc from The Four Men (© Hilaire Belloc, 1983) is reproduced by permission of PFD (www. pfd.co.uk). Grateful acknowledgements to the Rt. Hon. Tony Benn for extracts from his diaries; Henry Hardy and the Isaiah Berlin Literary Trustees for an extract from a letter by Sir Isaiah Berlin; an extract from the poem 'The Arrest of Oscar Wilde at the Cadogan Hotel' from Collected Poems © The Estate of John Betjeman 1955, 1958, 1962, 1964, 1968, 1970, 1979, 1981, 1982, 2001 is reproduced by permission of John Murray (Publishers); an extract from 'Summoned by Bells' by John Betjeman, Poetry © The Estate of John Betjeman 1960 is reproduced by permission of John Murray (Publishers); Christopher Booker for extracts from his letters and from A Looking Glass Tragedy (Duckworth) and The Neophiliacs (Collins); Lady Boothby for extracts from the papers of Lord Boothby; the Warden and Fellows of Wadham College, Oxford for an extract from Sir Maurice Bowra's poem The Statesman's Tragedy. Extracts from the

Journals of Collin Brooks, published in *Fleet Street, Press Barons and Politics: The Journals of Collin Brooks, 1932–1940*, edited by N. J. Crowson, Cambridge University Press, 1998, are published by permission of Cambridge University Press. Grateful acknowledgements to the Master and Fellows of Trinity College, Cambridge for an extract from the Lord Butler of Saffron Walden Papers; Dr David Butler for extracts from his papers at Nuffield College, Oxford; Dr Peter Catterall for extracts from his writings; W. D. G. Chalmers for a letter written by him. Extracts from the papers of Sir Austen Chamberlain and Neville Chamberlain are by permission of the University of Birmingham. Grateful thanks to Lord Hemingford for an extract from the papers of William Clark; Viscount Norwich for extracts from the diaries of Alfred Duff Cooper; Samuel B. Cunningham for letters by Sir Knox Cunningham; the British Library of Political and Economic Science for extracts from the diaries of Hugh Dalton. Extracts from the diaries and letters of the 9th Duke of Devonshire are reproduced by permission of the Duke of Devonshire. Lines from *A Warning to Politicians*, taken from Patric Dickinson *Selected Poems* published by Chatto & Windus are used by permission of the author's estate. Grateful acknowledgements to the Provost and Fellows of Eton College for material from the Eton College Archives; the Hon. Angus Fraser for material from the papers of Lord Fraser of Kilmorack held on microfilm at the Bodleian Library, Oxford. Extracts from letters by Lieutenant-General Sir James Gammell at the Imperial War Museum are by permission of the Gammell family. The extract from David Gascoyne's poem *Farewell Chorus* is by permission of Enitharmon Press as publishers of David Gascoyne's *Selected Poems* (Enitharmon Press, 1994). Grateful acknowledgements to Donald Haley for an extract from the papers of Sir William Haley, and the Master, Fellows and Scholars of Churchill College, Cambridge as custodians of the collection at Churchill College, Cambridge; the Borthwick Institute for Archives, the University of York, for extracts from the papers of Lord Halifax; Taylor & Francis Books (UK) for an extract from the diaries of Sir Robert Hall; Dominick Harrod for extracts from letters by Sir Roy Harrod. Extracts from the diaries of Sir Cuthbert Headlam, published in *Parliament and Politics in the Age of Baldwin and Macdonald: The Headlam Diaries 1923–1935*, edited by Stuart Ball, Cambridge University Press, 1999, are published by permission of Cambridge University Press. Grateful acknowledgements to the Earl of Home for extracts from the papers of Lord and Lady Home of the Hirsel. Unpublished writings of J. M. Keynes copyright The Provost and Scholars of King's College Cambridge 2010 are published by permission of the Provost and Scholars of King's College, Cambridge. An extract from *The General Theory of Employment Interest and Money* by J. M. Keynes, Macmillan & Co, 1936, is published with permission of Palgrave Macmillan. Grateful acknowledgements to Michael Bloch for an extract from the diaries of James Lees-Milne. Lines from *First School* from *The Complete Poems by C Day Lewis*, published by Sinclair-Stevenson (1992), Copyright © 1992 in this edition, the Estate of C Day Lewis, is reprinted by permission of the Random House Group Ltd. Grateful acknowledgements to the Trustees of the Selwyn Lloyd estate for extracts from the Selwyn Lloyd papers, and the Master, Fellows and Scholars of Churchill College, Cambridge as custodians of the collection, at Churchill College, Cambridge; Major Hugh Lunghi for extracts from his letters; the Hon. Sir Humphrey Maud for extracts from the diary of Lady Redcliffe-Maud; the Hon. Virginia Makins for letters by Roger Makins, Lord Sherfield; Leo McKinstry for extracts from *Rosebery: Statesman in Turmoil* (John Murray); Juliet Nicolson for an extract from the diaries of Sir Harold Nicolson; Lady Poole for a letter by Lord Poole. Extracts from the papers of J. Enoch Powell are published by permission of Lord Howard and the Trustees of the Powell Estate, and the Master, Fellows and Scholars of Churchill College, Cambridge as custodians of the collection, at Churchill College, Cambridge. Grateful acknowledgements to Julian Shuckburgh for an extract from the diary of Sir Evelyn Shuckburgh; Philip Snow, Stefanie Snow Waine and Peter Waine, literary executors of Lord Snow for a letter by C. P. Snow; Lord Swinton for an extract from the papers of the first Earl of Swinton, and the Master, Fellows and Scholars of Churchill College, Cambridge as custodians of the collection, at Churchill College, Cambridge; the Thorneycroft family for a letter by Peter Thorneycroft in the Thorneycroft papers at Southampton University; Lord Woolton for an extract from the diary of the first Earl of Woolton in the Woolton papers at the Bodleian Library, Oxford; Professor Blair Worden for extracts from the letters and papers of Hugh Trevor-Roper; Lord Egremont for material by John Wyndham.

Every effort has been made to trace and contact all holders of copyright in quotations and illustrations. If there are any inadvertent omissions or errors, the publishers will be pleased to correct these at the earliest opportunity.

Abbreviations

AA	Automobile Association
AAI	Army Analysis Intelligence
AC	Austen Chamberlain
ADC	aide-de-campe
AE	Anthony Eden
AFHQ	Allied Forces Headquarters
AMG	Allied Military Government
ANC	African National Congress
ANZUS	Australia, New Zealand and United States
BAOR	British Army on the Rhine
BBC	British Broadcasting Corporation
BEF	British Expeditionary Force
CBI	Confederation of British Industry
CC	Carlton Club
CENTO	Central Treaty Oganisation
CFNL	Comité français de la libération nationale
CIA	Central Intelligence Agency
CID	Committee of Imperial Defence
CIGS	Chief of the Imperial General Staff
CLNAI	Comitato di Liberazione Nazionale per l'Alto Italia
CND	Campaign for Nuclear Disarmament
CO	Colonial Office
CRO	Commonwealth Relations Office
DBFP	Documents on British Foreign Policy
DGFP	Documents on German Foreign Policy
DO	Dominions Office
DSO	Companion of the Distinguished Service Order
D (T) C	Defence (Transition) Committee
EAM	Ethnikon Apeleutherotikon Metopon
ECSC	European Coal-Steel Community
EDC	European Defence Community
EDES	Ethnikos Dimokratikos Ellinikos Syndesmos
EEC	European Economic Community
EFTA	European Free Trade Association
ELAS	Ethnikos Laikos Apeleftherotikos Stratos

ELEC	European League for Economic Co-operation
ENO	English National Opera
EOKA	Ethniki Organosis Kyprion Agoniston
ERNIE	Electronic Random Number Indicating Equipment
ETU	Electrical Trades Union
FCNL	French Committee of National Liberation
FDR	Franklin Delano Roosevelt
f-n	footnote
FO	Foreign Office
FS	Foreign Secretary
GATT	General Agreement on Tariffs and Trade
GCE	General Certificate of Education
GCSE	General Certificate of Secondary Education
GNP	Gross National Product
GOC	General Officer Commanding
GPRF	Gouvernement provisoire de la République français
GRU	Glavnoye Razvedyvatelnoe Upravleniye
HM	Harold Macmillan
HM	His/Her Majesty
HMG	His/Her Majesty's Government
HMSO	His/Her Majesty's Stationery Office
H of C	House of Commons
IBA	Independent Broadcasting Authority
ICI	Imperial Chemical Industries
IMF	International Monetary Fund
IRA	Irish Republican Army
IRBM	Intermediate Range Ballistic Missiles
ITA	Independent Television Authority
ITV	Independent Television
JIC	Joint Intelligence Committee
KG	Knight of the Garter
KGB	Komitet Gosudarstvennoi Bezopasnosti
KKE	Kommounistikon Komma Ellados
KRRC	King's Royal Rifle Corps
LCC	London County Council
LDV	Local Defence Volunteers
LG/L1.G	Lloyd George
MA	Master of Arts
MBE	Member of the British Empire
MC	Military Cross
MCC	Marylebone Cricket Club
MI5	Directorate of Military Intelligence

MI6	Secret Intelligence Service
MLF	Multi-Lateral Force
MP	Member of Parliament
NA	National Archives
NATO	North Atlantic Treaty Organisation
NEDC	National Economic Development Council
NC	Neville Chamberlain
NHS	National Health Service
NKD	Narodnyi Kommissariatt Vnutrennikh Del
NUR	National Union of Railwaymen
NY	New York
OE	Old Etonian
OEEC	Organisation for European Economic Co-operation
OM	Order of Merit
OUDS	Oxford University Dramatic Society
OUP	Oxford University Press
PCI	Partito Comunnista Italiano
PM	Prime Minister
PoW	Prisoner of War
PPS	Parliamentary Private Secretary
PRO	Public Record Office, now the National Archives
PUS	Permanent Under Secretary
RA	Royal Archives
RAB	R. A. Butler
RAC	Royal Automobile Club
RAF	Royal Air Force
RMS	Royal Mail Steamer
RNVR	Royal Naval Volunteer Reserve
RPM	Resale Price Maintenance
RSC	Royal Shakespeare Company
SB	Stanley Baldwin
SC	Stafford Cripps
SCUA	Suez Canal Users' Association
SEAC	South-East Asia Command
SEATO	South-East Asia Treaty Organisation
SHAEF	Supreme Headquarters Allied Expeditionary Force
SHAPE	Supreme Headquarters, Allied Powers, Europe
SIS	Secret Intelligence Service
SL	Selwyn Lloyd
SMERSH	Acronym for Smert Shpionam (Death to Spies)
SOE	Special Operations Executive
S of S	Secretary of State

TUC	Trades Union Congress
TW3	*That Was the Week that Was*
UK	United Kingdom
UNEF	United Nations Emergency Force
UNO	United Nations Organisation
US	United States
USA	United States of America
VIP	Very Important Person
WEU	Western European Union
WSC	Winston Spencer Churchill
YMCA	Young Men's Christian Association*

*Also used as the nickname for a group of young progressive Conservative backbenchers in the 1920s and 1930s who followed the ideas of Noel Skelton on 'the property-owning democracy'.

Index

Cabinet of, 361; view of Eisenhower and Dulles, 366; & Eisenhower's pre-election visit to Britain, 1959, 440; congratulates HM on 1959 election victory, 451; HM visits at Villa Nova, 494; declares Selwyn Lloyd to have been harshly treated by HM, 525; consulted by HM on succession, 567; HM seeks support of for political comeback, 600–601; relationship with HM, 601

Eden, Lady (*later* the Countess of Avon), 356, 409, 600; sympathises with Rab Butler on his disappointment, 360

EDES (National Republican Greek League), 198

Edgecombe, Johnny, 545

Edinburgh, 261

Edinburgh, Duke of, attends WSC's retirement dinner, 298; HM does not like robust opinions of, 393; & State Visit of de Gaulle, 466; & Mountbatten as family name for royals, 453, 488; attends dinner to celebrate 250th anniversary of Downing Street, 604

Education Act (1944), 318, 382

Education, in 1950s, 274, 382; comprehensive schools, 382, 443, 501; eleven plus, 383; grammar schools, 274, 382, 383, 384, 443; public schools, 278, 383; secondary modern schools, 382; higher education, & the Robbins Report, 501–502; & Colleges of Advanced Technology, 501

Edward VII Hospital, f-n 35

Edward VII, King, f-n 35; visits Sir Henry Campbell-Bannerman, 577

Edward VIII, King, 113; visits troops during Great War as Prince of Wales, 55; & Abdication Crisis (1936), 94; accedes to throne, 127

Egypt, 337, 349, 351, 352 353, 388, 478, 480; growth of Arab nationalism in, 263; HM visits on

Macmillan & Co. business, 592

Egypt Committee, 334, 340, 341

Eire, 382

Eisenhower, President Dwight D. ('Ike'), 5, 356, 387, 393, 413, 426, 444, 495, 615; in North Africa, 164, 165, 167–168, 169, 170, 176, 177, 179, 194, 366, 514, 616; in Italy, 191; relationship with HM, 167–168, 170, 175, 186–187, f-n 186–187, 286; & Bavaria, 214; & Suez Crisis, 336, 337, 343, 346–347, 350,351, 352; & 1956 Presidential Election, 339, 350; favours HM to succeed AE, 350–351; admits he was wrong over Suez, 366; & 1960 Presidential Election, 486; congratulates HM on becoming PM, 378; meets HM at Bermuda, 387–388; & disagreements with HM over Oman, 394; & repeal of McMahon Act, 395, 415; & co-operation with Britain over Jordan, 416; & pre-election visit to Britain, 1959, 4, 439–441; & Summit, 444; & Paris Summit, 463, 464, 465, 470–473; & U-2 spy planes, 470, 473; & Laos, 492

Eisenhower Doctrine, 391, 394

El Alamein, Battle of (1942), 160, 239,

ELAS (National People's Liberation Army), 185, 198, 200

Electricity Council, 513

Electronic Random Number Indicating Equipment (ERNIE), 328

Electrical Trades Union, 462

Eliot, T. S., 130, 275

Elizabeth I, Queen, 275

Elizabeth, Queen, Consort of George VI, *formerly* Duchess of York, later Queen Elizabeth the Queen Mother, 86, 135; describes Boothby as 'a bounder but not a cad', 93; listens to *Mrs Dale's Diary*, 276